American Government and Business

H. H. Liebhafsky
Juris. Dr., Ph.D.

**Professor of Economics
The University of Texas**

JOHN WILEY & SONS INC.

New York | London | Sydney | Toronto

To Nancy

Preface

This book has been designed for use in undergraduate and first-year graduate courses concerned with the study of political economy, that is, with a study of problems of the use of governmental power to promote and foster or to discourage and inhibit particular economic activities and forms of organization. The approach of this book is interdisciplinary, and it should, therefore, be useful to students majoring in economics, political science, or business administration.

It is widely recognized by teachers of courses in "Business and Government" that the field is too broad to be entirely covered in a single three-hour course. Different teachers emphasize different topics and select for class discussion those chapters from the available textbooks that fit into the courses offered. This book lends itself readily to this practice. Part I contains general background materials pertaining to the overall problem of the use of governmental power in relation to economic activity and organization in the United States. Parts II (mainly antitrust) and III (administrative regulation) are independent of one another but do assume that the student has some knowledge of the relevant background materials contained in Part I. The chapters have been written so that the teacher can select for class discussion those chapters that fit his particular course and can assign some of the others as outside reading. He can emphasize antitrust by making intensive use of Part II or

he can emphasize administrative regulation by making intensive use of Part III. He can assign the individual chapters in Part I for class discussion or for outside reading to suit his purposes.

Although this book is approximately the length of other leading books in this field, it possesses a feature that others do not. Most other books require supplementation by use of books of readings or by casebooks. In this book, excerpts from governmental working documents have been interwoven into the textual discussion to eliminate the need for such outside materials. Many schools do not have such materials in their libraries. Thus, although to the length and cost of other books must be added the four or five hundred pages plus the additional cost of a book of readings, no such adjustment is necessary in the instance of this book.

Aside from the obvious savings in cost and time, I believe that the procedure used herein adds much to the relevance and realism of the problems under discussion. Thus, for example, in Chapter 24, I have discussed the problems of the *rate structure* and the *rate level* in regulated industries in *general terms* in the chapter dealing with regulation of domestic surface transportation; I have also included an excerpt from a report by a Hearing Examiner to determine whether the Interstate Commerce Commission should use its rule-making power to adopt certain cost formulas developed by its cost-finding section. The evidence presented by the cost-finding section included definitions of fixed costs, variable costs, joint costs, and "compensatory costs"—concepts taken from the field of price theory. Excerpts from decisions by courts are also included where appropriate. And Chapter 32, the concluding chapter of this book, examines the results of a Congressional investigation into the question of standards of evaluation to be applied to returns from government investments relative to returns from private investments, a question first raised by Adam Smith in 1776 and which is raised also in this book for the first time in Chapter 1. Thus, the circle drawn by this book is closed in its final chapter by a return to a significant question posed in its opening chapter.

Some topics not hitherto covered in the literature are dealt with in this book. For example, Chapter 20 on antitrust remedies contains what I believe is the first organized treatment of this subject in a book of this kind. Similarly, the *verbal* description and discussion of the use as evidence of embryonic econometric models in the *Permian Basin Area Rate Cases* and in the *A. T. and T. Rate* case are probably the first such to be presented in this type of book. In addition, many new developments, including "Truth in Packaging," "Truth in Lending," automobile safety legislation, environmental pollution, the Neal and Stigler reports on antitrust policy, and empirical studies made available by various congressional committees, particularly by the Senate Subcommittee on Antitrust and Monopoly, are covered. Unfortunately, the long lead time required for production of a book from a final manuscript makes it impossible to take account of last-minute developments in a field as dynamic as political economy. But more material pertaining to recent developments is contained in this book than is currently elsewhere available in a similar format.

Obviously, this book owes much to the ideas of many. The ideas of others are freely acknowledged throughout the text. Indeed, several are critically analyzed. Despite the mystical opposition of some to the use of footnotes, the text is heavily footnoted, primarily to provide specific references for the reader who has an interest in further pursuing the ideas examined. In view of the extensive footnoting, no lists of "Selected Readings" are included at the ends of chapters. It has been my own experience that students are far more interested in reading original decisions of courts and government documents than in reading secondary sources pertaining to the topics in question.

I am grateful for the help and encouragement I have received from a large number of people. In this regard, I must mention Professor Walter Adams of Michigan State University, Professor Willard Mueller of the University of Wisconsin, Professor Emmette Redford of the University of Texas, Professor Henry Steele of the University of Houston, Professor Bullock Hyder of North Texas State University, Professor Peter Asch of Rutgers, Professor Clyde Carter of the University of North Carolina, and Professor Walter Neale of the University of Tennessee. Among my immediate colleagues at the University of Texas, I must mention Professors Clarence Ayres, Charles Butler, Wendell Gordon, Jared Hazelton, and Tom Jannuzi. Professor Stephen McDonald provided assistance at a critical time. My colleagues and fellow members of the Bar, Mr. Frank Giesber, Professor B. Joe Colwell, and Professor Eugene Nelson gave me the benefit of their legal training in comments on several chapters.

A number of my graduate students also offered helpful suggestions and comments. These included Mark Bader, John Burnham, Richard Flint, Frank Giesber, Gene Hasha, Carolyn Hooper, Joe LaFace, Jose Mendoza, Walter Mizell, Raymond Roback, Koren Sherrill, Joe Steele, Stan Smith, Jesus Turullols, and Gene Uselton. I must thank Mark Bader and Richard Flint especially for valuable library research assistance. Will Hooker assisted in reading the printer's proofs.

Early drafts of the manuscript were typed by Raymond Roback, Carolyn Hooper, Judy Snyder, Sharon McCown, Martha Reininger, and Jackie Wallace. Maxine Cooper worked long and hard hours typing much of the final manuscript, as did J. R. Oiesen.

I have been exceptionally fortunate in having the invaluable help of my assistant, Koren Sherrill, throughout the period of preparation of the final manuscript. In addition to typing much of the final copy, she edited the final manuscript for consistency in matters of usage and style and accuracy of quotations, and, in the course of her reading of the final typed copy, she made many useful suggestions for improvements. In addition, she did all the paste work and has assured me that rubber cement spray should not be mistaken for hair spray! This book owes much to her conscientious work.

My wife, Nancy, edited most of the chapters in an earlier draft of Parts I and II and checked the accuracy of the quotations used. She also made many suggestions for improvements, all of which appear in the final copy. Her artistic sense of form and balance is reflected in all the chapters of this book. I thank her also for having spent many Sunday afternoons working with me in the library of the University of Texas Law School and for her constant encouragement during the writing of this book.

I am greatly indebted to Professor Carey Thompson for his constant, cheerful, and confident support of my work and to the Administrative Secretary of our Department, Mrs. Betty Fitzsimmons, and her assistants, Ina Berry, Janet Murphy, and Mary Willenborg, for having given me the essential logistical support without which no author can succeed. This support, too, has always been given willingly and with a smile. It has meant a great deal.

Obviously the responsibility for what I have said is my own.

H. H. Liebhafsky

Austin, Texas, 1970

Acknowledgments

I thank the following authors and publishers for permission to quote or paraphrase: M. A. Adelman, "The Measurement of Industrial Concentration," *Review of Economics and Statistics*, Vol. XXXII, November, 1951, Cambridge; Thurman Arnold, *The Symbols of Government*, 1935, Estate of Thurman Arnold, Washington, D. C.; A. A. Berle Jr. and Gardner Means, *The Modern Corporation and Private Property*, 1932, Macmillan, New York; J. L. Brierly, *The Law of Nations*, 1928, Oxford University Press, London; Benjamin N. Cardozo, *The Nature of the Judicial Process*, 1921, Yale University Press, New Haven; J. M. Clark, *Competition as a Dynamic Process*, 1961, The Brookings Institution, Washington, D. C.; J. M. Clark, "Toward a Concept of Workable Competition," *American Economic Review*, Vol. XXX, June, 1940; B. Joe Colwell, "Natural Gas Area Pricing: Economic and Legal Considerations," *Social Science Quarterly*, September, 1967, Austin; John R. Commons, *Legal Foundations of Capitalism*, 1924, Macmillan, New York; John R. Commons, *Institutional Economics*, 1934, Macmillan, New York; John Dewey, *Experience and Nature*, 1929, W. W. Norton, New York; John Dewey and James H. Tufts, *Ethics*, 1932, Henry Holt, New York; Corwin Edwards, *Maintaining Competition*, 1949, McGraw-Hill, New York; Corwin Edwards, "Public Policy and Business Size," *Journal of Business*, Vol. XXIV, October, 1951, Chicago; C. E. Ferguson, *The Macroeconomic Theory of Workable Competition*, 1964, Duke University Press, Durham; Marvin W. Foote, "Some Further Observations on Sentencing," *Trial Judges' Journal*, Vol. V, April, 1966, Chicago; Felix Frankfurter, *The Commerce Clause under Marshall, Taney, and Waite*, 1937, University of North Carolina Press, Raleigh; Wolfang Friedmann, *Law in a Changing Society*, 1959, Stevens & Sons, London; J. K. Galbraith, *American Capitalism*, 1956, Houghton-Mifflin, Boston; Samuel Gompers, *Seventy Years of Life and Labor*, 1925, E. P. Dutton, New York; J. W. Gough, *The Social Contract: A Critical Study*, 1957, Oxford University Press, London; Clare Griffin, *An Economic Approach to Antitrust Problems*, 1951, American Enterprise Association, New York; Learned Hand, *The Bill of Rights*, 1960, Harvard University Press, Cambridge; Charles Hartshorne and Paul Weiss (eds.), *Collected Papers of Charles Sanders Peirce*, 1960, Harvard University Press, Cambridge; Walter W. Heller, *New Dimensions of Political Economy*, 1967, Harvard University Press, Cambridge; Charles J. Hitch and Roland N. McKean, *The Economics of Defense in the Nuclear Age*, 1960, The Rand Corporation, Santa Monica; William C. Hood, "Empirical Studies of Demand," *The Canadian Journal of Economics and Political Science*, Vol. XXI, August, 1951, Toronto; Alfred E. Kahn, "Standards for Antitrust Policy," *Harvard Law Review*, Vol. LXVII, 1953, Cambridge; Stanley Kelley, *Professional Public Relations and Political Power*, 1948, The Johns Hopkins Press, Baltimore; Hans

Kelsen, *General Theory of Law and the State,* 1945, Legal Philosophy Series No. 1, Harvard University Press, Cambridge; Simon Kuznets, "The Contribution of Wesley C. Mitchell," in C. E. Ayres et al., *Institutional Economics,* University of California Press, Berkeley; Cornelia Geer Le Boutiller, *American Democracy and Natural Law,* 1950, Columbia University Press, New York; Karl N. Leweylln, *The Bramble Bush,* 1951 ed., Oceana Publications, Dobbs Ferry, N. Y.; H. A. Liebhafsky, "Modern Analytical Chemistry: A Subjective View," *Analytical Chemistry,* Vol. XXXIV, June, 1962, Washington, D. C.; Jacques Maritain, *The Range of Reason,* 1952, Charles Scribner's Sons, New York; Edward S. Mason, "Current Status of the Monopoly Problem," *Harvard Law Review,* Vol. LXII, 1949, Cambridge; Edward S. Mason, "Preface" to Carl Kaysen and Donald Turner, *Antitrust Policy,* 1959, Harvard University Press, Cambridge; Ronald Meek, "Value Judgments in Economics," *British Journal for the Philosophy of Science,* Vol. XV, August, 1964, Cambridge University Press, New York; Ralph L. Nelson, *Concentration in Manufacturing Industries in the United States,* 1963, Yale University Press, New Haven; Shorey Peterson, "Antitrust and the Classic Model," *American Economic Review,* Vol. XLVII, March, 1957; Karl Polanyi, *The Great Transformation,* 1944, Holt, Rinehart & Winston, New York; Roscoe Pound, *Law Finding Through Experience and Reason,* 1960, University of Georgia Press, Athens; Bertrand Russell, *Human Society in Ethics and Politics,* 1952, 1954, 1955; Simon and Schuster, New York; Paul Samuelson, "Theory and Realism: A Reply," *American Economic Review,* Vol. LIV, September, 1964; Joseph A. Schumpeter, *Capitalism, Socialism, and Democracy,* 1960, Harper & Row, New York; Edward A. Shils and Henry Finch (trs. and eds.), Max Weber, *The Methodology of the Social Sciences,* 1949, Macmillan (The Free Press), New York; George Stigler, "Comments on the Report of the Attorney General's Committee on Antitrust Policy," *American Economic Review Supplement,* Vol. XLVI, May, 1956; George Stigler, *Five Lectures on Economic Problems,* 1964, Macmillan, New York; F. W. Taussig, *A Tariff History of the United States,* 1931, G. P. Putnam's Sons, New York; Gus Tyler, *A Legislative Campaign for a Federal Minimum Wage (1955),* 1960, Eagelton Institute Cases in Practical Politics, Eagelton Institute, Rutgers; Myron W. Watkins, "Review of Edward S. Mason: Economic Concentration and the Monopoly Problem," *American Economic Review,* Vol. XLVII, September, 1957.

Contents

PART III

Special Working Rules which Replace or Modify the Operation of Market Forces

Table of Cases

AMERICAN GOVERNMENT
AND BUSINESS

Part I

THE PHILOSOPHICAL, POLITICAL, LEGAL, AND ECONOMIC SETTING

The Concept of Political Economy

The Purpose of This Book

This book seeks to provide factual information and to stimulate critical thinking with respect to some particular questions of *Political Economy*. That is, it undertakes to provide the reader with background information relating to, and with an analysis of, some of the principal issues and problems which arise from the interaction between selected uses of governmental power and certain private economic activities and relations in the United States with a view to stimulating the reader's thoughts on these subjects.

"Principal" issues and "selected" uses are terms requiring one to make value judgments. Indeed, the value judgments of an author permeate the whole of what he writes. Although it should be emphasized that there is a difference between value judgments made by someone with a personal interest in the outcome of an event (or whose personal interests will be advanced by a particular solution to a given problem) and those made by someone who has no such interest, one cannot ignore the fact that value judgments are made in all attempts to solve problems. In the final analysis, "scientific inquiry" is nothing more than a constant and never-ending process of problem-solving in a context of self-correcting value judgments, above which a special halo has been raised.

Different writers handle the problem of the value judgments contained in their works differently. One not uncommon approach is to ignore the problem altogether, leaving the reader to discover for himself when and where such value judgments enter the picture and how they affect its presentation. Another approach is to state that one is presenting "all sides" of the issue "fairly" and again to leave it to the reader to discover when and where the inevitable likes and dislikes and the prejudices of the author make themselves felt. A third approach is for an author to present his interpretation of various views and to state which of them he accepts or rejects and, at the same time, to indicate his own. The third approach may also contain hidden judgments and assumptions of which the author is unaware, but it opens the door to responsible debate and leaves the reader with a challenge. It is the third approach which is self-consciously adopted in this book because this book seeks to stimulate thought on the part of the reader.

In the next chapter we will examine three philosophical rationalizations of political democracy. Before we undertake this interesting and knotty problem, however, it will be useful to consider more fully the meaning of the concept of *Political Economy* with which this book deals. That question is the principal concern of this chapter, and it is treated in the next subdivision. The concluding subdivision of this introductory chapter provides a survey of the remaining chapters of this Part I (which is concerned largely with the presentation of background materials pertaining to various aspects of the subject) and a somewhat briefer survey of the scope and organization of the rest of this book.

A. THE DEFINITION OF "POLITICAL ECONOMY"

"Political Economy" Becomes "Economics"

It was once quite common to refer to the group of topics studied by economists as *Political Economy*. Thus, for example, Adam Smith titled Book IV of the work (*An Inquiry into the Nature and Causes of the Wealth of Nations*) which marks the origin of the English School of Classical Economists, "Of Systems of Political Economy." In it he discussed two "different" systems, "the system of commerce" and "that of agriculture," and touched upon topics ranging from the system of laws "established for the management of our American and West Indian Colonies" to the effect of a governmental policy of giving "prizes to successful artists and manufacturers" in encouraging "extraordinary dexterity and ingenuity," that is, to the effect of incentives on technological development. Smith's book was published in 1776, the year in which the *Declaration of Independence* was signed in the United States. And, just as the *Declaration* was not merely an abstract philosophical statement but contained in its later paragraphs a statement of the specific complaints of the colonists against "the present King" (George III), so also was Adam Smith's book not merely an abstract treatise. Instead, it was a documented statement of what Smith thought British governmental policy with respect to numerous economic activities and entities ought to be, given his basic assumptions about the nature of production, consumption, and man, as well as his acceptance of Sir Isaac Newton's explanation of the mechanics of the universe and the secular natural law philosophy which had been so greatly influenced by Newton's ideas about physics.

It has been many times pointed out that Smith argued that a governmental policy which aimed to foster the spontaneous and unhindered action of individuals—controlled by the "unseen hand" of competition—was more conducive to an increase in the wealth of a nation than any other policy. But the Theory of the Unseen Hand was merely one aspect (as T. E. Cliffe Leslie later pointed out) of Smith's philosophy, although it was the aspect which was most often repeated and refined by later economists. The other aspect is found in his statements in Book IV that the system of "natural liberty" which he advocated left the sovereign three duties: (1) providing for national defense; (2) administering justice; and (3) "establishing and maintaining certain public works and certain public institutions" which it would not be in the interest of any individual or group of individuals to erect or maintain "because the profit could never repay the expense to any individual or small number of individuals, though it may frequently do much more than repay it to a great society."[1] The concept of the Great Society of the 1960's was clearly not a new idea.

Smith's widely quoted statement, of course, provides no guide to policy for it does not explain how either the "profit" or the "expenses" are to be measured, much less how the profits or expenses of individuals can be compared with those of the "Great Society." And contemporary economists—we will see—have made little progress in this particular direction. Any attempt to define such costs and benefits (profits) must quite clearly involve all sorts of value judgments, and attempts to state them in the "scientific language" of contemporary economics do not escape this problem.

Smith's successor to the leadership of the English Classical School was David Ricardo

---

[1] Adam Smith, *An Inquiry into the Nature and Causes of the Wealth of Nations* (2 vols.; London: printed for W. Strahan and T. Cadell in the Strand, 1776), Vol. II, p. 289.

(an English stockbroker), who published his *Principles of Political Economy and Taxation* in 1817. Ricardo undertook to discover "the natural course of rent, profit, and wages" by means of deductive reasoning. He argued that "in different stages of society, the proportions of the whole produce of the earth which will be allotted to each of these classes [landowners, capitalists, and labourers] under the different names of rent, profit, and wages, will be essentially different." They were dependent, he asserted, "mainly on the actual fertility of the soil, on the accumulation of capital and population, and on the skill, ingenuity and instruments employed in agriculture." In the work of Ricardo the problem thus became one of the use of governmental power *corresponding to* appropriate Natural Laws rather than one of the use of governmental power *to create* conditions under which certain results were believed to be sure to follow. Both in spirit and in the flesh, Ricardo's abstract analysis and model building had more in common with present day *economic theory* than did Adam Smith's approach.

But this is not to say that Ricardo was uninterested in governmental policy concerning economic activities. On the contrary, Ricardo's deductive analysis enabled him to conclude that laws prohibiting the importation of grain ("the Corn Laws") into England were bad laws; they kept cheap grain out of the country, thereby producing an increase in rent, the price of the use of land, as population increased and pressed against the land available for production of the domestic food supply. Wages, Ricardo argued, would rise—in money terms. But the amount of food which money could buy would fall, and so the workers would be no better off than before; while the capitalists would suffer a declining rate of profits since, in his system, capitalists received what was left after rent and wages had been paid. With respect to laws providing for subsistence payments to the poor, the War on Poverty of his day, Ricardo argued for their repeal. It was only by:

. . . impressing on the poor the value of independence, by teaching them that they must

look not to systematic or casual charity, but to their own exertions for support, that prudence and forethought are neither unnecessary nor unprofitable virtues, we shall by degrees approach a sounder and more healthful state.[2]

And his view, it may be noted, still has its adherents in the United States today. Ricardo, it has been said, was the father of the theory of income distribution, the theory of the way in which the final product is shared among the various contributing factors of production.

Not all of Ricardo's contemporary students of economics agreed with him. Parson Thomas Robert Malthus, who is probably more widely known to most people as the author of *An Essay on Population* (1798), published his *Principles of Political Economy* in 1823. He disagreed with Ricardo concerning the nature of rent and, in 1815, defended the Corn Laws arguing that the high price of food was not the result of restrictions on imports imposed by law but was rather the result of pressure of the population on the food supply.[3] Malthus also believed in the possibility of a *general glut* of the market, a failure of the total demand for goods, a failure which would result in depression. Such a possibility was denied by Ricardo. Today it has, of course, become a standard article of faith in contemporary macroeconomic theory that it is possible for the economy to be in "equilibrium" at a level of employment which is less than "full." And so, today, as we will see in later chapters, the use of governmental power to avoid a "general glut" is a widely accepted idea.

In 1848, John Stuart Mill published his *Principles of Political Economy with Some of their Applications to Social Philosophy* and argued that, while there were "true natural" laws of production, the problem of distribution of income was a matter of social policy. Mill thereby raised the ethical problems implicit in the question of the distribution of the total product of a society. He argued that the positive use of governmental power in relation to economic activities was necessary in certain instances. For example, he asserted:

. . . There are matters in which the interference of law is required, not to overrule the

---

[2] David Ricardo, *Principles of Political Economy and Taxation* (2d ed.; London: J. W. Murray, 1819), chapter IV, "On Wages."

[3] T. R. Malthus, *An Inquiry into the Nature and Progress of Rent* (London, 1815).

judgment of individuals respecting their own interest but to give effect to that judgment; they being unable to give effect to it except by concert, which concert again cannot be effectual unless it receives validity and sanction from the law.[4]

Contemporary examples include workmen's compensation and social security.

As is apparent from Mill's title, he discussed ethical questions in his work. At the same time, however, there were economists who advocated the elimination of ethical and political considerations from the study of economics; they argued that economics should concern itself with "quantitative" concepts such as "exchange value." Among these one finds writers such as Henry McLeod, who was graduated in 1843 from Cambridge with honors in Mathematics,[5] W. S. Jevons (*Theory of Political Economy*, 1871) and the French economist, Leon Walras (*Elements of Pure Economics*, 1874). The last named is generally considered to be the father of "general equilibrium economics," and it is to him that contemporary mathematical economics owes its greatest debt. Note the substitution of the phrase "Pure Economics" for "Political Economy" in his title.

Alfred Marshall, the greatest of the English Neo-Classical economists published his *Principles of Economics* in 1890. Marshall's great work was a synthesis of various earlier ideas and emphasized the interrelationship between prices in *input* or *factor* markets and those in *output* or *product* markets. Although his system was essentially mathematical, Marshall relegated most of his mathematics to a separate *Mathematical Appendix* at the end of his book and wrote his text in the vein of Smith and Mill, stating his own ethical positions at many places. Marshall's *Principles* became the principal economics textbook in the English-speaking world and remained so until the late 1920's, if not later.

In the United States, the American Economic Association held its first annual meeting and published the results in 1886. Most of its founders had received their graduate training in Germany from teachers who were inclined to take an historical approach rather than the purely deductive approach of Ricardo. Most of these founders had much more in common with Mill than with Ricardo. A majority of them clearly demonstrated that *Political Economy* was the principal area of their interest by adopting a four-point policy statement which, while it disavowed any intention of taking a "partisan attitude" in the study of "industrial and commercial policy," nevertheless concluded with the sentence: "We believe in a progressive development of economic conditions, which must be met by a corresponding development of legislative policy."[6]

But the term *Political Economy* smacks of an art and of subjectivity rather than of a science and of objectivity. In the course of time the example of Walras was followed and the qualifying adjective was dropped, with a few exceptions, by those playing the role of "theoretical economist" in contemporary society.

Economics Becomes Quantitative but Not Always Quantifiable

Sometime before World War II, economic *theorists* began to direct their attention more and more to quantitative (mathematically stated) but not necessarily always quantifiable (measurable) magnitudes as subjects for analysis and manipulation and even more completely to assume away all the political, social, and legal relationships which affect public policy. The reason for assuming them away was a widespread belief that these things cannot be quantified and to take them into account would make economics less "scientific." Indeed, much effort has since been devoted to attempts to produce static measures of "economic welfare" which will be free from value judgments. This problem, which in itself is a contradiction of terms, will be discussed further in Chapter 10 of this book.

Today some slight progress in the direction of quantification of economic concepts has been made while, in many cases, the

[4] John Stuart Mill, *Principles of Political Economy with Some of their Applications to Social Philosophy* (2 vols., 5th ed.; New York: D. Appleton Co., 1890), Vol. II, p. 585.

[5] Lewis H. Haney, *History of Economic Thought* (3rd ed.; New York: The Macmillan Co., 1936), p. 516.

[6] Richard T. Ely, "Report of the Organization of the American Economic Association," *Publications of the American Economic Association*, Vol. I (March, 1886), pp. 35–36.

practice of assuming away the political, social, and legal factors affecting economic activities has continued. But progress in actual quantification—for example, in the areas of demand for goods, of costs, of production conditions facing firms and industries, and in the motivation of firms— is far less than most of those who are not privy to the secrets of mathematical economics and econometrics believe. Not only are definitional problems involved in the statements of the concepts employed, but data gathering problems exist. Statistical techniques, though improving, are far from completely reliable, particularly where attempts are made to measure changes in the values of the variables through historical time. Writing in 1955 in a paper in which he had surveyed the econometric studies of demand up to that time, William C. Hood (a Canadian econometrician) remarked:

> The conclusion seems to emerge from this review of the literature that our progress in this field since the days of Allen, Bowley, and Schultz [Schultz published his study in 1938] has been modest indeed. The improvements in economic theory have not been fundamental; while there have been some advances of note in statistical methodology and theory, the techniques in use now are much the same as those of earlier writers. ... Conditional regression cannot yet be accepted without reservation. On the problem of assessing our results we have probably not advanced at all. ...
> ... analysis of information will always require art, though the widening of the scope of scientific analysis—not merely econometrics—is a gain to be prized. Let us, therefore, continue to be thankful for artists.[7]

The conclusion reached by Hood in 1955 was confirmed ten years later (in 1965) by Professor William J. Baumol, who also provided a useful survey of the problems involved in attempts to determine demand relationships statistically.[8]

A survey of empirical studies of costs of production of firms by John Johnston in 1960 similarly points up the many diffi-

culties and problems in that area of investigation.[9] And in the area of productivity studies, Professor Solomon Fabricant, widely recognized as an outstanding empirical worker and as the director of one of the oldest (and probably the leading) institutions of empirical research in economics, the National Bureau of Economic Research (NBER), testified before a Congressional committee in 1959:

> A general deficiency of all the measures of output—and thus of productivity—is their failure to take adequate account of change in the quality of output. ... And, to repeat, the indexes of output per unit of labor and tangible capital combined, though broader than any other indexes now available, fail to cover adequately the investment in education, science, technology, and social organization that serves to increase production. ...
> The technical questions (which I have selected from a host), are, of course, matters primarily for the producer rather than the user of productivity statistics. But for the user it is important to be aware of the sharp differences made in the rate of growth of productivity by technical choices not always specified . . . namely, whether output or input is defined in one way rather than another, or weights or components of output and input are determined by this rather than that method, or data are selected or estimated from one or another source.[10]

Somewhat later Professor Fabricant stated:

> With the statistics presently available we have been able to measure the direct effects, on output, of increase in labor time and increase in volume of capital. *The indirect effects of the increase in these resources, and the effects of all other causes, we have been forced to lump together under the heading of "productivity" and to measure as a whole.* The residue contains the contributions of the several forms of intangible capital that I mentioned, education, and so on; the economies resulting from increased specialization within and between industries to which Adam Smith referred, economies made possible by growth in the Nation's resources and its scale of operations generally; the improvement (or falling off) of the efficiency in the use of resources resulting from change in the

[7] William C. Hood, "Empirical Studies of Demand," *Canadian Journal of Economics and Political Science*, Vol. XXI, (August, 1955), pp. 309–327, at p. 327.

[8] William J. Baumol, *Economic Theory and Operations Analysis*, (2d ed.; Englewood Cliffs: Prentice-Hall, Inc., 1965), pp. 210 ff.

[9] John Johnston, *Statistical Cost Analysis* (New

York: McGraw-Hill Book Co., Inc., 1960).

[10] *Employment, Growth and Price Levels* (Hearings before the Joint Economic Committee, 86th Cong., 1st sess.) (Washington, D.C.: U.S. Government Printing Office, 1959), Part 2, "Historical and Comparative Rates of Production, Productivity and Prices," p. 353.

degree of competition, in volume, direction and character of government subsidies, in the nature of the tax system, and in other Government activities and regulations; and the greater (or smaller) benefits resulting from change in the volume, character, and freedom of commerce among nations.[11]

The study to which Fabricant referred was one which was subsequently published by John W. Kendrick. Its principal conclusion is that between 1899 and 1953 the "efficiency" or productivity of a combined unit of input consisting of unit of capital-and-labor services (computed according to a particular formula) increased at an average rate of about 1.7 percent during this period.[12] What does this result mean? According to Professor Fabricant's further testimony:

The simple calculation . . . does no more than suggest the high relative importance of the factors grouped under productivity. But this is significant. *It is*, as Dr. Abramovitz has pointed out in another national bureau study, a *"measure of our ignorance concerning the causes of economic growth, and an indication of where we need to concentrate our attention." It is well to know how far short we are of determining the sources of increase in national product.*[13]

That the problems to which Professor Fabricant had called attention in 1959 still existed in 1967 is a conclusion which can be inferred from an examination of the publication in 1967 of a series of papers and comments on the theory and empirical analysis of production presented at a conference sponsored by the National Bureau of Economic Research in 1965.[14]

More examples could be given, but the point has been made sufficiently. These statements come not from authors of works in the area of static welfare economics or from critics; they come from some of the leading contemporary econometricians. In pointing to the "improvement [or falling off] of the efficiency in the use of resources resulting from the change in the degree of competition," what Fabricant undoub-

tedly had in mind was the fact that the Gross National Product (GNP)—from which may be derived numerous related magnitudes such as National Income, Personal Income, and Disposable Income that are heavily relied on in analyses presented in the *Annual Report of the President's Council of Economic Advisors* (whose work will be discussed in greater detail later)—is officially defined as a measure of "the Nation's output of goods and services in terms of its *market value*."[15]

When this measure is "expressed in current prices," it "reflects the total dollar value of production"; when it is "expressed in constant dollars to eliminate the effect of price changes, it provides an overall index of the physical volume of goods and services produced by the economy."[16] Thus, to the extent that monopoly power or a lack of competition result in higher prices than would otherwise exist in some areas of the economy, the value figure for the products of that sector may be higher than it would be in the absence of such conditions. And, since the elimination of general price changes involves the use of price index numbers to produce the constant dollar figure which is taken as representative of the physical volume of output, whether or not and to what extent the prices of such products enter into the index will affect the final result. The use of such price indexes rests in turn upon the concepts of contemporary demand theory, and most particularly upon concepts developed in static-welfare economics by price theorists. Unfortunately, economists have not been able to solve the so-called "index number problem," a point which was made quite clear by Mr. Ewan Clague, formerly Commissioner of Labor Statistics, in 1961 in testimony before the Subcommittee on Economic Statistics of the Joint Economic Committee of the Congress. A report on government price statistics had been completed in 1961 by a committee of economists under the Chairmanship of Professor George

---

[11] *Ibid.*, p. 356. (Italics mine.)
[12] John W. Kendrick, *Productivity Trends in the United States* (Princeton, N.J.: Princeton University Press, 1961), esp. p. 60.
[13] *Employment, Growth and Price Levels, op. cit.*, p. 356. (Italics mine.)
[14] Murray Brown (ed.), *The Theory and Empirical Analysis of Production* (National Bureau of Economic

Research Studies in Income and Wealth No. 31) (New York: Columbia University Press, 1967).
[15] United States Department of Commerce, *A Supplement to the Survey of Current Business, National Income* (Washington, D.C.: U.S. Government Printing Office, 1954), p. 1. (Italics mine.)
[16] *Ibid.*

Stigler of the University of Chicago (a leading price theorist) under a contract with the Bureau of the Budget. It was with reference to this report that Mr. Clague (whose Bureau of Labor Statistics has the responsibility for preparing various index numbers for governmental and other use) said:

> The committee expresses the opinion that a "constant-utility" or "welfare" index would be superior to a consumer price index for most purposes and should be developed to supersede the present index. . . . The committee uses the terms "constant-utility" or "welfare" index in the sense of what theorists generally call a true cost-of-living index.
>
> . . . It is important to note that the committee's strong preference for a *welfare* index is the motivating force behind the various recommendations it makes. Thus, while some recommendations are pertinent to, and can be evaluated in terms of applicability to fixed-weight indexes, other recommendations are acceptable only if one first accepts the committee's overriding preference for the *welfare* index approach.[17]

In its Report the Subcommittee remarked, among other things:

> Statistics users from industry, labor, and agriculture appearing or represented at the hearings were generally opposed to trying to go very far in the direction of an index which puts *major emphasis on attempting to measure how much a given level of satisfaction, or welfare, costs* in one period of time against another. They based their opposition somewhat upon the concept of such an index but mostly upon the impossibility of finding proper measures for such satisfactions. The academic witnesses who appeared the last day of the hearings were more hopeful that something could be done in working toward a welfare index and that it would be worthwhile to devote research effort in that direction.[18]

Obviously, the problem of quantification is far from being solved in any area of economics.

The Current Tendency for "Economics" Again to Become "Political Economy"

Today many economists take the view that economic theory can and should be free from value judgments. Indeed, partly because of serious problems of definition and measurement (like those described above) and, even more so, because of the great emphasis which has been placed on problems of growth and development since World War II, more and more economists are coming to admit publicly that it is not possible to derive *from within the field of economic theory itself* the value judgments that are essential as the basis and terms of reference of any discussion of society as a "going concern." Economists actively working in the field of government policy today widely recognize that economic considerations represent only part of most problems. As Simon Kuznets, the inventor of the system of national income accounts, has remarked:

> In short, given the mutability of economic and social institutions . . . and the resulting changes in the nature of major economic policy problems, there is a great conflict today between the requirement that a comprehensive theory of economic behavior be based in large part on the statistical approach and the claim that such a theory will be available for guidance in the solution of policy problems. In the nature of the case, a really comprehensive and statistically founded theory cannot be available until long after any given set of major problems has emerged and been somehow resolved; and it would have been solved, if it was, with the help of the empirical evidence (necessarily partial) available at the time and with a variety of incomplete, partial hypotheses (many claiming more generality than they in fact possess) entertained while the evidence for testing them is still to be assembled. If one assumes . . . as most of us do, that it is next to impossible for economic scholars to ignore the major problems of the day, and if the complete, statistically based theory is something that one strives for but never attains, perhaps one should, in the service of policy problems, admit the necessary limitations of the statistical approach and assign a greater role to incomplete and partial theories that provide reasonable shortcuts. . . . They may be indispensible not only as the best solutions to changing policy problems but also as valuable leads to the qualitative distinctions that are so basic even in statistical measurement and empirical study.[19]

[17] *Government Price Statistics* (Report of and Hearings before the Subcommittee on Economic Statistics, Joint Economic Committee, 87th Cong., 1st sess.) (Washington, D.C.: U.S. Government Printing Office, 1961), Part II, p. 578. (Italics mine.)

[18] *Ibid.*, *Report*, p. 5. (Italics mine.)

[19] Simon Kuznets, "The Contribution of Wesley C. Mitchell," in C. E. Ayres, Neil W. Chamberlain, Josef Dorfman, R. A. Gordon, and Simon Kuznets, (eds.) *Institutional Economics* (Berkeley: University of California Press, 1963), p. 120.

The very fact of these recent developments, trends, and statements, like those by Kuznets earlier, raise interesting questions concerning the role of the economist *qua* economic theorist in the area of policy formulation, and this question will also be considered in greater detail in later chapters. As a wise man with a knowledge of specific facts, an economist may have a great deal to contribute to the solution of a particular problem, but the same statement can also be made of a wise political scientist, a wise psychologist, or any other wise man. In short, a notion that there is such a thing as a "purely economic solution" to a policy problem is both misleading and dangerous: there are economic *aspects* of policy problems just as there are other aspects, but the present state of development of economic theory does not justify giving economic *theory* a preeminent or decisive role in the area of policy formulation. This point has been clearly recognized by Professor Walter Heller (former Chairman of the Council of Economic Advisors) in his *New Dimensions of Political Economy*. (Note his title.)

Indeed, today more and more economists are coming to agree with Professor John H. Williams, who remarked in 1951 that he had serious reservations about the "dependability of theory as a guide to policy" and cautioned that "the most dangerous policy maker is the man who knows the answer because he can take it literally from his theory."[20] Other writers have also taken this position.[21]

The limitations stated by Williams apply, of course, to the advocacy of "sound economic policy" by economists. For the most part, economists are apt to emphasize goals such as "full and efficient employment of resources" in order to "maximize" output at "least cost," within a context of "a steady state of economic growth "as objectives of "economic" policy. Even if we accept all these goals—*no matter how we may personally define them*—as desirable, a problem arises of whether they are to be attained at the expense of other so-called "noneconomic" goals. About these, the economist *qua* economist has very little to say, given his present limited area of investigation and interest. (This point will be further discussed in Chapter 32.) Although today there is much discussion among some economists of the application of mathematical programming techniques to "economic problems," the problem of determining *the* "objective" to be maximized is not solved by the use of such techniques. These mathematical techniques all assume *the* "objective" to be given. What has been admitted in a recent book by Hitch and McKean, who advocate the application of the maximization principles of price theory to national defense problems, can be taken as applicable to other problems of public policy as well. They have remarked:

Even at relatively low levels, incommensurables are likely to be too important to ignore; and in some low level problems they are dominant. In other words, there are military problems at all levels in which a definitive economic calculus cannot be made because of the multiplicity, incommensurability, or nonmeasurability of the objectives or costs.[22]

In their book, Hitch and McKean conclude that "the right way to measure cost" in the long run is by the approximate "value of the alternatives that must be sacrificed." In the long run they would use the dollar value of resources as a measure, but in the short run they find that the difficulties of measurement are greater.[23]

Clearly, the concept of "alternative" or of "opportunity cost" employed by Hitch and McKean is an empty phrase in the absence of a specification of the methods of measuring the costs which accrue in, and the benefits to be obtained from, following this or that course of action. Because they have recognized this fact, they have employed the concept of the "dollar value of resources"—apparently without recognizing that such a concept itself involves an implicit assumption that actual market prices are a measure of the *social* value of the goods or inputs to which they are attached and therefore their use in this way involves an implicit ap-

[20] John H. Williams, *Economic Stability in a Changing World* (New York: Oxford University Press, Inc., 1953), p. 15.

[21] Harry N. Rosenfield, "Experts Are Never Right," *The Antioch Review*, Vol. IX (March, 1949),

pp. 3–15, at pp. 3 and 14.

[22] Charles J. Hitch and Roland N. McKean, *The Economics of Defense in the Nuclear Age* (Cambridge: Harvard University Press, 1960), p. 183.

[23] *Ibid.*, pp. 171–72.

proval of the *status quo in actual markets.* Thus, these authors have criticized the statement by a Cabinet officer—that his Department believed "that the costs of multiple-purpose . . . projects should be allocated on a basis that properly recognizes the added costs of including each separable function and a *fair* share of joint costs"—by italicizing the word *fair* and remarking that the use of this word involves "the unwarranted intrusion of ethical concepts into an economic calculus."

Indeed, they themselves have asserted *in the same context* that "dollars do, even if imperfectly, take account of the *value* in other uses of different skills and of factors of production other than labor."[24] Apparently in their minds the term *value* either involves no ethical considerations of the type involved in the word *fair* or else such minor ones that they can be ignored. In short, Hitch and McKean accept the view that actual market price *is* a measure of the social value of an activity. And, of course, it is their basic ethical assumption which has made it possible for their economics to become "quantitative." Clearly, the Hitch and McKean "defense economics" is in reality an application of mathematical techniques *in accordance with a given ethical assumption* and ignores many of the problems arising from the impact of expenditures for national defense.

The preceding discussion of the work of Hitch and McKean leads naturally to mention of "cost-benefit analysis." These words are used to identify attempts by economists and others to measure quantitatively the "costs" of various social investments and the "benefits" of these investments for purposes of making public policy decisions. Among the earliest attempts to make such measurements must be counted the activities of the United States Army Corps of Engineers under the Rivers and Harbors Act of 1902, which required the United States Army Corps of Engineers to report on river and harbor projects, taking into account the amount of commerce benefitted and the cost. Today, it is recognized that not only *direct*, but also *indirect* costs and benefits must be taken into

account. Thus, evaluation of an irrigation project may involve an estimate not only of the increase in agricultural output resulting from increased irrigation, but also the effect of the project on employment and income of grain millers and bakers. If the project involves building of a dam, the effect of the new dam on existing dams must also be considered, as well as the value of any recreational facilities produced as a by-product. Obviously, *evaluations* of this sort require many value judgments and also employ market prices as measures of social value. A useful survey of the literature in this field has been provided by A. R. Prest and R. Turvey; their conclusion, like that of Thomas Hood concerning statistical studies of demand, is that cost-benefit analysis is one of the "useful arts" as distinguished from a science.[25]

The use of market price as a measure of social value originated in economics partly from necessity, partly from a desire to rationalize the *status quo*, and partly from a desire to make economic analysis quantitative—a desire which, in turn, was based on a peculiar belief originating perhaps, in the seventeenth and eighteenth centuries that the terms "quantitative," "objective," and "ultimate truth" are synonymous, and partly from the adoption by some economists in their theoretical works of either a natural law philosophy or of one of logical positivism, with its accompanying cultural relativism, or of what has recently been more aptly termed (by C. E. Ayres) its "moral agnosticism." (These philosophical tendencies are further considered in the next chapter.)

Professor J. M. Clark one of the most eminent of American economists in the first half of this century (and the son of one of the leading economists of the last part of the last century and early part of this one), also directed his attention to the adoption of cultural relativism by economists and remarked in 1961:

. . . *Consumers' preferences, under the conditions in which they are generated and expressed, are certainly not authoritative standards of welfare, and to accept them as such—as theoretical "welfare economics" does— is to abdicate the problem. If no authoritative yard-*

[24] *Ibid.*, pp. 171–74. (Italics mine.)
[25] A. R. Prest and R. Turvey, "Cost-Benefit Analysis: A Survey," in *Surveys of Economic Theory,* Vol. III (New York: St. Martin's Press, 1966), pp. 155–207.

stick is available in a free and democratic society, it is at least possible to compare them with the conditions necessary to successful choosing and compare them with the conditions that exist in the current American economy. It may be easier to identify the conditions necessary and favorable for successful choosing than to define the choices that should result.[26]

As has just been noted, in the next chapter, the logical positivist position in philosophy will be more closely examined with particular reference to the way the logical positivist approach seeks to rationalize political democracy. In Chapter 3, we shall also examine the related tendency in legal philosophy which is called legal positivism or analytical jurisprudence.

It should be emphasized that what has been said above does not necessarily lead to the conclusion that the use of actual market prices as a measure of trends in the national income statistics and elsewhere can be readily abandoned. Indeed, in Chapter 8 and elsewhere in this book, such statistics will be employed in a survey of the changes which have occurred in certain economic magnitudes between 1789 and the present time. The present discussion does, however, seek to emphasize that, since actual market prices are a reflection of the *status quo* in markets, their use as a measure of social value does incorporate various value judgments which are often ignored and which are sometimes, as is clearly true in the case of the Hitch and McKean statement quoted earlier, not even recognized or admitted. Such a procedure may be productive of a kind of *apparent* certainty, but conclusions derived from indulging in it may be quite misleading. An awareness of the limitations involved in the employment of such measures ought always to accompany their use, whatever may be the significance of such awareness for the reputation of Economics as a "hard" science.

Writers who undertake to define and explain the meaning of the term *economic policy* inevitably end up explaining away their use of the term by pointing out that this term is, in their usage of it, sufficiently broad to mean "a complex of many related ends and means" and that broadly inter-

preted the phrase refers to a "group of policies." Such difficulties are, quite obviously, the result of the fact that the use of governmental power is almost never based on *purely* "economic" considerations and that there is no such thing as a "government economic policy" distinct from and independent of all other government policies. The real danger in the notion that there is such a *separate* "economic" policy concerning the use of governmental power is that this view suggests that there exists a policy which can be formulated on the basis of, or tested against, "economic principles" *alone* and that economists have some *special* talent or ability for formulating external norms or "social welfare functions" to be employed in selecting the "best" social policies.

It is only in economic models, built by economic theoreticians—for example, the one discussed and explained in Chapter 10—that individuals can be said to have purely economic motives; and in such models, as has been noted, it is almost always assumed that government does not exist, or that the use of governmental power can be ignored, and that the "existing institutional arrangements are given." Usually the justification for such assumptions consists of an assertion that to introduce the effects of the use of governmental power or of non-economic motives into the model would involve serious complications which might make it impossible for any conclusions at all to be drawn. Thus, for example, the authors of one economic theory book have defended the assumption that "businessmen" behave rationally to maximize profits" (the basic assumption of the orthodox static theory of the firm) on grounds that to "introduce a more realistic assumption would make economic theory very difficult" and, besides, "no one really knows what the correct assumption would be."[27]

More recently another economist has stated this position even more fully:

It is reasonable to believe that economic and (say) politico-philosophical objectives do not have an equal footing in any individual's hierarchy of wants. Bread and freedom are probably

[26] J. M. Clark, *Competition as a Dynamic Process* (Washington, D.C.: The Brookings Institution, 1961), p. 217. (Italics mine.)

[27] Alfred W. Stonier and Douglas C. Hague, *A Textbook of Economic Theory* (2d ed.; London: Longmans, Green and Co., Ltd., 1957), p. 2.

not equivalent objectives, although I would not presume to say which is paramount. In studying policy formulation within the context of a specific set of economic objectives, one simply recognizes that there are likely to be other aims, some of which are more important and others less important. Our conclusions accordingly hold for situations in which the objectives of higher order are equally satisfied. We have already alluded to this by stipulating that the choice of targets and techniques must not violate the more basic objectives and, in particular, that the process of choice must itself not be a value.

Whether these conditions are satisfied or can be satisfied is actually a moot question. Contemplating this point is exactly like contemplating the philosophical theorem about interpersonal utility comparisons. It presents a fascinating problem in logic; but if one complies with the logical conclusions, he is forced to renounce policy questions as insoluable by scientifically trained people. Therefore, we feel justified in proceeding *as if* these conditions were satisfied.[28]

It follows that, since the analysis contemplated in the quotation is conducted on the basis of the assumption that the other conditions *are* satisfied, *if they are not in fact satisfied*, the ensuing analysis reduces to a verbal solution of a nonexistent problem. The procedure adopted in the quotation above, a procedure not uncommon among economic *theorists*, seems in fact to be a perversion of a position once stated by Max Weber, a great German scholar, who wrote:

. . . The constructs of pure economics which are useful for analytical purposes cannot, however, be made the sources of practical value-judgments. Economic theory can tell us absolutely nothing more than that for the attainment of the given technical end, x, y is the sole appropriate means or is such together with y^1 and y^2 respectively; and that their application and thus the attainment of the end x requires that the "subsidiary consequences," z, z^1 and z^2 be taken into account. These are all merely reformulations of causal propositions, and to the extent that "evaluations" can be imputed to them, they are exclusively of the type which is concerned with the degree of rationality of a prospective action. The evaluations are unambiguous *only* when the economic end and the social context are definitely given and all that remains is to choose between several economic means, when these differ only with respect to their certainty, rapidity, and quantitative productiveness, and are completely identical in every other value-relevant aspect. It is only when these conditions have been met that we evaluate a given means as "technically most correct," and it is only then that the evaluation is unambiguous. In every other case, *i.e.*, in every case which is not purely a matter of technique, the evaluation ceases to be unambiguous and evaluations enter which are not determinable exclusively by economic analysis.[29]

To *assume* that the "social context is given," when it is not, may result in an evaluation which is ambiguous or meaningless if that which is assumed does not correspond to reality. Some writers, like Fritz Machlup and Milton Friedman, have, however, taken a different view. They have argued that even though the *assumptions* on which a theory is based *are* unrealistic, nevertheless, the theory can be made to yield meaningful conclusions which can serve as a basis for policy. Their position has recently been explicitly rejected by another leading American economist, Paul A. Samuelson, who has remarked:

. . . the doughnut of empirical correctness in a theory constitutes its worth, while its hole of untruth constitutes its weakness. *I regard it as a monstrous perversion of science to claim that a theory is all the better for its shortcomings;* and I notice that in the luckier exact sciences, no one dreams of making such a claim.

In connection with slavery, Thomas Jefferson said that, when he considered that there is a just God in Heaven, he trembled for his country. Well, in connection with the exaggerated claims that used to be made in economics for the power of deduction and *a priori* reasoning—by classical writers, by Carl Menger, by the 1932 Lionel Robbins (first edition of *The Nature and Significance of Economic Science*), by disciples of Frank Knight, by Ludwig von Mises—I tremble for the reputation of my subject.[30]

And there, as far as economists are concerned, the matter rests. The reader can take his choice as to which position he accepts as his own.

---

[28] Charles E. Ferguson, *A Macroeconomic Theory of Workable Competition* (Durham: Duke University Press, 1964), p. 56. (Italics his.)

[29] Edward A. Shils and Henry A. Finch (eds. and trs.), *The Methodology of the Social Sciences, Max Weber* (Glencoe, Ill.: The Free Press, 1949), pp. 37–38. (Italics his.)

[30] Paul A. Samuelson, "Theory and Realism: A Reply," *American Economic Review*, Vol. LIV (September, 1964), pp. 736–39, at p. 736. (Italics his and mine.) See also the further discussion in *American Economic Review*, Vol. LV (December, 1965), pp. 1153 ff.

A rejection of the notion that governments do have *purely* "economic policies" does *not* lead to the conclusion that use of governmental power has no effect on the economic activities of private individuals or on the various so-called "economic quantities" (prices, incomes, rates of growth, employment, etc.) to which contemporary economic theorists devote most of their attention. On the contrary, there are few if any areas of economic life and activity which are not affected by the use of governmental power. And this situation has always existed. For example, as Karl Polanyi pointed out, contrary to a contemporary myth, the market economy in England did not just "happen" after the Industrial Revolution had gotten underway; nor did it arise from men's "propensity to truck, barter, and exchange" as Adam Smith had asserted. Instead, the market economy was established by legislative and judicial action designed to change the existing institutional structure into one which would be compatible with a market economy, and much hardship was suffered by those who had hitherto been protected by the previously-existing institutional arrangements.[31]

Consider also that the Tennessee Valley Authority was established by Congress in 1933 for the specific purposes of: (1) "flood control"; (2) "navigation"; and (3) "maximum generation of electric power," to the extent that this objective was "consistent with flood control and navigation"; with the additional objective of improving, increasing, and cheapening "the production of fertilizer and fertilizer ingredients." These specific purposes were all in pursuance of a generally stated intention on the part of Congress to promote "the economic and social well-being" of the people living in the valley and "to conserve and develop" the valley's resources. An "economic" evaluation of such a multiple purpose project, that is, a cost-benefit analysis, would thus involve an "economic" measure of "social well being," and something more is needed than merely a static measure of "profitability" of production of electric power in terms of current money

values. Where there are multiple objectives (benefits or profits), the problem of identifying and allocating "common costs" can only be solved by some rule of thumb (habit based on experience) or by some arbitrary method, or else in a democratic reconciliation of competing interests, that is to say, by the political process.

Implicit in what has been said thus far is the proposition that the term *Political Economy* encompasses something more than merely bringing the most recent developments of *pure economic theory* to bear upon the various problems which are raised for consideration; that is, something more is involved than merely evaluating various policies by analyzing their effects on production, distribution, and consumption of goods and assuming that politico-philosophical objectives have been met, even if they have not been met.

John R. Commons on the Meaning of "Political Economy"

What *is* involved can, perhaps, be best explained by quoting the definition of *Political Economy* formulated by John R. Commons in 1924, which reads:

. . . the state also proportions the factors over which it has control. It opens up certain areas, localities or resources, instead of others. It does this, not directly as individuals do, but indirectly through working rules which guide the transactions of individuals. It encourages or protects certain businesses or classes of business, certain occupations or jobs, rather than others. It restrains certain activities deemed detrimental to the whole. Its proportioning of factors is the proportioning of inducements to individuals and associations of individuals to act in one direction rather than in other directions. This proportioning by means of working rules to individuals and associations is *Political Economy*.[32]

The *working rules* exist in many forms "such as the common law, statute law, shop rules, business ethics, business methods, norms of conduct," and so on; they "appear, in the history of the race, as the essential and ultimate means by which the members of a going concern are able to work together . . . and to exert their united

---

[31] Karl Polanyi, *The Great Transformation* (New York: Rinehart and Co., Inc., 1944).

[32] John R. Commons, *Legal Foundations of Capitalism*

(New York: The Macmillan Co., 1924), p. 387. Also in paperback, Madison: The University of Wisconsin Press, 1957.

power against other concerns."[33] Another name for working rules is "institutional arrangements." Such arrangements specify relationships *among men* and *between men and things*. These arrangements include norms of behavior. They may be formal (statutes, court decisions, codes, administrative orders); or they may be informal (traditions, customs, status relationships). Every price system exists within the context of such working rules. They lie behind the broad catch-all categories of "supply" and "demand" in the same way as they lie behind prices which are determined administratively, although the kinds of working rules applicable to these two broad classifications of the ways in which prices may be determined differ. Instead of being an ultimate standard of valuation to which the social order *ought* to conform, *actual* market prices are in reality a reflection of that social order which does exist. To accept *actual* market prices as a measure of social valuation is thus to accept the *status quo* in markets; and to argue that a particular configuration of prices *should* exist is tantamount to arguing that the social order which will produce that configuration *should* exist.

The subject of *Political Economy* is thus much broader than the "economic calculus" (used by Hitch and McKean or in cost-benefit analysis) which Walras called "Pure Economics"; it involves questions of philosophy, of law, of politics, of sociology, of history—in short, it involves all of the disciplines having to do with the explanation and analysis of the existing social order. And, since no one individual can expect to have a complete knowledge of all the fields encompassed, heavy reliance must be placed upon the work of many scholars working in many different fields. That this is the case is readily apparent in the following survey of the scope and organization of this book.

B. THE SCOPE AND PLAN OF THIS BOOK

This book is concerned primarily with an examination of some selected working rules of economic activity and organization in the United States today. The background materials in Part I have been included primarily because any intelligent discussion in later parts of this book of *specific* working rules must rest upon a knowledge of some essential elements of history, of constitutional law, and of the nature of the process by which social changes are incorporated in law, as well as of the nature of economic theory. Moreover, as already implied the philosophical tendencies evident in the policy positions taken by legal philosophers are reflections of tendencies and points of view in philosophy proper. The same is true of economists. The importance of understanding and identifying the philosophical biases of individuals lies in the fact that such knowledge provides a basis for insights into the real meanings of statements made by individuals about working rules and into the attitudes held toward, and the evaluations of, such rules by particular scholars and judges.

For example, the natural law philosophy of an earlier time—particularly as developed in the works of St. Thomas Aquinas—is apparently today being revived in contemporary jurisprudence with a variable definition of the term "natural." This philosophy provides one (but not the only) rationalization in defense of the proposition that the provisions concerning personal freedom in the First Ten Amendments to the Constitution are "absolutes." A secular natural law approach was also used by some to rationalize the trials of German war criminals on charges of having committed "Crimes against Humanity." That logical positivism in philosophy has its counterparts in positive or analytical jurisprudence has already been noted. And finally, that characteristic indigenous American philosophical development known as "pragmatism" or "instrumentalism" also has its counterparts in several theories of law and government regulation. Indeed, the underlying philosophical bias of the author of this book is that of instrumentalism.

In view of the existence of this state of affairs, Chapter 2, as has been mentioned, undertakes briefly to examine the ways in which three contemporary general philosophical tendencies undertake to rationalize political democracy and serves as back-

[33] *Ibid.*, pp. 6 and 68.

ground for the examination of particular philosophical tendencies in law in Chapter 3. For emphasis, it should be repeated that Part I consists of *general* background materials, while the rest of the book is concerned with the examination of *specific* working rules.

Parts II and III of this book are respectively concerned with an examination of the antitrust laws and of the activities of regulatory agencies. The antitrust laws and laws to protect consumers are working rules whose function is to strengthen the operation of market forces by creating conditions to insure that competition may serve to provide a set of economic checks and balances; that is, such laws may be thought of as laws to *enforce* and supplement competition. Regulatory commissions, on the other hand, have been created to enforce special working rules to deal with situations in which for various reasons, depending on the case being considered, market forces do not operate effectively either in controlling results in particular markets or in determining the direction of movement of and level of economic aggregates. Such working rules replace or modify the operation of market forces.

In both cases, much of the public policy is formally stated and implemented in the process of actual litigation, pretrial settlement of actual law suits, and in administrative proceedings. Some understanding of what lawyers think about the nature and functions of law and of the judicial process, as well as of how they think, is thus necessary to an intelligent discussion of working rules in these areas. Chapters 3 and 4 deal with these topics: Chapter 3 contains not only a discussion of different philosophies of law but also a discussion of types of law; Chapter 4 considers the process of judicial decision as a source of changes in law, including the question of "creative interpretation."

The law suits and administrative proceedings within which certain public policies and changes in law are formulated on a day-to-day basis by a process of trial and error inclusion and exclusion are, in turn, based on broad constitutional provisions and on constitution-like statutes. Moreover, executive action may also produce changes in law. Chapters 5 and 6 are thus concerned

with an examination of the philosophy of law and social change contained in the Constitution—in particular, the recognition given to the existence of lobbies and pressure groups by Madison in the *Federalist*—and with the activities of Congress and the President in the process of producing actual changes in law. Chapter 7 represents the capstone of the five background chapters dealing with the problems of law and social change and contains a survey of the contemporary policies of the Supreme Court with respect to the basic provisions of the Constitution. *The relationship between policies relative to civil and voting rights and those relative to working rules regulating economic activity is examined in detail.*

The use of governmental power to promote, control, guide, and direct economic activities and organization in the United States is not a twentieth century innovation. Governmental power has always been used for these purposes in the United States. Chapter 8 provides a broad survey of the growth of various economic quantities along with information on government policies seeking to promote or deter such growth since 1789.

Chapter 9, in turn, examines the particular question of the changes in the form and in the concentration of private economic power which have occurred since 1789. This chapter relies heavily on various investigations conducted by governmental agencies (including Congressional committees) for basic data, and also contains an examination of various merger movements.

Chapter 10 contains a verbal description of the general model of price theory and definitions of certain basic concepts, such as that of "perfect competition," employed by price theorists. This chapter has been designed primarily for readers who do *not* possess specialized training in economic theory. Chapter 11, the concluding chapter of Part I discusses various measures of market control and of resource control which have been devised by economists and also provides a survey of empirical studies of concentration of economic power in the hands of business associations. It concludes with a historical survey of the growth of the power of organized labor in the United States.

As is clear from the foregoing description,

Part I contains materials from many different fields, some of which will already be familiar to some readers and others of which will be familiar to other readers; but all these materials will probably be familiar to only a few readers. There will be fewer still who will have given much thought to the various interrelationships which exist among the philosophical, legal, and economic ideas which are discussed in Part I or to the question of how they are related to the working rules of economic activity and organization in the United States.

The remainder of the book, as has already been noted, is concerned with an examination of selected specific working rules of economic activity and organization. Not all of the specific working rules of the American economic system are considered in this book; any attempt to do so would extend this book beyond all reasonable limits. Moreover, even though they may not be identified as such, some specific working rules are dealt with in detail in various special courses. Thus, for example, working rules pertaining to labor organization, employment contracts, and conditions of employment are the subject of intensive study in courses in Labor Economics; working rules pertaining to the establishment of full employment and to the stabilization and growth of the economy are studied in courses in National Income Analysis and in Money and Banking; and working rules pertaining to international

economic activities and organization are the subject of courses in International Economics. Nevertheless, all such working rules are a part of Political Economy. In this book, because they are dealt with in detail in special courses, such rules will be treated much more briefly than will be working rules such as the antitrust laws and specific working rules pertaining to the regulation of particular industries and activities which are not dealt with in such special studies and which have traditionally, therefore, been the subject of books titled variously as "Business and Government" or "Social Control of Industry." Thus, as has been noted, Part II consists of several chapters dealing with the antitrust laws; Part III examines typical working rules pertaining to particular industries (e.g., transportation, communications, etc.), to particular activities (e.g., operations in securities markets, production of foods and drugs, etc.), and to the control of economic aggregates.

Chapter 12, the first chapter of Part II, contains a description of the scope and organization of Part II; while Chapter 23, the first chapter in Part III, contains an analogous description of the scope and organization of Part III.

The reader is now challenged to consider which, if any, of the three basic philosophical rationalizations of political democracy discussed in the next chapter comes closest to representing his own view.

2

Three Philosophical Rationalizations of Political Democracy

This chapter discusses the rationalizations of political democracy provided by three contemporary philosophical views: logical positivism; natural law philosophy; and instrumentalism or pragmatism. As has been noted, it is the last of these three positions which this writer prefers.

The first of the three views to be discussed, *logical or analytical positivism*, represents the views of writers who, while they do not constitute a "school," nevertheless have two basic beliefs in common: (1) formal philosophy should concern itself only with *Logical Analysis*, and not with statement of a "world view"; and (2) questions of ultimate value are not proper subjects for scientific analysis. The moral agnosticism expressed by these writers is probably more widely adopted by economists in their *theoretical* tracts dealing with "static welfare economics" than is any other view.

The moral agnosticism adopted by logical positivists has not gone unchallenged either by secular natural law philosophers or by those adopting the pragmatic and, especially, the instrumentalist point of view. The natural law conception of ultimate truth is not widely held in contemporary

economic theory, but it is being increasingly relied upon by legal philosophers in justification of "human rights," especially since the Nuremberg trials of German war criminals; and it has always been a bulwark in the defense of property rights, for example, in interpretations of the due process clauses of the Fifth and Fourteenth Amendments to the Constitution of the United States. For this reason, contemporary secular *natural law* philosophy, will be considered *second*.

The *third* philosophical tendency to be discussed below is *pragmatism*, with particular reference to instrumentalism. This tendency is important because, although contemporary economists generally adopt moral agnosticism in their *theoretical* works, practicing economists (especially those in government service) have always operated within a pragmatic context of self-correcting value judgments to make policy recommendations relating to goals which are instrumentally defined but never final. For example, the Council of Economic Advisors stated in 1964 in its discussion of the problem of poverty in the United States:

Poverty is costly not only to the poor but to

the whole society . . . the overriding objective is to improve the quality of life of individual human beings. For poverty deprives the individual not only of material comforts but of human dignity and fulfillment. Poverty is rarely a builder of character.[1]

The preceding statement clearly is *not* morally agnostic.

Even more to the point are the following statements by Professor Walter Heller, who served as Chairman of the Council during the Kennedy Administration and at the beginning of the Johnson Administration. On the basis of his own experience, Professor Heller has written:

. . . The detached, Olympian, take-it-or-leave-it approach to Presidential economic advice— the dream of the logical positivist— simply does not accord with the demands of relevance and realism and the requirements of the Employment Act.

. . . Unlike his academic colleague who can abstract from reality, deal with ultimates, and envision quantum jumps in our progress toward the ideal economic state, the economic practitioner has to operate deep in the heart of realism, has to deal with movement *toward* rather than *to* the ideal, and has to be at all times multidimensional in his objectives. The lump sum tax—economically the best of all taxes—will never replace the lump of taxes we now live with. And the principle that a change is good if the gainers could more than compensate the losers—the central policy precept of formal welfare economics—is a sterile guide when, in practice, the compensation can never be made. All this exaggerates my point, particularly since many academic economists are themselves at the forefront in providing realistic analysis and policy proposals. But it does illustrate the gulf that often separates economic science with its limitations, from economic practice, with its . . ., the gulf will never be entirely bridged. . . .

The economist on the firing line clearly has fewer options than the academic economist because he has to operate within the limits not only of his scientific knowledge but of political reality, public understanding, and institutional rigidities (like fixed exchange rates, a lengthy legislative process, and so forth).[2]

At the same time, Professor Heller thought it significant that "The advisor knows that he has to answer not only to

himself but to his profession as well." And so, understandably, he attributed the increased influence of economists over Presidents in recent years not only to "the conscious pursuit of national goals through economic policy by Presidents" but also to advances "of recent decades in positive economics and in economic knowledge." And thus, also, Professor Heller counseled that in cases in which the view of the economic advisors *did* diverge from that of the President, "the advisor's best defense of integrity and credibility" was to maintain a position of "Selective silence, publicly." (See the reference cited in footnote 2.)

A consideration of the three basic contemporary philosophical tendencies mentioned above is thus appropriate at this point in our study. Accordingly, the first three subdivisions below will deal with the rationalizations of political democracy provided by logical or analytical positivism, by natural law philosophy, and by instrumentalism, in that order. The fourth subdivision will undertake to discuss the relationship of instrumentalism to political economy.

A. LOGICAL OR ANALYTICAL POSITIVISM

Rudolph Carnap

Rudolf Carnap came to the United States from Vienna in 1936 after Hitler's rise to power and was employed as a professor at the University of Chicago. His works deal extensively with problems of probability and contain many references to economic theories and to well-known contemporary econometricians. In Vienna he had been a member of the "Vienna Circle," a group under the leadership of Moritz Schlick, which had adopted the view that philosophy should be concerned with the meaning of *propositions* rather than with the meaning of *life*. That is, this group—which had been greatly influenced by the views held at that time by Bertrand Russell and by Ludwig Wittgenstein (who later repudiated most of his *Tractatus Logico-Philo-*

[1] *Economic Report of the President together with the Annual Report of the Council of Economic Advisors* (Washington, D.C.: U.S. Government Printing Office, 1964), p. 55.

[2] Walter W. Heller, *The New Dimensions of Political Economy* (New York: W. W. Norton and Company, 1967), p. 15 and pp. 25–26.

sophicus)—adopted the view that "logical analysis" of *propositions* was the *only* proper task of philosophy. The group further took the view that propositions which could not possibly be verified empirically were "meaningless" and that all matters of ethics fell within the classification of meaningless propositions.

Thus, propositions like, "Thou shalt not kill" are really value judgments stated in the form of commands and to this proposition there corresponds the value judgment "Killing is evil." But, the argument continues, a value judgment is merely a wish; there is no way to "prove" that it is false.

Carnap's work is lavish in its use of mathematical symbols, and a calculus is employed to determine the meanings of statements.[3] For this reason, and also because the moral agnosticism of his work is consistent with the conception of price as a measure of social value, Carnap's work has appealed to some economists, particularly to those with a vested interest in a mathematical specification of the static conditions of "economic welfare." Since logical positivism does not itself provide any basis for moral judgments, logical positivists have generally relied upon Emotion as the foundation stone for their systems of ethics—it is the Emotions which become an Unquestioned Absolute in the system, a point which becomes clearly apparent when the works of Bertrand Russell are examined with care. Indeed, just as it is Emotion which has the status of a "given" in Russell's ethical system, so also do "Tastes" or "Consumer Sovereignty" acquire the same status in the economic version of this approach; and so also does the Basic Constitution or Basic Law (the "*Grundnorm*") acquire this position in the legal version (as we will see in the next chapter).

Bertrand Russell

As has been noted, in its inception logical positivism was greatly influenced by Bertrand Russell's then current views. His later position is somewhat ambiguous because of his use of the language of utilitarianism in his formal ethical system. Thus, he stated in 1952 the proposition that reason signified the choice of the "right means to an end that you wish to achieve" and added that reason had nothing whatever to do with the choice of ends.[4] He then defined "right conduct" as that which, "on the evidence," was likely to produce the "greatest balance of good over evil or the smallest balance of evil over good," where good and evil were considered as being equal "when a man is indifferent as to whether he experiences both or neither."[5] This view has much in common with Adam Smith's position concerning the conditions under which government *should* undertake economic activity, a point noted in the opening pages of Chapter 1. And the language is also quite like that of contemporary price theory.

Russell defined an action as "good" if "it has value on its own account, *independently of its effects*."[6] The qualifying phrase (which has *now* been italicized) constituted an outright rejection of the instrumentalist position, we will see below. Indeed, Russell substituted for the term "good" the term "intrinsic value." But he also further stated that certain acts whose effects aroused the *emotion* of "approval" were to be defined as "good" and those whose effects aroused the *emotion* of "disapproval" were to be defined as "bad." A "right" act is one of which, "on the available evidence, the effects are likely to be better than those of any other act that is possible in the circumstances." By definition, "we 'ought' to do . . . the act which is right." Finally, the coda: "It is right to feel approval of a right act and disapproval of a wrong act."[7] His position, Russell asserted, rested upon "the appeal . . . to the emotions and feelings which have given rise to the concepts of 'right' and 'wrong,' 'good' and 'bad.'"[8] Emotion, thus, became the ultimate basis of this system.

In 1959, Russell emphasized the point that questions of ultimate value cannot

---

[3] See, for example, his *Meaning and Necessity* (Chicago: University of Chicago Press, 1947) or his *Introduction to Semantics* (Cambridge: Harvard University Press, 1942).

[4] Bertrand Russell, *Human Society in Ethics and Politics* (New York: Simon and Schuster, Inc., 1952,

1954, 1955), p. vi. Permission to reproduce granted by Simon and Schuster, Inc.

[5] *Ibid.*, p. 30.

[6] *Ibid.*, p. 94. (Italics mine.)

[7] *Ibid.*, pp. 97–98.

[8] *Ibid.*, p. 100.

be dealt with by scientific methods and that logical analysis was the "main business of philosophy."[9]

In 1947, Russell was extremely critical of absolutism (Plato received particularly sharp criticism in his work). He also identified "pragmatism" (especially instrumentalism) as "systematic contempt for philosophy"; and he was skeptical of skepticism. Thus he also wrote that he adhered to an empirical theory of knowledge and emphasized the uncertainty of knowledge.[10]

Russell also argued in 1947 that his logical positivist views provided *the only* theoretical justification for democracy as a political philosophy. Thus, he wrote that *the only* philosophy which provided a philosophical justification for political democracy was empiricism because it calls attention to the uncertainty of knowledge. In short, since men may be mistaken all opinions must be considered.[11] It is worth noting that in 1948 Hans Kelsen, the legal positivist, took an almost identical position. Kelsen argued that it is *"only* philosophical relativism" which can admit that "what is right today may be wrong tomorrow"; and, therefore, he argued, "philosophical relativism" or moral agnosticism is the real basis of political democracy.[12] That Kelsen and Russell were in error in claiming this distinction as peculiarly a property of logical positivism will be seen in the following discussions of both the natural law and instrumentalist positions.

B. CONTEMPORARY NATURAL LAW PHILOSOPHY

Jacques Maritain

Jacques Maritain, perhaps one of the outstanding and most articulate natural law philosophers of the 20th century, undertook in 1952 in *The Range of Reason* to indicate what natural law philosophy may have to learn from other philosophical tendencies and what it has to give in return.

With respect to logical positivism, Maritain stated that the most important contributions of the logical positivists was their emphasis of the need for clarity[13] but he also asserted that science deals "only with the realm of what is sense-perceivable." Therefore, he added, "the crucial error" of the logical positivists was their belief that "whatever has no meaning for the *scientist* has *no* meaning *at all*."[14] And so, Maritain rejected cultural relativism and argued that there is such a thing as "moral knowledge" which is different from the "knowledge of speculative reason, the knowledge peculiar to the philosopher or scientist."[15] Natural law, he believed, is not merely that which is natural, but also that which is known through *connaturality* (through being inborn): natural law is known in an undemonstrable manner, and no exercise of human reason produces natural law, or causes it to be produced, although natural law is known to human reason. "*Natural Law* depends *only* on Divine Reason," he added, and it is precisely for this reason that it "binds men in conscience, and is the prime foundation of human law. . . ."[16]

He capitalized the words and thus wrote *natural law* as *Natural Law* because he rejected secular conceptions of natural law as "right reason"; that is, he rejected the notion that "the law of nature" can be discovered by means of reason and asserted that Natural Law *is* Divine Reason.

With respect to the question of the philosophical justification of democracy as a political philosophy, Maritain took the view that a *pluralistic* solution is necessary. What he meant by this term was that "men belonging to very different philosophical or religious creeds or lineages could and should co-operate in the common task and for the common welfare . . . provided they similarly assent to the charter and basic tenets of a society of free men."[17]

Moreover, he asserted that it is "normal" in a democratic society for diverse philo-

---

[9] Bertrand Russell, *A History of Western Philosophy* (New York: Simon and Schuster, Inc., 1959), pp. 834–836.

[10] Bertrand Russell, *Philosophy and Politics* (Cambridge: Cambridge University Press, 1947), p. 24.

[11] *Ibid.*, p. 20.

[12] Hans Kelsen, "Absolutism and Relativism in Philosophy and Politics," *American Political Science Review*, Vol. XLII (October, 1948), pp. 906–914.

[13] *The Range of Reason* (New York: Charles Scribner's Sons, 1952), p. 5.

[14] *Ibid.*, p. 6. (Italics his.)

[15] *Ibid.*, p. 16.

[16] *Ibid.*, p. 28.

[17] *Ibid.*, p. 166.

sophical or religious schools of thought to come into free competition. He welcomed the competition: "Let each school freely and fully assert its belief! But let no one try to impose it by force upon the others!" He believed that in such free competition "the Christian leaven would play an ever-growing part," and he also believed that "without genuine and vital reconciliation between democratic inspiration and evangelical inspiration, our hopes for the democratic culture will be frustrated."[18] But, since it is true that "supernatural faith does not provide" any particular social or political system, "supernatural faith must be complemented by sound practical philosophy, historical information, and social and political experience."[19]

Although Maritain did assert that there exists a "deep-seated antagonism" between natural law philosophy and pragmatism "that the best efforts cannot overcome," he would have incorporated pragmatism into natural law philosophy, "not at the level of metaphysics nor at the level of the philosophy of nature, but at the level of ethics and moral philosophy."

What will become apparent in the next subdivision is that, at the *moral* or ethical level, natural law philosophy and pragmatism (or instrumentalism) stand much more closely together than either stands to the moral agnosticism of logical positivism; however, neither would be prepared to subordinate itself to the other in the areas in which there is disagreement between them. Thus Maritain rejected a proposition he attributed to Sidney Hook that "democratic inspiration" can find "in 'scientific method' its highest source of authority," because even a "secular faith implies the commitment of the whole man . . . and draws its strength . . . from beliefs which go far beyond scientific method."[20]

Renée Williamson

So also has Renée de Visme Williamson (a political scientist) taken a natural law position in direct reply to Hans Kelsen's view (stated earlier) that "philosophical relativism" is the real basis of political democracy. Williamson has asserted that "it is not true that there are no values beyond man" and has argued that merely because it cannot be proven that such values exist does not of itself demonstrate that they do not exist. On the basis of this position, Williamson has also argued that the framers of the United States Constitution and the signers of the Declaration of Independence "were inspired by a philosophy that was completely alien to political relativism. They took a firm stand on absolute values and had the courage to be dogmatic."[21] He has added that the Founding Fathers "based themselves on self-evident truths, and not hypotheses."[22] (In Chapter 5, we will briefly consider further the political philosophies of the Founding Fathers—whose average age was thirty years.)

F. A. von Hayek

F. A. von Hayek, an Austrian, eventually returned to Germany after many years of teaching at the University of Chicago. After World War II he took the view that legal positivism, particularly views of legal philosophers like Hans Kelsen, had opened the doors to the victories of the fascists and bolshevists in Europe after World War I. An economist who has also written on other subjects, Hayek advocated a secular (nonreligious) natural law point of view in economics and in law. Writing in 1960, he saw many signs of a revival of faith in natural law as a basis for social order, particularly in Europe, and a decline in the influence of cultural relativism (a tendency which, of course, Hayek welcomed).[23]

Hayek's natural law argument is cast in secular terms, but also comes to rest on an absolutist position. Maritain remarked that "supernatural faith does not" specify any particular social or political system. And, on the basis of this conclusion, he argued that "supernatural faith must be complemented by sound practical philosophy, historical information, and social and

---

[18] *Ibid.*, p. 170.
[19] *Ibid.*, pp. 170–171.
[20] *Ibid.*, p. 168.
[21] Renée de Visme Williamson, "The Challenge of Political Relativism," *Journal of Politics*, Vol. IX (May, 1947), pp. 147–177, esp. pp. 159–1965. See also his *Independence and Involvement: A Christian*

Reorientation in Political Science (Baton Rouge: Louisiana State University Press, 1964).
[22] Williamson, "The Challenge of Political Relativism," *op. cit.*, p. 161.
[23] F. A. von Hayek, *The Constitution of Liberty* (Chicago: University of Chicago Press, 1960), pp. 238–239 and chap. xvi.

political experience" in political matters. It is the use of "sound practical philosophy, historical information, and social and political experience," among others, which the pragmatists and instrumentalists have emphasized, and it is to their views that attention will now be turned.

C. PRAGMATISM OR INSTRUMENTALISM

C. S. Peirce (1839–1914)

Charles Sanders Peirce was perhaps the first truly indigenous American philosopher. Although during his lifetime he published no books, his *Collected Papers* were published posthumously between 1931 and 1935. His emphasis of precision and clarity in the expression of ideas was an anticipation of logical positivist emphasis of the same subjects; and, at the same time, his philosophy served as a source of ideas to which William James and John Dewey owed much.

Peirce's emphasis on clarity in the expression of ideas was already apparent as early as 1878, when he published an essay called "How to Make Our Ideas Clear" in *Popular Science Monthly*. In this essay he argued that "to develop the meaning" of an idea, it is necessary to "determine what habits it produces, for what a thing means is simply what habits it involves."[24] Thus, he asserted, "Our idea of anything is our idea of its effects."[25] And the rule for attaining clarity was: one must consider the operational effects of his conceptions. The conception of the effects is the conception of the object.[26] In explanation of the operation of the rule, Peirce cited several examples. To say that something is "heavy," he said, was merely to say that "in the absence of opposing forces," it would fall. The "real" he defined as "that whose characters are independent of what anybody may think them to be. A dream has a real existence *as a mental phenomenon* if

somebody has really dreamt it; that he dreamt so and so does not depend on what anybody thinks was dreamt, but is completely independent of all opinion on the subject."[27] But the "thing dreamt" is not real. There is a difference between the *fact* of dreaming and "the thing dreamt" which by its very nature (by definition) cannot be real.

The emphasis upon the definition of an idea in terms of its *consequences* is an emphasis of the empirical source of knowledge. The proposition that "all solid bodies on earth fall in the absence of any upward forces or pressure" is "a safe basis for prediction" or "*corresponds* to reality" because it is known through experience.[28] So is weightlessness in outer space.

With respect to the question of what he called "Normative Sciences" (the conformity of "things to ends"), Peirce took the view that ethics was the study of what "ends of action we are deliberately prepared to adopt."[29] In other words, specifying the problem to be solved involves defining the standard of valuation to be employed in solving it. It is not a very long step from this proposition to John Dewey's position that "ends" are merely "ends-in-view" and are never final, because "ends-in-view" are "means" to other "ends-in-view," and that the whole question is one of a *process* and not one of ultimate, absolute, and static standards.

William James (1842–1910)

It was William James who called attention to the views of Peirce in a lecture in 1898,[30] as well as subsequently. In "What Pragmatism Means," James wrote in 1907 that a pragmatist turns his back on "verbal solutions" and looks towards action and consequences of action.[31]

James also contrasted the pragmatist with the rationalist. The former "clings to facts and concreteness, observes truth at its work in particular cases, and generalizes.

[24] Charles Hartshorne and Paul Weiss (eds.), *Collected Papers of Charles Sanders Peirce* (6 vols.; Cambridge: Harvard University Press, 1960), Vol. V–VI, "How to Make Our Ideas Clear," pp. 248–271, at p. 257.

[25] *Ibid.*, p. 528.

[26] *Ibid.*

[27] *Ibid.* (Italics mine.)

[28] *Ibid.*, "The Reality of Thirdness," pp. 64–69,

esp. pp. 64–65.

[29] *Ibid.*, "Ethical and Esthetical Goodness," pp. 82–86, esp. p. 83.

[30] William James, "Philosophical Conceptions and Practical Results," *Collected Essays and Reviews* (New York: Longmans, Green and Co., Inc., 1920), pp. 406–437.

[31] William James, *Pragmatism* (New York: Longmans, Green and Co., Inc., 1907), pp. 51–55.

Truth, for him, becomes a class-name for all sorts of definite working-values in experience." But for the rationalist, truth "remains a pure abstraction, a bare name to which we must defer." The typical "ultra-abstractionist fairly shudders at concreteness: other things equal, he positively prefers the pale and the spectral. If the two universes were offered, he would always choose the skinny outline rather than the rich thicket of reality."[32] Indeed, not only does he choose it, but he offers reasons why he prefers it and rejects "common sense."

John Dewey (1859–1952)

John Dewey called his philosophy "instrumentalism." One of the most respected intellectuals of his time, he held the view that the use of "intelligence" is the only "intelligent method" to be used in establishing a free society. On the one hand, he rejected absolutist conceptions; on the other, he rejected a "purely empirical theory" (such as that of Russell) also, on grounds that "it merely formulates and justifies the socially prevailing habit of regarding enjoyments as they are actually experienced as values in and of themselves."[33]

Dewey believed that values are subject to scientific analysis quite as much as are other concepts. Thus he stated as his main proposition that "Judgments about values are judgments about the conditions and results of experienced objects; judgments about that which should regulate the formation of our desires, affections, and enjoyments."[34] He specifically (in advance) rejected Russell's conception of values as determined by emotions, by pointing out that "a feeling of good or excellence is as far removed from goodness in fact as a feeling that objects are intellectually thus and so is removed from their being actually so."[35] His emphasis upon "ends-in-view" rather than upon final ends has already been noted. "Ends-in-view" are not ideal abstractions; they are "objects of conscious intent. When achieved in existence they

are ends because they are then conclusions attained through antecedent endeavor, much as a post is not a goal in itself, but becomes a goal in relation to the runner and his race."[36]

The emphasis upon change in Dewey's philosophy was the result of the early influence on his thought of the ideas of Hegel and Darwin. Dewey thought of man as being "*in* nature," *not* as being apart from it. He thought of science, including social science, as something to be employed deliberately in order to serve the "ends which we desire."

An illustration of this view can be given in terms of a contemporary problem. Atomic energy can be put to use to destroy civilization or to enrich our lives. Is it true that we cannot make a non-emotional choice between these two uses? Intelligence clearly points to the latter use, just as natural law philosophy points to the latter use. Only the moral agnosticism of logical positivism refuses to admit that a clear non-emotional choice is possible in such a case: to do so would involve an admission that the moral agnosticism of logical positivism represents an impossible philosophical position, a position devoted to playing a word-game.

Where logical positivists rationalize political democracy on grounds of uncertainty of knowledge and where natural law philosophers rationalize it on grounds that there exist, somewhere, somehow, absolute values above man, Dewey provided a functional justification; a belief in the power of "pooled and cooperative human experience."[37]

The instrumentalist justification of democracy is thus *functional*. The belief is *not* one that man is perfectable; it is *merely that he can learn. Democracy is a process, a method of testing policies by trial and error;* it involves a "positive toleration which amounts to sympathetic regard for the intelligence and personality of others, even if they hold views opposed to ours, and of scientific inquiry into facts and testing of ideas."[38]

---

[32] *Ibid.*, p. 68.

[33] John Dewey, *The Quest for Certainty* (New York: G. P. Putnam's Sons, 1929), p. 259.

[34] Dewey, *The Quest for Certainty*, p. 265.

[35] *Ibid.*

[36] John Dewey, *Experience and Nature* (2nd ed.; New York: W. W. Norton and Co., Inc., 1929), p. 112.

[37] John Dewey, "Democracy and Educational Administration," an address before the National Education Association, February 22, 1937, published in *School and Society*, Vol. XLV (April 3, 1937), pp. 457–462. at pp. 458–459.

[38] John Dewey and James H. Tufts, *Ethics* (rev. ed.; New York; Henry Holt and Co., Inc., 1932). 1932), p. 365.

The alternative is "an appeal to authority and precedent," including "natural law, supernatural law, the divine right of kings, the constitution, the received conventions, the private conscience, emotion, and the wisdom of ancestors." There is one feature common to all such appeals. In each of them, said Dewey, "there is an appeal to a final authority" precluding the need for further inquiry.[39]

And yet, instrumentalism does not completely reject the use of authority or of precedent. It considers them to be valuable instruments to be employed as tools of analysis, "*so long as no evidence is presented calling for a reexamination of their findings and theories.*"[40] Or, as Professor Galbraith has put it in a pungent sentence, "The enemy of conventional wisdom [defined by him as 'ideas which are esteemed at any time for their acceptability'] is not ideas but the march of events." The instrumentalist philosophy not only recognizes this fact but also takes the positive stand that political democracy is a functional device for dealing with the social impact of the march of events. Political democracy possesses the flexibility necessary to deal with those changes which are inevitable because our knowledge of things is never absolutely final.

Maritain's natural law philosophy accepts political democracy at the secular level on grounds that "the Christian leaven" will play an ever-growing part and in the somewhat pessimistic belief that "hopes for a democratic culture will be frustrated" unless there occurs a genuine and vital reconciliation between democratic inspiration and evangelical inspiration." Russell relied on the fact that "since men may be mistaken" they "should take account of this possibility in all their dealings with men of opinions different from their own." Instrumentalism takes a stronger position than either of these two and asserts positively that political democracy is an example of the continuous scientific process of trial-and-error judgment carried on in a context of change. Therefore, instrumentalism constitutes the adoption of a method of seeking solutions to specific existential problems, with "ends-in-view" or immediate standards of valuation which are never final, but which are derived from the problem under consideration at a particular time. It does not claim to have final answers or absolute standards.

D. INSTRUMENTALISM AND POLITICAL ECONOMY

Economists who have been directly and seriously concerned at the *operational* level with problems of Political Economy have by and large adopted the pragmatic or instrumentalist approach, although in some cases the language used to describe what they have been doing obscures that fact. That this is the case will become apparent not only in the consideration of the work of the Council of Economic Advisors in later chapters, but also in the discussion in Chapter 13 of various meanings which have been attached to the phrases "workable competition" and "workable economy." Phrases such as these cannot be operationally defined in general terms because they do not define absolutes; they can be defined only in terms of their applications to particular problems. The method adopted is essentially one of "judging" by responsible analysts on the basis of the best available evidence. And "judging" involves taking account of the consequences of the judgment in terms of the social policy which the judgment seeks to promote.

In criticizing the attempt to identify factors of "workable competition" in the *Report* of the Attorney General's National Committee to Study the Antitrust Laws (1955), some members of the Committee remarked:

... The "doctrine" of workable competition is only a rough and ready judgment by some economists, each for himself, that a particular industry is performing reasonably well—presumably relative to alternative industrial arrangements which are practically attainable.[41]

In the context in which this criticism was presented, as we will see in Chapter 13, it was probably justified, since the *Report*

[39] *Ibid.*
[40] *Ibid.*, p. 366. (Italics his.)

[41] *Report of the Attorney General's National Committee to Study the Antitrust Laws* (Washington, D.C.: U.S. Government Printing Office, 1955), p. 339.

was the product of a group in which some social interests were represented out of proportion to their importance in the system as a whole. But the criticism would have been much stronger if the critics had recognized frankly that the standard of valuation employed in a given case is never independent of the facts of that particular problem and that the concept of "workable competition" does *not* define an absolute standard but merely points to a *method* of dealing with problems in which a reconciliation of various competing social interests is attempted by responsible men, who are not committed in advance to a given conclusion and who have no personal interest in the outcome.

The definition of Political Economy by John Commons, quoted in the preceding chapter, is also an instrumentalist definition; that definition emphasizes the fact that the state is an instrument of control.[42]

According to Commons, when Peirce's pragmatism is applied to economics, the subject matter of economics becomes "the whole concern [the 'entity'] of which the individuals are members, and the activities investigated are their transactions governed," not by "a law of nature," but by "a working rule, for the time being of collective action."[43]

The working rules exist within a context of technological change which has an impact upon and which interacts with them. Nuclear proliferation treaties were unnecessary in a world which did not know atomic energy. But once atomic energy had been discovered, problems of control and of valuations of the uses, peaceful and otherwise, to which it may be put have arisen and must be answered. These answers cannot be found in the moral agnosticism of logical positivism or in the absolutism of secular natural law theories. If they can be found at all, they will have to be found—as Dewey has said—by means of "scientific inquiry into the facts and testing of ideas," and with a view to the consequences flowing from the different possible courses of action which may be chosen. Such a view is consistent at the *operational* level with Maritain's position that "supernatural faith must be complemented by sound practical philosophy, historical information, and social and political experience," as well as with his view that solutions must be attained by means of "practical rather than theoretical or dogmatic agreement."

Some of the remaining chapters of Part I present historical information and background materials pertaining to our social and political experience of the type mentioned by Maritain. The next chapter is concerned, in particular, with a brief survey of types of law and with a discussion of various contemporary philosophies of law. This discussion is followed by four chapters dealing with the general problem of law and social change and, most especially, with the mechanics of changes in working rules in the United States—including changes resulting from activities of judges, legislators, and pressure groups. Chapter 7 completes this series of four chapters on law and social change with a survey of some fundamental questions of United States Constitutional law. The four remaining chapters of Part I are concerned with the growth of economic magnitudes and the concentration of private control over economic activity. There is a brief discussion in Chapter 10 of some basic economic concepts.

[42] John R. Commons, *Legal Foundations of Capitalism* (New York: The Macmillan Co., 1924), p. 387.

[43] Commons, *Institutional Economics* (New York: The Macmillan Co., 1934), p. 227.

3

Types and Philosophies of Law

As has been mentioned, this chapter and the four following ones deal with the nature of law and the way in which changes in law occur. This chapter specifically describes various types of law and explains the essential elements of different contemporary philosophies of law. These different legal philosophies, are really particular applications of the three general contemporary philosophical views explained in the preceding chapter, and it is against the backdrop of the different legal philosophies, discussed in this chapter, that the role of judges in making changes in law will be discussed in the chapter that follows.

A. TYPES OF LAW

Common Law

Meaning of the Term Common Law. The term *common law* has several meanings, depending upon its usage. Some courts have defined the common law of the United States as that portion of the law of England (both court decisions and applicable acts of Parliament) which had been adopted and was in force in the United States at the time of the Revolution. Others have defined it as that part of the "common law" of England which has not been modified by judicial decision, statutory law, or constitutional provisions in the United States. The English common law consists of those principles and rules which derive their authority from usages and customs "of immemorial antiquity" or from decisions of courts recognizing and affirming such usages (since about the beginning of the thirteenth century).

The Federal Courts and Common Law. At one time our federal courts held that there existed a "federal common law" independently of the common law as it happened to be interpreted and applied in the individual states of the Union. However, in 1938 the Supreme Court held that there was no federal common law by saying:

Except in matters governed by the Federal Constitution or by Acts of Congress, the law to be applied in any case is the law of the State. And whether the law of the State shall be declared by its Legislature in a statute or by its highest court in a decision is not a matter of federal concern. *There is no federal general common law.* Congress has no power to declare substantive rules of common law applicable in a State whether they be local in their nature or "general," be they commercial law or a part of the law of torts. And no clause in the Constitution purports to confer such power upon the federal courts. . . .[1]

Thus, except in the cases indicated in the first sentence in the quotation above, federal courts apply the law of the state within which they have jurisdiction.

Method of the Common Law. Because the common law rests on custom and usages as well as on the rules of law decided in prior cases, it is often said that the system is rigid. The truth of this statement when applied to a particular instance, however, depends upon the extent to which the precedents in prior cases are followed. The scope of the rule that "precedents must be obeyed" will be considered in detail in the next chapter. It is to be noted now, however, that there is no particular reason why a common law system cannot be a flexible one. Indeed, as John Commons pointed out, the common law method is an experimental one,

... wherein each particular case, when decided, becomes itself a change in the code, constitution, or statute, because it has a lasting effect as a precedent. And then when a new case arises it is not merely a matter of going back to a fixed code or primordial principle that has always existed in law or economics, or even of discovering a previously unknown divine intent applied to that case. It is a matter of reasoning from many conflicting precedents or experiences, some of which would lead to a decision towards one side of the case, and others to a decision on the opposite side of the case. Thus in a common-law country the code, or statute, or constitution, itself changes experimentally with changes in the practices of the people and the decisions of disputes.[2]

Civil Law

The term *civil law* refers to the system of law which derives from Roman law, particularly from the Code of Justinian, promulgated by one of the Roman Emperors. The civil law system is the system of jurisprudence which applies throughout most of Continental Europe. In this system, much less attention is paid to precedent and much more attention is paid to the works of legal scholars. However, John Commons may have been taking an extreme position in asserting that the "distinction between codes and common law" is similar to the distinction between the deductive and the experimental methods of thinking both in economics and in law. For example, Professor Wolfgang Friedmann has cited the works of the French jurist, Gény, as well as interpretations of provisions in the French, German, Swiss, and Italian Civil Codes and has noted that, since the beginning of the present century, judges in these countries have also transformed particular code provisions "through creative interpretation in many vital respects."[3]

It is necessary to distinguish the term *civil law* from the term *civil action*. The latter is a term which applies to actions between private persons. A *civil action* must also be distinguished from a *criminal action*. The latter involves an offense against the state. Section 4 of the Clayton Act provides for triple damages to be awarded to a plaintiff who successfully demonstrates that he has been injured by a violation of the antitrust laws. Even though such an action springs from a criminal violation, it is nevertheless a civil action, since it is a suit between private parties. We will consider this aspect of the Sherman Act in Part II of this book.

Statutory Law

Statutory law means "written law," that is, a particular law or laws enacted by a legislative body. It exists both in civil law and in common law countries. Statutory law is sometimes referred to as "positive law," but the term "positive" is also

---

[1] *Erie R. R. Co.* v. *Tompkins*, 304 U.S. 64 (1938), at p. 79, overruling *Swift* v. *Tyson*, 16 Pet. 1 (1842). (Italics mine.) In *Banco Nacional de Cuba* v. *Sabbatino, Receiver, et. al.*, 376 U.S. 398 (1963), at p. 425, the Court held that "an issue concerned with a basic choice regarding the competence and function of the Judiciary and the National Executive in ordering our relationships with other members of the international community must be treated exclusively as an aspect of federal law." It also pointed out that there were "enclaves" where federal judge-made law governs, citing decisions involving federal statutes. All these cases can, of course, be encompassed under the opening sentence in the quotation given in the text.

[2] John R. Commons, *Institutional Economics* (New York: The Macmillan Co., 1934), p. 221.

[3] Compare Commons, *op. cit.*, pp. 221 ff. and Wolfgang Friedmann, *Law in a Changing Society* (London: Stevens and Sons, Ltd.; and Berkeley: University of California Press, 1959), pp. 24-25.

used to designate a particular philosophy of law and it is better to avoid confusion by not using this term in the former context. The process of statutory law-making will be discussed in Chapter 6 and requires no further discussion here.

Equity

Origin and Nature of Equity. The term *equity* refers to a body of rules developed in England in the fourteenth century to provide relief unobtainable in common law courts, whose formal procedures relative to the raising of issues and whose remedies were both limited both in nature and scope. The essential element of an action in equity was and is the absence of an adequate remedy at common law. Although the common law originally permitted various types of remedies, by the fourteenth century the common law courts were no longer equipped to order a person to take a particular kind of action or to refrain from doing so. Instead, the principal remedy available to a plaintiff was that of *damages.* Moreover, the procedures had become so rigid that, unless the plaintiff's case was put formally before the court in the specific *form* prescribed for that type of action, his case would be thrown out of court.

Originally, the plaintiff's right to sue arose out of the issuance in the name of the king of a writ to the plaintiff. The writ ordered the defendant to meet the plaintiff's demand or else to show cause in one of the king's courts as to why the defendant should not do so. Thus, the writ was an authorization for the court to proceed with the action. The writ itself described the controversy and stated the demand of the plaintiff for relief. The chancellor (who may be roughly described as the king's secretary) had custody of the seal of the king; that is, the chancellor issued the writs in the name of the king and stamped them with the king's seal. In the course of time, precedents were established and the procedure was regularized: the number or *types* of writs became limited; and, unless an action fell within the form of one of the existing types, there was no action because there was no writ—unless the chancellor saw fit to invent a new type of writ to cover the plaintiff's case. Eventually, there were approximately eight types of common law writs applicable to personal actions and four major types available under special circumstances. Table 3–1 contains the names of the writs, together with an approximate indication of their purposes.

Even a cursory glance at Table 3–1 will disclose that the distinctions among some of these forms of action were extremely fine ones. The difference between *Trespass* and *Trespass on the Case* (which has today become the basis for an action in negligence, for example, in the case of an automobile accident) lay in whether the injury was the result of direct or indirect action; and, similarly, the difference between *Replevin* and *Detinue* turned on the manner in which the defendant acquired possession of the goods allegedly wrongfully held by him. The plaintiff's lawyer thus carried a heavy burden: if he did not use the proper writ in framing the claim of the plaintiff, the case would be thrown out of court. Table 3–1 also shows clearly that in most cases the only remedy available to the plaintiff at common law was that of damages.

The crystallization of the common law procedures indicated in Table 3–1 prevented the common law from satisfying the social needs of the time. Thus, a new and independent body of rules based on popular conceptions of morality was developed to provide the required flexibility for continued social, economic, and legal development. At first the King's Council, and eventually the chancellor, exercised the king's power to administer the rules of "equity and good conscience". Eventually they were formally administered by a Court of Chancery. It is of some significance that the early chancellors were high officials of the Church. Thus, some of the procedures employed in equity were borrowed from the ecclesiastical courts; others were developed by the Star Chamber.[4] The chancellor was not bound by the technical rules of procedure and pleading employed in the common law courts; and he provided remedies in areas left untouched at common law—such as enforcement of trusts, issuance of injunctions, and orders for specific performance of contracts.

---

[4] See Harold Potter, *An Introduction to the History of Equity and Its Courts* (London: Sweet and Maxwell, Ltd., 1931).

Table 3-1

Types and Uses of Common Law Writs[a]

Private Writs— Personal Actions	Plaintiff's Claim	Type of Remedy
Trespass	Unlawful injury to his person, property or rights by immediate force or violence of defendant	Damages
Trespass on the Case	Injury to his person, property or rights not accompanied by immediate force or violence of defendant	Damages
Trover	Wrongful interference with or detention of his goods (a special form of trespass on the case)	Damages—recovery of *value* of converted goods
Replevin	Unlawful taking of his goods	Recovery of the specific goods
Detinue	Unlawful detention of his goods, the defendant having *first* lawfully come into possession of them	Recovery of the specific goods

Private Writs— Contractual Actions	Plaintiff's Claim	Type of Remedy
Debt	Defendant owes plaintiff specific sum of money	Payment of debt
Covenant	Breach of contract of record or under seal	Damages
Assumpsit	Breach of simple contract (not of record or under seal)	Damages

Extraordinary Writs	Plaintiff's Claim	Type of Remedy
Mandamus	Illegal deprivation by public official of plaintiff's right	Order from higher court to lower court or to inferior body or person to do or not to do the act which his office, trust or station requires
Habeas Corpus ad Subjiciendum	There are various forms of *Habeas Corpus;* the writ listed here is the one used for an illegal detention	Person detaining the prisoner directed to produce the prisoner in court, together with reasons for his detention for determination by court as to disposition
Prohibition	Inferior court is exceeding its jurisdiction (or has no jurisdiction)	Order from superior court to the inferior court to restrain the latter from exceeding its jurisdiction
Quo Warranto	Defendant has unlawfully usurped an office, franchise or liberty	Order to defendant to show by what authority he supports his claim to the office

[a] The reader who wishes to study the particular forms of the declarations required by these specific writs or typical cases setting forth the elements and natures of the actions involved may be referred to Edison R. Sunderland, *Judicial Administration: Its Scope and Methods* (National Casebook Series; Chicago: Callaghan and Co., 1937), pp. 387–599.

Inevitably, the common law courts became jealous of the jurisdiction of the Court of Chancery. Among other things, although the chancellor was careful not to assert his supremacy over the common law courts, he did not hesitate to order *persons* who had obtained judgments at common law not to enforce such judgments. That is, he did not tell the common law courts what *they* could or could not do; nor did he assert that *their* judgments were wrong. Instead, he prohibited *persons* who had won judgments in the common law courts from having such judgments enforced. The common law judges, naturally, objected to this procedure. The dispute came to a head under James I who, desiring to assert his supremacy over the common law courts and their judges, followed the advice of Bacon (who was then his attorney general) and issued a decree favoring the Court of Chancery. Thus, the power of equity courts was firmly established, although the dispute simmered on for a number of years.[5]

Present Status of Equity. And so, two systems of law grew up side by side. In the Judicature Acts of 1873 and 1875, Parliament abolished the existing system of independent common law and independent equity courts and undertook to unify the system. In the United States, the distinction between the two bodies of law has also existed. In recent times, however, numerous states and the federal courts have undertaken to abolish the distinctions between law and equity. Although procedural differences have largely disappeared, substantive differences remain. Thus, in the Federal Rules of Civil Procedure, it is now specified that "There shall be one form of action known as the 'civil action.'" The basic maxims of equity, nevertheless, remain to guide the court in "equitable proceedings." For example, the maxim "Equity regards that as done which ought to be done" serves as the basis for ordering "specific performance" of a contract where the damage remedy is deemed inadequate. (Would an art collector prefer the delivery to him of a Rembrandt painting according to an original contract of sale, or would he prefer monetary damages for breach of contract? A court might order the seller to deliver the painting, thus ordering "specific performance" of the contract—

a procedure developed in equity—on grounds that the legal remedy is inadequate.)

Importance of Equitable Remedies. The importance of the development of equity, insofar as this book is concerned, lies in the fact that the invention of equitable remedies introduced a needed flexibility into the law by providing procedures and types of relief which would otherwise have been unobtainable. Originally, the chancellor could—but was not required to—decide equity cases with a jury to find facts. Today the procedure in the several states differs. The Texas Constitution, for example, contains an explicit guaranty of jury trial in equity cases,[6] but the Seventh Amendment to the United States Constitution guarantees jury trial only "in suits at common law"; indeed, it has been held in the federal courts that, where a federal court issues an injunction (in a case in which facts are decided without a jury), it cannot give additional relief in the form of damages since the latter type of relief is a common law action, requiring a jury to determine the facts.[7]

From the point of view of this book, it should be noted that the equitable remedies are of very great importance as devices for implementing government policy both in the case of regulated industries and in the area of antitrust. Policies of administrative regulatory agencies as well as antitrust policies are often the subject of litigation in what would once have been called "equitable proceedings." For example, the Sherman (antitrust) Act provides not only for criminal actions, but also for actions in equity. That is, although Section 3 of the act contains criminal sanctions and although there is also a damage remedy,

---

[5] See W. S. Holdsworth, *A History of English Law* (12 vols.; 5th ed.; London: Methuen and Co., Ltd., 1942), Vol. V, esp. pp. 461 ff.; and F. W. Maitland, *Equity*, ed. by A. H. Chayton and J. Whittaker, rev. by John Brunyate (2d ed.; Cambridge: Cambridge University Press, 1949), p. 9. (The latter was first published in 1909.) Maurice Ashley in *England in the Seventeenth Century* (paperback; London: Penguin Books, Ltd., 1960), pp. 49–50, describes the struggle between the Lord Chief Justice Coke and Bacon. Coke saw the common law judges as intermediaries between parliament and the king; Bacon believed in maintaining the royal perogatives and in keeping the common law judges subordinate to the throne.

Ashley states that, although the king dismissed Coke from office in 1616, the latter had vindicated the independence of the judiciary. In the process, however, the flexibility of equity procedures (which were later to harden into as rigid a system as the common law) was embedded in the law of England.

[6] *Carter* v. *Carter*, 5 Tex. 93 (1894); *Tronzetti* v. *Tronzetti*, 120 S.W. 2d 123 (1938).

[7] *Norton* v. *Colusa Parrot Mining Co.*, 167 Fed. 202 (1908); see also *Dimick* v. *Schiedt*, 293 U.S. 474 (1934), at p. 487, where the Supreme Court held that the Seventh Amendment adopts the rules of the common law "in respect of trial by jury, as those rules existed in 1791."

Section 4 permits the institution of "proceedings in equity" and authorizes the relevant court "at any time to make such temporary restraining order or prohibition as shall be deemed just in the premises." The remedies of dissolution, divorcement, and divestiture (for the moment these words can be roughly translated as defining actions by a court to break up a business combination which has been found guilty of violating the Sherman Act) are all equitable remedies, and we will have an occasion to examine them in greater detail later on.

B. PHILOSOPHIES OF LAW

"A Law" versus "The Law"

The preceding section has been concerned with an explanation of different types of law and different legal systems. Writers in the field of jurisprudence (legal philosophy) generally distinguish between the concept of "a law" and that of "the law." *A law* is often defined as a particular working rule recognized as binding within a given jurisdiction. The plural of "a law" is *laws*. However, the term *the law* has many definitions, depending upon what particular philosophy the particular legal philosopher stating the definition happens to accept. Moreover, precisely how some of these legal philosophers distinguish their concept of "the law" from their concept of "the state" is not always clear, and at least one of them, Hans Kelsen (already identified as one of the leaders of the positivist school), makes no distinction between these two concepts.[8] Moreover, sooner or later, practically all writers in the field of jurisprudence explain why their definition of *the law* is superior to that of other writers. In this respect there seems to be little difference between the problem which they face and the problem faced by economists who try to define economics. Indeed, one definition

of economics as "what economists do" has long had its counterparts in statements by students of international law that "international law is the practice of states" and in statements by students of domestic law (like Karl N. Llewellyn in 1930) that "Law *is* to the community what law *does*."[9] As has already been noted, there are three basic contemporary philosophies of the nature of law and several variations of each of these basic themes. It is to a brief consideration of these three basic themes and variations that our attention will now be directed.

Legal Positivism: Law as the Expression of Political Power

Hobbes and Austin. In 1651 Thomas Hobbes, a forerunner of the so-called English empiricists, published an essay in which he wrote: "It is true, that Sovereigns are all subject to the Laws of Nature; because such Laws be Divine, and cannot by any Man, or Commonwealth be abrogated. But to those Laws which the Sovereign himself, that is, which the Commonwealth maketh, he is not subject."[10] For, Hobbes reasoned, if there were laws above the sovereign with a judge to interpret them, there would have to be laws above the judge with a judge having higher powers to interpret these laws, and laws above this judge with a judge having still higher power to interpret them, and so on *ad infinitum*.

So also, in the middle of the nineteenth century, the English lawyer, John Austin, stated "The subject matter of jurisprudence is positive law: law, simply and strictly so called: or law set by political superiors to political inferiors."[11] In a similar vein is Justice Holmes's remark made in 1909—in a case in which the Supreme Court denied the American Banana Company the right to sue the United Fruit Company (for triple damages under the Sherman Act) on grounds that United had instigated the government of Costa Rica to seize Ameri-

---

[8] Hans Kelsen, *General Theory of Law and State*, trans. Anders Wedberg (20th Century Legal Philosophy Series, Vol. I; Cambridge: Harvard University Press, 1945).

[9] Karl, N. Llewellyn *The Bramble Bush* (New York: Oceana Publications, 1951), p. 91. (Italics his.)

[10] Thomas Hobbes, *Leviathan* (1st ed.; London: printed for A. R. Crooke, 1651), chap. xxix. A useful reference is E. A. Burtt (ed.), *The English

Philosophers from Bacon to Mill (New York: Modern Library, Inc., 1939), pp. 129–234. Hobbes's views are similar to those of Jean Bodin, who wrote in 1556.

[11] John Austin, *Lectures on Jurisprudence or the Philosophy of Positive Law*, rev. and ed. by Robert Cambell (2 vols., 5th ed.; London: John Murray, 1929), Vol. I, p. 86. (Austin's lectures were first published in 1861.)

can's principal productive facilities in Costa Rica, thereby eliminating American from competition with United. Justice Holmes said:

The fundamental reason why persuading a sovereign power to do this or that cannot be a tort is not that the sovereign cannot be joined as a defendant or because it must be assumed to be acting lawfully. . . . The fundamental reason is that it is a contradiction in terms to say that, within its jurisdiction, it is unlawful to persuade a sovereign power to bring about a result that it declares by its conduct to be desirable and proper. It does not, and foreign courts cannot, admit that the influences were improper or the results bad. It makes the persuasion lawful by its own act. *The very meaning of sovereignty is that the decree of the sovereign makes law.*[12]

It is interesting to note that Justice Holmes denied that the "sovereign . . . must be assumed to be acting lawfully" but that he then argued that the idea that the sovereign can act unlawfully contradicts the concept of "a sovereign."

Hans Kelsen. The legal positivists take their guide line from the logical positivists discussed in Chapter 2. They argue that law is the command of the highest political authority within the state and consists essentially of technical rules and concepts to be analyzed. As already noted, one of the leading exponents of this view of law in recent times has been Professor Hans Kelsen.[13] As previously noted, legal positivists take the logical positivist view that ethical principles have no relevance to the study of law and that "facts" are a matter of legal sociology. Their concern is with the law "as it is" and not with the law "as it should be." That is, they take the view that value judgments have no place in law and that only propositions which can be verified "externally" have meaning.

According to Kelsen, "the derivation of the basic norms of a legal order from the basic norm of that order is performed by showing that the particular norms have been created in accordance with the basic norm."[14] It is legal for one individual to put another individual in jail *if* there is an individual norm, "a judicial decision,"

prescribing this act. The judicial decision is legal *if* it has been rendered "in conformity with a criminal statute." The statute is legal *if* it is in conformity with the constitution. The search for a basic norm (the *Grundnorm*) continues:

If we ask why the constitution is valid, perhaps we come upon an older constitution. Ultimately we reach some constitution that is the first historically and that was laid down by an individual usurper or by some kind of assembly. The validity of this first constitution is the last presupposition, the final postulate, upon which the validity of all the norms of our legal order depends.[15]

Kelsen argues that the "basic norm is not created in a legal procedure by a law-creating organ." Thus, once the philosopher rests his legal system on some assumption external to the legal system, his job is done. The basic norm is not created by law: "It is valid because it is presupposed to be valid; and it is presupposed to be valid because without this presupposition no human act could be interpreted as legal, especially as a norm-creating act."[16] Thus the basic norm derives its validity from the fact that without it there could be no legal positivism.

Although legal positivism was once widely accepted in the United States, it is today less widely accepted because, as we have seen, it provides no defense against and may even serve as a rationalization for the activities of dictators. For example, policies providing for the liquidation of Jews in Nazi Germany and for forced labor camps in Russia would have to be considered "law" by the legal positivists, a position which natural law philosophers sharply reject.

H. L. A. Hart. In the work of H. L. A. Hart (which he calls "analytical jurisprudence"), the *Grundnorm* (or basic norm) of Kelsen becomes a "rule of recognition." Hart postulates that the legal system consists of *primary* rules (statutes, court decisions, etc.) involving obligations imposed upon individuals and legal persons and *secondary* rules which have as their subject

---

[12] *American Banana Co.* v. *United Fruit Co.*, 213 U.S. 347 (1909), at p. 358. (Italics mine.) The word *tort* in quotation can be defined for present purposes as an act by the defendant which gives a private right of action to the plaintiff independent of the

existence of any contract.

[13] Kelsen, *op. cit.*

[14] *Ibid.*, p. 115.

[15] *Ibid.*

[16] *Ibid.*, p. 116.

matter the primary rules. These secondary rules, known as "rules of recognition," specify the "ways in which the primary rules may be conclusively ascertained, introduced, eliminated, varied, and the fact of their violation conclusively determined."[17] The basic rule of recognition may be carved in stone—like the Code of Hammurabi—or be a written document. The precise form of its existence is not important. What is important is "the acknowledgement of reference to the inscription or writing as *authoritative, i.e.*, as the *proper* way of disposing of doubts as to the existence of the rule."[18] Thus, Hart looks not to the source of the basic rule, but merely to the question of whether or not it exists and is accepted. His system, too, is a purely deductive one. Legal or analytical positivism thus has much in common with contemporary static price theory, and at least one writer in the field of jurisprudence has favorably compared legal positivism with Milton Friedman's positive economics.[19]

Natural Law Theories: Law as "Divine Justice" or as "A Reasonable Solution"

Historical Background. In an obvious reliance on the work of Sir Henry Maine (discussed further below), J. L. Brierly has pointed out that the natural law theories had their origin in the political thought of the Greeks and in the incorporation of Greek ideas into Roman law. From the Greek Stoics the Romans borrowed the philosophical conception of *jus naturale*, which meant "the sum of those principles which ought to control human conduct, because founded in the very nature of man as a rational and social being."[20] In the course of time, as Maine's studies had made clear, this idealistic conception was made synonymous with the Roman conception of *jus gentium*, which consisted of those principles which were regarded "as *so simple and reasonable* that . . . they must be recognized everywhere and by everyone."[21]

Medieval lawyers and theologians built upon these concepts to develop the notion that law is based on the law of nature, which, in turn, is an expression of the Divine Will. Thus, in the Middle Ages, St. Thomas Aquinas (one of the earliest natural law philosophers) defined law as "nothing else than an ordinance of reason for the common good, made by Him who has care of the community and promulgated."[22] This view, of course, sees the ultimate origin and final justification of law in God; since the law of nature *is* that part of the law of God discoverable by human reason, it necessarily possesses an authority superior to that of ordinances adopted by mere human beings. Even as late as the eighteenth century, the great English lawyer, Blackstone, said: "The will of the Maker is called the Law of Nature. . . . This law, being coeval with mankind and dictated by God Himself, is obligatory upon all. No human laws are of any validity if contrary to this, as they derive their force and authority from this original."[23]

Blackstone's *Commentaries* served as a major text for American lawyers even as late as the early twentieth century. The natural law theory is clearly evident in the following excerpt from an opinion written in 1822 by Judge Storey in a case involving the question of whether a schooner, the *La Jeune Eugenie* (which had been seized by a United States officer while engaged in the slave trade on the coast of Africa), should be surrendered to the French Government for disposition in accordance with French law. In deciding in favor of the surrender, Judge Storey said:

> Now in respect to the African slave trade, such as it has been described to be, and in fact is, in its origin, progress, and consummation, it cannot admit of serious question, that it is founded in a violation of some of the first principles, which ought to govern nations. It is repugnant to the great principles of christian duty, the dictates of natural religion, the

[17] H. L. A. Hart, *The Concept of Law* (London: Oxford University Press, 1961), p. 92.

[18] *Ibid.* (Italics mine.)

[19] Jerome Hall, *Studies in Jurisprudence and Criminal Theory* (New York: Oceana Publications, 1958), p. 14.

[20] J. L. Brierly, *The Law of Nations* (London: Oxford University Press, 1928), p. 10. (Italics mine.)

[21] *Ibid.* (Italics mine.)

[22] *Summa Theologica*, trans. by Fathers of the English Dominican Province (New York: Benziger Bros., Inc., 1947), Vol. I, First Part of the Second Part, Q.90, Article 4, p. 995.

[23] Sir William Blackstone, *Commentaries on the Laws of England*, ed. Wm. Hardcastle Browne (New York: L. K. Strouse and Co., 1892), pp. 7–8. (The *Commentaries* were originally given as lectures in 1758.)

obligations of good faith and morality, and the eternal maxims of social justice. When any trade can be truly said to have these ingredients, it is impossible that it can be consistent with any system of law, that purports to rest on the authority of reason or revelation. And it is sufficient to stamp any trade as interdicted by public law, when it can be justly affirmed that it is repugnant to the general principle of justice and humanity. . . . (*Sic.*)

I have come to the conclusion, that the slave trade is a trade prohibited by the universal law, and by the law of France, and . . . I feel myself, at perfect liberty, with the express consent of our own government, to decree, that the property be delivered over to the consular agent of the King of France, to be dealt with according to his own sense of duty and right. . . .[24] (*Sic.*)

It is an interesting question as to whether or not Judge Storey would have felt himself at "perfect liberty" had he not had the consent of the United States Government to his action; at the same time, it should be noted that his line of argument is: (1) the slave trade is against natural law; (2) natural law is universal; (3) the French law is a part of universal law; and (4) therefore, the slave trade is a trade which is prohibited by the law of France. Thus, the system of natural law transcends national boundaries. The language is that of the Age of Reason; the spirit of the decision is that of the Supreme Court in its twentieth century antisegregation decisions.

The doctrine of "paramount obligations" based upon "Christian duty," "natural religion," and similar appeals to absolute standards of valuation is not, of course, restricted to judicial decisions, and it may be used to oppose social change. Thus, for example, Judge Thurman Arnold has called attention to the resolution adopted in 1933 by the American Bar Association in opposition to the Child Labor Amendment to the United States Constitution. The resolution reads:

RESOLVED by the American Bar Association that the proposed Child Labor Amendment to the Constitution of the United States should be actively opposed as an unwarranted invasion by the Federal Government of a field in which the rights of the individual states and of the family are and should remain paramount.[25]

The resolution, of course, failed to come to grips with the problem which the amendment sought to solve; instead, it attacked the amendment by representing it as a threat to undefined "rights" which "are and should remain paramount."

Bentham and Blackstone. Jeremy Bentham, who espoused a utilitarian philosophy, severely criticized Blackstone's position. In the preface to his *Fragment on Government* (1776), Bentham characterized Blackstone's views as "a mechanical veneration of antiquity."[26] Moreover, said Bentham, "a great multitude of people are continually talking of the law of nature; and then they go on giving you their sentiments of what is right and wrong; and these sentiments, you are to understand, are so many chapters and sections of the law of nature."[27]

Writing about a hundred years later, John R. Commons summarized the opposing positions of Blackstone and Bentham by pointing to their common element:

. . . Blackstone wished the law to be as he conceived it to be, which to him seemed divine and natural. Bentham wished it to be different and said so. And this is the only alternative to a theory of change and experiment. For, in lieu of historic research founded on a theory of the novelty of changes in customs and of experimental adaptation to other changes, wherein the change itself is the subject-matter of investigation and experiment, the only basis left for law and economics is Wish. Blackstone and Bentham were wishers, not scientists.[28]

The Contemporary Natural Law Position. Today, natural law writers reject the notion that the content of natural law is specific, permanent, and unchangeable. Writers like Jacques Maritain think of natural law as unwritten law which is "attuned to the necessary ends of the human being."[29]

---

[24] *United States* v. *La Jeune Eugenie*, 2 Mason 409 (1822); 26 Federal Cases 832, at pp. 846 and 851.

[25] Quoted from Thurman Arnold, *The Symbols of Government* (New Haven: Yale University Press, 1935), p. 210.

[26] Jeremy Bentham, *A Fragment on Government*, ed. F. C. Montague (London: Oxford University Press, 1951), p. 101.

[27] Jeremy Bentham, *The Works of Jeremy Bentham* (22 vols.; Edinburgh: William Tate, 1838), Vol. I, *An Introduction to the Principles of Morals and Legislation*, *An Introduction to the Principles of Morals An Introductio* p. 18, n. 6.

[28] Commons, *op. cit.*, p. 220.

[29] For a discussion of contemporary natural law writers, see Edgar Bodenheimer, *Jurisprudence* (Cambridge: Harvard University Press, 1962), chap. ix; and Hall, *op. cit.*

When this notion is interpreted in the light of his attitude toward democracy briefly summarized in the preceding chapter, it again becomes apparent that Maritain's approach *at the operational level* is essentially pragmatic and flexible.

Secular Theories. Among the secular natural law theorists, one finds writers like Gustav Radbruch who took the view that the law requires some recognition of legal rights. An opponent of legal positivism (on grounds that it had created conditions for the rise of Nazi power in Germany), he argued that law which was totally unjust was "useless law." So also, J. L. Brierly undertook to distinguish contemporary natural law from the conceptions held by medieval writers by providing an experimental definition of natural law. Thus Brierly wrote:

> . . . what medieval writers did not always realize was that what is reasonable, or to use their own terminology, what the law of nature enjoins, cannot receive a final definition: it is always, and above all in the sphere of human conduct, relative to conditions of time and place. We realize, as they hardly ever did, that these conditions are never standing still . . . When a modern lawyer asks what is reasonable, he looks only for an answer that is valid now and here, and not for one that is finally true; whereas a medieval writer might have said that if ultimate truth eludes our grasp, it is not because it is undiscoverable, but because our reasoning is imperfect. Some modern writers have expressed this difference by saying that what we have a right to believe in today is a law of nature with *a variable content.*[30]

Professor Jerome Hall has asserted that there is today a tendency toward a new "natural law jurisprudence" in the United States; that is, there is a tendency to adopt the views that: (1) it is possible to discover "objectively better or worse solutions of legal problems"; (2) man is a rational creature even though he is motivated by powerful instincts and "deep rooted emotions"; and (3) "although the effect on law of fortuitous, irrational, and dictatorial forces must be recognized . . . value is an essential element."[31] Hall does not explain precisely what he means by "value"

in this context, but he quotes with approval a statement by a great English lawyer, Frederick Pollock, that "The Law of Nature . . . is a living embodiment of the collective reason of civilized mankind, and as such is adopted by the Common Law in substance though not always by name."[32]

If by "collective reason of civilized mankind" is meant the knowledge acquired experimentally (through trial and error, in a process of learning and doing), the meaning of the "Law of Nature" in the preceding quotation has been changed from a mystical to a functional or instrumentalist concept. Whether or not one calls such a functional approach "natural law" jurisprudence, this view seems closely related to instrumentalist views like that of Roscoe Pound. His work will be discussed later in this chapter; before doing so, it will be useful to mention briefly the historical approach to the study of law, for this approach has had an influence on a number of legal philosophies, which cannot be characterized either as legal positivist or as natural law theories.

The Historical School: Law as Custom and Tradition

The founder and leader of the historical school was the German jurist, Friedrich Karl von Savigny (1779–1861), who argued that law as not something that could be developed by a "mind that knows independently of experience" or a rule put forth arbitrarily by a political authority. Law could only be understood in terms of the history of the race.[33] His approach clearly challenged the natural law theories. In England, Sir Henry Maine further developed the historical thesis by arguing that law has grown in all societies by following certain patterns and passing through certain stages.

It was Maine's view that "Law was brought into harmony with society" by means of three instrumentalities: "Legal Fictions, Equity, and Legislation." Maine used the words "Legal Fiction" to describe "any assumption which conceals, or affects to conceal, the fact that a rule of law has undergone an alteration, its letter remaining

---

[30] Brierly, *op. cit.*, pp. 14–15. (Italics his.)

[31] Hall, *op. cit.*, p. 140.

[32] *Ibid.*, quoting from Frederick Pollock, "The Law of Reason," 2 *Mich. L. Rev.* 173 (1903).

[33] Friedrich Karl von Savigny, *Von Beruf unsrer Zeit für Gezetzgebung und Rechtswissenschaft* (3rd ed.; Freiburg: J. C. B. Mohr, 1892). (This was first published in 1814.)

unchanged, its operation being modified."[34] That equity proceedings did introduce flexibility into the law has already been shown in this chapter. Obviously, legislation produces changes in law; and so also may a judge produce changes in law by reliance on "legal fictions," as defined by Maine. His work has had an influence on several derivative philosophies of law to which attention will now be given.

Derivative Philosophies; Law as an Instrument of Social Order

Legal Realism. A view of the law in terms of the behavior of officials, particularly the behavior of judges, was widely accepted in the United States in the 1920's and 1930's. Among its principal spokesmen were Karl N. Llewellyn, Judge Jerome J. Frank, and Thurman Arnold. Adherents to this view argued that economic, sociological, and psychological factors explain the behavior of the officials charged with interpreting and enforcing the law and that what these officials do "about disputes" constitutes "law." Thus, these adherents rejected the external element upon which the natural law philosophers laid great stress.[35] Some writers have considered legal realism an offshoot of legal positivism. It is interesting to note that in 1951, about twenty years after he had first stated his well-known definition of law as "what officials do about disputes," Professor Llewellyn limited that definition by saying it was "at best" a part of the "whole truth." Thus he wrote in 1951:

. . . the words fail to take proper account either of the office of the institution of law as an instrument of conscious shaping or of the office and work of that institution as a machinery of sometimes almost unconscious questing for the ideal; and the words therefore need some such expansion and correction as this.[36]

By 1951, therefore, Llewellyn had traveled some distance in the direction of instrumentalism.

In a new preface to the 1962 paperback edition of his book, *The Symbols of Government*, Judge Thurman Arnold wrote: "I believe that the analysis of the symbols of government which were current in 1933 is still relevant thirty years later."[37] In this book, Arnold argued that jurisprudence consists of a vast and complicated amount of literature—read only by legal philosophers whose function is to write more unread literature—and that this literature serves the purpose of providing assurance to the practicing lawyer that *Somewhere, Someone* is working to reconcile the conflicts which appear in law and to provide a justification of the ideal of a rule of law above men. The existence of this vast body of literature serves, he asserted, the function of helping the man in the street "keep his faith that government is symmetrical and rational, that there exists somewhere, available to him if he only could get time to study it, a unified philosophy of science of law."[38] Thus, Judge Arnold said:

In the science of jurisprudence all of the various ideals which are significant to the man on the street must be given a place. It must prove that the law is certain and at the same time elastic; that it is just, yet benevolent; economically sound, yet morally logical. It must show that the law can be dignified and solemn, and at the same time efficient, universal and fundamental, and a set of particular directions. Jurisprudence must give a place to all of the economic, and also ethical, notions of important competing groups within our society, no matter how far apart these notions may be. In its method, it must make gestures of recognition to the techniques of each separate branch of learning which claims to have any relation with the conduct of individuals, no matter how different these techniques may be.

Such a task can only be accomplished by ceremony, and hence the writings of jurisprudence should be considered as ceremonial observances rather than as scientific observances. This is shown by the fact that the literature of jurisprudence performs its social task most effectively for those who encourage it, praise it, but do not read it. For those who study it today it is nothing but a troubling mass of conflicting ideas. However, it is not generally read, so that its troubles are known only to the few people who read it for the purpose of writing more of it. For most of those who reverence the law, the knowledge that there is a constant

---

[34] Sir Henry Maine, *Ancient Law: Its Connection with the Early History of Society and Its Relation to Modern Ideas*, with Sir Frederick Pollock's notes (London: John Murray, 1906), chap. ii.

[35] Llewellyn, *op. cit.*; Jerome J. Frank, *Law and the*

Modern Mind (New York: Brentano's, 1930); Arnold, *op. cit.*

[36] Llewellyn, *op. cit.*, p. 9.

[37] Arnold, *op. cit.*, p. v.

[38] *Ibid.*, p. 49.

search going on for logical principles is sufficient. . . . There is comfort in such a literature, but there is no progress and no discovery.[39]

And yet, Judge Arnold added, the existence of an "ideal element in the law" nevertheless serves the function of providing stability, permanence, and strength "which come from unquestioning public acceptance."

Sociological Jurisprudence. The most important name in the field of sociological jurisprudence is that of Dean Roscoe Pound, who first formulated his views in 1912.[40] His position was that the lawyer must be a "social engineer."[41] His views were greatly influenced by the philosophies of Peirce, James, and Dewey. In 1960, Pound formulated the task of sociological jurisprudence in terms of five points:

. . . (1) Study of the actual social effects of legal institutions, legal precepts, and legal doctrines; (2) study of the means of making legal precepts effective in action; (3) psychological study of the judicial, administrative, legislative, and juristic processes as well as philosophical study of the ideals; (4) study not merely of how doctrines have evolved considered solely as legal materials, but study also of what social effects the doctrines of law have produced in the past and how they have produced them; and (5) recognition of individualized application of legal precepts—of reasonable and just solution of individual cases.[42]

The view stated in the quotation is clearly that of an eclectic: items (1) and (2) involve pragmatism; item (3) is the view of the legal realists; item (4) involves the historical approach to law; and item (5) is a natural law concept. Pound's approach constitutes a rejection both of the purely analytical approach embodied in "legal positivism" and of the mysticism embodied in the eighteenth century natural law theories. Such an approach was perhaps first suggested by Holmes in 1880, when as Lowell Lecturer he said in an often quoted statement:

. . . The life of the law has not been logic; it has been experience. The felt necessities of the time, the prevalent moral and political theories, intuitions of public policy, avowed or unconscious, even the prejudices which judges share with their fellow-men, have had a good deal more to do than the syllogism in determining the rules by which men should be governed. The law embodies the story of a nation's development through many centuries and it cannot be dealt with as if it contained only the axioms and corollaries of a book of mathematics.[43]

Holmes's statement points to something more than the nature or source of the law. It points primarily to the fact that the law cannot be static and that it must change in response to many different and sometimes conflicting pressures, that is, to the "felt necessities of the times." Such a view is essentially instrumental or pragmatic, and one of today's most articulate spokesmen on behalf of this view is Wolfgang Friedmann.

Law as an Instrument of Social Order. In 1959, he restated a view he had taken in 1951 in a book called *Law and Social Change in Contemporary Britain.* He said he had earlier put forth the view that "law must, especially in contemporary conditions of articulate lawmaking by legislators, courts, and others respond to social change if it is to fulfill its function as a paramount instrument of social order."[44] In his 1959 work, he has expanded this view. Also in 1959, Friedmann said:

The scientific significance of the vast volume of discussion—learned and otherwise—about the meaning of the "rule of law" is of modest proportions.

In a purely formal sense, the rule of law means no more than organized public power. In that sense, any system of norms based on a hierarchy of orders, even the organized mass murders of the Nazi regime, qualifies as law. As the "science of law" is understood by positive theories—the rule of law means the rule of organization. Such a concept is as unassailable as it is empty.

It is about the rule of law in its ideological sense, as implying the yardstick by which to measure "good" against "bad" law that the discussion has centered. The difficulty, however, is that to give to the "rule of law" concept a

---

[39] *Ibid.,* pp. 70–71.

[40] Roscoe Pound, "The Scope and Purpose of Sociological Jurisprudence," 24 *Harvard L. Rev.* 591 (1911); 25 *Harvard L. Rev.* 140 (1912).

[41] Roscoe Pound, *Law Finding Through Experience and Reason* (Athens, Ga.: University of Georgia Press, 1960), pp. 42–43.

[42] *Ibid.,* p. 33.

[43] Oliver Wendell Holmes, Jr., *The Common Law* (Boston: Little, Brown and Co., Inc., 1881), p. 1.

[44] Friedmann, *op. cit.,* p. ix.

universally acceptable ideological content is as difficult as to achieve the same for "natural law." In fact, the two concepts converge. . . .

A democratic ideal of justice must rest on the three foundations of equality, liberty and ultimate control of government by the people. It is, however, far from easy to give these concepts a specific content.[45]

Friedmann's discussion of the content of these three concepts is much like that provided by John Dewey (which was quoted in Chapter 2). Friedmann has written:

. . . We can still not formulate the principle of equality in more specific terms than Aristotle who said that justice meant the equal treatment of those who are equal before the law. We can give to this apparent tautology a more concrete meaning by saying that a democratic ideal of justice demands that inequalities shall be inequalities of function and service but shall not be derived from distinctions based on race, religion, or other personal attributes. . . .

The meaning of "liberty" is hardly more easy to define. In terms of a democratic ideal of justice, liberty means certain rights of personal freedom which must be secure from interference by government. They include legal protection from arbitrary arrest, freedom of opinion and association, of contract, labour and many others. Briefly, they may be subsumed under the two broad categories of the freedom of the person and the freedom of the mind. . . .

Lastly, the principle of control by the people means that law must ultimately be the responsibility of the elected representatives of the people. This is, indeed, a vital principle but it can say little about the technique by which the modern legislator can discharge this function.[46]

A universal danger "to the principles of representative democracy" lies in the fact that the population explosion, increasing urbanization, and the "dulling impact of modern mass media of communication" are producing a "decline of active civic participation" in government. In this situation, the law must be "vigorous and rigorous in

its watch over abuses"; it can "help to maintain or restore the principles of control by the people," although the methods which are employed must vary "from country to country and from one situation to another." But the basic safeguard lies "only in a society whose members are imbued with their personal sense of responsibility."[47]

Moreover, Friedmann has concluded:

That the content of the rule of law cannot be determined for all time and all circumstances is not a matter for lament but for rejoicing. It would be tragic if the law were so petrified as to be unable to respond to the unending challenge of evolutionary or revolutionary changes in society.[48]

C. A CONCLUDING COMMENT

Our survey of different philosophies of law has now been completed. It has necessarily been brief and to the point. It is clear that the three basic philosophical tendencies of logical positivism, natural law philosophy, and instrumentalism or pragmatism have their counterparts in the field of jurisprudence. We will now turn to an examination of the general problem of law and social change which is clearly identified in the legal philosophies of Holmes, Pound, and Friedmann. In the chapter which follows we will consider the role of the judge in producing changes in law, as well as the nature of some technical aspects of the judicial process. Thereafter, we will consider also the roles in the American System of Political Economy of pressure groups, of Congress, and of the President. It may also be noted that the Appendix to this book contains a discussion of the extent to which the three basic philosophical views presented here exist also in policy positions taken by economists.

---

[45] *Ibid.*, pp. 489 and 491.
[46] *Ibid.*, pp. 491–493.

[47] *Ibid.*, pp. 494–495.
[48] *Ibid.*, p. 503.

4

Law and Social Change: the Judicial Process

This chapter examines the ways in which changes in law are produced by means of judicial activity. First it examines the role of the judge as a lawmaker and then describes briefly some technical aspects of the judicial process, such as the role of the jury and the purpose of the judge's charge to the jury, as well as the difference between direct and circumstantial evidence. A rudimentary understanding of these elements of the legal process is important to an understanding of the decisions of judges in particular cases—for example, to an understanding of some of the basic landmark decisions in the area of our Constitutional law (discussed in Chapter 7). In addition, for the same reason, the Appendix to this chapter provides a brief description of the organization and operation of the system of federal and state courts.

A. JUDGES AS LAWMAKERS

Some General Observations

The pressures for changes in law come from many sources. Where patterns or norms of social life have changed, judges must eventually take account of such

changes or the legal system will break down. Technological advances and new scientific knowledge, bringing with them new ways of doing things, requiring new institutional arrangements to exploit or control them and giving rise to new problems, eventually demand legal recognition. Such recognition may come in the form of legislation or in the form of court decisions or both. National emergencies, such as the Great Depression or World War II, produce crises of which the law must take account. A small group of individuals, far-sighted or self-interested—a "pressure group"—may undertake to mould public opinion into a demand for change which cannot be ignored.

For example, in explaining how the power of government was employed to establish the market economy in England after the Industrial Revolution, Karl Polanyi emphasized the fact that until the English middle class had forced its way to power in 1832 and had succeeded in abolishing the Speenhamland Law of 1795—which had guaranteed the poor an income (through subsidy) irrespective of their earnings—no labor market existed in England.[1] The Speenhamland Law had originally been adopted as an emergency,

---

[1] Karl Polanyi, *The Great Transformation: The Political and Economic Origins of Our Time* (New York: Rinehart and Co., Inc., 1944), pp. 77–85.

humanitarian measure to offset the initial effects of the Industrial Revolution. It was the War on Poverty of Ricardo's day. Instead of accomplishing its purpose, Polanyi argued, the Speenhamland Law together with laws prohibiting the organization of labor unions prevented wages from rising and "led to the ironical result that the financially implemented 'right to live' eventually ruined the people whom it was ostensibly designed to succor."[2] The reaction was inevitable: thirty-nine years later, in 1834, the law was repealed.

How quickly laws change depends on many different factors. In the case of the Speenhamland Law, Polanyi pointed out:

. . . But the contemporaries did not comprehend the order [the market economy] for which they were preparing the way. Only when a grave deterioration of the productive capacity of the masses resulted—a veritable national calamity which was obstructing the progress of machine civilization—did the necessity of abolishing the unconditional right of the poor to relief impose itself upon the consciousness of the community. The complicated economics of Speenhamland transcended the comprehension of even the most expert observers of the time; but the conclusion appeared only the more compelling that aid-in-wages must be inherently vicious, since it miraculously injured even those who received it.[3]

And so, once those interested in establishing the market economy perceived the working rule embodied in the Speenhamland Law as a barrier to their objective, they obtained political power and employed the authority of government to remove the barrier by changing that working rule. Thus, the market economy in England was established by means of political power acting through the form and agency of law, just as the immediately-preceding system of minute regulation of economic activity (known as "mercantilism") attacked by Adam Smith had similarly been so established. Note that the process was set in motion by changes in the existing technology and that the particular working rules which were adopted represented a conception of how the economy ought to be organized.

Circumstances such as the strength of myths and customs, understanding by the principal parties of the meanings of the events of the times, the constitutional structure, the extent of suffrage, and the interests of the personalities involved may act either to speed up or to delay the response of the law to technological and social pressures. As we will see in Chapter 7, in the United States in 1937 the Supreme Court began upholding the constitutionality of various measures adopted by Congress during the Roosevelt administration only after Justice Roberts, who had previously consistently voted against the validity of such legislation, changed his position and voted with the previous minority, thereby turning the previous four-man minority into a five-man majority. Subsequent vacancies were filled by new appointments, and, thereafter, many new pieces of legislation were upheld as constitutional.

Thus, not all changes result from legislation: changes may occur as a result of executive action combined with other action—from a combination of executive and legislative action and judicial interpretation; and changes may also occur in judge-made law alone. An example of the latter occurred in 1954 when the Supreme Court specifically overruled its own previous "equal but separate facilities" doctrine and thereby rejected the practice of establishment of a system of separate public schools for whites and Negroes. It had earlier permitted the establishment of segregated public facilities in another context in the decision of Plessy v. Ferguson in 1897.[4] On other occasions it has sharply limited some of its previous decisions, without specifically overruling them—for example, in cases involving the conflict between the monopoly rights given under the patent laws and the prohibition of monopolization contained in the Sherman Act,[5] a problem which we will also consider more closely in Part II.

The Scope and Nature of Judicial Activity

It is clear that judges do engage in some "creative" activity in interpreting statutes and in applying the established rules of

---

[2] Ibid., p. 81.
[3] Ibid., pp. 81–82.
[4] Brown v. Board of Education, 347 U.S. 483 (1954), 349 U.S. 294 (1954); and Plessy v. Ferguson, 163 U.S. 537 (1897).
[5] United States v. General Electric Co., 272 U.S. 476 (1926), limited by United States v. Line Material Co., 333 U.S. 287 (1948).

common law in specific cases. The crucial question is "how much freedom do they have?" A naïve view of this freedom of judicial interpretation is that the words of Chief Justice Hughes (spoken when he was still Governor of New York)—that "the Constitution is what the judges say it is"— are to be interpreted literally. The very fact that *these* words themselves require interpretation points up the nature of the problem facing the judge who must make a decision in a given case. A literal interpretation of Hughes's words ignores the fact that there are both internal (self-imposed) and external (not self-imposed) limitations upon the freedom of judges. It is to a consideration of some of these limitations that we turn now.

The Function of Precedent. We have seen in the preceding chapter that Bentham criticized Blackstone on grounds that the latter had exhibited a "mechanical veneration of antiquity." In effect, Bentham's position was that slavish attention to precedent—to general principles developed in earlier cases which may have involved a different social setting—constitutes a serious barrier to the adjustment of the law to meet new social problems. But, we have also seen from John Commons' analysis of the nature of common law—as a method of problem-solving by means of trial and error inclusion and exclusion—that there is no inevitable reason why the common law method must degenerate into such a barrier to social change. The problem which Bentham raised is that of *stare decisis*.

In its strictest form, the rule of *stare decisis et non quieta movere*—which means "to stand by settled precedents and not to disturb settled rules"—involves the proposition that a judicial rule which has been long accepted and established should not be disturbed except by legislative action. A strict interpretation of the rule involves the interesting proposition that what a previous *court* has once decided can thereafter be changed only by the *legislature*, on grounds: (1) that vested rights have been created by the prior court decision; or (2) that any other rule would introduce great uncertainty into the law; or (3) that it is

always open to the legislature to change the rule announced by the court if it wishes to do so—and apparently the longer the rule has been in effect without such action by the legislative branch, the more authority it ought to have. A second interpretation of the rule is that prior decisions must be accorded great weight, but, where previous decisions are out of line with "reason" and generally accepted contemporary principles of law, the highest court in the jurisdiction may change the rule. The third and most liberal view is that the principle is merely a social policy, not an inflexible rule of law,[6] and that precedents may be overruled in response to the "felt necessities of the times." This last view is instrumentalist in nature.

The reasons given by legal philosophers for the rule vary. All agree that it makes for certainty in the law; thus both private individuals and lawyers are able to act on the basis of the proposition that settled rules will continue to be enforced. Bodenheimer has pointed out also that the rule makes for efficient judicial administration, since it reduces the work load of the judges.[7] This would seem to be a rather peculiar justification, since it loses sight of one purpose for which courts are established. (A better solution would be more judges!) The most convincing reason for the rule is that it operates as a limitation upon the power of judges to "make law." Such a limitation can have both its good and its bad aspects. On the one hand, it may slow down the process of adjustment of the law to social changes; on the other, it does result in a uniformity of decisions on the part of courts, since it requires that they apply the principles as once-determined by the highest court within the relevant jurisdiction. Of course, lower courts are bound to follow such principles on pain of reversal in any case, but the law is clearly more certain and orderly because of the existence of the rule. Complete abandonment of the principle would widen the area for creative interpretation and judicial legislation.

The "Point of the Case" versus Dictum. Not every statement made in a decision by a court acquires the force of precedent. Only

[6] Roscoe Pound, *Law Finding Through Experience and Reason* (Athens, Ga.: University of Georgia Press, 1960), pp. 38–39.

[7] Edgar Bodenheimer, *Jurisprudence* (Cambridge: Harvard University Press, 1962), pp. 368–371.

those statements which acquire the status of "the point of the case"—*ratio decidendi*, "the ground of the decision"—are considered authoritative principles to be applied in later similar factual issues. Nonessential statements by the court are generally identified as *dicta* or *obiter dicta*. Unfortunately, legal scholars do not always agree as to what statements constitute the *ratio decidendi* and what statements constitute *dicta* in a given decision. And laymen are even more apt to confuse the two. The prevailing legal view seems to be that the *ratio decidendi* consists of that general principle announced by the court *which is necessary* to the decision of the actual issue between the litigants.[8] Nevertheless, what is necessary to a decision of the actual issue is a question about which responsible men may sometimes differ, with the result that *dicta* from an earlier case may be the source of changes in the law in later cases.

A Case Study of Dictum: "Monopoly Thrust Upon." Some interesting examples of the problem of deciding what is *ratio decidendi* can be found in recent cases in the field of antitrust involving the charge of monopolization. The Attorney General's National Committee to Study the Antitrust Laws flatly stated in 1955: "An individual company has not violated Section 2 of the Sherman Act [which prohibits "monopolization"] where monopoly power has been 'thrust upon it.'"[9]

The Committee cited in support of its position: a landmark decision in which Judge Learned Hand had found the Aluminum Company of America guilty of "monopolization" under the Sherman Act;[10] some language by the Supreme Court in a 1946 case in which it affirmed the holding of a lower court that several American tobacco companies had violated the Sherman Act;[11] and some language by Judge Wyzanski of Boston in a District Court opinion holding the United Shoe Machinery Corporation guilty of violating the Sherman Act.[12] (All these cases will also be considered more closely in Part II.)

In *none* of these cases did the Supreme Court *actually hold* that the defendant had acquired a monopoly innocently as a result of superior skill, foresight, or ability.

The "thrust upon" idea, referred to by the Attorney General's Committee, had been stated by Judge Learned Hand in 1945 in the *Alcoa* case. After he had held that Alcoa did have a monopoly in the production of aluminum ingot, Judge Hand said:

It does not follow because "Alcoa" had such a monopoly, that it "monopolized" the ingot market; it may not have achieved monopoly; *monopoly may have been thrust upon it.* If it had been a combination of existing smelters which united the whole industry and controlled the production of all aluminum ingot, it would certainly have "monopolized" the market. In several decisions the Supreme Court has decreed the dissolution of such combinations, although they have engaged in no unlawful trade practices. . . .[13]

Judge Hand then proceeded (*in the same paragraph*) to analyze numerous earlier decisions by the Supreme Court and to conclude:

. . . it is unquestionably true that from the very outset the courts have *at least kept in reserve the possibility that the origin of a monopoly may be critical in determining its legality* . . . The successful competitor, having been urged to compete, must not be turned upon when he wins. The most extreme expression of this view is in *United States* v. *United States Steel Corporation*, 251 U.S. 417, . . . which Sanford, J., in part repeated in *United States* v. *International Harvester Corporation*, 274 U.S. 293 . . . *It so chances that* in both instances the corporation had less than two-thirds of the production in its hands, and *the language quoted was not necessary to the decision; so that* even if it had not later been modified, *it has not the authority of an actual decision. But, whatever authority it does have was modified by* the gloss of *Cardozo, J., in United States* v. *Swift and Co.*, 286 U.S. 106, p. 116 . . . *when he said, "Mere size . . . is not an offense against the Sherman Act unless magnified to the point at which it amounts to a monopoly . . . but size carries with it an opportunity for abuse that is not to be ignored when the opportunity is proved to have been utilized in the past.*[14]

[8] *Ibid.*, pp. 377–378.
[9] *Report of the Attorney General's National Committee to Study the Anti-trust Laws* (Washington, D.C.: U.S. Government Printing Office, 1955), p. 56.
[10] *Aluminum Co. of America* v. *United States*, 148 F. 2d 416 (1945), at p. 429.

[11] *American Tobacco Co.* v. *United States*, 328 U.S. 781 (1946), at p. 786.
[12] *United States* v. *United Shoe Machinery Corp.*, 110 F. Supp. 295 (1953).
[13] *United States* v. *Aluminium Co. of America*, 148 F. 2d 416 (1945), at p. 429. (Italics mine.)
[14] *Ibid.*, pp. 429–430. (Italics mine.)

The plain language of Cardozo's statement is that *size is not an offense unless* magnified to the point at which *it amounts to monopoly, but size may be an offense, even when not so magnified, if there is proof that "the opportunity for abuse" deriving from that size has been utilized in the past.* Many subsequent writers have cited the *Swift* case for the proposition that "mere size is not an offense under the Sherman Act," but such a statement is clearly an oversimplified version of what Justice Cardozo *actually said* in this case.

Yet, the oversimplified version of the statement appears in the second of the cases cited as an authority by the Attorney General's National Committee in support of its assertion that the *dictum* concerning the "thrust upon" doctrine is really *ratio decidendi*. In *American Tobacco Company* v. *United States*,[15] Justice Burton wrote: "'Size carries with it an opportunity for abuse that is not to be ignored when the opportunity is proved to have been utilized in the past.' *United States* v. *Swift and Co.*, 286 U.S. 106, 116. An intent to use this power to maintain a monopoly was found by the jury in these cases."[16] (In *United States* v. *Griffith*, Justice Douglas also cited this statement as Cardozo's opinion.[17]) But a comparison of Justice Burton's version of Cardozo's statement with the *exact* quotation reproduced by Judge Hand given previously (note that they cite the same page) discloses that Justice Burton had changed the plain meaning of Cardozo's statement. Cardozo's statement implies that monopoly is an offense and size *may be* if other facts are also present. It was probably with regard to situations like this that Dean Edward Levi said of *ratio decidendi*: "It is not what a prior judge intended that is of importance; rather it is what the present judge, attempting to see the law as a fairly consistent whole, thinks should be the determining classification."[18]

In the *American Tobacco Company* case, Justice Burton also cited with approval several passages from Judge Hand's opinion in the *Alcoa* case. Among these passages is the "thrust upon" passage quoted earlier. However, Justice Burton also then said in the *American Tobacco* case:

. . . Because of the presence of that element [a finding of fact that a combination or conspiracy to monopolize existed], we *do not have* here *the hypothetical case of* parties who themselves have not "achieved" monopoly but have had monopoly "*thrust upon*" them. See *United States* v. *Aluminum Co. of America*, 148 F. 2d 416, 429.

The present cases are not comparable to cases where the parties, for example, merely have made a new discovery or an original entry into a new field and unexpectedly or unavoidably have found themselves enjoying a monopoly coupled with power and intent to maintain it.[19]

Since the case was a "hypothetical" one, obviously the Court did not decide it.

Two years later, in *United States* v. *Griffith*, Justice Douglas also referred to the *Alcoa* case by saying:

. . . So it is that monopoly power, *whether lawfully or unlawfully acquired, may* itself constitute an evil and *stand condemned* under Section 2 *even though it remains unexercised.* For Section 2 of the Act is aimed, *inter alia*, at the acquisition or retention of effective market control. See *United States* v. *Aluminum Co. of America* . . . Hence the existence of power "to exclude competition when it is desired to do so" is itself a violation of Section 2, provided it is coupled with the purpose or intent to exercise that power. . . . It follows *a fortiori* that the *use of monopoly power, however lawfully acquired*, to foreclose competition, to gain a competitive advantage, or to destroy a competitor, *is unlawful.*[20]

According to this view, lawful acquisition would *not* be a complete defense; it is *use* of monopoly power in certain ways which is unlawful.

The third case cited by the Attorney General's Committee was the *United Shoe Machinery* case. In that case, District Judge Wyzanski analyzed both the *Alcoa* and *Griffith* case statements quoted above and asserted that "taken as a whole, the evidence" against the United Shoe Machinery Corporation satisfies "*both* Griffith and Aluminum." Therefore, Judge Wyzanski found it "*unnecessary to choose*" between

15 328 U.S. 781 (1946).

16 *Ibid.*, at p. 796.

17 *United States* v. *Griffith*, 334 U.S. 100 (1948), p. 107, n. 10.

18 Edward H. Levi, *An Introduction to Legal Reasoning* (Chicago: University of Chicago Press, 1949), p. 2.

19 *American Tobacco Co.* v. *United States*, 328 U.S. 781 (1946), at p. 786. (Italics mine.) Note that p. 429 of Judge Hand's decision was cited.

20 *United States* v. *Griffith*, 334 U.S. 100 (1948), at p. 107. (Italics mine.)

these two approaches.[21] His decision was affirmed by seven of the Supreme Court Justices without an opinion in 1954, one year before the Attorney General's Committee rendered its *Report*. The Court said simply: "the Court being satisfied that the findings of the District Court are justified by the evidence and support the decree, the judgment is affirmed."[22] It is of interest now to consider how the Court treated the "monopoly thrust upon doctrine" in the *du Pont Cellophane* case decided in 1956, one year *after* the Attorney General's Committee had asserted that this phrase identified a defense against the charge of monopolization under the Sherman Act.

A Related Case Study of Dictum: The du Pont Cellophane Case. In 1953, the government brought an action against du Pont on grounds that the latter had monopolized cellophane production and sales. Judge Leahy, the District Judge, framed the issues before the trial court by saying:

The charge here is duPont monopolizes cellophane. The charge involves two questions: 1. does duPont possess monopoly powers; and 2., if so has it achieved such powers by "monopolizing" within the meaning of the Act and under United States v. Aluminum Company of America. . . . Unless the first is decided against defendant, the second is *not* reached.[23] (*Sic.*)

One hundred forty pages later in his Finding of Fact Number 838 (the case was tried without a jury), Judge Leahy held:

The record establishes plain cellophane and moistureproof cellophane are each flexible packaging materials which are functionally interchangeable with other flexible packaging materials and sold at same time to same customers for same purposes *at competitive prices*; there is no cellophane market distinct and separate from the market for flexible packaging materials; the market for flexible packaging materials is the relevant market for determining nature and extent of duPont's market control; and *duPont has at all times competed with other cellophane producers and manufacturers* of other flexible packaging materials *in all aspects of its cellophane business.*[24] (*Sic.*)

Three pages later Judge Leahy reinforced his position: "Facts, in large part uncontested, demonstrate duPont cellophane is sold under such intense competitive conditions acquisition of market control or monopoly power is a practical impossibility. . . ."[25] (*Sic.*)

According to his own statement of the issues and of their significance, one would expect such findings to settle the case: Judge Leahy had found that du Pont did not have a monopoly, and his second question "is not reached." However, Judge Leahy, nevertheless, proceeded also to discuss at length the answer to his second question. Perhaps his reason for doing so is to be found in his statement:

. . . I think excellence of corporate function in this country, whether it be small, or big business, calls for a critical re-examination by the Congress, after a half-a-century of the enforcement of the Sherman and allied Acts.[26] (*Sic.*)

In any event, *although he had already held* in his Finding of Fact Number 838 *that du Pont did not have a monopoly*, Judge Leahy said:

. . . Its "monopoly" was "thrust upon" it within the true meaning of the decisions and, wholly apart from the existence of the moistureproof patent, the facts as to how duPont achieved its position constitutes a defense to the charge of "monopolization."[27] (*Sic.*)

Indeed, Judge Leahy felt that even stronger language stating his own economic analysis was called for:

I am able, after critical examination of the record, to determine duPont's position is the result of research, business skill and competitive activity. Much of duPont's evidence was designed to show research, price and sales policies of that Company are responsible for its success and these policies were conceived and carried forward in a coordinated fashion with skill, gaining for duPont substantial recognition in the packaging industry.

. . . The record reflects not the dead hand of monopoly but rapidly declining prices, expanding production, intense competition stimulated by creative research, the development of new

[21] *United States* v. *United Shoe Machinery Corp.*, 110 F. Supp. 295 (1953), at p. 343. (Italics mine.)

[22] *United Shoe Machinery Corp.* v. *United States*, 347 U.S. 521 (1954), at p. 521. (Justices Jackson and Clark did not participate.)

[23] *United States* v. *E.I. du Pont de Nemours and Co.*, 118 F. Suppl. 41 (1953), at p. 54. (Italics mine.)

[24] *Ibid.*, p. 194. (Italics mine.) See also Finding Number 58, at p. 63.

[25] *Ibid.*, pp. 197–198.

[26] *Ibid.*, p. 213.

[27] *Ibid.*, p. 217.

Products and uses and other benefits of a free economy. DuPont nor any other American company similarly situated should be punished for its success. Nothing warrants intervention of this court of equity. The complaint should be dismissed.[28] (*Sic.*)

Now note: *none of the praise heaped on du Pont* by Judge Leahy (much less his recognition of the excellence "of corporate function"), once he found that it did not have a monopoly, *is essential to the decision. It is all obiter dictum*, an interesting insight into and reflection of Judge Leahy's personal opinions, but *not an authoritative source of principle.*

The case was appealed to the Supreme Court by the government. In 1956, the Court upheld Judge Leahy's Finding of Fact Number 838 by a vote of 4 to 3 (with Justices Clark and Harlan not participating). The majority opinion was written by Justice Reed, while Justice Frankfurter wrote a short concurring opinion. Justice Reed rested the relatively short majority opinion entirely upon the fact that the majority accepted the lower court's finding of fact that du Pont did not possess a monopoly in the relevant market and concluded by saying: ". . . it seems to us that du Pont should not be found to monopolize cellophane when that product has the competition and interchangeability with other wrappings that this record shows."[29]

He also said, with reference to the possibility of the existence of an exception to Section 2 (the monopoly section) of the Sherman Act: "This exception to the Sherman Act prohibitions of monopoly power is perhaps the monopoly 'thrust upon' one of *United States* v. *Aluminum Co. of America*, 148 F. 2d 416, 429, *left as an undecided possibility by American Tobacco Co.* v. *United States.*"[30] Moreover, he added: "Section 2 requires application of a reasonable approach in determining the *existence* of monopoly power. . . . *This* of course *does not mean there can be a reasonable monopoly.*"[31] Thus, according to Justice Reed, the "thrust upon" doctrine was an undecided question in 1956, a year *after*

publication of the *Report* of the Attorney General's National Committee. And a fair reading of the relevant portion of Justice Burton's opinion (quoted earlier) in *American Tobacco* does lead to the conclusion that Justice Reed was correct in his assessment of Justice Burton's meaning. The "thrust upon" case was a "hypothetical one" insofar as *American Tobacco* was concerned, and the question was therefore left undecided, just as Justice Reed later pointed out.

The minority dissenting opinion in the *du Pont Cellophane* case was written by Chief Justice Warren (with Justices Black and Douglas concurring) and reads in part:

This case . . . turns upon the proper definition of the market. . . . We cannot agree that cellophane . . . is "the selfsame product" as glassine, greaseproof and vegetable parchment papers, waxed papers, sulphite papers, aluminum foil, cellulose acetate, and Pliofilm and other films.
. . . Du Pont was not "the passive beneficiary of a monopoly" . . .
. . . Du Pont cannot bear "the burden of proving that it owes its monopoly *solely* to superior skill. . . ."
If competition is at the core of the Sherman Act, we cannot agree that it was consistent with that Act for the enormously lucrative cellophane industry to have no more than two sellers from 1924 to 1951. . . . The public should not be left to rely upon the dispensations of management in order to obtain the benefits which normally accompany competition.[32]

The minority thus used the "thrust upon" doctrine as an intellectual ploy. By the minority's own assertion, the case does not turn on this point, since this point is not essential to the decision of the issue. Perhaps the minority was chiding the trial court (the minority twice asserted in its dissenting opinion that the trial court had erred or misconceived the antitrust laws).

Justice Frankfurter, who had concurred in the acceptance of the lower court's finding of fact (that du Pont did not have a monopoly in cellophane), wrote a concurring opinion calling attention to the relevant issues. He said:

Mr. Justice Reed has pithily defined the conflicting claims in this case. "The charge was monopolization of cellophane. The defense, that

[28] *Ibid.*, p. 217 and p. 233.
[29] *United States* v. *E.I. du Pont de Nemours and Co.*, 351 U.S. 377 (1956), at p. 404.

[30] *Ibid.*, pp. 390–391. (Italics mine. Note that again p. 429 of *Aloca* was cited.)
[31] *Ibid.*, at p. 393. (Italics mine.)
[32] *Ibid.*, at pp. 414–415; pp. 425–426.

cellophane was merely a part of the relevant market for flexible packaging materials." Since this defense is sustained, the judgment below must be affirmed and it becomes unnecessary to consider whether du Pont's power over trade in cellophane would, had the defense failed, come within the prohibition of "monopolizing" under Section 2 of the Sherman Act. *Needless disquisition on the difficult subject of single-firm monopoly should be avoided since the case may be disposed of without consideration of this problem.*

The boundary between the course of events by which a business may reach a powerful position in an industry without offending the outlawry of "monopolizing" under Section 2 of the Sherman Act and the course of events which brings the attainment of that result within the condemnation of that section, cannot be established by general phrases.[33]

It is clear, therefore, that in 1956 the Supreme Court had not yet itself decided what the *dictum*—monopoly "thrust upon" a defendant—meant and that the Attorney General's Committee was in error in asserting this *dictum* as an existing rule of law. So far there has been no Supreme Court decision in which a defendant has been found to have acquired a monopoly by having had it "thrust upon" him.

In 1964, in a case involving very special facts, a Louisiana District Court cited Judge Leahy's opinion in the *du Pont* case as a precedent. [*Clark Marine Corporation* v. *Cargill, Inc.*, 226 F. Supp. 103 (1964)]. The plaintiff had brought a treble damage action alleging that the defendant had monopolized the business of fleeting and switching grain barges and injured the plaintiff's business. The Court found as facts that the plaintiff had suffered because of the lack of his own business ability and that the "superior position" of the defendant was due to its "superior skill and effective business activity." *At no point* did the Court *hold* that the defendant possessed a monopoly. Hence, not only because it is merely the decision of a district court but also because the Court did *not* make the relevant finding of fact, this case does not stand for the proposition that "monopoly thrust upon a defendant is lawful."

The Lessons to Be Learned from These Case Studies. One *lesson* to be learned from careful study of these decisions is, of course, that whether or not a defendant can safely rely on a defense of "monopoly thrust upon" in a Sherman Act case is still an "undecided" question. The meaning of the *du Pont Cellophane* case is simply as Justice Frankfurter clearly pointed out: the trial court found that du Pont did not have a monopoly within the meaning of the Sherman Act, and a majority of the Supreme Court Justices deciding the case agreed with this finding of fact. At the same time, the Attorney General's National Committee and Judge Leahy both treated the "thrust upon" doctrine as a rule of law, and so, in effect (although for a different reason), did the dissenting Justices. On the other hand, neither Justice Reed—speaking for the majority—nor Justice Frankfurter believed that the question of "thrust upon" had yet been decided, because no case had arisen to require such a decision.

A second lesson to be learned from the examination of these decisions is that one must be careful not to read too much into any court decision; most particularly, the novice must be careful to try to avoid quoting *dicta* from cases as rules of law because they happen to represent his belief as to "what the law should be." *Dicta* are sometimes an accidental and sometimes a premeditated source of change in the law. In other words, as we have seen from these excerpts, judges and lawyers are not themselves immune from reading their own beliefs and wishes into prior decisions.

The "Doctrine of Judicial Restraint." That the courts inevitably must perform a creative function in "applying" laws is clear, despite many naive arguments that they ought to restrict themselves to performing a purely grammatical function. In part, the objection to the proposition that the courts should take an active part in readjusting the law to meet changes in social conditions stems from those who believe that such practices introduce uncertainty into the law; and, in part, it stems from those whose particular and special interests are disturbed by such readjustments and who believe that they will be able to delay such changes if the task of making them is thrown upon the legislatures, particularly in the United States upon the state legislatures. In short, many of the objections to creative interpretation arise out of a conflict of interests and a clash of values. Sometimes

---

[33] *Ibid.*, p. 413. (Italics mine.)

these objections take the form of an assertion that the courts should "apply" but not "make" the law; and, at others, that the courts, and especially the Supreme Court, should practice the doctrine of "judicial restraint."

Such a position was taken in 1958 by the Conference of Chief Justices (of state courts), which, by a vote of 38 to 8, adopted a resolution (based on a *Report* written by five members of the University of Chicago Law School) urging the Supreme Court to "exercise the power of judicial self-restraint —by recognizing and giving effect to the difference" between "that which . . . the Constitution may prescribe or permit and that which . . . a majority of the Supreme Court, as from time to time constituted, may deem desirable or undesirable."[34] It is interesting to note, in this connection, that many of the Chief Justices of State Supreme Courts obtain their offices by election rather than by appointment and that their terms are of limited duration. There may exist a difference between the amount of political independence enjoyed by such elected judges as compared with federal judges, who are appointed for life (during good behavior).

Indeed, in *The Federalist* (No. 78), Alexander Hamilton argued that "complete independence of the courts of justice is essential in a limited Constitution" (one which contains certain specified exceptions, such as prohibitions against bills of attainder or *ex-post-facto* laws), on grounds that "limitations of this kind can be preserved in practice no other way than through the medium of courts of justice, whose duty it must be to declare all acts contrary to the *manifest tenor* of the Constitution void."[35] Hamilton took a strong position in support of the power of the courts to declare statutes unconstitutional and denied that such a position implied "a superiority of the judicial power to the legislative power." All that this position implies, he argued, is:

. . . that the power of the people is superior to both; and where the will of the legislature,

declared in its statutes, stands in opposition to that of the people, declared in the Constitution, the judges ought to be governed by the latter rather than the former. They ought to regulate their decisions by the fundamental laws, rather than by those which are not fundamental.[36]

Hamilton also referred to the exercise of judicial discretion in determining which of two contradictory statutes is to be held controlling. In such a case he asserted:

. . . it is the province of the courts to liquidate and fix their meaning and operation. So far as they can, by any fair construction, be reconciled to each other, reason and law conspire to dictate that this should be done; where this is impracticable, it becomes a matter of necessity to give effect to one, in exclusion of the other. The rule which has obtained in the courts for determining their relative validity is, that the last in order of time shall be preferred to the first. But this is a mere rule of construction, not derived from any positive law, but from the nature and reason of the thing. It is a rule not enjoined upon the courts by legislative provision, but adopted by themselves, as consonant to truth and propriety, for the direction of their conduct as interpreters of the law. They thought it reasonable, that *between the interfering acts of an equal authority, that which was the last indication of its will should have the preference.*[37]

But, he added, since the Constitution represented a "superior" authority, in the case of a conflict between a statute and the Constitution the latter must be followed. It is the will of the people (which Hamilton argued is declared in the Constitution) which must control; but *it is that will based on deliberate reflection and on information and not a momentary response to demagogic appeals* which he had in mind, since he also stated that:

. . . This independence of the judges is equally requisite to guard the Constitution and the rights of individuals from the effects of those ill humors, which the arts of designing men, or the influence of particular conjunctures, sometimes disseminate among the people themselves, and which, though they speedily give place to better information, and more deliberate reflection, have a tendency, in the meantime, to

[34] Conference of Chief Justices, *Report of the Committee on Federal-State Relationships as Affected by Judicial Decisions, Adopted August, 1958, Pasadena, Printed and distributed as a public service by The Virginia Commission on Constitutional Government* (Richmond, 1959); and *New York Times*, August 24, 1958, p. 42.

[35] *The Federalist*, of the New Constitution, written in 1788, by Mr. Hamilton, Mr. Jay, and Mr. Madison (A New Edition; Philadelphia: Benjamin Warner, 1818). (Numerous more recent editions are available to the student, including a Modern Library edition and several paperback editions.)

[36] *Ibid.*

[37] *Ibid.* (Italics mine.)

occasion dangerous innovations in the government, and serious oppressions of the minor party in the community.[38]

When Hamilton wrote, the Constitution had not yet been ratified, much less had it been the subject of Supreme Court decisions. Today, the Constitution must be said to consist not only of the language employed by its framers but also of the Amendments to it and of the interpretations made of it by the Supreme Court in the course of historical time and during a period of technological change not envisioned by the Founding Fathers. A literal interpretation of the original Constitution in the modern world is literally impossible.

Thus, with respect to the view that the Supreme Court should interpret the Constitution today as it "was intended to be interpreted by those who wrote it," Judge Learned Hand remarked in 1958:

... it would be fatuous to attempt imaginatively to concoct how the Founding Fathers would have applied them [the First, Eighth, and the Fourteenth Amendments to the Constitution] to the regulation of modern society. Not only is it true that, "if by the statement that what the Constitution meant at the time of its adoption is what it means today it is intended to say that the great clauses of the Constitution must be confined to the interpretation which the framers, with the conditions and outlook of their time, would have placed upon them, the statement carries its own refutation," but it is also impossible to fabricate how the "Framers" would have answered the problems that arise in modern society had they been reared in a civilization which has produced these problems. We should indeed have to be sorcerers to conjure up how they would have responded.[39]

In another work, Judge Hand pointed out that the problem of literal versus creative interpretation was merely another aspect of the doctrine of separation of powers,[40] the rather naive notion that there are clearly distinct and separate law-making, law-interpreting, and law-enforcing branches of government. (This question will occupy us further in the next chapter.)

Another great judge, Justice Benjamin Cardozo, remarked that the judge "is to exercise discretion informed by tradition, methodized by analogy, disciplined by system, and subordinated to the 'primordial necessity' of order in social life."[41] But, somewhat later, in a much-quoted statement, he added, "Deep below consciousness are other forces, the likes and the dislikes, the predilections and the prejudices, the complex of instincts and emotions and habits, which make the man, whether he be litigant or judge."[42]

The issue, thus, is not one of *literal* versus *creative* interpretation. The fact that judges do "make" law and inevitably must "make" law is clearly with us. At the same time, it must be recognized that they are not completely free to make law as they see fit and that they are freer to exercise their discretion in some areas than in others. Or, to quote again from Justice Cardozo's book: "Some fields of law there are, indeed, where there is freer scope for subjective vision. ... The personal element, whatever its scope in other spheres, should have little, if any, sway in determining the limits of judicial power."[43]

Probably the greatest limitation on creative interpretation is the fact that judges must subordinate their desires to what Cardozo called "the 'primordial necessity' of order in social life." For, without that order, there would not only be no rule of law and hence no function for the courts to perform, but no courts. The Constitution is *not* just what the Supreme Court says it is; the Constitution is what the Supreme Court says it is, subject to the judicial traditions and the facts of life which obtain at the time the Court renders its decision. In this regard, it is important to keep in mind that the violence with which a radical or extremist minority group may object to particular decisions of the Supreme Court is not necessarily an index of the extent to which the populace as a whole is prepared to accept or reject such decisions.

[38] *Ibid.*

[39] Learned Hand, *The Bill of Rights* (Cambridge: Harvard University Press, 1960), pp. 34–35.

[40] Learned Hand, "How Far Is a Judge Free in Rendering a Decision?" reproduced in Irving Dilliard (ed.), *The Spirit of Liberty: Papers and Addresses of Learned Hand* (New York: Alfred A.

Knopf, Inc., 1953), p. 109.

[41] Benjamin N. Cardozo, *The Nature of the Judicial Process* (New Haven: Yale University Press, 1921), p. 141.

[42] *Ibid.*, p. 167.

[43] *Ibid.*, p. 109.

The unanimous 1954 decision by the Court holding unconstitutional segregation in the public schools,[44] followed by its decision eight years later prohibiting the teaching of religion in the public schools,[45] and its decisions pertaining to the treatment of suspects in criminal cases, apparently including cases involving tax evasions,[46] subjected the Court to violent attacks by those opposed to these decisions, but the Court has continued to be a respected institution.

In describing the judicial process, Bodenheimer has emphasized the fact that a judge seeks to synthesize materials at hand and not to manufacture something entirely new. That is, the judge consciously seeks to rest his decision on formal and informal sources considered by the legal profession to be legitimate.[47] In short, a judge "may make changes in law" but he cannot himself "tear down the edifice of the law. . . . For fundamental structural changes in the legal system . . . he must rely on outside help."[48]

Wolfgang Friedmann has taken a similar position. He has emphasized that judging involves "careful evaluation of conflicting interests," and that the matter is not one of infallible knowledge.[49]

B. SOME TECHNICAL ASPECTS OF THE JUDICIAL PROCESS

In this section we will briefly consider some of the more technical aspects of the judicial process: the role of the jury, the function of the judge's charge to the jury, types of evidence, and the basis of judicial review. A rudimentary knowledge of these matters is important to anyone who wishes to understand and evaluate court decisions.

The Jury as Fact Finder

Originally the jury was a body of witnesses called upon to swear to some question of fact of which the jurors were supposed to have personal knowledge. In the latter part of the seventeenth century, the character of the *petit* or *trial jury* began to change to what it is today: a body of twelve men—with no previously formed opinions about the case—sworn in a district court to try and determine by a unanimous verdict questions of fact. The *grand jury*, which consists of a larger number—usually 13 to 23—than the petit jury (hence the name *grand*), is a body summoned by the sheriff and has the function of receiving complaints and accusations for the purpose of determining whether a criminal trial should be held. That is, the grand jury does not find a person guilty or innocent; it merely determines whether or not a trial should occur. The petit jury determines guilt or innocence. Grand jury proceedings are secret; petit juries usually listen to testimony in open court.

Judge Jerome Frank was, before his death, one of the most severe critics of the jury system. He pointed out that it was a naive view that "juries find facts while judges determine the law." Citing from his own long experience on the bench, he pointed out that juries often try to state what they think "the law should be" in their verdicts. Another theory is that the jury tries the lawyers and not the clients.[50] Still others have argued that the real function of the jury is to provide the citizenry with confidence in the courts or to give citizens a sense of participation in government or to serve as a buffer between the judge and the general public in the case of an unpopular verdict.

Judge Wyzanski, however, has defended the jury system and has argued that certain cases, such as defamation cases and tort cases involving family disputes, are much better left to a jury than decided by the judge. However, in cases involving "regulatory statutes," he says "there is reason to hold the jury by a much tighter rein."[51]

[44] *Brown* v. *Board of Education of Topeka*, 347 U.S. 483 (1954).

[45] *Engel* v. *Vitale*, 370 U.S. 421 (1962).

[46] The subject of due process is discussed in detail in Chapter 7.

[47] Bodenheimer, *op. cit.*, p. 386.

[48] *Ibid.*, p. 62.

[49] Wolfgang Friedmann, *Law in a Changing Society* (London: Stevens and Sons, Ltd.; and Berkeley: University of California Press, 1959), pp. 61–2.

[50] Jerome J. Frank, *Courts on Trial* (Princeton: Princeton University Press, 1949), pp. 110–137. Judge Robert Traver's novel, *Anatomy of a Murder* (New York: Dell Pub. Co., Inc., 1959), adopts the theory that in murder cases the jury tries the murdered man.

[51] Charles E. Wyzanski, Jr., "A Trial Judge's Freedom and Responsibility," 65 *Harvard L. Rev.* 1281 (1952).

Cases under the antitrust laws, for example, may involve many strands and threads of complicated testimony and much documentary evidence of a highly technical kind, and such cases also normally require very long periods of time for trial. Recall that the crucial finding of fact in Judge Leahy's *du Pont Cellophane* case decision was numbered 838! For all these reasons, there is a tendency for the parties to have the judge determine the facts in such cases. Where civil actions involving equity matters are concerned, the federal courts are not required to use juries.

The Judge's Charge to the Jury: His Definition of the Law

The judge has the function of instructing the jury as to "what the law is"; in many cases, appeals are based upon the claim that the judge has erred in his definition or statement of the law in charging the jury. An understanding of this point is helpful in reading some antitrust cases, particularly older ones. Even where there is no jury, the judge generally states *his understanding* of the prevailing rule of law, as, for example, in the first quotation earlier from Judge Leahy's decision in the *du Pont Cellophane* case—in which he stated that there were two questions involved, of which the second was not reached if the first was answered in the negative.

Rules of Evidence: Circumstantial versus Direct Evidence; Statistical Inference. The rules pertaining to admissibility of evidence will be of little concern in later chapters; but it may be useful to point out that the origin of the rules can be traced to the belief of the common law judges at the end of the seventeenth century that such rules were necessary to prevent jurors from being misled by irrelevant, biased, or fraudulent testimony. The rules are not arbitrary; they are the result of long experience and are mainly rules excluding certain types of evidence.

The difference between *direct* and *indirect* (or "circumstantial") evidence is of some importance in the field of antitrust law. Often the existence of a conspiracy under the Sherman Act can be proved only by the use of "circumstantial" or indirect evidence, that is, by evidence of facts which give rise to an inference that a conspiracy exists. Circumstantial evidence involves deductive reasoning. We will have an occasion to consider this matter again in Part II in considering the meaning of the so-called "conscious parallelism" doctrine in relation to the question of price leadership. Direct evidence is that which tends to establish the matter in question by means of direct experience gained through sense perception. Either type may serve as a basis for a finding of fact.

It is interesting, in this connection, to note that Judge Wyzanski stated that in the *United Shoe Machinery* case—in which one of the issues was the effect of the corporation's acts upon its customers and competitors—the court asked the parties to obtain depositions from forty-five customers, "arbitrarily selected from a standard directory of shoe manufacturers," by taking the first fifteen names under the first, eleventh and twenty-first letters of of the alphabet.[52] Both the plaintiff's and the defendant's lawyers conducted cross examinations. Judge Wyzanski indicated that, in his view, the judge can perform a useful function by making provision in antitrust cases for the use of statistical sampling techniques to determine the effects of conduct. The information gained from the use of such statistical techniques is clearly circumstantial, since the whole problem of statistical inference is involved.

Another interesting use of statistical techniques in an antitrust case is that employed by economists and lawyers for the defense in a case involving a merger of Chicago banks. The experts undertook to show that the "market" for bank loans consisted of a "retail" (local) market and a "wholesale" (national) market and made extensive use of statistical techniques for testing relationships among various variables.[53] In an article describing their procedures, the users noted that their analysis would be open to attack by opposing counsel and remarked that statistical tech-

---

[52] *United States* v. *United Shoe Machinery Corp.*, 110 F. Supp. 295 (1953), at p. 305. The sample covered three percent of the shoe manufacturers.

[53] Harold H. Lozowick, Peter O. Steiner, and Roger Miller, "Law and Quantitative Multivariate Analysis: An Encounter" 66 *Michigan Law Review* 1641 (June, 1968).

niques would be of use in cases involving "indirect evidence"; that is, in cases involving "facts" resting on circumstantial evidence.

The real question of the use of this procedure is whether or not the "facts" of the case are established with a higher degree of reliability by the statistical technique employed than they would be if more conventional judicial methods were employed. Since any number of witnesses may be called, it does seem clear that sampling techniques *to select witnesses* ought to be employed only if both sides to the lawsuit agree and that attorneys for each side ought to be given ample opportunity for questioning of witnesses selected by such random sampling methods.

Note must be taken at this point of the 1968 decision of the Supreme Court of California in *People* v. *Collins*.[54] In this case, two defendants had been convicted of second-degree robbery. Witnesses were unable to identify positively the defendants as the persons whom the witnesses had seen at the scene of the crime. The witnesses did, however, testify concerning certain characteristics possessed by the perpetrators of the offense. These characteristics were specified to consist of the following items: (A) Negro man with beard; (B) man with mustache; (C) girl with blond hair; (D) girl with ponytail; (E) partly yellow automobile; (F) interracial couple in an escape car. The prosecuting attorney called as an expert witness an instructor of mathematics and sought to establish that there was an overwhelming probability that, since the accused defendants possessed all of the characteristics specified by the witnesses, the defendants were guilty of committing the crime as charged. The expert mathematician-witness testified that the probability of the joint occurrence of a number of independent events is equal to the product of the individual probabilities that each will occur. Then, without presenting any evidence in support of the individual probabilities, the prosecutor had the expert witness *assume* probabilities for the occurrence of each event and produce the probability that there was only one chance in 12 million that the defendants were innocent and that another couple possessing the same characteristics could have committed the robbery. Unable to establish factually the probabilities applicable to the events in question, the prosecutor, nevertheless, offered some unsupported opinions of his own and invited the jury to make its own estimates. A verdict of guilty was returned.

On appeal, the Supreme Court of California reversed and remanded the case for a new trial. Aside from the fact of admission into evidence of statements made by the defendants before they had been fully appraised of their legal rights, the Supreme Court pointed out that the probabilities used in the computations were unfounded assumptions and that no factual basis had been laid for their use; moreover, the prosecution had failed to prove that the various events or characteristics identified by the witnesses were independent. In fact, in an Appendix, Justice Sullivan employed the probabilities suggested by the prosecution to demonstrate that there was a 41 percent chance of the existence of another interracial couple possessing the defendants' characteristics.[55]

The court thus clearly recognized that the theory of probability is a tool, not an answer, and that the use of this theory in a given case must be explicitly supported by evidence. In short, the determination of each of the probabilities was a question of fact to be determined on the basis of the evidence *by the finder of fact*, just as was the issue of independence of the characteristics whose probabilities were to be estimated. In Part III of this book we will consider the question of the introduction into evidence in a rate proceeding before the Federal Power Commission of an econometric model pertaining to natural gas prices. The data employed in producing results by means of such a model, as well as the functional relationships postulated in such a model, are all questions of fact. Independent findings of fact on the basis of evidence offered in support of such models are necessary, unless the trier of facts is to abandon his duty of fact-finding to the model builder. In short, the introduction of an econometric model into evidence by either party to an action ought to entitle the other party to full rights of cross exa-

[54] 438 P. 2d 33 (1968).

[55] *Ibid.*, p. 38.

mination and to a designation of the model and of the expert testimony supporting it as that of a "hostile witness", with the protection of whatever legal consequences follow from such a designation. Results produced by such a model constitute *circumstantial evidence,* not a finding of fact.

It is interesting also to note that in 1966 a United States Court of Appeals was faced with the question of deciding the extent to which citation by the Federal Trade Commission of general economic works—which had not been introduced into the record and thus could not be subjected to cross examination or refutation by the defendant—constituted a denial of procedural due process of law. The relevant part of the court's opinion reads:

Procter asserts that the Commission's decision was based upon economic theories drawn from extra-record writings and was therefore violative of due process. It states that the decision was premised and critically based upon 85 citations of 43 extra-record writings which purport to deal with economic, political and social concepts.

These cited writings were general in nature. None of them dealt with the facts in the present case. At no place in its opinion did the Commission regard the citations as evidence. There was no citation of any economic writings by the hearing examiner in his second initial decision, which adopted findings of fact and comprises about 88 pages of the record. The hearing examiner's first initial decision cites no such authority. The Commission apparently cited these writings to demonstrate that its decision comported with economic authority. The Supreme Court has cited and relied on economic writings in its consideration of Section 7 cases. *F.T.C.* v. *Consolidated Foods,* 380 U.S. 592 (1965); *United States* v. *Penn-Olin Chem. Co.,* 378 U.S. 158 (1964); *United States* v. *Philadelphia Nat'l. Bank,* 374 U.S. 321 (1963); *Brown Shoe Co.* v. *F.T.C.,* 347 F. 2d 745 (7th Cir., 1965); *Crown Zellerbach Corp.* v. *F.T.C.,* 296 F. 2d 800 (9th Cir., 1961). We find no error in this respect.[56]

The holding of the court is interesting, since it constitutes a finding of fact by an appellate court that the Commission *did not rely* on the general economic works it cited in making its decision. By implication, if the Commission had relied upon them, presumably a reversible error would have been made, since the defendant was not given an opportunity to challenge the assumptions of and reasoning in these works at any stage in the proceeding. One challenge would, of course, have consisted of an attack on the assumptions made in such works, particularly if no factual foundation had first been laid for them by the evidence introduced into the record.

The Basis of Judicial Review

Subject to the qualifications mentioned below, it may be said that appellate courts review the "law" and not the "findings of fact" made by lower courts or commissions. In the early days of administrative commissions, courts often reviewed both the "law" and "findings of fact" of such administrative tribunals, thereby duplicating the efforts of the latter and often nullifying their "expert" opinions. However, in 1910 the Supreme Court held that the courts should not set aside administrative orders by usurping administrative functions. Instead, it indicated that judicial review should be confined to: (1) "questions of constitutional power and right"; (2) "whether the administrative order is within the scope of the statutory authority under which it purports to have been made"; and (3) whether, "even if the order is within the scope of the statute in form, it is also within its scope in substance"—that is to say, whether it constitutes an unreasonable or arbitrary exercise of power, lacking in procedural due process.[57] These rules were codified in the Administrative Procedure Act of 1946.

Nevertheless, as we have seen in the excerpt from the dissenting Supreme Court opinion in the *du Pont Cellophane* case given earlier in this chapter, the three dissenting Justices disagreed with Judge Leahy's Finding of Fact Number 838 and would have reversed his decision on that ground. In general, the courts require that administrative commissions and lower courts have *some* "reasonable" amount of evidence on which to base their findings of fact, but they do not ordinarily reverse lower court findings of fact in cases about which reasonable men could differ. Occasionally, however, the appellate courts may reverse in such a case. Thus, in one case involving

---

[56] *The Procter and Gamble Co.* v. *Federal Trade Commission,* 358 F. 2d 74 (1966), at pp. 76–78.

[57] *Interstate Commerce Commission* v. *Illinois Central R.R.,* 215 U.S. 452 (1910), at p. 470.

the question of whether a trade association had engaged in price-fixing in violation of the Federal Trade Commission Act, a United States Court of Appeals reversed the Commission's finding of fact by saying:

... We believe that such findings are unsupported by the evidence or by any reasonable inferences to be drawn therefrom. We say this with full recognition of our limited scope of review of findings of fact by the Commission.[58]

On the other hand, in 1966 the Supreme Court repeated the proposition that the test is whether the action of the Commission is supported by "substantial evidence," a test which the Court presumably employed in 1945 in upholding a cease and desist order by the FTC to prohibit the A. E. Staley Company from using a discriminatory (basing point) pricing system, by saying:

Congress has left to the Commission the determination of fact in each case whether the person, charged with making discriminatory prices, acted in good faith to meet a competitor's equally low prices. The determination of this fact from evidence is for the Commission. ... In the present case, the Commission's finding that the respondent's price discriminations were not made to meet a "lower" price and consequently were not in good faith, is amply supported by the record.[59]

The use of the words, "amply supported by the record," in the preceding quotation is of interest in the light of a decision handed down in 1966 by the Supreme Court reversing a judgment of a three-judge District Court in which orders of the Interstate Commerce Commission were set aside. The ICC had originally granted the applications of seven railroads to furnish additional rail service to the Lake Calumet Harbor Port (near the southern limits of Chicago) which was being developed as a major deep-water port facility for traffic via the St. Lawrence Seaway. The District Court, with one judge dissenting, rejected— on grounds that there was not "ample support in the record"—the finding of the Commission that the additional service was

required by the "public convenience and necessity." The Supreme Court reversed the District Court, saying:

... The test on judicial review is, of course, whether the action of the Commission is supported by "substantial evidence" on the record viewed as a whole. ... Substantial evidence is "enough to justify, if the trial were to a jury, a refusal to direct a verdict when the conclusion sought to be drawn from it is one of fact for the jury." ... A careful reading of the opinion leads us to conclude that the court was applying the test of substantiality. Indeed, at four separate places in the opinion it uses the term "substantial evidence" as being the necessary requirement. As unfortunate as it is that the "ample support" language crept into the decision, we do not believe that the court was creating a "novel formulation" . . .[60]

Thus, the District Court, in fact, applied the "substantial evidence" test. However, it applied the test incorrectly, since:

... "the possibility of drawing two inconsistent conclusions from the evidence does not prevent an administrative agency's finding from being supported by substantial evidence." It is not for the court to strike down conclusions that are reasonably drawn from the evidence and findings in the case. Its duty is to determine whether the evidence supporting the Commission's findings is substantial ... it was not the District Court's function to substitute its own conclusions for those which the Commission had fairly drawn. . . .[61]

The Court has shown a strong tendency to allow administrative agencies wide latitude in the exercise of discretion. Thus, in upholding action by the Federal Trade Commission to refuse to grant a delay in enforcement of one of its orders, the Court said in 1967:

... the Commission alone is empowered to develop that enforcement policy best calculated to achieve the ends contemplated by Congress and to allocate its available funds and personnel in such a way as to execute its policy efficiently and economically.[62]

At the same time, however, the Court has broadly interpreted the provisions per-

---

[58] *Tag Manufacturing Institute et. al. v. Federal Trade Commission*, 174 F. 2d 452 (1949) at p. 463.

[59] *Federal Trade Commission v. A. E. Staley Manufacturing Co. and Staley Sales Corp.*, 324 U.S. 746 (1945), at p. 758.

[60] *Illinois Central Railroad Co. et. al. v. Norfolk and Western Railway Co. et. al.*, 385 U.S. 57 (1966), at

p. 66.

[61] *Ibid.*, at p. 69.

[62] *FTC v. Universal-Rundle Corp.*, 387 U.S. 244 (1967) at p. 251. See also *Hardin v. Kentucky Utilities Co.*, 390 U.S. 1 (1968) and *Udall v. FPC*, 387 U.S. 428 (1967).

taining to judicial review contained in the Administrative Procedure Act—which applies to proceedings before all of the federal agencies—by saying:

... the Administrative Procedure Act ... embodies the basic presumption of judicial review to one "suffering legal wrong because of agency action, or adversely affected or aggrieved by agency action within the meaning of the relevant statute," 5 U.S.C. #702, so long as no statute precludes such relief or the action is not one committed by law to agency discretion, 5 U.S.C. #701 (a). The Administrative Procedure Act provides specifically not only for review of "Agency action made reviewable by statute" but also for review of "final agency action for which there is no other adequate remedy in a court." 5 U.S.C. #704. . . .
... this Court has echoed ... [Congress] that the Administrative Procedure Act's generous review provisions must be given a "hospitable" interpretation [cases cited]. . . . Only upon a showing of "clear and convincing evidence" of a contrary legislative intent should the courts restrict access to judicial review.[63]

The "liberal provisions concerning judicial review" in the Administrative Procedure Act state that "the court shall review the whole record or such portions thereof as may be cited by either party."

Questions of "Fact" versus Questions of "Law"

The discussion in this chapter has so far been carried on as if the distinction between questions of fact and questions of law were a clear one, easily identified. Indeed, questions of fact are generally said to be concerned with matters to be established by the evidence, while questions of law are said to be essentially statements of legal policy. But the difference between what is a question of "fact" and what is a question of "law" may be a difficult one to define in borderline cases.

For example, although the dissenting Justices in the *du Pont Cellophane* case phrased their argument in terms of a disagreement with Judge Leahy's Finding of Fact Number 838 (that other wrapping materials were "functionally interchangeable" with cellophane and hence no monopoly existed), they may really have been stating their view that "functional interchangeability" is *not the proper legal test* to be employed under the Sherman Act. In short, they may have disagreed with the policy adopted by the majority in this case. Such a disagreement is sometimes termed a disagreement about "substantive" issues (as distinct from "procedural" issues, a distinction which will be further discussed in detail in Chapter 7 in connection with the due process clauses in the Constitution). In some cases in the antitrust area, appellate courts have sometimes been criticized for having rendered apparently inconsistent decisions. However, those making these criticisms have sometimes failed to see that the decisions of the appellate courts in question turned precisely on the fact that these appellate courts felt themselves limited by the lower court's finding of fact or by the way in which the question raised in the appeal had been framed for presentation.

In some areas of the law, basic meanings and policies have become fixed; in such cases it is said that "meanings have become settled." Thus, terms such as "bankruptcy" and "issue" do not currently admit of much discretionary definition by the courts. So also, we will see in Part II, various *per se* offenses (price-fixing agreements, agreements to divide markets, or agreements to limit output) exist under the antitrust laws, and it is not open to the courts to find that prices have been fixed at "reasonable" levels or that markets have been divided "reasonably." But even in the area of settled meanings, as Friedmann has pointed out, rapid changes are occurring.[64]

However, as has become apparent in the preceding section of this chapter, it is in the areas of law in which meanings are most unsettled at a given time and in which few if any precedents exist that one is most likely to find the courts engaging in creative interpretation. In such cases, one often finds the Justices of the Supreme Court differing. As was true in the *du Pont Cellophane* case, one finds concurring, dissenting "concurring in part," or "dissenting in part" opinions, along with the majority opinion in such cases. Thus, for example, the issuance by President Truman of an Executive Order directing the Secretary of Commerce to take possession of and to

---

[63] *Abbott Laboratories* v. *Gardner*, 387 U.S. 136 (1967), at pp. 140–41.

[64] Friedmann, *op. cit.*, p. 30.

operate most of the nation's steel mills (in the course of a nationwide steel strike during the Korean Emergency) gave rise to a decision by the Supreme Court invalidating the Order. There were no precedents for the Court to follow: three of the nine Justices dissented from the majority opinion, and there were five separate additional opinions concurring in the majority opinion, producing a total of seven opinions.[65] (We will consider this case more closely in Chapter 6.) The diversity of opinions written by the majority in invalidating the President's Order can be looked upon as the result of an attempt by the Justices to make articulate the issues involved in the conflict which the decision undertook to resolve.

In this chapter, we have primarily considered the scope and nature of the judicial process as a method of producing orderly changes in law in response to changing social conditions. The Appendix to this chapter provides a brief description of the organization and operation of the federal and state courts and explains for the interested reader the difference between *appeal* and a *writ of certiorari* as methods of bringing cases to the attention of the Supreme Court. In the next chapter, we will consider the ways in which private interest groups may operate to bring about changes in law either by attempting to influence the legislative, executive, or administrative processes directly or by creating a climate of "grass roots" opinion favorable to the position which the particular group happens to favor.

---

[65] *Youngstown Sheet and Tube Co.* v. *Sawyer*, 343 U.S. 579 (1951). Justices Black, Jackson, Douglas, Frankfurter, Burton, Clark, and Vinson all wrote opinions.

Appendix: Organization and Operation of the Judicial System

A. THE SYSTEM OF FEDERAL COURTS

All federal judges, both of superior and inferior courts, are appointed and hold their offices during good behavior (at a compensation which cannot be diminished while they are in office) under Article III of the Constitution, which thereby sought to establish an independent judicial branch of the federal government. This objective has been largely attained.

Chart 4-1 shows the organization of the system of federal courts; it is self-explanatory. The special courts will not be discussed. The following discussion of the court system will consist of a brief explanation of the organization and jurisdiction of the various federal courts and of a brief consideration of the grounds for appealing a lower court decision to the Supreme Court.

The Supreme Court

Organization. The Supreme Court exists by virtue of Article III, Section 1, of the Constitution. It was organized on February 2, 1790 under the Judiciary Act of September 24, 1789 (1 *Stat.* 73). Congress has the power to fix the number of Associate Justices; all the Justices (including the Chief Justice) are nominated by the President and appointed by him with the advice and consent of the Senate. Six of the current nine members constitute a quorum. Since 1944, if no quorum is possible, the Supreme Court may designate one of the Courts of Appeals to serve in the capacity of a court of last resort (58 *Stat.* 272); this procedure

was followed in the *Alcoa* case discussed earlier in this chapter.

Jurisdiction. The Supreme Court has original jurisdiction in all cases "affecting Ambassadors, other public Ministers and Consuls, and those in which a State shall be a Party." As we will see in Chapter 7, the question of original jurisdiction of the Court has been an important one in the history of our Constitutional law. The Court also has appellate jurisdiction, subject to such exceptions and regulations as Congress may impose, in all cases in law and equity which arise under the Constitution or out of statutes or treaties made under it (that is, cases involving a Federal question) or in which the plaintiff and defendant are citizens of different states (diversity of citizenship). There is a general jurisdictional limit which requires that a sum of money in excess of $10,000 be involved, but there are exceptions to this jurisdictional requirement, for example, in civil liberties cases. The Supreme Court has also been authorized by Congress to fix the rules of procedure to be followed in lower federal courts. It has the advice of a continuing Advisory Committee on the Rules of Civil Procedure in determining the content of such rules.

Mandatory and Discretionary Review by the Supreme Court. At common law there were a number of different ways in which a case might be brought from an inferior court before a superior court for review. For example, at common law the term *appeal* meant that a superior court could review the entire case, the facts as well as the law.

Chart 4-1

The System of Federal Courts

U.S. SUPREME COURT

Chief Justice
8 Associate Justices

U.S. COURTS OF APPEALS

11 Judicial Circuits
3 to 9 Judges each
     (97 in all)
1 Justice of the Supreme Court

SPECIAL COURTS

U.S. Court of Claims
Chief Judge
6 Associate Judges

U.S. DISTRICT COURTS

90 District Courts
1 to 24 District Judges each
     (333 in all)

U.S. Court of Customs and Patent Appeals
Chief Judge
8 Associate Judges

U.S. Court of Military Appeals
Chief Judge
2 Associate Judges

Source: General Services Administration, Office of the Federal Register, *United States Government Organization Manual, 1969–70* (Washington, D.C.: U.S. Government Printing Office, 1969), pp. 44–54.

The term *writ of error*, however, referred to a process under which only questions of law were removed to the superior court for review.[66] Today there is a tendency to ignore this distinction, and the meaning of the term *appeal*, as used in contemporary statutes, must be determined from the language of the statute in which the term is employed. In the past, however, the way in which a case has come up for review may have had an effect on the outcome. The *Colgate* case, discussed in Chapter 14 *infra*, is an example; in that case the Supreme Court held itself to be bound on review by the lower court's interpretation of the original indictment because the case had been brought up for review on a *writ of error*. At common law a *writ of certiorari* was an order from a superior court to an inferior court to send up the record in some pending proceeding or all of the record in a case before a verdict had been rendered, but by statute it may be used after a verdict. As has been noted above, Congress has no

power to determine or change the original jurisdiction of the Supreme Court since this is defined in Article III, Section 1, of the Constitution. The appellate jurisdiction of the Supreme Court is, however, fixed by Congress, and the statute currently in force is found in 28 U.S.C.A. 1251–1257. A general description of this legislation, emphasizing the difference between an *appeal* from a decision of a highest state court and *certiorari*, will now be given, although a detailed legalistic discussion will not be attempted. It is to be noted first that today, where the process of appeal exists, *appeal* is a matter of *right* on the part of the parties, while *certiorari* is a matter of *discretion* on the part of the Supreme Court.[67] Under 28 U.S.C. 1252, any party may appeal from a decree or order of any court of the United States holding an Act of Congress unconstitutional. An appeal can also be made to the Supreme Court, under 28 U.S.C. 1254, from a decision of a Court of Appeals if the appeals court holds a

[66] *United States* v. *Godwin*, 7 Cranch 108 (1824).
[67] *Radio Corp. of America* v. *United States*, 341 U.S.

412 (1950). See also *Revised Supreme Court Rules*, 388 U.S. 931 (1967).

state statute unconstitutional. The Supreme Court may grant *certiorari* in a case heard by a Court of Appeals and will usually do so if two different Courts of Appeals arrive at conflicting decisions in similar cases. A Court of Appeals may also certify to the Supreme Court questions in response to which instructions are desired. The removal of causes of action from highest state courts to the Supreme Court is dealt with by 28 U.S.C. 1257. An *appeal* may be had in any case where a decision in a highest *state* court is against the validity of a treaty or statute of the United States or where a highest *state* court upholds a state statute in the face of a claim that it is repugnant to the Constitution or to treaties or laws of the United States. The Supreme Court may grant *certiorari* in any case in which the validity of a treaty or federal statute is questioned (even if the decision of the highest state court is in favor of its validity) or in any case in which a state statute is questioned as being repugnant to the Constitution or a treaty or law of the United States. Since the granting of *certiorari* is a discretionary matter on the part of the Supreme Court, and since a denial of *certiorari* does not involve a review of the case, a denial of *certiorari* is without prejudice and does not imply approval of a lower court decision; thus, a denial of *certiorari* (a newspaper reporter's comments in a particular instance to the contrary notwithstanding) merely means that, for undisclosed reasons, the Supreme Court has decided not to review the case. Some of these undisclosed reasons may lie in the fact that the case involves an inconsistency with the Supreme Court's own informal limitations on the scope of judicial review. These informal rules are further briefly discussed below.

Limitations on the Exercise of Judicial Review. Congress fixes the limits of the appellate jurisdiction of the Supreme Court. And, in addition to the formal rules of the Supreme Court, there are certain informal rules (which are more fully explained in Chapter 7). For example, the Court will not render Advisory Opinions, but it will review cases arising out of state and federal declaratory judgments acts.[68] Suffice it to say here that among the more important informal rules are these: the Court will pass on the constitutionality of a statute only if such a decision is necessary to the disposition of the case before it; the Court will ordinarily not formulate rules broader than necessary to dispose of the precise facts before it—it is this latter rule which lies at the heart of Justice Frankfurter's concurring opinion in the *du Pont Cellophane* case quoted in the first section of this chapter. In recent cases, however, the Court has shown some tendency to relax these informal rules in civil rights cases.

United States Courts of Appeals

United States Courts of Appeals hear appeals from final and some interlocutory decisions of District Courts, although in a few cases—for example, where injunction orders are issued by special three-judge District Courts—the Supreme Court reviews District Court decisions directly. The fifty states, the District of Columbia, and the U.S. territories are divided into eleven circuits, and each Court of Appeals has from three to nine judges. These Courts generally hear cases with three judges sitting but may hear cases *en banc* with all judges present. One of the justices of the Supreme Court is assigned as circuit justice for each circuit. The circuit judge with the senior commission is the chief judge of the circuit. These courts also review and enforce orders of many administrative regulatory commissions; for example, orders of the Federal Trade Commission under Section 5 of the FTC Act (discussed in Chapter 18 *infra*).

United States District Courts

The District Courts have original jurisdiction in those matters of federal jurisdiction which are not within the original jurisdiction of the Supreme Court. There are 90 District Courts, and each District Court has from one to 24 judges. Only one judge is usually required to hear and decide a case. The judge with the senior commission is the chief judge. The District Courts are trial courts; they may apply the rules of law or of equity, depending on the nature of the case. Each District Court has a clerk

---

[68] *Muskrat* v. *United States*, 219 U.S. 346 (1911); and *Nashville, Chattanooga and St. Louis Ry. Co.* v. *Wallace*, 288 U.S. 249 (1933). The federal provision is found in 28 U.S.C. 2201 and 2202.

with his assistants, a United States attorney, a United States marshal, commissioners, referees in bankruptcy, and probation officers.

B. THE STATE COURT SYSTEMS

State courts are created by state constitutions and state legislatures, and different states have different systems. In general, there are inferior trial courts (county courts), appellate courts, and courts of last resort. In some states there may be one court of last resort for criminal cases and another for purely civil matters. In addition, there are specialized courts, such as juvenile courts, probate courts, etc.

5

Law and Social Change: the Social Contract in a Context of Factions and Images

This chapter continues the general survey of the problem of law and social change begun in the preceding chapter. Specifically, this chapter considers (1) some elements of seventeenth and eighteenth century political philosophy with particular reference to the language employed in official documents by the "Founding Fathers"; (2) the problems created by the fact that legislators, executive officials, and administrators operate within a context in which lobbies, special interest groups, and pressure groups—designated as "factions" by Madison in *The Federalist* (No. 10)—spend large (and largely undisclosed) sums of money to influence the legislative, executive, and administrative processes within which contemporary working rules are formulated and implemented; and (3) the extent to which public relations techniques—which have been successful in "merchandising commodities"—are being successfully employed in "selling *men* and *measures*" to grass roots voters.[1]

[1] The words in quotation marks in this sentence are attributed to Clem Whitaker (of Whitaker and Baxter, a leading California public relations firm) in an address before the Los Angeles Area Chapter of the Public Relations Society of America, July 13, 1948, by Stanley Kelley, Jr., in *Professional Public*

It is, perhaps, worthwhile pointing out that it is the lifetime tenure of federal judges which largely insulates them from the *direct* effects of factional pressures and makes it possible for them to render "unpopular" decisions—which sometimes become the subject of much factional criticism. In this regard, it is interesting to note that Donald Blaisdell, in a scholarly study published in 1941, for the Temporary National Economic Committee, remarked that it "is difficult, almost impossible, to offer satisfactory documentation for the statement that pressure groups do not stop with Congress, the President, or the administrative agencies in the achievement of their aims. . . . Yet pertinent material is available, meager though it is."[2] In evidence, Blaisdell wrote:

When the Supreme Court decided in 1936 that Congress did not have the power to deal with economic problems as it had attempted to do in the 1933 A.A.A., it ruled on a matter in which many citizen groups had filed briefs as

Relations and Political Power (Baltimore: The Johns Hopkins Press, 1956), p. 39. (Italics his.)

[2] Donald B. Blaisdell, *Economic Power and Political Pressures* (Temporary National Economic Committee Monograph No. 26) (Washington, D.C.: U.S. Government Printing Office, 1941), p. 76.

friends of the court. Briefs supporting the validity of the act were filed by representatives of the League for Economic Equality, American Farm Bureau Federation, National Beet Growers' Association, the Mountain States Beet Growers' Marketing Association, Farmers' National Grain Corporation, and the Texas Agricultural Association. Briefs challenging the validity of the act were filed by Hygrade Food Products Corporation, American Nut Co., Berks Packing Co., et al., General Mills et al., the National Association of Cotton Manufacturers, and the Farmers' Independence Council of America. The latter organization was set up and financed by the American Liberty League, an anti-New Deal propaganda agency established in 1934.[3]

But to say that the Court is subjected to pressures is not to say that it succumbs to them. Instances in which "leaks" occur as to impending decisions of the Supreme Court are nonexistent, but "leaks" as to what occurs when Congressional Committees meet in "executive sessions" from which the public and the press are excluded are a regular, habitual occurrence. And, most important of all is the fact that a legal proceeding *is* an adversary proceeding: the lawyers on the opposing sides are in fact recognized as *advocates*, and the entire trial is carried on according to well-established rules. In short, as we have seen in the preceding chapter, it is of the essence of "judging" to be subjected to pressure by interested claimants, and Blaisdell's evidence merely illustrates this point.

A. EIGHTEENTH CENTURY POLITICAL PHILOSOPHY AND THE CONSTITUTION

Legal versus Political Theory

Although no separation of legal and political theory exists in the works of the ancient Greek philosophers, and although some writers have argued convincingly that such a separation makes no sense in today's world, it is nevertheless true that the subjects of politics and government are today, almost without exception, taught in Colleges of Arts and Sciences and not in Schools of Law. Today, however, several leading law schools have added medical

doctors, mainly psychiatrists, and economists to their faculties in an attempt to broaden their curricula. Emphasis on vocational aspects of law, however, continues to be a dominant element.[4]

As is true in the cases of law and of economics, attempts to define precisely the subject matter of the field of political theory have been largely unsuccessful. One approach is to state that "power" is the subject matter of political theory; the relationship of such a view to the legal positivist position discussed in Chapters 2 and 3 is obvious. Another approach holds that "decision-making" is the proper subject; this view seems to have much in common with and, perhaps, to be derived from concepts developed in Schools of Business Administration and in courses in "managerial economics." It lends itself to a certain amount of quantitative statement, although the problems of quantification (measurement) are formidable. There is also a "group theory"; it, too, lends itself to algebraic statement.

The lack of precise definitions in this area need not be a source of despair. Instead, this lack is merely evidence of the interrelation of all human activities and evidence that attempts to segregate particular activities as controlling and independent of all others involve artificial classifications and may produce half-truths. A similar process of soul-searching is currently characteristic of the so-called physical sciences. For example, one well-known analytical chemist remarked in an address delivered at the annual meeting of the American Chemical Society in 1962:

Let me be really subjective in closing. As a reserve officer, I lived through the mechanization of the field artillery. With this painful but necessary process, the current revolution in analytical chemistry has much in common, emotionally and factually, for mechanization resembles instrumentation or automation. I believe that it is foolish to resist such revolutions and sensible to turn them to good account. If modern analytical chemistry suffers at all, it suffers because the characterization and control of materials is too big an assignment for a single discipline. If this is so, we may surely say of analytical chemistry what the National Archives

---

[3] *Ibid.*, p. 78.

[4] For a strong argument that political and legal theory should be unified, see Jerome Hall, *Studies in Jurisprudence and Criminal Theory* (New York: Oceana Publications, 1958), chap. IV.

Building says of the nation: "What is past is prologue.[5]

The Formal Organization of the United States Government

A traditional conception of the organization of the United States Government holds that there are three separate but equal branches of government whose powers are derived from a fundamental law of the land laid down in the Constitution. Yet, this clear and precise conception is an ideal abstraction, a model which may, in fact, obscure our view of the realities. As we have already seen a constitution requires interpretation by courts; and, therefore, it is misleading to suggest that any constitution always stands above the judiciary or for that matter above the legislative or executive branches of a government. It is also to be recalled from the Appendix to Chapter 4 that, in the United States, the President appoints federal judges with the consent of Congress and that Congress has the power to specify the number of Associate Justices of the Supreme Court. It is more realistic to think of the Constitution, statutes, and Supreme Court decisions as as well as the traditions, customs, and beliefs of the nation as standing at the same level. Moreover, the model totally ignores the existence of political parties, pressure groups, and the employment of public relations experts. The purely formal and idealistic presentation of the model is really a hangover from the past, a reflection of natural law philosophy combined with the doctrines of "separation of powers" and of "the social contract," which dominated the minds of the seventeenth and eighteenth century political philosophers whose language appears in the Constitution and in the *Declaration of Independence*. Some consideration of these ideas is necessary.

The Doctrine of Separation of Powers of Government

The fact that the Constitution establishes three not-so-separate branches of government at the federal level (a scheme of organization also generally adopted in state constitutions) is generally attributed to the influence of Baron de Montesquieu's *The Spirit of Laws*. Montesquieu (1689–1775) had relied upon his analysis of the English Constitution to argue that the judicial, executive, and legislative powers ought to be separate and distinct.[6] But this separation of powers in the United States is not, nor according to Madison's discussion of this question in *The Federalist* (Nos. 47 and 48) was it ever intended to be, as distinct and complete as popular belief generally holds. Thus, Madison first pointed out that "the oracle" who was always "consulted" in this context was Montesquieu; and then Madison made his own examination of the British Constitution from which Montesquieu had derived his conclusions:

On the slightest view of the British Constitution, we must perceive that the legislative, executive, and judiciary departments are by no means totally separate and distinct from each other. The executive magistrate forms an integral part of the legislative authority. . . . One branch of the legislative department forms also a great constitutional council to the executive chief. . . . The judges again are so far connected with the legislative department, as often to attend and participate in its deliberations, though not admitted to a legislative vote.[7]

Montesquieu, said Madison, "did not mean that these departments ought to have no partial agency in, or no control over, the acts of each other." What Montesquieu really meant was that in no case should one department be controlled *wholly* by one who has also the "whole power of another department." The various state constitutions then in existence, said Madison, also involved a mixture of powers.

In Essay 48 of *The Federalist*, Madison stated the affirmative side of his argument, namely, "that unless these departments be so far connected and blended as to give

[5] Herman A. Liebhafsky, "Modern Analytical Chemistry: A Subjective View," Fisher Award Address, reprinted in *Analytical Chemistry*, Vol. XXXIV (June, 1962), pp. 23A–33A, at p. 33A. Copyright American Chemical Society. Reprinted by permission of copyright holder.

[6] M. de Secondat, Baron de Montesquieu, *The Spirit of Laws*, trans. M. Nugent (2 vols., 2d ed.; London: printed for J. Nourse and P. Vaillant in the Strand, 1752), Vol. I, Bk. XI, chap. vi, "Of the Constitution of England."

[7] *The Federalist*, of the New Constitution, written in 1788, by Mr. Hamilton, Mr. Jay, and Mr. Madison (A New Edition; Philadelphia: Benjamin Warner, 1818), No. 47. (Numerous more recent editions of this work are, of course, available to the student, including a Modern Library edition and a Mentor paperback edition.)

each a constitutional control over the others, the degree of separation" which Montesquieu's maxim specified "can never in practice be duly maintained." The problem, Madison argued, was one of "providing some practical security for each department, against the invasion of the others." A limitation on the term of the office of the executive and a judiciary without an enforcement power were not to be feared so much as a legislative department, which—through control of the taxing and spending powers, and in other ways—might encroach upon the other two. Thus, Madison stated the groundwork for the system of checks and balances: the veto power, the power to override the veto, the difficult methods of amending the Constitution, and all the rest. What is of interest from the point of view of this book is the realism of Madison's approach to the problem, given the environment in which he wrote. He approached the problem from a pragmatic point of view. In the more complex world of today, the same kind of realism is required on the part of the citizens if the functions of government are to be performed effectively.

The Doctrine of Social Contract

The doctrine of "social contract" goes back at least as far as Plato who referred to it in Book II of *The Republic*. It is essentially a notion that, wherever government exists, government must *in some sense or other* rest upon the consent of those governed or upon that of those who make up the society in which the government exists—although *the sense* is undefined. Such a notion can be made compatible with almost any philosophy of government except that of government by Divine Right. There are two basic forms of the notion, an absolutist version and a democratic version. Both will be discussed below.

Thomas Hobbes (1588–1679) and the Absolutist Version of "Social Contract." In *Leviathan* ("The Mortal God") in 1651, Hobbes, consistently with his legal positivism, argued that the nature of man was such that he was motivated by a lust for

power (competition and glory) or by a lack of confidence in or fear of all other men (diffidence). For these reasons, as long as "men live without a common Power to keep them all in awe, they are in that condition called Warre." Thus, in the course of time, "men agree amongst themselves to submit to some man, or assembly of men, voluntarily, on confidence to be protected by him against all others." The agreement to submit, Hobbes argued, was a "covenant," a social contract, "of everyone with everyone." This argument, moreover, bound not only those who made the original covenant but also bound their children and their children's children. The obligation of the subject to the sovereign terminated only when the sovereign no longer had the power to protect his subjects.[8]

Hobbes's system was a forerunner of the philosophies of contemporary dictatorships. It will be noted that he published *Leviathan* immediately after a period of civil war in England; that is, he wrote during the period of Cromwell and the Interregnum, following the Civil War and the execution of Charles the First. Hobbes's views were timely.

John Locke (1632–1704) and the Democratic Version of "Social Contract". Locke's *Two Treatises of Government* provided a rationalization for the "Grand and Glorious" Revolution of 1688 in England which resulted in the deposition of James II and the signature of the Bill of Rights by his successor, William of Orange, in 1689. In January of 1689, the House of Commons voted that "King James II had 'endeavoured to subvert the constitution by breaking the original contract between king and people'" and that he had therefore "abdicated" the throne.[9] Therefore, it invited William to succeed James II. Locke's version of the social contract theory was consistent with the ensuing parliamentary supremacy over the king. His equally timely doctrine became popular.

"Absolute Monarchy," wrote Locke, "is indeed inconsistent with Civil Society, and so can be no Form of Civil Government at

---

[8] Thomas Hobbes, *Leviathan* (1st ed.; London: printed for A. R. Crooke, 1651), esp. chaps. XIII, XVII, and XXI. A readily available source is E. A. Burtt (ed.), *The English Philosophers from Bacon to Mill*

(New York: Modern Library, Inc., 1939), pp. 129–234.

[9] Maurice Ashley, *England in the Seventeenth Century* (paperback; London: Penguin Books, Ltd., 1960), p. 177.

all."[10] Thereupon Locke adopted the democratic "contract among men" version of the idea by writing: "And thus every Man, by consenting with others to make one Body Politic under one Government, puts himself under an Obligation to every one of that Society, to submit to the determination of the Majority and to be concluded by it."[11] His point of departure was the proposition that "the Natural Liberty of Man is to be free from any Superior Authority on Earth" and "to have only the Law of Nature for his Rule." But men united themselves in commonwealths by mutual consent for the "great and chief End" of preserving "their Property." Thus, the "great End of Men's entering into Society" was "the Enjoyment of their Properties in Peace and Safety." And, the supreme power placed by the people in any person or assembly "is only temporary." Therefore, "upon forfeiture [because of a miscarriage by those in authority], or at the determination of" a "time set, the Supreme Power reverts to the Society; and the People have a Right to act as Supreme, and continue the Legislative in themselves; or place it in a New Form, or New Hands, as they think Good."[12] This, indeed, is the philosophy of revolution. Clearly the "Grand and Glorious" Revolution was not only successful, it was *just*.

The American Version: The Declaration of Independence and The Federalist. Locke's doctrine of consent and revolution against despotism permeates the *Declaration of Independence*. Written by Thomas Jefferson and edited by the other lawyers of the Continental Congress, the first two paragraphs of the *Declaration* assert:

When, in the course of human events, it becomes necessary for one people to dissolve the political bands which have connected them with another, and to assume, among the powers of the earth, the separate and equal station to which the *laws of nature and nature's God* entitle them, a decent respect to the opinions of mankind requires that they should declare the causes which impel them to separation.

We hold these truths to be self-evident:— That all men are created equal; that they are created by their Creator with certain unalienable rights; that among these are life, liberty, and the pursuit of happiness. That, to secure these rights, *governments are instituted* among men, *deriving their just powers from the consent of the governed;* that, whenever any form of government becomes destructive of these ends, it is the right of the people to alter or to abolish it, and to institute a new government, laying its foundation on such principles, and organizing its powers in such form, as to them shall seem most likely to effect their safety and happiness. Prudence, indeed, will dictate, that governments long established should not be changed for light and transient causes; and accordingly all experience hath shown that mankind are more disposed to suffer while evils are sufferable, than to right themselves by abolishing forms to which they are accustomed. But when a long train of abuses and usurpations, pursuing invariably the same object, evinces a design to reduce them under absolute despotism, it is their right, it is their duty, to throw off such government, and to provide new guards for their future security. . . .[13]

Note that these paragraphs state a set of general principles. The complaints of the colonists against George III represented the occasion for the statement; but, in the *Declaration*, Jefferson undertook first to assert the philosophy of Locke as a *general* proposition. He also asserted Jean Jacques Rousseau's version of Locke's ideas: The "Sovereignty of the people" is Supreme, and it is "against the nature of the body politic for the Sovereign to impose on itself a law which it cannot infringe." It can "never bind itself" or "alienate any part of itself." That is, a ruler who does not recognize the "Sovereignty" of the people violates the social compact and the people have a "natural right" to overthrow him.[14]

Similarly, John Jay wrote in the second of *The Federalist* essays, "Nothing is more certain than the indispensible necessity of

---

[10] John Locke, *Two Treatises of Government* (2d ed. corrected; London: printed for Awnsham and John Churchill at the Black Swan in Pater-noster Row, 1694), "An Essay Concerning the True, Original, Extent and End of Civil-Government," par. 90. (A more readily available edition is Burtt, *op. cit.,* pp. 403–503.)

[11] *Ibid.,* par. 97.

[12] *Ibid.,* par. 243.

[13] Italics mine.

[14] Jean Jacques Rousseau, *A Dissertation on Political Economy: to Which Is Added, a Treatise on the Social Compact* (1st Amer. ed.; Albany: Barber and Southwick, 1797), esp. Bk. I, chap. VII. The standard translation is that by G. D. H. Cole, *Rousseau: The Social Contract and Discourses* (Everyman's Library No. 660; London: J. M. Dent and Sons, Ltd., 1913).

government, and it is equally undeniable, that whenever and however it is instituted, the people must cede to it some of their natural rights, in order to vest it with requisite powers."

As an historical proposition, the "social contract" doctrine cannot be supported by the evidence. Men simply did not depart from a "state of nature" by making an agreement with each other under a great oak –which had grown from a small acorn —or some other romantic type of tree. Nor did all the authors of the Constitution accept the unqualified form of the statement of the doctrine which Jefferson had incorporated into the *Declaration.* Hamilton's opening paragraph in the first of *The Federalist* essays is adequate testimony to establish this proposition. He wrote:

It seems to have been reserved to the people of this country, by their conduct and example, to decide the important question, whether societies of men really are capable or not of establishing good government from reflection and choice, or whether they are forever destined for their political considerations on accident and truth.

Whether Hamilton realized it or not, the answer to this question given by the Constitutional Convention could not be final. The issue continues to be determined ever anew: he had stated the problem of the continuous choice of the voting members of a democratic society in terms of the *consequences* of that choice. He asserted in italics that the ensuing *Federalist* essays proposed to discuss:

. . . *The utility of the UNION to your political prosperity.* . . . *The insufficiency of the present Confederation to preserve that Union* . . . *necessity of a government at least equally energetic with the one proposed, to the attainment of this object* . . . *The conformity of the proposed Constitution to the true principles of republican government* . . . *Its analogy to your own State constitution* . . . *and lastly, The additional security which its adoption will afford to the preservation of that species of government, to liberty, and to property.*

The appeal is cast in essentially utilitarian and pragmatic terms. In 1913, Charles Beard pointed out that a majority of the members of the Constitutional Convention were lawyers by profession, that small farming and artisan interests were unrepresented, that most held government bonds whose value they wished to protect, some were land speculators with an interest in strong government, and others were slaveholders and merchants.[15] Twenty-four years later however, Charles Warren challenged the thesis that the property interests of the members of the Convention exerted a substantial influence on their work, and Beard's book was also criticized by Robert E. Brown in 1956.[16] But, whatever the motivating factors, *that* issue is important *only* if one holds to a fundamentalist and basically unrealistic static view that "the Constitution today means what it did when it was written." Any view which holds that the "past is prologue" must consider the motivating factors irrelevant. It is the present and future that demand attention.

The defense of the federal system (in contrast to systems of confederation—which involve a weak central authority) in the essays of *The Federalist* (Essays 17 to 21) rests almost entirely upon historical examples. Thus, Hamilton and Madison opened Essay 19 with the statement, "The examples of ancient confederacies, cited in my last paper have not yet exhausted the source of *experimental instruction* on the subject." (Italics mine.) A more concise statement of the instrumentalist thesis of problem-solving could hardly be made. However, even though the right to vote was still restricted, Essay 22 concludes with these two sentences:

The fabric of American empire ought to rest on the solid basis of *the consent of the American people.* The streams of national power ought to flow immediately from that pure, original fountain of all legitimate authority.

And the italicized words appear in the original. What, then, are we to make of the social contract or consent doctrine today?

A Contemporary View of the Social Contract. The contract theory cuts both ways. Beginning with the Kentucky Resolution drafted by Vice-President Thomas Jefferson in 1798

[15] Charles A. Beard, *An Economic Interpretation of the Constitution of the United States* (New York: The Macmillan Co., 1913).
[16] Charles Warren, *The Making of the Constitution*

(Boston: Little, Brown and Co., Inc., 1937); and Robert E. Brown, *Charles Beard and the Constitution* (Princeton: Princeton University Press, 1956).

(in opposition to the first of a number of similar waves of intolerance to sweep this country in the form of the Alien and Sedition Acts—a wave sponsored by absolutists who favored the establishment of an American aristocracy and who saw an opportunity to capitalize on the excesses of the French Revolution to strengthen their position by frightening the populace temporarily out of its better judgment), the contract theory was employed to bolster the doctrine of State's Rights and as a rationalization of a threatened secession. The notion of the right of a state to secede from the Union, which was made moot by the Civil War, is clearly implicit in the contract theory of the Constitution. But if that question *is* moot, the social contract doctrine cannot stand.

Yet an idea which has persisted so long and which appears in so many documents pertaining to freedom and liberty must have some significance. What is it? J. W. Gough, whose historical study of the concept of the social contract is perhaps the most authoritative in existence, has concluded as follows:

The ultimate *raison d'être* for the contract theory, all through its history, has been to reconcile the apparently conflicting claims of liberty and law. The demands of government could be explained and justified, it was thought, if they were based on the consent of the governed: people would freely obey a government they had themselves created and undertaken to obey. This was a useful practical weapon in the struggle against the tyranny of absolute monarchs, but when kings have been replaced by constitutional or parliamentary governments, the contractual formula cannot be applied without notorious intellectual difficulties. . . .

The great drawback to kings who claimed to rule by divine right was that, though they often admitted that they had duties to perform, they acknowledged no responsibility except to God, and there was no earthly means of calling them to account except rebellion. Constitutional government, on the other hand—representation, popular elections, and so on—provides a mechanism for ensuring that ministers, and persons put in authority under them, are responsible to the electorate for their actions. If we want a formula to express this responsibility, the metaphor of trusteeship, which Locke and others employed, seems to me preferable to that of contract, for it is free from many of the misleading associations of the contract theory.[17]

Another view holds that the words "social contract" refer to the moral obligations of an individual living in an organized society,[18] a moral obligation whose existence it is to be noted, logical positivism denies or ignores.

The meaning which will be attached to the democratic version of the doctrine of social contract in this book is thus a complex one, consisting of the idea of (1) trusteeship and the moral obligation implicit in the individual's living in society, rather than contract in the legal or legalistic sense of the term, coupled with (2) a recognition of the historical role which the concept has played in the establishment of parliamentarian government. Such a meaning is consistent with the Thomist position as expressed by Maritain, with the instrumentalism of Dewey, and with the idea of law as an instrument of social order developed by Friedmann. It follows that a fundamentalist position of adopting a conception of the doctrine of consent—with the term left undefined—as a logically convenient but empty absolute or a legalistic standard for evaluation of the particular working rules, examined later in this book, is rejected.

Natural Law in the Declaration of Independence and in the Constitution

Renée de Visme Williamson—whose fundamentalist natural law position in opposition to the morally agnostic, logical positivist position of Kelsen has been discussed in Chapter 2—has taken the position that the moral relativists base their version of democracy on the reference to "consent of the governed" in the second paragraph of the *Declaration of Independence*. Williamson has argued, in a completely legalistic way, that the "true intention" of the authors of the *Declaration* was to make the *second* paragraph subservient to the *first*; and he has asserted that, since the words "laws of nature and nature's God" appear in the *first* paragraph, it is clear that the Founding Fathers "specifically based their claim to independence not on the consent of the

---

[17] J. W. Gough, *The Social Contract: A Critical Study of Its Development* (2d ed.; London: Oxford University Press, 1957), pp. 254–255.

[18] Charles Frankel, *The Social Contract* (New York: Hafner Pub. Co., Inc., 1947), p. xxi.

governed nor on the will of the thirteen colonies but on 'the laws of nature and of nature's God.'"[19] Williamson's argument appears in a relatively brief essay. A much more detailed and documented study of the role played by the natural law concept in our history was undertaken by Cornelia Le Boutiller in 1950. She has written:

The free institutions of democracy, it should not be denied, owe a great deal to the doctrine of natural law, as it has come down to us from ancient times. It may be questioned, however, whether they owe it to the doctrine of natural law intellectualized into a metaphysical principle. ... Rather it is here proposed, democracy's debt is to what has been noted as a shifting phenomenon, namely that a limit has been built up in the minds of freedom-loving men—not always the same, perhaps, but always on the alert—beyond which it is not safe for men to go. . . .

Whatever Americans may say or may have said about the law of nature, about a "higher law," they appear to have meant, not a transcendental essence, but *a practical plan*. This is the plan to make possible individual, free, righteous development within a happy and prosperous commonwealth.[20]

What Madam Le Boutiller has identified as the "practical plan" is, of course, what Holmes meant when he referred to the "life of the law" as "experience"; and it is what Commons had in mind when he asserted that "the state . . . proportions the factors over which it has control . . . indirectly . . . through working rules which guide the transactions of individuals." It is what James meant when he asserted that the pragmatic approach is "an attitude of looking away from first things, principles, 'categories,' supposed necessities; and of looking towards last things, fruits, consequences, facts." It is also what Dewey meant when he asserted that alternative approaches involve a belief that "there is some voice so authoritative as to preclude the need for inquiry." It is, in short, a conception of political democracy as a process of trial and error experimentation, a process of constant adjustment and readjustment, rather than as an end in itself.

It is in the light of such a conception that the contemporary problems of "factions" and the political activities of public relations agencies will now be considered.

B. THE PROBLEM OF "FACTIONS"

Madison on "Factions"

Probably the earliest treatment of the problem of "factions" in relation to the government of the United States occurs in Madison's Essay 10 of *The Federalist*. He wrote:

Among the numerous advantages promised by a well-constructed Union, none deserves to be more accurately developed than its tendency to break and control the violence of faction. . . . The valuable improvements made by the American constitutions on the popular models, both ancient and modern, cannot certainly be too much admired; but it would be an unwarrantable partiality to contend that they have as effectually obviated the danger on this side, as was wished and expected. . . .

By a faction, I understand a number of citizens, whether amounting to a majority or minority of the whole, who are united and actuated by some common impulse of passion, or of interest, adverse to the rights of other citizens, or to the permanent and aggregate interests of the community.

Some Facts about Factions

No one knows the total number of pressure and interest groups operating in the United States at the federal and state levels, nor how much they spend. One expert estimated the number of lobbyists operating in 1963 in Washington, D.C. alone at more than 4,500, consisting of about 3,800 individuals, about 230 public relations and law firms, and about 550 organizations.[21] He also pointed out that the total cumulative number of lobbyists who had registered (under a federal law adopted in 1946) was 6,504 in 1962, but that many did not file statements of expenditures.

Those who do not file statements, such as the National Association of Manufacturers

[19] Renee de Visme Williamson, "The Challenge of Political Relativism," *Journal of Politics*, Vol. IX (May, 1947), pp. 147–177, esp. pp. 159–161.

[20] Cornelia Geer La Boutiller, *American Democracy and Natural Law* (New York: Columbia University Press, 1950), pp. 134–135 and p. 184. (Italics mine.)

But see also Wesley Frank Craven, *The Legend of the Founding Fathers* (New York: New York University Press, 1956).

[21] Felton West, "The Patient Persuaders," in the *Houston Post*, reproduced in the *Congressional Record*, Vol. 109, pp. 4805 ff. (March 25, 1963).

(NAM) and the Americans for Constitutional Action, rely on the 1954 decision of the Supreme Court in *United States* v. *Harriss*[22] which limited the application of the 1946 law to registration by those who engage in "direct communication" with members of Congress for the "principal purpose" of influencing legislation. Organizations which do not register claim that they do not engage in such "direct communication" or do not have as a "principal purpose" the influencing of legislation, and the Department of Justice has brought no action against them to test these claims.

The 1946 Regulation of Lobbying Act merely requires that professional lobbyists, who undertake to influence the decisions of Congress, must register and provide some limited information about themselves and must also submit quarterly reports of receipts and expenditures. These reports are published on a quarterly basis in the *Congressional Record*. The law contains no provisions relating to analysis of the expenditures; nor does it require detailed reports of sources of funds or disbursements. As we will see later, some writers have argued that the law may actually give a false impression that regulation of lobbies exists where in fact there is no regulation. (The subject of regulation will be further discussed later in this section.)

About all the data that can be obtained from the quarterly reports appearing in the *Congressional Record* are the names of those organizations which did in fact register in the period in question and the total amounts which were officially reported spent. Thus, study of the relevant issues of the *Record* for 1962, 1963, and 1964 discloses that in 1963, among others, the Coordinating Committee for Fundamental American Freedoms reported that it had spent $127,826.73 (in opposing civil rights legislation in 1963), while the Citizens Committee for a Nuclear Test Ban spent $61,240.64 (in seeking approval of the 1963 atomic test ban treaty). Similarly, the United Federation of Postal Clerks reported

expenditures in 1963 of $202,996.97 (in support of a bill providing for a pay increase for government workers in 1964), and the Business Committee for Tax Reduction reported expenditures in 1963 of $182,292.83 (in support of the $11.5 billion tax cut legislation adopted in 1964). While the American Farm Bureau reported expenditures in 1963 of $118,284 (in support of legislation deemed favorable to the interests of farmers), the American Legion reported expenditures in 1963 of $117,274.97 (in the interest of legislation for the benefit of veterans), and the American Medical Association (AMA) reported expenditures in 1962 of $83,075.87 (in opposing legislation to provide medical care for the aged). Moreover, the AMA reported spending nearly a million dollars in the *first quarter* of 1965 alone (for the same purpose).[23] Obviously, many different and conflicting interests are represented, and the sums spent are large. But as we will see later, the sums officially reported probably represent only a fraction of total expenditures, and much lobbying takes place "indirectly," as the following two case studies demonstrate.

Two Case Studies of Lobbying Activities

The two case studies now to be presented represent the activities of two pressure groups which have long opposed each other on the national political scene. One of these groups is the NAM, and the other is the AFL-CIO. In 1965, professors Monsen and Cannon provided a useful case study of the campaign of the NAM to secure adoption of the Taft-Hartley Act (amending the National Labor Relations Act) in 1947.[24] Basically, as Monsen and Cannon point out, the NAM's economic philosophy has changed very little in the course of time. Both that philosophy and the technique of "indirect communication" with Congress, on which the NAM has relied in its refusal to register under the existing legislation, are illustrated in the following description of its activities.

The NAM's Fight against the Wagner Act.

[22] 347 U.S. 612 (1954).

[23] Information such as that given in parentheses above does not appear in the quarterly reports but can be obtained from examination of statements of the organizations in question; often such information does appear elsewhere in the *Record*, having been

placed there on behalf of such organizations by members of Congress. It can also be determined from committee hearings.

[24] R. Joseph Monsen and Mark W. Cannon, *The Makers of Public Policy* (New York: McGraw-Hill Book Co., Inc., 1965), pp. 56–60.

Donald Blaisdell has described the activities of the NAM in opposing the Wagner Act—which established the National Labor Relations Board—in 1935 as follows:

Immediately [upon introduction of the Wagner bill] the N.A.M. galvanized into action. James A. Emery, addressing the National Metal Trades Association, called Senator Wagner's bill "lynch law," and Ernest T. Weir asked members of the Union League Club of Chicago to "urge your employees and your fellow-citizens to register their will down in Washington" and "to be vigilant in the fight, carry it to your people, make them see the fallacy of radicalism, and the folly of the demands for over-night change emanating from Washington." Upon announcement of public hearings, to commence on March 11, the N.A.M. sent a call, through its news letter of March 4, to all industrialists who would like to appear in opposition to this bill, to communicate immediately with its New York office. On March 29, C. L. Bardo, president of the association, *suggested that members advise their suppliers and dealers of the importance of this bill to the company*, register their opposition with their Senators and Representatives, and request groups with which they were affiliated to take similar action. On the following day he again urged manufacturers to write to their Senators and to "bring the bill to the attention of your local board of trade, other business groups, and individual employers, urging them to take similar action."

On the same day Walter B. Weisenburger wrote executives of the employers' associations affiliated with the National Industrial Council, suggesting "Washington pilgrimages" by industrialists. "Of course, one of the most effective means of combating this legislation is the 'come to Washington' idea," he wrote. He offered to meet with local delegations in Washington before their calls and "check over the presentation of material." He also urged distribution of pamphlets prepared by the National Industrial Council in collaboration with the N.A.M. to stir up local campaigns against legislation pending in Congress. . . .[25]

The AFL-CIO Campaign for an Increased Minimum Wage in 1955. The use of indirect pressure has also been employed by organized labor. Our second case study is concerned with labor's successful campaign for an increase in the minimum wage in

1955 as described by Gus Tyler, who was then a director of the Political Department of the International Ladies Garment Workers' Union.[26]

In order to direct the campaign, a Joint Minimum Wage Committee was set up under Arthur Goldberg, who was a prominent labor attorney at the time (and who later served as the United States Ambassador to the United Nations after having served for a short time as an Associate Justice of the Supreme Court). A fund of about $20,000 was provided to the Committee by the interested unions and was spent "largely for rent (offices and meeting places), phone, mail, secretarial and clerical staff. The legislative representatives were paid by their respective unions and so reported to Congress under the Regulation of Lobbying Act."[27]

The Committee's approach to the problem involved first of all a "summit conference of union presidents with the President [Eisenhower]," on March 7, 1955, which "had one positive value: it produced press coverage to help get the campaign 'off the ground.' But it failed to persuade Eisenhower."[28] Union leaders next conferred with the Senate Majority Leader (Lyndon Johnson) and the Speaker of the House (Sam Rayburn), and then "the regular legislative offices of both the AFL and the CIO" informed "Congressmen in general" that "the unions meant business in the matter of the minimum wage."[29] The Joint Committee also decided that it would be essential to create a "favorable climate of opinion for the measure." Thus, "although the minimum-wage campaign started as a Washington operation, by mid-March the main effort was at the local level." The "standard procedure" ordinarily adopted by interest groups in such cases has been described by Tyler as follows:

It is standard procedure for unions—like any other interest group—to urge their affiliates to write to Congress supporting the passage of group legislation endorsed by the group. Such calls result in greater or lesser mail pouring or

[25] Blaisdell, *op. cit.*, pp. 100–101. (Italics mine.)
[26] This section draws on Gus Tyler, *A Legislative Campaign for a Federal Minimum Wage (1955)* (Case No. 4 in the *Eagleton Institute Cases in Practical Politics*) (New York: McGraw-Hill Book Co., Inc., 1960).

(The Eagleton Institute is located at Rutgers University.)
[27] *Ibid.*, p. 2.
[28] *Ibid.*, p. 4.
[29] *Ibid.*, p. 3.

trickling into Congressional offices, usually identical in wording, often printed and mimeographed. The impact of mass-produced mail, where the citizen does nothing more than sign his name, is minimal.[30]

But, instead of following the "standard procedure" described above, the Joint Committee undertook to get "'*communities*' to communicate with Congressmen rather than trade unionists alone. The Joint Committee assumed . . . that the role of the unions was to motivate the community to voice that interest."[31]

"In addition," said Tyler, "the local unions were given an educational job; that is, creating a body of opinion."[32] Moreover, this decision was a "master stroke," because the "effect of spontaneity" was achieved by it. Thus, he wrote:

. . . Locally, the campaign was an almost totally unprofessional operation. . . . petitions were mimeographed. Trade unionist volunteers circulated the petitions. Post cards and letters were, almost always, paid for by the individuals sending the same to his or her representative. The press releases, except original "model releases," were not turned out by the professional journalists but by union activists, very often a local union president who was also a worker in the shop.

The unprofessional, almost amateur, flavor of the campaign gave it a fresh quality. The "pros" initiated, planned, sparked. The amateurs did the job. . . . tens of thousands of letters. . . . did not talk about the issue in general, but about the circumstances of the individual worker—name, place, and state of suffering—in detail. The postcards contained many spelling inaccuracies and precisely that vice became a virtue, lending the communique authenticity and credibility.

Some of these local communities even did original research: names of factories that had fled to low-wage zones leaving behind a ruin of unemployment; names of families on economic shoals; the number of workers in an area earning no more than 75 cents an hour. This raw research found its way into the local press and, at a later point, into Congressional testimony.[33]

Local delegations also undertook to see their local Congressman during the Easter recess of Congress when Congressmen were in their home districts. "A quickie guide of 'do's and dont's' was provided for Congressional conversations, a compound of Emily Post and Dale Carnegie."[34]

Eventually, the bill providing for a one dollar minimum wage was passed. But a possibility existed that President Eisenhower might veto the legislation. The Joint Committee "felt that the ranks ought to be alerted to communicate directly with the White House." This action was taken. And, wrote Tyler:

How much mail arrived at the White House on this issue the Joint Committee never knew. But, if the reports of the locals were accurate, the President received as much mail as all of Congress in the previous months.

On August 12, 1955, the bill was signed and became law.[35]

Political scientists disagree about the question of whether or not pressure groups ought to be controlled—and if so, to what extent. It is to different views of this problem that attention will be given next.

Madison on "Curing the Mischiefs of Faction"

In Essay 10 of *The Federalist*, Madison also wrote: "There are two methods of curing the mischiefs of faction: the one, by removing its causes; the other, by controlling its effects."

Insofar as the removal of the causes was concerned, Madison saw two ways of doing so: (1) to destroy the liberty which every pressure group needs in order to operate; or (2) to create a society in which every citizen holds the "same opinions, the same passions, and the same interests." But neither of these methods is consistent with the concept of an open society, and so Madison rejected both. Consequently, he asserted, the solution provided in the Constitution of "controlling the effects" of faction was clearly the right one.

That solution lay in the establishment of a republican form of government, one in which "the representatives were raised to a certain number so as to guard against the cabals of a few," while at the same time the number was made small enough "to guard against confusion." Madison argued that "in a pure democracy," by which he meant "a society consisting of a small

[30] *Ibid.*, p. 10.
[31] *Ibid.* (Italics in the original.)
[32] *Ibid.*

[33] *Ibid.*, pp. 15–16.
[34] *Ibid.*, pp. 20–21.
[35] *Ibid.*, p. 31.

number of citizens who assemble and administer the government in person," there was no cure for the "mischiefs of faction." But in a republic, he continued, a solution was possible, primarily because in such a governmental form power was delegated to a "small number of citizens elected by the rest," and a "greater number of citizens, and a greater sphere of country" could be governed. However, Madison also pointed out, control of factions by means of the adoption of a republican form was more likely to be successful in a large than in a small republic, because in a large republic:

. . . you take in a greater variety of parties and interests; you make it less probable that a majority of the whole will have a common motive to invade the rights of other citizens; or if such a common motive exists, it will be more difficult for all who feel it to discover their own strength, and to act in unison with each other. Besides other impediments, it may be remarked that, where there is a consciousness of unjust or dishonorable purposes, communication is almost always checked by distrust in proportion to the number whose concurrence is necessary.

Thus, Madison put his trust into a "safety in numbers" and an accompanying "diversity of interests" argument. Even if the "influence of factious leaders" was able to "kindle a flame within their particular States," they would be "unable to spread a general conflagration through the other States." And even if a "religious sect" degenerated "into a political faction in a part of the Confederacy," the "variety of sects dispersed over the entire face of it" would "secure the national council against danger from that source."

The Contemporary "Group" Theory and Its Critics

Some contemporary political scientists, perhaps taking Madison's essay as their point of departure, have postulated that there is a universal "grouping process" in democratic societies and that control over government action becomes the principal focus of interest of such groups, because it is government which establishes the "work-

ing rules" according to which the interests of groups are determined.[36] Moreover, it is held, individuals are members of more than one group; therefore, it is unlikely that any single group will eventually dominate. Some of these writers have also taken the position that pressure groups really insure that there is functional—according to particular interests—rather than mere geographical representation in the legislative body. Other writers have suggested that lobbyists perform useful functions since they are able to provide professional assistance to congressmen on complex matters, including assistance in drawing up pieces of legislation, thereby assuring that more than one voice will be heard and saving taxpayers the money involved in providing professional legislative assistance to legislators. But it is clear that such a position comes close to flying in the face of the maxim stated by Madison: "No man is allowed to be a judge in his own cause, because his interest would certainly bias his judgment, and, not improbably, corrupt his integrity."

Recently, in a desire to throw light on many of these issues, Lester Milbrath has published the results of a comprehensive research study in which he has examined the role of Washington lobbyists as "political actors" and lobbying as a "communications process." Among other things, his study examined the salaries of lobbyists, as well as their personality traits, their experience, and their educational backgrounds. Basing his conclusions largely on answers in questionnaires directed to the lobbyists themselves, Milbrath has asserted that present-day lobbying is a "clean" game and that the "little" dirt (corruption) that is present is merely evidence of the fact that there are a "few" corrupt individual lobbyists. He has also concluded that the "creative" function performed by lobbyists in calling attention of legislators to all the various alternative courses of action open to them in particular cases far outweighs any other costs involved in lobbying.[37]

But the group theorists and admirers of the creativity of lobbyists also have their

---

[36] See David B. Truman, *The Governmental Process* (New York: Alfred A. Knopf, Inc., 1951); and E. E. Schatteschneider, *The Semi-Sovereign People* (New York: Holt, Rinehart and Winston, Inc., 1960).

[37] Lester Milbrath, *The Washington Lobbyists* (Chicago: Rand McNally and Co., 1964), pp. 297 ff. and p. 313.

opponents. Daniel Berman for example has taken a somewhat less optimistic view. He has pointed out that pressure groups may "not be representative of the entire nation" (citing the fact that "it is business groups that dominate the pressure system") and that "many individual pressure groups are far from being representative of their own memberships."[38]

In support of Berman's argument, it may be noted that the *Wall Street Journal* reported in February of 1965 that the American Medical Association (AMA) consisted of about 162,000 dues-paying members with another 42,000 dues-exempt members (mainly in government service) and intended to spend about $25 million to influence legislation—a figure which may be compared with its officially reported lobbying expenditures of $83,075.87 in 1962 as well as with the $9.6 million budget for 1965 of the AFL-CIO which had about 16 million members and officially reported expenditures of $149,212.22 in 1962. The income of the AMA consisted of dues of $45 per year from physician members (which accounted for $7.2 million) income from advertising in the weekly *Journal of the American Medical Association* (about $10 million), and income from investments and other sources.[39] According to the *Report* of the McClellan Committee (Senate), the AMA began in 1948 to impose annual dues payments of $25 on all member doctors and in this way financed expenditures of about $4 million paid to Whitaker and Baxter, a California public-relations firm, in 1948 and thereafter, to create a climate of public opinion unfavourable to compulsory national health insurance legislation. This *Report* also states that the Committee on Political Action (COPE) of the AFL-CIO had available funds of about $1.2 million in 1956, obtained largely from one dollar contributions by individual union members, from an "educational fund" maintained by unions out of union dues, and from a general fund maintained by the AFL-CIO.[40]

It is also worth noting that Blaisdell's report of the activities of the NAM in 1935

and Tyler's report of the activities of the Joint Minimum Wage Committee in 1955 indicate that organizational directives came down from the top in both campaigns. However the upper echelon of the NAM suggested in 1935 to the member industrialists that "members [of the NAM] *advise their suppliers and dealers of the importance of this bill to the company*" and that the industrialists should make "Washington pilgrimages" (note the picture called up by the language employed), apparently at their own or their companies' expense. (How such expenditures are to be entered into the calculations lying behind the depictions by economic theorists of cost curves of individual firms operating under competitive conditions is not altogether clear, and the standard procedure is to assume that such expenditures are either nonexistent or unusual.) In the case of the Joint Committee, the labor unions made effective use of visits by Congressmen to their home districts during the Easter recess of the Congress because the union members could not afford trips to Washington, trips which presumably could not have been taken on company time with expenses paid.

Thus, Berman's criticism of the group theory is not to be lightly dismissed.

Berman has also pointed out that the "new lobby" technique is more sophisticated than the old; apparently lobbyists, too, learn from experience. Indeed, some today are paid on a contingent fee basis; that is, the payment of their fees is made contingent upon their success in influencing the outcome of a legislative action which favors their employers. And many have learned that it is cheaper and easier to concentrate their efforts on members of key committees in the House and Senate to kill off legislation to which they are opposed—by never having it reach the floor, a point to be considered in greater detail in the next chapter.

Regulation of Lobbies

Madison, as we have seen, put his trust in the idea of "safety in numbers," believing that a diversity of interests would be

[38] Daniel M. Berman, *In Congress Assembled* (New York: The Macmillan Co., 1964), pp. 108–109. See also Schattschneider, *op. cit.*, pp. 31 ff.

[39] *Wall Street Journal*, February 8, 1965, p. 1.

[40] *Final Report of the Special Committee* (Report of the Special Committee to Investigate Political Activities, Lobbying, and Campaign Contributions, Senate Report No. 395, 85th Cong., 1st sess.) (Washington, D.C.: U.S. Government Printing Office, 1957), pp. 47 and 116.

enough to safeguard against the dominance of particular interest groups. Most contemporary regulatory statutes, including those adopted by the various states, embody some type of disclosure principle. On this point, part of the opinion of Chief Justice Warren in the *Harriss* case is worth noting:

Present-day legislative complexities are such that individual Members of Congress cannot be expected to explore the myriad pressures to which they are regularly subjected. Yet full realization of the American ideal of government by elected representatives depends to no small extent on their ability to properly evaluate such pressures. Otherwise, the voice of the people may all too easily be drowned out by the voice of special-interest groups seeking favored treatment while masquerading as proponents of the public weal. This is the evil which the Lobbying Act was designed to help prevent.

Toward that end, Congress has not sought to prohibit these pressures. It has merely provided for a modicum of information from those who for hire attempt to influence legislation or who collect or spend funds for that purpose. It wants only to know who is being hired, who is putting up the money, and how much. It acted in the same spirit and for a similar purpose in passing the Federal Corrupt Practices Act to maintain the integrity of a basic governmental process.[41]

It may be remarked in passing that Justices Douglas, Black, and Jackson dissented from the majority opinion in the *Harriss* case on grounds that even the severe limitation placed upon the operation of the lobbying law by the majority (restricting it to cases involving "direct communication" for the "principal purpose" of influencing legislation) was insufficient to validate the law under the First Amendment to the Constitution.

One Senate Committee has, however, remarked concerning the problem of regulation:

Disclosure is like an antibiotic which can deal with ethical sickness in the field of public affairs. There was perhaps more general agreement upon this principle of disclosing full information to the public and upon its general effectiveness than upon any other proposal. It is hardly a sanction and certainly not a penalty. It avoids difficult

conclusions as to what may be right or wrong. In this sense it is not even diagnostic; yet there is confidence that it will be helpful in dealing with questionable or improper practices. It would sharpen men's own judgments of right and wrong if they knew these acts would be challenged.[42]

But this solution is seen as too idealistic by many writers. Edgar Lane, who has made a pioneering study of lobbying at the state level, also quotes this portion of the *Report* but points out that the paragraph rests on the assumption that the "public" will make use of the knowledge disclosed. That assumption may not be warranted. Lane suggests that disclosure plus "management" is required but does not explain what he has in mind.[43] One element of management might, of course, be government publication of detailed and complete information concerning total amounts spent, together with some analysis of the purposes for which the sums were spent and statements indicating to whom the money was paid.

Lane has also pointed out, as have many others, that a disclosure law may in fact be bad if it gives the impression, as the present federal law may, that there is regulation where in fact no real regulation exists. In 1966 in its *Final Report*, the Joint Committee on the Organization of Congress made a number of recommendations which would go far in the direction of providing real regulation of lobbying. Unfortunately, Congress adjourned without acting on the recommendations.[44]

But the problem does not necessarily end with control of lobbying. Indeed, today the lobbying problem may be less important than the problem of "imagery" to which attention is given next.

C. THE CREATION OF IMAGES OF MEASURES AND OF MEN

Machiavelli on Imagery

In 1513, Niccolo Machiavelli wrote *The Prince* and became the forerunner of

---

[41] *United States* v. *Harriss*, 347 U.S. 612 (1954), at p. 625.

[42] *Ethical Standards in Government* (Report of the Subcommittee on the Establishment of a Commission on Ethics in Government, Senate Committee on Labor and Public Welfare, 82d Cong., 1st sess.) (Washington, D.C.: U.S. Government Printing Office, 1951), p. 37.

[43] Edgar Lane, *Lobbying and the Law* (Berkeley: University of California Press, 1964), p. 187.

[44] *Organization of Congress* (Final Report of the Joint Committee on the Organization of the Congress, Senate Report No. 1414, 89th Cong., 2d sess.) (Washington, D.C.: U.S. Government Printing Office, 1966).

writers who concern themselves with the problem of political techniques and means of acquiring and holding political power as distinct from that of the objects of the uses of that power. He argued that it was important that a ruler "should *seem* to be all mercy, faith, integrity, humanity, and religion." Indeed, he asserted that it was more necessary "to *seem* to have" these qualities than actually to have them, since actually possessing them might be a hindrance on occasion: "I would even be bold to say that to possess them and always to observe them is dangerous, but to *appear* to possess them is useful."[45]

The Public Relations Technique in Politics

The technique defined by Machiavelli has today become an important element in the formulation of working rules and in the election of candidates to office, both at the state and national levels. There is probably only one way in which its effects can be neutralized in a democratic society: by widespread recognition and understanding on the part of the population of the existence and use of this technique. It has become more effective in recent years because of the development of television, but Stanley Kelley has suggested that matters of public relations began to become an important concern of "giant corporate enterprises" beginning about 1900, as a reaction against attacks on business in the press and periodicals, against the various attempts at national and state regulation of the period, and against the growth of labor union memberships.[46] Beginning in 1948, techniques which had previously been used to sell goods and services were, for a time, successfully employed on behalf of the AMA by Whitaker and Baxter to "sell" the views of the AMA in its fight against compulsory national health insurance. Since 1952, these techniques have been employed on a massive scale in Presidential elections and by various groups interested in supporting or opposing particular measures. As Kelley has clearly noted, the object of the use of the public relations technique is to mould the views of voters at the grass roots level, a process which is far more expensive and time-consuming than that of direct lobbying, but whose results, if successful, are likely to be much longer lasting.[47]

According to Kelley's valuable pioneering study, the basic technique employed by public relations firms is to draw up a "campaign plan." Such a plan involves development of four basic concepts: (1) the selection of a "simple theme" which involves an attack upon the opponent's position and at the same time provides an emotional appeal to the *unthinking* listener or reader on the theory that the average American "doesn't want to improve his mind" and "doesn't want to work, consciously, at being a good citizen"; (2) the adoption of a "gimmick" or some "attention-getting novelty or trick"; (3) the use of an "appeal that is beyond politics" on the theory that, since the various major communications media are used largely for entertainment purposes, politics must itself become "a form of entertainment" to compete successfully for the attention of the viewer or listener; and (4) careful attention to "timing" of the campaign, with the result that most of the money is spent in the last three weeks before an election or before a crucial vote on a measure is to occur.[48]

Public Relations and the "Merchandising of Measures": Two Case Studies

The AMA. A Special Senate Committee set up in 1957 under the chairmanship of Senator McClellan has provided some interesting data concerning the operations of Whitaker and Baxter after 1948 on behalf of the AMA's position in opposition to compulsory health insurance legislation. The Committee reported:

The firm of Whitaker and Baxter was retained in December 1948 and opened offices for the campaign in Chicago in January 1949. With a nucleus from its own organization, the firm recruited a staff of 42 to run the campaign from the Chicago office. The firm registered and reported under the Lobbying Act, although it allegedly made no contacts with Congress and confined its activities to public-relations work at the grassroots levels.

The campaign against compulsory health-

---

45 Niccolo Machiavelli, *The Prince*, trans. W. K. Mariotte (London: J. M. Dent and Sons, Ltd., 1908), p. 143. (Italics mine.)

46 Kelley, *op. cit.*, p. 2.
47 *Ibid.*, p. 44.
48 *Ibid.*, pp. 44–59.

insurance legislation was conducted in some 3,000 counties in the 48 States. Each State, county, and local medical society was active in arousing the interest of doctor members and their families, nurses, pharmacists, druggists, and others interested in or affiliated with the medical profession. As a result, a large volunteer group was organized.[49]

In his description of this particular campaign, Kelley found that it is common practice to mobilize "natural allies," namely, related groups which also have a financial interest in the outcome or which stand in a subservient relation to the principal pressure group.[50]

The McClellan Committee also reported:

Through publicity in the press, speeches by local doctors to various organizations and groups, and wide distribution of literature, a great deal of outside support was developed. By the time the campaign ended, AMA had succeeded in obtaining the support of some 12,000 organizations in its opposition to the legislation. All forms of media were used in the campaign to present to the public the case against the proposed legislation, including television, radio advertising, and extensive distribution of literature. Thousands of speeches were delivered and an intensive effort was made to secure formal endorsements from numerous organizations, with excellent results.

The campaign also received the benefit of over $2 million worth of newspaper advertising paid for voluntarily by thousands of advertisers who were so impressed with the advertising made in AMA's behalf that they adopted it and ran ads in the same vein at their own expense.[51]

Kelley also investigated this aspect of the program. He reported that much of the tie-in advertising was prepared by Whitaker and Baxter and that "partial or complete mats for tie-in ads were sent to newspaper advertising directors."[52] Thus, apparently, the newspaper advertising directors also acquired a stake in the campaign.

The McClellan Committee further reported:

The compensation paid to Whitaker and Baxter for the 3½ years of their services amounted to $325,000 out of which the firm bore its own very extensive traveling expenses. The expenses of the Chicago office maintained by the Whitaker firm were borne by AMA. Fees and salaries of

the Chicago staff for 3½ years came to about $700,000.

Other expenses to AMA were $297,000 for national magazine advertising, $587,000 for newspaper advertising, $405,000 for broadcasts, $1,356,000 for printing, $102,000 for charges covering fieldmen, and $95,000 for staff travel expenses. The total cost of the campaign to AMA was $4,678,157.33.[53]

The election of President Johnson in 1964 assured the defeat of the AMA's program of opposition to health insurance for the aged. Yet, according to the February 8, 1965 issue of the *Wall Street Journal*, despite its defeat on this issue "the AMA has become an increasingly powerful force in the economics of medicine and public health. A year-round lobbying effort in Washington and surprisingly effective grassroots pressure are providing it with growing political influence, and it is being listened to each year on dozens of pieces of legislation."[54] Indeed, its Washington office in 1964 was reported to have analyzed 836 bills of interest to doctors and to have testified "before Congressional committees on many of them."[55] Moreover, the AMA had created a national committee, the American Medical Political Action Committee (AMPAC), which was estimated to have spent between $2 and $3 million on campaigns for seats for about 100 members of the House of Representatives, most of whom lost in the wake of President Johnson's great vote-getting ability. However, among those Representatives whom the AMPAC supported and who won were "Representatives Burleson (D. Texas), Baring (D. Nevada), Wyatt (R. Oregon), Wilson (R. California), and Hall (R. Missouri)."[56]

The Harris-Fulbright Bill. Methods similar to those used by the AMA were employed both by opponents and by supporters of the Harris-Fulbright Bill to amend the Natural Gas Act by exempting natural gas producers from regulation by the Federal Power Commission in 1954. Among the opponents of the legislation was the Council of Local Gas Companies, which established a Washington office staffed in part with personnel supplied by interested gas

49 Senate Report No. 395, *op. cit.*. pp. 47–48.
50 Kelley, *op. cit.*, p. 58.
51 Senate Report No. 395, *op. cit.*, p. 48.
52 Kelley, *op. cit.*, pp. 85–86.

53 Senate Report No. 395, *op. cit.*, p. 48.
54 *Wall Street Journal*, February 8, 1965, p. 1.
55 *Ibid.*
56 *Ibid.*, p. 6.

companies. The Council spent $27,699.36 for various purposes. The bill was also opposed by the United Automobile, Aircraft, and Agricultural Workers Union which spent $38,762 on newspaper advertisements and spot radio announcements.[57] Major oil companies supporting the legislation, in turn, organized the Natural Gas and Oil Resources Committee (NGO), financed by "contributions based on a formula keyed to production. Contributions aggregating $1,950,000 were received from over 1,000 contributors," but about $1,646,500 came from 26 firms. The McClellan Committee reported:

At the outset of its work, NGO retained the public relations firm of Hill and Knowlton, Inc., to furnish an outline of a complete program of operations.

The manpower which enabled NGO to carry out its extensive program nationally [distribution of over 5 million pieces of literature] was furnished by various firms in the industry without charge. . . .

The expenses of NGO from October 1954 until March 31, 1956 amounted to $1,753,513.70. The sum of $798,304.59 had been expended for newspaper and magazine advertising and $499,181.77 was spent for printed materials. The remaining sum, amounting to something less than $500,000, went to pay for administration expense ($234,732.62), national publicity ($87,032.89), Hill and Knowlton, Inc. ($85,160), and lesser items.[58]

Moreover, as was true in the case of some of the contributions to the Council of Local Gas Companies, the expenses contributed to the Natural Gas and Oil Resources Committee were charged as operating expenses by the contributing companies and listed as such for income tax purposes.[59] (Again the problem of precisely how such expenditures are to be included in the cost curves in the contemporary theory of the firm employed in static price theory is not altogether clear, and, for this reason, such public relations expenditures are also usually treated as nonexistent or as not representative of the "typical" case.)

Public Relations and the "Merchandising of Men" (1952–1968)

Presidential Campaigns. The merchandising of a political candidate is a more difficult problem for the public relations firm than the merchandising of a measure or of opposition to a measure. The public relations expert must always reckon with the possibility of the unguarded remark by the candidate and with the fact that the candidate may have a mind of his own, making it difficult to build his "image." Thus, the New York Times reported on September 28, 1964 concerning the candidates in the 1964 Presidential election:

Mr. Johnson seems to enjoy and to see value in news conferences, but he does not say much that is startling. Mr. Goldwater's assistants have a horror of news conferences and he has not given one since the campaign began. But, when he does speak to reporters, he usually says something provocative.[60]

In the 1952 Presidential campaign, the Republicans employed the Kudner Agency and Batten, Barton, Durstine, and Osborn (BBD and O) to handle their advertising, and Robert Humphreys served as the Public Relations Director of the Republican National Committee. Robert Duffy, President of BBD and O, conceived of the problem as one of "merchandising Eisenhower's frankness, honesty and integrity, his sincere and wholesome approach."[61] The Joseph Katz Company of Baltimore and the Erwin Wasey Agency (Chicago office) handled the advertising for the Democrats. Stanley Kelley has concluded that "For good or ill, it appears that the Democratic candidate's [Adlai Stevenson] speeches owed little to the advice of public relations men." The public relations men thereupon identified Stevenson's approach as "The Blunt Truth Technique."[62] The Republicans were reported to have spent $2 million in a radio-TV campaign (a rate of $34 million a year) during the final three weeks of the campaign. Spot radio announcements were used at a saturation rate. The Democrats spent about $77,000 on spot commercials.

Kelley, whose book is worth careful attention, has concluded:

The strategy, treatment of issues, use of media, budgeting, and pacing of the Eisenhower campaign showed the pervasive influence of professional propagandists. The Democrats used

[57] Senate Report No. 395, *op. cit.*, pp. 27–31.
[58] *Ibid.*, p. 14.
[59] *Ibid.*, p. 15; see also p. 82.

[60] *New York Times*, September 28, 1964, p. 12.
[61] Quoted in Kelley, *op. cit.*, p. 156.
[62] *Ibid.*, p. 172.

fewer professionals, were less apt to draw upon commercial and industrial public relations experience in their thinking, and their publicity men had less of a voice in the policy decisions of the campaign.[63]

In the Presidential campaign of 1960, according to *Advertising Age*, the Democrats spent $6.2 million and the Republicans $7.5 million on radio and television time.[64] And in 1964, according to Leonard Sloane of the *New York Times*, a sum of about $9 million was spent by each party on all media.[65] The Democrats employed the Doyle Dane Bernback Agency, which had also assisted in planning the arrangements for the Democratic National Convention in Atlantic City.[66] The Republicans employed Erwin Wasey (note that the Chicago office of this firm had worked for the Democrats in 1952) and Ruthraff and Ryan, Inc. The Republicans spent about $4.8 million on radio and television and about $200,000 on an eight-page ad in the October issue of *Reader's Digest*, placed by the Leo Burnett Company which had been the Republicans advertising agency until it was replaced by Erwin Wasey in August of 1964, following the Goldwater nomination.[67] The Democrats spent about $4 million on radio and television advertising, with $1.7 million being spent on network television broadcasts and the remainder being spent for twenty-second and one and five-minute spot broadcasts.[68] The Leo Burnett Company was apparently the agency which developed the principal Republican campaign slogan, "In your heart, you know he's right."

The Republicans operated on a budget of $20 million during the 1968 Presidential campaign, while the Democrats had a budget of about $10 million.[69] President Nixon originally began with a small advertising agency, Feeley and Wheeler, which was replaced by the New York public relations firm of Fuller, Smith, and Ross.[70] About 30 percent of the budget

was devoted to radio. The agency began as early as February to purchase prime television time, and the entire campaign was characterized by the smoothness of its public relations activities.

Candidate Humphrey began with the agency of Doyle, Dane, and Bernbank, which demanded payment at the standard 15 percent commission rate. The Democrats then switched to the use of the firm of Lennon and Newell on a fixed fee basis. Mary Wells Lawrence and Stuart Greene of Wells, Rich, and Greene also assisted in planning the Democratic campaign.[71]

The third party candidate, Governor Wallace, was represented by Luckie and Forney, a Birmingham, Alabama, firm. Wallace's campaign cost was estimated at between $5 and $10 million.[72]

In the case of the Republican primary elections, it was estimated that Governor Rockefeller and President Nixon spent $5 million each, while in the Democratic primaries, Senator McCarthy was reported to have spent between $5 and $7 million and Senator Robert Kennedy's expenditures, prior to his tragic death, reportedly amounted to $4 million.[73]

Congressional Campaigns. The merchandising of candidates occurs also at the state level. Kelley has fully analyzed the classic case of the "merchandising of doubt" in the Maryland Senatorial election of 1950, in which Senator John Butler defeated then-incumbent Senator Millard Tydings. A Chicago public relations expert, Jon N. Jonkel, later indicted and fined $5,000 for violating the Maryland election laws, was employed by the Republican candidate, Butler. Jonkel selected the issue of "doubt" as the "gimmick" to be employed in defeating the Democratic candidate for reelection. According to Jonkel's testimony before a United States Senate Committee established to investigate the conduct of the election, his conception of the campaign was as follows:

---

[63] *Ibid.*, p. 195.

[64] *Advertising Age*, September 17, 1964, p. 1.

[65] *New York Times*, September 27, 1964, sec. 3, p. 16F.

[66] *Advertising Age*, September 17, 1964, p. 1.

[67] *New York Times*, September 27, 1964, sec. 3, p. 16F.

[68] *Ibid.*

[69] I am indebted to Mr. John Burnham for the

collection of most of the data pertaining to the 1968 Presidential election contained herein. See also, Joe McGiniss, *The Selling of the President—1968* (New York: Trident Press, 1969).

[70] *Wall Street Journal*, October 4, 1968, p. 22.

[71] *Advertising Age*, October 7, 1968.

[72] *Wall Street Journal*, October 24, 1968, p. 8; and *Advertising Age*, October 7, 1968, p. 100.

[73] *Wall Street Journal*, October 8, 1968, p. 8.

He [Butler] campaigned . . . on the fact that Senator Tydings had been the chairman of a subcommittee which investigated the loyalty of the State Department employees.

. . . he [Butler] would say, for instance, that "Russia boasts that all over the world it is going to take over the world by force, by trickery, or by this or that. This is our country. We have seen it happen in other countries. You are a father, you are a mother, do you believe that we are well organized here? Do you feel that you know for sure that there are not Communists or Communist influence in the top levels of our Government?"

You just asked them those questions. Those are the questions he asked. That is the way he campaigned. We never had anything personal against Senator Tydings.[74]

As Kelley has pointed out, Tydings was thus faced with the "impossible task of proving absolute certainty." Jonkel had employed the doubt technique "to achieve that 'brevity and clarity'" which most public relations firms seek.[75]

Expenditures on public relations activities in state elections are also increasing. For example, in the 1964 Senatorial election in New York, Senator Kenneth Keating, a Republican who had refused to support the National Goldwater-Miller ticket, reportedly had a budget of $1 million, which was expected to increase to $1.5 million, and employed Weiss and Gellar of New York City, Vandecar and Port of Albany, and the Rumrill Agency of Rochester to handle his public relations matters. Senator Robert Kennedy was similarly reported to have had in 1964 a budget of from $1 to $1.5 million and employed Pappert, Koenig, and Lois as his advertising firm.

The Federal Communications Commission undertakes to publish by political parties the radio and television station charges for political broadcasts. In the case of the 1966 elections, total charges both in primary and general election campaigns to the Republican Party amounted to more than $12 million, while charges to the Democrats amounted to about $18.5 million. The charges to candidates other than those of the two major parties amounted to about $1.4 million.[76]

The Engineering of Consent

One of the pioneers of the public relations profession, Mr. Edward Bernays, has sought to provide a philosophical basis for the political role played by the public relations expert. According to Bernays, the public relations counsel must be constantly aware of his power to influence public opinion and therefore he must avoid "the propagation of antisocial or otherwise harmful movements or ideas."[77]

The use of public relations firms in order to create images has not been limited to cases involving real world politicians. After the 1936 Presidential election many of the major business enterprises in the United States began to employ public relations firms to present management's point of view in labor disputes and in attacks upon the new regulatory agencies which were being created at the federal level.

An interesting example of a letter of solicitation used by the public relations firm of Hill and Knowlton in 1937 appeared as an exhibit in the hearings titled *Violations of Free Speech and Rights of Labor* conducted by a Senate subcommittee in 1939. In part, the letter of solicitation read:

April 22nd, 1937.

Bender Body Company,
    W. 62nd and Barberton Ave., Cleveland, Ohio.

Gentlemen: At the suggestion of Mr. Parsons of Wm. J. Mericka and Co., we are making you the following proposal for developing and handling a program of publicity and public relations for your company:

PURPOSES

The purposes of a publicity and public relations program are:

(a) To make a company more widely known and its name more familiar to the general public throughout the country.

---

[74] *Hearings on the Maryland Senatorial Election of 1950* (Hearings of the Subcommittee on Privileges and Elections, Senate Committee on Rules and Administration, 82d Cong., 1st sess.) (Washington, D.C.: U.S. Government Printing Office, 1951), pl 305. Also quoted in Kelley, *op. cit.*, p. 124. Kelley provides a detailed analysis of the entire campaign, pp. 107–143.

[75] Kelley, *op. cit.*, p. 139.

[76] *Annual Report of the Federal Communications Commission for Fiscal Year 1967*, (Washington, D.C.: U.S. Government Printing Office, 1968), p. 193.

[77] Edward L. Bernays, *Crystallizing Public Opinion* (new ed.; New York: Liveright Pub. Corp., 1961), pp. 214–15.

(b) To assist in the sales promotion of specific products.

(c) To see to it that facts and news about the company are *correctly reported* in the newspapers and magazines.

Your company should, we believe, be interested in all of these objectives.

It would be to your advantage to have more people throughout the United States familiar with the name of your company and with its products. This would be beneficial both from the sales standpoint and from the standpoint of the standing and reputation of the company. It would be especially important when and as the stock of the company is listed on the exchange.

On the product promotion side, publicity in newspapers and magazines, particularly on trailers, would be a substantial aid in sales promotion.

From time to time there is news arising in your company in which newspapers are interested as a matter of course, and which *you want to be sure is correctly presented*. Included in such material would be news concerning earnings, personnel changes or promotions, announcements regarding new products, *or anything that might develop in the labor situation. News material of this sort should be properly prepared* and given to the newspapers *so that it will be correctly reported.*

FUNCTION OF OUR ORGANIZATION

The firm of Hill and Knowlton is set up for the purpose of handling publicity and public relations for corporations and business organizations.

We act as a clearing house for all of the news arising in a company which we serve, and in addition create for our clients a large amount of material appearing in newspapers and magazines, which otherwise would not appear.

Our experience covers a rather broad field of industrial activity. We have offices in both Cleveland and New York. In the Cleveland territory we have among our clients, Republic Steel Corporation, The Warner and Swasey Company, The Austin Company, The Standard Oil Co. of Ohio, and a number of other concerns of comparable size. In our New York office we handle public relations for the American Iron and Steel Institute.[78]

It is to be noted that the firm prepared news materials "properly" so that they would be "correctly reported" and included news pertaining to the labor situation among the items to be dealt with, particularly, in

the cases of firms in the steel industry, during the steel strikes of the 1930's. But how James Madison would have assessed the increasing influence of the men from Madison Avenue, had he conceived of it, is, unfortunately, an unanswerable hypothetical question. Nevertheless, Madison did reject as one of the solutions to the problem of "factions" that of creating a society in which every citizen had "the same opinions, the same passions, and the same interests." That the corporation, described by Pope Innocent as *persona ficta* and by Justice John Marshall as an "invisible, intangible creature," should have created for itself an artificial personality does not, however, seem illogical.

In the field of "merchandizing measures and men," Congress considered an Election Reform Act in 1967. Under the Corrupt Practices Act of 1925, a limited amount of reporting of campaign expenditures to the Clerk of the House and to the Secretary of the Senate is currently required. But unless news services choose to make use of the information filed in this way, the public is not likely to obtain such information. Nor is there any provision in the law for analysis of expenditures. In 1967, S. 1880, containing stringent reporting and disclosure provisions and providing for publicity concerning an analysis of expenditures of candidates, passed the Senate but was prevented from reaching the floor of the House by the House Rules Committee. Clearly, modern legislation to deal with the problem is needed and should be enacted. The present legislation was adopted even before radio had become an important means of communication; much less does it concern itself with problems created by the development of television or the widespread use of public relations firms. But there is no sign that such legislation or further legislation pertaining to lobbying will be enacted in the near future. Indeed, Congress has permitted income tax deductions to be taken for lobbying expenses incurred as a result of seeking to influence legislation "of direct interest to the taxpayer." The economic theory of the firm does not ordinarily consider explicitly the

---

[78] *Violations of Free Speech and Rights of Labor* (Hearings before a Subcommittee of the Senate Committee on Education and Labor, 76th Cong., 1st sess., 1939) (Washington, D.C.: U.S. Government Printing Office, 1939), p. 15. (Italics mine.)

question of how expenses incurred by firms in financing public relations and lobbying activities are to be treated. To the extent that such expenses are covered by the final prices charged by such firms for their products, any statistical or econometric study which makes use of such prices as a measure of the "value of the resources used" must rest either on an assumption that such expenses are so unimportant that they can be ignored or else on an assumption that these expenses are socially valuable and properly included within the statistical measure of value employed. The point, of course, is that while such measures cannot be abandoned without giving up the ability of economists to quantify such magnitudes, they can be used in a given case as a basis for policy recommendations only with great care and with the qualification that the use of the measure in itself involves a subjective judgment on the part of the user.

The next chapter will deal with the subject of the legislative, executive, and administrative processes as a source of change in law, within the context of lobbies and pressure groups as described in this chapter.

6

Law and Social Change: Legislative, Executive, and Administrative Processes

This chapter continues the consideration of the problem of law and social change begun in Chapter 4. Specifically, this chapter discusses briefly the mechanics, as well as the formal sources of changes in working rules as the result of legislative, executive, and administrative actions at the federal level. The emphasis of this chapter is upon the *context* within which such changes occur. Accordingly, the first major subdivision of this chapter is concerned with a discussion of the activities and organization of Congress; the second major subdivision undertakes an analogous discussion of the Executive Branch; and the third major subdivision is concerned with a consideration of similar problems in the case of administrative agencies.

A. CHANGES IN LAW:
THE LEGISLATIVE BRANCH

The Great Compromise and Its Aftermath

Article I, Section 1, of the Constitution vests "all legislative power" in the Senate and the House of Representatives. Yet, as will become apparent shortly, the President

also possesses much legislative power. Article I, of course, contains the "Great Compromise" of the Constitution under which Members of the House are chosen for two year terms on the basis of population and Senators are chosen for six year periods, two from every state. This method of selection was a compromise between representatives to the Constitutional Convention from heavily populated and from less populated states. Those from the more heavily populated states wished representation in the Congress to be based on population; those from the less populated states demanded equal representation for all states. The compromise has produced some inevitable differences both in the powers of the two Houses of Congress and in the ways in which they are organized. Some of the differences between the powers of and procedures employed in the House and Senate require further discussion.

For example, since representation in the House of Representatives is based on population and since the terms of Members of the House are for periods of two years only, bills concerning the raising of revenue must originate in the House, on the theory that tax legislation will thus be made more responsive to the voice of the electorate. But, as we will see later, such tax legislation may actually originate in policy recommendations made to the President by some executive agency such as the Council of Economic Advisors or the Department of State (tariff laws.) The House Ways and Means Committee, however, has a decisive voice in determining whether or not legislation will be considered and is, therefore, one of the most powerful of the Congressional Committees. The impact of its decisions—and particularly, as we will see, the views of its chairman—on economic activity thus can be and often are very great. (The House also has the sole power of impeachment; that is, the House has the power to institute a written accusation against a public official; and the Senate acts as a court to try an official upon the charges contained in the accusation presented by the House. But these matters are of less interest within the terms of reference of this book.)

The Senate may approve or disapprove most formal Presidential appointments (for example, appointments of individuals as federal judges or to regulatory commissions) and must concur in treaties by a two-thirds majority vote. The Senate does not *ratify* treaties; *ratification* is an act of validation of a treaty performed by the President with the approval of the Senate. The Senate thus has important power in the area of international economic relationships. For example, the proposal for establishment of an International Trade Organization by an international treaty was buried in a Republican-dominated Senate committee after World War II, thereby frustrating the Democratic Truman administration's attempt to establish an international forum for discussion of ways and means of changing working rules relative to international trade.

The Presiding Officers of the Senate and the House

The presiding officer of the Senate is, of course, the Vice President of the United States. However since he represents the Executive Branch and can vote only in the case of a tie, he has little real power in Congress.

The presiding officer of the House is the Speaker, and he is always a member of the majority party. The Speaker has substantial power. Among other things, he appoints members of special committees refers bills to the standing committees, can recognize or refuse to recognize members, and decides when a bill—which has been cleared by the Rules Committee or has been in its hands for 21 days—is to be brought up on the floor. Because of this power, his views carry great weight with the other members of his party. Occasionally, when an important issue is at stake, the Speaker may take the floor to state his position formally; often, however, he merely makes his views known informally. But his powers are not unlimited, since committee chairmen also have great power.

The Committees of Congress

Between ten and twenty thousand bills are introduced at every session of Congress. Many of these are nominal; the members introducing them often have neither the intention nor the desire to see all these bills enacted into law. In some cases, they may indicate as much to the other members by prefacing their statements introducing a particular bill with a remark that they are introducing it "at the request" of some named constituent. Many other bills are "private bills" usually to settle individual claims against the government.

Important bills are ordinarily introduced by senior members or by committee chairmen. Legislation important to the program of the President is generally introduced by the relevant committee chairman, if the President enjoys a Congressional majority. If he does not, such legislation is usually introduced by the ranking minority member of the relevant committee. Support of the proposed bill by the relevant committee chairman, we will see, is important in any case. Hence there may be a great emphasis on "bi-partisanship," particularly by Presidents who do not enjoy a Congressional majority and in the area of foreign affairs where "unity" is believed to be an important factor.

Because of the complexities of the tasks facing Congress and because of the pressures to which Congressmen are subject, most of the real work of the Congress is done in standing committees, whose chairmen have a decisive voice in determining whether or not bills referred to their committees will reach the floor. In addition, the House Rules Committee has also often had great power in this regard. In 1969 there were 19 standing committees in the Senate and 21 in the House, as indicated in Table 6-1.

In addition, there were (and are) special committees, joint congressional commissions, and joint committees (composed of members of both Houses). Standing committees may also establish subcommittees; for example, the Subcommittee on Antitrust and Monopoly of the Senate Judiciary Committee has held many hearings on the

Table 6-1

Committees of Congress, 91st Congress, 1st Session (1969)

Senate	Members	House	Members
Standing Committees:		*Standing Committees:*	
Aeronautical and Space Services	15	Agriculture	36
Agriculture and Forestry	17	Appropriations	50
Appropriations	27	Armed Services	37
Armed Services	17	Banking and Currency	31
Banking and Currency	15	District of Columbia	25
Commerce	18	Education and Labor	31
District of Columbia	7	Foreign Affairs	33
Finance	17	Government Operations	31
Foreign Relations	17	House Administration	25
Government Operations	15	Interior and Insular Affairs	33
Interior and Insular Affairs	17	Internal Security	9
Judiciary	15	Interstate and Foreign Commerce	33
Labor and Public Welfare	15	Judiciary	35
Nutrition and Human Needs	14	Merchant Marine and Fisheries	31
Organization of Congress	6	Official Conduct	12
Post Office and Civil Service	9	Post Office and Civil Service	25
Public Works	17	Public Works	34
Rules and Administration	9	Rules	15
Standards and Conduct	6	Science and Astronautics	31
		Veterans Affairs	25
Select and Special Committees:		Ways and Means	25
Small Business	17		
Aging	21	*Select and Special Committees:*	
Democratic Policy Committee	9	House Beauty Shop	3
Republican Policy Committee	14	On Small Business	13
		Parking	3
		Recording Studio	3

Joint Committees	Members
Atomic Energy	18
Defense Production	10
Disposition of Executive Papers	4
Economic Committee	16
Immigration and Nationality Policy	10
Internal Revenue Taxation	10
Library	10
Navajo-Hopi Indian Administration	6
Reduction of Federal Expenditures	12
Printing	6

Source: Compiled from *Congressional Directory* (91st Cong., 1st sess.) (Washington, D.C.: U.S. Government Printing Office, 1969), pp. 252–285.

problem of concentration of economic power and its effect on the economy.

The members of the standing committees of each House are ostensibly chosen by a vote of the entire membership of that House; members of other committees are appointed by the presiding officers. However, although there are exceptions in a few cases, membership on committees is apportioned between the two major political parties in the ratio in which they hold seats in each chamber, and the allocation of the membership assignments within each party is not only determined differently by the Republicans and Democrats but also is determined differently within the parties in each House. There are thus four methods of selection. The Democratic Committee on Committees in the House, which is made up of that party's members of the House Ways and Means Committee, allocates committee seats to House Democrats; Democratic membership of the House Ways and Means Committee is determined by a vote of all the Democrats in the House. The Republicans in the House employ a Republican Committee on Committees whose membership consists of one member from each of the states, selected by the Representatives from that state. Democrats are assigned to committees in the Senate by the Democratic Floor Leader (Majority or Minority Leader, depending on the situation) who is chosen by a vote of all Democrats in the Senate (the caucus); and Republicans are assigned to committees in the Senate by the chairman of the party conference which consists of all Republican Senators.[1] Thus, the party system is loosely tied to the legislative system through the device of committee memberships.

Although the party caucuses or conferences (the membership of the party in each House) represent the political aspect of the legislative branch, the conferences have not often been successful in producing responsible party leadership. One of the few instances in which *party discipline* was enforced occurred on January 2, 1965, when the Democratic caucus (by a reported vote of 157 to 115) removed Representative John Bell Williams of Mississippi from his second place position on the House Interstate and Foreign Commerce Committee and placed his name on the bottom of the seniority list, behind that of newly-elected members, and similarly deprived Representative Albert W. Watson of South Carolina of his seniority rights. Watson had had only two years of service in the House. Both men had openly supported the Republican candidate for the Presidency in 1964. But such instances of *party discipline* are rare, and, in general, although the caucuses do select the official party leaders in both Houses and are the governing bodies of the *political parties* in Congress, their power over individuals is limited. The seniority system of committee memberships makes the task of appointment of committee members less important than it might otherwise be; most members serve continuously on the same committees. And in neither party are the members of the party bound without exception by the policy decisions made by the party caucus. The lack of strong responsible party control and the seniority system combine to make the chairmen of the standing committees the most powerful men in Congress. During the first session of the 89th Congress, both the House and the Senate disciplined individual members for misconduct. This discipline related to moral and ethical matters and not to matters involving membership in either major political party. Thus Representative Adam Clayton Powell was excluded from his seat on grounds of "misconduct." His expulsion was the first in 46 years and the fourth since the First Congress.[2] Powell was subsequently reelected and in June 1969, the Supreme Court held that the House had no power to deny a seat to an elected member, although a right to discipline did exist.

Senator Thomas Dodd was censured by the Senate, also in 1967, although he did not lose his seniority or the chairmanship of the Internal Revenue Subcommittee. Dodd was the sixth Senator to have been censured in this way. That committee chairmen have great power has been asserted above. It is to this topic that we must now turn.

[1] For a detailed analysis of this system of assignments, see Daniel M. Berman, *In Congress Assembled* (New York: The Macmillan Co., 1964), pp. 136–150.

[2] *Congressional Record*, Vol. 113, pp. 918–57, March 2, 1967.

The Powers of Committee Chairmen

Seniority and membership in the majority party are the sole determinants of committee chairmanships. And, since rank is determined by the length of a member's continuous service on a committee, those members who come from "safe" constituencies are the ones most likely to be found holding the committee chairmanships. "Safe" constituencies are those which do not often change hands; they are constituencies in which the two-party system does not exist as an effective force. The result is that when the Democrats are the majority party the Old Confederacy enjoys power in committees far out of proportion to its importance in the Union. When the Republicans control Congress, the Midwest has a powerful voice in Congress. Thus, as many observers have noted, to the extent that these sections of the country do not represent truly national attitudes (the attitude in most states of the Old Confederacy toward the issue of civil rights and the traditional isolationist tendencies of the Midwest require little comment), Congress has often reflected sectional rather than national views and attitudes. Members of Congress are not themselves in agreement on the subject of the merits of the seniority system.[3]

Bills which have been introduced are referred to committees by the presiding officer; although rulings concerning the jurisdiction of committees may be overturned by a majority vote, such action is rarely taken. Once a bill has been referred to a committee, what happens to it depends largely on the attitude of the committee chairman toward the proposed legislation. Although committees are supposed to meet regularly, the chairman may decide not to call committee meetings in order to prevent action on some bill which he opposes. The chairman also has control of hearings conducted by his committee and can decide who shall and who shall not be heard during them. This power extends even to his recognition of other members of the committee itself. In addition, the chairman has control over the committee staff and its

funds. In general, Congress appropriates money *to the committee* (hence, for the use of the committee chairman) and not to its subcommittees.

Although subcommittees may be established directly with specific jurisdiction by each House, committee chairmen often insist that subcommittees shall not have any specialized jurisdiction. In this way, a chairman may prevent establishment of centers of power within the committee itself, preventing subcommittee chairmen from becoming experts in particular subjects or acquiring interests in them. Moreover, the committee chairmen decide upon the sizes of subcommittees, who shall be on them, and whether or not to allocate funds to them.

Finally, when a bill is actually reported from a committee with a recommendation for its enactment, the chairman of the committee may control the legislative management of that bill—that is, who shall speak on the floor, how much time is to be given to whom, etc. And, in cases in which there is disagreement between the House and Senate with respect to a particular piece of legislation, so that a conference committee (consisting of members from both Houses) must be established to iron out the differences between two versions of a bill passed in each House separately, the chairman is generally the head of the group representing his particular House in the conference committee.[4]

Although committee chairmen are powerful, procedures do exist for forcing them to release proposed legislation for consideration on the floor. In the case of the House, a discharge petition relative to a particular bill can be filed by any Member. If a majority of the membership of the House signs the petition and a majority vote favors it, the bill may be brought forth from the committee. In the Senate a similar procedure exists, although no petition is required. But procedural rules (designation of particular time periods when such petitions may be made, etc.) and other devices have operated to prevent extensive use of these procedures.

---

[3] See *Organization of Congress, op. cit.,* Part 1, pp. 121–138.

[4] There are many descriptions of the power of

committee chairmen in the literature. One of the most useful and penetrating is that given by Berman, *op. cit.,* pp. 117 ff.

Supervisory and Investigatory Functions of Committees

Aside from their activities with respect to legislation, committees also perform a watchdog function relative to administrative agencies and to the Executive Branch of the government. Thus, a department of government which depends for its funds upon Congress may be called to account by a Congressional committee and made to justify its actions. Often this supervision takes the form of an investigation of the agency by means of public as well as closed hearings. For example, the National Stockpile and Naval Petroleum Reserves Subcommittee of the Senate Committee on Armed Services conducted an extensive investigation of the strategic and critical materials stockpiling policy of the United States in 1962 and 1963—partly to determine the extent to which the program had been utilized since 1953 to subsidize domestic producers of such materials, rather than for its ostensible purpose of supporting the national defense effort.[5]

The power to investigate is extremely broad. Indeed, the scope and nature of the investigative power of Congressional committees were defined by Justice Warren in 1957 as follows:

. . . The power of Congress to conduct investigations is inherent in the legislative process. That power is broad. It encompasses inquiries concerning the administration of existing laws as well as proposed or possibly needed statutes. It includes surveys of defects in our social, economic or political system for the purpose of enabling Congress to remedy them. It comprehends probes into departments of the Federal Government to expose corruption, inefficiency or waste. But, broad as is this power of inquiry, it is not unlimited. There is no general authority to expose the private affairs of individuals without justification in terms of the functions of Congress. . . . Nor is the Congress a law enforcement or trial agency. . . . No inquiry is an end in itself; it must be related to, and in furtherance of, a legitimate task of the Congress. Investigations conducted solely for the personal aggrandizement of the investigators or to "punish" those investigated are indefensible.[6]

The history of the policy of the Supreme Court with respect to this power was also neatly summarized by Justice Warren, when he wrote:

In *Kilbourn* v. *Thompson*, 103 U.S. 163, decided in 1881, an investigation had been authorized by the House of Representatives to learn the circumstances surrounding the bankruptcy of Jay Cooke and Company, in which the United States had deposited funds. The committee became particularly interested in a private real estate pool which was part of the financial structure. The Court found that the subject matter of the inquiry was "in its nature clearly judicial and therefore one in respect to which no valid legislation could be enacted." The House had thereby exceeded the limits of its own authority.

Subsequent to the decision in *Kilbourn*, until recent times, there were very few cases dealing with the investigative power. The matter came to the fore again when the Senate undertook to study corruption in handling of oil leases in the 1920's. In *McGrain* v. *Daugherty*, 273 U.S. 135 and *Sinclair* v. *United States*, 279 U.S. 263, the Court applied the precepts of *Kilbourn* to uphold the authority of the Congress to conduct the challenged investigations. The Court recognized the danger to effective and honest conduct of Government if the legislature's power to probe corruption in the executive branch were unduly hampered.

Following these important decisions, there was . . . a lull in judicial review of investigations. . . .

In the decade following World War II, there appeared a new kind of congressional inquiry unknown in prior periods of American history. Principally this was the result of the various investigations into the threat of subversion of the United States Government, but other subjects of congressional interest also contributed to the changed scene. This new phase of legislative inquiry involved a broad-scale intrusion into the lives and affairs of private citizens. It brought before the courts the novel questions of the appropriate limits of congressional inquiry.[7]

Although the investigative power of Congress has been used extensively in investigations of Communist or alleged Communist activity, it can be (and has been) used to investigate labor unions and private

---

[5] *Inquiry into the Strategic and Critical Material Stockpile of the United States* (Draft Report of the Subcommittee on National Stockpiles and Naval Petroleum Reserves, Senate Committee on Armed Services, 88th Cong., 1st sess.) (Washington, D.C.:

U.S. Government Printing Office, 1963).

[6] *Watkins* v. *United States*, 354 U.S. 178 (1957), at p. 187.

[7] *Ibid.*, at pp. 193–195.

businessmen and their affairs. The *Kilbourn* case involved captains of high finance, and the *McGrain* and *Sinclair* cases were the result of scandals arising out of graft in the making of oil leases by businessmen and Cabinet Members during the Harding administration. However, it should be noted that sometimes Congressional investigations are held primarily to gain publicity for members of the committee and its chairman. Witnesses who refuse to testify may be cited for contempt of Congress, and headlines may be made. A citation of contempt by a Congressional committee is upheld as a matter of course by the other members of the relevant House. Cases involving such citations are prosecuted by the Department of Justice, and trial is held in the federal courts. In some instances, the power to investigate has been employed to "try" individuals in the eyes of the public without giving them the safeguards of procedural due process to which they would be entitled in a regular judicial proceeding (the right of cross examination of other witnesses and other fundamental procedural rights which will be discussed in detail in the next chapter).

The problem involved in all such investigations is, as Justice Warren pointed out in the *Watkins* case, that:

> Abuses of the investigative process may imperceptibly lead to abridgement of protected freedoms. The mere summoning of a witness and compelling him to testify against his will, about his beliefs, expressions or associations is a measure of governmental interference. And when these forced revelations concern matters that are unorthodox, unpopular or even hateful to the general public, the reaction in the life of the witness may be disastrous. This effect is even more harsh when it is past beliefs, expressions, or associations that are disclosed and judged by current standards rather than those contemporary with the matters exposed.[8]

In the *Watkins* case, which involved the refusal of a defendant to disclose to the House Un-American Activities Committee (now called the Internal Security Committee) the names of others involved in collaboration with the Communist Party (although he had admitted his own acti-

vity), the Court, with one Justice (Clark) dissenting and two (Burton and Whittaker) absent, said that:

> We have no doubt that *there is no congressional power to expose for the sake of exposure*. The public is, of course, entitled to be informed concerning the workings of its government. That cannot be inflated into a general power to expose where the predominant result can only be an invasion of the private rights of individuals. . . .
>
> . . . It is the responsibility of the Congress, in the first instance, to insure that compulsory process is used only in furtherance of a legislative purpose. That requires that the instructions to an investigating committee spell out that group's jurisdiction and purpose with sufficient particularity. Those instructions are embodied in the authorizing resolution.[9]

In 1959 and 1961, however, the Court sustained convictions of contempt of Congress in actions involving this committee, by a five to four majority.[10] But in 1963, the Court held that in one case the Committee had violated its own rules of procedure; and in 1966 it unanimously held that an essential element of a contempt conviction in such a case is a showing of "a clear line of authority from the House to the questioning body" that the particular investigation being challenged is authorized.[11] These two cases represent a return to the principle of the *Watkins* case.

An interesting case involving alleged interference by two congressional committees with the judicial aspect of the power of the Federal Trade Commission was decided by the Court of Appeals for the Fifth Circuit in 1966. Congressional committees do not necessarily restrict their activities to investigation of alleged subversive activities but may also embark upon investigations of business firms, and precedents set in one type of case may apply also to the other. The 1966 case involved the question of whether or not acquisition by the Pillsbury Company of several competitors' assets violated the antitrust laws. In the words of the Court of Appeals the case involved a number of different issues. Of these issues:

> . . . The third question is whether there were other violations of procedural due process of

---

[8] *Ibid.*, at p. 197.

[9] *Ibid.*, at pp. 200–201. (Italics mine.)

[10] See *Barenblatt* v. *United States*, 360 U.S. 110 (1959); *Braden* v. *United States*, 365 U.S. 431 (1961);

Wilkinson v. *United States*, 365 U.S. 399 (1961).

[11] *Yellin* v. *United States*, 374 U.S. 109 (1963) and *Gojack* v. *United States*, 384 U.S. 702 (1966).

such a nature as to seriously infect the proceedings in such a manner as to require a reversal of the Commission's order. . . .

Since a resolution of one of the attacks made under the procedural due process heading, if decided favorably to Pillsbury, would make unnecessary our consideration of any of the other matters, we shall deal with that first. It is the alleged improper interference by committees of Congress with the decisional process of the Federal Trade Commission while the *Pillsbury* case was pending before it. The alleged interference, we hasten to add, was not alleged improper influence behind closed doors but was rather interference in the nature of questions and statements made by members of two Senate and House subcommittees having responsibility for legislation dealing with antitrust matters all clearly spread upon the record.

Briefly stated, the criticism of the conduct of the members of the House and Senate arises in this manner: following the filing of the complaint against Pillsbury on June 16, 1952, the Government undertook to make out its case in chief. On April 22, 1953, the hearing examiner granted Pillsbury's motion to dismiss. . . . On appeal, the Commission reversed by an order dated December 21, 1953. Thereafter, the Pillsbury Company undertook to introduce its evidence, and evidence for both parties continued to be received for the next several years.

During the months of May and June, 1955, hearings were held before the subcommittee on antitrust and monopoly of the Committee of the Judiciary of the United States Senate, and before the antitrust subcommittee of the Committee on Judiciary of the House of Representatives. At these hearings, Mr. Howrey, the then Chairman of the Commission, and several of the members of his staff, appeared including Mr. Kintner, the then General Counsel and later Chairman of the Commission, who wrote the final opinion from which this appeal is prosecuted.

It is to be noted that these hearings were held after the Commission had issued its interlocutory order, but long before the examiner made his Initial Decision on the merits, and, of course, before the Commission made its Final Decision in 1960.

In this interlocutory opinion of the Commission, reversing the dismissal of the Pillsbury case by the examiner, the Commission rejected an argument made by the Government (counsel supporting the complaint) to the effect that where a showing that a company in the field having a substantial share of the business of the industry acquires the assets of competitors so that the resulting merged entity would meet the "substantiality" test of *Standard Oil Co. of California* v. *United States*, 337 U.S. 293, no further proof need be introduced in support of the complaint. This is what will be hereafter spoken of as the "per se" doctrine. The Commission in its order reversing the order of dismissal rejected this contention and expressly held that the per se doctrine did not apply under Section 7, as amended.

The posture of the case at the time of Mr. Howrey's appearance before the Senate Committee, therefore, was that the Commission had found sufficient evidence to make a prima facie case of acquisition of competitors by a company having a substantial share of the business in the specified fields of industry, and a prima facie case of other conditions in the industry to make out an affirmative case of a "substantial lessening of competition." The Commission had, thus, given Pillsbury an opportunity to introduce countervailing evidence. Some had already been introduced and the prospects were that this would continue for a considerable period of time.

When Chairman Howrey appeared before the Senate subcommittee on June 1, 1955, he met a barrage of questioning by the members of the committee challenging his view of the requirements of Section 7 and the application of the per se doctrine announced by the Supreme Court in the *Standard Stations* case, *Standard Oil Co. of California* v. *United States*, 337 U.S. 293 (1949), in a Clayton Act Section 3 case, to Section 7 proceedings. A number of the members of the committee challenged the correctness of his and the Commission's position in holding that a mere showing of a substantial increase in the share of the market after merger would not be sufficient to satisfy the requirement of Section 7 of a showing that "the effect of such acquisition may be substantially to lessen competition."

Much of the questioning criticized by the petitioner here is in the nature of questions and comments by members of the committee in which they forcefully expressed their own opinions that the per se doctrine should apply and that it was the intent of Congress that it should apply.

The thrust of the comments and questions was that there was no need to carry on the long and complicated inquiry into all of the surrounding matters reflecting on the conditions in the industry if the Commission should determine that there was a substantial acquisition by a substantial member of the industry; that monopolies ought to be stopped quickly, and that Congress did not intend the Commission to apply the "rule of reason" in Section 7 proceedings.

The questions were so probing that Mr. Howrey, the chairman of the Commission, announced to chairman Kefauver of the subcommittee that he would have to disqualify himself from further participation in the Pillsbury case. . . .[12]

After considering in detail the Senate and House subcommittee hearings referred to above, the Court of Appeals held:

> In view of the inordinate lapse of time in this proceeding, brought to undo what was done by mergers completed in 1951, we are naturally loathe to frustrate the proceedings at this late date. However, common justice to a litigant requires that we invalidate the order entered by a quasi-judicial tribunal that was importuned by members of the United States Senate, however innocent they intended their conduct to be, to arrive at the ultimate conclusion which they did reach.[13]

In general, despite this case, the powers of Congressional investigatory committees must be included among the working rules according to which economic activity is undertaken, and such investigations are often the source of much data concerning the actual activities of labor unions and business firms in the United States. The discussion of the activities of the natural gas producers with respect to the Kerr-Mills Bill in the preceding chapter, for example, was based entirely on materials resulting from such an investigation. Congressional investigations and reports based on them are also often a source of information concerning the activities of regulatory agencies. Sometimes, however, the final reports are merely self-serving political documents, and a reader is well-advised to examine carefully the hearings on which they are based.

Procedural Obstacles

The fact that committee chairmen are very powerful is not the only obstacle to the enactment of legislation in the Congress, Even though procedures exist for discharge of a bill from a recalcitrant committee, it does not follow that the bill will thereafter come to a vote in the relevant chamber. Other procedural obstacles must also be overcome. The most important of these are the power of the Rules Committee in the House and the provisions of the cloture rule (for limiting debate) in the Senate.

The House Rules Committee. Because of the very size of the House (435 members), the conditions under which legislation is to be considered on the floor must be determined by some sort of rules. Consequently, in the case of most bills (exceptions include the important category of bills which have been referred to the Appropriations and to the Ways and Means Committees, commonly referred to as "money bills"), a procedure has been adopted under which bills are referred to the Committee on Rules. This committee has at times had the sole power to decide upon the questions of whether or not, and, if so, under what conditions, a bill would be considered. Thus, the House Rules Committee has in the past often been and may again in the future be in a strategic position to kill off legislation which its members (and especially its chairman) do not like or to require sponsors of a bill to accept amendments in order to guarantee that the Rules Committee will act favorably on the bill and recommend that it be considered on the floor. Berman has pointed out that it does not necessarily follow that the Chairman of the House Rules Committee has been an unpopular fellow; on the contrary, a congressman who may not personally be in favor of a piece of legislation which his constituents strongly support may even importune the Rules Committee to bury a bill in order to avoid having to commit himself on the measure.[14] For this reason, attempts to limit the power of the Rules Committee have always resulted in bitter floor fights.

In the past, various devices have existed for freeing a bill from control by the Rules Committee and for bringing it to the floor. Most of these have required a majority vote of the House (which is difficult to obtain on controversial measures) or have been subject to delaying tactics on the part of opponents of the legislation involved.[15] Most observers have noted that, since 1937, a coalition of Southern Democrats and conservative Republicans has existed in the House Rules Committee, and although the power of the Committee was somewhat curtailed in 1965, this coalition successfully

[12] *The Pillsbury Co.* v. *Federal Trade Commission,* 354 F. 2d 952 (1966), pp. 954–956.

[13] *Ibid.,* pp. 9–10.

[14] Berman, *op. cit.,* pp. 205 ff.

[15] For a discussion of these procedures and the difficulties involved in attempting to use them, see William R. MacKaye, *A New Coalition Takes Control: The House Rules Committee Fight of 1961* (Case No. 29 in the *Eagleton Institute Cases in Practical Politics*) (New York: McGraw-Hill Book Co., Inc., 1963), p. 6.

blocked many measures proposed by the incumbent administrations.

In 1949, a Democratic majority in the House succeeded in forcing an amendment to the rules under which chairmen of the relevant legislative committees were allowed two days each month in which to call up for consideration on the floor any bills which had been in the hands of the Rules Committee for 21 days without having been assigned a rule of procedure. But, in 1951, this so-called "21 day rule" was repealed when a more conservative group had again attained control over the House. However, on January 4, 1965, the Speaker was given power to call up bills which have been in the hands of the Rules Committee for 21 days.[16] On the basis of past experience, one may conclude that the type of rule in force at any time depends on the political complexion of the House at the time the rules for a particular Congress are adopted.

Other devices have also been employed in an attempt to insure that legislation is not bottled up or killed off by a recalcitrant Rules Committee. In 1961, when the 21 day rule was not in force, largely as a result of pressures exerted by the Speaker of the House (then 79 year-old) Sam Rayburn— who actually took the floor and staked his own prestige on the outcome and eventually won—and the Kennedy Administration, membership of the House Rules Committee was increased to fifteen members despite the bitter opposition of the committee's chairman (then 78 year old) Howard W. Smith, a Democrat from Virginia who worked closely with the Minority Leader, Republican Charles Halleck. Among those who were reported as opposed to the increase in membership and in support of the conservative position—the position of no change —were the "National Association of Manufacturers, the United States Chamber of Commerce, the American Farm Bureau Federation and the Southern States Industrial Council . . . the American Medical Association and the National Association of Real Estate Boards," while among those reported as supporting the Rayburn position were the "AFL-CIO, the National

Education Association and other less influential lobbying groups."[17]

The decision to increase the number of members of the Rules Committee—rather than to attempt to "purge" conservative committee members opposed to the administration's programs, that is, to have the party caucus remove them from the Committee and replace them by members who were more likely to support the Democratic leadership—was believed by the party leaders to be less likely to produce long-lasting resentments.[18] But, as MacKaye pointed out, this change in the size of the Rules Committee produced no change in its powers.[19] This Committee has, therefore, remained a powerful voice in the determination of contemporary working rules according to which economic activity is undertaken in the United States today, although its power is somewhat less in sessions in which a "21 day rule" like that adopted in 1965 is in force.

The Cloture Rule in the Senate. The Senate operates differently from the House. In the Senate, there is a rule that debate is to be unlimited unless "cloture" is invoked. The present cloture rule (Senate Rule XXII) is as follows: a petition signed by sixteen Senators may be filed that a limitation be imposed on debate in the Senate. Two days after the petition is filed, the Senate votes on question. *If two-thirds of those present and voting* support the petition, further comments on the proposed legislation and on any amendments to it are limited to one hour on the part of any single Senator. In the absence of cloture, filibusters can be and have been employed by Senators opposing the enactment of particular pieces of legislation. (The object of a filibuster is, of course, to prevent a vote from being taken by not allowing the Senate to transact any business until the bill, to which those conducting the filibuster object, is laid aside.) There have been numerous attempts to change the conditions under which cloture can be imposed—for example, several attempts have been made to make it possible to limit debate by a simple majority of those present and voting rather than by a

---

[16] *Congressional Record,* Vol. III, pp. 19–23 (Jan. 4, 1965).

[17] MacKaye, *op. cit.,* pp. 22–23.

[18] *Ibid.,* p. 13 ff.

[19] *Ibid.,* p. 28. Although the "Rayburn Resolution" was effective only during the 87th Congress, the change was made permanent on January 9, 1963.

two-thirds majority—but none of these has succeeded.[20]

Thus, in the Senate, it is possible for a determined minority to frustrate the will of a *simple* majority. It is not, however, possible for such a minority to frustrate the will of a *two-thirds* majority, and cloture was imposed during the debate on legislation to create a private minopoly to exploit space communications in 1962, as well as during debate on civil rights legislation in 1964 and 1965 and during debate on open housing legislation in 1968. In the past, opponents of civil rights legislation have relied on the rule to oppose such legislation. Those favoring such legislation have, therefore, been strongly opposed to the rule. Thus, enactment of the 1964 Civil Rights Act somewhat diminished opposition to the rule from this source, although objections arising from other sources still exist. Some observers have argued that, if the will of a minority is to be overridden, it ought to be clearly demonstrated that that minority is very small; and therefore—particularly in the light of the fact that cloture was actually imposed according to the present rule in 1962, 1964, 1965, and 1968—the two-thirds majority rule is a sound one.

In any case, it is apparent that the procedures of the House Rules Committee and the difficulty of limiting debate in the Senate may operate to frustrate proposals stemming from the Executive Branch. Since Members of the House tend primarily to represent the narrow, sectional interests of the district to which they owe their positions and since, perhaps to a somewhat lesser extent, Senators also do so on many issues, these procedural rules do constitute a device by means of which the programs proposed by a President may be defeated. The President, of course, depends for his election to office upon his appeal to voters in tho.e states which have a majority of electoral votes rather than upon the support of voters in a single state or in a particular congressional district within a state, and therefore he must inevitably represent a much broader interest. Thus he must conceive of himself as "President of all the people."

The Congressional Record; Congressional Agencies

The *Congressional Record* contains the proceedings of Congress and is issued daily when Congress is in session. Not everything which appears in the *Record* is spoken on the floor of the Houses of Congress; often a member will obtain unanimous consent (according to a routine procedure) to have his remarks printed in the *Record* as though they had been delivered on the floor in person. (He may also include materials supplied to him by pressure groups.) The following statement by Representative O'Hara describing the *Record* is in point:

3. *The Congressional Record*

The *Congressional Record* is a shambles, full of utterances never uttered and statements never made. It can be read only by an accomplished speed reader who then would experience great difficulty in distinguishing fact from fiction.

The state of the Congressional Record not only makes it difficult for interested observers to assess the actions of the Congress but forces reliance upon contemporary accounts which are themselves often based upon incomplete information, faulty evaluation, and the personal political preferences of their authors. Worse, it places the executive and judicial branches of our Government in great difficulty when they seek to define the intention of Congress in applying the laws.

To remedy these failures it is necessary to make the Congressional Record more readable and to make it more accurately reflect our proceedings. These objectives can be obtained by:

A. Limiting the body of the Record to a verbatim report of the proceedings. To further this objective, remarks made before the House and Senate should be transcribed by the Reporters of Debate and by tape recording which could be used as the primary and authoritative source and erased after any doubts about the actual transcript have been removed.

B. A revised digest of the Record indicating in chronological sequence the names of Members speaking on each subject and briefly summarizing the arguments made by them and the conclusions reached by them.

---

[20] For a description of one of these attempts, as well as for the history of the question of whether the cloture rule applies to the adoption of rules for a new session, see Alan Rosenthal, *Toward Majority*

Rule in the United States Senate (Case No. 25 in the *Eagleton Institute Cases in Practical Politics*) (New York: McGraw-Hill Book Co., Inc., 1962).

C. Printing of the Record in larger, more readable type.

A separate section of the Record could be reserved for statements made in a context other than in debate and amendment of the legislation under consideration and for statements with regard to the bill under consideration but not actually delivered.[21]

Thus, although the student should be aware of the limitations involved in making use of it, he should nevertheless know that the *Record* is an original source of much information concerning the work of Congress and he should be familiar with it. Various unofficial commercial publications, such as the *Congressional Quarterly* and the *Congressional Digest*, are also available; these contain information concerning pending legislation and other materials (reports of lobbying expenditures, appropriations of funds to committees, action on legislation, etc.).

Among the more important Congressional agencies are the General Accounting Office ("created to assist the Congress in providing legislative control over the receipt, disbursement, and application of public funds"); the Government Printing Office (which handles the printing and sale of all official government documents); the Library of Congress (a national library, whose "Reference Service" is often the source of speeches by members of Congress); and the Tariff Commission (which "investigates and reports upon tariff and trade matters" primarily with a view to determining "injury" to American producers from foreign imports "at the request of the President, either branch of Congress, the House Committee on Ways and Means or the Senate Committee on Finance").

B. CHANGES IN LAW: THE EXECUTIVE BRANCH

The Nature and Scope of the Presidency

In 1963, Theodore Sorenson (who was then Special Counsel to President Kennedy) emphasized the fact that White House decision-making was an *art and not a science*. He emphasized the importance of judgment in the exercise of this art and rejected the idea that guides to decision-making in private business could be used by the President—on grounds that the scope of Presidential decision-making could not be matched in any large corporation.[22]

Probably one of the outstanding academic authorities on the powers and functions of the President is Clinton Rossiter. He has identified the following ten functions performed by the President: (1) Chief of State (by acting as the ceremonial head of government); (2) Chief Executive (in supervising the day-to-day activities of the Executive Branch); (3) Commander-in-Chief (of the military forces); (4) Chief Diplomat (in formulating and executing foreign policy and conducting foreign affairs); (5) Chief Legislator (by guiding Congress in its law-making activity); (6) Chief of the Party (by serving as number one political boss in his party); (7) Voice of the People (in calling the attention of the nation to its "unfinished business"); (8) Protector of the Peace (in taking actions in times of national disaster to restore domestic order); (9) Manager of Prosperity (by seeking to maintain full employment, high level production, a high rate of growth, price stability, etc.); and (10) World Leader (in serving as the leader of the "Free World").[23]

All these functions are important. However, from the point of view of the subject matter of this chapter, the President's function as Manager of Prosperity may involve action on his part to induce the Congress to adopt new legislation, and his role as Chief Diplomat may require executive action involving negotiation of an international Executive Agreement. Therefore, the roles of the President as Chief Legislator and as Chief Executive are of paramount importance in any examination of the formal sources of change and the techniques by means of which changes in working rules occur in the United States. It is these two roles which will be examined in detail shortly.

The office of the Presidency is often

---

[21] *Organization of Congress, op. cit.*, Part 4, p. 570.

[22] Theodore C. Sorenson, *Decision-Making in the White House* (New York: Columbia University Press, 1963), pp. 10–11. This book contains a foreword by President Kennedy.

[23] Clinton P. Rossiter, *The American Presidency* (2d ed.: New York: Harcourt, Brace and World, Inc., 1960).

referred to as "the world's most demanding job." Obviously the President cannot be familiar with the detailed operation of every government department, program, or agency, and he must rely on advisors and assistants. In 1939, numerous agencies were transferred to the Executive Office of the President. One of the subdivisions of the latter is the White House Office. According to the *United States Government Organization Manual*, this office "facilitates and maintains communications with the Congress" as well as with the heads of the executive departments and agencies and with the press. What the language in quotation marks really means is that this office does the President's lobbying in Congress. From the point of view of this book, the Bureau of the Budget, the Council of Economic Advisors, and the Office for Trade Negotiations also require additional attention, and they, too, will be considered later in the chapter. There are 12 Executive Departments. The newest is the Department of Transportation, created in October 1966. Its principal, but not sole, predecessor was the Office of the Undersecretary of Commerce for Transportation. (This new Executive Department is discussed further in Chapter 26 of this book.) The others include the Department of State, of the Treasury, of Defense, of Justice, of Agriculture, of Commerce, of Labor, of Health, Education and Welfare, of Housing and Urban Development, of Interior, and the Post Office Department.

The President as Chief Legislator

Although the President has the power to submit proposals for legislation to Congress, he has no formal authority to force Congress to adopt his proposals. He is thus driven to the use of informal techniques, including persuasion, granting favors or withholding them, and television broadcasts to induce the electorate to exert pressure upon members of Congress.[24] If he enjoys a majority in both Houses of Congress and if he has swept that majority into office with him, the President may enjoy a "honeymoon" period of friendly relations with the Congress during the early part of his administration; but "honeymoons" do not last forever, and sometimes they do not even begin.

Origin and Clearance of Proposed Legislation in the Executive Branch: The Bureau of the Budget. Within the Executive Branch, proposals for legislation may arise within any of the Departments or agencies. Also, under existing legislation, bills introduced in the Congress without prior consultation with the Executive Branch must be sent by the relevant committee chairman to the relevant agencies for comment.

In 1921 Congress created the Bureau of the Budget within the Department of the Treasury, and in 1939 this agency was made a part of the Executive Office of the President. Initially, the Bureau was "launched with a dual type of responsibility. Its functions were to be administrative as well as budgetary." Under the direction of its first head, Charles G. Dawes, the Bureau undertook almost immediately "to examine the President's legislative proposals for their fiscal implications."[25] After the Bureau was transferred to the Executive Office of the President, its administrative functions expanded to include an examination of *all* legislation, and among its contemporary duties is that of assisting the President "by clearing and coordinating departmental advice on proposed legislation and by making recommendations as to Presidential action on legislative enactments." Thus, positions on all proposed or pending legislation (irrespective of how it originated) taken by various Departments within the Executive Branch are coordinated, and differences are ironed out, if possible, under the leadership of officials of the Bureau of the Budget. The Bureau undertakes to insure, insofar as it is possible, that the administration will speak with a single voice to the Congress. But it is not always successful in attaining this objective.

A Case Study of an Inter-Agency Dispute. A case in point is that of the attempt by the Eisenhower administration and especially by its Budget Director, Joseph Dodge, to limit the expansion of the electric power production facilities of the Tennessee Valley Authority (TVA) between 1953 and 1955. The Administration opposed the proposed expansion and in 1953 reduced the TVA's budget request for funds to build additional steam generating facilities. Gordon Clapp,

---

who was then head of the TVA, suggested a compromise, under which the Atomic Energy Commission (AEC) would purchase power from private sources, releasing to the TVA, for supply elsewhere, power which was currently being used by the AEC. The Administration (under the leadership of Dodge) developed an alternative plan under which private utility companies (who feared the future competition of cheap electric power which would be produced by TVA if its steam generating facilities were expanded) would contract with the AEC but would actually deliver the power to the TVA for use at Memphis (the point of ultimate consumption). The effect of this proposal would have been to limit the TVA's future operations to that of an electric power *distribution* company which purchased power from private producing companies rather than to enable it to expand production as originally requested. Such a profitable compromise was acceptable to the private power companies interested in limiting the future expansion of TVA's productive facilities.

The result of these maneuvers was a battle in Congress and sharp disputes among various agencies within the Executive Branch. Charges of conflict of interest, graft, and corruption were made. The final outcome was the TVA Revenue Bond Act of 1959 under which the TVA must now seek funds for expansion in the open market, while, at the same time, expansion of its productive facilities is limited by the amount of capital it can raise in this way. In other words, the ultimate solution was a compromise, according to which TVA is no longer dependent upon Congress (or upon requests submitted through the Bureau of the Budget for funds for capital expansion), but at the same time its power to expand is limited by the capital market.[26] The compromise thus involved the adoption of market price as a measure of the social value of additional TVA facilities.

However, in 1968 the Supreme Court interpreted this legislation, which barred the TVA from expanding its sales outside "the area for which the Corporation [TVA]

or its distributors were the primary source of supply on July 1, 1957." The Court held that the purpose of this language was to "control" but not to prohibit altogether the expansion of TVA's services and that the matter of whether or not an "area" fell within the terms of the exception specified by the statute might be determined administratively by the TVA itself; such a determination would be upheld if it "fell within the permissible range of choices contemplated by the statute" and was supported by "reasonable economic and technical evidence."[27]

The types of pressures which the President may exert are, for the most part, independent of the objectives which the use of those pressures seeks to attain. They can be exerted in an attempt to secure civil rights legislation; and they can be used to induce Congress to combat poverty or to reduce (or raise) taxes in accordance with an administration's belief that such tax reductions will stimulate employment and growth. Development of policies to accomplish the last objectives may originate from the activities of the Council of Economic Advisors, although the latter is not solely responsible for developing them.

The Council of Economic Advisors. The Council of Economic Advisors was created by the Employment Act of 1946 and consists of three members appointed by the President with the advice and consent of the Senate. In recent years the Council has been becoming more influential, particularly in gaining acceptance by the President and Congress of its recommendations: President Johnson's War Against Poverty was announced in the *Annual Economic Report* of January 1964, and the tax cut legislation of 1964 was strongly advocated in the same document as it had been in the *Report* for 1963.

Section 2 of the Employment Act of 1946 states that:

... it is the continuing policy and responsibility of the Federal Government to use all practicable means consistent with its needs and obligations and other essential considerations of national policy, with the assistance and cooperation of industry, agriculture, labor, and

[26] An interesting account of the struggle between the opposing forces and of the possible conflict of interest involved can be found in Aaron Wildavsky, *Dixon-Yates: A Study in Power Politics* (New Haven:

Yale University Press, 1962).

[27] *Hardin* v. *Kentucky Utilities Co.*, 390 U.S. 1 (1968), pp. 8–13.

State and local governments, to coordinate and utilize all its plans, functions, and resources for the purpose of creating and maintaining, in a manner calculated to foster and promote free competitive enterprise and the general welfare, conditions under which there will be afforded useful employment opportunities, including self-employment, for those able, willing, and seeking to work, and to promote maximum employment, production, and purchasing power.[28]

This language is obviously that of compromise. The policy specified is one of the use of "all practicable means consistent with . . . needs and obligations," a phrase which can mean all things to all men. Similarly, the policy envisages the "assistance and cooperation" of every major economic interest group and of governmental units at every level. The final Act was less explicit than those who strongly advocated it had hoped it would be; but it was more explicit than those who opposed it had wished it to be. Except for the establishment of the Council of Economic Advisors as part of the President's staff, the Act contained no provisions for implementing a policy of full employment. To the extent that the administration in power adopts measures recommended by the Council to attain full employment, the decision to adopt the measures has been a normal incident of the political process rather than a direct result of the 1946 legislation. Indeed, many of the same policies might have been adopted without the existence of such legislation. During the Kennedy and Johnson administrations the Council became a much more significant influence than it had been in earlier administrations. (Many observers assert that it was Professor Walter Heller who converted both Presidents Kennedy and Johnson to a belief in the "New Economics.")

Since one of our concerns in this chapter is the role of the President as Chief Legislator, our mention of the Council of Economic Advisors has been limited to a consideration of the *role and position* of the Council within the Executive Branch and its function as a source or an originator of legislation. Later, in Part III of this book we will consider some of the substantive aspects of the work of the Council. A new agency, the Environmental Quality Coun-

cil, was added to the President's staff by law in 1970. Its work is discussed in Chapter 28 later.

The techniques of originating and obtaining support for legislation desired by the Executive Branch ("the President") but which Congress must eventually adopt or reject have occupied our attention thus far in this chapter. There is also another sense in which the President may engage in legislative activity: he may issue orders and legislate directly in performing his functions. This fact is nowhere more evident than in his performance of the function of Chief Executive.

The President as Chief Executive: Legislation by Executive Order and Agreement

Executive Orders. In addition to the duties mentioned earlier, the Bureau of the Budget has the responsibility for securing agreement among the various departments to the texts of proposed Executive Orders and Proclamations and, where necessary, of preparing such orders. Executive Orders are themselves legislative acts performed by the Executive Branch. That is, Congress often adopts broad legislative policy statements and delegates the authority for the implementation of such policies to the President. This implementation generally takes the form of an Executive Order, published in the *Federal Register* which is issued daily. Thus, for example, on January 3, 1951, President Truman issued Executive Order 10200, "Establishing the Defense Production Administration," a new agency, pursuant to the Defense Production Act of 1950, in order to deal with certain production problems arising out of the Korean emergency.[29]

Presidential Prerogative. The President also has power to issue Executive Orders by virtue of Article II of the Constitution which makes him Commander-in-Chief of the Army and Navy of the United States. But precisely how far the Supreme Court will sustain an Executive Order not based on a specific Congressional delegation of authority is an unsettled issue. As has been noted in Chapter 4, in 1952, during the Korean war, a labor dispute between the major steel producers and their employees

[28] Public Law 304, 79th Cong., 2d sess. (1946).

[29] 16 *Federal Register* 61 (Jan. 3, 1951).

concerning the content of collective bargaining agreements resulted in the calling of a nationwide steel strike, despite efforts on the part of the government to bring about a settlement. President Truman, *without relying on any specific delegation of power from the Congress*, issued an order directing the Secretary of Commerce to take possession of and to operate the steel mills. As noted in Chapter 4, in holding the Executive Order unconstitutional, the members of the Supreme Court offered six concurring opinions and a dissenting opinion in a six to three decision.[30] Justice Black, who took the view that the Order was unconstitutional, wrote, among other things:

The President's order does not direct that a congressional policy be executed in a manner prescribed by Congress—it directs that a presidential policy be executed in a manner prescribed by the President. The preamble of the order itself, like that of many statutes, sets out reasons why the President believes certain policies should be adopted, proclaims these policies as rules of conduct to be followed, and again, like a statute, authorizes a government official to promulgate additional rules and regulations consistent with the policy proclaimed and needed to carry that policy into execution. . . . The Constitution does not subject . . . lawmaking power of Congress to presidential or military supervision or control.[31]

That the issue was not finally settled by this case is clear from Justice Frankfurter's concurring opinion. He wrote:

The issue before us can be met, and therefore should be, without attempting to define the President's powers comprehensively. I shall not attempt to delineate what belongs to him by virtue of his office beyond the power even of Congress to contract; what authority belongs to him until Congress acts; what kind of problems may be dealt with either by the Congress or by both . . .; what power must be exercised by Congress and cannot be delegated to the President. . . . The judiciary may, as this case proves, have to intervene in determining where authority lies between the democratic forces in our scheme of government.[32]

Executive Agreements. The conduct of the foreign relations of this country is also an Executive function; and, therefore, the President has the power to enter into certain types of international agreements without the specific approval of Congress or of the Senate in particular. Such international agreements are known as "self-executing" Executive Agreements. (Agreements settling private claims are an example.) In addition, there may be international Executive Agreements made pursuant to some express delegation of power by the Congress.

In exercising the power to make Executive Agreements of these two types, the President engages in legislative functions which often produce changes in working rules. Indeed, the entire reciprocal trade agreements program has been implemented by means of an Executive Agreement known as the General Agreement on Tariffs and Trade (GATT). This program has become so important in recent years that the Office of the Special Representative for Trade Negotiations was established within the Executive Office of the President in 1963 to assist the President in carrying out the trade agreements program and in dealing with matters involving international commodity agreements. The tariff negotiations which have been conducted under the General Agreement have been undertaken pursuant to a delegation of authority contained in an amendment to the Tariff Act of 1934, a matter which will be considered further in Chapter 8.

In general, the Supreme Court has been willing to go quite far to sustain delegations of authority by Congress to the President to make such international agreements. Thus, for example, in 1936 the Court sustained the validity of an Executive Order prohibiting exportation of arms and ammunition from the United States to Bolivia. The Order (a Proclamation) had been issued by the President pursuant to a Joint Resolution of Congress providing him with that authority.[33]

Another example of the way in which international Presidential legislation may affect the working rules of economic activity can be found in the following

---

[30] *Youngstown Sheet and Tube Co.* v. *Sawyer*, 343 U.S. 579 (1951). Justices Black, Jackson, Douglas, Frankfurter, Burton, and Clark wrote concurring opinions, and Justice Vinson wrote a dissenting opinion in which Justices Reed and Minton joined.

[31] *Ibid.*, at pp. 587–588.
[32] *Ibid.*, at p. 597.
[33] *United States* v. *Curtiss-Wright Export Corp.*, 299 U.S. 304 (1936).

occurrence: in December 1950 President Truman and Prime Minister Attlee (England) conferred with respect to the then-current problem of shortage of raw materials (occasioned by the Korean emergency and United States stockpile policy) and produced an agreement which resulted in the establishment of the International Materials Conference, an arrangement under which steps were taken to allocate internationally according to principles of "equitable distribution" those raw materials which were then in short supply.[34]

Thus, it is clear that changes in law do result from activities of the Executive Branch. The pure separation of powers theory, discussed in the preceding chapter, has no meaning in the real world of political life in the United States. And the following examination of the activities of the administrative regulatory agencies demonstrates that such agencies, too, not only engage in legislative activities but also perform judicial functions to produce changes in law.

C. CHANGES IN LAW: ADMINISTRATIVE AGENCIES

Vagueness of the Classification

The table of contents of the *United States Government Organization Manual* contains an enumeration of "independent offices and establishments." But, except for such a specific enumeration the term "independent" is meaningless, just as the term "regulatory" agency is also incapable of precise definition. One might, for example, select the Interstate Commerce Commission (ICC), the Civil Aeronautics Board (CAB), the Federal Power Commission (FPC), the Federal Communications Commission (FCC), the Federal Trade Commission (FTC), the National Labor Relations Board (NLRB), and the Securities and Exchange Commission (SEC) for study. This specific group was in fact selected for study by Judge James M. Landis in his *Report on Regulatory Agencies to the President-*

Elect (Kennedy) in 1960.[35] Other writers list all or most of the federal agencies under the heading of "Planning Agencies"; and still others list the seven agencies named above, plus the Federal Reserve Board (FRB) and such other agencies as strike their fancies.

The agencies listed above do have some particular problems in common; and along with certain offices that are within Executive Departments, such as the Food and Drug Administration (FDA) of the Department of Health, Education, and Welfare and the Commodity Exchange Authority (CEA) of the Department of Agriculture, they all engage in legislative, executive, and judicial functions. They are all also concerned primarily with regulating the activities of particular industries or groups of industries. Establishments such as the Tennessee Valley Authority (TVA) and the Atomic Energy Commission (AEC) are actually owners of or contractors for productive facilities rather than regulatory bodies, while the General Services Administration (GSA) is in fact the housekeeping and purchasing agent for the government. Any classification of "independent" agencies must be misleading, since any attempt to specify "regulatory" agencies must eventually end up in an arbitrary list. None of these agencies is really completely independent of the President nor of Congress and all exercise some degree of executive, legislative, and judicial power: even the Board of Commissioners of the District of Columbia exercises the usual authority of a municipal government. In Parts II and III of this book, there will be further detailed discussion of most of the agencies and establishments mentioned above.

Relationship to Executive and Legislative Branches

These agencies are all related to the Executive Branch in at least five different ways: (1) the President appoints the commissioners, but according to a 1934 Supreme Court case, if the relevant statute expressly prohibits their removal except for "cause,"

---

[34] See my article, "The International Materials Conference in Retrospect," *Quarterly Journal of Economics*, Vol. LXXI (May, 1957), pp. 267–288.

[35] James M. Landis, *Report on Regulatory Agencies to the President-Elect* (reproduced as a Committee

Print by the Subcommittee on Administrative Practice and Procedure, Senate Judiciary Committee, 86th Cong., 2d sess.) (Washington, D.C.: U.S. Government Printing Office, 1960).

he cannot remove them on "capricious" grounds.[36] The terms of office of commissioners are staggered, and some officials submit their resignations as a matter of course whenever a newly-elected President is inaugurated. (2) Except in the case of the TVA under the TVA Revenue Bond Act of 1959, the Bureau of the Budget controls the budget requests of these agencies. (3) Legislative proposals originating in the various agencies and establishments must be submitted to Congress through the Bureau of the Budget. (4) In many cases, the President has the power to designate one of the commissioners as Chairman of the Commission. Finally, (5) there may be informal consultation between the White House and individual commissioners or the chairman of a commission.

It must also be noted in the present context that in his January 1969 *Economic Report*, President Johnson recommended to Congress that "The term of the Chairman of the Federal Reserve Board should be appropriately geared to that of the President to provide further assurance of harmonious policy coordination," that is, to insure that the Board would adopt administration policy with regard to monetary controls and not adopt monetary policies contrary to the fiscal policies adopted by the administration as it has on some occasions in the past, a matter further discussed in Chapter 31.

In August 1969, President Nixon sent Reorganization Plan No. 1 to Congress calling for reorganization of the Interstate Commerce Commission. Under the plan, the President would, for the first time, have the power to appoint the Chairman of the Commission.

Obviously, neither President Johnson nor President Nixon believed that the administrative agencies should really be independent of the executive branch.

These agencies are all also subject to supervision by Congress in much the same way as that in which the twelve Executive Departments are subject to such supervision; and, with the partial exception in the case of the TVA mentioned above and also with the exception of the Federal Reserve Board, they depend on Congress for funds. Thus, these agencies are each related to Congress through *at least* two different committees: the Appropriations or Finance Committees; and the Senate and House standing committees having jurisdiction over the subject matter with which the particular agency is concerned.

The Nature of the Regulatory Process

Lack of Coordinated Policies. "The process of regulation," says Marver Bernstein, "is unavoidably political."[37] In some cases, Congress has been unable or unwilling to specify the goals of regulation, and the agencies have failed, accordingly, to develop broad policies in such areas. Moreover, in some areas—for example, in the area of communications—numerous agencies such as the Federal Communications Commission, the Department of State, the National Aeronautics and Space Administration, the Department of Defense, and the Federal Aeronautics Administration all have an interest in the solution of problems. Yet effective interagency coordination does not always exist.

It may be, however, that the lack of broad policies in some cases is merely a reflection of the confusion which arises out of the fiction that these agencies really are independent at the policy-making level. Aside from the instances in which policy is made in the course of adversary proceedings in cases contesting a particular commission's order or rulings, a frank and wide-spread recognition of the political nature at the policy level of the regulatory process has long been overdue. The solution to the problem of expansion of the TVA's productive facilities, discussed earlier in this chapter, was brought about as a compromise of conflicting interests in the political arena, and it may be that a similar compromise solution to the problem of formulation of basic regulatory policies is the only one possible. (This question will also be considered further in Part III.)

Influence of Lobbies and Pressure Groups. In the absence of basic solutions of this sort,

[36] *Humphrey's Executor* v. *United States*, 195 U.S. 602 (1934). And see also *Wiener* v. *United States*, 357 U.S. 349 (1958), for the extent to which the Court is willing to go to read such a prohibition into the statute.

[37] Marver Bernstein, *Regulating Business by Independent Commission* (Princeton: Princeton University Press, 1955), p. 248.

the same kinds of conflicts of interests and pressures which have existed in the past will probably continue to be present. In speaking of the problem of such pressures, Judge Landis wrote in 1960:

Much attention has recently been centered on efforts, unfortunately too frequently successful, to sway the judgment of the members of regulatory agencies by so-called *ex parte* approaches or arguments, usually personalized, made off the record in proceedings that should be decided on the record. The extent of these *ex parte* approaches has only partially been revealed. They come from various sources—the office of the President, members of Congress, and the regulated industries. Some are made in good faith; others to further a personal desire regardless of the public interest. Many of them emanate from lawyers striving to press their clients' cause, indeed, one of the worst phases of this situation is the existence of groups of lawyers, concentrated in Washington itself, who implicitly hold out to clients that they have means of access to various regulatory agencies off the record that are more important than those that can be made on the record. . . .

Instances have also recently been uncovered of actual malfeasance in the sense of bribery among high administrative officials. More serious than these are the subtle but pervasive methods pursued by the regulated industries to influence regulatory agencies by social favors, promises of later employment in the industry itself, and other similar means.[38]

An interesting example of the way in which pressure may be exerted upon a regulatory agency by members of an industry appears in testimony concerning the Food and Drug Administration before a Congressional Committee given by Dr. Barbara Moulton in 1960. She said:

No one in the Bureau of Medicine would deny the value of occasional conferences with industry, particularly about technical details in the new drug applications. However, when a company representative spends 3 or 4 days a week in the New Drug Branch Offices, arguing each point step by step, wanting to know and being told exactly where the application is at all times and which chemists and which pharmacologists are assisting in its review, I submit that the medical officer responsible for making a wise decision in the interest of the public is suffering under an almost insurmountable handicap.[39]

We have already considered an example

of Congressional pressure in the *Pillsbury* case in the first subdivision of this chapter.

Lawmaking by Administrative Agencies

It has been noted that the principal regulatory commissions mentioned earlier all engage in legislative and judicial activities. A ready example can be found in the Federal Trade Commission's *Manual of Organization, Procedures, Rules of Practice and Statutes*. The manual contains sections setting forth: (1) the procedure to be followed in obtaining advisory opinions concerning whether or not proposed courses of action, "if pursued, would probably violate any laws administered by the Commission"; (2) procedures to be followed in formulating informal trade practice rules (voluntary rules agreed to by the members of an industry), and trade regulation rules to give effect to statutory provisions, as well as quantity limit rules (fixing the maximum quantities of commodities upon which price discounts may be given without running afoul of the Robinson-Patman Act); (3) procedures for making consent agreements (which contain orders and waivers of certain procedural requirements); (4) rules of practice for adjudicative proceedings (formal proceedings conducted under statutes administered by the Commission); (5) a specification of the content of an initial decision by a Hearing Examiner ("findings and conclusions as well as the reasons or basis therefor, upon all the material issues of fact, law, or discretion presented on the record" and "an appropriate order" disposing of the case); as well as (6) a statement of procedures to be followed in appealing from such an initial decision to the Commission.

The preceding paragraph—which indicates the various types of judicial and legislative law-making functions undertaken within one regulatory agency—may, however, be somewhat misleading because it is too neatly put. For one thing, neither the Commission's manual nor its statements of procedures answers the question: *who really produces the changes in law which emanate from activities of the regulatory commissions?* In speaking of this question in relation to

---

[38] Landis, *op. cit.*, pp. 13–14.

[39] *Administered Prices in the Drug Industry* (Hearings before the Subcommittee on Antitrust and Monopoly,

Senate Committee on the Judiciary, 86th Cong., 2d sess.) (Washington, D.C.: U.S. Government Printing Office, 1960), Part 22, p. 12025.

the activities of the Interstate Commerce Commission, Judge Landis pithily remarked in 1960: "Opinions of the Interstate Commerce Commission are presently in the poorest category of all administrative agency opinions. Their source is unknown and the practice has grown up of parsimony in discussing the applicable law in making a determination."[40] With respect to the question of opinions handed down by regulatory commissions in general, Judge Landis wrote:

. . . Unlike the judges of the federal judiciary, members of administrative commissions do not do their own work. The fact is that they simply cannot do it. In adjudicatory matters, the drafting of opinions is delegated to opinion writing sections or assistants so that the rationalization upon which a purportedly informed decision rests is not truly their own. One can well imagine the morass which would characterize our constitutional law dealing with "due process" had the Justices of the Supreme Court for the last half century had their opinions drafted by clerks and issued anonymously. . . . Yet, this is substantially the state of the law emanating from thousands of decisions issued by the Civil Aeronautics Board, the Interstate Commerce Commission, the Securities and Exchange Commission, the Federal Power Commission and the National Labor Relations Board. But worse than this, it is a general belief, founded on considerable evidence, that briefs of counsel, findings of hearing examiners, relevant portions of the basic records, are rarely read by the individuals rhetorically responsible for ultimate decision. It is difficult for them to do otherwise, for as the analysis of the work load of one commissioner indicated, he had to make a decision during his work-day every five minutes, or as another commissioner recently testified, he made 18,000 decisions in five years. The fact is that delegation on a wide scale, not patently recognized by the law, characterizes the work of substantially all the regulatory agencies and certainly all the major ones. Absent such

delegation, the work of these agencies would grind to a stop.[41]

From the point of view of this chapter, however, discovery of the immediate sources of changes in law produced by administrative agencies is less important than establishing the proposition that such changes do in fact occur as the result of the operations of these agencies.

Since the *Landis Report* was published in 1960, most of the commissions have undertaken to improve their procedures and to speed up the handling of cases. Thus, the Federal Power Commission has adopted a procedure of fixing maximum producing *area* rates for natural gas instead of attempting the almost impossible task of fixing rates on the basis of the costs of thousands of *individual* producers, and its power to do so was upheld, as we will see in Part III, by the Supreme Court in 1968.[42]

As has been several times noted, the work of numerous specific regulatory agencies is discussed in detail in Part III of this book, and the work of the Federal Trade Commission will be discussed in Chapters 12 and 18 of Part II. Chapter 23 in Part III contains a general discussion of the regulatory process and some readers may want to read Chapter 23 at this time.

Although the present background materials will not be complete until consideration has been given to some elements of our economic history, to the problems of the forms of business associations, and the extent of concentration of economic power, there remains also one final topic to be considered in the general area of law and social change. This topic, an examination of some relevant landmark cases in United States Constitutional law, is the subject of the next chapter.

[40] Landis, *op. cit.*, p. 39.
[41] *Ibid.*, pp. 19–20.

[42] *Permian Basin Area Rate Cases* 390 U.S. 747 (1968).

Some Landmarks of United States Constitutional Law

In 1937 Justice Felix Frankfurter, who was then Professor of Law at Harvard, remarked: "More than any other branch of law, the judicial application of the Constitution is a function of the dominant forces of our society."[1]

Earlier, in 1924, John R. Commons had referred to the Supreme Court as the "first authoritative faculty of political economy in the world's history." Both the statement by Frankfurter and the statement by Commons recognize what has already been discussed at length in Chapter 4: courts do and must engage in the process of creative interpretation, and the economic and political philosophies of judges are inevitably reflected in their opinions. Yet, as we have also seen in Chapter 4, judges are not completely free to make law as they see fit. They can make some changes in the law, but in order to make fundamental structural changes, they must rely on outside help. Within this context, the Supreme Court has always played a most important role in the formulation of working rules according to which economic activity has

been and is carried on in the United States, and an understanding of the past and present policies of the Court concerning the nature and scope of the powers of the federal and state governments to regulate economic activities is essential if one is to understand those working rules and how they have operated in the past.

That judges must and do engage in creative interpretation is nowhere more evident than in the opinions written by Chief Justice John Marshall between 1801 and 1835. Although he was not the first Chief Justice, it was during his tenure that some of the basic issues of our Constitutional law were first formulated. As we will see, Marshall was a Federalist and believed in a strong central government; his decisions reflect this view and are still cited by the Court today.

Indeed, the power of the Supreme Court to declare laws of Congress unconstitutional, asserted by Marshall in 1803, has been exercised by the Supreme Court ever since Marshall made that crucial decision.[2] In the case in question, the Court held that

[1] Felix Frankfurter, *The Commerce Clause under Marshall, Taney and Waite* (Chapel Hill: University of North Carolina Press, 1937), pp. 2–3.

[2] *Marbury* v. *Madison*, 1 Cranch 137 (1803).

Congress did not have power to confer upon the Court new forms of original jurisdiction and that the original jurisdiction possessed by the Court was limited to that specified in the Constitution.

In the discussion which follows shortly, we will examine the extent to which the interpretation of various *specific* clauses of the Constitution by the Court have reflected both the prevailing economic and political views of the times and the economic and political views of particular Justices.

The types of cases and the methods of bringing them before the Court when a constitutional question is involved have already been indicated in the Appendix to Chapter 4. Brief mention has also been made there of some of the informal rules of judicial restraint which the Court has adopted in the course of time because of its recognition of the extraordinary power to declare laws unconstitutional which it has possessed since 1803.[3] Most of these rules together with the reasons for them (where the reasons are not obvious) were summarized by Justice Brandeis in 1936 in the following language:

1. The Court will not pass upon the constitutionality of legislation in a friendly, non-adversary, proceeding. ... "It never was the thought that, by means of a friendly suit, a party beaten in the legislature could transfer to the courts an inquiry as to the constitutionality of a legislative act."

2. The Court will not "anticipate a question of constitutional law in advance of the necessity of deciding it."

3. The Court will not "formulate a rule of constitutional law broader than is required by the precise facts to which it is to be applied."

4. The Court will not pass upon a constitutional question although properly presented by the record, if there is also present some other ground upon which the case may be disposed of.

5. The Court will not pass upon the validity of a statute upon a complaint of one who fails to show that he is injured by its operation.

6. The Court will not pass upon the constitutionality of a statute at the instance of one who has availed himself of its benefits.

7. "When the validity of an act of the Congress is drawn into question, and even if a serious doubt of constitutionality is raised, it is a cardinal principle that this Court will first ascertain whether a construction of the statute is fairly possible by which the question may be avoided.[4]

These rules of self-restraint indicate generally the Court's awareness of its power over governmental policy in the United States. The rules are designed to avoid fixing policy on a broader base than is necessary for the determination of the issues presented. In recent years there has been a tendency to relax some of these informal rules, particularly in civil rights cases and as a result of declaratory judgment acts. Nevertheless, taken as a whole, the rules do represent a pragmatic approach to the use of the great power of judicial review.

With this background information firmly in mind, we are now ready to turn to a discussion of the following topics in the order indicated: (1) the policy of the Court concerning the power of Congress under the Commerce Clause; (2) the use of the Contract Clause to protect and limit vested interests; (3) the development of policy concerning the Privileges and Immunities Clause; (4) the use of the Due Process and Equal Protection Clauses to limit legislative policies; (5) policies relative to the scope of the taxing and spending powers and the General Welfare Clause; and (6) policies concerning implied powers and other miscellaneous powers and limitations.

A. THE COMMERCE CLAUSE

Article I, Section 8, of the Constitution contains the powers delegated to the Congress, and its third clause states that Congress shall have the power "To regulate Commerce with foreign Nations, among the several States, and with the Indian Tribes." This clause involves both the power of Congress to regulate affirmatively in the sense of "promoting" commerce and limitations upon the power of the states to regulate. It thus involves questions concerning the so-called "federal-state relation," the relationship between the powers of the federal government on the one hand, and of the states on the other. Cases involving this question were among the first raised before the Court with regard

---

[3] See the Appendix to Chapter 4.
[4] *Ashwander* v. *Tennessee Valley Authority*, 297 U.S.

288 (1936), concurring opinion at pp. 346–48.

to the Commerce Clause. In time, the Court was also confronted with cases requiring it to determine the extent of the affirmative power of Congress to regulate under this clause. The first great case involving the Commerce Clause came before the Court in 1825. In 1942, Justice Jackson commented on this early decision by remarking that "At the beginning Chief Justice Marshall described the federal commerce power with a breadth never yet exceeded."[5] It is to Marshall's important decision in this case "at the beginning" that we turn now.

Gibbons v. Ogden (1824): The Basic Issues Are Raised

The essential facts in the case were these: the New York Legislature granted an exclusive right to navigate the waters of that state by steam vessels to certain persons. Ogden, who held the privilege, objected to competition (not authorized by the statute) undertaken by Gibbons and sought an injunction against the latter to prevent him from using his boats within the State of New York. There existed at the time a federal law providing for the licensing of coastal ships. A New York equity court granted the injunction, and the defendant (Gibbons) appealed from the decision of a New York appeals court which had sustained the lower court's position. The Supreme Court held the New York statute to be unconstitutional. (Daniel Webster represented Gibbons.)

Chief Justice Marshall began his opinion by defining commerce: "Commerce, undoubtedly, is traffic, but it is something more; it is intercourse. It describes the *commercial* intercourse between nations and parts of nations. . . ." (Italics mine.) It is a short step from the words "commercial intercourse" to the words "economic activity" used in 1942 by the Court in *Wickard* v. *Filburn*, but more than a century of decisions lies between these two definitions of "commerce" by the Court. Marshall had no trouble in finding that "navigation" lay within the meaning of the term "commerce." He followed a normal judicial procedure of pointing out that the word "commerce" had "always been understood to comprehend" navigation "within its

meaning; and a power to regulate navigation is as expressly granted as if the term had been added to the word 'commerce.'"[6]

Nor did Marshall have any great difficulty in stating the scope of the power. The words "with foreign Nations, . . . and with the Indian tribes," he asserted, "comprehend every species of commercial intercourse between the United States and foreign nations. No sort of trade can be carried on between this country and any other, to which this power does not extend." And, in the phrase, "among the several States," the word "among" means "intermingled with. . . . Commerce among the States cannot stop at the external boundary line of each State, but may be introduced into the interior." This does not mean that these words "comprehend that commerce which is completely internal" to a given state, however. What is involved is "commerce that concerns more States than one." Thus, he wrote:

. . . The genius and character of the whole government seem to be, that its action is to be applied to all the external concerns of the nation, and to those internal concerns which affect the States generally; but not to those which are completely within a particular State, which do not affect other States, and with which it is not necessary to interfere, for the purpose of executing some of the general powers of government.[7]

Clearly, Marshall contemplated a national policy involving the present wide use of the federal authority. The language quoted above is broad enough to sustain all of the present-day federal regulatory activities and federal operations in the area of economic and business activity.

With respect to the extent of the Congressional power, Marshall's position was equally broad. He wrote:

It is the power to regulate; that is, to prescribe the rule by which commerce is to be governed. This power, like all others vested in Congress, is complete in itself, may be exercised to its utmost extent, and acknowledges no limitations, other than are prescribed in the constitution. These are expressed in plain terms, and do not affect the questions which arise in this case, or which have been discussed at the bar. *If, as has always been understood, the sovereignty of*

[5] *Wickard* v. *Filburn* 317 U.S. 111 (1942) at p. 120.
[6] *Gibbons* v. *Ogden*, 9 Wheaton 1 (1824), at pp. 189–91.
[7] *Ibid.*, at p. 195.

Congress, though limited to specified objects, is plenary as to those objects, the power over commerce with foreign nations, and among the several States, is vested in Congress as absolutely as it would be in a single government, having in its constitution the same restrictions on the exercise of the power as are found in the constitution of the United States. The wisdom and discretion of Congress, their identity with the people, and the influence which their constituents possess at election, are, in this, as in many other instances, as that, for example, of declaring war, the sole restraints on which they have relied to secure them from its abuse. They are the restraints on which the people must often rely solely, in all representative governments.[8]

Thus, the Congressional authority was complete and full. There remained the further question of whether the states might have concurrent jurisdiction over a particular type of interstate commerce until such time as Congress had exercised the power. Marshall saw no reason to decide this policy issue in this case because, according to the facts of the case, Congress had already exercised the power by the legislation providing for the licensing of coastal ships. As Justice Jackson had written in 1942, Marshall described the commerce power "with a breadth never yet exceeded." But, at the same time, he too followed the pragmatic and conservative maxim of "not formulating a rule of Constitutional law broader than required by the precise facts to which" it was to be applied, thereby leaving it to future experience to provide additional content.

Permissibility of State Actions to Restrict Interstate Commerce

Marshall's View. Three years after *Gibbons* v. *Ogden*, Marshall held unconstitutional a Maryland statute which imposed a license fee upon importers and others selling imported foreign articles or commodities. He relied upon the fact that Congress had adopted legislation relative to imports and upon the second paragraph of Article I, Section 10, of the Constitution which prohibits a state from imposing import duties without the consent of Congress except "what may be absolutely necessary

for executing its inspection Laws"; and he *also* relied upon the Commerce Clause. In this case he laid down the rule of thumb that goods which were "the property of the importer, in his warehouse, in the original form or package in which" they were imported were in interstate commerce.[9] Thus, they could not be taxed by the states. From the point of view of the present discussion, the case is important because it illustrates Marshall's attempt to broaden his interpretation of the Commerce Clause to include a limitation on the taxing power of the states; and therefore the case also raises implicitly the question of whether other powers of the states, such as the police power, may represent qualifications of the broad doctrine of the exclusive power of the Congress over interstate commerce. The "original package doctrine" laid down in the case, it may be noted in passing, today really means that the goods being taxed shall not have become "commingled" with the general mass of goods within a state. For example, in 1967, the Court denied the State of Illinois the right to impose a use tax upon a mail order seller from Missouri in a case in which the seller relied solely on the United States Postal Service in carrying out his business.[10]

In 1829 Marshall upheld the right of the State of Delaware to construct a dam obstructing navigation in the absence of Congressional legislation to the contrary, on grounds that the Act providing for its construction would "not be considered as repugnant to the power of Congress to regulate commerce *in its dormant state,* or as being in conflict with any law passed on the subject."[11] In doing so, he further opened the door to the development of a national policy allowing use of the police power by the states as a device for imposing restrictions upon interstate commerce.

Taney's View. Marshall died in 1835, and Roger B. Taney, a Jacksonian Democrat, became the new Chief Justice. Most of the Justices at this time held to Marshall's point of view, but Taney did not. Consequently, the decisions under the Com-

---

[8] *Ibid.,* at pp. 195–97. (Italics mine.)
[9] *Brown* v. *Maryland,* 12 Wheaton 419 (1827), at p. 442.
[10] *National Nellas Hess Inc.* v. *Department of Internal*

Revenue of the State of Illinois, 386 U.S. 753 (1967).
[11] *Willson* v. *Black Bird Creek Marsh Co.,* 2 Peters 245 (1829). (Italics mine.)

merce Clause produced during the period of Taney's tenure constituted compromises between two different points of view as to what the national policy should be. In 1847 in *The License Cases* (upholding state laws requiring licenses for the sale of imported liquor), Taney stated his position:

It is well known that upon this subject a difference of opinion has existed, and still exists, among the members of this court. But with every respect for the opinion of my brethren with whom I do not agree, it appears to me to be very clear, that the mere grant of power to the general government cannot, upon any just principles of construction, be construed to be an absolute prohibition to the exercise of any power over the same subject by the States. The controlling and supreme power over commerce with foreign nations and the several States is undoubtedly conferred upon the Congress. Yet, in my judgment, the State may nevertheless, for the safety or convenience of trade, or for the protection of the health of its citizens, make regulations of commerce for its own ports and harbors, and for its own territory; and such regulations are valid unless they come in conflict with a law of Congress.[12]

Thus Taney denied flatly that the power had been *exclusively* granted to Congress. He adopted a provisional, partially concurrent power theory instead; and he also further pointed to a way (although his decision did not rest on this ground) in which the states could regulate interstate commerce through the police power.

The Contemporary View. Finally, in 1851 in the *Cooley* case, Justice Curtis wrote a compromise opinion upholding the right of Pennsylvania to impose regulations upon ships putting into port in Philadelphia despite the existence of the federal statute which had been at issue in *Gibbons* v. *Ogden*. He wrote:

. . . the power to regulate commerce embraces a vast field, containing not only many, but exceedingly various subjects, quite unlike in their nature; some imperatively demanding a single uniform rule, operating equally on the commerce of the United States . . . and some, like the subject now in question, as imperatively demanding that diversity, which alone can meet the local necessities of navigation.

Either absolutely to affirm, or deny, that the nature of this power requires exclusive legislation by Congress, is to lose sight of the nature of the subjects of this power, and to assert concerning all of them, what is really applicable but to a part. *Whatever subjects of this power are in their nature national, or admit only of one uniform system, or plan of regulation, may justly be said to be of such a nature as to require exclusive legislation by Congress.*[13]

The *Cooley* case continues to represent the prevailing policy: where the Court believes that the subject is one requiring a system of national regulation, it will hold that the power belongs exclusively to Congress; but where it believes that local regulation is more appropriate, it will uphold the state regulation as a valid exercise of the police power. The real basis of decision in the last group of cases is whether the Court believes that the state regulation is discriminatory legislation adopted to benefit solely the citizens of that state or whether it believes that the regulation is a legitimate attempt to protect public health and safety. For example, it has invalidated a state statute imposing an inspection fee on the sale of imported oysters[14] and sustained a state statute prohibiting the sale of oleomargarine deceptively packaged to pass as butter;[15] but it has also invalidated a state statute requiring all oleomargarine sold in the state, irrespective of where it had been produced, to be colored pink.[16] In *Buck* v. *Kuykendall* (1925), the Court invalidated a Washington statute which sought to regulate motor transportation between Seattle (Washington) and Portland (Oregon) on the ground that the primary purpose of the statute was "not regulation with a view of safety or to conservation of the highways, but the prohibition of competition."[17] Among more recent decisions, one finds a 1952 case in which the Court has invalidated a Mississippi tax imposed upon vehicles employed in the laundry business not licensed in the State of Mississippi, where the cleaning establishment was located in Memphis, Tennessee, but business was carried on both in Tennessee and in Mississippi.[18] And in 1963, the Court

---

[12] *The License Cases*, 5 Howard 504 (1847), at p. 579.

[13] *Cooley* v. *Board of Wardens of the Port of Philadelphia*, 12 Howard 299 (1851), at p. 319. (Italics mine.)

[14] *Foote* v. *Stanley*, 232 U.S. 494 (1914).

[15] *Plumley* v. *Massachusetts*, 155 U.S. 461 (1894).

[16] *Collins* v. *New Hampshire*, 171 U.S. 30 (1898).

[17] 267 U.S. 307 (1925), at p. 315.

[18] *Memphis Steam Laundry Cleaner* v. *Stone*, 342 U.S. 389 (1952).

invalidated a Florida law requiring a processor and distributor of fluid milk and milk products to favor Florida milk producers, where the processor and distributor had previously been obtaining about 70 percent of its requirements from milk producers and brokers in other states. The Court stated that the "exclusion of foreign milk from a major portion of the Florida market cannot be justified as an economic measure to protect the welfare of Florida dairy farmers or as a health measure designed to insure the existence of a wholesome supply of milk."[19]

The Meaning of the "Silence of Congress": Past and Present Policy. The fact that Congress has not legislated on a particular subject (the "silence of Congress")—a problem first raised by Webster in *Gibbons* v. *Ogden*—has been interpreted differently by different judges. In *Leisy* v. *Hardin* (1890), the Court invalidated an Iowa statute prohibiting the keeping or sale of any intoxicating liquor, where the defendant had imported the liquor from Illinois and sold it in the original package.[20] This decision has been taken by many to represent a preference on the part of the 1890 Court for a *laissez faire* economy, since the position leads to the result that, until Congress acts, no regulation of the subject matter occurs. The same position had been taken earlier (1886) by the Court in *Wabash, St. Louis and Pacific Railway* v. *Illinois*, when it invalidated an Illinois statute permitting the state to regulate railway rates.[21] The *Wabash* decision was one of a number of factors leading to the enactment of the Act to Regulate Interstate Commerce (1887) by the Congress, legislation to which the Court pointed the way in its opinion since it suggested that Congress should act to solve the problem.

The present state of the law is illustrated by *Morgan* v. *Virginia* (1946) in which the Court invalidated a West Virginia statute requiring racial segregation in the case of interstate and intrastate motor vehicles. Speaking for the majority, Justice Reed wrote:

. . . *state legislation is invalid if it unduly burdens*

. . . *commerce in matters where uniformity is necessary— necessary in the constitutional sense of useful in accomplishing a permitted purpose.* Where uniformity is essential for the functioning of commerce, a state may not interpose its local regulation. *Too true it is that the principle lacks in precision . . .*[22]

There were three concurrences and one dissent. In his concurring opinion, Justice Black said of the "undue burden" test: "I think that whether state legislation imposes an 'undue burden' on interstate commerce raises pure questions of policy, which the Constitution intended should be resolved by the Congress."[23]

Historical Development of the Affirmative Use of the Commerce Clause by Congress

To 1937. It was not until 1887 and the adoption of the Act to Regulate Interstate Commerce that *Congress* began to assert positive influence on American economic life under the Commerce Clause. In *The Daniel Ball* (1871), the Court had upheld a federal statute providing for the licensing and inspection of steam vessels carrying passengers or merchandise on the navigable waters of the United States, but it had refused to express an opinion in the case "upon the power of Congress over interstate commerce when carried on by land transportation."[24] However, in 1886, as noted above, the Court in its decision in the *Wabash* case issued an invitation to Congress to act in the area of railway regulation, by saying "the regulation can only appropriately exist by general rules and principles, which demand that it be done by the Congress of the United States under the commerce clause of the Constitution."[25] The establishment in 1887 of the Interstate Commerce Commission preceded the establishment of the next "independent regulatory commission," the Federal Trade Commission, by more than 25 years. It is apparent, then, why in this period much of the law of the affirmative power of Congress to regulate was developed in the field of transportation.

For example, in 1911, in the *Southern Railway* case, the Court upheld the power of

---

[19] *Polar Ice Cream and Creamery Co.* v. *Andrews*, 375 U.S. 361 (1963).
[20] *Leisy* v. *Hardin*, 135 U.S. 100 (1890), at p. 109. (Italics mine.) Gray, Harlan, and Brewer dissented.
[21] 118 U.S. 557 (1886).
[22] *Morgan* v. *Virginia*, 328 U.S. 373 (1946), at p.

377. (Italics mine.)
[23] *Ibid.*, at p. 387.
[24] *The Daniel Ball*, 10 Wallace 557 (1871), p. 566.
[25] *Wabash, St. Louis and Pacific Ry. Co.* v. *Illinois*, 118 U.S. 557 (1886), p. 577.

Congress to require safety coupling devices to be installed on railroad cars moving wholly in intrastate commerce but using an interstate "railway highway."[26] Thus the power to remove intrastate burdens upon interstate commerce, where there was a *real and substantial* relation between the two, was upheld. Then, in 1914 the Interstate Commerce Commission was permitted to require an intrastate railway to increase its rates to a level of interstate rates which had been found to be "reasonable" by the Commission, despite the fact that the intrastate railway pleaded that its lower rates were fixed in accordance with an order by the Texas Railroad Commission.[27] Thus the power of Congress to remove obstructions to commerce imposed by the states themselves was sustained.

However, in areas other than transportation, the Court for a long time adopted a restrictive attitude toward the use by Congress of the Commerce Clause to regulate intrastate activities. Thus, in 1895 in *United States* v. *E. C. Knight Company*,[28] the Court refused to permit the Sherman Act to be employed in an action against the American Sugar Refining Company which controlled about "90 percent of the sugar refined and sold in this country." This case has sometimes been cited to show the opposition of the Court to the Sherman Act in particular; however, the Court did permit the Act to be applied two years later and thereafter where there was a clear showing that interstate commerce was affected.[29] It is therefore more accurate to look upon the *Knight* case as being one in a line of many in which the Court held to a restrictive interpretation of the Commerce Clause insofar as Congressional power was concerned. In this case the Court held that *even conceding* the fact that a monopoly existed, Congress had no power to act because "manufacturing is not commerce." Other cases in which the Court subsequently restricted the use of the commerce power

included: (1) a denial of the power of Congress in 1908 to impose liability on common carriers for injuries caused by defective equipment or negligence on the part of the carriers—on grounds that the law was too broad;[30] (2) a declaration in 1918 in *Hamner* v. *Degenhart* that a federal statute prohibiting child labor was unconstitutional—on grounds that commerce did not include manufacturing, the same grounds which had been employed in the *Knight* case;[31] (3) a holding in 1935 that the Railroad Retirement Act was unconstitutional—because compulsory retirement pensions were thought to have no relationship to the efficiency of the railway system;[32] (4) invalidation in 1935 of the National Industrial Recovery Act of 1933—partly on grounds of an "excessive delegation of power to the President" and partly on grounds that the regulation exceeded the commerce power;[33] and (5) invalidation in 1936 in *Carter* v. *Carter Coal Company* of another New Deal measure, the Bituminous Coal Conservation Act of 1935—again on grounds that manufacturing was not commerce, citing *United States* v. *E. C. Knight Company*, as well as *Hamner* v. *Degenhart* and other cases mentioned above.[34] In addition, between 1933 and 1936, other pieces of state social legislation and legislation sponsored by the Roosevelt administration had also been held unconstitutional on other grounds. These included the Agricultural Adjustment Act[35] and the New York minimum wage law for women.[36]

Roosevelt and the Court in 1937. Because he believed the five-man majority of the Court (Chief Justice Hughes and Justices Stone, Cardozo, and Brandeis appear often as dissenting Justices in the cases cited above) was opposed to his recovery program, President Roosevelt in 1937 requested Congress to reorganize the judiciary. His plan was for Congress to adopt legislation making it possible to appoint an additional number of judges in all federal courts (in-

---

[26] *Southern Railway Co.* v. *United States*, 222 U.S. 20 (1911).

[27] *Houston, East and West Texas Ry. Co.* v. *United States (Shreveport Rate Case)*, 234 U.S. 342 (1914).

[28] 156 U.S. 1 (1895).

[29] See, in particular, *United States* v. *Trans-Missouri Freight Assn.*, 166 U.S. 290 (1897); and *Addyston Pipe and Steel Co.* v. *United States*, 175 U.S. 211 (1899). (Both cases are considered more fully in Part II *infra*.)

[30] *Employer's Liability Cases*, 207 U.S. 463 (1908).

[31] *Hamner* v. *Degenhart*, 247 U.S. 251 (1918).

[32] *Railroad Retirement Board* v. *Alton R.R.*, 295 U.S. 330 (1935).

[33] *Schechter Poultry Corp.* v. *United States*, 295 U.S. 495 (1935).

[34] *Carter* v. *Carter Coal Co.*, 298 U.S. 238 (1936).

[35] *United States* v. *Butler*, 297 U.S. 1 (1936).

[36] *Morehead* v. *Tipaldo*, 298 U.S. 587 (1936).

cluding the Supreme Court) where there were incumbent judges of retirement age who were unwilling to resign or retire. At the time, no mandatory retirement law existed in the case of federal judges, and it was believed by many that conservative judges were remaining in office beyond their retirement ages in order to hamper the adoption of New Deal legislation. The proposal was defeated in Congress after a bitter struggle. Justice Van Devanter, a member of the majority group, resigned in 1937 and was succeeded by Justice Black, and the effects of this retirement and new appointment were to convert the previous majority into a minority and to convert the previous minority into a majority.

1937 to 1942. However, even *before* the retirement of Justice Van Devanter, the Court began to uphold the validity of New Deal legislation. In March of 1937, it upheld a minimum wage law enacted by the State of Washington, although a few months before—as has already been noted— it had invalidated a minimum wage law enacted by the State of New York. In the earlier New York case, Justices Cardozo, Hughes, Stone, and Brandeis had dissented; while Justice Roberts, Sutherland, Van Devanter, McReynolds, and Butler had constituted the majority. In the 1937 Washington case, Justice Roberts (the youngest of the Justices) voted with Cardozo, Hughes, Stone, and Brandeis to constitute a new majority.[37] Before the year had ended, the Court had upheld much New Deal legislation, including the Social Security Act and the National Labor Relations Act.[38] In upholding the latter, the Court finally rejected the argument that "manufacturing is not commerce." Then, in 1941 in *United States* v. *Darby*,[39] the Court sustained the Fair Labor Standards Act in a case involving a Georgia lumber manufacturer. In doing so, the Court specifically overruled *Hamner* v. *Degenhart*, which has been mentioned earlier as the case in 1918 in which the Court had refused to permit Congress to prohibit child labor on grounds that manufacturing was not

commerce. In upholding social legislation under the Commerce Clause between 1937 and 1942, the Court often relied on the concepts, developed in the *Southern Railway* and the *Shreveport Rate* cases, of "activities having a substantial relation to interstate commerce" and of "protecting and fostering interstate commerce." Moreover, as has been noted, after the *Knight* case, the Court did apply the Sherman Act in a number of cases where there was a clear showing that interstate commerce was involved; such cases will be discussed further in Part II of this book.

Present Policy concerning the Affirmative Use of the Commerce Clause by Congress

Three cases illustrating the present policy of the Court relative to the power of Congress under the Commerce Clause will be considered now. This policy was established in 1942. It will become apparent in the discussion that the present policy is nothing more or less than an application of the broad interpretation first given to the clause by Marshall in *Gibbons* v. *Ogden* in 1824.

Wickard v. *Filburn (1942).* The facts in the 1942 case were these: Filburn owned and operated a small farm in Ohio. He maintained a herd of dairy cattle, raised poultry, and sold milk, poultry, and eggs. He also planted winter wheat, sold part of the crop, and fed some of it to livestock on his farm; in addition, he used some of the wheat to make flour and kept the rest for the following seeding. In July of 1940, under the Agricultural Adjustment Act of 1938, Filburn received an acreage allotment based on an estimate of yield. However, he sowed an acreage in excess of his allotment and harvested an excess acreage. Doing so subjected him to a monetary penalty under the Act—which he did not pay—and the County Marketing Committee thereupon refused to issue him the marketing card which he required under the existing regulations. Filburn then sought an injunction to prevent the enforcement of the penalty ($117.11) against him, and he also

---

[37] See Robert H. Jackson (who later became a Justice and wrote the decision in the *Wickard* case), *The Struggle for Judicial Supremacy* (New York: Alfred A. Knopf, Inc., 1941). The Washington case referred to in the text is *West Coast Hotel Co.* v. *Parrish*, 300 U.S. 379 (1937); the New York case is *Morehead*

v. *Tipaldo*, 298 U.S. 587 (1936).
[38] The Social Security Act was at issue in *Steward Machine Co.* v. *Davis*, 301 U.S. 548 (1937); the National Labor Relations Act was upheld in *NLRB* v. *Jones and Laughlin Steel Corp.*, 301 U.S. 1 (1937).
[39] 312 U.S. 100 (1941).

sought a declaratory judgment to the effect that the wheat marketing provisions of the Act were unconstitutional under the Commerce and Due Process Clauses of the Constitution.

Justice Jackson, speaking for the Court, pointed out that under the *Darby* case the issue would be settled, were it not for the fact that the Agricultural Adjustment Act extended federal regulation "to production not intended in any part for commerce but wholly for consumption on the farm." Pointing out that consumption of home-grown wheat on the farm affects the demand for the wheat crop and remarking that the principle was not affected by the fact that the appellee's "own contribution to the demand for wheat may be trivial by itself," Justice Jackson held the Act constitutional, saying:

> Whether the subject of the regulation in question was "production," "consumption," or "marketing" is, therefore, not material for purposes of deciding the question of federal power before us. That an activity is of a local character may help in a doubtful case to determine whether Congress intended to reach it. The same consideration might help in determining whether in the absence of Congressional action it would be permissable for the state to exert its power on the subject matter, even though in so doing it to some degree affected interstate commerce. *But even if appellee's activity be local and though it may not be regarded as commerce, it may still, whatever its nature, be reached by Congress if it exerts a substantial economic effect in interstate commerce, and this irrespective of whether such effect is what might at some earlier time have been defined as "direct" or "indirect."*
>
> . . . It is of the essence of regulation that it lays a restraining hand on the self-interest of the regulated and that advantages from the regulation commonly fall to others. *The conflicts of economic interest between the regulated and those who advantage by it are wisely left under our system to resolution by the Congress under its more flexible and responsible legislative process. Such conflicts rarely lend themselves to judicial determination. And with the wisdom, workability, or fairness, of the plan of regulation we have nothing to do.*[40]

Thus by 1942 full circle had been reached. Marshall had said in *Gibbons* v. *Ogden* that the "genius and character of the whole government seem to be that its action is to be applied . . . to those internal concerns which affect the States generally." *Wickard* v. *Filburn* was merely the logical consequence of this assertion. And so were the first cases under the 1964 Civil Rights Act which will be considered next.

Heart of Atlanta Motel, Inc. v. *United States (1964).* In upholding Title II of the Civil Rights Act of 1964 (78 Stat. 241), Justice Tom Clark, writing for the majority relied heavily upon *Gibbons* v. *Ogden* and *Wickard* v. *Filburn,* although he also cited several other cases mentioned earlier.

The *Heart of Atlanta* case involved the question of whether a motel doing an interstate business (including national advertising) could be prevented from discriminating because of race or color under the accommodations section of the Civil Rights Act. Although Justice Clark noted that Congress had based the Act upon Section 5 of the Fourteenth Amendment (an "enabling" clause authorizing Congress to enforce that Amendment by appropriate legislation) and upon the Equal Protection Clause (both will be considered further in subsequent sections below) as well as upon the Commerce Clause, *he rested his decision entirely upon the latter.* Thus, he asserted that "the principles which we apply today are those first formulated by Chief Justice Marshall in *Gibbons* v. *Ogden,*" and he quoted many of the sections of Marshall's opinion which have been reproduced above. Justice Clark then summarized the position of the majority by asserting:

> . . . In short, the determinative test of the exercise of power by the Congress under the Commerce Clause is simply *whether the activity sought to be regulated is "commerce which concerns more States than one" and has a real and substantial relation to the national interest.*[41]

To the argument that the motel's activity was "purely local," Justice Clark replied by quoting *United States* v. *Darby,* in which the Court had overruled *Hamner* v. *Degenhart* and had held that manufacturing was included within the commerce power.

Katzenbach v. *McClung (1964).* In the second case under the 1964 Civil Rights Act, *Katzenbach* v. *McClung,* the defendants (Ollie McClung, Sr. and Ollie McClung, Jr.) owned a restaurant (Ollie's Barbecue) which employed 36 persons and which

---

[40] *Wickard* v. *Filburn,* 317 U.S. 111 (1942), at pp. 124–25 and 129. (Italics mine.)

[41] *Heart of Atlanta Motel, Inc.* v. *United States,* 379 U.S. 241 (1964), at p. 255. (Italics mine.)

purchased 46 percent of its meat supply from a local supplier who had purchased it out of state. The District Court had "expressly found that a substantial portion of the food *served in the restaurant* had moved in interstate commerce." (Italics mine.)

Justice Clark rejected as irrelevant an argument that the amount of food served by this particular restaurant was an insignificant part of *the total amount of interstate commerce* and quoted the following from Justce Jackson's opinion in *Wickard* v. *Filburn*:

. . . That the appellee's own contribution to the demand for wheat may be trivial by itself is not enough to remove him from the scope of federal regulation, where, as here, his contribution, taken together with that of many others similarly situated, is far from trivial.[42]

There were also several concurring opinions in the case. Justice Douglas stated his reluctance to rest the decision solely on the Commerce Clause and indicated that he would rest it on Section 5 of the Fourteenth Amendment. (Section 5 will be discussed later.) Justice Black, who cited the *Shreveport Rate* case discussed above indicated he would use both the commerce power and the Necessary and Proper Clause of the Constitution in Article I, Section 8. Justice Goldberg stated that the matter was one of human dignity and not of economics and that he would rest the decision both on the Commerce Clause and on Section 5 of the Fourteenth Amendment.

It is at any rate clear that, since *Wickard* v. *Filburn*, the federal regulatory power has been held to be very broad and that Congress has by no means exhausted its power under the Commerce Clause as a basis for regulation. *The key phrase now is "national interest."* Marshall's conception of the scope of the federal power became a reality with the *Filburn* case, and the Court has shown no inclination to retreat from this position. Instead, in 1968 in *Maryland* v. *Wirtz*[43] the Court held that Congress has power to regulate the activities of a State in a case in which the state engages in economic activities that are validly regulated by the Federal Government when they are engaged in by private persons.

B. THE CONTRACT CLAUSE

In employing the Commerce Clause to limit state power, Marshall was interested in protecting national free trade as well as property; as a Federalist his respect for vested interests was also very great. He also adopted a policy of employing the Contract Clause of the Constitution to protect them. Taney, the Jacksonian, on the other hand, saw an opportunity to weaken the protection accorded by Marshall and made use of that opportunity.

Article I, Section 10, Paragraph 1, of the Constitution states that, among other things, "No State shall . . . pass any . . . Law impairing the Obligation of Contracts. . . ." The primary purpose of the provision was to prevent states from relieving debtors. Marshall, however, applied the clause in the celebrated *Dartmouth College* case to a corporate charter and held that a grant of power to the Trustees of Dartmouth College in the original charter providing for the establishment of the college could not be revoked by the state legislature.[44] The effect of the decision was to define a corporate charter as a contract containing fixed rights which could not be changed by actions of legislative bodies. However, in 1837 in the *Charles River Bridge* case, under Taney the Court held that "in grants by the public nothing passes by implication." That is, the Court held that nothing could be read into a corporate charter by implication; a corporation possessed no rights which were not explicitly stated in its charter.[45]

This view still stands as the contemporary policy, and subsequent cases have been concerned largely with the scope of the power reserved in public contracts and with legislation relative to private contracts. All legislation in force at a time a contract is made is, of course, a part of every contract; and the Court has held that a state does have a right to interfere with a contract by an exercise of the police power. For example, in 1934, a Minnesota moratorium statute enacted during the Depression (providing for postponement of mortgage foreclosures and forced sales) was upheld by the Court

[42] *Katzenbach* v. *McClung*, 379 U.S. 294 (1964), at p. 301.
[43] 392 U.S. 183, (1968).
[44] *Trustees of Dartmouth College* v. *Woodward*, 4 Wheaton 518 (1819).
[45] *Proprietors of the Charles River Bridge* v. *Proprietors of the Warren Bridge*, 11 Peters 420 (1837), at p. 545.

on grounds that "the State continues to possess authority to safeguard the vital interests of its people. It does not matter that legislation appropriate to that end 'has the result of modifying or abrogating contracts already in effect.'"[46] Moreover, today, it may be noted, the Court will apply the test of "reasonableness" to such abrogations or modifications.[47]

C. PRIVILEGES AND IMMUNITIES OF CITIZENS

The Two Privileges and Immunities Clauses

Article IV, Section 2, of the Constitution provides that "The *Citizens* of each State shall be entitled to all the Privileges and Immunities of Citizens in the several States." The first sentence of Section 1 of the Fourteenth Amendment states, "All *persons* born or naturalized in the United States . . . are citizens of the United States and of the State wherein they reside." The second sentence reads in part, "No State shall make or enforce any law which shall abridge the privileges or immunities of citizens of the United States; . . ." Corporations cannot claim immunity from local regulation under either of these provisions and so these clauses do not constitute a barrier against reasonable regulation of out-of-state corporations by states. A knowledge of the interpretation of these clauses by the Court is helpful in understanding: (1) how and why, from the Civil War until about 1937, the Court employed other clauses of the Fifth and Fourteenth Amendments to strike down federal and state legislative policies *regulating property and contractual rights* with which it disagreed and (2) the way in which since 1937 it has continued to use the other clauses of the Fourteenth Amendment to protect the *civil liberties* guaranteed in the Bill of Rights against encroachments by *state* legislatures and *state* officials, as will be fully explained below.

The Policy Adopted Relative to "Privileges and Immunities"

Article IV, Section 2. In 1823 Justice Bushrod Washington (a Justice of the Supreme Court) wrote a Circuit Court opinion in which he defined the "privileges and immunities" referred to in Article IV of the Constitution as confined "to those which are fundamental . . . and which have *at all times been enjoyed by the citizens of the several states*," but he excluded therefrom "rights which belong *exclusively to the citizens of any other particular* State."[48] Subsequently, in *Paul* v. *Virginia*, the Supreme Court approved this position and also held that a corporation was not a "citizen" within the meaning of this clause.[49] Consequently, the word *citizen* as used in Article IV refers to *state* citizenship, and a state is permitted to impose reasonable regulations on out-of-state corporations doing business within its jurisdiction.[50]

Section 1 of the Fourteenth Amendment. As has just been noted, under the *Corfield* and *Paul* cases, the word "citizen" in Article IV had been interpreted to refer to *state* citizenship. In the *Slaughter-House Cases* in 1873, the Court recognized that the first sentence of Section 1 of the Fourteenth Amendment for the first time specifically created *national* citizenship, but the Court continued to interpret the Privileges and Immunities Clause of the second sentence of Section 1 of the Amendment as applicable only to *state* citizenship! In this case, the Court upheld the power of the State of Louisiana to establish a monopoly in the slaughterhouse business in the face of an objection by New Orleans butchers that the statute was unconstitutional because it: (1) abridged their privileges and immunities as "citizens of the United States"; (2) denied them "equal protection of the law"; (3) deprived them of their property "without due process" of law; and (4) constituted "involuntary servitude" under the then recently-adopted Thirteenth Amendment. The Civil War Amendments had thus reached the Court.

In holding that although the first sentence of Section 1 of the Fourteenth Amendment created for the first time a "national citizenship," nevertheless, the meaning of "citizens" in the second sentence of this section of the Amendment was the same as that in

---

[46] *Home Building and Loan Assn.* v. *Blaisdell*, 290 U.S. 398 (1934), at pp. 434–435.
[47] *El Paso* v. *Simmons*, 379 U.S. 497 (1965), at p. 515.

[48] *Corfield* v. *Coryell*, 4 Wash. C.C. 371 (1825). (Italics mine.)
[49] *Paul* v. *Virginia*, 8 Wallace 168 (1869).
[50] *Blake* v. *McClung*, 172 U.S. 239 (1898).

Article IV, Section 2, under *Paul* v. *Virginia* (and that therefore the term referred to state citizenship), the Court reached in the *Slaughter-House Cases* a result consistent with contemporary policy concerning the scope of the police power of the state (a point to be discussed further below). However, in reaching this result, it effectively destroyed the possibility that this clause in the Fourteenth Amendment could at that time be used as a basis for federal civil rights legislation. The clause created no rights "placed under the special care of the Federal government." In addition, the Court rejected all of the plaintiff's other contentions, saying that the Thirteenth and Fourteenth Amendments had been adopted to eliminate discrimination against Negroes and hence did not apply to private business activities. Indeed, the Court remarked with respect to these arguments: "We doubt very much whether any action of a State not directed by way of discrimination against the negroes as a class, or on account of their race, will ever be held to come within the purview" of these provisions of these amendments.[51] How badly it misjudged its own future development of policy under the Fourteenth Amendment will soon become apparent. Indeed, as we will see, the Court has read much of the Bill of Rights into the Fourteenth Amendment in civil liberties cases.

D. THE DUE PROCESS OF LAW AND EQUAL PROTECTION CLAUSES

As has already been noted, from sometime after the Civil War up until about 1934, the Court utilized the Due Process Clauses of the Fifth and Fourteenth Amendments and sometimes the Equal Protection Clause of the Fourteenth Amendment as devices for substituting its own judgment for that of state legislatures and the Congress in cases involving the regulation of *property* and *contractual* rights. And, as has also been mentioned, the Court has continued to utilize the Due Process and Equal Protection Clauses of the Fourteenth Amendment as devices for protecting against state action

the civil liberties guaranteed under the Bill of Rights. In 1934, the Court sharply reversed its policy relative to the use of the Due Process and occasionally the Equal Protection Clauses in striking down legislative enactments concerning *property* and *contractual* rights, although between 1934 and 1937 it continued to hold unconstitutional several New Deal economic and social measures on other grounds (see the discussion of the Commerce Clause above). In many state courts, however, the practice persists of examining the substantive nature of state legislative acts relative to property by reliance on the concept of "substantive due process of law." We will see shortly that this phrase identifies a meaningless concept which can also be defined merely as "higher law as seen by the judges deciding the case."[52]

This subdivision examines the process by which the Court established itself in such a strong position of judicial superiority for evaluating proposed or intended legislative changes in working rules concerning property. In order for the Due Process and Equal Protection Clauses to be employed in this way to protect property and contractual rights, it was necessary for the Court: (1) to interpret the word "persons" in the Fourteenth and Fifth Amendments to include corporations; and (2) to change the meaning of the term "due process." Why and how this result was accomplished will now be described.

Differences of Language in the Fifth and Fourteenth Amendments

There are two Due Process Clauses in the Constitution. *One* appears in the Fifth Amendment and is a part of the Bill of Rights—adopted as a compromise measure on the basis of a recommendation by John Hancock (Jefferson was also a strong proponent) to insure ratification of the Constitution by reluctant states, most notably Massachusetts and Virginia. This Due Process Clause states that "No *person* shall . . . be deprived of life, liberty, or property without due process of law." (Italics mine.)

[51] *Slaughter-House Cases*, 16 Wallace 36 (1873), at p. 81.
[52] See, for example, Monrad G. Paulsen, "The Persistence of Substantive Due Process in the

States," 34 *Minn. L. Rev.* 91 (1950); and Richard V. Carpenter, "Economic Due Process and State Courts," 35 *A. B. A. Jour.* 1027 (1959).

The *second* Due Process Clause appears in the second sentence of Section 1 of the Fourteenth Amendment, which contains also an Equal Protection Clause in addition to the Privileges and Immunities Clause mentioned earlier. The Due Process and Equal Protection Clauses in the Fourteenth Amendment respectively read: "... nor shall any *State* deprive any *person* of life, liberty, or property without due process of law"; and "nor [shall any *State*] deny to any *person* within its jurisdiction the equal protection of the laws." (Italics mine.) The language of the Fourteenth Amendment is thus cast in terms of limitations upon the actions of *states* rather than in terms of the establishment of rights of *persons*.

The Fourteenth Amendment as a Limitation on State Action

Since the Privileges and Immunities, Due Process, and Equal Protection Clauses of the Fourteenth Amendment are stated in language which places restrictions upon the actions of *state* legislatures and *state* officials, the Court accordingly held in 1883 in the *Civil Rights Cases* that the enabling clause (Section 5) of the Fourteenth Amendment permitted Congress to adopt legislation "correcting the effect of prohibited *State* laws and *State* acts" but not to "create a code of municipal law for the regulation of *private* rights."[53] The restriction placed upon Congress by this language explains why the majority of the Court in the *Heart of Atlanta* and *McClung* cases rested the constitutionality of Section II of the Civil Rights Act of 1964 on the Commerce Clause rather than on the enabling clause of the Fourteenth Amendment. However, in 1966 the Court asserted that the "state action" concept includes cases in which the state action is merely peripheral or indirect and that a private individual is acting under "color of state law" when he conspires with state officials. Indeed, the Court has further held that Congress has the power under the enabling clause to prohibit the enforcement

of a state law; and in 1968 it held that Congress had power under the Thirteenth Amendment to "reach beyond state action to regulate the conduct of private individuals" to abolish "the badges and incidents of slavery in the United States."[54]

It has been noted that in order to apply the Fourteenth Amendment to protect corporations from legislative regulation the Court was forced, among other things, to bring corporations within the meaning of the word "persons" as used in the due process clause. It did so summarily in *Santa Clara County* v. *Southern Pacific Railroad*. In that case, Justice Waite said during the oral argument:

The court does not wish to hear argument on the question whether the provision in the Fourteenth Amendment to the Constitution, which forbids a State to deny to any person within its jurisdiction the equal protection of the laws, applies to these corporations. *We are all of the opinion that it does.*[55]

The Court was also forced to change the traditional meaning of the concept, "due process of law" into a natural law concept, a process which began at least as early as 1877 in *Munn* v. *Illinois*,[56] a case discussed further below.

The Original Meaning of "Due Process of Law": Reasonable or Fair Procedure

The Sixth Amendment guarantees the accused in *criminal* cases: (1) a speedy and public trial (free from massive publicity), (2) by an impartial jury of the state and district where the crime was committed; (3) a right to be informed of the nature and cause of the accusation; (4) a right to be confronted by witnesses against him; (5) a right to compel witnesses in his favor to attend the trial; and (6) a right to counsel— which, in cases from 1964 to 1968, the Court held includes the right to consult counsel while he is being interrogated by police and the right to freedom from having his conversations with his attorney montored by police. The amendment applies also in juvenile proceedings.[57]

[53] *Civil Rights Cases*, 109 U.S. 3 (1883), at p. 11. (Italics mine.)
[54] *United States* v. *Guest*, 383 U.S. 745 (1966); *United States* v. *Price*, 383 U.S. 787 (1966); *Jones* v. *Mayer Co.*, 392 U.S. 409 (1968).
[55] 118 U.S. 394 (1886), at p. 396. (Italics mine.)
[56] 94 U.S. 113 (1877).
[57] *Sheppard* v. *Maxwell, Warden*, 384 U.S. 333

(1966); *Turner* v. *Louisiana*, 379 U.S. 466 (1965); *Pointer* v. *Texas*, 380 U.S. 400 (1965); *Douglas* v. *Alabama*, 380 U.S. 415 (1965); *Miranda* v. *Arizona*, 384 U.S. 436 (1966); *Escobedo* v. *Illinois*, 378 U.S. 478 (1964); *Black* v. *United States*, 385 U.S. 26 (1966); *In re Gault*, 387 U.S. 1 (1967); and *Smith* v. *Illinois*. 390 U.S. 129 (1968).

Originally, the term "due process of law" meant "reasonable" or "fair" *procedure*. Courts and lawyers, consistently with the instrumentalist approach of the common law, have refused to define the term—either in criminal or civil cases—with precision. The prevailing attitude is still the pragmatic one evidenced by Justice Miller when he remarked in 1877:

... apart from the imminent risk of a failure to give any definition which would be at once perspicuous, comprehensive, and satisfactory, there is wisdom, we think, in the ascertaining of the intent and application of such an important phrase in the Federal Constitution, by the gradual process of judicial inclusion and exclusion, as the cases presented for decision shall require, with the reasoning on which such decisions may be founded.[58]

What is to be understood by the term *procedural due process* can perhaps be conveyed by the following statement by Justice Curtis in 1855 in a case involving the question of whether or not property could be taken by the Treasury Department under a statute in satisfaction of its claims without a prior *judicial* determination of the facts on which to base its power to issue such a warrant. Speaking for the Court, Justice Curtis wrote:

That the warrant now in question is legal process, is not denied. It was issued in conformity with an act of Congress. But is it "due process of law?" The Constitution contains no description of those processes which it was intended to allow or forbid. It does not even declare what principles are to be applied to ascertain whether it be due process. It is manifest that it was not left to the legislative power to enact any process which might be devised. The article is a restraint on the legislative as well as on the executive and judicial powers of the government, and cannot be so construed as to leave Congress free to make any process "due process of law," by its mere will. *To what principles, then, are we to resort to ascertain whether this process*, enacted by Congress, *is due process?* To this the answer must be twofold. *We must examine the constitution itself, to see whether this process be in conflict with any of its provisions. If not found to be so, we must look to those settled usages and modes of proceeding existing in*

the common and statute law of England, before the emigration of our ancestors, and which are shown not to have been unsuited to their civil and political condition by having been enacted on by them after the settlement of this country. . . .

. . . "due process of law" generally implies and includes actor [plaintiff], reus [defendant], judex [judge], regular allegations, opportunity to answer, and a trial according to some settled course of judicial proceedings . . . yet, this is not universally true.[59]

The right to be represented by counsel in an impartial tribunal and to cross examine witnesses are all elements of procedural due process—elements which, it is to be recalled from Chapter 6, are peculiarly lacking in some Congressional investigations. On the other hand, due process in the sense of "reasonable procedure" does not require the states "to establish ideal systems for the administration of justice, with every modern improvement and with provision against every possible hardship that may befall."[60] However, "notice and hearing are preliminary steps essential to the passing of an enforceable judgment," and "they, together with a legally competent tribunal having jurisdiction of the case, constitute basic elements of the constitutional requirement of due process of law."[61]

In 1908 the Court cited with approval an opinion by Justice Matthews written in 1884 in *Hurtado* v. *California*[62] and remarked:

. . . It does not follow, however, that a procedure settled in English law at the time of the emigration, and brought to this country and practiced by our ancestors, is an essential element of due process of law. If that were so the procedure of the first half of the seventeenth century would be fastened upon American jurisprudence like a straightjacket, only to be unloosed by constitutional amendment. That, said Mr. Justice Matthews, . . . "would be to deny every quality of the law but its age, and to render it incapable of progress or improvement.[63]

The 1884 *Hurtado* case was singled out by John Commons in 1924 as the first instance in which the Supreme Court departed from the traditional meaning of due process as

---

[58] *Davidson* v. *New Orleans*, 96 U.S. 97 (1877), at p. 104.

[59] *Murray's Lessee* v. *Hoboken Land and Improvement Co.*, 18 Howard 272 (1856), at pp. 276–77 and 280, (Italics mine.)

[60] *Owenby* v. *Morgan*, 256 U.S. 94 (1921), at pp.

110–111.

[61] *Powell* v. *Alabama*, 287 U.S. 45 (1932), at p. 68.

[62] 110 U.S. 516 (1884).

[63] *Twinning* v. *New Jersey*, 211 U.S. 78 (1908), at p. 101.

due procedure and in which it adopted a new meaning of *due purpose*.[64] That case involved a decision by the Supreme Court that "procedural due process" does not prevent a state from dispensing with the Grand Jury (which—as has been noted in Chapter 4—had always been used at common law and which is required under the Fifth Amendment in federal criminal cases) as a method of indictment, in favor of the adoption of different methods not known to the common law.

The difference between Commons' two terms, *due procedure* and *due purpose*, is significant. If due process means merely *due procedure*, it is not for the courts to pass upon the wisdom of legislation; it is the function of the courts merely to determine whether regular, fair, or reasonable procedures have been adopted by the legislature in the attainment of whatever end it seeks to accomplish. But if due process means *due purpose*, the courts also have the power to substitute their own judgment for that of the legislature in evaluating the *purposes* of the legislation; that is, they then have the right to examine the *purpose* of the legislation *as well as the procedures* employed to attain that purpose.

The Concept of "Substantive" Due Process: "Due Purpose"

What Commons identified as *due purpose* is alternatively known as *substantive due process*. This new meaning of the concept together with the holding by the Court in 1886 that corporations were included in the term "persons" in the Fifth and Fourteenth Amendments served as one of the principal vehicles by means of which a *laissez faire* economic philosophy was established as the basic working rule of the American economy between about 1877 and 1937.

Commons' identification of the *Hurtado* case in 1884 as the specific case in which the new definition of due process was introduced into our Constitutional law may be too precise. It is likely that the development of "substantive due process," the concept of a "higher law" known only to the Justices by unexplained means, was an outgrowth of natural law economic and

legal philosophies held by judges even as late as the early part of the twentieth century. The sources of these ideas—the works of the legal philosophers of the seventeenth and eighteenth centuries—have already been discussed in Chapter 3. Blackstone's influence was great.

In any case, the "substantive" due process idea was the device employed by the judges in pronouncing upon the fitness or unfitness of legislative acts pertaining to property and contractual rights from about 1877 until 1934; and, as has been noted, this concept still serves as the basis for one theory of civil liberties held by some of the Justices. The further development of the *procedural* due process concept during this period was carried on largely in decisions involving criminal actions, while the *substantive* concept was developed largely in cases involving the regulation of economic activities. And *Munn* v. *Illinois* in 1877—to be discussed next—is one of the earliest cases in which the substantive concept appears, although it appears there as a *dictum*.

Munn v. *Illinois* (1877): "Property Affected with a Public Interest" and "Due Purpose"

In *Munn* v. *Illinois*,[65] Chief Justice Waite upheld the right of the State of Illinois to regulate charges for the storage of grain in warehouses at Chicago and other points within that state. Those objecting to the regulation argued that the statute providing for it was unconstitutional under the Due Process Clause of the Fourteenth Amendment. Justice Waite replied by pointing out that a similar provision existed in the Fifth Amendment and that, despite the provision, Congress had in 1820:

... conferred power upon the City of Washington "to regulate . . . the rates of wharfage at private wharves, . . . the sweeping of chimneys, and to fix the rates of fees therefor, . . . and the weight and quality of bread," . . . and, in 1848, "to make all necessary regulations respecting hackney carriages and the rates of fare of the same, and the rates of hauling by cartmen, wagoners, carmen, and draymen, and the rates of commission of auctioneers," . . .

From this it is apparent that, down to the time of the adoption of the Fourteenth Amendment, it was not supposed that statutes regulating the

---

[64] John R. Commons, *Legal Foundations of Capitalism* (New York: The Macmillan Co., 1924), p. 333 ff.

[65] 94 U.S. 113 (1877).

use, or even the price of the use, of private property *necessarily* deprived an owner of his property without due process of law. . . . *The amendment does not change the law in this particular; it simply prevents the States from doing that which will operate as such a deprivation.*[66]

Justice Waite then proceeded to examine the circumstances under which such regulation was permitted. He concluded (by reference to an essay written by Lord Hale two hundred years earlier) that "when private property is affected with a public interest," it ceases to be private property only. Accordingly, it was not a violation of due process for the state to regulate charges for the use of "property affected with a public interest." By implication, therefore, it followed that state regulations affecting the use of property "not affected with a public interest" would be unconstitutional because they would be a violation of the Due Process Clause. Otherwise, what was the reason for the use of the phrase, 'affected with a public interest"? Due process had come to have a substantive connotation. The "natural rights" philosophy, discussed in Chapters 2 and 3, is clearly apparent in Justice Field's dissenting opinion. He asserted that the majority view was "subversive of the rights of private property, heretofore believed to be protected by constitutional guaranties against legislative interference."[67] As has been noted in Chapter 4, *dicta* and dissenting opinions may also point the way to changes in law.

The Employment of "Substantive" Due Process to Protect Property and Contractual Rights

It was in 1897 in the *Allgeyer* case that the Court first asserted positively the substantive due process concept as a basis for insuring "liberty of contract" against legislative interference.[68] In that case, the Court held unconstitutional a Louisiana statute prohibiting individuals within that state from making contracts of insurance with corporations doing business in New York. Thereafter, the Court began regularly to substitute its judgment for both that of Congress and the state legislatures, some-

times upholding—but often also denying—the legitimacy of legislative action in the area of regulation of property rights.

In 1898, for example, the Court had before it a Utah statute regulating working hours in local mines and smelters. In their argument the plaintiff's lawyers cited Book I, Chapter 10, of Adam Smith's *Wealth of Nations* as one of the "authorities" to be consulted in interpreting the statute.[69] But, in this case, the Court held that the statute was constitutional (despite the plaintiff's reliance on Adam Smith's work), on grounds that the state "legislature had adjudged that a limitation was necessary for the preservation of the health of the employees, *and there are reasonable grounds for believing that such a determination is supported by the facts.*"[70] In other words, a majority of the Court agreed with the purpose of the legislation. However, in 1905 in *Lochner* v. *New York*, the Court invalidated a New York statute regulating the hours of work of bakery employees. Arguing that the conditions for a valid exercise of the police power (which the Court had found to exist in the Utah case) were lacking in the New York case, Justice Peckham noted that "labor, even in any department, may carry with it the seeds of unhealthiness." Besides, he argued, working in a bakery was less unhealthful than working in some other occupations. And he also asked a question which revealed the true state of his mind: "*But are we all, on that account, at the mercy of legislative majorities?*"[71] Clearly Justice Peckham did not feel that "we" ought to be. The Supreme Court was really supreme in his mind.

Following the *Lochner* case, the decisions continued to be sometimes in favor of and sometimes in opposition to the constitutionality of such legislation. The theory of the *Allgeyer* case was often used to strike down legislation favorable to labor unions. In 1915, for example, the Court held unconstitutional under the Fourteenth Amendment a Kansas statute prohibiting employers from making use of "yellow-dog" contracts (contracts in which employees agree not to join labor unions),[72] and in 1923 the Court invalidated under the Fifth

---

[66] *Ibid.*, at p. 125. (Italics mine.)
[67] *Ibid.*, at p. 136.
[68] *Allgeyer* v. *Louisiana*, 165 U.S. 578 (1897).
[69] *Holden* v. *Hardy*, 169 U.S. 366 (1898), at p. 378.

[70] *Ibid.*, at p. 398. (Italics mine.)
[71] *Lochner* v. *New York*, 198 U.S. 45 (1905), at p. 59. (Italics mine.)
[72] *Coppage* v. *Kansas*, 236 U.S. 1 (1915).

Amendment a federal law providing a minimum wage for women employed in Washington, D.C.[73] Dissenting opinions appeared often in these cases under the names of Holmes, Hughes, Brandeis, and Cardozo. But before we examine the decision which establishes the current policy of due process in relation to legislative regulation of economic activities, it will be useful to examine also the other aspect of the thread which began to unravel with *Munn* v. *Illinois*, namely, the fate of the concept of a "business affected with a public interest." This concept was discarded in 1934 in the same decision as that in which due "purpose" relative to legislative regulation of economic activities was recognized as a meaningless category.

"Affected with a Public Interest" (1877 to 1934)

That the phrase "affected with a public interest" is a meaningless phrase or, at most, means "those businesses which the Court thinks are subject to regulation" is clearly evident in the decisions in which the phrase was used after 1877. Sometimes the Court upheld legislative regulations on grounds that the business which was being regulated "was affected with a public interest," and at other times it did not do so. And so in 1894 the Court upheld control over prices of grain elevators in North Dakota,[74] but it prohibited regulation of the ice business in Oklahoma in 1932,[75] just as it had earlier held unconstitutional a Kansas statute providing for the fixing of wages in the meat packing industry under a system of control of certain businesses which the Kansas legislature had declared were "affected with a public interest."[76] The opinion of Chief Justice Taft in the *Wolff Packing Company* case probably contains one of the most outstanding collections of meaningless words written in any judicial opinion. In defining the categories of "businesses affected with a public interest," the Chief Justice said:

Businesses said to be clothed with a public interest justifying some public regulation may be divided into three classes:

(1) Those which are carried on under the authority of a public grant of privileges which either expressly or impliedly imposes the affirmative duty of rendering a public service demanded by any members of the public. Such are the railroads, other common carriers and public utilities.

(2) Certain occupations, regarded as exceptional, the public interest attaching to which, recognized from earliest times, has survived the period of arbitrary laws by Parliament or Colonial legislatures for regulating all trades and callings. Such are those of the keepers of inns, cabs and grist mills. . . .

(3) Businesses which though not public at their inception may be fairly said to have risen to be such and have become subject in consequence to some government regulation. They have come to hold such a peculiar relation to the public that this is superimposed upon them. In the language of the cases, the owner by devoting his business to the public use, in effect grants the public an interest in that use and subjects himself to public regulation to the extent of that interest although the property continues to belong to its private owner and to be entitled to protection accordingly. . . .

It is manifest from an examination of . . . the third head that *the mere declaration by a legislature that a business is affected with a public interest is not conclusive* of the question whether its attempted regulation on that ground is justified.[77]

What did the Chief Justice really say in this quotation? Nothing more than that the phrase "business affected with a public interest" refers merely to those businesses which *are* currently being regulated, either because they have been regulated in the dim past or because they have become regulated industries at some time more recent than in the dim past, provided that the Court agrees with the legislative decision to regulate. On the basis of this statement, however, he drew the conclusion that the question involved was "always a subject of judicial inquiry." The intellectual kinship between Chief Justice Taft's statement that "the mere declaration by a legislature that a business has become affected with a public interest is not conclusive" and Justice Peckham's question "But are we all, on that account, at the mercy of legislative majorities?" is close indeed. The Supreme Court was truly supreme. But all this,

[73] *Adkins* v. *Children's Hospital*, 261 U.S. 525 (1923).
[74] *Brass* v. *North Dakota*, 153 U.S. 391 (1894).
[75] *New State Ice Co.* v. *Liebmann*, 285 U.S. 262 (1932).

[76] *Wolff Packing Co.* v. *Court of Industrial Relations of the State of Kansas*, 262 U.S. 522 (1923).
[77] *Ibid.*, at pp. 535–36. (Italics mine.)

together with the judicial policy of using the Due Process Clause to frustrate legislative policies relative to the establishment of working rules for economic activity, was swept away in 1934, however much those sympathetic to these views may have wished or continue to wish it to be otherwise.

Due "Purpose" with Respect to Property Again Becomes Due "Procedure"

Nebbia v. New York (1934). In 1933 the State of New York adopted a statute under which a Milk Control Board was empowered to fix maximum and minimum retail prices of milk. The Board fixed the price at nine cents a quart. Nebbia, owner of a grocery store in Rochester, sold two quarts of milk and a five-cent loaf of bread for eighteen cents and was convicted of violating the Board's order. The case was appealed to the Supreme Court on grounds that the statute and the order contravened the Due Process and Equal Protection Clauses of the Fourteenth Amendment.

The majority opinion was written by Justice Roberts, with Justices McReynolds, Van Devanter, Sutherland, and Butler joining in a dissenting opinion. Among other things, in upholding the New York statute, Justice Roberts wrote:

The Fifth Amendment, in the field of federal activity, and the Fourteenth, as respects state action, do not prohibit governmental regulation for the public welfare. They merely condition the exertion of the admitted power, by securing that the end shall be accomplished by methods consistent with due process. *And the guaranty of due process, as has often been held, demands only that the law shall not be unreasonable, arbitrary or capricious, and that the means selected shall have a real and substantial relation to the object sought to be attained.*[78]

Note that the quotation represents a return to the concept of due process as *due procedure* and that the decision was handed down in 1934—by the so-called pre-Roosevelt Court. Justice Roberts also said:

It is clear that there is no closed class or category of businesses affected with a public interest, and the function of courts in the application of the Fifth and Fourteenth Amendments is to determine in each case whether circumstances vindicate the challenged regulation as a reasonable exertion of governmental

authority or condemn it as arbitrary or discriminatory. *Wolff Packing Co.* v. *Industrial Court,* 262 U.S. 522, 535. [The pages cited by Roberts indicate that he has cited Taft's classification *in support* of the argument that there "is no closed category," that is, in precisely the reverse of the way in which Taft intended that the classification be used!] *The phrase "affected with a public interest" can, in the nature of things, mean no more than that an industry, for adequate reason, is subject to control for the public good. . . .*

So far as the requirement of *due process is concerned, and in the absence of other constitutional restriction, a state is free to adopt whatever economic policy may reasonably be deemed to promote public welfare, and to enforce that policy by legislation adapted to its purpose. The courts are without authority either to declare such policy, or, when it is declared by the legislature, to override it. If the laws passed are seen to have a reasonable relation to a proper legislative purpose, and are neither arbitrary nor discriminatory, the requirements of due process are satisfied, and judicial determination to that effect renders a court functus officio. . . . And it is* equally clear that if the legislative policy be to curb unrestrained and harmful competition by measures which are not arbitrary or discriminatory it does not lie with the courts to determine that the rule is unwise. *With the wisdom of the policy adopted, with the adequacy or practicability of the law enacted to forward it, the courts are both incompetent and unauthorized to deal.*[79]

Two points in these two quotations should be emphatically noted: (first) Justice Roberts had called attention to the emptiness of Taft's classification and recognized that the courts have no authority to determine legislative policies respecting economic activites; and (second) Justice Roberts had returned to the application of the concept of *procedural* due process and abandoned the concept of *substantive* due process in a case involving *property* rights.

There is today no *substantive* due process limitation on the power of legislatures to establish working rules relating to economic activities. There is a *procedural* due process limitation only. *State* legislatures are free to adopt whatever regulations of economic activity they see fit to adopt—provided, of course, that such regulations do not come in conflict with other provisions of the Constitution, such as the plenary power of Congress to regulate interstate commerce. The scope of *state* action in that area under

---

[78] *Nebbia* v. *New York,* 291 U.S. 502 (1934), at p. 525. (Italics mine.)

[79] *Ibid.,* at pp. 536–37. (Italics mine.)

the police power has already been considered in this chapter. Moreover, with the decision in *Wickard* v. *Filburn* in 1942, *Congressional* power to establish the working rules of economic activity under the Commerce Clause without fear of judicial intervention was also established on a very broad base. In the area of regulation of economic activities, the present period is thus one of legislative superiority, just as the period between the end of the Civil War and *Nebbia* in 1934 was one of judicial superiority.

"Substantive" Due Process in Civil Liberties Cases

Although the *Nebbia* case destroyed the concept of substantive due process as applied to the legislative regulation of economic activities, it has not done so in the area of regulation of civil liberties. The present members of the Court hold two different theories concerning the extent to which the Bill of Rights is applicable to *state* actions under the Due Process Clause of the Fourteenth Amendment. On the one hand, there is the "balance of interests" theory held by some members of the Court; on the other, there is the view that the Constitution *absolutely* limits governmental action in some areas.

An example is a 1964 case involving a libel action brought by one of the Commissioners of the City of Montgomery, Alabama against the *New York Times* for having published a paid advertisement requesting contributions for the civil rights movement. The Court held that action by a state court awarding such damages in a civil action constituted "State action" within the meaning of the Fourteenth Amendment. The majority took the position that a public official has no right to damages "for defamatory falsehood relating to his official conduct" unless he proves "actual malice," namely, that the statement was made with knowledge that it was not true or with a reckless disregard for truth. Justice Black concurred in the result but wrote a separate opinion in which he asserted: "An unconditional right to say what one pleases

about public affairs is what I consider to be the minimum guarantee of the First Amendment."[80] Justices Goldberg and Douglas also concurred in the result. In his concurring opinion (joined by Justice Douglas), Justice Goldberg wrote:

> In my view, the First and Fourteenth Amendments to the Constitution afford to the citizen and to the press an absolute, unconditional privilege to criticize official conduct despite the harm which may flow from excesses and abuses.[81]

In 1965 Justice Black again stated his position flatly and provided a useful bibliography of the many dissenting opinions he has written in support of his views: "I have previously had a number of occasions to dissent from judgments of this Court balancing away the First Amendment's unequivocally guaranteed rights of free speech, press, assembly, and petition."[82]

But, in 1965, the Court was faced with a Louisiana case involving a statute prohibiting the picketing of a Louisiana courthouse by civil rights advocates, and in one of these cases Justices Black and Goldberg may have qualified their positions somewhat.[83] This case was the *Cox* case.

Justice Goldberg wrote the majority opinion in this case, while Justices *Black*, Clark, White, and Harlan dissented. Justice Goldberg wrote:

> We hold that this statute on its face is a valid law dealing with conduct subject to regulation so as to vindicate important interests of society and that the fact that free speech is intermingled with such conduct does not bring with it constitutional protection.[84]

Thus, the majority *upheld* the statute. In a dissenting opinion, Justice Black indicated that, although he dissented on the facts in this case, he too agreed that the statute was valid:

> The First and Fourteenth Amendments, I think, take away from government, state and federal, all power to restrict freedom of speech, press, and assembly *where people have a right to be for such purposes*. This does not mean, however, that these amendments also grant a constitutional right to engage in the conduct of picketing

---

[80] *New York Times Co.* v. *Sullivan*, 376 U.S. 254 (1964), at p. 297.

[81] *Ibid.*, at p. 298.

[82] *El Paso* v. *Simmons*, 379 U.S. 497 (1965), at p. 517. See n. 1, p. 517, for a list of cases containing

Black's dissenting opinions.

[83] *Cox* v. *Louisiana*, 379 U.S. 559 (1965).

[84] *Ibid.*, at p. 564. See also *Cameron* v. *Johnson*, 390 U.S. 611 (1938).

or patrolling, whether on publicly owned streets or on privately owned property. . . . Were the law otherwise, people on the streets, in their homes and anywhere else could be compelled to listen against their will to speakers they did not want to hear. Picketing, though it may be utilized to communicate ideas, is not speech, and therefore is not of itself protected by the First Amendment.[85]

In a related case, Justice Goldberg, the former labor lawyer who has since returned to private practice, asserted in a majority opinion:

We emphatically reject the notion urged by the appellant that the First and Fourteenth Amendments afford the same kind of freedom to those who would communicate ideas by conduct such as patrolling, marching, and picketing on streets and highways, as these amendments afford to those who communicate ideas by pure speech.[86]

This language is significant because it shows the extent to which the Court has changed its position on picketing since 1940. The Court had held in 1940 in *Thornhill* v. *Alabama* that an Alabama statute prohibiting picketing by labor of business establishments was unconstitutional and had asserted that "The freedom of speech and of the press, which are secured by the First Amendment . . . are among the fundamental personal rights and liberties . . . secured to all persons by the Fourteenth Amendment against abridgment by a State."[87] In the *Thornhill* case, Justice Murphy had also said: "In the circumstances of our times the dissemination of information concerning the facts of a labor dispute must be regarded as within that area of free discussion that is guaranteed by the Constitution." This statement had been widely interpreted to mean that "picketing is free speech." After 1940, the Court limited the doctrine in numerous ways; for example, by holding that picketing must be carried on in a peaceful context.[88]

In the *Cox* case, the fact that a courthouse was being picketed may account in part for the positions taken by the various Justices. Indeed, in 1966 Justice Black wrote a majority opinion in a 5 to 4 decision in which the Court upheld the convictions of civil rights demonstrators under a Florida statute, where the demonstration occurred in the driveway of a county jail.[89] It is also interesting, given the earlier *Thornhill* decision, that Justice Goldberg, whose previous position as an important labor attorney has already been noted in Chapter 6 and elsewhere, was chosen to write the majority opinion in the *Cox case*.

The application of the First Amendment to the states under the Fourteenth Amendment has also arisen in cases concerned with religious freedom.[90] And ramifications of these decisions have, in turn, brought challenges to laws requiring the closing of business establishments on Sundays. Such laws are, of course, primarily aimed at the operations of "discount" houses. In two cases decided in 1961, the Court apparently declared itself in favor of a six-day week and upheld such Sunday closing laws on grounds that they were within the police power of the state and represented merely a public policy of insuring one day of rest each week rather than being an interference with religious freedom under the First Amendment.[91] Since then, some discount houses have adopted a policy of closing one day a week but remaining open on Sundays.

It should thus by now be apparent to the reader, both from the discussion of Locke's theory—that the chief end of civil government is to permit men to enjoy the use of their property in peace (discussed at length in Chapter 5)—and from the discussion thus far in this chapter, that the problems of the regulation of economic activities and of civil liberties are not unrelated in our Constitutional history. Just as the decision in the *Cox* case concerning

[85] *Ibid.*, at p. 578. (Italics his.)

[86] *Cox* v. *Louisiana*, 379 U.S. 536 (1965), at p. 555.

[87] *Thornhill* v. *Alabama*, 310 U.S. 88 (1940), at p. 95.

[88] *Milk Wagon Drivers' Union* v. *Meadowmoor Dairies, Inc.*, 312 U.S. 287 (1941). See also *International Brotherhood of Teamsters* v. *Vogt*, 354 U.S. 284 (1957).

[89] *Adderly* v. *Florida*, 385 U.S. 39 (1966). Justices

Douglas, Warren, Brennan, and Fortas dissented.

[90] See, for example, *Cantwell* v. *Connecticut*, 310 U.S. 96 (1940); *Illinois ex. rel. McCollum* v. *Board of Education*, 333 U.S. 203 (1948); *Zorach* v. *Clauson*, 343 U.S. 306 (1952); and *Engel* v. *Vitale*, 370 U.S. 421 (1962).

[91] *McGowan* v. *Maryland*, 366 U.S. 420 (1961); and *Two Guys from Harrison-Allentown, Inc.* v. *McGinley*, 366 U.S. 582 (1961).

the picketing of a courthouse by a group of civil rights workers may eventually affect activities by labor unions, so does the decision in *Sanford* v. *Texas* invalidating the seizure of personal property under a *general* search warrant (one which does not describe with particularity the things to be seized) have implications for freedom of business firms from similar searches. In the *Sanford* case also decided in 1965, the Court repeated what it had previously said, namely, that the Fourth Amendment provisions are made binding upon the states by the Due Process Clause of the Fourteenth Amendment. Police "fishing expeditions" are unconstitutional. Justice Stewart spoke for a unanimous Court when he said:

It is now settled that the fundamental protections of the Fourth Amendment are guaranteed by the Fourteenth Amendment against invasion by the States. . . . The Fourth Amendment provides that "no Warrants shall issue, but upon probable cause, supported by Oath or affirmation, and *particularly describing* the place to be searched, and the persons or *things to be seized*." (Emphasis supplied.)

These words are precise and clear. They reflect the determination of those who wrote the Bill of Rights that the people of this new Nation should forever "be secure in their persons, houses, papers, and effects" from intrusion and seizure by officers acting under the unbridled authority of a general warrant. Vivid in the memory of the newly independent Americans were those general warrants known as writs of assistance under which officers of the Crown had so bedeviled the colonists. The hated writs of assistance had given customs officials blanket authority to search where they pleased for goods imported in violation of the British tax laws.[92]

The decision in the *Sanford* case subjects state agencies to the same kinds of limitations as those which have long existed in the case of activities of the federal agencies under the Fourth Amendment. State law enforcement agencies and advocates of States Rights have complained loudly concerning some of the Court's recent decisions in this area. It is therefore worth noting that these same limitations apply to the securing of evidence from business firms in antitrust cases and in cases involving tax evasions. As Justice Stewart pointed out in the quotation from the *Sanford* case given above, the injunction against general search warrants contained in the Fourth Amendment was placed in the Bill of Rights because of the vivid memory on the part of the Founding Fathers of the arbitrary acts of "officers of the Crown" undertaken during their search "for goods imported in violation of the British tax laws." Indeed, in 1968, the Court held that the procedural safeguards of due process apply to tax investigations, which frequently lead to criminal prosecutions.[93]

At a more general level, it may be noted that Justice Black argued in 1947 that "the specific guarantees of the Bill of Rights should be carried over intact into the first section of the Fourteenth Amendment" and that he would accomplish this result by "reliance upon the original purpose of the Fourteenth Amendment."[94] That the Court has taken a very long step in this direction since 1947 is readily apparent in its opinion in *Gideon* v. *Wainwright*, decided in 1962. In that case, which upheld the right of the accused to be represented by counsel in a criminal proceeding in a state court under the Sixth Amendment, the Court said that parts of the First, Fourth, Fifth, Sixth, and Eighth Amendments had in previous cases been made applicable to the states under the Due Process Clause of the Fourteenth Amendment.[95] And in 1965 in a concurring opinion in a Texas case in which the Court held that an accused in a state court has a right to confront witnesses against him under the Sixth Amendment, a right "made obligatory on the States by the Fourteenth Amendment," Justice Goldberg wrote:

. . . the Court has held that the Fourteenth Amendment guarantees against infringement by the States the liberties of the First Amendment, the Fourth Amendment, the Just Compensation Clause of the Fifth Amendment, the Fifth Amendment's privilege against self-incrimination, the Eighth Amendment's prohibition of cruel and unusual punishments, and the Sixth Amendment's guarantee of the assistance of counsel for an accused in a criminal prosecution.

---

[92] *Sanford* v. *Texas*, 379 U.S. 476 (1965), at p. 481. (Italics his.)

[93] *Mathis* v. *United States*, 391 U.S. 1 (1968).

[94] *Adamson* v. *California*, 332 U.S. 46 (1947), at pp. 124 and 90.

[95] *Gideon* v. *Wainwright*, 372 U.S. 335 (1962), at p. 341.

I adhere to and support the process of absorption by means of which the Court holds that certain fundamental guarantees of the Bill of Rights are made obligatory on the States through the Fourteenth Amendment. Although, as this case illustrates, there are differences among the members of the Court as to the theory by which the Fourteenth Amendment protects the fundamental liberties of individual citizens, it is noteworthy that there is a large area of agreement, both here and in other cases, that certain basic rights are fundamental—not to be denied the individual by either the state or federal governments under the Constitution.[96]

Thus, the limitations imposed upon the states under the Fourteenth Amendment in civil liberties cases are today substantial. And although, under the *Nebbia* case, the Court will no longer interfere with legislative policies pertaining to the regulation of economic activities, it has clearly continued to retain and even broaden its power to supervise procedural safeguards relative to the formulation and execution of legislative policies in the civil liberties area. It has also retained substantive control over such legislative policies. Some general conclusions concerning this point will be given at the end of this chapter. It will be useful now, however, to examine some decisions under the Equal Protection Clause of the Fourteenth Amendment and to consider how these decisions are related to those under the Due Process Clause.

The Equal Protection Clause

In the same volume of the *United States Reports* in which is found Chief Justice Waite's assertion—that the Court did not wish to hear argument on the question of whether the word "person" in the Fourteenth Amendment included corporations— is found the case of *Yick Wo* v. *Hopkins*.[97] In this case, the Court applied the Fourteenth Amendment to a case involving Chinese operators of a laundry in San Francisco and held unconstitutional, on grounds that the real purpose of the ordinance was discrimination, a municipal ordinance requiring licensing of laundry operators. Thus the Court, in this case, also rejected the "Negro-race theory" of the *Slaughter-House Cases*. If the Court had not had its substantive version of the Due Process Clause, it could probably have employed the Equal Protection Clause of the Fourteenth Amendment to restrict the activities of legislatures relative to property and contractual rights in the same way. In some cases, the Court has employed a strict interpretation of the Equal Protection Clause to that end.[98] In general, however, it has permitted the states to regulate certain economic activities where the basis of the classification has been found to be not discriminatory; moreover, it has seldom allowed the Equal Protection Clause to be used to strike down state tax laws.[99]

In general, the policy of the Court relative to the Equal Protection Clause was summarized by Justice Van Devanter in 1910 in the following language:

1. The equal protection clause of the Fourteenth Amendment does not take from the State the power to classify in the adoption of police laws, but admits of the exercise of a wide scope of discretion in that regard, and avoids what is done only when it is without any reasonable basis and therefore is purely arbitrary. 2. A classification having some reasonable basis does not offend against that clause merely because it is not made with mathematical nicety or because in practice it results in some inequality. 3. When the classification in such a law is called in question, if any state of facts reasonably can be conceived that would sustain it, the existence of that state of facts at the time the law was enacted must be assumed. 4. One who assails the classification in such a law must carry the burden of showing that it does not rest upon any reasonable basis, but is essentially arbitrary.[100]

In recent years the Equal Protection Clause has been applied often in legislative reapportionment and civil rights cases.[101]

In the context of this book, the various reapportionment and civil rights decisions under the Equal Protection Clause, like those under the Due Process Clause, derive their importance from the fact that they illustrate use of a mechanism by means of

[96] *Pointer* v. *Texas*, 380 U.S. 400 (1965), at pp. 411–12 and p. 414.

[97] 118 U.S. 356 (1886).

[98] *Cotting* v. *Kansas City Stockyards*, 183 U.S. 79 (1901).

[99] *Great Atlantic and Pacific Co.* v. *Grosjean*, 301 U.S. 412 (1937); *General Motors* v. *Washington*, 377 U.S. 436 (1964).

[100] *Lindsley* v. *Natural Carbonic Gas Co.*, 220 U.S. 61 (1911), at pp. 78–79.

[101] *Baker* v. *Carr*, 369 U.S. 186 (1962); *Anderson* v. *Martin*, 375 U.S. 218 (1964); *McLaughlin* v. *Florida*, 379 U.S. 184 (1964).

which a redistribution of political power has been accomplished. Indeed, the effect of the reapportionment decisions in shifting power from rural groups to urban groups was officially noticed in a 1968 publication issued by the House Agriculture Committee.[102] But it is still too early to assess the full impact of these decisions.

E. THE TAXING, BORROWING, SPENDING, AND PROMOTION OF GENERAL WELFARE POWERS

Article I, Section 8, Clause 1, of the Constitution authorizes Congress to levy and collect taxes (duties, imports, and excises must be uniform throughout the United States) "to pay the debts and provide for the common defense and general welfare of the United States." The second clause of Section 8 authorizes Congress to "borrow money on the credit of the United States." The use of fiscal policy to produce full employment rests on these two provisions and on the Sixteenth Amendment—which was adopted in 1913 because the Court had held in 1895 that the income tax was a "direct tax" (one which must be apportioned according to population), thereby making it impossible to tax incomes at the federal level.[103] Two aspects of the fiscal and general welfare powers are of interest from the point of view of this book: (1) the use of taxes as regulatory devices; and (2) the limitations or lack of them on the power to spend "for the general welfare." Both will be briefly examined below.

Taxes as Regulatory Devices

The power to tax is, of course, not a power to regulate any particular activity. However, the general policy which has been adopted by the Court relative to regulatory taxes is that, *if* Congress has the authority to regulate activities in a particular area, the fact that the *method* of regulation chosen is a tax measure is immaterial. This policy was laid down in 1869 and remains the law today. The case in which this basic policy was adopted involved the question of the

validity of a federal tax of ten percent of their face value imposed upon bank notes issued by state banks.[104] The tax had been imposed by Congress in 1866 for the purpose of driving the state banks out of business and strengthening the newly-created national banking system. The Court held that since Congress had the power "to provide a circulation of coin," it had the power to establish the national banking system and "to provide a system of currency for the whole country." The tax in question was thus merely a regulatory device employed to give effect to a legitimate regulatory power which existed elsewhere in the Constitution.

Occasionally, however, the Court has held in such cases that Congress does not possess a particular regulatory power. Thus, in 1922 the Court invalidated the second attempt by Congress to regulate by a tax measure the employment of child labor (after, as has been noted, the Court had invalidated the first attempt in *Hamner* v. *Degenhart* in 1918).[105] These cases thus stand for the proposition that whenever a tax law is employed as a regulatory device, the power to regulate must be found *by the Court* to exist in the Constitution *in some place other than in the taxing power*.

Borrowing and Spending to "Promote the General Welfare"; The Tenth Amendment

Power to Borrow. The only legal limit on the power of Congress to borrow is "the credit of the United States." Some, of course, do not like this proposition. Keynesian economists, on the other hand, assuming rational behavior on the part of investors, generally argue that the credit will be good as long as interest payments on the debt can be met and, further, that interest payments can be met as long as the increase in national income exceeds the increase in interest payments. This proposition assumes that a number of "other things remain equal," and probably no one knows the precise limit: for one thing, the answer also depends upon whether one assumes continuation of the existing institutional arrangements and income distribution.

[102]*Agricultural Legislation in the 90th Congress* (90th Cong., 2d sess., 1968) (Washington, D.C.: U.S. Government Printing Office, 1968), p. 1.

[103] *Pollock* v. *Farmer's Loan and Trust Co.*, 157 U.S.

429; 158 U.S. 601 (1895).

[104] *Veazie Bank* v. *Fenno*, 8 Wallace 533 (1869).

[105] *Bailey* v. *Drexel Furniture Co.*, 259 U.S. 20 (1922).

The Tenth Amendment; "Powers Reserved to the States." The nature of the spending power was discussed by the Court at length in 1936 in *United States* v. *Butler* in which it held the first Agricultural Adjustment Act unconstitutional on grounds that the Act constituted an invasion of the power reserved to the states under the Tenth Amendment.[106] This aspect of the case is today merely a piece of history, since, in *United States* v. *Darby* (upholding the Fair Labor Standards Act in 1941), Chief Justice Stone remarked that "the Tenth Amendment . . . states but a truism that all is retained which has not been surrendered."[107] Today this Amendment (this "truism") represents no limitation on the power of the federal government relative to that of the states.

The Spending and "General Welfare" Powers. The *Butler* case is today significant primarily for the proposition that the "power to tax and to appropriate" is limited only by the "requirement that it shall be exercised to provide for the general welfare of the United States."[108] The Court has never fully construed the meaning of the General Welfare Clause. However, as early as 1840 it upheld the power of Congress to dispose of federal property under Article IV, Section 3,[109] a power without which tremendous subsidies, in the nineteenth century in the form of grants of public lands to the railroads or the disposal of government aluminum and synthetic rubber plants to private industry after World War II, would have been impossible.

In 1937, the Court upheld the Social Security Act, pointing out that the problem of old age benefits was "national in area and dimensions" and could not be adequately be dealt with by the states alone.[110]

In this area, as is true of the other Constitutional cases discussed so far, it is apparent that the Court has gone a long way in the direction of extending the power of the federal government as compared with that of the states. It has, in short, adopted in most of these areas Marshall's view expressed in *Gibbons* v. *Ogden* that the action of the national government "is to be applied to all the external concerns of the nation, and to those internal concerns which affect the States generally." The same can be said of the "implied powers" doctrine and of the other miscellaneous powers of Congress, some of which are so obviously national in scope that little discussion of them is necessary in that which follows.

F. IMPLIED POWERS; WAR POWERS; OTHER POWERS

Implied Powers

Not only was Marshall's influence on the interpretation of the Constitution important in regard to: (1) the commerce power; (2) the federal-state relationship and (3) the Contract Clause; but also (4) his decision in *McCulloch* v. *Maryland* in 1819 laid the basis for the development of the implied powers doctrine (the interpretation of Article I, Section 8, Clause 18—which authorizes Congress to "make all laws which shall be necessary and proper" for carrying out the other powers enumerated in Section 8 and elsewhere in the Constitution).

In the *McCulloch* case, Marshall held that the Necessary and Proper Clause was *added to* the expressly enumerated powers. He held that the power to establish the Second Bank of the United States was implied by the fiscal powers expressly enumerated in the Constitution. The Necessary and Proper Clause, he asserted, "must allow to the national legislature that discretion, with respect to the means by which the powers it [the clause] confers are to be carried into execution, which will enable the body to perform the high duties assigned to it, in the manner most beneficial to the people." As long as "the end be legitimate" and within the scope of the Constitution, "all means which are appropriate, which are plainly adapted to that end, which are not prohibited" are also constitutional.[111] This position has prevailed in the Court's

---

106 *United States* v. *Butler*, 279 U.S. 1 (1936).

107 *United States* v. *Darby*, 312 U.S. 100 (1941), at p. 117. (This case has already been discussed in this chapter under the topic of the affirmative use of the Commerce Clause.)

108 *United States* v. *Butler*, 297 U.S. 1 (1936), at

pp. 65–66.

109 *United States* v. *Gratiot*, 14 Peters 526 :(1840).

110 *Helvering* v. *Davis*, 301 U.S. 619 (1937); *Steward Machine Co.* v. *Davis*, 301 U.S. 548 (1937).

111 *McCulloch* v. *Maryland*, 4 Wheaton 316 (1819), at p. 421.

decisions, particularly since the *Darby* case in which, as noted above, the Tenth Amendment was made meaningless.

The War Power and Other Powers

The War Power. In general, in time of war the Court has been willing to go very far in the direction of sustaining action by the national government under Article I, Section 8, Clause 11, and other provisions. During periods of total war widespread economic controls have been adopted (*e.g.*, during World War II), and civil liberties (particularly of those opposed to the war and of those related to the opposing race or nationality) have suffered during such periods. The economic controls will be further considered in Chapter 32 of this book.

Uniform Naturalization and Bankruptcy Laws. Clause 4 of Article I, Section 8, authorizes Congress to exercise the powers named in the above heading. In the case of naturalization, immigration laws—which their attendant effect on labor supplies—are included in the power.[112] This power also encompasses control over aliens after they enter the United States—for example, regulations pertaining to Mexican farm workers (*Braceros*). The theory of bankruptcy legislation was changed during the Depression. Where previously the emphasis was upon protection of creditors, the Chandler Act (1938) now also includes emphasis upon reestablishing the assets of the debtor as a going concern. It embodies the view that his assets may be worth less as scrap or in a forced sale than if his business can be revitalized by means of negotiated settlements with the creditors. For example, a railway tunnel of a bankrupt railway may not be worth much as scrap, but it may retain at least a part of its value if the railway system can be maintained in operation as a going concern.

Other Powers. There are, of course, numerous other powers also explicitly stated in Article I, Section 8, including the power to coin money, to punish piracy, numerous military powers, etc. Of those not discussed so far, either in this chapter or in earlier chapters (for example, the power to create courts inferior to the Supreme Court has already been discussed

in Chapter 4), one is of enough interest to warrant special mention at this time. Under Clause 8, Congress is authorized "To promote the progress of science and the useful arts by securing for limited times to authors and inventors the exclusive right to their respective writings and discoveries." This power is the basis of the patent and copyright laws which will be considered in detail in Chapter 19. These laws provide for establishment of legal monopolies and embody a policy which, on its face, is inconsistent with the policy embodied in the antitrust laws.

G. CONCLUDING REMARKS

In this chapter, many of the aspects of the process of judicial law-making which were first discussed in Chapter 4 have been illustrated in the course of our discussion of numerous decisions of the Supreme Court relative to the powers conferred upon the federal government and the basic rights guaranteed to individuals in the Constitution. It is of course true that the *laissez-faire* attitude of a majority of the Justices of the Supreme Court between the end of the Civil War and 1937 resulted in a situation in which they themselves determined the specific content of many of the working rules of economic activity in the United States during that period. It is probably also true that during most of the early part of that period their views were merely a reflection of the views of what Justice Frankfurter had described in 1937 as the "dominant forces of society." The Justices employed various Constitutional clauses to strike down as unconstitutional Congressional and state legislative attempts to establish working rules with which the Justices did not agree. But, in the early 1930's a majority of the Court no longer reflected the views of the "dominant forces." Eventually the Court was forced to change its position.

Since 1937 the Court has adopted an attitude of "judicial restraint" with respect to the regulation of property and contractual rights, and it has gone far in adopting Marshall's view that the federal government has full power to regulate

---

[112] *Chinese Exclusion Case*, 130 U.S. 581 (1889).

subjects which are of "national interest" and not purely local. This acceptance may merely be evidence of a recognition by the Court that life has become complex and that national and international interdependencies are great. But even though the national and state legislative bodies have been left relatively free to formulate working rules in the area of economic activity, they have not been left free to do so in the area of civil liberties and voting requirements. Judicial supremacy continues to be a fact of life in these areas.

In June 1969, Chief Justice Earl Warren retired. Justice Abe Fortas had resigned earlier in 1969. In October 1969 an eight member Supreme Court met with the new Chief Justice Warren Burger presiding. The vacancy resulting from Justice Fortas's resignation had not yet been filled. Of the seven members other than the new Chief Justice, who had not yet participated in any Supreme Court decisions, six (Justices Douglas, Black, Brennan, Marshall, White, and Stewart) had either accepted the majority view or written majority opinions in which they had accepted the "incorporation theory" that the first eight Amendments (the Ninth and Tenth are not relevant to the present discussion) in whole or in part applied to the states by virtue of their incorporation in the Fourteenth. Justice Harlan alone had continued to reject the theory explicitly. Justice Blackmun did not, of course, take his seat until June 1970. In April 1970, Justice Burger joined in a majority opinion upholding the right of a trial judge to expel from the courtroom a defendant who engaged in disruptive conduct during the trial. This decision involved a reliance on the incorporation theory [*Illinois* v. *Allen*, 397 U.S. 337 (1970)].

The decisions of the Court pertaining to the rights of suspects in criminal cases were the subject of much bitter controversy in 1968 and 1969. These cases always involve two questions. The first question is the constitutional question just discussed, concerning the "incorporation" theory that the Bill of Rights in whole or in part applies to the states by virtue of the Fourteenth Amendment. The second question is that of the point in time at which an accused's right becomes fixed. That is, for example,

granting that an accused has a right to counsel, is he entitled to counsel when he is first arrested, or when he is first made to appear in a "line-up"; or does the right arise later when he is arraigned? With regard to this question, there has been a division of opinion on the part of the Court, stemming largely from differences concerning the consequences on effective law enforcement of holding one way or another. With regard to this issue, one of *implementation* of a constitutional right rather than one of the *existence* of the right, the possibility of a change in the present law resulting from changes in membership of the Court seems more likely than it does in the case of the issue of the *existence* of the basic constitutional right. Justice Harlan, it must be emphasised, has not denied the validity of the right; instead, in cases involving actions by state officials, he has rested the existence of the right on the due process clause of the Fourteenth Amendment alone and has rejected the rationalization of the right by means of the "incorporation" theory.

Another group of opinions which has been the source of bitter criticism of and propaganda attacking the Court, is that having to do with the enforcement of state and federal laws pertaining to the regulation of the sale and distribution of "obscene" literature. In the case of these opinions also there is one issue pertaining to the rationalization of the basic constitutional right and another pertaining to its implementation.

We have already seen that some members of the Court hold to an absolutist doctrine in the case of the First Amendment and also adopt an incorporation theory that the First Amendment applies to the states by virtue of the Fourteenth Amendment. It should also be noted that in April 1969, the Court unanimously held that the First Amendment, as made applicable to the states by incorporation in the Fourteenth, prohibits making the mere private possession of obscene material a crime.[113] Insofar as cases involving "obscene" material are concerned, it also seems unlikely that changes in the membership of the Court will result in any change in the basic constitutional doctrine that the guarantees of

---

[113] *Stanley* v. *Georgia*, 394 U.S. 557 (1969).

the First Amendment apply in the case of state action by virtue of their incorporation into the Fourteenth Amendment. What seems more likely is that any changes in law which may be forthcoming will be concerned with the implementation of the basic rights by a redefinition of "obscenity." The doctrine of judicial supremacy in the area of civil liberties will thus probably continue to be a basic policy of the Court. This policy, it should be emphasized, protects businessmen in the conduct of their affairs as much as it does any other individuals.

There is some justification for the division of power and of labor in the existence, side-by-side, of the doctrines of legislative superiority in regard to economic regulation and of judicial superiority in regard to matters of civil liberties, whatever may be the so-called "inner logic" of this state of affairs. By adopting a policy of legislative supremacy with regard to the working rules of economic activity. the Court has in effect taken the position that in this area it is the will of the people as expressed by (or to the extent that it is expressed by) legislative representatives which should prevail. But as has been noted in Chapter 4, this position postulates a will based on deliberate reflection and on information and not on a momentary response to a demagogic appeal.

By continuing to assert the policy of judicial supremacy in the civil liberties area and in the area of voter qualifications, the Court has recognized that it can serve as a brake upon "dangerous innovations" on the one hand (for example, in the case of extensions of the power of Congressional investigating committees and experimentation with the elements of procedural due process) : and, on the other, that it can serve as an instrument for producing a legislative branch which is, perhaps, more responsive to the wishes of the electorate. The civil rights and reapportionment decisions since 1954 are examples. It is also true that the Court cannot take positive action to produce "dangerous innovations" of its own accord: as has been noted in Chapter 4, judges cannot alone tear down the structure of the law, even though they may be able to make changes in it. In the cases of such changes, the legislative process and, beyond that, the process of amending the Constitution are both available to wipe out the effects.

The examination of the problem of law and social change, which was begun in Chapter 4, has now been completed. The next four chapters—the final ones in this introductory Part I—are respectively concerned with: (1) a presentation of background materials concerning the growth and development of the United States economy in the light of the institutional processes discussed so far; (2) a discussion of background materials concerning the forms of business association; (3) an examination of some basic concepts of price theory; and (4) an explanation of a number of measures of economic power and a survey of empirical studies making use of such measures.

8

Some Uses of Governmental Power to Promote Economic Activity Since 1789

The preceding chapters have given some indication of the nature of several contemporary working rules of economic activity in the United States, but those chapters have been concerned primarily with the ways in which such rules have been and are being formulated. In this chapter, another topic is introduced: the growth of some selected economic magnitudes—which may be taken as representative of the growth of economic activities since 1789.

In this regard, it is worth-while recalling at the outset Solomon Fabricant's remarks (quoted in Chapter 1) concerning John Kendrick's conclusion that the productivity of a combined unit of labor and capital had increased in the United States by an annual average amount of 1.7 percent since 1899 and that the annual rate of growth of output had been about 3.5 percent. These percentage figures, Fabricant had remarked are a measure of the "indirect effects of the increases in these resources" [capital and labor] and of "all other causes" including "contributions of the several forms of intangible capital . . . education, and so on; the economies resulting from increased

specialization . . ., economies made possible by growth in the Nation's resources and its scale of operations generally" as well as those resulting from economies or diseconomies produced by the "change in degree of competition, in volume, direction and character of governmental subsidies, in the nature of the tax system, and in other Government activities and regulations"; moreover, they include "the greater (or smaller) benefits resulting from change in the volume, character, and freedom of commerce among nations."

What Fabricant's candid remarks mean is, of course, that economic growth cannot be explained merely by attention to a few "strategic" economic variables. As has already become clear, our economic growth has taken place in a social and political context, not in a vacuum. Any meaningful discussion of particular contemporary working rules in subsequent parts of this book must rest on an assumption that the reader has some knowledge of the extent to which and the ways in which the power of government has been employed to further or to discourage one interest or another in the past.

This chapter, therefore, seeks to provide a description of the growth of some selected economic magnitudes and of some specific uses of governmental power which have accompanied that growth. Emphasis will be placed on peacetime activities, because hot and cold war policies and activities are separate topics in themselves. The changes in the form and degree of private concentrations of power over economic activity that have taken place, mainly since the last decade of the nineteenth century, will be treated in the next chapter. In this chapter, the following topics will be examined in the order indicated: (1) the territorial expansion of the United States and population growth, together with a brief examination of the growth of the labor force; (2) the development of the transportation industry and its promotion by government subsidization; (3) government subsidization of other industries and the growth of gross national product; (4) government policies relative to banking and finance; (5) the position of the United States in the international economy; and (6) a brief examination of the nature of the growth of federal government expenditures, employment, and obligations. A concluding comment appears at the end of the chapter. The background material contained in this chapter is organized according to particular topics rather than according to periods of historical time; however, within each topical subdivision, the treatment will be roughly subdivided into time periods where such subdivision seems useful.

A. TERRITORIAL EXPANSION AND THE GROWTH OF POPULATION

Territorial Expansion and Public Land Policy of the United States Since 1789

In 1790 the center of population of the United States was located 23 miles east of Baltimore. By 1960 the center had shifted to about 4 miles east of Salem, Marion County, Illinois. These two simple facts are in themselves a summary of the westward expansion of the United States and an indication of its growth.

The contiguous contemporary area of the United States lying between the Atlantic and Pacific Oceans and between the Canadian and Mexican borders had been virtually acquired by 1853, prior to the Civil War. The addition of Alaska in 1867, shortly after the Civil War, completed the acquisition of the continental United States; and the island territories (including the present State of Hawaii) were largely acquired at the end of the Spanish-American War.

It is noteworthy that the Louisiana Purchase of 1803 almost doubled the gross area of the United States less that two decades after the First Congress met. It should come as no great surprise, then, that the population per square mile of land actually decreased between 1800 and 1810, even though total population actually increased by nearly two million persons during this period.

The westward territorial expansion of the United States after 1789 was partly the result of good fortune, partly the result of boldness on the part of individuals (when Jefferson agreed to the Louisiana Purchase, he did so without any specific Constitutional authority), partly the result of ignorance (when California was ceded to the United States in 1848, neither the Mexican nor the American negotiators knew that gold had been discovered there a few days earlier), partly the result of war (the acquisitions of territories at the close of the Mexican and Spanish-American wars are clear examples of cases in which the territorial expansion was furthered as a result of armed conflict), and partly the result of a widely-held belief on the part of Americans that westward expansion to the Pacific was our "manifest destiny." Along with these factors, there were various technological developments, economic factors, attitudes, and motivations. Indeed, historians sometimes emphasize one factor, sometimes another.[1]

But, whatever the explanation of a particular acquisition of territory, the fact that each resulted in an addition to the public domain meant that a public policy

---

[1] See, for example, Warren H. Goodman, "The Origins of the War of 1812: A Survey of Changing Interpretations," *Mississippi Valley Historical Review*, Vol. XXVII (1941), pp. 171–186. Unless specifically footnoted, data in this chapter are from various statistical publications of the United States Bureau of the Census.

with respect to that acquisition was necessary. The policy of disposal of public lands to private citizens which was adopted served, perhaps, as a precedent for subsequent policies of disposal of government-owned surplus war-time productive facilities, for example, for the disposal of synthetic rubber plants to private companies after World War II. Space does not permit a detailed description of the disputes between Easterners and Westerners concerning the terms on which the public lands were sold to private individuals; but the Western support of Jackson's successful candidacy for a second term as President was reflected in the liberalization in 1832 of the terms on which public land could be purchased.[2]

In addition to policies concerning the disposal of public lands to private individuals, various measures were subsequently adopted to provide for the use of the fruits of public lands by private citizens. Thus measures were subsequently adopted to provide for the use of timber, stone, and water from public lands; grazing rights have been leased to ranchers; and gas and oil rights have been made available to private individuals. Large grants of land also have been made available to the states for purposes such as these: establishment of educational institutions (land grant colleges, among others); establishment of penal or other public institutions; payment for buildings; payment for bridges, reservoirs, and reclamation of swamp or arid lands; repayment of bonds issued by local governments for various purposes; and establishment of wildlife and forestry areas. But perhaps one of the most significant uses of the public lands has been that of subsidizing various forms of transportion.

Beginning in about 1823, very large land grants were made by the federal government to subsidize transportation facilities in the United States. The Federal Coordinator of Transportation estimated in 1938 that the total of federal and state grants of lands to the railroads alone amounted to approximately 7.65 percent more than the area of the State of Texas or 9.46 percent of the area of the continental United States (excluding Alaska). The estimated area of the federal grants of land to the railroads alone amounted to 6.93 percent of the area of the continental United States or to an area equivalent to the combined areas of Indiana, Illinois, Michigan, and Wisconsin.[3] About 183 million acres having a value estimated at $429 million were given to the railroads.

But the railroads were not the only form of transportation to be subsidized. Nor was subsidization through grants of the public lands the only form of subsidization of production of what has come today to be known (in an economic term of art) as "social overhead" capital. Before discussing this question further below, however, it will be helpful to examine the growth of population.

Population Growth and Immigration Policy

The Period of "Free" Immigration (to 1880). Population density has continued to increase since 1803, and the proportion of people living in urban areas first exceeded those living in rural areas in about 1920 and has continued to do so. Moreover, despite a slight decline in the last decade, the median age of 27.8 in 1967 was considerably higher than the median age of 15.9 in 1790.

In the 147 years between 1820 and 1967, nearly forty-four million immigrants entered the United States. Of this total, 35.35 million were Europeans, about 7.34 million were from Canada, South and Central America, and only 1.29 million were from Asia. Although in the early period of our history the annual number of immigrants represented a small proportion of the annual population increase (between 1820 and 1821 population increased by about 320,000 persons, but the total number of immigrants in 1820 was only about eight thousand persons), at a crucial point, immigration did represent a substantial part of the increase. Thus, following a famine in Ireland and failure of the wheat crop in Germany, along with political repression in the latter country, large numbers of Irish

---

[2] See Ross M. Robertson, *History of the American Economy* (New York: Harcourt, Brace and World, Inc., 1964), esp. pp. 99ff.

[3] Federal Coordinator of Transportation, *Public*

Aids to Transportation (3 vols.; Washington, D.C.: U.S. Government Printing Office, 1939), Vol. II, Part I, p. 33.

and German immigrants entered the United States in the 1840's. Between 1830 and 1840 more than six hundred thousand immigrants came. In the next decade this number increased to 1.7 million; and between 1850 and 1860 the number jumped to about 2.6 million. For the most part, the Germans became farmers in the Midwest, and the Irish provided a labor force in Eastern cities. The proportion of businessman and professional people who entered the country in this period was quite small.

The influx of immigrants during this period created problems for the principal port cities along the Atlantic coastline. At this time the only federal law governing immigration was one adopted in 1819, and it had been concerned largely with the problem of overcrowding ships transporting immigrants: the law required that such ships must have at least five tons for every two persons carried and that reports of immigrants landing in the United States be made to the federal government.[4]

In 1847 Congress adopted further legislation. It did not, however, change the basic policy but merely undertook to protect the immigrants from unscrupulous shippers who crowded their vessels and did not allow sufficient space for each passenger. Many of the passengers suffered from disease, and the mortality rate at sea amounted to about six percent.[5] The port cities of entry, such as New Orleans, New York, and Philadelphia, undertook to impose taxes on passengers coming into the city and to use the proceeds to provide medical services for the immigrants.[6] But, as has been noted in the preceding chapter, a majority of the Supreme Court in 1849 still held strongly to Marshall's view of the supremacy of the federal power under the Commerce Clause; and the tax laws were declared unconstitutional despite a strong dissenting opinion by Chief Justice Taney—who argued that they were a valid exercise of the police power.[7] The states then adopted a procedure of requiring masters of vessels to indemnify them against any expenses resulting from an immigrant's becoming a public charge and permitted payment of a cash fee in place of posting a bond. This method of regulation of immigration by individual states was the only one used until about 1880, when the period of "free" (free from federal control) immigration ended. It is thus an interesting question as to precisely who bore the "social cost" of this aspect of our economic development.

Restricted Immigration After 1880. Beginning about 1890 the principal sources of immigrants were Italy, Austria-Hungary, and Russia, or the countries of Eastern and Southern Europe rather than the countries of Northwestern and Central Europe. Changing European conditions had produced a significant shift in the cultural patterns being imported into the United States to be absorbed and slowly intermingled with those already existing here. But the new immigrants did not fuse easily with the earlier ones. Demands for restrictions on immigration were then made upon Congress. In 1879 Congress had already been faced with pressure from Western states (notably California) to limit immigration of Chinese, large numbers of whom had been imported to work on the railroads and in the mines by owners seeking a "cheap and docile" labor supply.[8] Congress, in fact, had already adopted the first restrictive immigration legislation in 1875. Ever more restrictive measures were adopted thereafter. A restriction adopted in 1921 limited each country's quota to three percent of the number of people born in that country who were residing in the United States according to the 1910 census of population. Thereafter, until Congress wrote new legislation in 1965, ever more restrictive limitations were adopted.

After 1920, although European immigration was still important, Canadian and Latin American immigration became more important. An influx of displaced persons coming to the United States after World War II resulted in large figures for 1950.

Effect of Immigration upon Population Growth. Although the influence of net immigration on population growth was generally positive between 1875 and 1966, its importance

[4] Marcus Lee Hansen, *The Atlantic Migration, 1607–1860* (Cambridge: Harvard University Press, 1945), p. 102.

[5] *Ibid.*, p. 253.

[6] *Ibid.*

[7] *The Passenger Cases*, 7 Howard 283 (1849).

[8] Marion T. Bennett, *American Immigration Policies* (Washington, D.C.: Public Affairs Press, 1963), pp. 15 ff.

relative to the natural increase in population was less than that of the natural increase in every overlapping decade after 1915. Not only did the United States adopt a more restrictive immigration policy particularly in the 1920's, but also in the Depression of the 1930's many of the aliens left to return to their native land or to go elsewhere. In any case, however, in addition to contributing to the kind of an expanding market which is essential to the establishment and continued existence of mass production industries, the influx of immigrants also provided occupants for western farm lands and a labor supply in urban areas. The adoption of the policy of "free" immigration until about 1880 represents the adoption of a particular type of working rule conducive to the expansion of economic activity in a particular situation; and the adoption of ever more restrictive policies from that date to 1965 has similarly had economic effects.

Growth of the Labor Force

In governmental statistics used in this book, the "labor force" is defined as "persons fourteen years or older." The proportion of population in the labor force has increased since 1890. Many additional women entered the employed labor force during World War II; once the war had ended, a substantial number of them stopped working.

Massive unemployment existed during the Great Depression between 1931 and 1940. Peak unemployment was reached in 1933, when approximately 25 percent of the labor force was unemployed: *thus one out of each four persons* in the labor force was unemployed in 1933. The existence of such massive unemployment explains in a rather dramatic way why the Roosevelt administration undertook many experimental measures in 1933 in an attempt to bring about a recovery.

When it is remembered that in 1933 the type of economic analysis currently employed by the Council of Economic Advisors and the various national income concepts and theories of income determination which are today commonplace in elementary economics textbooks had not

yet been formulated, the experimentation with working rules which occurred during this period becomes quite comprehensible. For example, legislation favorable to organized labor was adopted in this period. In the absence of any meaningful solution to the unemployment problem by economists, those in charge of the government experimented with various measures: the problems facing those holding political power were pressing and real. It was not until 1936 that John Maynard Keynes published *The General Theory of Employment, Interest, and Money*. And he began his contribution with an attack on the unrealistic assumptions so widely accepted by the economic theorists of that day. Thus, Chapter 1 of his work consisted of a single paragraph, the concluding sentence of which asserted that classical economics dealt with a "special case."[9]

One of the New Deal measures did in fact involve an abandonment of a philosophy of competition in favor of a philosophy of detailed "self-regulation" of industry. This program, established by the National Industrial Recovery Act (NIRA), will be described in the next chapter. It has been the subject of much criticism by economists, but less often is it recognized or admitted in such criticisms that meaningful policy recommendations by economists about how to solve the problem of unemployment were lacking and that the NIRA was merely *one* of a number of experimental measures undertaken at this time, some of which—like the Reciprocal Trade Agreements Act discussed later—have generally been strongly approved by economists.

B. GOVERNMENT AND THE SUBSIDIZATION OF THE TRANSPORTATION INDUSTRY

The Growth of Transportation Facilities: Basic Data

The rapid westward movement of population and the economic development of the United States could not have proceeded as rapidly as they did had not the federal as well as the state and municipal

---

[9] John Maynard Keynes, *The General Theory of Employment, Interest, and Money* (New York: Harcourt, Brace and Co., Inc., 1936), p. 3.

governments adopted policies favorable to the development of those forms of transportation which had at a particular time become feasible. Table 8-1 gives some indication of the growth of transportation facilities in the United States. Note that as new forms of transportation have been developed, the *relative* importance of older forms has decreased; that is, we see that the railroad mileage operated was at a maximum when domestic airline service was nonexistent. We now turn to a brief survey of federal assistance to the development of transportation.

Table 8-1

Water, Land, and Air Transportation Facilities, 1789-1966

Year	Tons of Shipping; Documented Vessels (Thousands)	Surfaced Roads (Thousands of Miles)	Total Railway Mileage Operated (Thousands of Miles)	Domestic Airline Route Mileage (Thousands of Miles)
1789	202	0	0	0
1800	972	1.2	0	0
1820	1,280	9.6	0.022	0
1840	2,181	64.4	2.8	0
1860	5,354	88.3	30.6	0
1880	4,068	96.1	93.3	0
1900	5,165	128.5	258.8	0
1920	16,234	369.1	406.6	. . .
1940	14,018	1,367.0	406.0	42.8
1960	28,581	2,371.0ᵃ	381.7	101.4
1963	25,691	. . .	374.5	. . .
1964	26,160	. . .	372.3	104.8
1965	26,516	. . .	370.6	104.9
1966	26,522	2,831.0	370.1	104.7

a 1957 figure.

Sources: Data compiled from U.S. Bureau of the Census, *Historical Statistics of the United States, 1789–1945* (Washington, D.C.: U.S. Government Printing Office, 1949); *idem, Historical Statistics from Colonial Times to 1957;* and *idem, Statistical Abstract, 1968.*

Albert Gallatin's Plan for Development of a Transportation Network (1808)

The interest of the federal government in the development of transportation facilities was clearly evident at a very early period in our history. In 1807, the Senate requested Secretary of the Treasury Albert Gallatin to prepare a plan for the development of transportation facilities in the United States which would make use "of such means as are within the power of Congress."[10]

Gallatin sent his plan to the First Session of the Tenth Congress in 1808. Although Congress did not adopt all of his proposals, in the course of time nearly all of them have become realities. Gallatin advocated the use of the federal power: (1) to assist in the establishment of coastal canals from north to south to open inland navigation for sea vessels from Massachusetts to North Carolina, as well as to establish a "great turnpike road" from Maine to Georgia along the entire Atlantic seacoast; (2) to improve east to west navigation on rivers and to assist in building canals around rapids and waterfalls, as well as four turnpike roads from the Appalachian mountains to the Mississippi River; and (3) to develop what has now become known as the St. Lawrence Seaway, making it possible to navigate inland along this route from the Atlantic Ocean to the Great

[10] For a complete discussion, see Carter Goodrich, *Government Promotion of American Canals and Railroads,* *1800–1890* (New York: Columbia University Press, 1960), p. 27.

Lakes. He recommended that Congress appropriate $20 million for these developments.[11]

Actions by the Federal and State Governments to Foster Road and Canal Building

Even prior to making his *Report*, Gallatin had recommended to Congress that part of the revenue from sale of public lands be used to finance the establishment of internal transportation facilities and, when Ohio came into the Union in 1803, the policy of using such revenues for road building was incorporated into the enabling legislation. In 1806 Congress authorized the building of the Cumberland Road,[12] which extended by 1838 from Cumberland, Maryland to Vandalia, Illinois. Moreover, many states (*e.g.*, Virginia, Maryland, and New York) had already themselves undertaken canal building and road development projects. The drain on federal finances during the War of 1812 temporarily delayed further developments; but, after the war, agitation for internal improvements again increased.[13] Indeed, in supporting the charter of the Second Bank of the United States (to be further discussed later), John C. Calhoun proposed to use the federal government's share of the income for internal improvements. Several projects were undertaken at the federal level, but Goodrich has pointed out that an unwillingness on the part of Congress to raise the necessary tax revenues, combined with opposition by Jacksonian forces in the 1830's, further combined with sectional and state differences and disagreements, all operated to keep the role of the federal government in the building of turnpikes and canals in this period a secondary and indirect one.[14]

Jerome Cranmer has pointed out that between 1815 and 1860 two types of investments in canals occurred. Canals were considered worth-while projects in this period if they either: (1) stimulated the economic life of an economic region ("developmental projects"), even though they were not in themselves profitable; or (2) if they were profitable ("exploitative projects"), even though built in already developed regions.[15] He has cited the well-known Erie Canal as an example of the first type and various canals built in the Trans-Allegheny mountain region (*e.g.*, the Chesapeake and Ohio) as examples of the second. He has also estimated that the amount of private investment in exploitative canals on the Eastern Seaboard in this period greatly exceeded the amount invested by the states in development projects. In the Trans-Allegheny area the proportions were reversed, with state government investments far exceeding private investments. And he has also concluded that "Public expenditures dominated in the West, 89 percent of canal expenditure being accomplished on state account," while in the South "87 percent of investment was by private companies."[16]

Government and the Development of Rivers and Harbors

Prior to the development of the steamboat, river transportation was conducted by means of flatboats and barges. Steamboat operations were begun on the Ohio and Mississippi Rivers in 1811, and regular service was established in 1817. Although little was done until after the Civil War to improve the channels of the Mississippi River system (Mississippi, Ohio, and Missouri Rivers and tributaries), traffic steadily increased from about 67 thousand tons to more than 2 million tons between 1814 and 1860, as measured by receipts at New Orleans.[17] During the Civil War, practically all traffic other than military traffic ceased. After the Civil War, competition from railroads and an excess of boats left over from the military uses of the war produced a situation in which not more than half of the existing fleet could find

[11] Albert Gallatin, "Report to Congress on Roads and Canals, 1808," *American State Papers* (Washington, D.C.: Gales and Seaton, 1832), *Miscellaneous Series*, Vol. I, pp. 724 ff.

[12] Goodrich, *op. cit.*, pp. 23 ff.

[13] *Ibid.*, p. 37.

[14] *Ibid.*, pp. 37–47.

[15] H. Jerome Cranmer, "Canal Investment, 1815–1860," in National Bureau of Economic Research,

Trends in the American Economy in the Nineteenth Century (Princeton: Princeton University Press, 1960), pp. 547–570, at p. 557.

[16] *Ibid.*, pp. 558–564. (By "West," he means the Trans-Allegheny area.)

[17] This section draws heavily upon material to be found in *Public Aids to Transportation, op. cit.*, Vol. III, pp. 15 ff.

profitable employment. Where, previous to the war, individual ownership and operation of boats had been the rule, after the war the "through" and "long" haul business was taken over largely by pools and joint stock associations.

After the enactment of the Transportation Act of 1920, occasioned by the discontinuance of the federal wartime operation and the return of the railroads to private owners, interest in inland water transportation, particularly on the Mississippi River, increased. The 1920 Act provided for numerous financial aids to water transportation companies, and additional aid was provided under the Inland Waterways Corporation Act of 1924.

By 1936 total federal expenditures appropriated and alloted for both river and harbor improvements amounted to about 2.9 billion dollars; of this total, 77 percent had been made available since 1910, 64 percent since 1920, and 33 percent since 1933. The grand total of federal, state, and local expenditures on water terminals amounted to slightly less than a billion dollars in 1932. Total expenditures made under the direction of the Chief of Engineers of the United States Army for maintenance and improvement of rivers, harbors, flood control, and other miscellaneous works amounted to about one billion dollars in the year 1962 or to about one-third of the total expended up to 1936.

Government Subsidization of the Railroads

The peak of the canal-building era was reached between 1830 and 1840 and, as has been noted, the importance of the Mississippi River system as a transportation facility declined after the Civil War, although this is not to say that shipping by means of inland waterways was not important thereafter. As has also been noted above, one principal factor accounting for the decline in the relative importance of inland water transportation was the development of the railroads. In 1820 there were perhaps not more than 22 miles of railroad being used in the United States, probably as tramways.[18] By the time of the

Civil War, there were about 31 thousand miles of road being operated. The period of greatest subsidization of the railroads occurred in the twenty years following 1850.

In 1851 the Erie Railroad was completed; it was the first railroad to make a connection with the Great Lakes; the preceding year had marked the beginning of the system of land grant subsidization of railroads with a grant by Congress to the State of Illinois to assist in the building of the Illinois Central Railroad and to the States of Mississippi and Alabama to aid in the extension of the line from the Ohio River to Mobile.[19] In 1862 the Union and Central Pacific Railways were chartered by Congress and given large grants of land. They formed the first transcontinental railway; the last link in the road was completed in 1869. Thereafter, the Northern Pacific was completed in 1883, having been chartered and subsidized in 1864; the Southern Pacific had similarly been chartered in 1866. By 1893, there were five transcontinental lines. States also made land grants; Texas, for example, granted about 35 million acres for railway construction.[20]

Aside from the very large land grants which have already been mentioned, tariffs on railway iron were suspended, loans were guaranteed both by states and municipalities, cash and materials were contributed, banking privileges were made available, and various other forms of assistance were given. In 1938, the Federal Coordinator of Transportation estimated that the public aids given the railroads up to 1936 amounted to 1,443 million dollars.

Thus, in the early period of railroad development, there was much public assistance to the railroads; but by the late 1860's, for numerous reasons which will be considered more fully in Part III, demands for regulation and some abortive attempts at railroad regulation, particularly in the Midwest, had made their appearance. These demands culminated in the Act to Regulate Interstate Commerce of 1887 and the establishment of the Interstate Commerce Commission. Much of the

[18] Philip Locklin, *Economics of Transportation* (3rd ed.; Homewood, Ill.: Richard D. Irwin, Inc., 1947), p. 89.

[19] *Public Aids to Transportation, op. cit.,* Vol. II, pp. 12ff.
[20] *Public Aids to Transportation, op. cit.,* Vol. I, Part 1, p. 13.

regulatory experience accumulated in the course of operations of this agency was subsequently embodied in legislation establishing additional federal regulatory commissions in the 1930's.

Government Subsidization of Ocean Shipping

Shipbuilding and ocean transportation have been important industries almost from the beginning of our history; these related industries served as a substantial source of foreign exchange earnings. In 1800, for example, 995 vessels were built in the United States, and in no year between 1815 and 1939 were fewer than 500 ships built. In many cases, especially after 1945, the number has exceeded 1,500 annually. The importance and significance of American clipper ships to the economic development of New England and the Middle Atlantic States in particular were very great.

Aside from the assistance given to inland shipping in the form of subsidies to canals and expenditures for river and harbor improvements, the federal government has, almost since it was first organized, provided much assistance to ocean shipping. The First Congress provided assistance by permitting registration under the American flag only of ships built in the United States and owned by American citizens; it also provided for a ten percent reduction of duties and imposed a tonnage tax in favor of American shipping in the first tariff law.

In 1845 Congress provided for further subsidization of ocean shipping by means of mail contracts, with preference given to steamships which could be converted into vessels of war. Between 1847 and 1858 the amount spent on subsidization of steamship lines to Bremen, LeHavre, Liverpool, Panama, Oregon, and Cuba amounted to $14.4 million. Subsidization was discontinued between 1858 and 1867 but revived in that year and continued to 1874 when a graft scandal brought about its discontinuance. In 1891 Congress passed the Ocean Mail Act which provided a basis for expenditure of $29.6 million by 1928, with more than half going to the American Line in particular. Mail subsidies gradually increased from $9 million in 1929 to $29

million in 1934. The Merchant Marine Act of 1920 also provided for a loan fund of $25 million to assist in construction of new ships and this sum was increased to $250 million in 1928.[21] Subsidization of the cost of construction by payment of a differential to cover the excess of cost of construction in United States shipyards over cost in foreign yards was authorized in 1936, and similar operating differentials were also established. In addition, half of United States Government financed cargoes must be transported in United States Flagships, and the coastwise trade has long been reserved exclusively for United States shipping.[22]

Government Subsidization of Airlines

Subsidization of domestic air carriers was begun under the Air Mail Act of 1925 with the result that payments to air mail carriers exceeded revenue from air mail stamps by nearly $7 million in 1929. In 1930, the Watres Act provided for payments to airmail carriers; the total amount increased from $17 million in 1931 to about $20 million in 1932. Under further legislation, payments amounted to about $14 million in 1938. The contemporary subsidization procedure is provided for in Section 406 of the Federal Aviation Act of 1958, under which (as will be discussed in Part III) the size of payments is determined by the Civil Aeronautics Board after a hearing and in accordance with statutory provisions. Moreover, air carriers also receive government assistance in the form of navigation aids, aeronautical research and development expenditures by government in very large amounts, and the use of airport and airway facilities. Total federal aid for the airport program alone from 1947 to 1963 amounted to more than $798 million; in 1966 alone, the federal government contributed about $18 million. The Airport Facilities Expansion and Improvement Act of 1969 provided for extensive additional subsidization.

Government Expenditures for Highways

Total federal and state funds spent on highway improvements have, of course,

[21] *Subsidy and Subsidy-Effect Programs of the U.S. Government* (Materials Prepared for the Joint Economic Committee, 89th Cong., 1st sess.) (Washington, D.C.: U.S. Government Printing Office, 1965), p. 43.

[22] *Ibid.*, see esp. pp. 46 ff.

shown a substantial increase since widespread use of the automobile has become a fact of American life. In 1922, for example, the total combined expenditures amounted to only about $186 million, but in 1966 the figure for total contracts awarded was $5.4 billion.

Although the statistics could be multiplied and given in finer detail, what has been said is sufficient to establish the fact that federal assistance to all forms of transportation has been massive, varied, and continuous throughout our history and that the indirect effects of this policy must be taken into account along with the direct effects in explaining the growth of total output in the American economy since 1789.

C. GOVERNMENT SUBSIDIZATION OF OTHER INDUSTRIES; GROWTH OF GROSS NATIONAL PRODUCT

Growth of Gross National Product

There are no reliable estimates of gross national product prior to 1869. However, in 1960, Robert Gallman provided estimates of the growth of total commodity output between 1839 and 1899.[23] According to Gallman's study, commodity output (defined as the sum of the values added to products by agriculture, mining and manufacturing, and construction) increased elevenfold between 1839 and 1899; and, since population during this period increased less than half as rapidly as commodity output, output per capita (the ratio of the value of commodity output to population) in 1899 was about two and a half times higher than in 1839. It may also be noted that measured at 1958 prices gross national product amounted to 706.9 billion dollars in 1958, while in 1933 during the depth of the Great Depression gross national product, also measured at 1958 prices, amounted to only 141.5 billion dollars. The comparable figure for the year 1929 is 203.6 and that for 1941 is 263.7. Obviously, there has been much growth in the American economy since the beginning of World War II.

The Shift from Agricultural to Industrial Production

According to Gallman's study, the percentage of total commodity output accounted for by agriculture decreased consistently from 72 percent of the total in 1839 to 53 percent in 1869, while the proportion accounted for by mining increased from one to two percent and that attributable to manufacturing increased from 17 to 33 percent.[24] A similar shift in the relative importance of these sectors continued after 1869 and the importance of federal, state, and local governments as a source of gross national product also increased. In national income accounting statistics, the contribution of government is generally measured at cost, while the contribution of the private sector is measured at market prices; this difference in treatment arises out of the lack of measures of the "market value" of government's contribution and reflects a value judgment on the part of the producer of the statistics.

Government and Technological Developments

Among the principal technological developments which occurred prior to the Civil War were the invention of the cotton gin by Eli Whitney in 1794, the application of steam power to water transportation by Robert Fulton in 1807, the building of the Baltimore and Ohio Railroad in 1828, the patenting of the reaper by Cyrus McCormick in 1834, the patenting of the revolver (the "six-shooter") by Samuel Colt in 1836, the introduction of the steel plow by John Deere in 1837, the accidental discovery of the process for vulcanization of rubber by Charles Goodyear in 1839, the transmission of the first telegraph message by Samuel Morse in 1844, the patenting of the sewing machine by Elias Howe in 1846, and the opening (for a short time) of a transatlantic cable in 1858. Moreover, gold was discovered in California in 1848, and the modern oil industry was born with the drilling of Drake's petroleum well near Titusville, Pennsylvania in 1859.

All these events, as well as many others,

[23] Robert E. Gallman, "Commodity Output, 1839–1899" in National Bureau of Economic Research, *Trends in American Economy in the Nineteenth Century, op. cit.*, pp. 13–71, esp. p. 15.

[24] *Ibid.*, p. 24.

it has been noted, exerted significant influences upon the course of our economic development as well as upon the shift from agricultural to industrial production. Among the significant developments between the Civil War and World War I were, of course, the development of new flour-milling processes in 1874, the patenting of barbed wire and the telephone in 1876, Edison's invention of the incandescent light in 1879, and Ottmar Mergenthaler's invention of the linotype in 1885. In 1903, the Wright brothers demonstrated their aeroplane at Kitty Hawk, and in 1909 Henry Ford announced that his company would thereafter manufacture only the Model T, making an individual means of motor transportation available on a mass basis. The present developments of atomic energy, space travel, television, and automation are merely the logical further consequences of prior technological achievements in a continuing process of putting together things and ideas into new relationships. And just as the past developments have had their effect upon the relationships of men to men and of men to things, so can those which will occur in the future be expected to have similar effects.

For example, the decrease in the relative importance of agriculture has in no small degree been the result of increased efficiency arising from the technological developments mentioned above. This increased efficiency has been also partly the result of the fact that:

... For almost a century, research in agriculture has been sponsored and largely financed by the Federal Government through the Department of Agriculture and the State experimental stations. The results of this research have been widely disseminated by the Government both in technical publications and in nontechnical instructions to operating farmers. The results show, for example, in the rate of increase of output per man-hour in agriculture, which has grown by about 6 percent a year over the past two decades, or about double the rate in nonagricultural industries.[25]

Whether or not legislation adopted in 1965 to assist small business also in this way will have its intended effect remains to be seen.

Aside from the monopoly privilege provided under patent and copyright laws (which will be considered more fully in Part II), the federal government has also come to play a major role in the financing of industrial research and development. Of approximately $16.6 billion spent by private industry for research and development in 1968, $8.8 billion or more than half of the total was federally financed.

Although the federal government is the largest provider of funds, by far the largest recipient of funds has been private industry. The use of government funds by private industry has been primarily for development, with applied research next in importance. Expenditures for basic research have been relatively smaller. One estimate has put the estimated total of 1968 federal government obligations for research and development at about $16.7 billion, with $2.33 billion assigned to basic research, about $4.0 billion allocated to applied research, and more than $10.34 billion assigned to development.[26]

Although the data do not permit precise quantitative estimates, it is clear that in this area of economic activity, as in the others which have been discussed, the role of the federal government is important; moreover, the importance of the role of the federal government as a provider of funds has been increasing, particularly in the case of industrial research and development.

Government Actions to Aid Agriculture, Especially Since World War I

The decline in the relative importance of agriculture, combined with the problem of a large farm population, a large part of which falls within the "low income" or poverty category, has produced the so-called "agricultural problem" in the United States. Some of the methods of dealing with the problem reflect the fact that the agricultural areas are strongly represented in the Congress and that the number of "agricultural" votes in Congress has not been proportional to the population of the agricultural areas. Decisions of the Supreme Court relative to the question of legislative

[25] *Annual Report of the Joint Economic Committee on the January 1962 Economic Report of the President* (87th Cong., 2d sess.) (Washington, D.C.: U.S. Government Printing Office, 1962), p. 75.

[26] United States Department of Commerce, Bureau of the Census, *Statistical Abstract, 1968* (Washington, D.C.: U.S. Government Printing Office, 1968), Table 774, p. 526.

reapportionment, as has already been noted in Chapters 4 and 7, may be expected to have a direct effect on this aspect of the matter in the future.

It has been widely recognized that, in the absence of governmental control programs, agriculture is a much more highly competitive sector of the economy than is the industrial sector. Numerous studies, beginning with one in 1935 by Gardiner C. Means, have also shown that agricultural prices fluctuate much more widely than do industrial prices.[27] Thus, farm incomes have tended to fluctuate, while the prices of nonfarm items purchased by farmers have tended to remain relatively stable.

A decline in farm prices following World War I—an inevitable reaction to the high levels of output and prices which existed during the war—resulted in the Capper-Volstead Act of 1922 which granted agricultural associations and cooperatives an exemption from the antitrust laws and the right to process, prepare, handle, and market goods in interstate commerce. Special farm credit facilities were established in 1923; and between 1924 and 1928 Congress several times adopted tariff laws favoring domestic agricultural production, but these were vetoed by the President. In 1925, Congress also adopted the Hoch-Smith Resolution directing the Interstate Commerce Commission to prescribe the lowest possible rates for transportation of agricultural products.[28] However, the Supreme Court interpreted the resolution as "more in the nature of a hopeful characterization of an object deemed desirable, than of a rule intended to control rate making."[29]

Then in June of 1929, during the Hoover administration and just a few months prior to the stock market crash, the Agricultural Marketing Act was enacted. The Act provided for producers to form marketing cooperatives owned and controlled by themselves, thereby eliminating competi-

tion among them, which would operate to stabilize prices. A Federal Farm Board, capitalized at $500 million, was created to make loans to these cooperatives. The beginning of the federal program of stabilization of farm prices thus antedates the programs of the Roosevelt administration by several years, although this fact is often ignored.

Since 1929 (as we have seen in the discussion of *Wickard* v. *Filburn* in the preceding chapter), there have been various programs to reduce output or to restrict the marketing of surpluses, as well as programs to remove surplus output from the market, commodity price support programs to fix minimum prices of selected commodities, and programs to raise prices of agricultural commodities relative to those of industrial products. It has been estimated that between 1932 and 1959 the total cost of programs aimed primarily at stabilization of farm prices and incomes amounted to about $17.7 billion.[30]

Other types of assistance to farmers, some of which have already been mentioned, have included the credit terms embodied in the public land policies, the establishment of land-grant colleges, and the support of agricultural research programs. Programs for conservation of agricultural resources, including forest service programs, accounted for about $7 billion between 1932 and 1959; credit and related programs for rural electrification and telephone facilities amounted to about $1.6 billion; various research and marketing activities, as well as educational facilities, totaled $3.24 billion; and farm credit programs accounted for $0.5 billion in the same period.[31]

Government Aids to and Subsidization of Business Since 1789

Hamilton's Report on Manufactures. The private business sector of the economy represented by nonagricultural output has also been the recipient of much assistance

[27] See particularly, Saul Nelson and Walter G. Keim, *Price Behavior and Business Policy*, Temporary National Economic Committee Monograph No. 1 (Washington, D.C.: U.S. Government Printing Office, 1949). Gardiner Means's study was made for the Department of Agriculture and published as *Industrial Prices and Their Relative Inflexibility* (Senate Document No. 13, 74th Cong., 1st sess.) (Washington, D.C.: U.S. Government Printing Office, 1935).

[28] See W. H. Wagner, *The Hoch-Smith Resolution* (Washington, D.C.: W. H. Wagner, 1929).

[29] *Ann Arbor Railroad Co. v. United States*, 281 U.S. 658 (1930).

[30] *Subsidy and Subsidylike Programs* (Materials Prepared for the Joint Economic Committee, 86th Cong., 2d sess.) (Washington, D.C.: U.S. Government Printing Office, 1960), p. 28.

[31] *Ibid.*

and numerous subsidies in addition to the subsidies given in the cases of transportation and agriculture. Indeed, the demand of some elements of this sector for protection from competition by imports has been strong ever since the First Congress met. On April 11, 1789, shortly after it had convened, the First Congress was petitioned by the "tradesmen and mechanics of Baltimore for a protective tariff." As a matter of fact, the first four documents in Volume 1 of the "Finance Series" of *American State Papers* are petitions from citizens in Baltimore, New York, Philadelphia, and Boston respectively petitioning for protection from competition by imports.[32]

Alexander Hamilton's often-mentioned *Report on Manufactures* was submitted to the Second Session of the First Congress in 1791. In it he proposed many things: the encouragement of immigration, the encouragement of research, measures to facilitate transportation of goods, a system of "judicious regulations for inspection of manufactured commodities" (for the purpose of preventing "fraud and improving the quality and preserving the character of the goods"), and a protective tariff.[33] To some extent, the recommendation for inspection of manufactured products may be considered a forerunner of contemporary legislation such as the Food and Drug Act and of some of the powers of the Federal Trade Commission (to be further discussed in Part II), but even partial implementation of this recommendation was not undertaken until the 1900's by Congress with the adoption of the Federal Pure Food and Drug Act in 1906. (The recommendation can also be interpreted as evidence that Hamilton was a mercantilist.)

The Embargo of 1808 and the Rise of the Protective Tariff. Congress did not act immediately upon Hamilton's recommendation for a protective tariff. Prior to Hamilton's *Report*, Congress had adopted a weak protective tariff law in 1789. Frank Taussig, whose book, *The Tariff History of the United States* (first edition published in 1892), has acquired the status of a classic, pointed to the fact that up to 1808 the French Revolution and its accompanying

wars "opened to this country profitable markets for its agricultural products" as well as "profitable employment for its shipping" with corresponding prosperity; consequently, the existing prosperity "prevented the growth of any strong feeling in favor of assisting manufactures" by means of a protective tariff.

However, as Taussig also pointed out, during the Napleonic Wars, England and France sought to deny each other the benefits of trade with the United States, and each country undertook to blockade the trade of the other (Napoleon by the Berlin and Milan Decrees and England by the Orders in Council). Jefferson, who had by now become President, induced Congress to adopt the Embargo Act (December 22, 1807), under which the departure of ships from American ports for foreign ports was completely prohibited, in the hope of bringing about an understanding with the European powers. But no understanding was reached, and the effect of the Act was to reduce foreign exchange earnings from shipping, to destroy the market for agricultural products, and to reduce the supply of imported manufactured products. The Embargo Act was repealed in 1809 during Madison's administration because it had not brought England and France to terms. This law was followed a few months later by the Non-Intercourse Law which permitted commerce with all countries except France and England. And, eventually in 1812, war was declared on England. During the war, all trade with England was prohibited, and duties were doubled, largely in the hope of increasing revenue.

The effect of this series of events, according to Taussig, was to give "an enormous stimulus to those branches of industry whose products had before been imported." Among others, he cited manufacture of "cotton goods, woolen cloths, iron, glass, pottery, and many other articles" as being greatly stimulated; he also provided case studies of the stimulation of cotton, wool, and iron production in particular, and noted that "the restrictive legislation of 1808–15 was, for the time being, equivalent to extreme protection."[34]

[32] *American State Papers, op. cit., Finance Series*, Vol. 1, pp. 5ff.
[33] *Ibid.*, p. 123.

[34] F. W. Taussig, *The Tariff History of the United States* (8th ed.; New York: G. W. Putnam and Sons, 1931), pp. 16–17.

The basis for a movement for a strong protective tariff was thus laid by "the rise of a considerable class of manufacturers" during the events surrounding the Napoleonic Wars and the War of 1812, a class of manufacturers "whose success was dependent largely on the continuance of protection." Thus, political action was taken: new working rules were adopted. Beginning with the Tariff Act of 1816, Congress enacted successively more protectionist measures up until about 1828.

At the same time, the South had been turning more and more toward cotton production based upon the institution of slavery. Whitney had patented the cotton gin in 1794; thereafter cotton production had increased rapidly, from about 17 thousand bales in 1794 to 764 thousand bales in 1829. Because the Southern economy was based on agriculture, the South felt no great need for a protective tariff for its products and objected to the high tariff on manufactured products which produced higher prices and benefited only the North. At the same time, the "Westward Movement" was taking place on a broad front: by 1819 there were twenty-two states in the union—Kentucky, Tennessee, Vermont, Louisiana, Mississippi, Alabama, Indiana, and Illinois had been added to the original thirteen plus Ohio (which, it has already been noted, had been admitted as the fourteenth state in 1803). By 1819, therefore, the agricultural South and the industrial North each consisted of eleven states (there were eleven states north of the Mason Dixon Line and eleven states south of it), with an equal voice in the Senate. The effect of the admission of the twenty-third state, as Herbert Agar has pointed out, would be to destroy this political equilibrium. Each group of states possessed "appendages" from which new states might be formed.[35] Thus, under the Missouri Compromise, Maine was admitted as a free state in 1820 and Missouri as a slave state in 1821. The equilibrium was maintained.

At this time, the West needed transportation facilities, and pressure for a system of internal improvements stemming from that section of the country was strong. In addition, pressure for a liberal land policy was also strong. In this situation, Cranmer's conclusion that 89 percent of the canal expenditures in the Trans-Allegheny region between 1815 and 1860 were financed by state action should come as no surprise; nor should there by any surprise at the fact that the federal public land policies were being constantly liberalized as time passed.

Henry Clay sought to reconcile the various competing interests with his "American System," under which he would have encouraged manufactures in the North by a high protective tariff, thereby also creating a market for the raw materials produced by the South and West, and at the same time he would have financed the building of transportation facilities to the West with federal expenditures. Thus he (along with Calhoun, as has already been noted) favored the establishment of the Second Bank of the United States and the use of federal income derived therefrom for purposes of internal improvement, despite the fact that the Jeffersonian agrarians had been strongly opposed to Hamilton's First Bank of the United States. A way now existed for the Bank to be of service to agricultural interests as well as to business interests.

The Tariff Act of 1828 was the most protectionist measure enacted up to that date. It was followed by a reduced, but still protective, tariff act in 1832, and there occurred the well-known "nullification controversy." The 1828 Tariff Act had been known as the "Tariff of Abominations"; and in South Carolina a state convention asserted the right to declare the tariff laws of 1828 and 1832 unconstitutional. President Jackson, whose election in 1828 represented a triumph for the West, was not impressed and asserted the federal authority firmly. Henry Clay thereupon introduced a compromise measure in 1833. It provided for a gradual reduction in tariffs until 1842, and a general decline in tariffs followed—with an exception between 1842 and 1844—until the Civil War.

By 1853 the territorial expansion had been completed: Texas had been admitted to the Union; the Mexican War had been fought; the sectional controversies concerning the admission of new states had

[35] See Herbert Agar, *The Price of Union* (Boston: Houghton Mifflin Co., 1950), pp. 186 ff.

continued to give rise to compromises (such as that of 1850 under which California was to be admitted as a free state and the remaining territories acquired from Mexico were to be admitted as free or slave as their constitutions provided); the Kansas-Nebraska Act (1854) had repealed the Missouri Compromise; and the stage was set for Lincoln's election and the Civil War which followed.

After the Civil War, the South was no longer able to voice effective opposition to the tariff in the Congress, and with an occasional exception (*e.g.*, in 1885 during the administration of Grover Cleveland, the first Democrat elected to the Presidency after the Civil War), high tariffs were the rule until about 1913. Then, during the Wilson administration, the Underwood Act was adopted by a Congress completely controlled by the Democrats (at a special session called by President Wilson for that purpose).[36] According to Taussig's computations, in 1900 the effective average rate of duties was about 49 percent of dutiable imports; but in 1918, while the Underwood Act was in effect, the rate stood at about 24 percent of dutiable imports.[37]

In 1921, however, the Republicans regained control, and an Emergency Tariff Act was adopted raising duties. In 1922 the Fordney-McCumber Tariff Act was passed. The latter contained the highest rates in American tariff history. And, although the idea had been advanced earlier in debates, the 1922 Act adopted for the first time the "principle" that the costs of production of American and foreign production were to be "equalized," with the term "equalization" being understood to mean that American goods were to be protected. The Act provided for the Tariff Commission (which had been created in 1916) to investigate costs of production and to recommend to the President in particular cases that he either raise or lower duties for purposes of "equalizing" costs. This task was itself an impossible one, given the problems involved in making precise economic measurements. In fact, according to Taussig, the Commission "pretended to achieve the impossible—figures exact to a fraction of a cent." Moreover, although the Commission was supposed to be a "judicial body, standing aloof from any controversial question," it was clear that "its leading members were actuated in their conclusions by a wish to make protection higher, and to shape and interpret the cost figures so as to bring about higher duties."[38] (As has been noted in Chapter 6, many career members of the Executive Branch still consider the Tariff Commission a protectionist agency.)

Protectionism thus remained ascendent. Then, in 1930, the Smoot-Hawley Tariff Act raised duties even higher. In many cases, duties were raised 50 to 100 percent higher than they had been fixed in 1922. By the end of 1931, more than 25 countries had retaliated by imposing restrictions on United States imports. World trade had completely deteriorated.

The Reciprocal Trade Agreements Program: Trade Policy Since 1934. June 1934 marked the end of the policy of extreme protectionism which the United States had previously espoused. On June 12, an Amendment was adopted to Section 350 of the Tariff Act. The Amendment authorized the President to negotiate reciprocal trade agreements in a process of trading reductions in our own trade restrictions in exchange for reductions in restrictions by the other party to such an agreement. The Act was not based on a philosophy of "free trade," and there was no reference in it to the traditional economic theory of comparative advantage—according to which increased specialization made possible by increased international trade leads to an increase in total world output without an increased use of inputs, hence at a lower cost. The purpose of the Act was stated to be to expand "the foreign markets of the United States," and it was adopted with a view to increasing employment in our export industries. From the point of view of those who held political power, the Act was another of the many experimental attempts to overcome the problems created by the Depression.

The Act itself did not specifically limit the negotiation of trade agreements to negotiations between the United States and a *single* other party. Consequently, in

[36] Taussig, *op. cit.*, pp. 415 ff.
[37] *Ibid.*, p. 528.

[38] *Ibid.*, pp. 522–533.

1947 the procedure of negotiations was generalized in the General Agreement on Tariffs and Trade (GATT) so that multilateral tariff reduction negotiating sessions have become the general rule. Instead of being a bilateral agreement, the GATT is a multilateral agreement, and reductions in trade restrictions negotiated between any two of its parties are immediately generalized to apply to all of the parties.[39] Moreover (as noted in Chapter 6), the GATT is an Executive Agreement negotiated according to the delegation of authority given to the President in the Trade Agreements Act of 1934; thus it required *no* Senate approval after it had been negotiated, at least not to the extent that its provisions could be implemented by the President without Congressional action.

Once the President had exhausted the power to reduce tariffs granted in the original legislation on some items (originally he could negotiate reductions up to 50 percent of the existing tariffs), if he wished to employ these items in further bargains, he was forced to return to the Congress with a request for additional power to reduce tariffs on such items. The postwar battles in Congress relative to the trade agreements program since World War II have been concerned largely with how much additional power (subject to what limitations or "escape" clauses) should be delegated for what time period with respect to what goods. But what is important in the present context is that since the First Congress met in 1789, business—and also labor—interests have demanded and often obtained protection from foreign competition. And, as we will see in the next chapter, the tariff was considered at the turn of the century by many to be the reason for the rise of the business trusts. The present form of the trade agreements program is an excellent illustration of the way in which the working rules of economic activity may be changed by action of the Executive Branch under a delegation of power by the Legislative Branch.

The Postal Subsidy to Business. In addition to the protection obtained from tariff barriers, American business has also bene-fited from United States policy with respect to the carriage of the mails. The greatest dollar loss experienced in operations of the Post Office has consistently been in second class mail, which consists primarily of newspapers and periodicals. Low rates in this class have benefited publishers of newspapers and magazines and those advertising in them. Third and fourth class mail [which consists of merchandise, printed matter, and other mailable material which is not in the first (letters) and second classes] has also been carried at a considerable loss to the benefit of various business firms using advertisements distributed in this way. In these days of instant coffee and instant bank loans, some of this material may well deserve the designation of "instant waste." In fiscal year 1963, the deficit from second, third, and fourth class mail and from rural operations combined, totaled $916.1 million compared with the total postal deficit of $819.4 million. "The lower *total* revenue deficit resulted primarily from the fact that the first class mail had revenues totaling $138.8 million *greater* than its apportioned revenue."[40] Lower class mail was thus carried at the expense of first class mail. As a result of an unprecedented postal strike early in 1970, Congress increased postal rates to cover the cost of higher wages. Serious consideration was also given in 1970 to changing the status of the Post Office Department to that of a government-owned corporation.

With the adoption of the Postal Revenue Act of 1967, Congress undertook to increase postal rates on all classes of mail, despite a massive lobbying effort on the part of interests representing third class mail users. Those opposing the rate increase in the case of third class mail included representatives of *Esquire, Inc.,* and of the Boy Scouts of America. After the rate increases, it was anticipated that only 72 to 75 percent of the cost of third class mail deliveries would be covered; in short, although the cost to third class users was increased from its previous level of 61 percent of actual cost to about 72 percent of actual cost, the new legislation continues to involve substantial subsidization of third class mail.

[39] For a history of the General Agreement and of operations under it during the first ten years of its existence, see my article, "Ten Years of GATT," *Southern Economic Journal,* Vol. XXV (July, 1958), pp. 74–87.

[40] *Subsidy and Subsidy-Effect Programs, op. cit.,* p. 66. (Italics mine.)

Other Forms of Aids to Business. Many new forms of aids to business have also been devised, particularly since the beginning of World War II. Accelerated tax amortization of defense facilities was instituted during World War II and again permitted during the Korean Emergency. Under such a program, if one assumes that tax rates and rates of return remain unchanged for the normal life of the facility being amortized, since the facility may be depreciated for tax purposes during the first five years of its existence, a corporation pays lower taxes during those five years and has the additional funds thus retained available for investment purposes. It may use these funds to obtain even greater income during this period. About $5.7 billion of tax amortization certificates were issued during World War II; and between November 1950 and December 1959, about $23.3 billion worth of facilities were certified as elegible for participation in this scheme. The Treasury estimated in 1955 that the loss of tax revenues to the federal government between 1950 and 1959 resulting from this program amounted to about $5.2 billion.

Various price support schemes to subsidize minerals producers have also made their appearance from time to time. The use of the stockpile for this purpose during the Eisenhower administrations has already been noted in Chapter 6. The ultimate cost of this use has been put at $284.9 million by the General Services Administration.[41] One of the earliest of such arrangements was that with respect to silver begun with the Bland-Allison Act of 1878, under which the Treasury was required to buy specific quantities of silver every month, the stock being added to the money stock. The price was subsequently raised several times, most recently in 1946; but the program was discontinued during the Kennedy administration in 1963.[42] Other current forms of aid to business include special depreciation provisions in the tax laws for particular types of business enterprises (mainly for producers of oil and minerals) and government loans both by the RFC during its existence and, more recently, by the Small Business Corporation. And, as has already been noted, business firms also enjoy the

protection of a legal monopoly under the patent or copyright laws and federal subsidization of research and development programs.

As we have also already seen in the preceding chapter, the Supreme Court adopted a *laissez faire* policy relative to legislative regulation of economic activities after the Civil War. In the following chapter, we will see that this action was also an important factor in the development of the present forms and degrees of private control over economic power in the United States. In addition to the position taken by the Court, a further important factor was the use of governmental power to permit the adoption of new forms of business association which, on the one hand, allowed the establishment of large firms and made possible the widespread introduction of mass production techniques and, on the other, permitted the existence of concentrations of financial power having little if anything to do with the economies of large-scale production. The very great importance of these factors requires that the question of concentration of economic power be discussed separately, mainly in Chapter 11.

A Summary View of Current Subsidy and Subsidy-Effect Programs

Table 8-2 contains data showing net expenditures on subsidy programs by the federal government for selected years. Particularly worthy of note are the figures preceded by minus signs in the table. Negative magnitudes indicate instances in which receipts exceeded expenditures. The principal federal assets envisaged by the table are inventories of critical and strategic materials and stocks of farm commodities held by the Commodity Credit Corporation. Among the private assets listed are payments for improvements of farms, grants-in-aid for building hospitals and other facilities, and construction subsidies for merchant ships. The "homeowners and tenants" category includes items pertaining to the Federal Housing Administration, to urban renewal, and to public housing.

Although the data could be presented in finer detail for all the major categories of beneficiaries indicated in Table 8-2, little

41 *Ibid.*, p. 74.

42 *Ibid.*, p. 70.

Table 8-2

Net Expenditures on Subsidy and Subsidylike Programs of the Federal Government:
Selected Years, 1955–1970 (in Millions of Dollars)

Net Current Expenses	1955	1960	1965	1970 Estimate
Payments for Aid and Special Services:				
To agriculture	944	3,707	5,483	8,346
To business	741	1,278	1,483	1,357
To labor	269	324	465	842
To homeowners and tenants	−105	30	−62	1,481
Additions to Major Commodity Inventories:	1,552	1,032	−433	239
Additions to Civil Private Physical Assets:	322	836	946	1,092
Totals	3,723	5,726	6,597	9,770

Source: U.S. Bureau of the Census, *Statistical Abstract, 1969* (Washington, D.C.: U.S. Government Printing Office, 1969), pp. 383–384.

real purpose would be served by doing so at this point. Enough has already been said to indicate that numerous sectors of the economy have received much help both in the form of outright subsidies and in the form of favorable working rules and that neither the shift from agricultural to industrial production nor the present high levels of output in these sectors were achieved without a considerable use of governmental power through our history. Nor has there been a lack of the use of governmental power in the area of money and banking.

D. GOVERNMENT AND MONEY, BANKING, AND FINANCE

Hamilton and the First Bank of the United States

In December of 1790, even before his *Report in Manufactures*, Hamilton sent to the Congress his recommendation for establishment of the First Bank of the United States. He argued that such a bank would "augment" the active and productive capital of the country, serve as a facility to the government in obtaining pecuniary aid in time of emergency, and provide a device for facilitating payment of taxes.[43] Total capital of the Bank was fixed at ten million

dollars, with four-fifths of this amount to be subscribed by private investors and the remaining one-fifth to be provided by the federal government. The establishment of the Bank with a 20 year charter was in keeping with the Federalist philosophy (as were the other financial and fiscal measures recommended by Hamilton) quite as much as were Marshall's decisions establishing the supremacy of the federal government discussed in the preceding chapter. When the Bank was eventually liquidated in 1811, it paid off its stockholders above par.[44] It had made a profit.

Growth of State Banks: Sources of Opposition to the First Bank of the United States

The first private bank in the United States was the Bank of North America in Philadelphia. It was chartered by the Continental Congress in 1781 and operated by Robert Morris, who had grown rich while in charge of the financial operations of the government during the Revolutionary War. This bank was rechartered by Pennsylvania in 1782 when doubt arose as to the authority of the Continental Congress to issue such a charter. In 1784 the Bank of Massachusetts was chartered by that state in Boston, and the Bank of New York (Hamilton's enterprise) was chartered in the same year. Thus, there were three state

[43] *American State Papers, op. cit., Finance* Series, Vol. 1, pp. 67 ff.

[44] Agar, *op. cit.*, p. 70.

banks in operation by 1784.[45] By 1811 there were 88 state banks, and by 1830 there were 329.[46] These private banks received their charters as a result of special legislative enactments. Some of these banks were located in remote areas primarily so that holders of notes would find it difficult to redeem their holdings (they were located in "wildcat" territory); the practice of making loans to officers and stockholders was also common. In some cases the notes circulated at a discount. Such state banks were one source of strong opposition to the renewal of the charter of the First Bank of the United States in 1811. Among other things, the owners of the state banks believed that they would become the government's banking agent (at a profit) if the First Bank were not rechartered; the First Bank had also refused to accept the notes of some of the state banks (those which did not redeem their notes in specie on demand). In addition, Jeffersonians opposed the bank because they considered it a "Federalist" institution which concentrated economic power in the hands of a few—who would use it primarily to support business rather than agricultural interests. And so, the charter was not renewed.

The Second Bank of the United States

In 1816, however, the Second Bank of the United States was chartered; again four-fifths of the stock was publicly subscribed with the remaining one-fifth subscribed by the federal government, and again the charter was for a twenty-year period. Total capital was set at $35 million. The Second Bank had the power to certify whether or not bank notes issued by state banks were acceptable in payment of government debts; it also possessed power to control the money supply by making loans in accordance with business needs and by transferring funds among areas. In the South, and especially in the West, there was a strong opposition to the restrictions which it placed on monetary expansion: the expanding West was essentially in favor of an inflationary monetary policy, but the established East was basically in favor of "hard money." State banks also, of course, opposed the Bank because of the control which it exercised over their operations. Thus, various states undertook to levy taxes against the operations of branches of the Second Bank of the United States, and the stage was set for Marshall's decision in *McCullough* v. *Maryland*[47] (already discussed fully in the preceding chapter) that the federal government possessed the implied power under the "Necessary and Proper" Clause of the Constitution to establish the Second Bank and hence the state tax laws were unconstitutional.

In 1832 Nicholas Biddle, the President of the Bank, succumbed to pressure from political enemies of Jackson and sought to recharter the Bank (in advance of the time when such action was absolutely necessary), thereby making the question of the recharter an issue in the Presidential election of 1832. When Jackson was re-elected for his second term in 1832, the demise of the bank, as soon as its charter expired, was thus assured.

Among other things, in destroying the Bank, Jackson in 1833 withdrew the government's deposits from the Bank and placed them in selected state banks, thereby providing them with reserves which they promptly utilized to expand speculative loans, particularly for the purchase of land. The bursting of this speculative bubble in 1837 produced the crisis of that year, with losses to the Treasury.

An "Independent Treasury" system was then adopted by the Congress: under this scheme, government funds were to be kept in a number of "strong" banks throughout the country and payments of government obligations were to be made in cash.

The National Banking System

By 1860 there were about 1,500 state banks in the country. Then, in 1864 Congress adopted legislation providing for the establishment of a system of National

---

[45] This entire section draws heavily on material contained in *Bank Mergers and Concentration of Banking Facilities* (Staff Report of Subcommittee No. 5 of the House Committee on the Judiciary, 82nd Cong., 2nd sess.) (Washington, D.C.: U.S. Government Printing Office, 1952), pp. 1 ff. See also Harold F. Williamson, "Money and Commercial Banking, 1789–1865," in Williamson (ed.), *op. cit.*, pp. 227–235.

[46] U.S. Bureau of the Census, *Historical Statistics of the United States from Colonial Times to 1957* (Washington, D.C.: U.S. Government Printing Office, 1961), p. 623.

[47] 4 Wheaton 316 (1819), at p. 421.

Banks. The notes of the National Banks were to be secured partly with government bonds, a measure which, when the legislation was first proposed by Salmon Chase (Lincoln's Secretary of the Treasury), would have increased the market for United States Government bonds and thus have assisted in the financing of the Civil War. State banks did not rush to receive charters as National Banks, however, and in 1865 Congress adopted tax legislation amounting to ten percent yearly upon notes issued by state banks. As we have also seen in the preceding chapter, this regulatory tax legislation was upheld by the Supreme Court in *Veazie Bank* v. *Fenno* in 1869. Thus, although there were only 467 National Banks and more than 1,400 Non-National Banks in 1863, by 1870 there were 1,600 National Banks and only 325 Non-National Banks. The era of issue of notes by "wildcat" banks was largely ended. However, the practice of making speculative loans, with the attendant danger of bank failure, continued.

Establishment of the Federal Reserve System

The system of National Banks left much to be desired. The volume of notes issued, being based partly on gold and partly on government bonds, was tied to the size of the public debt rather than to the needs of business. Moreover, since each National Bank was itself a profit-making institution, there was no disinterested central bank control over the money supply. Finally, under the Independent Treasury System, the Treasury sometimes deposited government funds in certain National Banks and thereby exerted a degree of control over the money supply which varied in intensity according to the views of the particular individual who happened to be the Secretary of the Treasury.[48]

Substantial numbers of bank suspensions, particularly in 1893 (496 banks) and in 1908 (105 banks), led eventually to Congressional investigation of the banking system and the enactment of the Federal Reserve Act in 1913 during the Wilson administration. The Federal Reserve Act represented a compromise between outright government regulation and purely private "regulation." Regional Federal Reserve Banks were established, owned by private banks, but with boards of directors containing representatives also of nonbanking interests; and the Board of Governors of the Federal Reserve System was established to coordinate policy. The Federal Reserve Banks have power to control the reserves of member banks and thereby to exert an indirect effect on the money supply. Federal reserve deposits were, until recently, backed by fractional gold reserves and by commercial paper (securities created in the process of making loans and investments). Thus, an elastic money supply geared to the needs of business was established: an increase in the volume of business increases the quantity of commercial paper available for backing for Federal Reserve Notes; and so the availability of hand-to-hand money was and is tied to the need for it.

The Banking Crisis of 1933 and the Banking Measures of the Roosevelt Administration

Despite the powers which it possessed, the Federal Reserve Board was unable to prevent the use of extensive credit facilities for speculative purposes in the stock market and the eventual market crash in 1929. The period of the late 1920's was one of naïve boom or bust psychology. And, in 1932 the election of President Roosevelt gave rise to many rumors that the United States would abandon the gold standard after his inauguration. In 1930 about 1,300 banks suspended payments; the number reached 2,200 in 1931 and about 4,000 in 1933. On February 14, 1933 all banks in the State of Michigan closed. So-called bank holidays spread from state to state. On March 4, 1933 when President Roosevelt was inaugurated, the banking business was at a virtual standstill.

Two days later the President acted: he declared a national bank holiday to last for four days and placed an embargo on exports of gold on the theory that the gold reserves had to be protected. In his First Inaugural Address, he had informed the nation that the "only thing to fear is fear itself." He set about restoring the confidence of the nation in itself. Thus he accepted the many roles which the President must play and which have already been identified in Chapter 6.

---

[48] See Kenyon E. Poole, "Money and Banking, 1865–1919," in Williamson (ed.), *op. cit.*, pp. 551 ff.

On March 9, Congress convened in special session and validated the President's action with respect to the banks by adopting the Emergency Banking Act. Among other things, the Act authorized the Comptroller of the Currency to take over insolvent banks. A week later, sound banks began to reopen their doors. Then followed the Banking Act of 1933 (in June), giving additional authority over bank reserves to the Federal Reserve Board; this Act also created the Federal Bank Deposit Insurance Corporation to insure deposits and provided for regulation of speculative activities by banks. The Act was amended in 1934 by the Bank Insurance Act which extended the deposit insurance coverage, and this coverage has since been several times extended.

Obviously, legislation pertaining to banking in 1933 to 1934 clearly illustrates still another way in which power to establish working rules has been employed by the President and the Congress in order to affect economic activity. Other New Deal measures regulating securities markets and public utilities will be mentioned in the next chapter and in Part III.

The Monetary Standard

Hamilton's recommendations for the establishment of a mint and for the adoption of a decimal system of coinage were adopted by the Congress in 1791.[49] He recommended the adoption of a dual gold and silver standard on grounds that a greater supply of money would thereby be made possible. By 1834 the country was operating in fact upon gold basis.[50] During the Civil War the government suspended specie payment, and more than $400 million of paper money ("Greenbacks") were issued. The problem of redeeming this paper money and the attendant effect of redemption on price levels brought about a conflict between creditors and debtors. The latter wished the inflationary trend to continue, so that they might pay off their debts in "cheap money"; the former quite naturally wanted "hard money." A return to a metallic standard by resumption of specie redemption of "Greenbacks" would amount to a hard money policy.

Silver producers aligned themselves with the debtors, because in 1873 silver dollars were no longer being coined. The silver producers rightly believed that unlimited coinage of silver would increase the demand for their output; at the same time such coinage would increase the money supply, tending to make for "cheap" money. In 1878 Congress, as has already been noted, adopted the Bland-Allison Act providing for inclusion of some silver coins in the money supply. In 1890 the Sherman Silver Purchase Act was adopted, substantially increasing the Treasury's demand for silver; however, in 1893 the Act was repealed during the depression of that year. Meanwhile, most of the rest of the world had officially adopted the gold standard. (The United States had again been on a *de facto* gold standard since about 1879).

The inflationists captured control of one branch of the Democratic Party in 1896. William Jennings Bryan, a fundamentalist enemy of the views of Darwin and the party's nominee for President, was selected after he asserted in a speech that he and his followers would answer the demand (national and international) for a law adopting the gold standard by saying to those who supported it: "You shall not press down upon the brow of labor this crown of thorns, you shall not crucify mankind upon a cross of gold."[51]

But Bryan lost the election to McKinley, and in 1900 the Gold Standard Act was adopted to formalize what already was true in fact.

Successful operation of a gold standard in international trade involves a willingness on the part of all the trading partners to follow the same working rules. In their simplest form, the rules require that inflows of gold in settlement of favorable balances of payments must be permitted to affect domestic price levels and employment and to reduce exports and increase imports in order to reverse the inflow; similarly, outflows of gold in settlement of unfavorable balances must be permitted to change prices and affect income and employment, while increasing exports and reducing imports to reverse the outflow. During the period

[49] *American State Papers, op. cit., Finance* Series, Vol. 1, pp. 91 ff.
[50] Williamson, "Money and Commercial Banking, 1789–1865," in Williamson (ed.), *op. cit.*, pp. 227 ff.

[51] Bryan's speech appears in *Official Proceedings of the Democratic National Convention, 1896* (Logansport, Indiana: Wilson, Humphreys and Co., 1896), pp. 226–234. The quotation given is from page 234.

between World Wars I and II, most of the countries of the world abandoned the gold standard because of their unwillingness to subject their domestic economies to the fluctuations in domestic income, prices, and employment required for the successful operation of that standard. Moreover, with the rise of fascist governments in some countries of Europe and the general fear of war, so-called flights of capital from Europe to the United States occurred, with the result that a disproportionate share of the world's gold supply came into the hands of this country.

Devaluation—a reduction in the gold content of the dollar—occurred in 1934. President Roosevelt followed the advice of an economist, Professor Charles Warren of Cornell, in ordering the devaluation. Warren, like practically all other economists of that period, held to the so-called quantity theory of money, which, in its most naïve form states that the general price level (P) is nothing more than the ratio between the quantity of money (M), multiplied by the number of times it changes hands (V), divided by some measure of total output (O), or $MV/O = P$. According to this view, which—in another form—implies that money derives its value from the metal or commodity in reserve behind it, an increase in the quantity of money must produce an increase in the general price level. Such an increase in the price level was thought desirable in 1934 as one means of creating optimism and thereby bringing the United States out of the Depression. Unfortunately, however, the theory did not work. After the devaluation, prices did not behave as they were supposed to behave. Subsequent post mortems indicated that a mere increase in the money supply was not enough in a period of deep pessimism. It is the propensity to spend, the velocity of circulation of money $(V$ in the equation), which is of at least equal significance; and this magnitude (V) cannot be assumed to remain constant. Even though the money supply had increased people were not eager to buy goods.

The instance is important because it demonstrates quite clearly that experimentation may show that even a widely held and long-accepted economic doctrine may be in error. After this event and until

the 1960's, there were few reputable economists who accepted either the naïve quantity theory of money or the commodity theory of money (the theory that money derives its value from what lies behind it). Today, however, a group of monetary economists led by Professor Milton Friedman has sought to revive the quantity theory of money and to emphasize the role of monetary policy as an important determinant of the level of economic activity.

Since 1934 the United States has been on a modified "gold bullion" standard. Gold is available for certain purposes in large amounts under license from the Treasury; it is not available for general use as a monetary medium. In the period immediately following World War II, most of the rest of the world, of which a large part had been devastated by that war, experienced a dollar shortage: the need for imports from the United States was great, and the capacity to pay for these imports with export earnings was slight. But, beginning in the late 1950's, with the restoration of productive facilities abroad completed, the United States experienced gold outflows for numerous reasons (including, during the early 1960's, political activities by General Charles de Gaulle). The principal reason for the gold outflow, however, was a very large amount of unilateral transfers. "Unilateral transfers" can be defined merely as one-way movements of funds from the United States to other countries, movements which may result either from United States Government economic or military aid programs abroad or from private business investments abroad.

Proposals for imposition of restrictions upon United States travel abroad and for taxes upon United States foreign investments, as well as speeches by Members of Congress (such as Senator Fulbright) in the early 1960's urging Americans not to travel abroad, represent official attempts to influence economic activities through the operations of working rules. The purpose of such working rules is to insulate the domestic economy somewhat from the impact of gold movements and short-term capital movements, on grounds that domestic price stability and a high level of income and employment are valid goals; but, in the final analysis, they are results of under-lying political policies. This point will become even clearer in the discussion of the behavior of some selected international trade and financial statistics which follows.

E. THE UNITED STATES AND THE WORLD ECONOMY

The industrial development of the United States is clearly reflected in the facts that in 1820 about 61 percent of our exports consisted of raw materials and only 6 percent were made up of finished manufactures, but in 1960 about 57 percent of our exports consisted of finished manufactures and only about 19 percent consisted of raw materials. Similarly, in 1790 our net international liabilities amounted to about $60 million, but in 1960 our investments abroad exceeded foreign investments in the United States by more than $26 billion. However, in 1968 there was a net inflow of $5.2 billion.

During World War I the United States became a creditor nation with attendant international responsibilities which, unfortunately, were not always recognized between the two World Wars. Following World War II, unilateral transfers were undertaken (foreign aid programs such as the Marshall Plan) to assist much of the rest of the world to regain its economic feet. Since then, the cold war has resulted in further transfers of this type, although there has been much argument about whether either the economic development or the military aid programs constitute sound policy. It is to be noted that the value of exports of goods and services exceeded that of imports of goods and services slightly in 1968; these figures, however, exclude the negative (outflow) figure for unilateral transfers in the same year. Such transfers have been large since the end of World War II.

The nature of and the reasons for the large United States unilateral transfers since the end of World War II are worth serious consideration. As has been noted, these transfers have not been the result of inevitable economic forces; they have been the result of consciously adopted inter-national political policies. Aid to Europe after World War II may have been prompted partly by humanitarian motives, but it may also have been prompted by a recognition that, unless it was forthcoming, the spread of Russian power throughout the world would be greatly increased. So also unilateral transfers of economic and military aid to various parts of the world have been as much a result of ideological and political conflict as of any other factors. It is for this reason that an analysis of such matters which confines itself purely to a consideration of "economic" variables alone cannot be definitive. It is to the growth of government activity that we turn next.

F. GROWTH OF GOVERNMENT EMPLOYMENT, EXPENDITURES, AND FINANCES

Fabricant's Study

In 1952, Solomon Fabricant published the results of a study made for the National Bureau of Economic Research concerning the trend of government activity in the United States since 1900.[52] Among other things, he concluded that "in 1900, one out of 24 workers was on a government payroll, in 1920, one out of 15, and in 1940, one out of 11." In 1949 he found the ratio to be one out of 8. These figures are based on *total federal and state government employment, including military personnel* and do *not* refer merely to federal employees.[53] That is, they include the military services as well as state and local government employees (school teachers and the like).

Although the general trend in the total numbers of federal, state, and local government workers has been upward, *federal* government *civilian* employment as a percentage of the labor force actually decreased between 1952-1964 and, in 1964, it was far below its 1944 wartime peak.

Federal Government Expenditures

Federal government expenditures have always risen sharply in times of war and national emergency. Thus the figures for 1865, 1919, 1944, and since 1952 are large in relation to peace time periods. Interest

[52] Solomon Fabricant, *The Trend of Government Activity in the United States Since 1900* (New York: National Bureau of Economic Research, 1952).
[53] *Ibid.*, p. 14.

Table 8-3

Selected Data Pertaining to the Federal Administrative Budget; 1955, 1962, and 1969 (in Millions of Dollars)

Source and Function	1955	1962	1969[a]
Selected Revenue Items			
Individual income taxes	28,747	45,571	84,400
Corporate income taxes	17,861	20,523	38,100
Excise taxes	9,131	9,585	10,325
Employment taxes	5,587	12,561	34,842
Selected Expenditure Items			
National defense	40,695	51,103	80,999
International affairs and finance	2,181	2,817	3,938
Space research and technology	74	1,257	4,247
Agriculture and agricultural resources (including subsidies)	4,388	5,881	5,448
Natural resources	1,203	2,147	1,898
Commerce and transportation	1,225	2,774	8,048
Regulation of business	38	74	109
Housing and community development	136	349	2,313
Health, labor and welfare	2,165	8,328	50,350
Education	377	1,076	4,282
Veterans' benefits and services	4,522	5,403	7,692
Interest	6,438	9,198	15,171
General government			
Legislative functions	60	135	199
Judicial functions	31	57	105
Executive direction and management	12	22	33

[a] Estimated.

Sources: U.S. Bureau of the Census, *Statistical Abstract, 1964* (Washington, D.C.: U.S. Government Printing Office, 1964), Table 523, pp. 392–393; *Statistical Abstract, 1969*, p. 378.

on the public debt and veterans' benefits can both also be legitimately considered to be national defense expenditures. The interest payments are largely the result of money borrowed during periods of national emergency. Indeed, government interest payments are excluded from the national income figures on grounds that the debt is "not productive" by the Department of Commerce for this very reason.

As a matter of fact, the origin of the public debt lies in the Revolutionary War and in Hamilton's Message to Congress urging that the federal government assume the responsibility for the Revolutionary War debts. Hamilton said of the debt: "It was the price of liberty."[54] Since World War II, the continuing cold war and a reliance in the 1960's upon deficit financing at the federal level have caused the debt to continue to rise.

A detailed breakdown for selected years of some of the expenditures of the federal government is presented in Table 8-3, which also contains data pertaining to some of the principal (but not to all) sources of federal revenue. Corporate and individual income taxes are, of course, the principal federal revenue sources, with excise and employment taxes also serving as substantial sources.

The italicized items in Table 8-3 are of particular interest. In relation to the total, expenditures for "Regulation of business," under the "Commerce and transportation" heading, represent a very small amount; and the same is true of the expenditures under the "General government" heading for the "Legislative functions," "Judicial functions," and "Executive direction and management." It seems clear enough from the data that movements aimed at economy in government must be directed at functions other than these if such movements are to be

[54] *American State Papers, op. cit., Finance Series*, Vol. 1, p. 15. (His motives, of course, are irrelevant in the present context.)

successful in attaining their objectives of cutting costs of government. It is to Department of Defense procurement that attention must now be given, since "National defense" represents the largest single item in Table 8-3.

The Impact of Department of Defense Procurement Activities on the Economy

Between 1951 and 1965, the net value of military procurement from private business firms in the United States amounted to more than $331 *billion*, with about $26 billion being spent in 1964 alone. Of this total in 1956, only 14.8 percent was spent by formal advertising methods—that is, by competitive bidding. The remaining 86.6 percent was spent by a process of negotiation, and in 1966 the figure was 85 percent. Part of the latter (less than 30 percent) *may* involve competitive pricing. Reasons for the lack of price competition in the remainder include the propositions that it is: (1) impracticable to secure competition by formal advertising; (2) some of the negotiated procurement involves experimental, developmental, test, or research activity of a highly specialized nature; and (3) the remainder of the negotiated procurement involves "Technical or specialized supplies requiring substantial initial investment or extended period of preparation for manufacture."[55]

In fiscal year 1967, the Lockhead Aircraft Corporation ranked third, but in fiscal year 1964, the Lockhead Aircraft Corporation and its subsidiaries received the largest dollar volume ($1.4554 billion) of military prime contract awards. This sum amounted to 5.8 per cent of the United States total and represented 75 percent of the total sales of Lockhead in the calendar year 1963. Apparently, three out of every four dollars of sales income received by the company came from the federal government. The company ranked 30th in total sales among United States industrial corporations in 1967. The General Electric Company, which ranked fourth in total sales among United States industrial cor-

porations in 1967, received about 18 percent of its total sales revenue from such military prime contract awards in 1963 and ranked fourth in government sales in 1967. Other United States companies included in the top 29 industrial companies— all of whom received more than $200 million each of government contracts in 1963—included American Telephone and Telegraph Company ($635.6 million), General Tire and Rubber Company ($364.4 million), International Business Machines Corporation ($332.4 million), General Motors Corporation ($255.8 million), and Ford Motor Company (which, together with its subsidiary, Philco Corporation, received $211.2 million). In 1966, the Lockhead Corporation and the General Electric Company also ranked first and second, respectively, but in 1967, McDonnell Douglas Corporation and General Dynamics, Inc. were first and second.[56] National defense is an expensive undertaking. The total amount to be spent for "Regulation of business" in 1968 in Table 8-3, it may be recalled, was estimated at only $100 million. Elimination of this entire expenditure would amount to a mere drop in the bucket insofar as reduction of total federal government expenditures is concerned.

That the Department of Defense by means of its procurement policies not only affects the *level* of business activity but also may affect the *structure* of American industry is obvious from the above discussion. This point will concern us further later in this book.

G. GOVERNMENTAL POWER AND ECONOMIC ACTIVITY: A CONCLUDING COMMENT

That governmental power has always been employed to affect both the general direction as well as the nature of economic activity in the United States has become clearly apparent in the preceding chapters and in the description of the growth of

[55] *Background Material on Economic Impact of Federal Procurement—1965* (Materials Prepared for the Subcommittee on Federal Procurement and Regulation of the Joint Economic Committee, 89th Cong., 1st sess.) (Washington, D.C.: U.S. Government Printing Office, 1965), pp. 21 ff; and *Background Material on Economy in Government* (Materials Pre-

pared for the Subcommittee on Economy in Government of the Joint Economic Committee, 90th Cong., 1st sess.) (Washington, D.C.: U.S. Government Printing Office, 1967), p. 49.

[56] The data can be found in the two publications cited in the preceding footnote.

particular economic magnitudes contained in this chapter. Moreover, as will be seen in the next chapter, the nature of private control over economic activity has also been affected by the use of governmental power. It does not follow, of course, that all uses of governmental power can necessarily be explained by economic motives. But it is true that far from being a neutral or merely a passive force—one which has been used solely to establish law and order and to provide for the security of property and of the person—governmental power has always been and is being employed in the United States to create inducements and sanctions leading to this or that allocation of resources, quite as much as governmental power was employed in England to establish the market economy and to destroy mercantilism (a point noted in Chapter 4). Sometimes governmental power has been or is employed to substitute administrative controls for the operation of market forces. A protective tariff is such an administrative control. In some areas, governmental power has been or is employed directly in the market process. Examples are the purchase of silver to subsidize silver producers and also defense procurement. Governmental power has also been and is being employed to create working rules to favor one group or another. In the 1930's, legislation favorable to the organization of labor unions was adopted; at an earlier time the Sherman Antitrust Act had been used to destroy some unions. In the same way, general incorporation statutes, as well as laws authorizing the establishment of holding companies, were adopted in the nineteenth century; while, in the twentieth, a law to control particular types of holding companies was enacted. Such laws have affected and do affect the degree of concentration of private control over economic activity.

Governmental authority also has been and is being employed to prohibit some kinds of economic activity: state banking at one point in our history; importation of Chinese labor under the immigration laws after 1880; and prohibitions of entry of British secretaries in the 1960's. And governmental power has been and is being employed to encourage other types of activity. In short, the notion that American economic growth can be explained as the result of the operation of "pure market forces" or as the result of the unaided genius of private businessmen is a fiction.

There will, of course, always be some who decry the role of governmental power by asserting that "the government is getting to be too big" or "the government is becoming too powerful" or something equally vague and meaningless. Such statements are really nothing more than an expression on the part of the speaker that he does not like the way in which governmental power is presently being employed. It is legitimate to debate particular uses of governmental power. But it is idle chatter to denounce "the government" as if it were a faceless monster or an evil spirit conjured up by a witch doctor. In every organized society, governmental power exists. That is the meaning of an "organized society." The question is thus not one of the existence of governmental power but one of how it should be employed.

To be sure, not all of the important economic magnitudes which might be considered have been examined in this chapter. No data have been presented concerning the growth of communications facilities or of changes in the use of energy-producing substances. Nor have periods of wartime controls been singled out for special consideration. Such a detailed inclusion of all sorts of additional data and information would merely lengthen this chapter without adding much to the general picture which has already been given. In subsequent parts of this book, some additional historical data will be included in appropriate places.

In the following chapter, we will consider the changes in the forms of business associations which have occurred since the Civil War. The problems of enforcement of the antitrust laws which are to be discussed in Part II of this book and those which confront the regulatory agencies to be considered in Part III are largely problems of the development of appropriate working rules to deal with problems arising out of increases in the sizes of establishments and changes in forms and their implications. Increases in the sizes are the subject of Chapter 11, but changes in the forms will be discussed in the next chapter.

9

Forms of Business Associations; the Merger Movements

The growth of the selected economic magnitudes discussed in the preceding chapter has been accompanied by significant changes in the forms of organization of business activities, that is, by changes in the forms of business associations. This chapter consists of two subdivisions. The first contains an examination of the various types of business association forms which have been utilized and which exist in the United States; the second major subdivision contains a discussion of the various merger movements which have occurred in the United States, including the merger movement which seems to be currently in process.

A. TYPES OF PRIVATE BUSINESS ASSOCIATIONS AND ARRANGEMENTS

In 1789, by far the largest part of the economic activity of the nation was being carried on in small scale enterprises by single proprietors and by partners. The total number of business corporations which had been organized in the United States by 1800 was 335; and, of this number, 255 were concerned with transportation and public service facilities (turnpike, bridge, and canal companies, or were companies furnishing dock facilities or fire protection or water); 67 were engaged in banking, and only six were manufacturing enterprises.[1] In the year 1800, no new corporations were chartered in Maryland or Pennsylvania while, in the same year, only two were chartered in New Jersey and five were chartered in New York.[2] But in the year 1875, 78 corporations were chartered in Maryland, 137 were chartered in New Jersey, 149 were chartered in New York, and 333 were chartered in Pennsylvania.[3] And, by 1962, of 387,000 new business units formed, 182,000 were corporations.

There were more than 1.4 million corporations in the United States by 1965. There were also about 9 million single

---

[1] Joseph S. Davis, *Essays in the Earlier History of American Corporations* (4 vols.; Cambridge: Harvard University Press, 1917), Vol. II, p. 24.

[2] G. H. Evans, Jr., *Business Incorporations in the*

United States, 1800–1943 (New York: National Bureau of Economic Research, 1948), Table 6, p. 12.

[3] *Ibid.*

proprietorships and about 9 hundred thousand partnerships. However, although the number of single proprietorships far exceeded the number of corporations in 1965, in the same year, corporate businesses were the source of about $430.7 billion of national income while unincorporated enterprises accounted for about $354.3 billion. Clearly, in terms of the sources of national income, the corporate form is the more important today. Before we undertake to examine the reasons for the increased importance of the corporate form, it will be useful to examine briefly various forms of business associations and combinations.

Single Proprietorships and Partnerships

The single or sole proprietorship is, of course, the simplest form of business organization. In the absence of statutory provisions to the contrary, a single proprietor simply invests his capital and begins to do business. He has sole control over his affairs, makes his own decisions, and his activities are limited only by his ability, his credit, and his luck.

A partnership is a matter of contract. This form of business association has been defined in the Uniform Partnership Act as "an association of two or more persons to carry on as co-owners a business for profit." The essential element in a partnership is assent of the parties to an express or implied agreement; however, two or more individuals may so conduct themselves as to be liable to third parties as partners when in fact no partnership exists.[4]

Because partnerships are created by means of a contract, they are subject to all of the legal incidents attaching to a contract, including termination by death of one of the parties. And, of course, partnerships are limited in the amount of capital which they can raise by the personal credit of the partners, but there is unlimited liability for debt; and in general, either partner may bind the other in dealings with third parties. Today, many partnerships are still found in the wholesale and retail trades and in the areas of finance, insurance, and real estate activities, as well as in professional services—particularly in the cases of lawyers, doctors, and dentists.

Joint Stock Companies or Associations and Joint Ventures (Adventures)

At common law the term *association* referred to an unincorporated society, a "company," a union of persons who acted together without a charter but employed the methods and forms of corporations for some common purpose. A joint stock company was occasionally referred to as a "quasi corporation," particularly in some early statutes and was sometimes identified as a "hybrid, midway between a partnership and a corporation." Shares were transferable, but there was unlimited liability for debts, and such a company came into existence without a charter. It might have articles of association which, however, had the characteristics of a contract among the shareholders. Since there was transferability of shares, the company was not terminated by the death of one of its members.

The joint stock association form was a popular one in England in the early part of the eighteenth century and was employed in many speculative undertakings. As a result, Parliament enacted the Bubble Act of 1719 in an attempt to regulate this form.[5] The principal effect of the legislation was, however, to emphasize that the grant of a corporate charter was *a matter of privilege and not a right* of those seeking it.

At common law, *joint ventures* (adventures) were merely informal partnerships having generally limited scope and duration. For example, in a case in which several individuals joined together for the purchase and sale of specific securities for a profit, a Connecticut court held in 1932 that they were engaged in a joint venture.[6] Today, however, the usage of the term has changed and refers also to jointly owned subsidiaries established, usually, by two parent corporations.

Joint ventures are also often used as a kind of "trial marriage" by some companies contemplating merger. For example, prior to the merger in 1954 of the Olin Industries and the Mathieson Chemical Corporation,

---

[4] *Phillips* v. *Phillips*, 49 Ill. 437 (1863).

[5] See A. B. Dubois, *The English Business Company after the Bubble Act, 1720–1800* (New York: Commonwealth Fund, 1938).

[6] *Lesser* v. *Smith*, 160 Atl. 302 (1932).

the two companies engaged in a joint venture (1953) by establishing the Matholin Corporation to conduct developmental work relating to rocket fuel. Such joint ventures are also utilized by several companies on the annual list of 100 largest companies receiving the largest dollar volume of prime military contract awards.

Antitrust problems may arise with respect to joint ventures, whether or not they are eventually consummated by actual mergers. Legal actions have arisen involving joint foreign ventures of American companies just as they have arisen with respect to domestic joint ventures. These problems will be considered further in Part II of this book.

The Corporation

Concept of the Corporation According to Roman Law. In 1917, Charles Sherman remarked that the "true corporate personality is a gift of Roman law."[7] There were no restrictions on the formation of such business associations in Rome until 64 B.C., when some legislation was adopted and then suspended. However in 57 B.C., the *lex Julia de collegiia* (a law of Augustus Caesar), provided for the authorization of corporate associations. The application for the authority to incorporate required a showing that the "object" of the association would be "helpful to the state or beneficial to the public." At least three persons were needed to organize such a corporate association, although the association was not terminated by the death of one or more of the parties. These associations did not issue transferable shares of stock but they were controlled by majority vote, could hold property, could sue and be sued, incur obligations, alienate property, and make contracts.

The principal restriction placed upon individuals forming such associations was one to the effect that a person could be a member of only one such corporation at a time.[8] This restriction was adopted to prevent the accumulation of great wealth in the hands of a few persons—an idea not unrelated to the concept of interlocking directorates (to be discussed later). In 1917, Charles Sherman concluded his study of the corporation under Roman law by noting that modern corporation law was merely Roman corporation law modernized.[9]

Concept of the Corporation in the Middle Ages and at Common Law. According to Holdsworth, Pope Innocent IV in 1243 was the first to conceive of a group of persons as *persona ficta*, an artificial person.[10] The occasion for this identification was as follows. Legal problems existed in the Middle Ages in the cases of ecclesiastical bodies. Abbots ruled communities of monks, who were dead persons in the eyes of the law. Though the church property belonged to monastic orders, the abbots sometimes had occasion to secure legal enforcement of the rights of their orders, particularly when a prior abbot had been guilty of fraud or some other *delictum*. And so the notion developed that the Pope could create an artificial person with attendant legal and property rights. Thus was the logic of the law kept pure.[11] In England, during the reign of Henry VIII, the common law lawyers were assisted in the development of their own logical concept of the corporation as an artificial legal person by the theory of creation of artificial persons developed in canon law.[12] By 1615, Coke was able to state in the *Case of Sutton's Hospital* that the first essential for a valid corporation was a "lawful authority of incorporation,"[13] one capable of creating an artificial person. The common law, Parliament, royal charter, and prescription (the assertion of a right or title on the ground of having had the uninterrupted and "immemorial" enjoyment of it) were such "lawful authorities."

The well-known conception of the corporation as an "artificial being," invisible, intangible, and existing only in the eyes of the law" thus antedates Justice Marshall's description of it in those words in 1819

---

[7] Charles P. Sherman, *Roman Law* (3 vols.; Boston; The Boston Book Co., 1917), Vol. II, p. 124.

[8] *Ibid.*, pp. 125–131.

[9] *Ibid.*, p. 132.

[10] Sir John Holdsworth, *A History of English Law* (12 vols.; fifth ed.; London: Meuthuen and Co.,

Ltd., 1942), Vol. III, pp. 409 ff.

[11] *Ibid.*, p. 475.

[12] *Ibid.*, p. 477, citing Y.B. 14, Hy. VIII, Mich. pl. 2.

[13] *Ibid.*, Vol. IX, p. 46, citing 10 Co. Rep. at f. 29b.

by many centuries.[14] That conception, we have seen, arose as a result of the "felt necessities" of the times during the Middle Ages. The conception really constitutes a mystical statement of a working rule, a disguised social policy of permitting groups of private individuals to form separate associations within the state. To be sure, some corporations were formed as subdivisions of governments and were the predecessors of present day "municipal corporations." But many private business associations were also formed.

In all cases, the sanction of an "Authority" (the state or the Pope) was required for establishment of a corporation. This procedure represented a particular public policy. Holdsworth remarked that the reasons for the law to recognize the crime of conspiracy are the same as those which make it necessary to regulate the activities of groups of men who may acquire great power by organizing in the corporate form.[15] This position was specifically taken in a legal argument by Sir Robert Sawyer in 1682 when he asserted that if it were not possible to punish a corporation for its wrongful acts, the effect would be to set up independent commonwealths within the kingdom which would rival the Crown in power.[16]

In the eyes of the law, incorporation has thus *always* been a matter of *privilege* and *not* one of *right*. Moreover, throughout the history of the corporate idea, both in Roman law and at common law, it is apparent that the law makers were concerned with the fundamental problem of reconciling the need for, and benefits of, this legal form of private business association with the dangers inherent in the concentration of private economic power—which might come to rival the governmental power. As we will see in a later chapter, the existence within the Union of 50 States and of numerous "independent commonwealths" (to use Sir Robert Sawyer's term) have led to suggestions by some contemporary students of the subject (like Walter Adams) that there should be limitations on the absolute sizes of business associations

as well as to suggestions for the adoption of a federal incorporation statute. At the present time in the United States, incorporation is a privilege granted by the various states rather than by the federal government, although some of the corporations chartered in some states operate, quite naturally, in interstate commerce and have assets and revenues exceeding those of the particular state governments which have issued charters to such corporations. The states began by issuing special charters.

The Period of Special Incorporation Acts (to about 1875) in the United States. Special incorporation acts are precisely what the name implies, a grant of the privilege of a corporate charter by the legislature to specific persons for stated purposes. Inherent in the process of adoption of such a special grant of the privilege by the legislature are a host of problems: delay of the grant, lobbying, possible graft and corruption, public criticism, and delay of other important legislative activities. But, although general incorporation statutes (defined below) existed in several states, not until about 1875 had constitutional provisions requiring incorporation under general laws become commonplace.[17] Laws containing some of the features of general incorporation acts were adopted by North Carolina in 1795 and by Massachusetts in 1799, while New York adopted a general incorporation statute for manufacturing enterprises in 1811. By 1850 a number of states had adopted general incorporation statutes.[18]

Two factors were primarily responsible for the eventual widespread adoption of general incorporation acts—and for the inclusion of provisions in state constitutions prohibiting the issuance of special charters. One of these was a widespread recognition of the many business advantages of the corporate form as a legal device for private control of large scale enterprises at a time when large scale business operations were first being undertaken—during and shortly after the Civil War. The second was public fear of possible favoritism on the part of the state legislatures in the issuance of special charters. This fear was buttressed

---

[14] *Dartmouth College* v. *Woodward*, 4 Wheat. 518 (1819) (discussed in Chapter 7 preceding).

[15] Holdsworth, *op. cit.*, p. 46.

[16] 8 S.T. 1039 (1682) at p. 1178, cited in Holds-

worth, *op. cit.*, Vol. IX, p. 46.

[17] Evans, *op. cit.*, p. 10.

[18] Davis, *op. cit.*, Vol. II, pp. 17–20; and Evans, *op. cit.*, pp. 10 ff.

to some extent by dissatisfaction concerning the procedure of special incorporation as it had operated in the past.

General Incorporation Acts. A general incorporation statute is one which offers the privilege of incorporation to all members of a specified class on the same terms. One major distinction between municipal and private corporations is drawn in state statutes. Private corporations are often further subdivided according to their natures; thus there may be separate statutes according to which banks, trust companies, various types of utilities, manufacturing companies, and commercial corporations, respectively, are to be incorporated. In addition, there may be further statutes pertaining to the special incorporation of religious bodies, educational associations, and non-profit ("educational" or "charitable") organizations.

Typical general incorporation statutes contain provisions allowing a specified number of persons (in some cases, one person) to incorporate for specified privileged purposes. To do so, they must file certain documents (the most important of which is generally known as the "articles of incorporation") and pay certain fees (which may be substantial in some states). When they are approved, the "articles of incorporation" become the charter, the "contract" between the state and the corporation according to the decision of Justice Marshall and as modified by subsequent decisions relative to the relationship between police power and the Contract Clause of the Constitution (already discussed in Chapter 7).

The Relationship Among Charter, Stockholders, Directors and Managers. The corporate charter is usually required by law to contain the name of the corporation, the location of an office within the state which can be served with notice of legal actions against the corporation, a statement of the purposes of the corporation, and a description of all the types of stock to be issued. Common stock always carries with it a right to vote, usually one vote per share; other types of stock may have a right to vote if that right is expressly stated in the charter. In an ideal situation, a majority of the stockholders elect directors who hold meetings at which they determine basic corporate policies and appoint managers, in accordance with by-laws which are generally adopted at the first corporate meeting. In reality, there are many instances in which the ideal situation does not exist; this topic is an important one and will be treated in Sub-division *E* later in this chapter. Before doing so, let us examine some other types of business associations which have been employed in the United States.

The Pool

Not all business associations in the United States have been of a formal nature. Some have been quite informal. In the period after the Civil War, many of the newly-formed corporations engaged in such informal extra-legal associations with other newly-formed corporations. The name "pool" has been given to numerous types of such informal arrangements. The United States Industrial Commission (a non-partisan commission consisting of five members from each House of Congress and nine members who were to represent "fairly different industries and employments"), established by Congress in 1898, reported on one such pool in 1900 in these words:

The first combinations among distillers [of whiskey], beginning in 1882, were in the form of pools. The number of barrels to be produced by each distillery, and the prices were regulated by agreement. From 70 to 80 distilleries usually joined, and production was limited to about 50 percent of their capacity. One of these pools was known as the Western Exporter's Association. It determined the producing capacity of each distillery and divided the consuming capacity of the country pro rata. [No figures are given in the "testimony" concerning the "consuming capacity" figures assumed.] Distilleries producing in excess were required to export at their own cost, while any surplus arising fortuitously was exported at the expense of the association, the loss being met by assessment. The pools were frequently broken by violation of the agreement by members or by new distilleries; there were no penalties. Business became so unprofitable when broken that they could usually be reorganized soon.[19]

[19] *Report of the United States Industrial Commission* (19 vols.; Washington, D.C.: U.S. Government Printing Office, 1900–1902), Vol. 1, p. 76. (See pages 168, 169, and 200 for the testimony on which the summary is based.)

Similar informal arrangements existed in many other industries as well as in the field of railway transportation and as we will see in Part II, after the adoption of the Sherman Antitrust Act in 1890, many pools were held illegal by the Supreme Court.

Testimony taken by the Industrial Commission from a former president of the National Cordage Company contains the statement that such pools were formed in the cordage industry as early as 1860.[20]

Because the pooling arrangements were largely unsuccessful and impermanent, other arrangements were adopted. In some cases, even where pooling arrangements had not been tried, elimination of competition or of competitors was also achieved effectively by the use of methods to be considered next.

The Simple Trust and the Voting Trust

The first successor in point of time to the pool was a more formal arrangement known as a *trust*. To quote again from the contemporary record of the period, the *First Report* of the Industrial Commission in 1901:

The form of organization that has given them their name "trusts" was the one started by the Standard Oil Trust in 1882, afterwards followed by the Whiskey combination—the Distillers and Cattle Feeders' Trust—and by the Sugar Trust—the American Sugar Refineries Company. The plan of that organization was as follows: The stockholders of the different corporations entering the combination assigned their stock in trust to a board of trustees without the power of revocation. That board of trustees then held the voting power of the stocks of the different companies, and was thus enabled, through the election of directors, to control them absolutely. In place of the stock thus received the trustees issued trust certificates upon which the former holders of the stock drew their dividends, these being paid upon the certificate regardless of what disposition was made of the plants of the different corporations. Owing largely to hostile legislation and to the bitter feeling against the trusts above named, these trusts, after some adverse decisions of the courts, went out of existence, reorganizing as a single corporation in most cases, and none at the present time remain.[21]

A variation on this theme was the voting trust. The purpose of a voting trust was not, however, to unite various corporations under one management. The majority stockholders in a given corporation would merely turn their stocks over to a trustee for voting purposes only, in order to secure an agreed upon policy without "danger of sales by individual stockholders." The voting trust seems to have been largely a defensive measure—such a trust was said to have been established by the majority stockholders of the Pure Oil Company at a time when the Standard Oil Company was seeking to gain majority control of the former.[22]

The trust form soon became an object of public criticism and legal action. In some cases, legislation was enacted to make trusts illegal; in others they were held illegal in actions of state courts. In New York, for example, it was held that the action of organizing the Sugar Trust was *ultra vires*, an act outside the scope of the powers of the organizing corporations as defined by their own corporate charters. Three new types of arrangements were thereafter employed for the same purpose, but one of these, the "community" or "harmony" of interest, employed by the Standard Oil Company, did not have a very long life. Under the "harmony of interest" arrangement, the trust property was distributed among twenty corporations in 1892, but the control over these corporations was held by the former nine trustees of the original trust agreement, and a unity of policy and management were maintained by their common consent and action. Eventually, however, as we will see below, the Standard Oil Company of New Jersey adopted a different legal device to eliminate competition.

Mergers

Strictly speaking, a merger of corporations involves the union of two or more corporations by means of a transfer of all the property to one of them and dissolution of the others, while a *consolidation* involves the creation of a new corporation to hold the assets. In either case, a *fusion* of the pre-

---

[21] *Ibid.*, Vol. 1, p. 10.
[20] *Ibid.*, Vol. 13, p. XLV, p. 126, p. 137.

[22] *Ibid.*

viously-existing entities occurs, accompanied by a loss of identity of all or all but one of the firms. Acquisition of a controlling stock interest by one firm in another usually involves use of a legal device known as the holding company (to be explained below). However, the statistics available from the Federal Trade Commission pertaining to "mergers" and the economists of the Federal Trade Commission generally employ the term "merger" to refer to all of these devices and, in the antitrust area, the term has now come to have this broader meaning. In general, in this book, *the term merger will therefore be given that broader meaning.*

Nature of the Process. Consolidation of the assets of the firms which had previously been associated in the trusts was the most widely used form of combination in the last years of the nineteenth century and in the first two or three of the twentieth. The Industrial Commission reported in 1900:

The form of organization which seems most common at the present time is that of the single large corporation, which owns outright the different plants. A combination of this kind is formed by the purchase of all of the plants of the different corporations or individuals who enter into it, the corporations then dissolving as separate corporations. Often payments for the plants are made largely in stock of the new corporation, so that many of the former owners maintain their interest in the business. The affairs are then managed entirely by the stockholders of the one corporation through their board of directors in the ordinary way. It is usual for these larger corporations to choose a very liberal form of charter.[23]

The Commission also pointed out that most of the larger corporations "have, within the last few years been organized in New Jersey." The reasons were numerous: (1) the New Jersey tax rate was moderate and decreased as the amount of capital increased; (2) the form of the charter was extremely liberal (it permitted unlimited capital, unlimited indebtedness; and "practically unlimited" powers to the corporation); (3) there was less liability on stockholders than in several other states; (4) the liability of directors was also less: where stock was issued in exchange for property, "the judgment of the directors" was "conclusive" as to the value of the property

taken, unless there was "evidence of fraud," and stock issued in this way was "considered fully paid up." Delaware and West Virginia had also recently adopted very liberal laws, particularly with respect to taxation. Neither state required that stockholders' meetings be held in the state, and West Virginia did not even require that an office be maintained in the state, although it did limit the total capitalization to $5 million.[24]

Watered Stock and Overcapitalization. The fact that the judgment of the directors was "conclusive" with respect to the value of property taken in exchange for stock in the New Jersey law provided an opportunity for overcapitalization. It was utilized. The Commission found that the American Sugar Refining Company had been "capitalized at a sum at least twice as large as the cost of reconstruction of the plants themselves." In the case of the Distilling and Cattle Feeding Company, which had been organized as a corporation in 1890 and had taken over 81 distilleries from the trust, the par value of the stock issued was six times the actual value of the distilling properties.[25] In general, the Commission concluded that overcapitalization in the organization of the large corporations was the normal procedure rather than the exception. It remarked: "In cases that are considered fairly conservative, the amount [value] of stock issued, including both preferred and common stock, is more than two or three times" the actual value of the assets while "in not a few instances . . . the capital stock seems to bear little relation to actual value of plants and patents."[26]

Profits of Promoters and Underwriters. The promoter is the person (or group) who conceives of the merger; the underwriter or the underwriting syndicate, is the man (or group)—sometimes also known as an investment banker—who undertakes to guarantee the sale of the securities and to provide the cash for the financing of the enterprise.

The pay of the promoters and underwriters was often very high in the mergers of the turn of the century and that promoter's profits were at least one strong incentive to combination is clear from the

23 *Ibid.*, p. 10.
24 *Ibid.*, pp. 11–12.
25 *Ibid.*, p. 177.
26 *Ibid.*, p. 16.

evidence. In the case of the United States Steel Corporation, which was organized as a holding company, John Moody reported in 1904 that J. P. Morgan and Company, who had promoted and underwritten that enterprise, received $62,000,000.[27] The holding company was the second major device employed as a successor to the trust arrangement, and it will be discussed shortly. Before doing so, it will be useful to define and classify several different types of mergers and to illustrate them with examples taken from a Congressional investigation of the subject held in the 1960's.

Types of Mergers

Contemporary literature generally contains a classification of three basic types of mergers: namely, *horizontal, vertical* and *conglomerate.* Conglomerate mergers may themselves be subject to sub-classifications. At the working level, the problems of fitting actual cases into these classifications, may, however, become difficult. Thus, Harrison Houghton, then Assistant to the Director of the Bureau of Economics of the Federal Trade Commission submitted a statement of his "private views" to a Senate subcommittee in 1964. He said:

. . . It should be pointed out that the classification of particular mergers into . . . three broad categories is often not as easy as it may seem. *Horizontal* mergers are those which bring together members of the same line of business, marketing their products in the same or similar geographic areas. *Vertical* mergers may be backward toward a raw material or earlier stage of production or fabrication, or forward in the direction of the ultimate markets. The *conglomerate* merger involves the absorption of a firm in a new line or market.

Sometimes the distinctions become fuzzy. For example, an aquisition of a firm manufacturing the same product but selling in a different geographical area is horizontal in one sense and conglomerate in another. It is horizontal in respect to identity of the product involved but conglomerate in terms of the geographic market. Such a merger is, thus, often referred to as a *"market extension".* Similarly, mergers might involve *"product extensions."* A merger bringing together functionally related products which are not, however, close substitutes could be regarded as another variant of the conventional horizontal merger, but if the firms deal in unrelated products their merger would be conglomerate. For our purposes, however, market and product extensions have been classified as conglomerate. Without detailed information as to products and markets, moreover, only approximate designations may be made. And, finally, the first merger in a particular line may be conglomerate and subsequent acquisitions in the same line would be horizontal.[28]

Chart 9-1 is a duplication of one put into evidence by Mr. Houghton. (Note that he defined a merger to include the case of acquisition of stock.) The chart depicts the acquisitions of Minnesota Mining and Manufacturing Company from 1950 to 1964. Among industrial corporations, this company was listed as having ranked 65th according to assets in 1967.

This company is, of course best known for its manufacture of "Scotch" tape and of magnetic recording tape. Since 1950 it has acquired (among others) a competing manufacturer of adhesives (indicated as a horizontal combination in Chart 9-1), a producer of stone, sand, and gravel (indicated as both backward vertical and conglomerate because the producer of stone and gravel also produced ready mixed concrete), and numerous producers of unrelated products, such as a metal stamping firm; and the Mutual Broadcasting Company (indicated as conglomerate in Chart 9-1). Note that *within* the category of "electrical insulating" the acquisitions were horizontal, indicating that numerous electrical insulating material producers were acquired. Mr. Houghton pointed out that the Mutual Broadcasting Company, which has 458 affiliated radio stations, was the principal outlet for sound recording tape produced by Minnesota Mining and so "in some respects could be classified as a 'forward vertical'" acquisition.[29] An alternative classification might be that of captive buyer.

As we have already seen, the Industrial Commission had reported that most of the

---

[27] John Moody, *The Truth about the Trusts* (New York: Moody Publishing Co., 1904), p. 103.

[28] *Economic Concentration* (Hearings before the Subcommittee on Antitrust and Monopoly, Senate Committee on the Judiciary, 88th Cong., 2nd sess.) (Washington, D.C.: U.S. Government Printing Office, 1964), Part I, "Overall and Conglomerate Aspects," pp. 162-4. (Italics mine.)

[29] *Economic Concentration, op. cit.,* Part I, p. 165.

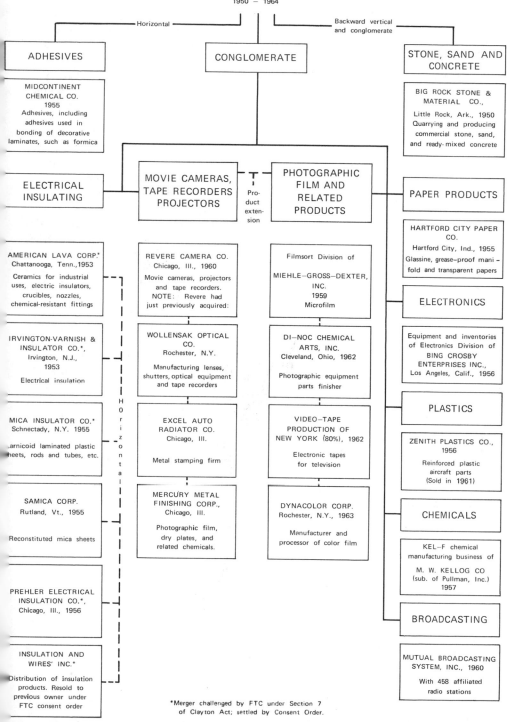

Chart 9-1

ACQUISITIONS OF
MINNESOTA MINING AND MANUFACTURING
1950 — 1964

*Merger challenged by FTC under Section 7
of Clayton Act; settled by Consent Order.

Source: Economic Concentration (Hearings before the Subcommittee on Antitrust and Monopoly, Senate Judiciary Committee, 88th Cong., 2d sess., 1964) (Washington, D.C.: U.S. Government Printing Office, 1964), Part I, p. 163.

combinations at the turn of the century had resulted from consolidations, that is, from the dissolution of the acquired companies and the acquisition of their assets by the new company. Such consolidations are, of course, still occurring. Another form of combination involves acquisition of a controlling interest in the stock of another corporation without a dissolution of the acquired company, or the establishment of a holding company. This form, too, is still in use, as Chart 9-1 indicates.

The Holding Company

Nature of the Holding Company. Bonbright and Means cite instances of holding companies created by special charters of state legislatures as early as 1823, but it was the amendments to the New Jersey corporation laws between 1888 and 1893, at a time when the trust device for elininating competition was coming under heavy legal attack and public censure, that created the opportunity for the use of this legal device as a means for control of corporate combinations.[30] These amendments to the New Jersey law (or changes in the working rules of economic organization) made it possible for one corporation to own stock in another. The use of this legal device was described by the Industrial Commission in 1900:

A third form of organization, *which is in many particulars quite like the original trust form,* is that which has been taken by the Federal Steel Company, by the Distilling Company of America, and others. In this form the central company, instead of purchasing the plants of the different corporations which it is proposed to unite, simply buys a majority of the stock, or possibly the entire stock of each one of the corporations. The separate corporations keep in separate existence, but a majority of the stock being held by the one larger corporation, its officers, of course, elect the boards of directors of all the separate corporations, and in this way hold ultimately complete control. It is usually true that the separate corporations manage their own affairs *practically* independently, *although* they are furnished information regarding the workings of the other establishments in the combination through the central officers, *and are doubtless largely directed in their policy in this way.*[31]

The comparison of the holding company to the trust by the Industrial Commission was an apt one and explains why consolidations primarily took the form of a "fusion" or of a merger of assets rather than that of the use of the holding company device. Bonbright and Means assert that the employment of this device by Standard Oil interests "gave impetus to its more extensive use."[32] Standard Oil Company of New Jersey had become a holding company by 1899; according to Eliot Jones: "the trust had simply hung out a new sign."[33] Thereafter, for a time, almost as many combinations occurred by use of the holding company device as by fusion. In 1904, however, a divided Supreme Court held that this device was a violation of the Sherman Act when it was used in a monopolistic setting,[34] and its use in industrial combinations thereafter declined. Nevertheless, the General Motors Company was organized as a holding company in 1908 when it acquired the controlling interest in the Buick, Cadillac, Cartercar, Elmore, Ewing, McLaughlin, Marquette, Oakland, Olds, Randolph, Welch, and Weston-Mott companies, as well as in companies producing parts. By 1909 General Motors controlled about 53.5 percent of total automobile production.[35] No antitrust action arose, however, and in 1916 General Motors Corporation was organized, and the assets of the former subsidiaries were acquired directly. Today it is a $13 billion dollar (asset) industrial corporation and ranked second in terms of assets in 1967. With sales of more than $20 billion in 1967, it ranked first in that category.

The Difference between Pure and Mixed Holding Companies. A *pure holding company* is one which owns the controlling interest in other companies but which does not itself directly operate facilities in order

---

[30] James C. Bonbright and Gardiner C. Means, *The Holding Company* (New York: McGraw-Hill Book Co., Inc., 1932), pp. 55–65.

[31] *Report of the Industrial Commission, op. cit.,* Vol. I, pp. 10–11. (Italics mine.)

[32] Bonbright and Means, *op. cit.,* p. 70.

[33] Eliot Jones, *The Trust Problem in the United States* (New York: The Macmillan Co., 1922), p. 57.

[34] *Northern Securities Company* v. *United States,* 193 U.S. 197 (1904).

[35] Based on production data contained in Willard Thorp and Walter Crowder, *The Structure of American Industry* (Temporary National Economic Committee Monograph No. 27) (Washington, D.C.: U.S. Government Printing Office, 1941), p. 244.

to produce products and services for sale to others. The United States Steel Corporation was formed as a pure holding company in 1901 by a process of exchange of its stock for the stock of: (1) the Carnegie Company (the largest independent producer of steel at that time); (2) the Federal Steel Company (the principal competitor of Carnegie and a Morgan company); (3) the National Steel Company (the third largest producer, and itself the result of the consolidation of a number of steel producing companies in Ohio); (4) the American Tin Plate Company (which had been formed from the combination of 39 plants and was commonly referred to as "the tin plate trust"); (5) the American Steel and Wire Company (an integrated company known as "the wire trust," also the result of a previous combination, controlling about 80 percent of the market for nails and wire fencing in the United States); (6) the National Tube Company (known as "the tube trust"); (7) the American Steel Hoop Company (formed as a result of the combination of 9 other firms); (8) and the American Sheet Steel Company (known as the "sheet steel trust," also organized as a consolidation of previous competitors in the production of sheet metal.)[36] Since then, however, United States Steel has also become an operating company, so that today it is a mixed holding company. In 1967 it had assets of more than $5.6 billion and sales of about $4.0 billion, ranking 10th in sales among industrial corporations. In terms of assets it was the seventh largest industrial corporation in the United States in 1967.

A *mixed holding company* has been implicitly defined above as one which not only holds the controlling interest in other companies but also serves as an operating company. The Standard Oil Company of New Jersey was originally organized as such a mixed holding company: in addition to holding the controlling interest in the twenty companies which had comprised the original trust, it also refined and marketed oil on its own account. This combination was formally dissolved as the result of an antitrust action in 1911, a matter which will be considered further in Part II of this

book. In 1967, Standard Oil of New Jersey had sales of more than $13 billion and assets of about $15.1 billion. Among industrial corporations, it ranked second in sales and first in assets in that year. American Telephone and Telegraph became a mixed holding company in 1900. In 1967, it easily outranked all utilities both in operating revenues and total assets. In fact, it also outranked all other corporations, including banks and life insurance companies, in the United States (Prudential had assets of $25.1 billion in 1967) as well as all of the foreign industrial corporations in assets. The assets of A. T. and T. in 1967 were about $37.6 billion, and its operating revenues were about $13.0 billion.[37]

Pyramiding within the Holding Company. *Pyramiding* is the name given to a process of establishing layers of holding companies between a parent holding company and its operating companies to make possible the control of large amounts of capital with a small initial investment. An example of the process is contained in Chart 9-2 which may be explained as follows.

Suppose that A and B, having access to a million dollars of capital wish to obtain control of operating companies with common stock outstanding worth $32 million. Suppose also that A and B first create Holding Company X_1, which issues common stock worth $2 million, of which A and B purchase $1 million, the remaining $1 million being sold to the public. (See Chart 9-2.) Holding Company X_1, now has $2 million. Next A and B create Holding Company X_2, which issues $4 million of common stock, of which Holding Company X_1 purchases $2 million, the remaining $2 million being sold to the public. Holding Company X_2 now has $4 million of assets. Next, A and B create Holding Company X_3, which issues $8 million of common stock, of which Holding Company X_2 purchases $4 million, with $4 million being sold to the public. Holding Company X_3 now has $8 million of assets. Next A and B create Holding Company X_4, which issues $16 million of common stock, of which Holding Company X_3 purchases $8 million, the remaining $8 million being sold to the public. Holding Company X_4, with $16

---

[36] Jones, *op. cit.*, chap. ix.
[37] See the *Fortune Magazine Annual Directory* for data of this type.

Chart 9-2

Example of a Holding Company Pyramiding Operation

Operating Properties
$32 million of common stock outstanding

Holding Company X_4
$16 million of common stock outstanding

Holding Company X_3
$8 million of common stock outstanding

Holding Company X_2
$4 million of common stock outstanding

Holding Company X_1
$2 million of common stock outstanding

A and B
$1 million bank loan

---

million of assets, purchases the controlling interest (50 percent in this case) in the operating companies which have a total of $32 million of common stock outstanding. The structure of the entire system would then appear as in Chart 9-2. Clearly, the structure is that of an inverted pyramid; it rests on a rather narrow base: A and B's bank loan. If nonvoting securities are added to the financial structure, an even greater amount of capital can be controlled with the initial $1 million bank loan. Moreover, as we will see later, it is seldom necessary to purchase 50 percent of the stock for control.

Bonbright and Means found few instances of pyramiding among industrial corporations but many instances of extreme pyramiding in the railroad and public utility areas during the 1920's. For example, making use of information in a report of the House Committee on Interstate and Foreign Commerce, they cited the case of the Van Sweringens who were enabled— by a complex system of pyramiding—to control a number of railroads with assets of over two and a half billion dollars with an initial investment of twenty million. They also cited the Cities Service Company,

a pure holding company which, with a million dollar issue of voting preferred stock, controlled more than 65 public utilities at the end of 1930, having assets of over a billion and a quarter dollars.[38] In the case of the Associated Gas and Electric System, which consisted of "three or four hundred corporations," Bonbright and Means cited the fact that one of its vice-presidents was unable to recall in what companies he was director or officer or what was the nature of the business transacted by some of the companies.[39]

In 1935, the Securities and Exchange Commission completed a 101 volume study[40] of utility corporations and found that 3 large utility systems controlled about 45 percent of the total output of the privately owned electrical utility industry, with 12 other large systems controlling another 35 percent. It further found that 11 holding company systems controlled 80 percent of the total mileage of natural gas pipelines, and 20 holding company systems controlled 98.5 percent of the transmission

[38] Bonbright and Means, *op. cit.*, p. 262 and p. 114.
[39] *Ibid.*, p. 119.
[40] Securities and Exchange Commission, *Utility Corporations* (Washington, D.C.: U.S. Government Printing Office, 1935).

of electrical energy.[41] In 1935 Congress enacted the Public Utility Holding Company Act authorizing the Securities and Exchange Commission to order corporate reorganizations of public utility systems and prohibiting the existence of holding companies beyond the second degree, in what some of the utility holding companies denounced as an unwarranted governmental interference and an extension of socialistic tendencies. Under this law there can be no utility holding companies beyond the second degree, that is, beyond X_2 in Chart 9-2. (The Act of 1935 is considered more fully later in this book.)

Interlocking Directorates

The term *interlocking directorate* may be broadly defined as a situation in which a director or official of one corporation is also a member of the board of directors of another corporation. An exhaustive Congressional committee staff study of the existence of interlocking directorates in the United States was published in 1965. The study classified such interlocking directorates into two different types in the following language:

1. *Horizontal:* Common director or directors link two or more companies that presently are, or potentially may be, competitors in the same industry. . . .
2. *Vertical:* Common director or directors link two or more corporations which deal with each other but are at different levels in the same industry, as manufacturer-supplier or a manufacturer-distributor. Vertical interlocks may also exist between different industries where one corporation provides a service to the other, as in the case of transportation services, and banking or other financial services.[42]

Both basic types of interlocking directorates defined above may be either (a) direct or (b) indirect. *Direct* interlocking

directorates involve the case of a "common director or directors on the board of each of the companies involved." *Indirect* relationships are of various kinds: (1) cases where enterprises are linked in such a way that, even though they have no directors in common, each may have one or more directors on the board of a third corporation; (2) cases in which a third company may have representatives on the boards of two or more competing enterprises; and (3) cases in which one company has a director on the board of a second which, in turn, has directors on the board of a third company with which the first company is in competition.

The legal and economic problems involved in interlocking directorates will be considered further in Part II of this book. Our interest in this chapter is merely in their extent and scope. It should be obvious that an interlocking director may be in a position to "serve as a liaison officer between two companies and to insure that the pursuit of the best interests of the one is not seriously detrimental to that of the other" and that "he is also in a position to bring about a measure of common action and, if the proportion of interlocking directors is sufficient, competition between the two firms may be eliminated entirely."[43] Indeed, it may not even be a question of the number of interlocking directors but of their power and influence. An interlocking directorate between, say, one of the ten largest corporations in the United States and the 399th might very well be weighted in the direction of the former; particularly so if the 399th corporation were a supplier of the larger corporation.

Table 9-1 is based on data contained in the Staff Report of the Congressional Subcommittee on Antitrust of the House Judiciary Committee referred to above. Apparently the high score in the sample of 29 leading corporations goes to the only nonindustrial corporation in the sample, namely, the American Telephone and Telegraph Company. Since A. T. and T. owned 99.82 percent of the stock of the Western Electric Company, which also appears on the list, it had interlocking relationships with 29 banks and financial institutions, 27 insurance companies, 81

---

[41] Securities and Exchange Commission, *The Public Utility Holding Company Act of 1935*, reproduced in *Study of Monopoly Power* (Hearings before the Subcommittee on Study of Monopoly Power, House Judiciary Committee, 81st Cong., 1st sess.) (Washington, D.C.: U.S. Government Printing Office, 1949) Serial No. 14, Part 2–B, pp. 1460 ff., at p. 1460.

[42] *Interlocks in Corporate Management* (Staff Report to the Antitrust Subcommittee, House Committee on the Judiciary, 89th Cong., 1st sess.) (Washington, D.C.: U.S. Government Printing Office, 1965), pp. 9–10.

[43] *Ibid.*, p. 7.

Table 9-1

Summary of Management Interlocks Among 29 Leading Corporations, December 31, 1962

Name of Company	Rank in 1962 (According to Assets)	Banks and Financial Institutions	Insurance Companies	Industrial and Commercial Companies	Other Companies	Grand Total
General Motors Corp.	2	23	4	33	3	63
Standard Oil Co. (N.J.)	1	3	1	2	1	7
Ford Motor Co.	3	12	3	39	3	57
General Electric Co.	11	20	14	47	3	50
Secony Mobil Oil Co.	7	11	2	7	1	21
U.S. Steel Corp.	4	20	10	58	1	89
Texaco Inc.	6	16	7	25	3	51
Gulf Oil Corp.	5	5	1	24	1	31
Western Electric Co.	15[a]	7[a]	11[a]	18[a]	1[a]	37[a]
Swift and Co.	77	18	5	16	0	39
E.I. du Pont de Nemours	10	5	1	12	0	18
Chrysler Corp.	21	12	9	32	2	55
Standard Oil (Calif.)	8	8	1	13		
Standard Oil (Ind.)	9	6	3	3	1	13
Bethlehem Steel Corp.	12	0	0	0	0	0
Shell Oil Co.	14	2	5	15	0	15
Westinghouse Electric Corp.	19	19	7	62	3	89
Int. Bus. Mach. Corp.	13	20	5	31	2	58
General Dynamics Corp.	61	16	5	39	4	64
Armour and Co.	100	12	5	22	3	42
Lockheed Aircraft Corp.	47	11	2	19	10	42
North American Aviation, Inc.	58	7	5	23	0	35
Phillips Petroleum Co.	17	3	0	7	0	10
Sinclair Oil Corp.	22	9	0	26	3	38
United Aircraft Corp.	64	11	14	14	0	39
American Motors Corp.	111	10	2	21	0	33
Continental Oil Co.	26	14	1	46	2	63
Douglas Aircraft Corp.	116	7	1	28	1	37
Amer. Tel. and Tel. Co.	—	22[a]	16[a]	63[a]	3[a]	104[a]

[a] Amer. Tel. & Tel. Co. owns 99.82 percent of Western Electric Co.
Sources: Based on data from *Interlocks in Corporate Management* (A Staff Report to the Antitrust Subcommittee, House Committee on the Judiciary, 89th Cong., 1st sess.) (Washington, D.C.: U.S. Government Printing Office, 1965), pp. 117 ff.; and Table 9–11 *infra.*

industrial and commercial corporations and 4 other companies, for a total of 141 interlocking directorates.

The Staff Report also examined the extent of interlocking directorates among commercial banks, among commercial banks and insurance companies, among commercial banks and industrial and commercial companies, and among life insurance companies. In the category of interlocks among 15 commercial banks and industrial and commercial companies it found more than 1200 management ties and remarked, "Bank of America, with 108 management interlocks with industrial and commercial corporations, was typical of the major commercial banks."[44] The Bank of America is the largest commercial bank in the United States (deposits of more than $19 billion in 1967) and had direct interlocks with 3 other commercial banks. The Chemical Bank New York Trust Co., sixth largest bank in the United States, had direct interlocks with 11 other banks.[45] Similar interlocking relationships were found to exist in the case of all the 15 largest commercial banks in the United States as of December 31, 1962; and there is little reason to think that the picture has

[44] *Ibid.*, p. 183.

[45] *Ibid.*, pp. 178–180.

changed much since that time. In the field of insurance companies, the study disclosed that officers and directors of the 20 largest life and fire insurance companies held 1,512 directorships or other management offices in other corporations.[46] As has been noted, since—under certain conditions— interlocking directorates may involve violations of the antitrust laws. this question will be the subject of further consideration in Part II.

Industrial Self-Government

"Industrial self-government" is an interesting and quaint notion that businessmen should be permitted to "regulate themselves," free from governmental "interferences." The pools which preceded the trusts were an embryonic form of "industrial self-government." When "industrial self-government" is undertaken on an international scale by means of cooperation of enterprises in two different countries, the resulting pool is called a cartel. It is interesting to note that in the 1880's the whiskey distillers' pool adopted the name of Western Exporters' Association, and the wallpaper pool called itself the American Wall Paper Manufacturers' Association. Trade associations today do not ordinarily behave as did the earlier pools but, occasionally, trade associations do engage in anticompetitive activities. They also played an important role in the writing of industry codes under the National Industrial Recovery Act during the early part of the depression and a lesser role in supplying personnel for work (often without compensation) in defense agencies created under the Defense Production Act of 1950 during the Korean emergency.

The Trade Association. There are many thousands of trade associations in the United States today. The most exhaustive study of trade association activities is one published in 1941 by the Temporary National Economic Committee—hereafter TNEC—which was created by Congress in 1937 "to make a full and complete study and investigation with respect to the concentration of economic power in, and financial control over, production and distribution of goods and services." The TNEC consisted of 3 Senators, 3 Repre-

sentatives, and 6 members from the Executive Branch and, in many ways, undertook in the 1930's the kind of work which had been done earlier by the Industrial Commission. Its 1941 study of trade associations concluded with an analysis of the activities and objectives of the American Association of Manufacturers (already covered in Chapter 6 of this book) and of the Chamber of Commerce of the United States, and described them as "the two foremost federations in the trade association field." Both organizations, we have seen, engage in lobbying and, in addition to having large numbers of individuals and firms as members, both have large numbers of national, state, and local trade association members.[47]

Trade associations were defined in the TNEC study as "voluntary, non profit organizations of enterprises engaged in a particular kind of business." Information was obtained from 1,311 associations in response to a questionnaire. Approximately 54 percent of the trade associations reported that they were themselves incorporated.[48] Moreover, "nearly 48 percent of the associations received 40 percent or more of their income, and 30 percent received 60 percent or more of their income, from their four largest contributors." Although only 2 reported their origin as prior to 1860, 8 had been organized during the 1860's, and 50 had been organized between 1870 and 1889. But by far the largest number were organized after World War I and nearly 23 percent were organized during the 3 year period from 1933 to 1935, when the National Recovery Administration was in operation. Responses to a question asking the associations to rank their activities in order of importance were summarized as follows:

... activity in the field of Government relations easily outranks other trade association activities. Over 80 percent of the associations reported some activity in this field, and it is the only activity which over 50 percent of the associations reported as of major significance. Trade promotion is next in rank; approximately 70 percent of the associations reported this

[46] *Ibid.,* p. 191.

[47] Charles A. Pearce, *Trade Association Survey* (Temporary National Economic Committee, Monograph No. 18) (Washington, D.C.: U.S. Government Printing Office, 1941), pp. 339–41.

[48] *Ibid.,* p. 2 and p. 9.

activity, and only about 50 percent indicated that it was a major activity. The only other activities that were reported as of major importance by a third or more of the associations are standardization and simplification, conventions, trade practices, and trade statistics.[49]

There have been numerous antitrust cases involving price reporting and trade statistics activities of trade associations. The TNEC study analyzed 125 cases acted upon by the Federal Trade Commission and the Department of Justice in the period from June 1, 1935 to October 1, 1939. Of the 125 cases brought, 92 involved trade associations, and the defendants in the remaining 33 cases were not formally organized. It is interesting that 85 of the 125 cases involved attempts to eliminate price competition, while 38 involved "elimination of competitors."[50] One of these cases, it may be remarked, involved the American Medical Association and was dismissed by the District Court on grounds that the defendants were not engaged in trade or commerce within the meaning of the Sherman Act.

The question was also asked in the TNEC survey: "If there were no legal limitation or area of doubt, what additional activity or activities would you endeavour to develop with the expectation that they would significantly benefit your membership?" Of the 202 associations replying to this question, 13 indicated that they would take active steps to combat "unfair" competition or "unfair" trade practices, and "nearly all the remaining associations expressed a desire for price or production control, in connection with which the participation of Federal agencies was not infrequently urged or invited."[51]

In another TNEC study, Clair Wilcox presented a list of 217 references to instances in which "trade associations, industrial institutes, and other common agencies" were said "to be exercising some form of control over production, price and terms of sale, or organizing boycotts in national or regional markets from 1920 to 1940."[52]

It should not be concluded that (though the pool idea is clearly not completely dead) all trade associations engage in such practices. By far the largest number have never been charged with any violation of the antitrust laws. Trade associations may perform useful functions in the areas of market surveys, industrial research, mutual insurance, and publication of trade journals, as well as in presenting the points of view of their members; at the same time, where they engage in price reporting activities, whether or not their conduct constitutes circumstantial evidence of activity to fix prices has presented great difficulties in antitrust cases, as we will see in Part II.

Trade Associations and the National Industrial Recovery Act: Codes. It has been noted that organization of trade associations increased greatly during the period of the NRA. Indeed, the fact that many trade associations responded to the TNEC questionnaire by urging price or production controls in which federal agencies would participate was probably partly due to their recollection of their NRA experiences. As we have seen in the preceding chapter, at the bottom of the depression, unemployment had reached a level of 25 percent of the labor force, and the first Agricultural Adjustment Act had been adopted in May of 1933 in an attempt to aid farmers. The National Industrial Recovery Act (NIRA) was an early attempt to solve the problem of depressed industrial output and employment. It was a compromise measure incorporating: (1) the demands for "industrial self-government" which had been advanced by Gerard Swope of the General Electrical Company, the Chamber of Commerce of the United States, and others; and (2) the demands of labor for "spreading the work" by reducing hours and for a right to bargain collectively.

What is of primary interest in the present context is the fact that the Act authorized the President to approve "codes of fair competition" upon application by trade associations or groups, and that codes drawn up by these groups were then exempt from prosecution under the anti-

---

[49] *Ibid.*, p. 26.

[50] *Ibid.*, pp. 67–69.
[51] *Ibid.*, pp. 64–65.
[52] Clair Wilcox, *Competition and Monopoly in American Industry* (Temporary National Economic Committee Monograph No. 21) (Washington, D.C.:

U.S. Government Printing Office, 1940), pp. 235–240. For a description of some trade association activities, see Arthur R. Burns, *The Decline of Competition* (New York: McGraw-Hill book Co., 1936), pp. 47–55.

trust laws. The principal concession to labor in the Act was a requirement that every code contain provisions providing for the right of employees to organize and bargain collectively through representatives of their own choosing, a proposition which was subsequently embodied in the Wagner Labor Relations Act. The working rules were bent in a new direction.

Clair Wilcox's survey (with William Loucks and Kermit Gordon) of NRA code provisions for the TNEC in 1940 is still the best compact treatment of this subject. He remarked:

The N.R.A. . . . conferred new powers and immunities on strong associations, invigorated weak associations, aroused moribund associations, consolidated small associations, and called some eight hundred new associations into life. . . .

The N.R.A. approved 557 basic codes, 189 supplementary codes, 109 divisional codes, and 19 joint N.R.A.—A.A.A. codes, a grand total of 874. All of these codes contained provisions which governed the terms and conditions of sale, subjecting to detailed regulation in various combinations such matters as quotation, bid, order, contract, and invoice forms, bidding and awarding procedures, customer classifications, trade, quantity, and cash discounts, bill datings, credit practices, installment sales, deferred payments, interest charges, guarantees of quality, guarantees against price declines, long-term contracts, time and form of payments, returns of merchandise, sales on consignment, sales on trial or approval, cancellation of contracts, trade-in allowances, advertising allowances, supplementary services, combination sales, rebates, premiums, free deals, containers, coupons, samples, prizes, absorption of freight, delivery of better qualities or larger quantities than those specified, sale of seconds and of used, damaged, rebuilt, overhauled, obsolete, and discontinued goods, the payments of fees and commissions, and the maintenance of resale prices.

Of the first 677 codes, 560 contained some provision for the direct or indirect control of price. . . .

Four hundred and twenty-two codes provided for the establishment of open-price reporting systems. Most of these systems were of a character that would probably have been outlawed under the earlier decisions of the Supreme Court. . . .

A number of codes contained provisions which were designed to effect an allocation of markets among members of a trade. . . .

Ninety-one codes provided for the restriction of output and the distribution of available business among the firms in a trade. . . .[53]

The simple pools of the 1860's had become sophisticated and—more importantly —they were now backed by the power of government. A corporate state had been born. But its life was short. In 1935, we have seen, the Supreme Court invalidated the Act primarily on grounds that it was an unlawful delegation of legislative authority to the President.[54] But, by then, even the administrators had begun to lose faith in this particular experiment. And so, the novel approach of enforcement of the antitrust laws was then adopted.

Other particular stabilization schemes affecting particular industries were, however, continued—for example, the Bituminous Coal Act and legislation to assist states to regulate the production of crude oil. And, in some industries, the cooperation which had been learned during the NRA period continued to be practiced; for example, in 1940 the Supreme Court upheld a lower court Sherman Act conviction of certain oil companies whose price fixing activities had originated in NRA codes.[55]

Trade Associations and the Korean Emergency. The Defense Production Act of 1950 as amended,[56] contains in Section 708(a) an authorization for the President to consult with representatives of business, industry, labor, agriculture "and other interests" with a view to encouraging the making of "voluntary agreements to further" the national defense program. Under Section 708(b) such voluntary agreements may constitute exceptions from the antitrust acts. Some safeguards are now built into the Act but, when it was first adopted, there were none; and it was "the overall policy of the Act to encourage voluntary cooperation between business and Government." This cooperation took an interesting form in 1950 and 1951. Many industry advisory committees were created in order to assist in the planning of the defense effort. For example, the Aluminum Producers' Industry Advisory Committee consisted of representatives of

[53] Wilcox, *op. cit.*, pp. 260–266.
[54] *Schecter Poultry Corporation* v. *United States*, 295 U.S. 495 (1935).
[55] *United States* v. *Socony-Vacuum Oil Co.*, 310 U.S. 150 (1940).
[56] 50 U.S.C. 2061–2166.

the three primary producers of aluminum; and the Administrator of the National Production Authority (NPA)—an agency which had the function of issuing defense priority ratings for the use of materials as well as allocation of some basic raw materials—saw no reason to include fabricators (customers of the primary producers), because the three primary producer-representatives "constituted" the industry. According to one Congressional committee, when these agencies were first staffed:

On December 20, 1951, at the instance of Alan Valentine, then administrator of the Economic Stabilization Agency, Otto Seyforth, president of the United States Chamber of Commerce, typed and addressed a number of letters which were mailed *at Chamber expense* to the presidents of a *select* list of large corporations soliciting personnel to staff important positions in Washington wartime agencies.[57]

The committee noted that selection of these individuals, who were known as WOC's— because most came to Washington without governmental compensation—was apparently on a "company basis rather than on an individual basis." Such WOC's were assigned to important positions: in the Petroleum Administration for Defense, WOC's were at the heads of ten divisions and at least half of the commodity divisions of the NPA had WOC's as their division directors. Testimony of government officials concerning the ability, unselfishness, and devotion to duty of the WOC's was clear and unequivocal. The committee did, however, call attention to one instance in which a priority in the use of basic materials had been given to one very large firm (a General Motors subsidiary) "while the applications made by all other locomotive builders for comparable relief were inexplicably lost, not once but twice."[58]

What this instance pointed up was the possibility of discrimination in the allocation of raw materials in short supply. Large firms might be favored at the expense of small firms. It should be noted that in times of emergency it is inevitable that the

government call upon individuals from private industry to assume important positions. Often-times employees of large firms are the only ones with relevant know-how. But, usually, in such periods, sales people are sent to Washington. The problem is one of insuring that, inadvertently or otherwise, policies adopted during such an emergency do not lead to favoritism strengthening the relative positions of those firms who are called to serve the common cause. One safeguard in such a situation would be adoption of a rule that the head of each division or bureau must be a full time career government servant. As a result of the investigations of various Congressional committees—and it is to be noted that supervision by Congressional investigations may be the only real safeguard in such situations—the practice of using WOC's was discontinued.

A related problem which has arisen is, as noted in the preceding chapter, procurement by the Department of Defense and the impact of that activity upon the structure of competition in the United States.

Contractual Arrangements

There are, of course, many types of contractual arrangements which may be employed by business associations. These may range from resale price maintenance contracts (under which retailers agree as a matter of contract to fix resale prices at levels determined by manufacturers, thereby eliminating competition among themselves) to patent licensing contracts. The latter rest upon the fact that in most countries the owner of a patent is given a private monopoly position by law within the relevant jurisdiction. There are many instances of market sharing and price fixing arrangements based on such underlying patent agreements. Tying arrangements, under which patent licensees may be required to purchase supplies not subject to the patent from the patent holder, are also common. These contractual arrangements and the theory of the patent monopoly will be more fully described in Part II, in the course of an examination of actual antitrust cases involving them. All these arrangements, of course, rest on a basic working rule that patent monopolies

[57] *The Mobilization Program* (Report of the Subcommittee on the Study of Monopoly Power of the House Committee on the Judiciary, 82nd Cong., 1st sess.) (Washington, D.C.: U.S. Government Printing Office, 1951), p. 82. (Italics mine.)

[58] *Ibid.*, p. 89.

are socially desirable. This working rule will also be considered further in Part II.

Tax-Exempt Foundations

The tax-exempt foundation is a relatively recently-developed form of business organization. As a general rule, such organizations are exempt from gift taxes, and bequests or gifts to them are deductible for tax purposes by the donor. These organizations are also allowed a tax free status. Some are incorporated; others are not. The reasons for creation of such foundations vary and are not always matters of pure philanthropy. Business considerations other than the fact that substantial tax reductions are achieved also enter into the interlude of their creation. Almost all are the progeny of planned parenthood. For example, it may be possible for a small group to retain control of an enterprise by transferring its stock to such a foundation. In the case of the Ford Foundation, for instance, voting shares of the Ford family were transferred to the Foundation, while additional voting shares were created and sold to the public by the Foundation subject to limitations on the right of any one person to hold more than a certain number of shares. With the income from the new (limited ownership) voting shares sold to the public, the Foundation was able to diversify its holdings, while at the same time the Ford family was insured control over the enterprise.

Since 1962, the House Small Business Committee has conducted investigations into the activities of such tax-exempt foundations. Among other things, it reported:

. . . substantial parts of the great fortunes of those who have profited by the enormous expansion of American industry have found their way into tax exempt foundations. These foundations have already passed and will continue to pass—by right of inheritance—to the control of heirs or their trustees. This enables a few individuals to control ever-increasing wealth.

In 1948 the Treasury Department estimated that there were about 10,000 such foundations in this country. . . .

. . . on May 16, 1963 Commissioner Caplin made a speech in Cleveland in which he said there were "roughly 15,000 actual foundations . . ."

The $1.044 billion received by 546 tax-exempt foundations in 1960 was substantially more—in fact, 17 percent more—than the $864,435,000 combined net operating earnings, after taxes, of the 50 largest banks in the United States.

The 546 foundations had assets of no less than $10.3 billion at the end of 1960.

To date, the granting of Federal tax exemption to foundations has been a mere formality. The record proves that, as far as the Treasury is concerned, an organization becomes "charitable" by merely describing itself as such. Once such exemption has been granted, there is little or no check on the foundation's activities. No less than 55 percent of the 546 foundations examined by the Subcommittee failed to comply with certain Treasury regulations during one or more years.[59]

The Subcommittee also found that of 546 foundations studied, one-hundred-eleven "owned ten percent or more of at least one class of stock in one or more of 263 different corporations on December 31, 1960."[60]

There has been some evidence that in some cases—generally involving foundations whose names are not before the public daily—stocks in the hands of the foundations have been utilized by one side or another in proxy fights and that foundations have made loans at favorable interest rates to some borrowers, in some cases, for speculative purposes. The Internal Revenue Service has no real power over the foundations other than the revocation of the tax-exempt status. The Acting Commissioner of the Internal Revenue Service testified in 1964 on the impact of the great increase in number of such foundations in recent years:

It certainly indicates also that so far as the Revenue Service is concerned, and assuming we continue our present role of examining these foundations for tax consequences, that we need to continue to devote the efforts that we have been devoting to this problem over the last three years, and if possible within the limitations of our budget, increase the funds available to us for making these examinations.

This is all apart and aside from the more fundamental question which the Chairman and Mr. Roosevelt [Representative James Roosevelt] raised as to whether or not there needs to be

---

[59] *Tax-Exempt Foundations: Their Impact on Small Business* (Hearings before Subcommittee No. 1 on Foundations of the House Select Small Business Committee, 88th Cong., 2d sess.) (Washington, D.C.: U.S. Government Printing Office, 1964), pp. 3–5.

[60] *Ibid.*, p. 5.

some type of super police organization established which would have the responsibility for auditing these corporations, these foundations, for all aspects of their activity involving all responsibilities which they have under the laws of this country.[61]

It may be remarked that the activities of the largest foundations eventually become identified with the business corporations out of whose earnings they were established and may, like a servo-mechanism, feed back prestige to these corporations or provide them with adverse publicity. A Ford Foundation investigation into civil liberties is a case in point; those opposed to such studies were extremely critical.

Because the role of the tax-exempt foundation in American economic and social (particularly academic) life is increasing, it is clear that some form of regulation may eventually become necessary. That some abuses have occurred and that some foundations have propaganda purposes is certain. One has recently had its lifeline cut by revocation of its tax-exempt status for this reason. But the number of foundations that have been involved in such abuses has not been established. At the moment, the information is much too sketchy for any real conclusions to be drawn or any new policies to be formulated. It is quite likely that the information problem will be at least partially overcome by means of Congressional investigations, in due course, if not in other ways, perhaps by studies financed by foundations themselves. In the United States, abuses of power have inevitably resulted in reaction and regulation.

The Communications Satellite Corporation: A Government-Created Private Monopoly

Probably the most interesting innovation in the forms of business associations in the United States is that of the government-created, private, profit-seeking monopoly. So far only one such organization has been established, the Communications Satellite Corporation under the Communications Satellite Act of 1962.[62] This private, profit-seeking monopoly enjoys a "chosen instrument" status in the area of international space communications; that is, it is a private

corporation "chosen" to carry out certain United States foreign policy aims. The Act providing for the establishment of the corporation was opposed by a number of Senators and was enacted after cloture had been imposed by the Senate (as described in chapter 6) to ward off a filibuster threatened by Senator Wayne Morse. Decisions pertaining to regulation of the activities of the corporation by the Federal Communications Commission will be examined in Part III of this book.

For the moment, it will be enough merely to give a brief description of this rather interesting form of business organization. The history of its development is as follows. In 1961, President Kennedy issued a "Statement of Communications Satellite Policy" in which he announced a United States policy of establishment of a global and nondiscriminatory satellite communications system involving participation as soon as possible by other countries. On February 7, 1962 the President sent to Congress a proposal for creation of a privately-owned communications satellite corporation. The initial proposal contemplated financing of the corporation by sale of two classes of stock: Class A stock sold to the public would carry voting rights and earn dividends; Class B stock would be sold only to approved "communications carriers" and would earn dividends but have no voting rights.[63] However, communications carriers (such as A. T. and T.) would also be permitted to purchase limited amounts of Class A (voting) stock. The bill was amended by the Senate Aeronautical and Space Sciences Committee to authorize the corporation "to issue, in such amounts as it shall determine, shares of capital stock without par value, which *shall carry voting rights* and be eligible for dividends." (Italics mine.) In addition, the committee amendment provided that "50 percent of the shares of voting stock issued at any time by the corporation shall be reserved for purchase by communications common carriers authorized by the Federal Communications Commission to own shares in

---

[61] *Ibid.*, p. 277.

[62] Public Law 87–624, 87th Cong., 2d sess. (1962).

[63] *Communications Satellite Act of 1962* (Report of the Senate Committee on Aeronautical and Space Sciences, 87th Cong., 2d sess., Senate Report 1319) (Washington, D.C.: U.S. Government Printing Office, 1962), p. 2.

the corporation" subject to a proviso that the aggregate of the shares of voting stock of the corporation held by the carriers should not at any time exceed 50 percent of the voting shares of the corporation which were issued and outstanding.[64] The committee felt that this arrangement provided "a good balance, with the public holding half the outstanding voting stock and the carriers owning half."[65] This arrangement was eventually adopted in the legislation.

The legislation also provided for 15 directors, 3 to be appointed by the President, 6 to be elected by the public, and 6 to be elected by the common carriers. In addition, the legislation provided for regulatory authority on the part of the Federal Communications Commission and for assistance to the corporation by the National Aeronautics and Space Administration (NASA) "on a reimbursable basis in the launching of satellites" and other services. It may be noted in this regard that A. T. and T. paid to NASA the total sum of $2,689,982.00 for the launching of Telstar, one of the earlier experimental communications satellites. The communications carriers have, of course, provided data calling attention to their very great expenditures on research in the development of the satellites—as distinct from the launch vehicles—as additional costs which they have borne. Indeed, in their testimony before the Senate Aeronautics and Space Committee, they pointed to the objections to the administration proposal that the carriers purchase Class B (nonvoting) stock because they "could see no benefit to be derived from the purchase of Class B stock." In fact, it was asserted that the purchase of Class B stock "would increase the rate base, pricing such carriers out of the market and forcing them to lose business to their competitors."[66] (It was also testified that the Bell System operates about 98 percent of all facilities used to provide long-distance telephone service in the country.) The Committee thereupon concluded that the "purchase of such stock would be speculative." It is interesting to note that when the corporation issued 10,000,000 shares of

common stock at a price of $20.00 per share in the Spring of 1964, the issue was over-subscribed; and by August 11, 1964, the price was $35.00 a share.[67]

As has been noted, under the legislation as finally adopted, 50 percent of the voting shares of common stock were reserved to the common carriers, with the Federal Communications Commission having the job of allocating these shares among approved carriers. Of the initial issue of ten million shares of common stock, five million were thus set aside (reserved) for the communications carriers and distributed.

In 1964, three of the 15 directors of the corporation were A. T. and T. employees, 2 were elected by I. T. and T., and 1 was elected by the other communications carriers.[68] In February of 1965 the corporation was reported to have had more than 137,000 stockholders.[69]

B. THE MERGER MOVEMENTS

Table 9-2 contains data pertaining to mergers in mining and manufacturing since 1895. It is to be noted that there are two peaks in the data between 1895 and 1954 and that, since 1954, mergers have been taking place at a high rate. The first peak occurred in 1899, and the second occurred in 1929. Whether a third peak is yet to be attained remains to be determined. In any case, the total of 2,442 in 1968 was the largest number in the series. In 1969, the number declined by 7 percent to 2,246. However, these figures refer to mining and manufacturing firms only. The merger of all types of firms increased from 3,932 in 1968 to 4,291 in 1969, with the largest increase occurring in service industries.

The First Merger Movement: 1890–1902

As we have already seen in the discussion of the forms of business organization and associations above, the last decade of the nineteenth century was one during which a

---

[64] *Ibid.*, p. 7.

[65] *Ibid.*

[66] *Ibid.*, p. 7.

[67] *Satellite Communications* (Hearings before a Subcommittee of the House Committee on Government Operations, 88th Cong., 2d sess.) (Washington, D.C.: U.S. Government Printing Office, 1964), Part 2, pp. 691–92.

[68] *New York Times*, May 12, 1964, p. 65, col. 2.

[69] *Ibid.*, February 17, 1965, p. 64, col. 3.

Table 9-2

Recorded Mergers in Making and Manufacturing in the United States, 1895–1969

Year	Number	Year	Number	Year	Number	Year	Number
1895	43	1914	39	1932	203	1951	235
1896	26	1915	71	1933	120	1952	288
1897	69	1916	117	1934	101	1953	295
1898	303	1918	71	1935	130	1954	397
1899	1,208	1919a	171	1936	126	1955c	683
1900	340	1920a	206	1937	124	1956	673
1901	423	1919b	438	1938	110	1957	585
1902	379	1920b	760	1939	87	1958	589
1903	142	1921	487	1940	140	1859	835
1904	79	1922	309	1941	111	1960	844
1905	226	1923	311	1942	118	1961	954
1906	128	1924	368	1943	213	1962	853
1907	87	1925	544	1944	324	1963	861
1908	50	1926	856	1945	333	1964	854
1909	49	1927	870	1946	419	1965	1,008
1910	142	1928	1,058	1947	404	1966	955
1911	103	1929	1,245	1948	223	1967	1,496
1912	82	1930	799	1949	126	1968	2,442
1913	85	1931	464	1950	219	1969	2,246

a Comparable with earlier years; b comparable with later years; c 1955 and after from Federal Trade Commission revised figures of 1965.

Sources: Department of Commerce, U.S. Bureau of the Census, *Historical Statistics of the United States from Colonial Times to 1957* (Washington, D.C.: U.S. Government Printing Office, 1961), p. 572; and Federal Trade Commission, *Current Trends in Merger Activity, 1969* (March 1970), p. 9.

number of our best-known and largest corporations were founded. In addition to the United States Steel Corporation (1901), Standard Oil Company of New Jersey (1899)—from which the various other Standard Oil Companies were created after the Supreme Court decreed dissolution of the company in 1911—and American Telephone and Telegraph Company (1900) were formed. Others dating from this period include: American Can Company (1901), International Harvester Company (1902), Eastman Kodak Company (1901), E. I. du Pont de Nemours Powder Company (1903), United Shoe Machinery Company (1899), National Lead Company (1891), American Tobacco Company (1890), Pittsburgh Plate Glass Company (1895), and United States Rubber Company (1892).[70] All are included among the 200 largest industrial corporations in the United States in terms of assets (A. T. and T. is counted as an industrial corporation for the present purpose), and all but 2 are included in the 100 largest by the same measure.

[70] *Report of the Industrial Commission*, Vol. 19, pp. 1127 ff.

Most of the combinations formed during this period were horizontal combinations, and many grew out of pooling practices or trust arrangements. According to the *Report of the Industrial Commission*, the principal reason for the creation of these combinations was "the desire to lessen too vigorous competition" which "naturally brings them together."[71] A second reason was "the various economies which they think will come by combination," including "regulation of production," ability to carry reduced inventories, full time operation of plants, increased specialization, and a reduction in selling costs "for example, in the number of travelling salesmen."[72] Another reason which was given by "one or two witnesses" was the protective tariff, although several other witnesses also believed that the tariff was merely a "contributing factor." In addition, one should mention the profits of the promoters which, as we have seen, were great. Willard Thorp has cited with

[71] *Ibid.*, Vol. 1, p. v.

[72] *Ibid.*, pp. v–vi.

approval, in this regard, a statement by Seager and Gulick that the movement was possible "only because a group of shrewd, plausible, and aggressive promoters was at hand to make fullest use of the favorable business situation."[73] By 1904, however, the situation had changed and the wave had subsided.

In a thorough study of mergers made in 1959, Ralph Nelson stated that the first merger wave was the most important because it transformed the structure of American industry from one of small and medium size enterprises into one in which one or a few very large firms dominated particular industries.[74] That this characterization is accurate has become apparent in the historical description of the development of forms of business associations in the preceding section. But it may be true also that the current merger movement (to be examined shortly), which involves further significant structural changes, may prove to be of equal significance.

The Second Merger Movement: 1925–1930

Although there was a flurry of mergers in the early 1920's, the second merger movement really dates from about 1925 and reached a peak in 1929. The data in Table 9-2 relate to mergers in mining and manufacturing only; many large public utility mergers also occurred during this period which marked a high point in the use of the holding company. Thorp stated that, in 1926, a total "of 1,029 public utility enterprises disappeared through merger or acquisition." Moreover, he remarked, the "same basic forces were present in the twenties as in the earlier period. . . . Promoters were extremely active, new issues of stock were floated where the total exceeded the parts."[75] In other words, there was more watered stock. Mention has already been made in the discussion of the holding company of the fact that overcapitalization was characteristic of the public utility sector in the 1920's, just as it was of industrial enterprises in the earlier merger period. In view of the way in which the promoters

were paid—by issues of stock—it is readily apparent that in both these periods the amount of overcapitalization is a measure of the activity of promoters. In fact, as has also already been pointed out, in the early 1930's pyramiding reached an all-time high in the United States, and concentration of control over public utility operating companies by means of the holding company device had also reached an extreme degree.

In the area of manufacturing and mining there were both horizontal and vertical mergers. The horizontal mergers did not often involve the largest firms in the industry but, instead, those in the tier just below them: the third and fourth largest. Vertical mergers involved acquisition of medium size firms producing parts and components. In 1925 the Chrysler Corporation was formed out of the Maxwell and Chalmers Corporations. In 1928 it acquired the Dodge Company, and it immediately became one of the "big three." Various motion picture-distributor-exhibitor companies were also organized in the 1920's.[76] And the National Dairy Products Corporation was incorporated in 1923; between 1923 and 1932 it acquired control of 331 separate dairy companies, 194 directly and the remainder as subsidiaries of the acquired companies. One of its best known subsidiaries is the Kraft Cheese Company. The Borden Company, although originally incorporated in 1899, began an acquisition program in 1928; and between 1928 and 1932 this company had acquired 207 separate dairy enterprises.[77]

But, as Thorp put it, in the public utility area, after the high point had been reached, the merger movement could proceed no farther because there were very few firms left to be acquired. In other areas, the stock market crash of 1929 helped to cause the wave to subside, so that in 1934, there were only 101 mergers in mining and manufacturing as compared with

---

[73] Willard Thorp and Walter Crowder, op. cit., p. 231.

[74] Ralph L. Nelson, *Merger Movements in American Industry, 1895–1956* (Princeton: Princeton University Press, 1959), p. 5.

[75] *Ibid.*

[76] See Daniel Bertrand, et. al., *The Motion Picture Industry—A Pattern of Control* (Temporary National Economic Committee Monograph No. 43) (Washington, D.C.: U.S. Government Printing Office, 1941), *Appendix* I.

[77] A. C. Hoffman, *Large Scale Organization in the Food Industries* (Temporary National Economic Committee Monograph No. 35) (Washington, D.C.: U.S. Government Printing Office, 1940), pp. 27–28.

1,245 in 1929. The crash also squeezed some of the water out of the stock.

The Present Merger Movement

Some Basic Data. Reference to Table 9-2 discloses that mergers in mining and manufacturing have exceeded 800 in every year since 1959 and reached 2,442 in 1968. Moreover, according to a study published by the Federal Trade Commission in 1969:

The number of large acquisitions, those involving acquired firms with assets of $10 million or more . . . increased in 1968, totaling 192 as compared to 169 in 1967. . . . The total value of large acquired assets equaled $12.6 billion, 50 percent greater than in 1967, and three times greater than the total for 1966. The most striking development, however, is the continued increase in size and frequency of the large acquisitions.[78]

Importance of Conglomerate Mergers in the Present Movement. There is much evidence that the present merger movement is dominated by conglomerate mergers. Thus, the Commission also reported in 1969:

From the standpoint of public policy the most unique aspect of the current merger movement is its conglomerate character. In 1968 these mergers accounted for 84 percent of the number and 89 percent of the assets of all acquisitions. . . . These proportions are higher than those of 1967 and continue the upward trend of recent years. The unique development of 1968 with respect to conglomerate mergers was their dramatic change in character and average size. . . . Virtually all of the increased larger merger activity of 1968 involved expanded patterns of diversification.[79]

Thus, the nature of the present merger wave differs from that of the previous waves.

Economic Theory and the Conglomerate Firm. From the points of view of economic theory and public policy, Professor Corwin Ed-

wards summed up the present situation when he remarked as follows:

Conglomerate enterprise does not have a well-defined place either in public policy or in economic theory. . . . Until recently, neither lawmakers nor economists were concerned with conditions in which the size and power of a business enterprise depends, not on possession of a large share of a single market, but on operation across a considerable number of markets.

. . . Doubtless some conglomerate mergers are harmless; some may even be useful. But the merger of unrelated activities seldom offers much prospect of efficiency, and hence, where there is reason to object to such a merger, prevention of it is unlikely to be disadvantageous to the economy. In a good many instances, the merger of noncompeting enterprises would eliminate significant potential competition, and should be prevented on this ground.

As I understand recent merger decisions, the antitrust agencies have made a beginning. . . .[80]

In his statement, Edwards also indicated certain specific business practices which should be prohibited. These practices and the larger problem of the "conglomerate enterprise" are both considered more fully later in Chapter 17 in the discussion of the "recent merger decisions" by the Supreme Court to which he referred. Questions pertaining to the measurement of "economic power" to which Edwards also referred will be discussed later in Chapter 11. Before we turn to that subject, it will be useful to examine the general circular flow model of price theory and to consider some basic price theory concepts. The data and information provided in this chapter should enable the reader to judge for himself the extent to which the assumptions of the model described in the next chapter correspond to reality. For example, is the assumption that no firm is large enough to affect the price of the product it sells warranted? It is to a verbal discussion of the general model of price theory that we now turn.

[78] *Current Trends in Merger Activity, 1968* (Federal Trade Commission lithoprint, March 1969), pp. 1–7.

[79] *Ibid.*, p. 3.

[80] *Economic Concentration, op. cit.*, p. 36 ff.

Static Welfare Economics and "Economic Efficiency"; the Circular Flow

In recent years the language of price theory has begun to make its appearance in court decisions dealing with the antitrust laws. As a case in point, one may cite more of the opinion of Justice Reed in the *du Pont Cellophane* case (already considered in another context in Chapter 4). He said:

An element for consideration as to cross-elasticity of demand between products is the responsiveness of sales of one product to price changes of the other. If a slight decrease in the price of cellophane causes a considerable number of customers of other flexible wrappings to switch to cellophane, it would be an indication that a high cross-elasticity of demand exists between them; that the products compete in the same market. The court below held that the "[g]reat sensitivity of customers in the flexible packaging markets to price or quality changes" prevented du Pont from possessing monopoly control over price. . . . The record sustains these findings.[1]

Since one way of defining the "cross price elasticity of demand" is to say that "it is a measure of the responsiveness of sales of one product to price changes of

the other," the first sentence in the quotation above may be paraphrased to read: "An element for consideration as to cross-elasticity of demand is the economic meaning of the concept of cross-elasticity of demand." So paraphrased, the sentence is seen to be as redundant as it is unexceptionable. The use of such language in this Supreme Court opinion suggests that some knowledge of the basic language of price theory is useful to anyone interested in a study of current legal policies relative to the antitrust laws. A complete explanation of this language cannot be given in a few words and the task will not be attempted in this book. *This* chapter is limited to a verbal discussion of basic concepts and is intended merely to introduce the reader to the subject.

As we shall see in later chapters, some economists hold the view that the principles of static welfare economics developed by price theorists can be usefully employed as a *norm* against which public policies relative to economic activities can be tested. But at the same time, as we shall also see in later

---

[1] *United States* v. *E. I. du Pont de Nemours and Co.*, 351 U.S. 377 (1956).

chapters, criticisms of this view have been voiced on several grounds; and it has been rejected outright by perhaps even more economists. For example, the Attorney General's Committee to Study the Antitrust Laws asserted in 1955 that:

> ... the economist's terms "pure" and "perfect" competition ... are technical terms identifying theoretical models which have defined conditions of equilibrium with logical precision and completeness. They do not purport to indicate ideal conditions. Whatever their views on public policy, economists are in agreement that departures from the model of "pure" or "perfect" competition do not necessarily involve monopoly power or substantial lessening of competition in the sense of being a problem for public policy. *We do not regard these models as offering any basis for antitrust policy.* Indeed, departures from conditions of pure or perfect competition are inevitable, pervasive and many of them useful to competition as a dynamic process.[2]

The alternative suggested by the Committee, the idea of "workable competition," will be discussed in depth in Chapter 13, as will be the derivative concepts of "economic performance," "economic structure," and other alternative approaches to the problem.

The conditions of an "optimum" according to static welfare economics can be reduced to two fundamental propositions and a value judgment or two, namely, assuming the distribution of income as given and that prices are a measure of the social value (utility) to consumers of goods, economic welfare will be at a maximum: (1) when all consumers within the economy are maximizing the total utility available from their given money incomes; and (2) when all firms are operating at the long-run least average cost under conditions of perfect competition or, what amounts to the same thing, at the point of "economic efficiency," making "normal" profits only.

In order to understand why the Attorney General's Committee and most economists who are actively working in the field of antitrust, of regulated industries, and in areas involving other real world problems have made little or no specific use of the model of perfect competition *as a norm*, even though they may extensively employ the language of price theory, it is necessary to know what this model involves, as well as to know some of the basic concepts used by economists.

A. SOME BASIC ECONOMIC CONCEPTS

The Concept of "Perfect Competition"

Various writers use the term "competition" differently. *Perfect competition* may be rigorously defined as a situation characterized by the following conditions: (1) there exists a large number of buyers and sellers, none of whom thinks he can influence the price of a commodity through his own individual actions; (2) all commodities of a given class are homogenous (perfectly interchangeable); (3) all buyers and sellers have perfect knowledge of the situation confronting them and of their alternatives; (4) all economic entities (buyers and sellers, producers and consumers, etc.) behave rationally to maximize their own self-interests (however these may be defined); and (5) there exist freedom of entry into the market and perfect mobility of inputs.

So defined, *perfect competition* is a conception of an ideal type. It does not exist in the real world. *Pure competition* is a less inclusive concept than *perfect* competition and may involve an absence of "ideal fluidity or mobility of factors" or of a lack of "perfect knowledge of the future and the consequent absence of uncertainty."[3] Nevertheless, it is also an ideal type or an abstraction from real world conditions.

The Concept of "Equilibrium"; "Economic" Variables; Comparative Statics

A *stable equilibrium position* is defined as one from which there is no tendency to move, or as one to whose values the dependent variables assumed in the analysis have a tendency to return after a slight disturbance. *Partial equilibrium* analysis involves changing the value of one independent variable, while holding "other

---

[2] *Report of the Attorney General's National Committee to Study the Antitrust Laws* (Washington, D.C.: U.S. Government Printing Office, 1955), p. 316. (Italics mine.)

[3] See, for example, E. H. Chamberlin, *The Theory of Monopolistic Competition* (fifth ed.; Cambridge: Harvard University Press, 1947), p. 6.

things constant" to determine the effect of this change on the dependent variable. *General equilibrium* analysis is not completely general, but allows the other economic variables in the problem to "change equally." What variables are to be considered *economic variables* is a matter which must be specified by the analyst. In 1890, Alfred Marshall asserted that economics concerns itself chiefly with motives which "affect . . . man's conduct in the business part of his life."[4] Accordingly, he thought economics could be a "hard" science. But he also argued that we ought not to trouble ourselves with "scholastic inquiries" as to whether the variables being considered were "economic" variables or not.[5]

In the areas of economic history and economic development, as Professor Walter Neale has pointed out, particularly where questions involving nonmarket economies are concerned, the Marshallian definition cannot be used. Neale has suggested that a substantive definition is more appropriate and that such a substantive definition can be framed in terms of materiality; thus according to Neale, the word *economic* means in a substantive sense "those technological and social processes which supply men with material means to action or the satisfaction of wants."[6] This kind of a definition, of course, is related to the definition by Commons already given in Chapter 1, since "social processess" can here be interpreted to mean "working rules." In the area of orthodox price theory, however, the narrower definition of Marshall holds undisputed sway.

Contemporary price (or microeconomic) theory is almost without exception concerned with static rather than dynamic situations. *Comparative statics* is the name given to the method of analysis used, which involves comparing the initial values of the dependent variables in an initial equilibrium position with the new values of the dependent variables in a new equilibrium position after some change in an independent variable. Nothing is said in the analysis about the path of adjustment or about the way in which the adjustment

occurs. The application of the results of such an analysis to a dynamic real world situation is thus sharply limited by the method of analysis employed. What this method of analysis provides is a frame of reference. In addition, microeconomics provides a "grand scheme" of economic organization to be described next.

The Circular Flow Model of the Economy

Figure 10-1 depicts a model of a stationary economy. All individuals in this model are assumed to wear two "hats" (among all their others). They are both consumers of products (outputs) and suppliers of services of factors of production (inputs). As consumers they spend their money incomes for products and thus demand them. In a free enterprise system (or under decentralized state socialism), firms purchase inputs or factor services in the factor markets and transform them into products or outputs. These are sold in the product markets. Thus, firms demand inputs and supply outputs. The source of the inputs is the individuals who own them. In exchange for their inputs, the individuals receive incomes. The amount of income received is equal to the prices paid by the firms (their costs) for these inputs multiplied by the quantities of these inputs supplied by the individuals. The amounts of the inputs owned by the individuals are assumed to be determined by existing institutional arrangements and are thus excluded from economic analysis.

Two sets of markets are depicted in Figure 10-1. There are both: (1) *product or output markets* and (2) *input or factor markets*. In each market, prices are determined by supply and demand according to the assumptions one makes. If one assumes perfect competition, in the long run, the prices which consumers pay for goods will be equal to the average cost (including a "normal" profit) of producing and selling these goods. These prices will, in turn, be just equal to the addition to costs of producing and to the addition to revenue from selling *additional* units of the goods (that is, "marginal cost" will equal "marginal revenue" as well as price and average cost).

[4] Alfred Marshall, *Principles of Economics* (eighth ed.; London: The MacMillan Co., Ltd., 1938), p. 14.
[5] *Ibid.*, p. 27.
[6] Walter C. Neale, "On Defining 'Labor' and 'Services' for Comparative Studies," *The American Anthropologist*, Vol. 66 (1964), pp. 1300–1307, at p. 1302.

Figure 10-1

The Circular Flow

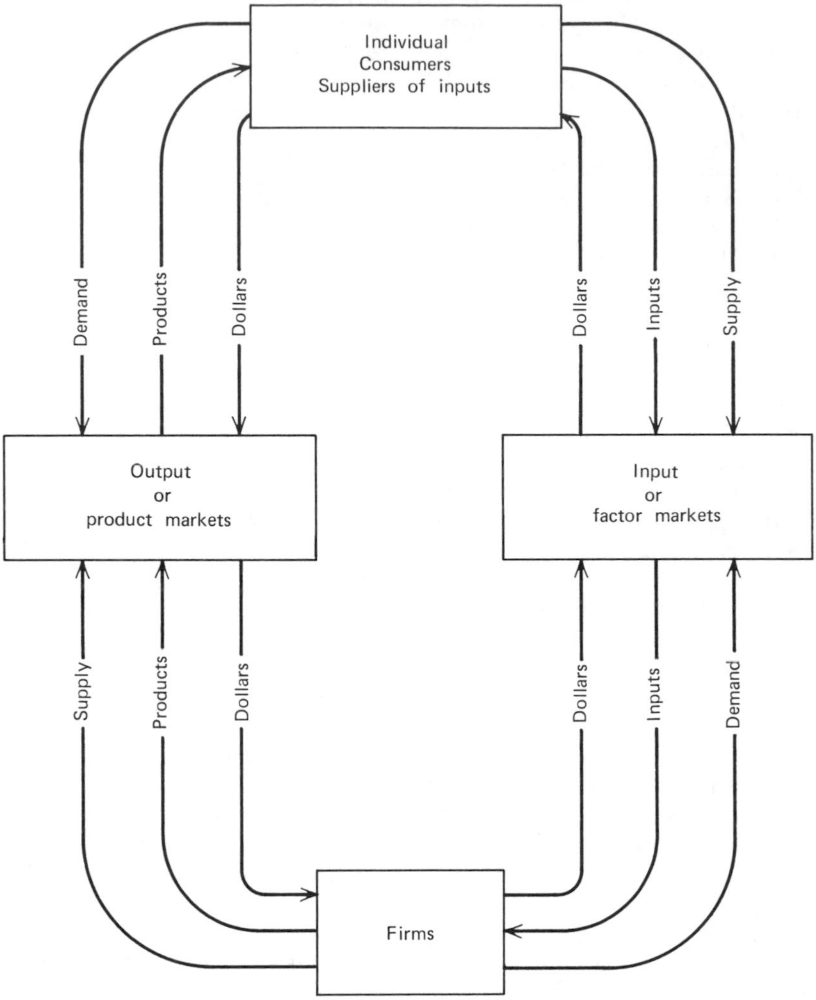

If consumers' wants are taken as data (compare the reliance of legal positivists on the *Grundnorm*, as described in Chapter 3), and if prices actually do reflect consumers' preferences, if one assumes that the distribution of income is *given* (fixed), he can assert that welfare is at a maximum in such a society. That is, a state of *relative* "economic efficiency is being attained in this society. Whether or not welfare would be greater under some other scheme of social organization or as a result of a redistribution of income (for example, a "War on Poverty") cannot be determined by use of this model.

The word *inputs* has been employed in our description, but it is useful to use also the term which was employed by the neoclassical economists. They used the word *factors*. The "factors of production," or the agents of production, were classified broadly as land, labor, capital, and the "entrepreneur" (the promoter and undertaker of the enterprise). Each of the factor or input services has a price. The payment for the service of land is called rent, the payment for labor service (including the service of routine management) is wages, and that for the use of capital is called interest. What is left over, the remainder, if any—the difference between the total of the three preceding payments and the firm's total sales revenue is designated as either profits or losses, and this is the amount payable to the entrepreneur. He is thus a risk-taker.

The Relationship between Macroeconomics and Price Theory

In Figure 10-1 outputs are sold by firms to individuals, and input services are sold by individuals to firms in never ending streams. In the opposite direction, money is paid by individuals to firms, and then back again to individuals as income. There are opposite flows of money and goods. Thus Figure 10-1 depicts a "circular flow."

This diagram depicts both the macro-economic and the microeconomic approaches to economic analysis. For example, it is possible to analyze the aggregate opposite flows of money and of goods. One can then define "inflation" as a situation in which the aggregate flow of dollars increases relative to the aggregate flow of goods. By making the model more complex, one can break down aggregate consumers' incomes into saving and consumer expenditure and analyze effects of changes in consumer spending. One can also insert into the stream of dollars the effects of actions by central banks to increase or decrease the money supply. This problem is considered in Chapter 31. Similarly, it is possible to show the government as a consumer in product or factor markets or as a borrower of funds. These questions, too, are examined in Chapter 31. And, it is possible to analyze by means of this model the effects of international transactions on the flow of goods and on the flow of money. All these matters are the concern of "macroeconomics," which deals with the *level* of operation of the system.

Price theory, on the other hand, concerns itself with the "micro-economic aspects" of the system. In price theory it is assumed generally that the system is operating at a full employment level. What determines the prices of the inputs and of the products? What costs are relevant? How are prices and outputs affected if the degree of competition is decreased? How do rational consumers determine the quantities of products which they purchase? These are some of the questions raised. Thus, price theory is concerned with an analysis in detail of the various determinants of, and of the relationships among, the elements of the system. Instead of taking an overall view of the system, its elements are analyzed in detail.

However, the two methods of analysis are concerned with an attempt to explain the *same* economic system. Figure 10-1 makes this point clear. They merely emphasize different aspects of the system and the two methods of analysis are related.

B. THE FUNCTIONS OF AN ECONOMIC SYSTEM

Types of Functions of an Economic System

The following functions must be performed in an economic system: (1) decisions must be made as to the kinds and amounts of products to be produced; (2) decisions must be made as to the quantities and kinds of inputs which are to be used and the proportions in which they are to be used to produce particular outputs; (3) decisions must be made as to how the total final output of products is to be distributed; and (4) some provision must be made for the maintenance and growth of the system. In the model depicted by Figure 10-1, if the total output is completely consumed in period after period without any provision for replacement of the capital equipment which is depreciated in the production of products, eventually the system must come to rest. Its capital will be exhausted. But if such provision is made, the system can continue to operate indefinitely at a given level. Consequently, some provision for maintenance of the system is an essential condition to its continued existence. Growth involves an expansion in the level of operations of the system.

The Nature of Price Theory; The Relation between Product and Factor Markets

Price theory seeks to study the principles according to which the functions of an economic system are or will be performed by making assumptions about the amount and kind of competition and concerning the rationality of the behavior of producers and consumers and the knowledge had by them, in the absence of governmental intervention. Thus, price theory devotes itself primarily to an analysis of the principal determinants of prices in both the output and in the input markets. The prices offered in the product markets are interpreted to be evidence of the preferences of the consumers and to serve as guides to producers in their allocation of resources to the production of products. The prices determined in the factor markets are identified as the costs to the producers of the resources they employ. There are two markets, and prices and their determinants in each market must be considered.

The analysis of the process by which consumers' valuations are reflected in the prices which they are willing to pay for the products is called the theory of demand. Consumers will allocate their incomes in such a way that the additional satisfaction obtained from an additional (marginal) unit of expenditure is the same in each use. Changes in consumers' valuations will be reflected in changes in the prices they are willing to pay. In the model, decisions as to what is to be produced are made by consumers and evidenced in the prices which they are willing to pay. Consumer sovereignty reigns. Goods for which there is no demand will not command a price. Producers will not, in the long run, be able to produce such goods because the prices received for the products which they produce determine the abilities of the producers to cover their costs. The costs of the producers are, however, the prices of the services of the factors of production which are used to produce the products. Thus the factors are employed to produce those products for which consumers will pay, and the relatively most "valuable" factors will command the highest prices. The two sets of prices are related. Factor prices depend on product prices. The demand for factors is "derived" from the demand for products.

But if consumers' valuations are *not* independent of the other variables in the system, that is, if advertising expenditures and promotional selling activities of firms exert any influence on consumers' absolute or relative valuations of goods, the decisions as to what products are to be produced are not made by consumers alone. In this case, prices will still reflect the relative valuations which consumers place on the products, but these valuations are clearly *not* independent of other variables in the system. Such valuations must now be considered to be the product of actions by firms to create

demand. Recognition of this fact does *not* destroy the theory of demand, but it does seriously weaken the welfare conclusions which are derived from the general circular flow model of the economy.

In a free enterprise system, by and large, decisions as to the quantities of factors or inputs used and concerning the proportions in which they are to be devoted to the production of particular products are made by managers of firms. These decisions can, of course, be influenced by governmental policies, as we will see later. However, under conditions of perfect competition, and in the absence of governmental action, since no firm thinks it can by its own actions affect the price of the product which it sells, there would be no need for advertising and no selling expenses. In such a situation also, firms would be guided only by the prices paid for products in the product markets; and assuming they were seeking to maximize their profits and behaved rationally, firms would also seek to make use of the least costly methods of production. Competition would drive the least efficient firms out of business; competition would also insure that no firms made greater than normal profits in the long run, for freedom of entry is one of the conditions of perfect competion, and thus, new firms would enter industries in which greater than normal profits were being made, driving profits down to a "normal" level.

But, in the real world, there are difficulties of definition. The term "profits" is difficult to define. Do firms maximize their long-run or their short-run profits? Do firms maximize profits at all? Some may seek a fixed percentage return on the capital investment. Professor Baumol has suggested that one reasonable hypothesis is that a firm's managers maximize sales revenue subject to a minimum profit constraint (that is, subject to a recognition by the managers that stockholders will require a minimum profit to remain "happy") because salaries of executives are more closely correlated with sales revenues than with profits. Indeed, some firms may seek only to become large or to eliminate competition. And some may seek only to keep their share of a market unchanged.

Thus, when the model is made more

realistic, when it is recognized that firms are large and do influence the prices of products by their own actions and often make decisions on "noneconomic" grounds, and when it is recognized that firms which produce joint products (for example, the production of many transportation services by a railroad) do not know the full cost of producing individual products and often follow a procedure of allocating expenses to particular products on the basis of revenues obtained from their sales, or some other arbitrary procedure, further questions of the usefulness of the general model as an *explanation* of reality arise. Its usefulness is thus primarily analytical. It provides a "pure case" for reference, not a description of reality as we will see in Chapter 11. It tells us what the real world is not!

We have seen that the prices which firms pay for the factors of production which they employ to produce products are costs to the firms. When the prices paid for the factors are multiplied by the amounts of the factors used, the resulting figures are the incomes earned by the relevant factors of production. Thus, the income of an individual depends both on the prices of the relevant factors and on the quantities of them which he owns. We have said that the quantities of the factors owned by the individuals are determined by the institutional arrangements of the society in question. The prices which are paid for the factors depend on the supplies of the factors and on the "derived" demands for them which arise out of their usefulness in the production of final products. Supply and demand are both important. The extent of competition among firms bidding for factors and the extent to which competition exists among suppliers of factors thus influences the prices which are paid for the use of such factors.

In general, the explanation of payments for factors of production or of the "functional distribution of income" is as follows. Under perfect competition, in the long run, the price paid for the use of a unit of a given factor of production is exactly equal to the additional sales revenue which results from the use of an additional unit of such a factor of production. In the long run, profits in such a situation will be "normal,"

which means that they are just sufficient to keep the "proper" amount of entrepreneurship engaged in the production of the final products. Thus, the price paid for an additional unit of a factor is equal both to its value to the firm and to its value to society.

Maintenance of the system is provided by including in the cost of the final product an amount just sufficient to replace the capital equipment which is "used up"; thus depreciation allowances are functionally a proper inclusion in the cost of the final product.

In this analysis, temporary profits greater than "normal" are justified by some on functional grounds by making the system dynamic. Thus they argue: if, for one reason or another, profits in the production of one type of products or of a new type of products become greater than normal, this fact is a signal for additional entrepreneurs to enter the field and to bid inputs away from their existing uses, and to use them to increase the production of the given products. In this way, the supply of the relatively more desirable products is increased, while that of the relatively less desirable products is decreased. Eventually only normal profits will once more be made in all industries and the economy find itself in a new position of stable equilibrium, perhaps at a higher level of output than before. In this way change and growth are explained by these writers. In Chapter 13 we will consider the problem of innovation in relation to the size of the firm.

The statement of the ways in which the functions of an economic system are performed involves a factual judgment with regard to the question of whether or not consumers' valuations of products are or are not independent of the other variables in the system. To assume that they are *completely* independent (and this is the usual assumption) is to introduce an unrealistic assumption into the model, just as to assume perfect competition is unrealistic. A model which makes these unrealistic assumptions explains the ways in which the functions of the economic system *would be* performed *if* its assumptions *were* valid, but it does *not* explain how they are actually performed in our own system today. Such a model provides a point of reference, a system of classification, not a description of the world as it is. It cannot serve as a practically attainable goal.

But the model does contain grains of truth. Perhaps its most important service is its emphasis of the complex nature of the market process and its demonstration that there are *two* sets of markets and *two* sets of prices to be considered. And, although the Attorney General's National Committee explicitly rejected the use of the model of perfect competition as a *norm* for the enforcement of the antitrust laws, as we will see in Chapter 13, many of the basic ideas embodied in our circular flow model are embedded also in various interpretations of the concept of "workable competition," and in evaluations by economists of the "conduct, structure, and performance" of particular industries.

However, in the next chapter we will consider a topic related to those discussed in the preceding chapter and this one, namely the extent to which economic power is concentrated in the hands of private business firms and labor unions. Such concentrations of power, of course, are inconsistent with the assumption of perfect competition.[7]

---

[7] The reader who requires a rigorous treatment of price theory is referred to my *The Nature of Price Theory* (Revised edition; Homewood: The Dorsey Press, 1968).

11

Concentrations of Economic Power: Business Associations and Labor Unions

This chapter undertakes: (1) to explain measures of "market control" employed by economists, largely in dealing with data reported to the Bureau of the Census by business firms; (2) to explain related measures of "resource control" used in analyzing information reported to the Securities and Exchange Commission and to the Internal Revenue Service; (3) to study problems of separation of ownership and control in large corporations; and (4) to present some basic information concerning the growth of the power of organized labor. However, the special working rules applicable to labor are a subject studied in courses in labor economics, and this topic is treated separately (briefly) in Chapter 29. Empirical studies of concentration are summarized where it is appropriate to do so. This chapter thus consists of four subdivisions dealing, respectively, with the topics enumerated above.

A. THE MEASUREMENT OF MARKET CONTROL

There are two basic types of measures of economic power but there is no accepted terminology for distinguishing between them. The pioneering studies in which these two measures were developed were both made by Gardiner Means, whose work on the holding company has already been mentioned.[1] One group of measures of economic power purports to measure the share of the market controlled by a particular firm or firms. Such measures will be called *Market Control Measures* in this book. This group will be discussed in this subdivision. The second group of measures seeks to determine the legal control of a firm or group of firms over the instruments of production; that is, over the productive resources employed. This group will be labelled *Resource Control Measures* and will be

[1] See National Resources Committee, *The Structure of the American Economy* (Washington, D.C.: U.S. Government Printing Office, 1939), Part I (which was prepared under his direction); and Adolph A. Berle, Jr. and Gardiner C. Means, *The Modern Corporation and Private Property* (New York: The Macmillan Company, 1932).

discussed in the next subdivision. Moreover, the discussion will be limited to a consideration of measures which have in fact been employed; measures suggested by theoretical economists which have not been or cannot be quantified (even though they may be quantitatively stated by means of mathematical symbols) will not be discussed.[2] Nor will we consider measures involving knowledge of highly sophisticated statistical techniques. Instead, we will consider the measures most often used.

The Theoretical Basis of Market Control Measures

The theory of perfect competition discussed in the preceding chapter rests on an assumption (among several others) that each seller's influence in the market is so insignificant that he takes the market price as given in his calculations; that is, *he knows* that he cannot influence the price of the product which he sells. Preferences on the part of a buyer for products of a particular seller are thus ruled out by assumption, since an assumption that such preferences exist would be inconsistent with the assumption that the seller cannot influence his price. Thus, products must be assumed to be homogenous (interchangeable), and it also must be assumed that no advertising or other selling costs are incurred. On the other hand, the theory of monopoly assumes that there is a single seller who is the sole supplier of the market and that no substitutes for the product he sells exist. Market measures of economic power often seek to determine the extent of the divergence of the actual market situation from the mental construct of perfect competition. Mere computation of such a measure does not of course, involve the conception of the perfectly competitive economy of pure theory as a "norm"; and the use of the measure does not necessarily imply logical acceptance of perfect competition as a norm. But in practice, as we will see shortly. it usually does.

Various economic quantities can be used as indicators of the share of the market possessed by a particular firm: the ratio of employment of the firm to total employment devoted to production in a particular

market (but this measure assumes that the output is sold and may not be a good measure in industries which involve a high capital investment); the ratio of total sales of the firm to total sales in the market (but this measure assumes no inter-firm sales); or the ratio of "value added by manufacture" within the given firm to the total value added by manufacture within the given market. If the ratio is infinitely small, it follows that the individual seller is an insignificant influence in the market. The ratio is usually multiplied by 100 and expressed as a percentage figure.

Bureau of Census as Source of Data: Standard Industrial Classification (SIC)

In the Census of Manufactures, individual manufacturing *plants* report their shipments in terms of *products* to the Bureau of the Census which then classifies the plants themselves. The Bureau also classifies the data which it receives according to the Standard Industrial Classification (SIC). In this system of classification, all manufacturing industry in the United States is classified into 21 *major industry* groups. These 21 *major industry* groups are known as "2-digit" groups. Thus in Table 11-1, "Food and kindred products" is a major industry group bearing the "2-digit" code number 20.

There are 21 such major industry groups, but since the first of these (code number 19) relates to armaments and other items of military and national defense significance, no data concerning this group are published. (They are probably Top Secret and result in the exclusion of Hughes Aircraft Corporation from the top 200 corporations.) The 20 "2-digit" major industry groups are then further broken down into other classifications. Thus, there are 447 "4-digit" *industry* and *product* groups. In Table 11-1, "meat packing" is an *industry* identified by the code number 2011 within the *major industry* group "food and kindred products" already identified by the number 20. When shipments are "aggregated into 4-digit totals without regard to the industry classification of the plants making such shipments, the term used is 'product group.'" There are also about 1,000 "5-digit" *product classes* such as "fresh beef"

---

[2] For a description of some of these, see Fritz Machlup, *The Political Economy of Monopoly* (Balti-

more: The Johns Hopkins Press, 1952), chap. xii. They are largely of academic interest.

Table 11-1

The Standard Industrial Classification (SIC) Illustrated

Name	Designation	SIC Code	Designation in the Vernacular
Food and kindred products	Major industry group	20	"2-digit"
Meat products	Industry group	201	"3-digit"
Meat packing	Industry	2011	"4-digit"
Fresh beef	Product class	20111	"5-digit"
Whole carcass beef	Product	2011112	"7-digit"

Source: Adapted from *Concentration Ratios in Manufacturing Industry, 1958* (Report prepared by the Bureau of the Census for the Senate Subcommittee on Antitrust and Monopoly, 87th Cong., 2d sess.) (Washington, D.C.: U.S. Government Printing Office, 1962), Part 1, p. 2.

which carries the number 20111 in Table 11-1. Further subsidisions are also made, as indicated in Table 11-1.

As has been noted, sales or value of shipments may be an unsatisfactory category for some purposes since there may be duplication as a result of inter-plant shipments. In such cases the Bureau uses the "value added by manufacture" category, thereby isolating the activities of single plants.

The Bureau defines a "company" to include also the affiliates and subsidiaries over which a firm acknowledges control. Since it receives the reports on a plant basis, it then groups the data on a company basis and distributes them according to industries. Thus, the total shipments of a given company are not assigned to just one industry except in the unlikely case usually postulated by contemporary price theory textbooks in which a company produces only a single product. A conglomerate firm, such as Olin-Matheson or Minnesota Mining, is therefore *treated statistically as if it were several firms*, since it is represented in more than one industry classification. That empirical studies of market measures of economic power based on such data must rest on a rather strong and quite unrealistic assumption that the economic power of a given firm in a particular market is independent of the absolute size of the firm or of its power in any other market is clearly apparent from this system of classifications. That is, the system ignores the existence of conglomerate firms. Since the data are classified by the Bureau for numerous uses rather than for purposes of measuring market power exclusively, other limitations upon the use of these data also exist. In the words of the Bureau:

In essence, the system seeks to establish spheres of economic activity which are *unique* and *distinguishable* from other spheres *because of a composite of similar characteristics* which they have in common. These characteristics include similarity of products in terms of their uses and the bringing together of plants which specialize in making these products and account for a significant proportion of their total shipments. They also include similarity of processes, similarity of materials used, and the bringing together of a group of plants which are economically significant in terms of their number, value added by manufacture, value of shipments, and number of employees.[3]

In other words, like the jack of all trades, the classification serves all purposes, generally speaking, but serves no specific purpose.

Moreover, under the law, the Bureau is not permitted to disclose data of the type here under discussion for individual firms; but it may publish aggregate figures for four or more firms. It is this limitation which has given rise to the statistical definition of the economic concept of the "concentration ratio," the most-widely used measure of market control. The economic theory of oligopoly (a few sellers) has thus come to be the "theory of the four firms" in the hands of some of the more empirically-minded.

---

[3] *Concentration Ratios in Manufacturing Industry, 1958* (Report prepared by the Bureau of the Census for the Senate Subcommittee on Antitrust and Monopoly, 87th Cong., 2d sess.) (Washington, D.C.: U.S. Government Printing Office, 1962), p. 3. (Italics mine.)

The Concentration Ratio

The *concentration ratio* is therefore conveniently defined as the percentage of the total shipments (or value added, as the case may be) of the four largest firms of the total shipments (or other relevant magnitude) in the relevant classification. In most cases the "4-digit" industry and product group class is used. This concentration ratio, it should be emphasized, shows the contribution of the four largest firms to the total without identification of individual companies and without reference to the size of any one firm in relation to the sizes of other firms in the economy as a whole. And so, the artificial person has now also become anonymous. Since 1935, numerous comprehensive tabulations of concentration ratios have been published, most of them based on Bureau of the Census data, and many of these have been the work of government agencies.[4] In addition, there have been numerous other studies, not always based on Census data. These are also considered below.

Estimates of Market Control

Up to World War II. Beginning with the *First Report* of the Industrial Commission, various quantitative statements of the qualitative judgments of individuals about the extent of monopoly or of market control have appeared in the literature. For example, testimony developed by the Commission in 1900 put the percentage of output controlled by the Standard Oil Company at between 81.4 and 95 percent, depending on whether it was taken from officials of the company or from its "opponents." The president of the American Sugar Refining Company candidly, or perhaps proudly, put the control over output of his company at about 90 percent.[5] All such statements are clearly quantitative statements of qualitative judgments. But, given the problems of definition and of classification inherent in the Census Bureau data, there is no particular reason to believe that estimates based on its data are any more or less meaningful than the quantitative statements of qualitative judgments made by witnesses before the Industrial Commission. Estimates of the qualitative-quantitative type were also made by John Moody in 1904.[6] In 1912, Charles Van Hise produced estimates based largely on census data;[7] and in 1922, Eliot Jones produced estimates for various industries based on such diverse sources as the reports of the Commissioner of Corporations and on statistical reports of the American Iron and Steel (trade) Association.[8] And there have also been others. In a 1941 study for the TNEC, Clair Wilcox employed various materials (including complaints filed by the Department of Justice and the testimony before the TNEC) in classifying industries as competitive, monopolistic, and so on; and he also provided concentration ratios from another TNEC study.[9]

Near the end of his study, Professor Wilcox cautiously remarked:

No sort of an estimate concerning the comparative extent of competition and monopoly in American markets is justified by the available evidence. Such an estimate must wait upon the articulation of usable definitions, the development of techniques of measurement, and the collection of a body of data much larger than anything that is now at hand. Indeed, it may be doubted if such an estimate can ever be made with any assurance.[10]

Since World War II. Nevertheless, since about 1949, numerous estimates and studies both of the relative roles of competition and monopoly in the United States in particular years and of the trend of concentration have appeared. One by George Stigler was apparently among the first. It consisted largely of a comparison of estimates provided by Moody and other earlier writers with the estimates provided by Clair Wilcox. Stigler used Wilcox's results in a way in

---

[4] Seven of the early studies are identified by Ralph L. Nelson, *Concentration in the Manufacturing Industries of the United States* (New Haven: Yale University Press, 1963), Table 2–1, p. 18.

[5] *Report of the Industrial Commission* (19 vols.; Washington, D.C.: U.S. Government Printing Office, 1900–1902), Vol. 1, pp. 17–18.

[6] John Moody, *The Truth about the Trusts* (New York: Moody Publishing Co., 1904).

[7] Charles Van Hise, *Concentration and Control* (New York: The Macmillan Co., 1914).

[8] Eliot Jones, *The Trust Problem in the United States* (New York: The Macmillan Co., 1922).

[9] Clair Wilcox, *Competition and Monopoly in American Industry* (Temporary National Economic Committee Monograph No. 21) (Washington, D.C.: U.S. Government Printing Office, 1940).

[10] Wilcox, *op. cit.*, p. 308.

which Wilcox himself had refused to use them and concluded that between the "beginning of the twentieth century" and the "nineteen-thirties" there had been substantial decreases in concentration in 14 industries, minor changes in concentration in 4, and substantial increases in concentration in 2 (automobiles and copper manufacturing). With respect to the case of electrical equipment, one of the industries in which he found "minor changes in concentration," Professor Stigler certified his conclusion by writing: "In 1902, General Electric 'Divides easily 90 percent of the field with the Westinghouse concerns, with which it has various working Agreements' (Moody, p. 249n.). They account for a somewhat smaller percentage in the 'thirties (Monograph 21, p. 114)."[11] [Monograph 21 is the TNEC number of the Wilcox study.] Interestingly enough, in 1960, when the Department of Justice brought a price fixing charge against 29 firms in the electrical equipment industry (including General Electric, Westinghouse, Allis Chalmers and others), the defendant companies and individuals who were also charged either pleaded guilty or *nolo contendere*; fines were levied and some individuals were imprisoned. For the years in which the conspiracy was in operation, therefore, one would have to consider that, even if the concentration ratio computed on the basis of individual companies was small, a high degree of control over the market existed. Similarly, in the case of tobacco, Stigler included this industry in his list of those in which concentration had "substantially decreased" between 1900 and the 1930's. Yet, in 1946 the Supreme Court upheld a lower court conviction of the three major tobacco producers after a jury had found that "a combination or conspiracy existed among" them "from 1937 to 1940, with power and intent to exclude competitors."[12] Some qualifications of Stigler's conclusions may therefore be warranted.

Another study which undertook to provide a quantitative estimate of the trend of monopoly from 1899 to 1937–39 was one published by G. Warren Nutter in 1951. Making use of previous estimates published by Moody, Van Hise, the Industrial Commission, the Census of Manufactures of 1899, and others—as well as of Wilcox's study—Nutter concluded that "in 1899, monopolistic [concentration ratio of 50 percent or more] industries accounted for 32.0 per cent of manufacturing income."[13] He also produced for 1937 one indicator of monopoly (based again on a concentration ratio of 50 percent); and a second indicator for 1937 which consisted of all the industries classified as monopolistic in Wilcox's study and all additional manufacturing census industries with concentration ratios of 50 percent or more and of "major" census products (by value) with concentration ratios of 75 percent or more. According to the first measure, monopoly declined from 32 percent to 28 percent between 1899 and 1937. According to the second, it increased from 32 percent to 38.3 percent in the same period.

One critic of Nutter's work called attention to the fact that Nutter had identified transportation [excluding water transport] as "monopolized" in 1899 and as "potentially 'workably competitive,'" in 1937. If, the critic argued, transportation had been classified as either monopolized in both years or as "potentially 'workably competitive'" in both cases, the result would have been "spectacular: Monopoly now increases by four points."[14] As a matter of fact, the critic characterized the phrase "potentially 'workable competitive'" as "Pickwickian." Professor Nutter's reply to this point was that he had classified the railroads differently for the two periods "on the basis of a judgment that, without government supervision, they *would have* behaved competitively in 1937 but not in 1899."[15] He thus rightly pointed out that matters of subjective judgment are involved

---

[11] George J. Stigler, *Five Lectures on Economic Problems* (New York: The Macmillan Co., 1950), p. 64.

[12] *American Tobacco Co.* v. *United States*, 328 U.S. 781 (1946).

[13] G. Warren Nutter, *The Extent of Enterprise Monopoly in the United States, 1899–1939* (Chicago: University of Chicago Press, 1951), p. 45.

[14] Stanley Lebergott, "Has Monopoly Increased?" in *Review of Economics and Statistics*, Vol. XXXV (November 1953), pp. 349–51, at p. 350.

[15] G. Warren Nutter, "Reply to Mr. Lebergott," *Review of Economics and Statistics*, Vol. XXXV (November, 1953), pp. 352–53 at p. 352. (Italics mine.)

in all such studies: they involve "iffy" questions.

Probably the best known of all the studies of this type is one published by M. A. Adelman in 1951. Adelman made use of Nutter's estimates—which had been based on the Census of Manufactures of 1899 and on the quantitative statements of qualitative judgments by Moody, Van Hise, and others, as noted earlier—as well as of concentration ratios published by the Bureau of the Census in 1947. Adelman indicated that he was comparing "major industry groups" in 1899 and 1947 on the basis of the Bureau of Census SIC system.[16] It may be useful to note, in this connection, that the Bureau of the Census has itself called attention to the fact that revisions of the SIC may make the data not comparable for different years. And indeed, Adelman was aware of the limitations of the data he had employed. He said:

... in view of the roughness of the early data and the crudity of some estimates, it seems best to state conclusions as follows: The odds are better than even that there has actually been some decline in concentration. It is a good bet that there has at least been no actual increase; and the odds do seem high against any substantial increase.[17]

Another interesting study of concentration is that published by Ralph Nelson in 1963. Using census data, he concluded that between 1947 and 1954 the average "share of industry sales of the four largest firms, weighted by industry employment, increased from 34.6 percent in 1947 to 35.3 percent in 1954" for 375 manufacturing industries.[18] But "underlying this glacial movement in the average" he found many "relatively large movements in the concentration of individual industries." Nelson also found a considerable turnover in the ranks of the 50 largest companies of 1947; 15 of these were no longer among the top 50 in 1954. However, he added "most of the displacement of companies from the group of the 50 largest is attributable to the famine-to-feast growth of 7 aircraft companies, from the postwar doldrum year of 1947 to the high mobilization year of 1954."[19]

Another valuable study is one published by Professor William G. Shepherd in 1964. He produced a careful survey of recent findings, including new studies of his own. Particularly interesting is his study of "35 oligopolies," based in part upon the list originally produced by Stigler, Shepherd's conclusion in the case of these "oligopolies" was that "on the whole, concentration of these 35 'oligopolies' tended to remain the same or increase, rather than decline appreciably."[20] It is interesting to note that of 14 oligopolies identified by Stigler Shepherd's results indicated that concentration had increased in the case of 10, had not changed in one case, and had decreased in the case of 3. Shepherd also found, as had Nelson, that decreases in concentration were associated with growing industries.[21]

Subsequently, however, in testimony given before the Subcommittee on Antitrust and Monopoly, Professor Shepherd somewhat qualified his earlier conclusion concerning the relationship between decreases in concentration and growth and also pointed to the many problems involved in statistical determination of the causes of concentration by saying:

Ralph Nelson and I have both found a "statistically significant" relation between growth and declining concentration.

This came out last summer at the hearings of the subcommittee. But I would now argue that this is a slender reed on which to place hopes for future decreases in concentration. Neither of us "explained" more than 7 percent of concentration changes; Nelson's "coefficient of determination" (r^2) [which may be briefly defined as the percentage of change explained by the statistical study] was 4 percent, mine was 7 percent. Lesson 1: Growth was, among the many influences on concentration, a relatively minor one.

Nelson's coefficient suggests that a 100-percent growth (in employment) was associated with a 2.1 point decline in concentration over 7 years,

[16] M. A. Adelman, "The Measurement of Industrial Concentration," *Review of Economics and Statistics*, Vol. XXXII (November 1951), pp. 269–96, Table 14.

[17] *Ibid.*, p. 296. (Italics his.)

[18] Ralph L. Nelson, *Concentration in Manufacturing Industries in the United States* (New Haven: Yale University Press, 1963), p. 9.

[19] *Ibid.*, p. 13.

[20] William G. Shepherd, "Trends of Concentration in American Manufacturing Industries, 1947–1958," *Review of Economics and Statistics*, Vol. XLVI (May, 1964), pp. 200–212, at p. 211.

[21] Ralph L. Nelson, *Concentration in the Manufacturing Industries*, p. 10; Shepherd, *op. cit.*, p. 203.

from 1947 to 1954. My coefficient suggested a $3\frac{1}{2}$-percent decline for 100-percent growth. Now, employment grows much less rapidly than output (the usual "growth" variable). Therefore a coefficient relating changed concentration to output growth would be even smaller. That is, output would have to perhaps redouble, go up by 200 percent, in order to achieve concentration decline of 2 points or $3\frac{1}{2}$, whichever the case may have been.

So, lesson 2: It would take a thumping amount of growth to reduce concentration even by a sliver. And, for that matter, the statistical analyses themselves prove nothing about what is causing what. . . .

More recently I have tried a number of other variables which might also have influenced concentration, but employment growth remains so far as the only apparent "influence" toward changing concentration. Though these new results are only preliminary, it may be instructive to list some of the factors which might have been associated with a decrease in concentration but which apparently were not: high profits in the early years of the 1947–58 period, changes in the profit rate, a rise in the number of firms, disparity in the size of firms.

In view of what Professor Kottke said this morning, I should note, in agreeing with him, that the lack of any apparent statistical relation in any test that may be undertaken does not prove that no such association exists. All it proves is that that particular test did not come up with any association. . . .[22]

Prior to Professor Shepherd's appearance, Professor Frank Kottke testified concerning the limitations of statistical studies of concentration. His explanation of the usual procedure and some of its limitations was in layman's language:

Basically, correlation analysis is a two-step procedure. First, a relationship of a specific character is hypothesized. For example, the investigator might propose the existence of a linear relationship between the change in the number of plants in an industry and the change in the proportion of total output supplied by the four leading companies. The second step is a conventional test to determine whether the assumed relationship is compatible with the statistical record: A machine is given two sets of data, and the criteria for comparing them. Obviously a wrong conclusion may emerge when ambiguities in the data are overlooked. But the greater source of difficulty lies elsewhere; unless

meaningful relationships are proposed, the results will be unenlightening. The "answers" obtained through statistical correlation can be no better than the "questions" the researcher has asked.[23]

Among the particular difficulties to which Professor Kottke pointed are: (1) the difficulty of quantifying some relationships (for example, data pertaining to barriers to entry of new firms); (2) the problem of taking account of "random once-in-a-decade events" (which Kottke suggested as a major cause of shifts in the level of industry concentration); and (3) the problem created by the assumption (identified by David Hume a long time ago) underlying most such studies that "whatever relationship exists, holds over the full range of values of the data."

Professor Adelman, it may be remarked, had also appeared before the Subcommittee at an earlier date and presented an up-to-date version of his original thesis that concentration had not increased. It is interesting to note that the way one phrases the conclusion that concentration has remained relatively stable since 1947 may reflect one's attitude toward the nature of the problem. Relative stability of concentration can be treated as a case in which concentration "has not increased" thereby suggesting that the problem is not becoming worse and so no great cause for worry exists; but it can also be treated as a case in which concentration "has not declined," suggesting that the problem is serious and has not yet been solved.

Table 11-2 is a reproduction of one prepared by the Staff of the Subcommittee on Antitrust and Monopoly under the direction of its Chief Economist, Dr. John Blair, probably the leading expert on concentration ratios in the United States. The Minority Economist of the Subcommittee challenged the use (by the Staff of which he is a member) of 1958 as the year for selecting the "largest" corporations in the table and was thereupon invited by the Chairman to submit his own table. He did so, employing 1947 as the base year. His table showed no increases in concentra-

[22] *Economic Concentration* (Hearings before the Senate Subcommittee on Antitrust and Monopoly, 88th Cong., 2d sess., 1964) (Washington, D.C.: U.S. Government Printing Office, 1964), Part 2, p. 639.
[23] *Ibid.*, p. 623.

Table 11-2

Major Industries[a] with the 4 Largest Companies Accounting for More than
50 Percent and the 8 Largest for More than 75 Percent or More of the
Value of Shipments, 1958

Industry code	Industry	Percent of Value of Shipments Accounted for By—		4 Largest Companies change, 1947–58, Percentage Points
		4 Largest Companies	8 Largest Companies	
3723	Aircraft propellers	97	99	−1
3334	Primary aluminum	96[b]	100	−4
3741	Locomotives and parts	95	99	+4
3211	Flat glass	92	99	+2[c]
3651	Electric lamps (bulbs)	92	97	0
3664	Telephone and telegraph equipment	92	97	+2[c]
2841	Soap and glycerin	90	94	+11
2862	Softwood distillation	89	96	+3
2073	Chewing gum	88	95	+18
3272	Gypsum products	88	96	+3
3612	Carbon and graphite products	87	92	0
3511	Steam engines and turbines	87	97	−1
3692	Primary batteries	84	96	+8
2043	Cereal breakfast foods	83	95	+4
2274	Hard-surfaced floor coverings	83	d	+3
3411	Tin cans and other tinware	80	89	+2
2111	Cigarettes	79	99+	−11
2811	Sulfuric acid	79	93	−3[a]
2896	Compressed and liquefied gases	79	88	−4
3572	Typewriters	79	99	0
2825	Synthetic fibers	78	96	0
3352	Aluminum rolling and drawing	78	85	−16
2826	Explosives	77	89	−3
3571	Computing and related machines	77	85	+8
3663	Phonograph records	76	83	−3
2045	Flour mixes	75	86	+34
2216	Finishing wool textiles	75	85	e
3717	Motor vehicles and parts	75	81	+19
3011	Tires and inner tubes	74	88	−3
2094	Corn wet milling	73	92	−4
2141	Tobacco stemming and redrying	73	90	−15
2895	Carbon black	73	98	−5
3313	Electrometallurgical products	73	91	−15
2072	Chocolate and cocoa products	71	84	+3
3581	Domestic laundary equipment	71	90	+31
3615	Transformers	71	84	−2
3584	Vacuum cleaners	70	89	+9
2852	Inorganic color pigments	69	83	+2[a]
3521	Tractors	69	90	+2
2223	Threadmills	68	79	+3
3021	Rubber footwear	65	82	−16
3275	Mineral wool	65	79	+8
2812	Alkalies and chlorine	64	89	−6
2833	Medicinal chemicals, including botanicals	64	77	−8[c]
3229	Pressed and blown glass, not elsewhere classified	64	79	+13
3691	Storage batteries	64	81	+2
3641	Engine electrical equipment	63	79	−4
2093	Margarine	62	86	−2

Table 11-2–continued

3497	Metal foil	62	76	− 12c
2824	Synthetic rubber	60	86	+ 7c
3721	Aircraft	59	83	e
3292	Asbestos products	59	76	− 1c
3221	Glass containers	58	75	− 5
3742	Railroad and street cars	58	81	+ 2
2131	Chewing and smoking tobacco	57	82	− 4
3593	Ball and roller bearings	57	77	− 5
3722	Aircraft engines	56	77	− 16
2121	Cigars	54	75	+ 13
3261	Vitreous plumbing fixtures	54	75	− 4
3586	Measuring and dispensing pumps	52	85	+ 3

a Industries with a value of shipments in 1958 of more than $100,000,000.

b Percentage withheld by Bureau of the Census to avoid disclosing figure for individual companies. This figure was calculated from data in Standard & Poor's "Industry Surveys."

c 1954–58.

d Percentage withheld to avoid disclosing figure for individual companies.

e Not available.

Source: Reproduced from *Economic Concentration* (Hearings before the Senate Subcommittee on Antitrust and Monopoly, 88th Cong., 2d sess.) (Washington, D.C.: U.S. Government Printing Office, 1964), Part 1, p. 89.

tion.[24] Table 11-2 (Dr. Blair's version) shows that, in the case of those corporations having shipments in excess of $100 million in 1958, concentration had increased since 1947. Since 1958 was the most recent year for which data were available at the time the table was drawn up, from the public policy point of view, 1958 would seem to be a more appropriate base year than 1947. But it, too, rests on a belief that the future will be like the past.

Professor Wilcox was probably right when he remarked in his own study in 1941 that estimates of the type here considered must be used with very great care. At best, the concentration ratio provides partial information: a very high ratio may be more significant than a very low one from the public policy point of view, because a low ratio is quite consistent with collusion (which may be established by other evidence) while a high ratio indicates the existence of market power positions even without collusion. Economists working with the census data find themselves playing the role of a detective in attempting to guess at market shares in the production of broad "product classes" of individual firms because working rules concerning disclosure of information as well as basic policies

deriving from the Bill of Rights preclude publication of precisely that information which is essential to the formulation of public policies in this area. A problem of reconciling competing social interests thus exists.

In this regard, in 1965, Professor Joel B. Dirlam argued that the Securities and Exchange Act should be amended to require corporations to "disclose on a fuller basis than they now do their sales and operating income from the different activities in which they are engaged," and that such information should be available to investors and to the antitrust authorities.[25]

At the time, the Securities and Exchange Commission rejected the proposal, but in 1966 during hearings on the subject by the Senate Subcommittee on Antitrust and Monopoly, the Chairman of the Commission indicated that the Commission had changed its position. In doing so, he stated his belief that the Commission already had authority to require fuller disclosure under existing legislation, and that the "growing tendency toward absorption of separate industrial enterprises into large conglomerate enterprises" made such a step desirable. In July 1969, the Commission finally acted to require limited

[24] It can be found in *Economic Concentration, op. cit.,* Part 1, pp. 445 ff.

[25] *Economic Concentration, op. cit.,* Part 2, p. 770.

disclosure in the case of new stock registrations only. Several other witnesses had also pointed to the fact that a requirement that conglomerate firms report separately their profits pertaining to each of their divisions would provide information helpful in the enforcement of the antitrust laws.[26]

But even were there no policy problem concerning the information barrier, it is not likely that the problems posed by use of concentration ratios can be solved. The ratio rests on an assumption that it is possible to define clearly and precisely "the industry" or "the market" or "the product." It does not help much in this context to say that a rough definition of "the industry" as composed of firms producing related products will suffice—for if such a rough definition will suffice, why go to the trouble of computing a precise arithmetical statement such as is embodied in the concentration ratio? Indeed, the very precision with which such measures are presented may be misleading.

The Problem of Conglomerate Firms

With respect to this point, the testimony of Professor Carl Kaysen is interesting. He said, among other things:

Concentration measures for particular markets have more direct bearing on antitrust laws [than do measures of resource control to be considered below]. . . .

. . . market concentration measures can provide a useful guide to the antitrust enforcement agencies in allocating their efforts. Other things being equal, more concentrated markets deserve more attention than less concentrated ones, in terms of initial investigatory effort and enforcement activity where ostensible violations of the law appear. Other things are not equal: markets differ in size and economic importance; enforcement agencies must consider the complaints of businessmen who consider themselves injured by allegedly illegal practices of suppliers, customers, or rivals; some cases and situations are more important from the point of view of legal precedent than others. So market structure is one factor among many, but it remains one worth examining when enforcement agencies form judgments about what to do.

In merger cases, where enforcement activity is essentially preventive, concentration measurements may appropriately play a larger role. The recent Supreme Court decisions in horizontal merger cases, in which acquired and acquiring firms operate in the same market, have moved fairly far toward establishing a presumption of illegality for horizontal mergers involving firms with market shares totalling 20 percent or more. In *properly* defined markets, such a rule appears to me entirely appropriate on economic grounds, if the presumption of illegality is rebuttable by evidence that the merger involves substantial economies of scale not achievable by other means, or that the acquired firm was in a failing condition.

A somewhat similar rule, applying a rebuttable presumption of illegality for vertical mergers in which a firm with a market share of 20 percent or more acquires a substantial customer or supplier could also be justified on economic grounds.

No similarly simple formulation of a rule for conglomerate mergers in terms of concentration levels can be made. Indeed, for truly conglomerate mergers, single market concentration figures have no particular significance. The rationale for decisions in such situations must go beyond concentration figures and include at least such questions as the nature of entry barriers in the various markets involved, and how they would be affected by the merger, and the importance of the acquiring firm as a potential competitor in the markets in which the acquired firm operates.[27]

The problem of how to define a market "properly" as this word is used in the above quotation shows that the use of concentration ratios as a basis for a "rebuttable presumption" nevertheless involves preliminary basic value judgments with respect to the definition of the "appropriate market" before the rebuttable presumption can come into play in the case of horizontal or vertical mergers; and, in the case of conglomerate mergers, the items mentioned by Professor Kaysen are all matters of judgment.

Professor Jules Backman (who has served as a consultant to the National Association of Manufacturers and helped prepare that organization's economic arguments against enactment of the Employment Act of 1946)[28] sharply disagreed with Professor Kaysen. Professor Backman said:

[26] *Economic Concentration, op. cit.*, Part 5, pp. 1981 ff.
[27] *Economic Concentration, op. cit.*, Part 2, pp. 551–552. (Italics mine.)
[28] See Stephen Kemp Bailey, *Congress Makes a Law* (New York: Columbia University Press, 1950), pp. 136–38. Professor Backman's most recent publication is *Foreign Competition in Chemicals and Allied Products* (Washington, D.C.: Manufacturing Chemists' Association, Inc., 1965).

Despite the limitations inherent in concentration ratios, they have been used and misused by the antitrust agencies and the courts, particularly in connection with their evaluation of the competitive effects of mergers. Probably the outstanding illustration of the misuse of concentration ratios was in the *Philadelphia Bank* case. . . .

The Court also suggested that:

. . . A merger which produces a firm controlling an undue percentage share of the relevant market, and results in a significant increase in the concentration of firms in that market (provides a test which is) fully consistent with economic theory. That "competition is likely to be greatest where there are many sellers, none of which has any significant market share" is common ground among most economists . . .

This proposed test utilized is the standard of pure competition as outlined in theory. Such a standard has little or no relationship to competition as it exists in the real world. The number of industries which would meet such a test is extremely small. In terms of this test, almost any merger involving a medium or large-size company would have to be proscribed because of its effect on concentration ratios.[29]

Professor Kaysen's statement that "for truly conglomerate mergers, single market concentration figures have no particular significance" rests on a recognition of the fact that, for statistical purposes, the multiproduct firm is treated in the Census Bureau data as if it were several independent firms. Is it really true that the firm which operates in several different markets will behave in the same way as the firm which operates only in one? There is sharp disagreement on this point. Some economists, like Professor Adelman have asserted:

. . . concentration has nothing to do with the size of firms no matter by what name it is called, big business, colossal corporation, financial giantism, and so forth. . . . I think that most of my fellow economists would agree that absolute size is absolutely irrelevant.[30]

But others, like Professor Corwin Edwards (who was formerly a Chief Economist of the Federal Trade Commission), take a different view:

A big firm has advantages over a smaller rival just because it is big. Money is power. A big firm can outbid, outspend, and outlose a small firm. It can advertise more intensively, do more intensive or extensive research, buy up the inventions of others, demand its legal rights or alleged rights more thoroughly, bid higher for scarce resources, acquire the best locations and the best technicians and executives. If it overdoes the expenditures it can absorb losses that would bankrupt a small rival.[31]

And others are undecided or agnostic. Thus Professor Kaysen said:

I do not think that conglomeration as such, that is operating in a number of different markets, provides competitive advantages by itself that are undesirable. One of the features of competition that makes us value it is that it conduces to efficiency. It is not the only reason to value competition but it is an important reason. If integration over a number of markets, conglomeration, diversification, whatever you call it, makes for efficiency, that may indeed give a competitive advantage to the conglomerate firm. . . .

There may be other situations in which diversification is neutral. It doesn't provide any efficiency. It doesn't entail any extra costs in which you can view the firm in a certain sense as running an investment portfolio in which it puts its assets in different kinds of businesses.

I don't think that diversification as such creates a competitive advantage.

Now, however, there is another element in the question, and this is a more difficult element for me to deal with. I am not very confident about what I am about to say, and I will say it with tentativeness which my lack of knowledge demands. Very large firms, and by very large, I don't mean moderately large, I mean very large, may have competitive advantages which are not social gains. That is, there may be competitive advantages that are not translated into more outputs per unit of input or the same output with fewer inputs. . . .

. . . it has got to do with its size and not with its conglomeration.

. . . some of this gain is, in my judgment, a real economy of scale. Whether all of it or not is a matter in which I find myself undecided. I have thought about this a good bit. I think it is a difficult problem and I don't know the answer to it.[32]

The differences among these three positions can, perhaps, be explained by the extent to which the particular economist is committed to the use of pure economic

[29] *Economic Concentration, op. cit.*, Part 2, pp. 565–66.
[30] *Economic Concentration, op. cit.*, Part 1, p. 228.
[31] *Ibid.*, p. 42.
[32] *Ibid.*, Part 2, pp. 557–58.

theory, or alternatively of how far he is willing to consider the effect of variables other than those which have been traditionally dealt with by economists. The question of what is a "very large firm" has arisen in all of the quotations. Thus, it is the problem of measurement of control over resources that must now be examined.

B. THE MEASUREMENT OF RESOURCE CONTROL

Two ways are currently widely used to measure the control of a firm over resources. One of these undertakes to measure the contribution of the firm in terms of total value added by that firm to the total value added by all firms in the size classification in question. In the case of this measure it is assumed that firms which make significant contributions to total output must necessarily control a large amount of resources in order to produce such large volumes of output. The second measure seeks to measure the size of the firm in terms of total or net assets and to state its position in a

group of the largest 50, or 100, or 200. Both measures will be considered in this section.

The Percentage of Total Value Added Measure

Computation of the percentage of value added measure involves in practice taking the ratio of the sum of the values added by a given number of the largest firms to that of the total value added by manufacture by all manufacturing firms. Thus, this measure is an aggregate measure showing the relative importance of the given number of firms. It is based on the census data. Understatements exist in the census data because the Bureau of the Census treats joint ventures owned by two or more firms as separate, independent companies. The effect of this treatment is to exclude many joint ventures from lists of, say, the 50 or 100 largest manufacturing corporations. Table 11-3 shows the share of value added by manufactures accounted for by different size groups of firms in the indicated years. It is readily apparent that the share of every category, from the largest 50 companies through the largest 200 companies, increased substantially between 1947 and 1963.

Table 11-3

Percentage of Value Added by Manufacture by Selected Size Groups 1947–63

Company Ranking in Respective Years	Percent of Value Added by Manufacture				
	1947	1954	1958	1962	1963
Largest 200 Companies	30	37	38	40	41
Largest 150 Companies	27	34	35	36	37
Largest 100 Companies	23	30	30	32	33
Largest 50 Companies	17	23	23	24	25

Source: Reproduced from *Economic Concentration* (Hearings before the Senate Subcommittee on Antitrust and Monopoly, 88th Cong., 2d sess.) (Washington, D.C.: U.S. Government Printing Office, 1964), Part 1 p. 388. The data were compiled by the Bureau of the Census; a special tabulation was made for 1962 and added to previous data; *Concentration Ratios in Manufacturing Industry 1963* (Report prepared for the Senate Subcommittee on Antitrust and Monopoly 89th Cong., 2d sess.) (Washington, D.C.: U.S. Government Printing Office, 1966), p. 2.

Measurement of Resource Control in Terms of Assets

As has been mentioned, the pioneering work in the measurement of resource control by means of data pertaining to assets was done under the direction of Gardiner Means. In 1964, Dr. Means testified before

the Senate Subcommittee on Antitrust and Monopoly with respect to the first study done under his direction:

The most reliable figures we have on concentration in manufacturing are those reported in the study made by the National Resources Committee for 1929. Among the 200 largest corporations in that year, the Resources Committee report included 82 manufacturing corporations. It included the Western Electric Co., along with its parent, the American Telephone and Telegraph Co., and it presented unconsolidated data for 107 large industrial corporations for 1935. From these data I have derived two concentration estimates for the 100 large companies in 1929. According to these figures, 100 large companies in 1929 had legal control of approximately 40 percent of the total assets of all manufacturing corporations and 44 percent of their net capital assets.[33]

By "legal control" Dr. Means meant that the 100 largest corporations either directly owned or controlled more than 50 percent of the stock of the corporations which owned the assets. He further testified concerning the problems and sources of data used in making, and results obtained from, a similar study he had presented to the subcommittee in 1964:

Today much more information is publicly available than in 1929 but it would still be necessary to go into detailed information in the hands of the Government to make an estimate as reliable as that which we made in 1929. For my present estimates I have done the best I can with the information that has been made public . . . the figures . . . are those filed with the Securities and Exchange Commission and, for total assets, are indentical with those published in the Fortune magazine list of 500 largest American corporations . . . [adjusted] for intercorporate stockholding. . . .

On this basis I estimate that the 100 largest manufacturing corporations in 1962 controlled at least 49 percent of the assets of all manufacturing corporations (excluding stocks in other corporations) and 58 percent of the net capital assets—the net land, buildings, and equipment—of all manufacturing corporations.[34]

Thus, according to Dr. Means, the increase between 1929 and 1962 amounted to from 40 percent to 49 percent of total assets and from 44 to 58 percent of net assets.

Another source of data pertaining to assets is the Bureau of Internal Revenue, which makes public a portion of the corporate income tax returns. On the basis of an estimate based on these data, Dr. Means

said that his results were too crude to be worth publishing but that he believed that a careful study based on Bureau files would show that concentration for the economy as a whole was not less in 1964 than in 1929.[35] He indicated his belief that an official government agency study was needed.

In November 1969, the Federal Trade Commission did publish a study on corporate mergers in which it was noted that "By the end of 1968, the 200 largest industrial corporations controlled over 60 percent of the total assets held by all manufacturing corporations."[36] In fact, according to the study, "the share of manufacturing assets held by the 100 largest corporations in 1968 was greater than the share of manufacturing assets held by the 200 largest corporations in 1950," and "the 200 largest manufacturing corporations in 1968 controlled a share of assets equal to that held by the 1000 largest in 1941." The study attributed a "key role in this process of centralization" to the "current merger movement."

This study was made under the direction of the FTC's Chief Economist, Willard Mueller, who has since become a Professor of Economics and Law at the University of Wisconsin. Professor Mueller is held by many to have been a significant force in the adoption of "Guidelines" adopted for enforcement of antimerger activities by the Commission (discussed in Chapter 17). The report also called attention to the fact that the degree of centralized decision-making resulting from this concentration of economic power "posed a serious threat to America's democratic and social institutions."

Table 11-4 contains information pertaining to companies which had been among the 100 largest in one of the selected years but which were no longer among the 100 largest in 1962. However, several points in explanation of the reasons for the dropouts need to be made. First of all, Dr. John Blair pointed out that most of the dropouts were among the companies ranked at the bottom of the group of the 100:

---

[33] *Ibid.*, Part 1, p. 35.

[34] *Ibid.*, p. 17.

[35] *Ibid.*, p. 11. See R. J. Larner, "The 100 Largest Nonfinancial Corporations," *American Economic Review*, Vol. LVI (Sept. 1966), pp. 776–87.

[36] *Economic Report on Corporate Mergers* (Hearings before the Senate Subcommittee on Antitrust and Monopoly, 91st Cong., 1st sess., 1969), Part 8A of *Economic Concentration*, p. 3.

Table 11-4

Net Capital Assets, 100 Largest Manufacturing Corporations, Selected Years 1947–1962 with Rankings by Total Assets for Each Year
(In Millions of Dollars)

Company	1962	1960	1955	1950	1947
Standard Oil of New Jersey	6,875.1 (1)	6,061.3 (1)	3,873.0 (2)	2,125.4 (2)	1,524.1 (1)
General Motors	2,884.1 (2)	3,010.4 (2)	2,353.0 (1)	802.0 (1)	723.0 (2)
Ford Motor	2,140.2 (3)	1,515.7 (4)	1,192.4 (4)	460.8 (7)	386.2 (9)
United States Steel	2,820.1 (4)	2,787.6 (3)	1,873.6 (3)	1,386.6 (3)	940.5 (3)
Gulf Oil	2,458.7 (5)	2,185.1 (5)	1,144.8 (9)	704.7 (10)	574.1 (11)
Texaco	2,551.7 (6)	2,220.2 (6)	1,216.0 (8)	788.6 (8)	486.6 (7)
Socony Mobil	2,253.1 (7)	1,870.5 (7)	1,212.7 (6)	819.6 (6)	637.7 (5)
Standard Oil of California	2,273.5 (8)	1,864.0 (10)	1,270.3 (11)	852.5 (12)	606.0 (13)
Standard Oil of Indiana	2,172.3 (9)	1,976.1 (9)	1,554.9 (7)	1,049.1 (5)	797.7 (5)
E. I. du Pont	984.7 (10)	883.7 (8)	561.5 (5)	461.6 (4)	316.6 (6)
General Electric	712.9 (11)	693.7 (11)	584.8 (12)	276.5 (9)	206.8 (8)
Bethlehem Steel	978.9 (12)	980.3 (12)	736.8 (10)	572.4 (11)	441.1 (10)
International Business Machine	960.4 (13)	849.7 (17)	409.4 (34)	182.7 (60)	97.9 (73)
Shell Oil	1,281.4 (14)	1,136.9 (13)	728.5 (16)	343.4 (19)	276.7 (22)
Western Electric	888.0 (15)	759.2 (15)	294.8 (21)	186.4 (23)	132.7 (16)
Union Carbide	958.5 (16)	970.8 (14)	670.4 (13)	409.1 (14)	238.1 (14)
Phillips Petroleum	1,084.0 (17)	1,078.8)16)	875.8 (18)	464.4 (21)	290.4 (27)
Getty Oil Companies	1,093.1 (18)	629.1 (21)	597.0 (23)	351.8 (28)	255.9 (26)
Westinghouse Electric	367.8 (19)	355.3 (18)	311.1 (15)	162.3 (16)	132.8 (17)
International Harvester	424.5 (20)	434.6 (20)	323.6 (22)	278.8 (18)	206.2 (19)
Chrysler Corp.	398.9 (21)	510.4 (23)	458.0 (14)	169.9 (15)	103.6 (23)
Sinclair Oil	961.0 (22)	901.9 (19)	811.6 (17)	467.1 (17)	298.4 (20)
Cities Service	882.3 (23)	812.8 (24)	633.6 (19)	590.6 (13)	610.0 (12)
Aluminum Co. of America	821.1 (24)	868.2 (22)	663.4 (20)	324.0 (26)	209.5 (29)
Monsanto Chemical	769.9 (25)	615.7 (26)	327.8 (43)	102.3 (75)	84.0 (84)
Continental Oil	752.2 (26)	389.8 (44)	290.4 (58)	156.5 (64)	119.1 (61)
Goodyear Tire & Rubber	422.8 (27)	342.8 (29)	227.6 (26)	125.4 (29)	111.5 (30)
Anaconda	704.3 (28)	706.6 (27)	602.1 (24)	402.1 (20)	353.7 (18)
Republic Steel	644.7 (29)	610.7 (25)	334.7 (25)	260.3 (25)	237.3 (24)
Eastman Kodak	367.8 (30)	330.1 (33)	249.1 (31)	190.3 (38)	144.4 (33)
Radio Corp. of America	264.4 (31)	239.5 (45)	158.0 (29)	87.4 (48)	59.1 (59)
Procter & Gamble	414.4 (32)	389.5 (30)	280.8 (42)	156.8 (35)	101.2 (34)
Reynolds Tobacco	145.6 (33)	110.7 (35)	41.5 (39)	31.6 (27)	25.0 (25)
International Paper	583.9 (34)	573.5 (32)	331.3 (33)	204.2 (33)	147.7 (42)
Allied Chemical & Dye	678.0 (35)	474.8 (49)	446.0 (30)	159.1 (42)	100.4 (37)
Dow Chemical	577.9 (36)	619.7 (28)	376.4 (38)	280.3 (39)	178.2 (46)
Reynolds Metals	565.5 (37)	555.2 (36)	264.6 (60)	104.0 (86)	
Armco Steel	464.4 (38)	398.4 (31)	231.7 (47)	164.0 (43)	119.7 (52)
Boeing	114.9 (39)	88.8 (38)	24.7 (35)		
American Can	524.8 (40)	528.2 (39)	254.0 (62)	197.5 (53)	141.2 (51)
International Telephone & Telegraph	206.2 (41)	288.5 (55)	208.0 (55)	50.2 (83)	43.6 (74)
Firestone Tire & Rubber	302.9 (42)	273.7 (43)	194.1 (32)	104.3 (41)	88.9 (39)
Sperry Rand	251.2 (43)	288.9 (37)	138.8 (45)	47.0 (100)	33.2 (100)
Atlantic Refining	664.9 (44)	617.7 (46)	413.2 (40)	278.4 (37)	224.1 (38)
National Steel	564.4 (45)	531.8 (40)	320.6 (41)	183.6 (31)	173.5 (41)
Olin Mathieson	398.2 (46)	396.1 (41)	311.1 (37)		
Lockheed Aircraft	94.3 (47)	73.9 (68)	40.2 (78)		
Inland Steel	490.9 (48)	534.0 (48)	233.2 (52)	146.4 (47)	98.7 (48)
Sun Oil	549.2 (49)	493.1 (52)	370.7 (48)	197.3 (51)	136.3 (54)
American Tobacco	65.2 (50)	68.7 (42)	49.1 (27)	43.8 (22)	32.8 (15)
Kennecott Copper	434.1 (51)	404.8 (47)	251.0 (28)	225.7 (24)	201.4 (21)

Table 11-4 (Continued)

Company	1962	1960	1955	1950	1947
Jones & Laughlin	540.6 (52)	547.7 (50)	374.9 (36)	251.5 (32)	175.5 (36)
Continental Can	486.4 (53)	477.4 (51)	189.0 (80)	129.3 (73)	94.2 (64)
Union Oil of California	502.1 (54)	482.8 (56)	379.7 (49)	254.5 (49)	178.4 (45)
National Dairy Products	326.6 (55)	298.1 (57)	205.5 (59)	160.0 (46)	115.1 (44)
Youngstown Sheet & Tube	376.0 (56)	405.0 (54)	208.5 (46)	110.8 (44)	96.1 (43)
Brunswick	59.0 (57)	27.5 (77)			
North American Aviation	106.7 (58)	82.3 (81)	23.8 (68)		
Kaiser Industries	355.1 (59)	387.9 (53)	220.9 (85)	168.0 (71)	
W. R. Grace	326.7 (60)	275.3 (65)	138.6 (74)		
General Dynamics	170.8 (61)	191.5 (34)	39.0 (82)		
American Cynamid	311.6 (62)	321.8 (60)	203.8 (54)	102.6 (55)	84.5 (66)
United States Rubber	202.9 (63)	181.1 (59)	149.4 (44)	93.7 (45)	89.4 (35)
United Aircraft	134.9 (64)	124.3 (58)	75.1 (75)	35.2 (88)	29.1 (82)
Burlington Industries	252.7 (65)	243.8 (64)	187.7 (56)	77.6 (77)	38.3 (94)
Singer Manufacturing	88.4 (66)	89.4 (72)	53.5 (70)	33.1 (68)	18.9 (67)
B. F. Goodrich	218.4 (67)	175.5 (62)	138.2 (57)	81.7 (50)	72.4 (47)
John Deere	119.7 (68)	119.8 (67)	89.1 (67)	62.6 (56)	52.1 (57)
Pure Oil	432.7 (69)	380.1 (70)	298.7 (63)	207.2 (57)	157.0 (53)
National Distillers & Chemical	216.2 (70)	229.5 (76)	126.0 (76)	44.8 (65)	25.4 (60)
Weyerhaeuser	409.0 (71)	377.0 (63)	241.9 (73)	185.3 (62)	113.1 (71)
Caterpillar Tractor	260.0 (72)	274.1 (66)	130.7 (89)	69.2 (90)	
Pittsburgh Plate Glass	308.7 (73)	321.3 (61)	223.0 (53)	110.4 (61)	80.4 (65)
Crown Zellerbach	368.3 (74)	345.3 (69)	233.8 (69)	99.7 (79)	84.7 (78)
Marathon Oil (Ohio)	422.2 (75)	326.9 (82)	219.7 (83)	134.3 (76)	95.1 (79)
General Foods	193.2 (76)	147.9 (79)	95.5 (79)	73.0 (63)	54.5 (62)
Swift & Co.	242.7 (77)	241.5 (73)	225.0 (50)	63.0 (30)	120.9 (28)
Sunray DX Oil	408.5 (78)	428.8 (71)	337.5 (61)	212.1 (66)	
St. Regis Paper	284.6 (79)	290.8 (74)	134.4 (96)	91.6 (93)	72.9 (91)
Minnesota Mining & Manufacturing	217.3 (80)	186.2 (86)			
Martin-Marietta	241.4 (81)				
General Telephone & Electronic	157.4 (82)	142.8 (88)			
Ownes Illinois	255.6 (83)	211.2 (80)	111.2 (93)	93.2 (89)	82.6 (81)
Allis-Chalmers	129.1 (84)	121.8 (78)	94.5 (64)	53.4 (70)	44.7 (68)
Corn Products	204.1 (85)	201.9 (87)		78.6 (96)	42.5 (88)
Borden	208.7 (86)	173.3 (97)	128.1 (90)	109.6 (67)	89.3 (65)
General Tire & Rubber	137.0 (87)	99.7 (100)			
Seagrams (United States)	81.2 (88)	77.3 (85)	35.6 (77)	25.6 (52)	25.0 (55)
American Smelting & Refining	148.5 (89)	153.5 (84)	115.6 (72)	74.8 (54)	46.5 (49)
Georgia Pacific	167.3 (90)				
Borg-Warner	131.9 (91)	116.0 (89)	81.4 (84)	47.2 (80)	30.6 (87)
Schenley Industries	39.4 (92)	40.7 (83)	51.2 (81)	56.7 (40)	50.0 (40)
Celanese	182.8 (93)	170.3 (94)	166.7 (86)	149.4 (58)	118.0 (58)
National Cash Register	123.4 (94)				
Coca-Cola	145.1 (95)	129.4 (91)	65.0 (99)	58.0 (78)	44.4 (63)
General American Transportation	341.0 (96)	286.4 (93)		112.3 (98)	67.9 (98)
Phelps-Dodge	143.1 (97)	144.8 (90)	137.0 (71)	130.5 (59)	113.7 (50)
Kimberly-Clark	237.7 (98)				
National Lead	145.2 (99)	128.4 (99)	102.1 (87)	47.5 (81)	44.6 (80)
Armour	145.4 (100)	119.9 (96)	183.4 (65)	154.9 (34)	134.4 (31)
Plus jointly controlled large corporations:					
Richfield Oil	294.9	257.6	192.3	108.4	
Kaiser Aluminium & Chemical	491.0	534.4	237.1		

Table 11-4 (Continued)

Company	1962	1960	1955	1950	1947
Companies among 100 largest in previous years but not in 1962:					
Douglas Aircraft		57.4 (75)	39.3 (51)		
Standard Oil of Ohio		250.9 (92)	194.2 (88)	136.0 (72)	101.4 (72)
Bendix		85.8 (95)	49.5 (95)		
Liggett & Myers		35.1 (98)	30.6 (66)	25.3 (06)	11.9 (02)
J. P. Stevens			97.0 (91)	70.4 (87)	38.6 (83)
Curtiss Wright			31.4 (92)		25.6 (77)
Wheeling Steel			131.8 (94)	102.3 (82)	68.3 (76)
American Viscose			122.0 (97)	102.0 (69)	88.2 (69)
Campbell Soup			61.9 (98)	33.5 (95)	
Philip Morris			25.8 (100)	10.4 (74)	
Nash Kelvinator				44.6 (84)	29.7 (92)
American Radiator & Standard Sanitary				56.2 (85)	41.2 (86)
National Biscuit				86.4 (91)	54.9 (95)
United States Gypsum				79.3 (92)	63.6 (97)
Pullman				29.7 (94)	33.5 (70)
Crane				40.3 (97)	39.4 (90)
United Merchants & Manufacturers				39.4 (99)	30.4 (99)
American Car & Foundry					59.2 (75)
Wilson & Co.					43.5 (89)
Publicker Industries					24.1 (93)
Standard Brands					25.5 (95)
American Sugar Refining					50.6 (96)

Source: Economic Concentration (Hearings before the Subcommittee on Antitrust and Monopoly, 88th Cong., 2d sess.) (Washington, D.C.: U.S. Government Printing Office, 1964), Part 1, pp. 392–395.

"13 of the 18 disappearances between 1947 and 1962 ranked among the last 25 companies on the list." Note the class standings of the dropouts in Table 11-4. Moreover, "a third of the newcomers reached the top 100 directly as a result of defense contracts." Indeed, according to Dr. Blair, between 1947 and 1962 only two real "breakthroughs" into the ranks of the 100 largest occurred: Georgia Pacific, which had grown largely as a result of mergers; and Brunswick, which had acquired various unrelated activities ranging from roller skate and yacht production to school equipment. However, in the case of Brunswick, since nearly 75 percent of its assets were in the form of accounts and notes receivable in 1962, Dr. Blair raised the question as to whether this company might not be more properly classified as a finance company rather than as a manufacturing company.[37]

Thus far we have been concerned with measurements of market shares and of control over resources *by* large corporations. The question now arises: who controls the large corporations? It is to this question that attention must next be given.

C. SEPARATION OF OWNERSHIP AND CONTROL, AND CONCENTRATION OF CONTROL WITHIN THE LARGE CORPORATION

The Berle and Means Study of 1932

In addition to his pioneering work in the measurement of control over resources and (with James C. Bonbright) in the study of the holding company as a device for con-

[37] *Economic Concentration*, Part I, pp. 209–210.

centrating control over corporate activities, Gardiner Means has worked with A. A. Berle in calling attention to the problem of separation of ownership and control in large corporations. In 1932 Berle and Means published what has by now become a classic work: *The Modern Corporation and Private Property*.[38] It was in this work that Means first published in book form the results of his early statistical investigations into the concentration of control over resources. Professor Berle, a teacher of corporation law at Columbia University, contributed the legal analysis contained in this book.

Berle and Means distinguished five major types of control over corporate activity: (1) control through complete ownership; (2) majority control; (3) control through a legal device without majority ownership; (4) minority control; and (5) management control. Of these devices, the first two are relatively straightforward and require no explanation, while the third has already been partially explained in the discussion of the holding company earlier. The use of non-voting securities in a holding company arrangement, of course, increases the amount of capital which can be controlled by those who hold a decisive interest in the voting securities. In the case of the situation depicted in Chart 9-2, for example, if it is assumed that there is just as much non-voting preferred stock outstanding as there is common stock in the case of the operating companies and of each of the holding companies, A and B would be able to control exactly twice as much capital, or $64 million worth of operating properties by means of their initial $1 million bank loan.

Berle and Means defined *minority control* as a case in which "an individual or small group" held a "sufficient stock interest to be in a position to dominate a corporation by means of that stock interest." They further pointed out that such a minority control rested upon the ability of the minority group "to attract from scattered owners proxies [authorizations to represent and act for such owners] sufficient when combined with their substantial minority interest to control a majority of the votes

at the annual meetings."[39] Moreover, they noted: "the larger the company and the wider the distribution of its stock, the more difficult it appears to be to dislodge a controlling minority."

The case of *management control* was defined by Berle and Means as a situation in which ownership was "so widely distributed that no individual or small group" possesses even "a minority interest large enough to dominate the affairs of the company."[40] In such a case no stockholder would be in a position "through his holdings alone to place important pressure upon the management." In the case of such corporations they added:

... control will tend to be in the hands of those who select the proxy committee by whom, in turn, the election of directors for the ensuing period may be made. Since the proxy committee is appointed by the existing management, the latter can virtually dictate their own successors. Where ownership is sufficiently sub-divided, the management can thus become a self-perpetuating body even though its share in the ownership is negligible.[41]

According to the statistical investigations made by Berle and Means, in 1932, 44 percent of the 200 largest corporations were in the category of "management control"; 21 percent fell within the category of control by some "legal device"; 23 percent were controlled by minority interests, 5 percent were controlled by majority stockholders, and 6 percent were privately owned. Thus, 65 percent of the 200 largest non-financial corporations (130 in number) were controlled either by management or by a legal device. The significance of this point, according to Berle and Means in 1932, lay in the fact that the interests of ownership and control might not be the same: the traditional economic theory of the firm involves an assumption that ownership and control are unified functions.

The TNEC Study

In 1940 a study of control over the 200 largest non-financial corporations was published by the Temporary National Economic Committee. Of particular interest in this study is its conclusion that in 61

[38] See footnote 1.
[39] Berle and Means, *op. cit.*, p. 80.

[40] *Ibid.*, p. 84.
[41] *Ibid.*, pp. 87–88.

of the 200 largest non-financial corporations, no dominant controlling interest was located. In *this* group of the 200 there was "no visible center of ownership control." The study also noted that "in many of these corporations the chief officers, though owning but little stock, may well have been in a position of control, relying largely on the power of the proxy machinery."[42] The authors of the study also reported:

. . . The group of corporations without visible centers of ownership control included some of the largest and most widely held of the 200 corporations, e.g. American Telephone and Telegraph Co., Anaconda Cooper Mining Corporation, Bethlehem Steel Corporation, Eastman Kodak Co., General Electric Co., The B.F. Goodrich Co., The Goodyear Tire and Rubber Co., Montgomery Ward and Co., Inc., Paramount Pictures Inc., Radio Corporation of America, United States Steel Corporation, Union Carbide and Carbon Corporation, Westinghouse Electric and Manufacturing Co., the Atchison, Topeka and Sante Fe Railway Co., Pennsylvania Railroad Co., Southern Pacific Co., Union Pacific Railroad Co., and Consolidated Edison Co. of New York, Inc.[43]

The group thus included many of the firms which had first been organized as trusts at the turn of the century. Some writers have taken the position that "to the extent that corporate managerial capitalism has replaced management by capitalists *per se*, the system is fundamentally altered,"[44] while others have asserted to the contrary that "the compelling constraint—obvious, but often forgotten" is still the fact "that the firm's health, indeed its survival, depends on the relation within it of revenues and costs."[45] Our consideration of concentration of economic power in the hands of business firms has now been completed. It is useful now also to examine very briefly the extent to which the power of organized labor has increased along with the increase in the power of private business organizations.

D. GROWTH OF THE POWER OF ORGANIZED LABOR

As has been noted in the introduction to this chapter, this subdivision undertakes to provide a brief historical survey of the nature of the growth of the power of organized labor which has accompanied the growth of the power of private business organizations in the United States. An examination of contemporary labor legislation and its historical antecedents will be made later in Part III. Some background information pertaining to the present strength of organized labor is necessary at this point, however, since the discussions of some of the concepts of the "workable economy" considered in Chapter 13 (for example, the doctrine of "countervailing power" held by J. K. Galbraith) assume that the reader has already acquired some background information of this type.

From the Colonial Period through the Civil War

Guilds and Local Craft Unions to about 1837. The predecessors of labor unions in the United States were organizations comparable to the early English guilds. Organized along craft lines, these associations included masters, journeymen, and apprentices and attempted to regulate both prices and the quality of their output.[46] Selig Perlman dated the beginning of the labor movement in the United States from the year 1792, when the Philadelphia shoemakers organized. Subsequently other local craft unions organized in Philadelphia, New York, and elsewhere.[47] Even earlier, in 1786, the Philadelphia printers had engaged in a strike, and other strikes had also occurred. In 1827, the first "city central" association, composed of associations of craft unions in the building trades within Philadelphia, was organized as the "Mechanics Union of Trade Unions."[48] By 1836,

[42] Raymond W. Goldsmith, *The Distribution of Ownership in the 200 Largest Nonfinancial Corporations* (Temporary National Economic Committee Monograph No. 29) (Washington, D.C.: U.S. Government Printing Office, 1940), p. 103.

[43] *Ibid.*, pp. 103–104.

[44] Calvin B. Hoover, *The Economy, Liberty and the State* (New York: Twentieth Century Fund, 1959), p. 268.

[45] Shorey Peterson, "Corporate Control and Capitalism," *Quarterly Journal of Economics*, Vol. LXXIX (February, 1965), pp. 1–24, at p. 9.

[46] R. F. Hoxie, *Trade Unionism in the United States* (2d. ed.; New York: D. Appleton-Century Co., 1936), p. 78.

[47] Selig Perlman, *A History of Trade Unionism in the United States* (New York: The Macmillan Co., 1937), p. 4.

[48] Hoxie, *op. cit.*, p. 83.

more than 50 local unions were active in Philadelphia and New York City. Organization of union groups from seven cities was undertaken in 1834, when the National Trade's Union was formed. This and other attempts at national organization failed in 1837 during the panic of that year.[49]

Utopianism of the 1840's and Origin of National Unions. The period of the 1840's was marked by the "organization of producers' and consumers' cooperatives." Idealistic schemes for cooperative communities were also put into operation but failed. During the 1850's several national unions (printers, stonecutters, hat finishers, iron moulders, machinists, and locomotive engineers) were organized. "Collective bargaining between unions and management was . . . slowly becoming prevalent in several leading trades."[50] The English common law doctrine that labor unions constituted conspiracies was also imported into the United States at an early date, although by 1842 a few American courts were beginning to question its use in such cases.[51]

From the Civil War to the Great Depression

National Unions and the National Labor Union (NLU). The Civil War produced conditions favorable to the organization of craft unions in the Northern states: "In 1863 there were approximately 80 local unions in 20 Northern states; by 1864 there were almost 300 in the same area."[52] Thirteen national unions appeared between 1861 and 1865. In 1866, John Silvis, one of the leaders of the iron moulder's union, and others organized the National Labor Union—a federation of national, city, and local trade unions and of reform groups. The organization became involved in politics, internal dissension arose, and by 1872 it had virtually disappeared.[53] A federal "Bureau of Labor," which the

NLU had advocated, was established in 1884. It was the predecessor of the present Bureau of Labor Statistics.[54]

Knights of Labor (1869–1890). In 1869, Uriah S. Stevens organized a small local union of Philadelphia garment workers, which called itself the "Noble Order of the Knights of Labor." At first it operated as a secret society, but by 1881 it had abandoned its secret practices. Its membership grew from about 10,000 persons in 1879 to more than 700,000 by 1886. The Knights eventually were organized as a national body, which exercised control over district assemblies, composed in turn of local assemblies. It encompassed both local assemblies, consisting of workers of single crafts, and local assemblies containing members from various professions and occupations. The avowed aim of the Knights was establishment of a cooperative society to replace the existing one. In the 1880's the organization experienced considerable success in various strike activities, the most notable being a victory over the Gould railway system in 1885.[55] But eventually those members who believed in "practical unionism", or in the attainment of shorter hours and higher wages by means of the process of collective bargaining, rather than in establishment of a collective society, collided with those who believed in the latter objective; and so, in time, the organization fell apart. Its demise was, in part, a reflection of the rise of the philosophy of business unionism (unions should work for higher wages and improved working conditions within the existing economic system) held by the leaders of the newly-formed American Federation of Labor.

The American Federation of Labor (Period of Dominance: 1886 to 1935)

The American Federation of Labor (AFL) was organized in 1886 as a result of the efforts of six craft unions, which had

[49] U.S. Department of Labor, *A Brief History of the American Labor Movement* (Washington, D.C.: U.S. Government Printing Office, 1964), p. 5.

[50] *Ibid.*, pp. 6–7.

[51] See *Rex* v. *Journeymen-Taylors of Cambridge*, 8 Eng. Reprint 9 (1721); *Commonwealth* v. *Pullis* (1806) in John R. Commons and Associates, *A Documentary History of American Industrial Society* (11 volumes; Cleveland: The Arthur Clark Co., 1910), Vol. 3, pp. 234–35; and see also *Commonwealth* v. *Hunt*, 45 Mass. 111 (1842).

[52] U.S. Department of Labor, *Brief History of the American Labor Movement, op. cit.*, p. 7.

[53] Carroll R. Daughtery, *Labor Problems in American Industry* (Boston: Houghton-Mifflin Co., 1938), pp. 327 ff.

[54] U.S. Department of Labor, *Brief History of the American Labor Movement, op. cit.*, p. 9.

[55] See *Ibid.*, p. 11 ff.; and Perlman, *op. cit.*, p. 70.

first organized the Federation of Organized Trades and Labor Unions (FOTLU) in 1881. Because the Knights of Labor at its 1886 convention refused to respect the jurisdiction of these six craft unions, they formed their rival national federation, the AFL. Samuel Gompers was elected President of the new organization, which began with a membership of 138,000 in 1886. The philosophy of the AFL was business unionism: the attainment of limited objectives within the framework of the existing economic system.[56] Thus Gompers spoke to the Boston Convention of the AFL, after numerous attempts since 1890 by socialists to win control of the organization:

I want to tell you, Socialists, that I have studied your philosophy; read your works on economics, and not the meanest of them; studied your standard works, both in English and in German—have not only read but studied them. I have heard your orators and watched the work of your movement the world over. I have kept close watch upon your doctrines for thirty years; have been closely associated with many of you and know how you think and what you propose. And I want to say that I am entirely at variance with your philosophy. I declare it to you, I am not only at variance with your doctrines, but with your philosophy. Economically, you are unsound; socially you are wrong; industrially you are an impossibility.[57]

The rejection of socialist doctrines by Gompers and the commitment to the philosophy of business unionism have remained characteristics of the dominant segment of the American labor movement to the present time. But this is not to say that periods of labor strife and unrest have not existed. Indeed, in the 1890's and again in the 1930's, bitter and violent struggles occurred. Although injunctions prohibiting strikes were issued as early as the 1870's, one of the first instances of issuance of an injunction under the Sherman Act oc-

curred in 1893 in a case in which a union sought to compel the adoption of a closed shop in New Orleans.[58] Thereafter injunctions were issued against Eugene V. Debs and the American Railway Union in 1894 and in other cases. Although attempts were made to limit the use of such injunctions by Section 6 of the Clayton Act in 1914, it was not until the enactment of the Norris-La Guardia Act in 1932 that the use of the injunction by employers was successfully limited. Antitrust actions involving the assessment of treble damages against labor unions were also successfully brought, beginning with *Lawlor* v. *Loewe* in 1915;[59] but beginning in 1940, the Supreme Court limited the application of the Sherman Act to labor unions to cases in which the union conspires *with* an employer or a group of employers in restraint of trade. Thus in 1965 the Court said:

. . . a union may make agreements with a multi-employer bargaining unit and may in pursuance of its own union interests seek to obtain the same terms from other employers. No case under the antitrust laws could be made out on evidence limited to such union behavior.

But *we think a union forfeits its exemption from the antitrust laws when it is clearly shown that it has agreed with one set of employers to impose a certain wage scale on other bargaining units.*[60]

This question, too, will be discussed more fully later (in Chapter 14). Between 1890 and 1940, of 24 criminal cases involving penal sentences imposed by trial courts under the Sherman Act, eleven pertained to labor unions.[61] In addition, the use of strikebreakers, private detective agencies, and propaganda devices by employers was widespread in different industries at various times.[62]

Nevertheless, despite a decline between 1920 and 1933—when the twentieth century low point was reached—membership of

---

[56] See, for example, Samuel Gompers, *Seventy Years of Life and Labor* (2 vols.; New York: E. P. Dutton and Co., 1925); and John Mitchell, *Organized Labor* (Philadelphia: American Book and Bible House, 1903).

[57] Gompers, *op. cit.*, Vol. 1, p. 397.

[58] *United States* v. *Workingmen's Amalgamated Council of New Orleans*, 54 F. 994 (1893).

[59] *Lawlor* v. *Loewe*, 235 U.S. 522 (1915).

[60] *United Mine Workers* v. *Pennington*, 381 U.S. 657 (1965), at p. 665. (Italics mine.)

[61] Walton Hamilton and Irene Till, *Antitrust in Action* (Temporary National Economic Committee

Monograph No. 16 (Washington, D.C.: U.S. Government Printing Office, 1941), p. 78.

[62] See, for example, *Violations of Free Speech and Rights of Labor* (Hearings and Reports of the Committee on Education and Labor pursuant to S. Res. 266, 74th Cong., 2d sess.); *Strikebreaking Services* (Report No. 6, 76th Cong., 1st sess., 1939); *The Chicago Memorial Day Incident* (Report No. 46, Part 2, 75th Cong., 1st sess., 1937); *Industrial Espionage* (Report No. 46, Part 3, 75th Cong., 2d sess., 1938); *Labor Policies of Employers' Associations* (Report No. 6, Part 6, 76th Cong., 1st sess., 1939).

Table 11-5

Labor Union Membership, Selected Years, 1897–1962 (In thousands)

Year	Total, All Unions	American Federation of Labor		Congress of Industrial Organizations	Unaffiliated
1897	440	265			175
1900	791	548			243
1905	1,918	1,494			424
1910	2,116	1,562			554
1915	2,560	1,946			614
1920	5,034	4,079			955
1925	3,566	2,877			689
1930	3,632	2,961			671
1933	2,857	2,127			730
1935	3,728	3,045			683
1940	8,944	4,247		3,625	1,072
1945	14,796	6,931		6,000	1,865
1947	15,414	7,578		6,000	1,836
1953	17,860	10,778		5,252	1,830
1954	17,955	10,929		5,200	1,826
1955	17,749		16,062		1,688
1956	18,477		16,904		1,573
1957	18,431		16,954		1,476
1958	18,081		14,993		3,088
1959	18,169		15,124		3,044
1960	18,117		15,072		3,045
1961	17,328		14,572		2,756
1962	17,630		14,835		2,794

Source: Reproduced from United States Department of Labor, *Brief History of the American Labor Movement* (Bulletin 1000, 1964 ed.; Washington, D.C.: U.S. Government Printing Office, 1964).

the AFL continued to show an upward trend until 1955, when the AFL and the CIO merged. Table 11-5 shows labor union membership for selected years, 1897–1962.

From the Depression to the Present

Favourable Federal Legislation. The National Labor Relations Act of 1935 (Wagner Act) was the most significant piece of labor legislation enacted up to that time. It provided for free collective bargaining and for the right of labor unions to organize free from employer pressures, as well as for an enforcement board (NLRB). The impact of this legislation on union memberships is clearly evident in Table 11-5. Further discussion of this legislation as well as of minimum wage legislation, of amendments to the National Labor Relations Act (the Taft-Hartley Act of 1947), and of the Social Security Act will be undertaken in a later chapter.

Establishment of the Congress for Industrial

Organization (CIO). Beginning in 1934, a dispute arose within the AFL respecting future organizational policies. In 1935 matters came to a head when six AFL unions and the officers of two others created a "Committee for Industrial Organization (CIO)" whose object was to promote organization of workers in unorganized industries into unions without regard to classifications into crafts (skills). The AFL, it will be recalled, traditionally consisted of unions organized along craft lines. Eventually the CIO became a rival national labor federation, a competitor of the AFL. The two rivals both engaged extensively in a drive for increased union memberships; their success is documented in Table 11-5.

Merger of AFL-CIO. The election of new presidents of both the AFL and the CIO in 1952 created a condition under which earlier animosities and belligerent attitudes standing in the way of an amalgamation of the two national federations began to give way. After much negotiation and bargaining, in 1955 the two federations merged into the AFL-CIO, a single organization containing about 16 million workers. But it would be a mistake to consider the merger as an event ending all the problems which had previously existed. As Table 11-5 indicates, since 1957, membership in the federation has declined.

The employer counterpart of the AFL-CIO is not a particular industry like the automobile industry, or the steel industry, or the communications industry. Instead the employer counterparts are the National Association of Manufacturers, the Chamber of Commerce of the United States, and the Committee for Economic Development. This point has, of course, been noted in Chapter 5 earlier and elsewhere.

In 1957, the large and powerful Teamster's Union was expelled from the AFL-CIO on charges of corruption and the United Automobile Workers' Union withdrew from the Federation in July 1967. By 1968 these two unions had organized a rival federation called the Alliance for Labor Action (ALA) and a number of other industrial unions in the AFL-CIO were considering joining the new federation. The harmony which resulted from the combination of the AFL and the CIO was thus apparently a short-lived matter.

A Concluding Remark

Our presentation of basic background materials has now been completed. Chapter 12, which follows, contains an explanation of the scope and the organization of Part II which deals with the basic working rules to enforce competition, known as the "antitrust laws." Chapter 23 is the first chapter in Part III and similarly contains an explanation of the scope and organization of Part III which deals with working rules which replace or modify the operation of market forces in cases of particular industries, activities, and economic aggregates.

WORKING RULES THAT ENFORCE AND SUPPLEMENT COMPETITION: THE ANTITRUST AND CONSUMER PROTECTION LAWS

The Basic Antitrust Statutes and Their Administration; Legislation to Protect Consumers

The next several chapters are principally concerned with an examination of the specific working rules that enforce competition, known as the "antitrust laws," and with supplementary laws to protect consumers. The purpose of the present chapter is to provide a brief survey of the principal federal antitrust statutes and of recent legislation to protect consumers, as well as a brief description of the agencies charged with the administration of these laws. The following chapter (13) undertakes to explain various meanings of the concept of "workable competition" which are often employed by economists in their discussions of the operations of these laws. The remaining chapters in this Part II are concerned with an examination of particular problems under specific antitrust laws and of the permissibility of particular business practices under these laws.

There are four major subdivisions in the present chapter: (1) the first contains a survey of the basic legislation embodying

the specific working rules of antitrust and some special exemptions from them; (2) the second discusses legislation to protect consumers, and concludes with a summary outline of both types of laws and the relationships existing among them; (3) the third describes two federal government agencies primarily charged with enforcement and administration of this legislation; and (4) the fourth contains a short description of the scope of existing state antitrust laws.

A. THE BASIC FEDERAL ANTITRUST STATUTES AND RELATED LAWS

One of the most readily available and comprehensive compilations of the basic federal antitrust laws is a document published originally in 1950 and revised sporadically thereafter by the staff of the Subcommittee on Antitrust of the House Committee on the Judiciary.[1] This compilation not only contains the texts of the basic laws, such as

[1] *The Antitrust Laws* (A Staff Report to the Antitrust Subcommittee of the House Judiciary Committee, 88th Cong., 2d sess.) (Washington, D.C.: U.S. Government Printing Office, 1965).

the Sherman, Clayton, and Federal Trade Commission Acts and their principal amendments (discussed further below), but also itemizes relevant and related provisions of many other pieces of legislation, such as the Communications Satellite Act of 1962, the Flammable Fabrics Act, and the Interstate Oil and Gas Compact, many of which contain exemptions from the antitrust laws for particular activities or industries. More than 100 pieces of legislation fall in this category. Such a detailed survey of the legislation falls beyond the scope of this book for obvious reasons and is unnecessary. In what follows, four major pieces of legislation—the Sherman Act of 1890, the Clayton and Federal Trade Commission Acts of 1914, and the Fair Packaging and Labeling Act of 1966—together with such of their major amendments as may be necessary to an understanding of the overall legislative pattern, are discussed. Several of these major amendments are discussed separately below, partly because they are complicated and partly because some of them represent substantial additions to or changes in the original legislation. (Such, for example, is the case of the Robinson-Patman Act amending Section 2 of the Clayton Act.) In addition, brief attention will also be given to legislation enacted since 1966 to protect consumers. It is to the Sherman Act that attention will now be given.

The Sherman Act of 1890 (15 U.S.C. 1–7)

The Sherman Act contains two fundamental substantive provisions. Section 1 prohibits contracts, combinations, and conspiracies "in restraint of trade" and reads:

Section 1: Every contract, combination in form of trust or otherwise, or conspiracy, in restraint of trade or commerce among the several States, or with foreign nations, is hereby declared to be illegal. . . .

Seemingly straightforward, the meaning of this language (as we will see in Chapter 14) has provided the point of departure for many discussions of what antitrust policy ought to be, both in judicial decisions and by economists. This provision was made subject to a proviso adopted in 1937, in what is known as the Miller-Tydings Act. This amendment exempts from the Sherman Act resale (define as "retail") price main-

tenance contracts under which retailers agree with manufacturers to maintain retail prices at levels fixed by the manufacturers (for the purpose of eliminating price competition at the retail level) where such contracts are lawful according to the law of the state in which the retail sale is to be made or to which the commodity is to be transported for such retail sale. (Resale price maintenance laws are commonly referred to as "fair trade" laws.) A further piece of legislation (an amendment to the Federal Trade Commission Act), known as the McGuire-Keogh Act, was adopted by Congress in 1952 to permit such contracts to be made under state laws where the state laws provide that they may be enforced against third parties who have not signed such contracts ("non-signers"). Except for the specific legislation exempting such resale price maintenance contracts from the Sherman Act, they would constitute a violation of the law if made in interstate commerce. Depending on the methods used by manufacturers to induce retailers to make such contracts, these contracts may still fall within the original prohibition of the Sherman Act despite the language of the exemption laws—as we will see in Chapter 14. These two amendments will be briefly further examined below.

The other major substantive provision of the Sherman Act is contained in its second section, which reads:

Section 2: Every person who shall monopolize, or attempt to monopolize, or combine or conspire with any other person or persons, to monopolize any part of the trade or commerce among the several States, or with foreign nations, shall be deemed guilty of a misdemeanor. . . .

Section 2 thus lists three separate offenses: (1) the act of "monopolizing"; (2) "attempting to monopolize"; and (3) "combining or conspiring to monopolize." The elements of these three separate offenses are not the same; an "attempt" in criminal law is an offense even if there is no actual consummation of the thing "attempted." If the illegal act is consummated, the "attempt" merges with the act, and the criminal action proceeds on the basis of the completed act. This fact has not always been understood by some economists who have discussed this section of the law, as we will see in a later chapter.

Both sections of the Sherman Act are punishable by a "fine not exceeding fifty thousand dollars, or by imprisonment not exceeding one year" (the difference between a "felony" and a "misdemeanor" is to be found in many states in this length of imprisonment—one year or less is the punishment for a "misdemeanor"), or by both of these punishments "in the discretion of the court." (The original amount of the fine was five thousand dollars and was increased to fifty thousand dollars by a 1955 amendment to the law. In 1969 the Attorney General requested Congress to increase the fine to $500,000 in the case of corporations.)

Sections 1 and 2 of the Sherman Act clearly employ the language of a criminal statute. However, as has been noted in Chapter 3, the Act also contains a provision for actions in equity, and thus there may be what are known as "civil proceedings" under it. Section 4 vests the federal district courts with power to issue injunctions to prevent or restrain violations of the Act; and this section also places the duty of instituting such proceedings in equity upon the "several district attorneys of the United States, under the direction of the Attorney General."

Section 6 of the Act provides for the forfeiture to the United States of property owned under a contract in violation of Section 1; it has, however, not been much used. Section 7 originally provided for the recovery of treble damages by a person injured "by reason of anything forbidden in the antitrust acts," but this provision was repealed in 1955 and superseded by an amendment to Section 4 of the Clayton Act which continues this provision in effect but subjects it to a four-year statute of limitations. Moreover, a final judgment or decree in any civil or criminal proceeding under the antitrust laws to the effect that the defendant has violated such laws is *prima facie* evidence (evidence sufficiently strong so that the defendant may be called upon to rebut it) against the defendant in such a private damage action. At the same time, consent judgments or consent decrees (discussed in detail later and defined for the

moment merely as those made by agreement between the defendant and the governmental authorities and approved by a court) do not constitute such *prima facie* evidence. The advantages to a defendant from a consent decree in this area are thus plain, aside from other advantages which may also accrue to him.

The Miller-Tydings Act of 1937 and the McGuire-Keogh Act of 1952 (Public Law 314, 75th Cong. and Public Law 542, 82d Cong.)

It has been mentioned in the preceding paragraphs that the Miller-Tydings Act of 1937 amended Section 1 of the Sherman Act to permit contracts between manufacturers and retailers to fix resale prices—contracts whose purpose is to eliminate competition at the retail level—where state laws permit such contracts to be made. This exemption was adopted during the Great Depression largely as the result of the pressure group activities of trade associations, such as the National Association of Retail Druggists. Of thirteen witnesses who testified in favor of the legislation before the House subcommittee holding hearings on it, seven represented drug trade associations.[2]

Some of the state laws authorizing resale price maintenance contracts (in all such laws the enforcement provision consists of establishment of a right to a legal action by the parties for non-compliance) provide also for a right of action against third persons who fail to honor the terms of such contracts, even though these third persons are not parties to the contract. In *Schewegeman Brothers* v. *Calvert Distillers Corporation*,[3] the Supreme Court held in 1951 that the Miller-Tydings Act did not extend the exemption from the Sherman Act to such third party (or "non-signers") clauses. Accordingly, those trade associations which strongly favored the elimination of price competition at the retail level made possible by such contracts were successful in 1952 in securing adoption of the McGuire-Keogh Amendment to Section 5 of the Federal Trade Commission Act, extending the exemption from the antitrust laws also to such non-signers provisions. As we will see in Chapter 14, this amendment was upheld

---

[2] *Hearings on H.R. 1611* (Hearings of Subcommittee No. 3 of the House Judiciary Committee, 75th Cong., 1st sess.) (Washington, D.C.: U.S. Government Printing Office, 1937).

[3] 341 U.S. 384 (1951).

by the Supreme Court in 1964. But (as has been noted and as we will also further see in Chapter 14), depending on how such contracts are brought into existence in the first place, they may still be illegal under the Sherman Act. Thus, the Supreme Court has limited the scope of the McGuire-Keogh Act in several cases. The importance of resale price maintenance contracts as a method of reducing competition has probably also been declining in recent years because many state courts have invalidated either their entire resale price maintenance laws or certain parts of them. Between 1952 and 1959, the highest courts in sixteen states had taken such action.[4] Advocates of resale price maintenance legislation have thus sought to secure *federal* legislation authorizing such resale price maintenance contracts *irrespective of the status of state law* on the subject. Thus far, they have been unsuccessful in their quest for such legislation which has also been called by its supporters "quality stabilization" legislation, a euphemism adopted for obvious reasons.

The Clayton and Federal Trade Commission Acts of 1914 (15 U.S.C. 12 ff. and 15 U.S.C. 41 ff.)

There is disagreement among economic historians as to whether the Sherman Act was the response of Congress to strong public pressures or merely the result of tactical considerations of partisan politics, but no such similar doubts attach to the history of the enactment of the Clayton and Federal Trade Commission Acts in 1914. The histories of these two pieces of legislation are closely, almost inextricably, interrelated.

Nine years after the Sherman Act had been adopted, the first of a number of bills was proposed to amend it.[5] No action was taken by Congress on these early proposals. However, as we will see in greater detail in Chapter 14, in 1911, the Supreme Court held in two cases that only "unreasonable restraints of trade" were prohibited by Section 1 of the Sherman Act.[6] These decisions, together with the failure of the Sherman Act in general to cope with the

problem of increased private concentration of economic power, and the rise of what has been called "Progressivism"—in the Republican Party under the leadership of Theodore Roosevelt and in the Democratic Party under that of Woodrow Wilson—combined eventually to produce both the Clayton Act and the Federal Trade Commission Act in 1914.

Both the Clayton and the Federal Trade Commission Acts have by now been amended. The amendments are of sufficient importance to carry separate names. Moreover, although the original Clayton and Federal Trade Commission Acts had a common origin in President Wilson's Message to Congress of January 20, 1914, the amendments to these two laws had different origins and were the results of different pressures. The amendments will therefore be treated separately below, after the substantive provisions of the two laws as enacted in 1914 have been described.

Substantive Provisions of the Original Clayton Act of 1914. The original Clayton Act was described in its opening sentence as "An Act to supplement existing laws against unlawful restraints and monopolies, and for other purposes." Section 2 prohibited price discriminations (1) "where the effect of such discrimination may be substantially to lessen competition or to tend to create a monopoly in any line of commerce," (2) subject to a proviso that, aside from differences in grade, quality, or differences in selling or transportation costs, such discriminations were permissible when "made in good faith to meet competition," and (3) subject to a further proviso that sellers were not to be prohibited from "selecting their own customers in *bona fide* transactions and not in restraint of trade." This section was substantially amended by the Robinson-Patman Act in 1936; the latter will be briefly described later. In Chapter 15 *infra*, some judicial decisions under both the original and the amended sections will be examined. The defenses contained in the proviso are considered in Chapter 16.

---

[4] *Report No. 467 to Accompany H.R. 1253* (Report of the House Committee on Interstate and Foreign Commerce, 86th Cong., 1st sess.) (Washington, D.C.: U.S. Government Printing Office, 1959), p. 6.

[5] *Interlocks in Corporate Management* (Staff Report to the Antitrust Subcommittee of the House Judiciary

Committee, 89th Cong., 1st sess.) (Washington, D.C.: U.S. Government Printing Office, 1965), pp. 16 and 223 ff.

[6] *United States* v. *Standard Oil Co.*, 221 U.S. 1 (1911); *United States* v. *American Tobacco Co.*, 221 U.S. 6 (1911).

Section 3 of the original Clayton Act is still in force in its original form. It prohibits what are generally known as "tying agreements," agreements which may be roughly described for the present (pending an examination of decisions involving this section also in Chapter 15 *infra*) as arrangements under which a seller imposes additional conditions in conjunction with a lease or sale of either patented or unpatented goods where the effect of these additional conditions "may be to substantially lessen competition or tend to create a monopoly in any line of commerce."

Section 4 originally provided for a recovery of treble damages by a plaintiff in a private action, but has since been amended. The nature of the amendment has already been described in the discussion of the Sherman Act earlier, since the amendment also repealed the original treble damage section of that Act (Section 7) and now applies to all the antitrust laws. The damage remedy will be further examined in Chapter 20 *infra* which deals with the general problem of remedies.

Section 5 is procedural; Section 6 contains the statement that "The labor of a human being is not a commodity or article of commerce." It does not wholly exempt labor from the antitrust laws, as we will also see later.

Section 7 was amended by the Celler-Kefauver Act of 1950. The amended section will also be discussed more fully below. In its original form, this section prohibited the acquisition of "the whole or any part of the stock or other share capital of another corporation engaged also in commerce, where the effect of such acquisition may be to substantially lessen competition between the corporation whose stock is so acquired and the corporation making the acquisition, or to restrain such commerce in any section or community, or tend to create a monopoly in any line of commerce." Judicial decisions under both the original and the amended Section 7 are treated in Chapter 17 *infra*.

Section 8 of the Clayton Act has not been amended. Neither has it been the subject of much enforcement activity. Ironically, it is this section which prohibits interlocking directorates, and it was the disclosures by Congressional committees concerning the widespread existence of interlocking direc-torates which generated much of the popular support for the original enactment of the Clayton Act. That such interlocking directorates are still widespread throughout the fabric of business enterprise in the United States has been indicated in Chapter 9, particularly by Table 9-1. Section 8 will be further discussed in Chapter 17 also.

Substantive Provisions of the Original Federal Trade Commission Act. In its original form, the Federal Trade Commission Act provided for the establishment of the Federal Trade Commission, consisting of five commissioners (this number has not been changed) with a staff of employees qualified under Civil Service rules and regulations. The first sentence of Section 5 (the only significant substantive provision) of the original Act read: "Unfair methods of competition in commerce are hereby declared unlawful." This broad language obviously conferred discretion upon the commissioners subject to judicial review, as we will see more specifically in Chapter 18 *infra*. The Commission was also empowered in Section 5 to hold hearings, while observing the rules of procedural due process, and to issue orders. If those to whom the order was directed failed to obey, the Commission was authorized to apply to an appropriate court for the enforcement of its order. In the original legislation, the burden was thus upon the Commission to seek enforcement of its orders. Section 5 was amended by the Wheeler-Lea Act in 1938 and again, as has already been noted in the discussion of the Sherman Act, by the McGuire-Keogh Act (resale price maintenance) in 1952. Decisions under both the original and the amended sections will be examined further in Chapter 18, and the amendments themselves will be further described below.

What should be abundantly clear to the reader by now is that, in adopting the Clayton and Federal Trade Commission Acts in 1914, Congress did not produce specific legislation that tied neatly together, and with precision, the ends left hanging loose in the original Sherman Act of 1890. Instead, the 1914 legislation involved the adoption of additional broad, constitution-like provisions and the creation of an additional administrative authority to enforce the legislation. But if Congress did not specify with particularity what was and what was not illegal, it did take action which embodied the common law method of trial and error inclusion and exclusion into the basic working rules of antitrust. Moreover, the laws which were enacted were not adopted in response to pronouncements based upon models of pure economic theory. They were as much an expression of certain political views as of economic ones; and the very fact that they were adopted is evidence that they represented agreement upon certain language by a number of individuals representing competing social interests.

The Robinson-Patman Act of 1936 (Public Law 692, 74th Cong.)

Legislative History. As has been noted above, the Robinson-Patman Act was adopted as an amendment to Section 2 of the Clayton Act in 1936. Section 2 of the latter, it has been noted, prohibited price discriminations under certain conditions. As a result of various decisions by the courts, the Federal Trade Commission reported to Congress in 1934 that "during a period when chain stores were enjoying extensive growth based largely upon special price concessions from manufacturers, the Commission was prevented by court decisions from applying Section 2 of the Clayton Act to ameliorate the resultant competitive situation between the chains, the co-operatives, and the independents."[7] In these decisions among other things, the lower federal courts had held that the section permitted quantity discounts by sellers to large buyers "without regard to the amount of the seller's actual savings in cost" resulting from such quantity sales. The Commission accordingly recommended legislation making it unlawful for any person "directly or indirectly to discriminate unfairly or unjustly in price between different purchases" of like commodities purchased under like conditions.[8] In short, the Commission wanted broad, discretionary authority to control price discriminations. Congress responded by going far beyond the Commission's recommendation and, probably, in a direction not contemplated by the Commission. The result was the Robinson-Patman Act of 1936,

which amended the price discrimination section (2) of the Clayton Act.

Substantive Provisions of the Robinson-Patman Act. The Robinson-Patman Act is a complex law. For present purposes, it is enough to indicate that the Act: (1) prohibits price discriminations which have the effect of substantially lessening competition or tending to create a monopoly in any line of commerce or the effect of injuring, destroying, or preventing competition either with persons who grant or knowingly receive the benefits of such discrimination or with customers of either the grantor or grantee of the discrimination, provided that the right of sellers to select their own customers "in bona fide transactions and not in restraint of trade" is not limited by the law; but (2) allows price discriminations to be made "in good faith to meet the equally low price price of a competitor"; (3) prohibits brokerage payments to buyers outright; (4) prohibits advertising or sales allowances not made "on proportionally equal terms" to all purchasers; and (5) prohibits buyers from "knowingly receiving" or "knowingly inducing" such discriminations in prices.

Obviously, there is much language here whose meaning can be determined only on a case-by-case basis in the judicial process of exclusion and inclusion. As has been noted, cases involving these provisions will be discussed in Chapters 15 and 16.

The Celler-Kefauver Act of 1950 (Public Law 899, 81st Cong.)

In 1934, the Federal Trade Commission did not restrict itself merely to recommending an amendment to Section 2 of the Clayton Act. If anything, it devoted more space to a recommendation that Section 7 of that Act be amended also. In its original form, it has been noted, Section 7 prohibited the acquisition by one corporation of "the whole or any part of the stock" of another corporation where the effect of the acquisition "may be to substantially lessen competition between the corporation whose stock is so acquired and the corporation making the acquisition, or to restrain such commerce in any section or community, or tend to create a monopoly in any line of

---

[7] Federal Trade Commission, *Chain Stores: Final Report on the Chain Store Investigation* (Washington,

D.C.: U.S. Government Printing Office,1935), p. 90.
[8] *Ibid.*, pp. 96–97.

commerce." With respect to the effectiveness of this provision, the Commission remarked:

... section 7 does not purport to prohibit acquisitions and mergers of physical assets as distinguished from capital stock. So this obvious method of accomplishing the forbidden results by unforbidden means has frequently been resorted to. In a number of instances the fact that the section has no application to physical assets has led corporations to acquire stock in apparent violation of the section, vote the stock so as to accomplish merger of the assets, and then claim they were entitled to retain the fruits of their unlawful stock transactions.[9]

Moreover, the Commission pointed out that it had instituted proceedings in three cases of the type described in the quotation above. In one of the three, the acquiring corporation had not yet voted to sell to itself the assets by means of the controlling stock interest it had obtained in violation of the statute, and the Supreme Court had upheld the power of the Commission to prohibit the merger by ordering divestiture of the stock. But in the two others, in which the stock obtained in violation of the statute had been used to convey the assets before the Commission had filed its complaint, the Court had taken the view that it was "beyond the power of the Commission to order divestiture of the physical properties."[10]

Thus, the Commission asserted accurately:

It is apparent that section 7 has become a virtual nullity and that it is an easy matter for corporations desiring to acquire the stock of competitors to do so without subjecting themselves to an effective order of divestiture from the Commission. The Supreme Court does point out, however, that if any unlawful status results it may be attacked in the courts which are not limited in the nature of the relief they may administer. The decisions above discussed naturally affected not only the ability but the disposition of the Commission to institute proceedings for violation of section 7 during a period when mergers of competing corporations were being consumated on an extensive scale.[11]

The period in question was, of course, one in which the second wave of mergers described earlier in Chapter 9 was taking place. Motion picture chains, dairy companies, retail food establishments, and the like—it will be recalled—were undertaking mergers in this period, although by far the largest amount of activity occurred in the public utility area. Clearly, the policy adopted by the Court with respect to Section 7 has in these cases of the 1920's affected the organization and direction of economic activity in the United States.

For the reasons given above, the Commission recommended that Section 7 of the Clayton Act be amended by making it also illegal to acquire "the whole or a major part of the assets of another corporation engaged also in commerce and in competition with the acquiring corporation."

It was not until 1950, however, that Congress acted favorably upon this recommendation by adopting the Celler-Kefauver Act; when it did so, the legislation was probably less the result of the Federal Trade Commission recommendation of 1934 than the result of the efforts of Senator Kefauver and his supporters and of Representative Celler and his. The 1950 law followed substantially the 1934 recommendation of the Commission. Today, therefore, Section 7 as amended prohibits acquisition by a corporation of the "whole or any part of the stock . . . and the whole or any part of the assets" where "in any line of commerce in any section of the country, the effect of such acquisition may be substantially to lessen competition or to tend to create a monopoly." The examination of the policy adopted by the Supreme Court relative to Section 7 as amended constitutes the principal subject matter of Chapter 17 *infra*.

The Wheeler-Lea Act of 1938 (Public Law 447, 75th Cong.)

The Wheeler-Lea Act of 1938 made two significant changes in the Federal Trade Commission Act of 1914. Because the Supreme Court had placed a restrictive interpretation upon the scope of the power of the Commission to prohibit unfair or

[9] *Final Report on the Chain Store Investigation, op. cit.,* p. 88.

[10] *Ibid.,* pp. 88–89. The cases in question were *Federal Trade Commission* v. *Western Meat Co.,* 272 U.S. 554 (1926), divestiture permitted; and *Thatcher Mfg. Co.* v. *Federal Trade Commission,* and *Swift and Co.* v. *Federal Trade Commission,* both also 272 U.S. 554 (1926), which the Commission lost.

[11] *Final Report on the Chain Store Investigation, op. cit.,* pp. 89–90.

deceptive advertising under the original Section 5 of the Act by holding that the Commission had to show not only injury to the public but also injury to a competitor before it could issue a cease and desist order, Congress in 1938 changed the language of Section 5 so that it now not only prohibits "unfair methods of competition in commerce" (the original prohibition) but also prohibits "unfair or deceptive acts or practices" in commerce. In addition, where previously the Commission was forced to go to court to request that its orders be enforced (and thus to carry the burden of proof), since the passage of the Wheeler-Lea Act, an order issued by the Commission under Section 5 of the FTC Act becomes final unless the Commission itself decides to modify the order or unless the person to whom it is issued files a petition for review of the order within sixty days after having been served with it. The Federal Trade Commission Act, as amended, will be considered in detail in Chapter 18. Certain other pieces of legislation designed primarily to protect consumers and concerning specific powers granted to the FTC will also be discussed in Chapter 18. Other legislation and proposed legislation since 1962 to protect consumers, although it does not fall strictly within the definition of antitrust legislation, will be described later in the present chapter. Our immediate problem, however, is to note next that there have been numerous pieces of legislation providing for exemptions from the antitrust laws.

The Webb-Pomerene Act of 1918 (Public Law 126, 65th Cong.)

The Webb-Pomerene Act of 1918 was the first of many exemptions from the Sherman Act adopted by Congress. This law pertains to the application of the Sherman Act to the international activities of American firms rather than to their purely domestic activities. One factor which undoubtedly greatly contributed to the enactment of this legislation in 1918 was the report of an investigation by the Federal Trade Commission into conditions of competition facing United States firms seeking to do business abroad.

Congress implemented the recommendations made by the FTC in the early report mentioned above by adopting the Webb-

Pomerene Act in 1918, exempting from the provisions of the Sherman Act "associations entered into for the sole purpose of engaging in the export trade and actually engaged solely in such export trade" or agreements made in the course of such export trade by such an association. Moreover, an association formed under the exemption is required within 30 days after its creation to file with the Federal Trade Commission a copy of its articles of association or agreement, together with data pertaining to its participants. Although the Webb-Pomerene Act permits United States firms to form export associations in order to fight foreign cartels, it does not permit United States firms to join such international cartels for the purpose of restricting United States commerce. Cases involving this question are discussed in Chapter 21.

Miscellaneous Exemptions from the Antitrust Laws

Largely in response to the activities of pressure groups, Congress has from time to time adopted special legislation exempting particular industries and activities from the antitrust laws. Some, but not all, of these exemptions will be further discussed incidentally in the course of the detailed examination of the implementation of the basic antitrust laws in the chapters which follow, particularly in Chapter 22 and in Part III. It is enough for the purposes of this book, however, to include at this point a brief mention of some of these exemptions. For example, in the 1945 McCarran Act (61 Stat. 448), Congress provided that the antitrust laws should apply to the insurance business only "to the extent that such business is not regulated by State law," thereby making regulation of the insurance business a matter for state regulation. So also under various pieces of legislation has Congress exempted from the antitrust laws the activities of agricultural marketing associations [Capper-Volstead Act of 1922 (7 U.S.C. 291 and 292); Agricultural Marketing Agreement Act of 1926 (7 U.S.C. 451 ff.); Agricultural Marketing Agreement Act of 1938 (7 U.S.C. 471 ff.)] as well as associations pertaining to fishing activities. And in 1961, Congress provided for an exemption in the case of telecasts of professional sports contests (15 U.S.C. 1291 ff.).

In the area of professional sports generally, a judicial exemption has been created in the case of baseball [*Toolson* v. *N.Y. Yankees*, 348 U.S. 236 (1955)] while boxing and basketball are not exempt. Professional football has been granted a statutory exemption (Public Law 89–900, S.6). In 1966, Congress adopted special legislation applicable to banks in the Bank Merger Act of 1966, amending legislation adopted in 1960. The Act of 1966 raised the knotty question of the extent to which the antitrust laws apply in general to industries subject to regulation by special agencies, a topic more economically discussed in Chapter 22 in this book. The same is true of the topic of labor and the antitrust laws, which will be discussed further in Chapter 14, as will be the Bank Merger Act of 1966. But mention must also be made now of the fact that, in times of national emergency, Congress has often permitted exemptions from the antitrust laws upon a certification of a need therefor by the President. Such an exemption is contained in Section 708 of the Defense Production Act of 1950 (50 U.S.C. App. 2158). No general principles can be derived to explain the exemptions other than a statement that they represent a Congressional response to the activities of interest groups; the most appropriate unified treatment of these exemptions is thus to make a list of the affected industries and the relevant laws. Probably the most readily available source of such a list is the reference identified in Footnote 1 of this chapter, and the interested reader may be referred to that source.

B. ACTIONS AND PROPOSED ACTIONS TO PROTECT CONSUMERS SINCE 1962

President Kennedy's Message to Congress in 1962

Strictly speaking, the principal substantive change in the Federal Trade Commission Act made by the Wheeler-Lea Act was designed to protect consumers, and thus it falls outside the category of the subject matter of what may be termed "antitrust" legislation. Beginning in about

1961, new interest was evidenced by some members of Congress in the problem of protecting consumers. As early as June 1961, the Senate Subcommittee on Antitrust and Monopoly began holding hearings on the need for "truth in packaging" legislation. The problem of protection of consumers received added attention in March 1962, when President Kennedy sent a broad-ranging Message to Congress concerning "consumer interests," asking, among other things, for amendments to the Food and Drug Act and for legislation improving mass transit. He also called attention to the need for improvements in motor vehicle safety features and for "truth in credit" and "truth in packaging" legislation.[12]

In his Message to Congress, President Kennedy also stated that he was directing the Council of Economic Advisors to create a Consumers' Advisory Council to represent consumers' interests in issues of government policy and that he was also asking each executive department head whose activities "bear significantly on consumer welfare" to designate a special assistant in his office to advise him on such matters. Executive Order 11136 of January 3, 1964, issued during President Johnson's administration, established the President's Committee on Consumer Interests, which consists of representatives of 12 government agencies and of private citizens appointed by the President. The private citizens serving on this committee, in turn, constitute the Consumer Advisory Council also created by the same Executive Order. Consumer representation at the highest level of the Executive Branch was thus assured for the first time in our history by these actions of the Kennedy and Johnson Administrations. Congress has also acted by establishing Consumer Subcommittees.

Early Legislative Proposals

On September 24, 1964, Senator Hart introduced a packaging and labeling bill (S.3745) "for the purpose of receiving comments and suggestions of interested parties." After the receipt of these comments, on January 21, 1963 Senator Hart introduced S. 387, known as the "Truth in Packaging Bill." This bill was referred to the Senate

[12] *Congressional Record*, Vol. 108, pp. 3910–3911 (March 15, 1962).

Subcommittee on Antitrust and Monopoly for further legislative hearings and was reported to the Committee on the Judiciary in June of 1963, but it was not acted upon by the 88th Congress. This bill would have amended the Clayton Act by adding a new section [3(a)] for the purpose of prohibiting "restraint of trade carried into effect through the use of unfair and deceptive methods of packaging and labeling" certain consumer goods further identified in the bill.[13] The bill would have further provided for the issuance of *mandatory* regulations by the Secretary of Health, Education, and Welfare in the case of foods, drugs, devices, or cosmetics and by the Federal Trade Commission with respect to all other commodities. The regulations would have required: (1) a net quantity of content statement upon the front panel of packages and labels; (2) establishment of minimum standards concerning the prominence of such statements (including minimum type size and face); (3) prohibition of qualifying words or phrases to such statements; (4) prohibition of language which might reasonably be construed as involving price deception; and (5) prevention of the use of deceptive illustrations or other pictorial matter upon packages. Additional authority would have authorized the implementing agencies to issue regulations on a discretionary product-by-product basis. Provisions were also included to provide for due notice and an opportunity to be heard to persons affected by such regulations, and enforcement provisions were also provided. In addition, violation of any regulation issued under the law would have constituted an unfair trade practice under Section 5 of the Federal Trade Commission Act. Opposition to the proposed legislation (which, it has been noted, was not acted upon by the 88th Congress) was led in the Senate by Senators Dirksen and Hruska (Republican members of the subcommittee). They centered their attack upon arguments that: (1) the bill constituted an inclusion of a non-antitrust matter in Section 3 of the Clayton Act and was inappropriate for that reason; (2) the cost of the bill to packagers and hence to consumers would be very great; and (3) the legislation was unnecessary since the

FTC and the Food and Drug Administration already had "ample authority" under existing legislation to accomplish the purposes of the legislation.

The history of S. 387 (which died in committee) provides an interesting illustration of the device of "killing off" legislation in a legislative committee rather than waiting until it reaches the floor in order to try to defeat it, a device already discussed in Chapter 6 of this book.

However, notwithstanding this early defeat suffered by the proponents of legislation to protect consumers, a great deal of progress has been made since 1962. This progress, as well as some of the tasks yet to be accomplished were noted in a Message to Congress by President Johnson in 1968.

President Johnson's Message to Congress on the American Consumer in 1968

In February 1968, President Johnson sent to Congress "The Fourth Message on the American Consumer Enumerating the Steps Taken to Insure Present Progress and Setting Forth a Program for 1968." The record of "progress" included protection of the consumer against: "Impure and unwholesome meat; death and destruction on our highways; misleading labels and packages; clothing and blankets that are fireprone rather than fire-proof; hazardous appliances and products around the house; toys that endanger our children; substandard clinical laboratories; and unsafe tires." Some of these items referred to new legislation, and some were the result of actions by regulatory agencies, as we will see in later chapters. At the time of the Message, the "Truth in Lending Act of 1968" had been passed by both the House and the Senate. It has since become law and will be discussed in Chapter 18. The "Program for 1968" included a recommendation for a study of automobile insurance, recommendations for various other health and safety measures—such as a law to protect against the sale of unwholesome fish and poultry—and a call for the enactment of the Deceptive Sales Act of 1968 "to give new powers to the Federal Trade Commission." Some of these objectives were accomplished by the enactment of amend-

---

[13] *Truth in Packaging* (Report of the Subcommittee on Antitrust and Monopoly of the Senate Judiciary Committee, 88th Cong., 2d sess.) (Washington, D.C.: U.S. Government Printing Office, 1964), p. 4.

ments to existing legislation; some were not acted upon by the 90th Congress. This legislation, too, will be considered where appropriate in later chapters. President Nixon's Message to Congress on "Consumerism" next warrants our attention.

President Nixon's Message on "Consumerism" (October 30, 1969)

President Nixon in 1969 sent a Message to Congress calling for further legislation dealing with consumer problems. The antecedents of his Message were one informal and two formal studies of the Federal Trade Commission, discussed at the end of Chapter 18. In his Message, the President asked Congress to (1) establish an Office of Consumer Affairs within the Executive Office of the President; (2) to establish a Division of Consumer Protection to replace the Consumers' Counsel in the Department of Justice, with a status comparable to that of the Antitrust Division; (3) to pass a new law making it possible for consumers to sue in federal courts "for fraudulent and deceptive practices"; and (4) to adopt legislation enabling the Federal Trade Commission to obtain injunctions to prohibit unfair or deceptive practices prior to FTC decisions on the facts in such cases. In addition, the President stated that he was taking various actions which did not require new enabling legislation, including the appointment of a National Commission on Consumer Finance under the "Truth in Lending" Act, and a direction to the Special Assistant to the President for Consumer Affairs to publish periodically a *Consumer Bulletin*. Furthermore, he was asking the chairman-designate of the Federal Trade Commission and the Bureau of the Budget to "revitalize" the Commission with a view to increasing the Commission's activities in the field of consumer affairs. This increase would be accomplished by a reduction in some of the antimonopoly and antimerger activities of the Commission according to one recommendation made to the President by one of his advisory groups, although he did not mention this point in his Message and restricted himself to stating that he hoped the expanded consumer protection activities could be undertaken by means of "a more efficient use of personnel and finances."

This question, too, will be further considered in Chapter 18. It is interesting to note that President Nixon did not in his Message call for the establishment of a Cabinet-level Department of Consumer Affairs.

Proposals for Establishment of a Cabinet-level Department of Consumer Affairs

As early as 1959, a proposal for establishment of a Department of Consumer Affairs was embodied in a bill introduced by the late Senator Estes Kefauver. Similar legislation has been sporadically introduced in Congress since 1959. In 1969, for example, Representative Benjamin S. Rosenthal and Senator Gaylord Nelson introduced identical bills (H.R. 6037 and S. 860, respectively). Under the proposed legislation, all of the consumer protection activities currently scattered throughout some 30 government agencies would have been transferred to the new Department. Thus, the duties conferred upon the Federal Trade Commission and the Food and Drug Administration by the Fair Packaging and Labeling Act (to be discussed below) would have been transferred to the new Department, as would duties pertaining to the computation of cost of living indexes currently performed by the Bureau of Labor Statistics. The proposed legislation was, however, not enacted by the 91st Congress. Instead, opponents of the proposal for the establishment of a Cabinet-level agency sought to win support for a proposal for an "independent" consumer protection agency, one whose functions would be more limited than those proposed for the new Department. One such agency had already been created with sharply limited functions by the 90th Congress. This agency and the Fair Packaging and Labeling Act will now be discussed, in the order mentioned.

The National Commission on Product Safety (P.L. 90–146, 90th Cong., 1st sess., 1967)

In 1967 Congress created a National Commission on Product Safety. The nature of this Commission and its purpose were explained in testimony in support of the enacting legislation by Undersecretary of Commerce J. Herbert Hollomon in the following language:

This bill is in general accord with the President's recommendation to Congress in the consumer protection message. The bill recognizes the need for further inquiry into two aspects of product safety: The right of the consumer to be protected from unreasonable risk of bodily harm and the right of the manufacturer to a reasonable degree of uniformity in safety regulations.

This bill calls for the establishment of a Commission of seven members, appointed by the President, and charged with the task of carrying out "a comprehensive study and investigation of the scope and adequacy of measures now employed to protect consumers against unreasonable risk of injuries which may be caused by hazardous household products". . . .[14]

On December 20, 1967, Congress enacted Public Law 90–146 establishing the Commission, and President Johnson appointed its members in March 1968. The Commission was authorized an appropriation of $2,000,000 and was given power to subpoena witnesses and documentary evidence. Excluded from its sphere of investigation were products covered by other legislation, such as the Motor Vehicle Safety Act of 1966, the Flammable Fabrics Act, and the Hazardous Substances Act.

The Fair Packaging and Labeling Act of 1966 (P.L. 89–775, 89th Cong., 2d sess.)

The Fair Packaging and Labeling Act of 1966 places additional responsibilities upon the Federal Trade Commission and upon the Food and Drug Administration.

Legislative History of the Act. The arguments (described earlier) made against S. 387 in the 88th Congress presumably explain why the "Fair Packaging and Labeling Act of 1966" was not put forward as an amendment to any of the antitrust laws but was instead introduced during the 89th Congress under the general power of Congress to regulate interstate commerce. This legislation began as S. 985 and was considered and passed by the Senate on June 9, 1966. A companion bill, H.R. 15440, was considered, amended, and passed by the House on October 3, 1966. A Conference Committee report to reconcile differences between the Senate and House bills was agreed to by the House on October 16 and by the Senate on October 17, and the

bill became law on November 3, 1966. The substantive provisions will be briefly summarized below.

Substantive Provisions of the Act. The Act contains both packaging and labeling provisions which are quite similar to those contained in S. 387 described earlier. The House Committee on Interstate and Foreign Commerce amended the new bill (S. 985) which had been adopted by the Senate, and the nature of the amendments (concerning the *packaging* provisions will be explained below.[15] The law as finally enacted *directs* the Secretary of Health, Education, and Welfare (in the case of foods, drugs, devices, and cosmetics) and the Federal Trade Commission (in the case of all other commodities) to promulgate *labeling* regulations: (1) pertaining to identification (by means of a package label) of the commodity and its manufacturer, packer, or distributor; (2) pertaining to the location and legibility of a statement of net quantity of contents; and (3) pertaining to any description in terms of weight, volume, or size. It also *authorizes* the enforcement agencies to issue *labeling* regulations "to prevent consumer deception or to facilitate 'value' comparisons" and to determine what size packages may be represented by words such as "small," "medium," and "large." It further *authorizes* regulations to control, but not prohibit, promotional devices, such as "cents-off" or "economy" sizes of packages. In addition, it extends to non-food items the existing requirement for a listing in the order of decreasing predominance of commodity ingredients and authorizes regulations to prevent "nonfunctional slack fill" or "packaged air" (defined explicitly as "slack fill not necessitated by product protection or automatic machine packaging").

S. 985 and H.R. 15440, as originally introduced, both contained Section 5(d)— relating to *packaging* (rather than *labeling*)— which read as follows:

(d) Whenever the promulgating authority determines, after a hearing conducted in compliance with section 7 of the Administrative Procedure Act, that the weights or quantities

---

[14] *Flammable Fabrics Act and Product Safety Commission* (Hearings before the Senate Commerce Subcommittee, 90th Cong., 1st sess., 1967) (Washington, D.C.: U.S. Government Printing Office, 1967), p. 35.

[15] In general, see *Fair Packaging and Labeling Act* (Report and Hearings before the House Committee on Interstate and Foreign Commerce, 89th Cong., 2d sess.) (Washington, D.C.: U.S. Government Printing Office, 1966).

in which any consumer commodity is being distributed for retail sale are likely to impair the ability of consumers to make price per unit comparisons such authority shall:

(1) publish such determination in the Federal Register; and

(2) promulgate, subject to the provisions of subsections (e), (f), and (g), regulations effective to establish reasonable weights or quantities, and fractions or multiples thereof, in which any such customer commodity shall be distributed for retail sale.

The language of this *packaging* provision was changed by the House committee, and the amendment thus made was enacted into law in the final legislative proceedings. Section 5(d), as quoted above, originally contained authority for the enforcement agencies to make voluntary packaging standards binding or to issue binding packaging regulations of their own in the absence of industry agreement on voluntary packaging standards. For this *mandatory* provision, the House committee substituted a completely *voluntary* procedure. Under the amendment, after a determination by the Secretary of Commerce that there is "undue proliferation of the weights, measures or quantities" in which a commodity is being distributed, he is directed to request manufacturers, distributors, or packers "to participate in the development of a voluntary standard." If one year later he determines that no packaging standard will be published or that the agreed packaging standard is not being observed, he is to report that fact to Congress with a recommendation for specific legislation to deal with the situation. This change in the language of Section 5(d) was a concession made by supporters of the legislation to its opponents in order to secure the law's enactment. Thus, as finally enacted, the law contains *mandatory and discretionary labeling* provisions but *voluntary packaging* provisions. The effective date of the law was fixed as July 1, 1967, subject to a proviso in the case of certain items and certain findings by the Secretary of Health, Education, and Welfare and the Federal Trade Commission. Regulations issued pursuant to the law will be noted in Chapter 18.

The Office of Consumer Counsel

In his 1968 *State of the Union Message*, President Johnson announced that he was appointing a government attorney "to serve the consumers of this land." Accordingly, an Office of Consumer Counsel was created in the Department of Justice by administrative action of the Attorney General. No special statutory authority for the creation of such an office exists, and the Office of the Consumer Counsel is thus dependent upon the pleasure of the Attorney General for its existence. In a statement to the Federal Trade Commission in December, 1968, Mr. Paul Bauer, the Consumer Counsel, indicated what he thought the functions of the office should be. In addition to the functions of representing consumers in actions before regulatory agencies and formulating legislative proposals and administration positions on matters pertaining to consumer welfare, Mr. Bauer laid considerable stress upon the role the new office could play in protecting low-income consumers against fraudulent sellers and sellers of defective goods. Initially, the new office was staffed with lawyers assigned temporarily from other duties within the Department of Justice. Although the potential benefits from the establishment of this new office would seem to be great, it would probably become a much more significant force if it were given a permanent and formal status, either by the issuance of an Executive Order or by appropriate legislation. Indeed, the creation by Congress of an Administrative Agency for Consumer Protection with a budget and staff independent of those of the Department of Justice and able to speak independently for itself, free from domination by a political Cabinet Officer, would be a highly desirable step.

Summary Outline

The following is a brief outline of the principal federal antitrust statutes, major amendments, and some important related laws to protect consumers which have been mentioned in this chapter.

I. The Sherman Act of 1890, as amended

  A. Prohibits:

    1. Contracts, combinations, conspiracies in restraint of trade (Section 1)

    2. Monopolizing; attempting to monopolize, combinations or conspiracies to monopolize (Section 2)

  B. Exempts:

    1. Resale price maintenance contracts,

including those binding on third party non-signers (Miller-Tydings Act of 1937; McGuire-Keogh Act of 1952)

2. Export associations (Webb-Pomerene Act of 1918)

3. Miscellaneous activities, including activities subject to regulatory agency approval under specified conditions

II. The Clayton Act of 1914, as amended

A. Prohibits:

1. Brokerage *per se*, non-proportional advertising and sales allowances, and price discriminations, except where in good faith to meet equally low price of competitor, where effect is substantially to lessen competition or to tend to create a monopoly (Section 2, as amended by the Robinson-Patman Act of 1936)

2. Tying agreements (Section 3) under same conditions

3. Mergers either as result of acquisition of stock or of assets, where the effect may be substantially to lessen competition in any line of commerce in any section of the country (Section 7, as amended by the Cellar-Kefauver Act of 1950)

4. Interlocking directorates under specified conditions (Sections 8 and 10)

B. Exempts:

1. Labor from antitrust laws (Sections 6 and 20)

2. Certain transactions subject to approval of regulatory commissions (Sections 7 and 11)

III. The Federal Trade Commission Act of 1914, as amended

A. Creates Commission whose orders are binding if not appealed to court by the defendant.

B. Prohibits:

1. Unfair methods of competition (Section 5)

2. Unfair or deceptive practices in commerce (Section 5, as amended by the Wheeler-Lea Act of 1938)

IV. Legislation Since 1962 to Protect Consumers

A. The Fair Packaging and Labeling Act of 1966

1. Authorizes voluntary agreements fixing standards for packaging under direction of Secretary of Commerce.

2. Requires mandatory and discretionary standards for labeling under direction of Federal Trade Commission and Secretary of Health, Education, and Welfare.

B. Department of Transportation Act of 1966

1. Creates Department of Transportation as policy agency.

2. Directs Secretary of Transportation to carry out provisions of the National Traffic and Motor Vehicle Act of 1966 through a National Traffic Safety Bureau.

C. Legislation Creating National Product Safety Commission (1967)

D. Various Health and Safety Measures—Flammable Fabrics Act Amendment, 1967; Food Inspection Laws, etc.

E. Truth in Lending Act of 1968

1. Requires creditors to furnish each person to whom credit is extended, prior to the consummation of credit, a statement giving debtor detailed information, including percentage rate of interest charged per period.

2. Charges Board of Governors of Federal Reserve System with duty of promulgating rules and regulations to implement the law.

C. ENFORCEMENT AND ADMINISTRATION OF THE ANTITRUST LAWS

The two major federal government agencies charged with enforcement of the antitrust laws are the Antitrust Division of the Department of Justice and the Federal Trade Commission. Many of the regulatory commissions, such as the Interstate Commerce Commission and the Federal Communications Commission, also have some responsibilities in this area, but consideration of their activities is postponed to later chapters. In addition, the two permanent Congressional subcommittees having major responsibility in this area are the Subcommittee on Antitrust and Monopoly of the Senate Judiciary Committee and the Antitrust Subcommittee of the House Judiciary Committee. Finally, within the Economics Bureau of the Department of State, there exists an International Business Practices Division which has the responsibility of advising the Secretary of State with respect to certain matters involving the relationship between antitrust policy and foreign policy. However, this Division has no enforcement responsibilities or authority relative to the antitrust laws.

The Antitrust Division of the Department of Justice

Personnel and Funds. The Antitrust Division, under the direction of one of the several

Attorneys General, was established in 1903. Prior to that time, enforcement of the Sherman Act was handled by the Justice Department as part of its general law enforcement activities. In 1968, the professional staff of the Antitrust Division consisted of eleven litigating and administrative sections, with six temporary field offices. Included among these sections were an Economic Section, which had the function of advising "on economic problems and economic aspects of litigation and relief," and a Judgments and Judgment Enforcement Section, whose purpose was to advise on matters pertaining to remedies to be sought in antitrust actions as well as to negotiate consent judgments. The importance of consent judgments, whose nature will be further examined in Chapter 20, has increased significantly in recent years. Until 1940 there had never been more than 12 consent decrees entered in a single year; in 1940 the number jumped to 21; and, since 1954, with the exception of 1961 (in which there were 18), the number has always exceeded 20. In January 1970, a Patent Unit was created to deal with antitrust problems involving patents.

The Assistant Attorney General in charge of the Antitrust Division is responsible to the Attorney General. The extent to which there has been active enforcement of the antitrust laws has thus been partly determined by the attitude of the Attorney General and the attitude of the President in whose Cabinet he serves and partly by the willingness of Congress to appropriate funds. Appropriations for the Division did not reach the sum of a million dollars until 1940 but have substantially increased since then. On the other hand, salaries of government employees have also increased substantially since the end of World War II. The average salary of employees within the Division was $7,680 in 1959 and $10,476 in 1965. In September 1968, the Division employed 287 attorneys and 25 economists. Appropriations and staff of the Division are still inadequate to allow accomplishment of the tasks set before it. In fiscal year 1967, for example, 444 major staff investigations

were initiated and 390 were closed. Also in fiscal year 1967, 2,457 mergers were examined, and 176 of these were selected for further investigation.[16] As early as 1962, representatives of the Foreign Commerce Section worked with representatives of the International Business Practices Division of the Department of State and with representatives of other government agencies to coordinate United States policy concerning antitrust matters in the international sphere. (This problem is discussed further in Chapter 21 *infra*.) In 1967, a total of 53 antitrust cases was filed in federal district courts.

Political Influences versus Career Employees. Two factors operate upon the Antitrust Division. On the one hand, because it exists within the Department of Justice, whose head is a Member of the President's Cabinet,

. . . it has no immunity from the forces of policy, politics, and pressures which play upon the administration. The frequent shifts in attitude and policy have done much to confuse lines. What is frowned at under one regime is tolerated or even looked upon with favor by another. . . .

. . . Persons put under indictment may not take it lying down nor limit their response to an answer in court. They see Congressmen, put pressure upon the Executive, enlist all who-know-who in their cause, move heaven and earth to have the suit stayed or stopped. Major antitrust proceedings are things of great consequence; their ramifications run far and wide into the national economy; group, class, interest, not party to the controversy, may be seriously affected by its outcome.[17]

At the same time, however, in every government agency staffed at lower levels by career employees, there grows up a tradition and there exist hardened attitudes and lines of policy. Political appointees at the policy-making levels (such as the Attorney General and the Assistant Attorneys General) must rely upon the accumulated experience and knowledge of the core of civil servants which remains from one administration to the next. Some kind of continuity is thus maintained from one administration to another, even in small

[16] *Annual Report of the Attorney General of the United States: for the Fiscal Year Ended June 30, 1967* (1968), p. 98.

[17] Walton Hamilton and Irene Till, *Antitrust in Action*, Temporary National Economic Committee Monograph No. 16 (Washington, D.C.: U.S. Government Printing Office, 1941), pp. 28–29.

government agencies. In time, the policy-making officials absorb some of the traditions and customs of the agency itself. Those with access to the files and, more importantly, who have participated in the formulation of the contents of these files, are in a position to shape the views of those who are newcomers to the agency. However, they do not always prevail.

An interesting case study of the pressure described above appears in a 1959 report of the House Antitrust Subcommittee.[18] In 1949, shortly before the Korean Emergency, the Department of Justice filed a complaint under the Sherman Act charging A. T. and T. and its subsidiary, Western Electric, with conspiracy to restrain and monopolize and with monopolization of the manufacture, distribution, and sale of telephones, telephone apparatus, and equipment. The government sought separation of Western Electric from A. T. and T. and various other types of relief. While the action was pending, A. T. and T. enlisted the aid of the Department of Defense to secure postponement of the suit for the duration of the Korean Emergency, which had by then occurred. The Department of Defense advocated postponement—in various ways by representations to the Department of Justice. Indeed, when the Eisenhower administration came into office, the outgoing Department of Defense officials entrusted the task, "of preparation of a draft memorandum for the benefit of the new administration" explaining the situation, to an employee of A. T. and T.

With the new administration came a new Attorney General (Herbert Brownell). According to the subcommittee report:

As a first step, Mr. H. S. Dumas, then executive vice president of A. T. and T., sought out a friend of Attorney General Brownell—Mr. Bayard Pope, of New York, chairman of the board of the Marine Midland Corporation of New York, and a director of the New York Telephone Co., a Bell subsidiary—and asked him to arrange a meeting with the Attorney General for the purpose of discussing the case. Mr. Pope was successful in making the necessary arrangements, and set up a luncheon meeting between

Mr. Dumas and Attorney General Brownell at his (Mr. Pope's) room in the Statler Hotel in Washington, D.C., in the middle of April 1953.[19]

The Attorney General apparently "listened very politely" to the representations as to why the suit should be dropped but "was most uncommunicative" and "made no commitment of any kind."[20] Subsequently, however, on June 27, 1953, T. Brooke Price, A. T. and T.'s vice president and general counsel, conferred with the Attorney General alone in the manager's cottage at the Greenbrier Hotel, White Sulphur Springs, West Virginia.

Edward A. Foote, who had had six months' previous experience in the Antitrust Division, was then put in charge of the negotiations with A. T. and T., with direct responsibility to the Assistant Attorney General (Stanley Barnes) and to the Attorney General. In 1955 the case was settled without divestiture. But the chief of the trial staff within the Antitrust Division, Victor H. Kramer, who was then Chief of the Division's General Litigation Section and who had been a member of the Antitrust Division for almost 18 years, declined to sign the decree.[21]

So also, Walter D. Murphy, the chief government trial lawyer on the case, who had served in the Division for 13 years, stated that he would prefer not to sign the decree because the decree perpetuated the relationship between A. T. and T. and Western Electric. Murphy preferred a dismissal of the complaint—thereby leaving the question of this relationship open to future action. And also, W. D. Kilgore, Jr., Chief of the Division's Judgments and Judgment Enforcement Section, was opposed to the settlement finally made.[22] Obviously, the case was one involving a conflict between the career employees and the political appointees of the agency.

It is useful also to note at this time that, with the inauguration of President Nixon in 1969, there came a new Attorney General and a new Assistant Attorney General in Charge of Antitrust (Richard W. McLaren).

About six weeks after taking office, Mr.

[18] Consent Decree Program of the Department of Justice (Report of the Antitrust Subcommittee of the House Judiciary Committee, 86th Cong., 1st sess.) (Washington, D.C.: U.S. Government Printing Office, 1959).

[19] Ibid., p. 52.
[20] Ibid.
[21] Ibid., p. 84.
[22] Ibid., p. 85.

McLaren candidly discussed future antitrust policy in a speech delivered before the National Industrial Conference Board. Among other things, Mr. McLaren said that he was taking a different view from that of his predecessors "in the area of reciprocity." He added that where reciprocity programs were conducted by large diversified firms, these programs "substitute buying power considerations for the normal and accepted ways of selling," involving "foreclosure effects on smaller or less diversified competitors."[23] We will see in Chapter 14 that Mr. McLaren completed his successful attack on reciprocity in August 1969.

Complaints, Investigations, Grand Juries, and Trials. The number of complaints received far exceeds the number of actions instituted. Once a decision has been made to investigate a complaint (rather than to refer it to another agency, such as the Federal Trade Commission, or to take no action concerning it for one reason or another), the Antitrust Division must rely upon the Federal Bureau of Investigation for further investigation. In some cases, attorneys from the Division work with FBI agents in the actual investigation. If a cause of action is believed to exist, there may be further investigation or the case may be put before a Grand Jury for further investigation. Indictment by a Grand Jury is necessary if a criminal action is contemplated. In 1962, Congress adopted a statute providing the Attorney General with power to issue a Civil Investigative Demand, requiring the production of documentary material pertinent to a civil antitrust proceeding, fulfilling certain jurisdictional requirements, and also describing the material "to be produced thereunder with such definiteness and certainty as to permit such material to be fairly identified" by a prospective defendant. The material may be copied, and originals or copies are held by an "antitrust document custodian" for a specified period of time. If one upon whom such a Demand is served refuses to produce the material, the Attorney General may seek a court order requiring him to comply with the Demand. An additional

power of compelling production of documentary evidence thus was created, but its use depends upon the ability of the Attorney General to describe the material "with such definiteness and certainty as to permit such material to be fairly identified." Obviously, the knowledge of the existence of the document and a sufficient knowledge of its content so that it can be described as required are conditions precedent to issuance of an order for it to be produced. The Civil Investigative Demand thus cannot serve as a replacement for the previously-existing investigative procedures. Nevertheless, the new procedure has been put to active use: first used in November of 1962, it had been used 164 times by the end of fiscal year 1963. The procedure was used 106 times in fiscal year 1968.[24]

Once sufficient evidence is at hand, a complaint may be issued. A decision must be made as to whether to proceed with a civil or a criminal action, or with both at the same time, as well as what sort of remedy (disposition of the case if the action is successful) to seek. In 1953, the Assistant Attorney General in charge of the Antitrust Division stated that the choice between civil and criminal actions was based on the following considerations:

> In general, the following types of offenses are prosecuted criminally: (1) price fixing; (2) other violations of the Sherman Act where there is proof of a specific intent to restrain trade or to monopolize; (3) a less easily defined category of cases which might generally be described as involving proof of use of predatory practices (boycotts, for example) to accomplish the objective of the combination or conspiracy; (4) the fact that a defendant has previously been convicted of, or adjudged to have been, violating the antitrust laws may warrant indictment for a second offense.[25]

Table 12-1 contains a breakdown of types of cases filed and of the principal complaints made. According to the Attorney General's *Annual Report* for 1967, in fiscal year 1967, 26 civil actions involving price-fixing—as compared with 16 criminal actions—were filed, and so not every case of price-fixing brings with it a criminal charge, despite

[23] Mr. McLaren's remarks were delivered on March 6, 1969.

[24] *Annual Report of the Attorney General for the Fiscal Year 1968* (Washington, D.C.: U.S. Government

Printing Office, 1969), p. 33.

[25] *Report of the Attorney General's National Committee to Study the Antitrust Laws* (Washington, D.C.: U.S. Government Printing Office, 1955), p. 350.

Table 12-1

Comparative Analysis of Antitrust Cases Filed, 1958–1967

	1958	1959	1960	1961	1962	1963	1964	1967
Type of Action								
Civil	32	21	59	40	41	39	41	36
Criminal	22	42	27	22	32	23	23	17
Nature of Complaint								
Price-Fixing	35	49	59	29	58	33	27	42
Mergers	4	6	13	15	10	14	10	7
Monopolization	10	7	9	6	19	5	6	6

Source: Compiled from Annual Reports of the Attorney General (Washington, D.C.: U.S. Government Printing Office).

the Assistant Attorney General's statement. To some extent, the increased use of the civil procedure may be a result of a belief that some violations of the antitrust laws really ought not to be considered criminal offenses; and to some extent it may represent a belief that no real purpose would be served by a criminal action.

If a trial is held, it may last for years. If the question is one which has not previously faced the courts, the lower court's decision may be appealed to the Supreme Court. Throughout, the government will have been represented by a handful of civil service lawyers; the defendant, particularly where it is a major corporation, will probably have been represented by several of the most prominent law firms in the country. When the Supreme Court has finally handed down its decision, the working rules of economic activity and organization will either have been expanded by inclusion or contracted by exclusion. But debate in the learned journals about the decision, however it may stand, will inevitably follow; some of this debate may be helpful in the formulation of new working rules in the future; and some of it may be an empty assertion and counter-assertion about facts.

Jurisdiction. The Antitrust Division is charged with enforcement of the Sherman Act, the Clayton Act, and the criminal sections of the Robinson-Patman Act. It also has various enforcement responsibilities under related legislation. The Federal Trade Commission, too, has jurisdiction under all these laws; for example, (as we will see in Chapter 18 *infra*), the Supreme Court has adopted the view that violation

of the Sherman Act constitutes a method of "unfair competition" under Section 5 of the Federal Trade Commission Act, thereby reading the former into the latter. The Antitrust Division does not ordinarily bring actions under Sections 2 and 3 of the Clayton Act (the price discrimination and tying arrangement sections) unless the case also involves a Sherman Act charge. Cases involving only price discriminations or tying arrangements are thus handled by the Federal Trade Commission. In 1948, the two agencies agreed to keep each other informed in writing before undertaking any investigation, Grand Jury proceeding, or trade practice conference. The object of this agreement was to improve liaison between the two and to avoid duplicate efforts.

The Federal Trade Commission

Personnel and Funds. The Federal Trade Commission consists of the Commission and its subordinate units. The Commission is a quasi-judicial body and makes decisions on the basis of hearings and evidence on complaints. The Office of the General Counsel consists of four divisions. One division represents the Commission in the federal courts; another supervises preparation of consent orders (agreements between a defendant and the Commission as to settlement of a case); another drafts legislation and makes reports on proposed legislation; the fourth administers the Webb-Pomerene Act. In addition to undertaking adjudicatory proceedings based on complaints, the Commission maintains a Bureau of Industry Guidance which administers a program under which various business firms may agree upon trade practice rules; this Bureau also assists businessmen in obtaining advice on how to comply with the antitrust statutes. In other words, the function of this Bureau is to secure voluntary compliance with the law and perform a liaison function with industry.

The personnel of the Office of Hearing Examiners hold initial hearings and make decisions on the basis of evidence pertaining to complaints which have been issued. The decisions of a Hearing Examiner are subject to appeal to, and to review by, the Commission; and the Commission's decisions are, in turn, subject to review in the federal courts. Examples of the use of this procedure will be given in Chapter 18. (The role of a Hearing Examiner is discussed in detail in Chapter 23.)

The Bureau of Economics of the Commission consists of three divisions: (1) the Division of Economic Evidence seeks to assist the enforcement bureaus in the investigation and trial of cases; (2) the Division of Industry Analysis conducts general economic studies and investigations (for example, some of the data on mergers in Chapter 9 of this book were taken from reports by this division); and (3) the Division of Financial Statistics, working in conjunction with the Office of Statistical Standards of the Bureau of the Budget, accumulates financial statistics used to classify various industries and corporations according to their financial characteristics. It is to be noted that the Economics Bureau is not a decision-making unit in the sense in which Hearing Examiners or the commissioners are decision-makers. At the same time, members of this Bureau may have an impact on policy by making appropriate recommendations in the Commission's reports, by making statements in their appearances before Congressional committees, and by the way in which they present data for use by the enforcement bureaus.

Mention must also be made of the work of the Bureau of Restraint of Trade. Members of this Bureau are concerned with activities pertaining to enforcement of Section 5 of the Federal Trade Commission Act and various sections of the Clayton Act, as amended by the Robinson-Patman Act. The Bureau contains separate divisions concerned with problems involving mergers, general trade restraints, discriminatory practices, compliance, and accounting.

The Bureau of Textiles and Furs is concerned with enforcement of legislation pertaining to labeling of wool, textiles, and furs, and sale of flammable fabrics. Finally, the Division of Deceptive Practices is concerned with investigation and trial of all cases involving advertising practices and deceptive practices in general. We will consider the work of these bureaus and their divisions as well as the Commission's enforcement responsibilities in great detail in Chapter 18.

The Federal Trade Commission not only has long had a much larger staff but also has long received considerably larger sums for its operations than the Antitrust Division. For years, there has been a close relationship between the Economics Bureau and both the House Antitrust Subcommittee and the Senate Subcommittee on Antitrust and Monopoly. For example, Dr. John Blair, the chief economist of the Senate subcommittee, was previously an important member of the staff of the Economics Bureau of the Commission. There is little doubt that this close relationship has resulted in the production of various important studies which have been published in the hearings of the Senate subcommittee, some of which have been cited in Chapter 9.

Procedure of the FTC. An extremely useful and highly authoritative statement of the procedures followed by the Federal Trade Commission in enforcing the laws it administers was submitted to the House Committee on Interstate and Foreign Commerce by FTC Chairman Paul Rand Dixon in September 1966. Because it contains an explanation in simple language of the relatively timeless procedures set forth more formally in the FTC's *Rules of Practice*, the relevant portion of his statement is herewith reproduced:

The basic or principal authority which Congress has granted to the Commission is enforcement of section 5(a) of the Federal Trade Commission Act (15 U.S.C. 45 (a)). As you know, this section merely states: "Unfair methods of competition in commerce, and unfair or deceptive acts or practices in commerce, are hereby declared unlawful."

Investigations and inquiries by the Commission to determine whether there are violations of this section, or of any other law administered by the Commission, may be originated upon the request of the President, Congress, governmental agencies, the Attorney General, upon complaints by members of the public or by the Commission upon its own initiative. No particular forms or procedures are required to request such investigations. The only limitation as to investigations, other than those imposed by statute (i.e., the Commission has no jurisdiction over banks), is that the Commission does not initiate investigations, or take actions, upon alleged violations which relate to a private controversy and which do not tend to affect the public adversely.

The Commission encourages voluntary cooperation in its investigations, but where the public interest requires, the Commission may, in any matter investigated, invoke any or all the compulsory processes it is legally authorized to use. Any person under investigation, who is compelled or requested to furnish information or documentary evidence, is advised with respect to the purpose and scope of the investigation.

The Commission may issue subpoenas directing any party to appear before a designated representative of the Commission at a particular time and place to testify or produce documentary evidence or both, relating to any matter under investigation. The Commission also is authorized to conduct investigational hearings (which are to be distinguished from hearings in adjudicative proceedings). Any person compelled to testify in an investigational hearing may be accompanied and represented by counsel in the manner prescribed in the Commission's Rules of Practice.

Under section 5(b) of the Federal Trade Commission Act (15 U.S.C. 45 (b)) the Commission, whenever it has reason to believe that any party is violating section 5(a) of the act and it appears to the Commission that a proceeding by it in respect thereto would be in the interest of the public, is authorized to issue a complaint against the party.

However, where time, the nature of the proceeding and the public interest permit, the Commission serves a notice upon the party of the Commission's determination to institute a formal proceeding against him and with such notice, it sends a form of the complaint which the Commission intends to issue, together with a proposed form of order to cease and desist. Within ten days after the service of the notice, the party may file with the Secretary of the Commission a reply stating whether or not he is interested in having the proceedings disposed of by the entry of a consent order. If the reply is in the negative, or if no reply is filed within the specified time, the complaint will issue and be served in accordance with the rules of the Commission. If, on the other hand, the reply is in the affirmative, the party will be offered

an opportunity to execute an appropriate agreement for consideration by the Commission. The party may appear personally or be represented by proper counsel.

The adjudicative proceedings of the Commission are commenced by the issuance and service of a complaint. The rules of the Commission set forth what must be contained in the complaint, including a requirement that it give notice of the time and place of hearing, which time shall be at least thirty days after service of the complaint.

Where the respondent can make a reasonable showing that he cannot file a responsive answer to a complaint based on the allegations contained therein, he may move for a more definite statement of the charges against him before filing his answer; such motion must be filed within ten days after service of the complaint and shall point out the alleged defects in the complaint.

The respondent named in the complaint has thirty days after service of the complaint to file an answer to the charges contained therein; the Commission's rules set forth what is to be contained in the answer. Should the respondent elect not to contest the allegations of fact set forth in the complaint, he files, in effect, an admission answer, which constitutes a waiver of hearings as to the allegations of the complaint and it, together with the complaint, provides the record on the basis on which the hearing examiner shall file an initial decision.

If the answer is a denial of the allegations of fact contained in the complaint, the "case" then is heard by a hearing examiner of the Commission.

The hearing examiner acts, in a sense, as a trial judge; generally speaking, all motions concerning the case are addressed to him and he makes a ruling thereon. Under certain circumstances, as set forth in the rules of the Commission, interlocutory appeals may be made to the Commission from such rulings.

During the hearings, counsel supporting the complaint has the burden of proving the allegations contained in the complaint.

Within ninety days after completion of the reception of evidence in a proceeding or within such further time as the Commission may allow by order entered in the record, the hearing examiner files an initial decision which includes a statement of (1) findings (with specific page references to principal supporting items of evidence in the record) and conclusions, as well as the reasons or basis therefore, upon all the material issues of fact, law, or discretion presented on the record, and (2) an appropriate order.

Any party to a proceeding may appeal an initial decision to the Commission, or the

Commission itself on its own initiative may place the case on its own docket for review.

Upon appeal from, or review of, an initial decision, the Commission will consider such parts of the record as are cited or as may be necessary to resolve the issues presented; and in addition will, "to the extent necessary or desirable, exercise all the powers which it could have exercised if it had made the initial decision." In rendering its decision, the Commission adopts, modifies or sets aside the findings, conclusions and order contained in the initial decision, and includes in its decision a statement of the reasons for its action.

Any party required by an order of the Commission to cease and desist, may obtain a review of such order in a circuit court of appeals of the United States, within any circuit where the method of competition or the act or practice in question was used or where such person, partnership, or corporation resides or carries on business, by filing in the court, within sixty days from the date of the service of such order, a written petition praying that the order of the Commission be set aside. Upon the filing of the petition, the Commission files with the court a record of the proceeding.

The appellate court has the power to enter a decree, affirming, modifying or setting aside the Commission's order and enforcing the same to the extent that it affirms the Commission's order.

The statute (15 U.S.C. 45 (c)) provides that "The findings of the Commission as to the facts, if supported by evidence, shall be conclusive."

The judgment and decree of the appellate court is final except that it shall be subject to review by the Supreme Court upon certiorari, as provided in section 240 of the Judicial Code.

When an order to cease and desist of the Commission becomes final, either by failure to appeal within the time prescribed by the statute or through affirmance by court action, and it is violated, the respondent is subjected to a fine of $5,000 per day for each violation (15 U.S.C. 45 (1)) which is recovered by a civil action brought by the United States. Furthermore, if an order of the Commission is affirmed and adopted by an appellate court, so that the order of the Commission becomes the order of the court, a violation thereof would constitute "contempt of court."

In addition to the "consent" and "adjudicative" procedures which I have attempted to outline, the Commission, when it has information indicating that the party is engaging in a practice violative of a law administered by the Commission, may, if it deems the public interest will be fully safeguarded thereby, afford such party the opportunity to have the matter disposed of on an informal nonadjudicatory basis. In making this determination the Commission considers (1) the nature and gravity of the alleged violation; (2) the prior record and good faith of the parties involved; and (3) other factors, including, where appropriate, adequate assurance that the practice has been discontinued and will not be resumed.

Also the Commission seeks, wherever possible, by various methods to prevent being required to employ its formal procedures in order to prevent the continuation of acts or practices which may violate any of the laws it administers.

One of the methods is to permit any party to request advice from the Commission as to whether a proposed course of action may violate any of such laws. It is the Commission's policy to consider such requests, and, where practicable, to inform the requesting party of the Commission's views, which will bind the Commission, so that if it changes these views, it will notify the inquiring party and give him an opportunity to conform with the new views. However, a request is considered inappropriate (1) where the course of action is already being followed by the requesting party, (2) where the same or substantially the same course of action is under investigation or is the subject of a current proceeding by the Commission against the requesting party, (3) where the same or substantially the same course of action is under investigation by another governmental agency against the requesting party, or (4) where the proposed course of action is such that an informed decision could be made only after an extensive investigation.

Another method is that the Commission issues "Guides" which "are administrative interpretations of laws administered by the Commission" and have as their purpose guidance of not only the Commission's staff, but also of businessmen in evaluating certain types of practices which may be violative of laws administered by the Commission.

Still another method is the issuance by the Commission of "Trade Practice Rules" which are designed to eliminate and prevent, on a voluntary and industrywide basis, trade practices which are violative of such laws. They seek so interpret and inform businessmen of legal requirements applicable to practices of a particular industry, and thus provide the basis for voluntary and simultaneous abandonment of unlawful practices by industry members.

The rules of the Commission (Sec. 1.63 of the Commission's Rules of Practice) state that for the purpose of carrying out the provisions of the statutes administered by it the Commission "is empowered to promulgate rules and regulations applicable to unlawful trade practices" (Trade Regulation Rules).

These trade regulation rules "express the experience and judgment of the Commission, based on facts of which it has knowledge derived from studies, reports, investigations, hearings, and other proceedings, or within official notice, concerning the substantive requirements of the statutes which it administers."

They "may cover all applications of a particular statutory provision and may be nationwide in effect, or they may be limited to particular areas or industries or to particular product or geographic markets, as may be appropriate."

"Where a trade regulation rule is relevant to any issue involved in an adjudicative proceeding thereafter instituted, the Commission may rely upon the rule to resolve such issue, provided that the respondent shall have been given a fair hearing on the legality and propriety of applying the rule to the particular case.[26]

Political Influences versus Career Employees. The Act creating the Federal Trade Commission provides that not more than three of the five commissioners may be members of the same political party. Moreover, the President may remove commissioners only for "inefficiency, neglect of duty, or malfeasance in office." In a celebrated case, the Supreme Court held in 1935 that this language prevented the President from removing commissioners merely on grounds that he did not share their views.[27] This decision, while consistent with the language of the Act, dramatically illustrates what is probably a mistaken notion that the commission form of regulation is, in general, a "judicial process" completely above politics. As a matter of fact, the realities of the situation are probably otherwise. In recent years, it has become a matter of practice for existing chairmen of commissions to submit their resignations when a new President who did not appoint them takes office. Emmette Redford has noted that, when President Kennedy took office, the "chairmen of each of the commissions, excepting the Board of Governors [of the Federal Reserve], promptly submitted his resignation as chairman" and that, as a result of expiration of terms, death, and resignations, the President was able to appoint in the first year of his

administration "three of five [members] of the FTC," as well as numerous members of other commissions.[28] In the case of the FTC, Corwin Edwards, writing in 1949, emphasized the bipartisan character of the commission but deplored the lack of other qualifications of commissioners.[29]

That the philosophical preconceptions of individual commissioners do affect the working rules established by the Commission in some cases is clear. An example can be found in the various positions which were taken by the Commission in 1941 and 1951 with respect to the policy to be applied under Section 2(b) of the Robinson-Patman Act. The precise question involved was whether or not a seller may cut prices in a discriminatory way "in good faith to meet the equally low price of a competitor" irrespective of the effect of the price discrimination upon competition or of whether or not the effect of the price discrimination tends to create a monopoly. This question will be further considered in Chapter 16. For the moment, it is enough to note that in 1941 the Commission took the position that "good faith" was a complete defense; but held in 1946, with one member dissenting, that the defense that the discrimination was made "in good faith to meet the equally low price of a competitor" could be overthrown by a showing that the discrimination also injured competition.[30] The Commission order was upheld by the Circuit Court of Appeals.[31] Subsequently, in June 1949, the Commission stated in a letter to a Congressional committee that its members believed it would be preferable to make the "good faith meeting of competition" a complete defense.[30] Obviously, the Commission had again changed its position.

Thereafter, in 1951, the Supreme Court held, with Justices Reed, Black, and Vinson dissenting, that the defense was a complete defense—meaning that a price discrimination by a seller "in good faith to meet the equally low price of a competitor" was not unlawful under the statute, even if that

[26] *Fair Packaging and Labeling Act, op. cit.*, Hearings, pp. 218–221.

[27] *Humphrey's Executor* v. *United States*, 295 U.S. 602 (1935).

[28] Emmette S. Redford, "The President and the Regulatory Commissions," *Texas Law Review* (December, 1965), pp. 288–321, at p. 314.

[29] Corwin Edwards, *Maintaining Competition* (New York: McGraw-Hill Book Co., Inc., 1949), p. 302.

[30] 43 FTC 56 (1946).

[31] *Standard Oil Co.* v. *Federal Trade Commission*, 173 F. 2d 210 (1949).

[32] *Study of Monopoly Power, op. cit.*, (82d Cong., 1st sess., 1951), Serial No. 1, Part 5, pp. 2–3.

discrimination injured competition or tended to create a monopoly.[33]

The next episode was the introduction of legislation in Congress to codify the holding of the Supreme Court in the case in question. In 1951, the Subcommittee on Study of Monopoly Power of the House Judiciary Committee held hearings on the proposed legislation. Commissioner Stephen J. Spingarn delivered a prepared statement to the subcommittee which included the following:

The Commission can see no reason why the difficulties arising from an unqualified good faith defense which were pointed out in 1934 in the chain store report are not equally important in 1951. To reaffirm the good-faith proviso as a complete defense, regardless of the effects which may flow from discriminations, again raises the anomaly of monopoly power being permitted to use the same weapons to maintain itself which are denied to others for fear of creating a monopoly.[34]

In the question and answer session following the delivery of the prepared statement, there occurred this interchange:

MR. STEVENS. [Associate Counsel] Just one other question, Mr. Commissioner. Is it true that in 1949 the Commission unanimously expressed the opinion that on balance good faith should be a complete defense under the Robinson-Patman Act?

MR SPINGARN. That is correct. Of course it was a different Commission. There have been three changes in the Commission since that date.

MR. STEPHENS. And the view you express now is that of the three new Commissioners?

MR. SPINGARN. The view that I am expressing now is of the three new Commissioners, Chairman Mead, Commissioner Carson and myself. It is partly but not wholly shared by Commissioner Ayres.

MR. STEPHENS. I understand. . . .[35]

The dissenting opinion in the *Standard Oil* case carries a footnote pointing out that there was a difference of opinion [when the 1949 statement was made to Congress] between the commissioners and "other officials" of the Commission. Apparently, between 1951 and 1955 (with another change in personnel and a new Chairman appointed by President Eisenhower), the Commission again changed its position. The *Report* of the Attorney General's National Committee to Study the Antitrust Laws contains the following statement without citation of any authority: "As the Federal Trade Commission has recently recommended to Congress, 'the right to meet a lower price which a competitor is offering to a customer, when this is done in good faith, is the essence of competitive economy.'"[36] Since Edward F. Howery was Chairman of the FTC at the time the *Report* was published and was also a member of the Attorney General's National Committee, and since there were three FTC representatives named to maintain liaison with the Committee, the statement must surely represent the position of the Commission in 1955, when its personnel had again changed. Thus, the "expertness" of the commissioners does not exist in a vacuum and is not completely free from the attitudes which they hold relative to the private concentration of economic power. It is not a matter of "purely scientific economic analysis." A view that Section 2(b) constitutes an absolute defense—that is to say, that price discriminations made "in good faith to meet the equally low price of a competitor" are permissible without regard to their effect on competition or to their tendency to create monopoly—obviously must rest on a view that destruction of competition and tendencies toward monopoly are not to be viewed with any alarm. The same view, of course, lay behind the conflict between the political appointees and the civil servants in the case of the consent decree in the A. T. and T. case discussed earlier in this chapter. And whether the one view or the other is dominant at the policy-making level in a given agency at a given time does depend, in no small degree, on the President's choice of policy-making appointees to such agencies. This is not to say that either the Antitrust Division or the Federal Trade Commission are political footballs, nor that Hearing Examiners of the latter are not independent. But an idealized conception of either of these agencies as being completely free from the political philosophy of those dominant in the Executive Branch

---

[33] *Standard Oil Co. (Indiana) v. Federal Trade Commission*, 340 U.S. 231 (1951).

[34] *Study of Monopoly Power, op. cit.* (82d Cong., 1st sess., 1951), Serial No. 1, Part 5, p. 109.

[35] *Ibid.*, p. 122.

[36] *Report of the Attorney General's National Committee to Study the Antitrust Laws, op. cit.*, p. 181.

is misleading, if not dangerous, since it can lead to conclusions based on false assumptions. Our discussion shows that political influences make themselves felt through the mechanism of the President's power of appointment of men to key policy-making positions, despite the independence of the Hearing Examiners. In this regard, it is useful to recall that the question of interference by a Congressional committee with the Federal Trade Commission's decision-making process was raised by the defendant in the *Pillsbury* case in its appeal from a Federal Trade Commission order issued in the case of a complaint based on a merger and Section 7 of the Clayton Act as amended. This particular question and the *Pillsbury* case in which it was raised have already been discussed in Chapter 6 and, therefore, further discussion of the matter is unnecessary at this point.

Volume of Complaints, Investigations, and Informal Settlements. In 1964, the Commission received for review scripts of 511,102 radio and television commercials and 267,405 pages of printed advertisements. About 43,000 advertisements were selected for further action. In addition, it received about 4,600 letters requesting complaint forms, issued 161 cease and desist orders, filed 129 formal complaints, and received 298 assurances of compliance which it considered adequate.[37] During 1965, the Commission reviewed 632,167 radio and television commercials and 265,442 printed advertisements. Of the total, over 34,000 were set aside to be investigated further; of these, 6,089 advertisements for alcoholic beverages were referred by the Commission to the Internal Revenue Service which has special responsibilities in this area.[38] In recent years the Commission has sought to settle cases by means of consent proceedings rather than by formal adjudication. In fiscal year 1967, there were 96 cases on the Hearing Examiners' dockets, and 459 "days" were devoted to evidentiary hearings and prehearing conferences.

There has probably been more agreement within the Commission concerning matters of falsehood and deception than with respect to questions involving monopolistic practices. Everybody, apparently, is opposed to sin and lies. But, as we will see in Chapter 18 *infra*, there have been disagreements between the Commission and the courts concerning the power of the Commission under the F.T.C. Act to require positive statements or "informative" advertising, rather than only to prohibit false or misleading or deceptive statements.[39] Several examples illustrating this problem will be provided in Chapter 18.

D. STATE ANTITRUST LAWS

In 1934, the Federal Trade Commission published a comprehensive survey of state constitutional and legislative provisions pertaining to antitrust.[40] In this survey, the Commission reported:

Pursuant to the directions contained in the constitutions of many of the States, or in acquiescence to popular demand, 41 States enacted laws relating to monopolies, some of which provide penalties for violations. The statutory provisions are exceedingly numerous and range from the broad generalities of a statute which denounces agreements and combinations, whether reasonable or unreasonable, to the narrower application made by States which have singled out particular industries or products for special protection against monopolies. The Federal antitrust laws have served in many instances as models for the antitrust laws in the several States.[41]

Contemporary writers are not in full agreement with respect to the effectiveness or usefulness of state antitrust laws. Typical of the writers who take an optimistic view of the state antitrust approach is Earl W. Kintner, a former Chairman of the Federal Trade Commission under President Eisenhower. Kintner has asserted that antitrust enforcement at the local level provides opportunities for education and experimentation.[42]

Less optimistic about the desire of state employees to apply their antitrust laws

[37] *Annual Report of the Federal Trade Commission for the Fiscal Year 1964* (Washington, D.C.: U.S. Government Printing Office, 1965), p. 16.

[38] *Annual Report of the Federal Trade Commission for the Fiscal Year 1965*, pp. 13–14.

[39] See, for example, *Alberty et. al. v. Federal Trade Commission*, 182 F. 2d 36 (1950).

[40] *Final Report on the Chain Store Investigation, op. cit.*, p. 82 ff.

[41] *Ibid.*, pp. 83–84.

[42] Earl W. Kintner, *An Antitrust Primer* (New York: The MacMillan Co., 1964), pp. 157–58.

effectively is Mark Massel, who has re-marked that such local laws may actually be used to eliminate competition.[43] The question of the use of the state's police power to restrict competition raised by Massel has, of course, already been discussed in Chapter 7 of this book. State antitrust laws have in fact probably been less important than federal laws for two reasons: (1) given the size of some contemporary business associations and the fact that they may operate in several states simultaneously, it is obviously not possible for any single state to exercise effective control; (2) state laws represent the interests of regional groups and so does the enforcement of state legislation; federal law, on the other hand, is not usually geared to the satisfaction of the demands of a particular state-regional group. The grass roots experimentation advocated by Kintner may become grass roots protection, a point he ignores but which Massel has emphasized. One ought not to be too optimistic concerning the future effectiveness of state laws, given their past history and the nature of "grass roots" politics. A dramatic example of the inability of the states to deal with antitrust problems in the cases of defendants engaged in interstate commerce is provided by the case of *State* v. *Milwaukee Braves*,[42] decided by the Supreme Court of Wisconsin in 1966. This court held that the State of Wisconsin was not entitled to seek an injunction under the Wisconsin antitrust statute to prevent the charter of the Milwaukee Braves baseball team from being transferred from Milwaukee to Atlanta, Georgia, primarily on grounds that the State of Wisconsin could not regulate the interstate commerce involved. The Wisconsin Supreme Court also pointed out that under existing interpretations of the Sherman Act by the Supreme Court of the United States, organized baseball had been exempted from federal antitrust prosecution. The effect of the Wisconsin decision, given the state of federal law on the subject, was to leave organized baseball immune from prosecution under either federal or state laws. (In passing, it may be noted that professional basketball and ice hockey have not been exempted from prosecution under the Sherman Act, and that the situation with respect to the position of organized baseball is thus a paradoxical one.)

As has been noted earlier in this chapter, the McCarran Act exempted the insurance industry from the Sherman Act and left the problem of regulation to the individual states. In 1967, the Staff of the House Antitrust Subcommittee published a report of its study of the automobile insurance industry. This report contains material which strongly supports Massel's position and concludes in part:

. . . by any objective standard, performance of the automobile insurance business in the United States is unsatisfactory. The system is slow, incomplete, and expensive. The companies and organizations involved in furnishing this service to the public in many respects do a poor job.[45]

This study is worth careful attention on the part of anyone who is particularly interested in the problem of state regulation as a substitute for federal antitrust enforcement.

Our survey of the basic federal and state legislation has now been completed. In the next chapter we will examine the extent to which economic theory has provided or can provide a standard or norm for enforcement of such laws. In subsequent chapters, as has been noted, we will examine in detail the content given by the courts to the legislative enactments described in this chapter. That is, in subsequent chapters we will examine the ways in which the courts have either limited or added to the basic statutory working rules.

[43] Mark S. Massel, *Competition and Monopoly* (Washington, D.C.: The Brookings Institution, 1962), pp. 64–65.

[44] 144 N.W. 2d 1 (1966).

[45] *Automobile Insurance Study* (Report by the Staff of the House Antitrust Subcommittee, 90th Cong., 1st sess., 1967) (Washington, D.C.: U.S. Government Printing Office, 1967), p. 73.

Concepts of "Workable Competition"

Two phrases are today often employed by economists in their discussions of the antitrust laws: "workable competition" and "the workable economy." The first is more widely used and was invented by J. M. Clark, the second by J. K. Galbraith. This chapter examines what these phrases mean to different economists. We will see that although different economists attach different meanings to these words, what most writers who use these phrases have in common is: (1) a recognition of the fact that the model of perfect competition does not provide a norm for enforcement of the antitrust laws; and (2) a belief in the instrumental or pragmatic approach to problem solving rather than a belief in the existence of absolute standards. At the same time, although numerous writers also recognize that economic variables are not the only ones to be taken into account in dealing with problems under the antitrust laws, many explain the meanings which they themselves attach to the phrases "workable competition" and "the workable economy" largely in the professional, technical language of price theory.

This chapter consists of three major subdivisions: (1) the first contains a brief explanation of the origin of the phrase "workable competition" and a consideration of

the way in which this phrase was used in the *Report* of the Attorney General's National Committee to Study the Antitrust Laws; (2) the second section discusses various meanings which have been given to the words "workable competition" and "the workable economy" by economists; and (3) the third section consists of some brief concluding remarks.

A. "WORKABLE COMPETITION": ORIGIN OF THE PHRASE AND ITS USE IN THE REPORT OF THE ATTORNEY GENERAL'S NATIONAL COMMITTEE

In 1933, Professors E. H. Chamberlin and Joan Robinson developed independently economic theories which pointed to the conclusion that the concepts of "perfect competition" and "pure monopoly" represented extreme or limiting cases and that the real world consisted largely of cases involving various degrees of "competition and monopoly intermingled." The development of these theories produced a situation from which various points of departure were possible. On the one hand, one could accept the implications of these theories to the effect that, in the real world, firms either made profits which were not competed away or else that they made only "normal" profits but produced at a higher than least average cost. Thus one could argue that the antitrust laws ought to be stringently applied to create conditions of perfect competition under which resource allocation would be "optimized" in accordance with the theory of static welfare economics. On the other hand, one could also point to the purely static nature of these new theories and argue that in a dynamic world the existing situation was a "reasonable" one. Or, one could reject both these positions and take the view that a new approach was needed to the problems of antitrust. It was the choice of the last of these three ways which led Professor J. M. Clark in 1940 to write an essay called "Toward a Concept of Workable Competition."

J. M. Clark and the Origin of the Phrase: "Workable Competition"

In his 1940 essay, Clark rejected the use of the *model* of perfect competition as a standard for application of the antitrust laws and argued that a more realistic "standard" should be employed. This proposed "standard" he called "workable competition." Clark defined "workable competition" as a situation of:

. . . rivalry in selling goods in which each selling unit normally seeks maximum net revenue, under conditions such that the price or prices each seller can charge are effectively limited by the free option of the buyer to buy from a rival seller or sellers of what we think as 'the same' product, necessitating an effort by each seller to equal or exceed the attractiveness of the others' offerings to a sufficient number of buyers to accomplish the end in view.[1]

(Clark's later views will be discussed in the second part of this chapter.)

"Workable Competition" in the Hands of the Attorney General's Committee

Fifteen years later, the *Report* of the Attorney General's National Committee to Study the Antitrust Laws described the concept of "workable" competition as—

. . . a kind of economists's "Rule of Reason"— not, of course, to be confused with the legal rule of reason, but analogous to it in the sense that it is also an acknowledgment of the inevitability of the exercise of human judgment and discretion in classifying different forms of economic behavior.[2]

Thereupon the Committee proceeded to discuss a list of factors which, in its opinion, might or might not—depending on the facts in a particular case, and depending on other relevant considerations and other qualifications—be significant to a decision as to whether or not "workable competition" existed in that case. The factors included: (1) the number of sellers; (2) opportunity for entry; (3) independence of rivals; (4) predatory preclusive practices; (5) rate of growth of the industry or market; (6) character of market incentives to competitive moves; (7) product differentiation and product homogeneity; (8) price discrimination. The list includes a conglomeration of items pertaining to market structure, to performance of a firm, and to particular actions of a firm; and the discussion in the *Report* of the items in the list is a masterpiece of contingent statements.

Professor J. M. Clark himself commented in the *Report* on this list by saying:

. . . The attempt to select economic concepts which are usefully relevant to antitrust problems results in a presentation which is selective, not only as to concepts included, but as to views held by economists on these concepts; the difficulty arises from the fact that some key concepts—such as substantial lessening of competition are both economic and legal.[3]

Similar views were expressed by some other members of the Committee. Thus, the *Report* also contains this statement:

A few members stress that the "doctrine" of workable competition is only a rough and ready judgment by some economists, each for himself, that a particular industry is performing reasonably well—presumably relative to alternative industrial arrangements which are practically attainable. There are no objective criteria of workable competition, and such criteria as are proffered are at best intuitively reasonable modifications of the rigorous and abstract criteria of perfect competition.[4]

---

[1] J. M. Clark, "Toward a Concept of Workable Competition," *American Economic Review*, Vol. XXX (June, 1940), pp. 241–256, at p. 243.

[2] *Report of the Attorney General's National Committee to Study the Antitrust Laws* (Washington, D.C.: U.S. Government Printing Office, 1955), p. 320.

[3] *Ibid.*, p. 317.

[4] *Ibid.*, p. 339.

George Stigler, who was also a member of the Committee, expressed his "admiration for the felicity of" the language of these few members and also remarked that according to his understanding of the doctrine it included the proposition that:

To determine whether any industry is workably competitive, therefore, simply have any good graduate student write his dissertation on the industry and render a verdict. It is crucial to this test, of course, that no second graduate student be allowed to study the industry.[5]

A copy of the *Report* of the Attorney General's Committee was distributed to every federal judge in 1955. It has had some influence on antitrust decisions and is still cited in some opinions. Testimony with respect to the background of some of the Members of the Attorney General's Committee given before the Select Senate Small Business Committee is of some interest in this regard. Angus McDonald, representing the National Farmers Union, submitted a list of Members of the Attorney General's Committee and some of their affiliations to the Select Senate Committee. Thereupon the following statement was made by Senator Long:

Just this question is in my mind: I understand that 25 of 61 on this committee were attorneys who had represented the larger concerns in defending against the enforcement of antitrust laws, and, of course, a lot of these people were not attorneys. An attorney could have been involved one way or the other. Out of those who were attorneys, the great majority were those who had been on the defense side, the side defending against the enforcement of the antitrust laws.

There is nothing illegal about it, and I don't believe it would be violating anything in the code of legal ethics, but it does seem to me that it is rather inappropriate to sit on a committee where there is as much representation on one side of the issue. Of course, it may be that those people may have also had clients who are small people too, but if their activities have been against the enforcement of these laws, that would be some indication as to where their sentiments would be.

Here is the point that strikes me forcefully. Not to single out any particular man, but let us assume that I was the attorney for one particular large corporation, make it General Motors, make it just any one, but if I had defended on the side against the enforcement of the antitrust laws day in and day out, advising them day in and day out how they could avoid being prosecuted by those laws, it stands to reason that if I still represented them it would be rather inappropriate for me to be in the position of sitting on a committee to exercise more or less legislative responsibilities to vote to recommend what the law should be.[6]

A separate, privately-printed dissenting opinion by Professor of Law Louis B. Schwarz (Pennsylvania) was also reproduced by the Select Senate Committee. It asserted that "The Majority Report [of the Attorney General's National Committee] would weaken the antitrust laws in a number of respects, and, even more important, it fails to adopt necessary measures for strengthening the law." Indeed, "on 30 specific issues discussed in this dissent, the Report takes a position inimical to competition." The reason the dissenting opinion was privately printed appears in its opening statement, which reads as follows:

This dissenting opinion was printed and released independently, because the co-chairmen [Professor S. Chesterfield Oppenheim of the University of Michigan Law School and Assistant Attorney General in Charge of Antitrust Stanley N. Barnes, an Eisenhower appointee] of the committee refused to publish it as submitted. Instead the opinion has been dismembered, condensed and distributed through 350 pages of the majority report.

This frustrates the main purpose of the dissent, which was to demonstrate that the net effect of most of the interpretations and changes recommended by the majority is to weaken rather than strengthen the antitrust laws. The co-chairmen justify this unauthorized mutilation of the dissent on the ground that other committee members were content to have their differences noted at particular points in the report. This handling of dissents on particular issues fairly records the position of those who are in the main satisfied with the report. It does not fairly present the views of those who differ with its basic philosophy.

The following members of the committee have expressed concurrence in the central thesis

---

[5] George Stigler, "Comments on the Report of the Attorney General's Committee on Antitrust Policy," *American Economic Review*, Vol. XLVI (May, 1956), pp. 504–507, at p. 504.

[6] *Report of the Attorney General's National Committee*

to Study the Antitrust Laws (Hearings before the Senate Select Committee on Small Business, 84th Cong., 1st sess.) (Washington, D.C.: U.S. Government Printing Office, 1955), Part I, pp. 193–194.

of the dissenting opinion, that the report inadequately deals with the problem of bigness and that most of the specific recommendations tend to weaken rather than strengthen the antitrust laws. Each has important differences on some points, as noted in the majority report:

Prof. Walter Adams, Michigan State University

Prof. Alfred Kahn, Cornell University

Prof. Eugene V. Rostow, Yale Law School

Prof. George J. Stigler, Columbia University

In addition, Prof. J. M. Clark of Columbia University, and David W. Robinson, Esq. of Columbia, S.C., have noted their agreement with major segments of the dissent.[7]

Stigler's disenchantment with the Committee's concept of "workable competition" has been a fact of life for many (but not all) economists since 1955 when the *Report* was first issued. Among the economists on the Committee whose names were not affixed to the dissent were Professor Clare Griffin of the School of Business of the University of Michigan, Professor M. A. Adelman (whose studies of concentration of economic power have been discussed in a preceding chapter) and Dean Emeritus E. T. Grether of the School of Business of the University of California. (Adelman's comment on the dissent appears in 1 *Antitrust Bulletin* 71.) Professor George Stocking, on the other hand, had declined an invitation to serve on the Attorney General's Committee on grounds that he was at the time of the invitation engaged "in testing . . . [the *Report's*] hypothesis that the concept of workable competition administered under a rule of reason provided an acceptable standard in antitrust proceedings" and Stocking wished to be free from any restraints in drawing his conclusions.[8] (Eventually, we will see, he found the hypothesis unsatisfactory.)

What the critics of the concept of "workable competition," as this phrase is used in the *Report* of the Attorney General's National Committee, really object to is the fact that the phrase has been used in the *Report* as a rationalization of recommendations which would lead to changes in the laws, changes which—as we will see in later chapters—would operate to reduce the scope of application of these laws or to reduce the power of enforcement agencies. The specific language of the *Report* was itself a compromise—as every committee report always is—but, given the heavy representation of some social interests to the exclusion or very light representation of others, the compromises were largely *among* those who were in favor of weak rather than strong enforcement of the antitrust laws rather than *between* those who favored strong and those who favored weak enforcement of the laws. On the other hand, economists are themselves not in agreement as to what meaning is to be given to the phrase "workable competition" as evidenced by the fact that not all of the economists on the Committee signed the dissent prepared by Professor Schwarz. It is to the various competing meanings which different economists attach to this phrase that attention is given next.

B. VARIOUS MEANINGS ATTACHED TO "WORKABLE COMPETITION" BY ECONOMISTS

As has just been noted, the meaning given to the phrase "workable competition" by a majority of the Attorney General's Committee is but one of many which can be given to these words, particularly if they are mistakenly looked upon as defining some sort of external or absolute standard or norm for antitrust enforcement. At least six different approaches to the use of these words can be found in the works of economists (and there may be more than this number). These include the following: (1) Some economists have treated the concept of "workable competition" as imposing a test on the *structure* of the market. This group includes those who are inclined to accept the model of pure or perfect competition as a norm for antitrust, as well as those who do not believe that the market power of a firm is independent of its absolute size and those who believe this test

---

[7] *Ibid.*, p. 258. (The dissent is reproduced at pages 258–275; it also appears in 1 *Antitrust Bulletin* 37 (1955), together with a comment on the dissent by M. A. Adelman.)

[8] George Stocking, "On the Concept of Workable Competition as an Antitrust Guide," 2 *Antitrust Bulletin* 3 (1956), at p. 3. This article contains a useful history of the Committee, including the roles played by and views of Professor S. C. Oppenheim and Attorney Blackwell Smith, whose views were, in turn, adopted by the Business Advisory Council of the Department of Commerce.

to be more appropriate than any other in a political democracy. Among these economists, one may list Professors Willard Mueller, Corwin Edwards, Walter Adams, Horace Gray, and, perhaps, Ben Lewis. (2) Others have looked upon the concept, particularly as it has been developed in the *Report*, as imposing a test upon the *performance* of the firm. An example is Professor Clare Griffin of the University of Michigan School of Business. (3) Still others, like Dean Edward Mason—who in 1937 anticipated Clark's development of the concept[9]—and some of his former students have sought to combine the structure and performance tests. The position of this group is closely related to the traditional neoclassical position held by writers like Professor Shorey Peterson—who has argued that "present theories of workable competition, even when stretched to make room for elements of countervailing power" merely "particularize older thinking regarding feasible market operation under dynamic conditions"—especially the approach of Alfred Marshall and earlier works of J. B. Clark.[10] (4) Another group has rejected the concept of "workable competition," especially the sense in which the phrase has been used in the *Report* of the Attorney General's Committee, as a basis for antitrust enforcement and has proposed various types of tests to be used either in conjunction with or as alternatives to those of structure and performance. This group includes Professors Myron W. Watkins, Alfred E. Kahn, Joel B. Dirlam, George W. Stocking, and some of the writings of Carl Kaysen. (5) Still others, like J. A. Schumpeter and J. M. Clark (before their deaths), and David Lilienthal have advocated *dynamic performance* tests of the type Peterson has argued were already apparent in the works of neoclassical writers; and some, like J. K. Galbraith, have sought to combine the concept of "dynamic performance" with other concepts of their own (like "countervailing power") to produce a concept of "the workable economy." These concepts of "dynamic performance" and of "the workable economy" are really explicit value judgments to the effect that economic progress will proceed in the

United States at a faster rate if the working rules of economic activity and organization are such that private concentrations of economic power are left undisturbed, or even fostered, than if they are broken down. But advocates of the market structure test like Horace Gray argue equally forcefully that their test, too, leads to "the workable economy." Finally (6) still other economists have rejected all these ideas and tests and have tried to substitute a "macroeconomic approach" which, we will see upon closer inspection later, is really merely another performance test in which different objectives are postulated from those postulated in the more traditional performance tests. The "macroeconomic approach" is an approach taken largely by economic theorists particularly interested in macroeconomic models and in growth models. Among those taking this approach are some mathematical economists, who argue that the problem of determination of political and philosophical objectives cannot be settled by "scientific means" and who therefore conduct their analyses in terms of purely economic variables by *assuming* that the philosophical and political objectives have been met when the macroeconomic economic objectives (full employment, price stability, and so on) selected by them for maximization have been met. An example is C. E. Ferguson.

These various points of view will be discussed next. What they have in common, as Professor Stocking has remarked, is a recognition of the fact that "personal judgments obviously enter into the evaluation." What is perhaps unfortunate, however, is that not all writers make explicit the various competing social policy considerations which they are reconciling or ignoring in taking their positions; instead, many still state that they are restricting themselves to a consideration of "purely economic variables" in their writings and state their conclusions largely in the professional language of price theory even while they admit that other considerations must be taken into account. An exception to this procedure, however, exists in some of the works of writers like Walter Adams and Corwin

---

[9] Edward S. Mason, "Monopoly in Law and Economics," 47 *Yale Law Journal* 34 (1937).

[10] Shorey Peterson, "Antitrust and the Classic

Model," *American Economic Review*, Vol. XLVII (March, 1957), pp. 60–78, at p. 63.

Edwards, both advocates of the market structure test, and the problem has also been recognized by Shorey Peterson in his statement that "the nature of policy problems forces us back toward the looser approach of earlier economists, and indeed of competent lawyers and judges."[11] It is to a more detailed consideration of the various views outlined above that attention must now be given.

(1) The Market Structure Test of "Workable Competition"

It has been noted that emphasis upon market structure as a guideline for antitrust enforcement appeared as early as 1937 in an article by Dean Edward Mason; but today probably its best known advocates are Corwin Edwards (who it will be recalled from Chapter 9 served for many years as Chief Economist for the Federal Trade Commission) and Walter Adams.

Corwin Edwards. Edwards has pointed out that a market structure test does not "necessarily aim at an atomized competition such as was envisaged by the older economic theory." It is based not only on "dislike of restriction of output and of one-sided bargaining power, but also desire to prevent excessive concentration of wealth and power, desire to keep open the channels of opportunity, and concern lest monopolistic controls of business lead to political oligarchy."[12] Edwards and Adams are examples of those exceptional economists who do not rely exclusively on the language of price theory.

The market structure approach recognizes the interdependence of economic and political activities; it does not rest upon the logical positivist conditions of static welfare economics; nor does it invoke the natural law concept of an "invisible hand" to guarantee attainment of an "optimum." Neither does it seek an atomistic dissolution of existing business firms into a physically impossible large number of plants, none of which exerts any influence on prices, and each of which produces the same product.

This conception of antitrust policy has as its principal aim "to prevent the defects of social organization from being made worse by a deliberate adoption of restrictive policies designed to serve private interests." It does not rule out the use of "noncompetitive processes regulated by the state" in cases where these are deemed more appropriate to attain the immediate end-in-view. Although certain general desirable structural characteristics can be formulated, the application of these to any specific industry or firm can only be determined on a case-by-case basis. These structural characteristics have been identified by Edwards as follows:

1. There must be an appreciable number of sources of supply and an appreciable number of potential customers for the same product or service. Suppliers and customers do not need to be so numerous that each trader is entirely without influence, but their number must be great enough that persons on the other side of the market may readily turn away from any particular trader and may find a variety of other alternatives.

2. No trader must be so powerful as to be able to coerce his rivals, nor so large that the remaining traders lack the capacity to take over at least a substantial portion of his trade.

3. Traders must be responsive to incentives of profit and loss; that is, they must not be so large, so diversified, so devoted to political rather than commercial purposes, so subsidized, or otherwise so unconcerned with results in a particular market that their policies are not affected by ordinary commercial incentives arising out of that market.

4. Matters of commercial policy must be decided by each trader separately without agreement with his rivals.

5. New traders must have opportunity to enter the market without handicap other than that which is automatically created by the fact that the others are already well established there.

6. Access by traders on one side of the market to those on the other side of the market must be unimpaired except by obstacles not deliberately introduced, such as distance or ignorance of the available alternatives.

7. There must be no substantial preferential status within the market for any important trader or group of traders on the basis of law, politics, or commercial alliances.[13]

---

[11] *Ibid.*, p. 77.

[12] Corwin Edwards, *Maintaining Competition* (New York: McGraw-Hill Book Co., Inc., 1949), p. 9.

[13] From MAINTAINING COMPETITION by Corwin Edwards, pp. 9–10. Copyright 1949 by McGraw-Hill, Inc. Used with permission of McGraw-Hill Book Company.

In general, the list aims at the establishment of a situation in which the behavior of buyers and sellers within any *particular* market is subject to the checks and balances provided by the existence of *real* alternatives available to each of them. The market structure test thus places primary emphasis upon the limitation of economic power in the hands of private individuals. That is, it seeks to limit the existence of such private power by subjecting it to a system of private checks and balances while, at the same time, it seeks to employ governmental power to insure the continued existence of that system of private checks and balances.

Although some critics of the market structure test have interpreted it to state a norm which infers "economic performance" from market structure, this inference is only partly warranted. As Edwards has pointed out, "historically" the aims "antedate conceptions of the economic equilibrium and of the role of competition in achieving it." It seeks as much to secure a distribution of economic power subject to checks and balances for political reasons as it seeks a distribution of economic power subject to checks and balances for economic reasons.

Walter Adams. The market structure test thus takes the view that the absolute size of a firm must be considered and raises the question of the extent to which conglomerate firms may exercise, in one market, power based on their operations in unrelated markets. Moreover, the market structure test is conceived of as only one aspect of a total policy; in the hands of Walter Adams, other aspects of a national policy of achieving a distribution of economic power involve encouragement of small business activities, use of government procurement and surplus property disposal programs in such a way as to encourage establishment of competing firms, and imposition of taxes on advertising.[14] Nor, in the hands of Adams and Horace Gray, has action of the government to promote monopoly escaped analysis.[15]

Despite the fact that the advocates of the market structure approach place emphasis upon the significance of economic power, very few of them can be classified as belonging to the "Chicago School" of economists. Members of the latter currently tend to minimize the extent of the concentration of economic power in the hands of business and to direct their attack against the use of government power *per se* as well as against labor unions (*c. f.* the Appendix to this book), but the market structure advocates point to the concentration of economic power in the hands of business firms and argue that the economic power attributed to American unions is "more illusory than it is real." Instead of decrying or ignoring the use of government power, they realistically seek to call attention to cases in which it is currently being used to promote anticompetitive practices and seek to have it used in a different way to promote competition. Thus, Adams in 1949 advocated adoption of federal legislation under which corporations with assets in excess of $25,000,000 or corporations controlling more than 10 percent of the supply of a good or service in interstate commerce would be required to register with the Securities and Exchange Commission and file data to:

... enable the Commission to determine, case by case, whether the interests of investors and consumers, the public interest, and the maintenance of effective competition are adversely affected by the corporate structure of the firm, the firm's position in the industry, and the business policies and practices pursued by such firm.

... If the Commission finds that, in the light of section 1 and the standards provided in section 8, the efficiency of a concentrated industrial unit could be enhanced or the effectiveness of competition promoted, the Commission would issue an order dissolving the company into its component parts or requiring the divestiture thereby or divorcement therefrom of a portion of such company's assets or securities.[16]

This proposal, first made in about 1949, antedates an advocacy by Carl Kaysen and Donald Turner of the establishment of a

[14] Walter Adams (ed.), *The Structure of American Industry* (3rd ed.; New York: The Macmillan Co., 1961), pp. 554–560. See also his, "The 'Rule of Reason': Workable Competition or Workable Monopoly?", 63 *Yale L. J.* 348, 1954.

[15] Walter Adams and Horace M. Gray, *Monopoly in America: The Government as Promoter* (New York:

The Macmillan Co., 1955).

[16] Testimony of Walter Adams in *Study of Monopoly Power* (Hearings before the House Subcommittee on Study of Monopoly Power, 81st Cong., 1st sess.) (Washington, D.C.: U.S. Government Printing Office, 1949), Serial No. 14, Part 2–B, pp. 1313–1314.

rebuttable presumption based on market shares (particularly in merger cases) in antitrust actions.

(2) The "Pure" Economic Performance Test of "Workable Competition"

A leading advocate of the "pure" economic performance test has been Professor Clare Griffin of the School of Business of the University of Michigan. He has stated his criteria in the following language:

(1) Is the industry (or company) efficient? (2) Is it progressive? (3) Does it show a reasonable and socially useful profit pattern? (4) Does it have as high a degree of freedom of entry as the nature of the industry permits? (5) Is it well suited to serve national defense needs?[17]

The structuralist, Corwin Edwards, has flatly rejected tests such as the one stated by Griffin by saying:

If the test of social performance could be successfully applied, its application would be, not a new way to enforce competition, but a substitute for the safeguards of competition. Under the policy of competition, business behavior is free from government interference so long as competition is not itself impaired. The government's right to intervene is limited strictly to the scope necessary to maintain the system of competitive checks and balances. Under the standard of social performance, however, any business act would be forbidden if it appeared to the government to be detrimental to the public good. In the application of such a standard, the government's right of investigation and of intervention would necessarily be unlimited. The power to dissolve an enterprise or to enjoin its conduct if its acts were disapproved would give the government, in practice, authority to guide and advise business. The result would be a new and pervasive kind of government control. It would be a long step, not toward competition, but away from private enterprise.[18]

Since Edwards wrote, White House pressure on the steel, aluminum, and copper industries to prevent price increases during the Kennedy and Johnson administrations are examples of his predictions come true. Obviously, the use of governmental power to determine policies of price administration in large basic industries must inevitably produce a reaction on the part of such industries to obtain a definitive voice in the use of such power.

(3) "Reconciliation" of the Structure and Performance Tests

Edward Mason. Edward Mason has long advocated the use of a combination of the market structure and performance tests. In his view, these tests are not unrelated. Thus he wrote in 1949:

... Should it [public policy] attempt to bring about a structure of industrial markets and a set of business practices such that the scope of action of individual firms is severely limited by the action of rival firms in the economy? Or should the objective be the efficient use of economic resources, considering elements of market structure only when they can be shown to lead to effective business performance? ... neither objective can be set without regard to the other; ... the tests both of workable competition and effective business performance have merits and demerits; ... these tests must be used to complement rather than to exclude each other.[19]

Mason has, however, admitted that "market structure tests are more precise and lend themselves more readily to administrative and judicial application," and that it is extremely difficult to devise tests of performance which can be applied by the courts. He once summarized the tests proposed in the literature to include: (1) progressiveness of the firm in product and process innovation; (2) whether or not cost reductions are passed on to buyers promptly; (3) whether or not investment is excessive in relation to output; (4) whether profits are "continually and substantially higher than in industries exhibiting similar trends in sales, costs, innovations, etc."; (5) whether competitive effort is exhibited mainly by selling activities rather than by improvements in services and products and price reductions.

Ten years later he wrote:

Business performance, as the term is currently used, is a normative concept; performance is

---

[17] Clare E. Griffin, *An Economic Approach to Antitrust Problems* (New York: American Enterprise Assn., 1951), p. xiii.

[18] Corwin D. Edwards, "Public Policy and Business Size," *The Journal of Business of the University of Chicago,* Vol. XXIV (October, 1951), pp. 280–292,

at p. 286. Copyright 1951 the University of Chicago.

[19] Edward S. Mason, "Current Status of the Monopoly Problem," 62 *Harvard L. Rev.* 1265 (1949), at p. 1280. Copyright 1949 by Harvard Law Review Association.

either "good" or" bad". Goodness and badness obviously have to be judged with reference to their approach to—or departure from—some ideal type, and in the search for the ideal, one of two standards or both are customarily brought forth. The *first* is a performance consistent with the existence of pure competition or of some variant that may take account of a "real" desire on the part of buyers for some degree of product differentiation. The *second* is "progressiveness," "dynamism," or some rate of innovation.[20]

With respect to the first test of performance (consistency with the model of pure or perfect competition) Mason rightly pointed out: "Unfortunately, the situations and type of conduct we have to deal with are not static." With respect to the second test ("progressiveness," "dynamism," "or some rate of innovation") he asserted, "But the second type of ideal performance cannot even be defined."[21]

What the debate between proponents of the market structure test and those of the performance test points up is that the problem of concentration of economic power, particularly in basic industries, involves also considerations of price stability, full employment, economic progress, national defense, and one's attitude towards politics. Moreover, it emphasizes that policies relative to antitrust and regulated industries cannot be studied in a vacuum without reference to one's conception of the way in which the entire economy is or should be organized to achieve those "ends-in-view" which are never final. The proponents of market structure tests seem to be more aware of these things than the proponents of economic performance tests.

Shorey Peterson. It is this overall approach which Shorey Peterson has emphasized in stressing the fact that recognition of all these problems already existed in the works of writers like Alfred Marshall (who placed the mathematical basis of his theory in an appendix to his *Principles*) and J. B. Clark. Peterson has concluded:

. . . Even if we could measure degrees of deviation from pure competition, we would accomplish little unless pure competition were the market condition really desired—the condi-

tion that would promote a balanced achievement of diverse economic goals; and surely it is not. And even if we had a significant measurement, related to a truly optimum market norm, the policy question would remain: In a society in which ideal blueprints never materialize, what degree of departure from the norm is reasonably acceptable, in light of political as well as economic factors? More theory and more research will aid us; but there can be no answer except through the kind of experienced judgment always relied on in such matters.[22]

What all this implies is that economists are not in a position to provide the courts with a *specific* norm to be applied in antitrust actions. There are no absolutes and, in such a situation, the common law *method* of self-correcting value judgments is perhaps the only method which results in acquisition of the "experienced judgment" needed for dealing with the problem. A suggestion that what is required is agreement on a *method* for dealing with the problem rather than the determination of an absolute *standard* which will have universal application for all time and in all places is, of course, unacceptable to those who adopt the rationalist position, or to whom *the* rule of human action has already been revealed. But a careful study of the literature of "workable competition" suggests that what the participants in the debate are really talking about is the *nature of the method* to be employed in dealing with such problems, although many discuss this question in obscure language which pays much lip service to the concept of a "standard." And this remark holds true also for the works of those writers who either reject market structure and performance tests outright and who substitute tests (like "intent" and "conduct") of their own, or who advocate the use of such tests in addition to tests of structure and performance.

(4) "Intent" and "Conduct" as Tests; Combined Tests

Myron Watkins on "Intent." Myron W. Watkins is perhaps Mason's severest critic. In a review of a book containing Mason's principal essays on the subject (as of 1957), Watkins wrote that Mason:

[20] Edward S. Mason, "Preface" to Carl Kaysen and Donald Turner, *A Policy for Anti-Trust Law* (Cambridge: Harvard University Press, 1959), p. xvii.

[21] *Ibid.*
[22] Peterson, "Antitrust and the Classic Model," *op. cit.*, p. 77.

. . . so it appears to the reviewer, would have concentrated business power tested primarily by reference to its "performance" record (innovations, price policy, profit, etc.). A "good" performance merits a decree of "no cause of action." The reviewer, on the other hand, is prepared to acquiesce in what he regards as an established legal doctrine: that both the circumstances in which concentrated business power originated and the mode of its exercise are subject to examination simply as a clue to the intent of those responsible If observed *conduct* reveals an intent to monopolize (or restrain trade), an offense is proven and not otherwise. To some, the difference between these two views may seem slight. To the reviewer the difference is radical.[23]

According to Watkins, the market structure test is also inadequate because:

. . . it focuses the issue on the pattern of market structure, the possession of market power, and ignores the animus lying behind the development of that structural pattern. Intent provides an appropriate *primary* criterion of compliance with or violation of the law, because of the nature of antitrust law itself. The Sherman Act prescribes a rule of *conduct*. It does not condemn monopoly; it prohibits monopolizing. It penalizes a certain course of market conduct, not a market position (possession of market power), whether it be that of a single seller or of one among a "few.' 'As in every branch of criminal law and in much of the law of torts, intent is a crucial factor. Fatal shooting of another person is not murder; it must be premeditated. Acquisition of "market control" (a large share of the available business) is not monopolizing; it must be the fulfillment of a deliberate design to throttle competition.[24]

Watkins' discussion of the criminal law leaves something to be desired; moreover, his emphasis of "intent" and his consequent treatment of the Sherman Act as a purely criminal law ignores altogether the fact that the law permits civil actions, whose importance in terms of the number of cases brought by the government far exceeds the number of criminal actions. For example, the suggestion that "premeditation" is essential to the crime of murder is misleading at the very least. What is required is an intention to commit *a* (some) felony—no *specific* intent to take the life of another is essential if a *general* intention to commit *a* felony exists. This proposition also applies to the Sherman Act. As Judge Wyzanski put it in the *United Shoe Machinery* case:

So far nothing has been said in this opinion of defendant's *intent* in regard to its power and practices in the shoe machinery market. . . . Defendant intended to engage in the leasing practices and pricing policies which maintained its market power. That is all the intent which the law requires when both the complaint and the judgment rest on a charge of "monopolizing," not merely "attempting to monopolize." Defendant having willed the means, has willed the end.[25]

Instead of leading to a distinction between "good" and "bad" monopolies on the basis of performance, Watkins' interpretation of the "intent" element would lead to a distinction between "legal" and "illegal" monopolies on the basis of whether or not the monopoly power was acquired by *specific* "premeditation" or in some other way. The end result is that a high degree of monopoly power, which may involve a "bad" performance and a "poor" market structure according to Mason's view, is, nevertheless, beyond the reach of the law according to Watkins' standard.

In reality, Watkins sometimes seems to be talking only about one particular type of crime—that of "attempting to do that which the law prohibits." He says that "intent, in law, is always an inference drawn from *conduct*." But as a matter of fact, "intent" which does not amount to an "attempt" is not prohibited by law. The difficult problem in law is that which arises in trying to determine when the conduct of the defendant implies both a "purpose" and "an effort to carry that purpose into execution." When *both* elements are present the defendant is found guilty of "*attempt*."

We have seen in Chapter 12 that Section 2 of the Sherman Act reads: "Every person who shall monopolize, or attempt to monopolize or combine or conspire . . . to

---

[23] Myron W. Watkins, "Review of Edward S. Mason: Economic Concentration and the Monopoly Problem," *American Economic Review*, Vol. XLVII (September, 1957), pp. 747–753, at pp. 751–752. (Italics his.) [See also his "Economic and Legal Concepts in Antitrust Adjudication," 9 *Antitrust Bulletin* 347 (1964).]

[24] Watkins, "Review of Edward S. Mason: Economic Concentration and the Monopoly Problem," *op. cit.*, p. 751.

[25] *United States* v. *United Shoe Machinery Corp.*, 110 F. Supp. 295 (1953); affirmed *per curiam*, 347 U.S. 521 (1954). (Italics his.)

monopolize" is to be found guilty of a misdemeanor. *Three separate offenses* are thus stated, and these separate offenses are defined by different elements. It is necessary to show a *specific* intent in order to make a finding of "attempt." A successful attempt, however, *merges* with the act attempted; and, in such a case, it is necessary only to show a *general* intent. That is the full meaning of the excerpt from the *United Shoe Machinery* case quoted earlier (to which the reader may now wish once more to refer). Judge Wyzanski has stated in this excerpt what is true in criminal law generally—similar statements can be found in other criminal cases having nothing to do with antitrust. Watkins has implicitly defined "monopolize" and "combine or conspire to monopolize" as "attempting to monopolize" in his review of Mason's book. While it is true that "attempting to monopolize" merges with "monopolize" if the attempt is successful, the reverse is not true. An unsuccessful "attempt to monopolize" does not constitute monopolizing. Watkins has put the cart before the horse: A charge of "monopolization" does not require proof of the "attempt to monopolize." Thus he has apparently declared himself in favor of enforcement of *one* part of Section 2 of the Sherman Act only. At the same time, his discussion throws no particular light on the type of evidence required to prove a case under that section. That, of course, is a question of fact to be decided on the merits in each case by the trier of the fact, be he judge or jury.

Precisely what theory of criminal law (whether that of retributive justice, the theory of an "eye for an eye"; or of preventive justice, a theory that punishment of the violator will prevent others from violating the law; or of remedial justice, the theory that the criminal will be "rehabilitated,") lies behind Watkins' position is not made clear by him. Nor does his position give any indication as to what social policy he thinks it is that the law ought to effectuate—other than that those who "intend" (attempt) to violate the law, as evidenced by their conduct, "should" be punished. Indeed, his position seems to involve a tacit belief that monopoly, where it is the result of actions not showing an "intent" to monopolize, is socially acceptable if not desirable, irrespective of its effects.

Alfred E. Kahn on "Intent." Alfred Kahn's position on "intent" is somewhat similar to that of Watkins, since Kahn also confuses "intent" with "attempt." Indeed he has acknowledged "the inspiration of Myron W. Watkins." Kahn states specifically: "the law need only prevent the deliberate impairment, misdirection, or suppression of competition to protect both the public interest and the legitimate interests of business competitors."[26] The reason this is so according to Kahn is that, in the absence of "deliberate impairment, misdirection, or suppression of competition," it will be true "in most industries" that the "force of competition will be" strong enough to bring about the desired results. Kahn thinks that market structure tests may also supply guidance in special cases, but that market performance tests "look at the wrong end of the process." To him "the essential task of public policy . . . should be to preserve the framework of a fair field and no favors, letting the results take care of themselves."[27]

Like Watkins, Kahn sometimes confuses "intent" with "attempt." Thus he argues that it is essential that standards of "conduct" be adopted so that businessmen will have "fairly definite standards," and he further asserts that "The inescapable conclusion is that, from a practical standpoint, the criterion of intent alone fills the bill for a sensible antitrust policy in such cases." The essential thing is to find out "what" the business firms were doing, not "why they were doing it." And he concludes:

It does not follow that an intent to suppress competition is or should be either a sufficient or a necessary basis for condemnation. Intent *unaccompanied by overt action cannot be made a basis for judicial action.* It must be accompanied, first, by the power to restrain or exclude, and, second, by some evidence that the power has been, or, barring interference, will be exercised. . . . Indeed, where, in certain cases, the evidence of power and its exercise is clear, and where the consequences are both sufficiently manifest and plainly unobjectionable, it is not and should

[26] Alfred E. Kahn, "Standards for Antitrust Policy," 67 *Harvard L. Rev.* 28 (1953). See the footnote of acknowledgments. Copyright 1953 by Harvard Law Review Association.
[27] *Ibid.*, p. 39.
[28] *Ibid.*, p. 53. (Italics mine.)

not have been necessary to demonstrate a "specific" illegal intent.[28]

And so it is apparent: Kahn does not really postulate "intent" as a criterion any more than Watkins does. He flatly states that "intent unaccompanied by overt action cannot be made a basis for judicial action." When his position is boiled down to its essential elements, what remains is that Kahn would prohibit "attempts to monopolize" and "monopolization," as well as combinations or conspiracies to monopolize. In the concluding sentence quoted above, he implicitly recognizes that, while it is necessary to show a *specific* intent to prove an "attempt"—since in the case of a successful attempt there is a merger of the lesser act (attempt) with the act itself— no *specific* intent need be shown in the case of a charge of "monopolization." It is enough that a *general* intent be shown. In short, he believes the Sherman Act should be enforced. But, as is true in the case of Watkins' discussion, Kahn's remarks throw no light on the kinds of acts which are to be considered evidence of an "attempt." That, of course, is again a question of fact to be decided in each case on its merits; and, as Watkins rightly pointed out in 1964, economic *theory* alone cannot provide an answer unless, of course, one interprets the profit maximization assumption as an assumption that all business activity is an attempt to monopolize—an attempt which is always frustrated under perfect competition, at any rate, by the sheer number of those making the attempt independently.

With respect to the debate about "intent," Professor Mason has much the better of it when he states in reply to the criticisms of his position by Watkins and Kahn that:

> . . . If the rule of "intent" means merely that the legal significance of action is to be judged largely with reference to the market power of the actor, I have no fault to find with it, though I do not think that subsuming, and confusing, both elements under the term "intent" gets us very far forward. But that "intent to monopolize" inferred exclusively from conduct, either is, or should be, the law, I would strongly deny.[29]

But if the seemingly precise solutions offered by Watkins and Kahn are more apparent than real, nevertheless their positions, too, quite clearly demand an examination of the facts in particular cases and not the use of some sort of rigorously defined abstract model. The *method* which underlies these positions is the same as that envisaged by the market structure and performance tests: the standard of evaluation is seen to be inherent in the formulation of the problem and not to be a matter of definition or reliance on some sort of external absolute. In this respect, the position of Professor Stocking is clearly to the point.

George Stocking: Structure, Performance, and Conduct. Professor Stocking has been consistent in his explicit rejection of the concept of "workable competition" as a norm for antitrust enforcement.[30] Thus he stated flatly in 1957: "I do not regard the principle of workability as an acceptable guide in antitrust cases."[31] But when Professor Stocking states that he rejects "workability" the reader should understand his statement to mean that he is against the interpretation of "workable competition" as this concept has been used in the *Report* of the Attorney General's Committee and as he believes it will continue to be used on the basis of that *Report*.

Stocking also believes, despite his rejection of the position taken by that Committee, that "the criteria economists have developed for determining workability— structure, conduct, and performance"— serve a "perhaps indispensible" function in determining whether or not monopoly exists. He explicitly rejects *structure* or *performance* alone as norms for antitrust enforcement but, at the same time, he believes that these two elements—together with evidence of "business conduct"—can serve as *evidence* of antitrust violations. The essential element, in his scheme of things, is *evidence* pertaining to "business conduct." Thus he argues that, since businessmen "do not try to protect valueless positions," any action on their part to protect a position which "they believe possesses elements of monopoly . . .

---

[29] Mason, in "Preface" to Kaysen and Turner, *op. cit.*, p. xv.

[30] George W. Stocking, "Workable Competition as an Antitrust Guide," 2 *Antitrust Bulletin* 3 (September, 1956), at pp. 3–4 and esp. F. N. 5 of reference cited.

[31] George W. Stocking, "Economic Tests of Monopoly and the Concept of the Relevant Market," 2 *Antitrust Bulletin* 479 (March, 1957), p. 482.

is persuasive evidence" that monopoly power exists.[32] And so, Stocking's position is really a position concerning the *credibility* of certain types of evidence. The argument quoted above runs in terms of the inference to be drawn by a fact finder from specific actions of businessmen "to protect a position which they believe possesses elements of monopoly power." Where such actions are found as a fact to have been taken, Stocking would apparently interpret this finding of fact as giving rise to a presumption that "monopoly power exists." There is nothing in economic theory which provides the answer to this question since the *methodological* question posed is not dealt with by economic theory. Stocking has cast his argument largely in terms of economic variables; but underneath his formal argument there exists a strong current of distrust of private, uncontrolled, economic power and of arguments in its defense. Thus the Stocking position is related to the positions of Walter Adams and Corwin Edwards and to a long-standing tradition in American ideas.

In keeping with his position, Professor Stocking has undertaken to make case studies of the "facts" in the *du Pont Cellophane* case, as well as in cases involving the steel and tin can industries, and has concluded "on the facts" in each case that the judicial determination of the *factual* issue was incorrect.[33] One may agree with the conclusion reached by Professor Stocking without agreeing with his attempt in every case to rationalize the conclusion reached "on purely economic grounds." The attempt to do so, while it undoubtedly springs from a desire to create an "air-tight" case which can draw authority also from the conception that economics "is a science," probably weakens the precise argument he makes. The real value of his studies lies in the fact that they demonstrate effectively that, to the extent that the actual decisions in these cases purport to be based on "purely economic grounds," such a claim is no more valid when it is put forward as a support for these decisions than it is a basis for a valid criticism of them. And,

indeed, such an objective may in fact have been the real purpose of the studies Stocking has made. His attempt to test the "hypothesis" that "workable competition" provides an objective standard for antitrust enforcement can be most fairly interpreted as a demonstration that the proposition is one of a position or point of view and *not* of a testable hypothesis.

"Taking Improper Advantage of a Dominant Market Position." It is useful at this juncture to note that Article 86 of the European Economic Community Treaty (1958) prohibits the activity of "taking improper advantage of a dominant market position." The Commission, which makes investigations and determinations of facts under Article 86 with respect to the activities of business firms in the European Economic Community, has had as much difficulty in finding any universal meaning for this language as American writers have had in finding abstract criteria in the phrase "workable competition." For example, Dr. Eberhard Gunther, President of the Federal Cartel Control Authority of Berlin has said of the provision, among other things:

Considerations in connection with the problem of dominant position within the market tend to a result similar to that of the relevant market: There are, it is true, satisfactory abstract criteria, but the establishment of a dominant position must, by applying these criteria, be examined at all times on a case-by-case basis, i.e., the examination must cover market structure and market form, market share, size of profits, elasticity of demand, and market behavior, the market behavior having to be given a decisive importance. The examination must not be related to a single date; instead, it must cover a longer period of time, according to the special circumstances of the individual case. Furthermore, the problem of potential competition will also have to be taken into account. In this manner, it will be possible to establish, in an individual case, whether for lack of substantial competition a dominant influence on the market is actually being exercised on the market by one or several enterprises.[34]

In other words, by determining on a case-by-case basis whether or not a firm has taken "improper advantage of a dominant

[32] *Ibid.*, p. 485.
[33] George W. Stocking, "The Rule of Reason, Workable Competition, and Monopoly," 64 *Yale Law Journal* 1107 (July, 1955).
[34] *Antitrust Developments in the European Common Market* (Hearings before the Subcommittee on Antitrust and Monopoly of the Senate Judiciary Committee, 88th Cong., 1st sess.) (Washington, D.C.: U.S. Government Printing Office, 1963), Part I, p. 87.

position in a relevant market, it will be possible to determine" whether or not "a firm has taken improper advantage of a dominant position in a relevant market." Dr. Gunther has advocated use of a method, not adoption of a norm. What the quotation really demonstrates is that economic *theory* provides no general external standard or norm for deciding the problem under consideration and that the standard of valuation to be employed must arise out of the definition of the particular problem being considered. In short, again the problem is recognized to be one of "judging," as Shorey Peterson has suggested, a point to which further attention will be given at the end of this chapter. It is interesting to note that Dr. Gunther has combined in his statement practically all of the views discussed so far in this subdivision, including an emphasis of "the market behavior of the firm." Moreover, implicit in his statement is a notion that the behavior of the firm through time rather than at a given time must be taken into account. Similar notions have appeared in some of the other views discussed above. These ideas are a reflection of the influence of advocacy by some of "dynamic performance" tests..

(5) "Dynamic Performance" Tests: "Workable Competition" and "The Workable Economy"; Empirical Studies

J. A. Schumpeter and the Idea of "Creative Destruction." Schumpeter's rejection of the conclusions of the static model of price theorists as a basis for public policy provided his point of departure. Schumpeter's position was that:

Capitalism . . . is by nature a form or method of economic change and not only never is but never can be stationary. And this evolutionary character of the capitalist process is not merely due to the fact that economic life goes on in a social and natural environment which changes and by its change alters the data of economic action; this fact is important and these changes (wars, revolutions and so on) often condition industrial change, but they are not its prime industrial movers. . . . The fundamental impulse that sets and keeps the capitalist engine in motion comes from the new consumers' goods, the new method of production or transportation, the new markets, the new forms of industrial organization that capitalist enterprise creates.

. . . The opening up of new markets, foreign or domestic, and the organizational development from the craft shop and factory to such concerns as U.S. Steel illustrate the same process of industrial mutation—if I may use that biological term—that incessantly revolutionizes the economic structure *from within*, incessantly destroying the old one, incessantly creating a new one. This process of Creative Destruction is the essential fact about capitalism. It is what capitalism consists in and what every capitalist concern has got to live with.[35]

Thus, according to Schumpeter, business practices can be evaluated only against the background of the dynamic process of "Creative Destruction." Indeed, it is necessary to:

. . . recognize the further fact that restrictive practices . . ., as far as they are effective, acquire a new significance in the perennial gale of creative destruction, a significance which they would not have in a stationary state or in a state of slow and balanced growth.[36]

Also, according to Schumpeter, the impact of new things, "new technology for instance," reduces the scope of such restrictive practices in the long run, and the conclusions of contemporary static price theory are thus wrong because they deal with a static situation which has nothing to do with the world in which we live. Indeed, the free entry assumed under perfect competition "may make it impossible to enter at all." That is, "the introduction of new methods of production and new commodities is hardly conceivable with perfect—and perfectly prompt—competition from the start." Progress comes from research and development, which in turn are only undertaken by firms which can count on the certainty of short-run monopolistic positions in which to exploit their inventions. Schumpeter wrote before federal government expenditures for research and development constituted more than 60 percent of all such expenditures in the United States and he wrote also before the technological developments resulting from total and limited wars and from space programs and the like had provided various new processes and materials for commercial

[35] Joseph A. Schumpeter, *Capitalism, Socialism, and Democracy* (3d ed.; New York: Harper and Bros., 1950), pp. 82–83. (Italics his.)
[36] *Ibid.*, p. 87.

application and exploitation, a matter already discussed in Chapter 8. Moreover, he relied on his own version of American economic history, a version in which the role of government in other areas is totally ignored. For example, he asserted truly but, nevertheless, a half-truth:

... the contents of the laborer's budget, say from 1760 to 1940, did not simply grow on unchanging lines but they underwent a process of qualitative change. Similarly, the history of the productive apparatus of a typical farm, from the beginnings of the rationalization of crop rotation, plowing and fattening to the mechanized thing of today—linking up with elevators and railroads—is a history of revolutions. So is the history of the productive apparatus of the iron and steel industry from the charcoal furnace to our own type of furnace, or the history of the apparatus of power production from the overshot water wheel to the modern power plant, or the history of transportation from the mailcoach to the airplane. ... This process of Creative Destruction is the essential fact about capitalism.[37]

But, as we have seen in Chapter 8, these things did not occur in a vacuum. Government sponsored agricultural research, land grants to railroads, mail subsidies to airlines, and defense contracts for aircraft producers were a factor. The extent to which governmental power was employed and is still being employed in the area of economic activities has been partly indicated in Chapter 8, and Schumpeter would have been hard put to demonstrate that the described changes *would have occurred had it not been so employed.*

Others have followed Schumpeter. In the 1950's their view came to be known as that of the "New Competition" or of "Effective Competition." Thus David Lilienthal endorsed the Schumpeterian thesis in 1953,[38] and *Fortune Magazine* undertook to popularize it. Probably a majority of the Members of the Attorney General's National Committee to Study the Antitrust Laws subscribed to it. And the view was probably also held by a majority of the policy level officials of the Eisenhower Administration.

J. M. Clark: "Competition as a Dynamic Process." Professor J. M. Clark declared himself a partial, *but only partial,* convert to the Schumpeterian thesis in his *Competition as a Dynamic Process* in 1961, when he said:

It is the author's belief that, while competition as it used to be conceived has changed its character and has been dislodged from full control in important spheres, *competitive forces persist, more pervasively and effectively than existing theories give them credit for. The operation of these forces is loaded with imperfections and faces serious threats, and these should not be minimized.* One may remark in passing that these imperfections include some that are (imperfectly) reflected in the theorems of formal economic theory, plus some others. Yet if the constructive features of competitive forces can be preserved, they offer us something better than the models labeled "pure competition" by E. H. Chamberlin and "perfect competition" by Joan Robinson— better because they have somehow managed to combine competitive incentives with the mass production and applied science that are nowadays essential to dynamic progress. And for appraising dynamic progress, "perfection" is an irrelevant criterion.[39]

Thus, Clark's approval was *not* an unqualified one. He recognized the "imperfections" with which dynamic competitive forces were "loaded;" and he did *not* reject the continued application of the antitrust laws; but he *did* believe that if they were to be successful it was necessary that they "be supported by a widespread acceptance of the general idea of competition as a way of business life."[40]

A. A. Berle and Peter Drucker versus Ben Lewis on the "Corporate Conscience". Another rationalization of the benefits derived from the presence of large corporations in the American economy has been the invention of the "corporate conscience" by Professor of Law A. A. Berle, Jr. Berle has asserted that the very great power posessed by some corporations is forcing their officers to behave in a socially responsible way and pointed to the General Electric Company as an example. Peter Drucker has taken a similar position.[41] But Professor Ben Lewis has pointedly disagreed:

[37] *Ibid.*, p. 83.
[38] David Lilienthal, *Big Business: A New Era* (New York: Harper and Row, 1953). See also "The Ethics of Business Enterprise," *Annals of the American Academy of Political and Social Sciences*, Vol. 343 (September, 1962), pp. 1–141.

[39] J. M. Clark, *Competition as a Dynamic Process* (Washington, D.C.: The Brookings Institution, 1961), p. 2.
[40] *Ibid.*, p. 479.
[41] Peter Drucker, *The Concept of the Corporation* (New York: The John Day Co., Inc., 1964), p. 247.

Bigness today has made its way. It has arrived, and, generously, it has accepted and is doing the very best it can with the rest of the economy. It is bigger; in absolute terms, bigness today is really big. Its roots are deep into, indeed, they have become a part of, the foundation rock of the economy, and they are reaching into areas thought at one time to be unfriendly to their outgrowth. The behavior of bigness today is spotless, at least no spots remain unremoved for long; and its appearance and demeanor are attractive and ingratiating. Tutored by its attorneys, bathed, barbered and cosmeticized by Madison Avenue, nourished and sanctified by war and cold war, and enthroned by public opinion which sees only goodness in bigness that is well mannered and well behaved, bigness exhibits the supreme confidence and gracious assurance that bespeak stature, status, and a clear conscience. Bigness was once the bad boy in Sunday School; now it sits on the vestry. It may not yet have acquired a full-sized soul, but the contract has been let and the press has been alerted. Bigness spreads its protective arms benevolently over thousands of small, less favored firms, and dispenses justice among them as it is given to see justice. It keeps them alive—in the aggregate—and in the main tolerably happy—and in line.

It is urged that, along with the growth of the big corporation as the repository of great economic power, will come the growth of the corporate conscience. The great modern corporation must be recognized as a political institution upon which, as upon other great political institutions in the past, the flow of events is forcing a degree of public responsibility commensurate with its massive power—

> the corporation, almost against its will, it is said by Adolf Berle, has been compelled to assume in appreciable part the role of conscience carrier of 20th century American society.

A succinct comment would be: It isn't going to happen; if it did happen it wouldn't work; and if it did work it would still be intolerable to free men. I am willing to dream, perhaps selfishly, of a society of selfless men. Certainly, if those who direct our corporate concentrates are to be free from regulation either by competition or government, I can only hope that they will be conscientious, responsible, and kindly men; and I am prepared to be grateful if this proves to be the case. But, I shall still be uneasy

and a little ashamed, with others who are ashamed, to be living my economic life within the limits set by the gracious bounty of the precious few. If we are to have rulers, let them be men of good will; but above all, let us join in choosing our rulers—and in ruling them.[42]

A Case Study of the Corporate Conscience in Action: The Electric Cases of 1962. An interesting case study can be made of the thesis of the corporate conscience. In 1960 the Department of Justice filed a criminal complaint against Westinghouse Electric Corporation, Allis-Chalmers Manufacturing Company, Federal Pacific Company, General Electric Company, I-T-E Circuit Breaker Company, Lewis J. Burger, George E. Burens, Landon Fuller, H. F. Hentschel, Houston Jones, L. W. Long, Frank M. Nolan, A. W. Payne, Frank E. Stehlik, J. T. Thompson, A. F. Vinson, and David W. Webb charging the existence of a conspiracy in unreasonable restraint of trade in power switchgear assemblies beginning "at least as early as 1958."[43] The indictment was based on a grand jury investigation and the government later dropped A. F. Vinson's name from the list of defendants. In addition, 19 other indictments were handed down by the grand jury and eventually 29 electrical manufacturing companies and 45 of their executives were indicted. At first, General Electric and Westinghouse entered pleas of *not guilty*, but the others received permission to plead *nolo contendere* (a plea which admits for the purposes of the instant case only the allegations of the indictment but which cannot be used in evidence in other proceedings). Eventually, some of the defendants pleaded Guilty, some pleaded *nolo contendere*, several individuals were sentenced to jail sentences, fines were levied, and consent decrees were signed in civil proceedings filed at about the same time as the criminal complaints. The pleas of *nolo contendere* served the relevant defendants the purpose of preventing the taking of evidence concerning the conspiracy in open court and of making proof of private damage actions under the antitrust laws more difficult; and, since grand

---

[42] *Administered Price Inflation: Alternative Public Policies* (Hearings on Administered Prices before the Subcommittee on Antitrust and Monopoly of the Senate Judiciary Committee, 86th Cong., 1st sess.) (Washington, D.C.: U.S. Government Printing Office, 1959), Part 9, p. 4715 and p. 4717.

[43] *United States of America* v. *Westinghouse Corporation* (and other named defendants) United States District Court for the Eastern District of Pennsylvania, Criminal No. 20399, Filed June 22, 1960.

jury proceedings are secret, information concerning the details of the conspiracy are not available from that source either.

However, the Senate Subcommittee on Antitrust and Monopoly held hearings on the matter in 1961 and proceeded to bare most of the facts concerning the conspiracy.[44] Some of the testimony before the subcommittee suggests that the conscience of the corporation—a corporation having been defined (it will be recalled) by Pope Innocent IV in 1243 as *persona ficta* and by Chief Justice John Marshall in 1819 as "an artificial, invisible being, existing only in the eyes of the law" (which has become anonymous in the Bureau of Census statistics of manufacturing)—is also nonexistent at the operational level. For example, Mr. Frank E. Stehlik, former manager of the Low-Voltage Switchgear Department of the General Electric Company, testified in 1961 before the Senate subcommittee investigating the activities of the conspirators as follows:

Mr. Stehlik. They had this group, the group that met at the Traymore [hotel in Atlantic City], met three or four times in that interim [1958–59], and then the working groups of people who were familiar with the actual jobs met, I believe they met as frequently as weekly.

Senator Hruska. How effective were the meetings? How well did they work to give advantage to the low bidder? They did select the low bidder?

Mr. Stehlik. Well, actually, the main effort outside of the sealed bid—in my business there was only about 3 or 4 percent of the total business was sealed bid, but the main purpose of the meetings was to agree on the book price, which was the basic price everybody was supposed to bid.

But, then, in order that it wouldn't look like an absolute agreement, they rigged up this phase-of-the-moon arrangement so that they could stagger the prices. The phase-of-the-moon was supposed to stagger the price only sufficiently so that the normal pricing variations would seem to be still reflected.[45]

The *Hearings* also contain an exchange of letters between Senator Kefauver and the Attorney General in which the latter confirmed the former's understanding of these facts: Mr. Stehlik and others had claimed the defense of acting subject to orders of their superiors (which, incidentally, was also the defense employed by the German defendants during the Nuremburg War Crimes Trials) and these defendants "were given polygraph tests in Washington by the FBI and . . . there was no indication—as a result of the tests—that they were not telling the truth." It was also confirmed that "the superior, who allegedly ordered them to violate the antitrust laws was asked by the Justice Department to take a polygraph test but refused on advice of counsel."[46]

Top management personnel in several of the companies stated publicly that they had no knowledge of the conspiracy. Their innocence suggests either: (1) that top management does not know what is going on, a state of affairs which raises interesting questions concerning Professor Berle's explicit citation in his 1959 book (*Power Without Property*, p. 108) of the ability of the directors of the General Electric Company, in particular, to "chose a good slate of new managers," and to advance the social welfare generally, as a specific example in support of his thesis of the corporate conscience; or (2) that the corporate conscience thesis applies only to the top management members of the corporation and does not apply to those individuals who actually implement the policy and make the day to day operational decisions.

The defense of lack of knowledge was also used by the President of General Motors in admitting during a Senate hearing in 1966 that the corporation had hired a private detective agency to investigate Ralph Nader, an outspoken critic of the failure of automobile producers to incorporate safety features in new cars. Among other things, private detectives had investigated Nader's sex life and put him under surveillance while he was testifying before the Congressional committee.[47]

The question thus arises: does the corporate conscience in fact operate as a check upon the actual exercise of corporate power?

---

[44] *Price-Fixing and Bid-Rigging in the Electrical Manufacturing Industry* (Hearings on Administered Prices before the Subcommittee on Antitrust and Monopoly of the Senate Judiciary Committee, 87th Cong., 1st sess.) (Washington, D.C.: U.S. Government Printing Office, 1961), Parts 27 and 28.

[45] *Ibid.*, p. 16, 815.

[46] *Ibid.*, p. 16, 184.

[47] *Federal Role in Traffic Safety* (Hearings before the Senate Committee on Government Operations, 89th Cong., 2d sess., 1966) (Washington, D.C.: U.S. Government Printing Office, 1966), Part 4, p. 1390.

Indeed, it is difficult to understand how one can be possessed of innocence and of a conscience at the same time, but none of the advocates of the thesis of the corporate conscience seems so far to have devoted himself to explanation of this problem.

Galbraith: "Countervailing Power in an Affluent Industrial State" or the "Workable Economy". In his earlier works, Professor J. K. Galbraith stated that while his "analysis is in a tradition of economic theory different from" that of Schumpeter, "and one of which he [Schumpeter] was frequently critical," Galbraith and Schumpeter both believed that:

. . . a benign Providence who, so far, has loved us for our worries, has made the modern industry of a few large firms an excellent instrument for inducing technical change. It is admirably equipped for financing technical change. Its organization provides strong incentives for undertaking development and for putting it into use. The competition of the competitive model, by contrast, almost completely precludes technical development.

There is no more pleasant fiction than that technical change is the product of the matchless ingenuity of the small man forced by competition to employ his wits to better his neighbors. Unhappily it is a fiction.[48]

Galbraith noted that, by the early decades of the present century, the task of constructing" the model of the capitalist society (described in Chapter 10 of this book) "was virtually complete." Indeed:

It was an intellectual achievement of a high order. As a device, in theory, for ordering the economic relations between men, it was very nearly perfect. Socialist theorists—Enrico Barone, the great Italian scholar, and Oskar Lange, the equally notable Polish economist—used the theoretical performance of the competitive model as the goal of the socialist state. Few of the original architects of the competitive model would have defended it as a description of the world as it is—or was. For some the competitive model was a first approximation to reality—it departed from real life only to the extent that there was monopoly in industry or over natural resources, including land, or that government or custom interposed barriers to competition. For others it was the goal toward which capitalism might be expected to move or toward which it might be guided or a standard by which it might be appraised. For yet others the construction and refinement of the competitive model was a challenging intellectual exercise.[49]

But Galbraith added, unfortunately, the development of the theories of monopolistic and of imperfect competition by Professors Chamberlin and Robinson, independently of each other's work and the inconvenient occurrence of the Great Depression, together with the recognition of the fact of concentration of economic power, dealt this theory a devastating blow in the 1930's.[50] And by the beginning of World War II, "by evolution, from a system where nearly everything worked out for the best, economists found themselves with a system where nearly everything seemed to work out for the worst." Unable to find a satisfactory solution in the world of ideas, resort was had to a "miasma of words."

But the trouble was not with the economy. The trouble simply lay in the world of ideas. And the development of the concept of workable competition provided no solution to the problem of the world of ideas:

. . . the notion of workable competition takes cognizance of the sadly overlooked point that over-all consequences, which in theory are quite deplorable, are often in real life quite agreeable. The difficulty with the notion is that its authors have failed to make clear why what is unworkable in principle becomes workable in practice. This failure, as I shall show presently, lies in the preoccupation with competition. In the competitive model the restraint on the power of any producer was provided by the competition of other producers—it came from *the same side of the market*. . . . This preoccupation with competition kept the investigators from seeing the actual restraints on market power—restraints that made not competition but the economy workable.[52]

Thus is one led from "workable competition" to the *workable economy*. Galbraith's first "approximation" to his theory of countervailing power (whose groundwork was laid by his critique of orthodox economic theory) read as follows:

To begin with a broad and somewhat too dogmatically stated proposition, private economic power is held in check by the countervailing power of those who are subject to it.

[48] J. K. Galbraith, *American Capitalism* (Boston: Houghton Mifflin Co., 1952), p. 86.
[49] *Ibid.*, p. 16.
[50] *Ibid.*, p. 32.
[51] *Ibid.*, p. 48.
[52] *Ibid.*, p. 58. (Italics mine.)

The first begets the second. The long trend toward concentration of industrial enterprise in the hands of a relatively few firms has brought into existence not only strong sellers, as economists have supposed, but also strong buyers as they have failed to see. The two develop together, not in precise step, but in such manner that there can be no doubt that the one is in response to the other.[53]

Obviously, Galbraith thus produced a "group theory" of economic behavior which paralleled the hope Madison expressed for the results of the methods of control of factions in the New Constitution of 1789, already discussed in Chapter 5: "Divided we stand and prosper."

The operation of the doctrine of countervailing power, said Galbraith, is seen most clearly in the labor market in the opposition of strong unions to industrial giants. Also, the automobile industry buys from the steel industry. Galbraith admitted frankly that, if in periods of inflation, wage increases are simply passed along to consumers in the form of higher prices, his doctrine has less force than in periods of less than full employment. Some of the criticisms which have been leveled at Galbraith's position are probably unfair. He did not take the simple naïve position some have attributed to him. In the area of antitrust, for example, he asserted:

The rule to be followed by government is, in principle, a clear one. There can be very good reason for attacking positions of original market power in the economy if these are not effectively offset by countervailing power. There is at least a theoretical justification for attacking all positions of market power. There is no justification for attacking positions of countervailing power which leaves positions of original market power untouched. On the contrary, damage both in equity and to the most efficient operation of the economy will be a normal consequence of doing so.

The problems of practical application of such a rule are mostly in the field of the antitrust laws and they are a good deal more difficult than the simple articulation of the rule implies. However, a general distinction between original and countervailing power is, in fact, now made

in antitrust laws—it has been forced, against the accepted current of ideas concerning competition, by the practical reality of the phenomenon itself.[54]

One difficulty with Galbraith's position is the fact that, in the end, he restricted himself largely to a concept of "efficient operation of the economy" in terms of a dynamic performance test, ignoring altogether the political aspects and implications of the neo-feudalistic solution he proposed. There is nothing in his theory to prevent one side or the other from enlisting the aid of government on its behalf or from capturing governmental power. Presumably if that happens, as it has on occasion happened, the theory ceases to apply, since no effective countervailing power then exists. Moreover, the stand-off admittedly fails to materialize in periods of inflation; in such periods a tacit partnership between the giants who oppose each other apparently occurs. In the presence of actual or tacit conspiracy, the doctrine of countervailing power, like the fiction of the corporate conscience, breaks down. In such cases, Galbraith recognized in 1952 that there is still room for the antitrust laws. His doctrine of countervailing power thus involved a definition of the areas in which antitrust laws *should* be applied and perhaps, also, the proposition that governmental power must be used as a countervailing force in certain situations.

But by 1967 Galbraith's views had changed somewhat. In 1967, testifying before a Senate Subcommittee concerning his current views, he summarized some new basic ideas he had published earlier that year.[55] His argument of 1967 rested on the fundamental proposition that:

. . . by common agreement the heartland of the industrial economy is now dominated by large firms. The great bulk of American business is dominated by very large corporations.[56]

It next involved the proposition that:

If a firm is already large it is substantially immune under the antitrust laws.[57]

[53] *Ibid.*, p. 111.

[54] *Ibid.*, p. 138. For a criticism of Galbraith's thesis see Bernard Nossiter, *The Mythmakers* (Boston: Houghton Mifflin Co., 1964).

[55] J. K. Galbraith, *The New Industrial State* (Boston: Houghton Mifflin Co., 1967).

[56] *Planning, Regulation, and Competition*, (Hearings before Subcommittees of the Senate Select Committee on Small Business, Ninetieth Congress, 1st sess., 1967) (Washington, D.C.: U.S. Government Printing Office, 1967), p. 7.

[57] *Ibid.*, p. 7.

And so he argued that the antitrust laws are therefore a "charade," applied in a discriminatory way against firms which are seeking to become larger; these laws constitute a "facade" behind which "the big participants who have the most power bask in immunity."[58] The argument then continues: "Big business is inevitable," and, therefore, the problem is "how to come to terms with it." It would be "quixotic to ask for repeal of the antitrust laws" which "are part of the American folklore." It is enough to "withdraw our faith" from the laws and "to cease to imagine that there is any chance that they will affect the structure of American industry or its market power. Then we would face the real problem, which is how to live with the vast organizations."

Among the large firms included in the list of those possessing immunity from the antitrust laws by Professor Galbraith were General Motors, General Electric, du Pont, Bethlehem (steel company), and Procter and Gamble. It is interesting to note that each of these companies has been a defendant in an antitrust case since 1952, and each has been prevented from consummating some transaction or other in violation of the antitrust laws. Cases involving each of these companies will be discussed in the chapters which follow.

In any event, Galbraith's specific policy proposals in his various writings may be less important than his forceful criticism of the static model of price theory and his demand that attention must be given to the use, in this way or in that, of governmental power.

His theme and variations, as he himself pointed out, rest on a conception of technical progress related to that of Schumpeter: a belief that such technical progress can be performed effectively *only* in large firms. This belief is not universally held and remains to be validated—it is really an assertion about *how* technical change *should be* fostered in our society rather than a demonstration of how it *must be* fostered.

Empirical Studies of Firm Size and Innovation. There have been a number of empirical studies of the relationship between size of the firm and innovation. In 1964, Professor Jesse Markham surveyed several such studies and concluded that five of them supported a generalization that beyond some critical level of firm size, expenditures on research and development did not increase significantly with increases in the size of the firm and in some cases did not increase at all.[59]

In 1965, the Subcommittee on Antitrust and Monopoly of the Senate Judiciary Committee held hearings on and heard, among others, testimony from numerous economists who had made empirical studies of the subject of "Concentration, Innovation, and Invention."[60] Most of the witnesses tended to take the view which had been expressed earlier by Professor Markham. Thus, Professor F. M. Scherer presented the results of an empirical study in which he had examined the outlays on research and development (R and D) expenditures made in 1955 and the number of patents issued in 1959 to 448 of the largest industrial corporations in the United States according to a list of such corporations prepared by *Fortune Magazine* in 1955. He stated his conclusion as follows:

In conclusion, the best interpretation I can draw from my research results is that giant firm size is no prerequisite for the most vigorous inventive and innovative activity. There may be a size threshold below which firms are disadvantaged because they cannot reap all R. and D. scale economies, spread risks, or tap sufficiently large markets in spreading their research exploiting results. But if such a threshold exists, it has probably been surpassed already by the several hundred U.S. firms with sales exceeding $100 million. Bigness beyond this point is apparently no major advantage, and may well be an impediment, to technical progressiveness, although the handicaps of bigness can be overcome by especially effective and forward-looking management.[61]

Professor Robert Schlaifer also stated:

. . . I reached two conclusions. The first is that decisions to undertake, continue, or drop any project for radical innovation must usually be

---

[58] *Ibid.*, p. 8.
[59] Jesse W. Markham, "Market Structure, Business Conduct, and Innovation," *American Economic Review*, Proceedings, Vol. LV (May, 1965), pp. 323–332.
[60] *Economic Concentration* (Hearings before the

Subcommittee on Antitrust and Monopoly, Senate Judiciary Committee, 89th Cong., 1st sess., 1965) (Washington, D.C.: U.S. Government Printing Office, 1965), Part 3.
[61] *Ibid.*, p. 200.

made by top managers or by managers very near the top, whether the company considering the project is large, medium, or small. This means that the large companies in any industry, being necessarily few in number, simply cannot consider, let alone appropriately act on, all proposals for radical innovation in that industry that are worthy of careful consideration. It is for this reason, I believe, that the original development of many important innovations has been due to very small companies, and particularly to companies formed for the sole purpose of developing a single innovation.[62]

Professor Daniel Hamberg further testified as to the results of his empirical work in these words:

What does statistical analysis reveal? A bit surprisingly, perhaps, in no more than 2 of the 19 manufacturing industries [investigated] can a case be made for the proposition that the relative amount of R. and D. increases, among firms employing at least 5,000 people, with size of firm; and 5,000 is ordinarily well below the number of people employed by the so-called corporate giants. The two industries that did show positive association between R. and D. intensity and size of firm were petroleum and stone, clay, and glass products. Interestingly, the same tests showed that in the basic metals industry group, the relative amount of R. and D. decreased as the size of firm rose.[63]

In 1967, the Senate Subcommittee on Antitrust and Monopoly held hearings on the subject of "New Technologies and Concentration," and several papers were presented stressing the point that new technological advances could be effectively utilized in "small" plants. In the course of these hearings the Committee's economist, Dr. John Blair, presented the results of an interesting study he had made of the relation between plant and firm size in several industries. Chart 13-1 is a reproduction of one put into evidence by Dr. Blair.

Dr. Blair explained his chart (Chart 13-1) by saying:

On the basis of the 1963 Census of Manufactures it has been possible to measure the level of plant and company concentration and to determine the difference or "divergence" between the two for industries representing 78 percent of the value of shipments of all manufacturing industries. The data for company concentration are the concentration ratios for the four, eight, 20, and 50 largest producers

as published by the Bureau of the Census. . . .

The data on plant concentration were obtained partly from a special tabulation made by the Census Bureau for the subcommittee and partly from a special tabulation made by the Census Bureau for the Census Bureau's publication, "Size of Establishments." The measure of divergence was in terms of the percentage difference between the share held by the eight largest plants and the eight largest companies.

In the top grid [of Chart 13-1] are two industries, gypsum and soybeans in which the divergence is indeed "extreme."

Immediately below are the patterns for biscuits and crackers and computing machines; both are examples of "wide" divergence . . .

The next two industries, steam engines and turbines and photographic equipment are illustrative of "moderate" divergence . . .

Locomotives and parts and hard-surface floor coverings, shown at the bottom of the chart are examples of those industries in which the limit to deconcentration set by the level of plant concentration is so high as to make restructuring impossible. The plant and company concentration curves are virtually identical, yielding a divergence which is "narrow" by any standard. In both a reduction of company concentration to the level of plant concentration would still leave the four largest companies with nearly 90 percent of the output, assuming, of course, the continuation of the present technologies . . .

. . . What has been presented above should make clear that very significant results can be obtained by dissolution [by means of antitrust actions] directed against only a few large industries in which concentration in terms of ownership and control is far in excess of what is demanded by the requirements of technology. What has been presented earlier in these hearings concerning the direction of technological change should not only reinforce the implementation of a dissolution program [by means of active enforcement of antitrust]; it should also lend it intellectual credibility and acceptance.[64]

Dr. Blair's study was not concerned with the question of whether or not there is a correlation between firm size and technological progress but with the equally important question of the relationship between firm size and ability to make effective use of technological developments, whatever their source. The testimony of Galbraith concerning the inevitability of the rise of large firms was also attacked in 1965 by Horace Gray in testimony given before the

---

[62] *Ibid.*, p. 1235.
[63] *Ibid.*, p. 1285.

[64] *Economic Concentration, op. cit.*, Part 6, pp. 2970–2978.

Chart 13-1

Examples of Highly Concentrated Industries[1] with Varying Divergences Between Plant and Company Concentration, 1963

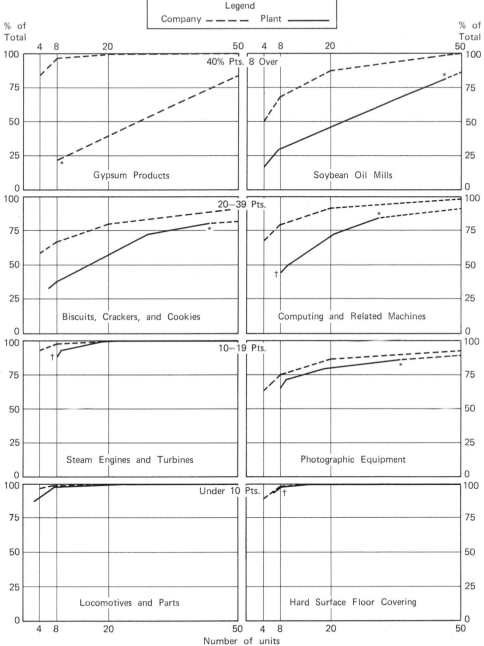

Source: Reproduced from *Economic Concentration* (Hearings before the Senate Subcommittee on Antitrust and Monopoly, 90th Cong., 1st sess.) (Washington, D.C.: U.S. Government Printing Office, 1967), Part 6, p. 2972.

Senate Subcommittee on Antitrust and Monopoly.

Horace Gray on the Relation between Technical Change and Size of Firms. Gray stated his position in these hearings by saying that "we have foolishly allowed scientific research, direction of technological development, and control of new technology to fall into the hands of the big business-military combine." Further, he argued, "it is the institutional power structure that determines the course of technological development, not the other way around."[65]

It is Gray's view that society, "for various institutional reasons" has defaulted "on its basic responsibility to control technological development in the public interest," and turned "the job over to great monopolistic corporations." And he adds, "if the results prove to be socially undesirable, the fault lies with the institutions, not fate or necessity, and the obvious remedy is to modify our institutional arrangements for management of the technological process."[66]

(6) The Macroeconomic Theory of "Workable Competition" and "The Workable Economy"

C. E. Ferguson. In Galbraith's doctrine of countervailing power the noun modified by the adjective *workable* was changed from "competition" to "economy." Thus Galbraith emphasized the words "workable economy" and rejected the words "workable competition." A similar substitution of the one noun for the other occurs in the works of those writers who seek to develop "macroeconomic theories of workable competition." An example is a 1964 book by an economic theorist who relies heavily on the use of mathematics, C. E. Ferguson.[67]

It has just been noted that Ferguson is an economic theorist given to the use of mathematics. It is not surprising, therefore, to find that his political philosophy seems to be stated in terms of plus and minus and to consist of a mixture, rather than of a compound, of logical positivism and natural law philosophy. His economic policy recommendations rest upon this mixture. Thus, he has written:

Government policy toward business is supposedly established by the Congress. To be sure, one might regard the Sherman Act, the Federal Trade Commission and the Clayton acts, the Robinson-Patman Act, the Miller-Tydings Act, and related measures as statements of principles governing public economic policy. Yet in reality these enactments are mere shadows; the substance of public policy is contained in the interpretations of the Federal Courts. Some observers would doubtless charge that the judiciary has usurped a function belonging exclusively to the legislature. [Donald] Dewey, on the contrary, says that the reluctance of Congress to legislate and the calculated vagueness of the laws enacted "have delegated the task of making the law of monopoly to the courts and the Federal Trade Commission." *Irrespective of the interpretation, the result is unquestionable: public policy toward business is made and enforced by nine men whose actions are not subject to popular approval.*[68]

(The reader may wish at this point to review the chapters devoted to the problem of law and social change appearing earlier in this book or to review some of the references there cited.) Ferguson summarizes his political philosophy by writing as follows:

In summary, I can only repeat what probably everyone knows. The legislative and judicial functions should be distinct. The function of the legislature is to determine policy and to express it in written laws; the courts are enforcement agencies. If judicial powers are expanded so that public policy is made by a plurality of nine justices, neither elected nor in any way responsible to public opinion, the government concerned sacrifices its representative character. This does not mean that the judiciary is not competent to enforce laws that are stated precisely enough. Indeed, whatever the policy toward business, its administration will probably have to lie in the hands of the courts, the Justice Department, or the Federal Trade Commission. But courts are not competent to legislate. My social welfare function is as "good" as yours, and I want it to be given equal weight in legislative decisions.[69]

Precisely how it is possible to give equal weight to everyone's social welfare function without the reapportionment or Civil Rights decisions (see the discussion in Chapter 7), which have been widely criticized as examples of "creative interpretation," is not considered by Professor Fer-

65 *Economic Concentration*, Part 3, pp. 1159–1160.
66 *Ibid.*, p. 1160.
67 C. E. Ferguson, *A Macroeconomic Theory of Workable Competition* (Durham: University of North

Carolina Press, 1964).
68 *Ibid.*, pp. 46–47. (Italics mine.)
69 *Ibid.*, p. 48.

guson. Indeed, his entire discussion of the nature of the judicial process is carried on without reference to any actual decisions of any court and without reference to the works of any legal scholar. With respect to Ferguson's mention of the question of separation of powers the reader may be referred to the discussion in Chapter 5 of this book of Madison's Essays 47 and 48 of the *Federalist*.

But the preceding quotations have *not* been given merely for the purpose of having Professor Ferguson speak for himself on subjects of political science and the law. In and of themselves his views on these topics are of little interest. The quotations have been given because they represent the *basis* of *his* rejection of the judicial process as an element in the formulation of the working rules of economic activity. This rejection, in turn, provides him with a rationalization for restricting his discussion solely to a consideration of certain *economic* "objectives" or "targets" to be attained in the Good Society whose blueprint he is making. His technique is typical of that of many economic theorists. Thus he has also written:

> . . . In a way, the control of business by the federal courts is based upon a social welfare function. The welfare function in question is merely the plurality of votes of the justices, or in other words, a social welfare function based upon votes cast by individuals in accord with their various ideas of national well-being. Although this method of decision doubtless renders the function inconsistent, it is nonetheless a social welfare function that may be used in formulating national policy.
> The difficulty is not the *lack* of a social welfare function; the function itself is at fault. In the first place, the method of determining the relevant criteria is not suitable in a nation whose citizens hold a pronounced democratic philosophy. As Henry Simons indefatigably urged, we want a government of laws, not men. Second, from a historical point of view, the actual results of judicial policy making have been piecemeal. The implications of the theory of second best have been ignored, and the courts have treated individual corporations as if they were virtually unrelated to the rest of the economy. Hence even if the method were acceptable but the historical procedures retained, the results would not insure social improvement.[70]

Ferguson thus rejects the "piecemeal" approach of self-correcting value judgments which is inherent, not only in the common law judicial process, but also in the democratic process itself. He advocates, instead, "a government of laws" *above men*, thereby mixing Henry Simons's faith in the "relatively absolute absolute" with his logical positivist belief in the equal weight to be attached to every individual's social welfare function. He does so in order that he may be left free, in accordance with current fashion in economic theory, to devote himself solely to an analysis of policies which will bring about the attainment of the four *economic* objectives (high and stable employment, "reasonable" stability of the price level, economic growth, and absence of "excessive market power") which he has chosen to discuss. He undertakes to validate his selection of these objectives on grounds that each "has had substantial endorsement in legislative *hearings* if not in legislative enactments."[71] He does not consider whether or not such imputed "legislative" social welfare functions are any more consistent than the judicially determined ones he has previously rejected as inconsistent and does not examine the question of whether or not his own social welfare function will receive an equal weight with that of everyone else in such legislative hearings or enactments in the world as it is. Of course, it is possible that, in principle, such will be the case—just as it is possible, in principle, to produce the same result in a judicial proceeding or even in a hereditary monarchy.

Ferguson frankly recognizes that "restricting the compass of targets to *economic* objectives may be subject to criticism." However, he then minimizes such criticism by pointing out that he has *stipulated in advance* that "the choice of targets and techniques must not violate the more basic [political and philosophical] objectives and, in particular, that *the process of choice* itself must *not* be a value."[72] And this, despite the fact that he has himself made the *process of choice* a value in the inception of his analysis by rejecting the judicial process as a method. Since the dilemma arising from this fact cannot be resolved, he simply ignores

---

[70] *Ibid.*, pp. 52–53.
[71] *Ibid.*, p. 52.

[72] *Ibid.*, p. 56. (Italics mine.)

it. Thus he takes the position which has already been remarked upon in Chapter 1 of this book:

> Whether these conditions [that the choice of economic targets must not violate more basic objectives and that the process of choice itself must not be a value] are satisfied or can be satisfied is actually a moot question. Contemplating this point is exactly like contemplating the philosophical theorem about interpersonal utility comparisons. It presents a fascinating problem in logic; but if one complies with the logical conclusions, he is forced to renounce policy questions as insoluable by scientifically trained people. Therefore, we feel justified in proceeding *as if* these conditions were satisfied.[73]

And so, the analysis provides its own justification. Ferguson produces a full circle and apparently defines "scientifically trained" in the same way as the eighteenth century rationalist philosophers did. His argument reduces to the propositions that: (1) since the logical conclusions cannot be complied with; and (2) since one would therefore be forced to renounce the attempt to solve policy problems by purely deductive reasoning if one attempted to comply with the underlying logical conclusions, (3) there is only one rational way to approach the problem and that is (4) to assume that the underlying logical conclusions have been complied with even though they have not been; (5) and in this way one can produce new logical conclusions about what policies *ought* to be adopted, just as if (6) the underlying logical conclusions had been complied with, even though they have not been. This methodology is something less than completely satisfying despite its widespread use in the building of economic models.

Reduced to its essentials, the macroeconomic theory of workable competition is another performance test, one in which a list is made of *economic* objectives which the analyst considers "desirable" and in which an analysis is made of how these objectives may be "maximized," assuming that the *economic* objectives are independent of all other objectives. Paradoxically, the "theory" illustrates dramatically that all these objectives are interrelated. In the area of antitrust in particular, Ferguson advocates the adoption of the following standard:

> To my view . . . excessive market power should be regulated so that no firm or union can set prices or wage rates that are not responsive to market forces. The reason for control, in other words is *not* to bring about some approximation to the allocative efficiency of perfect competition. Rather, the primary purpose of regulating market power should be to prevent individual economic units from establishing conditions that are inconsistent with other policy objectives.[74]

More specifically, he produces the following interesting "rule:" "The government should regulate business firms and labor unions in whatever way is required to achieve a stipulated set of national goals," leaving the word "whatever" conveniently undefined.

Ferguson also examines the question of whether or not the present structures of business firms and labor unions affect the attainment of his four targets. He points out that his data lead to the conclusion that this structure has no effect on employment or growth but that it does have an effect on price stability and—one is not surprised— on the existence of monopoly. And while his study does not lead to the inference "that government should favor the emergence of large size," he does conclude that "market structure seems to emerge as an adjustment to fundamental conditions of the market" and that "to the extent that it does, any change in structure imposed by outside authority is likely to have harmful effects."[75] The "harmful effects" here referred to are harmful effects on price stability of actions to break up concentrations of economic power. Since it is assumed at the outset that politico-philosophical objectives are met when the economic objectives have been met, existing concentrations of economic power thus become consistent with maximization of the politico-philosophical objectives by assumption and no real consideration of this problem is necessary. This then, is the scientific approach of the macroeconomic theory of workable competition, an approach which employs only macroeconomic variables.

---

[73] *Ibid.*, p. 56. (Italics his.)
[74] *Ibid.*, p. 62. (Italics his.)

[75] *Ibid.*, pp. xvii–xviii.

C. A CONCLUDING COMMENT

Many different interpretations of the phrases "workable competition" and "the workable economy" have been examined in this chapter. The question inevitably arises as to whether or not there is any real unity in all this diversity. The answer to this question is in the affirmative: what most of those (with the exception of C. E. Ferguson) who have attempted to put specific content into these phrases have in common is the rejection of what William James called the concept of truth as "a pure abstraction, a bare name to which we must defer." In doing so they take the position that "theories become instruments, not answers to enigmas, in which we can rest," and they adopt the attitude "of looking away from first things, principles, 'categories,' supposed necessities; and of looking towards last things, fruits, consequences, facts."[76]

Such an approach is not satisfactory to anyone who either believes that it is possible to achieve absolute certainty or who is driven into an attempt to achieve it as a matter of his personal emotional make-up. Obviously the instrumentalist approach will be rejected by anyone to whom "truth" has already been revealed or by anyone who is content with merely verbal solutions to imaginary problems. Those in these categories, as Dewey has pointed out, achieve their certainty by an appeal "to authority and precedent," including natural law, supernatural law, the divine right of kings, the constitution, the received conventions, the private conscience, emotion, and the wisdom of the ancestors. And in each of these approaches, "there is some voice so authoritative as to preclude the need of inquiry."[77] The "certainty" produced by these approaches comes at a high price.

Attempts to solve problems concerning the use of governmental power by reference to selected "economic" variables alone must inevitably produce purely verbal solutions or else they must degenerate into rationalizations of points of view which one holds for all sorts of undisclosed and perhaps conflicting reasons having nothing to do with the economic variables employed in the discussion. It is common practice among some economists faced with this problem to make the seemingly candid assertion that "value judgments must be stated" and then to proceed to make a "purely economic analysis" as a basis for "policy recommendations" by taking account only of such selected "strategic economic variables." Such a procedure is usually employed in the static welfare economics; it is also illustrated by Ferguson's technique in the development of his "macroeconomic theory of workable competition." But it is not enough that "value judgments be stated," in the sense in which this phrase is usually employed in current economic literature. Ferguson's typical "purely economic" analysis, it has been noted, stipulates that "the process of choice itself must not be a value." Yet, he himself makes the "process of choice itself" a *value in the inception* of his analysis by rejecting the judicial process as an element in the making of choices, even while he denies that the process of choice is a value. His analysis is then conducted "*as if*" the politico-philosophical objectives are simultaneously maximized when the economic variables he has selected for consideration, and justified by reference to legislative hearings and acts, are maximized—merely on grounds that failure to make this "*as if*" assumption would make it necessary to renounce the "scientific" method of analysis which he wishes to employ. But his analysis fails to come to grips with the issue of concentration of economic power in a democratic society.

An alternative to this procedure is to broaden the analysis to include as variables and as objectives those which have not traditionally been identified as "economic" and to show how these objectives and the competing social policy considerations attached to them are being reconciled by the analyst in question, recognizing at the same time that the solution offered may not be permanent and merely constitutes "a working value" in a process of continuous adjustment and change, a process within which the objectives may change even as the values of the variables included in the analysis change. Essentially the process is one of "judging" in the sense of seeking to

---

[76] William James, *Pragmatism* (New York: Longmans, Green and Co., Inc., 1907), pp. 51–55.

[77] John Dewey and James H. Tufts, *Ethics* (rev. ed.; New York: Henry Holt and Co., Inc., 1932), p. 365.

reconcile competing social interests in a system which is itself constantly changing and of explaining how the analyst has undertaken to bring about this reconciliation in his policy recommendations. Unfortunately, it does not produce absolute certainty.

Judge Leahy's opinion in the *du Pont Cellophane* case has been the subject of considerable criticism in previous chapters and has also been subjected to severe criticism by Professor Stocking. But, in the final analysis, although Leahy's *conclusion* may be rejected, the *procedure* which he employed of stating candidly the reason why he favored one social interest over another can only be admired: had he not done so, his position would be much less open to evaluation and criticism, but it would also have been obscure.

In general, those economists who have adopted the instrumentalist approach toward the antitrust laws have tended to be more or less conscious of the fact that a discussion in terms of purely economic variables is inadequate. Writers like Walter Adams, Corwin Edwards, Willard Mueller, Horace Gray, Shorey Peterson, and Ben Lewis have, perhaps, been the most forthright in openly recognizing that it is necessary to take account of variables other than those which are denominated "purely" economic. So have some of the advocates of the secular natural law or *laissez-faire* system. But not all.

Ferguson's "macroeconomic theory of workable competition" does serve the useful purpose of calling attention to the relationship which exists among economic as well as among economic and other goals. But his rejection of the judicial process as an element in the actual formulation of working rules on grounds that "the actual results of judicial policy have been piecemeal" clearly rests on a failure to recognize that the common law *method* is a way of producing orderly social change by giving specific content to general principles in a continuous stream of inclusions and exclusions through the medium of an adversary proceeding (according to procedural rules which have themselves been experimentally determined and which are also subject to change). Moreover, his position rests also on a naïve conception of the democratic process as it operates at the legislative and executive levels in the United States. In the matter of the number of social interests which are taken into account, the democratic political process is far more inclusive than is contemporary economic theory, particularly an economic theory which proceeds from the postulates of logical positivism or from those of a secular natural law philosophy.

Whether it is made operational by the common law method of judicial decision, by action in the legislative arena, or by action on the part of the Executive, the democratic process is basically an experimental approach, a "piecemeal" approach. Until a similar experimental approach becomes commonplace in economics, no reconciliation between law in a democratic society and theoretical economics in general, and in the area of antitrust in particular, seems likely. Those economists who have adopted an instrumentalist approach in economics have recognized this fact but, for the most part, economic theorists relying on economic models in which they manipulate "purely" economic variables have not done so. Accordingly, the influence of price theorists has been very limited.

It does not follow that decisions by judges in individual cases, or laws adopted by legislatures, or actions by the Executive are to be validated without qualification or that they are not to be subjected to criticism. On the contrary, it is only by examining such decisions, laws, or actions critically on the basis of available data that inconsistencies and conflicts, as well as conflicts of interest, can be discovered. But it does remain true that the judicial process is just as essential an element in the formulation of the working rules of economic activity in our society—despite the fact that it may result in delays, inconsistencies, and frustrations—as are the legislative or Executive processes, which may also produce these things. Often such delays, inconsistencies, and frustrations are merely evidence that a problem exists to which no agreed solution has yet been determined. The fact that this is true will become apparent in the examination of the policies which have been adopted by the courts and the Federal Trade Commission relative to the scope of the basic antitrust statutes, beginning with the study of the development of policies under the Sherman Act (in the next chapter).

14

The Sherman Act

This chapter undertakes: (1) to examine the common law background of the Sherman Act; (2) to discuss the prohibition of "restraints of trade" contained in Section 1 of the Act; and (3) to consider the "monopoly" provision contained in Section 2 of the Act. The reader may wish to review the discussion of the Sherman Act in Chapter 12.

A. THE SHERMAN ACT AND THE COMMON LAW

Status of the Common Law in 1890

As we have seen in Chapter 3, it was not until 1938 that the Supreme Court held that there was no such thing as a "federal common law" applicable in federal courts. But Senator Sherman apparently held this view in 1890. This fact explains why he asserted in his speech to the Senate in defense of his bill that the bill did not "announce a new principle of law" but applied "old and well recognized principles of the common law to the complicated jurisdiction of our State and Federal Governments." According to Senator Sherman, each state was already preventing

and controlling combinations within the limits of its jurisdiction and his bill did not propose to interfere with this practice. (Indeed it could not, under the Commerce Clause of the Constitution, as we have seen in Chapter 7.) Instead, his bill sought to confer jurisdiction upon the courts of the United States in the same kinds of cases.[1]

Mitchel v. Reynolds and the Rule of Reason

The landmark case of restraint of trade at common law is the English case of *Mitchel* v. *Reynolds*.[2] In this case, decided in 1711, a defendant had leased his bakery to the plaintiff for a period of five years and had agreed not to compete with the plaintiff in a specified area during this period of time. The English court held that the agreement not to compete was a valid ancillary agreement and that the main purpose of the contract was the lease of the bakery. In effect, it thus held that ancillary contracts, limited as to time and place, constituted reasonable restraints of trade. Note that the court was faced in this case with the possibility that the defendant might enrich himself through bad faith in the form of broken promises if it had held the restraint

[1] *Congressional Record*, Vol. 21, p. 2456 (March 21, 1890).

[2] 18 Eng. Rep. 347 (1711).

unreasonable and against public policy. On the other hand, the actual result in this case can be condemned on grounds that it clearly condones restrictions on competition.

Application of the Rule of Reason in 1890

The question of whether or not Congress intended to codify the common law by adopting the Sherman Act is today of little significance. What is significant is the contemporary policy of the Supreme Court relative to the scope of Section 1.

In a report prepared for the Temporary National Economic Committee (whose work and composition have already been described in Chapter 9), Professor Milton Handler concluded that there were a number of "discernible trends" in the state court cases decided prior to 1890. Some English and some American courts held that the "Rule of Reason" applied to horizontal agreements between competitors "which curbed, controlled, or eliminated competition," even though these agreements were not ancillary to another agreement. However, a second view regarded the Rule of Reason as inapplicable to such agreements or held the agreements of this type unlawful, without reference to the Rule. The prevailing view was probably that "all agreements among persons engaged in the same trade, industry or line of commerce, whereby competition was eliminated" by various devices, such as "fixation of prices, control of output, pooling of profits, division of markets," or other devices inconsistent with competitive institutions were unlawful. According to this view, it made no difference that the prices resulting might be "reasonable" or that the practices had been adopted to halt "ruinous competition." Handler discerned yet another position in the decided cases: "agreements by minority groups without control of the market were upheld if competition in the market itself remained unaffected." even though competition among the parties to the agreement had been eliminated. And finally, arrangements by those with monopoly power might be upheld by some courts if the prices fixed were "reasonable." Thus, there was not one but many different views at common law.[3]

B. "CONTRACTS, COMBINATIONS, AND CONSPIRACIES IN RESTRAINT OF TRADE"

Section 1 of the Sherman Act declares illegal "every contract, combination, and conspiracy in restraint of trade." The following major subdivision is devoted to a discussion of the meaning and application of that section.

The Rule of Reason versus Per Se Illegality

As we have seen in Chapter 7, the Supreme Court held in the *Knight* case, in 1895 that the Sherman Act could not be applied to the Sugar Trust, on the grounds that manufacturing was not commerce. Two years later, however, it had no difficulty in holding illegal a number of pooling arrangements in the railroad industry. In fact, in these early cases the Court explicitly rejected the view that Section 1 embodied the Rule of Reason although, as will become readily apparent below, the bases of rejection varied, depending upon the views of the different judges who wrote the majority opinions in the various cases. Thus in 1897, Justice Peckham wrote a majority opinion which held that the phrase "Every contract" did not have the "limited signification" which the defendants sought to attach to it. They had argued that at common law the phrase "contract in restraint of trade" meant "only such contracts as are in *unreasonable* restraint of trade," and consequently that the phrase in the Sherman Act did not include "all contracts in restraint of trade, but only those which are in *unreasonable* restraint of trade." Thus they argued that the Sherman Act codified that interpretation of the "common law" which would result in a decision in their favor.

Justice Peckham rejected this argument, saying that contracts in restraint of trade had "been known and spoken of for hundreds of years both in England and in this country, and the term includes [all] contracts which in fact restrain or may restrain trade." Some contracts of this kind, he asserted, had been held void because the

---

[3] Milton Handler, *A Study of the Construction and Enforcement of the Antitrust Laws*, (Temporary National Economic Committee Monograph No. 38) (Washing-

ton, D.C.: U.S. Government Printing Office, 1941), pp. 4–5.

restraint they embodied was unreasonable; others had been upheld because they were not unreasonable. Thus, a contract could be a "contract in restraint of trade" and still be valid at common law. But the word "Every" in the Sherman Act meant *all*, whether reasonable or not.[4]

Shortly thereafter, Justice Taft took the view that the common law rule was that all nonancillary restraints were unlawful. Thus he asserted the Rule of Reason meant that "the contract must be one in which there is a main purpose to which the covenant in restraint of trade is merely ancillary." In such a contract, the purpose of the "covenant in restraint of trade" was to protect one of the contracting parties "from the injury he might suffer from the unrestrained competition of the other," thereby being denied the fruits of the principal contract to which the restraint was merely ancillary.[5]

According to Justice Peckham, therefore, the word "Every" in Section 1 embodied the common law *definition* but prohibited *all* contracts in restraint of trade, whether ancillary or not; while Justice Taft held to the view that the statute "codified" the common law rule and prohibited only all nonancillary contracts of this type and that ancillary contracts were not unlawful under the statute because they were not unlawful at common law. But, according to Peckham, the Act modified the common law rule.

Such was the state of the law in 1911 when Justice White produced the Rule of Reason in the *Standard Oil* and *American Tobacco* cases. He not only believed that the statute "codified" the common law but also that, at common law, the Rule applied *both* to ancillary and nonancillary contracts. Thus, after holding that the *second section of the statute was merely a supplement to the first and did not state separate offenses, he* wrote:

. . . And, of course, when the second section is thus harmonized with and made as it was intended to be the complement of the first, it becomes obvious that the criteria to be resorted to in any given case for the purpose of ascertaining whether violations of the section have been committed, is the rule of reason guided by the established law and by the plain duty to enforce the prohibitions of the act and thus the public policy which its restrictions were obviously enacted to subserve.[6]

The Rule of Reason. In the *American Tobacco* case, the Rule was stated as follows:

. . . Applying the rule of reason to the construction of the statute, it was held in the *Standard Oil* case that as the words "restraint of trade" at common law and in the law of this country at the time of the adoption of the Antitrust Act only embraced acts or contracts or agreements or combinations which operated to the prejudice of the public interests by unduly restricting competition or unduly obstructing the due course of trade or which, either because of their inherent nature or effect or because of the evident purpose of the acts, etc., injuriously restrained trade, that the words used in the statute were designed to have and did have but a like significance. . . . In other words, it was held, not that acts which the statute prohibited could be removed from the control of its prohibitions by a finding that they were reasonable, but that the duty to interpret which inevitably arose from the general character of the term *restraint of trade* required that the words *restraint of trade* should be given a meaning which would not destroy the individual right to contract and render difficult if not impossible any movement of trade in the channels of interstate commerce—the free movement of which it was the purpose of the statute to protect.[7]

For purposes of marking the distinction between the Rule of Reason and the *per se* concept of illegality under the Sherman Act, it is useful to look upon the Rule as a matter of construction or of procedure. Under the Rule, once the prosecution has proved the existence of a restraint of trade, it is open to the defendant to show that the restraint is "reasonable," and thus to escape liability. In the case of the *per se* concept, however, it is enough merely that the prosecution prove the existence of the restraint, and it is not open to the defendant to show the "reasonableness" of the restraint. As we will see below, certain types

---

[4] *United States* v. *Trans-Missouri Freight Ass'n.*, 166 U.S. 290 (1897), at pp. 327–328.

[5] *Addyston Pipe & Steel Co.* v. *United States*, 85 Fed. 271 (1898), at p. 282.

[6] *Standard Oil Co. of New Jersey* v. *United States*, 221 U.S. 1 (1911), at pp. 61–62.

[7] *United States* v. *American Tobacco Co.*, 221 U.S. 106 (1911), at pp. 179–180. (Italics mine.)

[8] Compare A. D. Neale, *The Antitrust Laws of the U.S.A.* (London: Cambridge University Press, 1962), p. 21.

of conduct are now subject to the *per se* rule; price-fixing is an example.[8]

In 1941, Professor Milton Handler noted that "before 1911, all nonancillary restrictions of competition, such as combinations to fix prices, pool profits, share markets, and control output were unlawful restraints prohibited by the statute." After the adoption of the Rule of Reason, according to Handler, such agreements "continued to be unlawful, but now they were denominated 'unreasonable restraints of trade.' " Indeed, "conduct which prior to 1911 was condemned as an illegal restraint was held unreasonable *per se* thereafter." Thus, he concluded, the Rule of Reason resulted in a change in theory.[9]

Handler's view is interesting, particularly in the light of the treatment of this topic in the *Report of the Attorney General's National Committee to Study the Antitrust Laws*. The Committee took the view that the Rule of Reason is a general rule applicable to all Sherman Act cases. It further asserted that certain forms of conduct "such as agreements among competitors to fix market price or control production, are 'conclusively presumed to be illegal by reason of their nature or necessary effect.' " In such cases, the Committee maintained that "inquiry under the Rule of Reason is over once it has been decided that the conspiracy or agreement under review in fact constitutes price rigging or production control."[10]

The Committee thus sought to avoid admitting the *per se* thesis by treating the *per se* cases as a special case of the Rule of Reason, a practice which does not square with the history of the Act, whatever may be the psychological impact of the Committee's approach. Indeed, the Committee's statement apparently sought to minimize the seriousness of the *per se* violations and, perhaps, to further some Committee members' position that the law is uncertain. Rather than asserting "that inquiry under the Rule of Reason is over once . . ." one could argue with equal force, "In such cases, inquiry under the Rule of Reason never begins."

Per Se Illegality. In this regard it is interesting to consider the position of the Supreme Court three years after publication of the *Report*. Speaking for the majority in 1958, Justice Black said:

> . . . there are certain agreements or practices which because of their pernicious effect on competition and lack of any redeeming virtue are conclusively presumed to be unreasonable and therefore illegal without elaborate inquiry as to the precise harm they have caused or the business excuse for their use. This principle of *per se* unreasonableness not only makes the type of restraints which are proscribed by the Sherman Act more certain to the benefit of everyone concerned, but it also avoids the necessity for an incredibly complicated and prolonged economic investigation into the entire history of the industry involved, as well as related industries, in an effort to determine at large whether a particular restraint has been unreasonable—an inquiry so often wholly fruitless when undertaken. Among the practices which the courts have heretofore deemed to be unlawful in and of themselves are *price-fixing, United States* v. *Socony-Vacuum Oil Co.,* 310 U.S. 150, 210; *division of markets, United States* v. *Addyston Pipe & Steel Co.,* 85 F. 271, aff'd, 175 U.S. 211; *group boycotts, Fashion Originators' Guild* v. *Federal Trade Comm'n,* 312 U.S. 457; and *tying arrangements, International Salt Co.* v. *United States,* 332 U.S. 392.[11]

It is thus apparent that no real doubt today exists concerning the types of agreements which are *per se* illegal; it is to an examination of some specific cases in this category that attention will next be given.

"Reasonable" Price-Fixing. In 1927 the Supreme Court flatly asserted in a landmark case involving price-fixing:

> The aim and result of every price-fixing agreement, if effective, is the elimination of one form of competition. The power to fix prices, whether reasonably exercised or not, involves power to control the market and to fix arbitrary and unreasonable prices. The reasonable price today may through economic and business changes become the unreasonable price of tomorrow. Once established, it may be maintained unchanged because of the absence of competition secured by the agreement for a price reasonable when fixed.[12]

The case in question involved 23 corporations controlling 82 percent of the vitreous pottery in the United States. The defendants

---

[9] Handler, *op. cit.,* p. 8.

[10] *Report of the Attorney General's National Committee to Study the Antitrust Laws* (Washington, D.C.: U.S. Government Printing Office, 1955), p. 11.

[11] *Northern Pacific Railway Co.* v. *United States,* 356 U.S. 1 (1958), at p. 5. (Italics mine.)

[12] *United States* v. *Trenton Potteries,* 273 U.S. 392 (1927), at p. 397.

were charged with establishing a combination to fix prices in restraint of interstate commerce and to limit sales. It may be noted, in passing, that agreements to divide markets are often found to exist in conjunction with agreements to fix prices and are used as a method of implementing the latter. In 1940 the Court emphatically restated the rule of the *Trenton Potteries* case by holding unlawful a scheme among oil companies for taking "distress" supplies of gasoline off the market in an effort to raise prices. That is, in 1940, the Court said, among other things:

> . . . for over forty years this Court has consistently and without deviation adhered to the principle that price-fixing agreements are unlawful *per se* under the Sherman Act and that no showing of so-called competitive abuses or evils which those agreements were designed to eliminate or elleviate may be interposed as a defense.[13]

In the *Socony-Vacuum* case, the Court was forced to distinguish between practices adopted by the defendant oil companies and those engaged in by coal mining companies during the depression, because the Court had earlier held that the Sherman Act had *not* been violated by a plan of 187 coal producers to establish an exclusive selling agency whose apparent purpose was to enhance coal prices. In drawing a distinction between the two cases, Justice Douglas wrote in 1940 in the *Socony-Vacuum* case:

> . . . the only essential thing in common between the instant case and the *Appalachian Coals* case is the presence in each of so-called demoralizing or injurious practices. The methods of dealing with them were quite divergent. . . . The plan in the *Appalachian Coals* case was not designed to operate *vis-à-vis* the general consuming market and to fix the prices on that market. Furthermore, the effect, if any, of that plan on prices was not only wholly incidental but also highly conjectural. For the plan had not then been put into operation. Hence this Court expressly reserved jurisdiction in the District Court to take further proceedings if, *inter alia*, in "actual operation" the plan proved to be "an undue restraint upon interstate commerce." And as we have seen it would *per se* constitute such a restraint if price-fixing were involved.[14]

Whether or not one accepts the distinction between the two cases which Justice Douglas tried to draw, one thing does seem clear: agreements to fix prices are *per se* illegal under Section 1 of the Sherman Act, the *Appalachian Coals* case notwithstanding. No question of the reasonableness of the prices fixed exists in these cases.

Indeed, in 1968 the Supreme Court emphasized that fixing *maximum* prices was no less illegal than fixing *minimum* prices. The case in question involved also a grant of an exclusive dealership, and the defendants claimed that the fixing of maximum prices was necessary to protect consumers from the monopolistic power the defendant had placed in the hands of a dealer who had been granted an exclusive territory. Speaking for the majority, Justice White commented on this claim by saying, "The assertion that price-fixing is justified because it blunts the pernicious consequences of another distribution practice is unpersuasive."[15]

Various cases involving the legality of activities of trade associations under Section 1 of the Sherman Act are best understood as cases involving questions of fact as to whether or not actual price-fixing activities were being engaged in. These cases are considered next.

Trade Associations and Price-Fixing. The question of how far a trade association may go in facilitating exchanges among its members of information pertaining to prices, production, and markets has been the subject of some debate, particularly among lawyers. The trade association cases can be summarized as standing for the proposition that the use of the trade association form of organization for implementing an otherwise illegal agreement does not immunize the parties from a charge of price-fixing. The cases really turn on the question of whether or not price-fixing activities or agreements really are present. In other words, the issue in these cases is whether or not the activities in question constitute circumstantial evidence of price-fixing.

One of the earliest cases involving this question to come before the Supreme Court was the *American Column and Lumber* case. In

---

[13] *United States* v. *Socony-Vacuum Oil Co.*, 310 U.S. 150 (1940), at p. 218.
[14] *Ibid.*, at p. 216.

[15] *Albrecht* v. *Herald Co.*, 390 U.S. 145 (1968), at p. 154.

this case, a trade association required each of its members to submit six reports to its secretary, as follows: (1) a daily report of all actual sales; (2) a monthly shipping report with copies of invoices; (3) a monthly production report; (4) a monthly stock report; (5) a price list report; (6) an inspection report. All of these reports were, in turn, subject to a complete audit by the association, and the secretary supplied the members with market information. In addition, also, monthly meetings to discuss market conditions were held. In finding that this system constituted circumstantial evidence of the existence of a combination to fix prices, the Court said:

Genuine competitors do not make daily, weekly and monthly reports of the minutest details of their business to their rivals, as the defendants did; they do not contract, as was done here, to submit their books to the discretionary audit and their stocks to the discretionary inspection of their rivals for the purpose of successfully competing with them; and they do not submit the details of their business to the analysis of an expert, jointly employed, and obtain from him a "harmonized" estimate of the market as it is and as, in his specially and confidentially informed judgment, it promises to be. This is not the conduct of competitors but is so clearly that of men united in an agreement, express or implied, to act together and pursue a common purpose under a common guide that, if it did not stand confessed a combination to restrict production and increase prices in interstate commerce and as, therefore, a direct restraint upon that commerce, as we have seen that it is, that conclusion must inevitably have been inferred from the facts which were proved.[16]

Two years later, in the *American Linseed Oil* case a similar reporting scheme was held by the Court to constitute a price-fixing arrangement.[17] In 1925, however, two years later, in the *Maple Flooring* case, in which the trade statistics were of a different type and were also made available to the Department of Commerce, the Court was unable to find support "for an inference that the plan would" necessarily result in "concerted and prohibited" action. But it did limit its holding by saying:

We decide only that trade associations or combinations of persons or corporations which

openly and fairly gather and disseminate information as to the cost of their product, the volume of production, the actual price which the product has brought in past transactions, stocks of merchandise on hand, approximate cost of transportation from the principal point of shipment to the points of consumption . . . and who, as they did, meet and discuss such information and statistics without however reaching or attempting to reach any agreement or any concerted action with respect to prices or production or restraining competition, do not thereby engage in unlawful restraint of commerce.[18]

In this case, it is to be noted, there was neither any proof nor any allegation that any agreements had been made affecting prices or production. A similar lack of charges by the government concerning limitations on prices or output existed in the *Cement Manufacturers Protective Association* case in the same year, and thus no proof was offered that an agreement relative to prices or output existed. Again the Court refused to read into the record a Sherman Act violation.[19] These cases thus stand for the proposition that trade association activities are not necessarily illegal *per se* but may be held unlawful if it is both alleged and proved that they do in fact constitute an agreement in restraint of trade.

Among the more recent cases involving trade associations, note must be taken of the *Tag Institute* case, in which a Court of Appeals refused to sustain a cease and desist order by the Federal Trade Commission pertaining to certain price and other reporting activities by the Institute. The activities were an outgrowth of a Code of Fair Competition for the tag industry which had been put into effect under the N.I.R.A. (discussed in Chapter 9). The Court remarked:

. . . The evidence does not . . . warrant the Commission's finding that the effect of the Tag Industry Agreements "has resulted in a substantial uniformity of prices for tags and tag products among the respondent members." In the first place, this implies that instances of departure from uniformity are insignificant and unsubstantial—which certainly cannot be said. In the second place, there is no evidence that such uniformity as has existed is a result of the operation of the Tag Industry Agreements, for it

---

[16] *American Column and Lumber Co.* v. *United States*, 257 U.S. 377 (1921), at p. 410.

[17] *United States* v. *American Linseed Oil Co.*, 262 U.S. 371 (1923).

[18] *Maple Flooring Mfrs.' Ass'n.* v. *United States*, 268 U.S. 563 (1925), at p. 586.

[19] *Cement Mfrs.' Protective Ass'n. et. al.*, v. *United States*, 268 U.S. 588 (1925).

does not appear whether there has been an increase or decrease of uniformity either in list prices or in actual selling prices since the agreements have been in operation . . .

There has been some tendency to look askance at reporting agreements between competitors, where the information exchanged is reserved exclusively to themselves and withheld from buyers or the public generally. Presumably this is because such secrecy more readily suggests the inference that the agreement is inspired by some unlawful purpose and precludes the argument that the information thus secretly exchanged serves a function similar to that of market information made available through the activities of commodity exchanges, trade journals, etc. . . .

We have come to the conclusion that the reporting agreements herein, and the practices of petitioners thereunder, are lawful under the controlling authorities. . . . The Commission has endeavored to show that the agreement was . . . a price-fixing agreement having the purpose and actual effect of restraining and preventing price competition. We believe that such findings are unsupported by the evidence or by any reasonable inferences to be drawn therefrom. We say this with full recognition of our limited scope of review of findings of fact by the Commission.[20]

Labor Unions and Restraint of Trade. We have seen in a preceding chapter that Section 6 of the Clayton Act contains a provision ostensibly exempting labor unions from the antitrust laws. In general, the Court has held that the exemption is limited to union activities carried on in the course of a dispute *with* an employer and that a conspiracy *between* a union *and* an employer may involve illegal conduct under Section 1 of the Sherman Act. In 1964 the Supreme Court reviewed and restated its views on this subject in a case in which it held unlawful an agreement between a union and several employers to impose a given wage scale on various other employers for the purpose of eliminating some of them from the coal mining industry. In his review of the prior decisions, Justice White said:

The antitrust laws do not bar the existence and operation of labor unions as such. Moreover, Section 20 of the Clayton Act, 38 Stat. 738 and Section 4 of the Norris–LaGuardia Act, 47 Stat.

70, permit a union, acting alone, to engage in the conduct therein specified without violating the Sherman Act. *United States* v. *Hutcheson*, 312 U.S. 219; *United States* v. *International Hod Carriers Council*, 313 U.S. 539, affirming *per curiam* 37 F. Supp. 191 (D.C.N.D. Ill. 1941); *United States* v. *American Federation of Musicians*, 318 U.S. 741, affirming *per curiam*, 47 F. Supp. 304 (D.C.N.D. Ill. 1942).

But neither Section 20 nor Section 4 expressly deals with arrangements or agreements between unions and employers. Neither section tells us whether any or all such arrangements or agreements are barred or permitted by the anti-trust laws. Thus *Hutcheson* itself stated:

"So long as a union acts in its self-interest and *does not combine with non-labor groups*, the licit and the illicit under Section 20 are not to be distinguished by any judgment regarding the wisdom or unwisdom, the rightness or wrongness, the selfishness or unselfishness of the end of which the particular union activities are the means." 312 U.S., at 232. (Emphasis added.) And in *Allen Bradley Co.* v. *Union*, 325 U.S. 797, this Court made explicit what had been merely a qualifying expression in *Hutcheson* and held that "when the unions participated with a combination of businessmen who had complete power to eliminate all competition among themselves and to prevent all competition from others, a situation was created not included within the exemptions of the Clayton and Norris–LaGuardia Acts." *Id.*, at 809. . . . Subsequent cases have applied the *Allen Bradley* doctrine to such combinations without regard to whether they found expression in a collective bargaining agreement . . . and even though the mechanism for effecting the purpose of the combination was an agreement on wages.[21]

Agricultural Cooperatives and Restraint of Trade. The principle developed by the Supreme Court in cases involving labor unions has been employed in a parallel way by the Court in cases involving an exemption contained in the Capper-Volstead Act (7 U.S.C. 291) of the activities of agricultural cooperatives from the Sherman Act. In 1967, in a private action for treble damages the question of whether or not an agricultural cooperative could legally combine with privately-owned packing houses to engage in restrictive practices was answered in the negative.[22]

---

[20] *Tag Manufacturing Institute et al.* v. *Federal Trade Commission,* 174 F. 2d 452 (1949), at pp. 460, 462, 463.
[21] *United Mine Workers* v. *Pennington,* 381 U.S. 657 (1964) at pp. 661–663. In 1968 the Court held that orchestra leaders were a "labor group" and parties to

a "labor dispute" thus bringing them within the exemption. *Federation of Musicians* v. *Carroll,* 391 U.S. 99 (1968).
[22] *Case-Swayne Co.* v. *Sunkist Growers,* 389 U.S. 384 (1967).

The conclusion to be drawn from the cases involving labor unions and from those involving agricultural cooperatives is that the Court will not permit a party not included within one of the exemptions from the antitrust laws to avail himself of such an exemption merely by combining with a party who does have a legitimate claim to such an exemption.

The Nature and Proof of Conspiracy

The Definition of "Conspiracy." In 1842 a Massachusetts court defined "conspiracy" at common law in these words:

To constitute an indictable conspiracy there must be a combination of two or more persons by some concerted action to accomplish some criminal or unlawful purpose; or to accomplish some purpose not in itself criminal or unlawful by criminal or unlawful means.[23]

Thereupon the court held that a labor organization did not constitute a conspiracy at common law. This case, it may be noted in passing, is a landmark case in the field of labor law.

Proof of Conspiracy. The preceding discussion of cases involving price-fixing has already made apparent the fact that proof of the existence of a conspiracy is often a matter of circumstantial evidence. This fact was clearly recognized by the Court in 1914 in the *Eastern States Retail Lumber Dealers' Association* case, which involved the circulation among retail lumber dealers of a blacklist of wholesale dealers who also sold directly to consumers. The Court remarked:

. . . It is elementary . . . that conspiracies are seldom capable of proof by direct testimony and may be inferred from the things actually done, and when in this case by concerted action the names of wholesalers who were reported as having made sales to consumers were periodically reported to the other members of the associations, the conspiracy to accomplish that which was the natural consequence of such action may be readily inferred.[24]

A more recent leading case involving this question is the *Interstate Circuit* case. In this case, the defendants were distributors and exhibitors of motion picture films. Hoblitzelle and O'Donnell were the names of the president and general manager, respectively, of two of the defendant exhibitor corporations. According to the Court, in 1934, O'Donnell, the manager of Interstate and Consolidated (two exhibitor corporations), sent to each distributor a letter on Interstate letterhead, "each letter naming all of them as addressees, in which he demanded compliance with two demands as a condition of Interstate's continued exhibition of the distributor's films in its first-run theaters." The demands had to do with admission prices to be charged at all theaters and with the exhibition of the films in question as part of a double feature bill in subsequent-run theaters. In holding that a conspiracy existed among the defendants after the distributors complied with the demands in question, the Court remarked:

. . . As is usual in cases of alleged unlawful agreements to restrain commerce, the Government is without the aid of direct testimony that the distributors entered into any agreement with each other to impose the restrictions upon subsequent-run exhibitors. In order to establish agreement it is compelled to rely on inferences drawn from the course of conduct of the alleged conspirators.

The trial court drew the inference of agreement from the nature of the proposals made on behalf of Interstate and Consolidated; from the manner in which they were made; from the substantial unanimity of action taken upon them by the distributors; and from the fact that appellants did not call as witnesses any of the superior officials who negotiated the contracts. . . . This conclusion is challenged by appellants because not supported by subsidiary findings or by the evidence. We think this inference of the trial court was rightly drawn from the evidence.[25]

The fact that the existence of a conspiracy may be inferred from other facts and is often a matter of circumstantial evidence has given rise to the question of whether or not a situation in which a number of firms act on parallel lines solely because of business considerations may be one involving a violation of the Sherman Act. This situation has been denominated one of "conscious parallelism" by some writers; other writers, however, use this term to refer merely to the fact that the existence of a conspiracy may be established by circumstantial evidence. Circumstantial

[23] *Commonwealth* v. *Hunt*, 45 Mass. 111 (1842).
[24] *Eastern States Retail Lumber Dealers' Association et al.*, v. *United States*, 234 U.S. 600 (1914), at p. 612.
[25] *Interstate Circuit, Inc.* v. *United States*, 306 U.S. 208 (1939), at p. 221.

evidence can, of course, be rebutted, and a showing that the parallel action is not the result of a tacit or express agreement but is dictated by ordinary business considerations will serve as a defense in such cases. Thus in 1954, the Court held that a number of motion picture producers and distributors who restricted the showing of their first-run pictures to downtown theaters and who made available only "subsequent-run" pictures to suburban theaters, and whose policies were independently dictated by business considerations without collusion with each other, had not violated the antitrust laws. Speaking for the majority, Justice Clark wrote:

The crucial question is whether respondents' conduct . . . stemmed from independent decision or from an agreement, tacit or express. To be sure, business behavior is admissible circumstantial evidence from which the fact finder may infer agreement. . . . But this Court has never held that proof of parallel business behavior conclusively establishes agreement or, phrased differently, that such behavior itself constitutes a Sherman Act offense. Circumstantial evidence of consciously parallel behavior may have made heavy inroads into the traditional judicial attitude toward conspiracy; but "conscious parallelism" has not yet read conspiracy out of the Sherman Act entirely.[26]

In January 1969, the Court held that an agreement merely to exchange price information constituted a conspiracy, saying that the case was not merely one of parallel business behavior.[26a] Assistant Attorney General in Charge of Antitrust McLaren gave the Antitrust Division's interpretation of this decision in March 1969. He asserted that the case "stands for the proposition that checking with competitors, where it has become a prevailing market practice, violates the Sherman Act" and indicated that on similar facts in the future he would seek a criminal conviction.[26b]

Intra-Enterprise Conspiracy. The definition of conspiracy given earlier requires action or agreement by "two or more persons." Consequently, the question arises whether a parent and its subsidiary can conspire. A

leading case involving this question is the *Kiefer-Stewart* case, in which a jury found that the Seagram and Calvert Distilling Corporations, which are affiliated companies, had conspired to conduct a common (maximum) price policy and to impose this policy on other firms. Seagram owned the controlling interest in Calvert. The Court remarked:

Respondents next suggest that their status as "mere instrumentalities of a single manufacturing-merchandising unit" makes it impossible for them to have conspired in a manner forbidden by the Sherman Act. But this suggestion runs counter to our past decisions that common ownership and control does not liberate corporations from the impact of the antitrust laws. *E.g. United States* v. *Yellow Cab Co.*, 332 U.S. 218. The rule is especially applicable where, as here, respondents hold themselves out as competitors.[27]

In 1968 the Supreme Court decided an interesting case involving the problem at hand. The case involved a treble damage action by Perma Life Mufflers Corporation and several other muffler dealers against the International Parts Corporation and its subsidiary, Midas Muffler Corporation. The plaintiff alleged the existence of agreements between themselves and the defendants under which plaintiffs agreed to purchase only from the defendants and received in exchange an allocation of specific territories in which to sell. There was also an agreement to fix retail prices. The District Court and the Court of Appeals held that since the defendants had participated in the agreements, they had no standing to sue. The Supreme Court held, however, that since, after some time had passed, the defendants were *unwilling* participants in these agreements, their case should be tried.[28]

The case was thus remanded to the District Court for trial on the issues alleged of price-fixing, market allocation, and enforced tying agreements. Like the 1968 *Albrecht* case discussed earlier, the *Kiefer-Stewart* case, just discussed, involved a resale price maintenance agreement to fix *maximum*

[26] *Theater Enterprises* v. *Paramount Film Distributing Corp.*, 346 U.S. 537 (1954), at pp. 540–541.
[26a] *United States* v. *Container Corp.*, 393 U.S. 333 (1969).
[26b] *Address by Richard W. McLaren before the Antitrust Section of the American Bar Association*, (Lithoprint; Washington, D.C.: U.S. Department of Justice, March 27, 1969), p. 4.
[27] *Kiefer-Stewart Co.* v. *Joseph E. Seagram and Sons*, 340 U.S. 211 (1951), at p. 215.
[28] *Perma Mufflers* v. *Int'l. Parts Corp.*, 392 U.S. 134 (1968), at pp. 141–42.

resale prices. More often, however, such agreements involve the fixing of *minimum* resale prices, and attempts are often made to enforce them by refusals to deal and by boycotts. It is to cases of this type that we turn next.

Resale Price Maintenance, Refusals to Deal, and Boycotts under Section 1

Refusals to Deal and Resale Price Maintenance. As we have seen in Chapter 12, the Miller-Tydings Act provided an exemption from the Sherman Act for resale price maintenance contracts in cases where contracts or agreements of that description "are lawful in the state of resale." This amendment was necessary because the Court had earlier held in the *Dr. Miles* case that such agreements were unlawful where they eliminated competition among dealers.[29] After the *Dr. Miles* case in 1919, in the *Colgate* case, the Court was faced with a situation in which Colgate had announced uniform prices, urged its dealers to sell at these prices, and had also adopted a policy of refusing to sell to dealers who failed to adhere to the announced resale prices. The lower court interpreted the indictment as merely charging Colgate with a refusal to sell and not with making an agreement with dealers not to sell, and the Supreme Court considered itself on appeal to be bound by this interpretation. It thereupon held that a mere refusal to deal did not constitute a violation of Section 1. Justice McReynolds spoke for the majority and said:

. . . In the absence of any purpose to create or maintain a monopoly, the act does not restrict the long recognized right of a trader or manufacturer engaged in an entirely private business, freely to exercise his own independent discretion as to parties with whom he will deal. And, of course, he may announce in advance the circumstances under which he will refuse to sell.[30]

In a later case, the Court explained its decision in the *Colgate* case and undertook to reconcile *Colgate* with *Dr. Miles* as follows:

. . . [In the Colgate case] we were confronted with an uncertain interpretation of an indictment itself couched in rather vague and general

language, the meaning of the opinion and judgment of the court below being the subject of serious controversy. . . . We had no intention to overrule or modify the doctrine of the *Dr. Miles Medical Co.* case. Under the interpretation adopted by the trial court and necessarily accepted by us, the indictment failed to charge that the Colgate Company made agreements, either express or implied, which undertook to obligate vendees to observe specified resale prices; and it was treated as alleging only recognition of the manufacturer's undoubted right to specify resale prices and refuse to deal with anyone who fails to maintain the same.[31]

Then, in 1936, the Supreme Court upheld an Illinois statute authorizing resale price maintenance contracts in that state.[32] Congress thereupon adopted the Miller-Tydings Act, opening the door to a widespread adoption of such state statutes. But, as we have seen in Chapter 12, the Court then held that this exemption did not apply to the non-signer's type of state statute, whereupon Congress adopted the McGuire-Keogh Amendment to the Federal Trade Commission Act to extend the exemption also to this type of situation. In 1964 the Court upheld this amendment in *Hudson Distributors* v. *Eli Lily*.[33]

Boycotts. In 1960, in the *Parke Davis* case, the question of use of a boycott to enforce resale price maintenance in the absence of state legislation on the subject was again considered by the Court. In 1956, the Parke Davis Pharmaceutical Company had announced a resale price maintenance policy in its wholesalers' and retailers' catalogs which also contained a statement that it was Parke Davis' continuing policy to deal only with wholesalers who observed the schedule and sold only to retailers legitimately authorized to fill prescriptions. At that time, there was no statute authorizing resale price maintenance in Virginia or in the District of Columbia, and hence the Miller-Tydings Act did not apply in these areas. Drug retailers in Washington, D.C. and in Richmond, Virginia refused to follow the announced resale price maintenance schedule. Next, Parke Davis "representatives called contemporaneously upon the

---

[29] *Dr. Miles Medical Co.* v. *John D. Park and Sons Co.*, 220 U.S. 373 (1911).

[30] *United States* v. *Colgate*, 250 U.S. 300 (1919), at p. 307.

[31] *United States* v. *A. Shrader's Son Inc.*, 252 U.S. 85

(1920), at pp. 98–99.

[32] *Old Dearborn Distributing Co.* v. *Seagram Distillers Corp.*, 299 U.S. 83 (1936).

[33] 377 U.S. 386 (1964).

retailers involved, individually, and told each that if he did not observe the suggested minimum retail prices, Parke Davis would refuse to deal with him, and, furthermore, he would be unable to purchase any Parke Davis products from the wholesalers. Each of the retailers was also told that his competitors were being similarly informed."[34] The lower court held that "no violation of the Sherman Act had occurred because the actions of Parke Davis were unilateral and sanctioned by law under the doctrine laid down in the case of *United States* v. *Colgate*. . . ." The Supreme Court reversed the lower court and took the occasion to provide a review of the law on this subject. Speaking for the majority, Justice Brennan said:

The Government concedes for the purposes of this case that under the *Colgate* doctrine a manufacturer, having announced a price maintenance policy, may bring about adherence to it by refusing to deal with customers who do not observe that policy. The Government contends, however, that subsequent decisions of this Court compel the holding that what Parke Davis did here by entwining the wholesalers and retailers in a program to promote general compliance with its price maintenance policy went beyond mere customer selection and created combinations or conspiracies . . . in violation of Section 1 and Section 3 of the Sherman Act.

The history of the *Colgate* doctrine is best understood by reference to a case which preceded the *Colgate* decision, *Dr. Miles Medical Co.* v. *Park and Sons Co.* . . . Dr. Miles entered into written contracts with its customers obligating them to sell its medicine at prices fixed by it. The Court held that the contracts were void because they violated both the common law and the Sherman Act.

The *Colgate* decision distinguished *Dr. Miles* on the ground that the *Colgate* indictment did not charge that company with selling its products to dealers *under agreements* which obligated the latter not to resell except at prices fixed by the seller. The *Colgate* decision created some confusion and doubt as to the continuing vitality of the principles announced in *Dr. Miles*. This brought *United States* v. *Shrader's Son, Inc.* . . . to the Court. The case involved the prosecution of a components manufacturer for entering into price-fixing agreements with retailers, jobbers and manufacturers who used his products . . .

The next decision was *Frey and Son, Inc.* v. *Cudahy Packing Co.* . . . That was a treble damage suit alleging a conspiracy in violation of the Sherman Act between the manufacturer and jobbers to maintain resale prices. The plaintiff recovered a judgment. The Court of Appeals for the Fourth Circuit reversed on the authority of *Colgate*. The Court of Appeals concluded: "There was no formal written or oral agreement with jobbers for the maintenance of prices" and in that circumstance held that under *Colgate* the trial court should have directed a verdict for the defendant. In holding that the Court of Appeals erred, this Court referred to the decision in *Shrader* as holding that the "essential agreement, combination or conspiracy might be implied from a course of dealing or other circumstances," so that in *Cudahy*, "Having regard to the course of dealing and all the pertinent facts disclosed by the present record, we think whether there existed an unlawful combination or agreement between the manufacturer and jobbers was a question for the jury to decide, and that the Circuit Court of Appeals erred when it held otherwise . . ."

. . . Less than a year after *Cudahy* was handed down, the Court decided *Federal Trade Commission* v. *Beech-Nut Packing Co.*, 257 U.S. 441, which presented a situation bearing a marked resemblance to the Parke Davis program.

In *Beech-Nut* the company had adopted a policy of refusing to sell its products to wholesalers or retailers who did not adhere to a schedule of resale prices. Beech-Nut later implemented this policy by refusing to sell to wholesalers who sold to retailers who would not adhere to the policy. To detect violations the company utilized code numbers on its products and instituted a system of reporting. When an offender was cut off, he would be reinstated upon the giving of assurances that he would maintain prices in the future. The Court construed the Federal Trade Commission Act to authorize the Commission to forbid practices which had a "dangerous tendency unduly to hinder competition or to create monopoly." . . . The Sherman Act was held to be a guide to what constituted an unfair method of competition.

That *Beech-Nut* narrowly limited *Colgate* and announced principles which subject to Sherman Act liability the producer who secures his customers' adherence to his resale prices by methods which go beyond the simple refusal to sell to customers who will not resell at stated prices, was made clear in *United States* v. *Bausch and Lomb Optical Co.*, 321 U.S. 707, 722:

"The *Beech-Nut* case recognizes that a simple refusal to sell to others who do not maintain the first seller's fixed resale prices is lawful but adds as to the Sherman Act, 'He (the seller) may not, consistently with the act, go beyond the exercise of this right, and by contracts or combinations,

[34] *United States* v. *Parke Davis and Co.*, 362 U.S. 29 (1960), at pp. 33–34.

express or implied, unduly hinder or obstruct the free and natural flow of commerce in the channels of interstate trade.' 257 U.S. at 453. The Beech-Nut Company, without agreements, was found to suppress the freedom of competition by coercion of its customers through special agents of the company, by reports of competitors about customers who violated resale prices, and by boycotts of price cutters . . ."

. . . whatever uncertainty previously existed as to the scope of the *Colgate* doctrine, *Bausch and Lomb* and *Beech-Nut* plainly fashioned its dimensions as meaning no more than that a simple refusal to sell to customers who will not resell at prices suggested by the seller is permissible under the Sherman Act. In other words, an unlawful combination is not just such as arises from a price maintenance *agreement*, express or implied; such a combination is also organized if the producer secures adherence to his suggested prices by means which go beyond his mere declination to sell to a customer who will not observe his announced policy.

. . . When the manufacturer's actions, as here, go beyond mere announcement of his policy and the simple refusal to deal, and he employs other means which effect adherence to his resale prices . . . he has put together a combination in violation of the Sherman Act. . . .

. . . Parke Davis used the refusal to deal with the wholesalers in order to elicit their willingness to deny Parke Davis products to retailers and thereby help gain the retailers' adherence to its suggested minimum retail prices. The retailers who disregarded the price policy were promptly cut off when Parke Davis supplied the wholesalers with their names. . . . Parke Davis created a combination with the retailers and the wholesalers . . . and violated the Sherman Act.[35]

It is to be noted that the effect on price competition of a resale price maintenance program is the same whether that program is enforced by a unilateral refusal to deal, as in the *Colgate* case, or is a result of duress, as in the *Parke Davis* case. Moreover, as we have seen in Chapter 7, the long established right of a seller to refuse to deal has been qualified in cases involving racial discrimination under the Civil Rights Act of 1964. A similar qualification of the right to refuse to deal in cases in which this device is employed to achieve a result prohibited by the antitrust laws is thus long overdue. In short, considered in terms of its con-

sequences, the *Colgate* case should be overruled by the Court at the earliest opportunity.

In 1964, the Court extended the principle of the *Parke Davis* case to hold unlawful the fixing of retail prices of gasoline by a supplier who employed consignment agreements and retained title to the gasoline until it was sold at the retail level. The Court said, among other things, ". . . a consignment, no matter how lawful as a matter of private contract law, must give way before the federal antitrust policy."[36] This case will again be considered in chapter 19, when we consider the relationship between patent law and antitrust policy.

"Reasonableness" of Group Boycotts. The argument that a boycott is "reasonable" will not be accepted by the Court. In 1941, in the *Fashion Originators' Guild* case, a group of textile manufacturers and women's clothing manufacturers agreed among themselves not to sell to retailers who also purchased from other manufacturers who "pirated" the designs of those party to the agreement. The Court said that the defendants' argument that they were merely trying to protect themselves against the pirating of designs "is no more material than would be the reasonableness of the prices fixed by an unlawful combination."[37]

An interesting case illustrating what the Court itself described as "a classic conspiracy in restraint of trade"[38] was decided in May, 1966. The case involved actions taken by a number of conspirators, consisting of General Motors, some of its Los Angeles dealers, and an association of Los Angeles General Motors dealers, to force other General Motors dealers in the Los Angeles area to discontinue their practice of selling new General Motors automobiles at reduced prices through local discount houses. According to the Supreme Court:

The District Court decided . . . that the described events [the actions of the conspirators] did not add up to a combination or conspiracy violative of the antitrust laws. But its conclusion cannot be squared with its own specific findings of fact. These findings include the essentials of a conspiracy within Section 1 of the Sherman Act:

---

[35] *Ibid.*, pp. 37 ff.

[36] *Simpson* v. *Union Oil Company*, 377 U.S. 13 (1964), at pp. 19.

[37] *Fashion Originator's Guild of America* v. *Federal Trade Commission*, 312 U.S. 457 (1941), at pp. 465–67.

[38] *United States* v. *General Motors*, 384 U.S. 127 (1966), at p. 140.

That in the summer of 1960 the Losor Chevrolet Dealers Association, "through some of its dealer-members," complained to General Motors personnel about sales through discounters . . .; that at a Losor meeting in November 1960 the dealers there present agreed to embark on a letter-writing campaign directed at enlisting the aid of General Motors . . .; that in December and January General Motors personnel discussed the matter with every Chevrolet dealer in the Los Angeles area and elicited from each a promise not to do business with the discounters . . .; that representatives of the three associations of Chevrolet dealers met on December 15, 1960, and created a joint investigating committee . . .; that the three associations then undertook jointly to police the agreements obtained from each of the dealers by General Motors; that the associations supplied information to General Motors for use by it in bringing wayward dealers into line, and that Chevrolet's O'Conner asked the associations to do so . . .; that as a result of this collaborative effort, a number of Chevrolet dealers were induced to repurchase cars they had sold through discounters and to promise to abjure such sales in future. . . .

These findings by the trial judge compel the conclusion that a conspiracy to restrain trade was proved. The error of the trial court lies in its failure to apply the correct and established standard for ascertaining the existence of a combination or conspiracy under Section 1 of the Sherman Act. See *United States* v. *Parke, Davis and Co.*, 362 U.S. 29, 44–45.

. . . It is of no consequence, for purposes of determining whether there has been a combination or conspiracy under Section 1 of the Sherman Act, that each party acted in its own lawful interest. . . .

Neither individual dealers nor the associations acted independently or separately. The dealers collaborated, through the associations and otherwise, among themselves and with General Motors, both to enlist the aid of General Motors and to enforce dealers' promises to forsake the discounters. . . .

As Parke Davis had done, General Motors sought to elicit from all the dealers agreements, substantially interrelated and interdependent, that none of them would do business with the discounters. . . .

There can be no doubt that the effect of the combination or conspiracy here was to restrain trade and commerce within the meaning of the Sherman Act. Elimination, by joint collaborative action, of discounters from access to the market is a *per se* violation of the Act.

The protection of price competition from conspiratorial restraint is an object of special solicitude under the antitrust laws.[39]

As we have seen in the *Fashion Originator's Guild* case earlier, group boycotts are *per se* illegal under Section 1, and, as we will see later in this chapter, they *may* constitute a violation of Section 2 if they are part of an "attempt to monopolize."

Exclusive Dealing and Restraint of Trade

In a series of cases decided in 1967 and 1968, the Court was faced with the problem of the validity of exclusive dealing arrangements. A leading case is the *Schwinn* case.[40] According to the facts in the case, the Schwinn Company, a manufacturer of bicycles, maintained three different types of relationships with its distributors and retailers. In some cases, the company sold its product outright to distributors but imposed upon all its distributors a restriction allowing them to sell to *franchised retailers only in specified territories*; in other cases, the company shipped its product to retailers on an agency or consignment basis, retaining title; and in still other cases, the company sold to retailers by means of consignment or agency contracts with distributors. No issue concerning the use of the distribution methods as a way of fixing prices was raised, although the Court flatly stated that, if one had existed, the scheme would have constituted a *per se* violation of Section 1.[41] The Court held that the arrangement under which the distributors both acquired title and were subjected to a territorial limitation and to a limitation to sell to franchised dealers only constituted a *per se* violation of Section 1. However, the Court upheld the validity of the arrangements under which the distributors and retailers did not acquire title to the product but served merely as agents of the company. Speaking for the majority, Justice Fortas remarked:

. . . we are not prepared to introduce the inflexibility which a *per se* rule might bring if it were applied to prohibit all *vertical* restrictions of territory and all franchising, in the sense of designating specified distributors and retailers as the chosen instruments through which the manufacturer, *retaining ownership of the goods*, will distribute them to the public.[42]

---

[39] *Ibid.*, at pp. 140–148.
[40] *United States* v. *Arnold Schwinn and Co. et. al.*, 388 U.S. 365 (1967).

[41] *Ibid.*, p. 373.
[42] *Ibid.*, pp. 379–380. (Italics mine.)

In the *Schwinn* case, the government had not contended that the agency and consignment arrangements were *per se* illegal; instead it had argued that they were "unreasonable" restraints. But the Court did not agree, noting the absence of price-fixing and "the presence of alternative sources of products." It is to be noted that the *Schwinn* case involved a *"vertical* limitation" (running from manufacturer to distributors and retailers). The *Sealy* case, decided on the same day as the *Schwinn* case, involved a *horizontal* territorial allocation. Such an allocation is *per se* illegal, which we will now see.

The Sealy Company owns the licenses and trademarks under which a certain brand of mattress is distributed and sold in the United States. In turn, this company is owned by its licensees. Accordingly, the Court held that an arrangement under which maximum prices were fixed and sales territories were allocated among the licensees was a horizontal restraint and unlawful. Specifically, it found that "here, the arrangements for territorial limitations are part of an aggregation of trade restraints, including unlawful price fixing and policing."[43] Although the Court did not say so in explicit terms, it seems to have considered the Sealy Company itself to be a device utilized by potential competitors to eliminate competition. One is reminded of some of the reasons given by witnesses before the Industrial Commission for the rise of the corporate form of business association, a point developed at length in Chapter 9. The *Schwinn* case rule pertaining to exclusive dealerships in cases in which the manufacturer retains title, we will see in a later chapter, is similar to the rule applied in the case in which a single patent holder employs agents and consignees to distribute his product.

About six months after the *Schwinn* and *Sealy* decisions, the Court held that Oklahoma liquor retailers could secure an injunction based on Section 1 to prevent the division by wholesalers of that state into territories and the division of the market by brands.[44] The 1968 *Albrecht* case has already been cited to illustrate the proposition that the fixing of *maximum* prices is unlawful *per se.* This case also involved the fact that a newspaper publisher had granted an exclusive territory to a newspaper carrier; indeed, it will be recalled that the Court did not allow the defense to show that the imposition of a maximum price was necessary to protect subscribers because an exclusive territory free from competition had been granted! In regard to this point, in reversing the decision of the Court of Appeals which had accepted that argument, the Court said:

... on the record before us the Court of Appeals was not entitled to assume, as its reasoning necessarily did, that the exclusive rights granted by respondent [the newspaper publisher] were valid under S.1 of the Sherman Act, either alone or in conjunction with a price fixing scheme. See *United States* v. *Arnold Schwinn and Co.*[45]

Thus by 1968 the *Schwinn* case, decided in 1967, had become a precedent. Exclusive dealing arrangements are sometimes found in conjunction with tying arrangements. The latter may constitute violations of the Clayton Act, of the Federal Trade Commission Act, and of both sections of the Sherman Act.

Tying Arrangements as Restraints of Trade

Tying agreements are sometimes imposed on patent licensees by patent holders; a leading case involving such an illegal tying arrangement in conjunction with patented equipment is the *International Salt* case of 1947. Lessees of the defendant company's patented salt-dispensing machines also had to purchase their requirements of salt from the defendant as a condition of the lease. The government alleged that this condition in the lease contract violated Section 1 of the Sherman Act as well as Section 3 of the Clayton Act. Holding that a violation of the Sherman Act existed, the Court said:

The appellant's patents confer a limited monopoly of the invention they reward. From them appellant derives a right to restrain others from making, vending or using the patented machines. But the patents confer no right to restrain use of, or trade in, unpatented salt. By contracting to close this market for salt against

[43] *United States* v. *Sealy, Inc.,* 388 U.S. 350 (1967), at p. 357.
[44] *Burke, Ranch Liquors, et. al.* v. *Ford, All Brand Sales,* et. al., 389 U.S. 321 (1967).
[45] *Albrecht* v. *Herald Co.* 390 U.S. 145 (1968), at pp. 153–54.

competition, International has engaged in a restraint of trade for which its patents afford no immunity from the antitrust laws. . . . Not only is price-fixing unreasonable, *per se* . . . but also it is unreasonable, *per se*, to foreclose competitors from any substantial market. . . . The volume of business affected by these contracts cannot be said to be insignificant.[46]

The last sentence in the preceding quotation raises an issue known as that of "quantitative substantiality" under Section 3 of the Clayton Act, which prohibits tying agreements where the effect is "to substantially lessen competition or to tend to create a monopoly," and will be further discussed in the next chapter. For the present it is enough to note that, although the Court in 1953 apparently took the position that a tying agreement constitutes a violation of Section 1 of the Sherman Act when it is exacted by one who enjoys a lawful monopoly, the Court broadened its view in 1958. For example, in 1953 it said:

> . . . From the "tying" cases a perceptible pattern of illegality emerges: When the seller enjoys a monopolistic position in the market for the "tying" product . . . because for even a lawful monopolist it is "unreasonable, *per se*, to foreclose competitors from any substantial market," a tying arrangement is banned by Section 1 of the Sherman Act. . . .[47]

But in 1958, Justice Black spoke for the majority and said:

> While there is some language in the Times–Picayune opinion which speaks of "monopoly power" or "dominance" over the tying product as a necessary precondition for application of the rule of *per se* unreasonableness to tying arrangements, we do not construe this general language as requiring anything more than sufficient economic power to impose an appreciable restraint on free competition in the tied product, (assuming all the time, of course, that a "not insubstantial" amount of interstate commerce is affected).[48]

In 1969, the Court held that extension of credit could be a source of tying leverage, just as could sale of a product, and defined the concept of "substantial amount of commerce" for purposes of a tying arrangement under antitrust law by saying that "the

relevant figure is the total volume of sales tied by the sales policy under challenge, not the portion accounted for by the particular plaintiff."[48a] As has been noted, the question of "quantitative substantiality" just discussed arises also in cases involving tying arrangements under Section 3 of the Clayton Act, and will also be discussed in Chapter 15.

Another method of excluding competitors which is *per se* illegal is that of outright division of markets. This practice will be considered next.

Division of Markets, Joint Ventures, and Per Se Illegality

A survey of past decisions pertaining to outright division of markets and an argument that a joint venture (as defined in Chapter 9) may in fact be a mere cloak for an outright division of markets appears in the dissenting opinion in the *Penn-Olin* case of 1964. In 1960, "the Pennsalt Corporation and the Olin Mathieson Company signed a joint-venture agreement, each acquiring 50% of the newly formed Penn-Olin Company, which began producing sodium chlorate in 1961 in Kentucky."[49] The government claimed that the joint venture violated both Section 7 of the Clayton Act and Section 1 of the Sherman Act. The District Court held that neither statute had been violated; the majority opinion of the Supreme Court remanded the case for a retrial and a determination of the factual question of the effect on competition of the acquisition. The dissenting opinion took the position that a division of the market through the device of a joint venture had the effect of "substantially lessening competition" within the meaning of Section 7 of the Clayton Act; and in laying the basis for this position, Justice Douglas surveyed previous cases involving outright division of markets under Section 1 of the Sherman Act by saying:

> Agreements among competitors to divide markets are *per se* violations of the Sherman Act. The most detailed, grandiose scheme of that kind is disclosed in *Addyston Pipe and Steel Co.* v. *United*

[46] *International Salt Co.* v. *United States*, 332 U.S. 392 (1947), at pp. 395–396.

[47] *Times-Picayune Publishing Co.* v. *United States*, 345 U.S. 594 (1953), at pp. 608–609.

[48] *Northern Pacific Railway Co.* v. *United States*, 356

U.S. 1 (1958), at p. 11.

[48a] *Fortner Enterprises* v. *U.S. Steel*, 394 U.S. 495 (1969), at p. 502.

[49] *United States* v. *Penn–Olin Chemical Co.*, 378 U.S. 158 (1964).

States . . . where industrialists, acting like commissars in modern communist countries, determined what tonnage should be produced by each company and what territory was "free" and what was "bonus." The Court said: "Total suppression of the trade in the commodity is not necessary in order to render the combination one in restraint of trade. It is the effect of the combination in limiting and restricting the right of each of the members to transact business in the ordinary way, as well as its effect upon the volume or extent of the dealing in the commodity, that is regarded. . . ."

In *United States* v. *National Lead Co.* . . . a Sherman Act violation resulted from a division of world markets for titanium pigments, the key being allocation of territories through patent license agreements. A similar arrangement was struck down in *Timken Co.* v. *United States* . . . where world trade territories were allocated among an American, a British, and a French company through intercorporate arrangements called a "joint venture." *Nationwide Trailer Rental System, Inc.* v. *United States* . . . (affirming 156 F. Supp. 800), held violative of the antitrust laws an agreement establishing exclusive territories for each member of an organization set up to regulate the one-way trailer rental industry and empowering a member to prevent any other operator from becoming a member in his area. . . . what we have in substance [in this case] is two major companies who on the eve of competitive projects in the southeastern market join forces. In principle the case is no different from one where Pennsalt and Olin decide to divide the southeastern market as was done in *Addyston Pipe* and in the other division-of-market cases already summarized. Through the "joint venture" they do indeed divide it fifty-fifty. That division through the device of the "joint venture" is as plain and precise as though made in more formal agreements.[50]

The Section 7 (Clayton Act) aspect of this case will be further considered in Chapter 17. We have seen that agreements to divide markets are usually part of a larger scheme to fix prices. Such was the situation in the *Addyston Pipe and Steel* case. A more sophisticated method of eliminating competitors, we have seen in Chapter 9, is that of merger. The question of the legality of mergers under Section 1 of the Sherman Act thus arises. It is considered next.

Mergers as Restraints of Trade

The *E. C. Knight* case—in which, as we have seen in Chapter 7, the Supreme Court held that the Sherman Act could not be applied to the Sugar Trust in 1895— involved a merger; but since the case was disposed of on jurisdictional grounds, the substantive issue of legality of the merger was not reached. However, in 1904 in the *Northern Securities* case, the Court did hold it to be a violation of Section 1 for a holding company to acquire the controlling stock interest in two railroads which were in competition with each other. Four opinions were written in the *Northern Securities* case. This fact alone is a clear indication that the case presented new issues and that the Court lacked common law precedents upon which to base its opinion. The holding company device, after all, is a creature of statute and was unknown at common law. Indeed, it was not until 1964 and the *Lexington National Bank* case that the Court clarified its position on the status of mergers under Section 1 of the Sherman Act. Interestingly enough, in 1955 the Attorney General's National Committee remarked:

The application of Sections 1 and 2 of the Sherman Act . . . reveals no consistent pattern. . . . We believe that the 1948 Columbia Steel case . . . serves as a recent restatement of the law applicable to mergers under Section 1. Where mergers form part of a plan for monopolization, their role has already been analyzed under Section 2 of the Sherman Act . . . and more important for all practical purposes, the amended Section 7 of the Clayton Act is the primary provision to which the Department of Justice and the Federal Trade Commission will resort to test the legality of mergers.[51]

This statement represents the prevailing view in 1955, and the *Lexington National Bank* case of 1964 must thus have come as a distinct surprise to many, and especially to the authors of the *Report*. This case will be examined in detail below. Before doing so, however, it will be useful to consider briefly some of the earlier merger decisions (between 1904 and 1964).

In general, it may be said that the Court followed the *Northern Securities* case in a number of succeeding cases involving railroads, but that it applied the Rule of Reason to industrial combinations between 1904 and 1964, sometimes upholding the legality of the merger and sometimes not

---

[50] *Ibid.*, at pp. 177–180. See also *Zenith Corp.* v. *Hazeltine*, 395 U.S. 100 (1969).

[51] *Report of the Attorney General's National Committee to Study the Antitrust Laws, op. cit.*, p. 115, n. 1.

doing so, depending upon the finding of an existence of predatory practices or of an attempt to monopolize. Thus in 1911, in the *American Tobacco* and *Standard Oil* cases, the Court, as we have seen, announced the Rule of Reason but came to the conclusion that the predatory practices employed in establishing the power of these trusts warranted a conclusion that these trusts should be dissolved on grounds that they constituted unreasonable restraints of trade. Professor Handler commented on the *Standard Oil* case by noting that the grounds of the decision were not clearly stated and that Justice White seemed more concerned with "the profundities of the Rule of Reason." However, Handler did suggest that intent to monopolize and to maintain the monopoly by exclusion of competitors was "the element most stressed in the decision."[52]

After 1911 the Court consistently applied the Rule of Reason to industrial merger cases. In 1913 it refused to dissolve a combination called the United Shoe Machinery Company which consisted of a number of companies holding patents for the production of shoe machinery. Speaking for the Court, Justice Holmes asserted that the "combination was simply an effort after greater efficiency." He assumed that the success of the group was due to the fact that "their patents were the best," and noted that the patents conferred a monopoly on those who held them. The indictment did not charge that the companies had previously competed with one another, and it was admitted in argument that they did not. Under the circumstances, Justice Holmes *could* see nothing wrong with the combination.[53] And, in 1920, by a vote of four to three, the Court refused to dissolve the steel trust which had been put together, as we have seen in Chapter 9, in the form of a holding company, the United States Steel Corporation. Although the trust had engaged in price-fixing activities in the past, the Court found that it was not engaging in such practices at the time of the suit. The Court emphasized the fact that the holding company had not made a predatory use of its great power and asserted, "the law does not make mere size an offense or the

existence of unexerted power an offense."[54] Moreover, the Court found that the combination did not constitute a monopoly. The Court also "failed to see that the public interest would be served" by granting the government's request for dissolution. It did see a detriment to American foreign trade in granting the government's request.[55]

Thus by 1920, under the Rule of Reason, the Court had gone some distance in classifying the trusts as either "good" or "bad" on the basis of particular factual situations. Indeed, in 1941 Handler remarked at the conclusion of his survey of merger decisions under the Sherman Act:

It is apparent from this review of the Supreme Court cases that the course of decision in the field of mergers and consolidations has been erratic and unpredictable and that there is today virtually as much doubt and uncertainty regarding the permissive limits of capital combinations as there was in 1890.[56]

Handler's view was the prevailing one in 1948, when the *Columbia Steel* case was decided. That case involved the prayer of the government for an injunction, alleging a violation of both Sections 1 and 2 of the Sherman Act, to prevent United States Steel from acquiring the assets of the largest independent steel fabricator on the West Coast. At this time, it will be recalled from Chapter 12, Section 7 of the Clayton Act had been held by the Court to permit the acquisition of assets but not of stocks of another company "where the effect may be substantially to lessen competition or to tend to create a monopoly in any line of commerce," and hence the government could not seek relief under Section 7 in this case.

This case involved both horizontal and vertical integration; the horizontal integration was claimed by the government to lead to a violation of Section 1, while the vertical integration was attacked under Section 2 and will be discussed later, but not in the present context. The government introduced evidence to show that United States Steel possessed (prior to the merger) 13% of the "western market" and Consolidated (the name of the fabricating company

[52] Handler, *op. cit.*, p. 51.
[53] *United States* v. *Winslow*, 227 U.S. 202 (1913), at p. 217.
[54] *United States* v. *United States Steel Corp.*, 251 U.S.

417 (1920), at p. 451.
[55] *Ibid.*, at p. 457.
[56] Handler, *op. cit.*, p. 74.

which United States Steel sought to acquire) possessed 11%, so that after the merger United States Steel would control 24% of the market. The Supreme Court upheld the trial court's finding that the amount of competition which would be eliminated by the merger was too small to warrant a holding that the merger constituted a restraint of trade. Speaking for the majority, Justice Reed said:

> ... In determining what constitutes un-reasonable restraint, we do not think the dollar volume is in itself of compelling significance; we look rather to the percentage of business con-trolled, the strength of the remaining com-petition, whether the action springs from business requirements or purpose to monopolize, the probable development of the industry, consumer demands, and other characteristics of the market.[57]

The majority thus continued to hold that mergers under Section 1 were to be tested by the Rule of Reason. The approval of this decision in the quotation from the *Report* of the Attorney General's National Committee given earlier in this section thus amounts to advocacy of the continued application of the Rule in merger cases under Section 1.

However, as has been mentioned in Chapter 12, in 1950 Congress amended Section 7 of the Clayton Act to make the acquisition of assets of one corporation by another illegal where the effect would be "substantially to lessen competition or to tend to create a monopoly in any line of commerce in any section of the country," and this latest expression of the Con-gressional intention was undoubtedly in the mind of the majority when, in 1964, it decided the *Lexington National Bank* case, in which the Court apparently adopted as a test for mergers under Section 1 the question of whether or not significant competition would be *eliminated* by the merger.

According to the official report of the case, it involved a civil action by the government to prohibit "the consolidation of the largest and fourth largest of the six commercial banks in Fayette County, Kentucky."[58] Moreover, the "Comptroller of the Currency had approved the consolidation, although reports, required by the Bank Merger Act of

1960, from the Attorney General, the Federal Deposit Insurance Corporation, and the Board of Governors of the Federal Reserve System had all concluded it would adversely affect competition in the area."[59] The Court agreed with these findings of fact, and Justice Douglas spoke for the majority in stating the opinion. In this opinion he reviewed previous decisions which the Court apparently now considers applicable to horizontal mergers under Section 1 as follows:

> ... The case, we think, is governed by *Northern Securities Co.* v. *United States* ... and its progeny. The Northern Pacific and Great Northern operated parallel lines west of Chicago. A holding company acquired the controlling stock in each company. A violation of Section 1 was adjudged without reference to ... the extent to which the traffic of the combined roads was still subject to some competition. It was enough that the two roads competed, that their com-petition was not insubstantial, and that their combination put an end to it. ....
>
> *United States* v. *Union Pacific R. Co.* .... was in the same tradition. Acquisition by Union Pacific of a controlling stock interest in Southern Pacific was held to violate Section 1 of the Sherman Act. As in the *Northern Securities* case the Court held the combination illegal because of the elimination of the *inter se* competition between the merging companies, without reference to the strength or weakness of whatever competition remained. ....
>
> *United States* v. *Reading Co.* .... is the third of the series. There a holding company brought under common control two competing inter-state carriers and two competing coal companies. That was held "without more" to be a violation of Section 1 and Section 2 of the Sherman Act. ....
>
> The fourth of the series is *United States* v. *Southern Pacific Co.* .... in which the acquisition by Southern Pacific of stock of Central Pacific—a connecting link for transcontinental shipments by a competitor of Southern Pacific—was held to violate the Sherman Act. ....
>
> We need not go so far here as we went in *United States* v. *Yellow Cab Co.* .... where we said:
>
> "... the amount of interstate trade thus affected by the conspiracy is immaterial in determining whether a violation of the Sherman Act has been charged in the complaint. Section 1 of the Act outlaws unreasonable restraints in interstate commerce, regardless of the amount of commerce affected." The four railroad cases at least stand for the proposition that where merging

---

[57] *United States* v. *Columbia Steel*, 334 U.S. 495 (1948), at p. 527.
[58] *United States* v. *First National Bank and Trust Co. of*

Lexington et. al., 376 U.S. 665 (1964).
[59] *Ibid.*

companies are major competitive factors in a relevant market, the elimination of significant competition between them, by merger or consolidation, itself constitutes a violation of Section 1 of the Sherman Act. That standard was met in the present case in view of the fact that the two banks in question had such a large share of the relevant market.

It is said that *United States* v. *Columbia Steel* . . . is counter to this view. . . . The *Columbia Steel* case must be confined to its special facts. The Court said:

"In determining what constitutes unreasonable restraint, we do not think the dollar volume is in itself of compelling significance; we look rather to the percentage of business controlled, the strength of the remaining competition, whether the action springs from business requirements or purpose to monopolize, the probable development of the industry, consumer demands, and other characteristics of the market. We do not undertake to prescribe any set of percentage figures by which to measure the reasonableness of a corporations's enlargement of its activities by the purchase of the assets of a competitor. The relative effect of percentage command of a market varies with the setting in which that factor is placed. . . ."

In the present case all those factors clearly point the other way, as we have seen. *Where, as here, the merging companies are major competitive factors in a relevant market, the elimination of significant competition between them constitutes a violation of Section 1 of the Sherman Act.* In view of our conclusion under Section 1 of the Sherman Act, we do not reach the questions posed under Section 2.[60]

The decision in the *Lexington National Bank* case has the effect of making applicable to mergers generally under Section 1 of the Sherman Act the market structure test which is applicable under Section 7 of the Clayton Act as amended by the Celler-Kevauver Act of 1950, as we shall see in Chapter 17. However in February 1966, Congress adopted an amendment to the Bank Merger Act of 1960 for the ostensible purpose of exempting bank mergers from the Sherman Act.[61] Under this amendment, in the case of those bank mergers which are subject to challenge under the antitrust laws, a court must approve the merger if it finds that the "anticompetitive effects" of the merger are "clearly outweighed in the public interest by the probable effect of the transaction in meeting the needs of the community to be served." But in cases decided in 1967 and 1968, the Supreme Court held that the amendment created an exception from the antitrust laws and that the defendant banks seeking to merge had the burden of proving that the adverse effects of their merger were outweighed by considerations of public convenience and need. Indeed, in 1968 the Court interpreted its original 1967 opinion by saying:

. . . [In 1967] this Court interpreted the procedural provisions of the 1966 Act, holding that the Bank Merger Act provided for continued scrutiny of bank mergers under the Sherman Act and the Clayton Act, but had created a new defense with the merging banks having the burden of proving that defense. The task of the district courts was to inquire *de novo* into the validity of a bank merger and to determine, first whether the merger offended the antitrust laws, and second, if it did, whether the banks had established that the merger was nonetheless justified by "the convenience and needs of the community to be served."[62]

It has been argued, largely by banking interests, that the banking regulatory agencies—such as the Comptroller of the Currency, the Federal Reserve Board, and the Federal Deposit Insurance Corporation are better qualified than the courts to pass upon the validity of bank mergers and that the former will produce results which are socially more desirable than those which will be produced by adversary proceedings in open federal courts. Therefore, the past record of approvals and disapprovals of mergers by the regulatory agencies is illuminating. It is useful to note that between May 13, 1960 and May 12, 1965, the Federal Reserve Board approved 142 bank merger applications and denied 17, while one was withdrawn; the FDIC approved 173 of a total of 175 applications on which it acted; and the Comptroller of the Currency approved 450 of the 477 bank merger applications on which it acted, including, of course, the Lexington National Bank merger.[63] Apparently, in the minds of regulators the public convenience deriving

---

[60] *Ibid.*, pp. 670–673. (Italics mine.)

[61] Public Law 89–356 (February 21, 1966).

[62] *United States* v. *Third National Bank*, 390 U.S. 171 (1968), at p. 178. See also, *United States* v. *First City National Bank of Houston*, 386 U.S. 361 (1967).

[63] *Amend the Bank Merger Act of 1960* (Hearings before a Subcommittee of the Senate Banking and Currency Committee, 89th Cong., 1st sess.) (Washington, D.C.: U.S. Government Printing Office, 1965), pp. 15 ff.

from concentration of banking facilities far outweighs the benefits of competition in banking. Needless to say, the record is replete with instances of support for the 1966 legislation by the American Bankers Association, by various state banking associations, and by the Association of Registered Bank Holding Companies.[64] One broad issue raised by this legislation and cases involving it is that of the extent to which the antitrust laws are or should be applicable to economic activities and organizations subject to the jurisdiction of special regulatory agencies. This issue will be further considered in a later chapter. It is also to be noted that, having disposed of the 1964 *Lexington* case under Section 1, the Court did not consider the government's complaint under Section 2 of the Sherman Act. It is to cases involving Section 2 of the Sherman Act that the next major subdivision of this chapter is devoted.

C. MONOPOLIZING, ATTEMPTING TO MONOPOLIZE, AND CONSPIRING TO MONOPOLIZE

Section 2 of the Sherman Act declares illegal monopolizing, attempting to monopolize, and combining or conspiring to monopolize. It is these activities to which our attention is now directed.

Monopoly versus "Monopolization"

Elements of the Offense. Many writers draw a distinction between the *condition* of *monopoly* and the *act* of *monopolizing.* Thus they hold that Section 2 of the Sherman Act does not prohibit *monopoly* as such, and that the crime of *monopolizing* in Section 2 consists of the possession of monopoly power coupled with some deliberate but not necessarily *per se* unlawful act to achieve or maintain and make use of monopoly power. This position was taken in the *Report* of the Attorney General's National Committee to Study the Antitrust Laws. At common law, the term "monopoly" referred to grants by the crown "of something which before was of common right." A leading English common law case involving such a monopoly is that of *Darcy* v. *Allen.*[65] In this case, the

court held invalid the grant of a monopoly in the trade of playing cards by Queen Elizabeth to one Edward Darcy on grounds that monopolies resulted in higher prices, in deterioration of quality of the articles monopolized, and in unemployment as a result of restriction of output. These results of monopoly were cited by the court without benefit of the sophisticated analysis of contemporary price theory and were presumably based on experience rather than on deductive reasoning making use of economic models. Lying behind the decision was the struggle between the Crown and Parliament for supremacy, the fact that the common law judges were sympathetic to the position of Parliament and the fact that the practice of granting monopolistic privileges by the Crown provided it with a source of revenue independent of Parliamentary supervision and control. In 1623 Parliament adopted *The Statute of Monopolies* prohibiting monopolies and granting a treble damage remedy to those injured by monopoly. This provision was an antecedent of the damage remedy in our own law, which is further discussed in Chapter 20.

In a decision handed down in June 1966, Justice Douglas, speaking for the majority, apparently rejected the distinction which has been described above between "monopoly" and "monopolizing" and defined "monopoly" in precisely the way in which the Attorney General's National Committee had defined the crime of "monopolizing"; thus, without referring to the position of the Committee, Justice Douglas wrote:

The offense of monopoly under Section 2 of the Sherman Act has two elements: (1) the possession of monopoly power in the relevant market and (2) the willful acquisition or maintenance of that power as distinguished from growth or development as a consequence of a superior product, business acumen, or historic accident. . . . In *United States* v. *du Pont and Co.,* . . . we defined monopoly power as "the power to control prices or exclude competition." The existence of such power ordinarily may be inferred from the predominant share of the market.[66]

Section 2 and the Rule of Reason. It is to cases decided under Section 2 that we now turn. As we have already seen in this

---

[64] *Ibid.*
[65] 77 Eng, Rep. 1270 (1602).

[66] *United States* v. *Grinnell Corp.* 384 U.S. 563 (1966), at pp. 570–571.

chapter, in stating the Rule of Reason in the *Standard Oil* case in 1911, Justice White undertook to "harmonize" the second section of the Act with the first by making the second a "supplement" to the first.[67] Indeed, many of the cases discussed in the preceding section of this chapter have also involved not only an allegation by the government that the defendant was guilty of a violation of Section 1, but also an allegation of illegality based on Section 2. Thus, for example, in the *Standard Oil* case, the Court also held:

Giving to the facts . . . the weight which it was deemed they were entitled to, in the light afforded by the proof of other cognate facts and circumstances, the court below held that the acts and dealings established by the proof operated to destroy the "potentiality of competition" which otherwise would have existed to such an extent as to cause the transfers of stock which were made to the New Jersey corporation and the control which resulted over the many and various subsidiary corporations to be a combination or conspiracy in restraint of trade in violation of the first section of the act, but also to be an attempt to monopolize and monopolization bringing about a perennial violation of the second section.[68]

After 1911, the Court regularly applied the Rule of Reason to cases under Section 2 as well as to cases under Section 1. In the *United States Steel* case of 1920, the Court ignored altogether the fact that a holding company device had been used, and it did not find the fact that the purpose of the combination was "monopolization" enough to constitute a violation because the trust had failed to achieve monopoly power. Moreover the Court asserted in a dictum, "the law does not make mere size an offense or the existence of unexerted power an offense. It, we repeat, requires overt acts and trusts to its prohibition and its power to repress or punish them. It does not compel competition nor require all that is possible."[69]

In 1927, the Court refused to find International Harvester guilty of a violation of the Sherman Act, even though, as a result of consolidations, the company had acquired control of a large percent of the market and had employed exclusive dealing contracts with its dealers to eliminate competition. In this case the Court repeated the dictum from the *United States Steel* case by saying:

. . . The law, however, does not make the mere size of a corporation, however impressive, or the existence of unexerted power on its part, an offense, when unaccompanied by unlawful conduct in the exercise of its power.[70]

As we have seen in Chapter 4, in the case study of the defense of "monopoly thrust upon" as an example of dictum as a source of change in law, although the dictum that "Mere size alone is not an offense against the Sherman Act" has been widely repeated in economic and legal literature, Judge Hand clearly identified it as merely a limited dictum in his opinion, in the *Alcoa* case in 1945, when he said:

. . . It is unquestionably true that from the very outset the courts have kept in reserve the possibility that the origin of a monopoly may be critical in determining its legality. . . . The successful competitor, having been urged to compete, must not be turned upon when he wins. The most extreme expression of this view is in *United States* v. *United States Steel Corporation* . . . which Sanford, J., in part repeated in *United States* v. *International Harvester Corporation*. . . . It so chances that in both instances the corporation had less than two-thirds of the production in its hands, and the language quoted was not necessary to the decision; so that even if it had not later been modified, it has not the authority of an actual decision. But, whatever authority it does have was modified by the gloss of Cardozo, J., in *United States* v. *Swift and Co.* . . . when he said, "Mere size . . . is not an offense against the Sherman Act unless magnified to the point at which it amounts to a monopoly . . . but size carries with it an opportunity for abuse that is not to be ignored when the opportunity is proved to have been utilized in the past.[71]

Since this question has already been the subject of extended discussion in Chapter 4, the reader may be referred to that earlier discussion for citations to support the proposition that the Court has never held in an actual case that a firm has had monopoly "thrust upon it." Nor is it true that the

---

[67] *Standard Oil Co. of New Jersey* v. *United States*, 221 U.S. 1 (1911), at pp. 61–62.

[68] *Ibid.*, at pp. 72–74.

[69] *United States* v. *United States Steel Corp.*, 251 U.S. 417 (1920), at p. 451.

[70] *United States* v. *International Harvester Corp.*, 274 U.S. 693 (1927), at p. 708.

[71] *Aluminum Co. of America* v. *United States*, 148 F. 2d 416 (1945), at pp. 429–430.

"deliberateness" in the acquisition, maintenance, or use of monopoly power, which constitutes "monopolizing," necessarily involves conduct which would violate Section 1 in the absence of monopoly power. In the *Alcoa* case, Judge Hand held that Alcoa possessed a monopoly of the kind covered by Section 2, but he added, "It does not follow because Alcoa had a monopoly, that it 'monopolized' the ingot market." He then shifted the burden of proof to the defendant in such cases by saying: "Having proved that Alcoa had a monopoly of the domestic market for ingot, the plaintiff had gone far enough; if it was an excuse that Alcoa had not abused its power, it lay upon Alcoa to prove that it had not." With respect to the distinction between Sections 1 and 2 of the Act, Judge Hand wrote:

It is settled, at least as to Section 1, that there are some contracts restricting competition which are unlawful, no matter how beneficient they may be. . . . They are absolutely forbidden. . . . It will now scarcely be denied that the same notion originally extended to all contracts— "reasonable," or "unreasonable"—which restrict competition. . . . Starting . . . with the authoritative premise that all contracts fixing prices are unconditionally prohibited, the only possible difference between them and a monopoly is that while a monopoly necessarily involves an equal, or even greater, power to fix prices, its mere existence might be thought not to constitute an exercise of that power. That distinction is nevertheless purely formal; . . . it would disappear as soon as the monopoly began to operate; for, when it did—that is, as soon as it began to sell at all—it must sell at some price and the only price at which it could sell is a price which it itself fixed. Thereafter the power and its exercise must needs coalesce. . . .[72]

"Deliberateness" and "General Intent." The element of "deliberateness," the second element specified by Justice Douglas in the *Grinnell* case, is closely related to that of "general intent" but is not to be confused with .hat of "specific intent," already discussed in Chapter 13. Thus Judge Hand also wrote:

We disregard any question of "intent." Relatively early in the history of the Act—1905 . . . Holmes, J. . . . explained this aspect of the Act in a passage often quoted. Although the primary evil was monopoly, the Act also covered

preliminary steps, which, if continued, would lead to it. These may do no harm of themselves, but, if they are initial moves in a plan or scheme which, if carried out, will result in monopoly, they are dangerous and the law will nip them in the bud. For this reason, conduct falling short of monopoly, is not illegal unless it is part of a plan to monopolize, or to gain such other control in a market as is equally forbidden. To make it so, the plaintiff must prove what in criminal law is known as a "specific intent"; an intent which goes beyond the mere intent to do the act. . . . In order to fall within Section 2, the monopolist must have both the power to monopolize and the intent to monopolize. To read the passage as demanding any "specific" intent, makes nonsense of it, for no monopolist monopolizes unconscious of what he is doing. Alcoa meant to keep and did keep that complete and exclusive hold on the market with which it started. That was to "monopolize" that market, however innocently it otherwise proceeded.[73]

Evidence of Alcoa's general intention to maintain its monopoly position lay in the fact that it "effectively anticipated and forestalled all competition and succeeded in holding the field alone. . . . It was not inevitable that it should always anticipate increases in the demand for ingot and be prepared to supply them."[74]

The opinion of Judge Wyzanski in the *United Shoe Machinery* case in 1953 provides a second illustration of "deliberateness." In that case, it was established that United supplied 75% and more probably 85% of the current demand in the American shoe machinery market, and it was held that United's system of leasing its machines, rather than selling outright, "created barriers to the entry of competitors in the shoe machinery field." These leasing practices were not such as could "properly be described as the inevitable consequences of ability, natural forces, or law." Given its market power and the fact that that power was, in part, based on the leasing practices, United was guilty of "monopolization," even though the leasing practices, absent the monopoly power, might not have been unlawful. With regard to intent, as we have seen in Chapter 13, Judge Wyzanski wrote:

So far, nothing in this opinion has been said of defendant's *intent* in regard to its power and practices in the shoe machinery market. This point can be readily disposed of by reference once

[72] *Ibid.*, at pp. 427–428.
[73] *Ibid.*, at p. 431.

[74] *Ibid.*

more to *Aluminum*, 148 F. 2d at pages 431–432. Defendant intended to engage in the leasing practices and pricing policies which maintained its market power. That is all the intent which the law requires when both the complaint and the judgment rest on a charge of "monopolizing," not merely "attempting to monopolize." Defendant having willed the means, has willed the end.[75]

Definition of the Market. It is to be noted that before the question of "deliberateness" is reached, the question of whether or not monopoly power exists must be answered. This question cannot be answered without, in turn, first defining the relevant product and market. As we have seen in Chapter 10, in a few cases the Court has sought to deal with the problem of the definition of the market by making reference to price theory concepts, such as that of "cross elasticity" of demand. However, given the present state of empirical studies in demand theory, such language can largely be discounted as a case of "window dressing" in the decisions where it appears, and in some, as has been noted in the introductory paragraphs of Chapter 10, the way in which the language of price theory has been used in actual opinions suggests that the judges have not themselves fully understood the meaning of the language they have employed. There is no general abstract test for "substitutability" which can be used to answer specific factual questions in antitrust cases; to say that a product possesses substitutes at given prices is to make a factual statement about the behavior of buyers. Such statements have an empirical content and cannot be answered by a reliance on deductive reasoning alone. It is useful to examine in this respect the discussion of this question in the *Report* of the Attorney General's National Committee, which reads:

    . . . Most members would simply emphasize . . . that more than a limited number of buyers should be able within reasonable variations in prices to buy either the product or the substitute, for both commodities to be considered in the same market for Sherman Act purposes:

    "For every product, substitutes exist. But a relevant market cannot meaningfully encompass that infinite range. The circle must be drawn narrowly to exclude any other product to which within reasonable variations in price, only a limited number of buyers will turn; in technical terms, products whose 'cross elasticities of demand' are small."[76]

The quotation within the quotation above is from the opinion in the *Times-Picayune* case of 1953, in which the Court held that newspaper, radio, and television advertising were not part of the same market. The dissent on this point in the *Report* alleges:

    . . . the Committee's apparent approval of the quoted language from *Times–Picayune* may be unfortunate. If it is actually meaningful to say that the relevant market must be defined "narrowly to exclude any other product to which within reasonable variations in price, only a limited number of buyers will turn," it probably fails to reflect the realities of modern business. On the other hand, since there is no practical known method of measuring cross-elasticity of demand, the suggested test may well be meaningless and lead to arbitrary results.[77]

The problem of defining the relevant market is not unique to cases involving Section 2 of the Sherman Act but arises also under other provisions of the antitrust laws. Thus, for example, the antimerger provision in Section 7 of the Clayton Act, as amended, prohibits mergers "where the effect may be substantially to lessen competition or to tend to create a monopoly in any line of commerce in any section of the country." Largely as a result of cases tried under this provision, the Court has been tending more and more to adopt a pragmatic and empirical definition of "the market" in all of its antitrust decisions. Indeed, judges in the district courts have been leading the way in this direction. Thus in the *Brown Shoe* case, which involved the question of the legality of a vertical forward merger (as defined in Chapter 9) under Section 7 of the Clayton Act as amended in 1950, Judge Weber of the District Court said:

    An analysis of the maze of cases on the subject leads one to the conclusion that a "line of commerce" cannot be determined by any process of logic and should be determined by the process of observation. . . . In other words, determine how the industry itself and how the users, the public, treat the shoe product.[78]

---

[75] *United States* v. *United Shoe Machinery Corp.*, 110 F. Supp. 295 (1953), at p. 346.
[76] *Report of the Attorney General's National Committee to Study the Antitrust Laws, op. cit.*, p. 47.

[77] *Ibid.*, p. 47, n. 168.
[78] *United States* v. *Brown Shoe Co.*, 179 F. Supp. 721 (1962), at p. 730.

He thereupon held that men's, women's, and children's shoes were separate products. The Supreme Court affirmed his decision by holding that these separate "lines of commerce":

... are recognized by the public; each line is manufactured in separate plants; each has characteristics peculiar to itself rendering it generally noncompetitive with the others; and each is, of course, directed toward a distinct class of customers.[79]

Although the Court did not reach the Section 2 question in the *Lexington National Bank* case, the majority clearly applied a pragmatic definition of the market in finding that the merger constituted a violation of Section 1 by saying:

We agree with the District Court that commercial banking is one relevant market for determining the Section 1 issue in the case. In Fayette County commercial banks are the only financial institutions authorised to receive demand deposits and to offer checking accounts. They are also the only financial institutions in the county that accept time deposits from partnerships and corporations and that make single-payment loans to individuals and commercial and industrial loans to businesses. Moreover, commercial banks offer a wider variety of financial services than the other financial institutions, *e.g.*, deposit boxes, Christmas Clubs, correspondent bank facilities, collection services, and trust department services.[80]

Four of the Justices dissented from the opinion in the *Lexington National Bank* case. Justices Brennan and White agreed that Section 1 of the Sherman Act had been violated but would have rested the opinion on the fact that the factors cited by the Court in the *Columbia Steel* case (in the quotation given in the preceding subdivision of this chapter) compelled a different finding in the *Lexington* case from that made in the *Columbia Steel* case. Justices Harlan and Stewart took the view that those witnesses who testified that competition would not be substantially lessened by the merger should be believed.[81] Their dissent thus serves to illustrate the proposition that responsible men may differ in their interpretations of facts put into evidence.

Clearly, the definition of the market adopted by the majority is of great significance in antitrust cases. In the *Columbia Steel* case, the majority rejected the government's claim, that United States Steel was attempting to monopolize the markets in rolled and fabricated steel products, by rejecting the definition—offered by the government—of the market for fabricated products. This case, it will be recalled from our discussion in the preceding subdivision, involved allegations under both Sections 1 and 2 of the Sherman Act. United States Steel, having acquired government surplus steel production facilities in Utah, then sought to acquire the facilities of the largest independent steel fabricator, Consolidated Steel, on the West Coast as an outlet for the Utah production.

The case thus involved both a horizontal (fabricated steel) and a vertical (Consolidated's demand for rolled steel) aspect. The government argued that the merger would reduce competition in the sale of fabricated steel products and in the market for supplies of rolled steel as well. The government took the view that the relevant market was the 11-state area in which Consolidated normally sold its products. The defendants argued that both rolled and fabricated steel were sold in national markets and hence competition would not be eliminated by the merger. The Court held that the market for rolled steel was the 11-state area but that the market for fabricated steel was national. With regard to the vertical aspect of the merger, the Court said:

... Exclusive dealings for rolled steel between Consolidated and United States Steel brought about by vertical integration or otherwise, are not illegal, at any rate until the effect of such control is to unreasonably restrict the opportunities of competitors to market their product. ... It seems clear to us that vertical integration, as such without more, cannot be held violative of the Sherman Act.[82]

Moreover, since the acquisition did not constitute an unreasonable restraint of trade, and since the vertical integration was not illegal *per se*, the Court was unwilling to find on these facts an attempt to monopolize on the part of United States Steel. The

---

[79] *United States* v. *Brown Shoe Co.*, 370 U.S. 294 (1962), at p. 326.

[80] *United States* v. *First National Bank and Trust Co. of Lexington et. al.*, 376 U.S. 665 (1963), at pp. 667–668.

[81] *Ibid.*, p. 677.

[82] *United States* v. *Columbia Steel Co.*, 334 U.S. 495 (1948), at pp. 524–525.

government had failed to prove the *specific intent* which is an essential element of the charge of "attempt." In this case, the Court pointed out: "We recognize the difficulty of laying down a rule as to what products are competitive, one with another." It next proceeded to decide this question *"in this case and on this record,"* phraseology clearly indicating an empirical approach to the problem. And so it analyzed the government's market data for fabricated steel and concluded:

The figures on which the government relies demonstrate that at least in the past competition in structural steel products has been conducted on a national scale. . . . Purchasers of fabricated structural products have been able to secure bids from fabricators throughout the country, and therefore statistics showing the share of United States Steel and Consolidated in the total consumption of fabricated structural products in any prescribed area are of little probative value in ascertaining the extent to which consumers of these products would be injured through elimination of competition between the two companies.[83]

The importance of the definition of the market in Section 2 cases is also dramatically illustrated by the *Alcoa* and *du Pont Cellophane* cases. In the former, the District Court had excluded from the computation of Alcoa's percentage control of the market that part of Alcoa's ingot production which it itself fabricated but did not sell, but the District Court included "secondary" aluminum and arrived at a figure of 33 percent. Judge Hand, however, argued that "the ingot fabricated by Alcoa had an indirect effect on the market" because it eventually affected the supply of "secondary" aluminum. Thus he included what the District Court had excluded and arrived at a market share of 90 percent, frankly admitting that "There are various ways of computing Alcoa's control of the aluminum market—as distinct from its production—depending on what one regards as competing in that market." In this way he was able to provide a basis for his holding that Alcoa had a monopoly "of the kind covered by Section 2." As we have already seen in Chapter 4, Judge Leahy's Finding of Fact Number 838 in the *du Pont Cellophane* case was affirmed by the Court. That finding of fact reads:

The record establishes plain cellophane and moistureproof cellophane are each flexible packaging materials which are functionally interchangeable with other flexible packaging materials and sold at same time to same customers for same purpose at competitive prices; there is no cellophane market distinct and separate from the market for flexible packaging materials; the market for flexible packaging materials is the relevant market for determining nature and extent of du Pont's market control; and du Pont has at all times competed with other cellophane producers and manufacturers of other flexible packaging materials in all aspects of its cellophane business. (*Sic.*)[84]

Given this finding of fact, the conclusion that du Pont did not have a monopoly follows easily. Judge Leahy also rightly pointed out:

"Market control" or lack of "market control" are ultimate facts. They are determined by fact-finding processes, and on the basis of knowledge and analysis of all competitive factors which bear on a seller's power to raise prices, or to exclude competition. Existence of monopoly powers is not made on the basis of assumptions as to competitive markets. If the price, quantity of production and sale, and the quantity of a seller's product are determined by pressures exerted on him by buyers and sellers of another's product, the products and the sellers must, for purposes of any realistic analysis, be in the same "market" and must be in competition with each other.[85]

An economist with a knowledge of the ultimate facts may thus have something to contribute toward the solution of the problem; but one who has no factual knowledge applicable to the case at hand, and who undertakes to solve the problem by a reliance on deductive reasoning alone, would probably not make an effective "expert" witness in Judge Leahy's court.

The question of the definition of the market in merger cases under Section 7 of the Clayton Act as amended in 1950 is similar to that arising in Section 2 cases. It will occupy us further in Chapter 17, and we will there see the same tendency toward adoption of a pragmatic test that has already been illustrated in Section 2 cases under the Sherman Act in this chapter. Indeed, both the majority and the minority opinions in the *Grinnell* case discussed below noted that Section 2 of the Sherman Act involved the same kind of problem of definition of the

---

[83] *Ibid.*, pp. 511–513 ff.
[84] *United States* v. *E. I. du Pont de Nemours and Co.*,

118 F. Supp. 41 (1953), at p. 194.
[85] *Ibid.*, p. 197.

market as arises under Section 7 of the Clayton Act in a merger case. The dispute between the majority and the minority in the *Grinnell* case centered precisely upon the question of the proper definition of the product allegedly being monopolized. The essential facts pertaining to this issue were as follows: the Grinnell Corporation, a manufacturer of plumbing supplies and fire sprinkler systems, controlled three affiliated corporations which supplied subscribers with fire and burglar alarm services from central stations through automatic alarm systems installed on the subscribers' premises. These affiliates had participated in market allocation agreements, discriminatory pricing to forestall competition, and the acquisition of competitors, and had acquired 87 percent of the *insurance-company accredited central station service business* at the time of the government's action under Sections 1 and 2 of the Sherman Act. The District Court treated the "central station protective service" as the relevant product and the United States as the relevant geographic market. The defendants argued that protective services other than central station services were available to their subscribers on a local basis, that the proper geographic market was the local market; and that a proper definition of the product (service) would have to take account of the local substitutes. On this point, Justice Douglas spoke for the majority by saying:

Defendants earnestly urge that . . . they face competition from these other modes of protection. They seem to us seriously to overstate the degree of competition, but we recognize that . . . they "do not have unfettered power to control the price of their services . . . due to fringe competition of alarm or watchmen services." 236 F. Supp., at 254. What defendants overlook is that the high degree of differentiation between central station protection and the other forms means that for many customers, only central station protection will do. Though some customers may be willing to accept higher insurance rates in favor of cheaper forms of protection, others will not be willing or able to risk serious interruption to their businesses, even though covered by insurance, and will thus be unwilling to consider anything but central service protection.[86]

Justices Harlan, Fortas, and Stewart dissented. Justice Fortas wrote, in part:

. . . Because I believe that the definition of the relevant market here cannot be sustained, I would reverse and remand for a new determination of this basic issue, subject to proper standards.

. . . In the present case . . . the essence of the offense is monopolization, achieved or attempted, and the major relief is divestiture. For these purposes, "market" definition is of the essence, just as in Section 7 cases the kindred definition of the "line of commerce" is fundamental. We must define the area of commerce that is allegedly engrossed before we can determine its engrossment. . . .

In Section 2 cases, the search for "the relevant market" must be undertaken and pursued with relentless clarity. It is, in essence, an economic task put to the uses of the law. . . .

The trial court's definition of the "product" market even more dramatically demonstrates that its action has been Procrustean—that it has tailored the market to the dimensions of the defendants. It recognizes that a person seeking protective services has many alternative sources. . . .

But the court isolates from all of these alternatives only those services in which defendants engage. It eliminates all of the alternative sources despite its conscientious enumeration of them. . . .

I believe this approach has no justification in economics, reason or law. . . .[87]

The question, as these excerpts from the majority and from one of the dissenting opinions make clear, is thus one of fact; that is, it is one of what the evidence means. As Justice Fortas noted, the problem of definition of the market also exists in cases involving "attempts to monopolize," the next topic to be considered.

"Attempting to Monopolize"

Nature of the Offense. It has already been emphasized in Chapter 13, and in this one, that the crime of "attempting to monopolize" requires proof of the existence of a *specific intent. Often, but not always,* it also involves acts which constitute unreasonable restraints under Section 1. But that a violation of Section 1 need *not* be shown in order to make the case under Section 2 is clearly apparent from the opinion in the *Columbia Steel* case. In that case, the trial judge held that, since the purchase of Consolidated by United States Steel did not constitute a violation of Section 1, it could

---

[86] *United States* v. *Grinnell Corp.*, 384 U.S. 563 (1966), at p. 574.

[87] *Ibid.*, at pp. 586–592.

not constitute a violation of Section 2, since he believed every attempt to monopolize must also constitute an illegal restraint. The Supreme Court, however, said of the Section 2 allegation in this case: "We think the trial court applied too narrow a test of this charge; even though the restraint effected may be reasonable under Section 1, it may constitute an attempt to monopolize forbidden by Section 2 if a specific intent to monopolize may be shown."[88] Most of the cases now to be discussed do, however, involve acts like refusals to deal and tying agreements which have already been discussed in the context of Section 1 above. But before we turn to these cases, an interesting case terminated in August 1969 must be mentioned.

Attempting to Monopolize by Means of Reciprocal Selling Arrangements. In June 1969, in keeping with Assistant Attorney General McLaren's views already noted in Chapter 12, the Antitrust Division charged that United States Steel Company had used its purchasing power "since 1955 to promote sales in an attempt to monopolize the requirements of actual and potential supplier-customers for steel products, as well as cement, chemicals, and other products." In August 1969, the case was settled by entry of a consent decree prohibiting the defendant from engaging in the prohibited practices. The decree also ordered U. S. Steel to refrain "from membership and to prohibit its officers and employees from belonging to or participating in the activities of any association whose activities, programs or objectives" were "to promote trade relations involving reciprocal purchasing arrangements." In Chapter 17, we will consider a case involving the question of a reciprocal trading relationship within the context of a merger. The consent decree in this case represents an accretion to existing law. Our next problem is the consideration of attempts to monopolize by means of refusals to deal and boycotts.

"Attempting to Monopolize" by Means of Boycotts or Refusals to Deal. A leading case holding it unlawful to refuse to deal where the purpose of the refusal is an attempt to monopolize is the *Lorain Journal* case. In this case, the publisher of an Ohio newspaper refused to accept advertising from anyone who advertised or whom it believed to be about to advertise over a local radio station. From 1933 to 1948, when the radio station was licensed to operate, the newspaper publisher had enjoyed "a substantial monopoly" of the mass dissemination of news and advertising both of a local and national character. The Court held on these facts that the publisher was guilty of an attempt to monopolize under Section 2 of the Sherman Act.[89] The result is, of course, consistent with its holding in the *Parke-Davis* case that a group boycott to enforce resale price maintenance is an unreasonable restraint of trade. A similar result had been reached earlier (in 1927) in a case in which a defendant, who operated competing photographic stock houses, refused to supply at the regular discount the plaintiff after the plaintiff had refused to sell his business to the defendant. The plaintiff was permitted to recover treble damages on the theory that the defendant was attempting to monopolize.[90]

However, in the *Times-Picayune* case in 1953, the Court held that a newspaper publishing company was not guilty of an attempt to monopolize where it required its advertisers to purchase combined insertions in both its morning and evening papers and would not sell space for advertisements in either newspaper separately. The Court admitted that "tying arrangements flout the Sherman Act's policy that competition rule the marts of trade," but also held that the newspaper publishing company did not occupy a dominant position in the newspaper market in New Orleans, and further that advertising space in its two newspapers did not constitute separate products since there was no evidence that the readers of the newspapers consciously distinguished between the two papers. Moreover, according to the Court:

... With the advertising contracts in this proceeding viewed as in themselves lawful and no further elements of combination apparent in the case, Section 2 criteria must become dispositive here.

An insufficient showing of specific intent

---

[88] *United States* v. *Columbia Steel Co. et. al.*, 334 U.S. 495 (1948), at pp. 531–533.
[89] *Lorain Journal Co.* v. *United States*, 342 U.S. 143 (1951).
[90] *Eastman Kodak* v. *Southern Photo Materials Co.*, 273 U.S. 359 (1927).

vitiates this part of the Government's case. While
the completed offense of monopolization under
Section 2 demands only a general intent to do the
act, "for no monopolist monopolizes unconscious
of what he is doing," a specific intent to destroy
competition or build monopoly is essential to
guilt for the mere attempt now charged. . . . This
case does not demonstrate an attempt by a
monopolist established in one area to nose into a
second market, so that past monopolistic success
both enhances the probability of future harm and
supplies a motivation for further forays. . . .

We conclude, therefore, that this record does
not establish the charged violations of Section 1
and Section 2 of the Sherman Act.[91]

It has already been noted in Chapter 13
that a successful "attempt to monopolize"
merges with the crime of "monopolization."
In the same way, when a combination or
conspiracy to monopolize is charged, the
proof of the relevant "intent" merges with
the proof of the conspiracy or combination
and the purpose for which it was created.

Conspiracy to Monopolize

Nature of the Offense. A leading case
involving the charge of conspiracy to
monopolize is the *American Tobacco* case of
1946. The proof of the conspiracy to
monopolize proceeded along the following
lines. *First*, it was established that the
defendants possessed a dominant market
position when their respective shares of the
market were added together. *Next*, the jury
found that the defendants (American,
Reynolds, and Liggett Tobacco Companies)
conspired to fix prices and to exclude
undesired competition from "the distribution and sale of their products." The trial
judge charged the jury as follows:

Now, the term *"monopolize"* as used in Section
2 of the Sherman Act, as well as in the last three
counts of the Information, means the joint
acquisition or maintenance by the members of a
conspiracy formed for that purpose, of the
*power to control and dominate interstate trade and
commerce in a commodity to such an extent that they
are able, as a group, to exclude actual or potential
competitors from the field accompanied with the
intention and purpose to exercise such power.*[92]

The defendants appealed, claiming that
this instruction failed to make "actual

exclusion of competitors" a part of the crime.
(Milton Handler was one of the defendant's
lawyers.) The Supreme Court held, on
appeal, that the definition in the charge was
correct and that it was unnecessary to show
an actual exclusion of competitors if the
power to exclude them and the intent to do
so were both proved. Thus the Court said:

. . . A correct interpretation of the statute and
of the authorities makes it the crime of monopolizing, under Section 2 of the Sherman Act,
for parties, as in these cases, to combine or conspire to acquire or maintain the power to
exclude competitors from any part of the trade
or commerce among the several states or with
foreign nations, provided they also have such a
power that they are able, as a group, to exclude
actual or potential competition from the field and
provided that they have the intent and purpose to
exercise that power.[93]

In this case the Court also held that
Sections 1 and 2 state separate offenses.[94]

Vertical Integration. The problem of proof
of the existence of a conspiracy is similar in a
Section 2 case to that in a Section 1 case.
The question of intra-enterprise conspiracy
has arisen in Section 2 cases, just as it arose
in the *Kiefer-Stewart* case under Section 1
discussed earlier. One Section 2 case is the
"first" *Yellow Cab* case. According to the
Court:

. . . In January, 1929, one Morris Markin and
others commenced negotiations to merge the
more important cab operating companies in
Chicago, New York, and other cities. Markin
was then president . . . as well as the controlling
stockholder, of the Checker Cab Manufacturing
Corporation (CCM). That company was engaged in the business of manufacturing taxicabs
at its factory in Kalamazoo, Michigan, and
shipping them to purchasers in various states.[95]

By various methods, according to the
Court, by the end of 1932 Markin had
gained control of the three largest taxicab
companies operating in Chicago, and
through another subsidiary he had also
gained substantial footholds in the taxicab
business in New York City, Pittsburgh, and
Minneapolis. The government alleged the
existence of a conspiracy and combination
on the part of the relevant cab operating

[91] *Times–Picayune Publishing Co.* v. *United States,* 345
U.S. 594 (1953), at pp. 626–627.
[92] *American Tobacco Co.* v. *United States,* 328 U.S.
781 (1946), at pp. 784–785. (Italics his.)

[93] *Ibid.,* at p. 809.
[94] *Ibid.,* at pp. 788 ff.
[95] *United States* v. *Yellow Cab Co. et. al.,* 332 U.S. 218
(1946), at pp. 220 ff.

companies, CCM, and Markin relative to the control of the operation and purchase of taxicabs in the principal cities named above. It was argued by the defendants that their arrangement constituted a vertical integration and was not a combination or conspiracy under the Sherman Act. The Supreme Court, however, held:

The fact that these restraints occur in a setting described by the appellees as a vertically integrated enterprise does not necessarily remove the ban of the Sherman Act. The test of illegality under the Act is the presence or absence of an unreasonable restraint on interstate commerce. Such a restraint may result as readily from a conspiracy among those who are affiliated or integrated under common ownership as from a conspiracy among those who are otherwise independent. Similarly, any affiliation or integration ... cannot insulate the conspirators from the sanctions which Congress has imposed. The corporate interrelationships of the conspirators, in other words, are not determinative of the applicability of the Sherman Act. The statute is aimed at substance rather than form.[96]

The case was remanded to the District Court for a trial of the question of fact, and in the "second" *Yellow Cab* case the Court held that the government had failed to prove its allegations.[97]

It has been pointed out above that in the later *Columbia Steel* case the government made much of the fact that a vertical integration was involved. In dealing with this aspect of the government's case, the Court also further explained its holding in the *Yellow Cab* case as follows:

We do not construe our holding in the *Yellow Cab* case to make illegal the acquisition by United States Steel of this outlet [Columbia Steel] for its rolled steel without consideration of its effect on the opportunities of other competitor producers to market their rolled steel. In discussing the charge in the *Yellow Cab* case, we said that the fact that the conspirators were integrated did not insulate them from the act, not that corporate integration violated the act. ... Nothing in the *Yellow Cab* case supports the theory that all exclusive dealing arrangements are illegal *per se*.[98]

With the exception of the questions of the applicability of the Sherman Act to regulated industries, to the international activities of American business firms, in cases involving patents, and the problem of remedies, our discussion of the working rules of economic activity and organization embodied in this statute and court decisions under it is now virtually complete. The topics of "tying agreements," "price-fixing," and "proof of conspiracy" have, however, not yet been exhausted. Tying agreements are also unlawful under Section 3 of the Clayton Act; and the use of a multiple basing point system of pricing by a number of firms has been held to constitute a conspiracy by the Court. Such a system of pricing may also involve unlawful price discrimination under Section 2 of the Clayton Act. These topics are discussed in Chapter 15, which follows. Moreover, in Chapter 18 (which deals with the Federal Trade Commission Act) we will see that acts which would constitute a violation of the Sherman Act have also been held to constitute "unfair methods of competition" under Section 5 of the Federal Trade Commission Act—in other words, we will see in Chapter 18 that Sections 1 and 2 of the Sherman Act have been read into the Federal Trade Commission Act by the Court.

---

[96] *Ibid.*, at p. 227.

[97] *United States* v. *Yellow Cab Co. et. al.*, 338 U.S. 338 (1949).

[98] *United States* v. *Columbia Steel Co. et. al.*, 334 U.S. 495 (1948), at pp. 521–523.

Exclusive Dealing, Tying Arrangements, Price Discrimination, and Other Trade Practices under the Clayton Act as amended

This chapter is concerned: (1) with a study of tying arrangements and exclusive dealing under Section 3 of the Clayton Act; (2) with an examination of price discrimination under the original Section 2 of that law; and (3) with an analysis of price discrimination and other trade practices under Section 2 as amended by the Robinson-Patman Act in 1936.

A. TYING ARRANGEMENTS AND EXCLUSIVE DEALING UNDER THE CLAYTON ACT

The language of Section 3 of the Clayton Act is broad. The section has been held under specified conditions to prohibit tying arrangements, exclusive dealing arrangements, and certain "requirements" contracts, as we will now see.

The Scope of Section 3

Speaking for the Supreme Court, in 1949 Justice Frankfurter wrote:

Since the Clayton Act became effective, this Court has passed on the applicability of Section 3 in eight cases, in five of which it upheld determinations that the challenged agreement was violative of that Section. Three of these—*United Shoe Machinery Corp.* v. *United States; International Business Machines Corp.* v. *United States; International Salt Co.* v. *United States*—involved contracts tying to the use of a patented article all purchases of an unpatented ... article. The other two cases—*Standard Fashion Co.* v. *Magrane-Houston Co.; Fashion Originators' Guild* v. *Federal Trade Comm'n.*—involved requirements contracts. . . .[1]

The Concept of "Quantitative Substantiality"

Some of these cases, most notably the *International Salt* and *Fashion Originators' Guild* cases, have already been discussed in

---

[1] *Standard Oil Co. of California et. al.* v. *United States,* 337 U.S. 293 (1949), at p. 300.

the context of offenses against Section 1 of the Sherman Act in the preceding chapter, since many of the Clayton Act Section 3 cases involving tying arrangements have also involved charges of illegality under Section 1 of the Sherman Act. The *Standard Fashion* case of 1922 was the first case raising a question of an interpretation of Section 3 of the Clayton Act to come before the Court. It involved an action by the Standard Fashion Company to restrain the defendant (Magrane-Houston) department store from violating an exclusive dealing contract under which the defendant department store had agreed not to sell nor to permit to be sold on its premises during the term of the contract any other make of patterns. The lower court found as a fact that the pattern company controlled two-fifths of the pattern business in the United States. Given this finding of fact, the Supreme Court held that the tying contract was one which "probably" would lessen competition or tend to create a monopoly under Section 3. It added:

> Section 3 condemns sales or agreements where the effect of such sale or contract of sale "may" be to substantially lessen competition or tend to create monopoly. It thus deals with consequences to follow the making of the restrictive covenant limiting the right of the purchaser to deal in the goods of the seller only. But we do not think that the purpose in using the word "may" was to prohibit the *mere possibility* of the consequences described. It was intended to prevent such agreements as would under the circumstances disclosed *probably* lessen competition, or create an actual tendency to monopoly. That it was not intended to reach every remote lessening of competition is shown in the requirement that such lessening must be *substantial*.[2]

The question that the preceding quotation raises is whether the requirement that the "lessening [of competition] must be substantial" refers to the *percentage* of the market controlled or to an *absolute dollar volume or amount* of commerce. This question faced the Court in 1949 in the context of an "exclusive dealing" or "requirements" contract in the *Standard Oil Company of California and Standard Stations* case. In this case, Standard Oil of California had made contracts with its service-station dealers to

take their gasoline requirements and, in some cases, also their requirements of accessories (batteries, tires, etc.) only from Standard. Such contracts covered 16 percent of the gasoline service stations in Arizona, California, Idaho, Nevada, Oregon, Utah, and Washington—known as the "Western area." Standard itself accounted for 23 percent of the business in the area, and it was "undisputed" that all of Standard's major competitors employed similar contracts. The District Court held that "the contracts covered 'a substantial number of outlets and a substantial number of products, whether considered comparatively or not.' "[3] The Supreme Court sustained the holding of the lower court and said:

> We conclude, therefore, that the qualifying clause of Section 3 is satisfied by proof that competition has been foreclosed in a substantial share of the line of commerce affected.[4]

In arriving at this result, however, the Court drew a distinction between tying arrangements imposed on buyers by sellers who enjoyed a dominant position in the market and those who did not. The *International Salt* case, it will be recalled from the preceding chapter, involved the lease of patented machinery to which was tied the purchase of unpatented salt. The Court also said in the *Standard Stations* case:

> Requirements contracts, on the other hand, may well be of economic advantage to buyers as well as to sellers and thus indirectly of advantage to the consuming public. In the case of the buyer, they may assure supply, afford protection against rises in price, enable long-term planning on the basis of known costs, and obviate the expense and risk of storage in the quantity necessary for a commodity having a fluctuating demand. From the seller's point of view, requirements contracts may make possible the substantial reduction of selling expenses, give protection against price fluctuations, and—of particular advantage to a newcomer to the field to whom it is important to know what capital expenditures are justified—offer the possibility of a predictable market.[5]

The Court then went on to point out that these advantages of requirements contracts afforded "a weaker basis for the inference that competition may be lessened than would similar coverage by tying clauses, especially where use of the latter is com-

---

[2] *Standard Fashion Co.* v. *Magrane-Houston Co.*, 258 U.S. 346 (1922), at pp. 356–357. (Italics mine).

[3] *Standard Oil Co. of California et. al.* v. *United States*, 337 U.S. 293 (1949), at p. 298.

[4] *Ibid.*, at p. 314.

[5] *Ibid.*, at pp. 306–307.

bined with market control of the tying device."[6]

In 1961, in the *Tampa Electric* case, the Court upheld a requirements contract against attack under both Section 3 of the Clayton Act and Section 1 of the Sherman Act and cited the economic benefits of such contracts which it had mentioned in the earlier *Standard Stations* case. The *Tampa* case involved the validity of a contract under which the Tampa Electric Company agreed for a term of 20 years to purchase its requirements of coal for its steam boilers from the Nashville Coal Company. The Court found that the "challenged contract preempted competition" in less than one percent of the relevant market. More importantly, the Court added:

It may well be that in the context of antitrust legislation protracted requirements contracts are suspect, but they have not been declared illegal *per se*. Even though a single contract between single traders may fall within the initial broad proscription of the section [3], it must also suffer the qualifying disability, tendency to work a substantial—not remote—lessening of competition in the relevant competitive market. It is urged that the present contract pre-empts competition to the extent of purchases worth perhaps $128,000,000, and that this "is, of course, not insignificant or insubstantial." While $128,000,000 is a considerable sum of money, even in these days, the dollar volume, by itself, is not the test, as we have already pointed out. ... There is here neither a seller with a dominant position in the market as in *Standard Fashions* . . .; nor myriad outlets with substantial sales volume, coupled with an industry-wide practice of relying upon exclusive contracts, as in *Standard Oil* . . .; nor a plainly restrictive tying arrangement as in *International Salt*. . . . On the contrary, we seem to have only that type of contract which "may well be of economic advantage to buyers as well as to sellers." *Standard Oil Co.* v. *United States*. . . . In the case of . . . the seller it "may make possible the substantial reduction of selling expenses, give protection against price fluctuations, and . . . offer the possibility of a predictable market. . . ." In weighing the various factors, we have decided that in the competitive bituminous coal marketing area involved here, the contract sued upon does not tend to foreclose a substantial volume of competition.[7]

Alternatively, in the words of the Court, "In practical application, even though a contract is found to be an exclusive-dealing arrangement, it does not violate the section [3] unless the Court believes it probable that performance of the contract will foreclose competition in a substantial share of the line of commerce affected."[8] However, the Court has also said:

For our purposes, a tying arrangement may be defined as an agreement by a party to sell one product but only on the condition that the buyer also purchases a different (or tied) product, or at least agrees that he will not purchase that product from any other supplier. Where such conditions are successfully exacted, competition . . . with respect to the tied product is . . . curbed. Indeed "tying agreements serve hardly any purpose beyond the suppression of competition." *Standard Oil Co. of California* v. *United States*. . . . They deny competitors free access to the market for the tied product, not because the party imposing the tying requirements has a better product or a lower price but because of his power or leverage in another market. At the same time buyers are forced to forego their free choice between competing products. For these reasons "tying agreements fare harshly under the laws forbidding restraints of trade. . . ." They are unreasonable in and of themselves whenever a party has sufficient economic power with respect to the tying product . . . and a "not insubstantial" amount of . . . commerce is affected. . . . Of course where the seller has no control or dominance over the tying product so that it does not represent an effectual weapon to pressure buyers into taking the tied item, any restraint of trade attributable to such tying arrangements would obviously be insignificant at most.[9]

Thus, in 1949 a District Court properly found that the American Can Company had violated both the Sherman Act and Section 3 of the Clayton Act when the Court found that the company not only enjoyed a dominant position in the market but also had imposed a tying arrangement on lessees of its patented tin can closing machines, under which the lessees were forced to agree also to purchase their requirements of tin plate from the company.[10]

We have seen in Chapter 14 that in 1969

---

[6] *Ibid.*, at p. 307.
[7] *Tampa Electric Co.* v. *Nashville Coal Co. et. al.*, 365 U.S. 320 (1961), at pp. 333–335.
[8] *Ibid.*, at p. 327.

[9] *Northern Pacific Railway Co.* v. *United States*, 356 U.S. 1 (1958), at pp. 5–6.
[10] *United States* v. *American Can Co.*, 87 F. Supp. 18 (1949).

the Court pointed out that in cases under Section 1 of the Sherman Act, the test of "substantiality" was the *total volume of sales affected by the sales policy* and *not the amount sold to an individual purchaser*. In its opinion, the Court cited the *Standard Oil Company of California* case, a practice which suggests that the same test of quantitative substantiality applies both to Sherman Act and Clayton Act cases. Such a practice would be sound from both the economic and legal points of view. In the 1969 Sherman Act case in question,[10a] the Court remarked that the twin conditions that the seller have a "dominant position" *and* that a "substantial amount of commerce" be affected were essential to make out a case of *per se* illegality, but that a case of an unreasonable restraint of trade could be established by a finding of fact that there was "sufficient economic power," even though the defendant did not possess a monopoly or a dominant position throughout the market for the tying product. Moreover, the Court added that the significant question was whether a substantial *dollar volume* of business, large enough "so as not to be merely *de minimis*" was foreclosed to competitors.[10b]

Section 3 of the Clayton Act has not been changed since it was originally enacted in 1914. The price-discrimination section (2) of the Act, on the other hand, was substantially amended in 1936. The following discussion is devoted to a consideration of Section 2 in its original unamended form.

B. PRICE DISCRIMINATION UNDER THE ORIGINAL CLAYTON ACT

The Statutory Language

Section 2 of the Clayton Act originally read:

... It shall be unlawful for any person engaged in commerce, in the course of such commerce, either directly or indirectly, to discriminate in price between different purchasers of commodities, which commodities are sold for use, consumption, or resale within the United States or any Territory thereof or the District of Columbia or any insular possession or other place under the jurisdiction of the United States, where the effect of such discrimination may be to substantially lessen competition or tend to create a monopoly in any line of commerce: *Provided*, That nothing herein contained shall prevent discrimination in price between purchasers of commodities on account of differences in the grade, quality, or quantity of the commodity sold, or that makes only due allowance for difference in the cost of selling or transportation, or discrimination in price in the same or different communities made in good faith to meet competition: *And provided further*, That nothing herein contained shall prevent persons engaged in selling goods, wares, or merchandise in commerce from selecting their own customers in bona fide transactions and not in restraint of trade.[11]

The Level of Competition Affected

This provision was interpreted in 1923 and again in 1924 by a Court of Appeals to apply to a lessening of competition *between* a supplier and *his* competitors rather than to competition *among* purchasers *from* a supplier who discriminated among *them*.[12]

Of these two decisions, the Federal Trade Commission itself said in 1935:

In cases against the National Biscuit Co. and Loose-Wiles Biscuit Co., the Commission sought to prevent price discrimination in favor of chain-store purchasers as against purchasers of similar quantities acting for pools or cooperative associations of individual stores. It failed in this effort because on review by the Circuit Court of Appeals for the Second Circuit it was held in 1924 that the section had no application to a lessening of competition in the resale of a commodity. . . . Certiorari to review this decision was denied by the Supreme Court but the unsoundness of that view of the law was established by the Supreme Court in a private suit which reached it 5 years later (*Van Camp* v. *American Can Company et. al.*, 278 U.S. 245).[13]

The *Van Camp* case referred to by the Commission involved the following facts. The George Van Camp and Sons Company and the Van Camp Packing Company were both engaged in packing and selling food products in interstate commerce. The American Can Company supplied both

[10a] *Fortner Enterprises* v. *U.S. Steel*, 394 U.S. 495 (1969).
[10b] *Ibid.*, p. 501.
[11] 38 Stat. 730 (1914).
[12] *Mennen Co.* v. *Federal Trade Commission*, 288 Fed.

774 (1923); and *National Biscuit Co.* v. *Federal Trade Commission*, 289 Fed. 733 (1924).
[13] Federal Trade Commission, *Chain Stores: Final Report on the Chain Store Investigation* (Washington, D.C. U.S. Government Printing Office, 1935), p. 90.

companies with machines for sealing tin cans and a supply of tin cans, but it sold cans to the Van Camp Packing Company at a discount of 20 percent below the price at which it sold cans to the George Van Camp and Sons Company. Moreover, it charged the latter a fixed rental for the use of its can-closing machines but supplied such machines free of charge to the Van Camp Packing Company.[14] The Supreme Court held that the case fell within Section 2 because it affected competition between the two competing canning companies who were both purchasers from the price discriminator. It said specifically:

These facts bring the case within the terms of the statute, unless the words "in any line of commerce" are to be given a narrower meaning than a literal reading of them conveys. The phrase is comprehensive and means that if the forbidden effect or tendency is produced in *one* out of *all* the various lines of commerce, the words "in *any* line of commerce" literally are satisfied. The contention is that the words must be confined to the particular line of commerce in which the discriminator is engaged, and that they do not include a different line of commerce in which purchasers from the discriminator are engaged in competition with one another. . . . The fundamental policy of the legislation is that, in respect of persons engaged in the same line of interstate commerce, competition is desirable and that whatever substantially lessens it or tends to create a monopoly in such line of commerce is an evil.[15]

The Federal Trade Commission asserted in 1935:

Thus it appears that prior to the Van Camp decision, during a period when chain stores were enjoying an extensive growth based largely upon special price concessions from manufacturers, the Commission was prevented by court decisions from applying Section 2 of the Clayton Act to ameliorate the resultant competitive situation between the chains, the cooperatives, and the independents. Such decisions naturally discouraged the Commission with respect to the institution of further proceedings. As pointed out in the discussion of the legal status of price discrimination by and in favor of chain stores . . . the principal difficulties of enforcement grow out of the provisos regarding quantity, cost of selling, and meeting competition. . . .

Aside from the question whether the section requires that prices shall be made with "only due allowance" for differences in quantity, it may be that the effect of price discrimination which makes only such allowance will give to chain stores and other quantity buyers powerful advantages which may produce quite similar results, the only difference being that a longer period of time will be needed to appraise the effect.

. . . If the discrimination is "on account of differences in the grade, quality, or quantity of the commodity sold," or makes "only due allowance for difference in the cost of selling or transportation," or is "made in good faith to meet competition," it is not unlawful, even though the effect "may be to substantially lessen competition or tend to create a monopoly in any line of commerce." Discriminatory price concessions given to prevent the loss of a chain store's business to a competing manufacturer, to prevent it manufacturing its own goods, or to prevent it from discouraging in its stores the sale of a given manufacturer's goods, may be strongly urged by the manufacturer as "made in good faith to meet competition."

. . . Cost of selling is generally in inverse ratio to the quantity sold to a given customer. This means that both quantity and cost of selling tend to support a lower price to chains than to small competitors of the chains. If the section is taken to mean that *any* difference in quantity justifies *any* amount of discrimination, it is obvious that the section may be readily evaded.[61]

Accordingly, the Commission recommended that Section 2 be amended to make unlawful "unfair or unjust" price discriminations. However, as we have seen in Chapter 12, Congress went far beyond this recommendation and rewrote Section 2 entirely. In doing so, as we have also seen in Chapter 12, Congress had the assistance of the United States Wholesale Grocers' Association, "a national trade organization of independent wholesale food distributors with offices in Washington, D.C." The amended Section 2 contains a provision dealing with the payment of brokerage fees and also regulates advertising and promotional allowances; in addition, it makes illegal the *receipt* as well as the giving of price discriminations. All these trade practices had been mentioned by the Commission in its report on chain stores.[17] Decisions dealing with Section 2, as amended, are the subject of the next subdivision of this chapter.

---

[14] *Van Camp and Sons Co.* v. *American Can Co.*, 278 U.S. 245 (1929).

[15] *Ibid.*, at pp. 253–254. (Italics in the original.)

[16] *Final Report on the Chain Store Investigation, op. cit.*, pp. 90–91 and 64. (Italics mine.)

[17] *Ibid.*, pp. 61 ff.

C. PRICE DISCRIMINATION AND OTHER TRADE PRACTICES UNDER SECTION 2 AS AMENDED

Price Discrimination under Section 2(a)

After its amendment by the Robinson-Patman Act, Section 2 of the Clayton Act became Sections 2(a) to 2(f). Section 2(a) now prohibits direct and indirect discrimination "in price between different purchasers of commodities of like grade and quality, where either or any of the purchases involved in such discrimination are in commerce . . . and where the effect of such discrimination may be substantially to lessen competition or tend to create a monopoly in any line of commerce or to injure, destroy, or prevent competition with any person who either grants or knowingly receives the benefit of such discrimination or with customers of either of them" subject to certain provisos. The provisos raise the question of defenses against charges of price discrimination, and Section 2(b) of the amended law also deals with defenses. Since the defenses are discussed separately in Chapter 16 of this book, discussion of them will be omitted from the present chapter.

"Commodities of Like Grade and Quality." The "threshold question" concerning an action under Section 2(a) is that of the meaning of the words "of like grade and quality." A definitive decision involving them was handed down by the Supreme Court in 1966 in *Federal Trade Commission* v. *Borden Company*.[18] In the words of the Court, the facts were as follows:

The Borden Company, respondent here, produces and sells evaporated milk under the Borden name, a nationally advertised brand. At the same time Borden packs and markets evaporated milk under various private brands owned by its customers. This milk is physically and chemically identical with the milk it distributes under its own brand but it is sold at both the wholesale and retail level at prices regularly below those obtained for the Borden brand milk. The Federal Trade Commission found the milk sold under the Borden and the private labels to be of like grade and quality as required for the applicability of Section 2(a) of the Robinson–Patman Act, held the price differential to be discriminatory within the

meaning of the section, ascertained the requisite adverse effect on commerce, rejected Borden's claim of cost justification, and consequently issued a cease-and-desist order. The Court of Appeals set aside the Commission's order on the sole ground that as a matter of law, the customer label milk was not of the same grade and quality as the milk sold under the Borden brand. . . . Because of the importance of this issue, which bears on the reach and coverage of the Robinson–Patman Act, we granted certiorari. . . . We now reverse the decision of the Court of Appeals and remand the case to that court for the determination of the remaining issues. . . .[19]

The Court continued:

. . . The Commission's view is that labels do not differentiate products for the purpose of determining grade or quality, even though the one label may have more customer appeal and command a higher price in the marketplace from a substantial segment of the public. That this is the Commission's long-standing interpretation of the present Act, as well as of Section 2 of the Clayton Act before its amendment by the Robinson–Patman Act, may be gathered from the Commission's decisions dating back to 1936. . . .

During the 1936 hearings on the proposed amendments to Section 2 of the Clayton Act, the attention of Congress was specifically called to the question of the applicability of Section 2 to the practice of a manufacturer selling his product under his nationally advertised brand at a different price than he charged when the product was sold under a private label. Because it was feared that the Act would require the elimination of such price differentials, Hearings on H.R. 4995 before the House Committee on the Judiciary, 74th Cong., 2d Sess., p. 355, and because private brands "would [thus] be put out of business by the nationally advertised brands," it was suggested that the proposed Section 2(a) be amended so as to apply only to sales of commodities of "like grade, quality, and *brand*." (Emphasis added.) *Id.*, at 421. There was strong objection to the amendment and it was not adopted by the Committee. . . .[20]

The preceding quotation from the opinion bears the Court's footnote number 4. This footnote reads in part:—

Mr. H. B. Teegarden, who was then counsel to the United States Wholesale Grocers Association, and who apparently played a large part in drafting the bill, Hearings on H.R. 4995 before the House Committee on the Judiciary, 74th Cong., 1st Sess., p. 9, supplemented his oral

[18] 383 U.S. 637 (1966).
[19] *Ibid.*, at pp. 638–639.

[20] *Ibid.*, at pp. 640–641.

testimony with a letter addressed in part to the proposed amendment.[21]

This footnote is interesting since it suggests that, in its attempt to discover the "intention" of Congress, the Court is today not only looking at the actual Congressional proceedings but is also giving consideration to the views of the lobbyists and pressure groups who favored the legislation being interpreted. This procedure is apparently a new development in judicial technique.

The Level of Competition Affected under Amended Section 2. In June 1969, the Supreme Court decided a price-discrimination case involving the following facts. Standard Oil Company of California sold gasoline to Perkins, an independent distributor and retailer. Standard also sold gasoline at a lower price to Signal Oil Company, which in turn sold to Signal's subsidiary, Western Hyway. Western Hyway, in turn, sold to Regal, which owned retail outlets, major competitors of Perkins. Standard further sold gasoline to its own branded dealers at a lower price than it sold to Perkins. Perkins brought an action for treble damages alleging a violation of Section 2(a) of the Clayton Act. The Court of Appeals upheld the finding of damages in the case of Standard's sales to its own branded dealers but reversed the lower court's judgment that Perkins was also entitled to damages for the sales to Signal. The Court of Appeals thought that the relationship of Signal to Perkins was too remote to fall within Section 2(a).

The Supreme Court reversed the Court of Appeals decision, holding that there was no basis in Section 2(a) for holding that Standard's price discriminations were immunized "simply because the product in question passed through an additional formal exchange before reaching Perkins' actual competitor."[21a] In making this decision, the Court cited as a precedent the *Fred Meyer, Inc.* case, which involved discriminatory promotional allowances under another subparagraph of Section 2. The *Fred Meyer, Inc.* case will be discussed later in this chapter. For the moment, let us turn to consideration of the problem of predatory price discrimination.

Predatory Price Discrimination. Even before Section 2 of the Clayton Act was amended, predatory price discrimination (selling below cost) was held to be unlawful in the *Porto Rican American Tobacco* case in 1929. The case involved a situation in which, during a price war, American Tobacco Company sold its "Lucky Strike" cigarettes, manufactured in the United States, at a lower price (which constituted a loss) in Puerto Rico than that in the United States. The Port Rican American Tobacco Company sued for an injunction to compel the American Tobacco Company to discontinue its discriminatory pricing practices. A Court of Appeals held that the injunction would lie. Among other things, the Court of Appeals said:

. . . Ruinous competition, by lowering prices, constitutes an illegal medium of eliminating weaker competitors.[22]

In making the statement, the Court cited both the 1911 *Standard Oil* and *American Tobacco* cases, in which similar predatory practices had been involved.

In 1954, an interesting case was decided by the Supreme Court, *Moore* v. *Mead's Fine Bread.* In this case, Moore owned a bakery in Santa Rosa, New Mexico. All his business was intrastate. Mead's Fine Bread was a corporation in Clovis, New Mexico, which also operated plants at Lubbock and Big Spring, Texas, as well as at Hobbs, Roswell, and Clovis, New Mexico. The two competed for a time in Santa Rosa.

Then, after a threat by Moore to move his bakery elsewhere, Santa Rosa merchants began to do business only with him. The corporation labeled this action a boycott and cut the price of its bread in Santa Rosa only, eventually forcing Moore out of business. He then sued for treble damages, alleging a violation of Section 2(a) of the Robinson-Patman Act. The Court of Appeals held against Moore on appeal, but, on further appeal, the Supreme Court reversed the Court of Appeals, saying:

We think that the practices in the present case are also included within the scope of the antitrust laws. We have here an interstate industry

---

[21] *Ibid.*, pp. 641–642, n. 4.
[21a] *Perkins* v. *Standard Oil Company*, 395 U.S. 642 (1969).

[22] *Porto Rican American Tobacco Co.* v. *American Tobacco Co.*, 30 F. 2d 234 (1929), at p. 234.

increasing its domain through outlawed competitive practices. The victim, to be sure, is only a local merchant; and no interstate transactions are used to destroy him. But the beneficiary is an interstate business; the treasury used to finance the warfare is drawn from interstate, as well as local, sources which include not only respondent but also a group of interlocked companies engaged in the same line of business; and the prices on the interstate sales, both by respondent and by the other Mead companies, are kept high while the local prices are lowered. If this method of competition were approved, the pattern for growth of monopoly would be simple. As long as the price warfare was strictly intrastate, interstate business could grow and expand with impunity at the expense of local merchants. The competitive advantage would then be with the interstate combines, not by reason of their skills or efficiency but because of their strength and ability to wage price wars. The profits made in interstate activities would underwrite the losses of local price-cutting campaigns. No instrumentality of interstate commerce would be used to destroy the local merchant and expand the domain of the combine. But the opportunities afforded by interstate commerce would be employed to injure local trade. . . .

This type of price cutting was held to be "foreign to any legitimate commercial competition" even prior to the Robinson–Patman Act. See *Porto Rican American Tobacco Co.* v. *American Tobacco Co.* . . . It seems plain to us that Congress went at least that far in the Robinson–Patman Act. . . .[23]

Another interesting case involving predatory price discrimination was decided by the Court in 1967. In this case, the Utah Pie Company, a local bakery in Salt Lake City, sought treble damages from and an injunction against Continental Baking Company, the Carnation Company, and the Pet Milk Company. Among other things, Utah Pie Company claimed that the three defendants had discriminated in prices, charging less to retailers in Salt Lake City than elsewhere. In some cases, the defendants made sales below costs; nevertheless, the Utah Pie Company was able to charge the lowest prices in Salt Lake City because it had the advantage of a local plant. In the District Court, the jury found that the defendants had engaged in price discrimination, but the Court of Appeals reversed on grounds that there was insufficient evidence to support a finding of probable

injury to competition as a result of the price discrimination. The Supreme Court reversed the holding of the Court of Appeals, emphasizing the fact that a case of price discrimination is not merely a simple case of reducing prices but involves reducing prices *to some buyers and not to others.* The Court said:

Section 2(a) does not forbid price competition which will probably injure or lessen competition by eliminating competitors, discouraging entry into the market or enhancing shares of dominant sellers. But Congress has established some ground rules for the game. Sellers may not sell like goods to different purchasers at different prices if the result may be to injure competition in either the sellers' or the buyers' market unless such discriminations are justified as permitted by the Act. In this context, the Court of Appeals placed heavy emphasis on the fact that Utah Pie constantly increased its sales volume and continued to make a profit. But we disagree with its apparent view that there is no reasonably possible injury to competition as long as the volume of sales in a particular market is expanding and at least some of the competitors in the market continue to operate at a profit. . . . It is true that many of the primary line cases that have reached the courts have involved blatant predatory price discriminations with the hope of immediate destruction of a particular competitor. On the question of injury to competition such cases present courts with no difficulty, for such pricing is clearly within the heart of the proscription of the Act. Courts and commentators alike have noted that the existence of predatory intent might bear on the likelihood of injury to competition. In this case there was some evidence of predatory intent with respect to each of these respondents [defendants]. There was also other evidence upon which the jury could rationally find the requisite injury to competition. . . . We believe that the Act reaches price discrimination that erodes competition as much as it does price discrimination that is intended to have a destructive effect.[24]

The practice, especially on the part of large chain store companies, of discriminating in prices and of averaging profits among several stores was the subject of attention by the Federal Trade Commission long before the *Mead's Fine Bread* and *Utah Pie Company* cases were decided. Thus, in its *Final Report on the Chain Store Investigation*, the Commission had remarked:

[23] *Moore* v. *Mead's Fine Bread Corp.*, 348 U.S. 115 (1954), at pp. 119–120.

[24] *Utah Pie Company* v. *Continental Baking Company, et. al.*, 386 U.S. 685 (1967), at pp. 702–703.

. . . chains frequently sell the same quality goods at the same time at different prices in their various stores. This manifests itself in the form of leaders and so-called "loss leaders" at some stores, in the pricing of private brands, and in differences between the headquarters price and the branch-store price on many articles. The ability of chain stores to vary prices among their different branches, and thus to average their profit results in one of their chief advantages over independents. In other words, it is one of the chief elements in the growth of chain-store systems to their present dimensions and there is no ground for expecting a different effect upon their future growth. This means that chain-store systems will probably continue to increase in size and tend more and more toward a monopolistic position. . . .[25]

Thus, according to the FTC, the growth of giant chains was not to be explained by "economies of scale." The question of the legality of so-called "quantity discounts" naturally arises next.

Quantity Discounts. The *Porto Rican American Tobacco Company* and *Mead's Fine Bread* cases both involved injury to a competitor of the price discriminator; thus both cases involved what is known as "primary line competition." However, under the rule of the *Van Camp* case, which was codified in amended Section 2(a) by the use of the words "or with customers of either of them," Section 2(a) has been held to apply also to so-called "secondary line competition," that is, to competition among purchasers from the price discriminator. Such a situation existed in the landmark *Morton Salt* case, which involved the question of quantity discounts. The question has also arisen in cases involving basing point pricing, as well as in cases involving promotional allowances under Section 2(d), both discussed later. In the *Morton Salt* case, the salt company granted substantial discounts to largescale buyers. However, the evidence in the case showed that only five buyers had ever purchased sufficient quantities to benefit from the lowest price. The Court thereupon pointed out that "Theoretically, these discounts are equally available to all, but functionally they are not."[26] The Court added:

. . . The legislative history of the Robinson–Patman Act makes it abundantly clear that

Congress considered it to be an evil that a large buyer could secure a competitive advantage over a small buyer solely because of the large buyer's quantity purchasing ability. The Robinson–Patman Act was passed to deprive a large buyer of such advantages except to the extent that a lower price could be justified by reason of a seller's diminished costs due to quantity manufacture, delivery or sale, or by reason of the seller's good faith to meet a competitor's equally low price.

Section 2 of the original Clayton Act had . . . been construed as permitting quantity discounts, such as those here, without regard to the amount of the seller's actual savings in cost attributable to quantity sales or quantity deliveries. . . . The House Committee Report on the Robinson–Patman Act considered . . . the present Robinson–Patman amendment to Section 2 "of great importance." Its purpose was to limit "the use of quantity price differentials to the sphere of actual cost differences."[27]

In addition, in this case the Court held that the burden of proving the cost justification rested on the seller and that the Commission did not have to prove that competition had in fact been harmed but "only that there is a reasonable possibility that they [the discriminations] may" have such an effect. Specially, the Court asserted:

. . . It is urged that the evidence is inadequate to support the Commission's findings of injury to competition. As we have pointed out, however, the Commission is authorized by the Act to bar discriminatory prices upon the "reasonable possibility" that different prices for like goods to competing purchasers may have the defined effect on competition. That respondent's quantity discounts did result in price differentials between competing purchasers sufficient in amount to influence their resale price of salt was shown by the evidence. This showing in itself is adequate to support the Commission's appropriate findings. . . .[28]

An interesting case involving the principle of the *Morton Salt* case was decided by the Supreme Court in 1967. In this case, the Court upheld the power of the Commission to issue a cease-and-desist order to a seller of plumbing fixtures who offered a 10 per cent discount on purchases in truckload quantities. The Commission found that some customers were unable to purchase

---

[25] *Final Report on the Chain Store Investigation, op. cit.,* pp. 50–51.

[26] *Federal Trade Commission v. Morton Salt Co.,* 334

U.S. 37 (1948), at p. 42.

[27] *Ibid.,* at p. 43.

[28] *Ibid.,* at p. 47.

such large amounts. The defendant seller argued that, as a procedural matter, the Commission had no authority to issue the order since it had not preceded the order with a study showing that the discount policy did, in fact, have anticompetitive effects. The Supreme Court upheld the Commission's refusal to stay its cease-and-desist order, saying that the question of whether or not a postponement of a particular order would have an adverse effect on competition was a discretionary matter to be determined by the regulatory agency on the basis of its "specialized experienced judgment." This decision goes far in the direction of giving the Commission great power to determine whether or not a quantity discount arrangement is to be permitted.[29]

In the plumbing fixtures case just mentioned the defendant asserted a cost justification defense but did not undertake to prove his case; the issues involved in this defense—which was also raised in the *Morton Salt* case—will be further discussed in the next chapter. It is to the question of *administrative* limitation of quantiy discounts by FTC orders that attention will be given next.

Administrative Limitations of Quantity Discounts. In its *Final Report* on the chain stores in 1935, the Federal Trade Commission remarked:

Still another suggestion has been made aimed at prevention of price discrimination by manufacturers in favor of chain stores. It is that manufacturers be required to file their special prices and special discount schedules with the Federal Trade Commission, which would then be authorized to order discontinuance or modification of them if unfair or unreasonable as measured by the savings in cost of production or distribution. This would carry with it power to make the special allowances public in the Commission's discretion and to institute inquiries upon its own motion or complaint as to whether they reflected only due allowance for differences in cost. . . . This suggestion is made irrespective of the present powers of the Commission under section 6 to require reports or its powers under section 2 of the Clayton Act or section 5 of the Federal Trade Commission Act.

The proposed power to order discontinuance

or modification under the condition stated is nothing more than the Commission already has under Section 2 or which it may be given by an amendment thereof hereafter . . . recommended.

. . . the Commission attempted, during 1919 and 1920, to collect reports from concerns in the coal and steel industry. . . . Litigation ensued which prevented the action of the Commission for several years during which the unusual need for the data disappeared. When the Supreme Court finally disposed of the test case which had been prosecuted, the decision was not on the merits . . . the Supreme Court merely held that injunction would not lie against the Commission to prevent it from obtaining special reports. . . .[30]

The Commission then pointed out that amendment of Section 2 to deal with this problem was one possible solution. Section 2(a) of the Clayton Act, as amended, thus contains the following proviso:

. . . *provided however*, That the Federal Trade Commission may, after due investigation, and hearing to all interested parties, fix and establish quantity limits, and advise the same as it finds necessary, as to particular commodities or classes of commodities, where it finds that available purchasers in greater quantities are so few as to render differentials on account thereof unjustly discriminatory or promotive of monopoly in any line of commerce and the foregoing shall not then be construed to permit differentials based on differences in quantities greater than those so fixed and established. . . .

This provision was first utilized by the Commission in 1952, when it specified a quantity limit of 20,000 pounds for replacement tires and tubes as the maximum quantity which could be used to justify a quantity discount.[31] A Court of Appeals, however, held the order unenforceable on grounds that the proviso requires the Commission to find not only that there are few purchasers of large quantities, but also that the differentials are "unjustly discriminatory or promotive of monopoly."[32] The majority of the Attorney General's National Committee to Study the Antitrust Laws has remarked of this proviso:

We believe that any rational antitrust policy must leave the American business community free to explore new methods of distribution. Arrangements to impede competing distributive techniques have long been viewed as unreason-

---

[29] *FTC* v. *Universal-Rundle Corp.*, 387 U.S. 244 (1967).

[30] *Final Report on the Chain Store Investigation, op. cit.*, pp. 93–94.

[31] 17 *Federal Register* 113 (1952).

[32] *Federal Trade Commission* v. *B. F. Goodrich Co.*, 242 F. 2d 31 (1957), at p. 35.

able restraints of trade. Hence we deplore this singling out and penalizing of the quantity discount system. . . . Louis B. Schwartz and one other member . . . would add that "in absence of real experience," the majority seems to act "in unseemly haste in condemning a law that small-businessmen regard as important protection against discrimination."[33]

The problem raised by quantity discounts is not unrelated to the problem of growth by merger, the subject of Section 7 of the Clayton Act, as will become readily apparent in Chapter 17. This fact was recognized by the Federal Trade Commission in its *Final Report on the Chain Store Investigation* since it discussed both in the same context and called attention to the fact that there were "two conflicting conceptions" of public policy in this area:

One would prohibit and destroy monopoly at all hazards on the ground that its very existence either involves past absorption of independent businesses or precludes future diffusion of ownership of industry. . . . The other conception is that monopoly is not necessarily an evil, but becomes so only when its power is abused and that we must concern ourselves with the prevention of abuses and not with prevention of the power to abuse.[34]

One further type of price discrimination remains to be discussed in the present context, so-called basing point pricing. It is the subject of the next section.

Basing Point Pricing and the Robinson-Patman Act. A basing point system of pricing is one in which a seller adopts a price at some point of production as a base price and then quotes a "delivered" price consisting of the sum of this base price plus the cost of freight from this "basing point" to the point of delivery, irrespective of the actual cost at and freight from the point from which actual delivery is made. The *Corn Products Refining* case provides an illustration of this practice and of its illegality under Section 2(a). According to the Court:

. . . The Commission found from the evidence that petitioners have two plants for the manufacture of glucose or corn syrup, one at Argo, Illinois, within the Chicago switching district, and the other at Kansas City, Missouri. . . .

Petitioners' bulk sales of glucose are at delivered prices, which are computed, whether the shipments are from Chicago or Kansas City, at petitioners' Chicago prices, plus the freight rate from Chicago to the place of delivery. Thus purchasers in all places other than Chicago pay a higher price than do Chicago purchasers. And in the case of all shipments from Kansas City to purchasers in cities having a lower freight rate from Kansas City than from Chicago, the delivered price includes unearned or "phantom" freight, to the extent of the difference in freight rates. Conversely, when the freight from Kansas City to the point of delivery is more than that from Chicago, petitioners must "absorb" freight on shipments from Kansas City, to the extent of the difference in freight.[35]

The Commission found that this system of pricing constituted price discrimination under Section 2(a). The defendants argued that the system did not discriminate *among buyers at the same point of delivery*, but the Court rejected this argument, saying that "the purchasers of glucose from the petitioners are in competition with each other, *even though they are in different localities.* The injury to competition of purchasers in different localities is no less harmful than if they were in the same city."

The *Corn Products* case involved a single basing point; three years later, in the *Cement Institute* case, the Court held that a multiple basing point system of pricing also constituted a violation of Section 2(a). The Court said:

As commonly employed by respondents, the basing point system is not single but multiple. That is, instead of one basing point . . . a number of basing point localities are used. In the multiple basing point system, just as in the single basing point system, freight absorption or phantom freight is an element of the delivered price on all sales not governed by a basing point actually located at the seller's mill. And all sellers quote identical delivered prices in any given locality regardless of their different costs of production and their different freight expenses. Thus the multiple and single systems function in the same general manner and produce the same consequences—identity of prices and diversity of net returns. Such differences as there are in matters here pertinent are therefore differences of degree only.[36]

[33] *Report of the Attorney General's National Committee to Study the Antitrust Laws* (Washington, D.C.: U.S. Government Printing Office, 1955), p. 177.

[34] *Final Report on the Chain Store Investigation, op. cit.,* p. 86.

[35] *Corn Products Refining Co.* v. *Federal Trade Commission,* 324 U.S. 726 (1945), at pp. 730–731.

[36] *Federal Trade Commission* v. *Cement Institute et. al.,* 333 U.S. 683 (1948), at pp. 698–700.

In addition, the Court pointed out that the Commission had found as a fact that various predatory practices ranging from boycotts to price wars had been employed to insure universal adherence to the pricing system. Consequently, not only was the Commission correct in finding a violation of Section 2(a), but it was also correct in finding that the system constituted an unfair method of competition and a violation of Section 5 of the Federal Trade Commission Act. Said the Court:

> . . . We therefore hold that the Commission was not compelled to accept the views of respondents' economist-witnesses that active competition was bound to produce uniform cement prices. The Commission was authorized to find understanding, express or implied, from evidence that the industry's Institute actively worked, in cooperation with various of its members, to maintain the multiple basing point delivered price system; that this pricing system is calculated to produce, and has produced, uniform prices and terms of sale throughout the country; and that all of the respondents have sold their cement substantially in accord with the pattern required by the multiple basing point system.[37]

In June 1950 Congress adopted legislation to legalize basing point pricing, but on June 16 President Truman vetoed this legislation.[38]

Other Trade Practices [Sections 2(c) through 2(f)]

In its *Final Report on the Chain Store Investigation*, the Federal Trade Commission pointed to various trade practices, other than outright price discrimination, which favored the growth of the chains, by saying:

> . . . preferential treatments usually take the form of special discounts and allowances, sometimes given in consideration of promotional sales work or special service rendered by the chain-store receiving the concession.

> The preferences granted chains by manufacturers fall into the following general classifications: Volume allowances, promotional allowances, allowances in lieu of brokerage, freight allowances, and guarantees against price decline.

> Promotional allowances are classified as: Newspaper advertising allowances; window display allowances; counter display allowances; allowances for featuring and deals; and other advertising and promotional allowances. . . .

> Frequently money advanced for advertising was not used for that purpose at all but used for the purpose of reducing the price to the consumer. . . .

> . . . A number of the manufacturers in the grocery group stated that they give allowances in lieu of brokerage to certain chain customers. . . .

> . . . Seven manufacturers in the grocery group reported that they give free goods in one form or another. . . .

> There were interviews with 129 manufacturers in the grocery group, 76 of which admitted that preferential treatment in some form was given [to the chains]. . . . Thirty-three of the manufacturers interviewed stated positively that threats and coercion had been used by chainstore companies to obtain preferential treatment. . . .

> Fear of losing the business of certain chains through whom a large part of their output was marketed, and threat to manufacture a competing product were reasons assigned by some grocery manufacturers for acceding to the demand of chain-store buyers for special concessions. . . .[39]

These findings explain why Congress in the Robinson-Patman Act added Sections 2(c) to 2(f) to the original Section 2 of the Clayton Act. Section 2(c) contains a *per se* prohibition of the payment of brokerage to a buyer, while Sections 2(d) and 2(e) deal with the problem of promotional allowances, and Section 2(f) makes it unlawful for a *buyer knowingly* to induce or to receive a price discrimination. These provisions are discussed next.

Brokerage. According to the *Report* of the Attorney General's National Committee:

> Interpretation has developed Section 2(c) into a simple prohibition on payments to all distributive intermediaries except wholly "independent" brokers . . . the payment of middleman's commissions to any but pure "brokers" becomes *per se* illegal, even though valuable distributive services are performed, even when no adverse competitive effect results, and even where the challenged concession reflects actual savings in the seller's distribution costs.

> The Committee considers the prevailing interpretations of the "brokerage" clause at odds with broader antitrust objectives . . . the "broke-

---

[37] *Ibid.*, at p. 716.
[38] *Study of Monopoly Power* (Hearings before the Subcommittee on Study of Monopoly Power of the House Judiciary Committee, 82d Cong., 1st sess.) (Washington, D.C.: U.S. Government Printing Office, 1951), Serial No. 1, Part 5, pp. 253–255.
[39] *Final Report on the Chain Store Investigation, op. cit.*, pp. 59–63, 24, 26.

rage" clause as presently interpreted enacts a preferred position for the "independent" broker, thus discriminating against competing firms in distribution who are arbitrarily denied compensation for genuine marketing functions which they perform.[40]

A leading Court of Appeals decision illustrating the *per se* nature of the prohibition of brokerage in Section 2(c) is the *Southgate Brokerage* case. The brokerage company functioned both as a commission brokerage house and as a purchaser, warehouser, and distributor on its own account and accepted from sellers brokerage and allowances in lieu of brokerage on *all* its purchases. It claimed that with respect to the purchases made on its own account the brokerage and "in lieu of" allowances were made "for services rendered." The Court of Appeals held, however, that Section 2(c) prohibited payment of brokerage without regard to the other provisions of the Clayton Act. Moreover, the services which the company rendered were rendered to itself and not to the sellers, said the Court of Appeals.[41] In reaching this result, the Court relied on earlier decisions by other Courts of Appeals involving similar fact situations. In the *A & P* case in 1939, the Court of Appeals for the Third Circuit had specifically distinguished between Section 2(c) and the other provisions of the Robinson-Patman Act by saying:

... An examination of paragraph (a) shows that it deals with discriminations in price generally. Paragraph (c) upon other hand deals in particular with a trade practice which has frequently resulted in price discriminations and unfair competition. It is obvious that by its express language paragraph (c) must be applied only to transactions occurring in ... interstate commerce. ... The respective paragraphs must be read with due regard for the provisions of each.

The practice of paying brokerage, or sums in lieu of brokerage, to buyers or their agents by sellers was found by Congress to be an unfair trade practice resulting in damage to commerce. Paragraph (c) prohibits such practice. We conclude that Congress has properly exercised its power to the end that the named abuse may be done away with.[42]

Thus Section 2(c) defines a *per se* offense independently of the other provisions of the Act.

The Federal Trade Commission issues (free of charge on request) a *News Summary*. Interested readers may obtain copies by writing to the Commission. The following item concerning issuance of a consent order in a case involving Section 2(c) appeared in the *Summary* of May 6, 1967. It is reproduced here partly to give the reader some idea of the type of information contained in the *Summary* but primarily to illustrate the type of problem dealt with by the Commission under Section 2(c). The item reads as follows:

CONSENT ORDER (C–1201)
BROKERAGE (RP)   (Grocery Products)

A consent order issued by the Federal Trade Commission forbids a grocery products wholesaler and two brokerage concerns in Albany, N.Y., to receive illegal brokerage.

The following companies, all located at Dott and Railroad Aves., are cited in the agreed-to order: A. Greenhouse, Inc., Food Trends, Inc., and Consumer Motivation, Inc. The order also names Saul Greenhouse, president of A. Greenhouse; and Eugene Greenhouse, an officer of both Food Trends and Consumer Motivation.

The agreement is for settlement purposes only and does not constitute an admission by the respondents that they have violated the law.

According to the FTC's complaint, Eugene Greenhouse owns substantially all of the capital stock of Food Trends and Consumer Motivation, the brokers. On July 1, 1963, he ostensibly severed his connection as vice president of A. Greenhouse, the wholesaler, but has continued to act as the wholesaler's agent.

Food Trends and Consumer Motivation, the complaint continues, purportedly represent various seller-principals, but a substantial portion of their business consists of arranging sales to A. Greenhouse. They receive assistance from employees of A. Greenhouse.

The complaint alleges that Saul and Eugene Greenhouse frequently have made purchases for A. Greenhouse through Food Trends and Consumer Motivation, which received substantial brokerage commissions from the suppliers.

In view of this ownership and control, the complaint charges, the brokers have been acting for or have been subject to the control of the buyer, and consequently the respondent's receipt of brokerage on their own purchases is unlawful under Section 2(c) of the amended Clayton Act.

Commissioner Philip Elman dissented from the issuance of complaint.

5/5/67

---

[40] *Report of the Attorney General's National Committee to Study the Antitrust Laws, op. cit.,* pp. 188–191.
[41] *Southgate Brokerage Co.* v. *Federal Trade Commission,*

150 F. 2d 607 (1945), at p. 611.
[42] *Great Atlantic and Pacific Tea Co.* v. *Federal Trade Commission,* 106 F. 2d 667 (1939), at pp. 677–678.

It is obvious from the foregoing item that the Commission is prepared to look through form to the substance of the matter. It has adopted a similar attitude in dealing with promotional allowances under Sections 2(d) and 2(e) of the law.

Promotional Allowances and Services. Sections 2(d) and 2(e) have been interpreted by the courts in a parallel way. An early leading case is *Elizabeth Arden Sales Corporation* v. *Gus Blass Company.* In this case, the Elizabeth Arden Sales Company (defendent and appellant) made an oral agreement with the Gus Blass Company (plaintiff and appellee) under which the defendent agreed to pay one-half of the salary of a clerk in the plaintiff's department store, the clerk to be designated an "Elizabeth Arden demonstrator" with the duty of pushing the sale of the defendant's products. Unknown to the plaintiff, the defendent at the same time was paying the entire salary of a similar clerk in a department store operated by a competitor (M. M. Cohn Company) of the plaintiff. After about two years, the defendant discontinued the arrangement with the plaintiff and assigned the exclusive right to sell its products to the plaintiff's competitor. The plaintiff thereupon sued for treble damages under Sections 2(d) and 2(e) of the amended Clayton Act, which require that allowances and services must be made "on proportionately equal terms." As stated by the Court of Appeals:

The trial court found that "the defendant [appellant] discriminated in favor of M. M. Cohn Company against the plaintiff [appellee], both of whom bought commodities from the defendant for resale, by contracting to furnish or by contributing to the furnishing of services and facilities connected with the sale and offering for sale of such commodities so purchased from the defendant, such discrimination consisting of the payment of the entire salary of defendant's representative in the M. M. Cohn Company store and one-half salary to the defendant's representative in the plaintiff's store"; ... and that "the plaintiff has accordingly been damaged. ..."

The trial court thus appears to have treated the comparative arrangements with Cohn Co. and with appellee as constituting an unlawful discrimination ... under section 2(e) of the Clayton Act, as amended by the Robinson–Patman Act. ... The situation might alternatively have been regarded as a discriminatory payment of compensation by appellant for special clerk's services or facilities furnished by Cohn Co. and by appellee in demonstrating or pushing the sale of appellant's products, instead of as a furnishing of clerk's services or facilities by appellant to Cohn Co. and to appellee, and so to constitute a violation of section 2(d) of the Clayton Act, as amended by the Robinson–Patman Act. ...

Appellant contends, however, that whether subsection (e) or subsection (d) were applied, there was no illegal discrimination under either subsection, because on the basis of purchases made appellee had received clerk's services or clerk's salary "on proportionally equal terms" with Cohn Co. ...

But ... on the findings of the trial court and the evidence, appellant's furnishing of clerk's services or payment of clerk's salaries to appellee and Cohn Co. cannot be claimed to have ever had any established or determinable basis or standard whatever. The allowance had been fixed in both instances at the time the purchase of goods began, and there it simply remained. Its amount was arrived at by personal negotiation and individual agreement. There was no arrangement or provision for graduating it to the amount of goods purchased during any given period. Nor was it based upon any other guiding factor, such as a difference in the character of the stores and the type of facilities afforded for handling appellant's products, if that could have been made to constitute a valid legal distinction. ...

The agreement which appellant made with appellee provided no path on which appellee could travel to qualify or claim the right to have earned the additional services or salary which appellant was allowing Cohn Co. That appellant's whole policy was simply one of random and arbitrary arrangement was also made to appear from the varying customer allowances shown by its general records, which the court admitted in an effort that might justify the difference in treatment between appellee and Cohn Co. ...

We think it must be held that a seller engaged in commerce who furnishes a clerk's services or pays clerks' salaries in unequal amounts to customers competing in the distribution of its products, which amounts have no other basis or standard than the seller's discretion or favor, and as to which there is no competitive way for such customers to qualify for proportional or equal levels, is, to the extent of any differences in such amounts, guilty of a discrimination in the furnishing of services or facilities under subsection (e) or in the payment for services or facilities under subsection (d) of section 2 of the Clayton Act as amended by the Robinson–Patman Act. ... That which was discriminatory under the statute when done, because wholly unrelated to any proportionalized basis or standard, cannot subsequently, in order to enable the seller to escape damages for the discrimination, be artificially tailored into proportionally equal terms by fitting it to some imaginary basis or standard that has never in fact existed.[43]

Subsequently, in 1958 in a case involving the giving of "spot" promotional allowances by a distributor of imported meats to a chain store which were not equally available to all of the purchasers of meat from the distributor because they did not purchase specially for sale during certain holiday seasons, a Court of Appeals held:

That each allowance was the result of "a plan tailored exclusively to fit the desires of the two parties negotiating" and therefore could not have been made available on proportionally equal terms does not constitute a *per se* violation of Section 2(d). The mere showing that an allowance could not be offered to another competing purchaser is not the equivalent of proof that there in fact existed another such purchaser who was not offered the allowance. Nothing in the Robinson–Patman Act imposes upon a supplier an affirmative duty to sell to all potential customers. Absent monopolistic power, a seller may refuse to deal with anyone. . . . All that the Act requires is that a seller give fair and equal treatment to all those to whom he elects to sell products of like grade and quality.[44]

This Court was evidently not impressed by the Commission's argument that the Court's holding "would make the section very easy of evasion." The Commission thus has the burden of showing the actual existence of a competing purchaser who "was not offered the allowance."

This decision was handed down *after* publication of the *Report* of the Attorney General's National Committee to Study the Antitrust Laws. On the point in question, that Committee stated:

Sections 2(d) and 2(e), concerned with analogous marketing practices, have developed through parallel judicial interpretation. . . . The interpretive process thus interpolated into 2(e) the prerequisite of *competing* customers, and the interstate commerce requirement into Section 2(d). Decisions equally have not distinguished the "customers" of 2(d) from the "purchasers" of 2(e), and have considered allowances "available" and services "accorded" whenever openly offered to affected buyers.

The criterion of "proportionally equal terms" . . . has recently been construed by the Federal Trade Commission . . . the Commission has evolved a rule of thumb for testing the requisite proportional equality in allowances or services by comparing the promotional benefit with the dollar volume of purchases by various customers. In actual practice, proportional programs can thus conform to the law in three basic ways: (1) payment of a dollar allowance per unit of promotional service rendered by each buyer, up to a uniform maximum percentage of his dollar volume; (2) a simplified plan, granting each buyer a set dollar allowance per unit of merchandise bought, on condition that *he* perform a specified minimum quantum of promotional services; (3) the *seller's* direct furnishing of promotional services to the buyer, worth a uniform percentage of each buyer's volume. . . .

. . . the Committee disapproves the present disparity in the statutory consequences which attach to economically equivalent business practices. Today, "direct" or "indirect" price discriminations under Section 2(a) do not transgress the law unless they cause adverse market effects and unless unjustifiable under one of the defensive provisos. In contrast, "brokerage" concessions or "proportionally unequal" allowances or services are illegal *per se*. This legal quirk facilitates manipulation and fosters confusion, since the Act places a premium on cloaking any concession in terms of a desired legal result. . . .

For this reason, in order to reconcile the brokerage clause with "broader antitrust objectives," we favor legislation as necessary to restore the original vigor of the exception "for services rendered" in Section 2(c).

In contrast, Sections 2(d) and (e) seem amenable to interpretative reform. Hence we deem reconciliation of Sections 2(d) and (e) with "broader antitrust objectives" still feasible through reinterpretation short of amendment, and do not propose congressional action at this time.[45]

The Committee's term, "interpretative reform," is, of course, a euphemistic expression for "judicial legislation."

An interesting application of Section 2(d) can be found in the Commission's Final Order Number 8647, July 5, 1966. This order prohibited Clairol, Inc. from paying promotional allowances to beauty salons

---

[43] *Elizabeth Arden Sales Corp.* v. *Gus Blass Co.*, 150 F. 2d 988 (1945), at pp. 990, 993, 994.

[44] *Atlanta Trading Corp.* v. *Federal Trade Commission,*

258 F. 2d 365 (1958), at pp. 372–373.

[45] *Report of the Attorney General's National Committee to Study the Antitrust Laws, op. cit.,* pp. 189–193.

using hair-coloring preparations in a situation in which similar promotional allowances were not made available to retailers selling Clairol's hair care preparations to customers for home use.

In issuing its order in the *Clairol* case, the Commission referred to its earlier decision in the *Fred Meyer, Inc.* case. In the latter, the Commission had ruled in 1963 that wholesalers whose retailer customers competed directly with the Fred Meyer chain of supermarkets were entitled to a proportionally equal share of promotional allowances received by the Fred Meyer, Inc. chain from suppliers. However, in 1966, the Court of Appeals for the Ninth Circuit reversed the Commission's ruling, and an appeal was made by the Commission to the Supreme Court.

The Supreme Court handed down its decision in 1968. The Court held that the wholesalers were not in competition with the direct-buying retailer, Fred Meyer, Inc., but that the retailers who purchased from the wholesalers were in competition with Fred Meyer, Inc. and were entitled through the wholesalers to a proportionately equal share of the promotional allowances. In short, the Court held that although Section 2(d) did not apply in a case involving only wholesalers and a direct-buying retailer, Section 2(d) did prohibit the granting of promotional allowances to a corporate owner (Meyer) of a chain of supermarkets, a direct-buying retailer, without making available proportionately equal promotional allowances to wholesalers who sold to retailers in competition with the direct-buying retailer. The issue is one involving the "levels of competition" concept dealt with earlier in the *Van Camp* case. The Court held that the "level of competition" was a functional concept; since the retailers in competition with Meyer bought from wholesalers who were not given the promotional allowances given to Meyer, these retailers suffered a competitive disadvantage. The case stands for the proposition that the "levels of competitition" concept is a functional one.[46] This same functional concept was then used in 1969, we have already seen, in the *Perkins* case which involved the problem of price discrimination under Section 2(a).

The Supreme Court decision was implemented by the issuance of Modified Order 7492 by the FTC on June 20, 1968. On March 5, 1969, the FTC announced that its "Guides for Advertising Allowances and Other Merchandising Payments and Services," based on the *Meyer* decision, would take effect on May 1, 1969. The *Fred Meyer, Inc.* episode thus illustrates the way in which an initial decision by a Hearing Examiner may result eventually in a formal change in working rules.

Section 2(f) of the Clayton Act, as amended, makes it unlawful for "any person *knowingly* to induce or receive a discrimination in price." The landmark case interpreting this provision is the *Automatic Canteen Company* case, decided in 1953. The defendant company was a large buyer of candy and other confectionary products for resale through about 23,000 automatic vending machines located in 33 states and in the District of Columbia. According to the Court:

The Commission introduced evidence that petitioner [defendant] received, and in some instances solicited, prices it knew were as much as 33% lower than prices quoted other purchasers, but the Commission has not attempted to show that the price differentials exceeded any cost savings that sellers may have enjoyed in sales to petitioner. Petitioner moved to dismiss the complaint on the ground that the Commission had not made a prima facie case. This motion was denied; the Commission stated that a prima facie case of violation had been established by proof that the buyer received lower prices on like goods than other buyers, "*well knowing* that it was being favored over competing purchasers," under circumstances where the requisite effect on competition had been shown. . . .

Petitioner claims that the Commission has not, on this record, made a prima facie case of *knowing* inducement of prices that "made more 'than due allowance for' " cost differences, while the Commission contends that it has established a prima facie case, justifying entry of a cease and desist order where the buyer fails to introduce evidence. . . . Petitioner is saying in effect that, under the Commission's view, the burden of introducing evidence as to the seller's cost savings and the buyer's *knowledge* thereof is put on the buyer; this burden, petitioner insists, is so difficult to meet that it would be unreasonable to construe the language Congress has used as imposing it. . . .

---

[46] *FTC* v. *Fred Meyer, Inc., et. al.,* 390 U.S. 341 (1968).

No doubt the burden placed on petitioner to show his sellers' costs, under present Commission standards, is heavy. Added to the considerable burden that a seller himself may have in demonstrating costs is the fact that the data not only are not in the buyer's hands but are . . . obtainable even by the seller only after detailed investigation of the business. A subpoena of the seller's records is not likely to be adequate. It is not a question of obtaining information in the seller's hands. It is a matter of studying the seller's business. . . .

. . . Even if any price differential were to be comprehended within the term "discrimination in price," Section 2(f), which speaks of prohibited discriminations, cannot be read as declaring out of bounds price differentials within one or more of the "defenses" available to sellers, such as that the price differentials reflect cost differences, fluctuating market conditions, or bona fide attempts to meet competition, as those defenses are set out in the provisos of Section 2(a) and 2(b).

This is not to say . . . that the converse follows, for Section 2(f) does not reach all cases of buyer receipt of a prohibited discrimination in prices. *It limits itself to cases of knowing receipt* of such prices. The Commission seems to argue, in part, that the substantive violation occurs if the buyer knows only that the prices are lower than those offered other buyers. Such a reading not only distorts the language but would leave the word "knowingly" almost entirely without significance in Section 2(f). A buyer with no knowledge whatsoever of facts indicating the possibility that price differences were not based on cost differences would be liable if in fact they were not. . . .

Not only are the arguments of the Commission unsatisfying, but we think a fairer reading of the language and of what limited legislative elucidation we have points toward a reading of Section 2(f) making it unlawful only to induce or receive prices *known* to be prohibited discriminations. . . .

We therefore conclude that a buyer is not liable under Section 2(f) if the lower prices he induces are either within one of the seller's defenses such as the cost justification or not known by him not to be within one of those defenses.

. . . the Commission is, on this record, insisting that once knowledge of a price differential is shown, the burden of introducing evidence shifts to the buyer. The Commission's main reliance in this argument is Section 2(b). . . .

A confident answer cannot be given; some answer must be given. . . . It would not give fair effect to Section 2(b) to say that the burden of coming forward with evidence as to costs and the buyer's knowledge thereof shifts to the buyer as soon as it is shown that the buyer knew the prices differed.

. . . While this Court ought scrupulously to abstain from requiring of the Commission particularization of its findings so exacting as to make this Court in effect a court of review on the facts, it is no less important, since we are charged with the duty of reviewing the correctness of the standards which the Commission applies and the essential fairness of the mode by which it reaches its conclusions, that the Commission do not shelter behind uncritical generalities or such looseness of expression as to make it essentially impossible for us to determine what really lay behind the conclusions which we are to review.[47]

The meaning of a "prima facie" case will be discussed further in Chapter 16. The last paragraph of the opinion quoted above shows that the majority believed that the imposition upon the Commission of a requirement that it state clearly the grounds of its decisions was more important than the possible harm which might flow from the use of monopsonistic buying power. A sharp dissenting opinion took the opposite view.

The decision of the Court in the *Automatic Canteen* case has had a clear effect upon subsequent actions taken by the Commission under Section 2(f). Thus, for example, in January 1964, by Final Order 8039, the Commission prohibited 55 jobbers of automotive parts from *knowingly* inducing and receiving discriminatory prices from their suppliers by means of their establishment of a partnership, the National Parts Warehouse, which served as their joint purchasing agent.

A Concluding Comment

In this chapter we have been concerned primarily with the enforcement by the Federal Trade Commission of Section 2 of the Clayton Act as amended by the Robinson-Patman Act. The Commission's *Annual Report for the Fiscal Year Ended June* 30, 1967 contains the following summary of the casework of its Division of Discriminatory Practices, which performs this enforcement function, for the period in question:

Informal cases:	
Initiated	159
Disposed of during year	165
Pending June 30, 1967	310
Formal cases:	
Complaints issued	7

[47] *Automatic Canteen Co.* v. *Federal Trade Commission*, 346 U.S. 61 (1953), at pp. 62–81. (Italics mine.)

Contested orders	7
Consent orders	7
Dismissed	1
Cases pending litigation June 30, 1967	8

Also according to this report, 50 informal cases involving Sections 2(a), (c), (d), and (e) were settled by the use of informal procedures involving the giving of assurances by the defendants that the practices complained of would be discontinued.

In the course of our discussion of the working rules developed under the Robinson-Patman Act in this chapter, mention has necessarily occasionally been made of defenses contained in Sections 2(a) and 2(b) of the Act. Discussion and critical analysis of the provisions establishing these defenses are the subjects of the next chapter.

16

Defenses Against Charges of Discrimination Under the Robinson-Patman Act

As has been noted in the preceding chapter, the provisos of Sections 2(a) and 2(b) of the Clayton Act, as amended, contain certain "affirmative" defenses which the defendant can assert and prove in order to escape liability from charges of discrimination under the law. The relevant provisos in Section 2(a) read as follows:

2(a) ... *Provided*, That nothing herein contained shall prevent differentials which make only due allowance for differences in the cost of manufacture, sale, or delivery resulting from the differing methods or quantities in which such commodities are to such purchasers sold or delivered ... *And provided further*, That nothing herein contained shall prevent price changes from time to time where in response to changing conditions affecting the market for or the marketability of the goods concerned, such as but not limited to actual or imminent deterioration of perishable goods, obsolescence of seasonal goods, distress sales under court process, or sales in good faith in discontinuance of business in the goods concerned.

These provisos contain what have come to be known as the "cost justification" and "changing conditions" defenses and will be discussed first in this chapter. Section 2(b), on the other hand, contains the "good faith meeting of competition" defense and will be

discussed in the second and third major subdivisions below. Section 2(b) reads:

2(b) Upon proof being made, at any hearing on a complaint under this section, that there has been discrimination in price or services or facilities furnished, the burden of rebutting the prima facie case thus made by showing justification shall be upon the person charged with a violation of this section, and unless justification shall be affirmatively shown, the Commission is authorized to issue an order terminating the discrimination: *Provided, however*, That nothing herein contained shall prevent a seller rebutting the prima facie case thus made by showing that his lower price or the furnishing of services or facilities to any purchaser or purchasers was made in good faith to meet an equally low price of a competitor, or the services or facilities furnished by a competitor.

The above section does not apply to the brokerage provision contained in Section 2(c), but it does apply to the provisions concerning the furnishing of allowances or facilities under Sections 2(d) and 2(e). The question of the definition of a *prima facie* case has already been briefly considered in the preceding chapter but will be further discussed below. Another question requiring further consideration is whether the "meeting competition" defense is an "absolute" defense, that is, can a price discrimination be justified under this section, *even though* it tends substantially to lessen competition or to create a monopoly, if it is made in good faith to meet the "equally low price" of a competitor? Before considering these interesting questions further, however, it is useful to discuss the defenses contained in the proviso of Section 2(a) quoted above.

This chapter consists of three major subdivisions. As has been noted, the first examines the "changing conditions" and cost justification defenses stated in Section 2(a), and the second subdivision discusses the definition of a "prima facie" case under Section 2(b). The third and last subdivision analyzes the nature of the "meeting competition in good faith" defense provided in Section 2(b).

A. THE "CHANGING CONDITIONS" AND "COST JUSTIFICATION" DEFENSES OF SECTION 2(a)

"Changing Conditions"

In general, the last proviso of Section 2(a) seems to have been intended to deal with occasional and imminent distress situations and to permit a seller to revise his current price schedules in accordance with actual changes in market conditions resulting from "natural" market forces, irrespective of what those schedules may have stated in the recent past. The courts have rejected an attempt to bring this proviso into play in a case in which a seller sought to rely on it as a justification for his response to a boycott.[1] The proviso itself states examples drawn largely from cases involving distress conditions, situations which in and of themselves are not likely to lead to monopoly or to a reduction of competition as a result of action by a seller who is forced to rely on this proviso in justification of his price differential.

"Cost Justification"

The "cost justification" defense permitted under Section 2(a) has given rise to many difficult questions, and some reference has already been made to this defense in

connection with the *Morton Salt* and *Automatic Canteen Company* cases in preceding chapters. The *Morton Salt* case, it will be recalled, involved a holding by the Court that a quantity discount which was not functionally available to all buyers could be the subject of a cease-and-desist order by the Commission under Section 2(a). In this case, the Court put the burden of proving cost justification on the seller who is shown to have discriminated in price when the Court said:

. . . the general rule of statutory construction that the burden of proving justification or exemption under a special exception to the prohibitions of a statute generally rests on one who claims its benefits, requires that respondent [Morton Salt Co.] undertake this proof under the proviso of Section 2(a). Secondly, Section 2(b) of the Act specifically imposes the burden of showing justification upon one who is shown to have discriminated in prices. And the Senate committee report on the bill explained that the provisos of Section 2(a) throw "upon any who claim the benefit of those exceptions the burden of showing that their case falls within them."[2]

The difficulties inherent in proving "cost justification" were noted by the Court in its opinion in the *Automatic Canteen Company* case (in which, it will also be recalled from the preceding chapter, the Court held that the Commission must prove, among other things, that a buyer who received a price discrimination *knew* that the differential in price was not cost justified). The Court said, among other things:

. . . The elusiveness of cost data, which apparently cannot be obtained from ordinary business records, is reflected in proceedings against sellers. Such proceedings make us aware of how difficult these problems are. . . . It is sufficient to note that, whenever costs have been in issue, the Commission has not been content with accounting estimates; a study seems to be required, involving perhaps stop-watch studies of time spent by some personnel such as salesmen and truck drivers, numerical counts of invoices or bills and in some instances of the number of items or entries on such records, or other such quantitative measurement of the operation of a business.[3]

The Attorney General's National Committee to study the Antitrust Laws com-

---

[1] *Moore* v. *Mead Service Co.*, 190 F. 2d 540 (1951), at p. 541.
[2] *Federal Trade Commission* v. *Morton Salt Co.*, 334

U.S. 37 (1948), at pp. 44–45.
[3] *Automatic Canteen Co.* v. *Federal Trade Commission*, 346 U.S. 61 (1953), at p. 68.

312 THE ANTITRUST AND CONSUMER PROTECTION LAWS

mented upon the cost justification defense as follows:

> ... conspicuous has been the failure of past adjudications to evolve workable criteria by which the cost defense can attain its intended role. One District Court perceived the "ultimate fault" of an attempted cost defense in a failure to separate a seller's cost in dealing with each individual buyer; another District Court categorically rejected cost studies not based on individual transactions with individual customers. But on appeal one decision was reversed and the other affirmed, in opinions by appellate courts which admittedly disagreed with each other ... the Federal Trade Commission [has] indicated a readiness to accept cost studies "made in good faith and in accordance with sound accounting principles." However, no standards for testing the requisite "good faith" or "sound accounting principles" have as yet been promulgated. ... [4]

This statement was made in 1955, one year prior to the *Report* of the Special Advisory Committee (of Exports) on Cost Justification to the Federal Trade Commission which was made in 1956. The Commission today requires that cost studies take account both of variable and of fixed costs, but the specification or allocation of costs in the case of joint products continues to be a difficult problem of cost accounting. So does the allocation of distribution and selling costs.

One decision of interest in the present context is that of a Court of Appeals in 1956 in *Reid* v. *Harper and Brothers*. The plaintiff book seller, Reid, brought an action seeking treble damages against the defendant publishing company, alleging a price discrimination under Section 2(a). The defendant asserted the cost justification defense. In part, this defense rested on the following accounting procedure: Since the defendant had no cost records for the period from 1941 to 1950, the accountant making the cost study thereupon presented figures for this period by adjusting "backwards" the data for 1951. His adjustment involved the use of salary rates published by the Commerce and Industry Association of New York. In allowing this quasi-index number procedure, the Court of Appeals said:

> ... Although such an accounting method obviously lacks the full measure of desired precision, it appears to have been undertaken in good faith and to accord with the minimal requirements of sound accounting principles. Indeed, under the circumstances, it appears to have been the best available procedure. Both the courts and the Federal Trade Commission have recognized the dilemma confronting defendants in suits such as these, and have liberally accepted data derived from litigation-inspired accounting methods. [5]

Thus the Court of Appeals held that the trial court had correctly charged the jury that it was for the jury to decide whether or not it would accept or reject the assumptions made by the defendant's accountant in adopting this procedure. The question was one of fact and not of law. This case would, of course, have been even more interesting if the plaintiff had adopted a different index number and attacked the defendant's claim on that basis. In such a case, presumably the jury would have had the task of determining as a matter of fact which index number more accurately reflected the true situation—no mean task even for a trained economist.

B. THE "PRIMA FACIE" CASE OF SECTION 2(b)

Definition of Prima Facie Case

Section 2(b) states that the "burden of rebutting the prima facie case" made upon proof that there has been a discrimination in price "shall be on the person charged with a violation of this section." The question of the meaning of this language and the definition of "a prima facie case" has already been raised in the quotation from the opinion in the *Automatic Canteen Company* case in the preceding chapter. This question arises more naturally in actions involving charges of price discrimination against a seller under Section 2(a) than in cases involving a buyer under Section 2(f), but it also was a matter of issue under Section 2(f) in the *Automatic Canteen Company* case. Put in its simplest terms, the issue involved is this: Has the Commission established a *prima facie* case of price discrimination when it has proved that a price differential exists, so

---

[4] *Report of the Attorney General's National Committee to Study the Antitrust Laws* (Washington, D.C.: U.S. Government Printing Office, 1955), pp. 171–172.

[5] *Reid* v. *Harper and Brothers*, 235 F. 2d 420 (1956), at p. 422.

that the burden shifts to the defendant to prove one of his affirmative defenses, or must the Commission also show that competition has been adversely affected by the price discrimination? An early leading case involving this question is the *Moss* case. According to the Court of Appeals in that case:

The case was tried in part upon a stipulation declaring that in the eight instances mentioned in the findings, the respondent [defendant] sold rubber stamps to some of its customers at lower prices than it was selling the same stamps to other customers. The Commission's position was that, having proved this, Section 2(b) . . . put upon the petitioner the burden of justifying the discrimination; and warranted the order [to cease and desist], if it failed to do so. The petitioner did not prove affirmatively that the discrimination did not lessen competition or tend to prevent it; nor did it prove that its lower prices were only "to meet an equally low price of a competitor." On the contrary, it did not know its competitors' prices but merely bid low enough to get the business. This made it proper and indeed necessary for the Commission to make the findings it did. It is true that 2(a) makes price discrimination unlawful only in case it lessens, or tends to prevent, competition with the merchant who engages in the practice; and that no doubt means that the lower price must prevent, or tend to prevent, competitors from taking business away from the merchant which they might have got, had the merchant not lowered his price below what he was charging elsewhere. But that is often hard to prove; the accuser must show that there were competitors whom the higher of the two prices would, or might, not have defeated, but who could not meet the lower. Hence the Congress adopted the common device in such cases of shifting the burden of proof to anyone who sets two prices, and who probably knows why he has done so, and what has been the result. If he can prove that the lower price did not prevent or tend to prevent anyone from taking away the business, he will succeed, for the accuser will not then have brought him within the statute at all.
. . . we hold that the findings are supported by the evidence.[6]

Thus, the Commission's argument that the burden of proof shifted to the one who set two prices was sustained.

It was this argument under Section 2(a), which was the basis of the discussion in the

preceding chapter by the Supreme Court of the meaning of a "prima facie" case in the action against the Automatic Canteen Company under Section 2(f).

The relevant part of the statement of facts and of the opinion in that case reads as follows:

. . . the Commission stated that a prima facie case of violation had been established by proof that the buyer received lower prices on like goods than other buyers, "well knowing that it was being favored" . . . under circumstances where the . . . effect on competition had been shown. . . .

Petitioner claims that the Commission has not, on this record, made a prima facie case of *knowing* inducement of prices that "made more 'than due allowance for' " cost differences, while the Commission contends that it has established a prima facie case, justifying . . . a cease and desist order where the buyer fails to introduce evidence. . . .

. . . the Commission is, on this record, insisting that once knowledge of a price differential is shown, the burden of introducing evidence shifts to the buyer. The Commission's main reliance in this argument is Section 2(b), which . . . we interpreted in the *Morton Salt* case as putting the burden of coming forward with evidence of a cost justification on the seller, on the one, that is, who claimed the benefits of the justification.

. . . although Section 2(b) does speak not of the seller but of the "person charged with a violation of this section," other language in Section 2(b) and its proviso seems directed mainly to sellers . . . the legislative chronology of the various provisions ultimately resulting in the Robinson–Patman Act indicates that Section 2(b) was drafted with sellers in mind, and . . . the few cases so far decided have dealt only with sellers.

. . . We think we must read the . . . language of Section 2(b) as enacting . . . that ordinary rules of evidence were to apply to Robinson–Patman Act proceedings. If S. 2(b) is to apply to S. 2(f) *although we do not decide that it does because we reach the same result without it* we think it must so be read. . . . The reasons that have been given by legislators for the rule of S. 2(b) . . . is that the burden of justifying a price differential ought to be on the one who "has at his peculiar command the cost and other record data by which to justify such discriminations. Where, as here, such considerations are inapplicable, we think we must disregard whatever contrary indications may be drawn from a merely literal reading of the language Congress had used. . . .[7]

[6] *Samuel H. Moss, Inc.* v. *Federal Trade Commission,* 148 F. 2d 378 (1945), at p. 379.
[7] *Automatic Canteen Co.* v. *Federal Trade Commission,*

346 U.S. 61 (1953), at pp. 62–63, 67, 67–68. (Italics mine.)

In short, in a case involving a *buyer* under Section 2(f), a mere showing that a two price system existed did not lead to an inference that the *buyer* had *knowledge* that the price differential did *not* lie within one of the defenses available to the *seller*.

The *Automatic Canteen Company* case was decided in 1953. In 1954, the Federal Trade Commission itself said somewhat less than accurately: "The Federal Trade Commission has very generally held that under Section 2(a), counsel supporting the complaint has the burden of proof to establish the necessary competitive injury." More specifically, it also stated:

> The first part of Section 2(a) sets out the elements necessary to establish a violation of the law. They are: (1) discriminations in price between different purchasers of commodities of like grade and quality; (2) certain jurisdictional facts; and (3) competitive injury. Proof of all three is necessary to make out a prima facie case. It has often been pointed out that differences in price without competitive injury are not illegal.[8]

And so in 1954, the Commission adopted a position inconsistent with the holding in the *Moss* case. This position is, however, consistent with the discussion of price discrimination provided by the Attorney General's National Committee to Study the Antitrust Laws in 1955. This Committee stated:

> . . . Some types of price discrimination may stimulate effective competition; others may be evidence of effective monopoly, in the economic sense. Before proceeding to examine the differences among the various types of price discrimination, a word of preliminary warning is in order.
>
> Price discrimination as seen by an economist not only is not necessarily the same as "price discrimination" in the sense followed or applied in decisions under the Robinson–Patman Act, but it may be entirely antithetical. Furthermore, even when a price structure happens to be discriminatory in both senses, this may be evidence of either effectively monopolistic or effectively competitive forces, depending on its setting. Finally, even when price discrimination in an economic sense (whether or not in the sense proscribed under the Robinson–Patman Act) is evidence of departures from conditions of effective competition, it does not necessarily result in or denote violation of law.

Occasional statements in the economic literature that price discrimination is proof of the existence of monopoly elements have been widely misunderstood, and as misunderstood, repeated by noneconomists. Under pure competition (and *a fortiori* under perfect competition) no price discrimination could exist. Every seller would sell at the going price and would have no power to charge more and no need to take less. But any attempt to infer from this that price discrimination, in the economic sense, is "inherently monopolistic" or presumptively anti-competitive, is implicit acceptance of pure or perfect competition as a workable goal of public policy. We have already shown that the terms "pure" and "perfect" mean merely precise or complete in the theoretical sense, not ideal or desirable. We therefore repudiate pure and perfect competition as direct goals of antitrust policy . . . .[9]

Obviously, the legal definition of a prima facie case under Section 2(b) necessarily involves an implicit definition of the objectives of antitrust policy, a point which has not always been understood by those who have commented on this definition; so also does the position one takes on whether or not the "meeting competition" defense in 2(b) is an *absolute* defense imply a specific but implicit definition of the goals of antitrust.

C. THE "GOOD FAITH MEETING OF COMPETITION DEFENSE" OF SECTION 2(b)

Nature and Elements of the Defense

As has already been pointed out, Section 2(b) provides that "the prima facie case thus made" (however it may be defined) of a violation of Section 2(a) can be rebutted by a showing that the seller's price discrimination "was made in good faith to meet the equally low price of a competitor." The first major case involving an interpretation of this language by the Supreme Court was the *A. E. Staley* case, decided in 1945. This case was a basing point pricing case, involving facts similar to those of the *Corn Products Refining Company* case discussed in the preceding chapter. That is, the A. E. Staley Company was also a producer and distributor of glucose, was a competitor of the Corn Products Refining Company, and

---

[8] *In the Matter of General Foods Corporation*, 50 F.T.C. 885 (1954), at p. 890.

[9] *Report of the Attorney General's National Committee to Study the Antitrust Laws*, op. cit., pp. 333–334.

had adopted a basing point pricing system using Chicago as the basing point for products produced at Decatur, Illinois. The Federal Trade Commission charged that this system of pricing constituted a violation of Section 2(a) because it involved a price discrimination, and the Staley Company replied that it had adopted its basing point pricing system in "good faith" to meet the competition it was experiencing from the Corn Products Refining Company's use of a similar basing point pricing system. The Supreme Court, however, held that this defense did not apply in this case, since the basing point pricing system used by the Corn Products Company was itself illegal. Thus the Staley Company had failed to establish the element of "good faith" as required by Section 2(b). According to the Court:

... respondents argue that they have sustained their burden of proof, as prescribed by Section 2(b), by showing that they have adopted and followed the basing point system of their competitors. . . . It is the contention that a seller may justify a basing point delivered pricing system, which is otherwise outlawed by Section 2, because other competitors are in part violating the law by maintaining a like system. If respondent's argument is sound, it would seem to follow that even if the competitor's pricing system were wholly in violation of Section 2 of the Clayton Act, respondents could adopt and follow it with impunity.

This startling conclusion is admissible only upon the assumption that the statute permits a seller to maintain an otherwise unlawful system of discriminatory prices, merely because he had adopted it in its entirety, as a means of securing the benefits of a like unlawful system maintained by his competitors. . . .

Respondents have never attempted to establish their own nondiscriminatory price system, and then reduced their price when necessary to meet competition. Instead they have slavishly followed in the first instance a pricing policy which, in their case, resulted in systematic discriminations. . . .[10]

The opinion in the *Staley* case did not spell out the elements of the "meeting competition" defense, but it did suggest that *systematic* discrimination rather than a *sporadic* and *occasional* discrimination does not meet the test of "good faith." An argu-

ment similar to that employed by the Staley Company was used by the defendants in the *Cement Institute* case, which, it will be recalled, involved a multiple basing point system. In that case, the Court said:

The respondents contend that the differences in their net returns from sales in different localities which result from use of the multiple basing point delivered price system are not price discriminations within the meaning of Section 2(a). If held that these net return differences are price discriminations prohibited by Section 2(a), they contend that the discriminations were justified under Section 2(b) because "made in good faith to meet an equally low price of a competitor." Practically all the arguments presented by respondents in support of their contentions were considered by this Court and rejected in 1945 in *Corn Products Co.* v. *Federal Trade Comm'n* . . . and in the related case of *Federal Trade Comm'n* v. *Staley Co.* . . . . Consequently, we see no reason for again reviewing the questions that were there decided.[11]

These cases were followed in 1951 by the decision of the Supreme Court in the *Standard Oil of Indiana* case, in which the Court held that the "meeting competition" defense of Section 2(b) was an "absolute" defense; that is to say, the Court held that a defendant could escape liability under Section 2(a) for a price discrimination, *irrespective of the effect of the price discrimination on competition or its tendency to create a monopoly*, if he could show affirmatively that he had discriminated "in good faith to meet the equally low price of a competitor." This reading of the statute obviously also involves an implicit rejection of the models of pure or perfect competition as goals of antitrust policy. (The *Standard Oil of Indiana* case is also known in the literature as the "*Detroit Gasoline*" case.) The Supreme Court summarized the facts in this case on the basis of the Federal Trade Commission's findings as follows:

Since the effective date of the Robinson–Patman Act . . . petitioner has sold its Red Crown Gasoline to its "jobber" customers at its tankcar prices. Those prices have been 1 1/2¢ per gallon less than its tankwagon prices to service station customers for identical gasoline in the same area. In practice, the service stations have resold the gasoline at the prevailing retail service station prices. Each of the petitioner's so-

---

[10] *Federal Trade Commission* v. *A. E. Staley Mfg. Co.* 324 U.S. 746 (1945), at pp. 753–755.

[11] *Federal Trade Commission* v. *Cement Institute, et. al.,* 333 U.S. 683 (1948), at p. 722.

called "jobber" customers has been free to resell its gasoline at retail or wholesale. Each, at some time, has resold some of it at retail. . . . As to resale prices, two of the "jobbers" have resold their gasoline only at the prevailing wholesale or retail rates. The other two, however, have reflected, in varying degrees, petitioner's reductions in the cost of gasoline to them by reducing their resale prices of that gasoline below the prevailing rates. . . . The Commission found that such reduced resale prices "have resulted in injuring, destroying, and preventing competition between said favored dealers and retail dealers in respondent's [petitioner's] gasoline and other major brands of gasoline. . . ." While the cost of petitioner's sales and deliveries of gasoline to each of these four "jobbers" is no doubt less, per gallon, than the cost of its sales and deliveries of like gasoline to its service station customers in the same area, there is no finding that such difference accounts for the entire reduction in price made by petitioner to these "jobbers," and we proceed on the assumption that it does not entirely account for that difference.

Petitioner placed its reliance upon evidence offered to show that its lower price to each jobber was made in order to retain that jobber as a customer and in good faith to meet an equally low price offered by one or more competitors. The Commission, however, treated such evidence as not relevant. [Instead the Commission took the position]:

. . . "Even though the lower prices in question may have been made by respondent in good faith to meet the lower prices of competitors, this does not constitute a defense in the face of affirmative proof that the effect of the discrimination was to injure, destroy and prevent competition with the retail stations operated by the said named dealers and with stations operated by their retailer-customers." 41 F.T.C. 263, 281–282.[12]

The Court also asserted:

In addition, there has been widespread understanding that, under the Robinson–Patman Act, it is a complete defense to a charge of price discrimination for the seller to show that its price differential has been made in good faith to meet a lawful and equally low price of a competitor. This understanding is reflected in actions and statements of members and counsel of the Federal Trade Commission. Representatives of the Department of Justice have testified to the effectiveness and value of the defense under the Robinson–Patman Act. We see no reason to depart now from that interpretation.[13]

Thus the Court held that the defense was a complete or absolute defense, *irrespective of the effect of the price discrimination on competition or of its tendency to create monopoly.* The reference in the majority opinion to the position of the Federal Trade Commission is interesting, particularly in the light of testimony before Congress on this point of Commissioner Spingarn who pointed out in 1951 that there had been a difference of opinion in the Commission concerning this question and that the position of the Commission had changed as its membership had changed. In 1951, legislation was introduced in Congress to codify the holding of the Supreme Court in this case. Representative Walter, who sponsored this legislation in the House, testified in support of his bill before the House Subcommittee on Study of Monopoly Power, in part, as follows:

. . . business has been very much disturbed by the position that the Federal Trade Commission has indicated it has taken and will take. Business has been built up over the years according to certain practices. These practices may at times have gone over to the point where perhaps prosecutions should have been brought by the Department of Justice.

Nevertheless, business generally has come to the feeling that many of these legitimate practices are a part of our economy to such an extent that they ought not to be interfered with unless the general interest, of course, indicates that these practices are harmful.

But business has reason to be jittery over the gyrations of the Federal Trade Commission on this question of good faith meeting of competition as a complete defense. In 1941 the Federal Trade Commission took the position before the TNEC that good faith should be a complete defense, this opinion being uttered by no less a figure in this field than the late Walter Wooden. Now we turn the calendar forward a few years to the action by the Commission against the Standard Oil Co. of Indiana, where the position was taken that good faith was only a rebuttable defense. In June 1949 the Commission flip-flopped again in a letter addressed to me as chairman of the subcommittee then considering H. R. 2222, the so-called moratorium bill. In that letter the Commission said that all of its members on balance believed that good faith should be a complete defense. I am now somewhat surprised in having a preview of the Commission's statement, which will be delivered to this subcommittee immediately after my remarks, that

---

[12] *Standard Oil Co. (Indiana)* v. *Federal Trade Commission*, 340 U.S. 231 (1951), at pp. 235–236, 239.

[13] *Ibid.*, at pp. 246–247.

the Commission has again reversed itself, and with the exception of two of its members believes that good faith should be only a qualified defense. On the record of these drastic changes in view, it is little wonder that businessmen should be uncertain. . . .

Because of the position taken by the Federal Trade Commission, segments of industry are disturbed and have been disturbed. This is particularly true of steel and cement, and I say "particularly" advisedly.[14]

Opponents of the proposed legislation took the view that it was a thinly-disguised attempt to legalize the basing point system of pricing. The interest of the cement industry in securing the adoption of such legislation is easy to understand in the light of the decision in the *Cement Institute* case outlawing its system of multiple basing point pricing discussed in the previous chapter. Moreover, the steel industry had for years prior to the *Cement Institute* case also followed a basing point system of pricing known as "Pittsburgh Plus," and its system is fully described at page 697 in the opinion of the Court in the *Cement Institute* case, to which the interested reader may be referred for the details of that particular system.[15]

Among the strongest opponents of the proposed legislation was Representative Wright Patman, one of the original sponsors of the Robinson-Patman Act. His testimony before the subcommittee is interesting because it sets forth the "small business" point of view concerning the Robinson-Patman Act generally. In part he said:

Bear in mind, gentlemen, that our experience with discrimination long antedates the Robinson-Patman amendment. Price discrimination has always been the most potent weapon in the arsenal of the monopolist. Our experience of three-quarters of a century with the predatory practices of monopolists has made us thoroughly familiar with the evils of discrimination in both private business and public utilities. Seventy years ago the public clamor for relief against the "public be damned" attitude of big business led to restrictions on monopoly, first in the States and later by the Federal Government. It is significant that the Interstate Commerce Act of 1887 was directed primarily not at high railway rates but

at discriminatory rates. As the records of the old Standard Oil Trust, the Sugar Trust, the early steel pools, and many other monopolies were made public, it was realized how frequently price discrimination was used to gain and perpetuate monopoly power.

The Sherman Act unfortunately did not stop this practice. We need only to look at the evidence disclosed in the cases brought in the first decade of this century—such as those against the Beef trust, the Cash Register combine, the Standard Oil Co., the Tobacco Trust and many others—to recognize both the prevalence and the evil of price discrimination. By 1914 the American people were convinced that a new approach must be made to the problem of monopoly. The Clayton and the Federal Trade Commission Acts were the result. These statutes attempted to prevent the very creation of monopoly by striking at those practices by which monopoly was commonly achieved. Section 2 of the Clayton Act was aimed specifically at price discrimination.

But once again the will of Congress was thwarted by lack of clarity in legislative language. The courts decided that, by inserting the qualification that the act did not prevent discrimination if made in good faith to meet competition, Congress had not really intended to prohibit discrimination. By the thirties, section 2 of the Clayton Act had become virtually a dead letter. In the entire decade from 1927 to 1936 only one cease and desist order was issued by the Federal Trade Commission under this section.

Again the public became aroused and Congress responded by enacting the Robinson-Patman amendment in 1936. As one of the coauthors of that amendment, it is my honest and firm conviction that Congress intended to remove the weakness in the Clayton Act that had prevented its enforcement. We felt that we were reducing good faith to its proper role, namely as merely one factor among several, something that needs to be considered as a procedural matter but not as a full and final justification for discriminatory tactics.

For 15 years it appeared that Congress had finally succeeded in placing a ban on unjustifiable discrimination. In a long line of cases involving all kinds of discrimination we were successful in proceeding against this evil. From 1937 to 1950 the Federal Trade Commission issued some 315 complaints under section 2 of the Clayton Act. It was not until this latest decision in the *Standard Oil of Indiana* case that doubts have once more been cast on the real intent of Congress in enacting its antidiscrimination law.

Under this bill it will be possible for a large

[14] *Study of Monopoly Power* (Hearings before the Subcommittee on Study of Monopoly Power of the House Judiciary Committee, 82d Cong., 1st sess.) (Washington, D.C.: U.S. Government Printing Office, 1951), Serial No. 1, Part 5, pp. 2–3.

[15] *Federal Trade Commission* v. *Cement Institute el al.*, 333 U.S. 683 (1948), esp. at pp. 697 ff.

concern to enter any market where competition is keen, find a seller who has already cut prices and thereupon immediately launch a program of ruthless price cutting until all threats to its supremacy have been completely eliminated....[16]

The argument against the interpretation of Section 2(b) as an absolute defense is thus similar to the argument in favor of holding that quantity discounts must be functionally equally available to all, discussed in the preceding chapter. A similar controversy exists concerning the meaning and scope of the antimerger provision of Section 7 of the Clayton Act as amended in 1950, as we will see in the next chapter.

In 1963, the Supreme Court limited the *Standard Oil of Indiana* rule somewhat in the *Sun Oil* case by holding that the 2(b) defense did not apply to a price discrimination granted by a wholesaler to enable a retailer to meet competition *at the retail level*.[17] In effect, it thus held that the competition which may be met must be competition facing the price discriminator, the one who asserts the 2(b) defense. A year earlier, in 1962, the Court of Appeals for the Seventh Circuit had held that the defense could be employed by one who discriminated in price in order to gain *new* customers and was not restricted to cases involving discriminations in favor of *existing* customers.[18] Such a case seems to fall precisely within the terms of the example stated by Representative Patman in his testimony quoted earlier in this chapter.

However, still earlier, in 1959, the Court of Appeals for the Second Circuit had held that the 2(b) defense did not apply to such a situation. Accordingly, in 1962, after the decision of the Court of Appeals for the Seventh Circuit, the Commission issued a statement stating that it intended to follow the decision of the Court of Appeals for the Second Circuit, which had held that the 2(b) defense did *not* apply to a case of price discrimination designed to gain new customers; this, of course, was the position taken by the Commission in the *Sunshine Biscuits* case which the Court of Appeals for the Seventh Circuit had reversed. And there the matter rests, although it will surely eventually be resolved by the Supreme Court at the request of some defendant.

A Concluding Comment

Our examination of the price-discrimination and related provisions of the Clayton Act as amended by the Robinson-Patman Act has now been completed. One point in particular should stand out: by making the "good faith meeting of competition" defense an absolute defense, that is, by allowing a price discrimination to be justified irrespective of its effect on competition or of its tendency to create monopoly if the discrimination is made "in good faith to meet competition," the Supreme Court has held that Section 2(b) of the Act contains one provision which is inconsistent with the general spirit and objective of the Clayton Act. Two important remaining provisions of the Clayton Act will be discussed in the next chapter. These provisions are Section 8, prohibiting interlocking directorates under specified conditions, and Section 7 as amended in 1950, dealing with mergers. Section 8 has not been the object of much enforcement activity and will, therefore, be examined first.

---

[16] *Study of Monopoly Power, op. cit.,* at pp. 52–53.
[17] *Federal Trade Commission* v. *Sun Oil Co.,* 371 U.S. 505 (1963).

[18] *Sunshine Biscuits, Inc.* v. *Federal Trade Commission,* 306 F. 2d 48 (1962).

Interlocking Directorates and Mergers under the Clayton Act as Amended

As we have seen in Chapter 12, Section 7 of the Clayton Act was amended by the Celler-Kefauver Act in 1950. This section deals with mergers. The subject of interlocking directorates, as defined in Chapter 9, is dealt with by Sections 8 and 10 of the Clayton Act and is discussed in the first major subdivision of this chapter. The original unamended Section 7 of the Clayton Act and the treatment of mergers under this law are examined in the second major subdivision below. The bulk of this chapter, consisting of its third major subdivision, is devoted to a discussion of court decisions and actions by the Antitrust Division and the Federal Trade Commission relative to mergers under the 1950 amendment to Section 7.

A. INTERLOCKING DIRECTORATES UNDER THE CLAYTON ACT

The Statutory Provisions

The concept of "interlocking directorates" has already been extensively discussed in Chapter 9. Section 8 of the Clayton Act contains provisions (which have not

been changed since they were first enacted in 1914) prohibiting interlocking directorates in industrial and commercial corporations other than banks, banking associations, trust companies, and common carriers, as well as special provisions relating to banks, etc., which have been amended several times. Section 10 of the Clayton Act contains special provisions pertaining to interlocks in the case of common carriers. Also, various pieces of legislation pertaining to the regulation of particular industries, such as Section 409 of the Federal Aviation Act and Section 17(c) of the Public Utility Holding Company Act, prescribe conditions under which the relevant regulatory commissions may approve interlocking directorates in the industries in question.

The provision in Section 8 prohibiting interlocks in the case of industrial and commercial corporations "other than banks . . ." applies to cases in which one of the corporations involved has "capital, surplus, and undivided profits aggregating more than $1,000,000 if such corporations have been" competitors prior to the interlock "so that the elimination of competition by any agreement between them would constitute a violation of any of the provisions of any of the antitrust laws." The theory of this legislation is set forth in the following quotation from the House Committee Report to the 63rd Congress which enacted the law:

The idea that there are only a few men in any of our great corporations and industries who are capable of handling the affairs of the same is contrary to the spirit of our institutions. From an economic point of view, it is not possible that one individual, however capable, acting as a director in fifty corporations, can render as efficient and valuable service in directing the affairs of the several corporations under his control as can fifty capable men acting as single directors and devoting their entire time to directing the affairs of one of such corporations. The truth is that the only real service the same director in a great number of corporations renders is in maintaining uniform policies throughout the entire system for which he acts, which usually results to the advantage of the greater corporations and to the disadvantage of the smaller corporations which he dominates by reason of his prestige as a director and to the detriment of the public generally.[1]

Enforcement of the Statutory Provisions

According to one study of experience with this provision:

From its enactment on October 15, 1914, to January 1965, the FTC had filed a total of 13 complaints under section 8 of the Clayton Act. Only one of these complaints resulted in a cease-and-desist order, and this was by consent; the remainder were dismissed when the directors involved discontinued the prohibited relationship.

The Department of Justice did not undertake a systematic program with respect to interlocking directorates until after World War II, and the first cases to be litigated to a decision by a court were not filed until February 27, 1952, 38 years after enactment of the Clayton Act. As of January 1965, the Department of Justice had instituted a total of 10 cases to enforce section 8, and 5 cases to enforce section 10.

During the same period, the regulatory bodies, whose enabling statutes authorized enforcement of prohibitions against interlocks, tended to slump into a pattern where approval generally was granted to industry applications for otherwise prohibited interlocks. Over the years, the tendency for a regulatory body to become identified with the industry problems in which it

is immersed has manifested itself, insofar as the problem of interlocking managements are concerned, in sympathy for the industry viewpoint.[2]

Judicial Interpretation of Section 8. In 1952 in the *Weinberg* case, the Department of Justice brought an action under Section 8 to challenge the holding of a common directorship in Sears, Roebuck and Company and B. F. Goodrich Company by Sidney J. Weinberg. (It will be recalled from Chapter 15 that a contract between Sears and Goodrich for delivery of replacement tires had been the subject of an FTC order under the administrative quantity limit rule in Section 2(a) of the Clayton Act.) It was admitted that these corporations were competitors in seven product lines sold in interstate commerce. The defendants argued with considerable logic that the condition, contained in Section 8, that common directorships were prohibited in cases where "elimination of competition between the two companies by any agreement between them would lead to a violation of the provisions of any of the antitrust laws," meant that such common directorships were prohibited in any case in which a merger between the two companies would violate the antitrust laws. It is to be noted that this argument was made at a time when there had been very little litigation concerning the legality of mergers under Section 7 of the Clayton Act, as amended. The District Court, however, rejected this argument and took the view that the statute involved a *per se* test by specifying that it was to apply to all cases in which one of the competing corporations had capital, surplus, and undivided profits in excess of $1 million. The District Court also took the position that, since an agreement between Sears and Goodrich to divide markets would be *per se* illegal, the existence of an interlocking directorate between them was also *per se* illegal, given the fact that the one million dollar "substantiality" test was satisfied.[3]

Also in 1952, the Justice Department brought an action seeking to terminate a multiple interlock existing between W. T. Grant Company, S. H. Kress Company

---

[1] *Interlocks in Corporate Management* (Staff Report to the Antitrust Subcommittee of the House Judiciary Committee, 89th Cong., 1st sess.) (Washington, D.C.: U.S. Government Printing Office, 1965), p.

22 (quoting H. Rept. 627, 63d Cong., 2d sess., p. 19).
[2] *Ibid.*, pp. 57–58.
[3] *United States* v. *Sears, Roebuck and Co.*, 111 F. Supp. 614 (1953), at p. 616.

and Jewel Tea Company, in the form of a common directorship filled by John M. Hancock, a partner of Lehman Brothers, a banking firm. Prior to the actual trial, Mr. Hancock resigned his directorships in the Kress Company and in Bond Stores and was no longer a director of the Kroger Company. His attorneys then moved for dismissal of the case on grounds that it had become "moot." The trial court granted the motion, saying that it did not believe there was the "slightest threat" of any future violation of law by the defendant.[4]

It then refused to grant the requested injunction to restrain future violations. The government appealed to the Supreme Court, which noted that this case was the first involving a construction of Section 8 to come before it.[5] The Supreme Court pointed out that the power of the trial court to grant an injunction was not impaired by a holding that the case was "moot," but held against the government insofar as the issuance of an injunction on the particular facts in the case before it were concerned.[6]

After 1952 there seems to have been no further serious attempt on the part of the Antitrust Division to enforce Section 8 until June 1968, when a press release was issued stating that "interlocking directorates involving 16 companies, which the Department of Justice proposed to challenge as violations of antitrust law, are being eliminated."

The interlocks in question involved oil companies, automobile companies, and tire companies, as well as two Cleveland retail businesses both selling speciality items, such as cosmetics.[7] The interlocks were ended "through agreement by the directors and some of the companies." Moreover, "in the view of the Department [of Justice] this approach to the law best fulfills the purpose of Section 8, which is to maintain the independence of business decisions of competing companies." A policy of informal settlement was thus used in 1968. Although no actions were taken in 1969, in March 1970 a civil antitrust suit calling for The Cleveland Trust

Company to eliminate its interlocking directorates with certain major manufacturers of machine tools was filed.

Interlocking Directorates under Section 10. The Staff of the House Antitrust Subcommittee reported in 1965 on experience under Section 10 as follows:

As with section 8, during the period 1914 to the present, litigated decisions with respect to the provisions of section 10 of the Clayton Act have been sparse. The first proceeding did not reach the courts until 1935. All told, the Interstate Commerce Commission and the Attorney General have instituted five actions to enforce the prohibitions contained in section 10. . . . In addition, the statute has been construed in two private cases.[8]

In 1959, in one of the cases referred to above, the Supreme Court held that under Section 5(11) of the Interstate Commerce Act, the Interstate Commerce Commission had the authority to approve "in the public interest" transactions which might otherwise constitute a violation of Section 10 of the Clayton Act. The Court said:

Section 10 of the Clayton Act is, of course, an antitrust law, and much of what we have just said relative to the problem of accommodation of Section 5(2) of the Interstate Commerce Act and the antitrust laws is equally applicable to this contention. The evident purpose of Section 10 of the Clayton Act was to prohibit a corporation from abusing a carrier by palming off upon it securities, supplies and other articles without competitive bidding and at excessive prices through overreaching by, or other misfeasance of, common directors, to the financial injury of the carrier and the consequent impairment of its ability to serve the public interest.[9]

In March of 1965, the Supreme Court was faced with a "conflict of interest" case in which four officials of both the buying and selling corporations had been indicted under Section 10 for a sale of ten stainless steel railroad cars to the Boston and Maine Railroad but held that the section applied only to antitrust violations.[10]

Position of the Attorney General's Committee. The Attorney General's National Committee to Study the Antitrust Laws in 1955

[4] *United States* v. *W. T. Grant Co. et. al.*, 112 F Supp. 336 (1952), at p. 338.

[5] *United States* v. *W. T. Grant Co. et. al.*, 345 U.S. 629 (1953), at p. 633.

[6] *Ibid.*, at p. 635.

[7] Department of Justice, *Press Release*, June 27, 1968.

[8] *Interlocks in Corporate Management, op. cit.*, p. 65.

[9] *Minneapolis and St. Louis Railway Co.* v. *United States, et. al.*, 361 U.S. 173 (1959), at p. 190.

[10] *United States* v. *Boston and Maine Railroad et. al.*, 380 U.S. 157 (1965), at pp. 160–162.

relegated its discussion of Section 8 of the Clayton Act to a footnote in which it made the following observation:

A current study is needed to ascertain whether interlocking directorates are in fact an important problem affecting the competitive character of the economy. On the basis of such a study, Section 8 can be reappraised and appropriate conclusions and recommendations reached.[11]

In short, the Committee did not itself study the problem presented by Section 8. Instead, it pleaded lack of knowledge with respect to the effect of the practices dealt with by that section. The types and extent of contemporary interlocking directorates have already been described in Chapter 9. So have the types of mergers and scope of the current merger movement. It is to the law of mergers under Section 7 of the Clayton Act prior to its amendment that we turn next.

B. MERGERS UNDER ORIGINAL SECTION 7

The Original Statutory Language

Section 7 of the Clayton Act originally provided that:

No corporation engaged in commerce shall acquire, directly or indirectly, the whole or any part of the stock or other share capital of another corporation engaged also in commerce, where the effect of the acquisition may be substantially to lessen competition between the corporation whose stock is so acquired and the corporation making the acquisition, or to restrain such commerce in any section or community, or tend to create a monopoly of any line of commerce.

Experience under the Statute. In its *Final Report on the Chain Store Investigation*, the Federal Trade Commission recounted its experience in trying to enforce the prohibition contained in this section and described the section as a "virtual nullity."[12] It thereupon recommended an amendment of this section to include language which is very similar to that actually placed in this section by the Celler-Kefauver amendment of 1950.[13] Thus the Commission called attention to its problems under original

Section 7 by saying, among other things, in 1935:

The latest pronouncement of the Supreme Court regarding section 7 is found in the case of *Arrow, Hart and Hegeman Electric Co.* v. *Federal Trade Commission*, decided in March 1934. There the Commission had filed its complaint while the stock was in the hands of an acquiring holding company before it had been used to effect a merger of the physical assets of the two competing corporations. While the complaint was pending the holding company caused two new holding companies to be created, transferred the stock of one competing corporation to one of them and the stock of the other competing corporation to the other holding company and then brought about a merger of the physical assets. The lower court upheld the Commission's right to order divestiture of the assets under the principle of the *Western Meat Co.* case. The Supreme Court, with four justices dissenting, held that the Commission had no power to make such an order and that its power was limited strictly to divestiture of the stock originally acquired (291 U.S. 587).[14]

The Commission's recommendation for amendment of Section 7, accordingly, suggested that language be added to the section to prohibit the acquisition of the *assets* as well as of the *stock* of a competing corporation.

The du Pont-General Motors Case of 1957. The recommended change in the language of Section 7 was finally made in 1950, and cases under the amended law will be discussed below. Before doing so, however, it is useful to examine the *du Pont-General Motors* case, decided by the Court in 1957 under the original Section 7. The government's complaint was filed in 1949 under the original Section 7; hence the Court's decision was based on the unamended section but was handed down after the section had been amended. It seems likely, therefore, that the decision was not unaffected by the fact of the amendment.

The complaint in the *du Pont-General Motors* case was based upon the purchase by du Pont from 1917 to 1919 of a 23% stock interest in General Motors and an allegation that "du Pont's commanding position as General Motors' supplier of

---

[11] *Report of the Attorney General's National Committee to Study the Antitrust Laws* (Washington, D.C.: U.S. Government Printing Office, 1955), pp. 115–116, n. 1. The reference cited in footnote 1 of this chapter constitutes such a study.

[12] Federal Trade Commission, *Chain Stores: Final Report on the Chain Store Investigation* (Washington, D.C. U.S. Government Printing Office, 1935), p. 89.
[13] *Ibid.*, pp. 88–89.
[14] *Ibid.*, p. 89.

automotive finishes and fabrics was based on its acquisition of the stock" and the "consequent close relationship" between the two companies which led to the isolation of the General Motors market from free competition. The Court said:

> We are met at the threshold with the argument that Section 7, before its amendment in 1950, applied only to an acquisition of the stock of a competing corporation, and not to an acquisition by a supplier corporation of the stock of a customer corporation—in other words, that the statute applied only to *horizontal* and *not to vertical* acquisitions. . . .
>
> We hold that any acquisition by one corporation of all or any part of the stock of another corporation, competitor or not, is within the reach of the section whenever the reasonable likelihood appears that the acquisition will result in a restraint of commerce or in the creation of a monopoly in any line of commerce. Thus, although du Pont and General Motors are not competitors, a violation of the section has occurred if, as a result of the acquisition, there was at the time of suit a reasonable likelihood of a monopoly of any line of commerce. . . .[15]

The defendants also argued that there was "no basis for a finding of a probable restraint of trade or of monopoly within the meaning of Section 7 because the total General Motors market for finishes and fabrics constituted only a negligible percentage of the total market for these materials for *all* uses, including automotive uses."[16] To this argument the Court replied that "automobile finishes and fabrics have sufficient peculiar characteristics and uses" to constitute them "a line of commerce" within the meaning of the Clayton Act and cited the *Van Camp and Sons* case (discussed earlier in Chapter 15). It also pointed out that "the substantiality of General Motors' share" of the relevant market comprising the automobile industry was undisputed and asserted that "because General Motors accounts for almost one-half of the automobile industry's annual sales, its requirements for automotive finishes and fabrics represent approximately one-half of the relevant market for these materials."[17]

Moreover, since du Pont supplied the largest part of General Motors' requirements, du Pont possessed "a substantial share of the relevant market." And du Pont's "commanding position as a General Motors supplier was not achieved until shortly after its purchase of a sizeable block of General Motors stock in 1917."[18] As a matter of fact, the Justice Department placed in evidence in the trial court a memorandum to the du Pont Finance Committee from its Treasurer, dated December 19, 1917, concerning the proposed investment in General Motors stock. Item 5 of the summary section of this memorandum reads as follows:

> 5. Our interest in the General Motor Company will undoubtedly secure for us the entire Fabrikoid, Pyralin, paint and varnish business of those companies [under the control of General Motors], which is a substantial factor.[19]

The defense also argued that Section 7 was applicable only to the *acquisition* of stock and not to the *holding or subsequent use of* stock and that an action could not be brought in 1949 for a stock acquisition made 30 years earlier because it was barred by the statute of limitations. The Court, however, rejected this contention.[20]

Accordingly, the Court ordered that a divestiture plan be developed by the District Court. The broad language used by the Court in this opinion means that Section 7 can be used in the case of mergers completed after 1914, since the legality of the stock acquisition is to be tested by its effect *at the time the complaint is made* and *not as of the date of the acquisition* of the stock. This decision engendered dire predictions concerning the future of business organization in the United States. But the predictions have not come true, perhaps because the Government has chosen to proceed in merger cases under Section 7 as amended in 1950 rather than the original Section 7 and the rule of the *du Pont-General Motors* case. (In a footnote to its decision, the Court pointed out that the amendment to Section 7 applied

[15] *United States* v. *E. I. du Pont de Nemours and Co.*, 353 U.S. 586 (1957), at pp. 590, 592. (Italics mine.)

[16] *Ibid.*, at p. 593.

[17] *Ibid.*, at pp. 595–596.

[18] *Ibid.*, at pp. 596, 598–599.

[19] The entire Memorandum is reproduced in *A Study of the Antitrust Laws* (Hearings before the Sub-

committee on Antitrust and Monopoly of the Senate Committee on the Judiciary, 84th Cong., 1st sess., 1955) (Washington, D.C.: U.S. Government Printing Office, 1955), Part VI, pp. 2475 ff. The quotation above is from p. 2480.

[20] *United States* v. *E. I. du Pont de Nemours and Co.*, 353 U.S. 586 (1957), at pp. 597–598.

to mergers occurring after 1950.) It is to be noted that in *this* case the Court defined the "relevant market" much more narrowly than it had in the *du Pont Cellophane* case discussed in previous chapters. In that case it defined the market for cellophane as part of the "line of commerce" of "flexible packaging materials," but in the *du Pont-General Motors* case it defined the market for "automotive fabrics and finishes" as a separate line of commerce, thereby tying the relevant products to a particular use and foreshadowing its treatment of this problem under Section 7, as amended.

C. MERGERS UNDER SECTION 7 AS AMENDED

Early Experience

The Change in Statutory Language. Section 7, it has been noted, was amended in 1950. Since the amendment, acquisition of the stock *or of the assets* of a competitor is unlawful where the effect "may be substantially to lessen competition or to tend to create a monopoly *in any line of commerce in any section of the country.*" The italicized language is new and does not appear in the original Section 7. This language replaces the reference to competition between the "corporation whose stock is so acquired and the corporation making the acquisition" and the phrase "in any section or community," leaving no doubt that it applies not only to *horizontal* but also to *vertical* and *conglomerate* mergers.

The First Pillsbury Opinion and the Rule of Reason. An early case arising under amended Section 7 in 1953 was finally decided by a Court of Appeals in 1966. The case in question is the *Pillsbury Mills, Inc.* case. The original complaint charged Pillsbury with a violation of Section 7, as amended, because of its acquisition of the assets of two of its competitors, Ballard and Ballard Company and Duff's Baking Division of American Home Products Company. As a result of the acquisitions, Pillsbury moved from fifth to second place in the sale of family flour in the "southeastern area" of the United States and from third to first place in bakery flour. Pillsbury also increased its

share of the market for bakery flour to 45 percent, having already been in first place. The attorneys supporting the FTC complaint argued that amended Section 7 was satisfied by the same "substantiality" test as the tying arrangement cases under Section 3 and that the facts in the *Pillsbury* case were sufficient to satisfy this test as laid down in the *International Salt* and *Standard Oil of California and Standard Stations* cases, already discussed in Chapter 16. Without committing himself on the question of whether or not a Section 7 violation had occurred, the Hearing Examiner dismissed the complaint on the technical ground that the allegations in it were not supported by "reliable, probative, and substantial evidence" as required in administrative proceedings under the Administrative Procedure Act. On appeal from the Hearing Examiner's decision, the full Commission, however, held that a *prima facie* case had been made; thus it reversed the Hearing Examiner and remanded the case to him for further action. In doing so, the Commission asserted that tests which would satisfy the requirement that a "substantial amount of commerce" be affected under Section 3 were *not* applicable to Section 7 cases.[21] At the same time, the Commission rejected the application of Sherman Act tests to mergers under Section 7. Instead, it said, Section 7 involves "tests of its own" which are less strict than the Sherman Act tests. In the case at hand, the percentage market share of the large companies had steadily increased through merger, the number of mills had declined, there had been no new entries into the industry, and the number of competitors had been materially reduced by the acquisitions. For example, Ballard with 12 percent and Duff with 10.2 percent of the market had been eliminated. On this basis, although it rejected the "quantitative substantiality" test, the Commission felt that a prima facie case, open to rebuttal by the defendant, existed. Thus the case was remanded to the Hearing Examiner for further consideration.

Position of the Attorney General's Committee. The majority of the Attorney General's National Committee to Study the Antitrust Laws agreed with the Commission's position as of 1953 in the *Pillsbury* case, saying:

[21] *In the Matter of Pillsbury Mills, Inc.*, 50 F.T.C. 555 (1953), at pp. 564–565.

This Committee agrees with the decision in *Pillsbury* reversing the Examiner and remanding that case for further hearing. We also agree with *Pillsbury's* requirement that the effect of a merger must be tested with reference to carefully defined markets in regions where the merging companies do business. For Section 7 cannot be satisfied by a mere showing that the merging companies do a large dollar volume of business. Since that provision is concerned with probable substantial lessening of competition and tendency to monopoly, it applies only where such prospective adverse impact in defined markets can be shown.[22]

This position of the majority was, of course, consistent with its argument throughout the *Report* that "mere size is not an offense against the antitrust laws." Walter Adams, however, dissented from this majority position saying:

Section 7 condemns mergers not only where they lead in the direction of oligopoly or monopoly, but also where their effect "may be to substantially lessen competition." The test is whether the amount of competition *lost* is substantial, or whether competition has been foreclosed or eliminated from a significant segment of the market. The Clayton Act is a prohibitory, not a regulatory statute. By its enactment, Congress did not intend to authorize the courts or the Commission to determine whether particular mergers are good or bad or in the public interest. Instead, Congress acted on the presumption that a substantial foreclosure or elimination of competition was in itself a derogation of the public interest. Once we accept the notion that small companies may merge to compete more effectively with the large ones, or that large companies may merge to compete more effectively with the giants, we are in fact inviting the proliferation of oligopoly. This could hardly have been the intent of Congress, and I am persuaded that it was not.[23]

Professor Adams, it will be recalled from Chapter 13, has advocated the use of the market structure test in the application of the antitrust laws; his dissent as expressed above is consistent with this position. The difference between the positions of the majority and the minority of the Attorney General's Committee evident in these quotations has also appeared in the opinions of the majority and minority of the Supreme Court

relative to Section 7, as we will see below.

The Disposition of the Pillsbury Proceeding. The next step in the *Pillsbury* case occurred on February 19, 1959, when a second Hearing Examiner held that the acquisitions violated Section 7 with respect to some but not all of the lines of commerce involved. An appeal was taken from this holding to the full Commission, whose personnel had changed in the interim. On December 16, 1960, the Commission issued a Final Order requiring divestiture of Ballard and Duff assets by Pillsbury. Next, Pillsbury made an appeal to the courts, and on January 7, 1966, the Court of Appeals for the Fifth Circuit handed down its opinion[24] vacating the order and remanding the case to the Commission for further proceedings. On March 28, 1966, the Commission dismissed the complaint against Pillsbury. The opinion of the Commission supporting the dismissal order reads in part as follows:

. . . This proceeding has had a long, complex history. The case is fourteen years old. The record exceeds 40,000 pages in length. The evidence contained in the record pertains to market conditions which existed more than a decade ago. Whether the Commission could properly adjudicate the merits on the basis of the present record, without taking further evidence, is at least highly doubtful. Passage of time has also created serious uncertainty as to the availability of effective relief, even if the challenged acquisitions should be found unlawful. There are also in the case a number of procedural problems; thus, it is not unlikely that, upon a further court review, the substantive questions on the merits may not be reached.

Accordingly, in the light of all these considerations, the Commission, mindful of its responsibility to "develop that enforcement policy best calculated to achieve the ends contemplated by Congress and to allocate [the Commission's] available funds and personnel in such a way as to execute [that] policy efficiently and economically" . . . has determined that it would not be in the public interest to proceed further in this matter. The complaint will be dismissed. Continuing surveillance will be maintained, however, of future developments in this industry. Any future acquisitions by respondent will receive careful attention, and the Commission will take such action thereon as may be required in the public interest.[25]

---

[22] *Report of the Attorney General's National Committee to Study the Antitrust Laws, op. cit.,* p. 122.

[23] *Ibid.,* pp. 127–128.

[24] *The Pillsbury Co.* v. *Federal Trade Commission,* 354

F. 2d 952 (1966).

[25] *In the Matter of Pillsbury Mills, Inc.,* F.T.C. Docket 6000 (March 18, 1966).

Between the time of the first *Pillsbury* case in 1953 and that of the second decision in 1966, much law pertaining to the meaning of Section 7 had been written by the Court. It is to some of the cases involving this law that our attention must next be given.

The Formulation of Policy

The Youngstown-Bethlehem Steel Company Case. In 1956, the Antitrust Division brought an action seeking to prohibit the merger of the Bethlehem Steel Corporation and the Youngstown Sheet and Tube Company. Bethlehem was the second largest steel producer, and Youngstown ranked sixth. In 1958, a District Court granted the injunction in a 40-page opinion in which the trial judge adopted the pragmatic market definition approach which had been employed in the *du Pont-General Motors* case.[26] He asserted that, under Section 7, the "line of commerce" must be decided by the peculiar characteristics of the product or products which distinguish them from others. Accordingly, he refused to treat plastics and nonferrous metals as part of the same line of commerce as steel products. Industry and public recognition of the product were treated by him as significant factors in defining the product. Thus the pragmatic approach to the problem of the definition of the market, which has already been commented on in the discussion of recent merger cases under the Sherman Act in Chapter 14, has also been employed under amended Section 7 of the Clayton Act, almost from the outset. This approach dates back at least to the *du Pont-General Motors* case of 1957. Moreover, it was adopted by the Supreme Court in the first case to come before it under amended Section 7, the *Brown Shoe Company* case, discussed next.

The Brown Shoe Company Case and the "Pragmatic Definition" of the Market. An action under amended Section 7 involves: (1) a definition of the "line of commerce" (the product); (2) a definition of "any section of the country" (the geographic market); and (3) evidence of a substantial lessening of competition as a result of the merger in the relevant market (a condition which can be established by proof that, in

horizontal mergers, the acquiring and acquired firms have been or would have been substantial competitors *but for* the merger).

Let us now consider the treatment by the Court of these matters in the *Brown Shoe Company* case in 1962. The case involved an action by the government under Section 7 opposing the acquisition by the Brown Shoe Company, the fourth largest shoe *manufacturer* in the United States, of the Kinney Corporation, the largest *retailer* of shoes in the country. Prior to the merger, Brown was a minor factor in the *retail* market and Kinney was a minor *manufacturer*. The government argued that the effect of the merger would be substantially to lessen competition or to tend to create a monopoly in the production of shoes both in the national wholesale market *and* in the sale of shoes at retail. It defined the product broadly as "footwear," or "men's, women's, and children's shoes," and argued that the anticompetitive effect of the merger should be judged in the nation as a whole, or alternatively in each separate city, or city and its immediate surrounding area, in which the parties sold at retail. Brown objected to both these definitions, arguing that the first failed to take account of "price/quality and age/sex differences," factors tending to show that Brown and Kinney were not substantial competitors prior to the merger.

As tried, the case involved primarily a *vertical* integration (as defined in Chapter 9) of Brown's manufacturing facilities and Kinney's retail outlets, but there were also *horizontal* aspects. The District Court held that the *vertical* merger violated Section 7. With regard to the *vertical* merger, the Supreme Court said:

> ... in this industry, no merger between a manufacturer and an independent retailer could involve a larger potential market foreclosure. Moreover it is apparent both from past behavior of Brown and from the testimony of Brown's President, that Brown would use its ownership of Kinney to force Brown shoes into Kinney stores. Thus, in operation, this vertical arrangement would be quite analogous to one involving a tying clause.[27]

Consequently, in the light of the further finding of fact of a trend toward vertical

[26] *United States* v. *Bethlehem Steel Corp.*, 168 F. Supp. 576 (1958), at pp. 589–593.

[27] *Brown Shoe Co., Inc.* v. *United States*, 370 U.S. 294 (1962), at pp. 331–332.

integration in the industry, the Supreme Court found that the effect of the *vertical* merger would be "likely substantially to lessen competition." The defendant had also appealed from the District Court's finding of fact that the *horizontal* merger of *retail* outlets would tend substantially to lessen competition. The Supreme Court accepted the District Court's finding of fact concerning the effect of this *horizontal* merger.[28]

Because this case was the first involving amended Section 7 to come before the Court, the Supreme Court took the occasion to discuss at length the legislative history of the amendment and the "intention of Congress" in making the amendment. According to the Court:

The dominant theme pervading congressional consideration of the 1950 amendments was a fear of what was considered to be a rising tide of economic concentration in the American economy. . . . Through the recorded [legislative] discussion may be found examples of Congress' fear not only of accelerated concentration of economic power on economic grounds, but also of the threat to other values a trend toward concentration was thought to impose.

What were some of the factors, relevant to a judgment as to the validity of a given merger, specifically discussed by Congress in redrafting Section 7?

First, there is no doubt that Congress did wish to "plug the loophole" and to include within the coverage of the Act the acquisition of assets no less than the acquisition of stock.

Second, by the deletion of the "acquiring-acquired" language in the original text, it hoped to make plain that Section 7 applied not only to mergers between actual competitors, but also to vertical and conglomerate mergers whose effect may tend to lessen competition in any line of commerce in any section of the country.

Third, it is apparent that a keystone in the erection of a barrier to what Congress saw was the rising tide of economic concentration, was its provision of authority for arresting mergers at a time when the trend to a lessening of competition in a line of commerce was still in its incipiency. . . .

Fourth, and closely related to the third, Congress rejected, as inappropriate to the problem it sought to remedy, the application to Section 7 cases of the standards for judging the legality of business combinations adopted by the courts in dealing with cases arising under the Sherman Act, and which may have been applied to some early cases arising under original Section 7.

Fifth, at the same time that it sought an effective tool for preventing all mergers having demonstrable anticompetitive effects, Congress recognized the stimulation to competition that might flow from particular mergers. . . . Taken as a whole, the legislative history illuminates congressional concern with the protection of *competition*, not *competitors*. . . .

Sixth, Congress neither adopted nor rejected specifically any particular tests for measuring the relevant markets, either as defined in terms of product or in terms of geographic locus of competition, within which the anti-competitive effects of a merger were to be judged. Nor did it adopt a definition of the word "substantially," whether in quantitative terms of sales or assets or market shares or in designated qualitative terms, by which a merger's effect on competition were to be measured.

Seventh, while providing no definite quantitative or qualitative tests by which enforcement agencies could gauge the effects of a given merger to determine whether it may "substantially" lessen competition or tend toward monopoly, Congress indicated plainly that a merger had to be functionally viewed, in the context of its particular industry. . . .

Eighth, Congress used the words "*may be* substantially to lessen competition" (emphasis supplied), to indicate its concern was with probabilities, not certainties.[29]

The foregoing list is, of course, less important as an indication of what Congress had on its collective "mind" than as an indication of factors the Court considered important in 1962. Naïve arguments by some that the Court misinterpreted the "intention" of Congress in making this list imply that the proponent of such an argument can divine the collective Congressional "mind" more accurately than the Court did. That is a neat trick. Such criticisms really mean that the critic does not like the Court's list and would like to substitute his own list for that of the Court.

As has been noted, the District Court had held that "men's, women's, and children's shoes" were separate lines of commerce, but Brown had objected to this classification because it implied that competition had existed between Brown and Kinney prior to the acquisition. The Supreme Court upheld the District Court's finding of fact, saying: "Congress prescribed a pragmatic, factual approach to the definition of the relevant market, and not a formal, legalistic one."[30]

More specifically, the Court said:

The outer boundaries of a product market are determined by the reasonable interchangeability of use or the cross-elasticity of demand between the product itself and substitutes for it. However, within this broad market, well-defined submarkets may exist which, in themselves, constitute product markets for antitrust purposes. *United States v. E. I. du Pont de Nemours and Co.,* 353 U.S. 586, 593–595. *The boundaries of such a submarket may be determined by examining such practical indicia as industry or public recognition of the submarket as a separate economic entity, the product's peculiar characteristics and uses, unique production facilities, distinct customers, distinct prices, sensitivity to price changes, and specialized vendors.*[31]

The Court added that the language, "in any line of commerce," used in Section 7 might make it necessary to examine the effects of the merger in *each* submarket. It then upheld the District Court's finding that men's, women's, and children's shoes were the relevant "lines of commerce" in the case at hand. Moreover, the Court took the view that "the criteria to be used in determining the appropriate geographic market are essentially similar to those used to determine the relevant product market" and added that "just as a product submarket may have Section 7 significance as the proper 'line of commerce,' so may a geographic submarket be considered the appropriate 'section of the country.'"[32] This question will concern us further later in this chapter.

The Philadelphia National Bank Case and the Market Structure Test. We have already seen in Chapter 14 that in 1966, after the decision of the Court under the Sherman Act in the *Lexington National Bank* case in 1964, Congress adopted legislation providing a special defense in the case of bank mergers. A decision handed down in 1963 concerning bank mergers under Section 7 of the Clayton Act had also contributed to the pressures giving rise to this banking legislation. The Department of Justice had brought an action to enjoin the merger of the Philadelphia National Bank and Girard Trust Corn Exchange Bank, which were, re-

spectively, the second and third largest of the 42 commercial banks with head offices in the "Philadelphia metropolitan area," defined as the City of Philadelphia and its three contiguous counties in Philadelphia. The government's complaint alleged violations of Section 1 of the Sherman Act and of Section 7 of the Clayton Act. The Supreme Court held that there was a violation of Section 7 but did not find it necessary to decide the Section 1, Sherman Act, question. Under the 1960 Bank Merger Act, the Comptroller of the Currency was authorized to approve mergers of national banks after he had received reports on the effect of the proposed merger from the Federal Reserve Board, the Federal Deposit Insurance Corporation, and the Department of Justice. All three agencies had disapproved of the merger of the banks in this case, but the Comptroller, nevertheless, approved it. The Department of Justice then acted to enjoin the merger. The District Court dismissed the complaint, and the Department of Justice appealed.

The Supreme Court held that, despite the Bank Merger Act of 1960, Section 7 of the Clayton Act applied to the merger, saying that Section 7 reached both a "pure asset acquisition" and a "pure stock acquisition." Specifically, the Court stated:

Appellees contended below that the Bank Merger Act, by directing the banking agencies to consider competitive factors before approving mergers . . . immunizes approved mergers from challenge under the federal antitrust laws. We think the District Court was correct in rejecting this contention. No express immunity is conferred by the Act. Repeals of the antitrust laws by implication . . . are strongly disfavored, and have only been found in cases of plain repugnancy between the antitrust and regulatory provisions . . . the banking agencies have authority neither to enforce the antitrust laws . . . nor to grant immunity from those laws.[33]

The jurisdictional issue having been disposed of, the Court then turned to the question of whether the facts in the case warranted the issuance of an order under Section 7. Thus it said:

We have no difficulty in determining the "line of commerce" [relevant product or services

[30] *Ibid.,* at p. 336.
[31] *Ibid.,* at p. 325. (Italics mine.)
[32] *Ibid.,* p. 336.

[33] *United States v. Philadelphia National Bank et. al.,* 374 U.S. 321 (1963), at pp. 343, 350–351.

market] and "section of the country" [relevant geographical market] in which to appraise the probable competitive effects of appellee's proposed merger. We agree with the District Court that the cluster of products [various kinds of credit] and services [such as checking accounts and trust administration] denoted by the term "commercial banking" . . . composes a distinct line of commerce. Some commercial banking products or services are so distinctive that they are entirely free of effective competition from products or services of other financial institutions; the checking account is in this category. Others enjoy such cost advantages as to be insulated within a broad range from substitutes furnished by other institutions. For example, commercial banks compete with small-loan companies in the personal-loan market; but the small-loan companies' rates are invariably much higher than the banks', in part, it seems, because the companies' working capital consists in substantial part of bank loans. . . .

We part company with the District Court on the determination of the appropriate "section of the country." The proper question to be asked in this case is not where the parties to the merger do business or even where they compete, but where, within the area of competitive overlap, the effect of the merger on competition will be direct and immediate. . . . This depends upon "the geographic structure of supplier-customer relations. . . ." In banking, as in most service industries, convenience of location is essential to effective competition. . . . The factor of inconvenience localizes banking competition as effectively as high transportation costs in other industries. . . . Therefore . . . the "area of effective competition in the known line of commerce must be charted by careful selection of the market area in which the seller operates, *and to which the purchaser can practically turn for supplies,*" . . . the four-county area in which appellee's offices are located would seem to be the relevant geographic market. Cf. *Brown Shoe Co.* . . . In fact, the vast bulk of appellee's business originates in the four-county area. Theoretically, we should be concerned with the possibility that bank offices on the perimeter of the area may be in effective competition with bank offices within; actually, this seems to be a factor of little significance.[34]

Having satisfied itself with respect to the "line of commerce" and the "section of the country" involved in the case, the Court turned next to the question of "the effect on competition of the proposed merger." The comments on "economic investigation" in the following quotation should be particularly noted by the reader. The Court said:

Having determined the relevant market, we come to the ultimate question under Section 7: whether the effect of the merger "may be substantially to lessen competition" in the relevant market. Clearly, this is not the kind of question which is susceptible to a ready and precise answer in most cases. It requires not merely an appraisal of the immediate impact of the merger upon competition, but a prediction of its impact upon competitive conditions in the future; this is what is meant when it is said that the amended Section 7 was intended to arrest anticompetitive tendencies in their "incipiency." See *Brown Shoe Co.* . . . Such a prediction is sound only if it is based upon a firm understanding of the structure of the relevant market; yet the relevant economic data are both complex and elusive. . . . And unless businessmen can assess the legal consequences of a merger with some confidence, sound business planning is retarded. . . . So also, we must be alert to the danger of subverting congressional intent by permitting a too-broad economic investigation. . . . And so in any case in which it is possible, without doing violence to the congressional objective embodied in Section 7, to simplify the test of illegality, the courts ought to do so in the interest of sound and practical judicial administration. . . . This is such a case.

We noted in *Brown Shoe Co.* . . . that "[t]he dominant theme pervading congressional consideration of the 1950 amendments [to Section 7] was a fear of what was considered to be a rising tide of economic concentration in the American economy." This intense congressional concern with the trend toward concentration warrants dispensing, in certain cases, with elaborate proof of market structure, market behavior, or probably anticompetitive effects. Specifically, we think that a merger which produces a firm controlling an undue percentage share of the relevant market . . . is so inherently likely to lessen competition substantially that is must be enjoined in the absence of evidence clearly showing that the merger is not likely to have such anticompetitive effects.

Such a test lightens the burden of proving illegality only with respect to mergers whose size makes them inherently suspect in light of Congress' design in Section 7 to prevent undue concentration. Furthermore, the test is fully consonant with economic theory. [A footnote to this sentence cites works of Kaysen and Turner, of Stigler, and of Markham, generally taking a market structure point of view, discussed in Chapter 13 of this book.] That "[c]ompetition is likely to be greatest when there are many sellers, none of which has any significant market share," is common ground among most economists, and was undoubtedly a premise of congressional reasoning about the antimerger statute.

The merger of appelles will result in a single bank's controlling at least 30% of the commercial banking business in the four-county Philadelphia metropolitan area. Without attempting to specify the smallest market share which would still be considered to threaten undue concentration, we are clear that 30% presents that threat.[35]

The majority opinion thus clearly adopted the market structure test in this case. That this test is not universally adopted by economists has, of course, already been explained in Chapter 13 of this book. Justice Brennan wrote the majority opinion, Justice White did not participate, and Justices Harlan, Stewart, and Goldberg dissented on grounds that Section 7 did not apply to banks. As we will see from dissenting opinions in later cases, not all the Justices of the Supreme Court accepted the market structure test, although it was used by the majority in a number of Section 7 cases subsequent to the *Philadelphia National Bank* case.

Refinements in Later Cases

The El Paso Natural Gas Company Case and the Foreclosure of "Potential Competition." A second case involving the question of the application of Section 7 of the Clayton Act to a regulated industry was the *El Paso Natural Gas Company* case, decided in April of 1964. The government charged that Section 7 had been violated by the acquisition by El Paso Natural Gas Company of the stock and assets of Pacific Northwest Pipeline Corporation. At the time of the acquisition, El Paso was the sole out-of-state supplier of natural gas to California, and Pacific Northwest was one of the two major pipelines serving the trans-Rocky Mountain states and had made some unsuccessful attempts to enter the California market. By May 1957, El Paso had acquired 99.8% of Pacific Northwest's outstanding stock. The government filed its complaint charging a violation of Section 7 in July 1957. In August, El Paso applied to the Federal Power Commission for permission to acquire the assets of Pacific Northwest, and the Commission approved on December 23,

1959. A merger of assets was then effected on December 31, 1959. The Supreme Court set aside the Commission's order in 1962, holding that it should not have acted until the District Court had acted on the government's complaint under the Clayton Act. The government then amended its complaint to include the asset acquisition in the charge of a violation of Section 7. The District Court dismissed the government's complaint, and the government appealed.[36]

The Supreme Court quickly disposed of the "line of commerce" and "section of the country" questions, saying, "There can be no doubt that the production, transportation, and sale of natural gas is a 'line of commerce' within the meaning of Section 7" of the Clayton Act and "There can also be no doubt that California is a 'section of the country' as that phrase is used in Section 7."[37]

The sole question then was whether or not, on the "undisputed facts," the acquisition had a sufficient tendency to lessen competition to bring it within the proscription of Section 7. The District Court had found as facts that Pacific Northwest could not have entered the market because it could not have obtained a contract from the California distributors, could not have gotten supplies of gas, and could not have put together a project acceptable to the regulatory agencies to obtain their approval of such entry. The Supreme Court thought these findings of fact were "irrelevant." It held that, even though Pacific Northwest had no pipeline into California at the time of the merger, the record disclosed that the Company was a "substantial factor" in the California market. The "mere efforts of Pacific Northwest" to get into the California market had "a powerful influence on El Paso's business attitudes within the state." El Paso had responded to this *threat* by offering better terms and price concessions to its buyers. Thus the merger eliminated *potential* competition from the California market.[38]

The Supreme Court, accordingly, reversed the lower court. Justice White did not participate. A partly concurring, partly dissenting, opinion by Justice Harlan

[35] *Ibid.*, at pp. 362–364.
[36] *United States* v. *El Paso Natural Gas Co. et. al.*, 376 U.S. 651 (1964).
[37] *Ibid.*, at p. 657.
[38] *Ibid.*, pp. 661–662.

argued that the effect of this decision was to place "the Department of Justice in the driver's seat, even though Congress has lodged primary regulatory authority [over natural gas production and transmission] elsewhere [in the Federal Power Commission]." The application of the "elimination of *potential* competition" doctrine has not been limited to cases involving regulatory commissions. It arose also in the *Penn-Olin* joint venture case discussed next.

Penn-Olin: Joint Ventures and the Elimination of Potential Competition. The *Penn-Olin* joint venture case has already been discussed in Chapter 14 because it involved a complaint by the government based not only on Section 7 of the Clayton Act, but also on Section 1 of the Sherman Act. The Section 7 aspect of this case has, however, not yet been discussed. The case, it will be recalled, involved a joint venture agreement between the Pennsalt Chemicals Corporation and the Olin Mathieson Corporation under which each acquired a 50% interest in the newly formed Penn-Olin Chemical Company, which began producing sodium chlorate in 1961 in Kentucky. Again the Court had no difficulty in disposing of the "line of commerce" and "section of the country" questions:

At the outset it is well to note that some of the troublesome questions ordinarily found in antitrust cases have been eliminated by the parties. First, the line of commerce is a chemical known as sodium chlorate . . . used primarily in the pulp and paper industry to bleach the pulp, making for a brighter and higher quality paper. . . . Next, the relevant market is not disputed. It is the southeastern part of the United States. . . .[39]

The issue raised by the case was that of *potential* competition. The Court stated this issue as follows:

Appellees argue that Section 7 applies only where the acquired company is "engaged" in commerce and that it would not apply to a newly formed corporation, such as Penn-Olin. The test, they say, is whether the enterprise to be acquired is engaged in commerce—not whether a corporation formed as the instrumentality for the acquisition is itself engaged in commerce at the moment of its formation. We believe that this logic fails in the light of the wording of the section and its legislative background. . . . Certainly the formation of a joint venture and purchase by the organizers of its stock would substantially lessen competition—indeed foreclose it—as between them, both being engaged in commerce. This would be true whether they were in actual or potential competition with each other and even though the new corporation was formed to create a wholly new enterprise. Realistically, the parents would not compete with their progeny. Moreover, in this case the progeny was organized to further the business of its parents, already in commerce, and the fact that it was organized specifically to engage in commerce should bring it within the coverage of Section 7. . . . In any event, Penn-Olin was engaged in commerce at the time of suit and the economic effects of an acquisition are to be measured at that point rather than at the time of acquisition. . . .

This is the first case reaching this Court and on which we have written that directly involves the validity under Section 7 of the joint participation of two corporations in the creation of a third as a new domestic producing organization. We are, therefore, ploughing new ground. . . .

The joint venture, like the "merger" and the "conglomeration," often creates anticompetitive dangers. It is the chosen . . . instrument of two or more corporations previously acting independently and usually competitively with one another. . . . If the parent companies are in competition, or might compete absent the joint venture, it may be assumed that neither will compete with the progeny in its line of commerce. . . .

This is not to say that the joint venture is controlled by the same criteria as the merger or conglomeration. The merger eliminates one of the participating corporations from the market while a joint venture creates a new competitive force therein. . . . The rule of *United States* v. *El Paso Natural Gas Co.*, 376 U.S. 651 (1964), where a competitor sought to protect its market by acquiring a potential competitor, would, of course, apply to a joint venture where the same intent was present in the organization of the new corporation.

Overall, the same considerations apply to joint ventures as to mergers, for in each instance we are but expounding a national policy enunciated by the Congress to preserve and promote a free competitive economy.[40]

The District Court had found as a fact that Pennsalt and Olin each possessed the resources necessary to allow either to enter the southeastern market independently. But

[39] *United States* v. *Penn-Olin Chemical Co. et. al.*, 378 U.S. 158 (1964), at p. 161.

[40] *Ibid.*, pp. 167–170.

it also found it "impossible" to conclude "that as a matter of reasonable probability *both* Pennsalt and Olin would have built plants in the southeast if Penn-Olin had not been formed." Consequently, it declined to find that the joint venture had the effect of "substantially lessening competition." There was no basis, it said, for a finding that Penn-Olin would be a less effective competitor than "might have resulted if Pennsalt or Olin had been an individual market entrant."[41] The Supreme Court held that the District Court had erred in this regard and added:

> ... Certainly the sole test would not be the probability that *both* companies would have entered the market. Nor would the consideration be limited to the probability that one entered alone. There still remained for consideration the fact that Penn-Olin eliminated the potential competition of the corporation that might have remained at the edge of the market, continually threatening to enter. Just as a merger eliminates actual competition, this joint venture may well foreclose any prospect of competition between Olin and Pennsalt in the relevant sodium chlorate market. The difference, of course, is that the merger's foreclosure is present while the joint venture's is prospective. Nevertheless, "[p]otential competition ... as a substitute for ... [actual competition] may restrain producers from overcharging those to whom they sell or underpaying those from whom they buy. ... Potential competition, insofar as the threat survives [as it would have here in the absence of Penn–Olin], may compensate in part for the imperfection characteristic of actual competition in the great majority of competitive markets." Wilcox, *Competition and Monopoly in American Industry*, TNEC Monograph No. 21 (1940) 7–8. Potential competition cannot be put to a subjective test. It is not "susceptible of a ready and precise answer." As we found in *United States* v. *El Paso Natural Gas Co.* ... the "effect on competition ... is determined by the nature or extent of that market and by the nearness of the absorbed company to it, that company's eagerness to enter that market, its resourcefulness, and so on."[42]

The Supreme Court then reviewed the facts in the case but declined to disturb the trial court's finding that it was not possible to find a reasonable probability that *both* Pennsalt and Olin would have built plants in the relevant market area. But it remanded the case for the trial court to make a finding as to the "reasonable probability that *either* one of the corporations would have entered the market by building a plant, while the other would have remained a significant potential competitor." The trial court had said that this question need not be decided, but its basis for this statement, whether in the facts or in an error of law, was not clear.

On remand, the trial court found that changes in the competitive character of the market would have discouraged the entry of either company alone after 1961, and that neither would have done so. For this reason, the District Court thought it unnecessary to make a finding of fact of whether or not, if one company had entered the market alone, the other would have stayed at the edge of the market as a potential competitor. Thus the District Court dismissed the complaint. In 1961, it may be noted, Pittsburgh Plate Glass Company built a plant and entered the market as a competitor; and the price of sodium chlorate had decreased somewhat.[43]

1964–1967: Reciprocity; The "Line of Commerce"; The "Trend Toward Concentration." A number of other important Section 7 cases were decided by the Supreme Court in the period from 1964 to 1967, but space considerations prevent a detailed discussion of them. In all these cases, the majority of the Court clearly adopted the market structure test. In two cases decided in 1964, the Court prohibited firms dominant in one product line from acquiring firms producing "functionally [technologically] interchangeable" products in situations in which the acquired firms were *potential competitors* of the acquiring firms. Thus the Continental Can Company was prohibited from acquiring the Hazel Atlas Glass Company[44] and the Aluminum Company of America was prohibited from acquiring the Rome Cable Company.[45] Both cases were nominally decided in terms of the problem of defining "the line of

---

[41] *Ibid.*, at p. 173.

[42] *Ibid.*, at pp. 173–174.

[43] *United States* v. *Penn-Olin Chemical Co.*, 246 Fed. Supp. 917 (1965).

[44] *United States* v. *Continental Can Co. et. al.*, 378 U.S. 441 (1964). The majority consisted of Justices Black, Brennan, Clark, Douglas, Goldberg, Warren, and White.

[45] *United States* v. *Aluminum Company of America et. al.*, 377 U.S. 271 (1964). The majority consisted of Justices Black, Brennan, Clark, Douglas, Warren, and White.

commerce," and in both cases the lower court and the Supreme Court made much ostentatious use of the language of price theory. The effect of this use was to obscure the real bases of the decisions.

In 1965, the Court prohibited a large firm, owning food-processing plants and retail stores, from acquiring the assets of a firm holding a large share of the market for dehydrated onions and garlic, spices used as ingredients in the processing stage. The acquiring firm was also a large purchaser of processed foods from other producers who, in turn purchased supplies from the acquired firm. Such an arrangement involves a "reciprocal trading relationship," and the share of the market of the acquired firm unsurprisingly increased after the acquisition.

Then, in the *Pabst Brewing Company* and *Von's Grocery Company* cases[46] of 1966, the Court cited "the growing tendency toward concentration" in the markets in which the mergers occurred as a basis for prohibiting them. The *Pabst* case was formally cast in terms of the question of the meaning of the phrase, "any section of the country." But the real basis of the Court's decision can be found in the statement in the majority opinion that:

... Congress, in passing Section 7 and in amending it with the Celler–Kefauver Anti-Merger Amendment, was concerned with arresting concentration in the American economy, whatever its cause, in its incipiency. ... It passed and amended Section 7 on the premise that mergers do tend to accelerate concentration in an industry. Many believe that this assumption of Congress is wrong, and that the disappearance of small businesses with a correlative concentration of business in the hands of a few is bound to occur whether mergers are prohibited or not. But it is not for the courts to review the policy decision of Congress that mergers which may substantially lessen competition are forbidden, which in effect the courts would be doing should they now require proof of the congressional premise that mergers are a major cause of concentration. We hold that a trend toward concentration in an industry, *whatever its causes*, is a highly relevant factor in deciding how substantial the anticompetitive effect of a merger may be.[47]

This view was sharply criticized Justice Harlan. In the *Von's Grocery Company* case, a dissenting opinion was written by Justice Stewart and reads in part as follows:

The Court makes no efforts to appraise the competitive effects of this acquisition in terms of the contemporary economy of the retail food industry in the Los Angeles area. Instead, through a simple exercise in sums, it finds that the number of individual competitors in the market has decreased over the years, and apparently on the theory that the degree of competition is invariably proportional to the number of competitors, it holds that this historic reduction in the number of competing units is enough under Section 7 to invalidate a merger within the market, with no need to examine the economic concentration of market, the level of concentration in the market, or the potential adverse effect of the merger on competition. This startling *per se* rule is contrary not only to our previous decisions but contrary to the language of Section 7, contrary to the legislative history of the 1950 amendment, and contrary to economic reality.

... In the counting-of-heads game played today by the Court, the reduction in the number of single-store operators becomes a yardstick for automatic disposition of cases under Section 7.

Section 7 was never intended by Congress for use by the Court ... to roll back the supermarket revolution. Yet the Court's opinion is hardly more than a requiem for the so-called "Mom and Pop" grocery stores ... that are now economically and technologically obsolete in many parts of the country. ...

The emotional impact of a merger between the third and sixth largest competitors in a given market, however fragmented, is understandable, but that impact cannot substitute for the analysis of the effect of the merger on competition that Congress required by the 1950 amendment. Nothing in the present record indicates that there is more than an emphemeral possibility that the effect of this merger may be substantially to lessen competition.[48]

One solution might, of course, be to place on the defendant the burden of proving that a merger will not have the eventual effect of substantially lessening competition. There was no evidence offered in the case in question to establish this proposition. How one stands on this issue depends, of course, on whether or not he

---

[46] *United States* v. *Pabst Brewing Company, et. al.*, 384 U.S. 546 (1966); *United States* v. *Von's Grocery Company, et. al.*, 384 U.S. 270 (1966).

[47] *United States* v. *Pabst Brewing Company, et. al.*, 384 U.S. 546 (1966), at pp. 552–553. (Italics mine.)

There were no dissenting opinions but Justices Douglas, White, Fortas, Harlan, and Stewart concurred.
[48] *United States* v. *Von's Grocery Company, et. al.*, 384 U.S. 270 (1966), at pp. 282–304.

structure test. This test, ... n this chapter, is the one ...ase of various "guidelines" ...e Federal Trade Commis- ...ntitrust Division to assist ... businessmen in determining ...or not a prospective merger will ...prosecuted by these enforcement agencies.

The Procter and Gamble-Clorox Case and The "Product Extension" Merger. In 1967, the Supreme Court handed down what the Federal Trade Commission described as a "landmark decision" in a case involving a "product extension" merger. A *product extension* merger has been defined by the Commission as one in which the products of the acquired company are "comple-mentary to those of the acquiring company, may be produced with similar facilities, marketed through the same channels and in the same manner, and advertised by the same media." Thus product extension mergers possess some of the attributes of conglomerate mergers and some of hori-zontal mergers. The case in question involved the following facts. In 1957, Procter and Gamble (Procter), one of the nation's largest diversified manufacturers of household products, acquired the assets of Clorox Chemical Company, the leading manufacturer of liquid household bleach and the only one selling on a national basis. At the time, Clorox accounted for 48.8 percent of the national market, with higher percentages in some regional markets, and together with four other firms accounted for almost 80 percent of the national market, with the remaining 20 percent divided among nearly 200 small producers. In 1957 the amount of Procter's sales of soaps, detergents, and washing powders exceeded $1 billion, and it spent $80 million on advertising, receiving substantial discounts from the media because of its volume purchases. (Procter thus seems to have been not only the leading producer of soap but also the leading producer of "soap opera.") The FTC filed a complaint challenging the acquisition in October 1957. A Hearing Examiner held the acquisition to be a violation of Section 7 in an initial decision in June 1960. An appeal was then taken to the Commission which set aside the initial

decision in 1961 and remanded the case to the Hearing Examiner for the taking of additional evidence. A Hearing Examiner rendered a second initial decision, ordering divestiture, in February 1962. Again an appeal was taken to the Commission, which now adopted substantially the Hearing Examiner's findings. An appeal was then instituted by Procter in a Court of Appeals. (Between the time of the first and second appeals to the Commission, the personnel of the Commission itself had changed—a national election had occurred.) The Court of Appeals reversed the Commission's decision. The real basis of the Court of Appeals' decision can be found in the concluding paragraphs of its opinion. With italics supplied, these paragraphs read as follows:

The Commission recognized that complete guidelines for this type of merger have not yet been developed and that the case presented a challenge to it and to the courts "to devise tests more precisely adjusted to the special dangers to a competitive economy posed by the con-glomerate merger." *We do not believe these tests should involve application of a per se rule.*

The Supreme Court has not ruled that bigness is unlawful, or that a large company may not merge with a smaller one in a different market field. Yet the size of Procter and its legitimate, successful operations in related fields pervades the entire opinion of the Commission, and seems to be the motivating factor which influenced the Commission to rule that the acquisition was illegal.

Here Procter was merely adding another product to its line, which was somewhat akin to the products which it was already handling. They were all household items sold in grocery stores. It could have entered the market on its own, but decided not to do so.[49]

In 1967, the Supreme Court reversed the decision of the Court of Appeals and upheld the Commission's position. The Supreme Court did not consider the issue, raised by the Court of Appeals, of whether or not "bigness" was unlawful. It did, however, virtually adopt the views of the Commission and stated its understanding of the Commission's views by saying:

The Commission found that the acquisition might substantially lessen competition. The findings and reasoning of the Commission need be only briefly summarized. The Commission found that the substitution of Procter with its

---

[49] *The Procter and Gamble Co.* v. *Federal Trade Commission*, 358 F. 2d 74 (1966), at p. 78. (Italics mine.)

huge assets and advertising advantages for the already dominant Clorox would dissuade new entrants and discourage active competition from the firms already in the industry due to fear of retaliation by Procter. The Commission thought it relevant that retailers might be induced to give Clorox preferred shelf space since it would be manufactured by Procter, which also produced a number of other products marketed by the retailers. There was also danger that Procter might underprice Clorox in order to drive out competition, and subsidize the underpricing with revenue from other products. The Commission carefully reviewed the effect of the acquisition on the structure of the industry, noting that "the practical tendency of the merger . . . is to transform the liquid bleach industry into an arena of big business competition only, with the few small firms that have not disappeared through merger eventually falling by the wayside, unable to compete with their giant rivals." . . . Further, the merger would seriously diminish potential competition by eliminating Procter as a potential entrant into the industry. Prior to the merger, the Commission found that Procter was the most likely prospective entrant into the industry, and absent the merger would have remained on the periphery, restraining Clorox from exercising its market power. If Procter had actually entered, Clorox's dominant position would have been eroded and the concentration of the industry reduced. The Commission stated that it had not placed reliance on post-acquisition evidence in holding the merger unlawful.[50]

The extent to which the Supreme Court adopted the Commission's point of view can easily be seen in the statements by the Court that:

The anticompetitive effects with which this product-extension merger is fraught can easily be seen: (1) the substitution of the powerful acquiring firm for the smaller, but already dominant, firm may substantially reduce the competitive structure of the industry by raising entry barriers and by dissuading the smaller firms from aggressively competing; (2) the acquisition eliminates the potential competition of the acquiring firm. The liquid bleach industry was already oligopolistic before the acquisition and price competition was certainly not as vigorous as it would have been if the industry were competitive. . . . The interjection of Procter into the market considerably changed the situation. There is every reason to assume that the smaller firms would become more cautious

in competing due to their fear of retaliation by Procter. It is probable that Procter would become the price leader and that the oligopoly would become more rigid.[51]

Justice Harlan concurred in the decision but wrote a separate opinion in which he belabored the majority, asserting that it had not taken the opportunity afforded by this case to produce "guidelines" for determining the validity of conglomerate mergers. (Justices Fortas and Stewart did not participate; the members of the majority are listed in Footnote 50.)

In 1968, the Commission itself interpreted the Supreme Court's opinion by saying:

. . . In concluding that the merger might substantially lessen competition the Supreme Court considered the following factors to be of great importance: (1) excessive concentration in the industry involved at the time of the merger and the dominant position of the acquired company; (2) the relative disparity in size and strength as between the acquiring company and the remaining firms in the industry; (3) the dominant position of the acquiring company in other markets; (4) the nature of the production and distribution economies and advantages created by the merger; and (5) the elimination of the potential competition of the acquiring firm.[52]

Following the decision of the Supreme Court in the *Clorox* case, the Court of Appeals for the Third Circuit perfunctorily upheld the FTC's decision in the *General Foods-SOS* case, another case involving an attempted product extension merger. (386 Fed. 2d 936, 1967.) The FTC's opinion in the *General Foods* case (Docket No. 8600, March 11, 1966) contains a detailed comparison of the situation in the *General Foods* case and in the *Procter and Gamble* case, and rests the decision in the former almost entirely on the precedent set by the FTC's decision in the latter. The Supreme Court's decision in the *Procter and Gamble* case was thus crucial in determining the effectiveness of the Commission's policy toward product-extension mergers.

In the *Clorox* case, the majority of the Court again placed much emphasis upon the concept of market structure. Later, as has been noted, we will see that the *Guide-*

[50] *FTC* v. *Procter and Gamble Co.*, 386 U.S. 568, at pp. 574–75. (1967). The majority consisted of Justices Black, Brennan, Clark, Douglas, Warren, and White.

[51] *Ibid.*, p. 578.
[52] *Annual Report of the Federal Trade Commission for the Fiscal Year Ended June 30, 1967*, (Washington, D.C.: U.S. Government Printing Office, 1968), p. 83.

lines adopted by the Federal Trade Commission and those adopted by the Antitrust Division for testing the validity of mergers under Section 7 both employ the market structure test. Before considering these *Guidelines*, it is useful and interesting to consider one defense accepted both by the Court and the Commission in merger cases. This defense is known as the "failing company doctrine."

The International Shoe Company Case (1930), Dean Foods (1966), and the "Failing Company Doctrine." The *International Shoe Company* case was decided by the Supreme Court in 1930 under the original Section 7 of the Clayton Act. The case arose as follows. In 1921 the International Shoe Company acquired all or substantially all of the stock of the McElwain (shoe) Company. The Commission charged that the acquisition violated Section 7 of the Clayton Act. A majority of the Supreme Court held that "it appears that in respect of 95 percent of the business there was no competition in fact and no contest or observed tendency to contest, in the market for the same purchasers. . . ."[53] Given this finding of fact, the Court easily concluded that Section 7 was not violated by the acquisition. But the defendants had also raised a second objection to the Federal Trade Commission order, namely:

> . . . that at the time of the acquisition the financial condition of the McElwain Company was such as to necessitate liquidation or sale, and, therefore, the prospect for future competition or restraint was entirely eliminated.[54]

The majority stated with respect to this defense:

> . . . Beginning in 1920, there was a marked falling off in prices and sales of shoes, as there was in other commodities; and, because of excessive commitments which the McElwain Company had made for the purchase of hides as well as the possession of large stocks of shoes and inability to meet its indebtedness for large sums of borrowed money, the financial condition of the company became such that its officers, after long and careful consideration of the situation, concluded that the company was faced with financial ruin, and that the only alternatives presented were liquidation through a receiver or an outright sale. . . .[55]

Given this statement of the facts, the majority took the following position:

> In the light of the case thus disclosed of a corporation with resources so depleted and the prospect of rehabilitation so remote that it faced the grave *probability* of a business failure with resulting loss to stockholders and injury to the communities where its plants were operated, we hold that the purchase of its capital stock by a competitor (there being no other prospective purchaser) not with a purpose to lessen competition, but to facilitate the accumulated business of the purchaser and with the effect of mitigating seriously injurious consequences otherwise *probable*, is not in contemplation of law prejudicial to the public and does not substantially lessen competition or restrain commerce within the intent of the Clayton Act. To regard such a transaction as a violation of law . . . would "seem a distempered view of purchase and result.[56]

Justices Stone, Holmes, and Brandeis dissented from the majority opinion on the grounds that the two companies were in fact competitors, and that the "failing" McElwain Company was in fact "successfully competing" despite the impact of a general business depression which had cut the value of its gross sales in half.[57]

The argument between the majority and the minority in the *International Shoe Company* case was an argument about facts and not one about applicable principles of law. The discussion of the probable business failure of the acquired company was not necessary to the decision of the majority, given its holding that no competition existed between the two companies and the lack of any discussion of the effect of the merger on the structure of the market or of the trend toward concentration in the industry. Thus this language comes close to constituting a *dictum* which, however, the minority did not contest.

The failing company doctrine was the subject of a Commission opinion in 1966; in this opinion the Commission gave its interpretation of the "failing company doctrine" stated in the *International Shoe Company* case earlier. The case in question was the *Dean Foods* case. This case involved two points. In the early stages of the case, the Supreme Court held that the Federal

[53] *International Shoe Company* v. *Federal Trade Commission*, 280 U.S. 291 (1930), at p. 297.
[54] *Ibid.*, at p. 294.

[55] *Ibid.*, at p. 299.
[56] *Ibid.*, at p. 302–303. (Italics mine.)
[57] *Ibid.*, at p. 303–306.

Trade Commission has the right to seek a temporary injunction to prevent a prospective merger from being consummated.[58] A majority of the Court accepted the FTC's contention that unless an injunction was permitted, if the merger should eventually be found illegal under Section 7, the problem of "unscrambling" the merged companies might be so great as to be virtually impossible. The minority, however, argued that the question of whether or not an injunction should be issued would amount to a trial of the question of the legality of the merger on the merits of the case so that it would be impossible for the Commission to render an impartial decision in its later formal hearing.

The initial decision by the Hearing Examiner in this case was given in September 1966. The Examiner found as a fact that "Bowman [the acquired company] was a failing company without any prospect of rehabilitation and that its acquisition by Dean has not injured but strengthened competition. . . ."[59]

An appeal was taken to the Commission, which reversed the Hearing Examiner's decision in November 1966. There was one dissenting opinion. The majority took the view that "the significance of the *International Shoe* test is that it is premised on a business condition which could not easily be artificially produced by a company desiring to sell out to a competitor." The doctrine did not include cases of companies which were "merely suffering business reverses." Moreover, the majority took the view that even if Bowman's condition "were regarded as approaching serious dimensions, its acquisition by Dean nevertheless still had the prohibited anticompetitive effect." Thus the majority rejected the notion that the failing company doctrine constituted an *absolute* defense, irrespective of the effect on competition of the merger. Commissioner Elman dissented, not on grounds that he disagreed with the majority's interpretation of the *International Shoe* case, but on grounds that the merger did not have any anticompetitive effect.

Since the *Dean Foods* case, the Commission has often given premerger clearances

(in the form of an assurance that it would take no action to prevent the merger) on grounds of financial distress, imminent bankruptcy, and imminent insolvency. Thus, for example, in February 1968, six such premerger clearances were reported in the *News Summary*. The *Dean Foods* case was finally settled in 1967 when the parties agreed to a plan of divestiture and a Modified Order was issued by the Commission. The majority opinion discussed above shows that the Commission followed the market structure test in making its decision.

The Citizen Publishing Company Case (1969) and Limitation of the Failing Company Doctrine. In an interesting case decided in March 1969, the Supreme Court clarified and limited the failing company doctrine. The case involved the following situation. In 1940, the only two newspapers (the *Citizen* and the *Star*) in Tucson, Arizona, negotiated an agreement to fix prices and to pool and distribute profits in an agreed-on ratio, and also agreed that neither newspaper nor any of their stockholders would engage in any activities in the relevant county in conflict with the agreement. In 1953 the agreement was renewed, and in 1965 the *Citizen* acquired the controlling stock interest in the *Star*. The government brought an action alleging violations of Sections 1 and 2 of the Sherman Act and of Section 7 of the Clayton Act. The lower court found for the government. The defendants, who had asserted the failing company defense, appealed. The Supreme Court upheld the lower court decision.

Justice Douglas wrote a majority opinion in which he asserted that the failing company defense could not be applied unless it was established that the acquiring company was "the only available purchaser." Moreover, he added that no attempt had been made to reorganize the alleged failing company under the bankruptcy laws. He concluded by saying, "We confine the failing company doctrine to its present scope."[59a]

Thus not only must the acquiring company who uses this defense show that it is the only available purchaser, but also it

---

[58] *Federal Trade Commission v. Dean Foods Co., et. al.,* 384 U.S. 597 (1966).

[59] *Federal Trade Commission News Summary,* Septem-

ber 16, 1966, reporting Initial Decision (8674).

[59a] *Citizen Publishing Co. v. U.S.,* 394 U.S. 131 (1969), at pp. 138–139.

must show that no successful reorganization of the acquired company is possible.

Just as the Federal Trade Commission has used the market structure test in arriving at many of its Section 7 decisions, so has it used this test in establishing criteria for testing mergers in various specific industries, as we will now see.

Enforcement Agency Guidelines

Federal Trade Commission Enforcement Policy: Mergers in the Food Distribution Industry. On January 17, 1967, the Commission announced the criteria it would use "in identifying mergers warranting its attention and consideration" in the "Food Distribution Industry." The classes of mergers to be considered included the following (although smaller mergers might also be considered):

(1) Mergers and acquisitions by food chains resulting in combined annual food sales in excess of $500 million;

(2) Mergers and acquisitions by voluntary and cooperative groups of food retailers creating a volume of sales comparable to those of food chains with sales in excess of $500 million annually.

In justification of these criteria, the Commission cited the fact that ten or so retail companies with sales of $500 million or more had accounted for about one-half of all retail mergers occurring since 1948.

Federal Trade Commission Enforcement Policy: Vertical Mergers in the Cement Industry. Also on January 17, 1967, the Commission stated it would issue a complaint in every case in which a cement producer acquired a ready-mixed concrete firm ranking among the leading four nonintegrated ready-mix producers in any market, or acquired any ready-mixed producer regularly purchasing 500,000 or more barrels of cement annually. In support of these criteria, the Commission cited its own public hearings and industry studies.

Federal Trade Commission Enforcement Policy: Product Extension Mergers in Grocery Products Manufacturing. The Commission's third statement of enforcement policies was made May 15, 1968, and dealt with product extension mergers of the type dealt with in the *Clorox* case. The following criteria were laid down as a basis for investigation of such mergers:

(1) Both the acquired and the acquiring companies engage in the manufacture of grocery products, defined as products sold primarily in food stores;

(2) The combined company has assets in excess of $250 million;

(3) The acquiring company engages in extensive promotional efforts, sells highly differentiated consumer products, and produces a number of products, in some of which it holds a strong market position. A strong market position is defined as being one of the top four producers of a product in which the four top companies hold 40 percent or more of the values of shipments;

(4) The acquired company is either among the top eight producers of any one important grocery product, or has more than a five percent share of the relevant market.

In justification, the Commission referred to the *Clorox* case and to its own decisions in the *General Foods* case, the *Beatrice Foods* case and the *Foremost Dairies, Inc.* case, each of which involved a factual situation comparable to that in the *Clorox* case. Clearly, the market structure test was applied in the development of these criteria also.

Federal Trade Commission Enforcement Policy: Mergers in the Textile Mill Products Industry. The Commission's fourth statement of merger enforcement policy was issued in November, 1968. It, too, employed the market structure concept. Mergers which would warrant further attention by the Commission included those in which the sales or assets of the smaller firm exceeded $10 million, mergers of firms such that the combined firm would rank among the top four, or in which the combined market share amounted to 5 percent or more in any market in which the four largest firms accounted for 85 percent or more of the market. Various other criteria were also given, all involving the market structure concept.

On May 30, 1968, the Department of Justice had issued its own *Guidelines* outlining standards it would employ in determining whether or not to oppose mergers. These *Guidelines* are our next topic.

Antitrust Division Enforcement Policy: Merger Guidelines. Unlike the Federal Trade Commission, the Antitrust Division did not specify criteria to be applied to particular industries and activities. Instead, it provided a statement of "General Enforcement Policy," then discussed criteria in the cases of various types (horizontal, vertical, etc.) of mergers, and also made comments on particular problems, such as the failing company doctrine. These *Guidelines* fill 26 double-spaced typewritten pages and will not be discussed in detail in this book. Their general approach and philosophy can be adequately considered by an examination of the statement of "General Enforcement Policy," which opens forthrightly with the sentence: "Within the overall scheme of the Department's antitrust enforcement activity, the primary role of Section 7 enforcement is to preserve and promote market structures conducive to competition." The next sentence states even more explicitly: "Market structure is the primary focus of the Department's merger policy chiefly because the conduct of individual firms in the market tends to be controlled by the structure of the market, *i.e.*, by those market conditions which are fairly permanent or subject only to slow change (such as, principally, the number of substantial firms selling in the market, the relative sizes of their respective market shares, and the substantiality of barriers to the entry of new firms into the market)." Thus the market structure test is also the dominant concept behind the Antitrust Division's *Guidelines*.

The *Guidelines* were issued in 1968 under the Johnson Administration. After the Republicans came into office in 1969, Assistant Attorney General in Charge of Antitrust Richard McLaren commented on the *Guidelines* by saying that in his past public statements he had tried to warn businessmen that they could not rely on the *Guidelines* of his predecessors. Under his leadership, mergers might be challenged even though they satisfied the *Guidelines*. Therefore, to be safe, firms should learn of the Division's enforcement intentions by writing to the Division.[59b]

One of the most discussed actions brought under Section 7 by the Antitrust Division under the Nixon Administration was that involving the Ling-Temco-Vaught acquisition of Jones and Laughlin Steel Corporation. Ling-Temco-Vaught is the fourteenth largest industrial corporation in the nation and the eighth largest prime defense contractor. Jones and Laughlin Steel Company is the sixth largest steel producer in the United States and ranks as the eightieth largest in assets. The complaint charged that the merger would eliminate potential competition by Ling-Temco-Vaught with the steel industry, eliminate competition in products in which Ling-Temco-Vaught and Jones and Laughlin Steel were competing, and result in a combined firm with great possibilities for engaging in reciprocal selling relationships. Cases involving each of these situations have been discussed in the preceding paragraphs. All were won by the government. The case was terminated in June 1970 by a consent decree giving LTV the option of divesting itself of its interest in Jones and Laughlin or of divesting itself of interests in several other companies, including Braniff Airways, having assets in excess of $656 million.

Some Concluding Comments

In Chapter 13, we have seen that Professor Corwin Edwards (formerly the FTC's chief economist) has been an outspoken advocate of the market structure test; and some of his testimony before the Senate Subcommittee on Antitrust and Monopoly has been quoted in Chapter 9. Indeed, the situation presented by the *Clorox* case was one of those envisioned by Edwards in his testimony when, as we have seen, he remarked:

A big firm has advantages over a smaller rival just because it is big. Money is power. A big firm can outbid, outspend, and outlose a small firm. It can advertise more intensively, do more intensive and extensive research, buy up the inventions of others, defend its legal rights or alleged rights more thoroughly, bid higher for scarce resources, acquire the best locations and the best technicians and executives. If it overdoes its expenditures, it can absorb losses that would bankrupt a small rival.

Some of these advantages express economies of scale. They constitute real economies. Others are bargaining advantages which do not appear to have any particular advantage to the economy as a whole, and some of them are advantages of being able to live for a time on accumulated fat.

Such advantages . . . are derived from the total size of the enterprise, whether that size is attained in one market or in many. . . .

[59b] *Testimony before the House Ways and Means Committee*, March 12, 1969 (Washington, D.C.: U.S. Department of Justice, Lithoprint, 1969).

The power that is derived from dispersion of resources is peculiar to conglomerage enterprise. The aspects of such power that are most important have to do with:

(a) subsidization [of one product at the expense of another];

(b) reciprocity [as defined in the *Consolidated Foods* case];

(c) full line selling [as described in connection with tying agreements]; and

(d) the forebearance that prevails among large conglomerates [the mutual adoption of policies of "Live and Let Live"].

The best available way of coping with the anticompetitive possibilities of large conglomerates that we now have is by use of section 7 of the Clayton Act. Since much of conglomerate growth has taken place by acquisitions of going concerns, effective policing of conglomerate mergers could slow down that growth considerably. Doubtless some conglomerate mergers are harmless; some may even be useful. But the merger of unrelated activities seldom offers much prospect of efficiency, and hence, where there is reason to object to such a merger, prevention of it is unlikely to be disadvantageous to the economy.[60]

However, as we have also seen in Chapter 13, although there are many economists who advocate the market structure test, there are also some who reject it. For example, Professor M. A. Adelman followed Professor Edwards in testifying before the Senate Subcommittee on Antitrust and Monopoly and stated that he was "simply in conflict" with Professor Edwards in his views.[61] And there, as far as professional economists are concerned, the matter stands. The issue involves matters of policy and considerations which lie outside the traditional scope of economic theory as such. The nature of the underlying disagreement was clearly stated by Justice Douglas in his dissenting opinion in the *Columbia Steel* case, when he said, in part:

We have here the problem of bigness. Its lesson should by now have been burned into our memory by Brandeis. *The Curse of Bigness* shows how size can become a menace—both industrial and social. It can be an industrial menace because it creates gross inequalities against existing or putative competitors. It can be a social menace—because of its control of prices. Control of prices in the steel industry is powerful leverage on our economy. For the price of steel determines the price of hundreds of other articles. Our price level determines in large measure whether we have prosperity or depression—an economy of abundance or scarcity. Size in steel should therefore be jealously watched. In final analysis, size in steel is the measure of the power of a handful of men over our economy. That power can be utilized with lightening speed. It can be benign or it can be dangerous. The philosophy of the Sherman Act is that it should not exist. For all power tends to develop into a government in itself. Power that controls the economy should be in the hands of elected representatives of the people, not in the hands of an industrial oligarchy. Industrial power should be decentralized. It should be scattered into many hands so that the fortunes of the people will not be dependent on the whim or caprice, the political prejudices, the emotional stability of a few self-appointed men. The fact that they are not vicious men but respectable and social-minded is irrelevant. That is the philosophy . . . of the Sherman Act. It is founded on a theory of hostility to the concentration in private hands of power so great that only a government of the people should have it.[62]

Those who reject this argument assert that it is emotional and involves imprecise economic concepts. Unfortunately, often the alternative they propose is cast wholly in terms of precise but unquantifiable price theory concepts with no reference to the underlying philosophical basis of that approach. Indeed, in some instances, judges have, perhaps self-consciously, sought to write their opinions in the language of price theory in an obvious reaction to criticisms of prior decisions by economists. This tendency is to be only deplored, since it obscures the real bases of the decisions and fails to recognize that many criticisms by economists can be boiled down to a disagreement about the "facts" in the cases and the inferences to be drawn from them. The most competent judges in our society are those who frankly identify the competing social interests which they are seeking to reconcile in their decisions and who explicitly state why they have favored one interest rather than another in making their decision. In short, it is no accident that other writers trained *both* in law and in

---

[60] *Economic Concentration* (Hearings before the Subcommittee on Antitrust and Monopoly of the Senate Committee on the Judiciary, 88th Cong., 2d sess., 1964) (Washington, D.C.: U.S. Government Printing Office, 1964), Part 1, pp. 42–46.

[61] *Ibid.*, at p. 241.

[62] *United States* v. *Columbia Steel Co. et. al.*, 334 U.S. 495 (1948), at pp. 535–536. (Italics his.)

economics have placed their "purely theoretical economic" analyses in separate chapters on grounds that these analyses "have no immediate relationship" to legal decisions which involve "a valuable methodology of their own."[63]

The problem which arises in the case of conglomerate mergers (such as the one in the *Clorox* case) of the use in one market of power acquired or possessed in a second and different market has been held to constitute a method of unfair competition under Section 5 of the Federal Trade Commission Act, as we will see in the following chapter.

[63] See, for example, Eugene M. Singer, *Antitrust Economics* (Englewood Cliffs: Prentice-Hall, Inc., 1968), pp. vii–viii.

18

"Unfair Methods of Competition"; "Unfair or Deceptive Practices"; "Fair Packaging and Labeling"; and "Truth in Lending"

This chapter undertakes: (1) to discuss the prohibition of "unfair methods of competition" contained in Section 5 of the Federal Trade Commission Act; (2) to examine the rules pertaining to "unfair or deceptive practices," also adopted pursuant to Section 5; (3) to examine related legislation pertaining to advertising and labeling as enforced by the Federal Trade Commission; (4) to discuss the "Fair Packaging and Labeling Act" of 1966, (5) to note the Federal Trade Commission's responsibility under the "Truth in Lending Act" of 1968; and (6) to examine some studies evaluating the Federal Trade Commission.

A. "UNFAIR METHODS OF COMPETITION"

The Common Law and "Injury to a Competitor"

At common law, an action based on a complaint of "unfair competition" necessarily involved a showing of *injury to a competitor*. An illustrative case is that of *American Washboard Company* v. *Saginaw Manufacturing Company* (1900), in which the plaintiff, the sole manufacturer of washboards made of "genuine aluminum," sought an injunction to restrain the defendant from falsely stamping its washboards with the word "aluminum" even though they were made of zinc. The Court of Appeals pointed out that nowhere in his complaint had the plaintiff alleged that the defendant was "palming off its goods on the public as and for the goods of the plaintiff." The paintiff's argument that the injunction should lie because the defendant was deceiving the public, was then rejected by the court. Such a theory of the action, the Court of Appeals said:

. . . loses sight of the thoroughly established principle that the private right of action in such cases is not based upon fraud or imposition on the public, *but is maintained solely for the protection of the property rights of complainant.* It is true that in these cases it is an important factor that the public are deceived, but it is only where this deception induces the public to buy the goods as those of complainant that a private right of action arises.[1]

---

[1] *American Washboard Co.* v. *Saginaw Mfg. Co.*, 103 Fed. 281 (1900), at p. 285. (Italics mine.)

Thus *an essential element of a private action at common law was injury to a plaintiff-competitor.* As we will see below, the Supreme Court read the requirement of an element of injury to a competitor also into actions under Section 5 of the Federal Trade Commission Act in some of the earliest cases involving fraud and deception under that law. This section originally prohibited "unfair methods of competition."

The Development of Policy Concerning "Unfair Methods of Competition" and Section 5 of the FTC Act

The Gratz Case and the Doctrine of "Judicial Superiority." The words "unfair methods of competition" as used in Section 5 were not defined by Congress when the law was originally enacted in 1914. The Supreme Court held at an early date that it was for the courts and not for the Commission to give them meaning. The current meaning of the phrase has been developed in a trial and error process of self-correcting value judgments as a result of interaction of decisions by the Commission and the courts.

One of the earliest cases involving the original Section 5(a) was the *Gratz* case decided in 1920. The case arose as a result of a Federal Trade Commission complaint charging the defendants (respondents on appeal) with a violation of the prohibition of tying arrangements under Section 3 of the Clayton Act and with a violation of Section 5 of the FTC Act ("unfair methods of competition") as a result of the imposition by the respondent-sellers upon purchasers of their cotton ties of a requirement that the purchasers also buy a proportionate amount of cotton bagging. After a hearing, the Commission dropped the Section 3 Clayton Act charge on grounds of lack of evidence but found the defendants guilty of the Section 5 Federal Trade Commission Act charge. On appeal, the Court of Appeals anulled the Commission's order; the Commission then appealed to the Supreme Court. A majority of the Supreme Court upheld the decision of the Court of Appeals. The majority opinion asserted among other things:

The words "unfair method of competition" are not defined by the statute and their exact mean-

ing is in dispute. It is for the courts, not the commission, ultimately to determine as matter of law what they include. They are clearly inapplicable to practices never *heretofore* regarded as opposed to good morals because characterized by deception, bad faith, fraud or oppression, or as against public policy because of their dangerous tendency unduly to hinder competition or create monopoly. The act was certainly not intended to fetter free and fair competition as commonly understood and practiced by honorable opponents in trade.

Nothing is alleged which would justify the conclusion that the public suffered injury or that competitors had reasonable ground for complaint. All question of monopoly or combination being out of the way, a private merchant, acting with entire good faith, may properly refuse to sell except in conjunction, such closely associated articles as ties and bagging. . . .[2]

A dissenting opinion was written in this case by Justice Brandeis. He argued that the facts put in evidence in the *Gratz* case were sufficient to justify the Commission's finding. The *Gratz* case, we will see below, was subsequently overruled.

The Beech-Nut Case and the "Policy of the Sherman Act." In general, after the *Gratz* case, the Court was willing to hold that acts which *would constitute violations of the Sherman Act* would also constitute "unfair competition," but was less liberal in its interpretation of Section 5 in cases involving deceptive practices not amounting to Sherman Act violations. Thus, in the *Beech-Nut Packing Company* case in 1922, it upheld the Commission's finding of a violation of Section 5 in the resale price maintenance program of that company, where coercion and boycotts were employed to enforce the program, a type of practice already discussed in Chapter 14. The Court said specifically in the *Beech-Nut* case:

The Sherman Act is not involved here except in so far as it shows a declaration of public policy to be considered in determining what are unfair methods of competition, which the Federal Trade Commission is empowered to condemn and suppress. . . .[3]

The Klesner Case and "The Public Interest." However, in 1929, the Court refused to permit the Commission to issue an order in a case in which the defendant had adopted an approximation to a competitor's

---

[2] *Federal Trade Commission* v. *Gratz et. al.*, 253 U.S. 421 (1920), at pp. 427–428. (Italics mine.)

[3] *Federal Trade Commission* v. *Beech-Nut Packing Co.*, 257 U.S. 441 (1922), at p. 453.

name for his own store, with the result that some customers were misled into thinking that they were actually dealing with the competitor. The Court said:

While the Federal Trade Commission exercises under Section 5 the functions of both prosecutor and judge, the scope of its authority is strictly limited. A complaint may be filed only "if it shall appear to the Commission that a proceeding by it in respect thereof would be to the interest of the public." This requirement is not satisfied by proof that there has been misapprehension and confusion on the part of purchasers, or even that they have been deceived . . . to justify the Commission in filing a complaint under Section 5, the purpose must be protection of the public. The protection thereby afforded to private persons is the incident. Public interest may exist although the practice deemed unfair does not violate any private right. [The Court here cited the Beech-Nut case discussed above.][4]

The Raladam Case and "Injury to a Competitor." In the *Raladam* case, decided in 1931, the Court required (1) a showing that the methods involved "competition in commerce" in addition to (2) a showing that the methods were "unfair" and (3) that the proceeding was "in the interest of the public." This case involved the validity of a cease-and-desist order issued by the Commission to a respondent who had been advertising that his patent medicine was a safe and harmless way of removing "excess flesh of the human body," when, in fact, the Commission found, the preparation contained ingredients which might be harmful to health. The Court held in this case that, (1) since there was no evidence of *injury to a competitor* as a result of the false advertising, and (2) despite the fact that the product might be harmful to health, (3) the Commission had failed to make a case upon which the cease-and-desist order could be based. More specifically, the Court asserted:

By the plain words of the act, the power of the Commission to take steps looking to the issue of an order to desist depends upon the existence of three prerequisites: (1) that the methods complained of are *unfair*; (2) that they are methods of *competition* in commerce; and (3) that a proceeding by the Commission to prevent the use of the methods appears to be in the *interest of the public.*[5]

Moreover, the Court said:

. . . one of the facts necessary to support jurisdiction to make the final order to cease and desist, is the existence of competition; and the Commission cannot, by assuming the existence of competition, if in fact there be none, give itself jurisdiction to make such an order. . . .[6]

Thus, in the *Raladam* case, the Court made *injury to a competitor* an essential element of "unfair competition," just as this element had been required in a private action at common law in the *Washboard* case discussed earlier. The power of the Federal Trade Commission to inhibit false and deceptive practices was thus made contingent, among other things, upon its ability to show that the specific practices *actually* injured a competitor, and the Commission's power was accordingly limited. And so in its *Final Report on the Chain Store Investigation,* the FTC recommended that Congress amend Section 5 by also declaring "unfair or deceptive practices" in commerce unlawful (in addition to "unfair methods of competition in commerce"). This change in language was made by the Wheeler-Lea Act in 1938, as has been noted in Chapter 12 earlier. Cases subsequent to this amendment will be considered later in this chapter.

As we have just seen in the discussion of the *Beech-Nut* case above, the Court was willing, almost from the beginning, to permit the Commission to define "unfair methods of competition" by reference to the Court's decisions under the Sherman Act. This practice has continued to the present day and has been expanded also to include decisions under other antitrust statutes. Thus, in the *Cement Institute* case (discussed in Chapter 15), the Court found that the multiple basing point system of pricing constituted a violation both of Section 2(a) of the Robinson-Patman Act and of Section 5 of the Federal Trade Commission Act. The following three cases decided in 1965, 1966, and 1968 are also in point.

The Atlantic Refining Company Case and "Antitrust Guidelines" for Unfair Competition. The Atlantic Refining Company, a major producer and distributor of gasoline and oil products on the Eastern Seaboard, made

[4] *Federal Trade Commission* v. *Klesner,* 280 U.S. 19 (1929), at p. 27.
[5] *Federal Trade Commission* v. *Raladam Co.,* 283 U.S.

643 (1931), at pp. 646–647. (Italics in the original.)
[6] *Ibid.,* at p. 654.

an agreement prior to 1965 with the Goodyear Tire and Rubber Company to promote the sale of Goodyear products (batteries, tires, and tubes) to its wholesale and retail dealers and to assist in their resale, and in return it received a commission on all sales made to the wholesalers and dealers. The FTC found that Atlantic had used direct methods of coercion in the inauguration and promotion of the plan and, therefore, enjoined the use of these methods. There was no appeal taken from this particular finding or the order pertaining to it. However, the FTC also found that the sales-commission plan was "a classic example of the use of economic power in one market to destroy competition in another" and prohibited its use by Atlantic and Goodyear. The Court of Appeals affirmed the Commission's order; the Supreme Court also affirmed it in 1965. Among the important findings of fact in this aspect of the case were the following. Atlantic dealers were orally advised by sales officials of that oil company that their continued status as Atlantic dealers and lessees would be "in jeopardy" if they did not purchase "sufficient quantities" of Goodyear tires, batteries, and accessories. Some dealers, in fact, lost their leases when they did not comply with the Goodyear sales program. Moreover, the Court said: "Atlantic and its dealers did not bargain as equals. Among the sources of leverage in Atlantic's hands" were its "lease and equipment loan contracts with their cancellation and short-term provisions." Dealers were introduced to the program when they were visited by a *team* consisting of one Atlantic and one Goodyear sales representative. Goodyear had also made similar arrangements with 20 other oil companies. In upholding the Commission's cease-and-desist order, the Court said:

. . . We recognize that the Goodyear–Atlantic contract is not a tying arrangement. . . . But neither do we understand that either the Commission or the Court of Appeals held that the sales-commission arrangement was a tying scheme. What they did find was that the central competitive characteristic was the same in both cases—the utilization of economic power in one market to curtail competition in another. . . . As

our cases hold, all that is necessary in Section 5 proceedings to find a violation is to discover conduct that "runs counter to the public policy declared in the" Act. . . . But this is of necessity, and was intended to be, a standard to which the Commission would give substance. In doing so, its use as a guideline of recognized violations of the antitrust laws was, we believe, entirely appropriate. It has long been recognized that there are many unfair methods of competition that do not assume the proportions of antitrust violations. . . . When conduct does bear the characteristics of recognized antitrust violations it becomes suspect, and the Commission may properly look to cases applying those laws for guidance.

Although the Commission relied on such cases here, it expressly rejected a mechanical application of the law of tying arrangements. Rather it looked to the entire record as a basis for its conclusion that the activity of Goodyear and Atlantic impaired competition at three levels of the tires, batteries, and accessories industry. . . .

. . . the Commission was warranted in finding that the effect of the plan was *as though* Atlantic had agreed with Goodyear to require its dealers to buy Goodyear products and had done so. It is beyond question that the effect on commerce was not insubstantial. . . .[7]

The TBA Case and "Inherently Coercive" Marketing Systems. In 1968, the Court held that a marketing system under which Texaco, Inc. agreed with the Goodrich Company to promote the latter's products to the former's service dealers constituted a violation of Section 5, *even though* none of the coercive practices employed in the *Atlantic Refining Company* case were present. The Court stated that the FTC's determination of "unfair competition" was entitled to great weight, and that Texaco possessed "dominant economic power" over its dealers.[8] The *Texaco* case thus extended the principle of the *Atlantic Refining Company* case. Justice Stewart dissented from the majority opinion, but Justice Harlan concurred, saying, in effect, that although he had joined Justice Stewart in dissent in the *Atlantic Refining Company* case, he had now changed his mind and agreed with the majority view. The Court of Appeals issued its order in February 1969, and the Commission's final enforcement order was issued on March 19, 1969.

[7] *Atlantic Refining Co.* v. *Federal Trade Commission,* 381 U.S. 357 (1965), at pp. 369–370. (Italics in the original.)

[8] *Federal Trade Commission* v. *Texaco Inc., et. al.,* 393 U.S. 223 (1968).

Earlier, in 1966, the Court had referred in the *Second Brown Shoe Company* case with approval to its decision in the *Atlantic Refining Company* case and explained further the principle announced in the latter.

The Second Brown Shoe Company Case and "Trade Practices Which Conflict with the Basic Policy in the Sherman and Clayton Acts." In 1963, the Federal Trade Commission filed a complaint under Section 5 against the Brown Shoe Company, the country's second largest shoe manufacturer, alleging that it was an unfair trade practice for the company to make use of its "Franchise Stores Program" in selling its shoes to more than 650 retail shoe stores in the United States. The "Program" involved agreement by the retail shoe stores to sell Brown Shoe products, to refrain from selling the products of competitors, and also to adhere to Brown's resale price maintenance policy. In exchange for this agreement, the Brown Company provided the retail stores with various special services, including architectural services, a right to participate in group insurance at reduced rates, services of a field representative, and merchandising records. On the basis of these facts, the Commission held that the Program was an unfair method of competition under Section 5 and issued a cease-and-desist order. The Court of Appeals set aside the Commission's order on grounds that the Program did not represent an unfair method of competition in commerce. It also held that the Commission had not proved the existence of an exclusive dealing agreement which might violate Section 5. The Supreme Court reversed the Court of Appeals saying:

... We hold that the Commission has power to find, on the record here, such an anticompetitive practice unfair, subject of course to judicial review. . . .[9]

In announcing this holding, the Court cited the *Atlantic Refining Company* case, discussed above. Moreover, speaking for the majority, Justice Black remarked that the *Gratz* case (discussed earlier) had long since been overruled by the Court. He said:

In holding that the Federal Trade Commission lacked the power to declare Brown's program to be unfair the Court of Appeals was much

influenced by and quoted at length from this Court's opinion in *Federal Trade Comm'n* v. *Gratz.* . . . That case, decided shortly after the Federal Trade Commission Act was passed, construed the Act over a strong dissent by Mr. Justice Brandeis as giving the Commission very little power to declare any trade practice unfair. Later cases of this Court, however, have rejected the *Gratz* view and it is now recognized in line with the dissent of Mr. Justice Brandeis in *Gratz* that the Commission has broad powers to declare trade practices unfair [citing, among others, the *Cement Institute* and *Atlantic Refining Company* cases]. This broad power of the Commission is particularly well established with regard to trade practices which conflict with the basic policies of the Sherman and Clayton Acts even though such practices may not actually violate these laws. . . . [The Brown "Program"] obviously conflicts with the central policy of both Section 1 of the Sherman Act and Section 3 of the Clayton Act against contracts which take away freedom of purchasers to buy in an open market. Brown nevertheless contends that the Commission had no power to declare the franchise program unfair without proof that its effect "may be to substantially lessen competition or tend to create a monopoly" which of course would have to be proved if the Government were proceeding against Brown under Section 3 of the Clayton Act rather than Section 5 of the Federal Trade Commission Act. We reject the argument that proof of this Section 3 element must be made, for as we pointed out above, our cases hold that the Commission has power under Section 5 to arrest trade restraints in their incipence without proof that they amount to an outright violation of Section 3 of the Clayton Act or other provisions of the antitrust laws. This power of the Commission was emphatically stated in *F.T.C.* v. *Motion Picture Adv. Co.* . . . :

It is . . . clear that the Federal Trade Commission Act was designed to supplement and bolster the Sherman Act and the Clayton Act . . . to stop in their incipiency acts and practices which, when full blown, would violate those Acts . . . as well as to condemn as "unfair methods of competition" existing violations of them.[10]

The Phillips Petroleum Case and the "Joint Venture as Unfair Competition." The language of the *Second Brown Shoe* case confers broad discretionary authority upon the Commission in cases involving "the policy of the Sherman and Clayton Acts." And, as we have seen in Chapter 17, in the *Penn-Olin* case the Court had held that a joint venture

---

[9] *Federal Trade Commission* v. *Brown Shoe Co., Inc.*, 384 U.S. 316 (1966), at p. 320.

[10] *Ibid.*, at pp. 320–322.

constituted a merger in violation of Section 7 on the basis of the facts involved in that case. It follows under the doctrine of the *Second Brown Shoe* case that such a merger may also constitute a violation of Section 5 of the Federal Trade Commission Act. Accordingly, in August 1966, after its victory in the *Second Brown Shoe* case, the Commission signed a consent agreement with the Phillips Petroleum Company and the National Distillers and Chemical Corporation based both on Section 7 of the Clayton Act and on Section 5 of the FTC Act. The Commission's charge, in obvious reliance on the decision in the *Penn-Olin* case, included the specification that, *but for* a joint venture by Phillips Petroleum and National Distillers and Chemical (the leading producers of polyolefin resins), both firms would have *separately* entered into the production of polypropylene resin. The FTC order required not only dissolution of the joint venture but also divestiture of the assets of the joint venture. In addition, the FTC order banned future acquisitions without prior approval of the FTC by Phillips and National in the polyolefin field for a period of five to ten years.[11]

The FTC and Restraint of Trade by Pathologists and Blood Banks. Another interesting action by the FTC under Section 5 of the FTC Act, based also upon "the policy of the Sherman and Clayton Acts," was finally decided by the Commission in October 1966. In this case, the Commission upheld a finding of fact by a Hearing Examiner made in 1964 that the Community Blood Bank of the Kansas City Area, Inc., the Kansas City Area Hospital Association, and the hospital members of the association individually, as well as these hospitals' pathologists, had illegally conspired to restrain interstate commerce in whole human blood by refusing to accept blood from two properly licensed commercial blood banks in the Kansas City Area, with the objective of "inhibiting the operations of the commercial blood banks." The effect of the restraint so imposed was to prevent the commercial blood banks from supplying the major hospitals in the Kansas City area and to prevent them from forming donor's clubs or selling blood assurance or blood provider contracts. The real purpose of the restraint, according to the Commission, was to insure the success of the community-sponsored blood bank and to impose more rigid standards upon blood banks than those which were imposed by the official licensing agencies. Two of the Commissioners dissented from the majority opinion in this case on the grounds that the defendants were nonprofit organizations and were thus outside the Commission's jurisdiction, and that the evidence did not establish a *concerted* refusal to deal. Moreover, argued the dissenters, the defendants were acting on the basis of their "medical judgment" in imposing the standards which they set.[12] The argument was thus about what the evidence implied.

It is interesting to note also that the initial decision of the Hearing Examiner in this case in 1964 gave rise to the introduction of S. 2560 in the Senate. This bill was commonly called "the blood bank bill" and was designed to exempt from the antitrust laws the actions of nonprofit blood banks.[13] The proposed legislation was not enacted into law by the 88th Congress.

B. "UNFAIR OR DECEPTIVE ACTS OR PRACTICES IN COMMERCE"

Review of the Law Concerning "Unfair" or "Deceptive" Practices up to 1938

Prior to 1938, as we have seen in the preceding subdivision, cases involving "unfair" or "deceptive" practices were necessarily treated as cases of "unfair methods of competition" under Section 5 of the FTC Act. Moreover, under the *Raladam* and *Klesner* cases, the power of the Federal Trade Commission in this area was sharply limited by the requirements that *not only* a substantial public interest *but also* injury to a

---

[11] Federal Trade Commission Consent Order C-1088, reported in the FTC's *News Summary* of August 8, 1966. Actions of labor unions which would constitute violations of the Sherman Act are also unlawful under Section 5. See FTC I.D. 8691, April 18, 1968.

[12] Federal Trade Commission Final Order 8519,

reported in the FTC's *News Summary* of October 27, 1966.

[13] *Blood Banks and Antitrust Laws* (Hearings before the Subcommittee on Antitrust and Monopoly of the Senate Judiciary Committee, 88th Cong., 2d sess.) (Washington, D.C.: U.S. Government Printing Office, 1964), pp. 103–131.

competitor had to be shown. Thus, unless a deceptive practice injured a competitor, the practice could not be enjoined even though it might be harmful to the public. This limitation on the Commission's power was removed by the addition of the words "unfair or deceptive acts or practices in commerce" to the original prohibition in Section 5 by the Wheeler-Lea Act in 1938.

The Meaning of "In Commerce"

In 1941, the Supreme Court held that the use of the words "in commerce" did not mean "affecting commerce," and thereby prohibited the Commission from acting in deceptive practice cases involving purely local activities. The Commission had sought to prevent Bunte Bros. Candy Company from selling candy under circumstances involving a gambling feature. The Company's activities all occurred within the State of Illinois, but the Commission had prevented other candy sellers (who engaged in interstate commerce) from adopting similar selling schemes. The Commission claimed that the Bunte Brothers' activities competed with those of other sellers and thus the Commission had jurisdiction but, in a 6 to 3 decision, the Supreme Court held otherwise.[11a] The cases to be discussed next have to do with the power of the Commission under Section 5 as amended and thus interpreted.

Policy Concerning "Unfair" or "Deceptive" Practices Since the Wheeler-Lea Amendment

The Charles of the Ritz Case and "Irrelevance of Actual Deception." One question which arises under amended Section 5 is whether the Commission must show that there has been *actual* deception of purchasers before it can enjoin a practice. The courts have answered this question in the negative. Thus the action of the Commission was upheld when it issued an order to a producer of cosmetics to cease and desist from advertising its "Rejuvenescence [face] Cream" as one which restored "natural moisture necessary for a live healthy skin" and which restored youth or the appearance of youth. The defendant attacked the FTC's finding of fact that the preparation did not act as a rejuvenating agent and did

not restore or preserve the youthful appearance of the skin. According to the Court of Appeals: "Two medical experts testified for the Commission; and both affirmatively stated that there was nothing known to medical science which could bring about such results." This testimony was not contradicted; but the defendant argued that since "neither expert had ever used Rejuvenescence Cream or knew what it contained"—the defendant being unwilling to disclose its secret formula—the experts' testimony did not provide a sufficient basis for the finding of fact by the Commission that the defendant's claim was false. The defendant claimed also that the Commission had not produced a single witness who believed that the cream would actually rejuvenate, and therefore there was no deception! The Court of Appeals pointed out that the failure of the defendant to disclose the true formula of its preparation was "strong confirmation of the Commission's charges" and further that *actual* deception of the public *need not* be shown in such Federal Trade Commission cases. Specifically, the Court of Appeals said of the Federal Trade Commission Act:

That law was not "made for the protection of experts, but for the public—that vast multitude which includes the ignorant, the unthinking and the credulous". . . . The important criterion is the net impression which the advertisement is likely to make upon the general populace . . . while the wise and the wordly may well realize the falsity of any representations that the present product can roll back the years, there remains "that vast multitude" of others who, like Ponce De Leon, still seek a perpetual fountain of youth. As the Commission's expert further testified, the average woman, conditioned by talk in magazines and over the radio of "vitamins, hormones, and God knows what," might take "rejuvenescence" to mean that this "is one of the modern miracles" and is "something which would actually cause her youth to be restored." It is for this reason that the Commission may "insist upon the most literal truthfulness" in advertisements. . . .[14]

The Alberty Case and "Informative Advertising." Despite the statement in the *Charles of the Ritz* case quoted above that the Commission may "insist upon the most literal truthfulness," one Court of Appeals sub-

---

11a *FTC* v. *Bunte Brothers*, 312 U.S. 349 (1941).
14 *Charles of the Ritz Distributors Corp.* v. *Federal*   *Trade Commission*, 143 F. 2d 676 (1944), at pp. 679–680.

sequently held that the power to prohibit false advertising does not include the affirmative power to require additional advertising which the Commission "deems properly informative." In the *Alberty* case, the Commission found as a fact that the defendant was advertising certain pills produced by the defendant as a "tonic for the blood" but that the tablets in question had no beneficial effect except in cases of iron deficiency anemia. The Commission then prohibited the defendant from making certain claims in his advertisements and ordered him also to state in his advertisements that "the condition of lassitude is caused less frequently by simple iron deficiency anemia than by other causes and in such cases this preparation will not be effective in relieving or correcting it." A majority of the Court of Appeals held that the Commission did not have the power to impose such a requirement (calling for the inclusion of affirmative statements in this advertising) on the defendant. The majority stated:

Even if we give effect to the broadest possible concept of the power conferred by the Congress upon the Commission, we do not think that the Commission has the power here claimed. There is a limit to the Commission's power. It is not given a general charter to police the expenditure of the public's money or generally to do whatever is considered by it to be good and beneficial.[15]

The problem raised by the *Alberty* case is not unrelated to the problem of "truth in packaging and labeling," a topic which is discussed in Subdivision D of this chapter.

A more recent case involving issues related to those raised in the *Alberty* case was decided by the Commission in July 1966. This case is the *Vitasafe* case, in which a Hearing Examiner initially found that the marketers of "Vitasafe" and "Life Nutrition," vitamin-mineral preparations, were misrepresenting these preparations by claiming that they were a new scientific and medical discovery which would (1) increase and stimulate sexual activity, (2) be of value in preventing colds, (3) increase intelligence and mental alertness, (4) relieve or prevent melancholia and discomfort due

to menstruation, and (5) relieve or prevent fears or anxieties arising from contemplation of the onset of old age. In addition, the Hearing Examiner found that the defendants were falsely advertising that their capsules would be beneficial in treating and relieving tiredness, nervousness, depression, loss of happiness, loss of a sense of well-being, and similar symptoms. He further found that the capsules would be beneficial only in cases of a deficiency of Vitamins B_1, B_2, or C, or of niacinamide. The remaining 20 ingredients would be of no benefit in treating the symptoms itemized above. He also found that the advertisements were misleading in failing to reveal that in a great majority of cases the symptoms itemized above are not due to a lack of any of the ingredients contained in the capsules. The Commission upheld the Hearing Examiner's findings, and its cease-and-desist order permitted advertising representing the capsules as being beneficial in cases involving the itemized symptoms *only if* the advertising also was expressly limited to those cases due to a deficiency of the four ingredients listed above, *and if* the advertising clearly and conspicuously disclosed the material facts found.[16] Thus, instead of issuing an order requiring the defendant to make unconditional affirmative statements in his advertising, the Commission has found a way to escape the ruling of the *Alberty* case by specifying that the advertising in question is misleading *if* it fails to make certain disclosures of fact. The defendant is, of course, not required to advertise.

The Colgate-Palmolive Case and Deceptive Television Commercials. In April 1965, the Supreme Court handed down a significant decision affirming the broad discretionary power of the FTC to prohibit deceptive television commercials. The commercial in question "purported to give viewers visual proof that the advertiser's shaving cream could soften 'sandpaper,' but unknown to viewers the substance that appeared to be sandpaper . . . was in fact a simulated prop, or 'mock-up,' made of plexiglass to which sand had been applied."[17] The FTC had

---

[15] *Alberty et. al.* v. *Federal Trade Commission*, 182 F. 2d 36 (1950), at pp. 38–39.
[16] Federal Trade Commission Final Orders 8636 and 8637, reported in the FTC's *News Summary* of

July 20, 1966.
[17] *Federal Trade Commission* v. *Colgate-Palmolive Co. et. al.*, 380 U.S. 374 (1965), at p. 374.

held a hearing and issued an order which appeared to prohibit all use of undisclosed simulations in the defendant's television commercials. The Court of Appeals set the order aside on grounds that it was too broad, and the FTC then appealed to the Supreme Court. The Supreme Court reversed the Court of Appeals. In doing so, it said:

In reviewing the substantive issues in the case, it is well to remember the respective roles of the Commission and the courts in the administration of the Federal Trade Commission Act. When the Commission was created by Congress in 1914, it was directed by Section 5 to prevent "[u]nfair methods of competition in commerce." Congress amended the Act in 1938 to extend the Commission's jurisdiction to include "unfair or deceptive acts or practices in commerce"—a significant amendment showing Congress' concern for consumers as well as for competitors. It is important to note the generality of these standards of illegality; the proscriptions in Section 5 are flexible, "to be defined with particularity by the myriad of cases from the field of business." . . .

This statutory scheme necessarily gives the Commission an influential role in interpreting Section 5 and in applying it to the facts of particular cases arising out of unprecedented situations. Moreover, as an administrative agency which deals continually with cases in the area, the Commission is often in a better position than are courts to determine when a practice is "deceptive" within the meaning of the Act. This Court has frequently stated that the Commission's judgment is to be given great weight by reviewing courts. This admonition is especially true with respect to allegedly deceptive advertising since the finding of a Section 5 violation in this field rests so heavily on inference and pragmatic judgment. Nevertheless, while informed judicial determination is dependent upon enlightenment gained from administrative experience, in the last analysis the words "deceptive practices" set forth a legal standard and they must get their final meaning from judicial construction. . . .[18]

The Court then accepted the Commission's finding of fact as "warranted by the evidence." The case is important because it shows that the Court is prepared to go a long way in upholding the Commission in cases involving "deceptive practices."

Even before the Supreme Court's decision in the *Colgate-Palmolive* case, the FTC had acted in other cases to prohibit deceptive television commercials. Thus, in 1962 the Commission issued an order to prevent the makers of "Rise" shaving cream from unfavorably depicting competitors' products in television commercials by a chemical substance especially prepared to simulate "ordinary" shaving cream, a substance which was formulated in such a way as to come from the can "in a good puff" and then disappear quickly to give the impression of drying up rapidly, thereby conveying the impression that "Rise" shaving cream was a superior product which did not dry up as rapidly as did "ordinary" shaving cream. In issuing the order,[19] the Commission cited its own earlier order in the *Colgate-Palmolive* case which had been issued in 1961, even though the final Supreme Court decision upholding that order did not come until 1965. Also in 1962, a Hearing Examiner issued an order prohibiting General Motors and the Libbey-Owens-Ford Glass Company from using deceptive television camera techniques comparing optical distortions in automobile safety *plate* glass and automobile safety *sheet* glass. The commercials were designed to show that there is no perceptible distortion when objects are viewed through safety *plate* glass, but that there is distortion when the same objects are viewed through safety *sheet* glass. Some of the scenes of the sheet glass were photographed through a telephoto lens while some of those of plate glass were photographed through an ordinary lens. The telephoto lens magnified everything, *including the distortion*. Also, in several instances, the safety plate glass scenes were photographed through an open window containing *no* glass at all; such scenes, of course, showed no distortion. And, in a comparison of plate glass with home window glass, the latter was streaked with vaseline, giving the appearance of greater distortion. Again, the opinion in the *Colgate-Palmolive* case was cited.[20]

In the case of "Rise" shaving cream, the Commission's order applied not only to the manufacturer whose product was being deceptively advertised but also to the

---

[18] *Ibid.*, at pp. 384–385.
[19] Federal Trade Commission Order 7943, reported in the FTC's *News Summary* of May 9, 1962.

[20] Federal Trade Commission Initial Decision 7643, reported in the FTC's *News Summary* of August 7, 1962.

advertising firm which prepared the television commercial in question. In 1966 the Commission also issued an order to Merck and Company, Inc. and to its advertising agent to cease and desist from its false germ-killing and pain-relieving claims for "Sucrets" and "Children's Sucrets" in a television commercial. This commercial contained a depiction of the extinction of a flame, representing pain, to create an impression that the advertised product would be effective in removing the cause of pain by killing germs or helping to fight infection, thereby leading a viewer to believe that the product would provide more than temporary relief.[21]

The Commission has also used the procedure of accepting voluntary assurances of compliance to secure discontinuance of misleading television commercials. Thus, in March 1969, the Commission obtained such an assurance from Lever Brothers Company, Inc. The objectionable television commercial in question involved advertising of the laundry detergent "3B" All. The commercial began by showing an actor wearing a stained garment; he then poured "3B" All into a tank of rising water, commenting on the cleaning power of the substance and immersed himself in the tank to chin depth, emerging wearing a garment free from stain. The Commission learned that the stain was not removed by the immersion depicted but by washing it in the ordinary way in a washing machine.

Also in March 1969, the Commission announced that it had initiated an intensified program for the monitoring of advertising on national television networks, and in June 1969 it issued an order to the National Broadcasting Company to submit a report of commercials broadcast at certain times after this network "failed to comply satisfactorily" with the Commission's earlier request that all three networks voluntarily submit such reports.

The FTC and Misrepresentation of Television Audience Surveys. As early as 1962, the FTC began looking into the complex problem of measurement of the size of television audiences upon which the sale of sponsorship of particular television programs is often based. Consent orders were thereupon signed early in 1963 by C-E-I-R, Inc., the Pulse, Inc., and the A. C. Nielsen Company, in which these three concerns agreed not to misrepresent the accuracy of their audience measurements nor to use survey techniques causing error or bias in their survey reports.[22]

Indeed, the situation concerning claims of broadcast coverage had reached such a point in 1965 that the Commission felt it desirable to issue a statement concerning such claims and laying down guidelines including specification of sampling techniques to avoid deception and distortion.

The Mary Carter Paint Company Case and "Deceptive Pricing." An interesting case involving "deceptive pricing" was decided by the Supreme Court in November 1965. This case involved the validity of an FTC order requiring the Mary Carter Paint Company to discontinue its "deceptive 'free' and related" pricing claims. A majority of the Commission had found the following advertising claims to be false:

> "Buy only Half the Paint You Need"
> "Every Second Can Free of Extra Cost"
> "Buy 1 and get 1 Free"
> "I am satisfied with pennies per gallon! . . . You buy only half the paint you need! . . . The rest is free of extra cost"
> "These Mary Carter Paint Factories will be making free paint half the coming year."
> "ACRYLIC ROL-LATEX
> $2.25 Quart $6.98 Gallon
> Every 2nd CAN FREE OF EXTRA COST."

More specifically, the Commission had ruled that the *purported* regular price charged by the company for a *single* can was actually the *customary* price of *two* cans and that the second can was not a gift or gratuity as claimed in the advertising.[23]

The decision by the Commission in the *Mary Carter* case was appealed to a Court of Appeals which set aside the Commission's order but which was then itself reversed in November 1965 by the Supreme Court. The Supreme Court's majority opinion was brief and to the point. Among other things, the Court said in part:

[21] Federal Trade Commission Final Order 8635, reported in the FTC's *News Summary* of April 27, 1966.

[22] Federal Trade Commission Consent Orders C–289, C–290, and C–291, reported in the FTC's *News Summary* of January 10, 1963.

[23] Federal Trade Commission Order 8290, reported in the FTC's *News Summary* of July 17, 1962.

... In sum, the Commission found that Mary Carter had no history of selling single cans of paint; it was marketing twins, and in allocating what is in fact the price of two cans to one can, yet calling one "free," Mary Carter misrepresented ... it is arguable that any deception was limited to a representation that Mary Carter has a usual and customary price for single cans of paint, when it has no such price. However, it is not for courts to say whether this violates the Act. "[T]he Commission is often in a better position than are courts to determine when a practice is 'deceptive' within the meaning of the Act." ... There was substantial evidence in the record to support the Commission's finding. ...[24]

This decision also indicates the extent to which the Court is today prepared to recognize the "expertise" of the Commission, even in such matters as the meaning of "deception" under the law. In 1966, the Commission issued a new order finally settling the case.

The procedure and course of events in the *Mary Carter* case illustrate well the process by which specific working rules of economic activity are formulated in adversary proceedings and by interaction of regulatory commissions and courts. The problem of deceptive pricing, as illustrated by the *Mary Carter Paint* case, has also appeared in a different form in the case of the so-called "cents-off" pricing of groceries, a topic which will be further considered in connection with the Fair Packaging and Labeling Act of 1966, in Subdivision D of this chapter.

Montgomery Ward and the "Unconditional Guarantee." Another interesting case was the subject of a final order in August 1966. This case involved a decision by a majority of the Commission that Montgomery Ward and Company, Inc. had violated the FTC Act by advertising various products as *unconditionally guaranteed* and then furnishing the customer with a guarantee certificate subject to numerous limitations. The company's defense—that as a matter of policy, but unknown to its customers, it would honor guarantees as advertised, irrespective of limitations stated in the guarantee certificates—was rejected. In fact, the

Commission held that, in addition to being false and deceptive insofar as Ward's customers were concerned, the advertisements also constituted "unfair methods of competition" under Section 5 of the FTC Act.[25] In October 1966, the Commission denied Ward's petition for a rehearing on grounds that the petition raised no new issues which had not been considered in the earlier proceedings. The Commission's position in the *Montgomery Ward* case was affirmed by a Court of Appeals in 1967.[26] Neither in 1969, nor in 1970 were any deceptive practice cases decided by the Supreme Court.

The Deceptive Sales Practices Bill. In its *Annual Report for Fiscal Year 1967*, the Commission recommended to Congress that the FTC Act be amended to give the Commission power to obtain injunctions to prohibit deceptive practices whenever the Commission has issued or intends to issue a complaint. The injunction would thus be issued *in advance* of a formal finding by the Commission.

S. 3065 was introduced during the 90th Congress to implement the FTC's request. Although the Senate passed the bill, it was not enacted into law, despite strong Administration support for it.[27]

A formal statement in the form of a letter in support of the bill was sent to the Senate Commerce Committee by the Chairman of the FTC, Paul Rand Dixon. This formal statement is interesting for several reasons but for one in particular. In addition to expressing the reasons for enactment of the legislation, Chairman Dixon referred to various other statutes (discussed later in this chapter) authorizing the FTC to prohibit deceptive practices in specific cases and added the statement that "The Bureau of the Budget advises that enactment of this bill would be in accordance with the program of the President," a statement which throws some light on the extent to which the so-called "independent commissions" are in fact independent of the Executive Branch in regard to basic policy issues.[28]

[24] *Federal Trade Commission* v. *Mary Carter Paint Co. et. al.*, 382 U.S. 46 (1965), at pp. 48–49.

[25] Federal Trade Commission Final Order 8617, reported in the FTC's *News Summary* of August 8, 1966.

[26] *Montgomery Ward, Inc.* v. *FTC*, 379 F. 2d 666 (1967).

[27] *Unfair and Deceptive Practices in the Home Improvement Industry and Amendments to the FTC Act* (Hearings before the Senate Commerce Committee, 90th Cong., 2d sess., 1968) (Washington, D.C.: U.S. Government Printing Office, 1968).

[28] *Ibid.*, pp. 11–13.

C. SPECIAL LEGISLATION PERTAINING TO ADVERTISING AND LABELING ENFORCED BY THE FEDERAL TRADE COMMISSION

This Subdivision is concerned with an explanation of the way in which the original authority of the FTC pertaining to advertising and labeling has been affected by various special statutes *other than* the FTC Act, for example, by the Wool Products Act. In some cases, the FTC's power has been broadened; in others, it has been limited. The particular legislation involved is further identified in the description of its enforcement which follows.

Special Legislation Pertaining to Wool, Flammable Fabrics, Fur, and Textile Fiber Products

Four separate statutes dealing with the labeling of wool, flammable fabrics, fur, and textile fiber products are administered by the FTC's Bureau of Textiles and Furs. The nature of this special legislation was explained by FTC Chairman Paul Rand Dixon in the course of his testimony before Congress on the Fair Packaging and Labeling Act of 1966. Mr. Dixon said:

The Commission has been given specific authority by Congress to administer four labeling laws: the Wool Products Labeling Act, 1941; the Fur Products Labeling Act, 1952; the Flammable Fabrics Act, 1954; and the Textile Fiber Products Identification Act, 1960.

Gratifying results have been achieved from the enforcement of these laws in affording protection not only to consumers who purchase such products, but also to honest merchants and sellers.

The Wool Products Labeling Act covers the labeling of any product containing woolen fiber. It is the first act of this nature passed by Congress which provides for an affirmative act of labeling textile products. It covers both domestic and imported wool merchandise from the first manufacturing process applied to the wool until the wool is made into cloth and other end products.

Notable among the products covered would be men's, women's, and children's outer clothing, overcoats, jackets, mackinaws, skirts, slacks, sweaters, hosiery, wool hats, and even wool house slippers.

The Fur Products Labeling Act covers the labeling, invoicing, and advertising of fur products from the manufacturer right on through to their sale to consumers.

The Flammable Fabrics Act, effective in 1954, prohibits the introduction or movement in interstate commerce of articles of wearing apparel and fabrics which are so highly flammable as to be dangerous when worn by individuals.

The Textile Fiber Products Identification Act became effective in 1960 and it has by far the greatest coverage of any of the labeling acts. It covers items made of natural fibers other than wool, reprocessed wool, and reused wool, as well as products which are composed of synthetic fibers or blends of synthetic or natural fibers. The labeling requirements of the Fur Products Labeling Act are also present here in substantially the same general fashion.

... these acts ... have demonstrated the effectiveness of congressional action directing an administrative agency to issue regulations which are to have the effect of law. Once this is done and they are violated, it is a per se law violation.[29]

The Flammable Fabrics Act Amendment of 1967

The Flammable Fabrics Act was amended in 1967 to provide increased protection to consumers.[30] Some indication of the importance of this legislation can be gained by examining the testimony in 1967 in support of this legislation by FTC Chairman Paul Rand Dixon. Mr. Dixon said in part:

The bill would add an entire new section 14 which authorizes investigation and research. It provides that the Secretary of Health, Education, and Welfare, in cooperation with the Secretary of Commerce would annually study and investigate deaths, injuries, and economic losses resulting from accidental burning of products, fabrics, or related materials, and submit an annual report to the President and Congress.

This new section also authorizes the Secretary of Commerce to conduct research into the flammability of products, fabrics, and materials, conduct feasibility studies on reducing flammability, develop flammability test techniques, and offer appropriate flammability test training; he would also be required annually to report to Congress on the result of his research activities....

The Federal Trade Commission has gained considerable experience in administering the Flammable Fabrics Act. For example, since January 1, 1961, the Commission has issued 46

---

[29] *Fair Packaging and Labeling* (Hearings before the House Committee on Interstate and Foreign Commerce, 89th Cong., 2d sess.) (Washington, D.C.: U.S.

Government Printing Office, 1966), Part 1, pp. 38–41.

[30] P.L. 90–189, 90th Cong., 1st sess., December 14, 1967.

orders under the provisions of this act. During the period from April 1962 to date, the Commission has also accepted 261 assurances of voluntary compliance under this act. The orders pertain to such fabrics or wearing apparel as wood fibers, napped fleece fabrics, silk illusions, scarves, dresses, leis, bridal illusions, silk squares, and rayon fabrics. With the exception of napped fleece fabrics, the rest of those examples were on imported goods. The question was put, where do these dangerous goods come from? I might say with the exception of those cases that were napped fleece fabrics, I have been told by our Bureau Chief, that the rest of them are important. . . .

Recently, I am informed, a fire was caused by the ignition of a baby's cotton receiving blanket when the mother was lighting a cigarette. Fortunately, she was able to remove the blanket and there was no injury. There is little question but that such blankets, with a highly brushed surface, are dangerously flammable even under the tests set forth in the present act; however, the Commission has been unable to take action against them because it would not appear that these blankets come under the provisions of the existing law. They were read out during the hearings before the committee when the act was passed.

The staff of the Commission found that cotton and rayon pile bed blankets which have raised surfaces are highly flammable although not covered under the existing act. I think you held up a piece of that material.

I might add that the Department of Health, Education, and Welfare estimates that 2 million people are burned in the United States from all causes each year, and about 100,000 of these victims require hospitalization. Undoubtedly many of these fatalities and injuries are related to textiles and interior furnishings. . . .

The statistics already collected by the Department of Health, Education, and Welfare show many instances of children being burned because of wearing flammable clothing.

Therefore, we suggest that the Secretary of Health, Education, and Welfare, in cooperation with the Secretary of Commerce in its study and investigation of death and injuries resulting from the accidental burning of products, as provided by section 14 of S. 1003, keep the object of fire resistant clothing for children constantly in view. When there is a breakthrough by science in the development of a suitable means of providing such safety to our children, at a reasonable cost to their parents, appropriate recommendations may

be made to Congress for this type of legislation in addition to that proposed in S. 1003.

While we can give no assurance that enactment of S. 1003 will lead to immediate and startling reductions in the rate of death and injury from flammable products, we believe that such enactment will greatly strengthen the effectiveness of the Flammable Fabrics Act and again I reiterate the strong approval of this bill by the Federal Trade Commission.[31]

Examples of Special FTC Enforcement Activity

The nature of the FTC's work in relation to the special legislation dealing with particular types of products can be illustrated by some brief examples. In 1965, the FTC charged Waltham Athleticwear with not labeling its woolen samples and products with the information required by the Wool Products Labeling Act, and further charged that "some wool products contained substantially different amounts and types of fibers than represented on labels and invoices and in advertising," and that "required information was abbreviated on labels."[32] Also worth noting is the fact that the Commission eventually settled the case by means of a consent order; a practice (discussed in Chapter 20) which it has been increasingly using in such cases.

Action under the Flammable Fabrics Act is illustrated by an initial decision ordering Novik and Company to stop importing and selling dangerously flammable European silk bridal veil fabrics (illusion net), and to stop furnishing false guarantees to customers to the effect that these articles "are guaranteed to meet the tests required by the Flammable Fabrics Act." According to the Hearing Examiner, laboratory tests had been made on 20 samples of the material, and not one sample met the flammability requirements of Section 4 of the Act. The defendants argued that "silk illusion as used in a bridal veil is not an 'article of wearing apparel' as defined in the Act and is not subject to its provision." The Examiner held that "the evidence shows, and common knowledge indicates, that bridal veils have such proximity to the upper part of the

[31] *Flammable Fabrics Act Amendments of 1967* (Hearings before the Senate Committee on Commerce, 90th Cong., 1st sess., 1967) (Washington, D.C.: U.S. Government Printing Office, 1967), pp. 54–55.

[32] Federal Trade Commission Consent Order C–989, reported in the FTC's *News Summary* of September 22, 1965.

body as to constitute in the statutory language a 'covering for the neck, face, or shoulders.' "[33] It is interesting to note that in January 1967 the Commission rescinded its previous interpretation of Section 2(d) of the Act. The previous interpretation (issued in June 1954) was that ornamental millinery veils or veilings, when used in conjunction with or as part of a hat, were excluded from coverage by the law. Under the new interpretation, the question becomes one of fact to be determined in each specific case.

Action pertaining to fur products is illustrated by the issuance in 1969 of a consent order prohibiting Jack Felt, Inc., a manufacturer of fur trimmed ladies' apparel, from misbranding and falsely invoicing fur products.[34]

Consent orders are also used in cases involving textile fiber products. For example, the FTC charged Daly Brothers with using labels and advertising certain textile fiber products which did not contain the information required by the Textile Fiber Products Identification Act. Certain fibers were not named nor fiber content completely disclosed. The words "linen-look" and "Linen Weaves" falsely represented in the advertisements that linen fiber was present, and wearing apparel was advertised by a fiber trademark (such as "Arnel") without indicating the true generic name of the fiber or fibers. In addition, the FTC alleged that custom-made drapes sold by Daly Brothers were not labeled with required information. The case was settled by a consent agreement between the company and the Commission's counsel.[35]

The Drug Amendments of 1962

Since 1962, the FTC has voluntarily sought to reconcile the authority which it possesses under the Federal Trade Commission Act with the authority given to the Food and Drug Administration under the Federal Food, Drug, and Cosmetic Act of 1938, as amended by the passage of the Drug Amendments of 1962. In fact, the FTC took the position that "Congress, in the Drug Amendments of 1962, desired to avoid both regulatory gaps and regulatory conflicts in the policing of prescription-drug advertising by the Federal Trade Commission and the Food and Drug Administration." (The Food and Drug Administration and the relevant legislation under which it operates will be discussed later in this book.) In addition, according to the Commission: "The Drug Amendments of 1962 were clearly not intended to repeal the Commission's authority under Section 5 to proceed, where appropriate to prevent any regulatory gap, against unfair or deceptive representations in the marketing of prescription drugs." In practice, in cases in which the Food and Drug Administration asserted jurisdiction, the Federal Trade Commission deferred to such assertions and renounced its own claims to jurisdiction. It has remained free to act, however, under the food and drug sections (12 through 17) of the Federal Trade Commission Act, as well as under Section 5 of that Act, if the Food and Drug Administration does not assert a jurisdictional claim. The FTC has thus adopted what might be described as a policy of "amicable accommodation" in regard to the jurisdictional question, thereby avoiding a situation which might have given rise to an interagency dispute with a resulting loss of protection to the public.

For example, in October 1964 the FTC dismissed its charges against Chas. Pfizer and Company of having "misrepresented the extent of the clinical testing of its prescription drug 'Enarax,' used primarily in treating gastrointestinal disorders." (The FTC's original complaint had been filed in 1960, before the passage of the Drug Amendments.) In basing its dismissal "on the assertion by the Food and Drug Administration that it has jurisdiction over the advertising involved, the Commission stated it 'will take such further action in this area as may be warranted in the public interest' if the FDA's jurisdictional assertion proves to be in any way unfounded."[36]

[33] Federal Trade Commission Initial Decision 8452, reported in the FTC's *News Summary* of June 11, 1962.

[34] Federal Trade Commission Consent Order C–1506, reported in the FTC's *News Summary* of April 2, 1969.

[35] Federal Trade Commission Consent Order C–911, reported in the FTC's *News Summary* of July 2, 1965.

[36] See Federal Trade Commission Dismissal Order 7780 as reported in the FTC's *News Summary* of October 30, 1964.

Automobile Tires and the National Traffic and Motor Vehicle Safety Act of 1966

Prior to the adoption of automobile safety legislation in 1966, the FTC had concerned itself with the problem of advertising and labeling of automobile tires. Indeed, trade practice rules were first adopted in 1936, and tire advertising guides were promulgated in 1958. New Tire Advertising and Labeling Guides, pertaining to safety, grading, quality, and guarantees, were issued in August 1966 to take effect in February, 1967. The adoption of Section 201 of the National Traffic and Motor Vehicle Safety Act of September 1966, subsequent to the issuance of the FTC's August 1966 guides, placed responsibility for enforcement of certain labeling provisions in the hands of the Secretary of Commerce. The Department of Transportation Act of October 1966, in turn, provided that the Secretary of the newly created Department of Transportation was to establish a National Traffic Safety Bureau to which the enforcement responsibilities of the Secretary of Commerce were to be transferred. Pending the issuance of regulations by the latter, the Commission's guides were to remain in force. Moreover, the FTC retained the power to act to fill "regulatory gaps" in this area under the general provisions of Section 5 of the FTC Act in the same way as that in which it retained similar power under the Drug Amendments of 1962.

Special Legislation Pertaining to Cigarettes

Although at one time the Commission sought to regulate the advertising of cigarettes by requiring that cigarette labeling and advertising contain an affirmative warning of the health hazards of cigarette smoking, Congress sharply limited the FTC's authority in this area on July 27, 1965, by adopting the Federal Cigarette Labeling and Advertising Act. This Act required that after January 1, 1966, every package of cigarettes conspicuously display the following statement: "Caution: Cigarette Smoking May be Hazardous to Your Health." However, this Act also provided that no different statement relating to smoking and health "shall be required" on any cigarette package; and that for a period ending on July 1, 1969, no such statement "shall be required" in the advertising of any cigarettes the packages of which are labeled in accordance with the Act. The effect of this legislation was, of course, to limit the FTC's power to require affirmative statements in cigarette advertising for four years; however, the FTC continued to hold to the position, which was supported by an explicit statement in the new legislation, that its authority with respect to unfair or deceptive acts or practices in the advertising of cigarettes was unaffected by the Act. Indeed, the day after enactment of the new legislation, the Commission announced that it would continue to monitor current practices and methods of cigarette advertising and promotion and take all action, consistently with the new legislation, to prohibit all advertising which violated the FTC Act.[37]

As a matter of fact, the Commission subsequently took the position that "it is in the public interest to promote the dissemination of truthful information concerning cigarettes which may be material and desired by the consuming public." Accordingly, in November 1966 it scheduled a hearing on methods to be employed in determining tar and nicotine content in cigarettes.[38]

In December 1969, the Senate adopted a bill to prohibit advertising of cigarettes on radio or television after January 1, 1971. The proposed legislation would also require all packages of cigarettes to carry the following warning: "Cigarette smoking is dangerous to your health." Much earlier, in June 1967, the Federal Communications Commission ruled that television and radio stations must give time equal to that given to cigarette advertising to those opposing the use of tobacco, and in January 1969 the Commission announced it was going to consider a rule prohibiting the broadcasting of cigarette commercials by radio and television stations.

---

[37] Statement of the FTC, reported in the FTC's *News Summary* of August 10, 1965.

[38] The announcement appeared in the FTC's *News Summary* of November 4, 1966.

D. "FAIR PACKAGING AND LABELING"

The Declaration of Policy in the Act of 1966

The legislative history of the "Fair Packaging and Labeling Act" of 1966 has already been briefly given in Chapter 12, which also included a brief summary of its major substantive provisions. Section 2 of the law consists of a delaration of policy that emphasizes the fact that the theory of consumer sovereignty in a free enterprise system rests on an assumption that rational consumers will have access to accurate information on which to base their purchase decisions. Such an assumption, of course, also underlies the concept of static welfare economics, which has been described in Chapter 10. The "Declaration of Policy" reads:

Declaration of Policy

Sec. 2. Informed consumers are essential to the fair and efficient functioning of a free market economy. Packages and their labels should enable consumers to obtain accurate information as the quantity of the contents and should facilitate price comparisons. Therefore, it is hereby declared to be the policy of the Congress to assist consumers and manufacturers in reaching these goals in the marketing of consumer goods.

Although some of the proponents of the legislation at first referred to this legislation as "Truth in Packaging" legislation, such a designation was felt by some to carry with it an implication that producers and sellers engaged in widespread practices of fraud and deception, an implication which opponents of the legislation hotly denied. And so a compromise was reached: the problem, it was implicitly agreed, was not fraud and deception but confusion of consumers resulting from diverse practices and from the "packaging revolution resulting from a burst of 'creativity' in the packaging and labeling industry." The designation "fair labeling and packaging" law was therefore adopted.

The Substance of the Legislation

As has been pointed out in Chapter 12, the Fair Packaging and Labeling Act is based on the Commerce Clause of the Constitution. The reader who understands the detailed analysis given in Chapter 7 *supra* of the power of Congress under this clause should have no difficulty in concluding that the question of the constitutionality of this legislation presents no difficulties under the present broad interpretation of the commerce power by the Supreme Court. As has also been noted in Chapter 12, the 1966 law contains both mandatory and discretionary *labeling* provisions and voluntary *packaging* provisions. These provisions are reviewed below.

Mandatory Labeling Provisions. Section 4(a) prohibits the distribution in commerce by specified persons of any packaged consumer commodity unless in conformity with the regulations, specified in Section 4 and established according to procedures under Section 6(a), promulgated by the Secretary of Health, Education, and Welfare (HEW) in the case of foods, drugs, devices, or cosmetics or by the FTC in the case of all other consumer commodities. In Section 10, exceptions are provided in the case of meat and poultry products and other items which are subject to regulation under legislation administered by the Department of Agriculture. Section 7(a) states that violations of the prohibited acts in the case of foods, drugs, devices, or cosmetics shall also be deemed misbranded under the Federal Food, Drug, and Cosmetic Act, and Section 7(b) states that violations of the prohibited acts in the case of all other consumer commodities shall be deemed "unfair or deceptive acts or practices" under Section 5 of the Federal Trade Commission Act.

According to the law, the regulations to be issued by HEW and the FTC must provide for a label specifying: (1) the identity of the commodity and the name and place of business of the manufacturer, packer, or distributor and (2) a separate and accurate statement of the net quantity of contents in terms of weight, measure, or numerical count, placed in a uniform location upon the principal display panel of *that* label. If the package contains less than four pounds or one gallon, the statement of the net quantity of contents must be expressed both in ounces (with identification as to avoirdupois or fluid ounces) and, if applicable, in the largest whole unit (pounds, pints, quarts, or as appropriate), with any remainder in terms of ounces or common or decimal fractions of the whole unit. The purpose of these statements is, of course, to facilitate comparison of costs per unit by the consumer in order to enable him to make "value" comparisons. (During the hearings there was much talk of "price" comparisons as related to "value" comparisons, a point covered further below.) Analogous provisions pertain to consumer commodities labeled in terms of linear or area measures; and there is also a provision pertaining to "random" packages, defined as those of varying weights which are a part of a shipment or lot of a commodity which has no fixed weight pattern. Under Section 4(b), the use of qualifying words such as "jumbo" or "super" are prohibited from appearing in conjunction with the *separate* statement of net quantity of contents required under Section 4(a). Other descriptive terms may, however, appear elsewhere on the label. Under Section 5(b), the Secretary of HEW and the Federal Trade Commission are each given authority to make certain exemptions for "good and sufficient reasons."

Discretionary Labeling Provisions. Under Section 5(c), whenever the enforcement authority finds that regulations other than those specified in Section 4 are necessary to prevent deception or to facilitate "value" comparisons by consumers, it "shall" promulgate special regulations; these will be further explained below. The discretionary feature of this provision lies, of course, in the initial findings that the regulations are necessary to prevent deception or to facilitate *value* comparisons, since, once such findings have been made, the regulations "shall" be issued. It is of interest to note that the original Senate version of the law used the words "price comparisons" in Section 5(c) but that the words were changed to "value comparisons" in the House.

Although the Senate bill (S. 985) did not contain a provision pertaining to "nonfunctional slack fill," such a provision did appear in the substitute bill produced by the House Interstate and Foreign Commerce Committee, and this provision was eventually enacted into the law as Section 5(c)

(4). This provision has been described as a prohibition of the sale of "packaged air." According to the report of the House Interstate and Foreign Commerce Committee, "A package is non-functionally-slack filled if it is filled to substantially less than its capacity for reasons other than (A) the necessary protection of the contents of such package, or (B) the necessary requirements, in accordance with sound manufacturing practices, of machines used for enclosing such contents."[39]

Voluntary Packaging Provisions. S. 985 originally contained a provision in Section 5(d) under which the enforcement authorities would have had the power to prescribe packaging standards under certain conditions, but this section of the legislation was amended by the House Interstate and Foreign Commerce Committee which substituted a *completely voluntary* procedure for the original Section 5(d). By June 1968, both the Federal Trade Commission and the Food and Drug Administration had issued regulations to implement the new law.[40] In April 1969, the Commission began issuing a continuing series of "Interpretative Bulletins Relative to Compliance With the Fair Packaging and Labeling Act," and the reader who is interested in receiving these bulletins should write to the Office of Information of the Commission requesting that his name be placed on the mailing list. The bulletins are issued without charge.

E. THE FEDERAL TRADE COMMISSION AND "TRUTH IN LENDING"

Regulation Z

The "Truth in Lending Act of 1968" is part of the broader Consumer Credit Act of 1968. Other titles of the law deal with garnishment or attachment of wages by a creditor and create a National Commission on Consumer Finance. Congress assigned the responsibility for drafting the regulations to implement the "Truth in Lending" Act to the Federal Reserve Board but assigned enforcement responsibility to nine agencies,

---

[39] *Fair Packaging and Labeling Act* (Report No. 2076 (to accompany H.R. 15440) of the House Committee on Interstate and Foreign Commerce, 89th Cong.,

2d sess.) (Washington, D.C.: U.S. Government Printing Office, 1966), p. 12.
[40] 33 *Federal Register* 404; 4718.

including the Federal Trade Commission. The Board issued Regulation Z to implement the law in February 1969. Both the law and the regulation became effective July 1, 1969.

Under the Act and Regulation Z, consumer credit is defined as credit extended for personal, family, household, or agricultural purposes, and for which a finance charge is imposed or which is repayable in more than four installments. Transactions are classified into two types: open-end credit, which includes revolving charge accounts and transactions conducted by means of credit cards; and other credit, primarily of the instalment type usually employed to finance purchases of household durable goods.

The regulation embodies two disclosure concepts: the *annual percentage rate*, and the *finance charge*. It also specifies how both are to be computed and disclosed. These concepts are designed to enable a consumer to tell at a glance how much he is paying for credit. Advertising of credit is also regulated, and the regulation spells out the further disclosures a creditor must make. These disclosures include a statement of the conditions under which additional charges may be imposed and the method used in determining the charge made.[41]

The Federal Trade Commission's Role

The Commission has enforcement responsibilities pertaining to application of the regulation to department stores, retailers, and to all lenders not specifically under the control of one or another other regulatory agencies.

A "Truth in Lending" Section has been created within the Bureau of Deceptive Practices of the Commission to carry out the Commission's enforcement responsibilities. In 1968, members of this Section participated with representatives of the Federal Reserve Board in drafting the basic implementing regulation. The Section has available to it all the resources of the Commission (for example, the personnel devoted to monitoring television and radio advertising), as well as the various types of enforcement procedures developed by the Commission, ranging from cease-and-desist orders to agreements of voluntary compliance. It considers its most important target to be lending practices of small companies in urban poverty areas.

F. EVALUATIONS OF THE FEDERAL TRADE COMMISSION

Two official studies and one unofficial study of the Federal Trade Commission were published in 1969. The unofficial study was made by a group of law students and junior professors of law under the direction of Ralph Nader, who referred to himself as "the Consumer's Representative in Washington." One of the official studies was made by a committee created by the American Bar Association at the request of President Nixon; the other was made by a committee to study the antitrust laws created by President Nixon prior to the 1968 Presidential election; this committee submitted its report after the election and dealt with the Federal Trade Commission as part of its more general report. These three studies will now be briefly discussed.

The Nader Study of the FTC

The Nader study was made, as has been mentioned, by a group of young law students and law teachers who worked without compensation. Their study was rigidly limited to an examination of the FTC's activities in the field of consumer protection alone. Those making the study concluded that the Commission was failing to provide adequate protection to consumers and explained this failure largely by making various allegations about the way in which the affairs of the agency were conducted and by the "fact" that the personnel of the agency "were subservient" to the Commission's Chairman. The study was conducted with the cooperation of the Chairman and the agency, and much of the information contained in the study was provided by personal interviews with persons both within and outside the Commission.[42] The reports'

---

[41] Federal Reserve Board, *Press Release*, February 7, 1969 and Regulation Z, 12 CFR 226, effective July 1, 1969.

[42] This report is reproduced in *Establish a Depart-* *ment of Consumer Affairs* (Hearings before the Senate Subcommittee on Executive Reorganization, 91st Cong., 1st sess., 1969) (Washington, D.C.: U.S. Government Printing Office, 1969), p. 123 ff.

allegations of alcoholism and inefficiency on the part of the agency's personnel were based on interviews and given much publicity. Nowhere in the report, however, was there any mention of the antitrust activities of the Commission. The unfavorable publicity attending the publication of the Nader report was undoubtedly one of the factors which led President Nixon in April 1969 to request the American Bar Association to undertake a study of the agency.

The American Bar Association Study

The American Bar Association responded to the President's request by establishing a Commission to Study the Federal Trade Commission (hereafter referred to as the ABA Commission). This Commission made its report on September 15, 1969, as requested by the President.[43] (The discussion which follows is based on the Report of the Commission prior to its acceptance by the American Bar Association.) In general, the report concluded that the FTC was failing to plan its activities properly, underallocating resources to its consumer protection program and acting with too much delay. The report also found in many cases the existence of "incompetence" on the part of the Commission's staff. Although the ABA report mentioned the Nader study, it did so in a noncommital way. The ABA Commission's report recommended "a new and vigorous approach to consumer fraud" but left the operational details of what it had in mind unspecified. It also recommended that the existing allocation of enforcement duties between the FTC and the Antitrust Division (described in Chapter 12) be "re-examined and realigned in a manner more nearly consistent with the objectives of antitrust policy" but again left the details unspecified. It further recommended the establishment of priorities and planning goals in the case of FTC operations and recognition by the Commission of the problems of delay and conflict "at the Commissioner level between the functions of prosecutor and judge." The study also suggested that the function of making

economic studies should be separated from that of providing economic evidence in FTC proceedings. The ABA Commission's study was referred to by President Nixon in his Message to Congress on "Consumerism," mentioned in Chapter 12, as one source of his new proposals for reorganization of the FTC. The Stigler report which he had received earlier was, undoubtedly, another source.

The Stigler Report

As has been noted, prior to his election, President Nixon appointed a "Task Force on Productivity and Competition" under the chairmanship of Professor George Stigler, an economist at the University of Chicago.[44]

This Committee's report was made public after the election. The report was sharply critical of the FTC's general antitrust enforcement activities and *asserted, but did not prove*, that these activities are inimical to competition. Accordingly, the recommendation was made that the Commission's resources be redeployed in the direction of greater activity in the field of fraud and deceptive consumer practices and less antitrust enforcement activity.

A Concluding Comment

Insufficient attention was given in the Nader study to the antitrust enforcement activities of the FTC. This writer rejects the recommendation of the Stigler group that the FTC should engage in less antitrust activity. If more consumer protection is wanted, it would be obtained by an increase in appropriations and not by a reduction in antitrust activity. The ABA Commission's recommendations that the FTC speed up its procedures is obviously unexceptionable, but a larger staff and more funds might be necessary to accomplish that purpose. Whatever may be the internal problems of the FTC, the recognition that they exist should not result in a reduction of the Commission's antitrust activities. We have seen in this chapter that the Commission has been an active force in the antitrust field.

---

[43] *Report of the ABA Commission to Study the Federal Trade Commission* (Chicago: American Bar Association, 1969).

[44] The composition of the task force and its general recommendations are discussed more fully at the end

of Chapter 22 of this book. The Report can be found in *The Role of the Giant Corporation* (Hearings before the Subcommittee on Monopoly of the Senate Select Committee on Small Business, 91st Cong., 1st sess., 1969), p. 907 ff.

It has been faced with many obstacles in carrying out its duties. Nevertheless, in seeking to enforce Section 7 of the Clayton Act as amended, the Commission developed much of present day policy toward conglomerate mergers. Naturally, those who do not like this policy would like to see the Commission's antitrust activities curtailed. We have also seen in this chapter that the Commission has engaged in much work in the area of fraud and deceptive practices. In the area of fraud and deception, the work of the Commission, like that of many other regulatory agencies discussed in Part III, has served as a weapon in the War on Poverty and in helping to prevent the exploitation of the disadvantaged. The power to increase funds and personnel for this purpose lies with Congress.

In surveying its work during 1968, the Commission remarked in 1969:

The year's work involved much more than detecting dangers to fair competition and responding to complaints from victims of illegal business practices. Undertaken on its own initiative, and spurred by encouragement from Congress and the President, was a concerted effort to attack illegalities that would victimize consumers, particularly the elderly and the poorly paid who most needed to get full value for their money. Here the FTC's workload was generated less by its responsibility to maintain free and fair competition among businessmen than by its responsibility to protect the public from unfair and deceptive acts and practices. Here, it was necessary to attack evils whose economic effect fell hardest on those least able to afford them.[45]

This statement clearly recognizes the problem of the disadvantaged.

Our survey of business practices dealt with by the Federal Trade Commission under various pieces of legislation has now been completed. The next chapter is concerned with an equally important and interesting problem: the relationship between the policy expressed in the United States patent law and that expressed in the antitrust laws.

[45] *Annual Report of the Federal Trade Commission for 1968* (Washington, D.C.: U.S. Government Printing Office, 1969), p. 1.

19

Patents and Antitrust

This chapter undertakes: (1) to examine the nature and some of the rationalizations of the legal monopoly granted to a patent holder; (2) to discuss the relationship between patent policy and antitrust policy as spelled out in court decisions; and (3) to examine some particular problems concerning remedies which arise in patent-antitrust cases.

A. THE NATURE AND SCOPE OF UNITED STATES PATENT POLICY

Nature of Patent Privilege; Supremacy of Federal Law

In an interesting case involving the attempts of a plaintiff to recover damages from Sears, Roebuck and Company under an Illinois "unfair competition" law on grounds that Sears had copied the plaintiff's design for a "pole lamp," which admittedly was not patentable under federal law because the pole lamp did not satisfy the necessary requirements for issuance of a patent, was decided by the Supreme Court in 1964. The Court held that the Illinois statute could not provide a cause of action on these facts because to permit it to do so

would be tantamount to limiting the federal jurisdiction over patents by state action in an area in which the Constitution declares that federal law shall be the supreme law of the land. In the course of its opinion, the Court also provided a discussion of the history and nature of the patent privilege. It pointed out that prior to the Constitution, individual states had issued patents but that an exclusive power to do so had been conferred upon the federal government in Article I, Section 8, clause 8 of the Constitution "To promote the progress of science and the useful arts" by granting to authors and inventors the exclusive right to their respective writings and discoveries.[1] The power to issue patents is thus an *exclusive* power of the federal government. The question which arises next is that of the social policy which the use of this power is intended to promote. This question is our next topic.

Review of Judicial Policy: Definition of "Patentability"

In 1966, the Court reviewed its policy relative to the definition of "patentability." Congress had amended the Patent Act in 1952, and the case now to be discussed is

---

[1] *Sears, Roebuck and Co.* v. *Stiffel Co.*, 376 U.S. 325 (1964), at pp. 228–232.

the first in which the Court considered the effect of the amendments.[2]

Prior to 1952, two requirements had to be met for a patent to be issued: the requirements of "novelty" and "utility." The 1952 law added the test of "obviousness;" that is, the test of whether or not the subject matter sought to be patented is "such that the subject matter as a whole would have been obvious at the time the invention was made to a person having ordinary skill in the art to which the said subject matter pertains."[3]

According to the Court in the 1966 case, the 1952 law was designed to codify the existing judicial doctrine which had been announced in 1851 in the *Hotchkiss* case.[4] The court admitted that the test of "obviousness" was a difficult one to apply in practice but remarked that the "difficulties should be amenable to case-by-case development."

What is of particular interest in the case just mentioned is the emphasis placed by the Court upon the broad social policy which it sees behind the grant of the patent monopoly. The Court has clearly rejected the "natural law" approach in favor of the pragmatic approach; it is clearly interested in the *consequences* which attach to the definition of "patentability" and has framed its concept on this basis. Thus it has adopted a definition to which content is to be given on a "case-by-case" basis, thereby making it possible for changes to be taken into account and for mistakes to be corrected as new facts come to light.

With respect to the definition of "utility," the Court asserted in 1966 "a patent is not a hunting license. It is not a reward for the search, but compensation for its successful conclusion. 'A patent system must be related to the world of commerce rather than to the realm of philosophy.' "[5] Accordingly, the Court held that a new method of producing a chemical compound was not patentable in a situation in which it was not shown that the compound had actual uses, even though scientists were searching for possible uses for it. The process lacked "utility." This result is consistent with the view, expressed in the other cases discussed above, that the monopoly granted by the patent privilege is not to be "lightly conferred." So is the Court's holding, in a case decided in 1964, that a patentee may not collect royalties after the patent has expired. Specifically, the Court described the nature of a patent monopoly in the following language:

A patent empowers the owner to exact royalties as high as he can negotiate with the leverage of that monopoly. But to use that leverage to project those royalty payments beyond the life of the patent is analogous to an effort to enlarge the monopoly of the patent by tieing the sale or use of the patented article to the purchase or use of unpatented ones.[6]

Professor Machlup's "Economic Review" of the Patent System

It is appropriate in the present context now to consider briefly a study entitled *An Economic Review of the Patent System*, made at the request of and published in 1958 by the Subcommittee on Patents, Trademarks, and Copyrights of the Senate Judiciary Committee. This study by Professor Fritz Machlup, a widely recognized economic theorist, begins with a scholarly historical survey of the patent system dating back to 1624. According to Machlup, an "anti-patent movement" began in Germany in about 1850, but between 1873 and 1910 those advocating use of a patent system had prevailed, not only in Germany but also in a number of other countries.[7]

Part V of Machlup's study was concerned with an examination of the views of economists concerning the question of the benefits to be expected from, and reasons for, use of a "patent system." Machlup identified four positions on which advocates of a patent system have rested their cases: "the 'natural-law' thesis, the 'reward-by-monopoly' thesis, the 'monopoly-profit-incentive' thesis, and the 'exchange-for-secrets' thesis." Specifically, he stated:

The "natural-law" thesis assumes that man has a natural property right in his own ideas.

[2] *Graham et. al.* v. *John Deere Co. of Kansas City et. al.*, 383 U.S. 1 (1966), at pp. 3–19.

[3] *Ibid.*

[4] *Hotchkiss* v. *Greenwood*, 11 Howard 248 (1851).

[5] *Brenner, Commissioner of Patents* v. *Manson*, 383 U.S. 519 (1966), at p. 536.

[6] *Brulotte et. al.* v. *Thys Co.*, 379 U.S. 29 (1964), at p. 33.

[7] Fritz Machlup, *An Economic Review of the Patent System* (Study No. 15 of the Subcommittee on Patents, Trademarks, and Copyrights of the Senate Judiciary Committee, 85th Cong., 2d sess.) (Washington, D.C.: U.S. Government Printing Office, 1958), pp. 3–5.

Appropriation of his ideas by others, that is, their unauthorized use, must be condemned as stealing. . . .

The "reward-by-monopoly" thesis assumes that justice requires that a man receive reward for his services in proportion to their usefulness to society, and that, where needed, society must intervene to secure him such reward. . . .

The "monopoly-profit-incentive" thesis assumes that industrial progress is desirable, that inventions and their industrial exploitation are necessary for such progress, but that inventions and/or their exploitation will not be obtained in sufficient measure if inventors and capitalists can hope only for such profits as the competitive exploitation of all technical knowledge will permit. . . .

The "exchange-for-secrets" thesis presumes a bargain between inventor and society, the former surrendering the possession of secret knowledge in exchange for the protection of a temporary exclusivity in its industrial use.[8]

Machlup noted that economists are to be found on both sides of the issue of whether a society is better or worse off as a result of the existence of a patent system. After explaining the economic concepts of "social cost" and "social benefit" in general terms only, Machlup wrote as follows:

The analysis of the "increment of invention" [read the "marginal amount of invention"] attributable to the operation of the patent system, or to certain changes in the patent system, can only be highly speculative, because no experimental tests can be devised to isolate the effects of patent protection from all other changes that are going on in the economy. . . .

. . . The literature abounds with discussions of the "economic consequences" of the patent system, purporting to present definitive judgments, without even stating the assumptions on which the arguments are based, let alone submitting supporting evidence for the actual realization of these assumptions. No economist, on the basis of present knowledge, could possibly state with certainty that the patent system, as it now operates, confers a net benefit or a net loss upon society. The best he can do is to state assumptions and make guesses about the extent to which reality corresponds to these assumptions.

If one does not know whether a system "as a whole" (in contrast to certain features of it) is good or bad, the safest "policy conclusion" is to "muddle through"—either with it, if one has long lived with it, or without it, if one has lived without it. If we did not have a patent system, it would be irresponsible, on the basis of our present knowledge of its economic consequences, to recommend instituting one. But since we have had a patent system for a long time, it would be irresponsible, on the basis of our present knowledge, to recommend abolishing it. . . .

. . . While economic analysis does not yet provide a basis for choosing between "all or nothing," it does provide a sufficiently firm basis for decisions about "a little more or a little less" of various ingredients of the patent system. Factual data of various kinds may be needed even before some of these decisions can be made with confidence. . . .[9]

Economic analysis, thus, does not provide the answer.

The issues raised by Machlup's careful study of the economic rationalizations of the patent system are, of course, similar to those involved in the definition of "workable competition" and in the application of this phrase to the enforcement of the antitrust laws, a question already discussed in detail in Chapter 13. Indeed, what Machlup has identified as the "monopoly-profit-incentive" thesis is nothing other than the Schumpeterian theory of "creative destruction," an issue dealt with thoroughly in Chapter 13, and the reader may wish to review that discussion at this point.

Report of the President's Commission on the Patent System (1966)

It is also appropriate at this time to consider briefly the report made in 1966 by the President's Commission on the Patent System.[10] This Commission was appointed by an Executive Order in 1965 under the co-chairmanship of a well-known educator, Dr. Harry Huntt Ransom, and a jurist, Judge Simon H. Rifkind. Its membership was drawn from the public and from government agencies. The Commission apparently adopted a modified version of what Machlup labeled the "monopoly-profit-incentive" theory as the basis for its recommendations. Thus it reported, among other things:

The members of the Commission unanimously agreed that a patent system today is capable of continuing to provide an incentive to research, development, and innovation. They have dis-

---

[8] *Ibid.*, p. 21.

[9] *Ibid.*, pp. 62, 79–80.

[10] *To Promote Progress of the Useful Arts* (Report of the President's Commission on the Patent System) (Washington, D.C.: U.S. Government Printing Office, 1966).

covered no practical substitute for the unique service it renders.

First, a patent system provides an incentive to invent by offering the possibility of reward to the inventor and to those who support him. This prospect encourages the expenditure of time and private risk capital in research and development efforts.

Second, and complimentary to the first, a patent system stimulates the investment of additional capital needed for the further development and marketing of the invention. In return, the patent owner is given the right, for a limited period, to exclude others from making, using, or selling the invented product or process.[11]

This theory is modified in the report by the addition to it of the "exchange-for-secrets" thesis. This modification is stated in the following language:

Third, by affording protection, a patent system encourages early public disclosure of technological information, some of which might otherwise be kept secret. . . .

Fourth, a patent system promotes the beneficial exchange of products, services, and technological information across national boundaries by providing protection for industrial property of foreign nationals.[12]

Given this point of departure, it is not surprising that most of the Commission's recommendations were concerned with methods of making more effective the protection afforded the patent holder and reducing administrative delays involved in the process of issuing patents.[13] It also recommended that the term of a patent be extended to 20 years, thus adding three years to the present 17-year term.[14] It further recommended "clarification" of the "nature of the rights granted by a patent" and asserted that it did not favor "any proposal which would weaken the enforcement of the antitrust laws or which would curtail in any way the power of the courts to deny relief to a patent owner misusing the patent he seeks to enforce." Moreover, it warned against attempts to codify "the many decisions dealing with patent misuse." (The problem of misuse is discussed later in this chapter) It further asserted that its

recommendation was not intended to permit a patent to be used "to control commerce in subject matter beyond the scope of the patent" nor to permit a patent owner to "control commerce in one of the unpatented elements of his combination invention where his claims are to the whole invention."[15] In short, it did not consider the antitrust laws and the patent system to represent mutually exclusive systems. Finally, the Commission recorded its belief in an ultimate goal of "establishment of a universal patent, respected throughout the world," to be attained by means of international agreement.[16] The background materials upon which the Commission based its report were not published at the time the report was made, but the Commission promised to make these materials available at a later date.

With respect to the question of empirical studies of the relationship between patents, the size of the firm, and their contribution to the advancement of technology, the testimony in 1965 before the Senate Subcommittee on Antitrust and Monopoly of Professor Jacob Schmookler (who has made several pioneering empirical studies in this area) is instructive. He cited the results of several empirical studies by others which conclude that smaller firms "use commercially a much larger proportion of their patented inventions than do big firms."[17]

As a matter of fact, Schmookler also pointed out that some empirical studies contradict the conclusions of many arrived at by means of deductive reasoning alone:

The impression derived from the evidence . . . that, on the whole, very large firms contribute less to the advancement of technology in proportion to their size than do firms somewhat smaller is, of course, at variance with much contemporary opinion on the subject. To a considerable extent, the contemporary view that the larger the firm, the greater its relative contribution to the progress of technological knowledge rests on deductive logic. I do not wish to enter into that debate here. However, I would like to point out that deductive logic can contribute to our knowledge on the subject only to the extent

[11] *Ibid.*, p. 2.

[12] *Ibid.*, p. 3.

[13] *Ibid.*, pp. 5–32.

[14] *Ibid.*, p. 33.

[15] *Ibid.*, pp. 36–37.

[16] *Ibid.*, p. 55.

[17] *Economic Concentration* (Hearings before the Subcommittee on Antitrust and Monopoly of the Senate Judiciary Committee, 89th Cong., 1st sess.) (Washington, D.C.: U.S. Government Printing Office, 1965), Part 3, p. 1259.

that it begins from premises that approximate the salient facts. I submit that we do not yet know or understand all the salient facts, and that the logical briefs on behalf of the progressiveness of big firms ignore aspects of the problem which may be crucial.[18]

For these reasons, Professor Schmookler concluded that it would be a mistake to relax the antitrust laws in the hope of inducing a more rapid national rate of technological change.[19] This question is, of course, one important aspect of the more general problem of the relationship between patent policy and antitrust policy, discussed next.

B. PATENT POLICY AND ANTITRUST POLICY

The *General Electric* Case (1926) and the Basic Doctrine of Price-Fixing via Patents

Although the Supreme Court held in the *Bement* case as early as 1902 that a patent holder may fix the price at which one whom he has licensed to make and sell under the patent may sell the patented article,[20] the *General Electric* case of 1926 is usually cited as the landmark case involving the question of the relationship of the antitrust laws to the patent laws. The *General Electric* case involved two separate issues, and both will be discussed. The *first* charge involved the question of whether or not General Electric, which held the basic patent for the use of tungsten filaments in the production of incandescent light bulbs and other patents relating to the manufacture of electric light bulbs, could adopt a system of distribution for such products under which it fixed the resale prices charged by wholesalers and retailers for the bulbs. In regard to this question, the Court held that the contracts between GE and its distributors had the effect of appointing the latter as *mere agents* of the company and that ownership of the final products was retained by the company until they were sold to final consumers. Having disposed of the issue on this technical ground, the Court had no difficulty in finding that the company had the right to fix the final selling price and that it would

have had this right even in the absence of the patent monopoly which it possessed. Thus Justice Taft said:

We are of the opinion, therefore, that there is nothing as a matter of principle, or in the authorities, which requires us to hold that genuine contracts of agency like those before us, however comprehensive as a mass or whole in their effect, are violations of the Anti-Trust Act. The owner of an article, patented or otherwise, is not violating the common law, or the Anti-Trust law, by seeking to dispose of his article directly to the consumer and fixing the price by which his agents transfer the title from him directly to such consumer. The first charge in the bill can not be sustained.[21]

This aspect of the case thus did not turn on the question of the scope of the patent monopoly, but stands instead for the proposition that an owner may charge whatever price he can get for the articles he sells; the mere fact that the article is produced under a patent has no effect on this rule which applies, absent other facts constituting a violation of law, also to non-patented items. The crucial question in this aspect of the case was whether or not General Electric retained title and had merely appointed its dealers as agents; once this question was answered in the affirmative, the final decision followed logically. Nevertheless, as we will see later, in at least one subsequent case the Court refused to permit a perversion of this straightforward doctrine to be used as a defense in an antitrust-patent case.

The *second* charge in the *General Electric* case alleged that General Electric had a monopolistic purpose in its patent licensing arrangements with the Westinghouse Electric and Manufacturing Company and with the Westinghouse Lamp Manufacturing Company, a subsidiary of the latter. Under these licensing arrangements, General Electric licensed Westinghouse to make, use, and sell electric lamps under the GE patents but also required Westinghouse to adopt prices and terms of sale (in the distribution of the finished products), which were fixed by the General Electric Company. The Court held that such conditions might be legally imposed under

---

[18] *Ibid.*, p. 1260.
[19] *Ibid.*, p. 1264.
[20] *Bement* v. *National Harrow Co.*, 186 U.S. 70 (1902).

[21] *United States* v. *General Electric Co. et. al.*, 272 U.S. 476 (1926), at p. 488.

the patent monopoly possessed by GE, the antitrust laws notwithstanding. Justice Taft wrote:

The owner of a patent may assign it to another and convey, (1) the exclusive right to make, use and vend the invention throughout the United States, or, (2) an undivided part or share of that exclusive right, or (3) the exclusive right under the patent within and through a specific part of the United States. But any assignment or transfer short of one of these is a license, giving the licensee no title in the patent and no right to sue at law in his own name for an infringement. . . . Conveying less than title to the patent, or part of it, the patentee may grant a license to make, use and vend articles under the specifications of his patent for any royalty or upon any condition the performance of which is reasonably within the reward which the patentee by the grant of the patent is entitled to secure. It is well settled, as already said, that where a patentee makes the patented article and sells it, he can exercise no future control over what the purchaser may wish to do with the article after his purchase. It has passed beyond the scope of the patentee's rights. . . . But the question is a different one which arises when we consider what a patentee who grants a license to one to make and vend the patented article may do in limiting the licensee in the exercise of the right to sell. . . .

For the reasons given, we sustain the validity of the license granted by the Electric Company to the Westinghouse Company.[22]

Thus the basic law was laid down.

Limitations of the Basic *GE* Doctrine of Price-Fixing via Patents

After 1926, the federal courts began to impose limitations upon the basic doctrine announced in the *General Electric* case. Indeed, Justice Taft had pointed to one such limitation in the quotation given above when he said: "It is well settled, as already said, that where a patentee makes the patented article and sells it, he can exercise no future control over what the purchaser may wish to do" with the patented article. This principle was applied by the Circuit Court of Appeals for the Fifth Circuit in *Cummer-Graham Company* v. *Straight Side Basket Corporation* in 1944.[23] This case involved an action brought by a patent holder against a licensee on grounds that the licensee had failed to maintain

agreed prices on baskets, produced by means of the patented device. The Court held that although the patent granted the right to fix the price of the patented machine itself, it did not grant a right to fix the price of articles produced by the machine.[24]

The court also pointed out that in the *General Electric* case the tungsten filament light bulbs were *themselves* the things patented; and hence "the selling price of them was validly fixed in the licence to Westinghouse to make and sell them."[25]

A second limitation has also been applied to the basic *General Electric* case doctrine by limiting its application largely to the case of a *single licensor and a single licensee*, that is, by limiting application of the doctrine to the precise facts of the *General Electric* case. An illustration is found in the *Line Material* case of 1948. The opinion in this case resulted in a limitation of the second proposition dealt with in the *General Electric* case, namely, the validity of the price-fixing provision in the General Electric-Westinghouse licensing arrangements. Where this aspect of the General Electric case had involved a *single* patentee and a *single* licensee, the *Line Material* case involved *multiple* patentees and *numerous* licenses. The facts in the latter were as follows. Both the Line Material Company and the Southern States Company owned patents for the production of an electrical fuse device, and neither company could produce a device which contained all the advantages of the devices under all the different patents without the permission of the other company. The two companies accordingly made a cross-licensing agreement under which each licensed the other under the relevant patent. However, the cross-licensing arrangement also provided that the Line Material Company was to fix the price at which Southern States sold products under the combined patents and also permitted the Line Material Company to license other firms to produce under both patents and to fix their prices as well. The Supreme Court held that this case constituted a situation different from that involved in the *General Electric* case and that, therefore, the arrangement was not justified under the patent law. Specifically, Justice

---

[22] *Ibid.*, at pp. 489–490; 494.
[23] 142 F. 2d 646 (1944).

[24] *Ibid.*, at p. 647.
[25] *Ibid.*

Reed wrote in the majority opinion that it was necessary "to take into account the cumulative effect of such multiple agreements in establishing an intention to restrain. The obvious purpose and effect of the agreement was to enable Line to fix prices. . . ."[26] Justice Douglas wrote a concurring opinion, joined by Justices Black, Murphy, and Rutledge, in which he added that he would overrule the *General Electric* case.[27]

It will be recalled that the *General Electric* case also involved the question of price-fixing of the patented product in the hands of retailers, and that the Court disposed of this issue in that case by holding that the retailers were merely *agents* of General Electric and that General Electric, having retained the title to the product in the hands of its agent-retailers, had also retained the right to fix the price of such products. The *Masonite* case of 1942 involved an attempt to capitalize on *this* "agency" aspect of the *General Electric* case. The facts were as follows: The Masonite and the Celotex Corporations both possessed certain patents for the production of hardboard building materials. In 1928, Masonite claimed that Celotex had infringed Masonite's patents. In 1931, Masonite sued for infringement, and a District Court held that Masonite's patents was valid but had not been infringed. Masonite appealed, and the Court of Appeals held that the Masonite patent was both valid and infringed by Celotex. At this point, the two companies undertook negotiations and settled their respective claims by executing a so-called "agency agreement." Similar "agency agreements" were then made by Masonite with a number of other hardboard producing companies. Under these agreements, Masonite appointed the other party in each instance as Masonite's "agent" to sell Masonite's hardboard products. Masonite retained the power to fix the prices and terms of sale of its products, and the "agents" recognized the validity of Masonite's patents, *even though some of them held competing patents*. In effect, these agreements resulted in a situation in which Masonite became the sole producer, with the power to fix prices and terms of sale. The Supreme Court held that these arrangements constituted a conspiracy to fix prices in violation of the antitrust laws. Speaking for the majority, Justice Douglas said:

> We do not have here any question as to the validity of a license to manufacture and sell, since none of the "agents" exercised its option to acquire such a license from Masonite. Hence we need not reach the problems presented by *Bement* v. *National Harrow Co.* . . . and that part of the *General Electric* case which dealt with the license to Westinghouse Company. Rather, we are concerned here only with a license to vend. But it will not do to say that, since the patentee has the power to refuse a license, he has the lesser power to license on his own conditions. There are strict limitations on the power of the patentee to attach conditions to the use of the patented article.[28]

With respect to the question of conspiracy raised by this case, Justice Douglas noted that the agency agreements giving Masonite power to fix prices were illegal *per se*. Moreover, since each of the parties knew the scope and content of these agreements, a conspiracy existed.[29]

Thus in this case, a conspiracy existed not as a result of a combination of patents, but as a result of the "fixing of prices by one member of the group pursuant to express delegation, acquiescence, or understanding." A further limitation upon the use of agency or consignment agreements (under which the producer retains title until the products are sold at retail) was laid down by the Court in 1964 in *Simpson* v. *Union Oil Company*,[30] a case already mentioned in Chapter 14 of this book in the discussion of resale price maintenance under the Sherman Act. In this case, Union Oil Company leased service stations to operators and entered into "consignment" agreements with them under which the oil company retained title to the gasoline sold and paid the operators a commission. In the case in question, Union Oil Company allegedly used its leases and consignment agreements in a coercive manner to enforce maintenance

---

[26] *United States* v. *Line Material Co. et. al.*, 333 U.S. 287 (1948), pp. 312–313.

[27] *Ibid.*, at p. 316.

[28] *United States* v. *Masonite Corp. et. al.*, 316 U.S. 265 (1942), at p. 277.

[29] *Ibid.*, at pp. 274–275.

[30] *Simpson* v. *Union Oil Co.*, 377 U.S. 13 (1964).

of retail prices. And, it will be recalled, the Court then held that even though a consignment agreement might be lawful as a matter of private contract, if such an agreement was used in a coercive manner to violate the Sherman Act, the agreement was unlawful.[31]

The defendants sought to rely on the *General Electric* case rule, but the Court rejected this argument saying that in the *General Electric* case the Court particularly relied on the fact that patent rights "have long included licenses 'to make, use, and vend' the patented article for any royalty or upon any condition the performance of which is reasonably within" the monopoly position granted to the patentor by the patent.[32]

In 1966, relying on the decision in the *Union Oil Co.* case, the Department of Justice filed a civil action, again challenging the General Electric Company's system of retail price maintenance.[33] Almost four years after the complaint was filed, the case had not yet been decided.[34]

Some of the cases discussed above have involved actions by several firms. A case involving establishment of an industry-wide conspiracy by means of patent licensing will be considered next.

Conspiracy via Patent Licensing

The *United States Gypsum Company* case involved charges under both Sections 1 and 2 of the Sherman Act. The government claimed that the defendants acted in concert in entering into licensing arrangements covering the manufacture of gypsum board, in that United States Gypsum granted licenses to other producers who accepted the licenses *with the knowledge* that all other concerns in the industry would accept similar licenses, and that, as a result of such concerted action, competition was eliminated by fixing the price of patented board, eliminating the production of nonpatented board and regulating the production of patented board. In finding that the arrangement violated the Sherman Act, the Court said:

... Patents grant no privilege to their owners of organizing the use of those patents to monopolize an industry through price control, through royalties for the patents drawn from patent-free industry products and through regulation of distribution. ...

The *General Electric* case affords no cloak for the course of conduct revealed in the voluminous record in this case. That case gives no support for a patentee, acting in concert with all members of an industry, to issue substantially identical licenses to all members of the industry under the terms of which the industry is completely regimented, the production of competitive unpatented products suppressed, a class of distributors squeezed out, and prices on unpatented products stabilized. ...

... The rewards which flow to the patentee and his licensees from the suppression of competition through the regulation of an industry are not reasonably and normally adapted to secure pecuniary reward for the patentee's monopoly.[35]

"Monopolization" via Patent Pooling

The *Hartford-Empire Company* case of 1945 involved an attempted monopolization through the accumulation of patents covering automatic glassmaking machinery and allocation of certain types of business to particular participants. The facts in the case were complicated. The Hartford Empire Company had established a patent pool controlling more than 800 patents and by cross-licensing arrangements had gained control of the entire industry. Control over production (an allocation system) was then instituted.[36] The District Court found as a fact that, as a result of the pool, "the invention of glassmaking machinery had been discouraged," competition had been suppressed, and prices had been fixed. The Supreme Court held that the practices in question were unlawful under the Sherman Act and represented an example of a prohibited abuse of the restrictions incident to the ownership of patents.

Exclusion of Competitors via Patent Pooling

In May 1969, the Supreme Court was faced with a case involving the following facts. A Canadian patent pool was formed

[31] *Ibid.*, p. 18.

[32] *Ibid.*, pp. 23–24.

[33] Civil Action No. 66, Civ. 3118, United States District Court, Southern District of New York, September 27, 1966.

[34] Letter to author from Antitrust Division, dated January 21, 1970.

[35] *United States* v. *United States Gypsum Co. et. al.*, 333 U.S. 366 (1948), at pp. 400–401.

[36] *Hartford-Empire Co. et. al.* v. *United States*, 323 U.S. 386 (1945), at p. 400.

in 1926 by Canadian subsidiaries of the General Electric Company and Westinghouse Electric Company. This pool refused to license importers of television and radio equipment who had not purchased the pool's "standard" license "package." Zenith Radio Corporation refused to purchase the package and sold its products in Canada. On behalf of the pool an action claiming patent infringement was brought in the United States against Zenith. Zenith claimed, among other things, that the pool had violated the Sherman Act and that Zenith was entitled to treble damages. The Supreme Court upheld Zenith's claim.[37] Patents also often serve as a basis for illegal tying arrangements, as we will now see.

Tying Arrangements, Division of Markets, and the Patent Monopoly

As we have seen in Chapters 14 and 15 respectively, tying arrangements are prohibited both under Section 1 of the Sherman Act and under Section 3 of the Clayton Act. The reader may at this point wish to refer to the discussion of the *International Salt* case of 1947 which appeared in Chapter 14. That case, it will be recalled, involved a situation in which lessees of the patentee salt company's patented salt-dispensing machine were also required to purchase from the salt company their requirements of unpatented salt for use in the machine.[38] This arrangement was held to be a violation of the antitrust laws. Similarly, in the *International Business Machines Corporation* case, it had been held in 1936 that a requirement imposed by the patentee that its licensees purchase their supplies of unpatented tabulating cards for use in the patented business machines under the license was unlawful under Section 3 of the Clayton Act.[39] A division of international markets accomplished by means of patent licensing was held in 1947 to be a violation of the Sherman Act.[40]

Summary

It should by now be clear to the reader that any attempts to expand upon the

patent monopoly (1) through the pooling or aggregation of patents, or (2) by cross-licensing arrangements, or (3) by imposing conditions (such as price-fixing authority, tying clauses, or market or production controls in multiple licensing agreements) are looked upon with disfavor by the Supreme Court and will be held to constitute violations of the antitrust laws—the patent laws and the *General Electric* case of 1926 notwithstanding. The patent cases also involve some interesting questions pertaining to the nature of the judicial relief granted in cases in which a violation has been found. It is to the question of remedies employed by the courts in patent-antitrust cases that the next major subdivision of this chapter is devoted, but the question of *nonuse* requires discussion first.

Nonuse and Suppression of Patented Inventions

Before turning to the matter of remedies in patent antitrust cases, since one of these remedies both in such cases and in *nonuse* cases is that of *compulsory licensing*, it is useful to consider now one broad question of patent policy, which, however, is not strictly a patent-antitrust question. This problem is that of the *suppression* of a patented article *or* of the *nonuse* of a patent. An interesting discussion of the state of the law and the basic policy issues involved appears in the following statement by Justice Douglas written in 1945. In a dissenting opinion, Justice Douglas wrote:

The right of suppression of a patent came into the law over a century after the first patent act was passed. In 1886 Judge Blodgett had ruled that a patentee "is bound either to use the patent himself or allow others to use it on reasonable or equitable terms". . . . In 1896 that rule was repudiated by the Circuit Court of Appeals for the Sixth Circuit . . . where the court stated that a patentee's "title is exclusive, and so clearly within the constitutional provisions in respect of private property that he is neither bound to use his discovery himself, nor permit others to use it." That theory was adopted by this Court in . . . 1908 . . . [in] an infringement suit. One defense was that the patentee had suppressed the patent.

---

[37] *Zenith Radio Corporation* v. *Hazeltine Research Corp., Inc.*, 395 U.S. 100 (1969). This case involved various other complex technical legal issues not mentioned in the text.
[38] *International Salt Co., Inc.* v. *United States*, 332 U.S.

392 (1947).
[39] *International Business Machines Corp.* v. *United States*, 298 U.S. 131 (1936).
[40] *United States* v. *National Lead Co. et. al.*, 332 U.S. 319 (1947).

The Court held, Mr. Justice Harlan dissenting, that suppression of the patent was no defense; that the patentee's "right can only retain its attribute of exclusiveness by a prevention of its violation."

I think it is time to be rid of that rule. It is inconsistent with the Constitution and the patent legislation which Congress has enacted.

The result is that suppression of patents has become commonplace. Patents are multiplied to protect an economic barony or empire, not to put new discoveries to use for the common good. "It is common practice to make an invention and to secure a patent to block off a competitor's progress. By studying his ware and developing an improvement upon it, a concern may 'fence in' its rival; by a series of such moves, it may pin the trade enemy within a technology which rapidly becomes obsolete. As often as not such maneuvers retard, rather than promote, the progress of the useful arts. Invariably their effect is to enlarge and to prolong personal privilege within the public domain". . . . One patent is used merely to protect another. The use of a new patent is suppressed so as to preclude experimentation which might result in further invention by competitors. A whole technology is blocked off. The result is a clog to our economic machine and a barrier to an economy of abundance.

It is difficult to see how that use of patents can be reconciled with the purpose of the Constitution "to promote the progress of science and the useful arts." It is . . . difficult to see how suppression of patents can be reconciled with the provision of the statute which authorizes a grant of the "exclusive right to make, use, and vend the invention or discovery". . . . How may the words "to make, use, and vend" be read to mean "not to make, not to use, and not to vend?"[41]

In this case, the majority took the position:

This Court has consistently held that failure of the patentee to make use of a patented invention does not affect the validity of the patent. . . .

Congress has frequently been asked to change the policy of the statutes as interpreted by this Court by imposing a forfeiture or providing for compulsory licensing if the patent is not used within a specified time, but has not done so.[42]

These statements were made in a case in which the Court refused to hold that an intention—on the part of the one seeking the patent—to suppress the patented device was not sufficient grounds for a refusal by the Patent Office to issue the patent. At the same time, the Court has often undertaken to approve compulsory licensing of patents as an appropriate remedy when this device has been ordered by lower courts in patent antitrust cases. The related question of compulsory licensing as a remedy in cases of nonuse or suppression of patents was thoroughly examined in 1959 by Fredrik Neumeyer in a study prepared for the Subcommittee on Patents, Trademarks, and Copyrights of the Senate Judiciary Committee. In his study, Neumeyer pointed out that in 1790 a bill calling for compulsory licensing was introduced in Congress but failed to pass the House.[43] The proposed bill would have permitted any two Justices of the Supreme Court to hear complaints that a patent holder was not producing under his patent or was selling "at a price beyond what may be adjudged adequate compensation." If the allegations were found to be true, the Court could grant a license to the complainant.

Beginning in 1877, new attempts were made in Congress to introduce compulsory licensing provisions into the patent system, but all failed. The result is that since about 1945, compulsory licensing in the United States has been a judicial remedy employed largely in antitrust cases. European countries have adopted various approaches; some have put the compulsory licensing provisions into their patent laws, and others have incorporated such provisions into their cartel laws.

As Neumeyer noted in his study, in the United States compulsory licensing has been primarily employed as a remedy in patent-antitrust cases. It is to a discussion of this remedy in such cases that the following major subdivision is devoted.

C. REMEDIES IN PATENT-ANTITRUST CASES

Nature and Purpose of Compulsory Licensing and Related Remedies

Where a defendant patent holder has been found guilty of a violation of the

---

[41] *Special Equipment Co.* v. *Coe, Commissioner of Patents*, 324 U.S. 370 (1945), at pp. 380–383.

[42] *Ibid.*, at pp. 378–379.

[43] Fredrik Neumeyer, *Compulsory Licensing of Patents under Some Non-American Systems* (Study No. 19 of the Subcommittee on Patents, Trademarks, and Copyrights of the Senate Judiciary Committee, 85th Cong., 2d sess.) (Washington, D.C.: U.S. Government Printing Office, 1959), pp. 1–3.

antitrust laws, all of the remedies available in antitrust cases generally (discussed in detail in the next chapter) are available. However, four types of remedies have been more widely used in a patent-antitrust cases than have any of the others; and the discussion in this subdivision will be restricted to a consideration of these four. They are: (1) compulsory licensing at reasonable rates; (2) compulsory licensing royalty-free; (3) dedication to the public of the patent rights (in the same way that a real estate developer may dedicate part of his development to the public in the form of public parks or streets); and (4) injunction against the enforcement of patent rights. In effect, the last three remedies amount to the same thing, although the formalities involved are different. In none of these last three cases does the patent-holder derive any pecuniary compensation from the uses to which others may put the patented process, product, or device.

It has been noted that since 1945 compulsory licensing has been employed in antitrust cases by United States courts. As a matter of fact, in 1945 in the *Hartford-Empire* case (which has been discussed above as an example of monopolization under the Sherman Act by means of patent pooling), the Supreme Court upheld compulsory licensing at reasonable rates to be an appropriate remedy but rejected compulsory licensing on a royalty-free basis as confiscatory.[44] Subsequently, in 1947 in the *National Lead* case (cited earlier in this chapter as an example of a case involving a division of markets based on a patent licensing system), the Court replied to the government's request—that it modify the decree of a lower court calling for licensing on a reasonable royalty basis by substituting a compulsory royalty-free licensing provision—and also replied to the defendant's contention—that the Court had permanently rejected the royalty-free licensing remedy in the earlier *Hartford-Empire* case—

by saying that such a remedy was inappropriate in a civil proceeding.[45]

A majority of the Attorney General's National Committee to Study the Antitrust Laws interpreted these cases to mean that the Court's view is that royalty-free licensing and permanent injunction are "penal rather than remedial in character, and hence beyond the Sherman Act's authority to 'prevent and restrain' violations."[46]

However, the dissenting minority of the Attorney General's Committee took the view that "*Hartford-Empire* and *National Lead* pronounce no blanket statutory or constitutional ban on royalty-free licensing or dedication, but merely hold that a court will decree no more in any one case than is needed to achieve effective competition."[47] The cases support this view. As a matter of fact, a royalty-free licensing provision has been included in several consent decrees made in patent-antitrust cases since the *Report* of the Committee was published.[48] Moreover, dedication was required in one case terminated in 1953, *before* the Committee's *Report* was published.[49] And, in September, 1969, the Antitrust Division filed a consent decree requiring the four major automobile producers to make available to all applicants royalty free licences on air pollution control devices.

Extent and Effectiveness of Compulsory Licensing in Patent-Antitrust Cases

In 1960, the staff of the Senate Subcommittee on Patents, Trademarks, and Copyrights published a valuable and comprehensive study called *Compulsory Patent Licensing under Antitrust Judgments*. The study was undertaken "to determine how effective compulsory licensing in antitrust judgments has been 'in opening industry to competition, and what practical problems have arisen in the administration of such compulsory licensing.' "[50]

An appendix to the subcommittee study consists of the first list of its kind ever

[44] *Hartford-Empire Co. et. al.* v. *United States*, 323 U.S. 386 (1945), at pp. 415 ff.

[45] *United States* v. *National Lead Co. et. al.*, 332 U.S. 319 (1947), at pp. 338; 349.

[46] *Report of the Attorney General's National Committee to Study the Antitrust Laws* (Washington, D.C.: U.S. Government Printing Office, 1955), p. 256.

[47] *Ibid.*, p. 258.

[48] *United States* v. *Western Electric Co., Inc.* and *American Tel. and Tel. Co.*, Civ. 17–19, D.N.J. (1956);

and *United States* v. *Radio Corp. of America*, Civ. 97–38, S.D.N.Y. (1958).

[49] *United States* v. *General Electric Co. et. al.*, 82 F. Supp. 753 (1949); 115 F. Supp. 835 (1953).

[50] *Compulsory Patent Licensing under Antitrust Judgments* (Staff Report of the Subcommittee on Patents, Trademarks, and Copyrights of the Senate Judiciary Committee, 86th Cong., 2d sess.) (Washington D.C.: U.S. Government Printing Office, 1960), p. 1.

published of judgments containing patent relief and shows the fields covered by the patents which have been made available under such judgments.

The authors of the study estimated that since 1941, some 300 defendants ranging in size from the General Electric Company to "relatively small firms" were involved in these decrees, and that between 49,000 and 50,000 of the total of 600,000 patents issued were affected. The authors of the study also expressed their belief that the patent antitrust actions had resulted in the liberalization of licensing policies on the part of many patent holders.[51]

It is useful to note that the antitrust program covered by the study consisted of the entry between August 1941 and January 9, 1959, of 107 judgments (13 entered in litigated cases and 94 by consent).[52] But only 81 decrees were thoroughly studied. The authors of the study reported "mixed results" concerning the effects of the compulsory licensing provisions. The number of licensees under any one judgment varied from zero to 300. Many of the companies reporting that they had benefitted were small businesses without research facilities of their own.[53] According to the study, the decree in the *Line Material* case (discussed earlier) was an effective one.[54]

However, the subcommittee staff also discovered that, in 31 of the 81 cases actually surveyed, no licenses were issued even though the decrees in these 31 cases all required licenses to be issued at reasonable royalties.[55] Moreover, in most of these 31 cases not a single inquiry was received from a prospective licensee. Indeed, it was also learned that there were a number of additional cases in which the *licensees* thought the decrees had actually aided the defendants. Finally, the study also undertook to compare the effectiveness of compulsory licensing provisions contained in consent judgments (nonlitigated) with those contained in decrees resulting from litigation. Of the 81 cases for which information could be obtained, only 12 were litigated. The subcommittee staff determined that although 55 percent of the (nonlitigated) consent judgments were "ineffective," only 1 of the litigated judgments (or 9 percent of

them) was "ineffective."[56] It may be useful to note at this point that the 12 litigated cases in which the decree was "effective" included the *Line Material*, the *American Can*, the *National Lead*, the *Hartford-Empire*, the *United Shoe Machinery*, and the *General Electric* cases, all of which have been discussed either in this or in preceding chapters of this book.

The study also contains the conclusion of its authors that the consent decree in the A. T. and T. case (discussed in Chapter 12 of this book) merely legalized undesirable practices.[57] It will be recalled that A. T. and T. owns and controls Western Electric and that the consent decree in this case was made over the strong objections of some career officials in the Department of Justice under the circumstances set forth in detail in Chapter 12 earlier.

With respect to the general problem of consent decrees as compared with decrees entered after litigation, the study pointed out:

... antitrust decrees entered after a trial are more likely to provide effective relief than those entered by consent before there is any litigation. A trial defines the trade restraining practices of the defendant and makes a record of the specific complaints which have led to the institution of the action. These specific complaints furnish concrete illustrations of the evils which the relief sought is intended to cure. The trial court's opinion describes the conduct which is thought to violate the law and ordinarily indicates the kind of injunction that the court believes will provide effective relief. Without such a judicial evaluation of an antitrust complaint the framing of effective patent relief is extremely difficult.

... the secrecy with which consent decree negotiations are normally conducted tends to prevent the Antitrust Division from obtaining needed information about the value of patents from nonparties to the negotiations.[58]

The two preceding quotations point to the existence and nature of remedies other than compulsory patent licensing and to the difference between litigated and non-litigated decrees. These remedies and procedural matters are not peculiar to patent-antitrust cases but exist in antitrust cases in general. It is thus to the broad problem of remedies and procedures in general that the next chapter is devoted.

---

[51] *Ibid.*, p. 5.
[52] *Ibid.*, p. 1.
[53] *Ibid.*, pp. 5–6.
[54] *Ibid.*, pp. 10–11.

[55] *Ibid.*, p. 13.
[56] *Ibid.*, 18.
[57] *Ibid.*, pp. 46–47.
[58] *Ibid.*, p. 21.

The Problem of Remedies

Some indication has already inevitably been given in preceding chapters of the types of remedies which are available in antitrust cases. Since both criminal and civil actions may be brought under the Sherman Act, both criminal and civil remedies are employed in the final disposition of Sherman Act cases. Moreover, both public and private remedies are available in antitrust cases. Violation of a final cease-and-desist order issued by the Federal Trade Commission constitutes an offense for which a fine may be imposed; and failure to obey an order of a court affirming such an FTC order constitutes contempt of court and is also punishable. Finally, it is to be noted that settlement of a lawsuit without resort to actual litigation is among the oldest methods of resolving a legal conflict. Such settlement procedures are employed both by the Department of Justice and by the Federal Trade Commission, as the mention of consent decrees and consent orders in preceding chapters clearly indicates. This chapter undertakes to discuss in the following order: (1) criminal sanctions in antitrust cases; (2) public remedies in civil actions; and (3) remedies available to private persons in the form of damage suits and injunction proceedings.

A. CRIMINAL ANTITRUST PROCEEDINGS

The Statutory Provisions

Reference to the discussion of the Sherman Act in Chapter 12 will disclose that violations of the Sherman Act constitute misdemeanors punishable either by a sentence of one year in jail or a fine of $50,000 or both. Section 14 of the Clayton Act provides that, when a corporation is found guilty of a violation of a penal section of the antitrust laws, the directors, officers, or agents who have authorized, ordered, or done the unlawful acts are to be deemed guilty of a misdemeanor and are liable to a punishment of a year in prison or a fine not exceeding $5,000 or both. Section 6 of the Sherman Act provides for the forfeiture of property being transported in interstate or foreign commerce in violation of Section 1. The question which now arises is that of the theory which lies behind the imposition of sanctions in criminal cases generally and in criminal antitrust cases in particular.

Theories of Sanctions in Criminal Cases

The various theories lying behind the imposition of sanctions in criminal cases, as well as the problems facing the conscientious and responsible trial judge, have been clearly expressed by one wise and experienced trial judge, Marvin W. Foote, in the following way:

Trial judges need continually to worry the problem, as well as to worry with the problem, of sentencing.

The literature tells us that the purpose of sentencing should be punishment, deterrence, protection of the public, and rehabilitation. Punishment may be equated with chastisement or retribution. Our society has long abandoned the injunction of an "eye for an eye and a tooth for a tooth"—the *lex talonis*. Rather, punishment now sounds on making the individual responsible for, and accountable for, his acts.

The corollary to the existence of a scheme of punishment set out in legislative enactments is deterrence. There is no complete meeting of the minds on the part of criminologists, psychiatrists, psychologists, social scientists, jurists, legislators, and the public at large as to the dissuasive effect of a code of penalties. Suffice it to say that the law enforcement agencies and the judge on the bench, confronted with a statute or ordinance containing no sanctions for the violation, are furnished nothing to compel compliance. As yet no one has worked out a system of rewards for obedience to the law.

Protection of the public may require confinement of the lawbreaker. An individual or a gang running wild in the community must be brought to a halt in the name of public safety.

As an adjunct to the role of the public, there should be considered the therapeutic value of quarantining an individual. The breaking up of a pattern of behavior, the severing of relationships, and a complete change of environment may be imperative before it is possible to communicate effectively with the offender and make any kind of impression on him. . . .

Rehabilitation must be foremost in the mind of the sentencing judge. Unless the offender is reoriented so that he will accept the restrictions on conduct imposed by society acting through its governmental bodies, there is no hope for his becoming a law-abiding citizen.[1]

The Use of Criminal Sanctions and Antitrust

An interesting question can be raised in the light of Judge Foote's remarks as to whether the purpose of the criminal sanction in antitrust cases is punishment, retribution, deterrence, protection of the public, or rehabilitation.

Incarceration of Offenders. Up to 1950, no businessman had ever gone to jail for violating the Sherman Act. According to testimony in 1950 by the then-Assistant Attorney General in Charge of Antitrust:

A jail sentence was imposed once, so far as a violation by a businessman was concerned.

The serving of the sentence was suspended. The case was appealed, and I believe the case was reversed on appeal. No businessman has ever gone to jail for violation of the Sherman Act.[2]

Numerous trade union officials had, however, served jail sentences as a result of Sherman Act convictions by 1950.[3] This pattern was broken in 1959 when four businessmen were sentenced to 90-day jail terms each by an Ohio District Court.[4] This action was followed in 1960 in a case involving heavy electrical equipment manufacturers in which 31 jail sentences were imposed, of which seven were actually served, and fines totalling $1,926,000 were levied.[5] None of the cases reported by the Assistant Attorney General in Charge of the Antitrust Division as *filed* or *tried* in fiscal year 1967 or in fiscal year 1968 resulted in the *actual* serving of time in jail by a businessman. In one of the cases reported tried in 1968 the defendants pleaded *nolo contendere*, a plea explained further below, but all the defendants were either placed on probation or subjected to fines.[6]

Fines and Forfeitures. In fiscal year 1967, fines and recoveries totaled $2,341,245.53 including $1,639,635 collected as damages for the United States by the Division.[7] Thus the fine has continued to be the most important criminal remedy employed by the government in antitrust cases. In those cases in which actual jail sentences have been served, the Court has probably felt that an

---

[1] Marvin W. Foote, "Further Observations on Sentencing," *Trial Judges' Journal*, Vol. 5, No. 2 (April, 1966), p. 10. (Italics mine.) Judge Foote presides in the District Court of Littleton, Colorado.

[2] *Study of Monopoly Power* (Hearings before the Subcommittee on Study of Monopoly Power of the House Judiciary Committee, 81st Cong., 2d sess.) (Washington, D.C.: U.S. Government Printing Office, 1950), Serial 14, Part 3, p. 3.

[3] For a list see Antitrust in Action (Temporary National Economic Committee Monograph No. 16) (Washington, D.C.: U.S. Government Printing Office, 1941), p. 78.

[4] *United States* v. *McDonough Co. et. al.*, 180 F. Supp. 511 (1959).

[5] *Annual Report of the Attorney General of the United States for the Fiscal Year Ended June 30, 1961* (Washington, D.C.: U.S. Government Printing Office, 1962), p. 190.

[6] *Annual Report of the Attorney General for the Fiscal Year 1968* (Washington, D.C.: U.S. Government Printing Office, 1969), p. 82.

[7] *Ibid.*, p. 82. (The *Annual Report* for 1968, published in 1969, does not report comparable information.)

element of wanton, willful, disregard of law was present in the defendants' conduct. It has been noted in Chapter 12 that in 1955 the size of the fine imposed for a Sherman Act violation was increased by Congress from $5,000 per offense to $50,000 per offense. This increase was strongly supported both by the Attorney General in Charge of Antitrust and by the General Counsel of the Federal Trade Commission. Indeed, the former presented to the Congressional subcommittee holding hearings on the proposed legislation in 1950 a table showing the actual dollar amount of fines levied against certain major corporate defendants in the preceding 12 years and the net profits (both before and after taxes) of these defendants. In addition, the table showed the percentage of profits which a $50,000 fine *would have* represented in 1948. Thus, in the case of General Motors Corporation, five fines totalling $11,000 had been levied in the preceding 12 years. A $50,000 fine in 1948 would have represented only 0.011 percent of the corporation's net income after taxes and 0.006 percent of profits before taxes in that year! In the case of the General Electric Company, which had been fined six times for a total of $30,000, a $50,000 fine would have represented 0.023 percent of profits after taxes.[8] It is, thus, not surprising to find some of the supporters of stiffer penalties referring to the smaller $5,000 fine as a "license" to violate the law.[9]

The same point was dramatically made by Judge Simon Rifkind in the *National Lead* case (cited in the preceding chapter as an example of a patent-antitrust case). Judge Rifkind imposed the maximum fines then permitted under the law (the $5,000 limit applied at the time in question) and said:

I cannot even go through the formula of looking the defendant in the eye and saying, "Is there anything you wish to say before I pronounce sentence?" but I must confess that these amounts being substantially the maximum allowed by the statute, there is very little I can do or very little reflection I can give this matter except make the inevitable comment that a violation of the antitrust laws which persisted from some time in the early 1920's to the 1940's with

respect to which criminal liability is discharged by the payment of $5,000 on account hardly seems to me to be in the nature of a penalty which is likely to discourage violations of the antitrust laws as far as the criminal laws are concerned, but that is a problem for the Congress.[10]

It is, perhaps, also worthwhile noting at this point that in 1955 the Attorney General's National Committee recommended an increase in the size of the maximum fine only to $10,000 but some of the dissenters, including Professor (of Law) Louis B. Schwartz, advocated the $50,000 fine which Congress actually adopted in its amendment of the law in 1955.[11] As has been noted, in 1969 the Attorney General requested that the fine be increased to $500,000 in the case of corporations.

No cases were cited by the Assistant Attorney General in Charge of Antitrust in his reports for fiscal years 1967 and for 1968 in which the forfeiture provision in Section 6 of the Sherman Act was utilized.[12] In fact, the provision was utilized only three times in the first 50 years after enactment of the Sherman Act, and all three cases were settled out of court.[13] There is no reason to believe that this remedy will be more extensively used in the future.

Enforcement of FTC Orders. It should be obvious, but may be worth pointing out, that the Department of Justice can not itself impose criminal sanctions; at most, it can ask a court to do so. Nor does the Federal Trade Commission possess the power to impose such criminal sanctions. Its cease-and-desist orders constitute commands restraining or compelling certain actions on the part of defendants, subject to judicial review. Section 5(1) of the Federal Trade Commission Act provides for a fine of $5,000 for each violation of an FTC final order issued under Section 5 of the FTC Act, "while such order is in effect." It also defines *each day's continuance as a result of "failure or neglect"* as a separate offense. The ways in which an FTC order becomes "final" are stated in Section 5(g) of the FTC Act. In general, orders become "final" if a defendant fails to appeal within 60 days after the order is served upon him, or when

---

[8] *Study of Monopoly Power, op. cit.*, p. 38.

[9] *Ibid.*, p. 9.

[10] *Ibid.*, p. 16.

[11] *Report of the Attorney General's National Committee to Study the Antitrust Laws* (Washington, D.C.: U.S.

Government Printing Office, 1955), p. 352.

[12] *Report of the Attorney General for the Fiscal Year 1967, op. cit.*, pp. 81 ff. See also the *Annual Report* for 1968, *op. cit.*, published in 1969.

[13] *Antitrust in Action, op. cit.*, p. 81.

it is affirmed by an appropriate court. In 1959, similar provisions were made applicable to final orders issued by the FTC under the Clayton Act. These provisions are contained in Section 11(g) of the Clayton Act. In 1955, the Attorney General's Committee sharply criticized the provision which defines *each day's continuance* of a violation *as a result of "failure or neglect"* as a separate offense by saying that the provision could "result in a fine ruinous to all except the most affluent offenders."[14] An alternative, of course, is to obey the order.

Strictly speaking, a violation of an FTC order does not constitute an antitrust violation as such. The wrongful act in such a case is failure to obey the lawful final order. That is, once it is shown that an FTC lawful final order was issued and that the defendant failed to obey it, the government's case has been established. In cases in which an FTC final order has been affirmed by a court, failure to obey the order constitutes also a case of contempt of court. In both cases, prosecution is a duty of the Attorney General and his subordinates. It may be noted that Section 16 of the Clayton Act directs the Attorney General to bring "appropriate proceedings" in cases of violations of orders, and that fines are to be recovered in "civil actions" brought by the United States.

For example, in 1966, for the first time, a civil penalty procedure was employed to collect a fine of $10,000 in a case arising out of violation of an FTC cease-and-desist order issued in 1961 under the Flammable Fabrics Act. The U.S. District Court for the Southern District of New York entered a consent judgment in a compromise settlement of the suit instituted by the Department of Justice at the FTC's request. In addition to providing for the payment of the penalty, the judgment enjoined the defendants from further violation of the FTC's order.[15] (Sections 3(a) and 3(c) of the Flammable Fabrics Act, it may be noted by way of explanation, make the sale of articles of wearing apparel which are "so highly flammable as to be dangerous" an "unfair method of competition" under the Federal Trade Commission Act. Hence the cease-and-desist order in the case in question was issued pursuant to Section 5 of the FTC Act.) It should also be noted that under Section 15 of the Clayton Act, federal district courts are authorized to conduct proceedings in equity instituted by the Attorney General and his subordinates to restrain or prevent violations. Such civil proceedings are discussed further in the next major subdivision. Before doing so, however, it will be useful to consider the kinds of pleas which defendants may make in criminal actions.

The Defendant's Plea in Criminal Antitrust Cases

The Immunity Provision of 1903. One statute enacted in 1903 is worth mentioning at this point. This statute, known as the "Immunity Provision of 1903" (15 U.S.C. 32), provides an immunity from prosecution to persons who testify or produce evidence in "antitrust proceedings, suits, or prosecutions." An amendment to this law (15 U.S.C. 33) restricts the application of the law to "natural" persons; thus it does not apply to corporations.

Plea of "Not Guilty." A defendant who pleads "not guilty" in a criminal antitrust prosecution is protected by the procedural due process provisions of the Sixth Amendment—since these provisions have already been discussed in detail in Chapter 7, no further discussion is necessary here other than to note that the holdings of the Supreme Court in the 1960s concerning right to counsel (in cases of impoverished defendants) and admissibility of evidence (in cases of income tax evasion) apply equally to corporations and their officials on trial under the Sherman Act. A plea of "not guilty" places on the government the burden of establishing "beyond a reasonable doubt" the defendant's guilt. The government is not always successful in doing so. As a matter of fact, in 1940 Walton Hamilton listed 22 cases between 1890 and 1940 in which defendants were not convicted in criminal cases either as a result of a directed verdict, disagreement by the jury, or a verdict of "not guilty." In the same time period, four verdicts of "guilty" were

---

[14] *Report of the Attorney General's National Committee to Study the Antitrust Laws, op. cit.*, p. 373.

[15] The settlement is reported in the FTC's *News Summary* of December 16, 1966.

reversed.[16] More recently, in 1963, the Department of Justice filed an action against H. P. Hood and Co. and the Great Atlantic and Pacific Tea Company charging violations of the Sherman Act. After a 55-day trial the jury, having deliberated two and a half days, found both defendants not guilty of all charges.[17] Thus, contrary to the views of some, it is not true that in antitrust cases, "The Government always wins." On the other hand, a trial based on a Sherman Act charge of conspiracy to allocate customers, fix prices, and rig bids for removal of refuse in the Philadelphia area was concluded on October 16, 1964, with a verdict of "guilty" as to all defendants.[18]

Plea of "Guilty." The Assistant Attorney General in Charge of Antitrust did not report any cases in fiscal year 1968 in which a defendant pleaded "guilty." In the usual criminal case involving such a plea, the trial judge bears a heavy responsibility for insuring that the defendant's constitutional rights are guaranteed and that the defendant understands not only what his rights are but also the implications of such a plea. As one District Court has put it, a plea of "guilty" is an "express confession" in open court.[19] In antitrust cases, since the defendants are usually represented by leading members of the bar, the kinds of problems which exist in cases involving impoverished defendants do not usually arise. Although antitrust defendants do not often plead "guilty," they do often plead *nolo contendere*. As a matter of fact, it has been asserted that in recent years 79 percent of all criminal cases have been disposed of by pleas of *nolo contendere* and by pleas of "guilty."[20] Although there were no "guilty" pleas reported, a number of antitrust complaints filed in fiscal year 1968 resulted in pleas of *nolo contendere* by the defendants. The nature of such pleas is discussed next.

Plea of "Nolo Contendere." Some writers

draw what is in fact a superficial analogy between a consent decree in a civil action (explained further below) and a plea of *nolo contendere* in a criminal case. It is more appropriate to compare and contrast a plea of *nolo contendere* with a plea of "guilty" in a criminal case. As has been noted above, a plea of "guilty" has been properly characterized as an "express confession" in open court. A plea of *nolo contendere* has been similarly appropriately characterized as an *"implied* judicial confession."[21] Indeed, as early as 1869, a federal Court of Appeals pointed out that "the legal effect" of the pleas of *nolo contendere* and of "guilty" are the same *"as regards all the proceedings on the indictment."*[22] The decision as to whether or not to accept a plea of *nolo contendere* is a matter for the discretion of the trial court alone; such a plea may be accepted over the objections of the government. After accepting such a plea, the court may impose a fine, or a prison sentence, or both.[23] Thus, in fiscal year 1965, a plea of *nolo contendere* was accepted in an antitrust case by the District Court for the Eastern District of Pennsylvania over the government's objection, and, immediately after accepting the plea, the Court sentenced each defendant to pay the maximum fine of $50,000.[24] And in 1968, 13 corporations, 13 persons, and a trade association in Michigan pleaded *nolo contendere* to a charge of fixing bread prices and received sentences ranging from probation to fines of $45,000, with total fines reaching $211,500.[25]

In 1950, hearings were held by the House Subcommittee on the Study of Monopoly Power on H.R. 6987. This bill would have required the Attorney General to make periodic reports to the Congress with respect to consent decrees and pleas of *nolo contendere* in antitrust proceedings. But the bill did not become law. In testifying in opposition to the proposed legislation, then-Assistant

---

[16] *Antitrust in Action, op. cit.,* p. 90.

[17] *Annual Report of the Attorney General for the Fiscal Year 1965* (Washington, D.C.: U.S. Government Printing Office, 1966), p. 95.

[18] *Ibid.,* p. 90.

[19] *United States* v. *McDonough Co., et. al.,* 180 F. Supp. 511 (1959).

[20] Dominick R. Vetri, "A Note on Guilty Plea Bargaining," 112 *U. of Penn. Law Review* 865 (1964). This note also contains a useful statement of a suggested procedure to be followed by a trial judge in taking a "guilty" plea.

[21] *United States* v. *McDonough Co., et. al.,* 180 F. Supp. 511 (1959), at p. 515.

[22] *United States* v. *Hartwell,* 26 Fed. Cases 196 (1869), at p. 201. (Italics mine.)

[23] For a history of the plea and its characteristics, see *Hudson* v. *United States,* 272 U.S. 451 (1926).

[24] *Report of the Attorney General for the Fiscal Year 1965, op. cit.,* p. 93.

[25] *Annual Report of the Attorney General for 1968* (Washington, D.C.: U.S. Government Printing Office, 1969), p. 34.

THE PROBLEM OF REMEDIES

Attorney General in Charge of Antitrust, Herbert Bergson, emphasized the difference between consent decrees and pleas of *nolo contendere*, pointing out that the latter involved matters "which are entirely within the discretion of the Federal Courts."[26]

Specifically, Mr. Bergson stated:

. . . a *nolo contendere* plea is something over which the Department of Justice has no control. Such pleas are filed by the defendants with the court and complete discretion lies with the court either to accept or reject the plea. The same is true with respect to the fines levied by the court where such a plea is entered.[27]

Although acceptance or rejection of the plea is a matter for the discretion of the court alone, the Department of Justice does, of course, have some discretion in deciding whether or not to oppose or support the acceptance of such a plea. In the *Philadelphia Electrical Equipment* cases, after the Department had voiced an objection to the acceptance of the *nolo contendere* pleas tendered by the defendants, the Court rejected some of these pleas. Thereafter, some of the defendants changed their pleas to "guilty" and some were permitted by the Court to plead *nolo contendere*.

From the point of view of a defendant, a plea of *nolo contendere* possesses one advantage which arises out of the fact that decrees in civil or criminal cases entered "before any testimony is taken" do not constitute *prima facie* evidence against a defendant in private treble damage actions. Final decrees or judgments arising from litigation do constitute such *prima facie* evidence (which must be rebutted by the defendant). Moreover, consent decrees in public civil actions which result from negotiation without litigation are similarly not available to the plaintiff for use to establish a *prima facie* case in a private action. It is to public *civil* actions that we turn next.

B. GOVERNMENTAL CIVIL ACTIONS IN ANTITRUST CASES

Section 4 of the Sherman Act is the locus of authority for actions in equity on the part of the United States in Sherman Act antitrust cases. This section vests federal district courts with authority to prevent and restrain violations of the Sherman Act. Section 15 of the Clayton Act contains a related provision pertaining to the Clayton Act. As we have seen in Chapter 14 in the discussion of the *Pennington* case, Section 20 of the Clayton Act exempts *bona fide* labor disputes from this provision. In 1955, Congress amended Section 4 of the Clayton Act to provide (in Section 4a) for an action by the United States for the recovery of *actual* (not treble) damages in the case of an injury resulting from a violation of the antitrust laws. Also, as has been pointed out earlier, cease-and-desist orders by the FTC are similar to injunctions in their operation. Finally, both the Department of Justice and the FTC have developed procedures for the settlement of antitrust cases without resort to actual litigation. These remedies are discussed below.

Equity as a Method of Enforcement: Early Sherman Act and Section 7 Clayton Act Cases; Dissolution, Divorcement, and Divestiture

The government may bring *either* a criminal *or* a civil action or *both* in an antitrust case. An injunction by a court of equity may be either prohibitive or mandatory. That is, it may order a defendant to cease and desist from a particular practice, or it may order him to take some specific action. A clear statement by a Court of Appeals of the scope of the remedies available under Section 4 of the Sherman Act appears in *United States* v. *Great Lakes Towing Company*, decided in 1914.[28] This case involved a finding by the District Court that the Great Lakes Towing Company had monopolized the towing business on the Great Lakes by acquiring a controlling interest (through stock ownership) in all its competing companies and had engaged in predatory practices by discriminatory pricing and exclusive dealing contracts.[29] In discussing the remedy to be applied, the Court of Appeals stated that the "controlling inquiry" was: "What remedy promises the most effective relief against the evils found to exist?" Moreover, it pointed out that a

---

[26] *Study of Monopoly Power, op. cit.*, p. 68.
[27] *Ibid.*, p. 69. (Italics mine.)
[28] 217 Fed. 656 (1914), at p. 658.
[29] *United States* v. *Great Lakes Towing Co., et. al.*, 208 Fed. 733 (1913).

receivership might be employed when necessary but ought not to be used otherwise. In the case in question, the Court of Appeals thought that a prohibitive injunction enjoining "unfair" rate cutting and discrimination, as well as prohibiting exclusive dealing contracts would be adequate.[30]

In arriving at its position, the Court of Appeals had the benefit of a number of earlier Supreme Court opinions. For example, among the earliest cases in which *dissolution* (the dissolving of a company) was used was the *Northern Securities* case of 1904.[31] In this case, which involved the ownership of the stock of otherwise competing railroads by a holding company, the Court ordered the distribution of the stock of the competing railroads directly to the stockholders of the holding company, thereby, in effect, ordering the dissolution of the holding company. However, to the extent that the stockholders were able to unify their actions in a "harmony of interest" after the dissolution of the holding company, the effect of the decree on competition was obviously negligible. Dissolution was also employed as the remedy in the *Standard Oil*[32] and *American Tobacco*[33] cases of 1911.

In the *Standard Oil* case, a key phrase in the District Court's decree was this statement: "The defendants are not prohibited by this decree from distributing ratably to the shareholders of the principal company the shares to which they are equitably entitled in the stocks of the defendant corporations that are parties to the combination."[34] The dissolution plan in this case was thus analogous to that used in the *Northern Securities* case. The effect of the dissolution was to leave the controlling interests in the member companies in the hands of the persons who had controlled the original illegal trust. Most contemporary commentators thus considered the decree ineffective. In the *American Tobacco Company*

case, the decree involved not only the dissolution of the trust and the creation of new companies with a distribution of their stock to former shareholders of the original trust but also a series of injunctions pertaining to the acquisition of stock by any one company in another. Despite its complicated nature, however, this decree left the original organizers of the trust in effective control of the industry.[35]

In each of the three cases discussed so far, the remedy of *dissolution* was employed. In addition to *dissolution*, the remedies of *divestiture* and *divorcement* have also been used. These three remedies, *dissolution*, *divorcement*, and *divestiture* are often referred to as "the three *D's*" of antitrust. *Divorcement* and *divestiture* are related in that each involves an order to the defendant to dispose of either assets or stock holdings in a subsidiary, rather than the dissolving of the parent defendant company. An example of an early case involving divestiture is the *Union Pacific* case of 1913.[36] In this case, the Union Pacific Railroad Company was ordered to divest itself of a controlling stock interest in the Southern Pacific Railway held for Union Pacific by its subsidiary, the Oregon Short Line Railroad Company. The defendants originally proposed a plan involving a distribution of this stock to Union Pacific stockholders. However, the Supreme Court rejected this plan, which was obviously modeled upon those employed in the earlier cases discussed above.[37]

Indeed, the Court was willing to look through form to substance and thought it likely that under the proposed plan:

. . . the large stockholders could, by purchases and transfers of the stock, get into their own hands the power of choosing directors of both companies, and thus, though in a different manner, the Southern Pacific Company would continue to be in the practical control of the Union Pacific Company, which has been found to be a rival and competing company within the meaning of the law.[38]

---

[30] *United States* v. *Great Lakes Towing Co., et. al.,* 217 Fed. 656 (1914), at p. 659.

[31] *Northern Securities Co.* v. *United States,* 193 U.S. 197 (1904).

[32] 173 Fed. 177 (1909). The 1911 Supreme Court decision in the *Standard Oil* case upheld the District Court's dissolution decree with minor modifications. See *Standard Oil Co. of New Jersey* v. *United States,* 221 U.S. 1 (1911), at p. 82.

[33] 191 Fed. 371 (1911); *U.S.* v. *American Tobacco*

Co., 221 U.S. 106 (1911).

[34] *United States* v. *Standard Oil Co. of New Jersey,* 173 Fed. 177 (1909), at p. 199.

[35] *United States* v. *American Tobacco Co., et. al.,* 191 Fed. 371 (1911).

[36] *United States* v. *Union Pacific Railroad Co.,* 226 U.S. 470 (1913).

[37] *Ibid.,* at p. 474.

[38] *Ibid.,* at p. 476.

It is instructive also at this point to consider briefly certain aspects of the *International Harvester* case of 1918.[39] By 1918, it will be recalled from Chapter 12, the Federal Trade Commission Act had been enacted. Section 7 of that law provides that a trial court may appoint the FTC to act as a Master in Chancery to assist that court in framing the decree in an antitrust case. Under Section 6 of the FTC Act, the FTC is authorized on its own initiative to conduct investigations into the question of the manner of compliance with an antitrust decree.

In 1914, the combination known as the International Harvester Company was ordered dissolved.[40] A series of negotiations and maneuvers by the defendant followed; and in 1918, the government sought a modification of a consent decree which had been entered in the case earlier that year. In doing so, the government relied on a study of competitive conditions in the industry made by the FTC and requested that the defendant be split into three competing companies. The trial court rejected the government's request, asserting that competitive conditions already existed in the industry in 1918. On appeal, the Supreme Court commented on the government's reliance on the FTC study of the industry, a study whose conclusions were contrary to those subsequently stated by the trial court, by saying that the statements in the FTC study constituted "hearsay."[41]

As we have seen in Chapter 14, after the early Sherman Act cases, and particularly after the decision in the *United States Steel* case of 1920, until the *Alcoa* case of 1945, the Court did not often find mergers to be a violation of the Sherman Act. Indeed, Professor Walter Adams has remarked that the *United States Steel* and *International Harvester* opinions constituted "a virtual cease fire order on the divestiture front."[42] Although the Supreme Court permitted the FTC to order divestiture of stock illegally

owned under Section 7 of the Clayton Act in the *Western Meat Company* case in 1926,[43] the Court held in that same year in a number of companion cases that the FTC had no power to order divestiture of physical assets under Section 7, thereby making Section 7 what the FTC identified as "a virtual nullity."[44]

Equity as a Method of Enforcement: The Sherman Act Since 1945 and Section 7 Since 1950

As we have seen in Chapter 14, in the *Alcoa* case of 1945 the defendant was held guilty of "monopolizing" under Section 2 of the Sherman Act. At that time, the decision was hailed by some as evidence of a turning point in the application of the Sherman Act. The *Alcoa* case was remanded to the District Court for the formulation of a decree granting a remedy to the government. The occurrence of World War II postponed this action until after the end of the war. In 1947, following the disposal of the government's war surplus aluminium producing facilities to the Kaiser and Reynolds Companies, respectively, Alcoa petitioned the District Court to rule that competition now prevailed in the industry. The government, however, denied this claim and requested that a new company be created from Alcoa's existing facilities to compete with what would then remain of Alcoa after this divestiture, and with Kaiser and Reynolds. Judge Knox of the District Court refused to grant the government's request.[45]

Among other things, Judge Knox thought that it would be "a singular disservice to the public if the skill and technique of Alcoa's research department were impaired."[46] He further thought that if Alcoa were separated from its Canadian subsidiary, Alcan (Aluminium Company Limited of Canada), imports from Canada would provide "effective" competition in the United States for Alcoa, and, therefore, he required stockholders owning shares in both these

[39] *International Harvester Co., of New Jersey* v. *United States,* 248 U.S. 587 (1918).
[40] *United States* v. *International Harvester Co.,* 214 Fed. 987 (1914).
[41] *United States* v. *International Harvester Co.,* 274 U.S. 693 (1927), at p. 703.
[42] Walter Adams, "Dissolution, Divorcement, Divestiture: The Phyrric Victories of Antitrust," 27 *Ind. Law Journal* 1 (1951), at p. 3.

[43] *Federal Trade Commission* v. *Western Meat Co.,* 272 U.S. 554 (1926).
[44] Federal Trade Commission, *Chain Store: Final Report on the Chain Store Investigation* (Washington, D.C.: U.S. Government Printing Office, 1935), p. 89.
[45] *United States* v. *Aluminum Co. of America,* 91 F. Supp. 333 (1950), at p. 416.
[46] *Ibid.,* p. 418.

companies to divest themselves of their shares in one of the two.[47] At the same time, because Kaiser and Reynolds had been in operation only a short time, Judge Knox decided that the court should retain jurisdiction of the case for another five years. At the end of the five year period, another district court Judge (Cashin) concluded that competitive conditions in the industry were such that a further extension of time to request relief should be denied.[48]

In a number of other Sherman Act cases decided shortly after the end of World War II, the Supreme Court refused to order divestiture. Thus, in the *National Lead* case of 1947 (a patent licensing case discussed in the preceding chapter), the Court rejected the government's petition for divestiture because there was no evidence that the "physical properties" had been "acquired or used in a manner violative of the Sherman Act" except as an incident of the patent licensing agreements. Moreover, said the Court:

There is no showing that four major competing units would be preferable to two, or . . . that six would be better than four. Likewise there is no showing of the necessity for this divestiture of plants or of its practicality and fairness. . . . To separate the operating units of going concerns without more supporting evidence than has been presented here to establish either the need for, or the feasibility of, such separation would amount to an abuse of discretion.[49]

Quite obviously, the Court had not in 1947 gone as far in the direction of the market structure test as it did in its decisions under Section 7 of the Clayton Act in the early 1960s (as the discussion of these decisions in Chapter 17 makes clear). In 1951, the majority of the Court voted to delete, on grounds that the provision was unnecessary, a divestiture provision contained in the decree of the District Court in the *Timken* case (discussed further in the next chapter). The provision would have required an American company, the Timken Roller

Bearing Company, to divest itself of its controlling interests in a British and in a French subsidiary.[50]

Four years earlier, in 1947, the Supreme Court had approved, despite the government's objection, a decree of a district court permitting divestiture by the Pullman Company of its operating subsidiary to a combination representing the principal American railroads.[51] In 1943, the government had brought a Sherman Act civil action against Pullman Incorporated which controlled two subsidiaries, Pullman Standard Manufacturing Company (the producer of virtually all sleeping-car equipment then in use by American railroads) and Pullman Company (which owned and operated this equipment under various restrictive leasing arrangements).[52] The government sought divestiture by the parent of both subsidiaries. However, the lower court decreed that Pullman Incorporated should divest itself only of *one* of the two, either of the manufacturing company or of the operating subsidiary.[53] The company chose to divest itself of the operating subsidiary, and this choice was sustained, as noted above, by the Supreme Court in 1947.

One other divestiture decree dealt with by the Supreme Court in the years following the end of World War II must be noted. This decree was handed down by a lower court in the *Paramount Pictures* case in 1947 and made more stringent by the Supreme Court in 1948. The case arose as a result of (1) an allegation by the government that major producers of motion pictures were following restrictive practices (including the fixing of minimum admission charges) in the distribution of their films to exhibitors and (2) a request by the government that the producers be required to withdraw from the business of management and ownership of moving picture theaters. The District Court rejected this request because it did not believe that divestiture or divorcement were appropriate remedies in this case.[54] In 1948, the Supreme Court held that the

[47] *Ibid.*

[48] *United States* v. *Aluminum Co. of America*, 153 F. Supp. 132 (1957).

[49] *United States* v. *National Lead Co.*, 332 U.S. 319 (1947), at p. 352.

[50] *Timken Roller Bearing Co.* v. *United States*, 341 U.S. 593 (1951).

[51] *United States* v. *Pullman Co.*, 64 F. Supp. 108

(1946); 330 U.S. 806 (1947).

[52] *United States* v. *Pullman Co.*, 50 F. Supp. 123 (1943).

[53] *United States* v. *Pullman Co.*, 53 F. Supp. 908 (1944), at pp. 909–911.

[54] *United States* v. *Paramount Pictures*, 70 F. Supp. 53 (1947), at pp. 67–68.

government was entitled to the relief it had requested. Speaking for the majority, Justice Douglas wrote:

> We have gone into the record far enough to be confident that at least some of these acquisitions [of motion picture theaters] by the exhibitor-defendants were the unlawful practices which the defendants have inflicted on the industry. To the extent that these acquisitions were the fruits of monopolistic practices or restraints of trade, they should be divested. And no permission to buy out the other owner [in cases of joint ownership with independent owners] should be given a defendant. . . .
>
> Furthermore, if the joint ownership is an alliance with one who is or would be an operator but for the joint ownership, divorce should be decreed even though the affiliation was innocently acquired. For that joint ownership would afford opportunity to perpetuate the effects of the restraint of trade which the exhibitor-defendants have inflicted on the industry.[55]

In 1951, Professor Walter Adams (whose advocacy of the market structure test has been discussed in Chapter 13) surveyed most of the cases involving dissolution, divorcement, and divestiture between the end of World War II and 1951 and concluded that "the relief obtained by the Government in Section 2 cases under the Sherman Act" had been "inadequate."[56] According to Professor Adams, the *Paramount* case discussed above represented one exception, and the remedy employed in it represented an economic victory as well as a legal one. This decree was, of course, consistent with the market structure test advocated by Adams.

As we have already seen in Chapter 17, the Celler–Kefauver Act making acquisition of assets as well as of stock unlawful under stated conditions was adopted in 1950. The enactment of this legislation and the apparent Congressional intent embodied in it was not lost upon the courts. Since the late 1950s, the remedy of divestiture has been widely used to "unscramble" mergers consummated in violation of Section 7 as amended and also in some Section 2 Sherman Act cases. However, it should also be noted that dissolution was rejected in the *United Shoe Machinery* case (discussed in

Chapter 14) by District Judge Wyzanski in 1953. Judge Wyzanski wrote:

> The Government's proposal that the Court dissolve United into three separate manufacturing companies is unrealistic. United conducts all machine manufacture at one plant in Beverly, with one set of jigs and tools, one foundry, one laboratory for machinery problems, one managerial staff, and one labor force. It takes no Solomon to see that this organism cannot be cut into three equal and viable parts.
>
> A petition for dissolution should reflect greater attention to practical problems and should involve *supporting economic* data and *prophesies* such as are presented in corporate reorganization and public utility dissolution cases.[57]

At the same time, in addition to relief pertaining to United's leasing practices, Judge Wyzanski thought that:

> . . . United should be divested of its business of manufacturing and distributing . . . particular supplies [nails, tacks, and eyelets for the shoe machinery market] because this is the kind of dissolution which can be carried out practically, and which will also reduce monopoly power in each of the affected supply fields. . . .[58]

We will reconsider this decree later in this chapter.

The *du Pont–General Motors* decision, it will be recalled from the discussion in Chapter 17, was based on original Section 7 of the Clayton Act since the complaint was filed prior to 1950, even though the Supreme Court did not give its final opinion until 1957. The final decree in this case was not rendered until 1962 (1962 *Trade Cases*, Par. 70,245). It required du Pont and certain members of the du Pont family to divest themselves of the 60 million shares of General Motors stock being illegally held. In 1962, Congress adopted Public Law 87–493 to ease the tax burden which would fall on those having to dispose of the stock being held in violation of Section 7. This law had the stated purpose of amending the Internal Revenue Code "to provide that a distribution of stock made pursuant to an order enforcing the antitrust laws shall not be treated as a dividend distribution but as a return of capital," and

---

[55] *United States* v. *Paramount Pictures*, 334 U.S. 131 (1948), at pp. 152–153.

[56] Adams, *op. cit.*, p. 31.

[57] *United States* v. *United Shoe Machinery Corp.*, 110 F. Supp. 295 (1953), at p. 348. (Italics mine.)

[58] *Ibid.*, at p. 351.

thus be subject to a lower tax rate. The law applied to court orders rendered after January 1, 1961, if the case commenced before January 1, 1959. Thus the law was *specifically tailored* to fit the divestiture in the *du Pont* case!

As we have also seen in Chapter 17, the *Bethlehem–Youngstown Steel Company* case was the first case under amended Section 7 won by the Department of Justice. However, since the merger had not yet taken place, the District Court merely enjoined the merger and no divestiture order was necessary.[59]

The first case under Section 7 won by the Justice Department in which divestiture was actually ordered was the *Maryland and Virginia Milk Producers' Association* case, finally decided by a District Court in 1958 and affirmed by the Supreme Court in 1960.[60] Since then there have been many divestiture proceedings, including some provided for in consent decrees, a matter discussed further below. As we have also seen in Chapter 17, the *Pillsbury* case of 1953 was one of the earliest actions before the FTC involving a merger under amended Section 7, but the divestiture order in that case was finally vacated in 1966 by a Court of Appeals.[61] Action by the FTC will also be further discussed below.

One Section 2 Sherman Act case decided in 1966 in which the lower court's divestiture decree was affirmed by the Supreme Court is worth noting first. This case is the *Grinnell* case, also discussed in Chapter 14. Having held the defendants guilty of monopolization under Section 2 of the Sherman Act, the District Court enjoined them from engaging in certain practices and ordered the parent Grinnell Company to file not later than April 1, 1966, a plan of divestiture of the stock it held in a number of subsidiary companies. The company was given the option of selling the stock, of distributing it to its stockholders, or of using a combination of these methods. The government at first argued that this divestiture was inadequate

but later abandoned this position. This stock distribution plan, it may be noted, was not unlike those used in the early Sherman Act cases discussed above. However, the District Court also enjoined the defendants from ever again employing the President or Chairman of the Board of the Grinnel Corporation.[62] The Supreme Court eliminated the provision concerning employment from the decree, saying that, while such a provision might be appropriate in a case of conspicuous predatory conduct, such was not the case in this instance.[63] The Supreme Court did, however, sustain the divestiture and injunctive provisions of the decree, saying, "Dissolution of the combination is essential, as indicated by many of our cases, starting with *Standard Oil Co.* v. *United States.* . . ."[64]

An interesting and important procedural development concerning the framing of divestiture decrees occurred in 1967, when the Supreme Court held that Rule 24(a)(3) of the Federal Rules of Civil Procedure—which grants a right to intervene in a civil action to one who is "so situated as to be adversely affected by . . . disposition of property which is in custody of the court or an officer thereof"—applies to the framing of divestiture orders and is *not* limited to those *already* possessing an interest in the property.[65]

The case in question arose in the course of the framing of the divestiture decree which the Court had ordered in the *El Paso Natural Gas Co.* case, discussed in Chapter 17. Under the 1967 holding, parties who may be adversely affected by a dissolution decree now have a right to intervene in the proceedings to present their arguments to the court framing the decree.

In this case, the District Court had approved a divestiture plan under which a "New Company" was to be created as a new competitor. The Supreme Court, in remanding the case took the occasion to provide "Guidelines" for the divestiture decree under which the competitive position

[59] *United States* v. *Bethlehem Steel Corp.*, 168 F. Supp. 576 (1958).

[60] *United States* v. *Maryland and Virginia Milk Producers' Assn., Inc.*, 167 F. Supp. 45 (1958); 167 F. Supp. 799 (1958); 168 F. Supp. 880 (1959); and *Maryland and Virginia Milk Producers' Assn., Inc.* v. *United States*, 362 U.S. 458 (1960).

[61] *Pillsbury Co.* v. *Federal Trade Commission*, 354 F.

2d 952 (1966).

[62] *United States* v. *Grinnell Corp.*, 236 F. Supp. 244 (1965).

[63] *United States* v. *Grinnell Corp.*, 384 U.S. 563 (1966), at p. 579.

[64] *Ibid.*, p. 580.

[65] *Cascade Natural Gas Corp.* v. *El Paso Natural Gas Co., et. al.*, 386 U.S. 129 (1967).

of the "New Company" was to be no less favorable than that of the acquired company had been before "it was obliterated." A new decree was made by the District Court, and again an appeal was taken to the Supreme Court by a "consumer spokesman" under the prior decision.[65a] Again the Supreme Court vacated the District Court's decree and remanded the case, pointing out that under the second decree, the acquiring company had been given an interest in the "New Company" and, therefore, the "New Company" had not been put into the position enjoyed by the acquired company prior to the acquisition. This case is important since it demonstrates the "tough" policy adopted in 1969 by the Court in cases involving divestiture.

One other case involving divestiture is worth noting at this point, although— unlike the cases discussed so far—*this* case was settled by means of a consent decree, and a more complete discussion of consent decrees as a method of antitrust settlement must be postponed until later in this chapter. The case in point is the *United Fruit Company* case of 1958. The terms of the consent decree were such that United Fruit Company was required to create out of its assets a competitor capable of importing into the East Coast, the Gulf Coast, and/or the West Coast of the United States, approximately 9 million stems of bananas per year. Also United Fruit was required to divest itself of all stock or proprietary interest by June 30, 1966, in International Railways of Central America, either by private sale to purchasers having no relationship to or affiliation with United; on the open market on the London or New York stock exchanges; or by a combination of these two methods.[66] What is noteworthy in the *United Fruit* case is the fact that an attempt was made in this case in the *initial* decree to prevent control of the enterprise from being reacquired by the same persons who had originally had control of the enterprises when the antitrust violations had occurred. Failure to accomplish this result, it will be recalled from the discussion of the early Sherman Act decrees already given in this chapter, was considered a principal short-coming in these early decrees. In addition to the use of the remedies of dissolution, divorcement, and divestiture in the case of proceedings in equity resulting from complaints filed by the Department of Justice, it has been casually noted above that the Federal Trade Commission has also employed these remedies in its issuance of cease-and-desist orders. In the next section of this chapter, the use of such remedies by the FTC will be more closely considered.

FTC Orders as a Remedy in Section 7 Clayton Act Cases

In addition to civil actions filed by the Department of Justice and the use of the remedies described above in Sherman Act and Section 7 cases, the FTC, as we have seen, may order dissolution, divorcement, or divestiture in one of its final orders. Such orders may be appealed, and, as was true in the *Pillsbury* case mentioned above, the FTC order may eventually be overturned by a court. In recent years, as we will see now, the Commission seems increasingly to have relied on orders prohibiting *future* acquisitions by defendants and upon consent orders leading to divestiture. The total number of cases brought under Section 7 both by the Department of Justice and the FTC since 1950 is very large. For example, as early as October 1, 1962, 106 cases involving 599 acquisitions had been instituted since the 1950 amendment of Section 7 of the Clayton Act, and 47 cases had been concluded at the district court or Commission level.[67] Although no recent combined and cumulative statistics are available, the total number of cases has increased considerably since 1962. Between 1961 and 1967, the Department of Justice filed 77 merger cases, while in 1967 the FTC alone instituted 87 formal and informal cases. Under the circumstances, no real purpose would be served in this book by attempting to examine all the divestiture orders issued by the FTC in Section 7 cases since 1950. Instead, our procedure will be to consider a few typical cases.

[65a] *Utah Public Service Commission* v. *El Paso Natural Gas Company*, 395 U.S. 464 (1969).

[66] *United States* v. *United Fruit Co.*, 1958 Trade Cases No. 68941, Feb. 4, 1958. See especially Paragraphs VII and VIII of the decree.

[67] *Mergers and Superconcentration* (Staff Report of the House Select Committee on Small Business, 87th Cong., 2d sess.) (Washington, D.C.: U.S. Government Printing Office, 1962), p. 19.

One interesting case in 1965 involved the modification of a FTC order in accordance with a final order issued by the United States Court of Appeals for the Fifth Circuit. The modification order pertained to a divestiture order issued by the FTC in April 1962 against Foremost Dairies, Inc. Under the modified order, Foremost was forbidden to acquire any domestic manufacturer, processor, or seller of certain dairy products without FTC approval, and assets and properties to be divested by Foremost could not be disposed of to anyone not approved in advance as a buyer by the FTC. Moreover, the order contained an injunction prohibiting Foremost from acquiring a competing dairy company for a period of ten years without FTC approval.[68]

The technique of enjoining a defendant in a Section 7 case from acquiring any competitor in a given future time period used in the *Foremost Dairies* case was also employed by the Commission in 1966 when it issued an order to National Tea Company, the nation's fifth largest food chain, ordering it not to acquire any food retailer for ten years without prior approval by the Commission.[69]

The FTC has also used consent orders in merger cases; 11 consent orders were issued in formal merger cases in fiscal year 1967. For example, it signed consent orders in 1966 with the May Department Stores of St. Louis and with E. J. Korvette and Spartan Industries, both of New York City, in which the May Company agreed not to acquire any department store other than General Merchandise, Apparel and Furniture (GMAF) for ten years, and in which Korvette and Spartan agreed that, upon the consummation of their merger, the surviving corporation would not acquire for ten years, without FTC approval, any GMAF store.[70] Another Consent Order in 1966 required Ideal Cement Company of Denver to sell, within two years, Builder's Supply Company of Houston, Texas. This

vertical merger had involved a Portland cement producer (Ideal) and a producer of cement products (and hence a consumer of cement, Builder's Supply Company). Also in 1966, the Commission's Final Order in the *General Foods–S.O.S.* (product extension) merger case required General Foods to divest itself of S.O.S. within one year.[71]

Another interesting case in 1966 was that of the Kaiser Cement and Gypsum Corporation, a cement manufacturer and distributor which had acquired another cement manufacturing plant on the West Coast and merged the latter into its operations. The Commission issued a divestiture order in 1964 with divestiture required within three years. In 1966, a majority of the Commission approved divestiture to the Pittsburgh Plate Glass Company. Commissioners Reilly and Jones dissented from this approval on grounds that it amounted to fostering a conglomerate merger and made the Commission a "silent partner" in the conglomerate merger movement.[72]

Problems Involved in Divestiture; Premerger Notification

The problem of finding a buyer in a case in which divestiture is ordered is a difficult one. The problem is one of "unscrambling the merger." Several attempts to amend the law by requiring *premerger* notification and approval have run into strong opposition in Congress and it seems unlikely that any preventive legislation of this type will soon be adopted.[73]

However, although Congress has not adopted legislation requiring the FTC to be notified in advance by those planning mergers of their merger plans, Section 6 of the Federal Trade Commission Act already authorizes the FTC to conduct investigations and require written answers to questions and other information from business firms in conjunction with such investigations. In 1967, the Commission coupled its investigatory powers with a

[68] Federal Trade Commission Modified Order 6495, reported in the FTC's *News Summary* of March 12, 1965.

[69] Federal Trade Commission Order 7453, reported in the FTC's *News Summary* of March 22, 1966.

[70] Federal Trade Commission Consent Orders C–1105 and C–1106, September 12, 1966.

[71] Federal Trade Commission Final Order 8600, reported in the FTC's *News Summary* of March 26, 1966.

[72] The FTC's Approval Letter and the dissenting statements were reported in the FTC's *News Summary* of July 20, 1966.

[73] See, for example, *Premerger Notifications* (Hearings before the Antitrust Subcommittee of the House Judiciary Committee, 84th Cong., 2d sess.) (Washington, D.C.: U.S. Government Printing Office, 1956).

statement of guidelines pertaining to the Commission's enforcement policy concerning mergers in certain selected industries and required companies in these selected industries to notify the Commission at least 60 days in advance of the consummation of any merger of the specified type. In announcing this requirement (in which two commissioners did not concur), the Commission emphasized that the requirement did not mean that the firms in question had to request Commission *approval* prior to the actual consummation of the merger. Such a combination "Enforcement Policy *cum* Premerger Notification Statement" was issued by the FTC on January 18, 1967, in the case of "Food Distribution Industries" and on January 24, 1967, in the case of "Vertical Mergers in the Cement Industry." (The "guidelines" have already been noted in Chapter 17.) The novel procedure employed in the cases of these announcements would seem in fact to amount to a requirement of actual premerger *notification* even without the enactment of special legislation looking toward this end.

As a matter of fact, on April 8, 1969, the Commission adopted a resolution requiring firms undertaking corporate mergers involving firms with combined assets of $250 million or more to notify the Commission, and supply special reports within ten days after any merger agreement in principle is reached and no less than 60 days prior to (later changed to "as soon as possible") the actual consummation of such a merger. Reports are also required in cases of firms acquiring at least 10% of the voting stock of another corporation with assets of $10 million or more. The Commission was again careful to note that its reporting requirement did not mean that prior Commission approval was necessary in the case of mergers and cited Section 6 of the FTC Act as the basic authority for its action.

There seems to be no good reason why the reporting procedure under Section 6 and statements concerning enforcement policy cannot be extended to cases in a large number of other specific industries beyond the ones in which they have been so far used. Indeed, the reporting requirement under Section 6 could also be usefully employed in the settlement of Section 7 cases by consent decrees and by consent orders. It is to the nature of such non-litigated settlements that our attention will next be devoted.

Consent Decrees as a Method of Antitrust Enforcement

Nature of the Remedy. As has been noted in the discussion of the plea of *nolo contendere* earlier in this chapter, there is a significant difference between a plea of *nolo contendere* in a criminal case and settlement of a civil suit by a consent decree. Acceptance or rejection of a plea of *nolo contendere* is solely a matter of the discretion of the trial court and such pleas may be entered over the government's objection. A consent decree, on the other hand, is one entered by the consent of *both* parties and partakes of the nature of a contract made under the sanction of a court as a settlement of a lawsuit.[74] In 1964 in the *Ward Baking Company* case, the Supreme Court was faced with the precise question of stating the conditions under which a District Court could enter (without the agreement of the government) a consent decree in a civil antitrust case involving a charge of violation of Section 1 of the Sherman Act. The civil action had been preceded by a criminal action in which four of the defendants had pleaded *nolo contendere* to charges of conspiring to fix prices on sales of bread in sales on governmental accounts. In the civil action, the District Court entered a consent decree despite the government's objection. The Supreme Court then vacated the judgment below and remanded the case for trial. In doing so, Justice Goldberg spoke for the majority and said:

. . . where the Government seeks an item of relief to which evidence adduced at a trial may show that it is entitled, the District Court may not enter a "consent" judgment without the actual consent of the Government. There is nothing in the language or history of Section 5 of the Clayton Act indicating that Congress intended to give a defendant the privilege of rejecting the bona fide demands of the Government and at the same time avoiding an adjudication on the merits of the complaint.[75]

Section 5 of the Clayton Act provides that a final judgment or decree in a civil or

---

[74] *Kelly* v. *Town of Milan*, 21 F. 842 (1884).
[75] *United States* v. *Ward Baking Co.*, 376 U.S. 327 (1964), at p. 334.

criminal antitrust action by the United States shall be prima facie evidence (creating a rebuttable presumption) against a defendant in a private action to enforce the antitrust laws but excepts from this provision consent judgments or decrees entered "before any testimony has been taken," and so exempts consent decrees and pleas of *nolo contendere*. Thus a similarity does exist in the legal effect of consent decrees and pleas of *nolo contendere* in the antitrust field since both constitute exceptions to Section 5 of the Clayton Act. But this similarity is a product of statutory law only.

Although Section 5 of the Clayton Act is the only provision in any of the antitrust laws which contains mention of consent decrees, since a consent decree was first employed in the *Otis Elevator* case in 1906,[76] its use as a method of settling civil antitrust cases has increased to the point that this remedy is the one most often used.

The increased use dates from about the year 1940, when 21 such decrees were made. From 1906 to 1940, although ten decrees were made in 1927 and 12 were made in 1926, in no other year did the number exceed seven. On the other hand, the number has exceeded ten in every year since 1940 with the exception of 1947 when ten consent decrees were made, although no data are available for 1944–46 inclusive.[77] The *Annual Report of the Attorney General for the Fiscal Year Ended June 30, 1967* notes that consent decrees were signed by some but not all defendants in six cases but does not provide a total for the year. The *Annual Report* for 1969 provides no data of this kind.

Publication of Consent Decrees. With respect to the question of the publication of consent decrees, the following discussion of the matter (during a 1950 Congressional hearing on proposed legislation which would have required the Department of Justice to make annual reports to Congress both on consent decrees and on pleas of *nolo contendere*) is instructive. Mr. Herbert A. Bergson, who was then Assistant Attorney General in Charge of Antitrust, testified during the hearing. The exchange reads as follows:

. . . Mr. Chairman . . . you suggested that we might publish these decrees in the Federal Register. The decrees are published now by the Commerce Clearing House. They are matters of public record.

THE CHAIRMAN. Well, you must pay for getting the reports.

MR. BERGSON. Well whoever wants to buy the Commerce Clearing House Service can do so.

THE CHAIRMAN. I know, but if I have not got the money, I do not get Commerce Clearing House reports.

MR. BERGSON. It is available to all and sundry.

THE CHAIRMAN. That is not a public record.

MR. BERGSON. If what you desire to accomplish by this bill is to have copies of all decrees and copies of all complaints and have copies of all transcripts of the proceedings in which the decree is entered, we would be delighted to furnish them.

THE CHAIRMAN. Speaking of Commerce Clearing House, I do not know what the costs of their reports are, but—

MR. BERGSON. I have no objection to doing that.

THE CHAIRMAN. (continuing) I would not say that is a public record.

For example, I do not know how many newspapers get the Commerce Clearing House; certainly the small papers probably cannot afford to get the services of that sort, and similar services, so that there is no real publicity concerning these consent decrees. Yes, maybe the metropolitan dailies may have them, but not the other papers.

REPRESENTATIVE MICHENER. If these reports were filed, it might have the advantage of a report being filed with the Congress which is available to the press. The press would want publicity on it, and could take its time and read those reports and get the publicity. That is about it, is it not?

MR. BERGSON. Mr. Michener, every time a consent decree is entered, we hand 500 copies of that decree out to the press and you can comb all of the newspapers of the country to find more than a passing reference to the decree; and making them available here, I am sure, is not going to induce the press to publicize them any more.

We have never kept a consent decree from the press. We want them publicized. We give the press about 500 copies of them every time we enter one.[78]

The proposed legislation was, unfortunately, not enacted. It is difficult to understand why consent decrees approved by the courts

---

[76] Reproduced in Roger Shale, *Decrees and Judgments in Federal Antitrust Cases* (Washington, D.C.: U.S. Government Printing Office, 1918), p. 107.

[77] Data for the years 1906–1939 may be found in

Antitrust in Action, op. cit., Appendix D. (Subsequent consent decrees are published annually in Commerce Clearing House, *Trade cases.*)

[78] *Study of Monopoly Power, op. cit.,* pp. 52–53.

are not published in the *Federal Register* along with other official documents, particularly since FTC consent orders are published in this way. The description of the negotiation of the consent decree in the *A. T. & T.* case, given in Chapter 12 under the heading of "*Political Influences* v. *Career Employees in the Department of Justice,*" can usefully be reviewed at this time by the reader. In this regard, it is worth noting that:

As a general rule, consent decrees are accepted and signed by the court as a matter of purely formal routine. If the court, after a brief presentation by the defendant's counsel and the Antitrust Division attorneys, is satisfied that the parties are in agreement, he enters the order with but cursory examination. Ordinarily no record is made of the proceedings. Since no advance notice to the public or the trade of the presentation has been furnished, generally only counsel for the Government and the defendants are present.

In all cases under the prefiling negotiation procedures, the complaint and the decree are entered simultaneously. In some cases, although the complaint has been previously filed, it is superseded by a new complaint that is filed concurrently with the decree.

Findings of fact or conclusions of law are not made, nor are they required. Current procedure contains no procedure, contains no provision, to require the Department of Justice to prepare a written statement that sets forth the facts on which the Government based its case, what the terms of the decree are expected to accomplish or the reasons for the Government's acceptance of the particular compromise. Similarly, the court is not requested or required to render a written opinion.[79]

Thus the consent decree procedure, in effect, amounts to placing great *administrative* power concerning private economic organization and activity in the hands of the Antitrust Division. At the same time, in practice, this power is not subjected to the same safeguards which apply in the case of formal proceedings before administrative agencies like the Federal Trade Commission. Indeed, in 1954 the then Assistant Attorney General in Charge of Antitrust stated before the antitrust section of the American Bar Association:

Though consent judgments bind both parties and estop [bar] future *de novo* [new] proceedings involving matters covered, their provisions oftimes receive only cursory judicial scrutiny. In the ten year period from 1935 to 1945, approximately 106 consent antitrust actions ended in consent decrees. Of these, 80 were entered within 3 days after the complaint was filed. Indeed in many proceedings, decrees were entered at the same time complaints were filed. True, one judge held automobile-finance decrees under advisement for some 6 days, but even their judgments were entered unchanged. These facts, it seems clear, support one commentator's conclusion that consent procedure permits no conclusion of independent court determination.[80]

The House Antitrust Subcommittee thus fairly commented on the consent decree procedure in 1959 by saying:

. . . what has happened under the current consent decree procedures is that the judicial function has been superseded by an administrative procedure in which there are no administrative rules to safeguard the interests of the public or the interest of parties not privy to the Government's case. The consent decree practice has established an orbit in the twilight zone between established rules of administrative law and judicial procedures.[81]

In such a situation, obviously the underlying economic philosophies of those charged with enforcement of the consent program must play an important role, and sometimes a clash of the underlying economic philosophies of political appointees in the Department of Justice with those of its career appointees may result in conflict, a point which has already been illustrated in Chapter 12.

Modification. Either a defendant or the Government may take the initiative in opening negotiations leading up to the settlement of an antitrust action by consent decree. When the decree has been entered, certain legal consequences result. Defendants may not attack a consent decree in a future proceeding on grounds that it contains errors, and the Government is precluded from litigating the matters which have been concluded by the consent decree.[82] The Supreme Court has, however, remarked that the court entering the decree

---

[79] *Consent Decree Program of the Department of Justice* (Report of the Antitrust Subcommittee of the House Judiciary Committee, 86th Cong., 1st sess.) (Washington, D.C.: U.S. Government Printing Office, 1959),

p. 14.

[80] *Ibid.*

[81] *Ibid.*, p. 15.

[82] *United States* v. *Swift and Co.*, 286 U.S. 106 (1932).

has power to modify it "in adaptation of changed conditions."[83] An interesting example of a case involving this question is the *Swift and Co.* case of 1960, in which the defendants sought to modify a consent decree which had been made 40 years earlier. In 1920, the Government settled, by means of a consent decree, a Sherman Act case involving a charge of monopoly against five leading meat packers, Swift and Co., Armour and Co., Wilson and Co., the Morris Packing Company, and the Cudahy Packing Company, together with their subsidiaries and their chief officers.

It was this decree of 1920 which the defendants sought to modify in 1960. However, the Government opposed the modification, and the petition was denied by the District Court with the comment that the "usefulness of the decree is not exhausted or outworn so long as the petitioners retain the economic might they attained through the combination."[84] The mere passage of time alone is thus not enough to provide a basis for modification of a consent decree.

Judge Thurman Arnold (who was Assistant Attorney General in Charge of the Antitrust Division in the early 1940s and under whose leadership antitrust enforcement was infused with new vigor after the period of the N.R.A. Codes in the 1930s) took the position that the antitrust laws should be amended to prohibit the Department of Justice from making any consent decrees which do not terminate in three years. In testimony before the Senate Subcommittee on Antitrust and Monopoly in 1964, Judge Arnold stated his view in reply to a question by Senator Hart dealing with the problem of modification of consent decrees. Senator Hart's question and Judge Arnold's reply were as follows:

SENATOR HART. About these consent decrees, even though they have no expiration date, I take it it is possible for Justice to go to court and argue substantial changes in circumstances, or is it as a psychological matter a complete block?

MR. ARNOLD. The Supreme Court says they can go to court and a decree can be reopened. No decree has been reopened. I went to court on RCA. I was told it was a kind of contract, a consent decree. Now, of course, if the particular charge is one not included in the pleadings, then it is not *res judicata* [a thing or matter settled by law], but a particular charge always is. So if I wanted to amend the antitrust laws, I would just bring a proceeding on a broad base, settle it on a narrow base, and then I would have my amendment without any hearings or any trouble at all.[85]

Judge Arnold's testimony in July 1964 concerning his advocacy of a three year limitation on the duration of consent decrees was supported by a telling example based on his experience as Assistant Attorney General in Charge of Antitrust. His testimony reads:

MR. ARNOLD. I have a couple of suggestions for amendments which I have been making the past twenty years, and I would like to briefly put them in the record.

One of the ways in which the antitrust laws should be amended is to make it unlawful for the Department of Justice to enter into a consent decree for more than three years. The consent decree is, in all respects, a judgment of the Court and is *res judicata*.

I started a suit against General Motors, Ford, and Chrysler, and we convicted General Motors, and Ford and Chrysler pleaded *nolo*. At that time Ford and Chrysler were very happy about the suit. General Motors Acceptance Corp. gives General Motors a tremendous advantage because no General Motors dealer is going to deal with an independent finance company even if no pressure is put upon him. The pressure is just inevitably there because General Motors can cancel the dealer's franchise.

I brought suit to dissolve General Motors' ownership of the finance company. I was put on the bench [this is an apparent reference to Judge Arnold's appointment to the U.S. Court of Appeals for the District of Columbia rather than a slang expression] and promptly the Antitrust Division entered a consent decree with General Motors giving them a slap on the wrist and permitting them to keep their finance company.

The Supreme Court held in the very same case by a majority that the pressure of the large motor companies on its dealers whose franchise they could cancel did constitute a substantial interference with their selection of finance companies and I don't think anybody in his right mind could deny it.

And yet when they entered into that consent decree, General Motors has for all time to come an exemption from the operation of that Supreme

---

[83] *Ibid.*, at p. 114–115.

[84] *United States* v. *Swift and Co., Armour and Co., etc.*, 189 F. Supp. 885 (1960), at p. 193.

[85] *Foreign Trade and the Antitrust Laws* (Hearings before the Senate Subcommittee on Antitrust and Monopoly, 88th Cong. 2d sess.) (Washington, D.C.: U.S. Government Printing Office, 1964), Part 1, p. 131.

Court opinion because it [the matters dealt with by the consent decree] is *res judicata*.

And so the law at present is that General Motors can have a finance company but Ford and Chrysler cannot.

Well I would concede that having done that, the Department of Justice is in no moral position to go after Chrysler's formation of a finance company when they have excluded themselves from prosecuting General Motors, and that decree sits forever.[86]

Auto Financing Legislation (Hearings before the Senate Subcommittee on Antitrust and Monopoly, 86th Congress, 1st sess.) (Washington, D.C.: U.S. Government Printing Office, 1959).

However, it must be noted that in 1966 a District Court did grant a petition of the defendants for modification of an earlier decree to permit them to acquire motion picture theaters despite the government's contention that such a modification would substantially lessen competition and be inconsistent with the antimerger provisions of the Celler-Kefauver Act which had been enacted subsequent to the making of the original decree.[87]

Modification of Antitrust Decrees in General

In 1968, the Supreme Court handed down a significant decision concerning the problem of modification of antitrust decrees. It will be recalled from earlier discussion in this chapter that, in 1953, the United Shoe Machinery Company was held guilty of monopolization under Section 2 of the Sherman Act. The Government had requested that the company be divided into three separate companies, but the District Court had refused this request and had imposed conditions pertaining to the system of licensing shoe machinery then in effect. It had also included in its decree a provision that "On [January 1, 1965] both parties shall report to this court the effect of this decree, and may then petition for its modification, in view of its effect in establishing workable competition." [The influence of Professor (of economics) Carl Kaysen, who had been appointed a special consultant to the court in this case may be apparent in the use of the words "workable competition" in this decree.] Accordingly, on January 1, 1965, the Government

petitioned for further relief, asserting that "workable competition" had not been established and asked that the company be divided into two competing companies. The District Court denied this request, asserting that under the *Swift and Co.* case (discussed earlier in this chapter) there had been no clear showing of a "grievous wrong evoked by new and unforseen circumstances," and that the decree had merely sought to "move toward establishment of workable competition" and did not require that "workable competition" actually be established. Thus the District Court denied itself jurisdiction to deal with an obviously messy problem. (Given the many meanings of "workable competition" discussed in Chapter 13 earlier, defense counsel should have objected to the decree on grounds of vagueness!) However, the Supreme Court reversed and remanded the case, saying this case differed from the *Swift* case (in which the defendants had sought the modification) and that the District Court must now determine whether the relief granted had been adequate, and if it had not been, the decree would have to be modified.[88] A new era, involving modification of decrees already made whether by consent (as in the *Swift* case) or after litigation (as in the *United Shoe Machinery* case), may thus be at hand. The use of consent orders to settle cases by the Federal Trade Commission has also increased in recent years and it is to this topic that we turn next.

Consent Orders in Federal Trade Commission Cases

Numerous examples have been given in this chapter and in preceding chapters (particularly in Chapter 18) of the settlement of Federal Trade Commission cases by means of consent orders. A consent order of the Federal Trade Commission, however, stands on a different footing from the formal consent decrees entered in judicial proceedings in cases brought by the Department of Justice. The procedure for making "consent agreements" with the FTC is set forth in its *Rules of Practice*. FTC orders issued pursuant to such agreements have the same force and effect as, become final, and may be altered,

---

[86] *Ibid.*, p. 130. For further details and the texts of the decrees in these cases, the reader is referred to
[87] *United States* v. *Loew's Inc.*, 251 F. Supp. 201 (1966).
[88] *United States* v. *United Shoe Machinery Corporation*, 391 U.S. 244 (1968).

modified, or set aside in the same manner as and within the same time, as is provided by statute for other FTC orders. The agreement must contain a statement that the signing thereof "is for settlement purposes and does not constitute an admission by either party that the law has been violated." *Neither* the *agreement nor* the *order* has the standing of a decree issued by a court. The impetus for making such a consent agreement may come from the prospective defendant. The Commission may notify a person of its decision to issue a complaint and accompany this notice with a form of complaint and a proposed form of an order. The person served then has ten days within which to inform the Commission that he is interested in having the issue settled by entry of a consent order. If he does so inform the Commission, he is given an opportunity to execute an agreement for consideration by the Commission. *After* such an executed agreement is received, the Commission may then issue an appropriate complaint and order disposing of the matter, or it may reject the proposed agreement, issue a complaint, and proceed with a regular adjudication of the case. It is to be noted that the FTC issues its complaint *after* a proposed agreement has been received. This procedure differs from that used by the Department of Justice which normally first issues a complaint and then negotiates the consent decree on the basis of the complaint. The Attorney General's National Committee to Study the Antitrust Laws recommended in 1955 that the Department of Justice generally adopt "prefiling negotiations" as a method of procedure and noted that this procedure was in 1955 being used on an experimental basis.[89] ("Prefiling" means prior to filing a complaint.) Professor Louis B. Schwartz dissented from this recommendation, noting that:

. . . This procedure will whittle away the last remnants of judicial control and public scrutiny in this area . . . the proposal opens the possibility that the Government's complaint shall be modified so as to be consistent with the relief the defendant is prepared to consent to. The settlement of an antitrust suit ought not to be a simple matter of bargaining between the Department and the defendant.[90]

The same objections seem applicable to FTC consent orders; however, since the latter do not have the finality of consent decrees approved by a court of law, the practice of prefiling negotiations in the case of the FTC is probably less objectionable from the point of view of public control over the actions of an administrative agency. As a matter of fact, either the Commission or "any person subject to a decision containing a cease-and-desist order" may take the initiative in reopening a proceeding in which a final order has been made, except while the proceeding is pending in a United States Court of Appeals for review (after a transcript of the record has been filed in accordance with the appropriate statute) or in the United States Supreme Court.

In fiscal year 1967, 68 consent orders were issued by the FTC. As we have seen in Chapter 18, many such orders are issued in cases involving the various labeling statutes enforced by the Commission and under Section 5 of the FTC Act. As we have seen in this chapter, such orders are also used in Section 7 Clayton Act cases. The use of consent orders in the case of department store and Portland cement producer acquisitions has already been noted above. Such orders have also been used in cases involving acquisitions by paper and paperboard manufacturers. In two such cases in 1965, the orders required divestiture of acquisitions already completed and prohibited future acquisitions.[91]

The procedure of prohibiting acquisitions without FTC approval has often been used in consent orders. Another example can be found in the consent order issued in September 1968 to prohibit Frito–Lay, Inc., a potato chip manufacturer, and its parent, Pepsi Co., Inc. from acquiring manufacturers or wholesalers of certain soft drinks for a period of ten years without Commission approval.

Failure to comply with a consent order issued in a merger case may subject the

---

[89] *Report, op. cit.*, p. 360.

[90] *Ibid.*, p. 360.

[91] FTC Consent Order 7946 ordered Union Bag-Camp Paper Corp. to divest itself of six plants within 18 months and not to acquire without prior approval for ten years firms in the kraft paper and board

converting field. FTC Consent Order C–880 involved analogous restrictions in the case of the Mead Corp., one of the five largest paper and paperboard companies in the United States. Both orders were reported in the FTC's *News Summary* of March 1, 1965.

offender to a suit for civil penalties. Thus, in 1967, the FTC requested the Department of Justice to file a suit seeking an injunction against and penalties of $1,000 a day from the ABC Consolidated Corporation on grounds that the corporation had failed to complete divestiture under an order issued by the Commission pursuant to a consent agreement.

In 1966, the Commission amended its rules of practice to provide for the settlement of some cases in an informal way by means of "voluntary assurances of compliance" given by prospective defendants. In fiscal year 1967, 50 Robinson–Patman Act cases and 11 cases involving trade restraints were settled in this informal way. There remains now one type of public enforcement activity for discussion, the suit for damages by the Government. This type will be considered now.

Government Action for Damages

It has been pointed out in Chapter 12 that Section 7 of the Sherman Act, granting a right of damages to any person injured by a violation of the antitrust laws, was repealed in 1955 and that the damage remedy was placed in Section 4 of the Clayton Act. In 1955, Section 4(a) was added to give the United States a right to sue for actual (not treble) damages in such a case. This addition to the law was made necessary because of the decision of the Supreme Court in 1941 in *United States* v. *Cooper Corporation*. The Court had held in 1941 that the United States was not a "person" within the meaning of Section 7 of the Sherman Act or Section 4 of the Clayton Act and, therefore, had no standing in court to sue for damages in an antitrust case.[92] In the fiscal year ended June 30, 1965, the Antitrust Division collected $477,000 for the United States as a result of settlements of damage cases by the Division. In 1963, the Division collected $8,622,450 as a result of damage cases against members of the heavy electrical equipment industry.[93] The collections in 1963 exceeded the sum of $6,218,000 which Congress had appropriated for operation of the Division in that year. In fiscal year 1967, damage settlements

amounted to $1,639,635 and in 1969 the amount was about $1.3 million.

Although the Supreme Court had held in 1941 that the United States was not a "person" within the meaning of the treble damage provisions of the antitrust laws, in 1942 it *did* hold that a State was a "person" for such purposes.[94] What these holdings really mean, of course, is that the Court did not think it would be sound public policy to permit the United States to recover under the treble damage provision but that it thought it would be desirable to permit States to do so. The rationale of this distinction is not clear.

An example of a State damage suit arising out of the antitrust laws is found in the 1966 case of *Michigan* v. *Morton Salt Co. et. al.*, a case in which a number of Midwestern states (Illinois, Indiana, Iowa, Michigan, Minnesota, Missouri, and Wisconsin) sued a number of salt manufacturers alleging price-fixing in the sale of de-icing salt to public agencies.[95] Our discussion of *public* enforcement actions is now complete. We will next consider *private* actions for damages and injunctions.

C. PRIVATE ENFORCEMENT OF THE ANTITRUST LAWS

Nature and Scope of the Remedy

The private damage remedy is authorized, it has been noted, by Section 4 of the Clayton Act. And the provision, that final judgments or decrees rendered in *litigated* civil or criminal actions brought by the United States shall constitute *prima facie* evidence of the defendant's violation of the antitrust laws in private damage suits, is contained in Section 5 of that law. In addition, Section 16 of the Clayton Act provides for a right to injunctive relief in the case of threatened loss or damage resulting from a violation of the antitrust laws under the same conditions under which injunctive relief is granted by courts of equity in other (nonantitrust) civil actions. In an action for an injunction, it must be shown that the damage remedy is inadequate and that the "danger of irreparable loss is immediate," in keeping

[92] 312 U.S. 600 (1941).
[93] *Annual Report of the Attorney General of the United States for the Fiscal Year Ended June 30, 1965, op. cit.*, p. 84 and p. 100.
[94] *State of Georgia* v. *Evans*, 316 U.S. 159 (1942).
[95] 259 F. Supp. 35 (1966). Some of the cases were settled informally.

with the standard tests for equitable relief generally, a point noted earlier in Chapter 3.

Section 4(b) of the Clayton Act, it has been noted in Chapter 12, provides for a four year limitation on the commencement of any damage action under the antitrust laws, whether the action be public or private. The four year period commences from the date on which "the cause of action has accrued." This language means that the four year period commences on the date on which the wrongful act by the defendants giving rise to the claim of the plaintiffs has occurred. Section 5(b) of the Clayton Act provides for the tolling (suspending) of the operation of the statute of limitations during the pendency of and for a period of one year after any civil or criminal proceeding by the United States. This provision was the subject of two Supreme Court decisions in 1965. In the first of these cases, the Court held that the section operated to suspend the running of the statute of limitations even though there was not complete identity of the parties nor complete overlap of the time periods, nor coterminius geographic areas in the case of a conspiracy allegation in the Government complaint and a conspiracy allegation in the private damage action. It was enough that there was "substantial" identity in the two cases; in the case in question, six of the seven alleged conspirators in the private damage suit were also named in the Government's complaint.[96] The second decision by the Court in 1965 resulted in the proposition that the statute is tolled by a proceeding under Section 7 of the Clayton Act by the FTC, even though the FTC's case is settled by a consent order and even though consent decrees do not constitute *prima facie* evidence under Section 5(a) of the statute. Thus in this case the Court held that the provisions of Sections 5(a) and 5(b) of the Clayton Act are not wholly interdependent nor coextensive.[97]

It should be obvious that one who is a voluntary party to an antitrust violation has no standing in court to sue other parties to the violation for damages or for injunctive relief. A decision to this effect was handed down by a District Court in 1965.[98] It is interesting to note that although Section 16 of the Clayton Act specifically provides for injunctive relief in the case of threatened violations of Section 2 of the Clayton Act, in 1960, a District Court held that Section 2 (the price-discrimination prohibition) does not provide a basis for a treble damage action under Section 5 of that law.[99] Thus the treble damage remedy and the provision for private injunctive relief do not seem to be coextensive in their scope. Moreover, the requirement that the plaintiff must show a probability of immediate irreparable damage as a condition precedent to the issuance of an injunction has limited the use of Section 16 in antitrust cases. For example, in 1960, a District Court refused to grant such an injunction to a plaintiff motion picture theater lessee against a motion picture producer–distributor in an action in which the former claimed that he had been excluded from a fair opportunity to bid for the privilege of exhibiting certain films. The Court held that the plaintiff had failed to show that irreparable harm would result from a failure to grant the injunction.[100] Also in 1960, another District Court rejected the petition of a plaintiff for an injunction and denied his damage claim in a case in which the plaintiff argued that the defendant was refusing to supply him with cigarettes and tobacco which the plaintiff, in turn, wished to supply to the U.S. Navy. The plaintiff in this case was in the process of establishing a new business and had no previous record of such sales to the Navy, making it difficult to establish his damage claim.[101] It is interesting to note also that a private damage action was the basis of the *Pennington* case—which, it will be recalled, has already been extensively discussed under the heading of "*Labor Unions and Restraint of Trade.*" in Chapter 14. The concurring opinion of Justices Douglas, Black, and Clark reads in part:

. . . As we read the opinion of the Court, it . . . tells the trial judge:

First. On the new trial the jury should be instructed that if there was an industry-wide

[96] *Leh et. al.* v. *General Petroleum Corp., et. al.*, 382 U.S. 54 (1965).

[97] *Minnesota Mining and Manufacturing Co.* v. *New Jersey Wood Manufacturing Co.*, 381 U.S. 311 (1965).

[98] *Auto Supplies, Inc.* v. *Eco. Manufacturing Company*, 246 F. Supp. 224 (1965).

[99] *Englander Motors Inc.* v. *Ford Motor Co.*, 186 F. Supp. 82 (1960).

[100] *D. W. H. Corporation* v. *Twentieth Century Fox Film Corporation*, 182 F. Supp. 912 (1960).

[101] *Delaware Valley Marine Supply Co.* v. *American Tobacco Co.*, 184 F. Supp. 440 (1960).

collective bargaining agreement whereby employers and the union agreed on a wage scale that exceeded the financial ability of some of the operators to pay and that if it was made for the purpose of forcing some employers out of business, the union as well as the employers who participated in the arrangement should be found to have violated the antitrust laws.

Second. An industry-wide agreement containing those features is prima facie evidence of a violation.[102]

The Supreme Court then remanded the case for further proceedings consistent with its opinion. On remand, the District Court held that the plaintiffs had offered insufficient proof to establish a violation of the antitrust laws by the union or the large coal operators, but the District Court did permit the recovery of damages by two small coal operators who showed that they had been damaged by actions of the unions which also violated the law of Tennessee.[103] It is to be noted that, in this case, the plaintiffs did not have the benefit of a prior Government civil or criminal action to establish a *prima facie* case. Where the private damage suit does not rest upon a prior Government civil or criminal action, the plaintiff must, of course, also prove the fact that the defendant has violated the antitrust laws. Thus, in 1968, the Supreme Court affirmed a holding by a Court of Appeals that the District Court had correctly held that, since a case of conspiracy had not been proved by a plaintiff in such a private damage suit, the plaintiff could not recover.[104]

The Supreme Court also held in 1968, however, that a plaintiff in a private antitrust action can rely on the trial court's *opinion* and *finding as well as upon its decree* rendered in a prior Government antitrust action. Thus the Court permitted a plaintiff to recover treble damages from the United Shoe Machinery Company by showing that the trial judge in the Government's original suit against United Shoe Machinery Company had found United's leasing practices to constitute "monopolization" even though

he did not order dissolution of United in his final decree.[105] And as we have already seen in Chapter 14, in 1968 the Supreme Court held that one who was *forced* to participate in a conspiracy in violation of the antitrust laws is not barred from suing as a result of his involuntary participation in the conspiracy.[106]

Aside from the questions of whether or not there has been a violation of the antitrust laws, and of whether or not the plaintiff has been damaged as a result of the violation, the plaintiff also has the burden of proving the extent of the damage he claims. The courts have tended to be fairly liberal insofar as the matter of evidence of proof of actual damage is concerned in antitrust cases. Often the action of the defendant himself prevents a precise computation of damages in such cases and, in these instances, there has been a tendency for the courts to hold that although, as is true in damage actions generally, the jury may not render a verdict based on mere speculation or guesswork, it may make a reasonable estimate based on relevant data and may act on "probable or inferential evidence as well as upon direct and positive proof."[107]

In 1965, an economist examined the results of some private antitrust suits. This economist, Professor John D. Gulfoil, reported that between 1940 and 1963 only 57 awards were made in 1,539 reported private damage actions.[108] Gulfoil seemed to think that the low rate of recovery was in part due to past hostility on the part of the courts. The 1968 Supreme Court decisions discussed above are, however, definitely not hostile. Nor was the attitude of the Antitrust Division in 1969.

Attitude of the Antitrust Division Toward Private Damage Suits

In December 1969, Assistant Attorney General in Charge of Antitrust Richard McLaren stated that private antitrust proceedings "provide a meaningful deter-

[102] *United Mine Workers* v. *Pennington*, 381 U.S. 657 (1965), at pp. 672–673.

[103] *White Oak Coal Co.* v. *U.M.W.; Lewis* v. *Pennington*, 257 F. Supp. 815 (1966).

[104] *First National Bank of Arizona* v. *Cities Service Co.*, 391 U.S. 353 (1968).

[105] *Hanover Shoe Company* v. *United Shoe Machinery Corp.*, 392 U.S. 481 (1968).

[106] *Perma Mufflers* v. *Int'l Parts Corp.*, 392 U.S. 134 (1968).

[107] See for example, *Bigelow* v. *R.K.O. Theaters, Inc.*, 327 U.S. 251.

[108] John D. Gulfoil, "Private Enforcement of U.S. Antitrust Law," *Antitrust Bulletin*, Volume X (September–December, 1965).

rent to antitrust violations."[108a] He further pointed out that attorneys for private plaintiffs could employ subpoenas served upon defendants to require the latter to provide lists of the names of witnesses and documents presented in Grand Jury investigations, and in this way plaintiffs would have access to all the information developed by the Antitrust Division in such investigations. Mr. McLaren also asserted that it was the policy of the Division not to accept *nolo contendere* pleas in cases in which a guilty plea or a conviction after trial "will be of meaningful aid to private parties" who had suffered "substantial damages" as a result of the antitrust offense.

In addition, Mr. McLaren remarked that one seldom used aid to private plaintiffs was the inclusion in consent decrees of a provision enjoining the defendants from denying that the judgment was prima facie evidence of a violation in private antitrust actions. Such a provision had so far been included in only two consent decrees.[108b] Interestingly, however, the position of the Internal Revenue Service conflicts with that of the Antitrust Division.

Income Tax Deductibility of Antitrust Damage Payments as "Business Expenses"

In Revenue Ruling 64–224, the Internal Revenue Service held in 1964 that sums paid in damages in satisfaction of private antitrust judgments are deductible as "ordinary and necessary business expenses" for income tax purposes. This ruling was modified in 1966 by Revenue Ruling 66–330 to allow also the deduction of the cost of litigation involved in defending such suits, after the Supreme Court had held in *Commissioner* v. *Tellier* in 1966 that legal fees were deductible when paid in connection with a Government criminal or civil action.[109] The logic behind this Supreme Court decision was as follows: (1) the income tax is not a punitive tax; (2) legal expenses are "necessary and proper"; and (3) allowance of the deduction in the case at hand did not operate to frustrate any

public policy. However, the *Tellier* case did not involve an antitrust damage suit, and the question remains whether deductibility in antitrust cases does not operate to lighten the burden imposed upon the defendant, thereby frustrating antitrust policy. Some argue that the treble damage payment is not a punitive device; but if it is not, why, indeed, are *treble* rather than merely *actual* damages allowed? It is possible that some Congressional action to deny the deductibility in antitrust cases may eventually be forthcoming. But the outcome is far from clear.

What does seem clear is that any attempt to evaluate the effectiveness of the various remedies discussed in this chapter necessarily presupposes some standard of evaluation against which the actual use of the remedies in question can be tested. But the decision as to what standard is to be employed is, in fact, a fundamental value judgment which must be made by the analyst. That is, evaluations of this type almost always involve either an explicit or implicit adoption of one of the concepts of "workable competition" or of the "workable economy" described in Chapter 13 of this book. But there is also another approach to the problem.

That approach is, of course, to adopt, as the controlling question of the inquiry, the question posed by the Court of Appeals in the *Great Lakes Towing Company* case in 1914: "What remedy promises [or has achieved] the most effective relief in the light of the evils found to exist."[110] Such a study would involve an analysis of specific past decisions to determine "the nature of the evils found to exist" by the courts *in specific cases* and a comparison of these "evils" with the consequences resulting from the "remedies employed" *in these specific cases* to deal with the evils in question. Such an approach would not confuse the (1) question of whether or not the "evils found to exist" are in fact evils or "benefits" with the (2) question of whether or not the remedy actually employed fits the reason *given by the Court for*

[108a] *Address before the Philadelphia Bar Association* (Washington, D.C.: Department of Justice Lithoprint), December 11, 1969.

[108b] See *United States* v. *Bituminous Concrete Ass'n, Inc., 1960 Trade Cases,* Par. 69878 and *United States* v. *Lake Asphalt and Petroleum Co., 1960 Trade Cases,* Par. 69835.

[109] 383 U.S. 687 (1966); see also *Staff Study of Tax Treatment of Treble Damage Payments Under the Antitrust Laws* (Joint Committee on Internal Revenue Taxation, 89th Cong., 1st sess., 1965) (Washington, D.C.: U.S. Government Printing Office, 1965).

[110] *United States* v. *Great Lakes Towing Company et. al.,* 217 Fed. 656 (1914) at p. 659.

employing that remedy. Indeed, such an inquiry could be extended to a consideration of what other remedies might have been employed to deal with the "evils found to exist." But, in making this extension, one should be careful not to confuse his own conception of how the economy "ought ot be organized" with the objective test of the "evils found to exist" as stated by the Courts *in the decisions examined*. Had such a test been applied in the *Alcoa* case, the defendant would have had the burden of proving that after World War II, competitive conditions existed in the aluminium industry. This decision was termed an "economic defeat" by Professor Adams, (who employs the market structure test). Of course, it does not follow that such a defense would automatically carry with it a stamp approving the decision as the best possible one, given the "evils found to exist." In any event, one ought not to confuse his own position concerning the appropriate norms to be employed in applying the antitrust laws with the question of the appropriateness of the remedies actually adopted by the Courts *in specific cases*, given the norms that *the courts* have used in *their decisions* in such cases. The debate about the use of norms is a matter of value judgments, and the issues involved become even more complicated when one considers the problem of the application of the antitrust laws to the international activities of American business firms. So does the problem of remedies in such cases. These topics are discussed in the next chapter.

Antitrust and International Business Practices

This chapter undertakes to discuss various problems pertaining to the application of the antitrust laws to the international activities of American and foreign business firms and to examine United States policy relative to international action regarding antitrust matters. The following topics are examined in the order indicated: (1) the problem of jurisdiction, that is, of application of United States antitrust laws to international activities; (2) the question of the types of international business practices which may constitute antitrust violations; (3) the problem of enforcement of remedies in international antitrust cases; (4) the nature and scope of the exemption from antitrust contained in the Webb–Pomerene Act; and (5) a historical survey of United States policy pertaining to multilateral international actions relating to antitrust problems.

A. APPLICATION OF THE SHERMAN ACT TO INTERNATIONAL BUSINESS PRACTICES: JURISDICTION

American Banana Company v. United Fruit Company

The first case involving the application

of the Sherman Act to international activities of American business firms has already been mentioned in Chapter 3. This case involved an action for treble damage by the American Banana Company against the United Fruit Company.[1] The plaintiff (American Banana Company) alleged that United Fruit Company had induced the government of Costa Rica to seize American's productive facilities in Costa Rica, thereby eliminating the latter from competition with United. The Supreme Court held that American had no standing to bring an action under the Sherman Act on these allegations. Specifically, the Court said:

. . . the plaintiff's case depends on several rather startling propositions. In the first place, the acts causing the damage were done, so far as appears, outside the jurisdiction of the United States and within that of other states. It is surprising to hear it argued that they were governed by the act of Congress . . . the general and almost universal rule is that the character of an act must be determined by the law of the country where the act is done. . . .[2]

Not to be ignored in evaluating this decision is the fact that for the Court to have held otherwise would have amounted to the

---

[1] *American Banana Company* v. *United Fruit Company*, 213 U.S. 347 (1909).

[2] *Ibid.*, at pp. 355–356.

making of a foreign policy statement by the Court to the effect that legislation enacted by the government of Costa Rica was unlawful.

The *American Tobacco Company Case* of 1911

In 1911, the Court had no difficulty in applying the Sherman Act in the case of a conspiracy involving American and foreign corporations.[3] No action by a foreign government was involved in this case, hence no foreign policy problems were present. The Court held that acts in the United States by the foreign corporations were covered by the United States law.

The *Sisal Corporation Case*; *American Banana Company* Virtually Overruled

In 1927, in the *Sisal Corporation* case, despite an attempt by the Court to distinguish between the two cases, the Court virtually overruled its earlier *American Banana Company* decision. The *Sisal Corporation* case involved a conspiracy among three American banking firms, two American firms dealing in sisal, and a Mexican corporation to obtain legislation in Mexico establishing the Mexican corporation as the sole exporter of sisal from Mexico. Thereupon the American companies became the sole importers into the United States. In holding that the arrangement violated the Sherman Act, the Court said, in part:

The circumstances of the present controversy are radically different from those presented in *American Banana Company* v. *United Fruit Co., supra*, and the doctrine there approved is not controlling here. . . .

Here we have a contract, combination, and conspiracy *entered into by the parties within the United States and made effective by acts done therein.* The fundamental object was control of both importation and sale of sisal and complete monopoly of both internal and external trade and commerce therein. The United States complain of a violation of their laws within their own territory by parties subject to their jurisdiction, not merely of something done by another government at the instigation of the parties. True, the conspirators were aided by discriminating legislation, but *by their own acts here and elsewhere, they brought about forbidden results within*

the United States. They are within the jurisdiction of our courts and may be punished for offenses against our laws.[4]

It is to be noted that monopolization of the importation of bananas seems no less to affect the foreign commerce of the United States or to take effect there than does the monopolization of the importation of sisal. Both the *American Banana* and *Sisal* cases involved favorable legislation on the part of the foreign government involved. The difference between the two cases, if any exists, lies in the fact that *American Banana* involved a single defendant and the *Sisal* case involved a conspiracy among a number of defendants. But in both cases, United States imports were affected by the actions of the defendants and, as in the *American Tobacco* case, the acts took effect within the United States.

Jurisdictional Problems in Contemporary Cases

Since World War II, the Supreme Court has supplied a broad, lenient, answer to the jurisdictional question, an attitude completely consistent with its liberal interpretation of the Commerce Clause, already discussed in Chapter 7. A few cases will serve to illustrate the Court's attitude. In the *Alcoa* case of 1945, Justice Hand was faced with the question of the legality of the participation of Aluminium Company of Canada Limited (Alcan) in an European cartel, the "Alliance." The stock of Alcan was owned by the Alcoa common stockholders. The "Alliance" was a Swiss corporation owned by Alcan and French, British, and German corporations and undertook "from time to time to fix a quota of production" for each of its participants, as well as to purchase excess amounts of production from the participants at a fixed price, thereby engaging in a price-fixing scheme. In holding that the arrangement violated Section 1 of the Sherman Act, Judge Hand reviewed prior decisions pertaining to the applicability of the Sherman Act to international business practices and concluded by writing:

. . . we are concerned only with whether Congress chose to attach liability to conduct

---

[3] *U.S.* v. *American Tobacco Company*, 221 U.S. 106 (1911), at p. 120.

[4] *U.S.* v. *Sisal Sales Corporation, et. al.*, 274 U.S. 268 (1927), at pp. 275–276. (Italics mine.)

outside the United States of persons not in allegiance to it. That being so, the only question open is whether Congress intended to impose the liability and whether our own Constitution permitted it to do so: as a court of the United States, we cannot look beyond our own law. Nevertheless it is quite true that we are not to read general words such as those in this Act, without regard to the limitations customarily observed by nations upon the exercise of their powers; limitations which generally correspond to those fixed by the "Conflict of Laws." We should not impute to Congress an intent to punish all whom its courts can catch, for conduct which has no consequences within the United States. [Cases cited.] On the other hand, it is settled law—as "Limited" itself agrees—that a state may impose liabilities, even upon persons not within its allegiance, for conduct outside its borders that has consequences within its borders which the state reprehends; and these liabilities other states will ordinarily recognize. [Cases cited.][5]

Two interesting and complex jurisdictional questions were raised in 1955 in the *Swiss Watchmakers* case. The case involved among other defendants, one American corporation (Eterna, N.Y.) which did business in New York and was a subsidiary of a Swiss corporation (Eterna, A.G.), and two American Companies (Gruen and Longines) and their Swiss subsidiaries (Gruen S.A. and Wittnauer, S.A., respectively). The American parents had financial control of their Swiss subsidiaries but were alleged to have subjected themselves voluntarily to the control of the subsidiaries by permitting the subsidiaries to bind themselves to a "Collective Convention" and to become members of a Federation which exerted strict control over the Swiss watch industry. With respect to Eterna, A.G., the District Court held it had jurisdiction because this Swiss parent company had acted continuously within the jurisdiction *through* its subsidiary, Eterna, N.Y. The Court also held that it had jurisdiction over the Swiss subsidiaries of the American parents because the parents had voluntarily subordinated their policies to those of the subsidiaries, who could thus be considered to be present for jurisdictional

purposes.[6] Obviously, the courts in 1955 had become much more liberal in answering jurisdictional questions than they were in 1909. Our next problem is to examine the types of international business practices which may constitute antitrust violations.

B. TYPES OF UNLAWFUL INTERNATIONAL BUSINESS PRACTICES

Agreements to Limit Output, Divide Markets, and Fix Prices

Most of the antitrust cases involving the international business practices of United States firms have been characterized by arrangements between United States and foreign firms to divide markets, limit output, and fix prices; in short, by *per se* offenses under the Sherman Act. These agreements have often been made in conjunction with some other business arrangement, such as a patent-licensing agreement or creation of a jointly owned foreign subsidiary. In the 1911 *American Tobacco Company* case, there was a naked agreement (one made without the cover of any otherwise legal arrangement such as a patent license) between the Imperial Tobacco Company of Great Britain and Ireland and the American Tobacco Company under which the former limited its business to the United Kingdom and the latter limited its business to the United States. In addition, the two organized a jointly owned subsidiary to take over the export business of both. Although the agreement was made in England where it was lawful, it affected the foreign trade of the United States and hence constituted a violation of the Sherman Act.[7] The *Alkali Export Ass'n* case of 1949 similarly involved agreements made by an export association (whose members were the principal producers of alkali products in the United States) with foreign associations and companies dividing the market for such products, assigning quotas, and fixing prices in certain territories.[8] The quota system of controlling production used by the international aluminum "Alliance" and the role

[5] *U.S.* v. *Aluminium Co. of America*, 148 F. 2d 416 (1945), at p. 443.
[6] *U.S.* v. *Watchmakers of Switzerland Information Center*, 133 F. Supp. 40 (1955); 134 F. Supp. 710 (1955).

[7] *U.S.* v. *American Tobacco Company*, 221 U.S. 106 (1911).
[8] *U.S.* v. *United States Alkali Export Ass'n., Inc., et. al.*, 86 F. Supp. 59 (1949).

played by Alcan have already been noted in the preceding subdivision.[9] An example of the use of an international patent-licensing system as the basis for a market allocation and price-fixing agreement is provided by the *General Electric Incandescent Lamp* case of 1949.[10] A year earlier, there was a similar case involving the use of patents by the *General Electric Company* to fix prices in the case of tungsten carbide.[11] In 1947, the Supreme Court upheld a District Court's holding that National Lead Company and E. I. du Pont de Nemours and Company had utilized their patents as a basis for allocating markets in titanium products.[12]

In 1963, the same market practice appeared in a case involving the Singer Manufacturing Company and several foreign (Japanese and Italian) sewing machine producers.[13] Many additional cases could be mentioned, but we may conclude with mention of the *Zenith* case of May 1969, already discussed in Chapter 19. In that case, it will be recalled, an international patent pool was found to have excluded imports of products of the Zenith Corporation from the Canadian market.[13a] It will be instructive now to examine briefly the actual operations of one international cartel as an example of the kinds of activities in which such a cartel may engage.

A Brief Case Study: The International Electrical Equipment Cartel

A *cartel* is a form of business association by means of which firms of different nationalities agree to eliminate competition among themselves. The cartel system was an accepted way of doing business in several countries up until about the end of World War II.[14] The Electrical Equipment Cartel was organized as a result of negotiations among British, German, and Swiss companies manufacturing heavy electrical apparatus and representatives of two

American companies, Westinghouse Electric and Manufacturing Company and General Electric Company. These negotiations culminated in the signing by the parties of the "International Notification and Compensation Agreement" in December 1930 in Paris in the offices of International General Electric Company.[15]

The agreement involved two types of activities: (1) notification; and (2) compensation. The substance of the agreement with respect to notification required that upon receipt of an inquiry concerning the sale of equipment, each party to the agreement was required immediately to notify the secretary of the administrative staff set up by the agreement; the secretary had the function of then immediately informing every other party to the agreement of the receipt of the notification. Any order received by any member was also subject to the notification procedure. The notification procedure made it possible for all parties who might be interested in submitting a bid for the equipment in question to meet and agree upon the prices to be quoted. The party who actually received the order was required to pay compensation to the secretary and this compensation fund was then distributed among all the members and could be used to engage in cutthroat competition involving sales below cost in any case in which firms which were not parties to the agreement invaded territories of firms which were parties to the agreement. The amounts to be paid as compensation were determined by elaborate formulas, depending on the type of equipment being supplied; and the sums in question were included in the final price quoted the prospective purchaser. The members of the agreement made specific arrangements among themselves to allocate the business; these arrangements involved fixed bids on the part of the party who was actually to fill the order and fictitious higher

[9] *U.S.* v. *Aluminium Co. of America*, 148 Fed. (2d) 416 (1945).

[10] *U.S.* v. *General Electric Co.*, 82 F. Supp. 753 (1949).

[11] *U.S.* v. *General Electric Co.*, 80 F. Supp. 989 (1948).

[12] *U.S.* v. *National Lead Company*, 332 U.S. 319 (1947).

[13] *U.S.* v. *Singer Manufacturing Co.*, 374 U.S. 174 (1964).

[13a] *Zenith Corp.* v. *Hazeltine*, 395 U.S. 100 (1969).

[14] A classic study of international cartels and the

role they played just prior to and during World War II is Corwin Edwards, *Economic and Political Aspects of International Cartels* (Monograph No. 1, Senate Committee on Military Affairs, 87th Cong. 2d sess., 1946) (Washington, D.C.: U.S. Government Printing Office, 1946).

[15] This description of the cartel rests upon the FTC study, *Report of the Federal Trade Commission on International Electrical Equipment Cartels* (Washington, D.C.: U.S. Government Printing Office, 1948).

bids by the other parties. In 1947, Westinghouse Company and General Electric Company signed a consent decree—after a complaint had been filed by the Department of Justice alleging a Sherman Act violation —and agreed to terminate their participation in the International Notification and Compensation Agreement.

It is interesting to note in the present context that in 1960 Standard Oil Company (New Jersey) and Gulf Oil Company also signed consent decrees which barred them for 25 years from making any agreement to fix prices, divide markets, or allocate production of oil on the world market. This consent decree grew out of an investigation by the FTC in 1952 of the International Petroleum Cartel. Three of the other defendants charged in this case, Socony Mobil Oil Company, Texaco Inc., and Standard Oil Company of California, did not sign the decree at this time.[16] The decree contained an interesting provision that its clauses were not to take effect in any case in which they conflicted with any foreign law requiring performance of the activity proscribed by the decree. The problem of remedies in antitrust cases involving international business practices is thus more complex than in other cases, as we will see more clearly in the next subdivision. But there remain for consideration in the present context the questions of joint ventures and mergers.

Joint Ventures and Mergers

The question of legality of a "joint venture" as a device for dividing international markets arose in 1951 in the *Timken Roller Bearing* case.[17] Timken, an Ohio corporation, owned about 30% of the stock of British Timken, Ltd.; and an English businessman, Dewar, owned about 24%. In 1928, Timken (of Ohio) and Dewar organized "French Timken." From 1928 to 1951, the three companies kept alive agreements allocating trade territories among themselves, fixed prices, participated in cartels, and cooperated in eliminating competition from each other's territories. The District Court held that these acts

constituted a violation of Section 1 of the Sherman Act. The Supreme Court agreed and said, in part:

We cannot accept the "joint venture" contention . . . [argued by the defendants]. That the trade restraints were merely incidental to an otherwise legitimate "joint venture" is, to say the least, doubtful. The District Court found that the dominant purpose of the restrictive agreements into which appellant [Timken of Ohio], British Timken, and French Timken entered was to avoid all competition either among themselves or with others. Regardless of this, however, appellant's argument must be rejected. Our prior decisions plainly establish that agreements providing for aggregation of trade restraints such as those existing in this case are illegal. . . . The fact that there is common ownership or control of the contracting corporations does not liberate them from the impact of the antitrust laws. . . . Nor do we find any support in reason or authority for the proposition that agreements between legally separate persons and companies to suppress competition among themselves and others can be justified by labeling the project a "joint venture." Perhaps every agreement and combination to restrain trade could be so labeled.[18]

The *Minnesota Mining Company* case—in which American companies controlling four-fifths of United States export trade in abrasives established jointly owned factories abroad and refrained from exporting from the United States to countries by or in which the factories were located—is particularly interesting because of the argument advanced by the defendants in justification of their restriction of United States exports. The defendants argued that there was no violation of the Sherman Act because political and economic conditions in the countries in question prevented exports from being made from the United States. Therefore, they argued further, their action did not affect the foreign commerce of the United States. However, the District Court rejected this argument by making the following finding of fact:

In short, this Court finds as an ultimate fact that the defendant's decline in exports to the United Kingdom is attributable less to import and currency restrictions of that nation and to

---

[16] For a detailed description of the complex arrangements and activities of this cartel, see the FTC's study, *The International Petroleum Cartel* (Washington, D.C.: U.S. Government Printing

Office, 1952). The consent decrees may be found in *1960 Trade Cases*, paragraphs 69,849 and 69,851.

[17] *U.S.* v. *Timken Co.*, 341 U.S. 593 (1951).

[18] *Ibid.*, at pp. 597–598.

the preferential treatment afforded to British goods by British customers than to the defendant's desire to sell their British-made goods at a large profit rather than their American-made goods at a smaller profit and in a somewhat (but drastically) reduced volume.

The Canadian situation does not differ from the British in substance. . . .

It is no excuse for the violations of the Sherman Act that supplying foreign customers from foreign factories is more profitable. . . .[19]

Joint ventures are not, however, *per se* unlawful. Such was the holding of a District Court in the *Imperial Chemical Industries* case.[20] On the facts in this case, the Court did, however, hold that a series of patent licensing and other agreements involving a division of the world market constituted a violation of the Sherman Act.

In 1967, another interesting joint venture case was settled by a consent decree. In this case, the Antitrust Division had filed a complaint charging Monsanto Company and Farbenfabriken Bayer A.G. (a German company) with violating both Section 1 of the Sherman Act and Section 7 of the Clayton Act by establishing and operating a joint venture, Mobay Chemical Company, in the United States to produce raw materials essential to the production of certain plastics. Monsanto was required by the consent judgment to divest itself of its 50 percent interest in Mobay to Bayer. Thus this case involved action by a United States and a German firm *in the United States*.[21]

Another interesting case in 1967 involved a final judgment requiring the Joseph Schlitz Brewing Company to dispose of its stock interest in John LaBatt, Ltd., a London, Ontario company, and of the assets of the Burgermeister Brewing Corporation, which Schlitz had also acquired. It was held that these acquisitions would substantially lessen competition and that Schlitz's acquisition of LaBatt stock constituted an attempt to eliminate Canadian competition by halting the introduction of LaBatt beer into the United States.[22] The charge was filed under Section 7 of the Clayton Act. In this case, since the judgment operated on a

United States corporation, no enforcement problem existed. Nor did any problem arise in regard to the consent decree in the *Monsanto Company* case. It is to a consideration of the problem of remedies in cases involving international restrictive business practices under the antitrust laws that the next subdivision is devoted.

C. REMEDIES IN INTERNATIONAL ANTITRUST CASES

Decrees Affecting United States Companies

As is apparent from the discussion in the preceding subdivisions, many antitrust cases involving international activities of United States firms have been settled by consent decrees and some have been settled by means of litigated decrees. No jurisdictional problems arise in cases in which such decrees pertain to the activities of United States firms. Indeed, it will be recalled from the discussion of the problem of divestiture in Chapter 20 that the consent decree in the *United Fruit Company* case required United to divest itself of property *owned abroad*.[23] To the extent that a Court has jurisdiction over a defendant, no particular problems in enforcing a judgment arise. In the *United Fruit Company* case, even though the properties to be disposed of were outside the jurisdiction of the Court, United owned physical assets within the United States, its officials lived in the United States, and its main business was conducted in the United States.

Decrees Affecting Foreign Companies

To the extent that foreign companies are within a Court's jurisdiction, no problems concerning the making of a decree arise. Thus, in the *Monsanto* case discussed above, the decree required Monsanto to dispose of its 50 percent interest in Mobay to the German corporation, Bayer, A.G.

However, consider the situation in a case in which a United States court orders a foreign company to license its patents upon

[19] *U.S.* v. *Minnesota Mining and Manufacturing Co.*, 92 F. Supp. 947 (1950), at pp. 960–962.

[20] *U.S.* v. *Imperial Chemical Industries, Ltd.*, 100 F. Supp. 504 (1951).

[21] *Annual Report of the Attorney General of the United States for the Fiscal Year Ended June 30, 1967* (Washing-

ton, D.C.: U.S. Government Printing Office, 1968), p. 96.

[22] *Joseph Schlitz Brewing Co.* v. *United States, et. al.*, 253 F. Supp. 129 (1966); 385 U.S. 87 (1967).

[23] U.S. v. United Fruit Co., *1958 Trade Cases No. 68*, 941 (1958).

a reasonable royalty basis. Suppose that the foreign corporation then refuses to obey the terms of this decree *in its homeland* and that a company seeking a license there seeks an order *in a court of the homeland*, citing the United States court decree as a basis for its cause of action. In 1952, in the *Imperial Chemical Industries* case, a District Court ordered a British corporation (Imperial) to reassign to an American corporation (du Pont) patents under which the British corporation had already granted exclusive rights to another British corporation. The British grantee corporation (British Nylon Spinners, Ltd.) sought and obtained an injunction in an English court to prevent the British grantor (Imperial Chemical Industries, Ltd.) from complying with the decree of the United States District Court. The English court held that the decree of the American court constituted an assertion of extraterritorial jurisdiction and could not take effect in England.[24] It has already been noted above that in the *International Oil Cartel* case, the consent decree contained an escape clause providing that its provisions were not to take effect in any situation in which they conflicted with foreign law. In this case also, one of the defendants cited in the initial complaint claimed sovereign immunity on grounds that it was a corporation owned in large part by the British Government. After the Legal Advisor of the Department of State had advised the trial court to grant the claim, the court did so. Obviously, there is little reason for a court to claim jurisdiction over a defendant if it is obvious that no decree made by that court can be made effective. The problem of remedies in antitrust cases is thus inextricably intertwined with the problem of jurisdiction. Participation by American firms in international cartels has often been accomplished by use of export associations. In such cases, United States courts have often decreed dissolution of the export associations, despite the claim of the defendants that the use of such an association fell within the exemption from antitrust provided by the Webb–Pomerene Act, our next topic.

D. THE EXEMPTION CONTAINED IN THE WEBB–POMERENE ACT; EXPORT ASSOCIATIONS

Legislative History of the Webb–Pomerene Act (Public Law 126, 65th Cong.)

The Webb–Pomerene Act of 1918 was one of the earliest of many exemptions from the antitrust laws enacted by Congress. One factor which contributed greatly to the enactment of this legislation was a report by the FTC concerning the unfavorable conditions of competition with foreign cartels facing American firms doing business abroad.[25] Among those lobbying in support of the proposed legislation were the National Association of Manufacturers, the Chamber of Commerce of the United States, and the National Foreign Trade Council.[26] The President signed the law on April 10, 1918. It was titled, "An Act to Promote Export Trade and For Other Purposes." It is often called the "Webb Act" and is also known as the "Webb–Pomerene Act."

Scope and Enforcement of the Act

Section 2 of the law exempts from the Sherman Antitrust Act any association "established for the sole purpose of engaging in export trade." The exemption is limited in that the association may not undertake acts or agreements which: (1) restrain trade in the United States; (2) restrain the export trade of any domestic competitor or association; and (3) artificially influence prices within the United States of commodities of the class exported by the association. Associations formed under the Act are required to register with the Federal Trade Commission and to supply the Commission with relevant information upon request.

In 1955, the Commission issued a revision of an earlier guide pertaining to the legality of agreements made by such associations which reads in part:

. . . insofar as an export association enters into restrictive agreements with foreign competitors, those agreements will not be considered "in the course of foreign trade" within the meaning of

---

[24] *British Nylon Spinners, Ltd.* v. *Imperial Chemical Industries, Ltd.*, 3All England Law Reports 780 (1954).

[25] *Congressional Record*, Vol. 55, pp. 2576–3577

(June 13, 1917).

[26] *Webb-Pomerene Associations* (Report to the Federal Trade Commission by Its Staff) (Washington, D.C.: U.S. Government Printing Office, 1967), pp. 1–2.

the Webb Act and their lawfulness will be determined according to traditional Sherman Act criteria, as would similar conduct by an individual exporter. Whatever privileges the Webb Act extends to association activities "in the course of export trade" would be removed.[27]

Three of the antitrust cases discussed in the preceding subdivision involved unlawful activity on the part of export associations. The Electrical Equipment Cartel involved use of the Electrical Apparatus Export Association, an association employed by General Electric Company and Westinghouse Manufacturing Company to implement the International Notification and Compensation Agreement. The association was dissolved by the consent decree issued in this case. The *Minnesota Mining Company* case involved the use of the Durex Abrasives Corporation, an export association, which followed a policy of not exporting to foreign markets which could be supplied from manufacturing companies owned jointly abroad by the members of the association. In the *Alkali Export Association* case, the District Court held that the exemption contained in the Webb Act did not prohibit the Justice Department from bringing an action under the Sherman Act charging use of the association as a device to divide markets, thereby limiting United States trade.

In November 1968, for the first time, the Supreme Court was called upon to decide an antitrust case involving the meaning of the words "export trade" as used in the Webb–Pomerene Act. The case involved the question of whether sales by the Concentrated Phosphate Association, Inc., a Webb Act Association, to the Korean Government constituted sales made in the "export trade." The sales in question were financed by the United States Agency for International Development and the Korean Government buying agency involved was merely a nominal purchaser. The Supreme Court, accordingly, held that the sales were in fact sales by the Association on behalf of its members to a United States Government agency which was itself, in substance, the exporter of the products involved. Thus, looking through the form to the substance of the transaction, the Court held that the

sale was not one conducted in the export trade and that sales by the Association on behalf of the producers denied American taxpayers the benefits of competition. Prior to the time of this Sherman Act suit by the Government against the Association, the latter had voluntarily dissolved itself. The Government's position that the sale involved a violation of Section 1 of the Sherman Act was sustained, and the defendants' contention that the sale was exempt from Sherman Act prosecution under the Webb Act was rejected.[28]

In 1966, the Federal Trade Commission issued an interesting *advisory* opinion anticipating the decision in the *Phosphate Association* case, just mentioned, in which it held that although lawful ownership of foreign firms by an export association was permissible, artificial or intentional enhancement or depression of domestic prices were unlawful and outside the exemption of the Webb Act.[29]

Scope of Activity Under the Law; Proposals for Revision

There have been many studies of the operation of the Webb Act and some writers have argued for its repeal. The Senate Subcommittee on Antitrust and Monopoly held hearings from 1964 to 1967 concerning this question and on the problem of "antitrust and foreign trade." In 1964, the Federal Trade Commission submitted a statistical analysis of Webb Act activity to the Committee.

According to this statistical study, "Webb–Pomerene associations accounted for an average of about 7 percent of U.S. exports" up until 1948. Thereafter, the percentage varied, exceeding 10 percent "only in 1929, 1930, and 1931 when two Webb–Pomerene associations included in their memberships the dominant companies in the petroleum industry." The percentage declined to a low of 3.5 percent in 1953, and "in 1963, 33 associations accounted for approximately 4.8 percent of total U.S. exports." Also, "as of June 1, 1964, there were 33 active and registered export associations with 310 members." As a matter of fact, "although 120 export associations,

[27] *Ibid.*, p. 19.
[28] *United States* v. *Concentrated Phosphate Export Assn., Inc., et. al.*, 393 U.S. 199 (1968).

[29] Federal Trade Commission, *News Summary*, September 22, 1966.

representing 2,074 firms, were formed under the Webb–Pomerene Act between 1918 and 1943," their duration was brief. The maximum number of associations active during any one year was 43. In every period, some of the associations, though registered, were inactive.[30]

In 1967, Chairman of the FTC Paul Rand Dixon stated before the Senate Subcommittee on Antitrust and Monopoly that FTC studies indicated that the Webb Act had *not* provided "a unique shelter for small corporations in export trade"; *nor* was there any indication that large firms had used the exemption extensively. Use of the exemption was limited largely to cases "involving, for the most part, large firms operating in concentrated industries and marketing standardized products."[31]

With respect to the question of the Webb Act itself, Chairman Dixon did not think that the Act should be repealed. Instead, the Commission took the position that the exemption should be limited to cases involving "need" and in which the "probable effects" on competition would not be adverse.[32]

Chairman Dixon also asserted the law should be fitted into our "overall foreign economic policy." We come thus to the next major topic in this chapter: international antitrust agreements as an element of United States foreign economic policy.

E. INTERNATIONAL AGREEMENTS PERTAINING TO ANTITRUST

Chapter 5 of the Havana Charter

Near the end of World War II, much information became available concerning the extent to which the Axis powers had utilized international cartels to further their imperialistic aims. Accordingly, when a multilateral attempt was made after World War II to overcome the deterioration in international trade and commercial relations which had existed just prior to the war, the problem of international control over cartels was included in the list of those

to be considered. Proposals to deal with the cartel problem in a multilateral international agreement were put forth most strongly by the United States. The Havana Charter for an International Trade Organization was proposed as a device for improving overall international trade relations. This proposal was drafted at a conference held in Havana in 1947–48 under auspices of the Economic and Social Council of the United Nations. Chapter V of the Charter dealt with the subject of "international restrictive business practices" and contained provisions according to which a proposed International Trade Organization would investigate and publicize the results of its investigations into cases of alleged restrictive practices. The principal means to be relied upon for dealing with such restrictive practices was thus to be creation of adverse public opinion.

The United Nations Draft Agreement

However, isolationists succeeded in blocking Senate consideration of the question of United States membership in the proposed International Trade Organization and, eventually, President Truman withdrew from the Senate his request for approval of the proposed international agreement creating the ITO.

When it became apparent that the ITO Charter would not be implemented, the United States Representative took a leading part in having the Economic and Social Council of the United Nations establish an *Ad Hoc* Committee to draft a Proposed Agreement on Restrictive Business Practices. The *Ad Hoc* Committee submitted draft articles of such an agreement to the Council in July 1953. The substantive provisions of the new draft agreement were virtually identical to those contained in Chapter V of the ITO Charter, with the exception that the new draft agreement would have created a new agency to perform the investigatory functions which had been assigned in Chapter V to the ITO.[33]

[30] *Foreign Trade and the Antitrust Laws* (Hearings before the Senate Subcommittee on Antitrust and Monopoly, 88th Cong., 2d sess.) (Washington, D.C.: U.S. Government Printing Office, 1964), Part 1, p. 441.
[31] *International Aspects of Antitrust, 1967* (Hearings before the Senate Subcommittee on Antitrust and

Monopoly, 90th Cong., 1st sess.) (Washington, D.C.: U.S. Government Printing Office, 1967), p. 138.
[32] *Ibid.*, pp. 139–140.
[33] A useful source of historical information is *Restrictive Business Practices* (General Agreement on Tariffs and Trade) (Geneva, May 1959).

There was considerable international support for the draft agreement as reported by the *Ad Hoc* Committee to ECOSOC; however, in the United States, the Republican administration of Dwight Eisenhower had succeeded the Democratic administration of Harry Truman. The new administration did not favor the draft convention, despite the fact that the United States Representative to ECOSOC had played an important role in drafting the proposed agreement. In May 1955, the United States Representative to ECOSOC formally opposed adoption of the new draft agreement, thus insuring its demise.[34] Among those opposing United States support for the proposed draft agreement were the National Association of Manufacturers, the National Foreign Trade Council, and the American Bar Association.[35]

The Treaty of Rome: The European Economic Community

One viable multilateral international antitrust agreement of sorts does, however, exist, although the United States is not a party to it. This agreement is to be found in Articles 85 and 86 and in Regulation 17 of the treaty establishing the European Economic Community. The treaty was signed in 1957 by six European countries, including France, Italy, Germany, Belgium, the Netherlands, and Luxembourg. Article 85 prohibits agreements between enterprises "likely to affect trade between member states and which have the effect of preventing, restraining, or distorting competition in the Common Market." As has already been noted in Chapter 13, Article 86 prohibits "one or more enterprises [from abusing] a dominant position in the Common Market or any substantial portion of it." The Common Market Commission, the executive authority established under the treaty, is given authority to implement these provisions. Limited exceptions (where the effect of a market practice can be shown to benefit the Common Market) are allowed. In 1961, the Common Market Council issued Regulation 17, requiring Common Market firms to notify the Commission concerning existing agreements and practices and providing for review of Commission action by the Common Market High Court of Justice. The Commission may also issue "negative clearances," that is, declarations that particular agreements do *not* fall within the prohibited practices specified in Articles 85 and 86.

There is a Director-General of Competition under the Commission and he and his staff have the function of implementing and enforcing the articles and regulations. United States firms doing business in the Common Market, are, of course, subject to the Treaty and its implementing regulations. Some indication of the attitude of United States antitrust officials toward this European antitrust experiment, as well as of the nature of the experiment itself, appears in testimony given in 1966 by FTC Chairman Paul Rand Dixon before the Senate Subcommittee on Antitrust and Monopoly.

In his statement, Mr. Dixon first called attention to the antitrust provisions of the Treaty mentioned above and noted that the Common Market Commission had not been very active in the area of mergers but was engaged in developing its policies in this area in 1966. However, the Court of Justice had recently held that an exclusive distributor arrangement distorted competition and hence was outlawed by the Treaty.[36]

F. POLICY-MAKING AGENCIES AND UNITED STATES POLICY SINCE 1953

International Business Practices Division, Department of State

The Department of State possesses no antitrust enforcement authority. However, the International Business Practices Division of the Economics Bureau undertakes both formally and informally to insure consistency between foreign economic policy and domestic antitrust enforcement policy. Some of the aspects of this activity were detailed

---

[34] For this bit of history and the text of the statement of the U.S. Representative, see *Study of the Antitrust Laws* (Hearings before the Senate Subcommittee on Antitrust and Monopoly, 84th Cong., 1st sess.) (Washington, D.C.: U.S. Government Printing Office, 1956) Part 4, "Foreign Trade," pp. 1585 ff.

[35] *Ibid.*, pp. 1549 ff.

[36] *International Aspects of Antitrust* (Hearings before the Senate Subcommittee on Antitrust and Monopoly, 89th Cong., 1st sess.) (Washington, D.C.: U.S. Government Printing Office, 1967), Part 1, pp. 515–516.

by Assistant Secretary of State Anthony Solomon in testimony given before the Senate Subcommittee on Antitrust and Monopoly in 1966. The following description is based upon his testimony.[37]

The Department of State maintains close liaison with the Foreign Commerce Section of the Antitrust Division and with the Federal Trade Commission. It assists these agencies by compiling information on foreign antitrust laws and regulations and on international business activities. It also advises the enforcement agencies concerning foreign policy aspects of enforcement activities.

A special informal procedure has been established with Canada for regular two-way notification of impending antitrust actions and concerning restrictive private business practices which may give rise to such actions.

Finally, the Department undertakes to keep foreign governments advised of United States antitrust policies and activities affecting their interests and to promote consultations between American antitrust enforcement agency officials and those of foreign countries.

Foreign Commerce Section, Antitrust Division

The nature of the work of the Foreign Commerce Section of the Antitrust Division was detailed in testimony, also given before the Senate Subcommittee on Antitrust and Monopoly during its hearings, by the then Assistant Attorney General in Charge of Antitrust, Edwin M. Zimmerman. He noted that the Department of Justice consulted with other agencies whose interests might be affected by antitrust actions "in the foreign field," and called attention to the fact that the Foreign Commerce Section had been created in the Antitrust Division in 1962 to handle international aspects of antitrust problems.[38]

Division of Export Trade, Federal Trade Commission

Very little published information pertaining to the work of the Export Trade Division of the Federal Trade Commission exists. This division is located within the Office of

the General Counsel of the Commission and performs legal and administrative functions pertaining to the Webb–Pomerene Act. The work of this division is not, however, a subject of separate treatment in the Commission's annual reports, and the Division is not mentioned in the study of the Webb–Pomerene Act published in 1967 nor in testimony by FTC Chairman Paul Rand Dixon before the Senate Subcommittee on Antitrust and Monopoly in 1966.

United States Policy Since 1953

Since the sudden turnabout in 1953 in United States policy concerning a multilateral international agreement pertaining to international business practices, both the Department of State and the Justice Department have emphasized a policy of advocating that foreign countries adopt antitrust policies comparable to that of the United States. In his testimony before the Senate Subcommittee on Antitrust and Monopoly in 1966, Assistant Secretary of State Solomon reviewed the attempts which had been made in the past (discussed in preceding paragraphs) to obtain agreement on the text of a multilateral international convention dealing with restrictive business practices and then commented on why these attempts had failed. Among other things, he attributed the failure to dissimilarity of national laws, to problems pertaining to national sovereignty, and to the problem of the relationship of international procedures to domestic procedures and policies.[39]

Assistant Secretary Solomon also provided a statement of current United States policy. He asserted his belief that there was more hope of achieving agreement within the structure of the Organization for Economic Cooperation and Development (OECD), whose members had similar antitrust laws and policies, than in more diverse bodies.

Therefore, "the answer, at least for the near future," seemed to be a "system of informal cooperation among as many governments as possible, perhaps patterned on the US–Canadian procedure." Such cooperation could operate "under the aegis of and [be] reviewed in a multilateral organization such as the OECD." Secretary

---

[37] *Ibid.*, pp. 452–456.
[38] *Ibid.*, pp. 493–494.

[39] *Ibid.*, pp. 454–455.

Solomon concluded his statement by calling attention to the fact the United States has had a policy "ever since World War II [of negotiating] anti-restrictive business practice clauses in Friendship, Commerce, and Navigation Treaties, wherever possible." However, it may be noted, these clauses are weak in that under them, all that is provided for is "consultation" between the parties.

Assistant Attorney General Zimmerman's testimony was substantially the same as that of Secretary Solomon but did not provide an explanation of implementing procedures being utilized in 1966. He also emphasized the work of the OECD and the fact that its Committee on Restrictive Business Practices "meets twice a year in Paris and its subcommittees or working parties also meet at other times." This Committee is made up of antitrust officials from the participating countries, but its activities are largely restricted to making studies and recommendations; it has no operational policy functions.

The testimonies both of Assistant Secretary of State Solomon and of Assistant Attorney General Zimmerman make clear that the United States is today seeking to deal with international antitrust problems primarily by means of informal consultation and cooperation and that, although the concept of a formal international antitrust agreement has not been completely abandoned, the probability that any such an international agreement will be made in the near future is slight.

Our consideration of various aspects of the problems of "Antitrust and International Business Practices" has now been completed. There remain two final questions to be considered in our discussion of the special working rules of antitrust: (1) the problem of application of antitrust laws to firms and industries which are already subject to regulation under special legislation and (2) a brief critical survey of evaluations by various students of the effectiveness of antitrust laws. Both topics are discussed in the next chapter, the final chapter in Part II of this book.

CHAPTER

22

The Problem of Antitrust and Regulated Industries; Evaluations of Antitrust Policy

This chapter undertakes two different but related tasks. The first major subdivision is devoted to a consideration of the problem of the extent to which the antitrust laws apply to the activities and business practices of firms which are subject to regulation by specific commissions or agencies. The second major subdivision is concerned with a critical discussion of evaluations of the effectiveness of the antitrust laws by various writers.

A. THE PROBLEM OF ANTITRUST AND REGULATED INDUSTRIES

The Problem Defined

Some writers are content to deal with questions pertaining to the application of antitrust laws to industries subject to regulation by commissions and agencies by a simple exercise in classification. This exercise involves stating first that, in regulated industries, regulation is a substitute for competition; and stating, second, that the function of the antitrust laws is to preserve competition. Next, all industries can be classified into one of two categories: (1)

those subject to regulation and in which by definition the antitrust laws do not apply; and (2) those not subject to such special regulation in which the antitrust laws do apply. Such a neat and simple answer really evades the issue, since competition may be and is in fact relied upon in addition to regulation in most industries. The problem of the application of Section 7 of the Clayton Act to mergers in regulated industries has arisen in several cases decided since 1950, including the *Philadelphia National Bank* case already discussed in Chapter 17. Our discussion in the following paragraphs will undertake to examine the broad question of application of the antitrust laws to regulated industries in a number of different situations, as follows: (1) situations in which Congress has not provided for a specific exemption and in which reliance is placed upon the *mere existence* of a regulatory scheme and agency; (2) situations in which no specific statutory antitrust exemption exists but in which the agency has approved the action in question; (3) situations in which a statutory exemption may exist subject to agency approval but agency approval has *not* been obtained; and

(4) situations in which a statutory exemption apparently exists and agency approval has been given.

Situations of Reliance on Mere Existence of Regulatory Scheme and Agency

In cases in which Congress has not created an express exemption from the antitrust laws but in which a regulatory scheme and agency exist, the Supreme Court has held that the regulated industry is subject to antitrust action. This position is sometimes expressed in the statement, "immunity from the antitrust laws is not lightly implied."[1] [*Sic.*]

The position that the mere existence of a regulatory scheme is alone not sufficient to provide antitrust immunity dates back to one of the earliest cases won by the Government under the Sherman Act, the *Trans-Missouri Freight Association* case of 1897.[2]

This case involved a charge of price-fixing under the Sherman Act. At this time, the Interstate Commerce Commission was in existence, but the Act to Regulate Interstate Commerce did not contain a specific Sherman Act exemption, nor did the defendants plead that their acts had been done with agency approval. Instead, they argued that the public character of the railroads "and the peculiar power of control possessed by the State over the railroads" themselves resulted in an exemption from the Sherman Act. In other words, the defendants argued that the mere existence of a special regulatory scheme was *alone* sufficient to warrant an inference of an exemption from the antitrust laws. However, the Supreme Court rejected this argument, saying:

. . . The points of difference between the railroad and other corporations are great. . . . But the very character of a railroad would itself seem to call for special care by the legislature in regard to its conduct, so its business should be carried on with as much reference to the proper and fair interests of the public as possible. . . .[3]

A similar position was taken by the Court in later railroad cases; however, in the Transportation Act of 1920, Congress provided a basis for an exemption from antitrust in the case of railroad consolid-ations, and an actual exemption was contained in the Transportation Act of 1940,[4] as we will see later.

Situations Involving Lack of A Statutory Exemption But Agency Approval

Cases, in which the agency has approved an action which violates the antitrust laws but in which no express exemption exists, differ from those just discussed in that the defendant can claim that what he has done has been approved by the regulatory body which, presumably, possesses expertise to make the decision.

Among the earliest cases of this type was the *Texas and Pacific Railway Company* case.[5] This case was not an antitrust case, but was an action against a railway company by a shipper based on a claim of unjust and unreasonable rates. The company's defense was that the rate had been approved by the Interstate Commerce Commission and that, therefore, the shipper should resort to the procedure of making a claim before the Commission and could not sue in a court of law until such a claim had been dealt with by the Commission. The Supreme Court upheld this defense, relying heavily on the notion that the question of what was a "just and reasonable" rate was a question to be decided by the Commission on the basis of its expertise and not a matter to be decided in the first instance in a court. Thus the Supreme Court held that the matter was one primarily for the decision of the Commission in the first instance, and the principle thus stated is today known as the doctrine of *primary jurisdiction*—a doctrine which holds that in matters peculiarly within the expertise of a regulatory agency, resort must be had to an agency determination of the issue before the matter can be taken up in a court of law. In the antitrust field, the question thus arises: suppose there is a merger of a number of firms in a regulated industry. Is this a question of antitrust law or a question to be decided by the agency under the doctrine of primary jurisdiction? The bank merger cases decided by the Court under Section 7 of the Clayton Act, as amended, have all involved the

---

[1] See for example, *U.S.* v. *Philadelphia National Bank, et. al.*, 374 U.S. 321 (1963), at pp. 350–351.
[2] 166 U.S. 290 (1897).
[3] *Ibid.*, pp. 321–322.

[4] *Penn–Central Merger Cases*, 389 U.S. 486 (1968), at p. 492.
[5] *Texas and Pacific Ry. Co.* v. *Abilene Cotton Co.*, 204 U.S. 426 (1907).

question of primary jurisdiction; and, in most if not all of these cases, the relevant regulatory agencies have approved the mergers only to have them declared unlawful in subsequent antitrust actions.[6] In this class of cases, the Court has examined closely the extent to which the agency in question has taken account of competitive factors along with "public interest and convenience" in making its decision. Where competitive factors have not been given substantial and painstaking analysis and emphasis, antitrust adjudication has been allowed. Moreover, in 1967, in discussing the relationship of the Bank Merger Act of 1966 to antitrust law, the Supreme Court emphasized the fact that, in the area of application of antitrust law to actions by regulatory agencies, the rule does not apply that a factual determination made by an administrative agency will be accepted as binding upon the courts if supported by "substantial" evidence. This position was stated in the *First City Bank* case, a case in which a merger approved by the Comptroller of the Currency, but not by the Board of Governors of the Federal Reserve System, was challenged by the Antitrust Division. In part, the Court remarked:

. . . Prior to the 1966 Act, administrative approval of bank mergers was necessary. Yet in an antitrust action brought later to enjoin them we never stopped to consider what weight, if any, the agency's determination should have in the antitrust case. . . . Traditionally in antitrust action involving regulated industries, the courts have never given presumptive weight to a prior agency decision, for the simple reason that Congress put such suits on a different axis than was familiar in administrative procedure . . . immunity from the antitrust laws "is not lightly implied". . . . And the grant of administrative power to give immunity unless the agency's decision is arbitrary, capricious, or unsupported by substantial evidence would be a long step in that direction. . . . The appraisal of competitive factors is grist for the antitrust mill. . . . If the anticompetitive effect is adverse, then it is to be excused only "if the convenience and needs of the community to be served" *clearly* outweigh it.[7] (Italics in the original.)

The word *"clearly"* which the Court italicized in the preceding quotation must

be noted. As we will see later, various mergers approved by the Interstate Commerce Commission have been upheld by the Court. These mergers are exempt from antitrust action with agency approval. The deciding factor in most of the cases seems to have been the painstaking and detailed analysis which the Commission has made of the anticompetitive effects in relation to the "public convenience and necessity."

The *El Paso Natural Gas Company* case, also discussed in Chapter 17, raised the question of the application of Section 7 of the Clayton Act, as amended, to firms in the natural gas industry subject to regulation by the Federal Power Commission. The sequence of events in the preliminary stages of this case is also worth noting in the present context. In 1957, El Paso Natural Gas Company acquired 99.8 percent of the stock of the Pacific Northwest Pipeline Company, a potential competitor. In July 1957, the Justice Department brought an antitrust action alleging a violation of Section 7. In August 1957, El Paso applied to the Federal Power Commission for permission to acquire the assets of Pacific Northwest Company; and in December 1959, before the antitrust case was tried, the Commission granted the requested permission. The Supreme Court, however, set aside the Commission's order on grounds that it should not have acted until the District Court had decided the antitrust case.[8] Thereafter, the District Court decided in favor of the merger. However, as we have seen in Chapter 17, the Supreme Court reversed the lower court decision in 1964.[9]

It is clear, therefore, that in the absence of a specific statutory exemption from the antitrust laws pertaining to mergers, Section 7 of the Clayton Act, as amended, does apply to regulated industries.

A Situation in Which a Statutory Exemption May Exist, But the Agency Has Not Approved

Since 1932, the Supreme Court has been faced with a number of cases involving rate agreements by ocean carriers under the Shipping Act of 1916. The Act permits conferences (associations of carriers) to make

---

[6] *U.S.* v. *Philadelphia National Bank, et. al.*, 374 U.S. 321 (1963).

[7] *U.S.* v. *First City National Bank of Houston, et. al.*, 386 U.S. 361 (1967), at pp. 367–370.

[8] *California* v. *Federal Power Commission*, 369 U.S. 482 (1962).

[9] *U.S.* v. *El Paso Natural Gas Company, et. al.*, 373 U.S. 390 (1964).

rate agreements of various kinds and provides that such price-fixing agreements shall be immune from antitrust prosecution when they have been approved by the Federal Maritime Board. A 1966 case involving such a rate agreement will be considered shortly. Before doing so, it will be useful to consider the 1952 *Far East Conference* case. In this case, the conference in question had established a dual-rate system under which shippers who agreed to deal exclusively with the conference were given lower rates than were those who did not do so. In the *Far East* case, a *general* agreement *looking toward* the making of a specific rate-fixing agreement had been filed and approved by the Board. However, a specific dual-rate agreement was also made but *not* submitted to the Board. The Government brought an antitrust action, in which it sought an *injunction*, alleging that the dual-rate system had not been approved by the Board and, in fact, could not be approved by the Board because it violated the Shipping Act. The Supreme Court, however, held that the questions involved were of such a nature that they could be decided only by the Maritime Board itself and that the Attorney General should have submitted his complaint to the Board itself in the first instance. Speaking for the majority, Justice Frankfurter explained the decision by saying that the Court was relying on

. . . a principle, now firmly established, that in cases raising issues of fact not within the conventional experience of judges or cases requiring the exercise of administrative discretion, agencies created by Congress for regulating the subject matter should not be passed over. This is so even though the facts after they have been appraised by special competence serve as a premise for legal consequences to be judicially defined. Uniformity and consistency in the regulation of business entrusted to a particular agency are secured, and the limited function of review by the judiciary are more rationally exercised, by preliminary resort for ascertaining and interpreting the circumstances underlying the legal issues to agencies that are better equipped than courts by specialization, by insight gained through experience, and by a more flexible procedure.[10]

Twenty years before the *Far East* case, the Supreme Court had decided the *Cunard* case. In this case, a plaintiff shipper also sued for an *injunction* to prevent the defendants from continuing an alleged conspiracy in violation of the antitrust laws by maintaining a dual-rate system which had not been properly filed and duly approved by the regulatory agency. In this earlier case, the Court had also held that the shipper should have sought his remedy under the provisions of the Shipping Act by seeking damages in proceedings before the regulatory agency.[11]

However, in 1966 in the *Carnation* case, the Supreme Court did permit a plaintiff to sue for treble damages in a rate case under the antitrust laws, notwithstanding the earlier *Cunard* and *Far East* decisions.[12] In the *Carnation* case, two conferences consisting of carriers operating between the United States and the Far East had made a "treaty" or general agreement in 1952 *to be implemented* by *specific* rate agreements *later*. The 1952 general "agreement to make specific rate agreements" was filed with and approved by the Maritime Commission. (The "Board" was by now called the "Commission.") Subsequently, the two conferences made specific rate agreements which they did *not* file, and which were *not* approved by the Commission. The Carnation Company, a shipper, sued in 1966 claiming treble *damages* and that the rate agreements constituted a violation of the antitrust laws. The defendants relied on the *Far East* and *Cunard* cases and argued that the rate agreements were covered by the Commission's approval of the 1952 Conference agreement. The District Court dismissed the complaint and the Court of Appeals affirmed. The Supreme Court granted *certiorari*. After the granting of *certiorari*, but *before* the Supreme Court made its decision, the Federal Maritime Commission made its own investigation and concluded that the rate agreements were *not* included within the approval it had given to the earlier 1952 agreement and were thus unlawful. The Supreme Court cited all these events and reversed the decisions made by the lower courts. The majority opinion contained the

[10] *U.S.* v. *Far East Conference*, 342 U.S. 570 (1952), at pp. 574–575.
[11] *U.S. Navigation Company* v. *Cunard S.S. Company*, 284 U.S. 474 (1932).
[12] *Carnation Co.* v. *Pacific Westbound Conference, et. al.*, 383 U.S. 213 (1966).

following statements pertaining to the earlier *Far East* and *Cunard* cases:

This Court's decisions in *United States Navigation Co.* v. *Cunard Steamship Co.*, 284 U.S. 474, and *Far East Conference* v. *United States*, 342 U.S. 570, do not conflict with our interpretation of the Shipping Act. Those cases merely hold that the courts must refrain from imposing antitrust sanctions of debatable legality under the Shipping Act in order to avoid the possibility of conflict between the courts and the Commission.[13]

The Court then pointed out that the two earlier cases had both involved actions seeking *injunctions, not damages, as in the Carnation case*, and that in neither of the two earlier cases had the Commission ever determined the legality of the rate practices complained of. An award for damages in the *Carnation* case, based on past illegal conduct (failure to report the agreements to the Commission made the agreements illegal), the Court pointed out, would "not interfere with any future action of the Commission." Moreover, the Court could find in no provisions of the Shipping Act an "implied repeal" of the antitrust laws. Indeed, the Court added:

. . . We have recently said: "Repeals of the antitrust laws by implication from a regulatory statute are strongly disfavored and have only been found in cases of plain repugnancy between the antitrust and regulatory provisions". . . .[14]

Situations in Which a Statutory Exemption Exists and Agency Approval Has Been Given

As was noted earlier, the Transportation Act of 1920 authorized the Interstate Commerce Commission to make plans to consolidate the railroads into a limited number of systems, and the Transportation Act of 1940 repealed this provision but provided that the Commission might grant approval, carrying with it an antitrust exemption of mergers proposed by the carriers themselves. The *McLean Trucking Company* case was the first major case involving a Supreme Court decision pertaining to this policy of antitrust exemption.[15]

In this case, the Commission approved the consolidation of the seven largest eastern motor-carriers into one large company. The Commission found that, prior to the consolidation, the carriers competed with one another in about one-third of the area (measured by mileage) covered by their combined routes. However, it also concluded that after the merger there "would remain ample competitive motor-carrier service throughout the area served." In addition, it found that "shipment of freight would be simplified and expedited, equipment would be utilized more efficiently, terminal facilities improved, handling of shipments reduced, relations with shippers and public regulatory bodies simplified, safe operations promoted, and substantial economies achieved."[16] The case was appealed to the Supreme Court, which upheld the Commission's decision saying, in response to the argument that the Commission had failed to give sufficient weight to antitrust laws and policies in giving approval to the merger, that

. . . as a factor in determining the propriety of motor-carrier consolidations, the preservation of competition among carriers, although still a value, is significant chiefly as it aids in the attainment of the national transportation policy.

. . . the wisdom and experience of the Commission, not of the courts, must determine whether the proposed consolidation is "consistent with the public interest."[17]

In 1953 however, the Court refused to allow the Federal Communications Commission to authorize entry into the industry of a new firm to supply overseas radio telegraph services in a situation in which the Commission relied on vague generalities about the "national policy of competition" and did not make specific findings of fact pertaining to what effect such a new entrant might have on the market. Instead, the Court asserted that in such cases the Commission must "make specific findings, not of 'tangible benefit,' but merely to warrant, as it were, that competition would serve some beneficial purpose, such as maintaining good service and improving it."[18]

The emphasis given by the Supreme Court to the proposition that the regulatory

13 *Ibid.*, p. 220.
14 *Ibid.*, pp. 217–218.
15 *U.S.* v. *McLean Trucking Co.*, 321 U.S. 67 (1944).
16 *Ibid.*, p. 72.

17 *Ibid.*, pp. 85–88.
18 *Federal Communications Commission* v. *R. C. A. Communications, Inc.*, 346 U.S. 92 (1953).

agencies must base their actions upon *specific* findings of fact which is clearly apparent in the *R. C. A.* case just discussed appears also in the *Seaboard Air Line R. R. Company* case decided in 1965.[19] In this case the Department of Justice challenged a merger between two competing railroads, alleging that the merger violated Section 7 of the Clayton Act, despite the fact that the Interstate Commerce Commission had approved the merger. In approving the merger, the Commission had recognized that the merger would create a monopoly and eliminate competition in certain parts of Florida; but had also found that the merged lines carried only a small part of the total traffic involved, that ample rail competition would remain, and that the reduction in competition would have no appreciable effect upon shippers and communities.

In upholding the Commission's decision, the Supreme Court referred to and explained the decision in the *McLean Trucking Company* case and relied also on its previous decision in a 1959 case involving railroads by saying:

We believe that the District Court [which had ruled against the ICC] erred in its interpretation of the directions this Court set forth in *McLean Trucking Company* v. *United States*, 321 U.S. 67 (1944) and *Minneapolis and St. Louis R. Co.* v. *United States*, 361 U.S. 173 (1959). As we said in *Minneapolis* at 186:

"Although S. 5(11) [of the Interstate Commerce Act] does not authorize the Commission to 'ignore' the antitrust laws, *McLean Trucking Co.* v. *United States*, 321 U.S. 67, 80, there can be 'little doubt that the Commission is not to measure proposals for [acquisitions] by the . . . antitrust laws.' 321 U.S. 67, at 85–86. The problem is one of accommodation of S. 5(2) and the antitrust legislation. The Commission remains obligated to 'estimate the scope and appraise the effects of the curtailment of competition which will result from the proposed [acquisition] and consider them along with the advantages of improved service [and other matters in the public interest] to determine whether the [acquisition] will assist in effectuating the overall transportation policy.' 321 U.S. 67, at 87."

The same criteria should be applied here to the proposed merger. It matters not that the merger might otherwise violate the antitrust

laws; the Commission has been authorized by Congress to approve the merger of railroads in accordance with the criteria quoted above that such a merger would be "consistent with the public interest." 54 Stat. 906, 49 U.S.C. S. 5(2) (b) (1964 ed.).

Whether the Commission has confined itself within the statutory limits upon its discretion and has based its findings on substantial evidence are questions for the trial court in the first instance. . . .[20]

In 1967, the Court again emphasized the necessity for, and importance of, specific findings of fact by the Commission in the *Denver Railway* case.[21] In this case, the Commission approved *without a hearing* a sale of a quantity of authorized but previously unissued stock by Railway Express Agency (REA) to Greyhound Corporation. In part, the Supreme Court remarked, in holding the transaction raised questions under Section 7 of the Clayton Act:

Both the ICC and this Court have read terms such as "public interest" broadly, to require consideration of all important consequences, including anticompetitive effects. Thus the ICC is required to weigh anticompetitive effects in approving applications for merger or control under S. 5 of the Act authorizing the ICC to grant such applications only if consistent with the "public interest." *McLean Trucking Co.* v. *United States*, 321 U.S. 67. And similarly broad responsibilities are encompassed within like broad directives addressed to other agencies. *E.g.*, *National Broadcasting Co.* v. *United States*, 319 U.S. 190, 224; *FCC* v. *RCA Communications, Inc.*, 346 U.S. 86, 94; *California* v. *FPC*, 369 U.S. 482, 484–485.[22]

The fact that no hearing had been held invalidated the ICC's approval. The merger of the New York Central and Pennsylvania railroads probably constitutes the high point in the series of cases pertaining to railroad mergers, not only because of the size of the merger involved, but also because the Commission meticulously observed the directions given by the Court for the determination of merger cases. As has been noted earlier, the Transportation Act of 1920 authorized the Commission to make plans to consolidate the railroads of the United States into a limited number of systems but provided no authority for

[19] *Seaboard Air Line R. R. Co.* v. *U.S.*, 382 U.S. 154 (1965).

[20] *Ibid.*, pp. 156–157.

[21] *Denver and Rio Grande Western Railroad Co., et. al.*, v. *U.S.*, 387 U.S. 486 (1967).

[22] *Ibid.*, pp. 492–493. See also *Northern Lines Merger Cases*, 396 U.S. 491 (1970).

carrying out such plans. The Act of 1940 authorized the Commission to grant an antitrust exemption in the case of mergers proposed by the railroads themselves of which it approved. Although a problem of including in the conditions of the New York Central–Pennsylvania merger certain provisions pertaining to three weak railroads did arise in the early stages of the proceedings, once this problem had been met, the procedure followed came close to setting a model for action by regulatory agencies in such cases. In the words of the Court:

Examination of the record and the findings in the present case . . . satisfies us that the Commission has properly and lawfully discharged its duties with respect to the merits of the merger. In these elaborate and lengthy proceedings the Commission has considered evidence tendered by others and compiled by its own staff. Upon the aggressive suit of parties representing conflicting interests, it has analyzed every pertinent aspect of the merger. . . . It has weighed conflicting viewpoints on all of the fundamental issues and many more that are tangential.[23]

Thus the Court upheld the Commission's action, the guarantee of procedural due process having been met, and the issue having been disposed of in an adversary proceeding in which the anticompetitive effects were balanced against considerations of public convenience and necessity and the furtherance of the national transportation policy as defined by Congress.

There is no conflict between the Court's decisions pertaining to the granting of antitrust immunity by the Interstate Commerce Commission and the holdings of the Court in the various bank merger cases discussed earlier, although some spokesmen and apologists for the banking industry have claimed that a conflict exists. There is nowhere in the legislation pertaining to the regulation of banks a directive to the Comptroller of Currency or to the Federal Reserve Board or any other expression of Congressional policy to the effect that the regulatory authorities are authorized to grant antitrust immunity to proposals from or by banking firms to consolidate themselves into a limited number of systems. To

the contrary, in the case of the banking industry, as the Court has noted, Congress has provided that an antitrust action challenging a bank merger may be refuted by a clear showing by the merging banks that the merger is justified by the "convenience and need of the community." This point was clearly stated by the Court in 1968 in the following language explaining its holding in the *First City National Bank* case, discussed earlier. The Court said:

Last term, in *United States* v. *First City National Bank of Houston*, 386 U.S. 361 (1967), this Court interpreted the procedural provisions of the 1966 Act, holding that the Bank Merger Act provided for continued scrutiny of bank mergers under the Sherman Act and the Clayton Act, but created a new defense, *with the merging banks having the burden of proving that defense.* The task of the district courts was to inquire *de novo* into the validity of bank mergers approved by the relevant bank regulatory agency to determine, first, whether the merger offended the antitrust laws and, second, if it did, whether the banks had established that the merger was nonetheless justified by "the convenience and needs of the community to be served."[24]

That the burden of proof is on the regulated firms seeking an exemption from the antitrust laws is a proposition which the Court has also applied generally in cases involving agreements to fix rates and conditions of service made by such firms subject to agency approval. There are three statutes providing for immunization of such private agreements by agency approval: (1) there is the exemption in the case of the Shipping Act already mentioned;[25] (2) the Reed Bulwinkle Act provides for exemptions in the case of carriers regulated by the Interstate Commerce Commission;[26] and (3) the Civil Aeronautics Act also contains an exemption in the case of air carriers.[27]

Two cases decided in 1968 by the Supreme Court throw light upon the test to be employed by the regulatory agency in granting antitrust immunity to such a rate agreement. In one of these cases, the Federal Maritime Commission (FMC) refused to grant an exemption in a situation in which the members of two transatlantic

---

[23] *Penn–Central Merger Cases*, 389 U.S. 486 (1968), at p. 500.

[24] *U.S.* v. *Third National Bank in Nashville, et. al.*, 390 U.S. 171 (1968), at p. 178. (Italics mine.)

[25] 46 U.S.C., S. 814 (1952).

[26] 49 U.S.C., S. 5b (1952).

[27] 49 U.S.C., S. 492 (1952).

steamship conferences had adopted a "tying" rule under which they prohibited travel agents from booking passage on competing nonconference lines and from enforcing a "unanimity" rule under which unanimous consent of the members of one conference was required in order to make any change in the maximum commission rates payable to such agents (thereby making it more profitable for the agents to promote air travel from which they received greater remuneration). The Commission held hearings and disapproved both rules by applying a principle that "conference restraints which interfere with the policies of the antitrust laws will be approved only if the conferences can 'bring forth such facts as would demonstrate that the . . . rule was required by a serious transportation need, necessary to secure important public benefits or in furtherance of a valid regulatory purpose of the Shipping Act.' "[28]

The representatives of the conference appealed the Commission's decision, and the Court of Appeals set the order aside. However, the Supreme Court reversed the decision of the Court of Appeals, commenting upon the argument made by the steamship companies to the effect that the Commission had the burden of proving that the conference restrictions were not in the public interest by saying:

. . . Congress has, it is true, decided to confer antitrust immunity unless the agreement is found to violate certain statutory standards, but . . . antitrust concepts are intimately involved in the standard Congress chose. The Commission's approach does not make the promise of antitrust immunity meaningless [as the shipping companies had argued], because a restraint that would violate the antitrust laws will still be approved whenever a sufficient justification for it exists. Nor does the Commission's test, by requiring the Conference to come forward with justification for the restraint, improperly shift the burden of proof . . . once an antitrust violation is established, this alone will normally constitute substantial evidence that the agreement is "contrary to the public interest" unless other evidence in the record fairly detracts from the weight of this factor. It is not unreasonable to require that a conference adopting a particular rule to govern its own affairs, for reasons best known to the conference itself, must come forward and explain to the Commission what those reasons are. . . .[29]

A second case also decided in 1968 affirmed the proposition that exemptions would be allowed only in cases in which the burden of proof had been carried in favor of the exemption. In this case, the Pacific Maritime Association (PMA), consisting of Pacific Coast shipping employers, agreed with the International Longshoreman's and Warehouseman's Union to establish a fund to be used to combat the effects of technological unemployment resulting from the introduction of labor-saving machinery. The PMA undertook to raise the fund by levying charges upon its members based either on volume or on measurement of cargo, depending upon the manner in which the cargo had been manifested. In the case of automobiles, however, the assessment was based on measurement only, with the result that the Volkswagen Company was required to pay relatively higher fees to the terminal company unloading its cargo. The Company sought to invoke the jurisdiction of the Federal Maritime Commission, claiming a violation of the Shipping Act. However, the Commission refused to take jurisdiction, asserting, among other things, that the agreement was not of the type required to be registered and that the agreement did not effect competition. The Court of Appeals affirmed, but the Supreme Court reversed, (1) rejecting the Commission's contention that its interpretation of the Shipping Act minimized the potential number of antitrust exemptions; (2) asserting that "the Commission is required under S. 15 to consider antitrust implications;" and (3) citing the *Swedish Line* case just discussed.[30]

Summary and Conclusion

The preceding analysis demonstrates that (1) in situations involving firms in regulated industries in which no specific statutory antitrust exemption exists, and in which agency approval for the conduct in question has not been given, no antitrust exemption exists. That is, the Court will not infer the existence of an antitrust exemption from

---

[28] *Federal Maritime Commission et. al.* v. *Aktiebolaget Svenska Amerika Linien (Swedish American Line) et. al.*, 390 U.S. 238 (1968), at p. 243.

[29] *Ibid.*, pp. 245–246.
[30] *Volkswagenwerk Aktiengesellschaft* v. *Federal Maritime Commission, et. al.*, 390 U.S. 261 (1968), at p. 273.

the *mere* existence of a regulatory scheme and agency. (2) In situations in which no specific statutory exemption exists, but in which the conduct has been approved by the regulatory agency, the question is one to be tried *de novo* in the courts; and, specifically, in cases involving bank mergers, the Bank Merger Act of 1966 provides an additional defense which must, however, be affirmatively established by the defendant. (3) In situations in which an exemption apparently exists but agency approval has *not* been obtained, the case is not ripe for judicial determination, and the case will be remanded to the agency for determination of the factual issues involved. Finally, (4) in cases in which an exemption exists and agency approval has been given, the Court will carefully examine the agency's findings and handling of the case to insure that they conform to the statutory standards and that the burden of proving the exemption has been carried.

The Supreme Court has thus succeeded in employing procedural devices, in particular the placing of the burden of proof on the one seeking an exemption from the antitrust laws, thereby reconciling the structure and performance tests of workable competition, a procedure long advocated by Dean Edward S. Mason and explicitly proposed by Walter Adams in 1958.[31] This reconciliation has been accomplished and exists in the procedure of adopting, in the first instance, a presumption that "competition is the touchstone of economic regulation" even in situations in which a special regulatory agency has been established, but of allowing this presumption to be rebutted in particular cases in which the regulatory agency has been authorized by Congress to approve anticompetitive behavior in accordance with given statutory standards, usually by tests of "public convenience and necessity," tests which are essentially performance tests. The *Penn–Central Merger* cases constitute an outstanding example. And the following language from the opinion in these cases warrants attention in any discussion of antitrust and the regulated industries:

It is, of course, true that the policy of Congress, set forth in the Transportation Act, to consolidate the railroads of this nation into a "limited number of systems" is a variation from our traditional national policy, reflected in the antitrust laws, of insisting upon the primacy of competition as the touchstone of economic regulation. . . . This departure from the general and familiar standard of industrial regulation emphasizes the need for insistence that, before a rail merger is approved, there must be convincing evidence that it will serve the national interest and that terms are prescribed so that the Congressional objective of a rail system serving the public more effectively and efficiently will be carried out. Obviously not every merger or consolidation that may be agreed upon by private interests can pass the statutory test.[32]

In the *El Paso Natural Gas Company* case, discussed in Chapter 17 earlier, it may be noted, not only was there no statutory exemption, but there *was* evidence that the potential competition offered by the Northwest Pipeline Company *had* resulted in a reduction in prices of natural gas in California. And although the decisions of the Supreme Court in bank merger cases have been criticized by various apologists for the banking industry, when these criticisms are boiled down to their essence what remains is a rejection of findings of facts, facts about which responsible men may have different opinions. These facts are largely concerned with the actual or potential performance of large banks of the size of those contemplated by the merger in question.

B. EVALUATIONS OF ANTITRUST

It should be obvious, but may be worth noting, that one's evaluation of the antitrust laws depends upon the type of enforcement standard one employs. In this subdivision, we will undertake to examine some recent evaluations of the antitrust laws. The ones to be considered first were presented in the course of a discussion of "Planning, Regulation, and Competition," sponsored and published by the Senate Subcommittee on Monopoly of the Small Business Committee in 1967.

---

[31] See Edward S. Mason, "Current Status of the Monopoly Problem," 62 *Harvard Law Review* 1265 (1949), at p. 1280. Also see Walter Adams, "A Critical Evaluation of Regulation by Independent Commis-

sions," *American Economic Review*, "Papers and Proceedings," Vol. XLVIII, May 1958, pp. 527–543.

[32] *Penn–Central Merger Cases*, 389 U.S. 486 (1968), at pp. 499–500.

J. K. Galbraith: The Antitrust Laws as a "Charade"

The first panelist to present his point of view in the discussion mentioned above was Professor J. K. Galbraith; he utilized the occasion to explain further a thesis he had advanced in a recent book,[33] as part of his larger purpose in his book, to the effect that the antitrust laws were a "charade." In part he asserted:

. . . [Here] enters the element of charade in the antitrust laws. If a firm is already large, it is substantially immune under the antitrust laws. If you already have the basic requisite of market power, you are safe. . . .

. . . the antitrust laws are effective in two instances where the firms do not have market power, but are seeking to achieve it. Where firms are few and large they can, without overt collusion, establish and maintain a price that is generally satisfactory to all participants. . . . And this market power is legally immune or very nearly so. It is everyday practice in autos, steel, rubber, and virtually every other industry shared or dominated by, relatively, a few large firms. But if there are 20 or 30 or more significant firms in the industry, this kind of tacit price-making— this calculation as to what is mutually advantageous but without overt communication— becomes difficult, maybe very difficult. The same result can only be achieved by having a meeting or by exchanging information on prices and costs and price intentions. But this is illegal. It is also legally vulnerable. And it is, in fact, an everyday object of prosecution, as the Department of Justice will confirm. What the big firm in the concentrated industry can accomplish legally and effortlessly because of its size, the small firm in the unconcentrated industry does at the pain of civil, even criminal prosecution. . . .

The second manifestation of the charade has to do with mergers. If a firm is already large, it has as a practical matter nothing to fear under antimerger provisions of the Clayton Act. It will not be demerged. It can continue to grow from its own earnings; if discreet, it can even, from time to time, pick up a small impecunious competitor, for it can claim that this does little to alter the pattern of competition in the industry. But if two medium-sized firms unite in order to deal more effectively with the giant, the law will be on them like a tiger. Again, if you are large, you are exempt. If you seek to become as large, or even if you seek to become somewhat

larger, although still much smaller, you are in trouble. . . .

Here we have the nature of modern antitrust activity. It conducts a fairly effective war on small firms which seek the same market power that big firms already, by their nature, possess. Behind this impressive facade, the big participants who have the most power bask in nearly total immunity. And since the competitive market, like God and a sound family life, is something no sound businessman can oppose, even the smaller entrepreneurs who are the natural victims of this arrangement do not actively protest. . . .

. . . I readily concede that it would be quixotic to ask the repeal of the antitrust laws, although other industrial countries function quite competently without them. But the antitrust laws are part of the American folklore. They receive strong support from the legal profession and vice versa. They have a reserve value for dealing with extreme and sanguinary abuse of power as occasionally occurs. I would be content were we simply to withdraw our faith from the antitrust laws—were we to cease to imagine that there is any chance that they will affect the structure of American industry or its market power and, having in mind the present discrimination in their application, were we then to allow them quietly to atrophy. Then we would face the real problem, which is how to live with vast organizations—and the values they impose— that we have and will continue to have. . . .[34]

All this is consistent with Galbraith's concept of the "workable economy", explained in Chapter 13.

Walter Adams and the "Integrated Approach"

The second panelist, Professor Walter Adams, agreed with Galbraith's contention that "corporate giantism dominates American industry" but rejected Galbraith's conclusion. Thus Adams remarked:

It seems to me that Professor Galbraith keeps coming back to the charade of antitrust. But a competitive society is the product not simply of negative enforcement of antitrust laws; it is the product of a total integrated approach at all levels of government—legislative, administrative, and regulatory. An integrated national policy of promoting competition—and this means more than mere enforcement of the antitrust laws—is not only feasible but desirable. No economy can

---

[33] J. K. Galbraith, *The New Industrial State* (Boston: Houghton–Mifflin Co., 1967).

[34] *Planning, Regulation* and *Competition* (Hearings before the Subcommittee on Monopoly of the Senate

Small Business Committee, 90th Cong., 1st sess., 1967) (Washington, D.C.: U.S. Government Printing Office, 1967), pp. 7–11.

function without built-in checks and balances which tend to break down the bureaucratic preference for letting well enough alone—forces which erode, subvert, or render obsolete the conservative bias inherent in any organization devoid of competition. . . . The policy objective must be to promote market structures which will *compel* the conduct and performance which is in the public interest.[35]

Adams, it will be recalled from Chapter 13, advocates the market structure test of workable competition, and this test is merely one aspect of the "total policy" embodied in the integrated approach.

Willard Mueller: Galbraith Has Neglected His Homework

Professor Willard Mueller, at that time Chief Economist for the Federal Trade Commission, also rejected Galbraith's position, asserting flatly that Galbraith had not kept "abreast of contemporary antitrust policy or its effects." Thus Mueller stated the basis of his comment:

. . . Antimerger effort has been directed almost exclusively against the largest industrial concerns. . . . Over 60 percent of the largest, those with over a billion dollars and merely a third of the top 200 have been the subject of antitrust complaints. Practically all of these complaints have not involved the challenge of miniscule mergers, but rather have involved an attack upon mergers by large concerns. . . . My major conclusion is . . . that there has been an enormous effort. . . .

It is true that antitrust policy cannot easily— and certainly not quickly—solve problems of deeply entrenched power. Fifty years of ineffective public policy toward mergers resulted in unnecessarily high concentration in many industries. But recent developments show that much can be accomplished. I say categorically: Whether or not the market survives in the greater part of our economy, or is destroyed by vast aggregations of market power, will not be determined by technological imperatives but by public policy toward the achievement and retention of power. The market may well be destroyed in the next generation as Galbraith predicts, but not for his reasons. It will be a matter of public will or neglect, not technology.[36]

Donald Turner: Past Mistakes Need Not Be Repeated

The last of the panelists to comment on Professor Galbraith's position was the then Assistant Attorney General in Charge of Antitrust, Donald Turner. Turner took the position that:

On the impact of antitrust law, I think it is undeniable that it has been more active and vigorous in attacking price-fixing, other restrictive agreements, and mergers than in dealing directly with existing market power. . . .

Even assuming however . . . that our present relative inactivity in dealing with existing undue market power shall continue for the indefinite future, I do not agree that it is bad public policy or bad law or bad anything to continue to attack price fixing and other restrictive agreements and mergers in those areas in which we still have hope.

To put it somewhat differently, the fact that for historical reasons of one sort or another we have had to accept an unfortunate development in one or more areas of our economy does not mean, it seems to me, that we are compelled to make things worse by permitting more.

. . . In antitrust or in any other area of public policy it has always been true that even though we cannot undo the past we can try to do better in the future, and we cannot rationally measure prospective public policy by past mistakes. Past mistakes by no means compel repetition. . . .[37]

The "Secret" Neal Report on Antitrust (Johnson Administration)

Between 1967 and 1968, Presidents Nixon and Johnson appointed "secret" task forces to make recommendations concerning antitrust policy. The Johnson Task Force was under the Chairmanship of Dean Phil Neal of the University of Chicago Law School and consisted of three practicing lawyers, six professors of law, and three economists (Lee E. Preston, Paul W. McAvoy, and James W. McKie). One of the members (James A. Rahl) of this Task Force had previously served as a majority member of the Attorney General's National Committee to Study the Antitrust Laws. Although the *Report* of the Neal group had been kept secret by the Johnson Administration, after the Nixon Administration came into office, the *Report* was released in May 1969 by the Department of Justice.[38]

---

35 *Ibid.*, p. 16. (Italics his.)

36 *Ibid.*, pp. 34–35.

37 *Ibid.*, pp. 27–29.

38 See *The Role of Giant Corporations* (Hearings before the Subcommittee on Monopoly of the Senate Select Committee on Small Business, 91st Cong., 1st sess., 1969) (Washington, D.C.: U.S. Government Printing Office, 1969), Part 1A, pp. 877 ff. for a reproduction of the *Neal Report*.

Probably the most controversial recommendation of the Johnson Task Force was its proposal for enactment of a new law, *The Concentrated Industries Act.* This proposed law would require the Attorney General and the FTC to investigate and institute proceedings before a "Special Court" in cases of "oligopoly" industries. An "oligopoly" industry is defined in the proposed legislation as one in which four or fewer firms account for 70 percent or more of the sales in a market. Provision is made in the law for "deconcentration proceedings" before a "Special Court" to reduce the market share of any "oligopoly" firms possessing 15 percent or more of the market. The Special Court would consist of district judges and courts of appeal judges selected by the Chief Justice, and provision is made for the use of economists as "expert witnesses" in proceedings before the Special Court. "Oligopoly firms" would be given one year within which to achieve a voluntary reduction of their market shares.

The Task Force frankly stated that its report "focuses" on market structure. Thus, among others, the *Report* also contains a recommendation that acquisition by a conglomerate company of a company which is among the top four in its industry be prohibited but that acquisition of a non-dominant company not be prohibited. It also recommended that changes be made in the Robinson–Patman Act relative to price discrimination and in the patent laws to require nondiscriminatory licensing of patents.

The recommendations concerning mergers of conglomerate firms differ from the Antitrust Division's Guidelines discussed in Chapter 17, since some acquisitions by conglomerate firms subject to attack under the Guidelines would be permitted under the recommendations. No action was taken by President Johnson to implement the recommendations of the Task Force and the election of President Nixon assured that the recommendations would not be implemented. Instead, President Nixon appointed a new Task Force to make a study. In this regard it may be noted that newspaper reporters characterized Dean Phil Neal, the chairman of the Johnson Task Force, as a "liberal" and characterized Professor George Stigler (of the University of Chicago), chairman of Nixon's new Task Force, as a "conservative."

The "Secret" Stigler Report on Antitrust (Nixon Administration)

In 1968, President Nixon appointed a Task Force to study antitrust policy, called "The Task Force on Productivity and Competition," prior to his actual election to office. The Task Force reported shortly after his election. The Chairman of this group was Professor George Stigler (who had been a member of the Attorney General's National Committee, as had James Rahl of the Neal Task Force). The *Stigler Report* has been briefly mentioned in the final subdivision of Chapter 18.[39]

The Stigler group consisted of nine members. One third, that is, three of these (Professor Stigler, Professor Coase, and Professor Bowman) had an existing or past association with the Department of Economics of the University of Chicago. Peter Steiner of Michigan was a fourth economist-member. In addition to two lawyers (one from the University of Chicago and the other from the University of Michigan), there were two private businessmen on this Task Force, Alexander L. Stott, a Vice President of A. T. & T. (who predictably dissented from the group's recommendation that competition in regulated industries should be increased), and Raymond Mulford, President of Owens Illinois Glass Co. (who dissented from group's recommendation that the fine for antitrust violations be increased). Professor Richard Posner of Stanford was the ninth member.

The major Stigler Task Force recommendations differed substantially from those of the Neal Task Force, although the two Task Forces both recommended policies leading to increased competition in regulated industries and accepted the application of the *per se* rule to the cases in which it is currently applicable. The *Stigler Report*, in effect, rejected the *Neal Report* proposal for

---

[39] The *Stigler Report* was inserted in the *Congressional Record* by Senator Talmadge in June 1969, although it had not at the time been officially released by the Nixon Administration. Much of its content had, however, been "leaked" to the press. The Report is reproduced in *The Role of Giant Corporations*, *op. cit.*, Part 1A, pp. 906 ff.

a *Concentrated Industries Act*, saying that existing knowledge did not warrant support of such proposals. It further rejected the Antitrust Division's existing Guidelines in merger cases as too stringent, saying that the Division should not embark upon a vigorous program of action against conglomerate firms on the basis of "nebulous fears about size and economic power." The Stigler group also remarked that the FTC's merger guidelines were "as hard on economic theory as on mergers." The *Stigler Report* therefore proposed limiting the activities of the FTC to consumer protection and the making of economic studies and that the "increase in the Commission's appropriations be stopped." President Nixon's 1969 proposal for expanding the role of the FTC in consumer-protection activities and reducing its antimonopoly activities discussed in Chapter 18 apparently owes its origin to the *Stigler Report*, although such action to limit the functions of the FTC flies in the face of the legislative history of the FTC Act, discussed in Chapter 12. In fact, it can be stated that such action is really a device to reduce antitrust enforcement under the guise of providing increased consumer protection.

As in the case of the *Neal Report*, the *Stigler Report* recommends amendment of the Robinson–Patman Act, but the *Stigler Report* seeks to reduce the effectiveness of that legislation by broadening the cost justification and "good faith meeting of competition" defenses discussed in Chapter 16. In general, the *Neal Report* evidences more fear of concentration of economic power than does the *Stigler Report*. The *Neal Report*, it has been noted, emphasizes market structure tests; the *Stigler Report* rejects market structure tests but does not clearly specify which tests it employs.

A Concluding Comment

Galbraith's position during the Hearings on "Planning, Competition and Regulation," that the real problem is one of how to live with vast organizations and the values they impose, flows, of course, directly from his belief that vast organizations are the result of contemporary technological developments. The other three panelists participating in the discussion rejected this proposition. But all four of the discussants accepted the proposition that governmental

power may be and is, in fact, used to affect and influence the working rules of economic activity. Adams, Mueller, and Turner believe that governmental power ought to be used in one way, Galbraith thinks it should be used in another. We have seen in Chapter 9 in our discussion of the work of the Industrial Commission that many of today's corporate giants had their origin in a desire to eliminate competition and not in economic efficiency, a point Galbraith has ignored, just as he has ignored the effects of other governmental policies, discussed in Chapters 8 and 9, to which Adams has also pointed, on concentration of economic power. Moreover, Galbraith has ignored the evidence provided by Dr. Blair, which we have examined in Chapter 13, of the relationship between firm size and efficiency; and his opponents have rightly pointed to the large area in which the antitrust laws have been enforced against large firms, including cases involving price-fixing, other restrictive practices, and mergers, all analyzed in preceding chapters. It is true, as Turner has admitted, that the antitrust laws have not been used to break up existing enclaves of power possessed by large firms, but both Turner and Adams have proposed that such action should be taken. So did the *Neal Report*. What is needed is a careful and systematic analysis on a firm-by-firm basis of the relationships among firm sizes, plant sizes, and economic efficiency.

The discussion of divisional reporting in Chapter 9 indicates that the adoption of a meaningful requirement that firms report their activities on a divisional basis to the Securities and Exchange Commission might serve as an important first step in the development of a policy looking forward to implementation of the Adams and Turner proposals. The reporting requirements actually adopted by the Commission in July 1969 are inadequate since they do not require *regular, periodic* reporting by listed companies but merely require sporadic reports in cases of registrations of new securities. Moreover, the Commission has left it to the companies themselves to decide what is a "line of business" for the purpose of reporting with regard to their various divisions. The *Stigler Report*, it may be noted, rejected the deconcentration proposals of the *Neal Report* on grounds of inadequate knowledge, but the *Stigler Report* paid no attention to the problem it had raised— that of overcoming the inadequacy of knowledge which it alleged existed. Some attention to the problem of divisional reporting was surely called for in the *Stigler Report*.

Were effective and comprehensive divisional reporting procedures adopted, the data provided would make it possible for empirical analyses to be undertaken to estimate the effects of dissolution of large corporate giants into various independent operating units, thereby eliminating the possibility that power possessed in one market be used to gain control of other markets. In the meantime, the contemporary antitrust policy, particularly the policy respecting conglomerate mergers as adopted in the *Clorox* and *S.O.S.* cases discussed in Chapter 17 seems sound. Among the giant corporations identified by Galbraith as "immune from antitrust" were the following: "General Motors, Ford, the oil majors, United States Steel, General Electric, IBM, Western Electric, du Pont, Swift, Bethlehem, International Harvester, North American Aviation, Goodyear, Boeing, National Dairy Products, Procter and Gamble, Eastman Kodak, and all of comparable size and

scope." The reader is invited at this point to review in his mind's eye the extent to which one or more of the foregoing corporations has either been a defendant in an antitrust case discussed in the preceding chapters or has been listed in Chapter 8 as being among those receiving prime Government contracts on a noncompetitive basis, a problem ignored by both the Neal and Stigler studies. To say that large firms are "immune" from antitrust attack is misleading. As Professor Adams has pointed out, the problem of competitiveness of an economic system is a problem involving an integrated approach; the problem is, in fact, one of adopting an integrated approach to the use of governmental power to favor or to inhibit this particular type of business practice or association or that. And neither the *Neal Report* nor the *Stigler Report* dealt with the problem in these terms.

Our consideration of the special working rules of antitrust has now been completed. In the chapters which follow we will examine special working rules which replace or modify competition in the cases of particular industries, activities, and economic aggregates.

Part III

WORKING RULES WHICH REPLACE OR MODIFY THE OPERATION OF MARKET FORCES

Administrative Regulation: General Considerations

Some indication of the nature of the process of administrative regulation has already inevitably been given in preceding chapters. Indeed, in Chapter 6 it has been emphasized that the term "independent regulatory agency" is not capable of being defined with precision. The reader may at this point wish to review the discussion of administrative agencies as a source of changes in law as well as the discussion of the relationship of such agencies to the legislative, executive, and judicial branches of Government contained in Chapter 6. What has been said there need not be repeated here other than to emphasize the fact that administrative agencies perform administrative or executive functions, legislative functions (in making rules, for example, FTC rules to implement the Fair Packaging and Labeling Act), and judicial functions (in adversary proceedings conducted before hearing examiners, appealable to the relevant commission and eventually to the courts).

He may also wish to review the discussion of the concept of "procedural due process of law" discussed in the context of the *Nebbia* case in Chapter 7, in which the Supreme Court remarked that "there is no closed category of business in the public interest" and held that it was the function of the courts to examine agency decisions and orders from the point of view of procedural due process of law but that it *was not* an appropriate judicial function for the courts to decide the wisdom of any regulatory scheme adopted by the legislature. The reader may further wish to reread the discussion of the limitation in regard to judicial review imposed upon itself by the Supreme Court in the *Illinois Central* case (discussed in the section titled "*The Basis of Judicial Review*") in Chapter 4. We there saw that the Court has held that judicial review of agency action is limited to review of questions of: (1) constitutionality of the enabling statute; (2) conformity of the order or action with the enabling statute; and (3) abuse of discretion. We also saw that the Court will normally accept the "finding of fact" made by a lower court or an administrative agency if supported by "substantial evidence."

The Federal Trade Commission, whose work has been examined extensively in Chapters 12 and 18, is a regulatory commission. It has been discussed in Part II instead of being discussed in Part III because it is primarily an antitrust agency, although it also has a duty to supplement competition by implementing various laws to protect consumers. Some of the federal agencies to be discussed in the following chapters differ significantly from the Federal Trade Commission in that they have been charged with the exercise of power over rates (prices) and over long-run supply (by controlling entry into and exit from an industry of firms) *in specific industries.* Examples of such regulatory agencies are the Interstate Commerce Commission and the Federal Power Commission. Other regulatory agencies also to be discussed later have been charged with duties affecting industries in general (rather than specific industries), just as the Federal Trade Commission has been charged with various duties affecting industries in general. These agencies, like the Federal Trade Commission, have been given duties pertaining to specific *subjects*, such as the supervision of labor practices (National Labor Relations Board). However, the activities of *all* these agencies are subject to the requirements of procedural due process of law (discussed at length in Chapter 7), and their power to regulate is based on an affirmative use of the federal power to regulate interstate commerce (also discussed in Chapter 7).

Administrative regulation may take various forms and exists at all levels of government: municipal, state, and federal. Our discussion, however, will be limited to a discussion of administrative regulation at the federal level. The principles of regulation by commissions are essentially the same whether the agency is a federal or a state establishment. The *forms* of regulation may range from the issuance of licenses and franchises by municipal governments to full-fledged regulation by a commission under a broad constitution-like delegation of power.

No single hypothesis explains the existence of all forms of regulation; indeed, no single hypothesis explains all forms of regulation by commissions alone. The growth of administrative regulatory agencies is a response in the form of an institutional adjustment to the impact of technological changes on existing institutional arrangements and to the increasing economic interdependencies of the various sectors of the economy.

Each regulatory agency has its own history

and its own reason for being. A simple explanation that regulation is a substitute for competition in "naturally" monopolistic industries will not do. Regulation of the railroads by the Interstate Commerce Commission did arise in response to the abuse of their monopolistic positions by the railroads, but this fact does not explain the regulation also of the motor carrier industry by the Commission. Indeed, some have argued that the motor carrier industry is a competitive industry and should be freed from regulation. Such an argument, however, fails to consider the question of whether or not effective regulation of the railroads would today be possible if the railroads were subjected to competition from an unregulated motor carrier industry. In short, what the effect would be on national transportation policy of freeing the motor carriers from regulatory control is not easy to estimate and must be taken into account.

As has been mentioned, some of the regulatory agencies to be discussed in the following chapters exercise control over long-run supply (by controlling entry into and exit from the industry) and control over prices (rate control). In the case of these agencies, administrative regulation does, to a considerable extent, replace the operation of market forces. Other regulatory agencies implement working rules whose effect is merely to modify the operation of market forces. For example, the National Labor Relations Board has the function of promoting collective bargaining between employers and labor organizations. Such collective bargaining involves a modification of a market system in which individual workers bargain with employers. Also, the Food and Drug Administration undertakes to enforce working rules whose general objective is to insure that consumers will receive unadulterated foods and safe and effective drugs because whatever might be the case in an economic model based on an assumption of perfect competition, in the world as it is, experience has shown that the unaided operation of market forces will not achieve the desired consequence. The enforcement by the Securities and Exchange Commission of legislation requiring truthful disclosures to prospective investors and of legislation to prevent manipulation of markets by those in a position to do so is another example of modification of the operation of market forces. The enforcement of legislation to protect consumers by the Federal Trade Commission as a supplement to competition obviously also involves a modification of the operation of market forces, but for the reasons already given, this agency has been discussed in Part II.

Some writers suggest the proposition that "regulation is a substitute for competition in the case of public utilities and has been adopted to regulate public utilities." But this view is a narrow one, true only in an approximate sense, as we will soon see in the discussion of the "concept of a 'public utility'" in the first major subdivision of this chapter.

This chapter is organized as follows. The first major subdivision contains a development and review of some general concepts, such as the concept of a "public utility," and the current meaning of the phrase "affected with a public interest," whose historical development has been given in Chapter 7. In addition, a review of the process of "rule-making" and the process of "adjudication" as sources of changes in law is provided. The second subdivision undertakes to examine relevant provisions of the Administrative Procedure Act of 1946, as amended, and describes the function of the Administrative Conference of the United States. The third major subdivision contains a brief survey of the scope and organization of the remaining chapters in Part III, the final and concluding portion of this book.

A. BASIC GENERAL CONCEPTS AND LEGISLATION

The Concepts of a "Public Utility" and of "A Business Affected with a Public Interest"

Probably no *satisfactory operational* definition of the concept of a "public utility" can be given. None exists in the literature. In some cases, writers define a "public utility" as an industry having high fixed costs and in which a "natural monopoly" exists. Others treat the expression as identifying industries particularly concerned with performance of "transportation and distribution" functions. Still others emphasize a requirement that the public be served on a

nondiscriminatory basis; and most writers, particularly those who deem themselves specialists in the area of public utility economics, state that a "public utility" is "any industry which *is* being regulated," thereby limiting the scope of the subject matter with which these writers are concerned to a consideration of firms in industries already being regulated. Such a definition, of course, does not say anything about the issue of specifying the criteria to be employed in making a determination of whether or not an industry not already being regulated constitutes a "public utility" and hence "should" be regulated. Attempts to use the expression to identify industries which are "natural monopolies" (a term usually left undefined) and which have high fixed costs are sometimes outward expressions of a desire to limit the use of regulation by administrative commissions. At any rate, the reader should be careful in reading works in the area of "public utility" economics to discern the explicit or implicit definition being employed by the writer in question. The problem of whether or not a given industry "should" be regulated cannot be solved by the use of general phrases.

The difficulties inherent in any attempt to provide a general definition of the term "public utility" have not been overcome in the field of law anymore than they have been overcome by economists. As a result, the particular definition employed in a given case is dependent upon the nature of the problem being considered.

One popular textbook in the field of "public utility" economics quotes with approval the following statements made by Judge Vinson in a case involving the question of whether or not a warehouse company was a public utility and thus exempt from the federal price-control regulations imposed during World War II. Judge Vinson wrote:

If a business is (1) affected with a public interest, and (2) bears an intimate connection with the process of transportation and distribution, and (3) is under obligation to afford its facilities to the public on demand, at fair and nondiscriminatory rates, and (4) enjoys in a large measure an independence and freedom from business competition brought about either (a) by its acquirement of a monopolistic status, or (b) by the grant of a franchise or certificate from the State placing it in this position, it is . . . a public utility. . . .

It is these four attributes which make up the bundle of the public utility formula *to the extent to which I have promulgated it. The formula is a limited one.* It is designed only to provide an absolute test or standard by which one may *affirmatively* determine that a particular business is a public utility. I do not wish to be misunderstood as indicating that a business possessed of or operating under less than the total of these features may not be considered a public utility. The formula has *no negative or exclusive* implications. What I do say is that, at least, any business which does possess and practice and operate under each and all of these features, is, by a preponderance of considered judicial opinion, a business in the public utility class.[1]

This definition, obviously, does not provide a basis for determining whether or not an industry "should" be regulated. It does provide a basis for limiting the number of topics to be discussed in an economics course.

The statement by Judge Vinson that the business must be "affected with a public interest" is interesting, particularly in the light of the history of this phrase already given in Chapter 7. For the convenience of the reader, it will be useful to repeat here that part of the opinion of Justice Roberts in the *Nebbia* case of 1934 that states the Supreme Court's view of the phrase, "business affected with a public interest." As we have seen, Justice Roberts wrote:

It is clear that there is no closed class or category of businesses affected with a public interest, and the function of the courts in the application of the Fifth and Fourteenth Amendments is to determine *in each case* whether circumstances vindicate the challenged regulation as a reasonable exertion of governmental authority or condemn it as arbitrary or discriminatory. . . . The phrase "affected with a public interest can, in the nature of things mean no more than that an industry, for adequate reason, is subject to control for the public good. . . ."

So far as the requirement of due process is concerned, and in the absence of constitutional restriction, a state is free to adopt whatever economic policy may reasonably be deemed to promote public welfare, and to enforce that policy by legislation adapted to its purpose. The courts are without authority either to declare such policy, or, when it is declared by the legislature to override it. If laws passed are seen to have a reasonable relation to a proper legislative purpose, and are neither arbitrary nor discriminatory, the requirements of due process are satisfied. . . . And it is equally clear that if the legislative policy be to curb unrestrained or harmful competition by measures which are not arbitrary or discriminatory it does not lie with the courts to determine that the rule is unwise. With the wisdom of the policy adopted, with the adequacy or practicability of the law to forward it, the courts are both incompetent and unauthorized to deal.[2]

The definition of a "public utility" given by Judge Vinson is, of course, consistent with the language of Justice Roberts in the *Nebbia* case quoted above, since Vinson's definition cannot be employed by a court to strike down a legislative determination that a particular business is to be classified as a "public utility" or to limit an economic policy adopted by a legislature. Vinson specifically stated that his definition did *not* mean that a business "possessed of or operating under less" than a total of the characteristics he had specified "may not be considered a public utility." Thus Vinson's definition is open-ended and provides no operational basis for determining whether or not industries not in fact being regulated can or "should" be regulated.

The growth in the number of administrative agencies mentioned earlier, and the increase in administrative actions taken by executive departments as a result of New Deal legislation, resulted in numerous studies, hearings, and reports, both by private groups and by Congressional committees, of the problem of securing uniformity in procedural matters dealt with in such administrative proceedings.[3] Legislation to deal with this question was introduced in Congress in 1938, but the occurrence of World War II interrupted action on the matter. After the war, Congress adopted the Administrative Procedure Act of 1946.[4]

---

[1] *Davies Warehouse Co.* v. *Bowles*, 137 F. 2d 201 (1943), at pp. 212–217. Cited in Paul J. Garfield and Wallace Lovejoy, *Public Utility Economics* (Englewood Cliffs: Prentice–Hall, Inc., 1964), p. 11. (Italics mine.)

[2] *Nebbia* v. *New York*, 291 U.S. 502 (1934), at pp. 536–537. (Italics mine.)

[3] A survey of these studies can be found in U.S. Congress, *House Report* 1980 (79th Cong., 2d sess., 1946).

[4] 5 *U.S.C.A.* 500–559 (1964).

B. THE ADMINISTRATIVE PROCEDURE ACT AND THE ADMINISTRATIVE CONFERENCE OF THE UNITED STATES

The Administrative Procedure Act contains three broad groups of provisions pertaining to the procedural aspects of activities by regulatory agencies. These are: (1) provisions relative to the dissemination of information to the public concerning administrative rules and orders; (2) provisions prescribing procedures to be followed by administrative agencies in making rules and in adjudicatory proceedings; and (3) provisions concerning judicial review of actions taken by administrative agencies. Where relevant in the following pages, appropriate provisions of the Act will be quoted.

In 1964, Public Law 88-499 (the Administrative Conference Act) was enacted. This law authorized the establishment of a permanent, new federal agency called the Administrative Conference of the United States. The function of the Conference is to develop recommendations for improvements in the procedures by which federal departments and agencies establish rights and duties, and take actions concerning the interests of private persons and business firms "through administrative investigation, adjudication, licensing, rulemaking, ratemaking, claims determinations, and other procedures." The Act provides that the Conference shall consist of not more than 91 nor less than 75 members, of whom not more than 12 may be private citizens. The Chairman is appointed for a five-year term and is the only fulltime compensated member. In addition, there is a Council consisting of the Chairman and ten other members appointed by the President from government service and private life. The entire membership constitutes an Assembly, and the Chairman and Council develop subjects for consideration by committees of the Assembly. The Chairman is authorized to employ a fulltime staff of experts and consultants. Officials from all the major government agencies are included among the Government members. The following description of the nature and some of the functions of the Conference appeared in a statement issued by the Chairman's office in January 1968:

Because officials from all of the major agencies will be included in its membership, it is expected that Conference recommendations will be adopted in most instances where they are applicable. The Chairman is required by the Act to assist the agencies in putting recommendations into effect and to report at least once a year to Congress and to the President the recommendations made by the Conference and the extent of their implementation by the agencies. The power granted to the Conference is only the power to recommend. Full responsibility for the proper performance of agency functions remains with the agency heads. . . .

There are some thirty departments and agencies which conduct the bulk of administrative procedures affecting private rights. There is infinite variety to such proceedings. They range from the grant of a television license worth millions of dollars to the processing of applications for amateur or citizen band licenses; from the processing of an application to merge railroads of the magnitude of the New York Central and the Pennsylvania to authorizing truck transportation of a particular commodity over a particular route; or from the approval of a prospectus for a major new corporation to permitting cattle to graze on federal lands. Because of this steady flow of Federal agency determinations affecting our natural resources, transportation, power, finance, communications, commerce, securities, taxation, labor, credit, advertising, housing, veterans' benefits, the supply, quality, and price of food and fibers, public health, immigration, social welfare programs, drug control, and countless other areas of activity, the administrative process, in one way or another, continuously exerts its influence upon every citizen in his personal and business affairs. . . .[5]

A clearer statement of the many ways and areas in which the working rules of economic activity are made, to a not inconsiderable extent, by actions of administrative agencies would be difficult to find. Rule-making is a legislative process, it has been noted, and is one of the most important procedures employed by administrative agencies.

Rule-Making

The Administrative Procedure Act defines a *rule* as

. . . the whole or part of an agency statement of general or particular applicability and future

---

[5] Administrative Conference of the United States, *Information Concerning the Administrative Conference of the*

United States, January, 1968.

effect designed to implement, interpret or prescribe law or policy or describing the organization, procedure, or practice requirements of an agency and includes approval or prescription for the future of rates, wages, corporate or financial structures or reorganizations thereof, prices, facilities, appliances, services, or allowances therefor or of valuations, costs, or accounting, or practices bearing on any of the foregoing. . . .[6]

The term *rule-making* is defined simply as "agency process for formulating, amending or repealing a rule."

The procedure of rule-making is prescribed by the Act. The agency must give 30 days advance notice of proposed rule-making in the *Federal Register* or to individuals affected personally, and this notice must contain information pertaining to the time, place, and nature of the public rule-making activities. The notice must also identify the legal authority under which the proposed rule is to be made and contain a statement of the substance of the proposed rule or a description of the subjects and issues involved.

However, an exception from these requirements is allowed in cases involving rules made pursuant to statutes, if the rules are "interpretative rules," general statements of policy or of agency organization, practice, or procedure. An even more important exception is one involving cases "in which the agency for good cause finds (and incorporates the finding and a brief statement of the reasons therefor in the rules issued) that notice and public procedure are impracticable, unnecessary, or contrary to the public interest." This escape hatch is wide, indeed. In other cases, after the required notice has been given, interested parties must be given an opportunity to submit either written or oral data or arguments for consideration. Interested parties must also be given a right to petition for the issuance, amendment, or repeal of a rule. This last provision was added in 1966.

The nature and use of the rule-making power of the Federal Trade Commission (which may be taken as a "typical regulatory agency" in regard to this particular matter) is well illustrated by the following excerpt from an announcement of changes in the FTC's procedures, appearing in the

FTC's *News Summary* of May 16, 1962. The excerpt reads:

The Commission may initiate rulemaking proceedings on its own motion or upon petition of an interested party. Any proposed rule will be published in the Federal Register and interested parties will be given adequate time to present their written views on it. Then the Commission will formulate and publish a tentative rule, to which protests may be filed. A public hearing may be held if the FTC feels this is necessary to develop a proper rule. Following its consideration of all relevant matters, including protests, the Commission will adopt a rule in final form, to become effective 30 days or some other designated time after publication in the Federal Register.

Trade regulation rules will be based upon requirements of statutes administered by the Commission. They may be relied upon by the FTC in any adjudicative proceeding brought against a violator, provided that the respondent has been given a fair hearing on the legality and propriety of applying the rule to the particular case.

"Trade regulation rules," Chairman Dixon pointed out, "will not only enable businessmen to avoid legal pitfalls but also expedite disposition of our cases in which such rules are applicable by eliminating the necessity of proving again and again that the particular practice is unlawful."

Particularly to be noted in the preceding quotation is the assertion that trade regulation rules may be relied upon in any adjudicative proceeding brought against a violator, "provided that the respondent has been given a fair hearing on the legality and propriety of applying the rule to the particular case."

Adjudication

Adjudication is defined in the Act as "agency process for the formulation of an order," and an *order* is defined as "the whole or part of a final disposition, whether affirmative, negative, injunctive, or declaratory in form, of an agency in a matter other than rule making, but including licensing." Specific directions are given in Section 554 for the conduct of an adjudication. Much emphasis is placed upon procedural due process of law; those entitled to notice of a hearing must be "timely informed" not only of the time and place of the hearing

---

[6] 5 *U.S.C.A.* 551 (3) (1964).

but also of the matters of fact and law asserted. They must also be given an opportunity for "the submission and consideration of facts and arguments" whenever "time and the nature of the public interest permit." Provisions are included to prohibit the agency employee who makes the ultimate decision from consulting anyone concerning the case without giving notice to all parties to the proceeding. Employees who preside at hearings perform a judicial function; they may administer oaths and issue authorized subpoenas. Moreover, "any oral or documentary evidence may be received, but the agency as a matter of policy shall provide for the exclusion of irrelevant, immaterial or repetitious evidence." Transcripts of all testimony and exhibits must be made available to the parties.

Hearing Examiners; Initial Decisions; Appeals

The Act also provides for the appointment of Hearing Examiners "by and for" each agency. These examiners are largely independent of the agencies for which they are appointed: they are appointed from Civil Service registers and are removable "only for good cause established and determined by the Civil Service Commission" *and not by the agency itself.* Their compensation is prescribed by the Civil Service Commission independently of agency recommendations and ratings. Moreover, "agencies occasionally or temporarily insufficiently staffed may utilize examiners selected by the Civil Service Commission from and with the consent of other agencies." These Hearing Examiners function as presiding officers in hearings; there is in most cases a right of appeal from their decisions to the relevant Commission and from that Commission's decision to the courts. In the case of most of the federal regulatory agencies, the appeal is taken directly from the Commission's decision to a United States Court of Appeals and *not* to a District Court, in keeping with the concept that a finding of fact by an agency based on "substantial evidence" will not be overturned by the courts. District Courts are trial courts; they are largely concerned with finding "fact" and

applying "law"; Appellate Courts are primarily concerned with matters of legal policy. Thus, since an agency's finding of fact will usually be sustained if supported by "substantial evidence," by the time a Commission decision has been made, the status of the case is analogous to that of a case which has been tried in a district court, and the issue is "ripe" for appeal to and decision by an appellate court.

The reader may at this time wish to review the discussion of the attempt by a Congressional committee to influence the outcome of a decision made by the Federal Trade Commission in regard to the acquisition of assets of competing companies by the Pillsbury Company, discussed in Chapter 6 under the heading of *"Supervisory and Investigatory Powers of Committees"* [of Congress]. As we have seen in that discussion, the courts will not tolerate any attempt by Congressional committees to interfere with the judicial functions of regulatory agencies.

Agency "Expertise"

The term, *expertise*, is widely used but seldom defined. (A survey of 30 books dealing either with the general subject of "business and government" or with the specific topic of "public utility economics" has failed to reveal a single instance in which the word *expertise* is listed in the index.)

In 1952, in holding that the question of the legality of a discriminatory rate system under the Shipping Act of 1916 was a matter to be decided in the first instance by the Federal Maritime Board and not by a District Court, Justice Frankfurter remarked:

. . . the limited functions of review by the judiciary are more rationally exercised by preliminary resort for ascertaining and interpreting the circumstances underlying the legal issues to agencies that are better equipped by specialization, by insight gained through experience and by a more flexible procedure.[7]

For our purposes, the term *expertise* will be defined as the knowledge of an expert gained through a combination of special training, specialization, and insight obtained from experience by means of flexible procedures involving the making of self-

[7] *U.S.* v. *Far East Conference*, 342 U.S. 570 (1952), at pp. 574–575.

correcting value judgments such as those employed by regulatory agencies. The Commissioners, who are appointed by the President with the consent of Congress, we have noted, are often political appointees. They may or may not possess or acquire *expertise*. The hearing examiners appointed by and for the various agencies do not possess expertise; however, those who remain with an agency over a period of time do gain specialized experience. In this regard, it should be recalled that "agencies occasionally or temporarily insufficiently staffed may" be served by hearing examiners drawn from other agencies. The *expertise*, if it exists, must then lie in the *accumulated* experience and training possessed by an agency's staff, the Civil Service employees of an agency, whose period of employment is not terminated by charges in political appointments at the Commission level. But this accumulated experience does not consist merely of *personal* experience; it consists of the entire history of the organization, as embodied in its past activities and decisions, customs, procedures, and traditions, which is passed along from one generation of staff employees to the next. The relevant agency staff makes investigations and factual studies, prepares complaints or makes initial recommendations as appropriate, and represents the agency in formal hearings. In doing so, it draws on the accumulated experience of the agency.

Policy Statements, Press Releases, and Guidelines

Policy statements, press releases, and guidelines issued by agencies represent statements of the agency's intentions, attitudes, and interpretations of its statutory duties. Occasionally, an agency may issue guidelines resulting from informal hearings and after having received comments from interested parties. Such a procedure was followed by the Federal Trade Commission in issuing "Enforcement Guidelines" pertaining to mergers in selected industries. Similar guidelines pertaining to mergers issued by the Department of Justice were not the result of informal hearings, however. Such informal guidelines and policy statements do not have any formal legal effect; but they may be an important source of information to those affected by the policies announced in such statements and serve to give the agency's interpretation of the relevant law as well as some indication of how the agency intends to proceed to implement this legislation.

Proposed Amendment of the Administrative Procedure Act of 1946

The enactment of the Administrative Procedure Act of 1946 represented the culmination of efforts, directed toward enactment of such legislation, by the American Bar Association. In 1956, the House of Delegates of the Association (Delegates are elected from every state, and the House of Delegates is the principal policy-making organ of the Association) adopted a resolution calling for adoption of a revised Administrative Procedure Act. Since 1962, various bills to achieve such a revision have been introduced in Congress, and hearings have been held by the Subcommittee on Administrative Procedure of the Senate Judiciary Committee. In 1966, S. 1336 was passed by the Senate but not by the House. Next, S. 518 was introduced in the Senate in 1967. Among the changes in proposed new legislation were the elimination of various exemptions, such as the existing exemption of the power and policy of the Department of Interior over disposition of public lands and the exemption of proceedings before the National Labor Relations Board pertaining to certification of the winner in an employee representation election. The definition of the term "adjudication" would also be broadened, and the power of judicial review expanded. The net effect of the adoption of the revised Act would be to limit and delay activities of various government agencies, an object long close to the heart of those opposed to federal regulatory action *per se* as a matter of principle, irrespective of the consequences of such opposition. The following excerpt from the prepared statement of Wilber J. Cohen, Undersecretary of the Department of Health, Education, and Welfare throws some light on the far-reaching effect enactment of S. 518 would have had on the activities of that Department. Mr. Cohen stated, in part:

For one thing the bill, like its predecessor in the last Congress would formalize, complicate, and delay the hearing process in determining social security claims, where simplicity, informality, and speed are plainly needed.

The only requirements in the Social Security Act are that one whose claim is rejected be given opportunity for hearing, and that the decision be based on the hearing record. The present Administrative Procedure Act adds no requirement incompatible with the flexible and informal procedures we consider appropriate to this program. Its most important requirement, that a qualified hearing officer preside, is one that we have welcomed.

S. 518, on the other hand, would go far in likening these hearings to judicial trials. This, we think, not in the public interest. A social security hearing is not and should not be an adversary proceeding with Government pitted against the claimant, but has been consciously designed to assist the claimant—who may have the help of a lawyer but usually does not—to prove his entitlement if in fact he is entitled to benefits. The claimant, typically, is old and sick; often he is of limited education; sometimes his mental powers are failing; the last thing he wants or needs is the complexities of courtroom procedure. Why should he be required to file pleadings or a bill of exceptions? Why should he be required, as the bill would in effect require him, to hire a lawyer if he does not choose to do so? Why should the Government be required to file an answering pleading, and so routinely take a position of opposition to his claim?[8]

The scope of the bill was further outlined by Mr. Cohen. He added:

Let me turn next to the definition of "adjudication" and to the consequences of that definition. Although the change in definition itself would create an important ambiguity for the Food and Drug Administration in some of its rule-making operations, which our report asks you to remove, I will speak here only of its effects—whether intended, I do not know—which under this bill would flow from classifying as "adjudication" a great part of the day-to-day administration of our Department. Under present law it is not important that these activities technically constitute "adjudication" because no elaborate procedural rights attach to the characterization except where adjudication must be based on a hearing record. Under the bill, on the other hand, some distinctly disturbing consequences would attach to so-called informal adjudication. We cannot give you a complete catalogue of our activities that constitute informal "adjudication," but I should like to illustrate their range

and diversity. We read the definition as including every personnel action in the Department, every initial or reconsidered action on a social security benefit claim or on the qualifications of an institution to participate in medicare, every approval or denial under some 200 different programs, every disposition of surplus property, every admission of a patient to a Public Health Service hospital, every batch certification of a drug, every quarantine inspection, every detention of an imported food, drug, device, or cosmetic, probably the making of every procurement contract and every research contract, and as of next July every disclosure or refusal of information from our files.[9]

Other consequences which might result from enactment of the proposed legislation were also pinpointed by Mr. Cohen in these words:

S. 518, unlike its predecessor requires a showing of irreparable injury before an unauthorized proceeding or investigation may be enjoined. We do not condone unauthorized or irreparable injury to anyone, but we do suggest that in dealing with dangerous drugs, for instance, the concept of irreparable injury is a two-edged sword.

Let us suppose, as unfortunately happens from time to time, that a manufacturing error has led to the wide distribution of a dangerously adulterated drug in the guise of an innocuous product. If the manufacturer cannot or will not recapture every shipment and every bottle, the Food and Drug Administration must move into action at once, and to do that it must have access to the shipment records. The scope of its powers of inspection is unfortunately less clear than we would wish it were and section 9(a) of this bill would certainly tend to encourage resistance in any area of unclear authority. If litigation were brought to enjoin the inspection even the distraction of agency personnel to defend the litigation would be costly to the public; if a restraining order were to issue, the injury to the manufacturer, irreparable though it might be, would seem of small moment in comparison to the likelihood of injuries and deaths from consumption of the adulterated drug. Every day's delay in the corrective action would invite the most irreparable harm of all.[10]

What Mr. Cohen's statement makes clear is that an adversary proceeding is not an appropriate method to be employed in implementing various "action" programs

[8] *Administrative Procedure Act* (Hearings before the Senate Subcommittee on Administrative Practice and Procedure, 90th Cong., 1st sess., 1967) (Washington, D.C.: U.S. Government Printing Office, 1967), p. 151.

[9] *Ibid.*

[10] *Ibid.*, p. 153.

which Congress has adopted. The picture he has given of the aged, poverty-stricken, social security benefit claimant being opposed by government lawyers in an adversary proceeding is clearly to the point. The aged, poverty-stricken, claimant may prefer the actual benefit he is seeking to the empty guarantee in his particular case of procedural due process envisaged by the revision of the Administrative Procedure Act. Procedural due process is not an ultimate goal but is merely a means to an end that is itself not final. If one use of the new definitions in the proposed revision of the Administrative Procedure Act is to be that of frustrating the implementation of various pieces of social legislation enacted by Congress in the past, such a use is hardly a consequence "devoutly to be wished" except by those who are opposed to such legislation as a matter of principle.

In a prepared statement submitted to the Subcommittee, John Bagwell, General Counsel for the Department of Agriculture, argued that the proposed revision of the Administrative Procedure Act really amounted to a broad attack upon various government welfare programs in the guise of providing a "fair hearing." In part, his statement read:

Section 4(a) of the Administrative Procedure Act presently provides that, except where notice or hearing are required by statute, the notice provisions shall not apply to "interpretative rules, general statements of policy, rules of agency organization, procedure, or practice." S. 518 would delete such exception from the notice provision and would provide in S. 4(h) that advisory interpretations and rulings of particular applicability, minor exceptions from, revisions of, or refinements of rules which do not affect protected substantive rights, and rules of agency organization, are exempted from all the requirements of section 4.

These changes would appear to make informal rulemaking procedures applicable to interpretative rules, general statements of policy, and rules of procedure or practice which presently are not subject to such procedures. Subjecting interpretative rules and statements of policy, as well as rules of procedure and practice, to the procedures of section 4 for informal rulemaking can only complicate unnecessarily the administration of programs and discourage the issuance of interpretative rules and statements of policy

to the detriment of the affected members of the public. . . .

S. 518 would completely eliminate the exception for matters relating to public property, grants, benefits or contracts. The tremendous scope of governmental operations in these areas makes it essential that these functions not be burdened by rigid procedural requirements or exposed to unnecessary litigation with respect to procedures.

The amendments to section 4 of the Administrative Procedure Act, eliminating the present exemption from rulemaking requirements for programs involving contracts, loans, grants, benefits, control of public property, etc., would have an adverse effect upon the activities of this Department. The Department of Agriculture administers extensive programs relating to price supports, agricultural conservation, land diversion, loans, management of forest lands and national grasslands, and other activities which would be affected.

For the most part, administrative procedure has been the subject of legislation or of judicial review only where incident to governmental action which impinges on private rights. When engaging in activities such as contracting, management of public property, or making benefit payments or loans, or conferring other benefits or privileges, the agencies of the Government have been permitted to employ such procedures as they have found to be desirable or appropriate in the public interest. In instances in which Congress has felt a need for prescribing specific procedures, it has done so by statutory provision relating directly to the particular function involved.[11]

With regard to Mr. Bagwell's testimony quoted above, it should be noted that in October 1969, the Administrative Conference recommended that the Act be amended to remove the exemption in the case of rules promulgated in relation to "public property, loans, grants, benefits, or contracts." Presumably government contracts (*e.g.*, those let by the Department of Defense) would also be covered. The Conference also recommended that the agencies adopt procedures providing for public participation in the case of exempt categories "without waiting for" Congress to amend the law.

The case for subjecting agency personnel actions or policy statements to the public hearing procedure is, however, far from clear. In fact, the question of whether or not a particular policy should or should not

[11] *Ibid.*, pp. 199–200.

be adopted has already been subjected to an adversary proceeding in the very process of Congressional action upon the enabling legislation. To subject a policy which Congress has adopted in specific legislation to further debate in an administrative hearing would seem unnecessary. Congress itself can perform the watchdog function and does do so.

Some indication has already been given in general terms in this and in preceding chapters of the nature and scope of administrative regulation. In the chapters which follow, some specific areas and problems subject to such regulation will be examined.

C. THE SCOPE AND ORGANIZATION OF THE FOLLOWING CHAPTERS

It has been noted that Part III is devoted to a consideration of special working rules which replace or modify the operation of market forces in cases of particular industries, activities, and economic aggregates. Each of the regulatory agencies discussed in the following chapters has its own history and its own *raison d'être*. In carrying out the functions of adjudication and rule-making, these agencies are subject to the Administrative Procedure Act. In general, the discussion of the activities of the regulatory agencies in the following chapters involves a grouping of agencies having similar or related types of functions. Thus in Chapter 24 we will examine the regulation of domestic surface transportation by the Interstate Commerce Commission, and in Chapter 25 we will study the regulation of ocean transportation and of air transportation. Both Chapters 24 and 25 are concerned with regulatory agencies exercising price (rate) control functions and control over long-run supply (by controlling entry into and exit from the industry). Some competition exists among the various modes of transportation discussed in these two chapters, as it does among firms providing the service of a particular mode, but, for various reasons, replacement and supplementation of the operation of market forces has been undertaken. Chapter 26 deals with the activities and functions of the Department of Transportation in promoting transportation and in performing a safety

function. This Department does not possess regulatory functions of the type possessed by the agencies discussed in Chapters 24 and 25. In Chapter 27, we will consider the activities of two regulatory agencies which perform rate-making functions and exercise control over long-run supply in industries other than those performing transportation services; that is, we will study the economic regulation of the natural gas and hydroelectric power industries by the Federal Power Commission and the regulation of communications by the Federal Communications Commission. Chapter 28, however, deals with agencies which do not perform rate-making functions nor exercise control over long-run supply. Instead, the several agencies discussed are concerned with the performance of police functions in the respective areas of the physical environment, food and drugs, and in the securities markets. What these agencies have in common is the duty of performing a police function. In Chapter 29, we will examine the activities of the National Labor Relations Board in promoting and policing collective bargaining between unions and employers, and we will also examine the activities of various agencies within the Department of Labor concerned with enforcing statutory labor standards and with problems of effective utilization of manpower. Chapter 30 contains a description of the activities of the Small Business Administration in promoting the interests of "small business firms" and of those agencies within the Department of Agriculture which deal with agricultural problems. Special reference is given in the case of both to the relation of the activities examined to problems of rural and urban poverty.

Control of the money supply by the Federal Reserve System and macroeconomic policy formulation by the Council of Economic Admisors, already touched upon in Chapter 6, are the subjects of Chapter 31. Finally, Chapter 32 concludes this book with a brief survey of wartime controls from World War I to the present, with a discussion of government investment decisions, a problem already noted in the discussion of the work of Adam Smith in Chapter 1; and with a final subdivision containing Concluding Remarks.

24

Domestic Surface Transportation

Table 24–1 shows the extent to which various types of domestic transportation are subject to federal regulation. The various types of domestic surface transportation listed in the table are subject to economic regulation by the Interstate Commerce Commission (ICC). Although today the Commission is charged with the duty of regulating economic aspects of several different forms (modes) of transportation, originally, the Commission was created primarily to regulate the railroad industry.

We have already seen in Chapter 8 that government aid (both state and national) to the transportation industry has been massive and taken a variety of forms. At first, the attitude of the public toward the railroads (in particular) was one of warm support for the expansion westward of railroad lines and facilities. Eventually, however, this attitude changed into one of hostility toward the railroads and produced the establishment of the first of the great federal regulatory agencies, the Interstate Commerce Commission. This chapter undertakes to survey briefly the history of early attempts by states to regulate the railroads and the numerous pieces of federal legislation which have resulted in the present power of the Interstate Commerce Commission to regulate various modes of trans-

portation, as well as the nature of the problems currently confronted by the ICC. The first major subdivision of this chapter contains an examination of attempts by the states to regulate the railroads; the second traces the development of the federal regulatory scheme from the date of establishment of the Commission to the present; the third examines the problem of rate-making in general, a problem also faced by a number of other regulatory agencies discussed in the chapters that follow; and the last subdivision studies the problem of control over long-run supply.

A. REGULATION OF RAILROADS BY STATES PRIOR TO 1887

Regulation by Charter

The earliest railway corporations were established by *special* charters issued by state legislatures. (The nature and use of *special* charters has already been explained in Chapter 9.) In some cases, these charters contained specific schedules of maximum *rates*; others undertook to fix the maximum *rate of return*. However, these charter provisions were generally ineffective, since the rates fixed in them were high, and the

Table 24-1

Federally Regulated and Total Intercity Ton-Miles, 1966, by Type of Service[1]

Type	Federally Regulated[2]		Not Federally Regulated		Total	
	Billions	Percent	Billions	Percent	Billions	Percent
1. Rail	750.8	100.0	0	0	750.8	100
2. Motor[3]	*	*	*	*	380.9	100
3. Water[4]	71.0	14.0	436.1	86.0	507.1	100
4. Pipelines (oil)	285.9	85.9	47.0	14.1	332.9	100
5. Air	2.3	100.0	0	0	2.3	100
Total	*	*	*	*	1,974.0	100
Water traffic in U.S. waters with 1 foreign and 1 U.S. terminus, termed by engineers as "foreign" (not divided between regulated and other)					57.9	100
Grand Total					2,031.9	100

Source: Reproduced from *Annual Report of the Interstate Commerce Commission for 1968* (Washington, D.C.: U.S. Government Printing Office, 1969), p. 87.

* Not available.

[1] Some variance appears in totals because of rounding.

[2] Includes ton–miles by rail, by vehicles of class I–III intercity common and contract motor carriers, by pipelines (oil) subject to ICC regulations, and reported carried by class A and B water carriers plus an estimate for class C water carriers, and air ton–miles subject to regulation by the Civil Aeronautics Board. The data are published with a 2-year time lag. Data for 1967 can be found in the *Annual Report* for 1969, published in 1970.

[3] Preliminary.

[4] Includes coastal, inland waterways, intercoastal, and Great Lakes traffic, but not water traffic in U.S. waters with 1 foreign and 1 U.S. terminus, except for a very minor part of the ton–miles reported by ICC carriers.

railroads—which had monopoly power in many of the areas they served—were able to discriminate among shippers, commodities, and places (charging one class a lower rate than others) without violating the charters.

The Granger Movement and the Granger Laws

Factors Leading to Discriminatory Practices by the Railroads. A railroad is an industry having very high fixed costs. The capital investment in rights of way, track facilities, and rolling stock must necessarily be large. Moreover, in many cases, particularly where no competition from water transportation via river barges or canals existed, the early railroads were in a monopoly position. Competition existed at terminal points, such as St. Louis and Chicago, but all the routes from these terminal points to major eastern terminal cities did not pass through the same towns; thus many towns "along the way" were monopoly markets insofar as the railroads were concerned. The high

fixed charges also meant that a railroad would find it profitable at points of great competition to charge a rate just covering variable costs and to charge higher rates at the inbetween points. Discrimination took many forms: there was discrimination with regard to types of commodities hauled; with respect to places served; and with respect to classes of persons served. Lavish state and federal assistance to the railroads, together with various possibilities for graft in contracting practices, also resulted in an overbuilding of railroad capacity. All these factors set the stage for a demand for regulation.

The Granger Movement, the Granger Laws, and the Granger Cases. Moreover, in the 1870s and late 1860s, largely as a result of the aftermath of the Civil War—which ended the dominance of the farmers and placed the industrialists in a position of dominance—there was much farmer discontent. Low agricultural prices, and a drop in farm buying power added to the problem. The Granger Movement was a political expression of this discontent; the principal base of the power of this movement was the farmers of the midwestern states of Iowa, Illinois, Michigan, Minnesota, and Wisconsin. The farmers blamed "business monopoly, grain dealers, high and discriminatory railway rates, and monetary policy" (the farmers wanted "cheap money") for their troubles.

Accordingly, the legislatures of the Granger states enacted laws to regulate the railroads. Some of these laws prescribed maximum rates, as had the early special charters. Such provisions were uniformly ineffective. The Illinois and Minnesota laws of 1873 and 1874, however, set up commissions to fix maximum rates. Most of the laws also contained provisions preventing the railroads from charging more for a shorter haul than for a longer haul (a practice employed to meet competitive rates at terminal points by charging high rates for shorter hauls from inbetween points where no competition existed). Prohibitions of consolidations of railroads in an attempt to enforce competition were also common in these statutes.

In 1877, the Supreme Court decided the so-called *Granger Cases*. Five of these cases involved state statutes regulating railroads, and the sixth was *Munn* v. *Illinois*,[1] already discussed under the heading of *"Munn v. Illinois: 'Property Affected with a Public Interest' and 'Due Process'"* in Chapter 7. In that case, it will be recalled, the Supreme Court upheld the right of the state of Illinois to regulate operators of grain elevators on the grounds that the state could regulate "property affected with a public interest." In the *Munn* case, the Court was *not* troubled by the question of whether or not the Illinois statute constituted an attempt by a state to regulate interstate commerce. However, nine years later, in the *Wabash Railway* case in 1886, the Court invalidated an Illinois Granger law (regulating railroads) on these grounds,[2] as we have also seen in Chapter 7 in the discussion of the power of the states to regulate interstate commerce.

B. FEDERAL LEGISLATION SINCE 1887

The Act to Regulate Commerce of 1887

Legislative History. The decision of the Supreme Court in the *Wabash* case produced a situation in which there was no regulation of interstate operations of the railroads. The states were prohibited from regulation, and Congress had not yet acted to regulate. Even before 1886 and the *Wabash* decision, however, consideration had been given in congress to the problem of federal regulation. In 1872, a special Senate Committee, known as the Windom Committee, was created to investigate and study the problem. The Committee reported in 1874 and concluded that "the only means of securing and maintaining reliable and effective competition among railroads is through national or state ownership of one or more railroads, which being unable to enter into combinations will serve as regulators of other lines."[3] The Committee also recommended further development of waterways to serve as alternative methods of transportation. No action was taken concerning the proposals of this committee. Various bills providing for regulation did pass the House in subsequent years, but did not become law. Different bills were passed by the House and Senate in 1884, and the stalemate (neither side being willing to accept the legislation passed by the other) resulted in the appointment of another committee, known as the Cullom Committee, to study the problem. This Committee reported in favor of a system of regulation in 1886.[4] The Cullom Committee's recommendations resulted in the Act to Regulate Commerce of 1887.

Principal Provisions of the Act of 1887. This Act created the Interstate Commerce Commission, originally a commission of five members to be appointed by the President with the advice and consent of the Senate, to enforce and administer the other provisions of the legislation which applied to railroads and to rail and water carriers under common management. These other provisions prohibited various types

---

[1] 94 U.S. 113 (1877).

[2] *Wabash, St. Louis, and Pacific Railway* v. *Illinois*, 118 U.S. 557 (1886).

[3] *Transportation Routes to the Seaboard* (Senate Report 307, 43d Cong., 1st sess.) (Washington, D.C.: U.S.

Government Printing Office, 1874), p. 242.

[4] *Senate Report No. 46* (49th Cong., 1st sess., 1886) (Washington, D.C.: U.S. Government Printing Office, 1886).

of discrimination practiced by the carriers and required all rates to be "just and reasonable." The Act also prohibited carriers from charging less for a longer than for a shorter haul for traffic moving over the same line in the same direction *under substantially similar circumstances.*

In order to secure enforcement of its orders, the Commission was required to apply to a federal court for an injunction or writ of mandamus. Various penalizing provisions were also included in the original legislation.

In the beginning, the Act produced beneficial results. The carriers cooperated with the Commission; but in time, as a result of Supreme Court decisions, the Commission was stripped of much of its authority; Congress responded to these decisions by passing corrective legislation to restore the Commission's power. Much such legislation was enacted up to 1920, and the most significant of these laws will be examined next.

Corrective and Supporting Legislation up to 1920

Expediting Act of 1903. In order to overcome the problem of long delays in the judicial determination of cases involving the Commission, in 1903 Congress adopted the Expediting Act, which provided that cases under the Act to Regulate Commerce and under the Sherman Act were to be given precedence in federal courts upon certification by the Attorney General of the public importance of the case.

The Elkins Act of 1903. In 1903, Congress also strengthened the provisions pertaining to personal discrimination and made *solicitation* and *receipt* of rebates or concessions by shippers unlawful, thus extending the coverage of the law to the *users* of transportation services. This law is still in force.

In this regard, it is interesting to note that in fiscal year 1967 the Commission levied fines totalling $25,600 on Revlon, Inc. and its wholly owned subsidiary, Knomark, Inc. under the Elkins Act. Revlon, Inc. was charged with soliciting and receiving concessions from certain motor carriers and from the Pennsylvania Railroad, Inc. Knomark, Inc. was charged with aiding

and abetting a motor carrier in operating at lower rates over unauthorized routes.[5]

The Hepburn Act of 1906. Probably the most important piece of legislation adopted during this early period was the Hepburn Act. In addition to increasing the size of the Commission, the Act authorized the Commission to fix maximum rates, a power which the Supreme Court had held that the Commission did not have under the original legislation to prescribe "just and reasonable rates." In addition, the Hepburn Act also provided for a change in the enforcement procedure concerning the Commission's orders. Under the Hepburn Act, Commission orders were made binding upon the carriers, and a fine was imposed for their failure to obey any such an order. If a carrier refused to obey, the Commission could secure an injunction which was to be issued if the order had been "properly made and duly served." The Act further provided that the Commission's orders were to be binding on the carrier unless set aside by a court. Thus where, under the original Act, the *Commission* was forced to go into court with the burden of proof in each case to seek an injunction to enforce its orders, under the Hepburn Act, the *carriers* now had the burden of proving that the order was unlawful or improperly served, and hence not binding. In short, the Hepburn Act provided for a more efficient and quicker method of making effective the Commission's orders. The Hepburn Act also extended the jurisdiction of the Commission to include control over sleeping-car companies and pipeline companies transporting commodities other than water or gas. Thus the Commission now had jurisdiction over railroads, rail and water carriers under common management used for continuous carriage and shipment, and pipelines used to transport commodities other than gas and water. Finally, the Hepburn Act also included a "Commodities Clause" which prohibited a carrier from transporting in interstate commerce articles which it had produced or in which it had an interest. The practical effect of this provision was to prohibit the railroads from discriminating in rates in favor of coal or timber produced on railroad property.

[5] *Annual Report of the Interstate Commerce Commission for 1967* (Washington, D.C.: U.S. Government Printing Office, 1968), pp. 69–70.

The Mann–Elkins Act of 1910 and World War I. The original Act of 1887 provided that it was unlawful to charge a higher rate for a shorter haul than for a longer haul over the same line in the same direction *under substantially similar circumstances.* This long-haul–short-haul provision was designed to prevent discrimination by carriers against inbetween-points, by charging higher rates from such points (where a monopoly market existed) to terminal points than for shipments from one terminal point (where competition did exist) to another. In the *Alabama Midland* case[6] in 1897, the Supreme Court had made this clause meaningless by holding that the carriers themselves were to interpret the meaning of the words *under substantially similar circumstances.* The carriers promptly claimed that *similar circumstances* existed only at terminal points where competition existed and that their discriminatory rate policies were thus lawful under the Act. The Mann–Elkins Act of 1910 deleted the words *under substantially similar circumstances* from the law, thus making the discriminatory rate practice unlawful *per se.* This Act also authorized the Commission to suspend proposed rate changes pending its investigation of the reasonableness of the rates. Prior to this time, rate changes were merely put into effect immediately by the carriers, and if the Commission afterward found the rates unreasonable it could award reparation to those who had been subjected to damage by the unreasonable rates. The power to suspend rates thus constituted a further strengthening of the Commission's regulatory power. The Act also provided for establishment of a commission to study the problem of issuance of railroad securities.

There were various further pieces of legislation between 1910 and 1920, some pertaining to the organization of the Commission, but none of these is of major significance for our present purpose (which is merely to survey the problem and not to make a detailed study of the matter).

In 1917, the operation of the railroads was taken over by the Federal Government in order to further the World War I mobilization effort. The occasion of the return of the railroads to private management after the war provided an opportunity for a new evaluation of policy toward the railroads, and such a policy was embodied in legislation enacted in 1920.

The Transportation Act of 1920

Writers in the field of transportation economics generally emphasize that up to 1920 the policy of regulation which had been adopted was "too restrictive" because it emphasized the interests of shippers to the detriment of those of the carriers and failed to take account of the necessity for the carriers to earn a rate of return sufficiently high to attract new capital investments. The Act of 1920 did, however, take account of the interests of the carriers. It contained, among others, various provisions (of little importance to our present consideration of the problem of transport regulation) pertaining to the problem of returning the railroads to private control. It also contained provisions to expand the power of the Commission, and provisions designed to achieve "sound financial operation" of the railroads. (It also changed the name of the law to "Interstate Commerce Act.")

With regard to provisions aimed at putting the operation of the railroads on a "sound financial" basis, it should be noted that although a particular railroad may have possessed a monopoly at some points in 1920, there were probably other points along its lines at which it experienced competition from other railroads. (Today, of course, a railroad may be subject to competition from water, motor, and, usually, air transportation at all points along its lines.) The competition which existed in 1920 (and which has been magnified in our own time) meant that different rates could not be fixed for different individual railroads (as compared with those fixed for competing carriers). The individual rates so fixed would have been so high in the cases of some roads that these carriers would have been forced out of business. Accordingly, the 1920 Act took account of this problem by adding Section 15(a), "the rule of ratemaking" to the law. This provision stated:

In the exercise of its power to prescribe just and reasonable rates the Commission shall initiate, modify, establish, or adjust such rates so

---

[6] *Interstate Commerce Commission* v. *Alabama Midland Ry. Co.*, 168 U.S. 144 (1897).

that the carriers as a whole (or as a whole in each of such rate groups or territories as the Commission may from time to time designate) will, under honest, efficient, and economical management and reasonable expenditures for maintenance of way, structures, and equipment, earn an aggregate annual net railway operating income equal, as nearly as may be, to a fair return upon the aggregate value of railway property of such carriers held for and used in the service of transportation: Provided, That the Commission shall have reasonable latitude to modify or adjust any particular rate which it may find to be unjust or unreasonable and to prescribe different rates for different sections of the country.

It is to be emphasized that this new rule of ratemaking applied to the carriers *as a whole*. Because it was believed that the policy embodied in the new rule of ratemaking would give some carriers an excessive rate of return while causing others to operate at a loss, some elaborate provisions to assist the "weak" railroads by "recapturing" a part of the profits of the "strong" roads were also included in the law. However, detailed discussion of these provisions, which were abolished in 1933, would contribute little to the purpose of this chapter and may be left for detailed study in courses in Transportation Economics.

The Act of 1920 for the first time gave the Commission power to prescribe minimum rates as well as power to make rules pertaining to the division of joint rates. For the first time also, the Commission was given power to control the issuance of securities, as well as power to control abandonments of service and to control new construction. Indeed, upon making findings that such action was necessary in the public interest and that the action would not impair the ability of the carrier to perform its duty to the public, the Commission was also authorized to require a carrier to undertake new construction to extend its lines. Finally, although there were also other miscellaneous provisions which need not concern us now, the Act of 1920 directed the Commission to draw up and adopt a plan for consolidation of the railroad systems of the United States into a limited number of systems, although no authority to enforce such a plan was given. Thus, the Act of 1920 laid the foundation for the great railroad mergers of the 1960's.

The Act of 1920 (with its grant of control over new construction and over abandonments) gave the Commission power to control entry into and exit from the industry, while the rule of ratemaking combined with provisions to assist operations of weak roads at the expense of profits of strong roads was designed to insure the continued effective operation of the railroad system *as a whole*. The new rule of ratemaking recognized that a given railroad might experience competition from other railroads but was based on the assumption, true enough in 1920, that there existed a railroad monopoly of many transportation services. As we will see later, with the widespread development of motor, air, and pipeline methods of transportation by 1940, the assumption, that the railroads possessed a monopoly, was no longer valid; and a new rule of ratemaking had to be adopted to take account of the increased *intermodal* competition faced by the railroads.

Legislation from 1920 to 1940

The principal pieces of legislation between 1920 and 1940 pertained to the settlement of labor disputes and extended the regulatory power of the Interstate Commerce Commission to include regulation of motor carriers. Minor pieces of legislation included the Hoch–Smith Resolution of 1925, in which Congress sought to prescribe preferential treatment for agricultural commodities in the ratemaking process. However, the Supreme Court virtually nullified this legislation shortly after it was enacted and reduced it to a policy statement rather than a specific directive to the Commission. An amendment to the bankruptcy laws providing for participation by the Commission in cases involving reorganization of bankrupt railways was adopted in 1935, and an Emergency Transportation Act was passed in 1933, partly to help railroads meet the situation created by the Depression. This law also repealed the recapture provisions of the 1920 Act and submitted railroad holding companies to Commission control. In addition, the rule of ratemaking of Section 15(a) of the 1920 Act was amended by eliminating the "fair-return-on-the-fair-value" standard of the 1920 Act and substituting for it requirements that the Commission was to take account not only of the need of the railroads for revenue but was also to consider the effect of rates on movement of the traffic and the public's need for transportation service at a cost consistent with the furnishing of adequate service.

The Railway Labor Act of 1926 as Amended. The legislation pertaining to railway labor adopted in 1926 is important not only in its own right but also because it constituted the first federal legislation authorizing the election of labor representatives to represent labor interests in labor disputes. Under the law, as amended today, disputes between carriers and employees are to be settled, if possible in *conferences* of freely chosen representatives of each side. Provision is also made for settlement of disputes growing out of labor contracts by a National Railroad Adjustment Board of 36 members, 18 chosen by employers, and 18 chosen by railway labor unions. Provision is made for *voluntary* arbitration of disputes which the Mediation Board cannot settle. Finally, machinery is created for the establishment by the President of an Emergency Board to investigate and report disputes not settled by the other methods. However, an Emergency Board is created only for the purpose of dealing with a specific dispute and has a temporary life; there is no authority by means of which to enforce any recommendations it may make. The provisions of this law were used by President Nixon to avert a railway strike in December 1969 and in July 1970.

Enactment of the Motor Carrier Act of 1935. Reference to *Table 24–1* will disclose that 62 percent of the total of intercity ton-miles of transportation service performed in 1966 were performed by carriers that were federally regulated. Of this 62 percent, 37.8 percent consisted of motor traffic.

The motor transportation business differs sharply from the railroad business. Aside from the large volume of private motor transportation activity, commercial motor carriers do not find it necessary to provide and maintain their own rights of way and railroad lines, as do rail carriers, since the former use public highways. Moreover, there is much competition among motor carriers; and there exist a large number of carriers. In 1967, there were a total of 18,524 motor carriers of property and passengers to whom certificates or permits to operate had been granted by the Interstate Commerce Commission.[7]

The competition resulting from the very large number of motor carriers is the indirect result of the fact that capital investments necessary to enter the business are small compared with the sizes of those required to build new railroads. This fact is, in turn, a reflection of the fact that commercial motor carriers use public highways. The lack of high fixed capital investments, in turn, means that fixed costs are relatively less important than they are in the railroad business; variable costs, on the other hand, are relatively more important. *Table 24–2* provides a comparison of fixed investments and revenues for the various types of carriers subject to Commission regulation in 1967. It is to be noted that railroads accounted for 83.7 percent of the fixed investment and 51.0 percent of the revenue, while motor carriers of property and of passengers together accounted for only 5.9 percent of the fixed investment but for 39.4 percent of the revenues. Clearly the ratio of revenue to fixed investment was much higher in the case of the motor carriers and the absolute amount of fixed investment was smaller; but, the number of operators is large.

There are two main types of commercial carriers: (1) *common* carriers, which hold themselves out to the public as ready to serve all without discrimination; and (2) *contract* carriers, which operate for hire according to special contracts. An early attempt by the state of Michigan to regulate contract and common carriers as if there were no difference between the two types was nullified by the Supreme Court in 1925.[8] Much regulation at the state level is today concerned with the imposition of safety standards. As we have seen in Chapter 7, the Court has long rebuffed attempts by the states to regulate competition among motor carriers operating in interstate commerce.[9]

[7] *Annual Report of the Interstate Commerce Commission for 1967, op. cit.,* p. 105.

[8] *Michigan Public Utilities Commission* v. *Duke,* 266 U.S. 570 (1925).

[9] *Buck* v. *Kuykendall,* 267 U.S. 307 (1925), discussed in Chapter 7 under the heading of *"Permissibility of State Actions to Regulate Interstate Commerce."*

Table 24-2

Revenues, Net Investment, and Taxes, 1967 (Thousands)[1]

Kind of Carrier	Operating Revenues	Net Investment in Carrier Operating Property and Equipment, Dec. 31, 1966	Taxes Income and Excess Profits[11]	All Other
Class I line-haul railroads[2]	[3]$10,366,041	$24,333,754	[4]$66,317	$843,861
Motor carriers of property (class I intercity)	[10]8,009,642	[10]1,703,434	[5][10]92,369	[6]512,789
Motor carriers of passengers (class I intercity)	[10]666,530	[10]294,503	[5][10]30,393	[7]46,908
Water carriers (class A and class B)	[8][10]296,139	264,604	[5][10]11,686	[10]4,560
Oil pipelines[9]	[10]966,130	2,464,026	[4][10]124,235	[10]60,218
Total	20,304,482	29,060,321	325,000	1,468,336

	Percentage Distribution			
Class I line-haul railroads	51.0	83.7	20.4	57.5
Motor carriers of property	39.4	5.9	28.4	34.9
Motor carriers of passengers	3.3	1.0	9.4	3.2
Water carriers	1.5	0.9	3.6	1.3
Oil pipelines	4.8	8.5	38.2	4.1
Total	100.0	100.0	100.0	100.0

Source: Reproduced from Annual Report of the Interstate Commerce Commission for 1968 (Washington, D.C.: U.S. Government Printing Office, 1969), p. 138.

[1] Net investment in carrier property and equipment at the close of the preceding year.

[2] Effective Jan. 1, 1965, the revenue qualification of a class I railroad was increased from average annual operating revenues of $3,000,000 or more to $5,000,000 or more.

[3] Railway operating revenues.

[4] U.S. Government income and excess profits taxes only.

[5] U.S. and State taxes combined.

[6] From Quarterly Report Q–800.

[7] From Quarterly Report Q–750.

[8] Total waterline operating revenues.

[9] Does not include 5 pipeline departments.

[10] Preliminary.

[11] Excludes income taxes on extraordinary and prior period items.

The lack of power of the states to regulate motor transportation eventually resulted in federal regulation. The railroad companies strongly supported the concept of federal regulation in the belief that they would benefit from such regulation, while the motor carrier companies themselves were divided in their views. The Motor Carrier Act of 1935 was based on a report and recommendations made by the Office of the Federal Coordinator of Transportation, an agency which had been established by the Emergency Transportation Act of 1933 and whose functions had in time come to consist largely of the making of transport studies and the writing of reports.

The Act subjected interstate motor transportation to regulation by the Interstate Commerce Commission. Five classes of motor transport agencies were defined. These were: (1) common carriers; (2) contract carriers; (3) private carriers, or carriers used to transport goods owned by the carrier itself; (4) brokers, or firms which did not own transportation equipment but which sold transportation services; and

(5) exempt carriers, such as the farmer who uses his truck to haul his farm products to market.

Provisions of the Motor Carrier Act of 1935. The law provided for control over entry into the motor transport industry by requiring *common* carriers to secure *certificates of convenience and necessity* from the Commission and *contract* carriers to secure *permits*. A permit is issued upon a showing that the action will be in the "public interest," a less exacting requirement than that of a showing that such an action will satisfy "public convenience and necessity." Common carriers must provide insurance to cover goods carried; contract carriers need not do so. The Commission also has greater power over rates in the case of common carriers than it does in the case of contract carriers, as well as power over mergers and consolidations, issuance of securities, and adequacy of service. These powers will be discussed later.

A *grandfather clause* was included in the legislation to provide that those firms in operation at the time of enactment of the legislation would receive certificates or permits (as appropriate) *as a matter of right.*

The Transportation Act of 1940

Like the Act of 1920, the Act of 1940 represented a major overhaul of the legislation pertaining to the powers of the Commission. Part I of the Act of 1940 is the original Act to Regulate Commerce, as amended; Part II consists of the Motor Carrier Act of 1935. Part III consists of new legislation adopted in 1940 pertaining to the regulation of domestic water carriers and sets up a system to regulate them that is in many respects comparable to the system of regulation of railroads. The Declaration of Policy contained in the Act of 1940 reflects a new approach to the problem of regulation of transport as a whole and contained this important provision:

It is hereby declared to be the national transportation policy of the Congress to provide for the fair and impartial regulation of all modes of transportation subject to the provisions of the Act, so administered as to recognize and preserve the inherent advantages of each; . . . to the end of developing, coordinating, and preserving a national transportation system by water, highway, and rail, as well as by other means, adequate

to meet the needs of the commerce of the United States, of the Postal Service, and of the national defense. All of the provisions of this Act shall be administered and enforced with a view to carrying out the above declaration of policy.

Thus the 1940 Act visualized a transportation system consisting of various *modes* of transportation, a system in which the *inherent advantage of each mode* was to be recognized and preserved.

Among the substantive changes made by the 1940 Act, one of the most important was the amendment of the provision pertaining to consolidations which had been adopted in the Act of 1920. The Act of 1940 provided for the Commission to give approval to consolidations and mergers proposed by the carriers themselves if "consistent with the public interest," and subject to various other specific statutory standards. Several significant railroad mergers occurred in the late 1960s under the amended law, as we will see later. (The problem of application of the antitrust laws to railway mergers is discussed in Chapter 22.)

The rule of ratemaking was also amended to require the Commission to give consideration to the effect of rates on the movement of traffic *by the carrier or carriers for which the rates were prescribed.* The purpose of this provision was to prevent the Commission from prescribing rates for one carrier (motor) in such a way as to protect another type of carrier (railroad). Also, the burden of proof in any proceeding involving a change in rates was placed on the carrier. A Board of Investigation and Research to study transportation problems was also created by the 1940 Act.

Legislation from 1940 to 1966

The Railroad Modification Act of 1948. This law provided for a procedure for simplifying a railroad's financial structure in order to avoid a bankruptcy proceeding.

The Reed–Bulwinkle Act of 1948. This law provided for an exception from the antitrust laws for the use of railroad rate bureaus to fix rates, subject to Commission approval.

The Transportation Act of 1958. The Act of 1958 provided financial assistance to the railroads and made certain changes in the existing laws. A provision was included empowering the Commission to raise intrastate rates harmful to interstate commerce. The rule of ratemaking was also amended by adding the following new paragraph:

In a proceeding involving competition between carriers of different modes of transportation subject to this Act, the Commission, in determining whether a rate is lower than a reasonable minimum rate, shall consider the facts and circumstances attending the movement of the traffic by the carrier or carriers to which the rate is applicable. Rates of a carrier shall not be held up to a particular level to protect the traffic of any other mode of transportation, giving due consideration to the objectives of the National Transportation Act.

The Urban Mass Transportation Act of 1964. This law provided for direct grants by the Federal Government to states and local governments to assist the latter in solving mass urban transportation problems and also provided for low-interest rate loans to implement such plans.

The Department of Transportation Act of 1966

The Department of Transportation Act of 1966 will be discussed in detail in Chapter 26. For the moment, it is sufficient to note that this law transferred to the new Department from the Commission various functions, powers, and duties pertaining to railroad, motor, and pipeline safety, to safe transportation of explosives and other dangerous articles, and to daylight saving time and standard time zones. None of the powers pertaining to economic regulation of the various modes of domestic surface transportation were, however, affected by this law. A "memorandum of agreement" was signed by the Commission and the new Department to insure continuity of the functions being transferred from the Commission to the Department.[10]

Organization of the Commission

The Interstate Commerce Commission consists of the Commission and its supporting units. There are a number of Bureaus, subdivided into sections. Today, the Commission consists of 11 members appointed by the President with the advice and consent of the Senate. The Chairman is elected annually by the entire Commission. The Commission has created three divisions as follows: Division I deals with operating rights; Division II exercises authority over rates, tariffs, and valuations; and Division III performs functions pertaining to finance and service. Each division performs an appellate function pertaining to the areas of its responsibility.

General Description of Commission Operations

The following extract from the report of a Hearing Examiner in a Commission proceeding provides an authentic and informative description of the general method of operations of the Commission. The extract reads:

Carrier initiative and Commission functions.— Under our private enterprise system, even in the field of transportation, where freedom of action has been somewhat curtailed by regulation imposed in the public interest, the statutory scheme of ratemaking still generally leaves the initiative to the carriers. Indeed, it is their responsibility, in the first instance, to set appropriate rates and they are free to initiate such changes as they deem proper in their managerial discretion. The Commission is not, and was never meant to be, the manager of the operations of regulated carriers. Neither is it the Commission's function to pass upon the wisdom, as such, of a proposed course of action, nor to keep carriers from committing errors of judgment. The Commission does not have the task of forecasting, nor does it possess a crystal ball for predicting with exactitude, the ultimate practical outcome of every move a carrier may make, and save the latter from all improvident ventures. *Cf. Davis and Randall, Inc.* v. *United States,* 219 F. Supp. 673, 677 (W. D. N. Y. 1963). Rather, the duty of the Commission is confined to the determination of the lawfulness of carrier activities and practices when properly put in issue in general investigations or in particular and limited proceedings. Thus, the Commission may override any action taken by a carrier when found, based upon an evidentiary record, to be contrary to specific statutory standards or to be inconsistent with the general purposes of the national transportation policy.[11]

It is to the problems presented to the Commission in actions by carriers pertaining to rates that the next subdivision is devoted.

[10] *Annual Report of the Interstate Commerce Commission for 1967, op. cit.,* p. 9.
[11] *Rules to Govern the Assembling and Presenting of Cost Evidence,* Report and Order, Interstate Commerce Commission Docket 34013, October 10, 1966, pp. 64–65.

C. PROBLEMS OF RATEMAKING

Types of Ratemaking Problems

There are many different types of rate-making problems which must be dealt with by the Interstate Commerce Commission in performing its statutory duties. Moreover, similar ratemaking problems are faced by other regulatory agencies charged with ratemaking. For example, there are *rate structure* problems, that is, problems of rate relationships. In addition, there is a problem of *the level of rates*, or of the *rate of return*. This problem, in turn, involves the problem of determining a *rate base*. All these problems are further complicated in the field of transportation by the Congressional declaration of policy to the effect that the *inherent advantages* of each type of transportation service are to be preserved.

The Problem of the Rate Structure

The problem of the *rate structure* refers to the problem of the relationship of the rate charged for one type of service to the rate charged for another type. To take an extreme illustration, what is the relationship of a transportation rate of a certain sum per ton of coal to the rate per ton of diamonds? Also, what is the relationship of the rate per ton of gravel hauled by a railroad to the rate per ton of gravel hauled by a motor carrier? What is the relationship of the rates from two neighboring cities to some other city by any mode of transportation?

Two concepts are usually called into play in discussing rate structure problems. One of these is the *cost of service* concept, the other is the *value of service* concept.

Cost of Service. In order to understand the *cost of service* concept, it is necessary to know the various definitions of cost which are employed. *Total cost* is defined as the sum of all the costs (including a "normal" profit) incurred in furnishing the service. The short-run total cost is classified (in economics generally) into the categories of *fixed costs* and *variable costs*. *Fixed costs* are defined as those which are incurred whether the service is performed or not. They include a so-called "normal" profit. *Variable costs* are defined as those which vary with the volume of service rendered; sometimes in Transportation Economics, the variable costs are also called "out-of-pocket" costs.

The variable costs may be identifiable as being the result of offering particular services or they may not be identifiable. If they are not identifiable, they are termed *joint* or *common* variable costs. By definition, fixed costs are always joint or common. The allocation of joint or common costs to particular services is usually accomplished by some arbitrary means; one practice, for example, is to assign equal portions of these costs to all services, provided that no evidence calling for any other type of distribution exists. The *fully allocated costs* consist of the variable costs attributable to a particular service plus the amount of the joint or common costs (both fixed and variable) allocated to that service. In a sense, the "fully allocated cost" concept is related to the economist's concept of total cost; on a per unit basis it is analogous to full average cost per unit.

These definitions are employed in the ratemaking process. If there already exists a given productive capacity which will not be fully utilized if all rates are fixed at the level of the relevant full average cost, discrimination in rates is usually rationalized on some "reasonable" basis. It is often argued that discrimination is justifiable and "reasonable" if it leads to greater utilization of capacity at a lower cost per unit of service. Since some services will not be demanded if a rate equal to full average cost of production is charged for all services, a rate is usually considered to be "compensatory" if out-of-pocket or variable costs are covered or slightly exceeded. The argument on behalf of this procedure is that if the rate on a low-rated commodity is fixed equal to the variable cost of the service, while the rate on a high-rated commodity is not increased above the level it would be were the low-rated service not performed, such discriminatory pricing may be desirable since it results in fuller utilization of capacity. If, indeed, the rate on a low-rated service is fixed at slightly more than its variable or out-of-pocket cost, the low-rated service will make some contribution to the fixed cost and the high-rated service may be performed at a lower rate than it would be were the low-rated service priced at full average cost and thus priced out of the market. Accordingly, the variable or out-of-pocket cost, which can be identified as the result of performance of a particular service, sets a *floor* below which the rate cannot be permitted to fall. Such a rate, it has been noted, is called a *compensatory* rate.

Value of Service. Charging a rate equal to the *value of the service* to the user amounts to "charging what the traffic will bear" and sets the *upper* limit to any rate. Presumably, no user will purchase the service at a rate in excess of the value of the service to him. But to charge the full value of service would amount to exerting to the full the monopoly power possessed by the enterprise producing the service and to allowing the rate to be determined by demand alone. The "best" rate thus, ideally, lies somewhere between the *cost of the service* and the *value of the service*, at a level which, all the rates *as a whole* considered in the light of the rate base chosen, will allow a "fair return on the fair value" of the investment in the productive capacity. It is not necessary, however, that any given rate bear its full share of this "fair return." Several case studies of actual problems pertaining to the *structure* of rates will now be considered.

Case Studies of Transportation Rate Structure Problems

Case Studies of "Intermodal" Rate Structure Problems. The following excerpt from the *Annual Report of the Interstate Commerce Commission for 1967* illustrates the nature of intermodal competitive rate structure problems:

On further hearing, Division 2 in *Canned or Preserved Foodstuffs from Fla. to N. Y. and N. J.*, 326 I.C.C. 776, found a proposed rail door-to-door piggyback flat charge of $650 per flatcar of two trailerloads, and a proposed reduced motor-water-motor rate of Sea-Land Service, Inc., just and reasonable. The evidence showed that after the effective date of the piggyback charge, rail revenue on this traffic increased sharply. Destructive competition was not shown to exist, since rail rates were found to exceed out-of-pocket costs and Sea-Land did not show its competing service to be the low-cost mode. This proceeding was reopened by the Commission on its own motion and consolidated, for issuance of a single report, with two complaint proceedings, Nos. 34471 and 34471 (Sub-No. 1), both entitled *Sea-Land Service, Inc. v. Atlantic Coast Line Railroad Company, et. al.* The proceedings were later assigned for a limited further hearing.

In *Atchison, T. and S. F. Ry. v. Morris*, 329 I.C.C. 326, 26 railroads complained that the rates of numerous motor carriers on clay and drilling mud from origins in South Dakota and Wyoming to western points were unreasonably low. The complainants offered a cost study based on regional averages. After adjustments were made to the regional costs to reflect characteristics of the traffic, it was found that some of the rates were above and some were below out-of-pocket costs. In reversing the hearing examiner's refusal to consider such costs as representative, the Commission concluded that since the rates were published to many points in 12 States, regional average costs should be used to determine whether the assailed rates were compensatory, in the absence of more specific cost data. The defendants introduced no such data and the rates that were below the costs discussed were required to be canceled.[12]

A Case Study of an "Intramodal" Rate Structure Problem. Another excerpt from the same publication provides an example of a rate structure problem involving two carriers of the same type, an *intramodal* problem. It reads:

Docket No. 34303, *Seaboard Air Line R. Ro. v. Southern Ry. Co.*, 329 I.C.C. 17, was illustrative of the fact that competitive disputes are not confined to carriers of different modes, and that considerations other than cost at times are controlling. In this case, railroads in the South complained that local carload commodity rates on sand, gravel, and crushed stone between points in Southern States by carriers of the Southern Railway System were unreasonably low. Base rates were published on 100-ton minimum shipments in articulated cars (a coupling of two 50-ton hopper cars), and very low incentive rates on weight in excess of 100 tons per car. Noting that costs are not the sole criterion for determining rates, the Commission considered the facts (1) that transportation expense, being such a large percentage of the production-site value of such commodities, prevents their movement for any substantial distance; (2) that the complaining railroads' share of the traffic, despite increased production, had declined; (3) that under the rates the defendants had experienced an increase in volume and gross revenues; and (4) that there was no showing of direct or indirect injury to any person, including the complainants. Thus, the assailed rates were found not shown to be unjust and unreasonable. Subsequently, the Commission's decision was upheld in *Seaboard Air Line Railroad Co. v. United States, et. al.*, E.D. Va., 268 F. Supp. 500.[13]

---

[12] *Annual Report of the Interstate Commerce Commission for 1967, op. cit.*, pp. 15–16.

[13] *Ibid.*, pp. 16–17.

Fully Distributed Cost As a Measure of "Inherent Advantage." An interesting case involving the problem of intermodal competition was decided by the Supreme Court in 1968. The reader will recall that the Transportation Act of 1940 laid down a general policy of regulation to the effect that the *inherent advantages* of each mode of transportation were to be recognized and preserved. In the case study given above involving Sea–Land Service, Inc. and the New York Central Railroad Company, the Commission found that the Sea–Land company was participating in the traffic "at a rate which exceeded its own fully distributed costs."

The Supreme Court case now to be considered involved the question of whether "fully distributed" cost or "out-of-pocket" cost is the proper measure of *inherent advantage.* For our purposes, "fully distributed" cost means full average cost, including a proportionate contribution to fixed cost in which a share of "fair return on fair value" is counted, and "out-of-pocket" cost means variable cost. The case involved the following facts. From 1953 to 1968, ingot molds moved almost exclusively by combination barge-truck service from Nevile Island and Pittsburgh, Pa., to Steelton, Ky. The overall service charge was $5.11 per ton. In 1963, two railroad companies lowered their rates from $11.86 to $5.11 per ton. The barge lines complained to the Commission that this rate reduction destroyed their *inherent advantage* and thus violated the Interstate Commerce Act. The Commission held hearings and made findings that the "fully distributed" cost for the railroads was $7.59 per ton, while that for the truck-barge service was $5.19, and also that the "out-of-pocket" cost to the railroads was $4.69. The Commission then ordered the railroads to cancel their rate reduction pointing to the fact that it had always used "fully distributed" cost as the measure of *inherent advantage.* A lower court reversed the Commission's order, but on appeal to the Supreme Court the position taken by the Commission was upheld. In part, the Court remarked:

Unfortunately, the meaning of the term "inherent advantage", which is what the Commission is supposed to protect, is nowhere spelled out in the statute. The railroads argue, and the District Court held, that Congress intended by the term to refer to situations in which the carrier could transport goods at a lower incremental cost than another. The fallacy of this argument is that it renders the term "inherent advantage" essentially meaningless in the context of the language and history of the statute.

. . . the Commission pointed out that the principle proposed by the railroads would, if recognized, permit the railroads to capture all the traffic here that is presently carried by the barge-truck combination because the railroads' out-of-pocket costs were lower than those of the combined barge service. The District Court seems to have been impressed by the fact that the railroads were merely meeting the barge-truck rate, despite the uncontroverted evidence that given equal rates, all traffic would move by train. Given the service advantage, it does seem somewhat unrealistic to suggest that rate parity does not result in undercutting the competitor that does not possess that service advantage. In any event, regardless of the label used, it seems self-evident that a carrier's "inherent advantage" of being the low cost mode on a fully distributed cost basis is impaired when a competitor sets a rate that forces the carrier to lower its own rate below its fully distributed costs in order to retain traffic. In addition, when a rate war would be likely to eventually result in pushing rates to a level at which rates would no longer provide a fair profit, the Commission has traditionally, and properly taken the position that such a rate war should be prevented from occurring in the first place.[14]

However, the Court was also careful to point out that nothing in the opinion was to be construed as requiring the Commission to use fully distributed costs "as the only measure of inherent advantage in intermodal rate controversies."

Problems of Definition and Measurement of Costs

In 1962 and 1963, the Commission undertook to hold hearings concerning the question of whether or not it should use its rulemaking power to adopt certain cost formulas developed by the cost finding section of its Bureau of Accounts. The Hearing Examiner's report and order were handed down in October, 1966. The report of the Hearing Examiner contains much

[14] *American Commercial Lines, Inc., et. al.* v. *Louisville and Nashville Railroad Co., et. al.,* 392 U.S. 571 (1968), at pp. 581; 593–594.

useful information pertaining to the definitions and measurement of costs employed or proposed by the cost finding section. According to the report:

... the cost finding section has determined the out-of-pocket costs for general freight operations to approximate 80 percent for railroads and 90 percent for motor carriers of their respective total operating expenses, rents, and taxes, other than income taxes; plus an allowance for return on investment. The latter allowance is computed for railroads on the basis of a 4-percent return (after making provisions for Federal income taxes) on 50 percent of the depreciated value of railroad property, on service, and on working capital. For motor carriers of general commodities this allowance is based on 90 percent of a 5-percent return (without any provision for Federal income taxes) on property and on working capital.[15]

The Hearing Examiner's comment on this point was limited to description; no discussion of the logic of the computation of the percentage figures was given.

However, the method employed by the cost finding section of determining "fully distributed" cost was discussed in the report in these words:

According to the publications of the cost finding section, there are three levels of costs which, under various circumstances, are helpful in analyzing and testing the compensatory character of a rate. All three are said to provide a complete cost picture and to be necessary on occasion to explain carrier rates. The first and lowest cost level consists of those one-way out-of-pocket or variable expenses which are separable from the joint expenses incurred in the round-trip movement of the equipment, hereinafter referred to as the out-of-pocket level. The second level of cost includes the out-of-pocket or variable expense applicable to the operation as a whole. It embraces joint expenses (such as those applicable to line-haul equipment) which, while of a joint character for an individual segment of a carrier's operations are, nevertheless, variable with traffic volume when the operations are viewed as a whole. The third level of cost consists of the so-called fully distributed costs which are made up of the out-of-pocket or variable costs plus an apportionment of the constant expenses.

The economic significance of each of the above three levels of cost is summarized by the cost finding section as follows:

1. The bare out-of-pocket costs may serve as a minimum below which so-called "back-haul" rates cannot fall without incurring an out-of-pocket loss. Justification for rates approaching this low level of cost may exist where the conditions of demand vary widely by directions of movement, low rates being necessary to obtain a more efficient utilization of the equipment in the direction of the empty return. In such instances rates may be economically justified at a level but little above the separable expenses assignable to the one direction of movement. Such rates, however, are conditioned upon the ability of the remaining traffic handled on the round trip to cover all the joint costs for the trip not recovered from the low-rated traffic; otherwise, the carrier would incur an out-of-pocket loss for the round-trip movement taken as a whole. The principle involved is that the revenues derived from the performance of any segment of the operations, such as the round-trip movement, should normally equal the out-of-pocket expense incurred in performing such segment of the service. The cost finding section maintains that this lowest level of cost is usually of temporary or local significance and should not be used as a general yardstick in rate cases.

2. The second and broader concept of the out-of-pocket or variable costs, applicable to the operation as a whole, is that which is more commonly used. Such out-of-pocket costs provide a minimum below which rates having widespread or general application cannot fall without occasioning an out-of-pocket loss. Since such costs reflect the relative amount of transportation service received by the shipment, they provide a measure, generally in cents per 100 pounds, of the differences in the rates for shipments of varying sizes and lengths of hauls, which can be justified by differences in the cost of performing the service. Any remaining differences in the rates for the several kinds of traffic must be based on considerations other than cost.

3. The fully distributed costs, based on the out-of-pocket or variable costs plus an apportionment of the constant expenses, provide for comparisons of the relative cost of transportation for different regions or territories, separate agencies of transportation, or single carriers, based on total expenses. They also indicate the extent of the constant costs which are present in the operation and which must be recovered out of the revenues received over and above the out-of-pocket expenses. The fully distributed costs provide a standard or yardstick which is helpful in testing the longrun compensatory character not of particular rates, but of the rate structure as a whole.

The apportionment of the out-of-pocket costs is fundamentally based on the relative use which the traffic in question makes of the carrier's plant

[15] *Rules to Govern the Assembling and Presenting of Cost Evidence, op. cit.,* p. 9.

and facilities. The apportionment of the constant and joint costs is fundamentally based on a weighing of the effect which the rates themselves would have upon the movement of the traffic and the carrier's revenues. Of far-reaching significance in this latter connection has been the recognition and application of the principle that by reducing the rates on traffic having expansible volume (elastic demand), the contribution to the constant costs can be increased, within limits, beyond that attainable by limiting rate differentiation strictly to cost-of-service considerations.

In its presentation in this proceeding the cost finding section amplifies on its concept of the fully distributed cost level. It states that the fully distributed cost, sometimes also called "revenue need," is presumed to be that revenue level which is sufficient to cover all expenses, rents, taxes, and interest on investment. It has been used by the Commission for comparative purposes to determine the low-cost or the most economic mode of carriage. According to the cost finding section, this level is supposed to provide a return on investment which is sufficient to attract capital for payment of interest charges, dividends, and amounts for the replacement of equipment and facilities at a price level different from the one which was used when the assets were placed on the books of the company.

For railroads, the fully distributed costs comprise the out-of-pocket costs as previously described, plus the constant costs. These constant costs consist of the remaining 20 percent of the freight operating expenses, rents, and taxes (other than Federal income taxes); an allowance for return based on a rate of 4 percent (after provisions for Federal income taxes) on the depreciated value of the remaining 50 percent of road property; plus the passenger and less-than-carload deficits.

For motor carriers the fully distributed cost level is based on a procedure which involves the use of an operating ratio of 93 percent applied to (divided into) the total operating expenses, rents, and taxes (other than income taxes). The amount thus obtained is considered to be the fully distributed cost level. Thus, for motor carriers the fully distributed costs include the out-of-pocket costs, as heretofore defined, and constant costs. The latter is composed of, or is designed to cover, the remaining 10 percent (constant portion) of the total operating expenses, rents, and taxes (other than income taxes); the remaining 10 percent (constant portion) of the 5-percent return on depreciated investment and on working capital; and a so-called "allowance for profit."[16]

The preceding excerpt should be carefully studied by the reader. His ability to under-

stand it is a good index of his understanding of the concepts and relationships developed thus far in this chapter. Moreover, similar concepts are employed by other regulatory agencies in dealing with ratemaking problems.

The Hearing Examiner's report also contains a useful distinction between the problems of determining costs and those of setting rates, and notes that costs are becoming increasingly important as a decisive factor in the determination of rates, while value of service, although still an important consideration, is becoming relatively less influential.

In the quotation from the report of the Hearing Examiner, it will have been noted, the "fully allocated cost" used to test *inherent advantage* includes an allowance for profit. The question of the definition of profit or of a "fair rate of return" is a problem of the general *level* of rates, and to this problem we now turn.

The Problem of the Level of Rates

The problem of the *level* of transportation rates has been the subject of both judicial and statutory attention. Moreover, the principles applicable to the determination of the general level of rates laid down by the Supreme Court in cases involving one type of public service industry apply with equal force to cases involving other types of public service industries, as we will now see.

The "Fair Return on Fair Value" Concept. As early as 1886, at a time when the Court was still exercising judicial superiority in regard to matters of economic regulation (a topic already discussed in detail in Chapter 7), it also began to place limitations upon the power of administrative agencies to determine the general level of rates. Thus in 1886, the Court asserted:

From what has been said, it is not to be inferred that this power of regulation is itself without limit. This power to regulate is not a power to destroy, and limitation is not the equivalent of confiscation. Under pretence of regulating fares and freights, the State cannot require a railroad corporation to carry persons or property without reward; neither can it do that which in law amounts to taking of private property for public use without just compensation, or without due process of law.[17]

---

[16] *Ibid.*, pp. 11–13.

[17] *Stone* v. *Farmer's Loan and Trust Co.*, 116 U.S. 307 (1886), at p. 331.

The "due process" concept in this quotation is the "substantive due process" concept discussed in Chapter 7. To be noted is the fact that the quotation does not provide an operational definition of the phrase "that which in law amounts to a taking of private property for public use without just compensation. . . ." In 1890, however, the Court attempted to put some specific meaning into the idea conveyed by the phrase.

Smyth v. *Ames*: "Fair Return upon Fair Value." In 1890, in *Smyth* v. *Ames*, the Supreme Court said:

We hold . . . that the basis of all calculations as to reasonableness of rates to be charged by a corporation maintaining a highway under legislative sanction must be the fair value of the property being used by it for the convenience of the public. And in order to ascertain that value, the original cost of construction, the amount expended in permanent improvements, the amount [market value] of its bonds and stock, the present as compared with the original cost of construction, the probable earning capacity of the property under particular rates prescribed by statute and the sum required to meet operating expenses are all matters for consideration, and are to be given such weight as may be just and right in each case. We do not say that there may not be other matters to be regarded in estimating the value of the property. What the company is entitled to ask is a fair return on the value of what it employs for the public convenience. On the other hand, what the public is entitled to demand is that no more be exacted from it . . . than the services rendered by it are reasonably worth.[18]

Unfortunately, the list of elements which the Court listed as being worthy of consideration in determining "fair value" is not particularly helpful and, indeed, contains some contradictions. Particularly to be noted is the omission of an allowance for depreciation, although one might argue that this allowance is implicitly present in the phrase "the present as compared with the original cost of construction." However, the inclusion of the items "original cost" and "amount expended in permanent improvements," on the one hand, and the "present value," on the other, gave rise to a debate among economists as to whether *original cost* or *reproduction cost new* should be

the standard of "fair value." We will consider this debate further shortly. In 1909, the Supreme Court corrected the mistake it had made in its failure to include an allowance for depreciation in *Smyth* v. *Ames*.[19] This correction was made in a case involving regulation of a public service company at the municipal level. The principle of *Smyth* v. *Ames*, it is to be noted, applied to public service companies generally, whether regulated at the local or federal level, and qualifications of the doctrine also were stated in cases involving regulation of public service enterprises other than those in the field of transportation.

An additional point to be made in conjunction with the *Smyth* v. *Ames* doctrine is that a "fair return" can be measured either in dollars or in percent. The *rate of return* is a quotient and is equal to the earnings in dollars divided by the rate base in dollars, or in terms of a verbal formula:

Rate of Return (R) =

$$\frac{\text{Net Earnings in Dollars (E)}}{\text{Rate Base in Dollars (B)}} = R = \frac{E}{B}$$

It is obvious from the foregoing that $B = E/R$, namely that the earnings in dollars divided by the rate of return produces the rate base. For this reason, any attempt to use *market value* as a rate base must involve circular reasoning, since market value is equal to the capitalized value of the earnings, or to the earnings in dollars divided by some rate of return. This point was recognized by the Court in 1913, when it remarked, "The value in use, *as measured by the return*, cannot be the criterion when the return itself is in question."[20]

"Fair Return on Fair Value" and Original Cost versus Reproduction Cost New. The question of whether the rate base should be taken as equal to the original cost plus improvements less depreciation or as equal to the reproduction cost new was once the subject of extended debate among economists specializing in Transportation and in Public Utility Economics. On the one hand, it is to be noted that the original cost concept favors the public service company owners in

---

[18] *Smyth* v. *Ames*, 169 U.S. 466 (1896), at pp. 546–547.

[19] *Knoxville* v. *Knoxville Water Co.*, 212 U.S. 1 (1909),

at p. 10.

[20] *Minnesota Rate Cases*, 230 U.S. 352 (1913), at p. 461. (Italics mine.)

times of deflation, while the reproduction cost new concept favors these investors in times of inflation. Moreover, to the extent that graft and overcapitalization resulted in inflated asset values in the case of railroads, the reproduction cost new formula operated to produce a lower rate base than would otherwise have been the case. Original cost may be easier to compute. The Supreme Court tended from the time of *Smyth* v. *Ames* to 1944 to emphasize that reproduction cost new must be taken into account by regulatory agencies in determining the rate base. One landmark case usually cited in this regard is the *Bluefield Waterworks* case, in which the Court remarked, among other things:

The record clearly shows that the Commission in arriving at its final figure did not accord proper weight, if any, to the greatly enhanced costs of construction in 1920 over those prevailing about 1915 and before the war, as established by uncontradicted evidence; and the company's detailed estimated cost of reproduction new, less depreciation, at 1920 prices appears to have been wholly disregarded. This was erroneous.[21]

The *Smyth* v. *Ames* doctrine provided a way for the courts to substitute their own judgments for those of regulatory commissions in ratemaking cases, just as the substantive due process concept served this same purpose in regard to legislative economic regulation until the *Nebbia* case. However, in 1942, the Court began to hold that a commission was not required to use any particular formula or combination of formulas in determining the rate base; and in 1944 it adopted what has been called a "credit standard" in deciding ratemaking cases. Thus in the 1942 case the Court said:

The Constitution does not bind ratemaking bodies to the service of any single formula or combination of formulas. Agencies to whom this legislative power has been given are free, within the ambit of their statutory authority, to make the pragmatic adjustments which may be called for by particular circumstances. Once a fair hearing has been given, proper findings made, the other statutory requirements satisfied, the courts cannot intervene in the absence of a clear showing that the limits of due process have been overstepped. If the Commission's order, as applied

to the facts before it and viewed in its entirety, produces no arbitrary result, our inquiry is at an end.[22]

The acute reader will have noted that in 1942 the position of the Court concerning the question of administrative superiority in regard to ratemaking was thus made consistent with its position concerning legislative superiority in regard to economic regulation laid down in the *Nebbia* case in 1934, as explained in Chapter 7. The one position was obviously the consequence of the other, and the two decisions represent examples of the extent to which the Court has abandoned the concept of "substantive" due process in regard to economic regulation generally.

The Credit Standard and the Hope Natural Gas Company Case. The *Hope Natural Gas Company* case of 1944 was a logical consequence of the decision in the *Natural Gas Pipeline Company* case of 1942 and of the abandonment by the Court of the substantive due process concept in regard to economic regulation generally in various cases following the *Nebbia* case of 1934. In the *Hope* case, the Hope Natural Gas Company contended that its rates should be set at a level to bring it a return of 8 percent on a reproduction cost rate base of $66 million. The Federal Power Commission allowed a return of 6.5 percent on an original cost rate base of $33 million Rates set at this level would allow the company to pay 8 percent on its common stock, and it was able to borrow by issuing bonds at 3 percent.

The Supreme Court upheld the Commission's decision. In doing so, it said in part:

From the investor or company point of view it is important that there be enough revenue not only for operating expenses but also for the capital costs of the business. These include service on the debt and dividends on the stock. . . . By that standard the return to the equity owners should be commensurate with returns on investments in other enterprises having corresponding risks. That return, moreover, should be sufficient to assure confidence in the financial integrity of the enterprise, so as to maintain its credit and to attract capital.[23]

[21] *Bluefield Waterworks and Improvement Co.* v. *Public Service Commission of West Virginia*, 262 U.S. 678 (1923), at p. 689.
[22] *Federal Power Commission* v. *Natural Gas Pipeline*

Company, 315 U.S. 575 (1942), at p. 586.
[23] *Federal Power Commission* v. *Hope Natural Gas Company*, 320 U.S. 591 (1944), at p. 603.

Precisely how the appropriate rate of return is to be determined was not specified by the Court in the *Hope* case, but the case does stand for the proposition that the Court has committed matters of ratemaking far more to the discretion of administrative commissions than was the case prior to 1944. Moreover, attention has now shifted from the problem of the *rate base* to that of the *rate of return*. Instead of being bound by some precise formula to determine the rate base, administrative commissions are now free to adopt a trial and error method of self-correcting value judgments and thus to arrive at a rate of return whose consequence is the development of the service industry in question consistently with the public interest. In short, the effect of the *Hope* case has been to permit administrative agencies to utilize their special experience and competence more freely than was true prior to 1944.

Table 24-3 contains information pertaining to the actual rates of return experienced by the various modes of transportation from 1957 to 1966. These rates of return to stockholders were computed after charging the interest paid to bondholders as an item of expense.

Moreover, the rates of return in *Table 24-3* are rates of return to the carriers *as a whole* and not to any individual carrier; some individual carriers may have ex-

perienced higher rates of return, and others lower rates of return.

The reader may recall that Section 15 of the Transportation Act of 1920 dealt with ratemaking and provided that, subject to certain conditions, rates should be fixed at a level which would provide a fair return upon the "agregate value" of the property devoted to transportation service. This rule applied to the railroads *as a whole* and did not create any rights applicable to any individual carrier, but the source of the "fair return" language was obviously *Smyth* v. *Ames*, which did involve an individual carrier.

Some writers have adopted a "cost of capital" concept in discussing the problem of the rate level. The "cost of capital" may be defined as the weighted average cost of all the capital counted in the rate base. For example, assume that a company has outstanding $400,000 worth of bonds carrying a 5 percent interest charge and $100,000 par value of 6 percent preferred stock. Also assume that it has $500,000 worth (par value) of common stock outstanding. If we now further assume that common stock of *comparable* enterprises is making a 15 percent return, we can compute the cost of capital by multiplying each rate of return (the interest rate in the case of the bonds) by the proportion which that particular security represents of the total value of the capital

Table 24-3

Rates of Return, Various Modes of Transportation, 1957–1966

		Ratio of Net Income to Shareholders' and Proprietors' Equity			
Year	Class I Railroads	Motor Carriers of Property	Carriers by Inland and Costal Waterways	Maritime Carriers	Oil Pipeline Companies
1957	4.31	9.12	8.68	7.55	16.27
1958	3.51	6.64	6.21	3.67	16.30
1959	3.34	6.86	5.38	5.53	17.62
1960	2.57	6.18	5.73	1.74	15.71
1961	2.21	7.72	6.14	2.44	16.27
1962	3.25	8.58	7.65	6.24	17.57
1963	3.65	12.61	9.47	5.18	15.96
1964	3.96	13.76	13.40	7.21	15.97
1965	4.59	14.48	11.92	7.81	16.25
1966	4.97	17.09	12.45	8.38	16.50

Source: Compiled from *Annual Report of the Interstate Commerce Commission for 1967* (Washington, D.C.: U.S. Government Printing Office, 1968), Appendix G.

and summing the resulting products. That is, we have:

	Par Value	Proportion of Total	Rate of Return
Bonds	$400,000	0.4	5
Preferred stock	$100,000	0.1	6
Common stock	$500,000	0.5	15

Therefore, the cost of capital is equal to $(.4)(5) + (.1)(6) + (.5)(.5) = 10.1$ percent. If the company earns 10.1 percent on its capital of $1 million, it will earn $101,000, which is just exactly what is needed to pay each type of security at a rate equal to the relevant one listed above. But especially to be noted is the fact that the rate of return on common stock *has been arbitrarily assumed* and is not a matter of contract. It is usually determined subjectively by taking it as equal to the analogous return in "comparable industries."

In our example, an overall return of 10.1 percent will pay off the existing security holders at the rates assumed, but does *not* guarantee that *future* investors will be satisfied with equal rates of return. There is no magic formula by which the "proper" rate to satisfy the credit standard can be determined. What, for example, is the definition of a "comparable industry"? Ratemaking, as we have seen in one of the ercerpts from the report of the Hearing Examiner, is a problem of *judging* and *deciding*. The *general* problems faced in determining transportation rates exist also in determining natural gas rates and telephone rates, as we will see in later chapters.

The Special Case of Oil Pipeline Rates. Crude oil and products pipelines are overwhelmingly owned and controlled by major oil companies. In 1959, for example, "seventy-five percent of the pipeline facilities in the United States were operated by 89 pipeline companies." These 89 companies were, in turn, owned by 20 major oil companies.[24] Railroad rates for hauling crude oil are about five times the pipeline rates over comparable distances, since pipeline costs are low relative to those of railroads. No rate cases involving crude oil pipelines were instituted before the Interstate Commerce Commission in either 1966 or 1967. Indeed, from the time of the enactment of the Hepburn Act to 1959, only six rate cases involving pipelines had been decided by the Commission. The Commission has attributed the lack of complaints to the fact that the major oil companies are both the owners of the oil and of the pipelines in which it is transported,[25] and control over the cheapest means of transportation has been alleged by some to be a device utilized by the major oil producers to control the oil production industry.[26] In any case, the Commission is able to exercise few of the types of powers it has over the railroads and motor carriers in pipeline cases, in many instances because statutory authority to do so is lacking. That is, the Commission has no control over consolidations or mergers of pipeline companies, and the "commodities clause" does not apply to pipelines.

D. CONTROL OVER LONG-RUN SUPPLY

The Interstate Commerce Commission exercises control over long-run supply of most domestic surface transportation services through its control over entry into and exit from the industry. This control may take any one of a number of different forms. These forms will now be discussed.[27]

New Construction of Railroads and Motor Carrier Operations

In fiscal year 1967, the Commission authorized the construction of two small railroads involving a total of only 113 miles of track; it was concerned with a much greater volume of activity in the field of motor carrier operations, including the authorization of irregular route motor carriers to convert their service to regular route service and the processing of 13 applications under the "grandfather" clause made by motor carriers in Alaska and

---

[24] *Consent Decree Program of the Department of Justice* (Report of the House Antitrust Subcommittee, 86th Cong., 1st sess.) (Washington, D.C.: U.S. Government Printing Office, 1959), p. 122.

[25] *Ibid.*, p. 247.

[26] *Ibid.*, pp. 124 ff.

[27] This subdivision makes extensive use of data found in the *Annual Report of the Interstate Commerce Commission for 1967, op. cit.* Individual footnotes will not be used.

Hawaii. The new railroads, on the other hand, were intended primarily to service particular industrial areas.

Abandonments, Discontinuances, and Revocations

In fiscal year 1967, the Commission instituted 32 actions to revoke the permits of dormant water carriers and actually revoked 27 such permits. During the same period, it also received applications for discontinuance of 153 passenger trains, and permitted actual discontinuance of 36 passenger trains. Railroad abandonments involved short segments of trackage. An example of this is the approval of an application by the Chicago, Rock Island and Pacific Railway Company to abandon 87 miles of railroad line between Horton, Kansas, and Beatrice, Missouri. *Table 24-4* provides information concerning issuance of certificates of convenience and necessity for construction, abandonment, acquisition, and operation of lines of railroad from July 1, 1965 to June 30, 1967.

Consolidations and Mergers

Motor Carriers. In fiscal year 1967, the Commission received a total of 345 motor carrier applications involving purchase, control, and merger activities, and decided 313 of these cases. Concentration of control in this area of transportation service has increased markedly since 1957. In that year, only 0.97 percent of all the motor carriers had revenues exceeding $10 million, but by 1965 the figure had reached 2.46 percent; and in 1957, 31.22 percent of the carriers had revenues of less than $25,000, but in 1965 the percentage figure had fallen to 24.13 percent.

An example of a case in which the Commission approved the acquisition of several smaller buslines by a major busline is that of *Transcontinental Bus System—Control —Virginia Stage Lines.*[28] In this case, the Commission permitted Transcontinental Bus Systems, Inc. to acquire control of several eastern buslines in the Trailways system. Although the merger was hotly contested, the Commission found that the

Table 24-4

Certificates of Convenience and Necessity Issued for Abandonment, Construction, Acquisition, and Operation of Lines of Railroad under Sec. 1(18) of the Interstate Commerce Act, as Amended

	July 1, 1965 through June 30, 1966		July 1, 1965 through June 30, 1967	
	Applications	Miles	Applications	Miles
I. Abandonment applications filed	106	1,920.1	72	860.0
Certificates of abandonment:				
Granted	92	1,054.4	85	817.3
Denied	5	334.0	7	95.5
Dismissed	8	357.6	6	194.9
Abandonments permitted since effective date of act		52,777.9		52,595.2
II. Construction applications filed	20	166.0	15	142.1
Granted	15	127.4	20	201.6
Denied	1	14.8		
Dismissed	4	49.7	1	6.0
III. Acquisition and operation applications filed	10	111.6	13	202.6
Granted	9	63.3	5	42.8
Denied	2	62.5		
Dismissed	3	37.7	4	117.2

Source: Annual Report of the Interstate Commerce Commission for 1967 (Washington, D.C.: U.S. Government Printing Office, 1968), p. 106.

[28] 101 M.C.C. 529 (1967).

centralized control established by the merger would not eliminate competition but would "permit the establishment of an improved service for the travelling public."

It has been noted earlier that the Transportation Act of 1920 authorized the Commission to make plans to consolidate the railroads into a limited number of systems but provided no authority to carry out such plans and that the Act of 1940 authorized the Commission to approve plans for consolidations of common carriers proposed *by the carriers themselves*. The first case to arise under this provision was the *McLean Trucking Company* case of 1944. In this case, the Commission authorized the merger of the seven largest motor carriers into one large company, and the Supreme Court upheld the merger.[29] In doing so, the Court remarked that although competition was a value to be considered in merger cases under the Transportation Act of 1940, this value "is significant chiefly as it aids in the attainment of the national transportation policy." In this case, the Commission found that competition after the merger would be "ample" in the area being served and that "shipment of freight would be simplified and expedited, equipment would be utilized more efficiently, terminal facilities improved, handling of shipments reduced, relations with shippers and regulatory bodies simplified, safe operations promoted, and substantial economies achieved." This list of items provides some indication of the criteria which must be met by a proposed merger in the motor carrier industry.

Rail Mergers. The relatively low level of earnings of the railroads as a whole is clearly apparent in *Table 24–3*. The solution to this problem currently being advanced by the railroads themselves is that of merger and consolidation of railroad systems. A number of major mergers occurred in the late 1960s and others were pending. *Table 24–5* contains a summary of the principal merger and consolidation applications pending before the Commission as of June 30, 1968. Some of these mergers were substantially completed by June 30, 1968, most notably that of the Pennsylvania and New York Central railroads. Upon com-

pletion, the new merged company, the Pennsylvania–New York Central Transportation Company, became the nation's largest railroad measured either by mileage operated, revenues, or traffic. The approval of the Penn–Central merger was originally given by the Commission in 1966; at about the same time, the Commission denied an application for merger of the Great Northern Railway Company, the Northern Pacific Railway Company, the Chicago, Burlington and Seattle Railway Company, the Pacific Coast Railroad Company, and the Spokane, Portland and Quincy Railroad Company into a new company on grounds that the merger would present disadvantages outweighing the benefits to the carriers of the merger. Approval of mergers is thus not automatic.

In evaluating mergers, the Commission has in the past taken specific account of the effect of the merger on a number of other interests including: (1) effect on the public; (2) effect on other lines; (3) effect on railroad employees; (4) effect on railroad investors; and (5) effect on competition with other modes of transportation. The nature of the standards imposed by the relevant statute and the manner in which the Commission met these standards was discussed at length in the Supreme Court opinion upholding the validity of the Penn–Central merger in 1968. Among other things, the Court said:

With respect to the merits of the merger . . . our task is limited. We do not inquire whether the merger satisfies our own conception of the public interest. Determination of the factors relevant to the public interest is entrusted by the law primarily to the governing commission, subject to the standards of the governing statute. The judicial task is to determine whether the Commission has proceeded in accordance with law and whether its findings and conclusions accord with the statutory standards and are supported by substantial evidence. . . .

Section 5 of the Interstate Commerce Act, as amended by the Transportation Act of 1940, 54 Stat. 905, 49 U.S.C. S 5, sets forth the national transportation policy that is to guide the Commission in its scrutiny of mergers proposed by railroads. The Commission is to approve such proposals, pursuant to the terms of S 5(2)(b) of the Act, when they are made upon just and

---

[29] A more detailed discussion of this case appears in Chapter 22 under the heading "*Situations in Which*

an Exemption Exists and Agency Approval Has Been Given."

Table 24-5

Major Applications Pending for Unification of Railroads, June 30, 1968

Finance Docket Number	Nature of Transaction
21478	Consolidation of the Great Northern Pacific Ry. Co., Chicago, Burlington & Quincy RR. Co., and Pacific Coast RR. Co., into Great Northern Pacific & Burlington Lines, Inc., and lease by that company of Spokane, Portland & Seattle Ry. Co. Pending judicial review.
21989	Merger of New York Central RR. Co., into Pennsylvania RR. Co.—New Haven reorganization aspect.
22688	Chicago & North Western control—Chicago, Rock Island & Pacific.
23178	Acquisition by Chesapeake & Ohio Ry. Co. and Baltimore & Ohio RR. Co. of control of Western Maryland Ry. Co.
23285	Merger of Chicago, Rock Island & Pacific RR. Co., into Union Pacific RR Co.
23595	Purchase (portion) of Chicago, Rock Island & Pacific Co., by Southern Pacific Co.
23832	Merger of Chesapeake & Ohio Ry. Co. into Norfolk & Western Co.
23919	Purchase (portion) of Chicago, Rock Island & Pacific RR. Co. by Atchison, Topeka & Santa Fe Ry. Co.
24182	Consolidation of Chicago & North Western Ry. Co. and Chicago, Milwaukee, St. Paul & Pacific RR. Co. into Chicago, Milwaukee & North Western Transportation Co.
24785	Kansas City Southern Ry. Co. (control)—Joplin Union Depot Co.
24880	Seaboard Coast Line RR Co.—(merger)—Piedmont & Northern Ry. Co.
24907	Illinois Central RR Co. (control)—Waterloo RR Co.
25031	Louisville & Nashville RR. Co.–Chicago & Eastern Illinois RR. Co. (purchase-portion).
25070	St. Louis–San Francisco Ry. Co.–Birmingham Belt Railroad Co.—Merger.
25103	Illinois Central Gulf RR.—Acquisition of Gulf Mobile & Ohio RR. Co. and Illinois Central RR. Co.
24178	Control of Atchison, Topeka & Santa Fe Ry. Co. by Mississippi River Corp. and Missouri Pacific RR. Co. Application dismissed at request of applicants.

Source: Reproduced from *Annual Report of the Interstate Commerce Commission for 1968* (Washington, D.C.: U.S. Government Printing Office, 1969), p. 64.

reasonable terms and are "consistent with the public interest." In reaching its decision, the Commission is to give weight to a number of factors, such as: "(1) The effect of the proposed transaction upon adequate transportation service to the public; (2) the effect upon the public interest of the inclusion, or failure to include, other railroads in the territory involved in the proposed transaction; (3) the total fixed charges resulting from the proposed transaction; and (4) the interest of the carrier employees affected." 49 U.S.C. S 5(2)(c).

Examination of the record and findings in the present case satisfies us . . . that the Commission has properly and lawfully discharged its duties with respect to the merits of the merger. . . .

The Commission has carefully considered the implications of the fact that the Pennsylvania and New York Central, as individual systems, operated at a profit, and that there are reasonably good prospects for a continuation of such operation. But it was impressed by the fact that, as individual systems, these profits are not sufficient to put the roads in a position to make

improvements important to the national interest, including the maintenance of services which, although essential to the public, are not self-supporting, and furnishing assistance to other roads serving public needs in their general territory. The Commission emphasized that the merger would enable the unified company to "accelerate investments in plant and equipment . . . and provide more and better service." 327 I.C.C. 475, 501–502. And it pointed out that only by permitting the merger would it be possible for the Commission to compel Penn–Central to come to the rescue of New Haven. . . .

With respect to the lessening of competition where it now exists between the roads to be merged, the Commission pointed out that it will retain continuing power over reductions of services and facilities which are not specifically approved in the merger plans. Such consolidations and abandonments will have to be presented to the Commission for its approval and may be subjected to public criticism and hearings and to conditions or disapproval. It also noted that the rail service by the merged company will remain subject to vigorous competition from other roads, including the N and W and the C and O–B and O systems, and from motor, water, and air carriers. The Commission summarized some of the factors which would act as a restraint upon the merged company as follows:

"The power of shippers to direct the routing, the availability of numerous routes in a dense network of the interline routes, the influence of connecting carriers in preventing a deterioration in service on the joint routes in which they participate, the growing strength of the N and W and C and O–B and O systems, all stand to provide a check against any abuse of economic power by the merged applicants." 327 I.C.C. at 514.

Considering the record, and the findings and analysis of the Commission, we see no basis for reversal of the District Court's decision that the Commission's "public interest" conclusions are adequately supported and are in accordance with law.[30]

In June 1970 the merged Penn–Central Company filed a petition in bankruptcy, casting some doubt on the Commission's judgment in approving this merger.

The Department of Justice supported the Penn–Central merger. In 1965, however, the Antitrust Division had challenged the Commission's approval of a merger involving the Seaboard Air Line Railroad. In upholding the Commission's action in the *Seaboard* case, the Supreme Court had foreshadowed its holding in the *Penn–Central* case. The present era thus seems to be one in which mergers of large railroads has become the policy tool to be used in solving the railroad problem of low earnings on the part of some weak railroads. Indeed, in its *Annual Report for Fiscal Year 1968* (distributed in 1969), the Commission remarked:

Generally supported by the railroads, the concept of common ownership seems to be gaining a limited degree of favor among some members of other modes of transport.[31]

Diversification of investments seems also to be one current trend.

Diversification

Under Sections 20(a) and 214 of the Interstate Commerce Act, the Commission may authorize carriers to issue securities "which contribute to a soundly capitalized transportation industry, capable of adequate service at reasonable rates." Nothing in the statute, however, prevents a carrier from acquiring a noncarrier operation if the acquisition is made without the issuance of securities. Thus in 1966 the Pennsylvania Railroad Company acquired a west coast realty concern, and the New York Central Railroad acquired a manufacturer of van trailers. The reverse of this action arose in 1966 as a result of an application to the Commission by Pepsi Co., Inc. to acquire North American Van Lines, Inc. through an exchange of stock. However, an attempt by Greyhound, Inc. to acquire stock of Railway Express Agency, Inc. which had been approved by the Commission was frustrated when the Supreme Court overturned the Commission's approval on grounds that it had been given without holding a hearing and that the acquisition violated Section 7 of the Clayton Act. Attempts by railroad companies to diversify are thus subject to Section 7 of the Clayton Act and particularly, it would seem, to precedents set in cases involving conglomerate mergers under Section 7.

Concluding Remarks

The Interstate Commerce Commission is the oldest of the federal regulatory agencies; its powers have been expanded as a result of the interaction of court decisions and legislation enacted in response to recommendations made by the Commission (primarily in its *Annual Reports*) on the basis of its experience in dealing with specific regulatory problems. Moreover, both the organization and the operation of the Commission have provided models for the establishment of other regulatory agencies. Nowhere is this point more emphatically made than in the *Annual Report of the Civil Aeronautics Board for 1968*, issued upon the Board's Thirtieth Anniversary. The report contains the following statement:

. . . Of course the [Civil Aeronautics] act of 1938 was far more advanced than the industry it was designed to serve, since it was patterned on the regulatory provisions of the Interstate Commerce Act. Many provisions, in fact were

[30] *Penn–Central Merger and N and W Inclusion Cases*, 389 U.S. 486 (1968), at pp. 498–502.
[31] *Annual Report of the Interstate Commerce Commission*

for Fiscal Year 1968 (Washington, D.C.: U.S. Government Printing Office, 1969), p. 53.

taken over substantially verbatim. Thus the new statute was instantly supplied with the benefits of a half century of experience and refinement in the administrative regulation of large and significant transportation problems.[32]

But the transfer of benefits and of experience has not been a one-sided one. We have seen how the "fair return on fair value" concept developed in *Smyth* v. *Ames* was eventually replaced by the adoption of a credit standard in the *Hope Natural Gas Company* case. The broad general principles applicable to economic regulation which are not peculiar to the particular industry subject to regulation by a given agency have been developed by the courts not in cases involving actions of one regulatory agency alone but in various cases involving different agencies, both at the state and federal level.

As we have now seen, the Interstate Commerce Commission regulates domestic surface transportation activities; in the next chapter, we will consider the two agencies which regulate two modes of transportation not regulated by the Interstate Commerce Commission, namely, air and ocean transportation.

[32] *Annual Report of the Civil Aeronautics Board for 1968* (Washington, D.C.: U.S. Government Printing Office, December, 1968), p. 151.

Air and Ocean Transportation

This chapter is divided into two parts. The first major subdivision is concerned with a discussion of the economic regulation of both domestic and international air transportation by the Civil Aeronautics Board; the second is concerned with the economic regulation of ocean transportation by the Federal Maritime Board.

A. AIR TRANSPORTATION AND THE CIVIL AERONAUTICS BOARD

Legislation Prior to 1938

The first piece of legislation pertaining to regulation of civil aviation was the Air Commerce Act of 1926 (44 Stat. 568). This legislation imposed safety requirements but contained no provisions pertaining to economic regulation. Subsidization of domestic air carriers, it will be recalled from Chapter 8, was begun in 1925 and, as a practical matter, most airlines could, in this early period, be operated successfully only if they held air mail contracts. In this early period, there developed two general

types of air carriers: air mail contractors who flew regular established routes, hauling mail, persons, and property; and a group of "fixed base operators" who operated airports, flying schools, crop-dusting services, etc., and who conducted business on a single contract per trip basis.[1]

Further legislation in 1934 and 1935 pertaining to air mail rates gave certain regulatory powers to the Post Office Department and to the Interstate Commerce Commission. In addition, legislation enacted in 1934 created a Federal Aviation Commission to study the problem of regulation of air transportation and make recommendations to Congress.

The Civil Aeronautics Act of 1938 (52 Stat. 973)

The Federal Aviation Commission made its report and recommendations to Congress in 1935, and the Act of 1938 eventually was adopted. This Act created the Civil Aeronautics Authority as an independent regulatory agency. Within the Authority, two additional bodies were

---

[1] This subdivision rests, in part, on an informational memorandum distributed by the Civil Aeronautics Board to new employees to acquaint them with the functions and operations of the Board. The title of the memorandum (lithographed) is "Synopsis of Purposes and Provisions of the Federal Aviation Act in Relation to the Civil Aeronautics Board," revised, October 15, 1967. I am indebted to Mr. James F. Buske, Jr. for assistance in obtaining some of the material on which this chapter is based.

created. One of these, known as the Administrator, was to exercise promotional and developmental functions; the other, known as the Air Safety Board, performed functions pertaining to safety and accident prevention. The Act contained various provisions for economic regulation, including provisions for awarding certificates of convenience and necessity, subject to a "grandfather" clause (explained in Chapter 24), provisions for subsidy assistance, and power of control over rates. The original airmail carriers were awarded "grandfather" certificates and eventually became our contemporary trunk line airlines. The early fixed-base operators did not at first receive such certificates but were awarded exemptions; eventually, however, following action by Congress in 1962, they were awarded certificates of convenience and necessity and have evolved into the "air taxi" industry. The Authority itself, a five-member Board, exercised both judicial and legislative functions relative to awarding of routes and ratemaking.

The Reorganization Plan of 1940 (54 Stat. 1231)

In 1940, the agency was reorganized by Reorganization Plans III and IV. The Air Safety Board was abolished and its functions were transferred to the Authority, whose name was now changed to the Civil Aeronautics Board. The Administrator, whose organization eventually became the Federal Aviation Agency, was transferred to the Department of Commerce for administrative purposes only. The Board was also transferred to that Department for "housekeeping" purposes only; that is, it had independent agency status in regard to substantive matters.

The Federal Aviation Act of 1958 (72 Stat. 731)

The Act of 1958 left the provisions pertaining to economic regulation virtually untouched but transferred the Board's safety rulemaking powers to the Administrator and authorized the Administrator to revoke or suspend safety certificates subject to a right of appeal to the Board. Thus the effect of this Act was to separate the function of economic regulation further from the safety function.

The Department of Transportation Act of 1966 (80 Stat. 931)

This Act transferred the Federal Aviation Agency and its functions to the new Department of Transportation. The Act also transferred the accident-investigating functions to the National Transportation Safety Board of the new Department. Thus, today, the Civil Aeronautics Board has economic regulatory functions only. A virtually complete separation of the safety and economic regulatory functions has now been achieved.

Organization and Operations of the Civil Aeronautics Board

The Civil Aeronautics Board consists of the Board and its operating units. In general, the functions of the Board include: (1) granting, modifying, and withdrawing operating authority; (2) control over abandonment of services; (3) control over foreign operations of United States carriers subject to Presidential approval; (4) control over mergers and interlocking relationships; (5) control over rates; and (6) control over foreign companies operating in the United States. In the following paragraphs, we will examine these powers and duties more closely.

The Congressional Declaration of Policy in the Civil Aeronautics Act of 1958

Section 102 of the Civil Aeronautics Act of 1958 contains the following Congressional declaration of policy:

In the exercise and performance of its powers and duties under this Act, the Board shall consider the following, among other things, as being in the public interest, and in accordance with the public convenience and necessity:

(a) The encouragement and development of an air-transportation system properly adapted to the present and future needs of the foreign and domestic commerce of the United States, of the Postal Service, and of the national defense;

(b) The regulation of air transportation in such manner as to recognize and preserve the inherent advantages of, assure the highest degree of safety in, and foster sound economic conditions in, such transportation, and to improve the relations between, and coordinate transportation by, air carriers;

(c) The promotion of adequate, economical, and efficient service by air carriers at reasonable charges, without unjust discrimination, undue preferences or advantages, or unfair or destructive competitive practices;

(d) Competition to the extent necessary to assure the sound development of an air-transportation system properly adapted to the needs of the foreign and domestic commerce of the United States, of the Postal Service, and of the national defense;

(e) The promotion of safety in air commerce; and

(f) The promotion, encouragement, and development of civil aeronautics.

The Civil Aeronautics Board has interpreted subparagraph (a) in the preceding quotation to mean that the Board has the function of promoting the airline industry. Thus, the Chairman of the Board said in 1967:

I wish to emphasize the fact that we are charged with responsibility to promote as well as regulate transportation. We regard the promotional aspects of our work as very important. I would also note that the Act directs us to encourage competition to the extent necessary to assure the sound development of air transportation. This, too, is very important. The nature of the airline business is such that it is frequently possible to achieve the promotional and regulatory aims of the Act by authorizing competitive services. Generally, we would regard this as preferable to the use of mandatory processes.[2]

The emphasis upon competition in the Chairman's statement should be particularly noted by the reader.

Certificates of Public Convenience and Necessity: Control over Supply

Section 401 of Title IV of the Act prohibits carriers from operating without Board authorization, outlines standards and procedures for obtaining certificates, states duties of certified carriers, and establishes methods of revocation, suspension, and modification of such certificates. The Board requires a showing of ability to finance, inaugurate, and operate a service as a condition of issuance of a certificate. In cases of international operations of United States carriers or of operations in the United States of foreign carriers, the issuance of a certificate is conditioned upon the President's approval. The Board has the power to impose conditions upon the issuance of a certificate and makes use of this power by specifying service conditions, type of equipment, use of airports, and so on.

A total of 57 air carriers was certified as of 1968. This number included 11 domestic trunk line carriers (three of these also had international routes), two United States flag carriers flying international routes, 13 local service carriers serving medium and small cities, 13 supplemental carriers providing both domestic and international service (supplemental carriers were once known as unscheduled carriers), three "all cargo" carriers of which two had international routes, seven Alaskan carriers, two having routes between Alaska and the 48 continental states, one certified Caribbean carrier, three helicopter carriers, and a few firms whose operations were suspended in 1968.[3]

Certificates are issued after a public hearing; sometimes carriers, whose interests may be adversely affected, oppose the issuance of a certificate. The initial decision of the Hearing Examiner is subject to Board review. Most applications for certificates come from existing carriers seeking to change their existing routes. The Board has considered the effect on subsidy payments in recent proceedings involving local service carriers, as well as improvements in service factors. In the case of trunk line carriers, the effect on competition (increased competition being considered a favorable factor) has been taken into account. Another exceedingly important factor has been the effect on existing and potential airport congestion. The use of vertical take-off and short-landing equipment has been favored. Thus one proceeding in 1968, *Service to White Plains, New York*, involved new route segments from White Plains to Chicago, Cincinnati, Cleveland, Pittsburgh, and St. Louis; and it was hoped that the decision would have the effect of relieving the three major New York airports of some congestion.[4] The power of the Board respecting certification is broad: it may alter, modify, or suspend certificates at any time in whole or in part—if the public convenience and necessity so require. As a practical matter, however, the Board has itself taken the position that it will not use this broad power in such a way as to

[2] *The Civil Aeronautics Board Promotes and Regulates the Airline Industry* (Washington, D.C.: Civil Aeronautics Board, 1968), p. iii.

[3] *Ibid.*, pp. iii–iv.

produce "a basic alteration in the character of a carrier's system." But it is clear that the certification power possessed and used by the Board lends itself to a more effective employment than does the certification power in the case of other types of transportation services. Yet, there have been few Supreme Court decisions in the last ten or 15 years involving the use of this power. Perhaps the explanation lies in the fact that the broad power possessed by the Board has been utilized in an environment which includes promotion of the industry as a basic objective.

It has been noted that permits involving international operations of United States carriers require Presidential approval. An example is provided in a Press Release issued by the Board in December, 1968. The item reads as follows:

FOR RELEASE
CAB 68–143   IMMEDIATE
382–6031   DECEMBER 19, 1968

The Civil Aeronautics Board's decision in the *Bermuda Service Investigation* has been approved by President Lyndon B. Johnson.

The Board awarded:

(1) Northeast Airlines, Inc., a route between Boston, Mass., and Hamilton, Bermuda on a subsidy-ineligible basis. Northeast becomes the second nonstop United Carrier between Boston and Bermuda, the other carrier being Pan American World Airways.

(2) Eastern the first United States route between the coterminals Chicago, Illinois and Detroit, Michigan and the terminal point, Hamilton, Bermuda. At the same time the carrier's terminal points New York City and Washington, D.C. are redesignated as New York/Newark and Washington/Baltimore. The CAB thus made permanent Eastern's temporary authority to provide Bermuda service from Baltimore's Friendship Airport, in addition to Eastern's authority to provide Bermuda service through Dulles International Airport.

The CAB also amended the certificate of Pan American by redesignating the coterminal point New York, N.Y. as New York/Newark, and deleting the carrier's authority to serve Baltimore, Md., Norfolk, Va., or Charleston, S.C., as a coterminal point instead of New York or Boston when weather conditions render it necessary.

4 *Annual Report of the Civil Aeronautics Board*, 1968 (Washington, D.C.: U.S. Government Printing Office, 1968), pp. 9–15.
5 For a useful discussion of various economic and legal problems involving international aviation, see

The System of Bilateral International Air Route Agreements

Until 1940, the United States had negotiated bilateral agreements involving reciprocal operating rights for aircraft with only eight countries. An attempt to deal with the problem on a multilateral basis by establishment of an international organization in 1944 failed.[5] Thereupon the United States and Great Britain negotiated a bilateral agreement known as the Bermuda Agreement. This agreement has served as a model for all subsequent United States bilateral agreements; in 1968, the United States had 51 such agreements in force. The Board participates in the negotiation of such agreements by the Department of State. In general, these agreements provide for an exchange of air routes and that each country is to designate the carriers from that country to serve such routes. The carriers so-designated must then obtain operating permits from the relevant domestic regulatory authority of the country in which the operation is to be conducted. In the case of the United States, such permits are issued in adversary proceedings, but the Board gives great weight to the existence of a bilateral agreement, and there are no instances on record in which the Board has ever declined to issue a certificate of convenience and necessity or permit in a case in which a bilateral agreement has existed. In some cases, the Board has also issued permits to foreign carriers even though no bilateral agreement has existed, giving much weight in such cases to considerations of reciprocity with respect to United States carriers by the other country. In June 1968, 20 United States carriers were engaged in foreign operations, and served 167 points in 119 foreign countries, while 47 foreign carriers served 120 points in the United States.[6]

The Problem of Ratemaking

Sections 403–406 and Section 1002 of the Act are concerned with the Board's ratemaking powers. The rule of ratemaking reads as follows:

Charles M. Sackrey, "Overcapacity in the United States International Air Transport Industry," 32 *Journal of Air Law and Commerce* 1 (1966).
6 *Annual Report of the Civil Aeronautics Board for 1968, op. cit.*, pp. 30–39.

In exercising and performing its powers and duties with respect to the determination of rates for the carriage of persons or property, the Authority [Board] shall take into consideration among other factors—(1) the effect of such rates upon the movement of traffic; (2) the need in the public interest of adequate and efficient transportation of persons and property by air carriers at the lowest possible cost consistent with the furnishing of such service; (3) such standards respecting the character and quality of service rendered by air carriers as may be prescribed by or pursuant to law; (4) the inherent advantages of transportation by aircraft; and (5) the need of each carrier for revenue sufficient to enable such carrier, under honest, economical, and efficient management to provide adequate and efficient air carrier service.

The Board has power to fix rates for *domestic* service and prescribe maximum and minimum rates in *overseas* service. Rates must be "just and reasonable," and must be filed with the Board. "Unjust" discrimination and preferences are also prohibited. (The influence of the earlier Interstate Commerce Act is clearly evident in these provisions.)

The Rate Structure Problem. No final action pertaining to rate structures has ever been taken by the Board. However, a staff report, *A Study of Domestic Passenger Air Fare Structure,* was completed in 1968 and further studies were planned from which the Board hoped it might be able to produce policy directives in the future.[7]

Airmail Rates and Subsidization

The 1938 Act continued the policy of subsidization of air transportation by means of payments for transportation of airmail which had begun in 1925. Under the 1938 Act, the Postmaster General paid the total compensation on the basis of rates fixed by the Board. In 1953, however, the Board undertook to divide this compensation into two types: (1) a payment by the Postmaster General for the carriage of mail, known as a *service rate* based on cost of service; and (2) a subsidy equal to the difference between cost of service and the operating requirement, including a fair return on the investment, disbursed by the Board.

The trend of subsidy payments is today downward. In 1939, 16 trunk line carriers received subsidies amounting to about $12 million, or 70 percent of the total. In 1968, however, none of the 11 domestic trunk lines received any subsidy payments; a sum of about $13 million per year was being paid to local service carriers. The class rate technique (under which all carriers of a given class receive the same rate) has been employed since 1961, although prior to that time the rate was computed on an individual carrier basis. The 1968 subsidy estimate was $59.3 million, the lowest total dollar amount in nine years.[8]

The Board has followed a policy of reducing subsidies where possible by a judicious granting of operating rights. That is, in 1968:

The CAB allowed local service carriers more liberal operating authority and access to higher density markets on a subsidy-ineligible basis to improve route structure service and stimulate higher earnings.[9]

Thus, for example, in February 1969, the Board approved a request by Mohawk Airlines (a local service carrier) to amend its certificate to permit nonstop service between Albany and Buffalo, N. Y., on a subsidy-ineligible basis. The Board remarked, in part, ". . . Mohawk's operations . . . hold promise of achieving a subsidy need reduction." (CAB 682–6031)

In 1967, for the first time, an airmail rate proceeding was conducted on a formal hearing basis in the *Domestic Service Mail Rate Investigation.* This proceeding affected 22 airlines and resulted in a retroactive rate reduction.[10]

The Problem of International Rates

The *Annual Report* of the Board for 1968 contains the following statement: "The United States has accepted, as a practical matter, the International Air Transport Association (IATA) as a vehicle to deal with rates and fares" in international air transportation with the provision that the government may act in cases of extreme unacceptability of proposed rates and fares. The IATA was established at a conference attended by representatives of 41 airlines in 1945. It is a *private* international business association which fixes fares and conditions of service in international trans-

---

[7] *Ibid.,* p. 49.
[8] *Ibid.,* p. 1.

[9] *Ibid.,* p. 179.
[10] *Ibid.,* p. 52.

portation. One of its by-laws provides that rate agreements must be approved by the relevant governmental agency exercising such authority in the case of each member company. In the case of United States companies, this provision means that they must have Board approval of any international rate agreements in which these companies participate. However, in 1963, when the Board refused to approve a rate fixed in this way, several European governments, most notably Great Britain, threatened to seize the United States companies' aircraft upon their landing in those countries if the companies did not raise rates in accordance with the IATA agreement; the Board then withdrew its disapproval and permitted the United States companies to charge the new higher rates.[11] Thus, "for all practical purposes," the IATA fixes rates for international transportation. However, in 1964 the Board did disapprove a prohibition by the IATA of inflight entertainment on international flights.[12] Thus sometimes the Board does have an effective voice in matters decided by IATA, and sometimes it does not.

The Problem of the Rate Level

In 1960, the Board adopted a credit standard (as explained in Chapter 24) for determining the rate of return in proceedings titled *General Passenger Fare Investigation*.[13] Both the outcome of this proceeding as well as the Board's policy since that time were described in the following language by the Chairman of the Board in 1967:

In a landmark case in 1960, the Board determined that the best measure for determining the reasonableness of general rate levels is the rate of return the air carriers earn on their total investment. The Board also determined in that case that for the domestic trunks a fair and reasonable return on investment was 10.5%, taking into account the relative risk and volatility of the industry and the return that would be required for it to attract needed capital. The Board also determined that this return should be allowed over an extended period of time.

This decision was academic in a sense for several years because the industry's earnings were far below 10.5%. However, in 1965, earnings

passed that bench mark. Thereupon the Board adopted a general policy against allowing further fare increases, and began to encourage the airlines to institute promotional fares designed with a twofold objective: (1) to provide better travel opportunities to the public; and (2) to make more efficient use of the industry's plant and equipment by filling up empty seats, leveling out peaks and valleys in traffic volume and the like. We had a good response from the industry. They do now have major promotional fares, including a youth fare providing a 50% discount on a space available basis, a Discover America excursion fare which (subject to some restrictions), provides a 25% discount for round-trip travel, and a family plan. The complexity of the fare structure is a cause of irritation and concern. But, frankly, I see no way to eliminate it except to do away with discount fares; and I believe that would be too high a price to pay for fare simplification. Let me say that I do not believe doing away with the discount fares would make it possible to lower basic fares.[14]

The reader will recall (from the explanation of the "cost of capital" approach in Chapter 24) that this method involves making an assumption or an independent finding of fact concerning the rate of return required to produce both debt and equity capital and stating the rate of return as the weighted average of these two. Thus the cost of capital method involves the statement of an end result but does *not* provide an *operational* method of finding the various rates of return which are used in computing the weighted average.

The use of promotional or discount fares to fill empty seats is the result of an attempt to cope with excess capacity generated by the introduction of larger and faster jet aircraft with capacity exceeding the volume of traffic generated at regular basic rates. One student of international air transportation has pointed out that the use of similar lower fares on international routes to overcome excess capacity has been frustrated by the attitude of some foreign companies in the IATA.[15]

Mergers, Acquisitions, and Interlocking Relationships

Section 408 of the Act requires the carriers to obtain prior Board approval for

[11] Sackrey, *op. cit.*, pp. 42–43.
[12] *Annual Report of the Civil Aeronautics Board for 1968, op. cit.*, p. 178.
[13] 32 CAB 291 (1960).

[14] *The Civil Aeronautics Board Promotes and Regulates the Airline Industry*, 1969, *op. cit.*, pp. vii–viii.
[15] Sackery, *op. cit.*

mergers and consolidations. The Board may approve such arrangements only if it finds that they are not adverse to the public interest and will not create a monopoly. Section 409 prohibits various types of interlocking relationships.

Between 1938 and 1968, 42 mergers and acquisitions occurred with Board approval. The Board held in 1940 that a merger would not be permitted if it gave the merged airline

> . . . the degree of control of air transportation, or some phase thereof, within a particular section of the country, necessary to constitute a monopoly therein.[16]

Thus the creation of monopoly power in *any one* market area alone is sufficient to condemn a merger.

Furthermore, both the size and the competitive position of the merged company are important considerations. For example, in disapproving a proposal by American Airlines to acquire Mid–Continent Airlines, the Board said:

> These underlying circumstances of size and competitive position are critical factors in measuring the application now before us against the standards of public interest set forth in section 2 of the Act, in particular, the injunctions to promote sound economic conditions in air transportation [subsection (b)] and to consider in the public interest competition to the extent necessary to assure the sound development of an air transportation system properly adapted to our needs [subsection (d)].
> . . . it is part of the generally accepted business concept of goodwill that the company serving the larger number of customers to their satisfaction will on that account enjoy a competitive advantage in soliciting patronage for additional service. It is only human nature to elect a service or commodity of known value rather than to risk a choice of the less familiar. In this respect American, through the mere volume and geographical scope of its operations, inevitably holds a position of some favor over its competitors of more limited operation. . . .
> . . . the wider the geographical scope of a carrier's operations in comparison with a particular rival, the greater the competitive advantage which it will enjoy through its control of traffic

originating at or destined to points to which the other carrier does not have access.[17]

Earlier, in 1940, the acquisition of Western A. E. by United Airlines had been disapproved on grounds that "to allow one air carrier to obtain control of air transportation in the west coast area greatly in excess of that possessed by competitors would . . . greatly endanger the development of a properly balanced . . . system in this area."[18]

In 1961, however, the Board approved the merger of United and Capital Airlines on grounds that Capital was a failing company (on the verge of bankruptcy) and would disappear if the merger was not allowed.[19]

At the same time, in order to restore competition in some markets in which competition would be eliminated as a result of the United–Capital merger, the Board required American Airlines and Northwest Airlines to provide competitive service.[20] In the following year (1962), the Board announced its intention to disapprove a proposed merger of Eastern and American Airlines, and the parties thereupon abandoned their proposal to merge.[21]

The number of mergers in 1967 and 1968 was greater than that in any prior year. The 1967 mergers involved companies which did not have competitive routes prior to the merger, and the 1968 mergers involved mainly local service companies and were justified by the Board on grounds that the mergers would result in a substantial reduction in subsidy payments to the companies involved.

On the whole, it seems clear that in its merger decisions, the Board has followed a policy of enforcing and maintaining competition. A reliance on competition to the extent that such a reliance is possible, given the restrictive statutory provisions subject to which it must operate, has also been a characteristic of the *recent* policies adopted by the Federal Maritime Commission; and it is to a discussion of the regulation of ocean transportation by this agency that we turn now.

---

[16] *United Airlines–Western Air Express, Interchange of Equipment*, ICAA 723 (1940), at p. 734.

[17] *American Airlines Inc., Acquisition of Control of Mid-Continent Airlines, Inc.*, 7 CAB 365 (1946), at pp. 378–379.

[18] *Acquisition of Western A.E. by United A.L.*, 1 CAA

739 (1940), at p. 750.

[19] *United–Capital Merger Case*, CAB Docket 11699 (1961).

[20] *Annual Report of the Civil Aeronautics Board for 1968, op. cit.*, pp. 108–109.

[21] *Ibid.*, p. 177.

B. OCEAN TRANSPORTATION AND THE FEDERAL MARITIME COMMISSION

The reader must be careful to distinguish between two federal agencies concerned with maritime problems. One of these agencies, the Federal Maritime *Commission*, performs economic regulatory functions and is an independent agency; the other, the Federal Maritime *Administration*, is concerned with the promotion and development of the merchant marine and is a part of the Department of Commerce. The difference between these two agencies was explained clearly in 1966 by the Chairman of the Federal Maritime Commission in testimony before a Congressional committee in these words:

Prior to 1961 both promotional and regulatory functions were vested in the Federal Maritime Commission of the Department of Commerce. As a result of Reorganization Plan No. 7, effective August 12, 1961, all regulatory functions were transferred to an independent agency, the Federal Maritime Commission; all promotional functions were retained in the Maritime Administration. Therefore, the Federal Maritime Commission has jurisdiction over rates and practices of foreign and American flag-carriers as well as terminal operators and freight forwarders in the foreign and domestic offshore commerce. The Maritime Administration has responsibility, under the Secretary of Commerce, for the determination and award of operating and construction subsidies, research and development programs affecting the size and character of our merchant marine, the requirements for appropriations to support subsidy and related programs, the operation of our maritime academies, and the implementation of promotional programs, such as the "ship American" program.[22]

Organization and Operation of the Federal Maritime Commission

The Federal Maritime Commission consists of the Commission and its operating subdivisions. The Commission performs regulatory functions under a number of different pieces of legislation discussed further below. In general, the Commission has the functions (1) of regulating services, practices, and agreements by common carriers by water engaged in the foreign commerce of the United States; (2) of accepting, rejecting, or disapproving rates filed by such carriers; (3) of regulating rates, fares, charges, classifications, tariffs, and practices of *domestic* carriers by water operating in the offshore trade of the United States; and (4) of investigating discriminatory rates, charges, classifications, and practices in the water-borne offshore foreign and domestic commerce of the United States. More specifically with regard to "practices," the Commission approves or disapproves agreements filed by the carriers, including conference (associations of carriers) agreements and intercorporate working agreements and reviews the operation of approved agreements for compliance with existing law.

Statutory Authority

The Act to Regulate Commerce of 1887. The original Act to Regulate Commerce gave the Interstate Commerce Commission jurisdiction over carriers engaged in transportation "partly by railroad and partly by water in cases in which both were used under a common control, management, or arrangement for continuous carriage or shipment." This provision did not give port-to-port jurisdiction, but limited the Commission's control to joint water and rail traffic.

The Panama Canal Act of 1912. This law provided that a railroad could own a water carrier only with Commission approval and that the Commission could regulate any water carrier owned by a railroad in the same way as it regulated the railroad itself.

Shipping Conferences and the Shipping Act of 1916, as Amended. A shipping conference is an association of ocean carriers whose principal purpose is to eliminate competition. In the words of the Joint Economic Committee in 1965:

Shipping conferences are associations organized by formal agreements to control trade routes. Their basic purpose is to set freight rates and sailing schedules. Conferences are fully developed price-fixing agreements. Some go beyond price-fixing and include pooling agreements whereby each member is guaranteed a share of cargoes or revenues. . . .

---

[22] *Establish a Department of Transportation* (Hearings before the Senate Committee on Operations, 89th

Cong., 2d sess.) (Washington, D.C.: U.S. Government Printing Office, 1966), p. 401.

More than 100 active steamship conferences, including 30 pool conferences control U.S. foreign trade routes. In all but seven conferences, U.S. flag lines are greatly outnumbered by foreign-flag lines. The predominance of foreign-flag lines and deficiencies of regulation by our Government have enabled foreign lines, some of which are government-owned, to determine freight rates, sailing schedules, and other conditions vital to the expansion of American commerce.[23]

The legislative history and policy adopted in the Shipping Act of 1916 were also summarized by the Joint Economic Committee as follows:

In 1916 Congress passed the Shipping Act following a classical investigation that turned up evidence of typical monopoly abuses in many areas, including domination of shippers through systems of exclusive patronage enforced by deferred rebates, the use of fighting ships against independent carriers, discriminatory rates, and the like. There is no doubt that all these devices were illegal under the antitrust laws, and the Supreme Court was in the very act of striking them down when the outbreak of war rendered the issue moot. In legislating, the Congress heard persuasive voices arguing that absolute freedom of competition was impracticable in ocean shipping. Whatever the current merits of this argument, Congress at that time accorded antitrust immunity to shipping combinations. But it was willing to do so only by bringing them under controls that would provide some of the benefits of free competition. Unregulated steamship monopolies were not regarded as compatible with the public interest.[24]

The Act of 1916 created the United States Shipping Board and gave it jurisdiction over ocean carriers and common carriers operating on the Great Lakes. Water carriers operating over other inland waterways, however, remained subject to Interstate Commerce Commission jurisdiction.

Section 14 of the Act of 1916, as amended, prohibits: (1) the payment of deferred rebates [a deferred return of a portion of the money paid for the service, the return being conditioned upon compliance by the shipper with certain conditions]; (2) the use of "fighting ships" [ships used to reduce or eliminate competition of another carrier]; (3) discriminatory contracts based on volume; and (4) refusals to deal on grounds that a shipper has patronized another carrier. Section 15 requires carriers to file with the Commission copies of agreements with any other carrier or person subject to the Act and provides the Commission with power to approve or disapprove such agreements.

The Amendments of 1961

Some significant amendments to the law were enacted in 1961. The nature of these amendments has been clearly described by the Joint Economic Committee as follows:

The 1961 amendments to the Shipping Act gave the Federal Maritime Commission broad authority over ocean freight rates. In the first place, all common carriers in the foreign trade of the United States, and all conferences in that trade, must now file and abide by their published rates. Until this amendment to the Shipping Act, the law did not clearly prevent charging rates different from the published tariff, which was not required by statute to be filed. The shipper might be obliged to prove unjust discrimination or actual loss of business to a competitor. Now the filed rates must be adhered to; nor may increases be made without 30 days' notice unless special permission is given for good cause. Reductions are permitted upon filing, and this possible deficiency is a question for the new agency's continuing study since the slowing down of ratecutting would tend to preserve the stability that has generally been regarded as a desirable end in the international transportation of commodities.

A second provision of the Shipping Act, as amended in 1961, lays down explicitly that conference agreements must, as a condition of approval, be in the public interest. The previous tests, whether the agreements are discriminatory, detrimental to commerce, or in violation of the law, remain in force, but the law is strengthened by the special inclusion of the public-interest standard.

A third new provision of the Shipping Act added in 1961 directs the Federal Maritime Commission to disapprove rates so high or so low as to be detrimental to U.S. commerce. This is the only provision dealing with the level of rates as such, and is perhaps the strongest provision of the Shipping Act.

The final new provision of the Shipping Act grants statutory confirmation to the dual-rate system, provided certain conditions intended to make such contracts equitable to shippers are

---

[23] *Discriminatory Ocean Freight Rates and the Balance of Payments* (Report of the Joint Economic Committee, 89th Cong., 1st sess.) (Washington, D.C.: U.S.

Government Printing Office, 1965), p. 10.
[24] *Ibid.*, p. 21.

approved by the Federal Maritime Commission. The Maritime Commission was given 6 months from the enactment of the amendments on October 3, 1961, to review existing dual-rate contracts and to approve them if they meet the new statutory requirements. The Commission asked and was twice granted 1-year extensions. It was not until April 3, 1964, that the Commission issued the precise conditions under which it would approve such contracts.[25]

Dual rates, referred to in the quotation preceding, involve an arrangement under which a shipper who agrees to give all of his business to a particular carrier (or to carriers who are members of a particular conference) receives a lower rate than does a shipper who does not make such an agreement. In short, a dual rate system is a special type of "tying" arrangement.

Other Amendments

Between 1916 and 1961, there were various other pieces of legislation designed mainly to clarify the respective jurisdictions of the Maritime Commission and the Interstate Commerce Commission. Thus the Intercoastal Shipping Act of 1933 subjected both contract (as defined in Chapter 24) and common carriers operating in intercoastal commerce via the Panama Canal to the provisions of the Act of 1916, and Part III of the Transportation Act of 1940 codified the authority of the Interstate Commerce Commission over domestic water carriers. Domestic ocean commerce (between Hawaii and the United States and between Alaska and the United States) is subject to Maritime Commission regulation.

Regulatory Experience from 1916 to 1965

In 1965, the Joint Economic Committee characterized regulation under the Shipping Act up to 1963 as a failure, remarking:

Broadly speaking, the succession of regulatory agencies that have been charged with administration of the statute, each in its brief turn, have been poorly informed and ill-equipped. They have simply not known what was occurring in the industry, and have generally had no grasp of legal or technical principles. They proceeded on particular instances and established no positive rules of conduct. In the absence of general standards on national policy, the tendency became irresistible to permit what was on the

one hand adroitly advocated by special interest, and on the other hand, was not condemned under articulated guidelines. . . .[26]

Reorganization Plan No. 7 was put into effect in August 1961. As has been noted, it created the Federal Maritime Commission as an independent regulatory agency apart from the Federal Maritime Administration (which continues to be a part of the Department of Commerce and to administer the subsidy program). But neither the reorganization (which separated the promotional from the regulatory functions) nor the amendments of 1961 resulted in a policy of positive regulation. Indeed, not until the Joint Economic Committee had called the situation to the attention of the President in 1963 did a policy of positive regulation emerge. A narrative detailing this series of events was presented by the Joint Economic Committee in 1965 and reads as follows:

Foreign flag steamship lines, conferences and foreign governments vehemently opposed the amendments enacted in 1961. Britain, Canada, Denmark, France, Germany, Italy, the Netherlands, Sweden, and Norway formally protested to the Department of State that the Bonner Act violates international law and interferes with the business operations of foreign-owned steamship companies and foreign-based steamship conferences.

On the other hand, the American steamship lines themselves readily admitted before the Antitrust Subcommittee, the House Merchant Marine and Fisheries Committee, and the Senate Commerce Committee that regulation of steamship conferences and ocean transportation was in the best interest of the United States and the American merchant marine. . . .

While the Celler investigation and the Bonner bill caused great concern to the steamship industry, by 1963 it looked as though the tidal wave of concern had receded. First, the grand jury that had been called to investigate the violations discovered by the Celler subcommittee was abruptly dismissed. Second, the reorganized Federal Maritime Commission quietly subsided into the tradition of nonregulation, manifested not only by its request for extensions of the Bonner bill deadline for dual-rate approval, but also by its inadequate response to the inquiry of the Joint Economic Committee during its investigation of the steel price increases of 1963. The committee asked why it costs American exporters considerably more to ship steel products to Europe and Japan than it costs European and

---

[25] *Ibid.*, p. 26.

[26] *Ibid.*, p. 22.

Japanese exporters to ship their steel products to this country.

Representatives of the Commission not only failed to explain the rate disparities, but they admitted that the Commission, like its predecessors, had never investigated the problem even though the Merchant Marine Act of 1936 had ordered such an investigation and this was, as recently as 1961, reaffirmed in the very investigations that had led to the Commission's creation.

The then Chairman, Thomas E. Stakem, Jr., admitted to the committee in June 1963 that the Commission had not investigated the level of freight rates, the conference system of rate-making, the relationship between rates and trade movement, and the effects on the balance of payments of present ocean transportation practices. He further admitted that the Federal Maritime Commission had rarely disapproved a major conference agreement under section 15, and had never subjected a freight rate to the test of the new section 18.

Apart from pursuing its own investigation, the Committee felt obliged to inform the late President Kennedy of the ineptitude and neglect of the Federal Maritime Commission. The President responded by ordering the Bureau of the Budget to investigate. The Bureau recommended that the agency be restaffed and that a regulatory program setting forth priorities and objectives be formulated. It also recommended that a new chairman be designated. The President named Rear Adm. John Harllee, U.S. Navy (retired), as the new chairman on August 26, 1963, and the latter immediately appointed Mr. Timothy May as the new managing director. The Commission next proceeded to formulate a program of priorities and objectives. This became an official program on March 9, 1964.

Besides actions taken in response to . . . specific recommendations of the Joint Economic Committee, the Commission has taken other positive regulatory steps for the first time.

A. The Commission has refused to approve pooling agreements unless the proponents can prove that such an agreement is in the public interest of the United States. Prior to the chairmanship of Admiral Harllee, the Commission's policy was to approve pools routinely, without hearing unless demanded, and without determining their effects on U.S. foreign commerce whenever the carriers felt that it was in *their* best interest to have such an agreement. The Commission now demands that the effects of the pooling agreement on the public interest of the United States be known before it grants approval. For only the second time in nearly 50 years the Commission has recently disapproved

an important pool, and it currently has 18 major pools under investigation—more than half the pools connected with U.S. foreign commerce.

B. In two areas, quick action by the Commission greatly alleviated discrimination against American exporters. Last year, the two conferences governing trade from the east and west coast of the United States to the Far East imposed a surcharge of $10 a ton on all shipments to Manila because of alleged port difficulties. No other conferences serving Manila imposed a surcharge of such magnitude. The ships serving Canada and Mexico imposed no surcharge on shipments to Manila. As a result of the surcharge American exporters of cotton and paper products lost markets to Mexican and Canadian exporters of these products. . . .

Because of the high level of the surcharge and its effects on U.S. commerce, the Commission ordered an immediate investigation. The conferences quickly reduced the surcharge to $5 per ton.

In a similar situation involving the port of Chittagong, East Pakistan, a 40-percent surcharge was imposed by the conference from the United States. No other conferences from any country in the world imposed a surcharge. The Commission at once ordered an investigation and the surcharge was temporarily dropped. It was reimposed in April of this year, but again it was substantially reduced as a result of the Federal Maritime Commission's investigations. . . .

C. The Commission has begun investigations of (a) the conference system of ratemaking, (b) the conferences' methods of handling shipper complaints, and (c) the effectiveness of the neutral bodies of self-policing forces of conferences.

D. The Commission, in December of 1964, eliminated discrimination against United States and foreign shipping lines, when it imposed countervailing duties on imports from Uruguay. Uruguay gives rebates to shippers using ships of her registry. This action will offset this discrimination.

Every American exporter and every American taxpayer should congratulate the Federal Maritime Commission for the actions it has taken in the past year, and also for its sturdy resistance to the counterattacks launched by the industry. For the first time the Commission has begun to carry out the mandates of the Congress. We believe that this committee has shared in stimulating not only the vivification of an important agency of Government but a fresh appraisal of the regulatory function in our foreign trade. We hope, indeed, that these beginnings will develop the knowledge and skills without which important results cannot be

27 *Ibid.*, pp. 26–32.

obtained and sustained, and that the dignity and fortitude under fire the Commission has evidenced in these early stages will deepen into the confidence and surehandedness that command universal respect.[27]

Regulation since 1965; Alternatives to the Present System

Since 1965, the Commission has continued upon its course of positive regulation. Thus in 1965 it disapproved or modified several dual rate agreements; and in 1968, the Supreme Court upheld the Commission's adoption of a principle that restraints imposed by a shipping conference which would violate or interfere with the policies of the antitrust laws would be approved only if the conference carried the burden of proving that such restraints were required by a serious transportation need, were necessary to secure an important public benefit, or were in furtherance of a valid regulatory purpose of the Shipping Act.[28]

Another example of positive regulation is provided by the Commission's action in 1969 in disapproving a dual rate agreement and requiring amendment of the agreement in such a way that *separate* dual rate contracts be offered to shippers in *each* trade area served by the conference, thereby making it possible for shippers to use nonconference shippers in some areas (Docket 1092, January 7, 1969). The Commission has also claimed authority under the Shipping Act of 1916 to approve or disapprove mergers and was upheld in this claim by a Court of Appeals (Docket 66–45, January 4, 1968).

But obviously, the Commission is limited by the provisions of the Act of 1916 authorizing companies to hold membership in shipping conferences. Therefore, in 1966, the Joint Economic Committee suggested several alternatives to the present system of regulation, none of which, however, has been put into effect. The Committee said:

Even though the Federal Maritime Commission has begun to regulate our oceanbound foreign commerce, and even though we are convinced that the Commission will continue and obtain results, we are not certain that it is wise to continue to grant antitrust immunity to steamship operators. Although regulation can effectively control monopolistic abuses, we are not convinced that it can be effective in control, ling abuses by shipping conferences. Moreover-we are not convinced that American shippers and steamship operators are receiving more benefits under the current system than they would under a system of free competition.

Unlike all other present exemptions from the antitrust laws, thc Shipping Act docs not confer upon the Federal Maritime Commission power to fix reasonable rates in foreign trade. It may under section 17 correct unjust discriminations of a limited character, and under section 18 it may disapprove a rate that is so high or so low as to constitute a detriment to commerce, but these are narrower, and as yet unexercised powers. We would not be understood as implying that they do not reach the problem of the unbalanced rate structure at present prejudicing our exports. The fact remains that they fall markedly short of true ratemaking in domestic transportation.

The reason for this deficiency is, of course, the diffidence with which Congress has approached control of foreign trade. The right to regulate foreign carriers has really never been the issue; the persuasive argument has been that its exercise would be offensive to other nations, which might in retaliation do the same, with confusing results inimical to commerce. A recent example might be found in the direct orders several governments issued to their flag carriers not to comply with orders of the Federal Maritime Commission to submit certain financial data. Though contrary experience might be cited in other international fields, and though it might be thought possible to show the maritime powers their community of interest with us in sensible regulation of abuses (an effort we understand the Commission is pursuing at present), it is the case that national regulatory policy stops short at the water's edge. . . .

The expedients that naturally suggest themselves at once are (1) to repeal section 15 of the Shipping Act or (2) to confer full ratemaking jurisdiction on the Federal Maritime Commission. Thus we should restore competition outright or invoke our conventional system for procuring its economic equivalent. . . .

As for conferring rate powers on the Commission, the practical arguments against it are probably still insuperable. Even apart from the expected resistance of the maritime powers, the technical problems are complex, and the proceedings would certainly consume such immoderate amounts of time as would limit their utility, at least at the outset.

A third expedient, less drastic than repealing section 15 or extending regulation, strongly appeals to us.

It is simply to make our subsidized fleet more

---

[28] *Volkswagenwerk Aktiongesellschaft* v. *Federal Mari-* *time Commission, et. al.*, 390 U.S. 261 (1968).

competitive by directing their owners to withdraw from the conferences. This course requires no legislation, only an administrative order by the Secretary of Commerce under existing contracts. Without abolishing the conferences or otherwise disturbing current law affecting their operation, and without elaborate legal ritual, such a step instantly would procure some (perhaps most) of the benefits of free competition. . . .[29]

The reference in the preceding quotation to subsidization (by means of the Merchant Marine Act of 1936) should be noted. In the 90th Congress (1967–68), 15 bills were introduced in the House alone to provide for an increase both in the dollar amount and the scope of the program for subsidization of the shipping industry, but no final action was taken by Congress concerning these proposals, which, of course, contemplated administration of the program by the Federal Maritime Administration of the Department of Commerce. In none of these proposals, nor in the hearings held on these bills, was any attention given to the suggestion made in 1966 by the Joint Economic Committee that owners of the subsidized fleet should be required to withdraw from shipping conferences.

It is interesting to note that the Federal Maritime Administration is one of the few agencies concerned with promotion of a mode of transportation which was not transferred into the Department of Transportation upon creation of the latter. The Department of Transportation is primarily concerned with matters pertaining to safety and promotion of various modes of transportation and with overall transportation policy. With these remarks, we may conclude our discussion of agencies concerned with the *economic regulation* of transportation services begun in the preceding chapter and turn to a discussion of the functions and role of the Department of Transportation in the next one.

[29] *Discriminatory Ocean Freight Rates and the Balance of Payments* (Report of the Joint Economic Committee, 89th Cong., 2d sess.) (Washington, D.C.: U.S. Government Printing Office, 1966), pp. 19–21.

26

The Department of Transportation: Promotion and Safety Functions

This chapter consists of two major subdivisions. The first contains a discussion of the history of the legislation creating the Department of Transportation; the second is devoted to a description of the organization and functions of this new department.

A. LEGISLATIVE HISTORY OF THE DEPARTMENT OF TRANSPORTATION ACT

President Johnson's 1966 Message to Congress

In March 1966, President Johnson sent to Congress a Message calling for the establishment of a Cabinet-level Department of Transportation to perform the functions of promoting the transportation industry and increasing the safety of transportation services. His Message contained one paragraph citing the recommendation, made by many special study groups since 1936, that such a new

department be established, as well as paragraphs defining the scope of the proposed new department and calling for establishment of a National Transportation Safety Board.[1]

In his Message, the President also urged Congress to enact the Traffic Safety Act of 1966. He further recommended that the Department of Housing and Urban Development (HUD) continue to bear the responsibility for urban transportation but that the Secretaries of the new department and of HUD recommend to him within a year "the means and procedures" for achieving cooperation between the two departments in regard to urban transportation policy. He broadly stated the role of the new department in these words:

ROLE OF THE DEPARTMENT

The Department of Transportation will—
coordinate the principal programs that promote transportation in America;
bring new technology to a total transportation system, by promoting research and development in cooperation with private industry;

[1] *Creating a Department of Transportation* (Hearings before the House Committee on Government Operations, 89th Cong., 2d sess., 1966) (Washington, D.C.: U.S. Government Printing Office, 1966), pp. 39–40.

improve safety in every means of transportation;

encourage private enterprise to take full and prompt advantage of new technological opportunities;

encourage high-quality, low-cost service to the public;

conduct systems analyses and planning, to strengthen the weakest parts of today's system; and

develop investment criteria and standards, and analytical techniques to assist all levels of government and industry in their transportation investments.[2]

Moreover, it must be noted that the Message also explicitly stated that the establishment of the new department would not alter the economic regulatory functions performed by the Interstate Commerce Commission, the Civil Aeronautics Board, or the Federal Maritime Commission, although the function of determining investment criteria would, necessarily, have some effect upon the regulatory policies adopted by these three independent agencies.

Identical bills were thereupon introduced in both houses of Congress. These bills embodied the proposals made in President Johnson's Message and were introduced at the request of the Administration; indeed, these bills were drafted by the Administration, a practice common in cases of this type, in which the President is acting in the role of Chief Legislator, as described in Chapter 6.

Controversies Concerning the Administration's Proposals

In the course of extensive hearings on these bills by the relevant House and Senate Committees, a number of issues concerning, and objections to, specific provisions were raised. Two of the most important issues involved the question of whether or not the Federal Maritime Administration should be transferred from the Department of Commerce to the new department and the nature of the transportation investment standards to be developed. Both these issues will be further considered below. Before doing so, however, it will be useful to note some of the other issues raised during the hearings on the proposed legislation. These included:

"clarification" of the respective roles of the Secretary of Transportation and Congress in regard to formulation of national transportation policy; the question of how to assure continuity of the agencies to be transferred to the new department; assurance of the independence of the National Transportation Safety Board; questions concerning the location of programs pertaining to urban mass transportation; and various questions pertaining to the independence of existing agencies concerned with transportation problems.[3]

The way in which most of these issues were resolved in the legislation finally adopted will be clarified in conjunction with our examination (in Subdivision B) of the organization and functions of the new department. It is to be emphasized that one of the major issues involved concerned the question of the retention by various agencies, such as the Federal Maritime Administration, of an independent agency status and another major issue concerned the question of the determination of investment standards by the new Secretary of Transportation In the case of the Federal Maritime Administration, the question of independent agency status and that of investment standards were closely related. Both questions were dealt with by amendments to the legislation proposed by the Administration and require further discussion.

Exclusion of the Federal Maritime Administration. The Federal Maritime Administration was eventually excluded from the group of agencies transferred to the new department. This exclusion occurred as a result of an amendment to the proposed legislation adopted by the House. Both maritime management and maritime labor interests opposed the transfer of this agency from the Department of Commerce to the new department, and so the House voted in favor of an amendment to deny the new Secretary authority over the Maritime Administration, and that agency remained in the Department of Commerce. Indeed, while the hearings on the House bill were being conducted, the House Committee on Merchant Marine and Fisheries adopted a

---

[2] *Ibid.*, p. 42.

[3] *Establishing a Department of Transportation and for Other Purposes* (Report of the Senate Committee on Government Operations, 89th Cong., 2d sess., 1966) (Washington, D.C.: U.S. Government Printing Office, 1966), pp. 3–4.

resolution opposing transfer of the Maritime Administration to the new department and calling for legislation to establish the Maritime Administration as an independent agency. Both labor and management interests feared that transfer of the Maritime Administration to the new department would mean that maritime problems would be subordinated to problems pertaining to domestic transportation in the new agency and that the policy of subsidization of ocean transportation would be subjected to unfavorable changes.

The Problem of Investment Standards. The position of the Administration concerning investment criteria as well as the nature of the provisions pertaining to them, were outlined in testimony by Charles L. Schultze, an economist and President Johnson's Director of the Bureau of the Budget. Mr. Schultze first pointed to the "massive investments" which governments at the state and federal level had made in the transportation industry up to the present time, a point developed in detail in Chapter 8.

He then asserted that there were no common standards in existence for evaluating the effects of transportation investments. Accordingly, Section 7 of the proposed legislation would authorize the Secretary to develop standards and criteria for such investments, subject to Presidential approval. It would also require the Civil Aeronautics Board to take account of these criteria in determining airline subsidy payments.[4]

The question of government investment decisions in the transportation industry is, of course, merely one aspect of the general problem of government investment decisions. This topic is discussed in Chapter 32 in the context of a recent study by the Joint Economic Committee.

Opposition of Maritime and Domestic Water Transportation Interests. Maritime and domestic water transportation interests were strongly opposed many of the provisions of the proposed legislation although they did not oppose the mere creation of a Department of Transportation.[5] They expressed the view that inclusion of the promotional functions relative to their industries in the Department of Transportation "would obscure and hinder" the industries in question.[6] In short, they were afraid that the amounts of the subsidies they would receive would be lower under the proposed new organizational scheme than they were under existing arrangements.

Effect on Porkbarrel Legislation of Section 7. "Porkbarrel legislation" is legislation adopted for purposes of political patronage (generally in the form of appropriations for public works), for example, an appropriation for a local improvement designed to please the constituents of a particular legislator. The Chairman of the House Public Works Committee, Representative Fallon, also testified in opposition to the provisions of Section 7. He argued that "the unique evaluation of projects" was a function that ought to be performed by Congress after a recommendation was made by an appropriate committee of Congress which had heard testimony from the affected agencies of the Government and all interested organizations and persons.[7]

As we have seen earlier in this book, an economist's conception of "social value" invariably and inescapably incorporates the conception of market price as a measure of social value. In 1969, Julius Margolis noted that a conflict existed between administrators and economists in cases in which administrators do not accept the economist's view of the public interest, "a view defined by their [the economists'] profession in their scientific journals, *i.e.*, the aggregation of individual preferences."[7a] Representative Fallon's testimony is an example. Margolis also noted that the economist's position involved rejection "of an active role of the political process or administrative structure as formulators of the public interest," and Fallon's position, of course, emphasized the method of making the decision, a method rejected by the economist.

---

[4] *Creating a Department of Transportation, op. cit.*, pp. 59–60.

[5] See, for example, the testimony of Ralph Casey, President of the Merchant Marine Institute, *Creating a Department of Transportation, op. cit.*, pp. 316–317.

[6] *Creating a Department of Transportation, op. cit.*, pp. 581–584.

[7] *Creating a Department of Transportation, op. cit.*, pp. 234–235.

[7a] Julius Margolis, "Shadow Prices for Incorrect or Nonexistent Social Values," in *The Analysis and Evaluation of Public Expenditures: The PPB System* (A Compendium of Papers; Joint Subcommittee on Economy in Government, 91st Cong., 1st sess., 1969) (Washington, D.C.: U.S. Government Printing Office, 1969), p. 538.

Section 7 as Enacted

As finally enacted into law, Section 7 reads:

TRANSPORTATION INVESTMENT STANDARDS

SEC. 7(a). The Secretary, subject to the provisions of section 4 of this Act, shall develop and from time to time in the light of experience revise standards and criteria consistent with national transportation policies, for the formulation and economic evaluation of all proposals for the investment of Federal funds in transportation facilities or equipment, except such proposals as are concerned with (1) the acquisition of transportation facilities or equipment by Federal agencies in providing transportation services for their own use; (2) an inter-oceanic canal located outside the contiguous United States; (3) defense features included at the direction of the Department of Defense in the design and construction of civil air, sea, and land transportation; (4) programs of foreign assistance; (5) water resource projects; or (6) grant-in-aid programs authorized by law. The standards and criteria developed or revised pursuant to this subsection shall be promulgated by the Secretary upon their approval by the Congress.

The standards and criteria for economic evaluation of water resource projects shall be developed by the Water Resources Council established by Public Law 89–90. For the purpose of such standards and criteria, the primary direct navigation benefits of a water resource project are defined as the product of the savings to shippers using the waterway and the estimated traffic that would use the waterway; where the savings to shippers shall be construed to mean the difference between (a) the freight rates or charges prevailing at the time of the study for the movement by the alternative means and (b) those which would be charged on the proposed waterway; and where the estimate of traffic that would use the waterway will be based on such freight rates, taking into account projections of the economic growth of the area.

The Water Resources Council established under section 101 of Public Law 89–90 is hereby expanded to include the Secretary of Transportation on matters pertaining to navigation features of water resources projects.

(b) Every survey, plan, or report formulated by a Federal agency which includes a proposal as to which the Secretary has promulgated standards and criteria pursuant to subsection (a)

shall be (1) prepared in accord with such standards and criteria and upon the basis of information furnished by the Secretary with respect to projected growth of transportation needs and traffic in the affected area, the relative efficiency of various modes of transport, the available transportation services in the area, and the general effect of the proposed investment on existing modes, and on the regional and national economy; (2) coordinated by the proposing agency with the Secretary and, as appropriate, with other Federal agencies, States, and local units of government for inclusion of his and their views and comments; and (3) transmitted thereafter by the proposing agency to the President for disposition in accord with law and procedures established by him.[8]

To be noted, is the fact that six types of investment activities are excluded from coverage by the criteria to be developed by the Secretary of Transportation. Moreover, any criteria which are developed must be approved by Congress before they are promulgated. The exclusion of grants-in-aid has the effect of excluding the federal highway program; water resource projects are also exempt, but the new Secretary has been given a place on the Water Resources Council so that he can presumably exert some influence on decisions pertaining to water resource projects. Also to be noted in this regard is the fact that Congress has provided a definition of the concept of "direct navigation benefits" of such water resource projects. This definition is clearly subject to amendment by legislation, and those who do not approve of it have their remedy at the polls. The alternative course of action would have been for Congress to leave this definition to be made by the Secretary of Transportation by means of an administrative process involving reliance on the welfare functions of whatever particular economists were called in for consultation.

The application of Section 7 is narrowly limited by the language of Section 4, which requires the approval by Congress of "the adoption, revision, or implementation" of "any investment standards or criteria." Accordingly, the Department of Transportation has largely limited its activities under Section 7 to performing those functions resulting from the Secretary's membership on the Water Resources Council.

---

[8] Public Law 89–670, October 15, 1966.

B. ORGANIZATION AND OPERATIONS OF THE DEPARTMENT OF TRANSPORTATION

Organization

The Secretary. Section 2 of the proposed administration bill was amended in Congress to require the Secretary to make recommendations with respect to transportation policy to the President and to Congress to insure that he would function within the framework of existing transportation policy and not independently. In addition, although Section 4, as originally proposed, would have required the Secretary to *develop* policies and make recommendations, Congress changed the language of the bill to require him to *exercise leadership* in the development of such policies, thereby further limiting his power to act independently of existing policies. The Office of Secretary, as finally established, is thus a much less powerful one than the one envisaged by the administration bill.

The Administrations and the United States Coast Guard. The United States Coast Guard was transferred to the new department from the Department of the Treasury; and three new administrations were created and assigned, respectively, various promotional and safety functions previously performed by other agencies or bureaus within other departments. Thus, the Federal Aviation Administration was created in the new department and assigned the promotional and safety functions previously performed by the Federal Aviation Agency; the Federal Railroad Administration was created and assigned functions pertaining to railroad safety, research, and development previously performed elsewhere, largely by divisions of the Interstate Commerce Commission; and the Federal Highway Administration was created and performs various functions pertaining to highway construction and motor vehicle travel formerly performed by bureaus located in the Department of Commerce. The heads of these Administrations and the Commandant (of the United States Coast Guard) report to the Secretary, but also have statutory duties to perform and enjoy a certain amount of independence.

The Urban Mass Transportation Administration. It will be recalled that originally matters pertaining to urban transportation were left under the control of the Secretary of Health, Education, and Welfare. However, in July 1968, under the President's Reorganization Plan No. 2, most of the functions and programs established under the Mass Transportation Act of 1964 were transferred to the Department of Transportation to be performed by a new administration, the Urban Mass Transportation Administration. This agency undertakes research, development, and demonstration projects pertaining to urban mass transportation. It makes grants to public and private nonprofit institutions for research pertaining to the problems of its concern and may make grants and loans to assist communities in acquiring capital equipment to meet their local transportation needs. The loans are made at low interest rates and may be made directly or in cooperation with private lending agencies. Grants are also made to communities for the purpose of planning, designing, and engineering mass transportation systems. Its principal subdivisions are an Office of Research and an Office of Program Operations. In August 1969, as we will see below, President Nixon asked Congress for funds to expand greatly the operations and activities of this new agency.

The National Transportation Safety Board. This Board enjoys a statutory existence and functions independently of the Secretary. Provisions are included for making its actions consistent with those taken by the Administrations, as well as provisions insuring that the Administrative Procedure Act will apply to all proceedings before the Board. The Board consists of five members appointed by the President with the advice and consent of the Senate.

Alaska Railroad and St. Lawrence Seaway Corporation. The administration bill did not transfer either the Alaska Railroad or the St Lawrence Seaway Corporation to the new department, since administration officials believed that such a transfer could easily be accomplished under existing legislation by an executive order. Congress, however, included provisions in the final legislation transferring both these agencies (which perform proprietary functions) to the new department. In the case of the Corporation, the rationalization for the location of this agency within the department was that the Corporation would be "downgraded" if transferred by an executive order; in the case of the Railroad, the rationalization was that the management of the enterprise would be more efficient if supervised by transportation specialists located in the new department. Neither rationalization is particularly convincing.

Operations

The Department of Transportation officially came into existence on April 1, 1967, and issued its *Second Annual Report* (covering the period from July 1, 1967 to June 30, 1968), in June 1969. Its *Third Annual Report* was published in March, 1970.

The Secretary. The Secretary performs overall planning, directional, and control functions. The various Assistant Secretaries and the General Counsel are staff officers and also exercise departmental-wide functions. The principal operating units of the Department are the Administrators who head the various Administrations described above and the Commandant of the United States Coast Guard. The Department is thus highly decentralized; each of the Administrators and the Commandant possess line authority and exercise program responsibility, but are directly responsible to the Secretary. Although the functions of the various Administrations were transferred to the new department from other departments and agencies, these functions were performed without interruption throughout fiscal year 1967, as a result of special agreements pertaining to this matter between the Secretary and the various agencies from which the duties of the Administrations were transferred. During the first year of operations of the new department, the Secretary was thus primarily concerned with organizational matters and matters pertaining to the assurance of continuity during the transitional period of performance of the promotional and safety functions transferred to the Administrations.

The Federal Aviation Administration. This *Administration* performs all of the functions previously performed by the Federal Aviation *Agency*. Its main function is to insure aviation safety. This task is accomplished by the use of certification and enforcement procedures, including certification of aircraft, pilots, and mechanics. Safety standards are codified in the Federal Aviation Regulations, which are changed as technology advances or circumstances require. The Administration also exercises control over airspace and facilities (such as airports). The system currently in use is a manually operated one, employing radar, general purpose computers, and radio communications. Pilot studies and projects involving automated systems are under consideration, particularly in heavy traffic areas. Under these, aircraft would automatically report their altitudes, positions, and other flight data.

Among the most interesting and significant operations of the agency is the continuing Supersonic Transport Program (SST) for construction and operation of a titanium aircraft measuring 318 feet from nose to tip. The Federal Government sponsored the original research concerning, and development of, such aircraft. It is expected that 500 such aircraft will be in use by 1990, even if sonic boom limits their use to operations over water and sparsely populated areas. Each of these planes has a capacity of 280 passengers at a speed of 1,800 miles per hour for a distance of 4,000 miles.[9]

Federal Highway Administration. The Federal Highway Administration consists of several administrative units and three major operating bureaus. The Bureau of Public Roads administers construction of a 41,000-mile system of interstate and defense highways, and improvement of 860,000 miles of primary and secondary roads and their urban extensions. That is, it administers the federal aid highway program which amounts to $4.4 billion annually. It also conducts a Spot Improvement Program in conjunction with state highway departments to identify specific high-hazard accident locations. In its highway planning programs it attempts to take into account urban needs and problems and the need to relocate those whose homes or businesses have been or will be destroyed by execution of the road building program. It has also been directed by Congress to submit a report every two years, commencing in 1968, of the future

[9] *Annual Report of the Department of Transportation for 1967* (Washington, D.C.: U.S. Government Printing Office, 1968), Part II, pp. 51–53.

highway needs of the nation. The Highway Beautification Act of 1965 provided for funds for landscaping and scenic enhancement of rights of way. Under this law, 756 landscaping projects were under way at the end of fiscal year 1967, and 464 rest areas had been built.[10]

The Bureau of Motor Carrier Safety has the function of taking measures to reduce to a minimum the property damage and personal injuries and deaths resulting from operation of commercial motor carriers. Included among its activities are establishment and enforcement of regulations pertaining to commercial drivers and pertaining to inspection and maintenance of equipment.

The National Highway Safety Bureau administers provisions of the National Traffic and Motor Vehicle Safety Act of 1966 and of the National Highway Safety Act of 1966. Among its activities must be mentioned its reports and activities pertaining to motor vehicle recall campaigns. Under the National Motor Vehicle Safety Act of 1966, manufacturers of automobiles are required to notify by certified mail the first purchasers of automobiles of any safety defects in such automobiles subsequently discovered by the manufacturers. Manufacturers are also required to notify the Secretary of Transportation. The Bureau publishes a quarterly summary report concerning the results of such campaigns.

In addition to the motor vehicle recall campaigns, various other measures have been taken under the National Traffic and Motor Vehicle Safety Act and the Highway Safety Act. These measures include issuance of safety standards for new motor vehicles and motor vehicle equipment. The first such standards were issued in January 1967; additional standards were issued in January 1969. Proposals for safety standards applicable to used motor vehicles are under constant study, as is the use of grants-in-aid to assist states in establishing programs of annual state motor vehicle inspections. Continuing research into other factors pertaining to motor vehicle safety is also sponsored and conducted.[11]

The Federal Railroad Administration. This Administration is responsible for: operation of the Alaska Railroad; administration of the High Speed Ground Transportation Program; and performance of the railroad and oil pipeline safety functions formerly performed by the Interstate Commerce Commission, including jurisdiction over rail–highway grade crossings, transportation of hazardous substances, and inspection of locomotives.

The Office of High Speed Ground Transportation carries out the provisions of the High Speed Ground Transportation Act of 1965. Under this program, the Pennsylvania Railroad put into operation in January 1969 an improved rail passenger service in the Northeast Corridor between Washington, D.C., and New York City. Fifty electrically propelled cars at speeds up to 110 miles per hour with experimental telephone service, new baggage service, and use of two new suburban stations are involved in this service. Other experiments involve use of turbine engines, and an auto-train operating between Washington, D.C., and Jacksonville, Florida, to haul both passengers and their cars. Such new developments in railroad passenger service are being undertaken in an attempt to compete with air transportation. In short, within the new department, the concept of intermodal competition is a viable one.

The United States Coast Guard. In addition to its rescue and police functions, the United States Coast Guard performs the function of promoting safety of merchant vessels and develops, installs, and maintains navigational aids. Commercial vessels are subject to Coast Guard inspection and certification, and Coast Guard technical personnel review designs for new vessels. Safety of containerized cargo has been one topic of considerable Coast Guard attention. It has also issued guides pertaining to the use of automated ship-propulsion devices. The performance of such functions accounts for the transfer of the Coast Guard from the Treasury Department to the Department of Transportation, along with the rest of the various agencies responsible for safety and

[10] *Ibid.*, Part I, p. 69 ff.

[11] *Safety for Motor Vehicles in Use* (Report to the Congress from the Secretary of Transportation) (Washington, D.C.: U.S. Government Printing Office, 1968), p. 1 ff. See also, *Alcohol and Highway Safety* (Report to Congress from the Secretary of Transportation) (Washington, D.C.: U.S. Government Printing Office, 1968).

technological improvements in regard to modes of transportation other than maritime transportation.

The National Transportation Safety Board. This board, unlike the other elements of the Department of Transportation, is autonomous and reports to Congress independently of the Secretary of Transportation. It came into existence in April 1967, and most of its original staff consisted of personnel transferred from the Civil Aeronautics Board. During its first year of operations, the Board investigated major rail and aircraft accidents and made numerous recommendations pertaining to safety procedures and to subjects for further study to the Administrations of the Department and to the Secretary, including, for example, recommendations pertaining to problems of highway safety. The Board did not make any recommendations for additional legislation to Congress during the first year of its existence, but it did strongly support legislation advocated by the Administration pertaining to natural gas pipeline safety.

The Natural Gas Pipeline Safety Act. Prior to 1968, natural gas pipeline safety was largely regulated by voluntary compliance standards adopted by the natural gas industry and by various state statutes. These statutes were not, however, uniform. In addition, the Federal Power Commission possessed power to issue certificates of convenience and necessity concerning the building of interstate natural gas pipelines but not over distributional or gathering facilities and was authorized to include safety conditions as conditions of the issuance of such certificates.

In 1968, Congress adopted the Natural Gas Pipeline Safety Act. This law authorizes the Secretary of Transportation to prescribe safety standards for natural gas pipelines and imposes a penalty for violations of the standards he sets. Control over the building of new pipelines remains a function of the Federal Power Commission, since this problem also involves questions pertaining to the economic regulation of the natural gas industry. The legislation provides for establishment by the Secretary of Transportation of a Technical Pipeline Safety Standards Committee of 15 members. The Secretary must submit proposed standards to the Committee but is not bound by its decisions pertaining to such standards. If the Committee disapproves the standards, the Secretary must publish, together with the standards, his reasons for rejecting the Committee's point of view.

President Nixon's Message to Congress on Urban Transportation (1969)

On August 7, 1969, President Nixon sent to Congress a Message calling for an expenditure of $10 billion over a 12-year period to develop and improve urban mass transportation facilities. He pointed out that such facilities were presently dependent upon the demands of those "who *must* make use" of these services and that a problem of increasing the demand by others for such services by modernizing facilities and services existed. Accordingly, he proposed contract authorization starting with a first year authorization of $300 million and rising to $1 billion annually by 1975. Over the 12 year period, $9.5 billion would be spent on capital investments and $500 million for research and development. What the other $2 billion would be spent for was not specified.

A Concluding Comment

With the adoption of the pipeline legislation, safety regulation of all forms of transportation—marine, air, rail, public and private motor carrier, and oil and natural gas pipeline—has been centralized in the Department of Transportation. Most transportation research and promotional functions, as we have seen, have also become responsibilities of the various modal Administrations, although in the case of the maritime industry, these functions have been excluded from the control of the Department. This exclusion constitutes one shortcoming in the existing organizational scheme. Economic regulatory functions, however, have not been transferred to the new department, although arrangements do exist for coordination of activities of the regulatory agencies with those of the Department, particularly in cases in which subsidization policies adopted by the Department are related to rate problems dealt with by the various agencies, for example, in the case of air transportation.

This chapter concludes our consideration of the special working rules pertaining to the transportation industry. In the next chapter, we will consider the problems of federal economic regulation three industries not involving transportation services but in which the regulatory agencies are also concerned with problems of ratemaking and control over long-run supply, problems similar to those faced by the transportation regulatory agencies discussed in Chapters 24 and 25. That is, we will consider aspects of the interstate hydroelectric industry, the natural gas industry, and the communications industry.

Hydroelectric Power; Natural Gas; Communications

This chapter consists of two major subdivisions. The first contains a discussion of the problems of economic regulation of the interstate hydroelectric power and the natural gas industries by the Federal Power Commission. The second consists of a treatment of the problems of economic regulation of the communications industry by the Federal Communications Commission.

A. THE FEDERAL POWER COMMISSION

History, Organization, and General Survey of Operations

The Federal Power Commission was created by the Federal Power Act of 1920 to control the construction and operation of hydroelectric projects on federal lands and navigable waters of the United States. As established by this law, the Commission consisted of the Secretaries of War, Interior, and Agriculture. These Cabinet officers, in turn, delegated the actual performance of their duties on the Commission to their staff members, and the early activities of the Commission were confined almost entirely to the issuance of licenses for hydroelectric projects.

In 1930, the Commission was established as an independent agency of five commissioners; and the Public Utility Holding Company Act of 1935 granted the Commission power to control interstate transmission and *wholesale* rates charged for electrical energy sold in interstate commerce. Control over (retail) rates charged by distributors of electrical energy in intrastate commerce is exercised by the various states. The Commission was also given power to regulate issuance of securities, mergers, and acquisitions in the cases of companies over which it has jurisdiction. Under various amendments to the law, the Commission also approves rates for the sale of electric power from certain federal hydroelectric projects.

The Natural Gas Act of 1938 assigned the Commission jurisdiction over interstate transportation and sale of natural gas. The Commission originally believed that it did not possess power to regulate intrastate activities of independent producers pertaining to the production of natural gas which eventually moved in interstate commerce. However, in 1954, the Supreme Court ordered the Commission to regulate the activities of independent producers.[1] Various attempts were thereupon made by producers of natural gas to secure legislation exempting their activities from federal regulation. (Indeed, the activities of the lobbyists for the natural gas industry in regard to such legislation have already been discussed in Chapter 6 under the heading *"Public Relations and the Merchandising of Measures . . ."* and the reader may wish to refer to that discussion at this time.) Until the middle of the 1960s, the Commission devoted most of its effort to the natural gas industry and very little to the regulation of hydroelectric power rates; but, as we will see below, after that time it became more active in both areas. The Commission also issues certificates authorizing gas sales to and from interstate pipelines and for the construction and operation of pipeline facilities under this legislation and amendments to it. The responsibilities and authority of the Commission were further amended by the Water Resources Planning Act. Under this legislation, the Commission participates (through its Chairman) as a member of the Water Resources Council in reviewing comprehensive plans for development of river basins and related land resources.

In the 1960s, the Commission created a Division of Econometric Analysis within its Office of Economics. The presentation by personnel of this Division of an econometric model in a natural gas rate proceeding in 1965 will be further discussed later in this chapter. The Bureaus of Power and of Natural Gas must also be mentioned; these two bureaus are, respectively, concerned with problems pertaining to hydroelectric power and natural gas production and pipelines. It is to specific problems pertaining to hydroelectric power that we turn first.

Aspects of the Electric Power Industry

Three functions must be performed in the electric power industry: production of electric power by reliance upon some other source of energy, such as coal, natural gas, or water power; transmission of the electric power by means of high voltage lines and circuits; and distribution of the power to ultimate users. The distribution function may be performed by a company or organization other than the one which produces or transmits the electric power. Indeed,

many municipal companies purchase electric power from companies which transmit such power, the transmitters, in turn perhaps, having purchased the power from an original producer, including a government-owned producer. Federal control consists primarily of control over hydroelectric production plants and over wholesale sales to or by transmitter-producers. Retail sales to ultimate consumers or end-users are controlled by municipal authorities or by state public utility commissions. Thus a Court of Appeals held in 1968 that the Commission does not have authority with respect to acquisitions by hydroelectric companies of facilities used solely for local distribution (*Duke Power Co.* v. *FPC*, CADC 20578, June 28, 1968).

Hydroelectric Licenses and River Basin Development

Title I of the Federal Power Act consists of the Federal Water Power Act of 1920 and assigns to the Commission the responsibility for licensing nonfederal hydroelectric power projects on navigable waterways, on any streams over which Congress has jurisdiction in cases in which the project affects interstate commerce and on public lands or reservations of the United States. In 1965, the Supreme Court held that the Commission's authority included power to license a project on a stream located entirely within the State of Missouri, in a situation in which the power was produced for sale in interstate commerce and in which the power production facilities might affect the navigability of a river to which the Missouri stream was a tributary.[2] Justices Goldberg, Harlan, and Stewart dissented, pointing out that the question of control over the interstate *transmission* of electricity was not the basis for the licensing (of production) requirement. The majority, however, took the position that Congress intended to require a license for hydroelectric power projects utilizing the headwaters of a navigable stream, in cases in which the electric power was being generated for an interstate system. In general, it may be noted that the courts have been liberal in construing the Commission's power to license such projects and have defined

[1] *Phillips Natural Gas Company* v. *Wisconsin*, 347 U.S. 672 (1954).

[2] *Federal Power Commission* v. *Union Electric Company*, 381 U.S. 90 (1965).

"navigable" to mean "potentially navigable." It must also be noted, however, that in 1967 the Supreme Court held that the Commission must make findings under the law to the effect that private operation (as distinguished from federal operation) of the proposed project will be in the "public interest" and that the question of "public interest" cannot be decided without also taking evidence pertaining to the question of the effect on wildlife (fish) and recreational aspects of the matter of private versus federal development of a project.[3]

On June 30, 1968, there were 398 Commission hydroelectric power licenses in effect. The Federal Power Act also provides that the United States may recapture or relicense hydroelectric projects upon expiration of the Commission's licenses, which are valid for 50 years after they have been issued. The first report by the Commission to Congress concerning such a recapture was made in 1967. In this report the Commission recommended that the project in question not be recaptured.[4]

In issuing licenses, the Commission normally imposes general conditions requiring the firms licensed to provide free and nondiscriminatory public access and use of project property for recreational purposes, as well as facilities for conservation of fish and wildlife. Projects are inspected to insure that the conditions in the licenses are met.

The Commission thus, quite naturally, participates in the activities of the Water Resources Council. Title II of the Water Resources Act authorizes the establishment of regional river basin commissions to make plans for development of relevant river basins. Three such typical commissions are the Pacific Northwest River Basins Commission, the Great Lakes Basin Commission, and the New England River Basins Commission. The Federal Power Commission is represented by one of its regional engineers on each of these commissions.

Problems of Electric Power Ratemaking

Until 1935, neither the states nor the Commission possessed power to fix (whole-sale) rates for electric power transmitted in interstate commerce. In that year, Congress adopted Title II of the Public Utility Holding Company Act of 1935 authorizing the Commission to control such rates. Other legislation required the Commission to pass judgment upon rates charged by certain federal hydroelectric projects. Under this latter legislation, the Commission is concerned with 58 projects.

Some idea of the volume of work of the Commission can be gained from the fact that in fiscal year 1967, the Commission completed action on 1,963 private rate schedules out of a total of 2,006 filed. As has been noted, it has actively regulated electric power wholesale rates only since the beginning of the 1960s. Indeed, in its 1966 *Annual Report*, the Commission candidly remarked: "The Commission's revitalized rate regulation activity under Part II of the Federal Power Act led to many informal and formal complaints during the year." From 1963 to 1967, the dollar value of rate decreases exceeded the dollar value of rate increases, a point clearly shown by *Table 27–1*. Total reductions in 1968 amounted to more than $8 million, the largest amount in the Commission's history.[5] In its rate proceedings, the Commission primarily employs cost of service principles qualified by considerations looking toward continued growth in the use of electric power. Since it regulates rates at the *wholesale* level, it is sometimes faced with problems involving discriminations among different purchasers for resale, especially municipal purchasers, but it is not faced with the question of discriminations in rates among different ultimate consumers or end-users of power who buy from retailers.

The fact that the Commission finally embarked upon a course of serious regulation of hydroelectric wholesale rates in the early 1960s gave rise to the introduction in Congress of numerous bills to exempt various types of producers from the Commission's jurisdiction. The Commission opposed such legislation, and Congress did not enact it.

[3] *Udall* v. *Federal Power Commission*, 387 U.S. 428 (1967).
[4] *Annual Report of the Federal Power Commission for Fiscal Year 1967* (Washington, D.C.: U.S. Govern-ment Printing Office, 1968), p. 26 ff.
[5] *Annual Report of the Federal Power Commission for Fiscal Year 1968* (Washington, D.C.: U.S. Govern-ment Printing Office, 1969), p. 19.

Table 27-1

Federal Power Commission Hydroelectric Rate Actions, 1963–1967

| | Fiscal Year | | | | |
	1967	1966	1965	1964	1963
Filings received	2,006	2,649	2,576	1,295	1,882
Filings completed	1,963	2,798	2,686	1,323	1,494
Rate reductions	$4,284,777	$6,564,927	$8,024,782	$1,448,000	$1,240,880
Rate increases	$93,241	$55,928	$1,050,685	$395,200	$278,900

Source: *Annual Report of the Federal Power Commission for Fiscal Year 1967* (Washington, D.C.: U.S. Government Printing Office, 1968), p. 19.

Stock Issuances, Mergers, Interconnections, and Accounting

The Commission has jurisdiction over issuance of securities in the cases of companies not under the jurisdiction of the Securities and Exchange Commission under the Public Utility Holding Company Act of 1935 (already mentioned in Chapter 9) and those not regulated by state commissions. It has similar jurisdiction over mergers. In fiscal year 1967, the Commission reported that it had received 28 merger applications but did not indicate the nature of the actions taken. In December 1966, the Commission did, however, provide a statement of the considerations to be taken into account in approving a merger. It first pointed out that it was required to test mergers both by the provisions of the Federal Power Act and the Public Utility Holding Company Act (as described in Chapter 9 and again considered later in our discussion of the work of the Securities and Exchange Commission). Then the Commission stated, in the course of its opinion authorizing a merger, that it would take account of the following matters in considering merger applications: (1) effect of the proposed action on the applicants' costs and rate levels; (2) the contemplated accounting treatment; (3) the purchase price; (4) whether the acquiring utility had coerced the acquired utility into acceptance of the merger; (5) the effect the merger might have on the existing competitive situation; and finally, (6) whether the consolidation would impair effective regulation.[6]

Massive power failures in the Northeastern United States in 1965 and in the mid-Atlantic states in 1967 involving interruptions of service to several states resulted in studies by the Commission of reliability of service and in a Commission recommendation to Congress for enactment of an Electric Power Reliability Act, under which regional councils would be set up, exempt from the antitrust laws, consisting of representatives of power-producing firms in particular areas. Such councils would make plans for interconnection of systems and stand-by facilities to cope with cases in which power failures affecting large portions of the United States might otherwise occur as a result of cascading overloads.

One further highly important function of the Commission in this field must be noted. The Commission prescribes accounting systems to be followed in the case of licensed projects and determines the original cost, accrued depreciation, excess earnings and net investment figures of every licensed project. The "net investment" figure is intended to serve as the basis for determining the amount to be paid to the license holder if and when Congress should decide to exercise its recapture authority to take over the property upon expiration of the 50-year license.

Nature of the Natural Gas Industry

Natural gas may be produced either as a by-product in the production of oil or from natural gas wells. The search for natural gas is an undertaking involving uncertainty, and production is considered to be subject

[6] *Commonwealth Edison Company and Central Illinois Electric and Gas Company*, Opinion No. 507, 36 FPC 927 (1966), at p. 932.

to a very high degree of competition—there are several thousands of natural gas producers. In addition to the function of producing natural gas, there is a gathering function involving the use of a network of pipelines to carry the gas from the production site to a central transmission pipeline. There is also a transportation function involved in the transportation of the gas by means of a pipeline to the distribution site. Finally, there is a distribution function which must be performed to make the gas available to final end-users, be they residential consumers or industrial users. The existence of a very large number of producers of natural gas, it is usually asserted, results in a situation which differentiates the production aspect of the natural gas industry from most, if not all, of the other public service industries subject to regulation, either at the federal or state level. At the same time, as the Supreme Court has remarked, "The value to the public of the services they [natural gas producers] perform is measured by the quality and the quantity of the natural gas they produce and not by the resources they have expended in its search. . . ."

The distribution of gas is a retail function regulated by state commissions and cities. The transportation function is performed by pipeline companies, some of which are owned by distributors. There are many independent producers who sell to the pipeline companies. Also, some of the major integrated oil companies produce natural gas and transport it via their own pipelines in addition to their other operations. About 90 percent of the gas is produced by the independent producers and about 10 percent by the pipeline companies.

Control of Production and Gathering and of Independent Producers of Natural Gas

In fixing rates for integrated producers (those who not only own pipelines but who also own production and gathering facilities), the Commission has been forced to consider the production and gathering costs in determining the reasonableness of the rates charged to the distributors by the pipeline companies. It has generally used a cost of

service plus return on investment method. In the *Colorado Interstate* case in 1947, the Supreme Court upheld this practice, even though the companies claimed that their production and gathering activities constituted pure intrastate commerce.[7] And, in 1954, in the *Phillips* case, despite the Commission's position that it did not have jurisdiction over the production and gathering activities of *independent* producing companies, the Supreme Court held that the Commission did have such jurisdiction.[8] The effect of this decision was to increase the number of companies regulated by the Commission from about 150 to more than 4,300. The technique adopted for dealing with this great regulatory problem will be considered in detail later in this chapter.

Natural Gas Pipeline and Production Certificates of Convenience and Necessity

Under an amendment (1942) to the Natural Gas Act, the language of Section 7(c) now reads as follows:

No natural gas company . . . shall engage in the transportation or sale of natural gas . . . unless there is in force with respect to such natural gas company a certificate of public convenience and necessity issued by the Commission.

Other provisions of Section 7 authorize the Commission to control abandonments and to attach conditions required by the "public convenience and necessity" to the issuance of certificates. Under these provisions, the Commission issues certificates both to pipeline companies and to producers selling in interstate commerce.

In the case of *pipeline companies*, an applicant for a certificate must show: (1) that he possesses access to an adequate supply of natural gas; (2) that there exists a market for the gas; (3) that his proposed facilities are adequate to serve the market; and (4) that he possesses adequate financing to establish his proposed project. The Supreme Court has held that the refusal of a company to accept output from a producer in a contract dispute constitutes an abandonment of facilities subject to Commission approval even though the physical pipeline facilities have not in fact been disconnected.[9]

---

[7] *Interstate Natural Gas Company* v. *Federal Power Commission*, 331 U.S. 682 (1947).

[8] *Phillips Petroleum Company* v. *Wisconsin*, 347 U.S.

672 (1954).

[9] *United Gas Company* v. *Federal Power Commission*, 385 U.S. 83 (1966).

Some idea of the volume of Commission activity in this area can be gained from the fact that in fiscal year 1967 the Commission issued 298 pipeline certificates. Since 1966, the Commission has undertaken to afford gas distribution companies greater flexibility in seeking sources of supply and has issued a number of certificates to companies to serve areas already being served; thus, the Commission has undertaken to establish competitive conditions in the supply of natural gas to distributors. Certificate proceedings involving the establishment of competition of this nature are, of course, strongly contested by existing certificate holders, as well as by suppliers of competitive fuels, such as oil and coal.

A *producer of natural gas* must also obtain a certificate of public convenience and necessity before he makes a new sale of his output in interstate commerce. For all practical purposes, all independent producers (who sell to pipeline companies or to integrated producers) must thus obtain certificates if they wish to sell their output for resale in interstate commerce. Such a certificate proceeding involves a showing by the producer that the proposed price is consistent with both present and future "public convenience and necessity." As a matter of practice, the Commission has adopted a procedure of first issuing temporary certificates pending a final determination of a "just and reasonable" price (one approved by the Commission). A final or permanent certificate is then issued. Either a temporary or a permanent certificate may be (and often is) issued subject to conditions, particularly conditions pertaining to the maximum price which may be charged by the producer. (An alternative to a conditioned certificate would be for the Commission to issue a permanent certificate and then to institute a rate proceeding to determine whether the price is "just and reasonable.")

In 1957, the Supreme Court held that the Commission had erred in not issuing a conditioned certificate in a situation in which the Commission had allowed offshore Southern Louisiana gas production to be brought into interstate commerce at a price in excess of that which prevailed in the contiguous onshore Southern Louisiana producing area.[10] This case is known as the *CATC* case. As a matter of practice, the Commission has since fixed the prices in temporary certificates on an "in-line" basis, that is, the temporary price has been fixed at a level which is "in line" with other prices prevailing in the producing field in question, and no cost considerations have been taken into account. Some interesting cases have reached the courts as a result of this practice. In 1964, for example, the Supreme Court, in effect, held that the Commission could prescribe the actual price in issuing a temporary certificate. More specifically, the Court held that the Commission could impose a condition in a temporary certificate that the applicant should not increase his price pending a hearing on his petition for permanent certification.[11] (It is to be noted that, in general, producers may change their rates on their own initiative, subject to subsequent Commission approval or disapproval.)

An interesting case in 1965 grew out of the earlier 1964 decision in the *CATC* case mentioned above. Following the Supreme Court's decision that the Commission should have imposed conditions in the temporary certificates issued to the offshore Southern Louisiana producers, the Commission imposed conditions on the certificates granted: (1) requiring the producers to adhere to the "in-line" prices pending the final determination of "just and reasonable" prices; (2) ordering the producers to abstain from raising prices prior to a certain date; and (3) requiring the producers to refund to their customers the differences plus interest in the amounts collected under the original higher prices and the new temporary "in-line" prices. These conditions were upheld as a reasonable exercise of the Commission's power by the Supreme Court.[12] Finally, in 1968, in keeping with the trend of decision evident in the preceding cases, the Supreme Court held that the Commission could impose conditions on permanent certificates requiring producers to refund amounts collected under outstanding unconditioned temporary certificates in excess of the finally established price, and that parties other than the

---

[10] *The Atlantic Refining Company* v. *Federal Power Commission*, 360 U.S. 378 (1957).

[11] *Federal Power Commission* v. *Hunt*, 376 U.S. 515 (1964).

producer himself might challenge a temporary certificate at the time when a permanent certificate is applied for.[13] This decision obviously provides consumer representatives with excellent opportunities to seek redress for any errors made in the prices fixed in temporary certificates.

As we will see below, throughout this period, the Commission was working on the development of an industry-wide "area" pricing procedure for natural gas production. By 1967, this procedure had reached such an advanced stage of development that the Commission completed in that year only one producer proceeding employing an "in-line" price. It is to problems of ratemaking that we turn now.

Types of Natural Gas Ratemaking Problems

The Federal Power Commission is concerned with two types of natural gas ratemaking problems. One of these is the problem of natural gas *pipeline* rates; the other is the problem of natural gas *production* rates. In the case of integrated producers (who own natural gas production facilities as well as transmission facilities), the two problems are, of course, interrelated.

Natural Gas Pipeline Rates

In fixing natural gas pipeline rates, the Commission has largely relied on cost of service principles. In the case of integrated producers, it is necessary to make an allowance for the cost of production of the natural gas owned by the pipeline companies. One method which can be used is the rate base-rate of return method described in Chapter 24 in the discussion of the problem of determining the rate of return in the case of domestic surface transportation facilities. The *Hope Natural Gas* case, which it will be recalled laid the "fair return on fair value" doctrine of *Smyth* v. *Ames* to rest, involved a situation in which the Commission had used the original cost of natural gas production facilities in figuring the rate base to be used in a pipeline rate case. In the *Hope* case, the Court upheld the Commission's procedure, pointing out that the "end result" was the

significant question and that the Constitution did not require the Commission to adhere to any *particular* method of arriving at this end result.

An alternative method which the Commission has used, but which was not allowed to stand on appeal to a Court of Appeals is that of a "fair field price" based on the "fair market price for natural gas in the relevant field" as a basis for determining the cost of the pipeline's own production.[14] In the final analysis, the problem of determining the value of the gas produced by the pipeline company itself is not independent of the problem of determining the price of natural gas produced by independent producers, and we will see below that both problems have now been dealt with by an industry-wide area pricing approach. Proceedings looking to this result were instituted in 1966 and concluded in 1969. Indeed, in its *Annual Report for 1967*, the Commission reported its policy with regard to pipeline rates in this language:

> On April 13, 1966, the Commission initiated a new separate proceeding to determine whether the expense allowance for natural gas pipeline companies' own gas production should be based on an area price concept. Under present Commission policy, the cost allowance for the pipelines' gas production is determined by cost of service actually incurred, including a return on net investment.[15]

As an example of the Commission's workload in this area, it may be noted that during fiscal year 1967, 1,333 rate matters were filed by pipeline companies; ten of these were rate increase applications and 22 were rate reduction proposals. The rate reduction proposals resulted primarily from an opinion of the Commission requiring natural gas pipeline companies to pass on to their customers the tax savings resulting from the use by the companies of liberalized depreciation allowances in computing their federal income taxes.[16] The Commission's policy of requiring companies to pass tax savings along in the form of lower prices was upheld in a slightly different context by the Supreme Court in 1967. In the case in question, a regulated company was a

[12] *United Gas Improvement Company* v. *Callery Properties, Inc.*, 382 U.S. 223 (1965).

[13] *Federal Power Commission* v. *Sunray DX Oil Company*, 391 U.S. 9 (1968).

[14] *City of Detroit* v. *Federal Power Commission*, 230 F 2d 810 (1955).

[15] *Annual Report of the Federal Power Commission for Fiscal Year 1967*, op. cit., p. 47.

member of a group of consolidated companies, including two not subject to regulation which had suffered losses. A consolidated income tax return was filed, and the *actual* tax burden of the regulated company was thus less than it would have been had it filed a separate tax return. The company attempted to claim as its tax expense the amount it would have paid had it filed separately, but the Commission allowed it to claim only the *actual* amount of tax paid. The Commission's decision was upheld by the Supreme Court.[17]

Natural Gas Independent Producer Rates: Area Pricing

It has been noted that in 1954 the Supreme Court held that the Federal Power Commission had the duty to regulate independent producers of natural gas and that as a result of this decision the Commission was faced with the task of regulating many thousands of producers, although it had believed itself to be concerned only with the regulation of less than two hundred. An authoritative and penetrating analysis of the problems facing the Commission as a result of the *Phillips* case of 1954 and of the steps taken to deal with the problem has been provided by B. Joe Colwell. According to his account, after the *Phillips* decision:

. . . the FPC proceeded in an attempt to set wellhead gas prices on the traditional public utility individual company cost-of-service basis— the basis on which it had been regulating pipeline companies. The FPC considered the then contested rate increases and in 1960 disposed of the pre-1956 rate increases on the basis of Phillips' (the principal respondent) cost-of-service.

It had become obvious, however, that setting the price at which each individual producer could sell, based upon his cost, would be administratively impossible. . . . Therefore, on September 28, 1960, the Commission promulgated its Statement of General Policy 61–1 initiating area rate proceedings and setting tentative price levels which would serve as ceilings for new gas sales and price increases under existing contracts.[18]

The Permian Area Rate Cases

The Commission's Statement of General Policy 61–1 designated 11 pricing areas with respect to which proceedings were to be instituted. The *Permian Basin Area* proceeding was the first to be completed. This area consists of a gas producing area located partly in West Texas and partly in New Mexico. A Hearing Examiner began holding hearings in October 1961 and issued his order in September 1964. There were 384 parties represented in the proceeding, including 336 gas producers, and the final transcript contained more than 30,000 pages. An appeal was taken from the Hearing Examiner's order to the Commission which issued its decision in August, 1965. The decision was appealed eventually to the Supreme Court which decided the case in favor of the Commission in May, 1968.[19]

The Commission has itself described its *Permian Basin Area Opinion* as determining the following:

A two-price system for gas from the area, incorporating a separate price for new gas-well gas and a lower price for all other gas.

Specific standards for pipeline quality gas with deductions from the ceiling rate for gas of lesser quality, and upward and downward adjustments for variations in heat content.

A specific date, January 1, 1961, as the dividing line between new and flowing gas.

A minimum rate for gas provided it is of pipeline quality.[20]

Thus the Commission set a maximum *industry* price for gas produced from the area and adopted a two-price system (a higher price for new gas-well gas than for flowing gas) in recognition of the ability of firms in the industry to channel their exploratory activities either toward or away from the objective of discovering new sources of supply. This ability is referred to as *directionality*. By using the two-price system, the Commission sought to employ price functionally—as a policy tool to be used in encouraging firms to engage in a search for additional gas reserves.

[16] *Ibid.*, p. 46. (In 1968 the total number was 1,528.)

[17] *Federal Power Commission* v. *United Gas Pipeline Company*, 386 U.S. 237 (1967).

[18] B. Joe Colwell, "Natural Gas Area Pricing: Economic and Legal Considerations," *Social Science*

Quarterly (September, 1967), pp. 201–210, at p. 201.

[19] *Permian Basin Area Rate Cases*, 390 U.S. 747 (1968).

[20] *Annual Report of the Federal Power Commission for the Fiscal Year 1966* (Washington, D.C.: U.S. Government Printing Office, 1967), p. 130.

The maximum prices included a 12 per-cent return to producers on average production investments based on cost calculations made by the Commission's staff. The cost data in the case of new gas-well gas were composite cost data obtained from published sources and from the producers themselves by means of a series of questionnaires. The data were assembled and analyzed with a view to finding the national costs in 1960 of finding and producing gas-well gas. They were not intended to reflect conditions peculiar to the Permian Basin. In the case of all other gas, the composite costs used were the historical costs in the Permian Basin Area.

The Commission also required producers to make refunds of amounts collected in excess of the ceiling rates established. The total amount of such refunds was about $35 million.

The Supreme Court had little difficulty in upholding the Commission's industry-wide area pricing approach and cited cases of other regulatory agencies involving establishment of industry-wide maximum rates, as well as the *Nebbia* case discussed in Chapter 7.[21]

Colwell has concluded his analysis of this case by noting that the Commission's decision places it "even more solidly in the role of a regional economic planner." Indeed, he has continued:

The FPC has made another of those "prag-matic adjustments" that are supposed to characterize a liberal society and its economy. Hopefully this decision can provide a framework of regulation, primarily the setting of prices, and then allow the competitive elements of entre-preneurship to come to the fore. The Com-mission's avowed purpose is to allow for this development by providing a mandated price structure that relies on and encourages private initiative. Only time will tell if it is correct. And there is always the possibility that the "expert" judgment of the Commission is wrong. In this latter case, the Commission has provided a framework within which further adjustments can be made or, fortunately, it may abandon this framework and move to another, and still remain within the statutory and constitutional grounds.[22]

The correctness of Colwell's judgment, that the Commission has adopted the *method* of self-correcting value judgments in the determination of area rates, is emphasized by the fact that in May 1968, it issued a *Notice of Inquiry* in which it requested that all parties interested in area rate proceedings submit views and suggestions "as to what data collection system would be most appropriate for the *continuing review* of producer rates." In its *Annual Report for 1968* (published in 1969), the Commission also reported on various area rate proceedings which were nearing completion at the end of 1968.

The Use of an Econometric Model in the *Permian Basin Area Proceeding*

The *Permian Basin Area* proceeding is interesting not only because it involved a decision concerning a *maximum* industry-area price system but also because members of the Commission's Office of Economics put into evidence an econometric model which undertook to relate the price of natural gas to natural gas exploratory activity and to demands for natural gas for purposes of residential and commercial consumption.

An econometric model involves a mathe-matical specification of relationships thought to exist between one or more dependent variables and one or more independent variables and the use of various statistical techniques and procedures for attempting to determine from relevant data the validity and strength of the relationships postulated. Particularly to be noted is the fact that such a model can be put into evidence, where it is treated by the opposing side as the product of a hostile witness and subjected to attack, but that any attempt by a regulatory agency to make use of the results of such an econometric analysis without holding a hearing or observing the safeguards of procedural due process would be unlawful and constitute an abuse of discretion. Mathematical specification of relationships and the use of statistical techniques to produce strong circumstantial evidence upon which decisions may be based are clearly permissible when these techniques and the conclusions drawn from them are put into evidence where they may be subjected to cross-examination, but the advent of the age of the computer has not yet made obsolete the concept of procedural

---

[21] *Permian Area Rate Cases*, 390 U.S. 747 (1968), at pp. 768–770.

[22] Colwell, *op. cit.*, p. 210.

due process of law and one must be careful and not expect too much to result from the use of such econometric models.

The model put forward by the Commission's Staff in the *Permian Basin Area* case involved an assumption, strongly supported by circumstantial evidence in the form of statistical computations, that exploratory activity (measured by the number of exploratory wells drilled) was a function of seven independent variables, including an initial base price of natural gas, the wellhead price of crude oil, the marketed production of gas, the production of crude oil, the ratio of productive wells drilled to the total number of wells drilled, and time. Residential demand and industrial demand were similarly made functions of a number of independent variables.

These three equations were next related to one another through the price of natural gas.[23] Then, by inserting various assumed prices into these equations, the Commission's Staff witnesses undertook to forecast the probable (on the basis of their model) effects (of setting such prices) upon exploration and upon the demand for natural gas. Their model led them to the conclusion that an increase in the natural gas price would *reduce* both exploration and the demands for natural gas. The model did not, however, take account of "directionality."

The producers' advocates called on their own expert witnesses to attack not only the econometric techniques which had been employed but also to attack the knowledge of the natural gas industry possessed by the Commission's model builders. Moreover, the producers' advocates asserted rightly in their brief on appeal to the Commission:

The construction of an econometric model is not a purely mechanical procedure, but in every stage involves economic decisions requiring judgment. The greater part of the information used is of the subjective type. Use of subjective judgment was necessary in the selection of the relationships in the various equations, in the selection of the explanatory variables, in the choice of the mathematical forms of the equations, and in the choice of particular data used. In each instance the choice can have a great effect upon the relationships which are being measured and in most instances the choice required an intimate knowledge of the industry.[24]

The Hearing Examiner took the position that, since it ignored "directionality," the econometric model submitted by the Commission's Staff was not "relevant or material" to the problem—obviously, he had been convinced by the attack on the model (note that no attack was made upon the procedure of *use* of a model as an analytical device) by the producers' advocates. The Commission's opinion in the case completely ignored the econometric model.

What is to be concluded from all this is that, although an econometric model may be introduced into evidence by advocates of the position of one side or the other in a regulatory proceeding, the possibilities of cross-examination of the model builders and the use of other expert witnesses to refute the inferences drawn by the model builders should be retained; the mere use of mathematical formulations and of advanced statistical techniques does not provide instant absolute truth or instant solutions to the knotty problems facing those who must decide complex issues involving competing social interests. As a device for making clear underlying assumptions and relationships, the use of econometric techniques may be welcomed, but *not* at the expense of sacrificing the benefits of an adversary proceeding as a device for bringing to the forefront the competing social interests involved in every regulatory proceeding. It is for this reason that reliance upon the results of a model by a regulatory agency without holding a hearing in which the model could be subjected to challenges would constitute a denial of procedural due process.

Area Pricing and Pipeline Produced Natural Gas

In October 1969, the Commission decided that the area pricing procedure would be applied to all gas produced by integrated producers from new leases acquired after the date of the decisions.[25] A Hearing Examiner had decided in an initial decision that area rates would be applied to the first

[23] For a detailed description and analysis of this model see Joe Lee Steele, *A Critical Evaluation of the Uses of an Econometric Model in Cases Involving Natural Gas Rates* (microfilmed doctoral dissertation, The University of Texas at Austin, January, 1969.)

[24] Quoted in Steele, *op. cit.*, p. 64.

[25] Docket Number RP 66–24, Opinion Number 568, October 7, 1969.

10 percent of gas "produced off-system," but that with slight modifications, the cost of service method of determining rates should be continued.

A Concluding Comment

The problem of regulation of pipeline rates has inevitably forced the Commission to consider the rate to be applied to the integrated pipeline companies' own natural gas production. And from the adoption of this procedure it is a short step to the determination of rates for all natural gas production. Some writers have argued that natural gas production is a competitive industry which should not be subjected to Commission control; the use of *conditional* certificates of public convenience and necessity has, however, enabled the Commission to prevent the price of new gas from entering the market at levels far above those existing at the time of entry, thereby driving the price of all gas upward. Whether or not the 12 percent rate of return allowed in the *Permian Basin Area* case is high enough to result in a level of exploration to keep pace with increases in demands remains to be seen. This rate of return may very well be exceeded by those producers who have the good fortune to discover high quality reserves with small capital investments. In any case, the rate of return can be and presumably will be adjusted in either direction as experience dictates. In the case of the communications industry, federal control over entry is also exercised, but for technological rather than economic reasons in the case of broadcasting, as we will now see.

B. THE FEDERAL COMMUNICATIONS COMMISSION

Regulation Prior to 1934

In 1910, the Mann–Elkins Act (36 Stat. 544) conferred broad powers to regulate wire communications (telephone, telegraph, and cable) upon the Interstate Commerce Commission, but this "regulation proved largely nugatory partly by reason of the lack of an effective statutory mandate but also because of a lack of 'appropriations sufficient to carry on an investigation.'"[26] These powers were transferred to the Federal Communications Commission in 1934.

In 1927, Congress adopted legislation (44 Stat. 162) creating a Federal Radio Commission to license radio broadcasting stations, but this agency's life was at best an uncertain one, since it was created to function for one year, although its life was extended annually for additional one-year-periods by several subsequent statutes until 1930, when it was given permanent life. The functions of this agency were also transferred to the Federal Communications Commission in 1934.

The Federal Communications Commission: Organization and Functions in General

The Federal Communications Commission was created by Congress in 1934. The Commission was broadly charged with

. . . the purpose of regulating interstate and foreign commerce in communication by wire and radio so as to make available, so far as possible, to all people of the United States a rapid, efficient, nationwide, and worldwide wire and radio communication service with adequate facilities at reasonable charges, for the purpose of the national defense, for the purpose of promoting safety of life and property through the use of wire and radio communication, and for the purpose of securing a more effective execution of this policy by centralizing authority heretofore granted by law to several agencies and by granting additional authority with respect to interstate and foreign commerce in wire and radio communication.[27]

The Board performs judicial, legislative, and executive functions. The regulatory functions are performed chiefly by the four Bureaus. Thus the Common Carrier Bureau is concerned with regulation of common carriers by wire and radio; the Safety and Special Radio Bureau is concerned with licensing and regulation of a variety of radio stations not in the common carrier or broadcasting categories, for example, marine, aviation, and police radio stations. The Field Engineering Bureau performs monitoring and inspection functions, in-

---

[26] *Investigation of the Telephone Industry* (Report of the Federal Communications Commission, House Document 340, 76th Cong., 1st sess., 1939) (Washington, D.C.: U.S. Government Printing Office, 1939), p. 571.

[27] 350 Stat. 189, Sec. 1.

cluding examination of operators. The Broadcast Bureau is responsible for regulation of radio (AM and FM) and television stations. A special temporary Community Antenna Television (CATV) Task Force was also created in 1966 to study policy with respect to community antenna television (CATV) activities; as we will see later, the Supreme Court in 1968 upheld the power of the Commission to regulate such CATV systems.

General Description of Common Carriers

Included among the Common carriers subject to Commission regulation are firms carrying on interstate and foreign communications by wire, radio, cable, and satellites, including facsimile, telephoto, and broadcast transmissions. Communications common carriers are defined as those that provide public communications services for hire.

There are two types of common carriers. One group is fully regulated. The second is partially regulated and does not engage in interstate or foreign communications *except* through connection with the transmission services of nonaffiliated carriers. Broadcast stations are not included within the definition of common carriers.

The Commission controls construction, acquisition, discontinuance, merger, and curtailment of common carrier services. All charges, practices, classifications, and regulations of such common carriers must be "just and reasonable." All are required to file rate schedules for review and regulation by the Commission, which also prescribes record forms, accounting procedures, and depreciation rates. The most important area of common carrier regulation is that of the telephone industry.

Common Carriers: The Domestic Telephone Industry—The Bell System

The domestic telephone industry consists of about 2,250 independent companies and the Bell System. The Bell System consists of the telephone service, research, and supply companies controlled by the American Telephone and Telegraph Company which

has a virtual monopoly over interstate long distance telephone communication in the United States. This monopoly was established as a result of policies pertaining to the licensing of equipment manufactured under patents, the product of a deliberate plan of securing control of independent telephone companies. The history of A. T. & T. fills several volumes of hearings and reports published as House Documents and the interested reader may be referred to these sources for detailed information.[28] In brief, it may be noted that a policy was adopted of granting permanent licenses to independent companies to use telephone equipment produced under Bell System patents in exchange for a controlling stock interest in these companies which then, obviously, were no longer independent.

In 1934—and the picture has changed only slightly since then—the Federal Communications Commission described the Bell System structure in these words:

In the present corporate structure of the Bell System the American Telephone and Telegraph Co. is the parent organization, as well as the direct owner and operator of the interstate telephone facilities interconnecting the exchange and toll facilities of the associated and connecting companies. This company controls, through ownership of voting stock, 21 operating telephone companies commonly known as the associated companies. It also owns the Western Electric Co. which is the manufacturer and supplier for the system. The Bell Telephone Laboratories, Inc., jointly owned by the American Co. and the Western Electric Co., carries on research and development work for the system. Electrical Research Products, Inc., a wholly owned subsidiary of the Western Electric Co., licenses nontelephonic products under patents owned by the system. These are the more important component companies of the Bell System. There were in all, at the end of 1934, 273 corporations in which the American Co. either had direct or indirect ownership of 10 percent or more of the voting securities, or had potential control through various other means. In 181 of these companies the American Co.'s ownership of the outstanding voting securities was 50 percent or more. Of these 181 companies 29 were inactive; 104 were telephone companies; and 48 were engaged in various nontelephonic fields. Twenty-one of these nontelephonic subsidiaries operate in foreign countries. . . .

---

[28] See *Investigation of the Telephone Industry, op. cit.*; and *Report on Communications Companies* (House Report 1273, 73d Cong., 2d sess., 1934) (Washington, D.C.:

U.S. Government Printing Office, 1934). This report is sometimes referred to as the *Splawn Report*.

The relationship of the various instrumentalities constituting the Bell System is the result of stock ownership supplemented by agreements. The relationship of Western Electric Co. to the operating units of the Bell System is such that opportunity is afforded for pyramiding of profits. If Western Electric Co. has made excessive profits on its sales of materials and equipment for the construction of operating telephone plant and if rates for service are adequate to earn a fair return on the cost of such property, a double profit to the holding company will result; first, from the manufacture and sale of telephone equipment and, second, from the earnings of the operating company. The courts have held that Western Electric prices are not controlling in the determination of either investment, reproduction cost, or fair value of property of operating telephone companies in the Bell System; and that reasonable costs of manufacture plus a fair profit, rather than the prices charged by Western should be the controlling cost factors in determining fair value for rate making purposes. This declaration by the courts lays a foundation for the solution but does not solve the problem of determining the reasonableness of Western Electric prices, as they are reflected in investment accounts and reproduction cost estimates relating to individual operating companies, since the records of Western Electric do not readily lend themselves to analysis for this purpose.[29]

The Bell System is thus a clear example of a holding company system of the type illustrated in *Chart 9–3* in Chapter 9. In 1949 during the Truman Administration, the Department of Justice filed an antitrust complaint charging A. T. & T. and Western Electric with violating the Sherman Act in regard to the production and sale of telephone equipment. However, during the subsequent Eisenhower Administration, the case was settled by a consent decree according to whose terms A. T. & T. was permitted to retain its controlling interest in Western Electric. This decree had the effect —it has been noted in Chapter 12 in the subheading entitled, "*The Antitrust Division*" —of barring the United States from bringing any antitrust action in the future to require A. T. & T. to divest itself of its interest in Western Electric. Thus the arrangement was, so to speak, forever sanctified by the Eisenhower Administration.

The number of independent telephone companies has been decreasing, but few if any are being absorbed by the Bell System. Rather, the independent companies have been merging with one another. By far the largest of the independent companies, although it does not even remotely rival the Bell System in size, is the General Telephone and Electronics Company, which in 1959 controlled about one-third of all the independent telephone companies in the United States. This company is also a supplier of telephone equipment to other independent companies and a large defense contractor. In 1967, it had assets of about $5.4 billion as compared with A. T. & T.'s assets of about $37.6 billion. Standard Oil Company (New Jersey), the largest industrial corporation, had assets of around $13 billion the same year. Thus A. T. & T. was more than twice as large by this measure as the largest industrial corporation and about seven times as large as its closest competitor.

The A. T. & T. Rate Case of 1967

Prior to 1964, the Commission permitted the Bell System to maintain a 7 to 7.5 percent interstate earnings level. In 1965 earnings rose above 8 percent. In October, 1965, the Commission undertook to investigate the lawfulness of Bell rates. The final record of the case totalled more than 10,000 pages plus an additional 3,485 pages of exhibit material. The Commission's order of July 5, 1967 required Bell to reduce interstate rates by $120 million effective October 1, 1967, and affirmed the 7 to 7.5 percent rate of return policy which had previously been adopted. In September 1967, the Commission reconsidered its order and permitted $20 million of the rate reduction to be deferred, allowing A. T. & T. to include in its rate base $544 million of new plant under construction and set a new effective date of November 1, 1967.

A. T. & T. was represented before the Commission by a number of well-known economist-expert-witness-advocates, including Dr. Wm. J. Baumol, Dr. George L. Bach, and Dr. Paul W. McCracken who became Chairman of the Council of Economic Advisors in January 1969 at President Nixon's request. Testimony of all of the economists employed by A. T. & T. was on the whole favorable to the com-

[29] *Investigation of the Telephone Industry, op. cit.*, pp.575–576.

pany's point of view. Whether or not the costs of obtaining such expert testimony were included in the "necessary and proper" expenses of the company in figuring its cost of service does not appear in the final opinion.

The Econometric Model in the A. T. & T. Rate Case

An econometric model was put into evidence by an economist-expert-witness-advocate employed by the Commission. The Commission described the model by saying:

139. Dr. Myron J. Cordon, an FCC consultant utilized a unique approach using an econometric model, or price equation. According to Dr. Gordon, this established the relationship between market price, dividends, growth of dividends, the leverage or use of debt financing, and the stock financing rates. Coefficients were estimated on the basis of 49 electric utility companies, which Gordon found had no lesser risk than Respondents. Gordon found that the annual increase in Respondent's total assets had been about 8% in recent years and assumed that the Commission would authorize continuation of that rate of growth. At that rate of investment, he found 7%–7¼% to be the required rate of return.[30]

The Commission also employed several other economist-expert-witnesses to represent the Staff's position. In its opinion, the Commission commented on the testimony of one of these, Dr. Lionel W. Thatcher, as well as upon the econometric model put into evidence by Dr. Gordon in these words:

232. The two consultants retained by the Commission, Dr. [Lionel W.] Thatcher and Dr. [Myron J.] Gordon both propose a rate of return in the range of 6¾%–7¼%. Dr. Thatcher followed the cost of capital approach and utilized an imputed capital structure of 45% debt and 55% equity.

233. As we have already put forth, Dr. Gordon proposed a new and challenging approach to the question of fixing a rate of return in proceedings involving regulated entities. His econometric model, it appears to us, *has promise* of being a useful tool in this difficult and often vexing area of regulation.

234. We have found his approach and methods useful in analysis and evaluation of the effect of capital structure, i.e., the ratios of debt and equity upon the overall cost of capital. *It lends support to our conclusion* that a regulatory determination of revenue requirements can rely, in part, on announced and anticipated changes in capital structure.

235. *We have not had the opportunity to analyze, evaluate, and test fully his model to determine all of its implications insofar as fixing an overall rate of return is concerned.* However, we believe that it merits further attention as a means of making available more objective data and substantive support *for the exercise of subjective judgments in fixing a rate of return.* We would, therefore, encourage further study and refinement of the model to make it more useful in resolving the special problems which arise in the field of regulated entities.[31]

In the *A. T. & T.* case therefore, the Federal Communications Commission—unlike the Federal Power Commission in the *Permian Basin Area Rate* proceeding—did take notice of the econometric model offered in evidence by its Staff, although *in neither case was the decision based on the model.* In the *A. T. & T.* case, the model was also attacked both on technical grounds and on grounds that its content was subjective and unrealistic.

Particularly to be noted in the preceding quotation is the fact that the Commission recognized that the econometric model would merely provide an aid to a decision based on "subjective judgment." Indeed, Dr. Gordon's selection of 49 electric utility companies and his assumption that the risk of A. T. & T. was comparable to that experienced by these 49 companies also constituted the use of his own subjective judgment.

In any event, the Commission did not explicitly base its decision upon the model. In the final analysis, the key statement made by the Commission concerning its use of a 7 to 7.5 percent return was probably this one:

341. . . . Although we regard this range of return as appropriate on the basis of this record, we recognize that the facts and circumstances upon which our determination rests may change with time. We will, of course, continue to observe the trends in Respondents' interstate operating results and matters related thereto. As and when the going level of Respondents' inter-

---

[30] *In the Matter of American Telephone and Telegraph Company and the Associated Bell System Companies*, Docket No. 16258, Interim Decision and Order of the Federal Communications Commission, July 5, 1967, p. 45.

[31] *Ibid.*, pp. 49–50. (Italics mine.)

state earnings approaches either the upper or lower limits of this range, we will promptly consider what further action may be required in light of the then current conditions. This is not to be construed to mean that any level of earnings which exceeds 7.5% or falls below 7.0% will warrant immediate action looking toward rate adjustments. Whether or not remedial action will be required will depend upon all relevant circumstances obtaining at the time.[32]

Thus, obviously, the Commission adopted the instrumental *method* of self-correcting value judgments as the rationale for its decision. Indeed, hearings concerning A. T. & T.'s rate practices continued throughout 1968.

Common Carriers: Decline of the Telegraph Industry—Diversification of Western Union

Western Union's share of total domestic telegraph message service amounts to about 60 percent. The volume of domestic public messages had declined in 1966 by about 60 percent from its World War II level, however. In 1965, the Common Carrier Bureau of the Commission completed a report on the domestic telegraph industry and made a number of recommendations, most of which pertained to the continued diversification of Western Union and to the establishment of Western Union as an integrated message carrier. Western Union had in fact begun its program of diversification in 1945 when it opened the first public microwave (a very high frequency radio wave ranging from one to several inches in length) system between New York and Philadelphia. In 1964, Western Union completed a coast-to-coast microwave system.[33] Among the various new services offered by Western Union (in addition to services such as "Perfume by Wire"), mention must be made of its Telex (direct-dial printer exchange) service and its "Hot Line" service (which provides a subscriber with a permanent connection between telephone stations without the necessity for dialing). It also operates an automatic digital data network service (AUTODIN) for the Department of Defense. Western Union competes with the Bell System in the offering of some services; the Common

Carrier Bureau recommended in its report that Western Union be permitted to acquire the Bell System TWX (teletypewriter service) and to combine this service with its own Telex (dialprinter service). Despite the decline in the volume of domestic telegraph messages, the various new services offered have prevented Western Union's revenues from declining. In short, the solution to the problem of declining demand for telegraph message service has been found to lie in the offering of new services resulting from technological advances in the communications field and in the increasing use of high speed computers.

Characteristics of Wireless Communication

Wireless communications are carried on by the production of electromagnetic waves by a transmitting station and the reception and translation of these waves by a receiver. The frequencies of the waves are measured in numbers of waves per second, and the units of measurement are kilocycles (thousands of waves per second), megacycles (millions of waves per second) and gigacycles (thousands of millions or billions of waves per second). In standard or AM broadcasting, the *amplitude* of the waves is varied, and the Commission has assigned the frequency range of from 55 to 1600 kilocycles per second to this use. To insure that stations will not interfere with one another, it is necessary to assign a bandwidth of ten kilocycles to each station. The power and location of each station determine how many stations can be assigned to a specific frequency. Frequency modulation (FM radio) employs a technique of varying the *frequency* of the carrier wave while the amplitude is kept constant. The frequencies between 88 and 108 megacycles have been assigned to FM radio. Each station requires a bandwidth of 400 kilocycles, but transmission is relatively interference free. Low frequency waves, such as those assigned to AM radio radiate along the ground, but high frequency waves travel in straight lines, and for best reception it is necessary for the receiving antenna to be able to "see" the sending antenna. The Commission has allotted the frequencies of from 54 to 216 megacycles to VHF television broadcasting,

---

[32] *Ibid.*, pp. 106–107.
[33] This section is based on *Annual Reports of the*

Federal Communications Commission for 1966 and 1967. Individual footnotes will not be used.

and the frequency range of from 470 to 890 megacycles to UHF television broadcasting. The range of frequencies beyond 890 megacycles and ranging into the gigacycles is called the microwave spectrum. This band of frequencies is used for long distance telephone circuits and for communication by means of earth satellites. Microwave networks consist of an originating transmitting station and a series of relay stations, that is, a series of receiving–transmitting stations to send the transmission along to its final destination. Remote control television cameras used for on-the-spot telecasts often use microwaves to transmit to their base transmitter. Much use is made of the microwave band by government agencies, police, public utilities, and private business undertakings. Microwaves can also be used to operate equipment by remote control, and are being used in some household appliances, for example, in fireless cooking units.

Broadcasting

The term "broadcasting" is defined by the Commission as the dissemination of radio and television communications for public reception. The Commission does not regulate station rates. Stations are not common carriers and are not required to sell their time to everyone who requests it. However, the Commission does issue broadcast licenses, generally for three-year periods. Applicants must be legally, technically, and financially qualified and show that they will operate in the public interest. Up until January 1969, the Commission had never refused to renew a license granted to an existing broadcast station. At that time, however, the Commission rejected the application of Boston television station WHDH–TV for renewal and granted the license in question to another firm. The owners of the television station also owned a powerful radio station, an FM station, and a newspaper in Boston, and evidence introduced in the case disclosed that the television station had failed to broadcast a local news item so that the news value of the story in the newspaper would not be devalued. (Docket No. 8739, January 23, 1969.)

The Commission does not exercise control over program content; however, Section 315 of the Communications Act requires licensees to afford equal opportunity to use broadcast facilities to all legally qualified political candidates, and under the Commission's "fairness" doctrine, licensees must encourage the broadcast of various aspects of public issues.

In June 1969, the Commission's rules pertaining to the application of the "fairness" doctrine in cases of "personal attack" were upheld by the Supreme Court despite an argument that these rules constituted an abridgment of the First Amendment's guarantee of free speech.[33a] In its opinion, the Court remarked that the First Amendment guarantee applied to and protected the rights of the listening and viewing public and that it was these rights rather than those of the broadcaster which were "paramount."

The Commission does not ordinarily control the content of commercials. However, in February, 1969, it announced that it would consider a proposed rule which would ban the broadcast of cigarette commercials by television and radio (34 *Federal Register* 1959, February 11, 1969). Interested persons were given until July 7, 1969 to file reply comments concerning the proposed rule.

The Commission does limit the number of stations a single firm may own to seven AM, seven FM, and seven television stations. No more than five of the latter may be VHF.

Much of the Commission's regulatory activity in this area is devoted to technical matters, such as issuing licenses in such a way as to insure that stations operating on the same frequency are located in such a way and authorized to operate at an output level so that they will not interfere with one another, thereby minimizing "co-channel" interference; similar considerations must be taken into account in licensing stations operating on adjacent frequencies to reduce "adjacent" channel interference.

Attempts by the Commission to regulate program content or the content of commercials would, of course, raise knotty problems of censorship under the First Amendment. This fact explains the Com-

---

[33a] *Red Lion Broadcasting Co.* v. *FCC*, 395 U.S. 367 (1969).

mission's relative inaction in this area. It has, however, issued regulations restricting TV acquisitions in large markets in an attempt to insure competition and restricted network control over programming. In the top 50 markets, the rules regulating multiple ownership limit ownership by one owner to three stations, not more than two of which can be VHF. Among the limitations on the use of network-owned programs, rules have been proposed to limit the use of such programs to not more than 50 percent of prime time (6 to 11 p.m.).

In 1965, the Commission also issued a "Statement of Policy Concerning Loud Commercials." In some cases, it may be remarked, the loudness is incorporated in the recording supplied to the station and is not the result of action by the station; the Commission has placed the responsibility for detecting such cases involving pre-recorded commercials on the stations. Thus, subject to the free speech limitation of the First Amendment, the Commission has taken some actions in the area of broadcasting looking toward better service. However, the licensing function is essentially a techno-logical one, designed to control interference among stations and not a form of economic regulation. Problems of FM radio inter-ference with TV channels 7 to 13 also exist; in regard to these, the Commission has urged set manufacturers to install suitable filters and has itself undertaken to control such interference through the licensing function.

Subscription or "Pay" Television

The Commission first authorized over-the-air subscription television on an experi-mental basis in 1950. The method used involved the sending of a "scrambled signal" to be decoded by a special device attached to the subscriber's set. Several other experiments followed, and in 1966 the Commission's Subscription Television Com-mittee was created to study and report on the matter. The Committee reported in 1967; and the following excerpt from the Commission's *Annual Report for 1967* details the recommendations made:

Shortly after the close of the fiscal year, the Commission's Subscription Television Com-mittee issued its report on proposals for over-the-air pay-TV.

The report, submitted by Commissioners James J. Wadsworth (committe chairman), Robert E. Lee, and Kenneth A. Cox, for Commission consideration, consisted of a Fourth Report and Order (docket 11279) proposing establishment of over-the-air subscription tele-vision (STV) as a permanent broadcast service and a Second Further Notice of Proposed Rule-making, inviting comments on technical rules for equipment and system performance cap-ability. Oral argument on the Report and Order was held before the full Commission on October 2, 1967.

Under the terms of the Fourth Report and Order, STV authorizations would be granted to stations only in communities within the primary coverage area (grade A contour) of five or more commercial TV stations. The station of the STV applicant would be counted as one of the five. While there are no provisions for minimum or maximum hours of STV programing, the STV station would have to meet FCC requirements for minimum broadcast hours for non-STV programing.

STV would be permitted on both VHF and UHF stations but only one authorization would be allowed in any one community. There is no provision for any single, specific technical STV system.

Except where conditions do not permit, STV service would have to be provided in the primary coverage area to all persons desiring it. Charges, terms, and conditions of service would have to be applied uniformly and any subscriber classific-ations would have to be approved by the Commission. STV decoders, attached to sub-scribers' sets, would have to be leased, not sold to subscribers.

Regulations on broadcast material would prohibit the showing of feature films more than 2 years old. A limited number of feature films more than 10 years old would, however, be permitted each year. STV would not be per-mitted to broadcast sports events which were regularly televised in the community within 2 years preceding the proposed STV broadcast. These regulations are designed to prevent the "siphoning" of program material from free tele-vision.

In order to insure the presentation of at least a minimum amount of cultural and educational programing, STV rules would require that feature films and sports programing not exceed 90 percent of total program time.

No commercials would be permitted on STV.

Except as waived by the Commission, rules and policies applicable to conventional TV stations would apply to STV operations. STV authorizations would not be issued for periods longer than those of regular TV licensees.

CATV carriage and nonduplication rules

would apply to the conventional programing of an STV station. CATV systems, however, would not be required to carry STV programing. Subject to Commission approval, an STV station would be permitted to make arrangements with CATV systems within its grade B contour—the extreme range of its effective coverage—to have STV programs carried over the cable. No such arrangements would be permitted with CATV systems outside the grade B contour of the station. This aspect would be reserved for further study.

Cable STV and STV program origination by CATV systems would also be subject to further Commission investigation.

(On November 16, 1967, the House Interstate and Foreign Commerce Committee adopted a resolution asking the Commission to refrain from acting on the Fourth Report and Order for one year or until the Communications Act is amended to authorize STV.)[34]

Clearly, the Fourth Report and Order contemplated a higher degree of control over programming of STV stations than the Commission now exercises over "free" television stations. No amendment to the Communications Act has yet been adopted, and the final decision pertaining to this question is still pending.

Community Antenna Television Systems

Community Antenna Television Systems (CATV) are facilities which receive one or more broadcast signals from commercial stations and then amplify and distribute the amplified signals to subscribers. When first established, such systems were mainly for the purpose of serving remote communities unable to receive satisfactory signals. In recent years, however, CATV systems have been established within the primary service areas of licensed commercial stations. CATV systems can transmit signals on up to 12 channels, while licensed stations can transmit on only one. Problems of competition with licensed stations, of duplication of programs, and of origination of programs by firms operating CATV systems have thus arisen. The Commission has undertaken to control and regulate CATV systems primarily, as in the case of subscription TV, with a view to

insuring that already licensed stations are not driven out of business. In 1968, the Supreme Court upheld the power of the Commission to regulate this aspect of the communications industry under the Communications Act of 1934.[35] Interestingly enough, in the same year, the Court held that amplification and distribution of signals by CATV companies constituted *viewing* and not *performance* since the systems do no more than enhance the ability of subscribers to receive television broadcasts; and thus, the activities of the CATV companies do not fall within the provisions of the copyright laws.[36]

Educational Broadcasting; The Corporation for Public Broadcasting

In the Communications Act of 1934, Congress directed the FCC to study the question of making radio frequencies available for educational purposes, but (except for the issuance of a few licenses to university stations) little was done. With the expansion of FM broadcasting after World War II, the number of educational stations broadcasting primarily classical and semiclassical music increased. In June 1967, there were 127 educational television stations on the air; about two-thirds of these were owned by educational institutions, and the remainder were supported by community organizations. About two thirds of the stations were UHF.

Various plans and proposals for an educational television network have been made. The Ford Foundation has made large grants for this purpose, and a study financed by the Foundation proposed establishment of a domestic satellite system to link educational stations; unused channels would be leased to commercial stations, and the income would be used to provide financial assistance to the educational systems.

In 1967, Congress enacted The Public Broadcasting Act (P.L. 90–129). Title II of the Act provided for organization of a nonprofit corporation, the Corporation for Public Broadcasting, with the functions of assisting in the development of educational

[34] *Annual Report of the Federal Communications Commission for 1967* (Washington, D.C.: U.S. Government Printing Office, 1968), pp. 39–40.
[35] *United States* v. *Southwestern Cable Company,* 392

U.S. 157 (1968).
[36] *Fortnightly Corporation* v. *United Artists*, 392 U.S. 390 (1963).

programs of "high quality," and of assisting in the establishment and development of one or more educational television network systems. Assistance was also to be provided to educational radio broadcasting. An appropriation of $9 million for fiscal year 1968 was authorized, pending the development of a program of long range financing. The future of educational television stations is and will continue to be largely a matter dependent upon local support.

Regulation of the Communications Satellite Corporation (Comsat)

The history of the establishment of the Communications Satellite Corporation (Comsat) has already been given in Chapter 9 under the heading, "*The Communications Satellite Corporation: A Government-Created Private Monopoly*". It will be recalled that fears were expressed by some that the Corporation would not be effectively regulated by the Commission. During the Kennedy and Johnson Administrations, however, the Commission did actively undertake to regulate the Corporation: a rate investigation was begun in 1965. In February 1968, the Commission concluded that Comsat's earnings for calendar year 1968 would be "below the minimum level for a fair rate of return."

In 1964, a number of related international agreements were made providing a framework for ownership, establishment, and operation of a global communications satellite system. The product of these agreements was the International Telecommunications Satellite Communications Consortium (Intelsat), whose membership totalled 62 countries in 1968. The Communications Satellite Corporation (Comsat) is the United States representative in Intelsat; actions taken pursuant to Comsat's participation in the international organization are subject to Commission approval. Numerous communications satellites over both the Atlantic and Pacific Oceans now provide international television, telephone, and telegraph service and are used in support of the United States space exploration program.

In addition to its participation in Intelsat, Comsat has provided facilities for domestic use of satellites. Both A. T. & T. and Western Union have filed applications with the Commission for domestic satellite programs to provide service to all users, including television; in addition, the American Broadcasting Company filed an application, which the Commission rejected on grounds that it was technically defective, for establishment of a system to be employed for broadcast purposes. The question facing the Commission is thus one of whether or not to allow competition in the use of satellites for domestic purposes as an adjunct to its policy of rate regulation. A related problem is that of whether or not to allow joint ownership of such facilities by Comsat and common carriers. In 1966, the Commission authorized the joint ownership of earth stations. Since A. T. & T. (as we have seen in Chapter 9) owns about 29 percent of the stock of Comsat (the largest single block), one may question whether or not any real difference is made by this policy.

In January 1970, it should be noted, the Nixon Administration sent a Memorandum to the Chairman of the Federal Communications Commission urging that a policy of allowing competition (for example, by NBC, CBS, and ABC) with Comsat in the ownership and use of domestic communications satellites be adopted.[38] The Administration's Memorandum emphasized that a policy should be adopted of encouraging the development of domestic satellites "to the extent that private enterprise finds them economically and operationally feasible" but that there was no need to adopt a policy calling for immediate establishment of such a communications system.

In regulating Comsat, the Commission has adopted the view that the Corporation is primarily a carrier's carrier and should be allowed to serve noncarriers (including the Government) only in exceptional circumstances. The Commission has, moreover, undertaken to regulate Comsat as a monopoly and has prescribed the accounting procedures the Corporation is to follow. The order instituting rate investigations begun

---

[38] The memorandum is reproduced in *Assessment of Space Communications Technology* (Hearings before the House Subcommittee on Science and Applica-tions, 91st Cong., 2d sess., 1970) (Washington, D.C.: U.S. Government Printing Office, 1970), pp. 244–247.

in 1965 included a provision that certain revenues be placed in a deferred credit account until such time as the Commission orders the release of these revenues. It does not follow, of course, that the policies adopted and enforced by the Commission, whose members were largely appointed during the Kennedy and Johnson Administrations, will be continued by another Commission whose members have been appointed by an administration hostile to enforcement of regulation, and, to this extent, the fears expressed by those who opposed the establishment of Comsat as a privately owned monopoly in 1962 were justified.

A Concluding Comment

As we have seen in the preceding discussion, the Federal Communications Commission exercises broad authority over entry into and exit from the communications industry, but its power over rates does not include power to fix the rates of commercial broadcasting stations. In this respect its ratemaking activities are less extensive than are those of the Federal Power Commission. These two Commissions perform economic regulatory functions concerning the industries with which they are respectively concerned. And many of the aspects of this regulation can also be found in the regulation of domestic surface, ocean, and air transportation discussed in earlier chapters. Moreover, many of the same problems face state regulatory commissions which exercise authority over various public service industries at the local level.

In the chapters which follow, we will examine the activities of a number of other regulatory agencies and governmental organizations, but of the agencies to be discussed hereafter one only exercises price control (ratemaking power) and none exercises control over long-run supply (control over entry and exit). Our discussion of the performance at the federal level of these two economic regulatory functions has now been largely completed. In the next chapter we will be concerned with the activities of two federal agencies which are principally concerned with the elimination of fraud and deception on the part of sellers in security and product markets and of agencies concerned with controlling environmental pollution.

28

The Physical Environment; Foods, Drugs, and Cosmetics; Securities and Security Markets

This chapter undertakes to discuss the activities of various agencies primarily concerned with the exercise of police power functions in areas in which, even if perfect competition existed, the free market system would not operate to protect certain social interests whose protection is deemed vital to national welfare. The first major subdivision is devoted to a consideration of various agencies concerned with problems pertaining to pollution of the physical environment and includes a discussion of the Environmental Quality Council created by legislation signed into law by President Nixon in January 1970. The second major subdivision is concerned with a discussion of the activities of the Food and Drug Administration, an agency which exists as an entity within the Consumer Protection and Environmental Health Service of the Department of Health, Education, and Welfare. The third major subdivision is devoted to the Securities and Exchange Commission, whose police functions are analogous to those of the Food and Drug Administration.

A. THE PHYSICAL ENVIRONMENT

Nature of the Problem

Although the United States contains less than 6 percent of the world's population, it annually consumes about 40 percent of the world's resources. The very high levels of consumption and output enjoyed by the United States result in much pollution of the environment. It has been estimated that each year Americans discard about 76 billion glass and tin containers. Among the principal sources of air pollution is the internal combustion engine; carbon monoxide exhaust fumes from automobile exhaust systems are a principal source of air pollution in industrial areas. The world as a whole is faced with a population problem: in 1930 world population was estimated at 2 billion and, at present rates of increase, the figure is predicted to reach 7.5 billion by the year 2000.

The problem of maintaining the delicate balance between man and his physical environment has not much concerned economists, who have largely centered their attention on problems of economic growth, a growth which has carried with it various disturbances of that balance. Among the peripheral problems of economics has been the problem of *externalities*, a problem of the divergence between private and social costs of production. One of the earliest economists to deal with such problems was an English economist, A. C. Pigou. Pigou identified pollution of the environment as a case of external diseconomies of production in which firms make use of the environment at no cost to themselves to impose social costs of production upon society. The prices charged by such firms do not cover the cost to society of disposing of waste materials into the air or into streams because firms do not pay for the use of the environment. Thus the social cost of production of the products in question is greater than the actual private cost of production, and prices in this situation do not measure the social cost of the goods produced.

Various laws dealing with problems of pollution have been adopted by Congress and their enforcement has been made a responsibility of numerous different agencies. A significant attempt to coordinate existing policies and programs was undertaken both by Congress and the President in 1969–70. In the following paragraphs we will consider examples of both these actions.

Some Environmental Control Agencies

The Consumer Protection and Environmental Health Service. In July 1968, the Secretary of Health, Education, and Welfare established the Consumer Protection and Environmental Health Service within his Department. This Service consists of three operating Administrations; the National Air Pollution Control Administration; the Environmental Control Administration; and the Food and Drug Administration. The last-named agency has a long history and continues to operate as an entity within the Service. The work of this Administration thus warrants intensive discussion and the agency is treated separately in Subdivision B below.

In general, the new Service has the functions of conducting continuing research,

implementing existing programs, and making recommendations for further programs in the area of consumer health protection. Thus the National Air Pollution Administration has the function of administering the Clean Air Act of 1963, as amended, and the Air Quality Act of 1967. This legislation provides funds for research and developmental efforts in the area of air pollution generally and establishes national control over motor vehicle air pollution. The Administration has defined geographic air-quality control regions and air-quality criteria.[1] The geographic air-quality control regions serve as a basis for interstate compacts to deal with the problem at the local level. The Administration has also established air-quality monitoring programs and undertaken to coordinate federal and state air-pollution control activities. Eventually, the States will be assisted by the projection of air pollution trends and by technical engineering assistance.

The Environmental Control Administration is concerned with conducting research and implementing action programs in a broad group of topics, ranging from rat control in urban areas to the presence of radioactive matter in the atmosphere. It also performs the functions assigned to the Department in the area of water supply and sea resources.

The Federal Water Pollution Administration. Problems pertaining to water pollution are primarily a responsibility of the Department of the Interior under the Federal Water Pollution Act. The latter agency has established water quality standards after holding public hearings, and personnel of its Division of Technical Services assist local authorities in dealing with spot water pollution problems, for example, those caused by contamination of a bay with oil resulting from the breaking-up of a tanker.[2] The Water Pollution Control Administration has estimated that the cost of construction of local sewage plants to serve as alternatives to disposal of waste in streams and rivers will amount to $14.4 billions by 1980 measured in 1966 dollars. The estimated operation and treatment costs amount to $1.4 billion for a five-year period ending

---

[1] *Annual Report of the Department of Health, Education, and Welfare for 1968* (Washington, D.C.: U.S. Government Printing Office, 1969), p. 293 ff.

[2] *Its Your World* (United States Department of the Interior, 1969) (Washington, D.C.: U.S. Government Printing Office, 1969), p. 51 ff.

in 1973. The implementation of the Water Quality Act was assigned by Congress to an agency of the Department of the Interior rather than to the Department of Health, Education, and Welfare because the problem of water pollution is related to, and encompasses, a conservation aspect; and conservation of natural resources has traditionally been a function of the Department of the Interior.[2a]

The Forest Service. The Forest Service of the Department of Agriculture is responsible for administering 154 national forests and 19 grasslands projects. Twin policies of multiple use and sustained yield have been adopted. Watershed management to regulate the flow of streams and prevent erosion is practiced along with experimentation in methods of harvesting and growing timber. Wildlife and fish conservation practices are followed. The Service cooperates with state conservation agencies in carrying out its functions.

The Soil Conservation Service. Another agency within the Department of Agriculture concerned with conservation practices is the Soil Conservation Service, created in 1935. This agency also has responsibilities for watershed management and planning and conducts programs to prevent soil erosion, foster recreation, and protect wildlife.

The Agricultural Research Service. This agency, also within the Department of Agriculture, performs both research and regulatory functions. Among its regulatory functions is that of pesticide use control.

A detailed report on the relationship between the use of pesticides and environmental health was made at the end of 1969 to the Secretary of Health, Education, and Welfare by a special committee created by him to study the problem.[2b] Among other things, the committee recommended that approval of the Secretaries of the Departments of Health, Education, and Welfare and of the Interior be required, along with that of the Secretary of Agriculture, for all pesticide regulations. The committee pointed to a conflict between the objectives of increased agricultural output due to the use of pesticides and the effect on environmental health of such use. It also recommended elimination of all uses of DDD and DDT in the United States within two years, excepting in cases approved by the three Cabinet Officers mentioned above. These "hard" pesticides, the committee pointed out, are washed from fields into streams and then deposited in the bodies of fish eventually eaten by humans. Thus a pesticide chain is created with humans becoming the eventual depositories of such pesticides.[2c]

Other Agencies. Responsibility for administering programs affecting the environment is widely diffused throughout the Federal Government. Thus the Fish and Wildlife Service of the Department of Interior has certain responsibilities, and the Department of Transportation and the Department of Housing and Urban Affairs both have responsibilities pertaining to the changes produced in the environment as a result of highway-building programs in urban areas. New legislation enacted by Congress in December 1969 and signed by President Nixon in January 1970 is designed to try to bring some order out of the chaos and diffusion of responsibility and authority in this area.

The Environmental Policy Act and the Environmental Quality Council (83 Stat. 852)

The Environmental Policy Act, signed into law in 1970 by President Nixon, was modeled upon the Employment Act of 1946 and creates an Environmental Quality Council as a counterpart to the Council of Economic Advisors. Indeed, some of those advocating the passage of the new law thought of the new Council as a "counterweight" to the Council of Economic Advisors and argued that a conflict existed between the policies of continued growth of the economy and environmental balance.[2d]

The Environmental Policy Act. As has been noted, the Environmental Policy Act became law in 1970. Title I of this law contains a "national declaration of environmental policy." The first section of the law contains a declaration by Congress of a

---

[2a] *The Cost of Clean Water* (Department of the Interior) (Washington, D.C.: U.S. Government Printing Office, 1968), p. 3 ff.

[2b] *Report of the Secretary's Commission on Pesticides and Environmental Health* (Department of Health, Education, and Welfare) (Washington, D.C.: U.S. Government Printing Office, 1969).

[2c] *Ibid.*, pp. 7–19.

[2d] *Environmental Quality* (Hearings before the House Subcommittee on Fisheries and Wildlife Conservation, 91st Cong., 1st sess., 1969) (Washington, D.C.: U.S. Government Printing Office, 1969), p. 16 ff.

"continuing policy" of Congress "to use all practicable means . . . to create and maintain conditions under which man and nature can exist in productive harmony and fulfill the social, economic, and other requirements of present and future generations of Americans." Title II imposes upon federal agencies the duty of taking into account the environmental effects of existing and proposed programs. The agencies are directed to adopt an "interdisciplinary approach" to environmental problems and, in consultation with the Environmental Quality Control Council established by the Act, "to develop methods and procedures" which will insure that "presently unquantified environmental identities and values may be given appropriate consideration in decisionmaking along with economic and technical considerations." It is clear from the hearings on this legislation that those who sponsored it wished to emphasize non-economic variables and were not satisfied with the results which had so far been produced in our "dollar-directed economy." Price as a measure of social value had no place in their thoughts. It is not likely that economists will have the decisive voice in the formulation of environmental policy.

The Environmental Quality Council. The Act creates a three-member Council within the Executive Office of the President to assist him in making an annual Environmental Quality Report (commencing July 1, 1970), to make environmental studies, and to recommend environmental policies.

About one-third of President Nixon's 1970 *State of the Union Message to Congress* dealt with problems of pollution.[2e] Among other things, the President said:

We can no longer afford to consider air and water common property, free to be abused by anyone without regard to the consequences. Instead, we should now begin to treat them as scarce resources, which we are no more free to contaminate than we are free to throw garbage in our neighbor's yard. This requires comprehensive new regulations. It also requires that, to the extent possible, the price of goods should be made to include the costs of producing and disposing of them without damage to the environment.

On March 7, 1970, President Nixon issued Executive Order 11,514. This order had the effect of converting the newly established Environmental Quality Council from a *report-and-study staff agency* to a *direct action agency* and gave the Council, in the sphere of its activities, far more power than has ever been held by the Council of Economic Advisors. For example, the order directed the Council to issue guidelines to federal agencies in the area of environmental control and further directed the Council to issue such other instructions and require such reports from other federal agencies "as may be required to carry out the Council's responsibilities under the act." Centralization in the Council of authority over programs, policies, and proposals to deal with environmental problems was thus the central theme of the order.

The first steps have now been taken, and it seems clear that the federal police power will be extensively used and the federal activities will be greatly expanded in the area of environmental control in coming decades. These activities may well involve a redirection of some of our economic growth into channels to improve and maintain the environment. It is also clear that these activities will not be measured alone in terms of price as a measure of social value. Thus President Nixon also remarked in his *State of the Union Message*: "Our recognition of the truth that wealth and happiness are not the same thing requires us to measure success or failure by new criteria."

As has been noted, the Food and Drug Administration continues as an entity within the new Environmental Health Service and this Administration's work warrants detailed separate discussion.

B. THE FOOD AND DRUG ADMINISTRATION

History, Functions, and Organization

The agency today known as the Food and Drug Administration had its origin in the activities of the Bureau of Chemistry of the Department of Agriculture, beginning in the 1880s. This Bureau at first undertook

---

[2e] House Document 91–226, 91st Cong., 2d sess., 1970 (Washington, D.C.: U.S. Government Printing Office, 1970).

research on the subject of food preservatives and food adulteration but soon extended its work to include patent medicines and the quality and purity of drugs. It utilized the tool of publicity concerning its findings in an attempt to combat abusive practices and to secure from Congress the enactment of legislation providing for positive regulation.

The first proposal providing for such positive regulation was introduced in Congress in 1890, but it was not until 1906 that Congress responded to the activities of the Bureau by enacting the Food and Drug Act. This law prohibited adulteration and misbranding of foods and drugs sold in interstate commerce. Although it marked a first step, the law suffered from numerous weaknesses. It did not cover therapeutic devices and provided no authority for establishment of standards of identity for foods. In 1912, the law was amended to prohibit the making of statements which were "false and fraudulent," thereby requiring the enforcement authority to carry the difficult burden of proof of "fraudulent intent."

In 1927, the enforcement activities were transferred to a new unit in the Department of Agriculture called the Food, Drug, and Insecticide Administration. Various other laws related to the Food and Drug Act were enforced by this new Administration. The Import Tea Act of 1897, which had also previously been enforced by the Bureau of Chemistry, was one of these laws and required the inspection of imported tea and tea products. Another was the Insecticide Act of 1912; this law provided for the testing of insecticides and fungicides. Enforcement of the Caustic Poisons Act of 1927 was also a responsibility of the new agency; this law required warnings to be placed on labels of the products to which it pertained.

In the late 1920s and 1930s, pressures for adoption of new regulatory legislation mounted. The original 1906 law did not provide for fines sufficiently large to deter violations. Moreover, this law defined a product as "misbranded" if it failed to meet the "normal industry standard" for the product in question, thereby requiring the enforcement agency to prove what the "normal industry standard" was in each case. Finally, the cosmetic industry (which was not covered by the 1906 law) experienced much growth after 1906.

Accordingly, in 1938, Congress enacted the Pure Food, Drug, and Cosmetics Act. This act contained authority for the regulatory agency to regulate the cosmetics industry and also required producers of new drugs to obtain a permit to market them. Such a permit was to be issued only if the producer proved that the drug was safe to use as directed. Refusal of permission to inspect an establishment producing foods, drugs, or cosmetics was made a criminal offense; and provision was made for the establishment of minimum standards. Any food which failed to comply with such a standard was defined as "misbranded." Labeling regulations were also provided for. Finally, any drug was defined as "misbranded" if the label was false or misleading without regard to the fraudulent intent of the producer or distributor, and control over therapeutic devices was also established. In short, the 1938 law extended the coverage of the earlier legislation and provided for *positive* regulation, while the earlier laws had contained only *negative* provisions, prohibiting certain types of advertising and labeling. (The Wheeler-Lea Amendment to the Federal Trade Commission Act was also adopted in 1938 and authorized the Federal Trade Commission to exercise authority over false and deceptive advertising practices in interstate commerce.) Moreover, the penalty provisions of the law were made more severe and increased to include the possibility of a year in prison.

The name of the enforcement agency had been changed to Food and Drug Administration by the Agricultural Appropriations Act of 1931, prior to the 1938 legislation. In 1940, under Reorganization Plan IV, the Administration was transferred to the Federal Security Agency. This agency consisted of a grouping under one administration of all the federal agencies whose major purposes were to "promote social and economic security, educational opportunity, and the health of the citizens of the Nation." In 1953, Reorganization Plan I abolished the Federal Security Agency and established the Department of Health, Education, and Welfare, transferring to this new Executive Department all the functions and units of the Federal Security Agency, as well as other functions and agencies. One of the units thus transferred was the Food and Drug Administration.

The various administrative changes concerning the location of the Food and Drug Administration did not, however, prevent Congress from enacting further legislation pertaining to the substantive powers of the Administration. During the 1950s such legislation was primarily concerned with the regulation of food additives. In 1952, according to the report of a special House Committee created to investigate the problem, "There is hardly a food sold in the market place today which has not had chemicals used on or in it at some stage in its processing, packaging, transportation or storage."[3]

A number of chemical additives amendments were thereupon enacted, including the Pesticide Chemical Amendment of 1954, the Food Additives Amendment of 1954, the Food Additives Amendment of 1958, and the Color Additives Amendment of 1960. All embodied the "safety clearance principle," under which producers were required to carry the burden of proof that the use of the new chemicals would not endanger consumers.[4] Thus there has been a gradual evolution of the basic legislation, extending the "safety clearance principle" to pesticides, food additives, and colors.

During the 1960s, emphasis was given in new legislation to extending the safety clearance principle to new drugs and to control of advertising and use of hazardous substances, with special attention to the protection of children, as well as to the advertising and labeling of foods, drugs, and cosmetics.

From about 1959 to 1961, the Senate Subcommittee on Antitrust and Monopoly conducted hearings pertaining to prices, profits, and practices of the drug industry. These hearings disclosed that, since under the 1938 legislation a manufacturer was required to show that a new drug was *safe* but *not* that it was *effective*, the practice had developed that new chemical combinations were often being sold as new drugs without regard to their effectiveness. After the hearings in 1959–61, despite strong opposition by drug manufacturers, in 1962, Congress enacted the Kefauver Drug Amendments

Act. Under this legislation, among other things, *effectiveness* must be established by the sponsor before a new drug is approved. Moreover, drug labels must contain information pertaining to injurious side effects and must contain generic names in type at least half as large as the relevant trade name. Thus, if mystery ingredient "K745" is contained in a drug, if the generic name of this ingredient is "sodium chloride" (ordinary table salt), the label must also contain this information.

Earlier, in 1960, Congress had enacted the Hazardous Substances Labeling Act. This law provided for informative labeling of various dangerous household products. In 1965, Congress adopted the Drug Abuse Control Amendments to the Pure Food, Drug, and Cosmetics Act for the purpose of regulating stimulant and depressive drugs. In 1966, Congress changed the name of the Hazardous Substances Labeling Act to Hazardous Substances Act and provided for a prohibition from shipment in interstate commerce of substances for which no adequate warning label could be written, as well as for a prohibition of the sale of toys and other childrens' articles containing hazardous substances. Also in 1966, Congress adopted the Fair Packaging and Labeling Act and assigned enforcement authority partly to the Food and Drug Administration and partly to the Federal Trade Commission. (This law is described in Chapter 12.)

The reader should not assume that the preceding description of legislation concerning the functions of the Food and Drug Administration is a complete one. Our survey has been designed primarily to indicate the kinds of laws and the trend of legislation enforced by the Administration.

Today, it has been noted, the Food and Drug Administration is a component of the Consumer Protection and Environmental Health Service of the Department of Health, Education, and Welfare. The Administration is headed by an Administrator. The work of the Administration is carried on by the five bureaus and numerous field offices which compose it. The bureaus

[3] *Report of the House Select Committee to Investigate the Use of Chemicals in Food Products* (House Report No. 2356, 82d Cong., 2d sess., 1952) (Washington, D.C.: U.S. Government Printing Office, 1952), p. 4. I am indebted to Professor Stan Smith for this reference.

[4] *Annual Report of the Department of Health, Education, and Welfare for Fiscal Year 1961* (Washington, D.C.: U.S. Government Printing Office, 1962), p. 317.

are: Bureau of Medicine; Bureau of Regulatory Compliance; Bureau of Science; Bureau of Veterinary Medicine; and Bureau of Voluntary Compliance. For fiscal year 1969, the Administration's budget amounted to about $70.9 million (appropriated by Congress). Appropriations had amounted to only $5.664 million in 1952 and were reduced during the Eisenhower Administration in every year from 1952 through 1955, when they reached a low mark of $5.18 million. A reduction in positions from 1,000 in 1951 to a low of 877, in 1956 also occurred, with obvious effects upon the Food and Drug Administration's performance of its regulatory functions.

Operations

Obviously, in the light of the many different subjects and products dealt with in the legislation just discussed, the work of the Food and Drug Administration encompasses many different types of activities.[5] Thus in fiscal year 1967, the activities of the Administration ranged from evaluation of new drug applications to seizure of alleged therapeutic electrical gadgets claimed to be effective for "effortless reducing" and to the obtaining of an injunction to prohibit the sale of a "do-it-yourself" kit for home production of "giant firecrackers." In 1966, under the newly enacted Child Protection Act of 1966, the Administration seized several shipments of dangerously inflammable dolls and detained other shipments at the port—a total of 300,000 dolls was involved. In fiscal year 1967, Salmonella poisoning became a serious problem in the United States. (Salmonella poisoning causes an influenze-like illness and is often fatal in the cases of old people and young children.) It continued to be a serious problem in 1968, although the Administration undertook in 1967 an extensive campaign of inspections, analysis of samples, enforcement actions, industry education, and recalls of contaminated food and drug products in which the Salmonella bacteria were found. Among the mail-fraud cases in which the Administration participated were those involving nutritional quackery and, specifically, the following products: Air Force

Diet Manual (booklet); Bruce's Cancer and Sugar Cane (cancer cure); Con-Trol Cocktail (for weight reduction); and Crash Weight–Gain Formula No. 7 (to put on weight).

The problem of drug recall (on grounds of subpotency, misbranding, mislabeling, and failure to meet standards) has been increasing. In 1965, shipments of 340 drugs were recalled. In 1966, the number was 538 and in 1967 it was 651. Both large and small firms were involved; some recalls were instituted voluntarily by the drug producers themselves; others were the result of Administration orders. Some mention must also be made of the Administration's activities in the area of drug abuse control. In this area, its work has ranged from investigation and criminal prosecutions to research on psychological, social and physiological factors leading to drug abuse, and educational activities at various levels, including the university and college levels.

Today, only those color additives approved by the Administration may be used in foods. Each batch of color used must be tested and certified. In 1967, the quantity of color additives used amounted to more than 3.6 million pounds.

Skin "regenerators" and "hair growers" account for a large portion of the action in the cosmetics field. Products advertised as effective for such purposes are treated as "drugs" rather than as "cosmetics" under the law. In 1967, the Administration employed new chemical techniques to identify the various substances being used in lipsticks, suntan lotions, and perfumes. The Bureau of Medicine conducts continuing experimentation on the effects on the human body of chemicals used in foods, drugs, and cosmetics.

With the passage of the Fair Packaging and Labeling Act of 1966 and the issuance of regulations to enforce it by both the Federal Trade Commission and the Food and Drug Administration, the consumer economic protection activities of the Administration received increased emphasis. The Federal Trade Commission and the Food and Drug Administration have long worked both through formal and informal

---

[5] The information in these paragraphs is based upon those portions of the *Annual Reports* of the Department of Health, Education, and Welfare which pertain to the Food and Drug Administration; individual items will not be footnoted.

agreements in a cooperative spirit to reduce deception of buyers by sellers, and there is no reason to believe that this cooperation will not continue in the future; indeed, under the Fair Packaging and Labeling Act, further opportunities for extensive cooperation exist. In working to reduce deception of buyers by sellers, these agencies are, of course, working to create conditions under which buyers may maximize their self-interests according to the theory of rational consumer behavior. The Securities and Exchange Commission similarly plays an important role in seeking to reduce deception in the case of purchasers of securities. It is to a consideration of the work of this agency that the remainder of this chapter is devoted.

C. THE SECURITIES AND EXCHANGE COMMISSION

History, Functions, and Organization

On September 1, 1929, the value of all stocks listed on the New York Stock Exchange amounted to $89 billion; but by the middle of 1932, their value had declined to $15 million.[6] Subsequent investigations both by Congress and by the Securities and Exchange Commission disclosed the existence of many abuses on the part of those dealing in securities markets. For example, one abuse was artificial stimulation of security prices.[7] More than 100 of the stocks listed on the New York Stock Exchange were found to have been manipulated by means of pooling operations. The use of corporate information by corporate officials and other "insiders" was also a common practice, even though such action constituted a breach of a fiduciary duty to the corporation and its stockholders. Another abuse was the widespread and extensive use of credit to purchase securities, a factor which contributed to the speculative fever of the 1920s. The use of public utility holding companies and the issuance of stock whose value bore little relation to the value of the assets of the controlled operating companies, as described in Chapter 9, was still another abuse common in the 1920s.

The Securities Act of 1933. Congress reacted to the information uncovered by its investigations by enacting a number of laws, including the Securities Act of 1933. This law, whose enforcement was originally assigned to the Federal Trade Commission (since the Securities and Exchange Commission had not yet been created), had the primary purpose of providing for public disclosure of all financial and other data pertaining to the value of securities so that investors might realistically evaluate the worth of such securities. The law *did not* and *does not* guarantee the *value* of securities. It is aptly referred to as a "Truth in Securities Act."

The method of forcing full disclosure by sellers of facts pertaining to securities involves two steps: (1) a registration statement must be filed with the Securities and Exchange Commission containing certain financial and other information; (2) a prospectus containing information regarding the facts upon which a company's operations may be judged and its securities evaluated must be made available to all prospective purchasers who receive written offers through the mails.

The Securities Exchange Act of 1934. In 1934, Congress passed the Securities Exchange Act, creating the Securities and Exchange Commission and applying the disclosure principle also to every company having its securities listed on the exchanges. An attempt was also made to control trading by "insiders" by requiring officers, directors, and stockholders owning 10 percent or more of the stock of a listed corporation to report periodically to the Commission concerning their holdings and transactions in such stocks; and the law also requires management officials of listed companies to disclose certain information to stockholders from whom they solicit proxies. In addition, brokers and dealers are required to register with the Commission and so are the exchanges themselves. Control over margin requirements, that is, over the use of credit, was placed in the hands of the Board of Governors of the Federal Reserve System.

The Public Utility Holding Company Act. It has already been noted in Chapter 9 (in the discussion of the holding company) that in

---

[6] *A 25-year Summary of the Activities of the Securities and Exchange Commission* (Washington, D.C.: U.S.

Government Printing Office, 1960), p. xiv.

[7] *Ibid.*, p. xv.

1935 Congress enacted the Public Utility Holding Company Act. The purpose of this law was to free operating companies from the control of holding companies, and the task of breaking up the very large holding companies which existed during the 1920s into self-contained economic units was assigned to the Securities and Exchange Commission. The law required the financial structures of the units in question to be simplified, and the geographically widely dispersed properties owned by the parent or top holding companies to be integrated into smaller, economically viable units. (This law will be further discussed below.)

There have been numerous amendments to the basic laws of 1933 and 1934 since they were first enacted. Most of these amendments were enacted by Congress in response to recommendations made by the Commission after it had undertaken extensive special studies to determine the need for such additional legislation. Under the Holding Company Act of 1935, the Commission was enabled to conduct an investigation of investment trusts; and in 1940, Congress enacted the Investment Company Act. This law has the object of insuring that those in control of such investment trusts (as defined in Chapter 9) do not operate them to the detriment of the investing public and solely for their own advantage. The law prohibits excessive self-dealing and the taking of excessive profits by affiliated persons and companies. The types of securities which such companies may issue are limited, and an attempt is made to insure honest and adequate financial reporting to stockholders. Investment companies must file periodic reports of their transactions with the Commission.

The Investment Advisors Act. Also in 1940, Congress adopted the Investment Advisors Act. However, the Commission has little real power under this law; it cannot, for example, inspect the books of investment advisors or prescribe accounting procedures and records.

Other Legislation. The Trust Indenture Act and Chapter X of the National Bankruptcy Act also impose duties on the Commission. In regard to the former, the Commission examines trust indentures (deeds which serve as security for bondholders) to insure that trustees are independent of borrowers and that no conflicts of interest exist. Under the bankruptcy law, a court *must* in cases of corporate reorganizations involving an indebtedness of more than $3 million and *may* in any case request the Commission to report on a proposed reorganization plan. The Commission's report is, however, not binding on the court, and the Commission serves in an advisory capacity only.

Under various pieces of legislation, securities issued by the International Bank for Reconstruction and Development, by the Inter–American Development Bank, and by the Asian Development Bank are exempt from registration under both the Securities Act of 1933 and the Securities Exchange Act of 1934. The Commission does, however, require these international banks to file "appropriate" information.[8]

In 1963, the Commission completed a three-volume study of the securities markets and recommended that securities traded on the "over-the-counter" market (that is, securities not listed on the exchanges) be subjected to the requirements and regulations already being applied to securities listed on the exchanges under the existing legislation.[9] On the basis of its study, the Commission had concluded that purchasers of over-the-counter securities were inadequately protected and recommended amendment of the basic regulatory legislation to afford to investors in unlisted securities the protection which was already being given to investors in listed securities. Congress responded favorably to this recommendation by enacting the Securities Act Amendments of 1964. This legislation substantially increased the Commission's workload.

Organization. The Commission consists of five members; the Chairman is appointed by the President. The important operating units are the Division of Corporation Finance, the Division of Corporate Regulation, the Division of Trading and Markets, and the nine regional offices. To be noted also, is the existence of the Office of Opinions and Review. The staff of the

[8] *Annual Report of the Securities and Exchange Commission for 1968* (Washington, D.C.: U.S. Government Printing Office, 1969), pp. 56–57.

[9] *Report of Special Study of Securities Markets of the Securities and Exchange Commission* (Washington, D.C.: U.S. Government Printing Office, 1863), p. 541.

Commission amounted to 1,383 employees in 1968, and the *net* cost of the Commission's operations exceeded its appropriations for operations, with the difference being accounted for by fees collected for registration of securities and exchanges.

Operations

The following paragraphs contain a description of *typical* Commission activities, rather than an exhaustive detailed summary.[10]

The Securities Laws. The Commission has a number of different procedures which it can employ in enforcement actions: (1) it may institute administrative proceedings subject to the due process requirements of the Administrative Procedure Act; (2) it may refer the case to the Department of Justice for institution of criminal proceedings. Examples of action taken under the Securities and Exchange Act of 1934 are provided by the *Annual Report for 1968.* In *Richard Bruce and Co. Inc.*, the Commission found that the firm had solicited orders on the basis of unconfirmed extravagant reports and rumors for a speculative stock and had instructed its salesmen to "transmit such reports to persons . . . who could afford to lose money or would not complain if they did. . . ." In *Century Service Company and Billings Associates, Inc.*, the Commission found that brokers were engaging in a concerted high pressure sales effort, including the use of false representations and predictions to sell securities without regard to the financial needs or objectives of their customers. In both cases the Commission revoked the firms' broker–dealer registrations and prohibited the individuals involved from being associated with a broker or dealer.

It should also be noted that, among the administrative proceedings available to the Commission, the rulemaking power is one of the most important and is used extensively by the Commission in the performance of its duties under the various laws it enforces.

The Securities Act of 1933, it will be recalled, is implemented by requiring those who seek to raise capital by issuing new securities to provide both a registration statement and a prospectus.

A typical registration statement must disclose, among other things, such information as: the names of persons who participate in the management or control of the issuer's business; their security holdings and remuneration; the general character of the business; its capital structure, past history, and earnings; underwriter's commissions; payments to promoters, pending legal proceedings; and the purposes for which the proceeds of the issue are to be used. All this information is believed to be pertinent to the valuation of the security by a prospective purchaser.

The Commission's activity in this area is primarily concerned with the use of the rulemaking power to modify, simplify, and clarify informational requirements of the registration statement and the prospectus. Between June 30, 1938, and June 30, 1968, a total of 31,861 registration statements were filed by 13,398 different issuers. Of this total, 2,906 statements were filed in fiscal year 1968.

Under the relevant enabling legislation, the Commission utilized its rulemaking power in fiscal year 1968 to require certain disclosures in proxy statements pertaining to the interests of insiders. These statements are solicitations to stockholders to assign their voting rights to the issuer of a statement. A total of 5,244 proxy statements was filed during fiscal year 1968. Also during fiscal year 1968, 491 trust indentures were filed with the Commission under the Trust Indenture Act of 1939.

Under the Securities and Exchange Act of 1934, the Commission regulates 13 stock exchanges. These exchanges range in size from that of the New York Stock Exchange which accounted for 64.41 percent of total shares traded in 1968 to that of the Pittsburgh Stock Exchange which accounted for 0.02 of 1 percent of shares traded. The American Stock Exchange is the second largest exchange and accounted for 28.42 percent of shares traded in the same year. The percentage accounted for by the New York Stock Exchange has decreased steadily since 1935, when it amounted to 73.13 percent, while that of the American Stock Exchange has steadily increased during the same period, having amounted to only 12.42 percent in 1935.

---

[10] This section is based upon material found in the Commission's Annual Reports. Individual footnotes will not be used.

Under the Act of 1934, the Commission is responsible for determining the reasonableness of commission rates set by the exchanges. Until 1968, it left the matter of rate setting to be carried out by the exchanges themselves. However, in July 1968, the Commission conducted an extensive hearing to determine whether or not changes should be made in exchange rules, practices, or procedures. In September 1968, pending a long-term study of these questions, the Commission accepted a proposal by the New York Stock Exchange for an interim reduction in certain rates. This reduction was estimated to result in a reduction of charges by about $150 million, or by 7 percent of the total charges in 1967. Inspection of the security exchanges is carried on by the Commission's Division of Corporate Regulation.

On June 30, 1968, 4,831 stock and bond issues of 2,773 issuers were admitted to trading on the securities exchanges of the United States. Under the Amendments to the regulatory legislation adopted in 1964 requiring registration in the case of securities sold "over-the-counter," the total number of registration statements received by June 30, 1968, amounted to 3,168.

Brokers and dealers who use instrumentalities of interstate commerce in the conduct of an "over-the-counter" business must also register. By June 30, 1968, 4,397 such broker–dealers had registered. Investment advisors must also register under the Investment Advisors Act of 1940, and by June 30, 1968, the total number who had done so was 2,007. The Commission has adopted a procedure of surprise inspections of broker–dealers and investment advisors. In 1968, it conducted 514 broker–dealer inspections and found indications of 580 violations of the securities laws. Some broker–dealers apparently accounted for more than one violation. In the case of the 165 investment advisors inspected, there were 129 indications of violations. Clearly the 1964 amendments serve a necessary purpose.

Section 15A of the Securities Exchange Act provides for registration of associations of brokers and dealers with the Commission. The National Association of Securities Dealers (NASD) is the only registered

association in existence. The NASD practices self-regulation of its members, subject to Commission approval and supervision. Thus the Commission reviews all cases involving disciplinary action by the NASD pertaining to its members.

An investment company is an arrangement by means of which a group of persons invest funds in an entity which has the function of investing in securities. The activities of such companies are regulated by the Commission under the Investment Company Act of 1940. As of June 30, 1968, there were 967 active, registered investment companies. In fiscal year 1968, the Commission investigated 102 such investment companies. These investigations disclosed "violations not only of the Investment Company Act but also of other statutes administered by the Commission."

In 1967, the Commission proposed some amendments to the Investment Company Act of 1940. The amendments were primarily concerned with regulation of commission rates and charges for mutual fund sales. Although adopted with modifications by the Senate, the proposed legislation was shelved by House Committee on Interstate and Foreign Commerce.

In January 1969, the Commission won an important Supreme Court case in which the Court held that the McCarran–Ferguson Act (adopted to provide an exemption from the federal antitrust laws for the insurance business) did not apply to the relationship between insurance companies and *their* shareholders, thereby subjecting such companies to the provisions of the various acts regulating securities and to the rules promulgated thereunder by the Commission.[11]

In its *Special Study of the Securities Markets* in 1963, the Commission noted that institutional investment and trading by institutional investors (mutual funds, bank trust departments, pension funds, and others) had increased markedly in recent years. From 1957 to 1967, the total value of stocks held by major financial institutions rose from $29.5 billion to more than $113.5 billion (excluding trust funds, foundations, and college endowment funds). Transactions by institutions were estimated to account for approximately 50 percent of the trading

[11] *Securities and Exchange Commission* v. *National Securities et. al.*, 393 U.S. 453 (1969).

by nonmembers on the New York Stock Exchange. On July 29, 1968, a joint resolution by Congress was signed into law, authorizing the Commission to make a comprehensive study of institutional investment.

President Nixon (who was then a candidate) undertook to win support from leaders of the investment industry in 1968 by attacking not only the proposed Commission study but also by attacking the 1964 amendments—which, it will be recalled, were based upon an intensive study by the Commission.[12] This attack occurred on October 2, 1968, in a letter and policy statement circulated among leaders of the investment industry but not released for publication.[13]

Candidate Nixon asserted that a new study was needed by an "independent group" rather than by the Commission and said, in effect, that although the 90th Congress had authorized the Commission to make such a study, the Commission had already advanced proposals (impliedly without adequate study) "which would alter the basic character of the securities market . . ."[14]

Candidate Nixon somewhat stretched reality, it will be noted, since the 1964 Amendments were adopted after a three-volume report of a study had been issued by the Commission.[15] These amendments preceded by four years the 1968 Congressional Resolution authorizing a study of a different problem, but this point was ignored in the Nixon statement. That President Nixon and the Republican Party do not accept the idea that independent regulatory agencies are independent of the administration in power is clearly indicated in this policy statement by President Nixon's assertion that he intended to create a commission to study the question "of the proper role which those agencies now regulating our economic institutions are to play in insuring our nation's economic stability and growth." According to the *New York Times* report of the incident, the members of the investment industry to whom this statement was sent were all traditionally large contributors to political campaigns.

The Public Utility Holding Company Act. Since its creation, the Commission has continued to exercise responsibilities under the Public Utility Holding Company Act of 1935. Brief mention has already been made in Chapter 9 of the extent to which holding companies controlled the production of natural gas and electric power in 1929. According to a report by the Commission, the United Corporation group of (electric) companies controlled approximately 20 percent of the electrical energy generated in the United States, the Electric Bond and Share group controlled about 14 percent, and the Insull interests controlled about 10 percent. Thus three groups controlled 45 percent of the total privately owned electrical energy industry. In addition, 35 percent was controlled by 12 other companies, so that 15 companies controlled 80 percent. In the natural gas industry, 11 holding company systems controlled 80 percent of the natural gas pipeline mileage and 20 large holding companies controlled 98.5 percent of the transmission of electrical energy in interstate commerce.[16] The Act of 1935 defines a public utility "to mean an electric utility company or a gas utility company." Enforcement of Section 11, the principal provision of this law, is largely conducted by the Commission under its rulemaking power.

The law requires public utility holding companies to register with the Commission, and the Commission has the duty, after notice and hearing, of insuring compliance with the statutory standard of integrated operations and simplified financial structures. The "integration" requirement is in effect one of "regional cohesiveness and size."

Section 11(b) of the law limits the operation of each holding company system to a single integrated public utility system, subject to certain exceptions. Retention of additional integrated systems depends upon a showing that the additional system

---

[12] See the reference cited in Footnote 6 *supra.*

[13] The letter and statement were mentioned but not reproduced in *The New York Times* on October 2, 1968.

[14] Republican National Committee, *Release*, Washington, D.C., October 2, 1968.

[15] See Footnote 6 *supra.*

[16] *Securities and Exchange Commission Report on The Public Utility Holding Company Act of 1935* reproduced in *Study of Monopoly Power* (Hearings before the House Subcommittee on Study of Monopoly Power, 81st Cong., 1st sess., 1949) (Washington, D.C.: U.S. Government Printing Office, 1949) Serial No. 14, Part 2–B, p. 1460.

is small and unable to operate economically as a separate system. It must be located in a contiguous geographical area.

Section 11(b) of the law further requires the elimination of "undue or unnecessary" corporate complexities and that voting power be fairly distributed among stockholders. In addition, holding companies beyond the "second degree" (more than two tiers) are prohibited.

The Commission does not ordinarily specify how a company may comply with Section 11(b) but leaves this problem up to the companies themselves. The Commission merely orders compliance when necessary. Section 11(c) provides that if no voluntary plan is forthcoming in one year, the Commission may apply to a federal District Court for a compliance order under Section 11(d). If a company is not "dragging its feet," the Commission does not go to court. Since 1949, it has done so in only one case.

In the period from June 15, 1938, to June 30, 1949, a total of 2,152 companies (210 holding companies, 918 electric and gas utility companies, and 1,024 nonutility companies) came under the Commission's jurisdiction. In 1942, only 642 companies were still subject to Commission jurisdiction. Of the remaining 1,510 companies, 157 companies were exempted from the provisions of the Act by Commission order, and the rest "had been eliminated by sales, dissolutions, mergers, consolidations, and other means of divestment."[17]

Most of the data mentioned above represent the situation in 1942. About 25 years later, in fiscal year 1968, there were only 25 holding companies registered with the Commission. Moreover, the number of active systems was only 17, since four of the 25 holding companies were subholding companies within the 17 systems, and four were inactive. In the 17 active systems, there were 89 electric utility and gas or utility companies, 47 nonutility subsidiaries, and 15 inactive companies, or a total of 172 system companies. Since there were 2,152 companies subject to the Commission's jurisdiction in the period from 1938 to 1949, it is clear that the Commission has accomplished much of the monumental task put before it by Congress in 1938.

Nevertheless, cases involving the Commission's divestiture orders continue to reach the courts. Thus in 1968, the Supreme Court upheld the Commission's judgment in ordering the New England Electric System to divest itself of its gas properties and to limit itself to the operation of a single integrated system, despite the respondent's defense argument to the effect that the gas properties could not be independently operated without the loss of serious economies.[18] The case did not, however, involve any legal issues pertaining to the constitutionally of the basic legislation—these were all decided favorably many years ago insofar as the Commission's jurisdiction is concerned and the 1968 case raised merely the question of the validity of the evidence upon which the Commission had based its order.

Other Activities. The Commission does not consider it necessary or appropriate to participate in all cases under Chapter X of the Bankruptcy Act. Many of these cases involve only trade creditors and do not raise questions involving securities. Even so, in fiscal year 1968, the Commission participated in 22 new cases involving companies with aggregate assets of about $140 million and aggregate indebtedness of about $120 million.

One further activity of the Commission is worth noting in this survey of the operations of the agency. The reader will recall that in Chapter 9 the problem of disclosure of information pertaining to the activities of the various divisions of conglomerate firms has been mentioned. Following hearings by the Senate Subcommittee on Antitrust and Monopoly to investigate ways of dealing with this problem, the Commission, in September 1968, issued for public comment a proposal looking toward the issuance of a rule to revise the disclosure requirements under the various pieces of basic legislation. Under the proposed revision, reporting firms would be required to report both income and assets attributable *to each class* of their related or similar products.

A Concluding Comment

In this chapter, we have been largely but not exclusively examining the work of two

---

[17] *Ibid.*, pp. 160–164.

[18] *S.E.C.* v. *New England Electric System*, 390 U.S. 207 (1968).

agencies which are concerned with the use of governmental power to prevent fraud or deception on the part of sellers, although the Securities and Exchange Commission also exercises a minor price control function over the level of commission rates and charges by securities brokers. This Commission is concerned primarily with improving the operation of the capital market. We have also examined briefly the activities of some of the federal agencies concerned with problems of environmental pollution. In August 1970, the Council on Environmental Quality issued its first annual report.

In this report the Council recommended that there be established a federal Environmental Protection Agency in which the major environmental pollution control activities would be consolidated. This recommendation had been preceded by President Nixon's submission to Congress on July 9 of a reorganization plan to create the new agency. That there will be continuing federal action concerning environmental pollution control is a safe prediction. In the next chapter, we will examine the various uses of governmental power designed to affect the operation of the labor market.

Labor-Management Relations; Labor Standards and Economic Security; Manpower Policies and Programs

The reader will recall that a brief survey of the growth in the power of organized labor appears in the last subdivision of Chapter 11, and some readers may wish to review that discussion at this time. This chapter contains three major subdivisions. The first deals with the use of governmental power in the regulation of labor-management relations, largely through the activities of the National Labor Relations Board and of labor unions by agencies of the Department of Labor. The second major subdivision is concerned with an examination of the use of governmental power to establish and enforce fair labor standards, mainly under the Fair Labor Standards Act, and programs of economic security. The enforcement of labor standards legislation is also carried on by agencies of the Department of Labor. Finally, the third and last major subdivision of this chapter undertakes to examine policies and programs pertaining to disadvantaged workers and to structural unemployment. The question of the application of the antitrust laws to labor unions is an antitrust question and not a question in the areas of labor economics or labor law. That question has, accordingly, been treated in the second major subdivision of Chapter 14, under the heading "*Labor Unions and Restraint of Trade*," which some readers may now wish to read. In general, it may be stated that under presently prevailing law, when a union combines with a nonlabor group to violate the antitrust laws, the union loses its immunity from antitrust prosecution.

A. LABOR-MANAGEMENT RELATIONS AND REGULATION OF LABOR UNIONS

Labor and the Law Prior to 1932

As has been pointed out in Chapter 11, the English doctrine that labor unions constituted conspiracies was applied in the United States as early as 1806, but by about 1842, some state courts in the United States were beginning to question the applicability of this doctrine to labor unions.[1] However,

---

[1] See the references cited in Chapter 11.

in 1893, for the first time, a federal court issued an injunction to prohibit a union from engaging in a boycott on grounds that the boycott constituted a restraint of trade under the Sherman Act;[2] and thereafter, up until 1932, this law was used against labor unions as the basis both for actions seeking injunctions and for damages.[3]

In 1914, Congress adopted the Clayton Act. Section 6 of that Act *apparently* exempted labor unions from antitrust prosecution, but in 1921 in *Duplex Printing Company* v. *Deering*[4] the Supreme Court permitted an employer to obtain an injunction under Section 6 to prohibit a union from engaging in self-help practices, although under the original Sherman Act only the Federal Government had been able to bring such an action.

A *yellow-dog* contract is an agreement in which an employer exacts from an employee as a condition of employment that the employee will not join a labor union while an employee of the given employer. Such contracts were widely used as a basis for injunctions against activities of labor unions and against labor organizational activities until the 1930s. In 1915 (we have seen in Chapter 7), the Supreme Court held unconstitutional a Kansas statute outlawing the use of yellow-dog contracts,[5] and in 1917 in the *Hitchman Coal Company* case, the Court upheld the decision of a trial court which had issued an injunction to prohibit officials of the United Mine Workers Union from attempting to organize the plaintiff-employer's mine workers into a union on grounds that the defendants were attempting to induce the employees to breach their contract with the employer.[6] A dissenting opinion by Justice Brandeis in this case was written on the assumption that the yellow-dog contract was a binding contractual agreement but argued that the facts of the case did not show an attempt to induce the employees to breach their contract. It was not until 1932 that Congress acted to prohibit the issuance of injunctions on the basis of yellow-dog contracts. We will examine this legislation below. However, before we do so, it is useful to recall a matter mentioned in Chapter 24, namely, the enactment by Congress of the Railway Labor Act of 1926.

The provisions of the Railway Labor Act of 1926 have already been described in Chapter 24. What is significant in the present context is that this law established the rights of railway employees to join unions of their own choice and to be represented by those whom they selected and imposed a duty of good faith negotiation looking toward the making of a collective bargaining agreement upon the representatives of the workers and the employers. This principle of collective bargaining, we will see below, was also embodied in the National Industrial Recovery Act of 1933 and in the National Labor Relations Act of 1935 and has continued to constitute a basis for labor–management relations in industry generally since 1933.

The Norris–La Guardia (Anti-Injunction Act) of 1932 (29 U.S.C. 102)

In 1932, Congress acted to prohibit the issuance by federal courts of injunctions in cases involving self-help (strikes, organizational campaigns, boycotts, and picketing) activities in cases in which a *labor dispute* exists.

Crucial to the determination of whether or not this legislation applies in a given case is the determination of whether or not the facts disclose the existence of a *labor dispute*. This term is defined as any dispute over terms and conditions of employment or matters of representation of employees in collective bargaining, even though the parties involved do not stand in the relation of employer and employee. The courts have been liberal in their interpretation of what constitutes a labor dispute under this law. Thus it has been held that a labor dispute exists between union organizers (who are *not* employees of a given employer) and an employer, even though he has taken a poll of his employees and determined that none of them wishes to join a union.[7]

[2] *United States* v. *Workingmen's Amalgamated Council*, 57 Fed. 85 (1893).

[3] The first case in which a labor union was required to pay damages under the Sherman Act was *Loewe* v. *Lawlor*, 208 U.S. 274 (1908), usually identified as the "Danbury Hatter's Case." See also, 235 U.S. 522 (1915).

[4] 245 U.S. 445 (1921).

[5] *Coppage* v. *Kansas*, 36 U.S. 1 (1915).

[6] *Hitchman Coal Company* v. *Mitchell*, 245 U.S. 229 (1917).

[7] *Lauf* v. *E. G. Shinner and Company*, 303 U.S. 232 (1938).

Some of the instances in which issuance of an injunction was prohibited in the original 1932 law were modified by the Taft–Hartley Act of 1947 (discussed below); but originally the following activities were specified in the law:

(1) Ceasing or refusing to work
(2) Joining or continuing membership in a union
(3) Aiding or refusing to aid financially or by other lawful means any person interested in or participating in a labor dispute
(4) Giving publicity to the existence of facts involved in any labor dispute by advertising, speaking, patrolling, or by any other method not involving fraud or violence
(5) Assembling peaceably to act or to organize to act in promotion of their interests in a labor dispute
(6) Advising any person of intent to do any of the above, agreeing or refusing to do any of the above, or inducing others to do any of the above acts, without fraud or violence.[8]

This law was clearly far-reaching, and its enactment marks the beginning of an era of promotion of labor unions in the United States.

The NIRA and the National Labor Relations Act (29 U.S.C. 151)

We have seen in Chapter 9 that the National Industrial Recovery Act of 1933 was an attempt to combat the effects of the Great Depression by permitting the establishment of a system of anticompetitive controls in the United States. Section 7 of that law was adopted to win labor's support for the national program of codes and price-fixing adopted under this law and provided also that employees should have the right to bargain collectively through representatives of their own choosing. A National Labor Board was created to administer this section but was given no power to enforce its decisions. We have also seen in Chapter 7 that in 1935, the Supreme Court held the entire law unconstitutional. Congress then enacted the National Labor Relations Act (also known as the Wagner Act) and created the National Labor Relations Board to enforce this law. We will consider operations and activities of the

Board under the legislation, as amended since 1935, later in this subdivision. For the moment we will concentrate our attention on the other provisions of the Act, which has been called labor's Magna Charta. (It may be noted, in passing, that business interests engaged in a great deal of lobbying activity to oppose adoption of this legislation, a point illustrated in Chapter 5 under the heading, "*The NAM's Fight Against the Wagner Act*.") Section 7 of the Wagner Act guarantees employees "the right of self-organization" and the right to bargain collectively through representatives of their own choosing.

Section 8 of the Act prohibits five employer practices, designating them as "unfair labor practices." These include: (1) interfering with the right to employees to organize, bargain collectively, or engage in concerted action; (2) dominating or interfering with labor unions, including contributing financial support to them; (3) encouraging or discouraging labor union membership by means of employment practices; (4) retaliating against employees who file charges or testify against the employer; (5) refusing to bargain with the elected union representatives.

Employers did not at first pay much attention to the new law. Many corporation lawyers believed the law would be held unconstitutional by the Supreme Court and actually advised their firms to ignore it. In February 1937, the Senate Committee on Education and Labor published a *Preliminary Report* of its investigation of "violations of the right of free speech and assembly and interference with the right of labor to organize and bargain collectively." Among other things, the Report noted that employers were hiring strikebreakers and using methods of force and violence in attempts to overcome incipient labor organizations.[9]

In 1937, the Supreme Court upheld the constitutionality of the Wagner Act. In doing so, we have seen in Chapter 7, the Court rejected the argument that the Act was beyond the power of Congress under the Commerce Clause on grounds that it regulated manufacturing and not com-

---

[8] *Federal Labor Laws and Programs* (United States Department of Labor) (Washington, D.C.: U.S. Government Printing Office, 1964), p. 63.

[9] *Violations of Free Speech and Rights of Labor* (Pre-

liminary Report of the Senate Committee on Education and Labor, 76th Cong., 1st sess., 1937), (Washington, D.C.: U.S. Government Printing Office, 1937), Senate Report No. 46, p. 1.

merce.[10] Following this decision, labor union membership increased greatly, reaching a total of more than 17 million in 1962.

The Labor-Management Relations
(Taft–Hartley) Act of 1947 (29 U.S.C. 141; 171)

During World War II, unions did not press forward demands on behalf of their members; instead they supported the war effort by giving "no strike" assurances. But after the war ended, particularly in 1946, many strikes occurred, and threats were made of a railroad strike. The country was tired of the wartime controls and elected a Republican majority to Congress, even though the Democrats controlled the Presidency. This Congress hastened to abolish the wartime controls; inflation occurred; and union demands for salary increases resulted in strikes. The Republican-controlled 80th Congress (which met for the first time in January 1947) believed it had a mandate to amend the Wagner Act to reduce the power of labor unions. It adopted the Labor–Management Relations Act of 1947 (also known as the Taft–Hartley Act) over President Truman's veto in June 1947. Most of the Act is still in force.

The first paragraph of the statement of "Findings and Policy" in the Wagner Act of 1935 had consisted of an assertion that the "denial by employers of the right of employees to organize and the refusal of employers to accept the procedure of collective bargaining" had led to labor strife which burdened interstate commerce. This paragraph was followed by one asserting that the inequality of bargaining power of employees and employers had further harmful effects. Congress next asserted that experience had shown that "protection by law of the right of employees to organize and bargain collectively safeguards commerce from injury . . . and promotes the flow of commerce" and concluded with the statement that it was the policy of the United States to eliminate the cause of certain obstructions to commerce by "encouraging the practice and procedure of collective bargaining" by protecting the right of workers to organize and bargain with employers.

The emphasis in this statement of "Findings and Policy" in ⟨...⟩ was upon the rights to be ⟨...⟩ workers (who were cas⟨...⟩ underdogs); and the emp⟨...⟩ cast in the role of villain⟨...⟩

The statement of "F⟨...⟩ in the Taft–Hartley Act of 19⟨...⟩ much of the language contained in the Wagner Act, but adds a paragraph characterizing "some labor unions" as also being villains and lists a number of unfair union practices.

The Act contains five titles. Title IV creates a Congressional committee to study labor problems, and Title V contains definitions. Neither Title will be considered further in this book.

Title I consists of a group of substantial amendments to the Wagner Act. The five "unfair employer labor practices" stated in the Wagner Act are restated. However, *in addition*, a number of "unfair union labor union practices" are defined. These union practices are prohibited: (1) restraining or coercing employees in the exercise of their right to organize or refrain from organizing except in the case of a legitimate union shop agreement (that is, an agreement under which nonunion employees may be employed but are required to join the union within a specified period of time); (2) forcing an employer to discriminate against a worker for any reason other than failure of the worker to pay his union dues; (3) engaging in: a secondary boycott (bringing pressure to bear upon a neutral employer to induce him to exert his influence upon the primary employer to agree to the union's demands); a jurisdictional strike; or attempting to force the employer to deal with a union other than the one which has been accredited by the Board as the legitimate bargaining agent; (4) refusing to bargain collectively; (5) requiring payment of initiation fees found by the Board to be excessive or discriminatory; (6) engaging in featherbedding (causing an employer to pay for services not actually performed or to be performed).

In addition, the size of the National Labor Relations Board was increased from three to five members, and the General Counsel was made independent of the Board. Like Board Members, he is appointed

---

[10] *N.L.R.B.* v. *Jones and Laughlin Steel Corporation*, 301 U.S. 1 (1937).

the President with the advice and consent of the Senate. He has final authority with regard to the investigation of charges, issuance of complaints, and prosecution of unfair practices. The Board itself hears and decides cases. Thus it performs primarily a judicial function.

Supervisors and foremen were excluded from coverage; moreover under Section 14(b), if a state law prohibits a union from making membership in a union compulsory, a union and an employer are prohibited from making a union shop agreement. Under this provision, many states have passed so-called "right to work" laws. Also, employers have the right to petition the Board to hold an election to determine which of two or more unions claiming to be so actually is representative of a majority of the workers in a plant, and employers have a right to express their opinions concerning unionization to employees without being guilty of an unfair labor practice. (Prior to the Taft–Hartley Act, it had been held that for an employer to herd his employees into a plant auditorium on company time to propagandize against a union constituted an unfair labor practice.) So-called "hot-cargo" agreements are also prohibited in most industries. (Under these, unions agree with employers not to handle products of another employer engaged in a labor dispute.) The Taft–Hartley Act also contains specific provisions pertaining to collective bargaining and to the procedure employed by the Board in holding representation elections. For example, the Board has the duty of defining the appropriate bargaining "unit." All these provisions have, of course, been the subjects of many decisions both by the Board and by the courts, but to examine such rules and the decisions in detail would require a volume in itself.

Title II of the Taft–Hartley Act creates the Federal Mediation and Conciliation service as an independent agency headed by an administrator appointed by the President and approved by the Senate. There is a statutory requirement that a party to a collective bargaining agreement who intends to terminate or modify the agreement must serve upon the other party written notice of his intention 60 days prior to the termination date and 30 days after

such filing action must inform the Service that a labor dispute exists. The Service has no power to *compel* settlement of disputes, but it *may assist* the parties in making a settlement *by offering* its facilities for conciliation, mediation, and arbitration. It also undertakes to anticipate disputes and to assist the parties in developing procedures for settlement.

Title II is also the enacting legislation for procedures to be employed in cases of strikes or lockouts which may result in "national emergencies." If the President believes that an actual strike or lockout (action by an employer shutting down his plant) will imperil the national health or safety, he is authorized to create a Board of Inquiry to investigate and report on the matter without making any recommendations. One copy of the Board's report is filed with the Federal Mediation and Conciliation Service and made public. The President may then direct the Attorney General to seek an injunction to prohibit the strike or lockout. If a District Court finds that the strike or lockout will imperil the national health or safety, it may issue an injunction without regard to the provisions of the Norris–La Guardia Act. The parties to the dispute then have 60 days during which they must use the assistance of the Federal Mediation and Conciliation Service to try to settle the dispute. Meanwhile, the President may reconvene the Board of Inquiry. If the dispute is not settled in 60 days, the Board makes a new report which is made public and which must contain a statement of the employer's last offer of settlement. Within 15 days, the National Labor Relations Board must hold an election to determine whether or not the employees involved wish to accept the last offer of settlement. The results are then certified to the Attorney General who *must* ask the Court to vacate the injunction. After this request has been granted, the President must report the proceedings to Congress together with such recommendations as he chooses to make. The emergency provisions were invoked only six times in the five-year period from 1964 through 1968. The East Coast and Gulf longshore contracts expired on October 1, 1968; a brief strike occurred, and a Taft–Hartley injunction was issued but no agreement was reached while it was in effect and the strike resumed on December 20 and continued into the early months of 1969.[11]

In addition, Title II contains provisions pertaining to suits by and against labor organizations, provisions prohibiting political contributions both by corporations and unions in federal elections, and provisions pertaining to payment of fees and the making of loans by employers to representatives of that employer's employees. These last-mentioned provisions were designed to eliminate opportunities for graft, blackmail, and corruption on the part of union officials and were changed by new legislation adopted in 1959.

The Labor-Management Reporting and Disclosure (Landrum–Griffin) Act of 1959 (29 U.S.C. 401) and the Welfare and Pension Plans Disclosure Act, as Amended in 1962, (29 U.S.C. 302)

The Welfare and Pension Funds Disclosure Act, as amended in 1962, is primarily a disclosure act and has the purpose of safeguarding the funds of employee benefit plans. Administrators of such plans and funds are required to make available to participants and to file with the Department of Labor a description of the relevant plan and an annual report. Approximately 157,700 employee benefit plans were on file in the Department of Labor at the end of fiscal year 1968.

The Labor–Management Disclosure Act was enacted in 1959, after more than two years of hearings by the Senate Select Committee on Investigation of Improper Activities in Labor–Management Relations, popularly known as the McClellan Committee. The investigation produced the conclusions that democratic freedom was lacking in some labor unions, some union funds were being misused, and some racketeering was present in some labor union activities in that funds were sometimes extorted from management by some powerful labor leaders by threats of union activity.

Also known as the Landrum–Griffin Act, the law consists of seven titles in addition to one containing definitions and a statement of policy. Title I is called the Bill of Rights of Members of Labor Organizations and sets forth the rights which individual union members may enforce by bringing suits in federal courts. These rights are stated in six paragraphs, ranging from the first (which guarantees members equal right to attend, participate in, and vote at meetings and elections subject to reasonable union rules) to the sixth (which guarantees a right to notice and a fair hearing in the case of any disciplinary actions except those for nonpayment of dues).

Title II requires unions to adopt constitutions and by-laws and to file these, together with organizational and annual financial reports, with the Secretary of Labor. By the end of fiscal year 1968, 51,656 disclosure files of reporting labor organizations were considered active by the Department of Labor and approximately 13,000 investigations had been completed.[12] Union officials and employees must also report conflict of interest transactions, and employers must file reports of payments or loans to union officials or employees.

Title II further specifies the conditions under which a supervisory body may establish a "trusteeship" over a subordinate union and requires the filing of periodic reports concerning the purposes and nature of the "trusteeship" established. Title IV also pertains to the actions of national and international (parent) unions and specifies that officers must be elected every five years by secret ballots. This title also specifies the standards for conducting such elections.

Title V prescribes fiduciary responsibilities of officers, agents, stewards, or other union representatives, and requires that relevant officeholders be bonded in cases of unions with property or annual revenues in excess of $5,000.

Title VI contains miscellaneous provisions conferring on the Secretary of Labor power to inspect records to determine whether the act is being violated. This title also imposes criminal penalties for "extortionate picketing" (picketing designed to extract money for personal benefit from an employer other than for bona fide employee benefits). Violations of the law are also made subject to criminal action. In the Department of Labor, enforcement of both the Landrum–Griffin Act and of the Labor–

---

[11] *Annual Report of the Department of Labor for 1968* (Lithoprinted copy, March, 1969), pp. 21–22.

[12] *Ibid.*, p. 26.

Management Disclosure Act is placed in units under the jurisdiction of the Assistant Secretary for Labor–Management Relations.

Recapitulation

Our survey of the various statutes enacted since 1932 thus shows that the period from 1932 to about the end of World War II was one in which union activities were positively promoted through the use of governmental power; in 1947 a reaction occurred and governmental power was used to place limitations on the use of self help activities by labor unions; in 1959 the Landrum–Griffin Act was adopted, providing for the regulation by the Federal Government of *internal* union affairs. The National Labor Relations Board, created in 1935, is concerned not with the regulation of internal union affairs but with relations between management and labor. It is to a discussion of the work of this agency that we turn now.

Organization and Operations of the National Labor Relations Board (NLRB)

As has been mentioned earlier in this chapter, the National Labor Relations Board was created by the National Labor Relations Act of 1935 and administers that law as amended by the Taft–Hartley Act of 1947 and the Landrum–Griffin Act of 1959.

Under this basic legislation, the Board has two principal functions: (1) to determine by agency-conducted secret ballot elections whether employees wish to be represented by unions in collective bargaining and (2) to prevent and remedy unfair labor practices on the parts of unions and employers. In fiscal year 1968, the Board received 30,705 cases.[13] Of this number, 17,816 were unfair labor practice cases. Charges alleging violations by employers amounted to 11,892. In 1967, there were 2,971 charges of illegal union restraint and coercion; charges of illegal union secondary boycotts and jurisdictional disputes amounted to 1,815; unions were charged with illegal discrimination against employees 681 times, and there were 528 charges of illegal union picketing for organizational or recognition purposes. In 1967, unions filed 7,559 of the charges against employers and employers filed 2,942 charges against unions.

In dealing with unfair labor practices, the Board either employs a method of investigation and informal settlement or issues orders after a hearing. The agency has no independent statutory power of enforcement of its orders but must seek enforcement in a Court of Appeals.

The Agency is unique among federal regulatory agencies in that the General Counsel is appointed by the President, as are Board Members, and possesses statutory powers. He is responsible for the issuance and prosecution of formal complaints and supervises the regional offices.

Hearing Examiners issue intial decisions; appeals may be taken from their decisions to the Board; and decisions of the Board may be appealed to the courts.

A petition requesting the Board to certify a representative for collective bargaining purposes may be filed by an employee, a group of employees, any individual or labor organization or by an employer who has been presented with a request for recognition by any individual or organization claiming to represent his employees. If the Board finds that a representation question exists, it directs that a secret election be held and certifies the results. There are three types of elections: (1) *Representation* elections to determine the employee's choice of a bargaining agent; (2) *Decertification* elections to determine whether or not the employees wish to withdraw the bargaining authority of a labor organization previously elected; (3) *Deauthorization* polls to determine whether or not the employees wish to revoke the authority of their representative to make a union shop agreement. There were 8,183 elections of all kinds held in fiscal year 1967; 7,882 of these were representation elections; there were also 234 decertification elections and 67 deauthorization elections. Unions do not win all elections; of the 8,183 elections held, unions won 4,791 representation elections, or 59 percent of the total but in 1968, unions won only 57 percent of the total elections held.

---

[13] This subdivision is based on the annual reports of the National Labor Relations Board, especially upon the report for 1968, published in 1969. Individual footnotes will not be used.

B. LABOR STANDARDS AND ECONOMIC SECURITY

Wage and Hour Legislation

As we have seen in Chapter 7, early efforts by the states to regulate the conditions and terms of employment were regularly held unconstitutional by the Supreme Court until 1937. So were attempts by Congress to prohibit the use of child labor. Then, in 1937, the Court upheld minimum wage law enacted by the State of Washington.[14]

In 1938, Congress passed the Fair Labor Standards Act. As amended, this law fixes standards for minimum wages and for overtime pay. It also fixes standards for the employment of child labor. The law has been several times amended to increase the minimum wage and to increase the total number of employees covered. Under this legislation, control over hours of work is accomplished by controlling the length of the standard *workweek*; after the number of hours in the standard workweek has been worked, the overtime rates become applicable. In a 1969 report to Congress on the operation of the law, Willard Wirtz, the Secretary of Labor under President Johnson, recommended to Congress that the minimum wage be raised to $2.00 per hour.

The conclusions drawn by economic theorists concerning the effects on employment of minimum wage laws depend upon the assumptions made in such analyses about the degree of competition existing in the industry being analyzed. The use of such studies as a basis for policy is thus limited. Moreover, empirical studies often produce conflicting results. In 1969, in the report mentioned earlier, the Secretary of Labor also reported that there were only 63 cases of an "alleged plant shutdown or an employee layoff."[15]

Two years prior to the enactment of the Fair Labor Standards Act, Congress adopted the Walsh–Healy Public Contracts Act (41 U.S.C. 35–45). This law specifies that contracts by the Federal Government for supplies must contain provisions specifying labor standards for production of such supplies. Obviously such legislation involves the terms of a federal contract and did not run afoul of the then-prevailing (1936) Supreme Court interpretation of the Commerce Clause.

The Walsh–Healy Act created the Public Contracts Division within the Department of Labor as an agency to enforce the provisions of the law. The Wage and Hour Division was similarly created to enforce the provisions of the Fair Labor Standards Act by that law in 1938.

In the report mentioned above, the Secretary of Labor pointed to the Fair Labor Standards Act as a weapon to be used in the War on Poverty when he remarked that more than half of the 22 to 26 million people living in poverty in the United States "live there" because of low wages.[16]

Workmen's Compensation Laws

At common law, an action by a workman against his employer for compensation for an injury sustained in the course of his employment involved a proof that there was negligence *on the part of the employer* and that the employee had suffered damage as a result of *this* negligence. In any case in which an employee was injured by a fellow employee's negligence, the employer, accordingly, could not be held liable. This last stated proposition has been given the name of "fellow-servant" doctrine. Two defenses to a charge of negligence (and in borderline cases the two merge into a single defense) are the doctrine of contributory negligence and that of assumption of risk. The contributory negligence doctrine is merely the proposition that one cannot recover damages if he has himself been guilty of contributory negligence; the assumption of risk doctrine holds that one who is suing and alleging negligence cannot recover if the case involves a situation in which it can be shown that he assumed the risk of the injury causing the damage. He is presumed to have assumed the "foreseeable" risks only, however, not those which may be hidden or obscured and not apparent to an ordinary prudent person (which usually means "foreseeable" by the finder of fact).

[14] *West Coast Hotel Co.* v. *Parrish*, 300 U.S. 379 (1937).

[15] *Minimum Wage and Maximum Hours Standards under the Fair Labor Standards Act* (United States Department of Labor, Wage and Public Contracts Divisions) (Washington, D.C.: U.S. Government Printing Office, 1969), p. 8.

[16] *Ibid.*, p. 3.

Applied in cases involving employers and their employees, the assumption of risk doctrine, it has been noted by some, is simply a legal counterpart of the classical economic doctrine of free market regulation of the use of factors of production, since that economic doctrine assumes that the compensation paid the employee must be high enough to compensate for the risk involved in the employment. The contributory negligence doctrine, it may be remarked does not have a counterpart in economic theory.

Given the available defenses, many studies have shown that the employee's opportunity for compensation for an injury suffered while working was slight. One of the leaders in a movement for the enactment of social legislation to deal with this problem was John R. Commons, whose work has already been discussed in Chapter 1 and elsewhere.

In 1911, California, New Jersey, Washington, and Wisconsin adopted workmen's compensation laws upheld by the courts. Commons was instrumental in securing the enactment of the Wisconsin law.

Under these laws, although the amounts of compensation are different in the several states, employers are generally required to contribute to an "insurance fund," with premium payments based on the frequency with which accidents occur in their establishments; and employees are entitled to recover compensation as a matter of right according to stated schedules of compensation fixed by law for injuries. The problem of this type of compensation thus no longer involves the question of litigation based on an allegation of negligence nor the use of the three defenses mentioned earlier. There are also several federal workmen's compensation laws. Examples include one enacted to protect federal civil employees, and another to cover longshoremen, harbor workers, and all private employees in the District of Columbia. The state laws are administered by state agencies having various names, depending on the state; the federal laws are administered by agencies within the Department of Labor under the direction of the Assistant Secretary for Wage and Labor Standards. Some of these federal agencies also provide technical assistance and information to state agencies and prescribe safety standards for plants covered by federal laws.

Because the premiums paid by employers for unemployment compensation insurance vary depending upon the frequency with which accidents occur in their individual plants, in addition to providing compensation to workers, these laws have provided an inducement to employers to create relatively safe working conditions with the objective of preventing injuries and reducing premium payments.

Unemployment Insurance

In his book, *Institutional Economics*, published in 1934, John R. Commons discussed the topics of workmen's compensation legislation and unemployment compensation under a single subheading called: "Accidents and Unemployment—Insurance and Prevention."[17] This treatment emphasized an idea which Commons and his students had long held that in an industrial society the hazard of unemployment is comparable to industrial hazards and both types of hazards are costs which should be imposed upon employers and eventually passed on to consumers in prices charged for products. Accordingly, a merit system was proposed under which the cost of unemployment insurance to an individual employer was made a function of his employment record—employers who maintained the best employment records paid the lowest premiums.

The existing unemployment insurance program is a state-federal program originally established by the Social Security Act of 1935. Under this program, the Federal Government has imposed a tax on employers of four or more persons. This tax in 1969 amounted to 3.1 percent of wages paid up to a maximum of $3000 wages *per employee* paid by the employer. However, in any case in which a state has a federally approved unemployment compensation program (all 50 states do), employers in specified "covered" industries are allowed to credit against their federal tax liability an amount equal to 2.7 percent of the taxable wages paid. The Federal Government thus actually collects a sum equal to $3.1 - 2.7 = 0.4$ of

[17] John R. Commons, *Institutional Economics* (paperback reprint, Volume 2, Madison, Wisconsin: University of Wisconsin Press, 1961), p. 840.

1 percent of taxable wages paid by covered employers plus the entire tax from those not covered. This sum is returned to the states for administrative purposes. All of the state legislatures have enacted their own employment compensation tax laws, and the actual rates vary among the states. The actual rate paid by any given employer depends in all states upon his employment experience rating; the "merit" system advocated by Commons has thus been put into actual practice, although not without criticism by some. Among the sharpest criticisms are the argument that the "merit" rating system penalizes seasonal employers and that the system operates to increase tax rates during periods of general business decline or depression, that is, at precisely the time when tax rates should be reduced.

The constitutionality of this federal-state program was upheld by the Supreme Court in 1937 in *Steward Machine Company* v. *Davis*, a case already discussed at length in Subdivision F of Chapter 7, to which the reader may be referred at this point.

The industries covered by the law vary according to the various state laws, as do the benefits received. In order to collect compensation, a worker must be ready, willing, and able to work and be unemployed through no fault of his own. A worker may be denied benefits in most states if he refuses an offer to accept suitable work; such an offer may be made through the facilities of a state or federal employment service. Under a reorganization of the Department of Labor initiated in 1968 but implemented in 1969, *both* the Unemployment Insurance Service and the United States Training and Employment Service were, therefore, placed within the Manpower Administration of the Department. The work of this Administration will be discussed in detail in Subdivision C below. Before doing so, however, it is necessary to examine briefly the Social Security Program.

Social Security (Old Age, Disability and Survivor's "Insurance"; Medicare and Medicaid): Family Assistance Programs

In addition to providing for the nation-wide system of unemployment compensation just discussed, the Social Security Act of 1935 established a national system to protect wage earners and their dependents from loss of income resulting from old age and disability and to protect dependents in the case of death. The system established in 1935 is a federal system operated by the Security Administration of the Department of Health, Education, and Welfare.

The original Social Security Act has been many times amended to extend the coverage of the program, to vary the tax rates used in financing it, to vary the benefit payments made and, perhaps, most significantly in 1965 to include two separate health insurance programs for people 65 years old and over. The original Act provided for a tax of 2 percent on payrolls of enterprises in covered employments, 1 percent upon employees and 1 percent on employers. Many economists have argued that the tax imposed upon employers was actually also paid by employees in the form of reduced wages, and in some cases by consumers in the form of higher prices; in short, the tax was "shifted" by the employers. Under the original law, benefits were also deferred until 1942, since it was thought necessary to accumulate a fund from which benefits could be paid. In practice, however, a government-operated program of this kind needs no fund, since benefits can be paid to present recipients from the taxes collected from workers not yet eligible, who, in turn receive benefits from future workers, some perhaps not yet born.

In 1969, the Secretary of Health, Education, and Welfare emphasized the significance of the Social Security program in keeping a large number of people above the poverty level.[18]

Under existing law, the tax rate imposed upon employers was fixed to rise from 4.2 percent for retirement, survivors, and disability insurance plus 0.6 of 1 percent for hospital insurance in 1969–70 to 5.0 percent for the former plus 0.9 of 1 percent for hospital insurance in 1987 and after. The rate for self-employed people was fixed to increase from a total of 6.9 to a total of 7.9 percent in the same period.

In 1969, the outgoing Secretary of Health, Education, and Welfare recommended to

[18] *Annual Report of the Department of Health, Education, and Welfare for Fiscal Year 1968, Secretary's Introduction* (Washington, D.C., Lithoprint, 1969), pp. 60–61.

Congress that: (1) benefits be raised to a $100 minimum for an individual and $150 for a couple "over the next several years;" (2) that the maximum earnings base for computation of benefits ($7,800 in 1969–70) be completely eliminated in determining the employer's contribution; (3) that the employee's maximum earnings base for determining both benefits and contributions be raised to $15,000 per year; (4) that the ratio of the employer–employee contribution be changed from 50–50 to two-thirds for the employer and one-third for the employee in recognition of the fact that the employer can deduct his contributions as a business expense but the employee must pay an income tax on his deduction; and (5) that the maximum outside income which can be earned without loss of retirement benefits be raised from the 1969–70 limit of $1680 to $1800.[19] In December 1969, Congress responded by increasing benefits by 15 percent.

We have seen in Chapter 5 that the American Medical Association strongly opposed the adoption of any form of government sponsored health insurance in the United States. However, in 1965, following President Johnson's landslide victory, Congress amended the Social Security Act and established two separate but related health insurance programs (Medicare) for people 65 years of age or older.

One of these systems is the system of hospital insurance for the beneficiaries of retirement, survivors, and disability programs and those of the railroad retirement system. This program is financed by contributions of workers in the same way in which the other programs are financed. The other program of health insurance is one of supplementary medical insurance benefits involving payment of a monthly premium by the beneficiary, a payment matched by an equal contribution by the Government. In 1969, the premium was $4 per month. This program is voluntary, but the hospital insurance program is compulsory.

The Social Security Administration does not make contracts directly with hospitals or doctors. An intermediary, usually Blue Cross in the case of hospitals and Blue Shield in the case of doctors, is selected and the Administration deals with the intermediary. To be included in the program, hospitals must meet standards set by the Administration and the latter must pay hospitals "the reasonable cost" of hospital service plus 2 percent. The program thus involves administrative price control and hospitals under the program are, in effect, firms in a regulated industry. Fees paid to doctors must also be "reasonable," but there is no requirement that they must be uniform throughout the country or in the case of all payments. Two ways exist for payment to be made of the doctor's fee. In one case, a doctor may collect his entire bill from the patient who recovers 80 percent from the intermediary; and an alternative method is for the doctor to collect 20 percent from the patient and 80 percent from the intermediary.

The law also provides for federal medical assistance to states in providing medical services for the destitute who pass a "means" test. Such programs are administered by the states who make the payments to doctors and hospitals. This form of medical assistance is known as Medicaid.

In his 1969 report to Congress, the Secretary of Health, Education and Welfare recommended that Medicaid be extended to all totally disabled people, "no matter what their age."[20]

Family Assistance

About 9 million Americans receive public assistance payments, and about 7 million of these are either old (2 million), very young (4.2 million children), blind (85,000, or totally disabled (700,000). The average monthly check for an aged man or woman was $70.25 in 1969 and $162 for a family with three children.[21] In August 1969, President Nixon asked Congress to establish a federal aid program providing a minimum annual income of $1,600 for a family of four.

There are five types of federal–state public assistance programs: old age assistance to those over 65; aid to families with dependent children; aid to the needy blind; aid to the totally and permanently disabled; and Medicaid, described above.

---

[19] *Ibid.*, pp. 62–63.
[20] *Ibid.*, pp. 28–29.

[21] *Ibid.*, pp. 63–64.

The Federal Government sets standards for the programs and shares the cost of the programs with the states. However, the states have a decisive voice in deciding who shall receive aid and the amount of aid given. State practices vary widely. According to the report of the Secretary of Health, Education, and Welfare, too many states, "are still entangled in the 'quest for the worthy poor'" and a national standard should be developed. Moreover, the report pointed out: "We must concentrate on better training and better jobs for welfare recipients." This problem falls under the heading of the topic of "Manpower," to which we now turn.

C. MANPOWER POLICIES AND PROGRAMS

Manpower Policy

Contemporary microeconomic theory concerns itself largely with problems of "efficient" utilization of resources and assumes "the distribution of income is given." Accordingly, microeconomic theory has traditionally assumed that problems of poverty are of no concern to economic analysis. Discriminatory market practices are usually categorized as market imperfections, but seldom if ever has any real attempt been made to analyze them. Contemporary macroeconomic theory has traditionally concerned itself with an analysis of problems pertaining to the maintenance of a full employment economy and has assumed that the problems of frictional unemployment do not exist. Thus neither microeconomic nor macroeconomic theory has been concerned with the category of problems which is today encompassed by the term "manpower." Manpower policy was defined in 1964 as having the goals of: (1) developing workers' abilities; (2) creating jobs to make the most of these abilities; and (3) matching workers and jobs.[22]

Two events in 1957, the launching of Sputnik, and the persistence of a high level of unemployment, resulted in Congressional attention to manpower problems. In 1958, the National Defense Education Act was

passed, providing for a program of extensive federal aid to technical and scientific education; and the Area Redevelopment Act was enacted in 1961. The latter contained a provision for occupational training projects for unemployed workers in areas of substantial and persistent unemployment together with subsistence allowances for these workers and their families during training.

In 1962, Congress adopted the Manpower Development and Training Act, thereby laying the foundation for erection of a national manpower policy. This law provided for a nationwide program of occupational training for unemployed and underemployed workers, provided for expansion of research devoted to manpower problems, and made it possible to develop experimental and demonstration projects for the purpose of finding new ways of training disadvantaged workers. Although, manpower policy emphasized technical training to provide trained personnel for the coming space age, with the Declaration of the War on Poverty, emphasis has been placed primarily upon training and assisting disadvantaged workers. The original legislation has been many times amended and extended; amendments adopted in 1968 extended the operation of a number of training programs to 1972; states were given greater authority to initiate projects subject to standards set by the Department of Labor and that of Health, Education, and Welfare; and additional funds were authorized for new supplemental programs for the disadvantaged.

In addition to the Manpower Training and Development Act, provisions of the Civil Rights Act of 1964 play an important role in the attainment of the goal of matching workers and jobs. Title VI of the Act makes it an unfair labor practice for employers (of more than 25 employees), labor unions, or employment agencies to discriminate against anyone because of race, color, sex, religion, or national origin. The Age Discrimination in Employment Act of 1967 makes it unlawful to refuse to hire or to fire persons between 40 and 64 years of age on grounds of age alone. Title VII of the Civil Rights Act of 1964

---

[22] *Manpower Report of the President, 1969* (Washington, D.C.: U.S. Government Printing Office, 1969), p. 3. This subdivision rests largely on this source.

prohibits federal grants-in-aid for activities that involve discrimination prohibited by Title VI. The Civil Rights Act is implemented by the actions of the Equal Employment Opportunity Commission which had received more than 34,000 complaints by January 1969 and referred 18,000 of them for investigation. Title VII of the Act provides that the Commission may defer action in a case arising in a state with an enforceable fair employment practices law and the means to enforce it. As of 1967, the Commission deferred to 33 states, all located in the northern or western parts of the United States. A number of agencies and activities established prior to 1962 have also been incorporated into the manpower program by various means. An example is the agency formerly known as the United States Employment Service, created by the Wagner–Peyser Act in 1933, which was renamed the United States Employment and Training Service in 1969. The role of the Service will become apparent in the description of manpower programs which follows.

Manpower Programs

Programs to Develop Workers' Abilities. More than a million workers were enrolled in occupational training programs set up between August 1962 and June 1968. Most training has been carried on through vocational schools. On-the-job training programs have also been used. In 1968, the *JOBS (Job Opportunities in the Business Sector)* program was initiated. This program involves the cooperation of private business firms in the hiring and training of disadvantaged workers. Private firms bear most of the cost, while the Government underwrites those costs of the program which exceed those normally incurred in the hiring and training of new workers. The long-range goal is the employment of 500,000 disadvantaged workers by June 1971. The Vocational Education Acts of 1962 and 1963 have made possible greater utilization of vocational programs in public schools for manpower purposes. These programs are aimed at training young workers. Programs to train workers to read and write have been established (such as the *Adult Basic Education Program*) and programs to aid states in providing greater facilities

for higher education have also been the subject of special legislation. The *Concentrated Employment Program (CEP)* has been undertaken in slum areas to provide a variety of health, counseling, and training services. Special programs have also been undertaken to help handicapped workers become productive.

Programs to Create Jobs. Many of the programs devoted to the development of lagging areas and regions and to elimination of urban slum areas have manpower aspects. The Employment Act of 1946 establishes maximum employment as a national goal and thus also has an indirect manpower aspect. However, this legislation ignores the existence of men and women in the labor force who want and need jobs but who are not seeking work because of discouragement. Manpower programs directed to this group include *Operation Mainstream* to provide work experience for chronically unemployed adults, the *Neighborhood Youth Corps* involving arrangements to obtain jobs for young people to help them stay in school, and the *Job Corps* designed to serve young people "so underprivileged and alienated that they cannot profit from education and training without moving to a new environment." The *New Careers Program* undertakes to open job possibilities with career ladder possibilities for unemployed and underemployed persons.

Programs to Match Workers and Jobs. The agency formerly known as the United States Employment Service was renamed the United States Training and Employment Service in 1969 in recognition of the fact that this agency is an important tool of the Manpower Administration. The Service was originally created to give assistance in the establishment of public employment offices in the states but local employment offices have today become the chief manpower agencies in their communities. Today the Service does not wait for the jobless to request job seeking assistance but "actively seeks out those workers who most need help and arranges for the combination of services required by the individual." The Service has thus been reoriented in the direction of serving the most disadvantaged members of the community. Various programs have also been established to assist working mothers; for example, the Department of Health,

Education, and Welfare administers a program to provide day care for the children of working mothers. The activities of the Equal Employment Opportunity Commission in reducing job discrimination must also be considered activities designed to match workers to jobs.

The Manpower Administration

The central manpower policy-making agency is the Manpower Administration of the Department of Labor. In 1969, the Administration was reorganized in the line of command under an Assistant Secretary for Manpower. Regional Manpower Administrators directly responsible to the Manpower Administrator were made responsible for administering manpower programs in their regions. The United States Employment and Training Service was made responsible for administering all employment, work experience, and training programs. This centralization of authority and direction had become necessary because of the proliferation of programs. The Bureau of Unemployment Insurance Service, and the Bureau of Apprenticeship and Training are additional agencies responsible to the Manpower Administrator, who is directly responsible to the Assistant Secretary for Manpower.

A Concluding Comment

That important functions in the conduct of the War on Poverty should have devolved upon the Manpower Administration within the Department of Labor is, of course, logical and appropriate. However, this agency is not the only one dealing with problems of the disadvantaged. Programs to prevent deception and fraud in the case of the disadvantaged have been and are being undertaken by the Federal Trade Commission, particularly under the Federal Trade Commission Act and under the Truth in Lending Act. Moreover, programs implemented by the Department of Agriculture play an important role in combatting rural poverty, while some developed by the Small Business Administration are aimed both at rural and at urban poverty. It is to a discussion of the work of these last two agencies that the next chapter is devoted.

Agriculture; Small Business

We have seen in Chapter 1 that in Book IV of *The Wealth of Nations*, Adam Smith discussed two different "systems of political economy," "the system of commerce" and "the system of agriculture." In the United States today, the systems of agriculture and of commerce are intertwined and form a single system. We have also seen in Chapter 8 that a shift in the relative importances of agricultural and industrial production began as early as 1839 and continued thereafter, so that by the 1940s, agricultural production accounted for only 9.4 percent of our national income, with mining, manufacturing, trade, commerce, government, and finance accounting for the rest. Technological advances in agriculture from the time of the invention of the steel plow by John Deere in 1837 to the present have resulted in greatly increased agricultural productivity, producing a long-run decline in the prices of agricultural commodities relative to the prices of other goods and services.

In addition, we have seen in Chapter 11 that beginning at about the turn of the present century, many small business firms were beginning to disappear as a result of their merger with or acquisition by other firms and that a third merger wave is presently continuing to reduce the number of small business firms. Yet, some have pointed to the fact that increased investment in small business firms in both rural and urban communities would help to alleviate some of the poverty which exists in the United States.

This chapter consists of two major subdivisions. The first undertakes to examine contemporary uses of governmental power to promote the interests not only of agricultural producers but also of consumers of agricultural products; the second major subdivision analyzes contemporary uses of governmental power to promote the interests of "small" business firms, according to various legislative definitions of the word "small." In both areas, governmental power has been used to modify the operation of market forces. The relationship of programs in both areas to the War on Poverty will also be examined.

A. CONTEMPORARY USES OF GOVERNMENTAL POWER TO PROMOTE AGRICULTURAL INTERESTS

Aspects of "the Farm Problem"; Legislation Prior to 1961

We have already seen in Chapter 8 (in the discussion titled *Government Actions to Aid Agriculture* . . .) that agricultural prices fluctuate more widely than do industrial products prices. Neither the quantity of agricultural products supplied nor the quantity demanded is very responsive to price changes; moreover, the demand is subject to sudden changes; and the supply, which depends among other things on the weather, is also subject to sudden changes. Agricultural productivity has been high as the result of various technological changes in production techniques; output per man hour has risen greatly and thus agricultural prices have fallen relative to other prices over time.

The instability of prices has been one of the arguments for giving special governmental protection to agricultural producers. We have also seen in Chapter 8 that governmental aid to agriculture dates back to an early time in United States history. During the Depression, emphasis was placed upon various schemes to support prices and control production. Since 1961, although the central objective of increasing farm income has not changed, emphasis has now been placed in federal programs upon "supply management."

In 1968, Secretary of Agriculture Freeman called attention to the fact that the high price support programs of the 1930s had helped to stabilize farm incomes at the expense of a loss of foreign markets and the accumulation of surpluses. He noted that these programs had culminated in 1961 in "bulging stocks—with grain stored everywhere—even on ships—85 million tons of grain—1.4 million tons of wheat." It was then costing the Government about $1 million a day just to store these stocks.[1]

The programs of the 1930s all had their origin in the Agriculture Adjustment Act of 1933. This Depression legislation involved control over *acreage* devoted to production and a cash subsidy payment to farmers financed by a "processing" tax levied on farm products. The Act incorporated the "parity" principle, namely the idea that farm products prices should stand in the same relation to industrial products prices as that in which they had stood, on the average, in the period 1919 to 1929. Under this concept, if a bushel of wheat had an average price of $1.00 during the period

1919 to 1929, while a shirt cost $2.00 during the same period, two bushels of wheat should equal one shirt. Thus if in 1933 a bushel of wheat had a price of only $0.50, while a shirt still cost $2.00, the price of wheat would have to be doubled to achieve full parity. If prices were to be raised to only 90 percent of parity, the price of a bushel of wheat would have to be increased by only 40 cents.

The Supreme Court declared this law unconstitutional in 1936. However, Congress had in 1935 adopted the Soil Conservation and Domestic Allotment Act for the purpose of soil conversion, and after 1936, Congress amended this law to make possible payments to farmers for taking cropland out of production. There followed a wide variety of programs involving acreage restrictions, nonrecourse loans by the government (under which a farmer could use his crop, valued at a price above the market price, as security for a government loan and allow the government to acquire title by not repaying the loan—in substance a sale and not a loan), direct purchases to support prices, government export programs, and marketing quotas. The soil bank idea was also developed. Under it, farmers were paid to keep land out of production of *any* agricultural products. But all these programs suffered from the shortcoming that none of them prevented farmers from using new techniques to increase output from the reduced acreage devoted to production.

As noted by Secretary Freeman, the early programs to aid farmers had the result of producing large stocks in the hands of the Commodity Credit Corporation, the Government's purchasing agency. But, beginning in 1961, a new approach, known as "supply–management" was adopted.

The Concept of "Supply Management" After 1961

The new approach to farm problems adopted in 1961 was described by Secretary Freeman in testimony before the House Agriculture Committee in 1968. The approach was first embodied in the feed grain program in 1961 and subsequently extended to other commodities in the Food and

---

[1] *Extend the Food and Agriculture Act of 1965* (Hearings before the House Committee on Agriculture (90th

Cong., 2d sess., 1968) (Washington, D.C.: U.S. Government Printing Office, 1968), pp. 271–272.

Agriculture Act of 1965. Essentially, it involved direct payments to farmers for acreage voluntarily diverted to soil conserving or noncrop uses. In most cases, price supports were also added to the programs for specific commodities, and the Government loan rate was reduced to encourage farmers to pay off their loans.[2]

The Nature and Implementation of "Supply Management" Programs

The Commodity Credit Corporation and the Agricultural Stabilization and Conservation Service. The Commodity Credit Corporation was originally chartered in Delaware in 1933 and was given a permanent federal charter in 1948. It is an agency of the Federal Government, managed by a six-member board of directors, whose Chairman is the Secretary of Agriculture. The agency has a capital of $100 million and authority to borrow up to $14.5 billion to carry out price support and production stabilization programs. It purchases and disposes of agricultural commodities and makes payments to farmers for diverting cropland from production as designated by relevant legislation. The Corporation also undertakes to make storage arrangements for inventories of agricultural commodities when necessary. In carrying out its functions, the agency utilizes the personnel and facilities of the Agricultural Stabilization and Conservation Service, an agency established within the Department of Agriculture in 1953. Among the programs administered are the following.

Price Support Programs. Price support programs, under which attempts are made to maintain prices at some administratively determined level (usually at some percentage level of parity), include direct purchases from farmers and loans at a determined price with the crop serving as security for the loan. If the market price rises above the loan price, farmers can sell their crops and pay off the loans, pocketing the difference; if market prices remain below the loan price, farmers simply do not pay off their loans, leaving the Government with the agricultural products in question.

Mandatory price support programs were in effect in 1968 for wheat, corn, cotton, peanuts, rice, tobacco, tung nuts, barley, rye, oats, grain sorghum, butterfat, milk, wool, mohair, and honey. Discretionary authority existed in the cases of a few other commodities. Price support actions included incentive payments for wool and mohair, the latter two being commodities which must be imported to meet full domestic requirements.

Acreage Allotments and Marketing Quotas. Acreage allotments are used to limit output; in addition, if two-thirds of the producers voting in a referendum approve, marketing quotas are established. When such quotas are in effect, excess production of quota commodities is subject to penalties.

Land Conservation and Erosion Control Program (Appalachian Region). Under this special program, the Federal Government pays part of the cost of improving land located in the Appalachian Region.

Cropland Adjustment Program. This program involves the making of contracts for not less than five years nor more than ten years with farmers under which they are paid to divert land from production of designated crops to approved "conservation" uses.

Cropland Conversion Program. This program like the preceding one, involves diversion of cropland to noncrop uses, including recreation and wildlife development.

Agricultural Conservation Program. Under this program, the Government shares the costs of land improvement and provides technical assistance to farmers to improve their land and to prevent erosion (for example, by terracing).

Acreage Diversion Program. Under this program, farmers receive payments for diverting land from production of cotton, corn, and grain sorghums for conservation purposes. No program was in effect in 1968 for wheat, since the United States was seeking to increase wheat production to supply needy foreign countries in that year.

Other Activities. Other activities of the Corporation include inventory management, merchandising of government stocks in such a way as not to depress prices, and administration of international agreements and import quotas (for example in the case of wheat).

Results of "Supply Management"

Aside from the question of whether or not one believes that agricultural production in the United States should be subsidized, the "supply management" programs instituted since 1961 have been effective in attaining *their specific* objectives of reducing inventories in the hands of the Commodity Credit Corporation. Thus in 1968, the Corpoation's inventory and investment in agricultural commodities was less than $3.2 billion, as compared with nearly $8 billion in 1961. The inventory of commodities owned decreased from $6.1 billion in 1960 to $912 million in 1968. Storage costs, accordingly, also declined from the 1960 level of $476 million to $75 million in 1968.

Beneficiaries of the Farm Program

In 1968, during hearings on legislation to extend the Food and Agriculture Act of 1965, witnesses representing the Chamber of Commerce of the United States—who opposed the legislation—entered into evidence the results of a study of the operation of the existing legislation. The main thrust of their argument was that the existing programs benefitted large farmers rather than small ones.[3] The fact that large payments are made to large income recipients has resulted in much criticism but attempts to limit the amount paid to any one farmer have failed to secure Congressional approval.

The Federal Crop Insurance Corporation

This Corporation was created within the Department of Agriculture in 1938. It seeks to operate according to actuarial principles in providing crop insurance protection to farmers. Rates are, of course, not uniform. A total of 1,395 counties was served in 1968. The administrative cost of the program is not included in the premium and is paid by the Government.

Rural Poverty; Programs to Improve the Quality of Farm Life

In 1968, during Hearings on "Rural Renewal," Senator John Sparkman called attention to the fact that although much attention was being directed to the problem

of the urban poor, the problem of the poor living in rural areas had been neglected. As a matter of fact, Senator Sparkman estimated the number of rural poor at 14 million persons.[4]

The Office of Economic Opportunity administers programs of assistance for migrant workers and families with small incomes; in addition, a program of loans for rural families—provided under the Economic Opportunity Act of 1964—is administered by the Farmers Home Administration. The Department of Agriculture has also undertaken various programs to combat rural poverty as an adjunct to its programs to improve the quality of rural life. One agency employed for this purpose is the Rural Community Development Service which works closely with two action agencies, the Farmers Home Administration and the Rural Electrification Administration.

The Farmers Home Administration provides financial and management assistance to individuals, groups, and local organizations to improve the economies of relevant areas. Applicants must be unable to obtain needed credit elsewhere. The types of loans made include loans for the acquisition of titles, loans to carry on operations, rural housing loans, and loans to finance watershed protection and flood control programs. Thus, from January 1961 to June 1968, the Farmers Home Administration advanced nearly $600 million to rural communities to build water or sanitation systems. These loans were estimated to have created more than 200,000 man-years of on-site employment in the same period. Conservation work carried out with the aid of the Soil Conservation Service has also created much new employment. A program has also been established under which small groups, usually five or six, of families contribute unskilled labor to build their own housing under supervision of an experienced contractor. About 537 such projects existed in 1968. Another program has been one of assistance to about 47,000 rural landowners to establish income-producing outdoor recreation enterprises. Despite these activities, an estimated 5.9 million rural families still

[3] *Extend the Food and Agriculture Act of 1965, op. cit.*, pp. 382–385.
[4] *Rural Renewal* (Hearings before the Senate Select Committee on Small Business, 90th Cong., 2d sess., 1968) (Washington, D.C.: U.S. Government Printing Office, 1968), p. 1.

lack adequate water facilities and about 3.9 million lack adequate waste disposal facilities.

The Rural Electrification Administration was created in 1935. It makes loans to finance electric power generation, transmission, and distribution facilities in rural areas and also makes loans to furnish or improve telephone service in rural areas (defined on an area coverage basis). About 6 million establishments receive such electrical service, but there are still about 100,000 rural establishments which lack electric service. It is estimated that by 1974 there will be about 2.5 million rural telephone subscribers. The extension of the Administration's power facilities and telephone service involves, of course, increased employment opportunities in rural areas along with the improvements in the quality of farm life resulting from the expanded electric power and telephone services.

Among the methods used to attack the problem of rural, as well as urban, poverty is a program for distribution of food to needy families. The operation of this program is carried out by the Marketing and Consumer Service and two other agencies of the Department. Discussion of the activities of this Service and these agencies is our next topic.

Assistant Secretary for Marketing and Consumer Services

Three agencies of the Department report to the Secretary through an Assistant Secretary for Marketing and Consumer Services. The work of these agencies will now be examined.

The Marketing and Consumer Service. The Marketing and Consumer Service consists of 14 program divisions plus administrative divisions and is headed by an administrator. There are seven commodity divisions (Cotton, Dairy, Fruit and Vegetable, Grain, Livestock, Poultry, and Tobacco), which operate programs under various laws, as described below. In addition, there are a Livestock Slaughter Division, a Processed Meat Inspection Division, a Poultry Division, a Technical Services Division, a Transportation and Warehouse Division, a Commodity Distribution Division, a Food Stamp Division, a Food

Trades Division, and a Compliance and Evaluation Staff. The programs operated by these divisions will also be described.

Marketing Regulatory Programs. These programs are concerned with control over fraudulent or deceptive practices in the marketing of agricultural commodities, including control over labeling of packages containing seeds.

Marketing Agreements and Orders established in conjunction with price support activities of the Commodity Credit Corporation also fall within the jurisdiction of the Service.

Food Distribution Programs; Child Nutrition Programs. Under various pieces of legislation, stocks of agricultural commodities acquired under price support programs may be and are distributed to improve the diets of low income families. The Food Stamp Program is an arrangement under which food assistance is provided to needy persons in cooperation with activities of state welfare agencies. Participants exchange money for food stamps having a higher monetary value. The stamps may be exchanged at retail food stores for food. The retailers redeem the stamps at their banks, and the banks are reimbursed by the Federal Government. In some cases, the Office of Economic Opportunity participates in this program.

Several special programs to improve the nutrition of school children are also in operation. The school lunch program involves a federal contribution which must be matched by state funds to assist schools in operating nonprofit school lunch programs. A breakfast program was also authorized by Congress in 1966. The Special Milk Program, authorized by the Agriculture Act of 1954 is designed to increase the consumption of fluid milk by children. More than nineteen million children participated in the school lunch program in fiscal year 1968, and over 3 billion half-pints of milk were distributed under the milk program in the same year.

Meat and Poultry Inspection; Food Classification and Standardization. In 1967, Congress enacted the Wholesome Meat Act; in 1968, the Wholesome Poultry Products Act became law. These laws increased existing authority to inspect and control meat and poultry products and also provide for states to apply standards at least equal to federal standards in the cases of intrastate movement of these products. A system of voluntary agreements under which the Department of Agriculture provides technical and laboratory assistance in administering such regulations is authorized under these laws. In fiscal year 1968, such agreements existed in about half the states.

The Service establishes the grades used to classify the quality of a number of agricultural commodities. The quality of more than 500 million pounds of food and fiber was certified in fiscal year 1968. The total consisted of 21 billion pounds of meat and poultry; 62 billion pounds of fresh fruit and vegetables; 8.5 billion pounds of cotton; and 406 billion pounds of grain.

The Commodity Exchange Authority. In the Commodity Exchange Act of 1922, as amended, provision is made for regulation of trading and pricing on designated commodity exchanges. Enforcement of this legislation, with a primary object of prevention of manipulation is a function of the Commodity Exchange Authority. Among the exchanges regulated are the Chicago Board of Trade, the New York City Produce Market, and the New York Cotton Exchange. Regulation extends to 15 commodities: wheat, corn, oats, rye, flaxseed, soybeans, cotton, wool, wool tops, butter, eggs, potatoes, cottonseed oil, soybean oil, soybean meal.

The Packers and Stockyards Administration. This *Administration* was created in 1967 to replace the Packers and Stockyards *Division* for the purpose of carrying out the duties given to the Secretary of Agriculture by the Packers and Stockyards Act of 1921. This legislation is special antitrust-type legislation pertaining to meat, poultry, and meat and poultry products, and prohibits "unfair, deceptive, or unjustly discriminatory practices and practices aimed at controlling supplies, manipulating prices, and eliminating competition."

The Act of 1921 was the result of a report by the Federal Trade Commission in 1918 in which the Commission pointed to the high degree of control of markets for these products exercised by five large companies,

Swift, Armour, Cudhay, Wilson, and Morris. In part, this private market control was achieved by control of the facilities through which livestock sales took place.

Under the 1921 legislation, the Federal Trade Commission took the position that it had no jurisdiction to deal with cases involving packers. The matter came to a head in about 1956 when it was held in one case that a conglomerate firm, whose activities as a packer represented only a small part of its total business, was subject to regulation by the Secretary and that the Commission possessed no jurisdiction in such a case. Subsequent studies and Congressional hearings charged that the Secretary of Agriculture had been lax in performing the regulatory function and that the statute thus in fact conferred virtual antitrust immunity upon the packers.[5]

Various bills were thereupon introduced both in the House and in the Senate to deal with the matter, and Public Law 85–909 was enacted in September 1958 as a compromise between advocates of a strict antitrust policy and spokesmen for the packers. This Law provided that the Secretary of Agriculture was to have jurisdiction over all those activities of packers relating to livestock, meats, meat food products, livestock products in unmanufactured form, and poultry and poultry products, and that the Commission was to have jurisdiction over all other activities of packers. The legislation also authorized the Secretary to transfer jurisdiction to the Commission in any case he decides doing so is in the public interest. This legislation represents the outcome of a conflict between the advocates of strong regulation and the agricultural "bloc" in Congress. Within that "agricultural bloc," various groups exist, representing various interests and points of view, as we will now see.

Pressure Groups Representing Agricultural Interests

Three major organizations today seek to exert pressure on Congress in the interest of agricultural products producers. These three organizations are: (1) the American

---

[5] *Unfair Trade Practices in the Meat Industry* (Hearings before the Senate Subcommittee on Antitrust and Monopoly, 85th Cong., 1st sess., 1957) (Washington, D.C.: U.S. Government Printing Office, 1958).

Farm Bureau Federation, the largest and most powerful of the three; (2) the National Grange, the oldest of the three with roots in the Granger movement; and (3) the National Farmers' Union. The last named usually takes positions on various non farm issues parallel to those taken by the AFL–CIO; and the Farmers' Union emphasizes the position of the "family farm" in the system of agricultural production. The Farm Bureau Federation's views on many issues are similar to those of the National Association of Manufacturers, and the Farm Bureau speaks primarily for the large commercial farmers. The Grange takes a middle-of-the-road position between the other two organizations. The differences in the positions of the three major organizations is clearly apparent in the testimony representatives of each offered in 1968 before the House Committee on Agriculture concerning the question of extension of the Food and Agriculture Act of 1968.

The position of the American Farm Bureau Federation (AFBF) was presented by John C. Lynn, Legislative Representative (lobbyist) for the Federation. He stated that his organization opposed the concept of "supply management." The Bureau, it may be noted, claims a membership of 753,000 families.[6]

This testimony was followed later in the hearings by that of Harry L. Graham, Legislative Representative for the Grange who not only stated the Grange's positive support for the 1965 legislation but also commented specifically and critically on the statement offered on behalf of the Farm Bureau, saying that it employed the technique of the "big lie."[7]

Finally, in his statement on behalf of the National Farmers Union, Mr. Reuben L. Johnson not only emphasized the position of the Union that the *farm family unit* must be preserved but also called attention to the fact that the Farmers Union was seeking enactment of a law to be called the National Agricultural Bargaining Act which would allow producers to fix prices by means of bargaining committees.[8]

Secretary Freeman took the position concerning this proposed new legislation that it did not represent any real departure from the existing procedure, although he did not express either strong support for or strong opposition to the proposal. The proposed new legislation was not enacted into law by Congress, but the Food and Agriculture Act of 1965 was extended to December 31, 1970.

A Concluding Comment

Most economists, basing their conclusions upon an analysis of "economic" variables only, have been critical of the various farm programs, and many have advocated a return to a free market system. Such an advocacy, of course, amounts to a belief that governmental power should be used to establish the market as a regulator of agricultural prices and production. But those who advocate this solution have rarely given any attention to the problem of rural poverty or the extent to which an exodus of poor farmers from agriculture contributes to the problem of urban poverty, which has today also become a problem respectable enough to warrant attention by economists. To the extent that the present agricultural policies benefit primarily the large commercial agricultural producers, one may question the justification for the redistribution of income in their favor involved in the various subsidization programs. But any return to a free market system must surely contemplate (1) not only the continued presence of government demand for products distributed under the Food Stamp and other plans, (2) but also that the problem of rural poverty and unemployment will be attacked no less vigorously than the problem of urban poverty. Programs to stimulate rural employment as adjuncts of programs to improve the quality of farm life as undertaken by the Farmers Home Administration and the Rural Electrification Administration should be continued. And programs to stimulate investment in small business enterprises which will provide employment in rural areas must also be investigated further. Such programs will be considered in the discussion of problems of "small business" and the programs administered by the Small Business Administration, which now follows.

---

[6] *Extend the Food and Agriculture Act of 1965, op. cit.*, pp. 36–37; 67–68.

[7] *Ibid.*, pp. 99–100.
[8] *Ibid.*, pp. 255; 257–258.

B. USE OF GOVERNMENTAL POWER TO PROMOTE "SMALL" BUSINESS ENTERPRISES

The Problem of Definition of "Small" Business

Any discussion of the problems of "small" business is faced at the outset by the problem of definition. Precisely how "small" is a "small" business? Any definition which is adopted is necessarily arbitrary and depends peculiarly upon the problem being investigated or the policy being evaluated. For purposes of statistical study, the nature of the data may dictate a definition of "small" business firms as those employing less than some specified number of workers, those whose sales revenue is less than some arbitrary amount, or those having less than a certain dollar amount of assets. Or, one could specify that all firms are "small" which account for less than a certain percentage of the market, or less than a certain percentage of the total assets devoted to production of some particular product.[9]

In various legislative enactments by Congress (to be discussed below) dating from about 1944 to 1948, attempts were made to define the expression "small business." These definitions ranged from that of a small business firm as "one employing 250 employees or less" to a definition specifying that the number of employees was 500 or less, provided also that the firm was "independently owned and operated" and did not possess a "dominant" position in its market. The last-mentioned definition clearly places some discretion to make findings of "fact" in the administering authority. Finally, in 1953, Congress specified general criteria only, leaving the entire problem of implementation and application of the definition to the administering agency.

After its creation in 1953, the Small Business Administration adopted several different definitions, depending upon the particular program being implemented. Thus one definition has been employed for purposes of implementing programs to give financial assistance to small business firms, and another has been employed to implement programs designed to obtain for small business firms a larger share of government procurement contracts. In the area of policy formulation, the problem of definition becomes a problem of implementation of the policy itself. This proposition is clearly evident in a statement concerning the problem of definition of "small" business involved in the implementation of the small business investment program made by the Administrator of the Small Business Administration, who remarked in 1959 that the problem of definition must be approached from the standpoint of the purpose of the law.[10]

Quantitative Significance of Small Business Firms in the American Economy

In 1963, 99.7 percent of the number of business firms in the United States employed less than 500 employees and accounted for 52.9 percent of total employment. These firms were engaged primarily in wholesale and retail trade and in service industries, although a substantial number were also engaged in small manufacturing enterprises. Moreover, firms having less than 500 employees accounted for about 53.6 percent of the total value added by all manufacturing industries, although the importance of the small establishments was different in different industry subgroups.[11] Clearly, firms employing less than 500 employees constitute a significant element of the American economic system.

Federal Small Business Agencies Prior to 1953

In 1953, Congress created the Small Business Administration. The work of this agency will be considered further shortly. Prior to 1953, Congress had created two special agencies to deal with small business problems during periods of great demand

[9] For a detailed discussion not only of the problem of definition but also of policies toward small business generally, see Carolyn Nell Hooper, *Public Policy Toward Small Business: Implications for Efficient Utilization of Resources*, Ph.D. dissertation, microfilm (Ann Arbor: University of Michigan 1968).

[10] *Small Business Amendments of 1962* (Hearings before the Senate Committee on Banking and Currency, 86th Cong., 1st sess., 1959) (Washington, D.C.: U.S. Government Printing Office, 1959), p. 78. Also quoted in Hooper, *op. cit.*, p. 23.

[11] For a detailed description, see Hooper, *op. cit.*, Chapter 3.

for full utilization of resources for the production of military equipment as well as of goods and services required to maintain the domestic economy.

The Smaller War Plants Corporation. In 1942, in order to bring about fuller utilization of the resources commanded by small business firms for purposes of furthering the United States World War II effort, Congress passed the Smaller War Plants Corporation Act creating the Smaller War Plants Corporation: (1) to make loans to small business firms to enable them to convert their facilities to war production purposes; (2) to make contracts for military items; and (3) to make subcontracts with the object of performing the military procurement contracts. In addition, the Chairman of the War Production Board was explicitly directed to make use of the productive capacity of smaller plants in furthering the war effort.[12]

The purpose of the legislation and the function of the Corporation were not those of promoting the interests of small business firms as such; the primary purpose of the legislation was to mobilize the resources of small firms for purposes of carrying out the war effort. However, in 1945, at the close of the war, both the Senate and House committees concerned with problems of small business launched efforts to convert the wartime agency into a permanent and independent peacetime agency to promote the interests of small business firms. These efforts were opposed by the Department of Commerce and no legislation was enacted.[13] In December 1945, by Executive Order 9665, President Truman abolished the Smaller War Plants Corporation and transferred some of its functions to the Reconstruction Finance Corporation and others to the Department of Commerce for liquidation.

The Small Defense Plants Administration. Thereafter, up to the time of the Korean War in 1950, the Office of Small Business in the Department of Commerce was the principal agency concerned with small business. Upon the outbreak of the War, Congress enacted the Defense Production Act of 1950. This legislation created the

National Production Authority, discussed further in Chapter 32, whose function was to assign the available supply of raw materials to military and domestic requirements. A system for priority ratings involving the assignment of priorities in orders for materials needed for military production was instituted, and eventually allocation of a few critical raw materials was undertaken. The Office of Small Business was created within the Authority and conceived its task to be that of insuring that the interests of small business "would be adequately protected by the Federal agencies."[14] Note that this conception emphasizes *service to* small business firms rather than *contributions on the part* of such firms. The Office kept a watchful eye on developing raw material shortages to insure that small firms were not left without vital supplies and took various actions, largely in the form of making information available to increase the share of government procurement contracts going to small business. Funds were also made available from government sources to finance small business firms under restricted conditions; however, reliance was placed largely on the use of private sources of credit.

In 1951, Congress amended the Defense Production Act of 1950 and created a new federal agency, the Small Defense Plants Administration under the general direction and supervision of the President but not subject to any other agency or department of the Federal Government. The life of the new agency was to terminate on June 30, 1953, unless extended beyond that date. The new agency had the power to recommend to the Reconstruction Finance Corporation that the latter make loans to small business firms, but the law also provided that this Corporation was to apply its own standards and criteria in making such loans. Like its predecessor (the Smaller War Plants Corporation) the new Administration could make procurement contracts and also make subcontracts to fill its obligations under such procurement contracts. An important provision emphasizing that the contributions of small firms were to be taken into account was included in

[12] 56 Stat. 351.
[13] Hooper, *op. cit.*, p. 119.
[14] *First Annual Report of the Activities of the Joint Committee on Defense Production* (Washington, D.C.: U.S. Government Printing Office, 1951), p. 326.

the law, but another provision asserted that agencies of the Government were to insure that small firms received "fair and reasonable treatment."

Organization and Functions of the Small Business Administration

According to a study by Carolyn Hooper, the legislation resulting in the establishment of the Small Business Administration was the outcome of the efforts of one group in Congress seeking to establish a permanent independent agency to deal with small business problems and the efforts of another group seeking to liquidate the Reconstruction Finance Corporation.[15]

Whatever may have been the Congressional alignments involved, on July 31, 1953, Congress enacted the Small Business Act (15 U.S.C. 661) and created the present-day agency, the Small Business Administration.

This agency is headed by an Administrator. The Administrator appoints three Associate Administrators to execute specific functions of the agency. These three are: Administrator for Procurement and Management Assistance; Administrator for Financial Assistance; and Administrator for Investment. The agency also maintains area, regional, and branch offices in principal cities throughout the United States.

Operations and Activities of the Small Business Administration

The original authority granted to the Small Business Administration in the Small Business Act has been several times extended by amendments and by new legislation. In particular, the role of the agency as a tool in the War on Poverty has been recognized. Thus emphasis is now being placed upon Economic Opportunity loans under the Economic Opportunity Act, upon loans to small firms displaced by urban renewal projects, and upon loans to local development companies *both in urban and rural areas* with the object of providing help to the disadvantaged. Programs of this type are being carried on in addition to the programs of assisting small business firms owned by persons who are not generally classified as being below the poverty level of income or as members of a disadvantaged group. The various programs will now be somewhat more specifically considered.

Programs of Financial Assistance Under the Small Business Act. The Small Business Act authorizes the Small Business Administration to make loans to small business concerns to finance plant construction, conversion, or expansion, including the acquisition of equipment, facilities, materials, or supplies, and to supply such concerns with working capital. The Administration's specialists give such firms advice and assist them in dealings with financial institutions. During fiscal year 1968, the agency made a total of 9,476 loans having a total loan amount of 495.6 million. The cumulative total for the agency from 1954 to 1968 amounted to 85,285 loans granted and a total loan amount of $7,758.1 million.[16]

Regulation and Registration of Small Business Investment Companies. Under the Small Business Investment Act of 1958, the Small Business Administration licenses and regulates small business investment companies which are privately organized and operated. The Administration also makes financial assistance available to such companies. Between September 1958 and September 1967, such companies had provided more than 28,000 financings for a total of more than $1.25 billion.

Procurement Assistance

Government Liaison and Prime Contract Assistance. The Administration maintains close relations with federal procurement agencies, both civilian and military, constantly seeking to increase the share of government contracts alloted to small business firms. It is supported in this activity by the relevant Congressional committees on Small Business which occasionally investigate procurement activities of federal agencies with a view to determining how to increase the small business share. In fiscal year 1967, small business firms were reported to have accounted for 19.4 percent of the total dollar amount of all federal procurement, or for about $10.3 billion.[17] However, the share of small business firms in defense procurement has been declining.

---

[15] Hooper, *op. cit.*, pp. 130 ff.
[16] *Eighteenth Annual Report of the Activities of the Joint*

Committee on Defense Production (Washington, D.C.: U.S. Government Printing Office, 1969), p. 395.

The Small Business Administration is also authorized to issue "Certificates of Competency" certifying that a small business firm (or a group of small firms joined together in a pool) has the competency to perform government contracts, including research and development contracts. Primarily, however, the function of the agency in the procurement area is to serve as the small business advocate in government and as a source of information to small businessmen concerning government actions and plans.

Programs Used in the War on Poverty

The Administration provides a channel for technical and financial assistance and has undertaken various training programs which serve as weapons in the War on Poverty. Among the most important of the technical assistance programs is SCORE (Service Corps of Retired Executives), begun in October 1964. This is a volunteer program under which retired executives serve as advisors to small businessmen needing such help. By June 1968, nearly 44,000 small businessmen had taken advantage of this service.

The local development program is one of the most useful of the tools possessed by the Administration in carrying out its part of the War on Poverty. This program is also known as the "community development" program and is used both in rural and urban areas. Under this program, the citizens of a local community may secure help in financing local small business enterprises. First, they must raise 20 percent of the capital locally; then the Small Business Administration loans the remaining 80 percent. Loans may be as high as $350,000 at interest rates of from 4.5 to 5 percent for periods up to 25 years. This money can be used to help finance local small businesses in need of capital.[18] This program was expanded in 1967 under authority received under the Economic Opportunity Act into the Community Economic Development Program. Under the Community Economic Development Program, especially selected teams are sent

to "target areas" to live and work with the citizens of these areas for the purpose of *seeking out* opportunities for investments in small businesses in these areas.[19]

A Concluding Comment

The Small Business Administration which had its origin in a need to utilize fully the resources of small business during World War II has come to be an agency developing operational solutions to problems of the ghetto and of poverty both in rural and in urban parts of the United States. Subjected to an analysis making use of only "economic" variables and of an assumption that political and social objectives are maximized when the economic variables are maximized, it is possible that some of the programs implemented by action of the agency could not pass muster. Like many of the programs implemented by the Department of Agriculture, many of the programs administered by the Small Business Administration do involve a redistribution of income. These programs can neither be justified nor condemned without making value judgments and certainly not by an economic welfare analysis which makes at the outset an assumption that "the distribution of income is given" and cannot be changed. If these programs can be evaluated at all, that evaluation must be an instrumental one involving attention to the consequences of undertaking or not undertaking them. They both supplement and extend the manpower programs described in the preceding chapter. When an economy is beset by massive unemployment and a low level of output, problems of efficient utilization of manpower and of poverty are less apparent than they are in an affluent society with full employment. It is the problems of maintaining a high level of employment and of output and a high rate of growth which are the primary concern of the Board of Governors of the Federal Reserve System and of the Council of Economic Advisors. The operations and activities of these two agencies are the subjects of our next chapter.

[17] *Eighteenth Annual Report of the Senate Select Committee on Small Business* (Senate Report Number 1155, 90th Cong., 2d sess., 1968) (Washington, D.C.: U.S. Government Printing Office, 1968), p. 13.

[18] *Small Business Problems in Urban Areas* (Report of the House Select Committee on Small Business, 1966, 89th Cong., 2d sess., 1966) (Washington, D.C.: U.S.

Government Printing Office, 1966), pp. 4–5.

[19] *Rural Renewal* (Hearings before the Subcommittee on Finance and Investment of the Senate Select Small Business Committee, 90th Cong., 2d sess., 1968) (Washington, D.C.: U.S. Government Printing Office, 1968), pp. 4–5.

31

The Level and Direction of Movement of Economic Activity

This chapter contains a discussion of the work of two federal agencies concerned with the level and direction of economic activity as measured primarily by total output and employment. The first subdivision will be concerned with the role and functions of the Federal Reserve System relating to the supply of money and credit and the general price level. The second will undertake a discussion of the role of the Council of Economic Advisors.

A. THE FEDERAL RESERVE SYSTEM: MONEY, CREDIT, AND PRICES

The Federal Reserve System is concerned with controlling the supply of money and credit in relation to the level of output and employment. In addition, the System performs various service functions, such as the intercity collection and clearing of bank checks. The System was established in 1913, it will be recalled from Chapter 8. Although it is possible to analyze the functioning of private commercial banks in the abstract without reference to their participation in a central banking system such as the Federal Reserve System, our discussion below will be concerned with the banking system as it operates in the United States.

Structure of the Federal Reserve System

All national banks and many state commercial banks (a commercial bank is one which maintains deposit or checking accounts) are members of the Federal Reserve System. At the end of 1968, 4,716 national banks and 1,262 state banks were members of the System. These Member Banks own and maintain deposits in 12 Federal Reserve Districts into which the United States has been divided. The Federal Reserve Banks are "banker's banks." They are owned by, maintain deposits of, and make loans to Member Banks, and accept deposits from the United States Treasury but do not accept deposits from nor make loans to private individuals. Many of the Reserve Banks have branches. The qualifications of the Boards of Directors of Reserve Banks are specified by law and the Directors are supposed to represent broad community interests.

The Board of Governors of the Federal Reserve System consists of seven Members appointed by the President with the advice and consent of the Senate and has the duty of supervising the operations of the System. The Federal Open Market Committee is a statutory body consisting of the Federal Reserve Board and the presidents of five of the Member Banks. It formulates policies which the Member Banks must implement relative to open market operations (operations which will be explained below).[1] In addition, the Federal Reserve Act provides for the establishment of the Federal Advisory Council whose membership usually includes a representative banker selected from each Federal Reserve District. The Council confers annually with the Federal Reserve Board on business conditions and makes advisory recommendations concerning the operations of the System. In order to understand the way in which the volume of credit is controlled under the Federal Reserve System, it is necessary also to understand the "clearing principle" and the process of "creation of money" by commercial banks. Accordingly, these two topics are discussed next in the order mentioned above.

The Clearing Principle

Suppose that Mr. X and Mr. Y both maintain checking accounts in Bank A, and that Mr. X writes a check payable to Mr. Y who deposits it to his account in Bank A. The bank simply reduces Mr. X's deposit and increases that of Mr. Y.

Now suppose that Mr. X, having a deposit in Bank A, writes checks payable, respectively, to Mr. Y and Mr. Z, but that Mr. Y maintains his deposit in Bank B, while Mr. Z does business with Bank C. Suppose further that Mr. W writes a check payable to Mr. X, and that Mr. W also maintains his account in Bank C. At the end of the day, Bank A will have to pay off two checks to Banks B and C, respectively, but Bank C will also owe some money to Bank A. If these banks are all members of an intracity (within the city) clearing house, each will merely need to send its claims on all the other banks to a central clearing house and a settlement of any net sums due is all that will have to be made. Thus in our example, at the end of the day, Bank A will owe Bank B but as between A and C, whether Bank A owes Bank C or Bank C owes Bank A will depend on whether

Mr. X's check to Mr. Z was greater or less than that made payable by Mr. W to Mr. X. Since no checks were written against deposits in Bank B, obviously Bank B owes nothing but has a sum due from Bank A.

Suppose now that Mr. X lives in Los Angeles and Mr. Y lives in Seattle. In this case, the process of clearing the check will proceed through the Federal Reserve Bank for District 12 located in San Francisco, since (assuming Banks A (Los Angeles) and B (Seattle) are both Members of the System) both must by law maintain deposits in the Federal Reserve Bank for their district, and both Los Angeles and Seattle are in District 12. This case is simply that of a clearance when both the payor and the payee of the check maintain accounts in the same bank. The Federal Reserve Bank in San Francisco is thus a "central bank," a banker's bank.

Finally, suppose now that Mr. X lives in Los Angeles but Mr. Z lives in New York. These cities are located in different Federal Reserve Districts. In such a case, the Federal Reserve Banks in the two districts must themselves engage in a clearing operation, much as the different banks in a single city do so. Clearance and check collection involving different Federal Reserve Banks (different districts) are handled through a special account, the Interdistrict Settlement Fund, created for just this purpose.

The reader should note in considering the preceding examples that whenever Mr. X (a typical depositor in Bank A) writes a check on his account in Bank A payable to someone who maintains an account in some other bank, Bank A must pay that other bank by a reduction in its deposit in the Federal Reserve Bank in its district. Conversely, whenever a depositor of Bank A receives a check drawn on some bank other than on Bank A, the latter receives funds, again in the form of an increase in its deposit in the Federal Reserve Bank in its district. This point is of great significance in the discussion of control of credit which will be presented later in this chapter. Our next problem is

---

[1] This chapter draws upon *The Federal Reserve System: Purposes and Functions* (Federal Reserve Board: Washington, D.C.: U.S. Government Printing Office, 5th ed., 1967) and on annual reports of the Federal Reserve System, especially *Annual Report for 1968* (Washington, D.C.: U.S. Government Printing Office, 1969). Individual footnotes will not be used.

that of understanding how a private commercial bank actually creates money (deposits) by making loans and investments.

The Creation of Money (Deposits)

Checking accounts are money. (It does not follow that checks are "legal tender"— something which if tendered in payment of a debt constitutes a legally good faith offer to pay the debt.) But checks are in fact written in the conduct of business affairs and their dollar volume far exceeds that of the ordinary hand-to-hand money used in conducting business transactions.

Checking accounts may come into existence as a result of the deposit of currency in a bank, but most are created in the process by which a bank makes loans and investments. Suppose Mr. X secures a loan of $1000 from Bank A and gives the bank his note for this sum plus interest, leaving the $1000 due him on deposit in Bank A. His deposits will then increase by $1000 and the bank will have his promise to repay the loan. Now, if he writes a check for $1000 on his account payable to Mr. Y who maintains his account in Bank B, not only will Mr. A's deposits decrease, but also Bank A will have to pay Bank B, and Bank A's deposits in its Federal Reserve Bank will thereby be decreased while those of Bank B will be increased. One Member Bank may suffer a reduction in its deposits in the Federal Reserve Bank, but another Member Bank's deposits in its Federal Reserve Bank will always increase by an exactly offsetting amount. Thus the process of creating credit by a Member Bank is related to the size of its deposit in its Federal Reserve Bank. Just how much money can an individual Member Bank create by making loans? The answer to this question necessarily involves a consideration of the topic of bank reserves, to which we must turn next. But, before we do so, it may be useful to note that commercial banks which are not Members of the Federal Reserve System maintain deposits in banks which are Members and thus the non-member banks are indirectly included also.

The Nature and Function of Bank Reserves

Historically, bank reserves were required by law to protect depositors, but today protection is not their function. Com-mercial banks are in business to make profits, that is, to make as many loans and investments as possible. Unless there is a great loss of confidence in the bank and a "run on the bank" by its depositors, the bank does not need to keep reserves equal to 100 percent of its deposits. In the United States today, depositors are protected up to a limit by federal deposit insurance. Nevertheless, Member Banks are required to keep in reserve sums equal to fixed percentages (specified by the Federal Reserve Board) of their deposits. Note that the banks do *not* keep *a percentage of* their deposits in reserve. They keep sums *equal to specified percentages of* their deposits in reserve. These sums may consist of actual cash held or of deposits in Federal Reserve Banks. Thus the *required reserve* of a bank is defined as the legal percentage figure (the *reserve ratio*) multiplied by the bank's depoits. Let us assume that Bank A has total deposits of $10,000,000 and that the "reserve ratio" (legal required percentage) is 20 percent. The bank's required reserve is then (20 percent)($10,000,000) = $2,000,000. Of this total it may count part of its deposit, say $1,980,000, in its Federal Reserve Bank and $20,000 which we assume it has in cash.

The *actual reserve* of a Member Bank is precisely what it is called, the sum of the actual cash on hand, say $20,000 cash on hand and the amount on deposit of say $3,000,000 in its Federal Reserve Bank. Then it has an actual reserve of $3,020,000.

The *excess reserve* of a Member Bank is again exactly what its name says it is. The excess reserve is the sum by which the bank's actual reserve exceeds its required reserve. Thus: *Excess Reserve = Actual Reserve − Required Reserve*. In our example we have: $3,020,000 − $2,000,000 = $1,020,000 of Excess Reserve. Now by what sum can Bank A expand its deposits by making more loans and investments and still meet its reserve requirement? It is to this question that we turn next.

The Power of an Individual System Member Bank to Expand Deposits

We have seen that when an individual System Member Bank makes a loan or an investment, it expands its deposits. We have also seen that if the borrower uses the proceeds of his loan to write a check payable to a payee who maintains his deposits in a different bank, the deposit of the borrower falls *and* the deposit of the lending Member Bank in the Federal Reserve Bank also falls when the check is paid. Thus in such a case, the lending bank actually suffers a decline in its actual reserves. If a bank possesses excess reserves (reserves in excess of those it is required to have), by how much can it afford to have its actual reserves reduced? Obviously, by the amount of its excess reserves. Thus the individual Member Bank can make loans and create deposits until its *Excess Reserves* = 0. But, it cannot safely lend and invest, thus creating additional deposits, by more than the amount of its excess reserves, since to do so would mean that its actual reserves could fall below its required reserves. Thus we have a rule: An individual Member System Bank can lend up to the point at which it is fully "loaned up"; that is, it can lend up to the point at which its *Excess Reserves* = 0, or up to the point at which *Actual Reserve* equals *Required Reserve*. But we have also seen earlier that when one Member Bank's deposits in the relevant Federal Reserve Bank are reduced, another Member Bank's deposits are increased. Thus the total actual reserves in the System remain constant when an individual bank expands its deposits by making loans and investments. By how much can all the Member Banks in the System together expand their deposits?

The Power of All the Member Banks Together in the System to Expand Deposits

Suppose that Bank A were the only bank in the System. Then it would never suffer any adverse clearing balances and would never lose any reserves; its deposits in the Federal Reserve Bank would never change, and its actual reserves would remain constant. If it had excess reserves of $10,000, it could expand its deposits by loans and investments and doing so would not, by assumption, result in a reduction of its *actual* reserves. But its *required* reserves would increase, and this increase in its *required* reserves would *reduce* its *excess* reserves. If the reserve ratio were 25 per cent, for every dollar loaned and redeposited, required reserves would increase by $0.25. Therefore, if the bank had excess reserves of

$10,000, it could expand its deposits by a sum equal to *Excess Reserves* × 1/*Reserve Ratio* or by ($10,000)(1/0.25) = ($10,000)(4) = $40,000. We can check our answer by computing the amount of increase in the required reserve if the deposits were increased *by* $40,000. In this case the bank would have to have ($40,000)(0.25) = $10,000, or exactly the amount of its excess reserve.

Now the Federal Reserve System consists of many banks, not of just one bank. But since no reserves are ever lost to the Members of the System *as a whole* as a result of the clearing principle, the Members of the System *as a whole* are just like the one great bank in our example. Thus we have another rule: Even though an *individual* System bank can expand only by the amount of its excess reserves, the members of the *System as a whole* can expand by an amount equal to the total *System Excess Reserves* × *the Reciprocal of the Reserve Ratio*.

Of course, when the *reserve requirement* is increased, the possibilities for expansion are reduced. There are, in fact, various ways in which the Federal Reserve Banks can act to reduce or to increase the power of the Member Banks to make loans and investments, possibly even forcing them to call in loans or to sell investments. It is to a discussion of these actions that we will now proceed.

Control Over Member Bank Reserves

The Board of Governors (located in Washington, D.C.) stands at the apex of the Federal Reserve System and can take three types of actions to affect the ability of Member Banks to extend credit.

Changes in the Reserve Ratio. The most obvious and probably the most drastic measure which can be taken to affect the lending power of Member Banks is to make a change in the reserve ratio. Thus by increasing the reserve ratio, that is, by increasing the amount which constitutes a Member Bank's required reserve, that bank's excess reserves are reduced. An example of such action is that taken by the Board in December 1967, when it increased the reserve ratios of Member Banks having deposits in excess of $5 million by one-half of 1 percent.

Changing the Discount Rate. Member Banks

may borrow from Federal Reserve Banks. They may do so by issuing their own promissory notes, backed by approved collateral; or they may also rediscount short-term promissory notes thay have accepted as security for loans they have made. In practice, most loans to Member Banks are of the first type, secured by government securities, and usually for very short periods of time to overcome adverse clearing balances. An interest charge is, of course, made in the case of such loans. The proceeds of such loans are credited to the borrowing Member Bank's reserve (deposit) account in the Federal Reserve Bank making the loan. When the loan is repaid, it is repaid by a reduction in the reserve (deposit) account.

Each Federal Reserve Bank fixes, "subject to review and determination by the Board," the interest rate charged for such loans to Member Banks. Raising this "rediscount" or "discount" rate naturally makes Member Banks less eager to secure such loans— unless, of course, they can recoup the higher cost by raising their own interest rates to private borrowers. Lowering the rediscount rate has the opposite effect.

Open Market Operations. The Members of the Federal Reserve Board constitute a majority of the Open Market Committee, which includes the seven Board Members and presidents of five Federal Reserve Banks. The presidents of all 12 of the Reserve Banks participate in meetings of the Committee but five only have a right to vote. Trading in government securities and in foreign currencies authorized and directed to be conducted by the Open Market Committee are undertaken by the Federal Reserve Bank of New York, but each Reserve Bank participates in the holdings and earnings of the System Open Market Account.

If the Open Market Committee believes that the power of Member Banks to expand credit should be restricted, it orders that *sales* be made on behalf of the Account. Such sales of government securities are made at prices favorable to security dealers and other purchasers. The purchasers pay by means of checks written on their deposit accounts in their respective Member Banks. The Federal Reserve Banks collect these checks by reducing Member Banks' deposit (reserve) accounts. Such a sale of a security thus reduces directly the outstanding deposits of a Member Bank and at the same time reduces the actual reserve of the Member Bank. If the Open Market Committee believes that the power to extend credit of Member Banks should be increased, it orders that *purchases* be made for the System Open Market Account. Purchases of government securities are then made at prices favorable to the seller. He is paid by means of a check drawn by the Federal Reserve Bank. He deposits this check with his relevant Member Bank. When the check is collected, the Federal Reserve Bank increases the Member Bank's deposit (reserve) account. Thus such a purchase both increases private deposits in Member Banks and also increases Member Bank reserves.

Federal Reserve Notes

Federal Reserve Banks also issue Federal Reserve Notes—paper money, of which the reader may have some in his billfold even as he reads this sentence. Such currency is paid out to Member Banks on request by reducing their deposit (reserve) accounts in Federal Reserve Banks. Open market purchase operations are usually undertaken to offset such reductions in reserves when they occur on a nationwide bases, for example, during the Christmas shopping season. When Member Banks return such currency to the Federal Reserve Banks at the end of seasonal rush periods, the Member Banks' reserves are increased by these deposits. At such times, Open Market sales are undertaken to offset the increases in reserves. Thus both the supply of currency and Member Bank reserves are adjusted to the needs of business; hence, Federal Reserve Notes are sometimes called "elastic" currency.

Direct Control Functions

The control exercised by the Federal Reserve Board over Member Bank reserves obviously constitutes an indirect control over the supply of money. In addition to this power of control, the Board exercises a number of direct control functions, including supervision and examination of Member Banks and control over terms of credit granted to purchasers of securities (control over margin requirements). The power to control margin requirements is granted by the Securities and Exchange Act of 1934. Thus for example, on June 7, 1968, the Board increased the margin requirement for registered stocks from 70 to 80 percent.

Under the Defense Production Act of 1950, during the Korean Emergency, the Board was directed by Congress to fix the minimum size of down payments on installment loans and the length of time for the extension of such credit. This authority was repealed in 1953, but the Board has continued to engage in mobilization planning activities designed to insure the continuance of essential banking functions in times of national emergency, as have most other federal agencies at the request of the President and under the central direction of the Office of Emergency Planning.[2]

On July 1, 1969, Regulation Z of the Board of Governors of the Federal Reserve System implementing the Truth in Lending Act of 1968 became effective. Congress assigned responsibility for issuance of the implementing regulation to the Federal Reserve Board but assigned the enforcement responsibility to various regulatory agencies already having authority over the activities of particular lenders. Thus the Federal Home Loan Bank Board was given jurisdiction over savings and loan associations, and lenders not heretofore supervised by a federal agency (department store credit is one example) were placed under the jurisdiction of the Federal Trade Commission for enforcement purposes.

In addition to the various direct and indirect powers which may be exercised over Member Banks, there is also a rather nebulous power called "moral suasion" which means merely that the Federal Reserve authorities may strongly advise Member Banks concerning certain policies and activities.

The Federal Reserve System and the Federal Debt

Although we have discussed the various methods by means of which the volume of credit can be controlled, little has been said of the conditions under which an increase or a decrease in Member Bank reserves is

appropriate. Monetary policy is merely one aspect of the problem of maintaining total output and employment at full employment levels. Fiscal policy (the use of the taxing, spending, and borrowing powers of the Federal Government) plays an equally important role in this respect. Some aspects of fiscal policy will be further discussed in the next subdivision. However, it is useful to note first that a report published in 1968 by the Joint Economic Committee provides some interesting insights into, and a useful introduction to, the subject of the relationship between fiscal and monetary policies.

The Committee noted that monetary policy can be used to limit private spending by making private credit demand accomodate to government credit demand but that the "needs of the sovereign" for credit can not be denied by the monetary authorities. Fiscal policy, on the other hand, can either be supported or frustrated by the monetary policy adopted. Thus the Committee concluded, fiscal policy and monetary policy are complementary, not alternative instruments and should be used together as parts of "a coordinated economic policy."

For example, the Committee noted, if the executive branch undertook a large increase in public spending but Congress did not provide adequate tax revenues, the Federal Government would have to borrow by offering United States government securities for sale. In this situation, monetary policy would have to consist of measures to accomodate the public debt. If the public demand for loans were met, less credit would be available for use by the private sector. Federal Reserve System open market operations might be necessary in this situation. The System could follow one of two courses of action: (1) increase the supply of money while keeping interest rates at about the same level; or (2) hold the money stock fixed while allowing interest rates to rise. It might also compromise by permitting some increases both in the stock of money and in interest rates. But it could not stabilize both.

The magnitude of the Treasury's debt is a matter decided by the President and his advisors and by Congress; in this situation, the Federal Reserve System must *react*; it

---

[2] *Eighteenth Annual Report of the Joint Committee on Defense Production* (House Report 91–3, 91st Cong., 1st sess., 1969) (Washington, D.C.: U.S. Government Printing Office, 1969), p. 358 ff.

does *not determine* basic policy.[3] The report contains a suggestion in that the Treasury Department possesses a power to make decisions independently of the President, but this suggestion is somewhat misleading, since the Secretary of the Treasury is merely *one* of the President's Cabinet officers. The Secretary may strongly influence the President's decision; but the advice given to the President by the Director of the Bureau of the Budget and by the Council of Economic Advisors will probably also have influenced the President. The work of the Council will be discussed in the next subdivision, but before we take up this topic two others are worth considering: (1) regulation of banking by other federal agencies; and (2) the question of the independence from the President of the Federal Reserve Board.

Other Federal Agencies Regulating Banking

Office of Comptroller of the Currency. The Office of the Comptroller of the Currency was created by the law establishing the national banking system in 1863. The Comptroller exercises general supervision over the activities of national banks, including approval of mergers and creation of new national banks. Each national bank is examined three times every two years. His functions are those pertaining to national banks as banking firms, and he has no responsibilities concerning the total supply of credit analogous to those exercised by the Federal Reserve Board.

Federal Deposit Insurance Corporation. The Federal Deposit Insurance Corporation (FDIC) was created by an amendment to the Federal Reserve Act in 1933 but made subject to a separate law in 1950. The Corporation provides insurance up to a maximum amount of $15,000 per account for deposits in insured banks, imposing a premium payment upon such banks based on the total amount of deposits. It examines all participating banks which are not Members of the Federal Reserve System, pays off claims of depositors in cases of bank failures, and serves as a receiver in the cases of banks which have failed. It may also issue cease-and-desist orders to insured banks and impose a penalty of termination of insurance coverage in cases of non compliance. The Corporation has no credit control functions, although the existence of deposit insurance does, of course, make possible the use of lower reserve ratios by the Federal Reserve Board than might otherwise be the case.

The Independence of the Federal Reserve Board

The Federal Reserve System is a system of self-regulation by the banking industry. The expenses of the Board are financed by earnings of Federal Reserve Banks, and the Board is independent of the type of budgetary control exercised by Congress over other regulatory agencies. Members of the Board are appointed for 14-year terms, with the result that even a President who serves two terms may not have an opportunity to appoint a majority of Board Members. Moreover, the President ordinarily does not have an opportunity to appoint the Chairman of the Board. The presidents of the 12 Federal Reserve Banks are elected by the directors of their respective banks. Although these directors are supposed to represent the public, labor, and agriculture, as well as other interests along with the banking community, a 1964 study showed that 91 of the 108 directors of the 12 banks (nine per bank) were at that time or had been connected "with the banking industry they [were] supposed to regulate." Accordingly, Representative Wright Patman charged in 1965 that the System was "banker dominated."[4]

Up until 1964, the Federal Reserve Board generally adopted policies consistent with those adopted by the President. In 1964, however, Congress adopted the President's recommendation for a tax reduction to stimulate the economy (by making more money available for consumer expenditures), but in December 1964 the Federal Reserve Board (by a 4 to 3 vote) approved the action of the New York and Chicago Federal Reserve Banks to raise the rediscount rate, an action intended to restrict credit and reduce economic activity.

[3] *Standards for Guiding Monetary Action* (Report of the Joint Economic Committee, 90th Cong., 2d sess., 1968) (Washington, D.C.: U.S. Government Printing Office, 1968), pp. 3–4.

[4] *1965 Joint Economic Report* (Report of the Joint Economic Committee, 89th Cong., 1st sess., 1965) (Washington, D.C.: U.S. Government Printing Office, 1965), p. 35 ff.

The action of the Board contradicted that of the President and Congress. Accordingly, the Joint Economic Committee held hearings on the matter in December 1964 and early 1965. The testimony of Professor J. K. Galbraith pertaining to the history of the behavior of the Board prior to its 1964 action is interesting.

Professor Galbraith noted that the Federal Reserve System had been established in 1913 "during the closing moments of 19th century capitalism" and that for all practical purposes, power was left "residing in member banks." As long as government had not yet assumed responsibility for the level and stability of output, employment, and prices, Federal Reserve policy did not have to be coordinated with fiscal policy. But this situation has now changed. According to Galbraith, in 1965, the Federal Reserve System had not had independence for many years. Its Chairman regularly attended meetings on government policy, acquiesced in the interest rate policies there adopted, and insured their implementation by the System.[5]

But in December 1964, the Board's power was used to contradict the national policy, and sharp Congressional criticism followed. In his *January 1969 Economic Report*, President Johnson remarked that "the Administration and the Federal Reserve have worked well together" during the past year. He saw a need "for only a few reforms."[6]

And in its *1969 Joint Economic Report*, the Joint Economic Committee stated that it "firmly supported" the "reforms" recommended by President Johnson. Among other things, the "reforms" included a recommendation, noted in Chapter 6, "that the term of the Chairman of the Federal Reserve Board be appropriately geared to that of the President to provide further assurance of harmonious policy coordination," and one that Congress review the procedure for selecting the 12 presidents of the Reserve Banks, five of whom, it will be recalled, serve on the Open Market Committee.[7]

Clearly, these recommendations con-

stituted a reflection of the view of the President's Council of Economic Advisors that the privately regulated banking industry ought not to be permitted to pursue an independent course of action which might conflict with the fiscal policy adopted by the Administration in power. It is to the work of the Council that we turn next.

B. THE COUNCIL OF ECONOMIC ADVISORS

The role and position of the Council of Economic Advisors within the Executive Office of the President have already been described in Chapter 6. Moreover, it has also been noted that Professor Walter Heller has pointed out that the Council must be, among other things, a "consensus-seeker."

As we have also already seen, the Council was established by the Employment Act of 1946. When the Council was first established, there were differences of opinion as to whether or not it was to be a policy-formulating agency, as well as differences with respect to the question of how much independence it was to have. Fiscal fundamentalists (those who hold to a strong belief that the federal budget should be balanced upon an arbitrary basis according to a calendar invented by the Romans and who reject the concept of a budget balanced according to the level of output and employment) were suspicious of the Council. Eventually the Council encountered Congressional opposition, and its funds were reduced by the end of 1953. During the two Eisenhower Administrations, the Council served largely in a data-gathering and minor advisory capacity and sought to make itself noncontroversial. But during the Kennedy and Johnson Administrations, the Council became much more active. It was probably assisted in this respect by the fact that during the early part of this period the Chairman of the Joint Economic Committee was Senator Paul H. Douglas, a former Professor of Economics. Many observers also give credit to Professor Walter Heller,

[4] *Recent Federal Reserve Action and Economic Policy Coordination* (Hearings before the Joint Economic Committee, 89th Cong., 1st sess., 1965) (Washington, D.C.: U.S. Government Printing Office, 1965), p. 309 ff.

[6] *Economic Report of the President, January 1969*

(Washington, D.C.: U.S. Government Printing Office, 1969), p. 13.

[7] *1969 Joint Economic Report* (Report of the Joint Economic Committee, 91st Cong., 1st sess., 1969) (Washington, D.C.: U.S. Government Printing Office, 1969), p. 24.

Chairman of the Council during the Kennedy Administration, for having converted President Kennedy to a belief in the "New Economics."

A detailed discussion of the theory of determination of income and employment is beyond the scope of this book. Our interest is not that of an explanation nor of an evaluation of these theories; rather our interest in this book is that of understanding the role of the Council as a fountainhead of both formal (for example, changes in tax laws) and informal (for example, statements by the President urging private industry and labor to exercise restraint in price and wage changes) working rules. But many of the concepts employed by the Council and by macroeconomists do make their way into newspapers and news magazines. These concepts do, therefore, warrant our attention.

The System of National Accounts

In making recommendations for changes in working rules to the President, the Council relies heavily on estimates made by the Department of Commerce of the present and future magnitudes of a number of "economic aggregates." These aggregates will now be defined, although the methods employed in estimating them will not be discussed, since this problem could well be the subject of a book in itself.

The Gross National Product (GNP) is defined as the total value of the *flow* of the nation's output of goods and services during some specified period of time, usually a year or a quarter of a year. The total value of the output of goods and services can also be thought of as the sum of the values of the products of all amounts of goods and services produced multiplied by the final selling prices of these outputs. Such final selling prices include amounts to cover the depreciation of the capital equipment used in producing the output. Hence, the GNP does *not* represent a maintainable rate of consumption. If a nation consumes at a rate equal to its GNP, it will not be replacing the capital equipment used up in the production of the output, and eventually output must fall.

Gross National Product in Current Prices must be distinguished from Gross National Product measured in Constant Dollars. The latter is produced by dividing the former by an index of prices in order to eliminate the effect of price changes making it possible to compare the levels of GNP in different periods. Such comparisons, however, rest on an assumption that the qualities and kinds of products in the two periods are identical. The Potential Gross National Product is an estimate of the nation's output if its resources *were* fully utilized, that is to say if "full employment" existed. However, the term "full employment" does not mean 100 percent employment. Thus the Council remarked in 1969 that economic potential or capacity was not an absolute or technical ceiling on output. The concept allowed some margin for "unused human and physical resources." As a practical matter, a 4 percent level of unemployment was established as a target during the Kennedy Administration and this target has been kept since then. This target was thought to be one providing a reasonable balance of employment and price stability.[8]

Although GNP measures total output without allowing for depreciation, by subtracting the estimated amount of depreciation (Capital Consumption Allowance) from GNP, one produces Net National Product (NNP). Thus NNP *does* represent a maintainable rate of consumption. The NNP, however, includes the sums collected by government in the form of indirect taxes (additions to the final prices of the products) and the difference between the earnings of government enterprises and government subsidy payments. In order to obtain the National Income (NI), it is necessary to subtract these two items from NNP. National Income (NI) can also be defined as the sum of the earnings of the various factors of production (land, labor, capital, and entrepreneurs). However, not all of National Income is paid out to or received by individuals. For example, it is assumed in the accounting procedures that corporate taxes are paid out of corporate profits, while retained earnings by a corporation are obviously not paid out to individuals. Thus in order to arrive at an estimate of Personal Income (PI), adjustments of National Income figures are necessary. Personal Income (PI) is defined as the income

[8] *Ibid.*, p. 62; p. 64.

received by persons and it includes payments to individuals for welfare purposes by government. Individuals pay taxes. Thus individuals are not in a position either to spend or save *all* of their personal income. In order to compute their Disposable Income (DI) it is necessary to reduce Personal Income by Personal Taxes (PT). Finally, an individual can either spend or save his Disposable Income. Thus we define Disposable Income as consisting of Consumption Expenditures (CE) plus Savings (S). That is, finally, $DI = CE + S$.

Income from the Expenditure Point of View

The work and past recommendations of the Council can be more readily explained and understood if one further analyzes the Gross National Product in terms of the various expenditures which give rise to it. All income comes from expenditure. Thus Government Expenditure (GE) constitutes a source of income to some recipient. Government Expenditure, in turn, may be defined as equal to the sum of tax collections (T) plus the sum of government borrowing (Lg). Another source of income is Consumer Expenditure. What the reader spends on consumption (including such "consumer durables" as television sets and automobiles) represents income to a seller. Thus CE is another source of income. Also, what is spent putting resources to work to produce goods, that is investment, is also a source of income. When investment of depreciation allowances to replace worn out capital goods is included in the total investment figure, this *gross* amount is called Gross Private Domestic Investment (GPDI). Finally, if foreigners spend more on exports from the United States than Americans do on imports from abroad, income in the United States will be increased. But if Americans (including the Federal Government) spend more abroad than foreigners do in the United States, income will fall. Thus, Net Foreign Investment (NFI), the difference between the amount spent in the United States by foreigners and that spent by Americans abroad also affects income in the United States.[9]

We can now summarize the substance of the preceding paragraph by writing:

Gross National Product = Consumer Expenditure + Gross Private Domestic Investment + Government Expenditure + Net Foreign Investment.

Also, we have

Government Expenditure = Taxes + Government Borrowing.

Employment, Output, and Growth Policies; A Concluding Comment

In advising the President with respect to economic policy, the Council makes use of definitions such as those just explained. Suppose that there is agreement that the immediate goal is to adopt policies which will result in attainment of the estimated potential GNP, measured at a 4 percent level of unemployment, for an extended period of time (several years). Such a level of output means that economic growth will occur; as domestic investment increases, so will the stock of capital. The problem, then, is: given some estimated level of Government Expenditures (GE), and given a present actual level of GNP, what policies will produce the proper values for the variables, CE, GPDI, and NFI, to produce the desired value of GNP? Since the values of all the variables are measured in dollars, it is possible that some policies might produce an increase in GNP due solely to price rises rather than to increases in physical output. Obviously, such inflation is not our objective. The problem must be restated: What values of the variables will produce the desired level of GNP *with stable prices* while not allowing unemployment to fall below 4 percent?

Government Expenditures depend, to some extent, on international relations, but our estimate must be based on the forseeable future and a sudden change in GE could upset all the other plans. How do changes in Government Expenditures affect the other variables? When it is remembered that Government Expenditures = Taxes + Government Borrowing, does it make any difference how the Government Expenditures are financed? Our purpose in raising these questions is not to provide simple answers; instead it is to point up the very significant problems confronting the

[9] This definition of NFI is, of course, a loose one but sufficiently accurate for our present purposes.

Council. Even when policies are decided upon, the policies adopted may conflict with the objectives or values of one sector of the economy or another, and the Council may be confronted with a formidable task of convincing the President to adopt the policy the Council recommends, particularly if other strong voices in the executive branch counsel the President to adopt a different course of action.

For example in 1969, with a new Republican Administration taking office, there was much talk of a need to "cool off" the economy to reduce inflationary tendencies. Indeed, by 1969 it had become common talk that a choice had to be made between "a little more" unemployment or "a little more inflation." The term "trade-off" was coined by economic theorists to describe the idea that inflation could be reduced by reducing employment. The *Annual Report* of the outgoing Secretary of Labor in 1969 commented upon the "trade-off" idea by saying that it "may satisfy economic theory" but ignores social reality. The "trade-off" notion, the *Report* argued, amounted to favoring the affluent members of society by putting further burdens upon the "poor and the black." Social unrest would follow an increase in unemployment among the "hard core" unemployed.[10]

Even though the Council may believe that a tax increase is necessary to fight inflation, the President may find it difficult to convince Congress to adopt such legislation, particularly in an election year. And any proposal for a change in taxes implicitly involves a decision as to whether investors or consumers are to bear most of the burden or receive the benefit. A tax decrease intended to stimulate the economy can, for example, be given so that Consumer Expenditures increase, hopefully thereby indirectly stimulating Gross Private Domestic Investment; but such a reduction can also be given in such a way as to benefit investors in the hope of stimulating private investment directly and consumers indirectly as a result of an increase in income hopefully generated by the direct benefit to investors. The definition of Gross National Product as equal to the sum of total expenditures involves a recognition of the fact that governmental power can be employed directly by increasing Governmental Expenditures to generate income, or indirectly to stimulate the other variables upon which total income depends.

The Council does not operate in a vacuum. It confers regularly with other government agencies. Indeed, the Chairman of the Council, the Secretary of the Treasury, and the Director of the Bureau of the Budget form what is known as a "Troika" and prepare for the President joint, continuous assessments of the budgetary and economic outlook for the current and subsequent years; and the Troika, joined by the Chairman of the Federal Reserve Board is known as the "Quadriad" and meets with the President to discuss domestic and international monetary problems.

Problems pertaining to the determination of and analysis of the determinants of national income are topics dealt with in macroeconomic analysis. Much theoretical and empirical work has been done in attempts to isolate strategic variables and relationships among these variables. The Council has operated pragmatically or instrumentally. Had the tax cut of 1964 not been accompanied by an increase in output, the Council would surely have made further recommendations and advised the President to seek implementation of other programs; similarly, the increase in taxes imposed in 1968 upon the Council's recommendation was in the nature of a further judgment and a testing of an idea, namely that the high level of Government Expenditure, occasioned in large part by the War in Viet Nam, would result in continuing price increases unless Consumer Expenditures were directly reduced with hopeful indirect reductions in private investment. All three items, Government Expenditure, Consumer Expenditure, and Gross Private Domestic Investment are sources of income. A sharp increase in Government Expenditures at a time when the economy is operating at full employment levels must result in price increases by definition, since Gross National Product is defined as the sum of the products of the prices of all final products multiplied by the

[10] *Annual Report of the Secretary of Labor, January 1969* (Washington, D.C.: U.S. Department of Labor, 1969) (advance lithoprinted copy), pp. 31–32.

amounts of such products. If the amount of products remain constant and Gross National Product increases, such an increase can only be due to an increase in prices.

It has been argued by some that direct controls over wages and prices are an alternative to the use of tax measures in an attempt to offset the effects of increased Government Expenditures (and consequent reduction of products available to satisfy consumer demands). The most-widely accepted view is that in some cases the direct and indirect controls must be used together to supplement each other.

Direct controls were imposed during World War I, during World War II, and to some extent, during the Korean War. In the next chapter, the concluding chapter of this book, the use of direct controls will be briefly examined, as will be the problem of standards to be employed in evaluating the relative merits of government and private investments, a problem, it will be recalled from our discussion in Chapter 1, outlined in 1776 by Adam Smith.

32

Wartime Controls; Government Investment Decisions; Concluding Remarks

This chapter is the last one in this book. It contains three major subdivisions. The first is devoted to a brief discussion of direct controls or special working rules adopted during periods of war and of current planning for such controls in the event of total war in the future; the second contains a discussion of the problems of government investment decisions; and the third and final subdivision contains some concluding remarks and final observations.

A. WARTIME CONTROLS

Direct and Indirect Controls

During periods of war, government expenditures increase sharply, producing an increase in personal incomes. Satisfaction of the government demand for goods and services, on the other hand, reduces the quantities of these available to meet private demands precisely at the time when personal incomes are rising. The government expenditures may be financed by increased taxes, however; such taxes operate to reduce personal incomes. Also, government expenditures may be financed by the

sale of bonds; to the extent that these bonds are purchased by individuals, private savings increase and individual demands for goods are reduced. The measures used to finance the increased government expenditures are *indirect* controls.

Along with the *indirect* controls, it may be necessary to impose *direct* controls over wages and prices and to allocate both raw materials and finished products because the distribution of raw materials and products which would be accomplished by the market system may not be the appropriate one for conducting the maximum war effort. The administrative distribution of goods and services to final consumers is called *rationing*; the term *allocation* is used to refer to an administrative distribution of raw materials. One method of seeking to influence the use of materials which is less drastic than that of allocation is that of assigning administrative *priorities* to orders for goods; thus a certain manufacturer may be directed to fill all orders for military goods on a priority basis. Controls over maximum prices or over specific prices and wages may also be adopted.

World War I

The United States was unprepared when Congress declared war on Germany in April 1917. A Selective Service Act was adopted shortly thereafter; and a War Industries Board was put in charge of all government war purchases. Control was exercised over the distribution of food and fuel, and the price of grain was put under government control. The War Revenue Act was adopted, greatly increasing taxes. The authority of the War Industries Board was, however, not well defined and competition for supplies between the Army and Navy gave rise to problems in the assignment of priorities for production. In 1918, the Board was reconstituted with clear authority to establish military requirements, as well as to issue priority ratings. In this war, the United States did not produce a large amount of final products for military uses; instead, the United States furnished its partners with raw materials and semi-finished products and received finished goods in return. However, much was learned about running a wartime economy.

World War II

On September 1, 1939, Germany invaded Poland and World War II began. Opinion in the United States concerning eventual United States participation in the war was sharply divided until the Japanese attack on Pearl Harbor on December 7, 1941. This division of opinion hindered effective United States preparation for the inevitable entry of the United States into the war.

Despite strong opposition, in June 1940, Congress adopted a tax bill to raise funds for national defense expenditures and increased the ceiling on the national debt. The Selective Training and Service Act was adopted in September 1940; and in March 1941, Congress passed the Lend Lease Act empowering the President to provide goods and services to nations whose defense was deemed to be vital to the defense of the United States.

The United States economy was operating at a less than full employment level when the United States entered the war in December 1941. Shortly after the Declaration of War on December 8, 1941, Congress passed a $10 billion defense appropriations bill and extended the draft law. The War Production Board was established by President Roosevelt to supervise the armament program.

In January 1942, President Roosevelt set before Congress production goals greatly exceeding any similar goals set in the past: he called for production of 60,000 airplanes, 45,000 tanks, 20,000 antiaircraft guns, and 8,000,000 tons of shipping to be produced in 1942. The War Production Board undertook to issue priority orders and to plan production on a grand scale, prohibiting the use of materials for "nonessential purposes" and allocating materials to manufacturers. The War Powers Act of 1942 contained specific language authorizing the President to allocate materials upon "such conditions and to such an extent" as he deemed necessary or appropriate to promote national defense. The War Production Board was, however, not established and did not operate in such a way as to be clearly the final top authority in matters pertaining to operation of the defense effort and in 1943, the Office of War Mobilization was established as a "superagency" to exercise such final control. The Controlled Materials Plan adopted in 1942 was the principal method employed in controlling the use of materials. Allocations of steel, copper, and aluminum were made to manufacturers of final products on the basis of their requirements for essential production; these allocations were then transmitted "backwards" to the subcontractors producing the intermediate products used in making the final products. The requirements programs were revised each quarter by the allocating agency.

Government financing of new productive facilities was also undertaken in the cases of urgently needed war materials such as synthetic rubber, aluminum, and aviation gasoline.

Rationing of consumer goods was also undertaken; production of automobiles for private civilian use was virtually stopped; gasoline rationing was adopted.

The fact that the economy had been operating considerably below its full employment level at the time of the adoption of the earliest defense programs in 1939 meant that the *initial* increased government demand for goods and services could be met by putting hitherto unemployed resources to work and postponed the day when inflationary pressures began to make themselves felt. However, even in this situation, bottlenecks existed, and some materials were in much shorter supply than others. In these cases, price increases began to occur; and as the economy began to approach full employment in 1942, further inflationary pressures were felt. In January 1942, Congress passed the Emergency Price Control Act. It authorized the establishment on a statutory basis of the Office of Price Administration to exercise price controls and controls over rents in "defense rental areas." The agency at first sought to enforce selective price controls over wholesale prices, but prices continued to rise. In response to the President's request, Congress then enacted the Stabilization Act of 1942 in October of that year. The Act fixed prices in existence on September 15, 1942, as the level of maximum prices. Prices, nevertheless, continued to rise. In April 1943, the President issued a "hold the line" order, in which he directed the relevant agencies to make the price control regulations general and, if necessary, to "roll back" [reduce] prices. From this point on, until the end of the war, prices remained relatively stable. The experience gained during World War II was put to effective use five years later during the Korean War.

The Korean War

The invasion of the Republic of South Korea occurred on June 25, 1950. On July 19, President Truman sent to Congress a Message requesting partial mobilization of the United States. Congress responded by enacting the Defense Production Act of 1950 on September 8. In its amended form this law is still in force and constitutes the basis for current planning for defense mobilization, a topic further discussed below.

On September 9, 1950, Executive Order 10161 was issued.[1] The order provided for delegation to various executive departments of the authority for the establishment of priorities and allocations and expansion of domestic supply granted by the Defense Production Act and for creation of an Economic Stabilization Agency to enforce the price and wage-control provisions of the law. Among the most important of these

delegations of authority was that to the Department of Commerce which created the National Production Authority (NPA) to implement the priorities and allocation program.

In December 1950, the Office of Defense Mobilization was created to supervise and exercise control over the uses of the various powers which had earlier been delegated to the various executive agencies. The Director of Defense Mobilization, who headed this office, was thus the highest authority next to the President himself in the mobilization organization.

In July 1951, a Controlled Materials Plan (CMP) much like the one used during World War II was put into effect. The plan provided for complete allocation of copper, aluminum, and steel, including allocation for United States exports. This plan remained in effect until the Korean War ended; it was supplemented by the Defense Materials System (DMS) under which producers were required to set aside specified amounts of materials for the use of the Department of Defense and the Atomic Energy Commission.

Under the delegation of authority which it had received from the President, the Department of the Interior established the Defense Minerals Administration to exercise control over a number of metals and minerals up to the processing point at which the National Production Authority's orders became effective. The Secretary of Agriculture also exercised some authority over foods.

The National Production Authority operated subject to policy directives issued by the Defense Production Administration, an administration created in January 1951 to supervise the allocation and priority functions of the various defense agencies within the executive departments. The new agency, in turn, was responsible to the Director of Defense Mobilization. Within the Defense Production Administration, the Vital Materials Coordinating Committee was created. It consisted of representatives of the various executive agencies, including representatives of the National Production Authority (which was considered by many to be a spokesman for domestic business interests within the Department of Com-

---

[1] Federal Register 6105, September 9, 1950.

merce). This Committee formulated basic policies to be adopted in specific cases pertaining to expansion of supply, "balanced distribution of output," and limitation of "nonessential" uses. The Committee provided a forum within which the various "equal" executive agencies could reconcile their differences and come to agreement concerning policies to be adopted. Although the National Production Authority was the agency which implemented the various control arrangements over basic materials, within the context of the Vital Materials Coordinating Committee, the NPA had but one vote, as did each of the other executive agencies represented. Appeals from decisions of the Committee could be taken to the Director of Defense Mobilization, whose agency was a part of the staff of the President with, presumably, a direct channel of communication to the President. Appeals from the decisions of the Director could, of course, be taken by strong Cabinet Members to the President himself.

It has already been noted that Executive Order 10161 created the Economic Stabilization Agency. The basic legislation originally provided for compulsory price control only to the extent that economic stabilization objectives could not be attained by voluntary action. However by January 1951, prices had risen so much that the agency concluded that its voluntary stabilization program constituted a failure. An Office of Price Stabilization was created in January 1951 within the Economic Stabilization Agency. The latter immediately issued a General Price Ceiling Regulation which fixed prices for covered commodities at the level of the highest price charged by a particular seller during the period December 19, 1950, to January 24, 1950. Under General Overriding Regulation No. 9, commodities for which bonus price incentive schemes had been established to increase supplies were exempt from the General Price Ceiling Regulation. In time, General Overriding Regulation 44, issued March 17, 1953, ended all price controls after the Korean War had ended.

Problems of allocation of, and control of prices of, raw materials were complicated by

the fact that the General Services Administration was attempting to attain stockpile objectives (for critical and strategic materials) at a time when government demand for war material was also increasing. Moreover, under the Export Control Act of 1949, the Department of Commerce exercised control over exports both of strategic materials and of materials in short supply. Also, the Korean War was a limited war, and the United States had to seek the cooperation of foreign neutral exporting and importing countries in an attempt to prevent inflation of international raw materials prices and to insure that supplies of essential raw materials were made available to other Free World Nations. An international arrangement for voluntary cooperation in the purchase and sales of raw materials was thus made. Known as the International Materials Conference, this arrangement involved the use of a series of international commodity committees to estimate international supplies and requirements on a quarterly basis and succeeded in producing an orderly distribution of supplies of raw materials among Free World countries largely because of the self-restraint and good faith exercised by the United States in adjusting its stockpile purchase policy to prevailing economic conditions.[2]

It has been noted that price controls were ended in March 1953. The National Production Authority was abolished in October 1953, and its functions were transferred to the Business and Defense Services Administration within the Department of Commerce. This administration today continues to exercise the priority and allocations functions authorized by the Defense Production Act of 1950 as amended and extended.

Defense Activities and Planning Since the Korean War

The Defense Production Act of 1950 has been many times amended and extended. The provisions pertaining to authority for price and wage controls were terminated in 1953. The authority for establishment of a system of priorities and allocation of raw

[2] For a detailed discussion of the work of the International Materials Conference, see my article, "The International Materials Conference in Retro-spect," *Quarterly Journal of Economics*, Vol. 71 (May 1957), pp. 267–288.

materials has, however, continued in existence.

It has been noted that the Office of Defense Mobilization was the highest authority below the President in the defense organization during the Korean War. Both the name and the functions of this agency have undergone several changes.

In 1959, the Office of Defense Mobilization was consolidated with the Federal Civil Defense Administration to form the Office of Civil and Defense Mobilization.[3] Two years later in 1961, the Office of Civil and Defense Mobilization was reconstituted as a small staff agency, named the Office of Emergency Planning, located within the Executive Office of the President.

The various permanent executive departments of the Government and the regulatory agencies all have specific planning and operational functions to perform in the present defense organization scheme. The Joint Congressional Committee on Defense Production is the Congressional agency exercising a watchdog function; it publishes annually a report which contains as appendices the annual reports of the activities and operations of the various other elements of the Government under the Defense Production Act.

The Office of Emergency Planning has prepared alternative plans to meet various possible situations. Thus in its annual report to the Joint Committee on Defense Production in 1962, the Office noted that in the case of a "limited or conventional" war the federal government would continue to function and exercise control over the economy; however, in the case of a nuclear attack, local governments would be called upon to perform vital control functions until the central authority could once more be made effective. Thus planning had to be conducted to meet both types of situations.[4]

In 1968, the Defense Materials System and the priorities ratings assigned by the Business and Defense Services Administration were used to obtain materials for the atomic energy program, to implement programs of the Department of Transport-

ation and of the Department of Defense, and to obtain materials for use in the space programs of the National Aeronautics and Space Administration. This period was, of course, one in which a limited war—the Viet Nam War—was being carried on. In 1969, the Office of Emergency Planning defined its special emergency planning responsibilities to consist of a number of activities. These included making planning assumptions; developing emergency plans based on these assumptions; making plans for the functioning of the Federal Government under emergency conditions; representing the United States in North Atlantic Treaty Organization defense activities; and drafting legislation and executive orders to carry out the emergency functions of the Government.[5] Undoubtedly, the ration coupons to be issued to consumers during the next war have already been printed. Clearly, the preparedness for war of the United States is today much greater than it was in 1941 or in 1917. But it must be emphasized that that preparedness is not for an offensive war of agression; it is a preparedness against the event of nuclear attack upon the United States. And the agencies and some of the programs not only can be, but have been, used in cases of natural disasters, for example, in areas suffering damage and hardship as a result of floods or hurricanes.

B. GOVERNMENT INVESTMENT DECISIONS

Government Investment Decisions and Cost–Benefit Analysis

As we have seen in the opening pages of Chapter 1, Adam Smith argued that one of the duties of the sovereign was to establish and maintain certain public works and institutions which it would not be in the interest of any individual or group of individuals to erect or maintain "because the profit could never repay the expense to any individual or small group of individuals, though it may frequently do much more

---

[3] The information contained in this section is based on the Annual Reports of the Joint Committee on Defense Production (Washington, D.C.: U.S. Government Printing Office) for various years.

[4] *Twelfth Annual Report of the Joint Committee on Defense Production* (87th Cong., 2d sess., 1962)

(Washington, D.C.: U.S. Government Printing Office, 1962), p. 93.

[5] *Eighteenth Annual Report of the Joint Committee on Defense Production* (91st Cong., 1st sess., 1969) (Washington, D.C.: U.S. Government Printing Office, 1969), p. 101.

than repay it to a great society." It has also been noted in Chapter 1 that attempts by economists to measure the "costs" of social investments and the "benefits" of these investments involves what is known as "cost–benefit" analysis, a highly subjective attempt to utilize market prices as measures of social costs and values which has been characterized as an "art" rather than a "science."

Since 1967, various subcommittees of the Joint Economic Committee of Congress have conducted studies of the use of cost–benefit analyses, including the computation of "present values" of costs and benefits, in cases of government investments.

Planning–Programming–Budgeting System (PPBS)

For example, in 1967, the Joint Subcommittee on Economy in Government investigated the extent to which planning–programming–budgeting systems (which focus on output rather than on inputs) were being used in government agencies. Such systems involve the making of estimates of costs and benefits, both present and future, of various alternatives. The rates of return obtained from following various courses of action are estimated and compared as a basis for making decisions. In making estimates of future "returns" it is necessary to compute the "present values" of costs and benefits.

The "present value" of a given sum of money A due at the end of a specified number of time periods n is that sum V which if invested for the specified time at a specified rate of interest i will be equal to A. The formula for V is:

$$V = \frac{A}{(1+i)^n}.$$

The values for $A = \$1.00$ for given values of n and i are readily available in tables. Thus, the present value of \$1.00 discounted at 3 percent for a period of ten years can be obtained from such a table as equal to \$0.74409. If the discount rate is raised to 6 percent, the present value V decreases to \$0.31180; and if the period of time is increased to 20 years, while i remains equal to 3 percent, V also decreases to \$0.55368. To obtain the present value of \$100 under these assumptions, one merely multiplys the

present value of \$1.00 by 100. What these results mean is merely that if \$0.74409 is invested at 3 percent for a period of ten years, the principal and the interest will total \$1.00 at the end of the ten-year period. Therefore, \$74.409 invested at 3 percent for ten years will amount to \$100. And so on.

An investment which generates a stream of several income payments— which need not be equal in size—has a present value equal to the sum of those of the several income payments in the stream. Similarly, the present value of the cost of an investment which involves additional costs in each of the years of its life is equal to the sum of the present values of these several costs. And, of course, if the present value of the stream of benefits exceeds that of the stream of costs, the investment is "sound."

In the investigation mentioned earlier, the Joint Subcommittee on Economy in Government also examined the extent to which government agencies employ the method just described of computing the present values of costs and benefits estimated to flow from government investments. The Subcommittee reported that its hearings had disclosed that the economists testifying had generally agreed that the "appropriate" discount rate to be used in evaluating government investments was the "opportunity cost" of capital in the private sector, namely, the rate of return that the given amount of government investment could earn if it were employed in the private sector of the economy. Nevertheless, the Subcommittee added, within the government, a variety of actual rates was being used. These rates ranged from a zero rate in the case of many highway projects to a rate of 5 to 7 percent in poverty program evaluations.

The Subcommittee thereupon recommended that a *uniform* rate be used in evaluating all government investments and, more than this, that the rate used should reflect the "opportunity cost" as explained above. It also emphasized the fact that many of the cost–benefit studies made failed to take account of the indirect effects of the costs or benefits of the proposed investments and advocated that such indirect effects be estimated also. Unfortunately, it did not specify an operational procedure for making such estimates and this recommendation must be characterized as an empty one.

The Subcommittee also rejected a procedure which had earlier been specified in Senate Document No. 97 of the 87th Congress 2d Session. This document had provided for the discount rate in the case of water resource projects to be taken as equal to "the average rate of interest payable by the Treasury on interest-bearing securities outstanding at the end of the year." This rate, the Subcommittee argued, reflected only past history and did not reflect current costs. Moreover, this rate was far below the opportunity cost in the private sector. Finally, the Subcommittee asserted, "Government rates should be on a par with private sector rates, and . . . the current gap between the discount rates in the two sectors leads to resource misallocation."[6]

Thus the Subcommittee apparently adopted, without any real critical evaluation, the static welfare economics approach of equating market value with social value by adopting market price as a measure of social value.

Indeed, in a subsequent report the Subcommittee recommended that "no public investment be deemed 'economic' or 'efficient' if it fails to yield overall benefits which are at least as great as those same resources would have produced if left in the private sector."[7]

The problem of the "correct" rate to be used is, of course, a different one from that of the use of a *uniform* rate. The former question obviously involves a value judgment. And, as has been mentioned in Chapter 26, in 1969, Julius Margolis pointed out that economists have adopted a procedure for estimating social values which involves "aggregating individual values." According to also to Margolis, "Economists have accepted the task of generating support for this view of social welfare." He further pointed out that this approach involves "rejection of the legitimacy of an active role of the political process

or administrative structure as formulators of the public interest," with consequent tension between economists and administrators. The economists' position is rationalized by him as being "true to the principles of serving the public interest as defined by the profession in their scientific journals." That is, the economist "selects his models and criteria so as to maximize the professional view of the public interest."[8] Margolis's statement is, of course, accurate, but it comes close to stating that professional economists do and should see themselves in the roles of the philosopher–kings envisaged by Plato in *The Republic*.

The majority of the Subcommittee accepted the economists' criterion by accepting private opportunity cost as the measure of the discount rate. But Representative Wright Patman did not. Instead, in his dissenting statement, he stated numerous arguments for rejecting this view. He first pointed out that the basic premise of the majority position was that public investments could be valued in the same way as private investments and rejected this premise. He emphasized that government investments "to improve the quality of human life" do not lend themselves to measurement in dollars and cents. The noneconomic benefits of government investments cannot be measured by definition! Also, Representative Patman rejected the majority's underlying assumption that the size of national income "is the single and uppermost goal of our society." The majority's view, he noted meant that it believed society would benefit "more from a new gadget than from the construction of a new school or sewage system" because the immediate financial return on the former might be 5.5 percent on the gadget as compared with 5 percent on the school or sewage system.[9] In addition, Representative Patman pointed out that the interest rate in the private sector is determined in a market which is not competitive, yet the

[6] *Planning–Programming–Budgeting System: Progress and Potentials* (Report of the Joint Subcommittee on Economy in Government, 90th Cong., 1st sess., 1967) (Washington, D.C.: U.S. Government Printing Office, 1967), pp. 5–7.

[7] *Economic Analysis of Public Investment Decisions: Interest Rate Policy and Discount Analysis* (Report of the Joint Subcommittee on Economy in Government, 90th Cong., 2d sess., 1968) (Washington, D.C.: U.S.

Government Printing Office, 1968), p. 1.

[8] Julius Margolis, "Shadow Prices for Incorrect or Nonexistent Market Values" in *The Analysis and Evaluation of Public Expenditures: The PPB System* (A Compendium of Papers submitted to the Joint Subcommittee on Economy in Government, 91st Cong., 1st sess., 1969) (Washington, D.C.: U.S. Government Printing Office, 1969), p. 538.

[9] *Ibid.*, pp. 22–23.

majority view involved an assumption that competition did reign.

Although Representative Patman did not mention the point, it should also be noted that rejection of the political process as a method for determining investment decisions amounts to rejection of one way in which non-economic costs and benefits may be brought to bear on the final decision being made.

In its earlier report mentioned above, although the Subcommittee had accepted the opportunity cost test, the Subcommittee itself warned against the tendency to exaggerate "the potential of PPBS and the use of computers" in solving complex policy problems. It fully recognized the difficulties, if not impossibilities, of measuring intangible benefits or costs. It noted that the questions involved by their very nature were questions raising the burdens of one group in order to benefit another. Thus "many decisions remain beyond the reach of quantitative analysis." PPBS might be helpful in providing a basis for "a more rational and coherent" judgment, but it "does not help us much in deciding on ultimate goals for public policy or in deciding between alternative goals."[10]

Indeed, Aaron Wildavsky, a political scientist, has argued that PPBS leads to an emphasis of *programs* and to a neglect of *policy*. Thus he has asserted that "much attention should be paid to the political aspects of public decision-making and public policy-making instead of ignoring or condescendingly regarding political aspects."[11]

The position one takes on the opportunity cost issue just discussed is apt to be a reflection of the extent to which his personal political philosophy rests upon one or another of the three basic philosophical rationalizations of political democracy discussed in Chapter 2. Just as the legal philosophies held by contemporary lawyers reflect their underlying philosophical positions, a point noted in Chapter 3, so do the policy positions taken by economists often reflect also their underlying philosophical positions. We may thus end this book by making a few concluding remarks on this subject in the next and last major subdivision.

C. CONCLUDING REMARKS

It has been noted that how one stands on the opportunity cost issue raised in the positions taken by the majority and by Representative Patman may well be a reflection of the extent to which his own economic philosophy is a reflection of his personal adherence to a logical positivist, a natural law, or an instrumentalist philosophical position.

A logical positivist, for example, would strongly support the majority position that the rate of return earned in the private sector should be the decisive rate. He would do so on grounds that the rate determined in the private sector is a reflection of the emotionally determined preferences of the population as between current and future consumption. Thus the private rate is simply another form of the *Grundnorm* found in legal positivism.

One who holds strongly to a natural law point of view would also support the majority position on the theory that the rate of return in the private sector is in some sense or other the "natural" rate, a rate resulting from the operation of the forces of natural law in the marketplace. A natural law philosophy in economics is invariably found associated with an advocacy of a *laissez-faire* economic system.

Representative Patman's position, however, calls attention to the *consequences* of government investments and emphasizes that the evaluation of each investment must be conducted in terms of the problem the investment is intended to deal with. His is essentially a pragmatic or instrumentalist position, a position which rejects any appeal to "authority, custom, or tradition" including one cast in the form of an externally imposed control set by market forces. Note in particular, however, that the Patman position does not necessarily reject the proposition that use of a uniform rate of discount in the case of similar projects is desirable. That is not the issue. The issue is the *type* of uniform rate to be chosen.

What Representative Patman did not say, but what may also be worth pointing out, is that the debate about the use of

---

[10] *The Planning–Programming–Budgeting System, op. cit.*, pp. 9–10.

[11] "Rescuing Policy Analysis from PPBS," in

The Analysis and Evaluation of Public Expenditures: The PPBS System, op. cit., p. 835.

opportunity cost measured by the private market rate implies the existence of a higher degree of certainty and quantifiability than in fact exists. The Subcommittee has admitted that the costs and benefits are themselves difficult to quantify. The discount rate is thus applied to a set of numerical values which are themselves uncertain and are determined in a highly subjective fashion; and the use of such a rate will not overcome any errors of measurement made in the estimates of costs or benefits. Hence the use of the technique still "has a long way to go." It gives an illusion of certainty, but an illusion only.

In the opening paragraph of this book its purpose has been stated to be that of stimulating critical thinking with respect to some particular questions of Political Economy, with particular reference to the United States. Probably more questions have been asked than answers given. But, given our purpose, this is as it should be. The American System of Political Economy is not static and unchanging; at any given time, it is the result of a *continuous process* of self-correcting value judgments and changing goals. It derives its strength from its flexibility.

The landing of a man on the moon in July 1969 represented a significant technological achievement for the System. The fact that the extravehicular activities of the astronauts were viewed on television throughout the world was no less remarkable than the feat of the landing itself. A new era of exploration of the solar system whose implications cannot yet be clearly seen has opened. An economist making a cost–benefit analysis of expenditures involved in making the mission of Apollo 11 a success would surely have to draw heavily upon his imagination. What free market interest rate should be used? Yet, questions have been raised concerning the relative merits of expenditures upon the space program in comparison to the benefits which might be expected to flow from additional expenditures to eliminate poverty and to solve the problems of the urban areas in the United States, expenditures whose present and future monetary benefits are equally difficult to measure. It has been noted that all such expenditures have effects on the distribution of income. For this reason, the question of making them gives rise to controversy.

In May 1969, the Joint Subcommittee on Economy in Government published a group of papers by various academicians dealing with the problem of analysis and evaluation of public expenditure.[12] Some of these papers have already been mentioned in this chapter. Among the opening group of papers was one by Professor Peter O. Steiner, who concluded his scholarly search for a criterion or definition of the *public interest* by remarking that the analyst's function was really to "force an articulation of the . . . objectives served" and of the competing interests reconciled and that he (Steiner) would be willing to regard decisions arrived at in such a context as a "reasonable approximation" to the public interest.[13] Thus in effect, Professor Steiner concluded that the common law method of judging and of deciding cases was a process of continuously defining the "public interest" on a case by case basis. That view has, of course, been taken throughout this book.

There is, accordingly, no more appropriate note on which to close this book than by referring to a statement by David Hume quoted by Hamilton in Essay No. 5 of the *Federalist*:

> To balance a large society, whether monarchal or republican, on general laws, is a work of so great difficulty, that no human genius, however comprehensive, is able, by the mere dint of reason and reflection to effect it. The judgments of the many must unite in the work, experience must guide their labor; time must bring it perfection, and the feeling of inconveniences must correct the mistakes which they inevitably fall into in their first trials and experiments.

An instrumentalist point of view recognizes the validity of the ideas expressed in this quotation and goes on to argue that in a dynamic world there will be a continuous stream of "first trials and experiments"; thus this outlook leads to the conclusion that attempts to produce ultimate solutions or to derive "social welfare functions" based on individual emotional responses or preferences must ever be frustrated, and to an emphasis of the experimental *method* of

[12] *Analysis and Evaluation of Public Expenditures: The PBE System, op. cit.*

[13] *Ibid.*, p. 43.

self-correcting value judgments in which ideas are ever subject to correction by actual events. The individual, especially the academician, who seeks to substitute his judgment for that of a legislature or a court arrived at in an open and free reconciliation of competing interests has the burden of demonstrating that his method of producing his own evaluation is more reliable than is the process which was in fact employed and that the consequences of adopting his solution are more desirable than those actually resulting when tested by the problem which is being dealt with.

Logical Positivist, Natural Law, and Instrumentalist Philosophies in Economics

Although nearly all economists employ the same language in discussing policy problems, it does not follow that they hold the same value systems nor that they all agree on solutions to basic methodological problems. This Appendix undertakes to examine the extent to which pronouncements on public policies and approaches to policy problems by economists reflect their individual commitments to one of the three basic philosophies of logical positivism, natural law philosophy, or instrumentalism or pragmatism—which have been discussed in Chapter 2 and in terms of legal philosophies in Chapter 3. The following topics are discussed briefly in the order indicated in this Appendix: (1) logical positivism and static welfare economics; (2) secular natural law philosophy and advocacy of a *laissez-faire* system; and (3) instrumentalism (or pragmatism) and rejection of a *laissez-faire* system.

A. LOGICAL POSITIVISM AND STATIC WELFARE ECONOMICS

As has been noted in Chapter 2, although logical or analytical positivists do not constitute a "School," nevertheless they do hold two basic views in common, namely: (1) philosophy should concern itself prim-

arily with the meaning of propositions; and (2) questions of ultimate value are not proper subjects for scientific analysis. These same beliefs, we have also already seen in Chapter 3, permeate legal positivism and analytical jurisprudence. And these same beliefs are largely held by economists who attempt to make use in their writings of static welfare economics, described in Chapter 10, as a basis for evaluating or formulating public policies.

The counterpart in economics of logical positivism in philosophy and of legal positivism or analytical jurisprudence is Static Welfare Economics which, on the one hand, purports to make no real value judgments and to follow ideas expressed by the Italian economist, Vilfredo Pareto in about 1890, in specifying "scientific" conditions of "optimality," while on the other, it makes use of market price to measure the "social value" of economic activities.

Logical positivist advocates of the use of the concept of "economic efficiency"—as defined by long-run conditions of equilibrium such as those which *would be* attained in a perfectly competitive economy—adopt the emotionally determined wants of consumers as these are assumed to be reflected in prices as their *Grundnorm*. Thus *in effect*, they adopt a procedure similar to that of Bertrand Russell (described in Chapter 2), and define those actions of individuals which arouse the emotion of "approval" as "good" and those whose effects arouse the emotion of "disapproval" as "bad," with "approval" expressed by the market prices consumers are willing to pay for goods and "disapproval" expressed by a failure to purchase. Instead of avoiding a basic value judgment, this procedure merely amounts to the making of a basic value judgment that emotional approval as it is assumed to be expressed by prices is *the* test of "social value."

Some advocates of the use of the concept of "economic efficiency" as a norm take the view that *if* the economist has been given a "social welfare function," a term usually left undefined (although some rather naïve attempts have been made in a few instances to determine "*the* relevant social welfare" function), he will then be able to specify the conditions under which this function can be maximized. The specification of these conditions generally takes the form of a statement that the function will be maximized when the "social costs of additional units of output are equal to the social benefits of these units" and often ignores (assumes "away") the problems of measuring either of these while, at the same time, it is denied that value judgments are involved in the analysis. Indeed, this approach literally involves making policy pronouncements on the basis of an assumption that policies can be "evaluated" without making value judgments. A specific recent example of the ideas of an advocate of this approach will now be considered.

Ronald Meek on Static Welfare Economics

In 1963, the British Society for the Philosophy of Science invited numerous economists to discuss the question of "value judgments in economics" at its Annual Conference. Among those who were invited to present papers was Ronald Meek. He pointed to what he called "a new view of the basic function of economics" and asserted that if this view eventually predominated, it might very well eliminate the "intrusion of value-judgments" into econo-

mics. Among the developments to which he referred was:

... the development of the branch of economics known as 'welfare economics', a set of rules by which the various economic situations open to a society at any given time may be ordered and compared from the point of view of their relative desirability. *Now the interesting thing about these new developments is that they are mainly designed to help us make the 'right' economic choices in situations in which the price mechanism cannot be expected to make them for us automatically.*[1]

The sentence which has now been italicized in this quotation shows that Meek accepted the fundamental proposition that "the price mechanism makes the 'right' choices"—some of the time at any rate—and that the problem in other cases is merely one of making those choices which the existing price *system would have made had it been operating in accordance with his ideas.* At the same time, he suggested somewhat hopefully in his paper that "the intrusion of value-judgments" into economics was sure to decrease! Thus in his system, price *is* the measure of "social" value and price as determined in the free market makes the "right" choice "automatically" in some cases.

An Example of the Use of Static Welfare Economics

An interesting example of such a use of static welfare economics appeared in a paper in the March 1965 issue of the *American Economic Review.* In this paper, an economist undertook to determine by means of economic analysis *alone* "the appropriate rule for the compensation of persons damaged by accident."[2] The author in question first rejected the legal definition of "negligence" on grounds that it involved a "subjective judgment of judge or jury on how a hypothetical 'reasonable man' would act in like circumstances." He then asserted that economics applied a different standard, and this was the standard of the "maximizing man who is defined in terms that permit mensuration, at least in principle."

The author, moreover, assured the reader that the yield of resources devoted to

[1] Ronald L. Meek, "Value-Judgments in Economics," *British Journal for the Philosophy of Science*, Vol. XV (August, 1964), pp. 89–96 at p. 94. (Italics mine.) (New York: Cambridge University Press).

[2] Simon Rottenber, "Liability in Law and Economics," *American Economic Review*, Vol. LV (March 1965), pp. 107–114.

accident prevention could be measured by the "expected output of the marginal life saved, net of the expected lifetime consumption of the relevant person, discounted at an appropriate time rate" plus an amount equal to the "value put upon life by the deceased person." Thus the author computed the loss as equal to the "sum of the loss to the rest of society . . . *and the loss to the deceased himself.*"[3] This, then, is an example of Static Welfare Economics. Its *Grundnorm* constitutes its basic value judgment.

B. SECULAR NATURAL LAW PHILOSOPHY AND THE ADVOCACY OF A LAISSEZ-FAIRE SYSTEM

In 1870, T. E. Cliffe Leslie wrote an article for the *Fortnightly Review* containing what may still be the most penetrating description of the natural law point of view in economics, a view held today by one influential group of contemporary economists whose position will be discussed below. He remarked:

Mr. Lowe [M.P., in a speech] gave expression to the conception of *one school* of the followers of Adam Smith that Political Economy is, not what Adam Smith called his own treatise, *An Inquiry into the Nature and Causes of the Wealth of Nations,* but a final answer to the inquiry—a body of necessary and universal truth, founded on inviolable laws of nature, and deduced from the construction of the human mind.

. . . the fundamental conception is that their political economy *is* an ascertained body of laws of nature, is an offshoot of the ancient fiction of a Code of Nature, and a natural order of things, in a form given to that fiction in modern times by theology on the one hand, and a revolt against the tyranny of the fallacy and inequality of such human codes as the world had known on the other.

. . . The original foundation is in fact no other than that theory of nature which, descending through Roman jural philosophy from the speculations of Greece, taught that there is a simple Code of Nature which human institutions have disturbed, though its principles are distinctly visible through them, and a beneficial and harmonious natural order of things which appears wherever nature is left to itself. *In the last century this theory assumed a variety of forms and disguises, all of them, however, involving one fundamental fallacy of reasoning, a priori from assumptions obtained, not by the interrogation, but by the anticipation of nature; what is assumed as nature being at bottom a mere conjecture respecting its constitution and arrangements. The political philosophy flowing from this ideal source presents to us sometimes an assumed state of nature or of society in its natural simplicity; sometimes an assumed natural tendency or order of events, and sometimes a law or principle of human nature; and these different aspects greatly thicken the confusion perpetually arising between the real and the ideal,* between that which by the assumption ought to be, and that which actually is. The philosophy of Adam Smith, though combining an inductive investigation of the real order of things, is pervaded throughout by this theory of nature, in a form given to it by theology, by political history, and by the cast of his own mind.[4]

Von Hayek and von Mises

The current form of secular natural law philosophy in economics, particularly in the works of F. A. von Hayek, Ludwig von Mises, Henry C. Simons, and their followers invariably involves "an assumed natural tendency or order of events, and sometimes a law or principle of human nature" which, however, its various contemporary exponents generally call by some other name or identify with some other phrase. Indeed some of them (*e.g.,* von Mises) deny that theirs is such a natural law point of view— even while they are expounding it. For example, F. A. von Hayek has written on many aspects of economics, but his general theme is always the same: it amounts to a statement of his theory of individualism and that only a small part of the social order can be made "a conscious product of human reason." Thus the automatic price system is a "marvel."[5]

Thus also Ludwig von Mises is a writer who, on the one hand, deprecates positivism, instrumentalism, and the natural law points of view in philosophy but who, on the other, adopts a crude natural law point of view in a disguised form. He holds to a belief in the "regularity" of social phenomena "to which man must adjust his action."[6]

---

[3] *Ibid.,* p. 109. (Italics mine.)

[4] T. E. Cliffe Leslie, "The Political Economy of Adam Smith," *The Fortnightly Review,* Vol. XLIII, New Series (November 1, 1870), pp. 549–563, at pp. 549; 551–552. (Italics mine.)

[5] F. A. von Hayek, *Individualism and Economic Order* (Chicago: University of Cicago Press, 1958), p. 22, pp. 87–88.

[6] Ludwig von Mises, *Human Action* (New Haven: Yale University Press, 1949), pp. 1–2; pp. 38–40; p. 65; pp. 239–240; pp. 754–756.

The Chicago School

In a Prefatory Note to a posthumous publication of Henry C. Simons's best known essays, Aaron Director (of the University of Chicago Law School) noted that, prior to his death, Simons had been establishing himself as the head of a "School" at the University of Chicago.[7] Simons identified himself as belonging to the intellectual tradition of Adam Smith and Hayek. He frankly asserted that his Liberalism "postulated some invisible hand."

One question which naturally arises is that of whether or not there today actually exists a "School" of economists who have followed in Simons's footsteps (and in those of his contemporaries at the University of Chicago). This question was the subject of a series of papers published in 1962 in the *Journal of Political Economy*, a professional journal published by the Department of Economics of the University of Chicago. The first of these papers by H. Laurence Miller (whose Ph.D. is from Harvard) undertook to list the distinguishing characteristics of "the Chicago School of Economists"—which was loosely defined as consisting of economists who were teaching at Chicago or who had received graduate training there, or who held views similar to those of this group. Miller argued that "The Chicago School of economists is noteworthy, first and foremost for its advocacy of a private-enterprise economy and limited government," and that the distinguishing characteristics of this group of economists are that they: (1) take a "polar position among economists as advocates of" an individualistic market economy; (2) place great emphasis on the usefulness and relevance of neoclassical economic (price) theory; (3) equate the actual and ideal markets; (4) see and apply economics "in and to every nook and cranny of life"; and (5) put great emphasis on testing of hypotheses as a neglected element in positive economics.[8] Miller also pointed out that, while Henry Simons had attacked both private monopoly and concentrations of power in the hands of government, Milton "Friedman and other modern Chicagoans concentrate their attack almost entirely on government intervention."

Professor George Stigler of the School of Business of the University of Chicago (Ph. D. Chicago 1938) disagreed with Miller, denying the existence of a "School" and said that Miller had merely sketched the views of his friend, Milton Friedman (M. A. Chicago 1933, Ph. D. Columbia 1946; Professor, Chicago since 1941, and President of the American Economic Association in 1966). Stigler also asserted that Miller had not described "a unifying ethical or political philosophy or an articulate and reasonably specific program." Stigler thereby blithesomely ignored Miller's assertion that members of the so-called "School" took a "polar position among economists as advocates of" an individualist market economy,[9] a proposition which quite obviously describes a "unifying political and ethical philosophy."

Not all members of this "School" are located at the University of Chicago, and some have never studied there. Among its members one must also list Professor G. Warren Nutter of the University of Virginia (Ph. D. Chicago 1949) who, along with Professor Friedman, served as a principal economic advisor to Republican Senator Barry Goldwater during the latter's unsuccessful campaign for the Presidency in 1964, a position hardly to be considered inconsistent with a political philosophy of eighteenth or nineteenth century liberalism.[10] In 1968, Friedman served as an advisor to the Republican candidate, Richard Nixon. Latter day advocates of a *laissez-faire* system are apparently quite pragmatic in their recognition of the fact that the establishment of a basic working rule of unlimited individualism in the area of economic activities and organization also requires the use of governmental power and that the political and economic revolution which they seek is contingent upon their

---

[7] Henry C. Simons, *Economic Policy for a Free Society* (Chicago: University of Chicago Press, 1948), pp. v–vi.

[8] H. Laurence Miller, Jr., "On the 'Chicago School of Economics,'" *Journal of Political Economy*, Vol. LXX (February 1962), pp. 70–71.

[9] George Stigler, "Comment," *Journal of Political Economy*, Vol. LXX (February 1962), pp. 70–71.

[10] *New York Times*, March 31, 1964, 20:1; *ibid.*, Sept. 8, 1964, 1:6; *ibid.*, Oct. 8, 1964, 63:4; *ibid.*, Oct. 11, 1964, VI:35.

acquisition and use of political power. The issue they,pose is thus not one of *whether or not* governmental power should be used—although they often frame the issue in these terms—but of *how* it should be used *and for what purposes and whose benefit.* The contemporary advocates of the *laissez-faire* system are not really opposed to what they denounce by the use of their term "government intervention"; instead they seek a new kind of "intervention" and an abolition of the existing kind of "intervention" for the purpose of establishing the *laissez-faire* system in which they have great faith.

C. INSTRUMENTALISM AND THE REJECTION OF LAISSEZ-FAIRE

Static Welfare Economics and the natural law rationalization of the *laissez-faire* system are both purely deductive analyses. Where Reneé Descartes sought centuries ago to establish the existence of God by deductive reasoning and excluded the soul from topics of scientific investigation, thereby separating mind from body and hence science from religion, contemporary logical positivism in economics similarly establishes the conditions of "optimality" in a static economic system by deductive reasoning and purports to exclude value judgments, thereby apparently separating "positive economics" from "normative economics." Where also long ago Baruch Spinoza identified God and Nature as One and like Descartes sought to establish the existence of God by means of deductive reasoning, contemporary secular natural law philosophy in economics identifies its "relatively absolute absolute" of individualism with a *laissez-faire* system and similarly seeks to demonstrate the attainment of "freedom" in such a system by means of deductive reasoning. But instrumentalism offers a different way.

Ely and the Founders of the AEA

For the rationalist, as William James put it, "truth remains a pure abstraction." To the instrumentalist, on the other hand, "truth becomes a class-name for all sorts of definite working-values in experience." As

[11] Lafayette G. Harter, *John. R. Commons: His Assault on Laissez-Faire* (Corvallis: Oregon State University Press, 1962), p. 35.

has been noted in Chapter 1, when the American Economic Association was first organized in 1886, although its founders disavowed any intention of taking a "partisan attitude" in the study of industrial and commercial policy, nevertheless the pragmatists in the group, especially Richard T. Ely, put forth a policy statement including the sentence, "We believe in a progressive development of economic conditions, which must be met by a corresponding development of legislative policy."

Ely and his associates were men who had studied in Germany and who had been greatly influenced by the Historical School in the field of law (discussed in Chapter 3). In fact, Ely thought of economics as a "science of human relations."

Commons and Mitchell

In 1888, John R. Commons became a graduate student under Ely at Johns Hopkins. According to one writer, Ely's course in political economy included both sociology and political science along with the traditional economics of the day.[11] In time, Commons also acknowledged his deep indebtedness to Peirce and John Dewey.

Aside from achievements in the field of labor history and in the formulation of a concept of Political Economy as a study of the disposal and use of resources in an economy dominated by bargaining and collective action, Commons was a significant force in the adoption (in Wisconsin) of the first industrial workmen's compensation legislation, the first unemployment compensation legislation, and in an extension of the power of regulation of public utilities by means of administrative commissions.[12]

Commons was a self-conscious instrumentalist. Indeed, he wrote of Peirce:

Thus, Peirce's Pragmatism is none other than the scientific method of investigation. The charge is often brought against the so-called "philosophy" of Pragmatism that it is based on the fallacy that "whatever works" is true and right. . . . But Peirce's meaning was not so. He meant, *if a theory "works" when tested by experiments and verified by others, then the theory is true and right, so far as present knowledge is concerned and all the known facts are included.*

[12] *Ibid.*, pp. 89 ff. contains a useful discussion of the role played by Commons in the adoption of early social legislation in the United States.

. . . Peirce's Pragmatism, applied to . . . economics, is the scientific investigation of economic relations of citizens to citizens. Its subject-matter is the whole concern of which the individuals are members, and the activities investigated are their transactions governed by an entirely different law, not a law of nature but a working rule, for the time being, of collective action.[13]

Wesley C. Mitchell was also an instrumentalist and like Commons he, too, rejected the purely deductive approach and the *laissez-faire* system. Unlike Commons, Mitchell did not devote himself to an examination of the working rules of economic activity; instead he sought to employ statistical methods to determine the behavior of aggregate economic phenomena and hoped the results might provide a basis for policy. When the National Bureau of Economic Research was founded shortly after the first World War, Mitchell was its first director of research. Contemporary econometricians owe much to Mitchell's insistence upon empirical investigation of economic phenomena.

Mitchell's students at Columbia were well-respresented among the economists who served in federal government posts during the New Deal period and thereafter, and who exerted a significant influence on the actual formulation and implementation of many of our contemporary working rules of economic activity.

A Concluding Comment

As Simon Kuznets, the inventor of the national income accounts and statistical definitions of Gross National Product and other aggregates, which play such an important role in the work of the Council of Economic Advisors in the present day, said of Mitchell:

His views on the narrow institutional basis of much economic theorizing and of the influence on it of quick adaptation to pressing current problems should put us in a properly critical frame of mind in examining a "theory" in which economic growth is deduced from simple

relations of capital to output . . . or one in which a claim for successive stages of development is based either on merely terminological devices or on a few inadequately studied cases.[14]

Kuznets has characterized himself as one of Mitchell's "students and followers."

Another example can be found in Willard Thorp, who collaborated with Mitchell on a book about business cycles, and who in the period after World War II served as Assistant Secretary of State for Economic Affairs during the critical period of Marshall Plan aid to Europe and later negotiations under the General Agreement on Tariffs and Trade, in which (we have seen in Chapter 8) contemporary American international trade policy is embodied.

The Great Depression and the development of Keynesian national income analysis had the effect of pushing many contemporary economists in the direction of a *de facto* instrumentalist approach. A widespread recognition of the idea that the use of governmental power in the form of fiscal and monetary measures can and does affect the level of prices, employment, and output inevitably leads to a recognition of the fact that a simple belief in the balancing of the federal budget on the basis of a calendar year represents a mystical rather than a functional approach to the use of governmental power. It leads also to a consciousness of the proposition that use of governmental power inevitably affects the nature and control of economic power as well as the direction and level of economic activity and that *the important questions pertain to the way in which* governmental power is to be used *and to the consequences* which are likely to result from particular uses of such power, while the question of whether or not it is to be used is recognized to be moot.

Practice of the instrumentalist philosophy of Peirce, James, and Dewey and a rejection of the *laissez-faire* system—a rejection which Commons, Mitchell, and also Clarence Ayres[15] made explicit in their works—represents the prevailing *practice* of economists actually working the areas of public

[13] John R. Commons, *Institutional Economics* (New York: The Macmillan Co., 1934), pp. 156–157. (Italics his and mine.)

[14] Simon Kuznets, "The Contribution of Wesley C. Mitchell," in Joseph Dorfman, C. E. Ayres, Neil W. Chamberlain, Simon Kuznets, and R. A.

Gordon, *Institutional Economics* (A Series of Lectures) (Berkeley: University of California Press, 1963), p. 121.

[15] See C. E. Ayres, *The Theory of Economic Progress* (2d ed., New York: Schocken Books, 1962).

policy or in those concerning the use of governmental power, although their *theoretical* rationalizations of their activities still make use, in many cases, of logical positivist and natural law conceptions. The position, discussed in Chapter 32, of the majority of the Subcommittee on Economy in Government concerning the use of the opportunity cost of private investments as a standard *to* which government investments must mystically conform without regard to the consequences or results of applying such a test in particular cases is a clear example of what uncritical reliance upon the contemporary logical positivist and natural law conceptions produces. As Representative Wright Patman pointed out, the procedure can result in production of a new gadget rather than in a new sewage system or better education for the young. The reader, of course, is free to choose among the three positions.

Index